HISTORY OF ART

FIFTH EDITION REVISED
VOLUME II

HISTORY OF ART

FIFTH EDITION REVISED
VOLUME II

H. W. JANSON   ANTHONY F. JANSON

PRENTICE HALL, INC., AND HARRY N. ABRAMS, INC., PUBLISHERS

Project director: JULIA MOORE

Editor: JOANNE GREENSPUN

Assistant editor: MONICA MEHTA

Picture editor: JENNIFER BRIGHT

Art director: LYDIA GERSHEY

Designers:
LYDIA GERSHEY with YONAH SCHURINK
OF COMMUNIGRAPH

The Library of Congress has cataloged the trade edition of this book as follows:

Janson, H. W. (Horst Woldemar), 1913–
    History of art / H.W. Janson.—5th ed. revised Anthony F.
Janson.
       p.   cm.
    Includes bibliographical references and index.
    ISBN-0-8109-3442-6
    1. Art—History.   I. Janson, Anthony F.   II. Title.
  N5300.J3   1997
  709—dc21   96–49963

Prentice Hall ISBN for this book is 0–13–849233–6

Prentice Hall, Inc.
Simon & Schuster/A Viacom Company
Send inquiries to:
    Marketing Manager
    Humanities & Social Sciences, Prentice Hall, Inc.
    One Lake Street
    Upper Saddle River, N.J. 07458
    http://www.prenhall.com

Printed and bound in Japan

Note on the picture captions:

Each illustration is placed as close as possible to its first discussion in the text.
Measurements are given throughout, except for objects that are inherently large:
architecture, architectural sculpture, interiors, and wall paintings. Height precedes
width. A probable measuring error of more than one percent is indicated by
"approx." Titles of works are those designated by the institutions owning the works,
where applicable, or by custom. Dates are based on documentary evidence, unless
preceded by "c."

First Edition 1962, revised and enlarged, 1969
Second Edition 1977
Third Edition 1986
Fourth Edition 1991
Fifth Edition 1995, revised 1997

Front cover: Guido Reni. Detail of *Aurora*, a ceiling fresco in the Casino Rospiliosi, Rome. 1613.
Detail of figure 734

CONTENTS

PART FOUR
THE MODERN WORLD *650*
Map *656*

PREFACE AND ACKNOWLEDGMENTS
TO THE FIRST EDITION

The title of this book has a dual meaning: it refers both to the events that *make* the history of art, and to the scholarly discipline that deals with these events. Perhaps it is just as well that the record and its interpretation are thus designated by the same term. For the two cannot be separated, try as we may. There are no "plain facts" in the history of art—or in the history of anything else for that matter, only degrees of plausibility. Every statement, no matter how fully documented, is subject to doubt and remains a "fact" only so long as nobody questions it. To doubt what has been taken for granted, and to find a more plausible interpretation of the evidence, is every scholar's task. Nevertheless, there is always a large body of "facts" in any field of study; they are the sleeping dogs whose very inertness makes them landmarks on the scholarly terrain. Fortunately, only a minority of them can be aroused at the same time, otherwise we should lose our bearings; yet all are kept under surveillance to see which ones might be stirred into wakefulness and locomotion. It is these "facts" that fascinate the scholar. I believe they will also interest the general reader. In a survey such as this, the sleeping dogs are indispensable, but I have tried to emphasize that their condition is temporary, and to give the reader a fairly close look at some of the wakeful ones.

I am under no illusion that my account is adequate in every respect. The history of art is too vast a field for anyone to encompass all of it with equal competence. If the shortcomings of my book remain within tolerable limits, this is due to the many friends and colleagues who have permitted me to tax their kindness with inquiries, requests for favors, or discussions of doubtful points. I am particularly indebted to Bernard Bothmer, Richard Ettinghausen, M. S. İpşiroğlu, Richard Krautheimer, Max Loehr, Wolfgang Lotz, Alexander Marshack, and Meyer Schapiro, who reviewed various aspects of the book and generously helped in securing photographic material. I must also record my gratitude to the American Academy in Rome, which made it possible for me, as art historian in residence during the spring of 1960, to write the chapters on ancient art under ideal conditions, and to the Academy's indefatigable librarian, Nina Langobardi. Irene Gordon, Celia Butler, and Patricia Egan have improved the book in countless ways. Patricia Egan also deserves the chief credit for the reading list. I should like, finally, to acknowledge the admirable skill and patience of Philip Grushkin, who is responsible for the design and layout of the volume; my thanks go to him and to Adrienne Onderdonk, his assistant.

H. W. J.
1962

PREFACE AND ACKNOWLEDGMENTS
TO THE FIFTH EDITION REVISED

The Fifth Edition Revised of H. W. Janson's *History of Art* continues the process of broad change that was inaugurated in the previous edition. Whereas the changes to the Fifth Edition concentrated on art from Mannerism through the art of the twentieth century, this time the focus is on art before 1520. The differences are less sweeping, but readers familiar with earlier editions will note some significant changes in emphasis. I have brought the scholarship on ancient art up to date. In this regard I had the benefit of numerous suggestions made by Professor Andrew Stewart and Dr. Mary Ellen Soles. In several instances, however, I have followed an independent approach to ongoing controversies. Some of them are relatively minor (for example, Which battle does the *Nike of Samothrace* commemorate?). The most important, however, is the vexing question of the debt of Roman painting to Greek art, to which I devoted a year's study before siding with those specialists who see it as essentially Roman in character. I have also rethought a good deal of medieval art. I am indebted to the helpful comments of Professor Dale Kinney, who served as reader. Thus, I examined afresh the contribution of Abbot Suger in the formation of Gothic architecture, which has been undergoing a major re-evaluation of late, although again I have taken a different stand on the issue from many other writers. I have also emphasized what I regard as the critical role of Byzantium in preserving the heritage of Early Christian art and transmitting it to the Latin world, where it provided the foundation for the revolution in Gothic painting and sculpture. Finally, I have reorganized the historical background in the Introduction to Part Two and

included additional information within each chapter.

So far as the Renaissance is concerned, I have added more iconography than before, such as the inspiration of Poliziano in Botticelli's *Birth of Venus* and Raphael's *Galatea,* and the symbolism of Giorgione's *The Tempest.* The presentation of High Renaissance art has been altered, particularly in the case of Michelangelo, and more subtly where Leonardo and Raphael are considered.

This addition also completes the process of transforming the book into purely a history of Western art. It has been done with some regret, and I was especially reluctant to relinquish Islamic art. When that chapter was written, it represented the state of the art, and although our understanding has increased greatly in recent years, it would not have been difficult to bring the scholarship up to date. Nevertheless, I have decided to give it up in order to accommodate changes I felt were imperative to strengthen the treatment of other areas.

Perhaps the biggest change to the book has been the incorporation of new sections on the history of music and theater. They are frankly experimental, for although books on other disciplines have often included material on art, art-history surveys have avoided reciprocating the honor. I confess to misgivings about such an interdisciplinary approach, which is perhaps better suited to the expert than to the beginner, and about the risk of committing a naïveté often shown by colleagues in other fields when they have ventured into art. I have nonetheless decided to add them so as to suggest the larger cultural context in which the visual arts have existed. I have done so out of a deeply felt love for music and drama. However, my account is necessarily slanted to those aspects that illuminate the main content of this book. As this is by no means intended to be a general humanities book, I have placed less emphasis on the history of literature and philosophy, which are vast subjects in themselves, except insofar as they are directly relevant to the discussion.

I must also admit that I have tried to act as an advocate of modern music and theater because I appreciate the resistance that most people feel toward them, just as they do to modern art. I, too, have felt that resistance to modern culture, and I am more than sympathetic to the plight of many readers. From my own experience, I can attest that the only way to come to terms with these demanding art forms is to immerse oneself in them fully, however forbidding that may seem. The rewards are more than worth the effort.

In addition to the new sections on music and theater, the reader will also find a number of other boxed texts that appear throughout the book as supplements to the main text. These deal with such subjects as classical and Christian iconography, the religious orders, the guilds, and printmaking techniques. The Greek chapter, for example, includes discussions of the Greek gods and goddesses and the hero in Greek legend. In the chapter on Early Christian and Byzantine art, there are texts on the liturgy of the Mass, the various versions of the Bible, the life of Jesus, and biblical, church, and celestial beings. Monasticism is explored in the Romanesque art chapter, and the various printmaking techniques are explained

in the chapters on fifteenth- and nineteenth-century art.

Putting this book together is a mammoth undertaking. I can honestly say that this time around was by far the smoothest, thanks to the experienced and amicable "dream team" at Abrams, which has worked so well together on previous editions of this and other Janson volumes. Julia Moore served as project manager and developmental respondent and Joanne Greenspun as editor, with the assistance of project editor Monica Mehta and photo editor Jennifer Bright. Lydia Gershey and Yonah Schurink of Communigraph are responsible for the excellent design and prepress, and Shun Yamamoto oversaw the production process. Paul Gottlieb, Abrams' great publisher and editor-in-chief, was unfailingly supportive.

I would like to dedicate this edition to the memory of my father, who wrote the original survey of art history 35 years ago. I am keenly aware of the very broad changes I have introduced over the past several editions. He would undoubtedly be as surprised as I am by how extensive they are. They reflect changes in scholarship, as well as the inevitable differences in taste and outlook between two authors, no matter how closely related they may be. Yet my goal has always been to maintain the identity and integrity of the book as he originally conceived it. It is my hope that he would recognize the book as his. Fortunately, my mother is still alive, and since she played an integral role in its inception (not to mention mine), this edition is happily dedicated to her as well.

A. F. J.
1997

PRELUDE

The art-historical approach of this book is often labeled formalistic insofar as it is concerned with the evolution of style, yet this use of the label should not be taken to mean only the visual analysis of aesthetic qualities. It also draws on iconography, that is, the meaning of a work of art, and what Erwin Panofsky called iconology, its cultural context. Thus, it embodies what might be called the classical approach to art history as defined by three generations of mainly German-born scholars, including H. W. Janson, who was himself a student of Panofsky. It is well suited to introducing beginners to art history by providing the framework for how to look at and respond to art in museums and galleries—something both authors have themselves greatly enjoyed throughout their lifetimes.

Nonetheless, readers should be aware that there are other approaches that have benefited art history and are worthy of attention. The oldest is Marxism, which examines art in terms of the social and political conditions determined by the prevailing economic system. It has been especially useful in treating art since the Industrial Revolution, which created the historical circumstances analyzed so tellingly by Karl Marx in the middle of the nineteenth century. It remains to be seen what will become of Marxist art history in the wake of the collapse of communist governments in Russia and Eastern Europe.

Psychology, too, has added many insights to the private meaning that works of art have held for their creators, particularly when that meaning has been hidden even to the artists themselves. Although the more extreme attempts at psychoanalyzing Leonardo and Michelangelo, for instance, have caused some scholars to distrust this method, works such as Fuseli's *The Nightmare* (whose meaning was analyzed by H. W. Janson in a pioneering article) are incomprehensible without it. Another case in point: at my editor's suggestion, I have traced the theme of a woman holding a mirror from the sixteenth century to modern times as a "textbook" example of iconography, using works by Hans Baldung Grien, Simon Vouet, François Boucher, Pablo Picasso, Erich Heckel, and Cindy Sherman as examples. But the meaning of this fascinating image is vastly enriched by knowing that it is a classic representation of the anima, one of the psychological archetypes defined by Freud's former disciple Carl Jung, which personifies the feminine tendencies in the male psyche and acts as a guide to the inner realm. This discovery opens up a field of analysis that I invite readers to explore on their own.

Three new approaches—feminism, multiculturalism, and deconstruction—are perhaps the most radical of all. Feminism reexamines art history from the point of view of gender. Depictions of the woman with a mirror virtually call for a feminist treatment, which yields a very different understanding of their covert significance, as readers may readily ascertain by questioning these works themselves. Because it is embedded in current gender politics in Western society, there is risk that a major shift in social outlook might call some of its conclusions into question. In principle, however, feminist theory is applicable to the full scope of art history. It has certainly forced everyone to reconsider what is "good" art. After all, when this book first appeared, not a single woman artist was included—nor, I hasten to add, was one to be found in any other art-history survey. Today, such omissions seem nothing short of incredible.

Feminism in turn may be seen as part of the larger shift to multiculturalism, which itself addresses a very real gap in our understanding of the art of traditional and non-Western cultures. The representation of some African-American artists, for example, reflects the inclusion of artists who embody very different sensibilities from that of the European and American mainstreams. In these selections, I have taken a stand about what art I think is most significant, and not all readers will agree with it, since it favors universality over ethnocentricity. This position reflects in part my own sensitivities about the stereotyping that the latter fosters on both sides of the racial fence. In my opinion, it forces a cultural dead end, although I do not deny that art with a racial "edge" has a legitimate place. Feminism and multiculturalism have both attacked the "canon" of masterpieces in this and similar books as embodying a traditional chauvinism and colonialist attitudes. I leave readers to judge the issue for themselves.

Because they are so central to Postmodernist thought, I have attempted to summarize semiotics and deconstruction toward the end of this book, knowing full well that their followers will never be satisfied, partly because each treatment is necessarily brief and partly because I am not a convert to either cause. I took on the task in order to help the reader gain a little better understanding of the world of ideas we live in. I have to say that I enjoyed drinking from the cup of Postmodernism, even though it is ultimately not to my taste. It provided a brisk, refreshing tonic, hardly the poisonous brew that I might have expected. Rather than emerging gloomy from the experience, I find myself surprisingly optimistic as we fly headlong into the new millennium.

Let me add that I am fundamentally sympathetic to semiotics, which became an interest of mine more than 20 years ago, though I ultimately find Noam Chomsky's theory of linguistics to be more satisfying. Deconstruction has likewise made art historians reconsider meaning in new ways that have breathed fresh life into the field. Nevertheless, I know from classroom experience that semiotics is nearly impossible for the art-history novice to comprehend. Deconstruction, which has taken scholarship by storm in recent years, is even more taxing. What began as an internecine feud between two schools of French semiologists has spread to art history, where it pits older, mostly German-trained scholars against a younger generation using deconstruction as a way of finding their place in the sun. And that is perhaps the point. People are constantly recasting art history in their image. But if art history reflects our time, the reader may well wonder how it can have any claim to objectivity and, hence, validity. In actual fact, people's understanding of history has always changed with the times. How could it be otherwise? Indeed, it seems almost necessary for each generation to reinvent history to understand both the past and the present. The danger is that the intrusion of ideology, regardless of noble intent, will undermine the search for Truth, no matter how relative it may be. Such a thing happened during the 1930s, when scholarship was made to serve the political ends of dictatorships—and which led Panofsky and Janson to leave Germany.

Neither author of the present volume is an ideologue. Both are humanists who believe that the study of the humane letters is an enjoyable and enriching experience. Such a view carries with it the implicit charge (admittedly not always honored in the observance) that scholarly discourse be temperate, though it is rarely dispassionate. I would encourage the reader to examine all forms of art history with an open mind. One cannot view something so rich and complex from a single perspective any more than it is possible to see a diamond from one angle. Each approach has something to contribute to our understanding. To be sure, a plea for tolerance may seem an anachronism at a time when art history, like all fields, has become so contentious. In this regard, scholarship is simply the mirror of the rapid political change, social unrest, ideological intolerance, and religious fanaticism that characterize postindustrial society and the new world order that is emerging in its wake.

Let me end these rather personal remarks with a surprising admission. For nearly 40 years, both authors have given a great deal of thought to this book, which is written in the authoritative tones that intellectuals habitually adopt as their public voice. It is difficult, of course, to resist the temptation to pontificate—to hand down the "canon" as if it were immutable law. Yet, if the truth be told, the experience of surveying such a broad field as art history provides a lesson in humility. One becomes only too aware of the painful omissions and how little one knows about any given subject in this age of increasing specialization. If it requires the egotism of the gods to undertake such a project in the first place, in the end one sees it clearly for what it is: an act of hubris. It also requires a faith in the power of reason to produce such a synthesis, something that is in short supply in this skeptical era.

A. F. J.

INTRODUCTION

ART AND THE ARTIST

"What is art?" Few questions provoke such heated debate and provide so few satisfactory answers. If definitive conclusions are impossible, there is still a good deal that can be said. Art is first of all a *word*, which itself acknowledges both the idea and the fact of art. Without a word, one might well ask whether art exists in the first place. The term, after all, is not found in every society. Yet art is *made* everywhere. Art, therefore, is also an object, but it is not just any kind of object. Art is an *aesthetic object*. It is meant to be looked at and appreciated for its intrinsic value. Its special qualities set art apart, so that it is often placed away from everyday life—in museums, caves, or churches.

What does *aesthetic* mean? By definition, aesthetic is "that which concerns the beautiful." Of course, not all art is beautiful to each person's eyes, but it is art nonetheless. No matter how unsatisfactory, the term will have to do for lack of a better one. Aesthetics is, strictly speaking, a branch of philosophy which has occupied thinkers from Plato to the present day. Like all matters philosophical, it is subject to debate. During the last hundred years, aesthetics has also become a field of psychology, a field which has come to equally little agreement. Why should this be so? On the one hand, people the world over make much the same fundamental judgments. Our brains and nervous systems are the same because, according to recent theory, everyone is descended from one woman who lived in Africa a quarter-million years ago. On the other hand, taste is conditioned solely by culture, which is so varied that it is impossible to reduce art to any one set of precepts. It would seem, therefore, that absolute qualities in art must elude us, that we cannot escape viewing works of art in the context of time and circumstance, whether past or present. How indeed could it be otherwise, so long as art is still being created all around us, opening our eyes almost daily to new experiences and forcing us to readjust our understanding?

Imagination

We all dream. That is imagination at work. To imagine means simply to make an image—a picture—in our minds. Human beings are not the only creatures who have imagination. Even animals dream. However, there is a profound difference between human and animal imagination. Humans are the only creatures who can tell one another about imagination in words or pictures. No other animal has ever been observed to draw a recognizable image spontaneously in the wild. In fact, their only images have been produced under carefully controlled laboratory conditions that tell us more about the experimenter than they do about art. There can be little doubt, on the other hand, that people possess an artistic faculty. By the age of five every normal child has drawn a moon pie-face. The ability to make art is one of our most distinctive features; it separates us from all other creatures across an evolutionary gap that is unbridgeable.

Just as an embryo retraces much of the human evolutionary past, so budding artists reinvent the first stages of art. Soon, however, they complete that process and begin to respond to the culture around them. Thus even children's art is subject to the taste and outlook of the society that shapes his or her personality. In fact, children's art is generally judged according to the same criteria as adult art, only in appropriately simpler terms, and with good reason. The youngster must develop all the skills that go into adult art: coordination, intellect, personality, imagination, creativity, and aesthetic judgment. Seen this way, the making of a youthful artist is a process as fragile as growing up itself, and one that can be stunted at any step by the vicissitudes of life. No wonder that so few continue their creative aspirations into adulthood.

The imagination is one of our most mysterious facets. It can be regarded as the connector between the conscious and the subconscious, where most of our brain activity takes place. It is the very glue that holds our personality, intellect, and

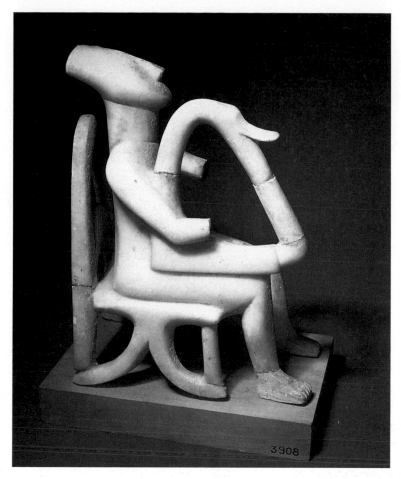

1. *Harpist*, so-called Orpheus. Marble statuette from Amorgos in the Cyclades. Latter part of the 3rd millennium B.C. Height 8¹/2" (21.5 cm). National Archaeological Museum, Athens

spirituality together. Because the imagination responds to all three, it acts in lawful, if unpredictable, ways that are determined by the psyche and the mind. Even the most private artistic statements can be understood on some level, if only an intuitive one. The imagination is important, as it allows us to conceive of all kinds of possibilities in the future and to understand the past in a way that has real survival value. It is an essential part of our makeup. The ability to make art, in contrast, must have been acquired relatively recently in the course of evolution. The record of the earliest art is lost. Human beings have been walking the earth for nearly 4.5 million years, although our own species (*homo sapiens*) is much younger than that. By comparison, the oldest known prehistoric art was made only about 35,000 years ago, but it was undoubtedly the culmination of a long development no longer traceable. Even the art found today in the simplest traditional culture represents a late stage of development within a stable society.

Who were the first artists? In all likelihood, they were shamans. Like the legendary Greek poet Orpheus, who sang his words while playing the lyre, they were magicians who were believed to have divine powers of inspiration and to be able to enter the underworld of the subconscious in a death-like trance, but, unlike ordinary mortals, they were then able

to return to the realm of the living. Just such a figure seems to be represented by *Harpist* (fig. 1) from nearly 5,000 years ago. A work of unprecedented complexity for its time, it was carved by a remarkably gifted artist who makes the beholder feel the visionary rapture of a bard as he sings his legend. With this unique ability to penetrate the unknown and rare talent for expressing it through art, the artist-shaman gained control over the forces hidden in human beings and nature. Even today the artist remains a magician whose work can mystify and move us—an embarrassing fact to civilized people, who do not readily relinquish their veneer of rational control.

In a larger sense art, like science and religion, fulfills humanity's innate urge to comprehend itself and the universe. This function makes art especially significant and, hence, worthy of our attention. Art has the power to penetrate to the core of our being, which recognizes itself in the creative act. For that reason, art represents its creator's deepest understanding and highest aspirations. At the same time, artists often play an important role as the articulators of our shared beliefs and values, which they express through an ongoing tradition to their audience.

Given the many factors that feed into it, art must play a very special role in the artist's personality. Sigmund Freud, the founder of modern psychiatry, conceived of art primarily in

2. Pablo Picasso. *Bull's Head*. 1943. Bronze cast bicycle parts, height 16¹/8" (41 cm). Musée Picasso, Paris

terms of sublimation outside of consciousness. Such a view hardly does justice to artistic creativity, since art is not simply a negative force at the mercy of our neuroses but a positive expression that integrates diverse aspects of personality. Indeed, when we look at the art of someone who is mentally ill, we may be struck by its vividness; but we instinctively sense that something is wrong, because the expression is incomplete. Artists may sometimes be tortured by the burden of their genius, but they can never be fully creative under the thrall of psychosis.

Creativity

What is meant by making art? At the very least, a work of art must be a tangible thing shaped by human hands. (This definition eliminates the confusion of treating as works of art such natural phenomena as flowers, seashells, or sunsets, which are raised to their status as art when they are depicted in still lifes and landscapes.) It is a far from sufficient definition, to be sure, since human beings make countless things other than works of art. Still, it will serve as a starting point. Now let us look at the striking *Bull's Head* by Picasso (fig. 2), which seems to consist of nothing but the seat and handlebars of an old bicycle. How meaningful is our formula here? Of course the materials used by Picasso are fabricated, but it would be absurd to insist that

Picasso must share the credit with the manufacturer, since the seat and handlebars in themselves are not works of art.

While we feel a certain jolt when we first recognize the ingredients of this visual pun, we also sense that it was a stroke of genius to put them together in this unique way, and we cannot very well deny that it is a work of art. Yet the handiwork—the mounting of the seat on the handlebars—is ridiculously simple. What is far from simple is the leap of the imagination by which Picasso recognized a bull's head in these unlikely objects. That is something only he could have done. Clearly, then, the making of a work of art should not be confused with manual skill or craftsmanship. Some works of art may demand a great deal of technical discipline; others do not. And even the most painstaking piece of craft does not deserve to be called a work of art unless it involves a leap of the imagination.

But if this is true, did not the real making of the *Bull's Head* take place in the artist's mind? No, that is not so, either. Suppose that, instead of actually putting the two pieces together and showing them to us, Picasso merely said, "You know, today I saw a bicycle seat and handlebars that looked just like a bull's head to me." Then there would be no work of art and his remark would not even strike us as an interesting bit of conversation. Moreover, Picasso himself would not have felt the satisfaction of having created something on the basis of his leap of the imagination alone. Once he had conceived his visual pun, he could never be sure that it would really work unless he put it into effect.

Thus the artist's hands, however modest the task they may have to perform, play an essential part in the creative process. Picasso's *Bull's Head* is, of course, an ideally simple case, involving only one leap of the imagination and a manual act in response to it: once the seat had been properly placed on the handlebars (and then cast in bronze), the job was done. The leap of the imagination is sometimes experienced as a flash of inspiration, but only rarely does a new idea emerge full-blown like the Greek goddess Athena from the head of her father, Zeus. Instead, it is usually preceded by a long gestation period in which all the hard work is done without finding the key to the solution to the problem. At the critical point, the imagination makes connections between seemingly unrelated parts and recombines them.

Ordinarily, artists do not work with ready-made parts but with materials that have little or no shape of their own. The creative process consists of a long series of leaps of the imagination and the artist's attempts to give them form by shaping the material. In painting, for example, the hand tries to carry out the commands of the imagination and puts down a brushstroke, but the result may not be quite what had been expected, partly because all matter resists the human will, partly because the image in the artist's mind is constantly shifting and changing, so that the commands of the imagination cannot be very precise. In fact, the mental image begins to come into focus only as the artist "draws the line somewhere." That line then becomes part—the only fixed part—of the image. The rest of the image, as yet unborn, remains fluid. Each time the artist adds another line, a new leap of the imagination is needed to incorporate that line into the ever-growing mental image. If the line cannot be incorporated, it is discarded and a new one put down.

In this way, by a constant flow of impulses back and forth between the mind and the partly shaped material, the artist gradually defines more and more of the image, until at last all of it has been given visible form. Needless to say, artistic creation is too subtle and intimate an experience to permit an exact step-by-step description. Only artists can observe it fully, but they are so absorbed by it that they have great difficulty explaining it to us. The metaphor of birth comes closer to the truth than would a description of the process in terms of a transfer or projection of the image from the artist's mind, for the making of a work of art is both joyous and painful, replete with surprises, and in no sense mechanical. There is, moreover, ample testimony that artists themselves tend to look upon their creation as living things. Perhaps that is why creativity was once a concept reserved for god, as only he could give material form to an idea. Indeed, the artist's labors are much like the Creation told in the Bible; but this divine ability was not fully realized until Michelangelo described the anguish and glory of the creative experience when he spoke of "liberating the figure from the marble that imprisons it." Evidently he started the process of carving a statue by trying to visualize a figure in the rough, rectilinear block as it came to him from the quarry. (At times he may even have done so while picking out his material on the spot.)

At first Michelangelo did not see the figure any more clearly than one can see an unborn child inside the womb, but he may have believed that he could see isolated "signs of life" within the marble—a knee or an elbow pressing against the surface. To get a firmer grip on this dimly felt, fluid image, he was in the habit of making numerous drawings, and sometimes small models in wax or clay, before he dared to assault the "marble prison" itself. For that, he knew, was the final contest between himself and his material. Once he started carving, every stroke of the chisel would commit him more and more to a specific conception of the figure hidden in the block, and the marble would permit him to free the figure whole only if his guess as to its shape was correct.

Sometimes he did not guess well enough. The stone refused to give up some essential part of its prisoner, and Michelangelo, defeated, left the work unfinished, as he did with his *Awakening Slave* (fig. 3), whose very gesture seems to record the vain struggle for liberation. Looking at the block, we may get some inkling of Michelangelo's difficulties here. But could he not have finished the statue in *some* fashion? Surely there is enough material left for that. Well, he probably could have, but perhaps not in the way he wanted, and so he abandoned the sculpture.

Clearly, then, the making of a work of art has little in common with what is ordinarily meant by "making." It is a strange and risky business in which the makers never quite know what they are making until they have actually made it. Or, to put it another way, it is a game of find-and-seek in which the seekers are not sure what they are looking for until they have found it. In the case of the *Bull's Head* it is the bold "finding" that impresses us most; in the *Awakening Slave*, the strenuous "seeking." To the non-artist, it seems hard to believe that this uncertainty, this need to take a chance, should be the essence of the artist's work. We all tend to think of "making" in terms of artisans or manufacturers who know exactly what they want to produce from the very outset, pick the tools best suited to the task, and are sure of what they are doing at every step. Such "making" is a two-phase affair: first, artisans make a plan, then they act on it. And because they—or their customers—have made all the important decisions in advance, they have to worry only about the means, rather than the ends, while carrying out this plan. There is thus comparatively little risk in their endeavors, which as a consequence tend to become routine. It may even be replaced by the mechanical labor of a machine.

No machine, on the other hand, can replace the artist. In art, conception and execution go hand in hand and are so completely interdependent that they cannot be separated from each other. Whereas artisans generally attempt what they know to be possible, artists are driven to attempt the impossible—or at least the improbable or seemingly unimaginable. Who, after all, would have conceived that a bull's head was hidden in the seat and handlebars of a bicycle until Picasso discovered it? Did he not, almost literally, "make a silk purse out of a sow's ear"? No wonder the artist's way of working is so resistant to any set rules, while the artisan's tends to encourage standardization and regularity. The difference is that the artist *creates* instead of merely *makes* something, although the word has been done to death by overuse, and every child and fashion designer is labeled "creative."

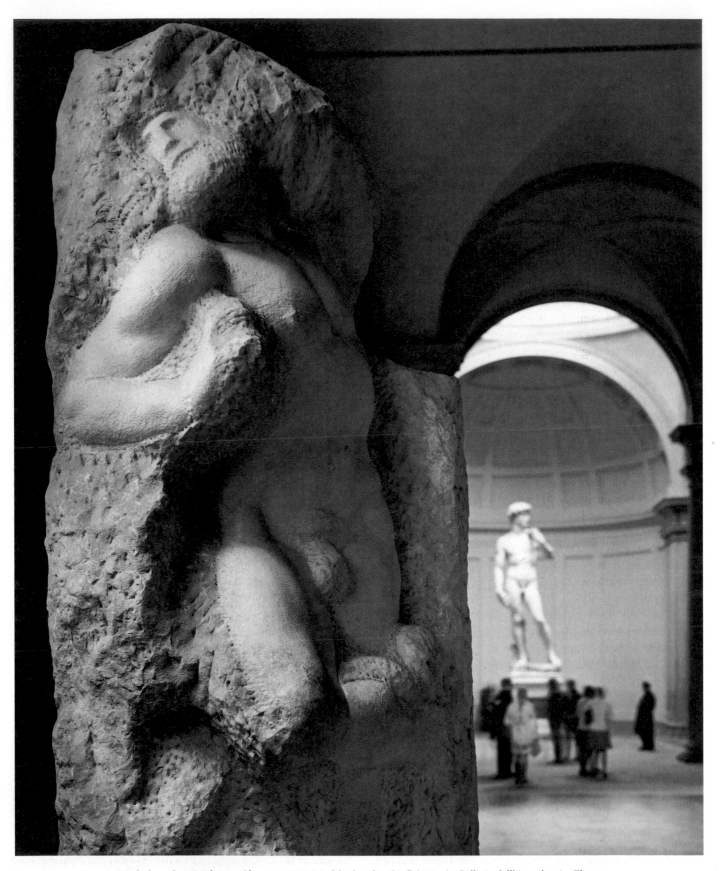

3. Michelangelo. *Awakening Slave.* c. 1525. Marble, height 8'11" (2.7 m). Galleria dell'Accademia, Florence

Needless to say, there have always been many more artisans than artists, since people's need for the familiar and expected far exceeds their capacity to absorb the original but often deeply unsettling experiences they get from works of art. The urge to penetrate unknown realms, to achieve something original, may be felt by every one of us now and then. To that extent, we can all fancy ourselves potential artists—mute, inglorious Miltons as it were. What sets the real artist apart is not so much the desire to *seek*, but that mysterious ability to *find*, which is called talent. It is often called a "gift," implying that it is a sort of present from some higher power; or as "genius," a term which originally meant that a higher power—a kind of "good demon"—inhabits and acts through the artist.

Talent must not be confused with aptitude. Aptitude is what the artisan needs. It means a better-than-average knack for doing something. An aptitude is fairly constant and specific. It can be measured with some success by means of tests that permit us to predict future performance. Creative talent, on the other hand, seems utterly unpredictable. It can be spotted only on the basis of *past* performance. Even past performance is not enough to ensure that a given artist will continue to produce on the same level. Some artists reach a creative peak quite early in their careers and then "go dry," while others, after a slow and unpromising start, may achieve astonishingly original work in middle age or even later.

Originality

Originality is what ultimately distinguishes art from craft. It is the yardstick of artistic greatness or importance. Unfortunately, it is also very hard to define. The usual synonyms—uniqueness, novelty, freshness—do not help us very much, and the dictionaries tell us only that an original work must not be a copy. If we want to rate works of art on an "originality scale," the problem does not lie in deciding whether or not a given work is original (the obvious copies and reproductions are for the most part easy enough to eliminate) but in establishing exactly *how* original it is.

Straightforward copies can usually be recognized as such on internal evidence alone. If the copyists are merely conscientious, they produce works of craft. The execution strikes us as pedestrian and out of tune with the conception of the work. There are also likely to be small slipups that can be spotted in much the same way as misprints in a text. But what happens when great artists copy each other? In such cases, they do not simply produce copies in the accepted sense of the word, since they do not try to achieve the effect of a duplicate. Rather, they do so purely for their own instruction, transcribing their models accurately, yet with their own inimitable rhythm, and are not the least constrained or intimidated by the other work of art. In other words, they "represent" (they do not copy) their models.

Ordinarily, though, the link is not immediately obvious. Édouard Manet's famous painting *Luncheon on the Grass* (*Le Déjeuner sur l'herbe*; fig. 4, page 22) seemed so revolutionary a work when first exhibited more than 130 years ago that it caused a scandal; the artist had dared to show an undressed young woman next to two men in fashionable contemporary dress. People assumed that Manet had intended to represent an actual event. Not until many years later did an art historian

discover the source of these figures: a group of classical deities from an engraving by Marcantonio Raimondi after a design supplied to him by Raphael (fig. 5). The relationship, so striking once it has been pointed out to us, had escaped attention, for Manet did not *copy* or *represent* the Raphael composition. He merely *borrowed* its main outlines while translating the figures into modern terms.

Had his contemporaries known of this, the *Luncheon* would have seemed a rather less disreputable kind of outing to them, since then the hallowed shade of Raphael could be seen to hover nearby as a sort of chaperon. For us, the main effect of the comparison is to make the cool, formal quality of Manet's figures even more conspicuous. But does it decrease our respect for his originality? True, he is "indebted" to Raphael; yet his way of bringing the forgotten old composition back to life is in itself so original and creative that he may be said to have more than repaid his debt. As a matter of fact, Raphael's figures are just as "derivative" as Manet's. They stem from still older sources which lead us back to ancient Roman art and beyond (compare the relief of *River Gods*, fig. 6).

Thus Manet, Raphael, and the Roman river-gods form three links in a chain of relationships that arises out of the distant past and continues into the future—for the *Luncheon* on *the Grass* has in turn served as a source of more recent works of art. Nor is this an exceptional case. All works of art anywhere—yes, even such works as Picasso's *Bull's Head*—are part of similar chains that link them to their predecessors. If it is true that "no man is an island," the same can be said of works of art. The sum total of these chains makes a web in which every work of art occupies its own specific place. This is known as *tradition*. Without tradition—the word means "that which has been handed down to us"—no originality would be possible. It is clear that Manet took tradition as his starting point and intended to link his painting to the past through well-hidden quotations in his "scandalous" group, as well as in the figure of the woman bathing and the landscape. Tradition provides, as it were, the firm platform from which artists make their leap of the imagination. The place where they land will then become part of the web and serve as a point of departure for further leaps.

And for us, too, the web of tradition is equally essential. Whether we are aware of it or not, tradition is the framework within which we inevitably form our opinions of works of art and assess their degree of originality. A masterpiece is a work that contributes to our vision of life and leaves us profoundly moved. Yet, it can also bear the closest scrutiny and withstand the test of time. Let us not forget, however, that such assessments should always remain subject to revision. In fact, tastes have varied greatly over time. Works that were once regarded as cornerstones of tradition have been discarded, while others that were ignored or even despised appear to be important works in their own right. Thus the "canon," or core body, of Western art is constantly shifting, rather than being static and immutable. One reason for this change is overexposure, which has reduced the greatest masterpieces to commodities through mass-merchandising in popular culture. Leonardo's *Mona Lisa*, Rodin's *The Thinker*, and Munch's *The Scream* are found everywhere in advertisements, humorous cards, and the like, so that they have become victims of their fame.

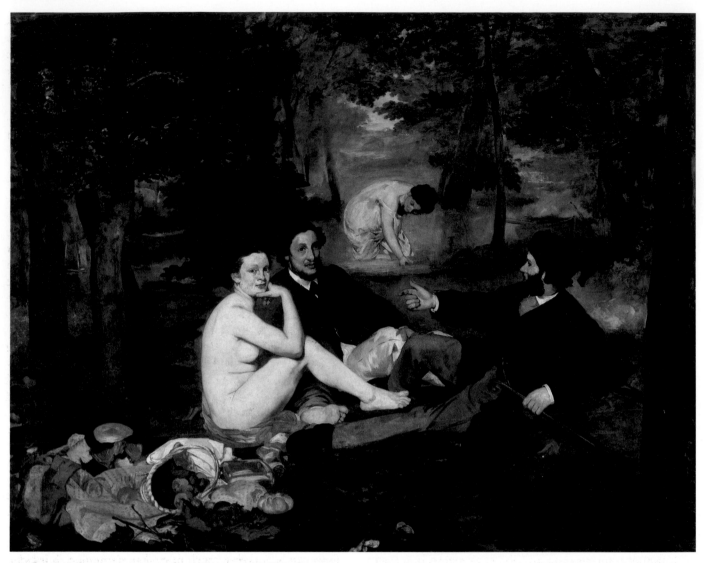

4. Édouard Manet. *Luncheon on the Grass (Le Déjeuner sur l'herbe).* 1863. Oil on canvas, 7' x 8'10" (2.1 x 2.6 m). Musée d'Orsay, Paris

5. Marcantonio Raimondi, after Raphael.
The Judgment of Paris (detail). c. 1520. Engraving.
The Metropolitan Museum of Art, New York

Rogers Fund, 1919

6. *River Gods.* Detail of Roman sarcophagus. 3rd century A.D.
Villa Medici, Rome

If originality distinguishes art from craft, tradition serves as the common meeting ground of the two. Most beginning artists start out on the level of craft by imitating other works of art. In this way, they gradually absorb the artistic tradition of their time and place until they have gained a firm footing in it. But only the truly gifted ever leave that stage of conventional competence and become creators in their own right. No one, after all, can be taught how to create—only how to go through the motions of creating. The aspiring artist of talent will eventually achieve the real thing. What the apprentice or art student learns are skills and techniques: established ways of drawing, painting, carving, designing—established ways of *seeing*.

Nevertheless, one of the attributes that distinguishes great artists is their consummate technical command. This superior talent is recognized by other artists, who admire their work and seek to emulate it. This is not to say that facility alone is sufficient. Far from it! The academic painters and sculptors of the nineteenth century were as a group among the most proficient artists in history—as well as the dullest. Still, complete technical command is a requisite of masterpieces, which are distinguished by their superior execution.

When would-be artists sense that their talents are not great enough to succeed in the fine arts as painters, sculptors, or architects, many of them take up one of the special fields known collectively as "the applied arts," for which they can be rewarded in less artistically risky work: illustration, typographic design, industrial design, and interior design, for example. The applied arts are more deeply enmeshed in our everyday lives and thus cater to a far wider public than do painting and sculpture. Their purpose, as the name suggests, is to beautify the useful—an important and valued end. They provide some scope for originality to their more ambitious practitioners, but the flow of creative endeavor is cramped by such factors as the cost and availability of materials or manufacturing processes, as well as accepted notions of what is useful, fitting, or desirable.

Nevertheless, it is often difficult to maintain the distinction between fine and applied art. Medieval painting, for instance, is to a large extent "applied," in the sense that it embellishes surfaces which serve other, practical purposes as well—walls, book pages, windows, furniture. The same may be said of much ancient and medieval sculpture. Greek vases, although functional pottery, were sometimes decorated by artists of very impressive talent. Indeed, the history of applied art is filled with artists of considerable stature. How can this be so, if art and the crafts are so separate? The reason is that what defines art is not any difference in materials or techniques from the applied arts but the willingness to take risks in the quest for bold, new ideas. In architecture the distinction between art and applied art breaks down altogether, since the design of every building, from country cottage to cathedral, reflects external limitations imposed upon it by the practical purpose of the structure, by the site, by cost factors, materials, and technology. (The only "pure" architecture is imaginary, unbuilt architecture.) Thus architecture is, almost by definition, an applied art, but it is also a major art (as against the other applied arts, which are often called the "minor arts").

The graphic arts, which comprise the pictorial arts outside painting, especially those that rely on line rather than color,

form a special case of their own. Drawings are original works of art; that is, they are entirely by the artist's own hand. With prints, however, the relationship between artist and image is more complex. Prints are not unique images but multiple impressions of images made by mechanical means on paper or other suitable material. Perhaps the distinction between original and copy is not so critical in printmaking after all. Printmakers must usually copy onto the plate a composition that was first worked out in a drawing, whether their own or someone else's. From the beginning, many prints have been made, at least in part, by artisans whose technical skill is necessary to ensure the outcome. Woodcuts and engraving in particular were traditionally dependent on craftsmanship, which may explain why so few creative geniuses have made them and have generally been content to let others produce prints from their designs. Although it does not require the artist's intervention at every step of the way, printmaking usually involves the artist's supervision and even active participation, so that the process can be thought of as a collaborative effort. *The Judgment of Paris* in figure 5 is an example of this type of work. Raphael had such admiration for Marcantonio's sensitive interpretations of his paintings that he began to make drawings for him to translate into engravings—a privilege enjoyed by no other printmaker. Because the design was conceived expressly with him in mind, Marcantonio's contribution was just as essential as, and hence no less original than, Raphael's.

Meaning and Style

Why do people create art? Surely one reason is an irresistible urge to adorn themselves and decorate the world around them. Both are part of a larger desire, not to remake the world in their image but to recast themselves and their environment in ideal form. Art is, however, much more than decoration. It is laden with meaning, even if that content is sometimes slender or obscure. What do we mean by content? The word encompasses not only the subject matter and literal meaning (its iconography) but its appearance as well, for the visual elements are themselves filled with significance. Art enables us to communicate our understanding in ways that cannot be expressed otherwise. In art, as in language, human beings are above all inventors of symbols that convey complex thoughts in new ways. We must think of art not in terms of everyday prose but of poetry, which is free to rearrange conventional vocabulary and syntax in order to convey new, often multiple, meanings and moods. A work of art likewise suggests much more than it states. It communicates partly by implying meanings through pose, facial expression, allegory, and the like. And like a poem, the value of art lies equally in what it says and how it says it.

But what is art trying to say? Artists often provide no clear explanation, since the work is the statement itself. If they could say what they mean in words, they would surely be writers instead. Fortunately, certain visual symbols and responses occur so regularly over time and place that they can be regarded as virtually universal. Nevertheless, their exact meaning is specific to each particular culture, giving rise to art's incredible diversity.

The meaning, or content, of art is inseparable from its formal qualities, its style. The word *style* is derived from *stilus*, the writing instrument of the ancient Romans. Originally, it referred to distinctive ways of writing—the shape of the letters as well as the choice of words. Now, style is used loosely to mean the distinctive way a thing is done in any field of human endeavor. It is a term of praise in most cases: "to have style" means to have distinction, to stand out. A thing that has style also has inner coherence, or unity.

In the visual arts, style means the particular way in which the forms that make up any given work of art are chosen and fitted together. To art historians the study of styles is of great importance. It not only enables them to find out, by means of careful analysis and comparison, when, where, and by whom something was produced, but it also leads them to understand the artist's intention as expressed through the work's style, the way it looks. This intention depends on both the artist's personality and the context of time and place. Accordingly, art historians speak of "period styles" if they are concerned with those features which distinguish, let us say, Egyptian art as a whole from Greek art. Within these broad period styles they in turn distinguish the styles of particular phases, such as the Egyptian Old Kingdom. And wherever it seems appropriate, they differentiate national or local styles within a period, until they arrive at the personal styles of individual artists. Even these may need to be subdivided further into the various phases of an artist's development. The extent to which they are able to categorize effectively depends on the degree of internal coherence, and on how much of a sense of continuity there is in the body of material they are dealing with. Thus art, like language, requires that we learn the style and outlook of a country, period, and artist if it is to be understood properly.

Style needs only be appropriate to the *intent* of the work. This idea is not always easy to accept. Westerners are accustomed to a tradition of naturalism, in which art imitates nature as closely as possible. But the accurate reproduction of visual phenomena, called illusionism, is just one vehicle for expressing an artist's understanding of reality. Truth, it seems, is indeed relative, for it is a matter not simply of what our eyes tell us but also of the concepts through which our perceptions are filtered. There is, then, no reason to place a premium on realism (a term that is sometimes taken to mean truth to life, in contradistinction to naturalism, though most people use them interchangeably). The advantage of realism at face value is that it *seems* easier to understand. The disadvantage is that representational art, like prose, is always bound to the literal meaning and appearance of the everyday world, at least to some extent. Actually, realism is exceptional in the history of art and is not even necessary to its purposes. Any image is a separate and self-contained reality which has its own ends and responds to its own imperatives as determined by the artist's creativity. Even the most convincing illusion is the product of the artist's imagination and understanding, so that we must always ask why this subject was chosen and made in this way rather than in some other way.

Self-Expression and Audience

The birth of a work of art is an intensely private experience, so much so that many artists can work only when completely alone and refuse to show their unfinished pieces to anyone. Yet it must, as a final step, be shared by the public in order for the birth to be successful. Artists do not create merely for their own satisfaction, but want their work validated by others. In fact, the creative process is not completed until the work has found an audience. In the end, works of art exist in order to be liked rather than to be debated.

This seeming paradox can be resolved once we understand what artists mean by "public." They are concerned not with *the* public as a statistical entity but with their particular public, their audience; quality rather than wide approval is what matters to them. At a minimum, this audience needs to consist of only one or two people whose opinions they value. Ordinarily, artists also need patrons among their audience who will purchase their work, thus combining moral and financial support. In contrast to customers of applied art, for example, who know from previous experience what they will get when they buy the products of craftsmanship, the "audience" for art merits such adjectives as critical, fickle, receptive, engaged. It is uncommitted, free to accept or reject, so that anything placed before it is on trial—nobody knows in advance how it will receive the work. Hence, there is a tension between artist and audience that has no counterpart in the relationship of artisan and customer.

The audience whose approval looms so large in artists' minds is a limited and special one. Its members may be other artists as well as patrons, friends, critics, and interested viewers. The one quality they all have in common is an informed love of works of art—an attitude at once discriminating and enthusiastic that lends particular weight to their judgments. They are, in a word, experts, people whose authority rests on experience and knowledge. In reality, there is no sharp break, no difference in kind, between the expert and the layperson, only a difference in degree.

Tastes

Deciding what is art and rating a work of art are two separate problems. If there were an absolute method for distinguishing art from non-art, it would not necessarily help in measuring quality. People tend to compound the two problems into one. Often when they ask, "Why is that art?" they mean, "Why is that *good* art?" How often have we heard this question asked before a strange, disquieting work in a museum or art exhibition? There usually is an undertone of exasperation, for the question implies that the viewer doesn't think he or she is looking at a work of art, but that the experts—the critics, museum curators, art historians—must suppose it to be one, or why else would they put it on public display? Clearly, their standards are very different from others. People wish for a few simple, clear-cut rules to go by. Then maybe they would learn to like what they see—they would know "why it is art." But the experts do not post exact rules, and the lay person is apt to fall back upon a final line of defense: "Well, I don't know anything about art, but I know what I like."

It is a formidable roadblock, this stock phrase, in the path of understanding between expert and lay audience. Until not so very long ago, there was no great need for the two parties to communicate with each other. The general public had little voice in matters of art and therefore could not challenge the judgment of the expert few. Today both sides are aware of the barrier between them and the need to level it. Let us examine the roadblock and the various unspoken assumptions that buttress it.

The fact that art is a complex and in many ways mysterious human activity about which even the experts can hope to offer only tentative and partial conclusions can be taken as confirming the belief that "I don't know anything about art." But are there really people who know nothing about art? The answer must be no for nearly all adults, who cannot help knowing *something* about it, just as everybody knows something about politics and economics, no matter how indifferent one may be to the issues of the day. Art is so much a part of the fabric of daily life that it is encountered all the time, even if the contacts are limited to magazine covers, advertising posters, war memorials, television, and the buildings where we live, work, and worship. Much of this art, to be sure, is pretty shoddy—art at third- and fourth-hand, worn out by endless repetition, representing the common denominator of popular taste. Still, it is art of a sort, and since it is the only art most people experience, it molds their ideas on art in general. When they say, "I know what I like," they may really mean, "I like what I know (and I am uncomfortable with whatever fails to match the things I am familiar with)." Such likes are not in truth so much theirs as those imposed by habit and culture without any personal choice. To like what we know and to distrust what we do not know is an age-old human trait. The past tends to be "the good old days," while the future seems fraught with danger.

But why should so many people cherish the notion of making personal choices in art when in fact they do not? There is another unspoken assumption at work here that goes something like this. "Since art is such an 'unruly' subject that even the experts keep disagreeing with each other, my opinion is as good as theirs. It's all a matter of subjective preference. In fact, my opinion may be better than theirs, because as a lay person I react to art in a direct, straightforward fashion, without having my view obstructed by a lot of complicated facts and theories. There must be something wrong with a work of art if it takes an expert to appreciate it." On the contrary, experts appreciate art more than other people precisely because of their greater knowledge. Expertise requires only an open mind and a capacity to absorb new experiences. So as their understanding grows, most people find themselves liking a great many more things than they had thought possible at the start. They gradually acquire the courage of their own convictions, until they are able to say, with some justice, that they know what they like.

LOOKING AT ART

The Visual Elements

We live in a sea of images conveying the culture and learning of modern civilization. Fostered by an unprecedented media explosion, this "visual background noise" has become so much a part of our daily lives that we take it for granted. In the process, we have become desensitized to art as well. Anyone can buy cheap paintings and reproductions to decorate a room, where they often hang virtually unnoticed, perhaps deservedly so. It is small wonder that we look at the art in museums with equal casualness. We pass rapidly from one object to another, sampling them like dishes in a cafeteria line. We may pause briefly before a famous masterpiece that we have been told we are supposed to admire, then ignore the gallery full of equally beautiful and important works around it. We will have seen the art but not really looked at it. Looking at great art is not such an easy task, for art rarely reveals its secrets readily. While the experience of a work can be immediately electrifying, we sometimes do not realize its impact until it has had time to filter through the recesses of our imaginations. It even happens that something that at first repelled or confounded us emerges only many years later as one of the most important artistic events of our lives. Because so much goes into art, it makes much the same demands on our faculties as it did on the person who created it. For that reason, we must be able to respond to it on many levels. If we are going to get the most out of art, we will have to learn how to look and think for ourselves in an intelligent way, which is perhaps the hardest task of all. After all, we will not always have someone at our side to help us. In the end, the confrontation of viewer and art remains a solitary act.

Understanding a work of art begins with a sensitive appreciation of its appearance. Art can be approached and appreciated for its purely visual elements: line, color, light, composition, form, and space. These may be present in any work of art. Their effects, however, vary widely according to medium (the physical materials of which the artwork is made) and technique, which together help to determine the possibilities and limitations of what the artist can achieve. For that reason, our discussion is merged with an introduction to four major arts: graphic arts, painting, sculpture, and architecture. (The technical aspects of the major mediums are treated in sections within the main body of the text and in the glossary toward the end of the book.) Just because line is discussed with drawing, however, does not mean that it is not equally important in painting and sculpture. And although form is introduced with sculpture, it is just as essential to painting, drawing, and architecture.

Visual analysis can help us to appreciate the beauty of a masterpiece, but we must be careful not to use a formulaic approach that would trivialize it. Every aesthetic "law" advanced so far has proven of dubious value, and usually gets in the way of our understanding. Even if a valid "law" were to be found—and none has yet been discovered—it would probably be so elementary as to prove useless in the face of art's complexity. We must also bear in mind that art appreciation is more than enjoyment of aesthetics. It is learning to understand the meaning of a work of art. And finally, let us remember that no work can be understood outside its historical context.

LINE. Line may be regarded as the most basic visual element. A majority of art is initially conceived in terms of contour line. Its presence is often implied even when it is not actually used to describe form. And because children start out by scribbling, line is generally considered the most rudimentary component of art—although as anyone knows who has watched a youngster struggle to make a stick figure with pencil or crayon, drawing is by no means as easy as it seems. Line

7. Rembrandt. *The Star of the Kings.* c. 1642. Pen and bistre, wash on paper, 8 x 12³/4" (20.3 x 32.4 cm).
The British Museum, London

has traditionally been admired for its descriptive value, so that its expressive potential is easily overlooked. Yet line is capable of creating a broad range of effects.

Drawings represent line in its purest form. The appreciation of drawings as works of art dates from the Renaissance, when the artist's creative genius first came to be valued and paper began to be made in quantity. Drawing style can be as personal as handwriting. In fact, the term *graphic art*, which designates drawings and prints, comes from the Greek word for writing, *graphos.* Collectors treasure drawings because they seem to reveal the artist's inspiration with unmatched freshness. Their role as records of artistic thought also makes drawings uniquely valuable to the art historian, for they help in documenting the evolution of a work from its inception to the finished piece.

Artists themselves commonly treat drawings as a form of note-taking. Some of these notes are discarded as fruitless, while others are tucked away to form a storehouse of motifs and studies for later use. Rembrandt was a prolific draftsman who was constantly jotting down observations of daily life and other ideas for further development. His use of line was highly expressive. Many of his sketches were done in pen and ink, a medium that captured his most intimate thoughts with admirable directness. In *The Star of the Kings* (fig. 7), one of his most elaborate sheets, Rembrandt rendered the essence of each pose and expression with remarkable succinctness—the dog, for example, consists of no more than a few strokes of the pen—yet every figure emerges as an individual character. Rembrandt's draftsmanship is so forceful that it allows us to

mentally trace the movements of the master's hand with astonishing vividness.

Once a basic idea is established, an artist may develop it into a more complete study. Michelangelo's studies (fig. 8) of the Libyan Sibyl for the Sistine Chapel ceiling is a drawing of great beauty. For this sheet, he chose the softer medium of red chalk over the scratchy line of pen and ink that he used in rough sketches. His chalk approximates the texture of flesh and captures the play of light and dark over the nude forms, giving the figure a greater sensuousness. The emphatic outline that defines each part of the form is so fundamental to the conceptual genesis and design process in all of Michelangelo's paintings and drawings that ever since his time line has been closely associated with the "intellectual" side of art.

In accordance with the practice of the day, it was Michelangelo's habit to base his female figures on male nudes drawn from life. To him, moreover, only the heroic male nude possessed the physical monumentality necessary to express the awesome power of figures such as this mythical prophetess. In common with other sheets like this by him, Michelangelo's focus here is on the torso. He studied the musculature at length before turning his attention to details like the hand and toes. Since there is no sign of hesitation in the pose, we can be sure that the artist already had the conception firmly in mind. (Probably it had been established in a preliminary drawing.) Why did he go to so much trouble when the finished sibyl is mostly clothed and must be viewed from a considerable distance below? Evidently Michelangelo believed that only by describing the anatomy completely

8. Michelangelo. *Studies for the Libyan Sibyl.* c. 1511. Red chalk on paper, 11³/₈ x 8³/₈" (28 x 21.3 cm). The Metropolitan Museum of Art, New York
Purchase, Joseph Pulitzer Bequest, 1924

9. Michelangelo. *Libyan Sibyl,* portion of the Sistine Ceiling. 1508–12.
Fresco. Sistine Chapel, The Vatican, Rome

could he be certain that the figure would be convincing. In the final painting (fig. 9) she communicates a superhuman strength, lifting her massive book of prophecies with the utmost ease.

COLOR. The world is alive with color, and because color is an adjunct element to graphics and sometimes sculpture, it is indispensable to virtually all forms of painting. This is true even of tonalism, which emphasizes dark, neutral hues like gray and brown. Of all the visual elements, color is undoubtedly the most expressive—as well as the most intractable. Perhaps for that reason, it has attracted the wide attention of researchers and theorists since the mid-nineteenth century. Along with the Post-Impressionists and, more recently, Op artists, color theorists have tried to set down their understanding of colors as perceptual and artistic laws equivalent to those of optical physics. Both Van Gogh and Seurat developed elaborate color systems, one entirely personal in its

meaning, the other claiming to be "scientific." We often read that red seems to advance, while blue recedes; or that the former is a violent or passionate color, the latter a sad one. Like a recalcitrant child, however, color in art refuses to be governed by any rules. They work only when the painter consciously applies them.

Notwithstanding this large body of theory, the role of color in art rests primarily on its sensuous and emotive appeal, in contrast to the more cerebral quality generally associated with line. The merits of line versus color have been the subject of a debate that first arose between partisans of Michelangelo and Titian, Michelangelo's great contemporary in Venice. Titian himself was a fine draftsman and absorbed the influence of Michelangelo. He nevertheless stands at the head of the coloristic tradition that descends through Rubens and Van Gogh to the Abstract Expressionists of the twentieth century. In fact, *Danäe* (fig. 10), painted in the middle of Titian's long career during a sojourn in Rome, shows the

10. Titian. *Danaë*. c. 1544–46. Oil on canvas, 47¼ x 67¾" (120 x 172 cm). Museo e Gallerie Nazionale di Capodimonte, Naples

impact of Michelangelo's figure of Night on the Tomb of Giuliano de' Medici (fig. 616). After seeing it, Michelangelo is said to have praised Titian's coloring and style but criticized his sense of design. We can readily understand Michelangelo's discomfort, for Titian has rephrased his sculpture in utterly sensuous terms through the painterly application of sonorous color that is characteristic of his work.

Though Titian no doubt worked out the essential features of the composition in preliminary drawings, none have survived. Nor evidently did he transfer the design onto the canvas but worked directly on the surface, making subtle adjustments as he went along. By varying the consistency of his pigments, the artist was able to capture the texture of Danäe's flesh with uncanny accuracy, while distinguishing it clearly from bed sheets and covers. To convey these tactile qualities, Titian built up his surface in thin coats, known as glazes. The interaction between these layers produces unrivaled richness and complexity of color; yet the medium is so filmy as to become nearly translucent as the cloud, in which guise Jupiter appears to the mortal young woman, trails off into the gossamer sky.

Color is so potent that it does not need a system to work its magic in art. From the heavy outlines, it is apparent that Picasso must have originally conceived *Girl Before a Mirror* (fig. 11) in terms of form; yet the picture makes no sense in black and white. He has treated his shapes much like the

11. Pablo Picasso. *Girl Before a Mirror*. March 1932. Oil on canvas, 64 x 51¼" (162.3 x 130.2 cm). The Museum of Modern Art, New York

Gift of Mrs. Simon Guggenheim

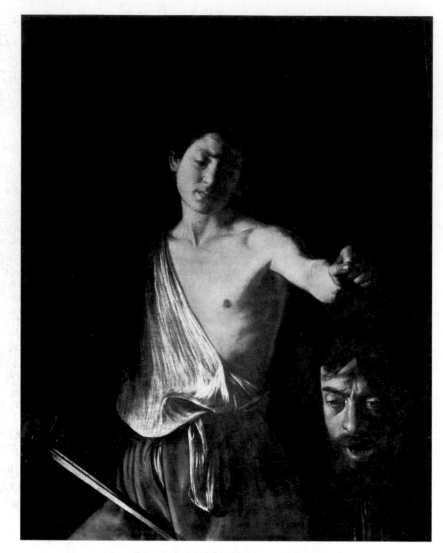

12. Caravaggio. *David with the Head of Goliath.* 1607 or 1609/10. Oil on canvas,
49¼ x 39⅜" (125.1 x 100.1 cm). Galleria Borghese, Rome

enclosed, flat panes of a stained-glass window to create a live-ly decorative pattern. The motif of a young woman contem-plating her beauty goes all the way back to antiquity, but rarely has it been depicted with such disturbing overtones. Picasso's girl is anything but serene. On the contrary, her face is divid-ed into two parts, one with a somber expression, the other with a masklike appearance whose color nevertheless betrays passionate feeling. She reaches out to touch the image in the mirror with a gesture of longing and apprehension.

Now we all feel a jolt when we unexpectedly see ourselves in a mirror, which often gives back a reflection that upsets our self-conception. Picasso here suggests this visionary truth in several ways. Much as a real mirror introduces changes of its own and does not reflect the simple truth, so this one alters the way the girl looks, revealing a deeper reality. She appears not so much to be examining her physical appearance as to be exploring her sexuality. The mirror is a sea of conflicting emo-tions signified above all by the color scheme of her reflection. Framed by strong blue, purple, and green hues, her features stare back at her with fiery intensity. Clearly discernible is a tear on her cheek. But it is the masterstroke of the green spot, shining like a beacon in the middle of her forehead, that con-veys the anguish of the girl's confrontation with her inner self. Picasso was probably aware of the theory that red and green are complementary colors which intensify each other. How-ever, this "law" can hardly have dictated his choice of green to stand for the girl's psyche. That was surely determined as a matter of pictorial and expressive necessity.

LIGHT. For the most part, art is concerned with reflected light effects rather than with radiant light. (Among the few exceptions are modern light installations such as laser dis-plays.) Artists have several ways of representing radiant light. Divine light, for example, is sometimes indicated by golden rays, at other times by a halo or aura. A candle or torch may be depicted as the source of light in a dark interior or night scene. The most common method is not to show radiant light directly but to suggest its presence through a change in the value of reflected light from dark to light. Sharp contrast (known as *chiaroscuro*, the Italian word for light-dark) is iden-tified with the Baroque artist Caravaggio, who made it the cor-nerstone of his style. In *David with the Head of Goliath* (fig. 12), he employed it to heighten the drama. An intense raking light from an unseen source at the left is used to model

13. Piet Mondrian. *Broadway Boogie Woogie.* 1942–43. Oil on canvas, 50 x 50" (127 x 127 cm).
The Museum of Modern Art, New York
Given anonymously

forms and create textures. The selective highlighting endows the lifesize figure of David and the gruesome head with a startling presence. Light here serves as a device to create the convincing illusion that David is standing before us. With its indeterminate depth, the pictorial space, which extends beyond the picture plane, becomes continuous with ours, despite the fact that the frame cuts off the figure. Thus the foreshortened arm with Goliath's head seems to extend out to the viewer from the dark background. For all its obvious theatricality, the painting is surprisingly muted: David seems to contemplate Goliath with a mixture of sadness and pity. The severed head is a self-portrait, and the disturbing image communicates a tragic personal vision that was soon fulfilled. Not long after the *David* was painted, Caravaggio killed another man in a duel, which forced him to spend the rest of his short life on the run.

Light can also be implied through color. Piet Mondrian uses white and the three primary colors—red, yellow, and blue—to signify radiant light in *Broadway Boogie Woogie* (fig. 13), a painting that immortalizes his fascination with the culture he found in America after emigrating from his native Holland during World War II. The play of color evokes with striking success the jaunty rhythms of light and music found in New York's nightclub district during the jazz age. *Broadway Boogie Woogie* is as flat as the canvas it is painted on. Mondrian has laid out his colored "tiles" along a grid system that appropriately resembles a city map. As in a medieval manuscript decoration (fig. 352), the composition relies entirely on surface pattern.

COMPOSITION. Composition is the organization of forms in art. It is of fundamental importance, because all art requires order. Otherwise its message would emerge as visually garbled. To accomplish this, the artist must control space within the framework of a unified composition. Moreover, pictorial space must work across the picture plane, as well as behind it. Since the Early Renaissance, we have become accustomed to experiencing paintings as windows onto separate illusionistic realities. The Renaissance invention of one-point perspective—also called linear or scientific perspective—provided a geometric system for the convincing representation of architectural and open-air settings. By having the orthogonals (shown as diagonal lines) converge at a vanishing point on the horizon, it enabled the artist to gain command over every aspect of his

14. Pieter de Hooch. *The Bedroom.* c. 1658–60. Oil on canvas,
20 x 23¹/₂" (51 x 60 cm). National Gallery of Art, Washington, D.C.
Widener Collection

15. Jean-Baptiste-Siméon Chardin. *Soap Bubbles.* c. 1733–34. Oil on canvas,
36⁵/₈ x 29³/₈" (93 x 74.6 cm). National Gallery of Art, Washington, D.C.
Gift of Mrs. John Simpson

16. *A Pond in a Garden.* Fragment of a wall painting, from the Tomb of Ramose, Thebes. c. 1400 B.C. The British Museum, London

composition, including the rate of recession and placement of figures. Pieter de Hooch, the Dutch Baroque artist, used one-point perspective in organizing *The Bedroom* (fig. 14). Nevertheless, the problems he faced in composing the three-dimensional space of his work were not so very different from those later confronted by Mondrian. (The surface geometry of De Hooch's painting is basically similar in design to *Broadway Boogie Woogie*.) Each part of the house is treated as a separate pocket of space and as a design element that is integrated into the scene as a whole.

Artists will usually dispense with aids like perspective and rely on their own eyes. This does not mean that they merely transcribe optical reality. *Soap Bubbles* by the French painter Jean-Baptiste-Siméon Chardin (fig. 15) depends in good measure on a satisfying composition for its success. The motif had been a popular one in earlier Dutch genre scenes, where bubbles symbolized life's brevity and, hence, the vanity of all earthly things. No such meaning can be attached to Chardin's picture, which is disarming in its simplicity. The interest lies solely in the seemingly insignificant subject and in the sense of enchantment imparted by the children's rapt attention to the moment. We know from a contemporary source that Chardin painted the youth "carefully from life and . . . tried hard to give him an ingenuous air." The results are anything but artless, however. The triangular shape of the boy leaning on the ledge gives stability to the painting, which helps to suspend the fleet-ing instant in time. To fill out the composition, the artist in-cludes the toddler peering intently over the ledge at the bubble, which is about the same size as his head. Chardin has carefully thought out every aspect of his arrangement. The honeysuckle in the upper left-hand corner, for example, echoes the contour of the adolescent's back, while the two straws are virtually parallel to each other. Even the crack in the stone ledge has a purpose: to draw attention to the glass of soap by setting it slightly apart.

Often artists paint not what they see but what they imag-ine. A wall painting from Thebes (fig. 16) presents a flattened view of a delightful garden in which everything is shown in profile except for the pond, which is seen from above. In order to provide the clearest, most complete idea of the scene, the Egyptian artist treated each element as an entity unto itself. Instead of using standard devices such as scale and overlap-ping, space is treated vertically, so that we read the trees at the bottom as being "closer" to us than those at the top, even though they are the same size. Despite the multiple vantage points and implausible bird's-eye view, the image works be-cause it constitutes a self-contained reality. The picture, more-over, has an aesthetically satisfying decorative unity. The geometry underlying the composition reminds us once more of *Broadway Boogie Woogie*. At the same time, the presentation has such clarity that we feel as if we were seeing nature with open eyes for the first time.

17. El Greco. *The Agony in the Garden*. 1597–1600. Oil on canvas,
40¹/₄ x 44³/₄" (102.2 x 113.6 cm). The Toledo Museum of Art, Toledo, Ohio
Gift of Edward Drummond Libbey

Pictorial space need not conform to either conceptual or visual reality. El Greco's *The Agony in the Garden* (fig. 17) uses contradictory, irrational space to help conjure up a mystical vision that instead represents a spiritual reality. Jesus, isolated against a large rock that echoes his shape, is comforted by the angel bearing a golden cup, symbol of the Passion (the suffering of Jesus in his last days). The angel appears to kneel on a mysterious oval cloud, which envelops the sleeping disciples. In the distance to the right we see Judas and the soldiers coming to arrest the Lord. The composition is balanced by two giant clouds on either side. The entire landscape resounds with Jesus' agitation, represented by the sweep of supernatural forces. The elongated forms, eerie moonlight, and expressive colors—all hallmarks of El Greco's style—help to heighten our sense of identification with Jesus' suffering.

FORM. Line creates shape. Every shape that we encounter in art is a counterpart to form. The only difference between them is that shape is flat, whereas form has volume, though it also has a characteristic shape defined by its contour. There is a vast difference between drawing or painting forms and sculpting them. The one transcribes, the other brings them to life, as it were. They require fundamentally different talents and atti-

18. *Alkestis Leaving Hades.* Lower column from the Temple
of Artemis, Ephesus. c. 340 B.C. Marble, height 71" (180.3 cm).
The British Museum, London

19. Praxiteles (attr.). *Standing Youth,* found in the sea off Marathon. c. 350–325 B.C. Bronze, height 51" (129.5 cm). National Archaeological Museum, Athens

20. Gianlorenzo Bernini. *Apollo and Daphne.* 1622–24. Marble, height 8' (2.43 m). Galleria Borghese, Rome

tudes toward material as well as subject matter. Although a number of artists have been competent in both painting and sculpture, only a handful managed to bridge the gap between them with complete success.

Sculpture is categorized according to whether it is carved or modeled and whether it is a relief or a free standing statue. Relief remains tied to the background, from which it only partially emerges, in contrast to free-standing sculpture, which is fully liberated from it. A further distinction is made between low (*bas*) relief and high (*alto*) relief, depending on how much the carving projects. However, since scale as well as depth must be taken into account, there is no single guideline, so that a third category, middle (*mezzo*) relief, is sometimes added.

Low reliefs often share characteristics with painting. In Egypt, where low-relief carving attained unsurpassed subtlety, many reliefs were originally painted and included elaborate settings. High reliefs largely preclude this kind of pictorialism. The figures on a column from a Greek temple (fig. 18) have become so detached from the background that the addition of landscape or architecture elements would be both unnecessary and unconvincing. The neutral setting, moreover, is in keep-

ing with the mythological subject, which takes place in an indeterminate time and place. In compensation, the sculptor has treated the limited free space atmospherically, yet the figures remain imprisoned in stone.

Free-standing sculpture—that is, sculpture that is carved or modeled fully in the round—is made by either of two methods. One is modeling, an additive process using soft materials such as plaster, clay, or wax. Since these materials are not very durable, they are usually cast in a more lasting medium: anything that can be poured, including molten metal, cement, even plastic. Modeling encourages "open" forms with the aid of metal armatures to support their extension into space. This in conjunction with the development of lightweight hollow-bronze casting enabled the Greeks to experiment with daring poses in monumental sculpture before attempting them in marble. In contrast to the figure of Hades on the column, the bronze youth in figure 19 is free to move about, lending him a lifelike presence that is further enhanced by his dancing pose. His inlaid eyes and soft patina, accentuated by oxidation and corrosion (he was found in the Aegean Sea off the coast of Greece, near Marathon), make him even more credible in a way that marble statues, with their

21. Frank Lloyd Wright. Solomon R. Guggenheim Museum, New York. 1956–59

seemingly cold and smooth finish, rarely equal, despite their more natural color (compare fig. 20).

Carving is the very opposite of modeling. It is a subtractive process that starts with a solid block, usually stone, which is highly resistant to the sculptor's chisel. The brittleness of stone and the difficulty of cutting it tend to result in the compact, "closed" forms seen in Michelangelo's *Awakening Slave* (fig. 3). One of the most daring attempts at overcoming the tyranny of mass over space is *Apollo and Daphne* by the Baroque sculptor Gianlorenzo Bernini (fig. 20). The dancelike pose of Apollo and graceful torsion of Daphne create the impression that they are moving in a carefully choreographed ballet. Time and motion have almost, but not quite, come to a standstill as the nymph begins to change into a tree rather than succumb to the god's amorous advances. The sculpture is an amazing technical achievement. Bernini is completely successful in distinguishing between the soft flesh of Daphne and the rough texture of the bark and leaves. The illusion of change is so convincing that we share Apollo's shock at the metamorphosis.

Like most monumental sculpture, *Apollo and Daphne* was intended for a specific location. It was originally placed along the wall to the left of the doorway, rather than in the middle of the room as now. Thus despite the fact that it is fully carved, the back side was never meant to be seen and provides little additional visual information. The statue demands our direct participation in order to experience the drama. The action unfolds gradually as we walk around the sculpture (our illustration shows the most characteristic view), reaching its climax almost directly in front of Daphne, where her transformation has its greatest "shock effect." Bernini's ingenuity in creating this theatrical display is fully characteristic of the Baroque.

SPACE. In our discussions of pictorial and sculptural space, we have repeatedly referred to architecture, for it is the principal means of organizing space. Of all the arts, it is also the most practical. Architecture's parameters are defined by utilitarian function and structural system, but there is almost always an aesthetic component as well, even when it consists of nothing more than a decorative veneer. A building proclaims the architect's concerns by the way in which it weaves these elements into a coherent program.

Architecture becomes memorable only when it expresses a transcendent vision, whether personal, social, or spiritual. Such buildings are almost always important public places that require the marshaling of significant resources and serve the

22. Interior of the Solomon R. Guggenheim Museum

purpose of bringing people together to share common goals, pursuits, and values. An extreme case is the Solomon R. Guggenheim Museum in New York by the architect Frank Lloyd Wright. Scorned when it was first erected in the late 1950s, it is a brilliant, if idiosyncratic, creation by one of the most original architectural minds of the century. The sculptural exterior (fig. 21) announces that this can only be a museum, for it is self-consciously a work of art in its own right. As a piece of design, the Guggenheim Museum is remarkably willful. In shape it is as defiantly individual as the architect himself and refuses to conform to the boxlike apartments around it. From the outside, the structure looks like a gigantic snail, reflecting Wright's interest in organic shapes. The office area forming the "head" to the left is connected by a narrow passageway to the "shell" containing the main body of the museum.

The outside gives us some idea of what to expect inside (fig. 22), yet nothing quite prepares us for the extraordinary sensation of light and air in the main hall after being ushered through the unassuming entrance. The radical design makes it clear that Wright had completely rethought the purpose of an art museum. The exhibition area is a kind of inverted dome with a huge glass-covered eye at the top. The vast, fluid space creates an atmosphere of quiet harmony while actively shaping our experience by determining how art shall be displayed. After taking an elevator to the top of the building, the visitor begins a leisurely descent down the gently sloping ramp. The continuous spiral provides for uninterrupted viewing, conducive to studying art. At the same time, the narrow confines of the galleries prevent us from becoming passive observers by forcing us into a direct confrontation with the works themselves. Sculpture takes on a heightened physical presence which demands that we look at it. Even paintings acquire a new prominence by protruding slightly from the curved walls, instead of receding into them. Viewing exhibitions at the Guggenheim is like being conducted through a predetermined stream of consciousness, where everything merges into a total unity. Whether one agrees with this approach or not, the building testifies to the strength of Wright's vision by precluding any other way of seeing the art.

Meaning in Context

Art has been called a visual dialogue, for though the object itself is mute, it expresses its creator's intention just as surely as if it were speaking to us. For there to be a dialogue, however, our active participation is required. If we cannot literally talk to a work of art, we can learn how to respond to it and question it in order to fathom its meaning. Finding the right answers usually involves asking the right questions. Even if we are not sure which question to ask, we can always start with, "What would happen if the artist had done it another way?" And when we are through, we must question our explanation according to the same test of adequate proof that applies to any investigation: have we taken into account *all* the available evidence, and arranged it in a logical and coherent way? There is, alas, no step-by-step method to guide us, but this does not mean that the process is entirely mysterious. We can illustrate it by looking at some examples together; the demonstration will help us gain courage to try the same analysis the next time we enter a museum.

The great Dutch painter Jan Vermeer has been called the Sphinx of Delft, for all his paintings have a degree of mystery. In *Woman Holding a Balance* (fig. 23), a young woman, richly dressed in at-home wear of the day, is contemplating a balance in her hand, with strings of pearls and gold coins spread out on the table before her. The canvas is painted entirely in gradations of cool, neutral tones, except for a bit of the red dress visible beneath her jacket. The soft light from the partly open window is concentrated on her face and the cap framing it. Other beads of light reflect from the pearls and her right hand. The serene atmosphere is sustained throughout the stable composition. Vermeer places us at an intimate distance within the relatively shallow space, which has been molded around the figure. The underlying grid of horizontals and verticals is modulated by the gentle curves of the woman's form and the heap of blue drapery in the foreground, as well as by the oblique angles of the mirror. The design is so perfect that we cannot move a single element without upsetting the delicate balance.

The composition is controlled in part by perspective. The vanishing point of the diagonals formed by the top of the mirror and the right side of the table lies at the juncture of the woman's little finger and the picture frame. If we look carefully at the bottom of the frame, we see that it is actually lower on the right than on the left, where it lies just below her hand. The effect is so carefully calculated that the artist must have wanted to guide our eye to the painting in the background. Though difficult to read at first, it depicts Christ at the Last Judgment, when every soul is weighed. The parallel of this subject to the woman's activity tells us that, contrary to our initial impression, this cannot be simply a scene of everyday life. The painting, then, is testimony to the artist's faith, for he was a Catholic living in Protestant Holland, where his religion was officially banned, although worship in private houses was tolerated.

The meaning is nevertheless far from clear. Because Vermeer treated forms as beads of light, it was assumed until recently that the balance holds items of jewelry and that the woman is weighing the worthlessness of earthly possessions in the face of death; hence, the painting was generally called *The Pearl Weigher* or *The Gold Weigher*. However, we can see that the pans actually contain nothing. This is confirmed by infrared photography, which also reveals that Vermeer changed the position of the balance: to make the picture more harmonious, he placed them parallel to the picture plane instead of allowing them to recede into space. What, then, is she doing? If she is weighing temporal against spiritual values, it can be only in a symbolic sense, because nothing about the figure or the setting betrays a sense of conflict. What accounts for this inner peace? Perhaps it is self-knowledge, symbolized here by the mirror. It may also be the promise of salvation through her faith. In *Woman Holding a Balance*, as in Caravaggio's *The Calling of St. Matthew* (fig. 726), light might therefore serve not only to illuminate the scene but also to represent religious revelation. In the end, we cannot be sure, because Vermeer's approach to his subject proves as subtle as his pictorial treatment. He avoids any anecdote or symbolism that might limit us to a single interpretation. There can be no doubt, however, about his fascination with light. Vermeer's mastery of light's expressive qualities elevates his concern for the reality of appearance to the level of poetry, and subsumes its visual and symbolic possibilities. Here, then, we have found the real "meaning" of Vermeer's art.

The ambiguity in *Woman Holding a Balance* serves to heighten our interest and pleasure, while the carefully organized composition expresses the artist's underlying concept with singular clarity. But what are we to do when a work deliberately seems devoid of apparent meaning? Modern artists can pose a gap between their intention and the viewer's understanding. The gap is, however, often more apparent than real, for the meaning is usually intelligible to the imagination at some level. Still, we feel we must comprehend intellectually what we perceive intuitively. We can partially solve the personal code in Jasper Johns' *Target with Four Faces* (fig. 24) by treating it somewhat like a rebus. Where did he begin? Surely with the target, which stands alone as an object, unlike the long box at the top, particularly when its hinged door is closed. Why a target in the first place? The size, texture, and colors inform us that this is not to be interpreted as a real target. The design is nevertheless attractive in its own right, and Johns must have chosen it for that reason. When the wooden door is up, the assemblage is transformed from a neutral into a loaded image, bringing out the nascent connotations of the target. Johns has used the same plaster cast four times, which lends the faces a curious anonymity. Then he cut them off at the eyes, "the windows of the soul," rendering them even more enigmatic. Finally, he crammed them into their compartments, so that they seem to press urgently out toward us. The results are disquieting, aesthetically as well as expressively.

Something so disturbing cannot be without significance— but what? We may be reminded of prisoners trying to look out from small cell windows, or perhaps "blindfolded" targets of execution. Whatever our impression, the claustrophobic image radiates an aura of menacing danger. Unlike Picasso's joining of a bicycle seat and handlebars to form a bull's head, *Target with Four Faces* combines two disparate components in an open conflict that we cannot reconcile, no matter how hard we try. The intrusion of this ominous meaning creates an extraordinary tension with the dispassionate investigation of the target's formal qualities. It is, then, this disparity between form and content that must have been Johns' goal.

How do we know we are right? After all, this is merely our "personal" interpretation, so we turn to the critics for help. We find them divided about the meaning of this work, although

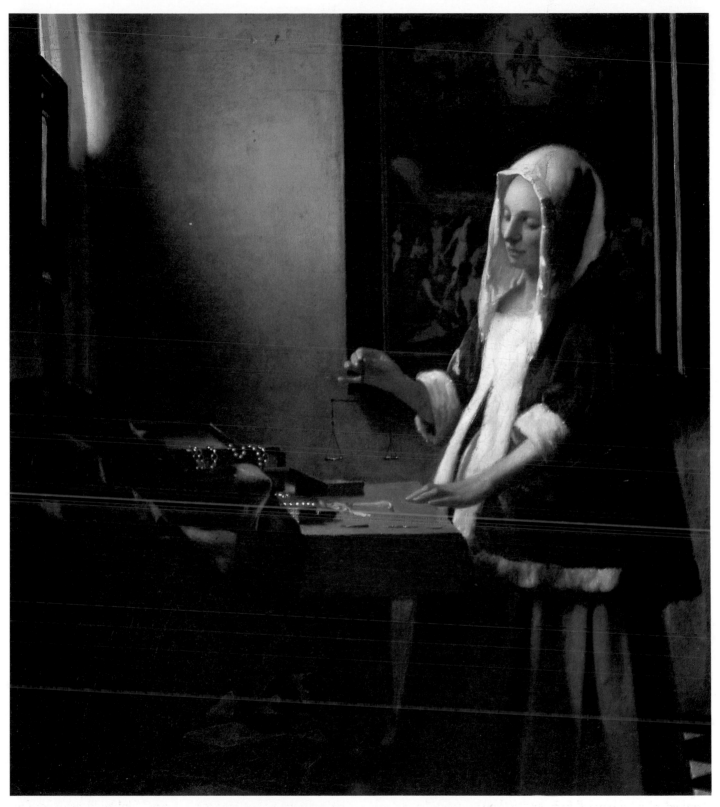

23. Jan Vermeer. *Woman Holding a Balance*. c. 1664. Oil on canvas,
16³/4 x 15" (42.5 x 38.1 cm). National Gallery of Art, Washington, D.C.
Widener Collection, 1942

24. Jasper Johns. *Target with Four Faces.* 1955. Assemblage: encaustic and collage on canvas with objects, 26 x 26" (66 x 66 cm) surmounted by four tinted plaster faces in wood box with hinged front. Box, closed 3³/4 x 26 x 3¹/2" (9.5 x 66 x 8.9 cm); overall dimensions with box open, 33⁵/8 x 26 x 3" (85.3 x 66 x 7.6 cm). The Museum of Modern Art, New York

Gift of Mr. and Mrs. Robert C. Scull

25. John Singleton Copley. *Paul Revere.* c. 1768–70.
Oil on canvas, 35 x 28¹/2" (88.9 x 72.3 cm). Museum of Fine Arts, Boston
Gift of Joseph W., William B., and Edward H. R. Revere

they agree it must have one. Johns, on the other hand, has insisted that there is none! Whom are we to believe, the critics or the artist himself? The more we think about it, the more likely it seems that both sides may be right. The artist is not always aware why he has made a work. That does not mean that there were no reasons, only that they were unconscious ones. Under these circumstances, the critic may well know the artist's mind better than he does and explain his creation more clearly. We can now understand that to Johns the leap of his imagination in *Target with Four Faces* remains as mysterious as it first seemed to us. Our account reconciles the artist's aesthetic concerns and the critics' search for meaning, and while we realize that no ultimate solution is possible, we have arrived at a satisfactory explanation by looking and thinking for ourselves.

It is all too easy to overlook the obvious, and this is especially true in looking at portraits. Those of famous people have a special appeal, for they seem to bridge a gap of time and place and to establish a personal link. In their faces we read a thousand insights about character which no amount of historical data can satisfy nearly as well. Our interest arises no doubt from the remnant of a primitive belief that an image captures not merely the likeness but also the soul of a sitter. In the age of photography, we have come to see portraits as mere likenesses, and we readily forget that they call on all our skill to grasp their meaning. *Paul Revere*, painted by the American artist John Singleton Copley around 1770 (fig. 25), gives rise to questions we cannot solve with on-the-spot observations, so we must look elsewhere to answer them. The fruit of our investigation must agree with our observations; otherwise we cannot be sure that we are right.

Silversmith, printmaker, businessman, and patriot, Revere has acquired legendary status thanks to Henry Wadsworth Longfellow's long poem about his midnight ride, and Copley's painting has become virtually an American icon. It has generally been treated as a workingman's portrait, so to speak. By all rights, however, such a portrait ought to be much more straightforward than this and, hence, less memorable. Revere has a penetrating glance and thoughtful pose which are heightened by the sharp light, lending him an unusually forceful presence. He looks out at us with astonishing directness, as if he were reading us with the same intensity that we bring to bear on his strongly modeled features. Clearly, Revere is a thinker possessing an active intelligence, and we will recognize the pose of hand on chin as an old device used since antiquity to represent philosophers. This is certainly no ordinary craftsman here, and we may also wonder whether this is really his working outfit. Surely no silversmith would have carried out his craft in what are probably Revere's best business clothes. Simply by looking at the picture we have raised enough doubts to challenge the traditional view of this famous painting.

26. John Singleton Copley. *Nathaniel Hurd*. c. 1765.
Oil on canvas, 30 x 25¹/2" (76.2 x 64.8 cm). The Cleveland Museum of Art
Gift of the John Huntington Art and Polytechnic Trust

At this point, our questioning of the picture's surface comes to an end, for the portrait fails to yield up further clues. Once we have posed the problem of this "artisan's" portrayal, we feel compelled to investigate it further. The more we pursue the matter, the more fascinating it becomes. Copley, we discover, had painted only a few years earlier a portrait of another Boston silversmith, Nathaniel Hurd (fig. 26). Yet this one is so different that we would never guess the sitter's trade. Hurd is wearing a casual robe and turban, and before him are two books, one of them devoted to heraldry from which he culled the coats of arms he needed for his work. Why, then, did Copley show Revere at a workbench with his engraving tools spread out before him, holding a teapot as the object of his contemplation and offering it to us for our inspection? In light of Hurd's portrait, Revere's work as a silversmith hardly explains these attributes and actions, natural as they seem. Oddly enough, the question has never been raised; yet surely the differences between the two paintings cannot be accidental.

Perhaps we can find the answer in the antecedents for each. Hurd's image can be traced back to informal portraits that originated in France in the early eighteenth century and soon became popular as well in England, where there was a rage for portraits of well-known men and women. This type of portrait was customarily reserved for artists, writers, and the like. In turn, the type gave rise to a distinctive offshoot that showed a sculptor at work in his studio with his tools prominently displayed (fig. 27). Sometimes an engraver is seen instead. There is another possible precedent: moralizing portraits, the descendants of pictures of St. Jerome, that show their subjects holding or pointing to skulls, much as Revere has the teapot in his hand. Copley was surely familiar with all of these kinds of images from the portrait engravings that we know he collected, but his exact sources for the Revere painting remain a mystery and may never be discovered. For after 1765 Copley freely adapted and combined motifs from different prints in his paintings, often disguising their origins so completely that we cannot be certain which they were. It is

27. Francis Xavier Vispré (attr.). *Portrait of Louis-François Roubiliac.*
c. 1750. Pastel on paper laid on canvas, 24¹/₂ x 21¹/₂" (62.2 x 54.6 cm).
Yale Center for British Art, New Haven, Connecticut
Paul Mellon Collection

likely that he conflated two or three in Revere's portrait. In any case, it is apparent that Copley has transformed Revere from a craftsman into an artist-philosopher.

Let us now look at this portrait in its larger historical and cultural context. In Europe, the artisan's inferior position to the artist had been asserted since the Renaissance, except in England, where the newly founded Royal Academy first drew the distinction in 1768, about when Copley painted Hurd's portrait. But in the Colonies there was, as Copley himself complained, no distinction between the trades of artist and artisan. Indeed, except for portraiture, it can be argued that the decorative arts *were* the fine arts of America.

It is significant that Copley's portrait probably dates from around the time of Revere's first efforts at making engravings, a form of art that arose, interestingly enough, out of silver- and goldsmith decorating during the late Middle Ages. Revere was then already involved with libertarianism, a cause which Copley himself did not share. This difference in their points of view did not prevent Copley from endowing Revere's portrait

with an ingenious significance and penetrating characterization. The painter and the silversmith must have known each other well. (Copley ordered various pieces of silver, and even false teeth, from Revere.) The portrait stands as Copley's compelling tribute to a fellow artist—and as an invaluable statement about the culture of the Colonial era.

Obviously, not everyone is in a position to undertake this kind of research. Only the art historian and the most interested lay person do. But this does not mean that "there must be something wrong with a work of art if it takes an expert to appreciate it." On the contrary, research serves only to affirm the portrait of Paul Revere as a masterpiece. Reacting to the portrait in "a direct, straightforward fashion," without the benefit of additional knowledge, precludes the understanding necessary for full appreciation. Critics, scholars, and curators are not the public's adversaries. In sharing their expertise and knowledge of art's broader contexts, they expand our general capacity for appreciating art, and provide a model for our own seek-and-find experiences.

PROLOGUE

The term *Gothic* was first coined for certain architecture of the twelfth century, and it is in architecture that the characteristics of the style are most easily recognized. The origin of our concept of Gothic art also suggests the way the new style actually grew. It began with architecture, and for a century—from about 1150 to 1250, during the Age of the Great Cathedrals—architecture retained its dominant role. Thereafter we find a gradual shift of emphasis from architecture to painting or, better perhaps, from architectural to pictorial qualities. Overlying this broad pattern was another one: international diffusion as against regional independence. Starting as a local development in the Île-de-France, Gothic art radiated from there to the rest of France and to all of Europe. As the new style gradually lost its imported flavor, regional variety began to reassert itself. Toward the middle of the fourteenth century, we notice a growing tendency for these regional achievements to influence each other until, about 1400, a surprisingly homogeneous "International Gothic" style prevailed almost everywhere. Shortly thereafter, this unity broke apart. Italy, with Florence in the lead, created a radically new art, that of the Early Renaissance, while north of the Alps, Flanders assumed an equally commanding position in the development of Late Gothic painting and sculpture. A century later, finally, the Italian Renaissance became the basis of another international style.

ARCHITECTURE

ST.-DENIS AND ABBOT SUGER. We can pinpoint the origin of no previous style as exactly as that of Gothic. It was born between 1137 and 1144 in the rebuilding by Abbot Suger of the royal Abbey Church of St.-Denis just outside the city of Paris. Suger, as chief adviser to Louis VI, championed the French monarchy not only in practical politics but also in "spiritual politics." By investing the royal office with religious significance and glorifying it as the strong right arm of justice, he sought to rally the nation behind the king. The abbey enjoyed a dual prestige that made it ideally suitable for Suger's purpose. It was the shrine of St.-Denis, the Apostle of France and special protector of the realm, as well as the chief memorial of the Carolingian dynasty. Suger wanted to make the abbey the spiritual center of France, a pilgrimage church to outshine the splendor of all the others, the focal point of religious as well as patriotic emotion. But in order to become the visible embodiment of such a goal, the old edifice had to be enlarged and rebuilt.

The great abbot himself has described the entire campaign in eloquent detail. Suger's account of the rebuilding of his church insistently stresses both the emphasis on strict geometric planning and the quest for luminosity as the highest values achieved in the new structure. "Harmony" (that is, the perfect relationship among parts in terms of mathematical proportions or ratios) is the source of all beauty, since it exemplifies the laws according to which divine reason has constructed the universe. The "miraculous" light that floods the choir through the "most sacred" windows becomes the Light Divine, a mystic revelation of the spirit of God. For Suger, the material realm was the stepping-stone for spiritual contemplation. Thus the actual experience of dark, jewellike light that disembodies the material world lies at the heart of Suger's mystical intent, which was to be transported to "some strange region of the universe which neither exists entirely in the slime of earth nor entirely in the purity of Heaven."

Suger's views shaped his mental image of the kind of struc-ture he wanted, we may assume, and determined his choice of a master as the chief architect. This great artist must have been singularly responsive to the abbot's ideas and instructions. For the master who built the choir of St.-Denis under Suger's supervision, the technical problems of vaulting must have been inextricably bound up with considerations of form (that is, of beauty, harmony, fitness, and so forth). But in order to know what constituted beauty, harmony, and fitness, the medieval architect needed the guidance of Suger. Together, they created the Gothic style. The success of the choir design at St.-Denis is proved not only by its inherent qualities but also by its extraordinary impact. Every visitor to St.-Denis, it seems, was overwhelmed by Suger's achievement, and within a few decades the new style had spread far beyond the confines of the Île-de-France.

NOTRE-DAME, PARIS. We know more about what Suger desired to achieve than we do about the final result, for most of St.-Denis is sadly mutilated today. Notre-Dame ("Our Lady," the Virgin Mary) at Paris, begun in 1163, reflects the salient features of St.-Denis more directly than does any other church.

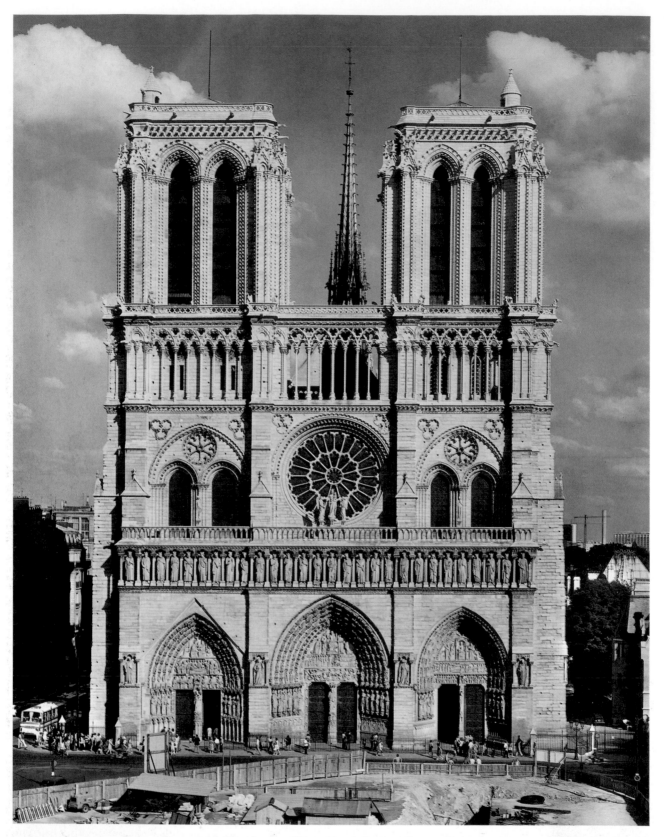

28. West facade of Notre-Dame, Paris. 1163–c. 1250

The most monumental aspect of the exterior of Notre-Dame is the west facade (Vol. Two, fig. 28). Except for its sculpture, which suffered heavily during the French Revolution and is for the most part restored, it retains its original appearance. The style is instantly recognizable. Although its elements derive from Romanesque architecture, all the details have been integrated into a wonderfully balanced and coherent whole. The meaning of Suger's emphasis on harmony, geometric order, and propor-tion here becomes strikingly evident. This formal discipline also embraces the sculpture, which has been assigned a precisely defined role within the architectural framework. At the same time, lacelike arcades, huge portals, and windows dissolve the continuity of the wall surfaces, so that the total effect approxi-mates that of an openwork screen.

The interior (Vol. Two, fig. 29) seems graceful, almost weightless, since the windows have been enlarged to the point

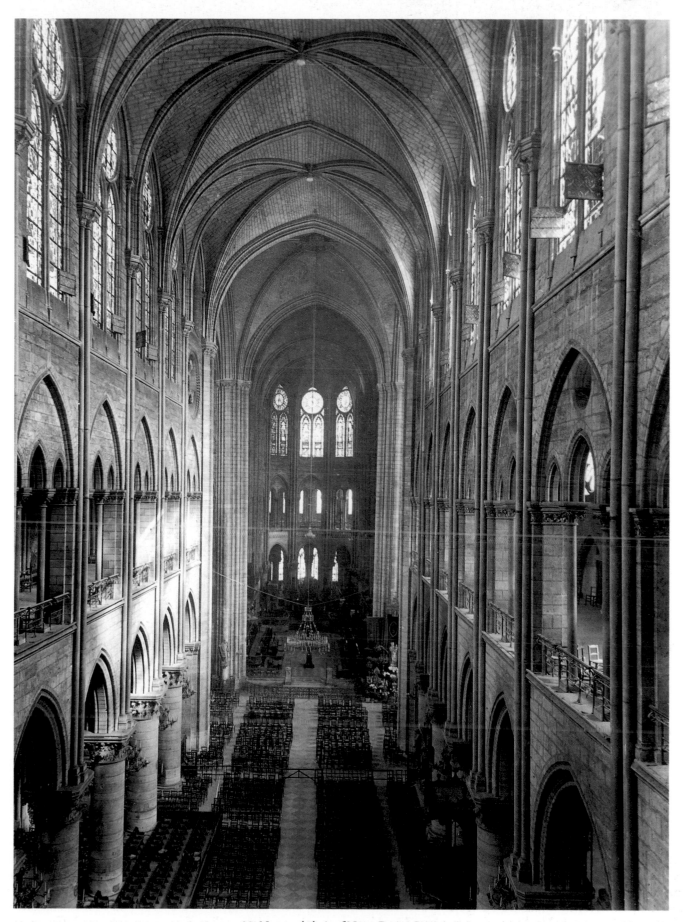

29. Nave and choir of Notre-Dame, Paris

30. Cimabue. *Madonna Enthroned.*
c. 1280–90. Tempera on panel, 12'7¹/₂" x 7'4" (3.9 x 2.2 m).
Galleria degli Uffizi, Florence

that they are no longer openings cut into a wall. They now fill the entire wall area, so that they themselves become translucent walls. Missing, however, are the original stained-glass windows, which endowed light with the poetic and symbolic values—the "miraculous light"—so highly praised by Abbot Suger. The ethereal light served to dissolve the physical solidity of the church and, hence, the distinction between the temporal and the divine realms. The intensely mystical experience it created lies at the heart of Gothic spirituality. Ribbed groin-vaulting based on the pointed arch is employed throughout. The outward pressure of the vaults is contained by heavy buttresses jutting from the walls, so that they are visible only from the outside. Above the aisles, these become flying buttresses—a characteristic feature of Gothic architecture—

arched bridges that reach upward to the critical spots between the clerestory windows where the outward thrust of the nave vault is concentrated. The lightness and slenderness of the forms help further to create the weightless effect that we associate with Gothic interiors. Gothic, too, is the verticality of the interior space. This depends less on the actual proportions of the nave than on the constant accenting of the verticals and on the soaring ease with which the sense of height is attained.

PAINTING
Italy

At the end of the thirteenth century, Italian painting produced an explosion of creative energy that had far-reaching

31. *Madonna Enthroned.* Late 13th century. Tempera on panel,
32 1/8 x 19 3/8" (81.9 x 49.3 cm). National Gallery of Art,
Washington, D.C.
Andrew Mellon Collection, 1937

impact upon the future. What were the conditions that made this possible? Medieval Italy, although strongly influenced by Northern art from Carolingian times on, had always maintained close contacts with Byzantine civilization. A new wave of Byzantine elements overwhelmed the lingering Romanesque elements in Italian painting. It is ironic that this neo-Byzantine (or "Greek manner," as the Italians called it) made its appearance soon after the conquest of Constantinople by the armies of the Fourth Crusade in 1204. Be that as it may, the Greek manner prevailed almost until the end of the thirteenth century, so that Italian painters were able to absorb the Byzantine tradition far more thoroughly than ever before. Eventually, toward 1300, Gothic influence spilled over into Italian painting as well, and it was the interaction of this

element with the neo-Byzantine that produced the revolutionary pictorial new style of which Giotto was the greatest exponent.

CIMABUE. Among the painters of the Greek manner, the Florentine master Cimabue (c. 1250–after 1300), who may have been Giotto's teacher, enjoyed special fame. His huge altar panel, *Madonna Enthroned* (Vol. Two, fig. 30), rivals the finest Byzantine icons (compare Vol. Two, fig. 31) or mosaics. What distinguishes it from icons is mainly a greater severity of design and expression, which befits its huge size. Panels on such a monumental scale had never been attempted in the East. Equally un-Byzantine is the picture's gabled shape and the way the throne of inlaid wood seems to echo it.

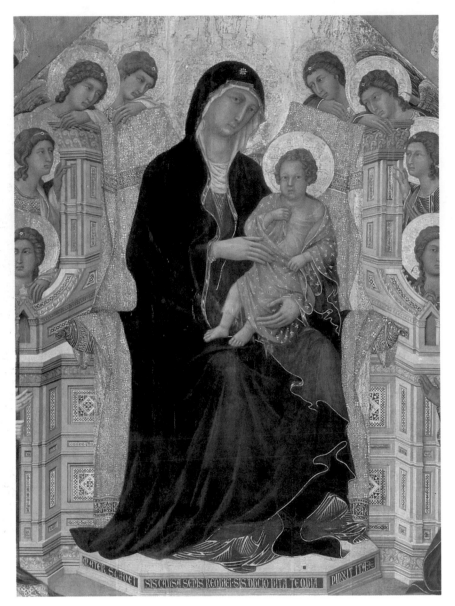

32. Duccio. *Madonna Enthroned,* detail from the center of the *Maestà Altar.* 1308–11. Tempera on panel, height 6'10¹/₂" (2.1 m). Museo dell'Opera del Duomo, Siena, Italy

DUCCIO. A quarter of a century after Cimabue painted his *Madonna Enthroned,* Duccio of Siena (c. 1255–before 1319) painted the main altar of Siena Cathedral (Vol. Two, fig. 32), which was honored by being called the *Maestà* (majesty) to identify the Virgin's role here as the Queen of Heaven surrounded by her celestial court of saints and angels. At first glance, the picture may seem much like Cimabue's, since both follow the same basic scheme. Yet the differences are important. They reflect not only two contrasting personalities and contrasting local tastes—the gentleness of Duccio is characteristic of Siena—but also the rapid evolution of style. In Duccio's hands, the Greek manner has become unfrozen. The rigid, angular draperies have given way to an undulating softness. The abstract shading-in-reverse with lines of gold is reduced to a minimum. The bodies, faces, and hands are

beginning to swell with a subtle three-dimensional life. Clearly, the heritage of Hellenistic-Roman illusionism that had always been part of the Byzantine tradition, however dormant or submerged, is asserting itself once more. But there is also a half-hidden Gothic element here. We sense it in the fluidity of the drapery folds, the appealing naturalness of the Infant Christ, and the tender glances by which the figures communicate with each other. The chief source of this Gothic influence must have been Giovanni Pisano, who was in Siena from 1285 to 1295 as the sculptor-architect in charge of the cathedral facade.

Apart from the *Madonna,* the *Maestà* includes many small compartments with scenes from the lives of Christ and the Virgin. In these panels, the most mature works of Duccio's career, the cross-fertilization of Gothic and Byzantine ele-

33. Duccio. *Annunciation of the Death of the Virgin,* from the *Maestà Altar*

ments has given rise to a development of fundamental importance: a new kind of picture space. The *Annunciation of the Death of the Virgin* (Vol. Two, fig. 33) shows us something we have never seen before in the history of painting: two figures enclosed by an architectural interior. Ancient painters and their Byzantine successors were quite unable to achieve this space. Their architectural settings always stay *behind* the figures, so that their indoor scenes tend to look as if they were taking place in an open-air theater, on a stage without a roof. Duccio's figures, in contrast, inhabit a space that is created and defined by the architecture, as if the artist had carved a niche into his panel. This spatial framework derives from the architectural "housing" of Gothic sculpture. Northern Gothic painters, too, had tried to reproduce these architectural settings, but they could do so only by flattening them out com

pletely. The Italian painters of Duccio's generation, on the other hand, trained as they were in the Greek manner, had acquired enough of the devices of Hellenistic-Roman illusionism to let them render such a framework without draining it of its three-dimensional qualities.

GIOTTO. Turning from Duccio to Giotto (1267?– 1336/7), we meet an artist of far bolder and more dramatic temper. Ten to 15 years younger, Giotto was less close to the Greek manner from the start, despite his probable apprenticeship under Cimabue. As a Florentine, he fell heir to Cimabue's sense of monumental scale, which made him a wall painter by instinct, rather than a panel painter. Of his surviving murals, those in the Arena Chapel in Padua, done in 1305–6, are the best preserved as well as the most characteristic. A single glance at

34. Giotto. *The Lamentation.* 1305–6. Fresco. Arena (Scrovegni) Chapel, Padua, Italy

Giotto's *Lamentation* (Vol. Two, fig. 34) will convince us that we are faced with a truly revolutionary development. It is a work of intense dramatic power. The tragic mood is brought home to us by the formal rhythm of the design as much as by the gestures and expressions of the participants. The very low center of gravity, and the hunched, bending figures communicate the somber quality of the scene and arouse our compassion even before we have grasped the specific meaning of the event depicted. With extraordinary boldness, Giotto sets off the frozen grief of the human mourners against the frantic movement of the weeping angels among the clouds, as if the figures on the ground were restrained by their collective duty to maintain the stability of the composition while the angels, small and weightless as birds, do not share this burden. The impact of the drama is heightened by the severely simple setting. The descending slope of the hill acts as a unifying element and at the same time directs our glance toward the heads of Christ and the Virgin, which are the focal point of the scene.

Giotto presents it in such a way that the beholder's eye level falls within the lower half of the picture. Thus we can imagine ourselves standing on the same ground plane as these painted figures, even though we see them from well below. He also endows his forms with a three-dimensional reality so forceful that the figures seem as solid and tangible as sculpture in the round. Yet Giotto's aim was not simply to transplant Gothic statuary into painting. By creating a radically new kind of picture space, he had also sharpened his awareness of the picture surface. His large, simple forms, the strong grouping of his figures, the limited depth of his "stage," all these factors help endow his scenes with an inner coherence such as we have never found before. To Giotto's contemporaries, the tactile quality of his art must have seemed a near-miracle. It was this quality that made them praise him as equal, or even superior, to the greatest of the ancient painters, because his forms looked so lifelike that they could be mistaken for reality itself. Equally significant are the stories linking Giotto with the claim that

35. Pietro Lorenzetti. *Birth of the Virgin*. 1342. Tempera on panel, 6'1 1/2" x 5'11 1/2" (1.9 x 1.8 m). Museo dell'Opera del Duomo, Siena

painting is superior to sculpture. This was not an idle boast, as it turned out, for Giotto does indeed mark the start of what might be called "the era of painting" in Western art.

The art of Giotto is so daringly original that its sources are far more difficult to trace than those of Duccio's style. Apart from his Florentine background as represented by the Greek manner of Cimabue, the young Giotto seems to have been familiar with the work of neo-Byzantine masters of Rome. There he must have become acquainted with Early Christian and ancient Roman mural decoration. Classical sculpture likewise left an impression on him. More fundamental than any of these, however, was the influence of the Pisanos—Nicola, and especially Giovanni. They were the chief intermediaries through whom Giotto first came in contact with the world of Northern Gothic art. And the latter remains the most important of all the elements that entered into Giotto's style. Without the knowledge, direct or indirect, of Northern works such as the *Death of the Virgin* from Strasbourg Cathedral (see Vol. Two, fig. 45), he could

never have achieved the emotional impact of his *Lamentation*.

THE LORENZETTI BROTHERS. There are few artists in the entire history of art who equal the stature of Giotto as a radical innovator. His very greatness, moreover, tended to dwarf the next generation of Florentine painters, which produced followers rather than new leaders. Their contemporaries in Siena were more fortunate in this respect, since Duccio never had the same overpowering impact. As a consequence, it was they, not the Florentines, who took the next decisive step in the development of Italian Gothic painting. The new closeness to everyday life depicted in the work of the brothers Pietro and Ambrogio Lorenzetti (both died 1348?) is coupled with Giotto's monumentality and Duccio's keen interest in problems of space. The boldest spatial experiment is Pietro's triptych of 1342, the *Birth of the Virgin* (Vol. Two, fig. 35), where the painted architecture has been correlated with the real architecture of the frame in such a way that the

36. Ambrogio Lorenzetti. *Good Government in the City.* 1338–40. Fresco, width of entire wall 46' (14 m). Palazzo Pubblico, Siena

two are seen as a single system. Moreover, the vaulted chamber where the birth takes place occupies two panels. It continues unbroken behind the column that divides the center from the right wing. The left wing represents an anteroom which leads to a large and only partially glimpsed architectural space suggesting the interior of a Gothic church. What Pietro Lorenzetti achieved here is the outcome of a development that began three decades earlier in the work of Duccio (compare Vol. Two, fig. 33): the conquest of pictorial space. Only now, however, does the painting surface assume the quality of a transparent window *through* which—not *on* which—we perceive the same kind of space we know from daily experience. Duccio's work alone is not sufficient to explain Pietro's aston-

ishing breakthrough. It became possible, rather, through a combination of the *architectural* picture space of Duccio and the *sculptural* picture space of Giotto.

The same procedure enabled Ambrogio Lorenzetti to unfold a comprehensive view of the entire town before our eyes in his frescoes of 1338–40 in the Siena city hall (Vol. Two, fig. 36). His mural forms part of an elaborate allegorical program depicting the contrast of good and bad government. The artist, in order to show the life of a well-ordered city-state, had to fill the streets and houses with teeming activity. The bustling crowd gives the architectural vista its striking reality by introducing the human scale. On the right, outside the city walls, the *Good Government* fresco provides a view of the

Sienese countryside, fringed by distant mountains. It is a true landscape—the first since ancient Roman times—full of sweeping depth yet with an ingrained orderliness, which lends it a domesticated air. Here the presence of people is not accidental. They have taken full possession of nature, terracing the hillsides with vineyards, patterning the valleys with the geometry of fields and pastures.

THE BLACK DEATH. The first four decades of the fourteenth century in Florence and Siena had been a period of political stability and economic expansion as well as of great artistic achievement. In the 1340s both cities suffered a series of catastrophes whose echoes were to be felt for many years.

Banks and merchants went bankrupt by the score, internal upheavals shook the government, there were repeated crop failures, and in 1348 the epidemic of bubonic plague—the Black Death—that spread throughout Europe wiped out more than half their urban population. The popular reaction to these calamitous events was mixed. Many people regarded them as signs of divine wrath, warnings to a sinful humanity to forsake the pleasures of this earth; in such people the Black Death engendered a mood of otherworldly exaltation. To others, such as the gay company in Boccaccio's *Decameron,* the fear of sudden death merely intensified the desire to enjoy life while there was yet time. These conflicting attitudes are reflected in the pictorial theme of the Triumph of Death.

37. Francesco Traini. *The Triumph of Death* (detail). c. 1325–50. Fresco. Camposanto, Pisa, Italy

TRAINI. The most impressive version of this subject is an enormous fresco, attributed to the Pisan master Francesco Traini (documented c. 1321–1363), in the Camposanto, the cemetery building next to Pisa Cathedral. In a particularly dramatic detail (Vol. Two, fig. 37), the elegantly costumed men and women on horseback have suddenly come upon three decaying corpses in open coffins. Even the animals are terrified by the sight and smell of rotting flesh. Only the hermit, having renounced all earthly pleasures, calmly points out the lesson of the scene. But will the living accept the lesson, or will they, like the characters of Boccaccio, turn away from the shocking spectacle more determined than ever to pursue their own hedonistic ways? The artist's own sympathies seem curiously divided. His style, far from being otherworldly, recalls the realism of Ambrogio Lorenzetti, although the forms are harsher and more expressive.

Northern Gothic Painting

We are now in a position to turn to Gothic painting north of the Alps. What happened there during the latter half of the

fourteenth century was determined in large measure by the influence of the great Italians, which was sometimes transmitted by Italian artists working on Northern soil. A major gateway of Italian influence was the city of Prague, which in 1347 became the residence of Emperor Charles IV and rapidly developed into an international cultural center second only to Paris. The *Death of the Virgin* (Vol. Two, fig. 38), made by an unknown Bohemian painter about 1360, again brings to mind the achievements of the great Sienese masters, although these were known to our artist only at second or third hand. The carefully articulated architectural interior betrays its descent from such works as Pietro Lorenzetti's *Birth of the Virgin* (Vol. Two, fig. 35), but lacks the spaciousness of its Italian models. Italian, too, is the vigorous modeling of the heads and the overlapping of the figures, which reinforce the three-dimensional quality of the design but raise the awkward question of what to do with the halos (a problem faced by Italian artists as well). Still, the Bohemian master's picture is not just an echo of Italian painting. The gestures and facial expressions convey an intensity of emotion that represents the finest

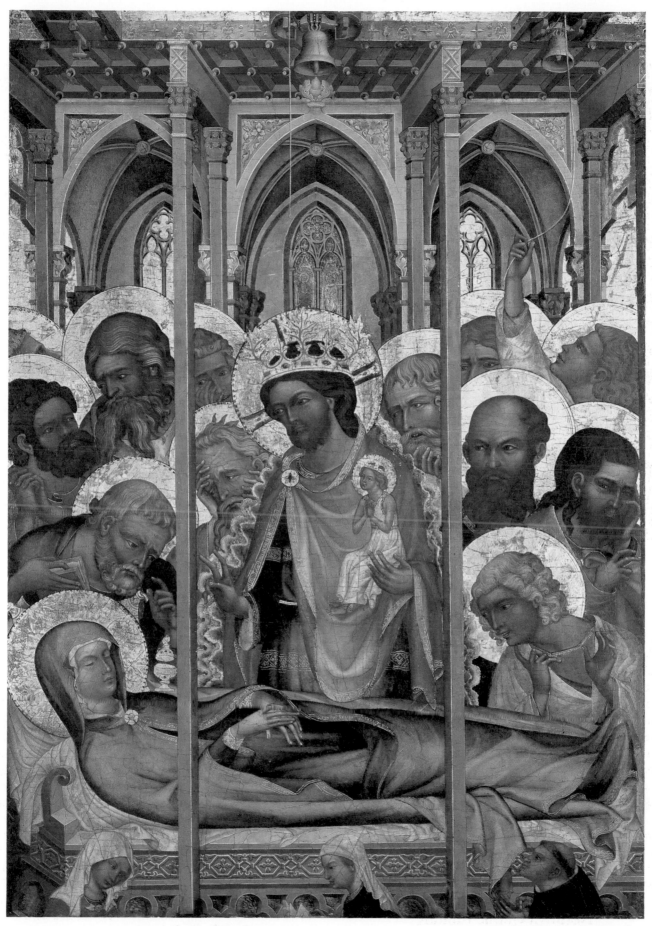

38. Bohemian Master. *Death of the Virgin*. 1350–60. Tempera on panel, 39 3/8 x 28" (100 x 71 cm). Museum of Fine Arts, Boston

William Francis Warden Fund; Seth K. Sweetser Fund, The Henry C. and Martha B. Angell Collection, Juliana Cheney Edwards Collection,

Gift of Martin Brimmer, and Mrs. Frederick Frothingham; by exchange

39. Melchior Broederlam. *Presentation in the Temple* and *Flight into Egypt.* 1394–99. Tempera on panel, 65³/4 x 49¹/4" (167 x 125 cm). Musée de la Ville, Dijon, France

heritage of Northern Gothic art. In this respect, our panel is far more akin to the *Death of the Virgin* at Strasbourg Cathedral (Vol. Two, fig. 45) than to any Italian work.

The International Style

BROEDERLAM. Toward the year 1400, the merging of Northern and Italian traditions gave rise to a single dominant style throughout western Europe. This International Style was not confined to painting, but painters clearly played the main role in its development. Among the most important was Melchior Broederlam (flourished c. 1387–1409), a Fleming who worked for the court of the duke of Burgundy in Dijon. His shutter for an altar shrine (Vol. Two, fig. 39) that he did between 1394 and 1399 is really two pictures within one frame. The temple of the *Presentation* and the landscape of the *Flight into Egypt* stand abruptly side by side, even though the artist has tried to suggest that the scene extends around the building. Compared to paintings by Pietro and Ambrogio Lorenzetti, Broederlam's picture space still strikes us as naïve in many ways. The architecture looks like a doll's house, and the details of the landscape are quite out of scale with the fig-

ures. Yet the panel conveys a strong feeling of depth. The reason for this is the subtlety of the modeling. The softly rounded shapes and the dark, velvety shadows create a sense of light and air that more than makes up for any shortcomings of scale or perspective. Our panel also exemplifies a chief characteristic of the International Style: its "realism of particulars." We find it in the carefully rendered foliage and flowers, in the delightful donkey (obviously drawn from life), and in the rustic figure of St. Joseph, who looks and behaves like a simple peasant and thus helps to emphasize the delicate, aristocratic beauty of the Virgin. This painstaking concentration on detail gives Broederlam's work the flavor of an enlarged miniature rather than of a large-scale painting, even though the panels are more than five feet tall.

THE LIMBOURG BROTHERS. Book illumination remained the leading form of painting in northern Europe at the time of the International Style, despite the growing importance of panel painting. Thus the International Style reached its most advanced phase in the luxurious book of hours known as *Les Très Riches Heures du Duc de Berry,* produced for the brother of the king of France, a man of far from admirable

40. The
Limbourg
Brothers.
February, from
*Les Très Riches
Heures du Duc
de Berry.*
1413–16.
Musée Condé,
Chantilly,
France

41. Gentile da Fabriano. *The Adoration of the Magi.* 1423.
Oil on panel, 9'10 1/8" x 9'3" (3 x 2.8 m). Galleria degli Uffizi, Florence

character but the most lavish art patron of his day. The artists were Pol de Limbourg and his two brothers, a group of Flemings who, like Broederlam, had settled in France. They must have visited Italy as well, for their work includes numerous motifs and whole compositions borrowed from the great masters of Tuscany.

The most remarkable pages of *Les Très Riches Heures* are those of the calendar, with their elaborate depiction of the life of humanity and nature throughout the months of the year. Such cycles, originally consisting of 12 single figures each performing an appropriate seasonal activity, had long been an established tradition in medieval art. The Limbourg brothers, however, integrated all these elements into a series of panoramas of human life *in* nature. Thus the February miniature (Vol. Two, fig. 40), the earliest snow landscape in the history of Western art, gives an enchantingly lyrical account of village

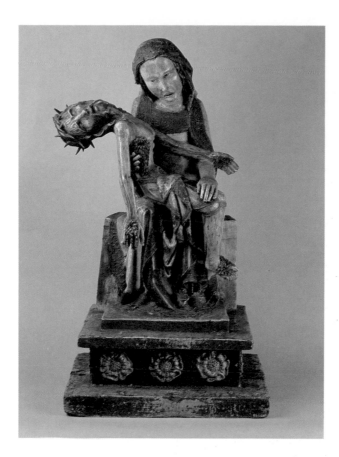

42. *Roettgen Pietà.*
Early 14th century.
Wood, height 34 1/2"
(87.5 cm).
Rheinisches
Landesmuseum,
Bonn, Germany

life in the dead of winter. We see the sheep huddled together in their fold, birds hungrily scratching in the barnyard, and a maid blowing on her frostbitten hands as she hurries to join her companions in the warm cottage. (The front wall has been omitted for our benefit.) In the middle distance is a villager cutting trees for firewood and another driving his laden donkey toward the houses among the hills. Here the promise of the Broederlam panels has been fulfilled, as it were: landscape, architectural interiors, and exteriors are harmoniously united in deep, atmospheric space. Even such intangible things as the frozen breath of the maid, the smoke curling from the chimney, and the clouds in the sky have become paintable.

GENTILE DA FABRIANO. During the later fourteenth century, it was in northern Italy, particularly hospitable to artistic influences from across the Alps, that the International Style found its greatest Italian representative in Gentile da Fabriano (c. 1370–1427). He worked mainly in Venice before moving to Florence, where he painted his masterpiece, *The Adoration of the Magi* (Vol. Two. fig. 41). In his altarpiece, the costumes are as colorful, the draperies as ample and softly rounded, as in Northern painting. The Holy Family on the left almost seems in danger of being overwhelmed by the festive pageant pouring down upon it from the hills in the distance. The foreground includes more than a dozen marvelously well-observed animals, not only the familiar ones but hunting leopards, camels, and monkeys. (Such creatures were eagerly collected by the princes of the period, many of whom kept private zoos.) The Oriental background of the Magi is further emphasized by the Mongolian facial cast of some of their companions. It is not these exotic touches, however, that mark our picture as the work of an Ital-

ian master but something else, a greater sense of weight, of physical substance, than we could hope to find among the Northern representatives of the International Style. Despite his love of fine detail, Gentile is obviously a painter used to working on a monumental scale, rather than a manuscript illuminator at heart.

SCULPTURE

THE PIETÀ. Gothic sculpture reflects a desire to endow the traditional themes of Christian art with an ever greater emotional appeal. Toward the end of the thirteenth century, this tendency gave rise to a new kind of religious imagery, designed to serve private devotion. It is often referred to by the German term *Andachtsbild* (contemplation image), since Germany played a leading part in its development. The most characteristic and widespread type of *Andachtsbild* was the *Pietà* (an Italian word derived from the Latin *pietas,* the root word for both pity and piety): a representation of the Virgin grieving over the dead Christ. No such scene occurs in the scriptural account of the Passion. The Pietà conflates two iconic types: the Madonna and Child and the Crucifixion, which were often paired as objects of veneration once they became familiar to Europeans following the conquest of Constantinople in 1204. Exactly where or when this imagery was invented we do not know, but it represents one of the Seven Sorrows of the Virgin, a tragic counterpart to the familiar motif of the Madonna and Child, which depicts one of her Seven Joys.

The *Pietà* reproduced here (Vol. Two, fig. 42) is carved of wood, with a vividly painted surface to enhance its impact. Like most such groups, this large cult statue was meant to be placed on an altar. The style, like the subject itself, responds to

43. Claus Sluter. *The Moses Well*. 1395–1406. Stone, height of figures approx. 6' (1.8 m). Chartreuse de Champmol, Dijon

the emotional fervor of lay religiosity, which emphasized a personal relationship with the deity as part of the tide of mysticism that swept the fourteenth century. Realism here has become purely a vehicle of expression to enhance its impact.

The agonized faces convey an unbearable pain and grief. The blood-encrusted wounds of Christ are enlarged and elaborated to an almost grotesque degree. The bodies and limbs have become puppetlike in their thinness and rigidity. The purpose

44. Nicola Pisano. *Nativity*, detail of pulpit. 1259–60. Marble. Baptistery, Pisa

of the work, clearly, is to arouse so overwhelming a sense of horror and pity that the faithful will share completely in Christ's suffering and identify their own feelings with those of the grief-stricken Mother of God. The ultimate goal of this emotional bond is a spiritual transformation that comprehends the central mystery of God in human form through compassion (which means "to suffer with"). The lean, "deflated" quality of form is the characteristic period flavor of Northern European art from the late thirteenth to the mid-fourteenth century. Only after 1350 do we again find an interest in weight and volume, coupled with a renewed impulse to explore tangible reality.

SLUTER. The climax of this new trend came around 1400, during the period of the International Style. Its greatest exponent was Claus Sluter, a sculptor of Netherlandish origin working for the duke of Burgundy at Dijon. Much of his work belongs to a category that, for lack of a better term, we must label church furniture (tombs, pulpits, and the like), which combine large-scale sculpture with a small-scale architectural setting. The most impressive of these is *The Moses Well* at the Chartreuse de Champmol (Vol. Two, fig. 43), which also housed Broederlam's altar wings. The majestic Moses epitomizes Sluter's statues. Soft, lavishly draped garments envelop the heavy-set body like an ample shell, and the swelling forms seem to reach out into the surrounding space, determined to capture as much of it as possible. (Note the

outward curve of the scroll, which reads, "The children of Israel do not listen to me.") The effect must have been heightened greatly by polychromy, which has unfortunately disappeared. At first glance, Moses seems a startling premonition of the Renaissance. (Compare Michelangelo's treatment of the same subject in fig. 608.) Only upon closer inspection do we realize that in his vocabulary Sluter remains firmly allied to the Gothic.

In the Isaiah, facing left in our illustration, what strikes us is the precise and masterful realism of every detail, from the minutiae of the costume to the texture of the wrinkled skin. The head, unlike that of Moses, has all the individuality of a portrait. Nor is this impression deceiving, for the sculptural development that culminated in Claus Sluter produced, from about 1350 on, the first genuine portraits since late antiquity. This attachment to the tangible and specific distinguishes his realism from that of the thirteenth century.

NICOLA AND GIOVANNI PISANO. Italian architects and sculptors followed a very different course from that of the painters. Untouched by the Greek manner, they were assimilating the Gothic style. The founder of Italian Gothic sculpture was Nicola Pisano (c. 1220/5 or before–1284?) who came to Tuscany from southern Italy around 1250. His work has been well defined as that of "the greatest—and in a sense the last—of medieval classicists." The narrative scenes, such as the *Nativity* (Vol. Two, fig. 44), on the marble pulpit he completed

45. *Death of the Virgin,* tympanum of the south transept portal, Strasbourg Cathedral, France. c. 1220

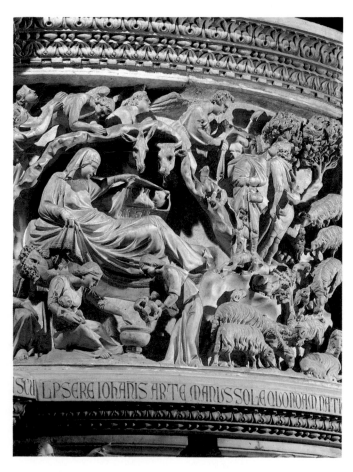

46. Giovanni Pisano. *Nativity,* detail of pulpit. 1302–10. Marble. Pisa Cathedral

in 1260 for the Baptistery of Pisa Cathedral, tell us that he must have been thoroughly familiar with Roman sarcophagi. The relief is treated as a shallow box filled almost to the bursting point with solid, convex shapes. This dense crowding of figures has no counterpart in Northern Gothic sculpture. On the other hand, it shares a striking Gothic quality of human feeling with the *Death of the Virgin* (Vol. Two, fig. 45) at Strasbourg Cathedral. The draperies, the facial types, and the movements and gestures in the Strasbourg relief have a classical flavor. The pathos also has classical roots, but what marks it as Gothic is the tenderness that pervades the entire scene. We sense a bond of shared emotion among the figures, and their ability to communicate by glance and gesture with moving eloquence.

Some 50 years later Nicola's son Giovanni (1245/50– after 1314), who was an equally gifted sculptor, carved a marble pulpit for Pisa Cathedral that also includes a *Nativity* (Vol. Two, fig. 46). Both panels have a good many things in common, as we might well expect. Yet Giovanni's slender, swaying figures, with their smoothly flowing draperies, recall neither classical antiquity nor the *Visitation* group at Reims. Instead, they reflect the elegant style of the royal court at Paris that had become the standard Gothic formula during the later thirteenth century. And with this change there has come about a new treatment of relief: to Giovanni Pisano, space is as important as plastic form. The figures are no longer tightly packed together. They are now spaced far enough apart to let us see the landscape setting that contains them, and each figure has been allotted its own pocket of space. If Nicola's *Nativity* strikes us as essentially an agglomeration of bulging, rounded masses, Giovanni's appears to be composed mainly of cavities and shadows. Here Giovanni Pisano is following the trend toward disembodiment found north of the Alps around 1300.

PART THREE

THE RENAISSANCE THROUGH THE ROCOCO

I n discussing the transition from classical antiquity to the Middle Ages, we were able to point to a great crisis—the rise of Islam—marking the separation between the two eras. No comparable event sets off the Middle Ages from the Renaissance. The fifteenth and sixteenth centuries, to be sure, witnessed far-reaching developments: the fall of Constantinople and the Turkish conquest of southeastern Europe; the journeys of exploration that led to the founding of overseas empires in the New World, in Africa and Asia, with the subsequent rivalry of Spain and England as the foremost colonial powers; and the deep spiritual crises of the Reformation and Counter Reformation. But none of these events, however great their effects, can be said to have produced the new era. By the time they happened, the Renaissance was well under way. Even if we disregard the minority of scholars who would deny the existence of the period altogether, we are left with an extraordinary diversity of views on the Renaissance. Perhaps the only essential point on which most experts agree is that the Renaissance had begun when people realized they were no longer living in the Middle Ages.

This statement is not as simple-minded as it sounds. It brings out the undeniable fact that the Renaissance was the first period in history to be aware of its own existence and to coin a label for itself. Medieval people did not think they belonged to an age distinct from classical antiquity. The past, to them, consisted simply of "B.C." and "A.D.," the era "under the Law" (that is, of the Old Testament) and the era "of Grace" (that is, after the birth of Jesus). From their point of view, then, history was made in Heaven rather than on earth. The Renaissance, by contrast, divided the past not according to the divine plan of salvation, but on the basis of human achievements. It saw classical antiquity as the era when civilization had reached the peak of its creative powers, an era brought to a sudden end by the barbarian invasions that destroyed the Roman Empire. During the thousand-year interval of "darkness" that followed, little was accomplished, but now, at last, this "time in-between" or "Middle Age" had been superseded by a revival of all those arts and sciences that flourished in classical antiquity. The present, the "New Age," could thus be fittingly labeled a "rebirth"—*rinascita* in Italian (from the Latin *renascere,* to be reborn), *renaissance* in French and, by adoption, in English.

The origin of this revolutionary view of history can be traced back to the 1330s in the writings of the Italian poet Francesco Petrarca, the first of the great individuals who made the Renaissance. Petrarch, as we call him, thought of the new era mainly as a "revival of the classics," limited to the restoration of Latin and Greek to their former purity and the return to the original texts of ancient authors. During the next two centuries, this concept of the rebirth of antiquity grew to embrace almost the entire range of cultural endeavor, including the visual arts. The latter, in fact, came to play a particularly important part in shaping the Renaissance, for reasons that we shall explore later.

That the new historic orientation (to which, let us remember, we owe our concepts of the Renaissance, the Middle Ages, and classical antiquity) should have had its start in the mind of one man is itself a telling comment on the new era, although it was soon taken up by many others. Individualism—a new self-awareness and self-assurance—enabled Petrarch to proclaim, against all established authority, his own conviction that the "age of faith" was actually an era of darkness, while the "benighted pagans" of antiquity really represented the most enlightened stage of history. Such readiness to question traditional beliefs and practices was to become profoundly characteristic of the Renaissance as a whole. Humanism, to Petrarch, meant a belief in the importance of what we still call "the humanities" or "humane letters" (rather than divine letters, or the study of Scripture): the pursuit of learning in languages, literature, history, and philosophy for its own end, in a secular rather than a religious framework.

We must not assume, however, that Petrarch and his successors wanted to revive classical antiquity lock, stock, and barrel. By interposing the concept of "a thousand years of darkness" between themselves and the ancients, they acknowledged (unlike the medieval classicists) that the Graeco-Roman world was irretrievably dead. Its glories could be revived only in the mind, by nostalgic and admiring contemplation across the barrier of the "dark ages," by rediscovering the full greatness of ancient achievements in art and thought, and by endeavoring to compete with these achievements on an ideal plane.

The aim of the Renaissance was not to duplicate the works of antiquity but to equal and, if possible, to surpass them. In practice, this meant that the authority granted to the ancient models was far from unlimited. Writers strove to express themselves with Ciceronian eloquence and precision, but not necessarily in Latin. Architects continued to build the churches demanded by Christian ritual, not to duplicate pagan temples; but their churches were designed *all'antica,* "in the manner of the ancients," using an architectural vocabulary based on the study of classical structures. The humanists, however great their enthusiasm for classical philosophy, did not become neo-pagans but went to great lengths trying to reconcile the heritage of the ancient thinkers with Christianity.

The people of the Renaissance, then, found themselves in the position of the legendary sorcerer's apprentice who set out to emulate his master's achievements and in the process released far greater energies than he had bargained for. But since their master was dead, rather than merely absent, they had to cope with these unfamiliar powers as best they could, until they became masters in their own right. This process of forced growth was replete with crises and tensions. The Renaissance must have been an uncomfortable, though intensely exciting, time to live in. Yet these very tensions, it seems, called forth an outpouring of creative energy such as the world had never experienced. It is a fundamental paradox that the desire to return to the classics, based on a rejection of the Middle Ages, brought to the new era not the rebirth of antiquity but the birth of modern civilization.

IRELAND

ENGLAND

NORTH SEA

AMSTERDAM
HAARLEM
LEYDEN
THE HAGUE
DELFT
ROTTERDAM
HERTOGENBOSCH

NETHERLANDS

UTRECHT

HOLLAND

HOLY ROMA

WOODSTOCK
OXFORD
OXFORDSHIRE
WINDSOR
LONDON
Thames R.

KASSEL •

BRUGES
FLANDERS
LILLE
DOUAI

ANTWERP
GHENT
BRUSSELS
BELGIUM
TOURNAI

BONN

Rhine R.

FRANKF
WÜRZB

ATLANTIC OCEAN

RHINELAND

BA

ENGLISH CHANNEL

CAEN
NORMANDY

CHANTILLY
VERSAILLES
CHARTRES
PARIS
MAISONS
FONTAINEBLEAU

REIMS

Meuse R.

Seine R.

ALSACE

KARLSR

STRASBOU

ISENHEIM
COLMAR
Lake Constance

BRITTANY

Loire R.

CHAMBORD

BERRY

DIJON

BURGUNDY

BASEL

SWITZERLAN

FRANCE

Lake Geneva

GENEVA

LO

MILA

BAY OF BISCAY

SAVOY

TURIN •

Rhône R.

AVIGNON

PROVENCE

PORTUGAL

Tagus R.

MADRID

TOLEDO

S P A I N

Guadalquivir R.

SEVILLE

GRANADA

MEDITERRANEAN SEA

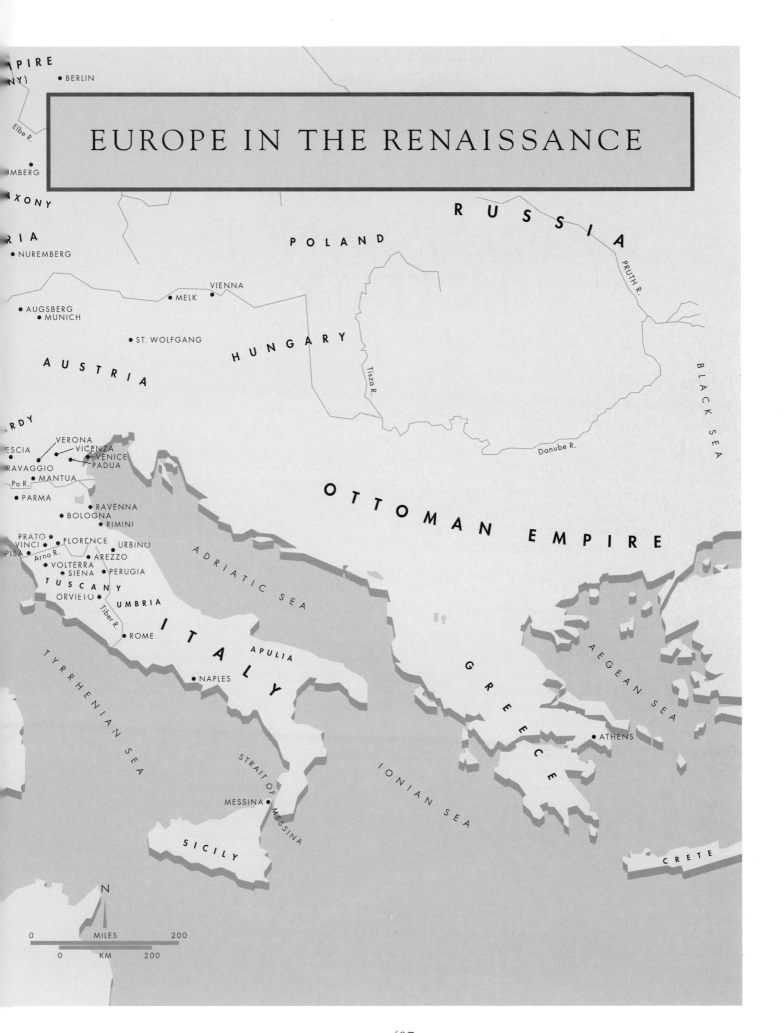

EUROPE IN THE RENAISSANCE

PIRE
NY)
• BERLIN

Elbe R.

MBERG

XONY

RIA
• NUREMBERG

RUSSIA

POLAND

PRUTH R.

• AUGSBERG
• MUNICH

MELK   VIENNA

• ST. WOLFGANG

AUSTRIA

HUNGARY

Tisza R.

BLACK SEA

RDY

Danube R.

VERONA
ESCIA   VICENZA
RAVAGGIO VENICE
        PADUA
Po R. MANTUA
• PARMA

OTTOMAN EMPIRE

• RAVENNA
• BOLOGNA
    • RIMINI

PRATO •
VINCI • • FLORENCE   • URBINO
PISA   • AREZZO
Arno R.
• VOLTERRA
• SIENA   • PERUGIA
TUSCANY
• ORVIETO

ADRIATIC SEA

UMBRIA

Tiber R.

ITALY

• ROME

APULIA

GREECE

AEGEAN SEA

TYRRHENIAN SEA

• NAPLES

STRAIT OF MESSINA

IONIAN SEA

ATHENS •

MESSINA •

SICILY

CRETE

N

0   MILES   200
0   KM   200

CHAPTER ONE

THE EARLY RENAISSANCE IN ITALY

As we narrow our focus from the Renaissance as a whole to the Renaissance in the fine arts, we are faced with some questions that are still under debate. When did Renaissance art begin? Did it, like Gothic art, originate in a specific center or in several places at the same time? Should we think of it as one coherent style or as an attitude that might be embodied in more than one style? "Renaissance-consciousness," we know, was an Italian idea, and there can be no doubt that Italy played the leading role in the development of Renaissance art, at least until the early sixteenth century. This fact does not necessarily mean, however, that the Renaissance was confined to the South.

So far as architecture and sculpture are concerned, modern scholarship agrees with the traditional view, first expressed more than 500 years ago, that the Renaissance began soon after 1400 in Florence. For painting, however, an even older tradition claims that the new era began with Giotto, who, as Boccaccio wrote about 1350, "restored to light this art which had been buried for many centuries." We cannot disregard such testimony. Yet if we accept it at face value, we must assume that the Renaissance in painting dawned about 1300, a full generation before Petrarch. Giotto himself certainly did not reject the past as an age of darkness. After all, the two chief sources of his own style were the Byzantine tradition and the influence of Northern Gothic. The artistic revolution he created from these elements does not inherently place him in a

new era, since revolutionary changes had occurred in medieval art before. Nor is it fair to credit this revolution to him alone, disregarding Duccio and the other great Sienese masters. Petrarch was well aware of the achievements of all these artists—he wrote admiringly of both Giotto and Simone Martini—but he never claimed that they had restored to light what had been buried during the centuries of darkness. And, in fact, such a thing was inherently impossible, because neither could have known classical painting.

How, then, do we account for Boccaccio's statement about Giotto? We must understand that Boccaccio (1313–1375), an ardent disciple of Petrarch, was chiefly concerned with advancing humanism in literature. In his defense of the status of poetry, he found it useful to draw analogies with painting. Had not the ancients themselves proclaimed that the two arts were alike, in Horace's famous dictum that art must conform to the example of poetry (*ut pictura poesis*)? Boccaccio thus cast Giotto in the role of "the Petrarch of painting," taking advantage of his already legendary fame. Boccaccio's view of Giotto as a Renaissance artist is, then, a bit of intellectual strategy, rather than a trustworthy reflection of Giotto's own attitude. Nevertheless, what he has to say interests us because he was the first to apply Petrarch's concept of "revival after the dark ages" to one of the visual arts, even though he did so somewhat prematurely.

Boccaccio's way of describing Giotto's achievement is also noteworthy. It was he who claimed that Giotto depicted every aspect of nature so truthfully that people often mistook his paintings for reality itself. Here he implies that the revival of antiquity means for painters an uncompromising realism. This, as we shall see, was to become a persistent theme in Renaissance thought, justifying the imitation of nature as part of the great movement "back to the classics" and tending to minimize the possible conflict between these two aims. After all, Classical Greek art was itself based on a synthesis of naturalism and ideal proportions.

FLORENCE: 1400–1450

There were special circumstances that help to explain why the Early Renaissance was born in Florence at the beginning of the fifteenth century, rather than elsewhere or at some other time. In the years around 1400, Florence faced an acute threat to its independence from the powerful duke of Milan, who was trying to bring all of Italy under his rule. He had already subjugated the Lombard plain and most of the Central Italian city-states. Florence remained the only serious obstacle to his ambition. The city put up a vigorous and successful defense on the military, diplomatic, and intellectual fronts. Of these three, the intellectual was by no means the least important. The duke had eloquent support as a new Caesar, bringing peace and order to the country. Florence, in turn, rallied public opinion by proclaiming itself as the champion of freedom against unchecked tyranny.

This propaganda war was waged on both sides by humanists, the heirs of Petrarch and Boccaccio, but the Florentines gave by far the better account of themselves. Their writings, such as *Praise of the City of Florence* (1402–3) by Leonardo Bruni (see fig. 577), give renewed focus to the Petrarchan ideal of a rebirth of the Classics. The humanist, speaking as the citizen of a free republic, asks why, among all the states of Italy, Florence alone had been able to defy the superior power of Milan. He finds the answer in her institutions, her cultural achievements, her geographical situation, the spirit of her people, and her descent from the city-states of ancient Etruria. Florence, he concludes, assumes the same role of political and intellectual leadership as that of Athens at the time of the Persian Wars.

The patriotic pride, the call to greatness, implicit in this image of Florence as the "new Athens" must have aroused a deep response throughout the city, for just when the forces of Milan threatened to engulf them, the Florentines embarked on an ambitious campaign to finish the great artistic enterprises begun a century before at the time of Giotto. Following the competition of 1401–2 for the bronze doors of the Baptistery of S. Giovanni, another extensive program continued the sculptural decoration of Florence Cathedral and other churches, while deliberations were resumed on how to build the dome of the Cathedral, the largest and most difficult project of all. The campaign lasted more than 30 years; it gradually petered out after the completion of the dome in 1436. Although difficult to express in present-day financial terms, its total cost was comparable to the cost of rebuilding the Acropolis in Athens. The huge investment was itself not a guarantee of artistic quality, but, stirred by such civic enthusiasm, it provided a splendid opportunity for the emergence of creative talent and the coining of a new style worthy of the "new Athens."

From the start, the visual arts were considered essential to the resurgence of the Florentine spirit. Throughout antiquity and the Middle Ages, they had been classed with the crafts, or "mechanical arts." It cannot be by chance that the first explicit statement claiming a place for them among the liberal arts occurs around 1400 in the writings of the Florentine chronicler Filippo Villani. A century later, this claim was to win general acceptance throughout most of the Western world. What does it imply? The liberal arts were defined by a tradition going back to Plato and comprised the intellectual disciplines necessary for a "gentleman's" education: mathematics (including musical theory), dialectics, grammar, rhetoric, and philosophy. The fine arts were excluded because they were "handiwork" lacking a theoretical basis. Thus when artists gained admission to this select group, the nature of their work had to be redefined. They were acknowledged as people of ideas, rather than mere manipulators of materials, and works of art came to be viewed more and more as the visible records of their creative minds. This meant that works of art need not—indeed, should not—be judged by fixed standards of craftsmanship. Soon everything that bore the imprint of a great master was eagerly collected, regardless of its incompleteness: drawings, sketches, fragments, unfinished pieces.

The outlook of artists, too, underwent important changes as well. Now in the company of scholars and poets, they themselves often became learned and literary. They might write poems, autobiographies, or theoretical treatises. As another consequence of their new social status, artists tended to develop into one of two contrasting personality types: the person of the world, self controlled, polished, at ease in aristocratic society; or the solitary genius, secretive, idiosyncratic, subject to fits of melancholy, and likely to be in conflict with patrons. It is remarkable how soon this modern view of art and artists became a living reality in the Florence of the Early Renaissance. However, such an attitude did not take immediate hold everywhere, nor did it apply equally to all artists. England, for example, was slow to grant them special status, and women in general were denied the professional training and opportunities available to men.

In addition to humanism and historical forces, we must acknowledge the decisive importance of individual genius in the birth of Renaissance art. It originated with three men of exceptional ability—Filippo Brunelleschi, Donatello, and Masaccio. It is hardly a coincidence that these founders knew each other. Moreover, they faced the same fundamental task: to reconcile Classical form with Christian content in creating the new style. Yet each possessed a unique artistic personality that enabled him to solve this problem in a distinctive way. Thanks to them, Florentine art retained the undisputed leadership of the movement during the first half of the fifteenth century, which became the heroic age of the Early Renaissance. To trace its beginnings, we must discuss sculpture first, for although Brunelleschi was perhaps the central figure, the sculptors had earlier and more plentiful opportunities than the architects or the painters to meet the challenge of the "new Athens."

527. Nanni di Banco. *Four Saints (Quattro Coronati).* c. 1410–14.
Marble, about lifesize. Or San Michele, Florence

Sculpture

GHIBERTI. The artistic campaign had opened with the competition for the Baptistery doors, and for some time it consisted mainly of sculptural projects. Ghiberti's trial relief, we recall, does not differ significantly from the International Gothic (see fig. 492); nor do the completed Baptistery doors, even though their execution took another 20 years. Only in the trial panel can Ghiberti's admiration for ancient art, as demonstrated by the torso of Isaac, be linked with the classicism of the Florentine humanists around 1400. Similar instances occur in other Florentine sculpture at that time. But such quotations of ancient sculpture, isolated and small in scale, merely recapture what Nicola Pisano had done a century before (see fig. 483).

NANNI DI BANCO. A decade after the trial relief, we find that this limited medieval classicism has been surpassed by a somewhat younger artist, Nanni di Banco (c. 1384–1421). The four saints, called the *Quattro Coronati* (fig. 527), which he made about 1410–14 for one of the niches on the exterior of the church of Or San Michele, demand to be compared not with the work of Nicola Pisano but with the Reims *Visitation* (see fig. 471). The saints represent four Christian sculptors who were executed for not carving the statue of a pagan god ordered by Diocletian—a story later conflated with that of four martyrs who refused to worship in the god's temple. The figures in both groups are approximately lifesize, yet Nanni's give the impression of being a good deal larger than those at Reims. Their quality of mass and monumentality was quite beyond the range of medieval sculpture, even though Nanni depended less directly on ancient models than had the sculptor of the *Visitation* or Nicola Pisano. Only the heads of the second and third of the *Coronati* directly recall examples of Roman sculpture, specifically those memorable portrait heads of the third century A.D. (see figs. 528 and 529). Nanni was obviously impressed by their realism and their agonized expressions. His ability to retain the essence of both these qualities indicates a new attitude toward ancient art, which unites classical form and content, instead of separating them as medieval classicists had done.

DONATELLO'S EARLY WORKS. Early Renaissance art sought an attitude toward the human body similar to that of classical antiquity. The artist who did most to reestablish this attitude was Donatello, the greatest sculptor of his time. Born in 1386, several years after Nanni di Banco, he died in 1466, outliving Nanni by 45 years. Among the founders of the new style, he alone survived well past the middle of the century. Together with Nanni, Donatello spent the early part of his career working on commissions for Florence Cathedral and Or San Michele. They often faced the same artistic problems, yet the personalities of the two masters had little in common.

Their different approaches are strikingly illustrated in Nanni's *Quattro Coronati* and Donatello's *St. Mark* (fig. 530). Both are located in deep Gothic niches, but Nanni's figures cannot be divorced from the architectural setting and still seem attached, like jamb statues, to the pilasters behind them. The *St. Mark,* however, no longer needs such shelter. Perfectly balanced and self-sustaining, he would lose nothing of his immense authority if he were deprived of his present enclosure. Here is the first statue since antiquity capable of standing by itself—or, to put it another way, the first statue to recapture the full meaning of the classical *contrapposto.* In a performance that truly marks an epoch, the young Donatello has mastered at one stroke the central achievement of ancient sculpture. He treats the human body as an articulated structure, capable of movement, and its drapery as a separate and secondary element that is determined by the shapes underneath rather than by patterns imposed from without. Unlike the *Coronati,* the *St. Mark* looks as if he could take off his clothes, yet he is not at all classicistic—that is, ancient motifs are not quoted as they are in Nanni's figures. Perhaps "classic" is a better word for him instead.

528. *Four Saints (Quattro Coronati),* head of second figure from left in fig. 527

529. *Portrait of a Roman.* Early 3rd century A.D. Marble, lifesize. Staatliche Museen zu Berlin, Antikensammlung

530. Donatello. *St. Mark.* 1411–13. Marble, 7'9" (2.4 m). Or San Michele, Florence

531. Donatello. St. George Tabernacle, from Or San Michele, Florence. c. 1415–17.
Marble, height of statue 6'10" (2.1 m). Museo Nazionale del Bargello, Florence

532. *St. George and the Dragon,* relief below *St. George* (fig. 531). Marble, height 15³/4" (40 cm)

A few years later, about 1415–17, Donatello carved another statue for Or San Michele, the famous *St. George* (fig. 531). The niche is shallower than that of the *St. Mark,* so that the young warrior saint actually protrudes from it slightly. Although encased in armor, his body and limbs are not rigid but wonderfully elastic. His stance, with the weight placed on the forward leg, conveys his readiness for combat. (The right hand originally held a lance or sword.) The controlled energy of his body is reflected in his eyes, which seem to scan the horizon for the approaching enemy. *St. George* is the Christian Soldier in his Early Renaissance version, spiritually akin to the *St. Theodore* at Chartres (see fig. 468), but he is also the proud defender of the "new Athens."

Below *St. George*'s niche is a relief panel (fig. 532) showing the hero's best-known exploit, the slaying of a dragon. (The maiden on the right is the captive princess whom the saint had come to liberate.) Here Donatello produces another revolutionary work, devising a new kind of relief that is physically shallow (called *schiacciato,* "flattened-out"). Yet it creates an illusion of infinite pictorial depth. This had already been achieved to some degree in certain Greek and Roman reliefs, as well as by Ghiberti (compare with figs. 197, 267–72, and 492). In all these cases, however, the actual carved depth is roughly proportional to the apparent depth of the space represented. The forms in the front plane are in very high relief, while those more distant become progressively lower, seemingly immersed in the background of the panel. Donatello discards this relationship altogether. Behind the figures, the amazing windswept landscape consists entirely of delicate surface modulations that cause the marble to catch light from varying angles. Every tiny ripple becomes endowed with a descriptive power infinitely greater than its real depth, and the chisel, like a painter's brush, becomes a tool for creating shades of light and dark. Yet Donatello cannot have borrowed his landscape from any painting, for no painter at the time he did the *St. George* relief had achieved so coherent and atmospheric a view of nature.

When the campanile of Florence Cathedral was built between 1334 and 1357, a row of tall Gothic niches had been designed for statues (barely visible above the rooftops in fig. 459). Half of these niches were still empty, but between 1416 and 1435 Donatello filled five of them. The most impressive statue of his series (fig. 533) is the unidentified prophet nicknamed *Zuccone* ("pumpkin-head"), made a dozen years after

533. Donatello. *Prophet (Zuccone),* on the campanile of Florence Cathedral. 1423–25. Marble, height 6'5" (2 m). Original now in the Museo dell'Opera del Duomo, Florence

the *St. Mark*. The figure has long enjoyed special fame as a striking example of the master's realism. There can be no question that it is indeed realistic, far more so than any ancient statue or its nearest rivals, the prophets on Sluter's *Moses Well* (see fig. 481). But, we may ask, what kind of realism have we here? Donatello has not followed the conventional image of a prophet (a bearded old man in Oriental-looking costume, holding a large scroll). Rather, he has invented an entirely new type, and it is difficult to account for his impulse in terms of realism. Why did he not simply reinterpret the old image from a realistic point of view, as Sluter had done? Donatello obviously felt that the established type was inadequate for his own conception of the subject. But how did he conceive it anew? Surely not by observing the people around him. More likely, he imagined the personalities of the prophets from what he had read about them in the Old Testament. He gained an impression, we may assume, of divinely inspired orators lecturing the multitude. This, in turn, reminded him of the Roman orators he had seen in ancient sculpture. Hence the classical costume of the *Zuccone,* whose mantle falls from one shoulder like those of the toga-clad patricians in figures 263 and 267. Hence, too, the fascinating head, ugly yet noble, like Roman portraits of the third century A.D. (compare figs. 280 and 281).

To shape all these elements into a coherent whole was a revolutionary feat that required an almost visible struggle. Donatello himself seems to have regarded the *Zuccone* as a particularly hard-won achievement. It is the first of his surviving works to carry his signature. He is said to have sworn "by the Zuccone" when he wanted to emphasize a statement and to have shouted at the statue while working on it, "Speak, speak, or the plague take you!"

Donatello had learned the technique of bronze sculpture as a youth by working under Ghiberti on the first Baptistery doors. By the 1420s, he began to rival his former teacher in that medium. *The Feast of Herod* (fig. 534), which he made about 1425 for the baptismal font of S. Giovanni (the Baptistery of Siena Cathedral), shows the same exquisite surface finish as Ghiberti's panels (see fig. 492), but also an expressive power that we could expect only of the master of the *Zuccone*. By classical or medieval standards, the main scene is poorly composed. The focus of the drama (the executioner presenting the head of St. John to Herod) is far to the left, while the dancing Salome and most of the spectators are massed on the right, and the center remains empty. Yet we see at once why Donatello created this gaping hole. It conveys, more effectively than the witnesses' gestures and expressions, the impact of the shocking sight. Moreover, the centrifugal movement of the figures helps persuade us that the picture space does not end within the panel but continues indefinitely in every direction. Hence the frame becomes a window through which we see this particular segment of unlimited, continuous reality. The arched openings within the panel serve to frame additional segments of the same reality, luring us farther into the depths of the palace.

SCIENTIFIC PERSPECTIVE. This architecture, with its round arches, its fluted columns and pilasters, is not Gothic at all, but reflects the new style launched by Filippo Brunelleschi, whose architectural achievements will occupy us soon. Although it is not certain, Brunelleschi probably also invent-

534. Donatello. *The Feast of Herod.* c. 1425. Gilt bronze, 23 1/2" (59.7 cm) square. Baptismal font, Siena Cathedral

ed linear, or scientific, perspective, and *The Feast of Herod* is seemingly the earliest surviving example of a picture space constructed by this method. The system is a geometric procedure for projecting space onto a plane, analogous to the way the lens of a photographic camera projects a perspective image on the film. Its central feature is the vanishing point, toward which any set of parallel lines will seem to converge. If these lines are perpendicular to the picture plane, their vanishing point will be on the horizon, corresponding exactly to the position of the beholder's eye. Brunelleschi's discovery in itself was scientific rather than artistic, but it immediately became highly important to Early Renaissance artists because, unlike the perspective practices of the past, it was objective, precise, and rational. In fact, it soon became an argument for upgrading the fine arts into the liberal arts.

While empirical methods could also yield striking results, scientific perspective made it possible now to represent three-dimensional space on a flat surface in such a way that all the distances remained measurable. This meant, in turn, that by reversing the procedure the plan could be derived from the perspective picture of a building. On the other hand, the scientific implications of the new perspective demanded that it be consistently applied, a requirement that artists could not always live up to, for practical as well as aesthetic reasons. Since the method presupposes that the beholder's eye occupies a fixed point in space, a perspective picture automatically tells us where we must stand to see it properly. Thus the artist who knows in advance that his work will be seen from above or below, rather than at ordinary eye level, ought to make his perspective construction correspond to these conditions. If, however, these are so abnormal that he must foreshorten his entire design to an extreme degree, he may disregard them and assume instead an ideal beholder, normally located. Such is the case in *The Feast of Herod*. Our eye should be on a line perpendicular to the center of the panel, but in the Baptistery we must crouch low to see it correctly, as the basin to which our relief is attached is only a few feet high. (For a further discussion of scientific perspective and the problems it raises, see pages 423–25.)

DONATELLO'S DAVID. Donatello's bronze *David* (fig. 535) is an equally revolutionary achievement: the first free-standing lifesize nude statue since antiquity. The Middle Ages would surely have condemned it as an idol, and Donatello's contemporaries must also have felt uneasy about it. For many years it remained the only work of its kind. The early history of the figure is unknown, but it must have been meant for an open space. It probably stood on top of a column in the garden of Cosimo de' Medici, the most powerful figure in Florence, where it would have been visible from every side.

The key to its significance is the elaborate helmet of Goliath with visor and wings, which was derived from depictions of the Roman wind god Zephyr, an evil and destructive figure who killed the young boy Hyacinth. This unique and otherwise implausible feature can only refer to the dukes of Milan, who had threatened Florence about 1400 and were now warring against it once more in the mid-1420s. The statue, then, must be understood as a civic-patriotic public monument identifying David—weak but favored by the Lord—with Florence, and Goliath with Milan. David's nudity is most readily explained as a reference to the classical origin of Florence, and his wreathed hat as the opposite of Goliath's helmet: peace versus war. Donatello chose to model an adolescent boy, not a full-grown youth like the athletes of Greece, so that the skeletal structure here is less fully enveloped in swelling muscles. Nor does he articulate the torso according to the classical pattern (compare figs. 182 and 183). Rather, he treats it with a soft sensuousness reminiscent of cult statues of the Roman youth Antinous (compare fig. 285, right). However, his *David* resembles an ancient statue mainly in its beautifully poised contrapposto. If the figure conveys a profoundly Classical air, the reason lies beyond its anatomical perfection. The impassive expression signifies the virtue humility, which triumphs over the sinful pride of Goliath. It was inspired by Classical examples, which equate the lowered gaze with modesty and virtue. As in ancient statues, it is nevertheless the body that speaks to us more eloquently than the face, which by Donatello's standards is strangly devoid of individuality.

DONATELLO'S GATTAMELATA. Donatello was invited to Padua in 1443 to produce the *Equestrian Monument of Gattamelata*, portraying the recently deceased commander of the Venetian armies (fig. 536). This statue, the artist's largest free-standing work in bronze, still occupies its original position on a tall pedestal near the facade of the church dedicated to St. Anthony of Padua. We already know its two chief precedents, the mounted *Marcus Aurelius* in Rome and the *Can Grande in Verona* (see figs. 279 and 489). Without directly imitating the former, the *Gattamelata* shares its material, its impressive scale, and its sense of balance and dignity. Donatello's horse, a heavy-set animal fit to carry a man in full armor, is so large that the rider must dominate it by his authority of command, rather than by physical force. The link with the Can Grande monument, though less obvious, is equally significant. Both statues were made to stand next to a church facade, and both are memorials to the military prowess of the deceased. But the *Gattamelata*, in the new Renaissance fashion, is not part of a tomb. It was designed solely to immortalize the fame of a great soldier. Nor is it the

535. Donatello. *David*. c. 1425–30. Bronze, height 62¼" (158 cm). Museo Nazionale del Bargello, Florence

self-glorifying statue of a sovereign, but a monument authorized by the Republic of Venice in special honor of distinguished and faithful service. To this purpose, Donatello has coined an image that is a complete union of the ideal and the real. The general's armor combines modern construction with classical detail, and the head is powerfully individual, yet endowed with a truly Roman nobility of character.

536. Donatello. *Equestrian Monument of Gattamelata.* 1445–50. Bronze, approx. 11' x 13' (3.35 x 3.96 m). Piazza del Santo, Padua

537. *(left)* Donatello. *Mary Magdalen.* c. 1455. Wood, partially gilded, height 6'2" (1.88 m). Museo dell'Opera del Duomo, Florence

538. *(opposite)* Lorenzo Ghiberti. *"Gates of Paradise,"* east doors of the Baptistery of S. Giovanni, Florence. c. 1435. Gilt bronze, height 15' (4.57 m)

DONATELLO'S LATER WORKS. When Donatello went home to Florence after a decade's absence, he must have felt like a stranger. The political and spiritual climate had changed, and so had the taste of artists and public (see page 409). His subsequent works, between 1453 and 1466, stand apart from the dominant trend. Perhaps that is why their fierce expressiveness and personal quality exceed anything the master had revealed before. The extreme individualism of his late works confirms Donatello's reputation as the earliest "solitary genius" among the artists of the new age.

In contrast to the *David* of some 20 years earlier, the wood *Mary Magdalen* (fig. 537) seems so far from Renaissance ideals that at first we are tempted to see in this statue a return to such Gothic devotional images as the Bonn *Pietà* (see fig. 479). But when we look back at the intensity of Donatello's *Zuccone* (fig. 533), we realize that it is not basically different from his earlier work. *Mary Magdalen* conveys a profound insight into religious experience: the ravaged features and wasted body make her the very embodiment of penitence, so that we fully share her anguish and longing for redemption.

GHIBERTI. At the same time that Donatello made *The Feast of Herod,* Ghiberti was commissioned to do a second pair of bronze doors for the Baptistery in Florence. This set (fig. 538), so beautiful that they were soon dubbed the "Gates of Paradise," is decorated with ten large reliefs in square frames, which provided a more generous field than the 28 small panels in quatrefoil frames of the earlier doors. They mark the artist's successful conversion, under the influence of Donatello and the other pioneers of the new style, to the Early Renaissance point of view. The only lingering elements of the Gothic style are to

539. Lorenzo Ghiberti. *The Story of Jacob and Esau,* panel of the *"Gates of Paradise."* c. 1435. Gilt bronze, 31¼" (79.5 cm) square. Baptistery of S. Giovanni, Florence

be found in the figures, whose gentle and graceful classicism still reminds us of the International Style. The *"Gates of Paradise"* show the new pictorialism that distinguishes Renaissance reliefs. The hint of spatial depth we saw in *The Sacrifice of Isaac* (fig. 492) has grown in *The Story of Jacob and Esau* (fig. 539)

540. Jacopo della Quercia. *The Creation of Adam*. c. 1430. Marble, 34 1/2 x 27 1/2" (87.7 x 69.8 cm). Main portal, S. Petronio, Bologna

541. *Adam in Paradise*, detail of an ivory diptych. c. 400 A.D. Museo Nazionale del Bargello, Florence

into a complete setting for the figures that goes back as far as the eye can reach. We can imagine the figures leaving the scene, for the deep, continuous space of this "pictorial relief" in no way depends on their presence. Ghiberti's spacious hall is a fine example of Early Renaissance architectural design reflecting the mature art of Brunelleschi. Because *The Story of Jacob and Esau* is about a decade later than *The Feast of Herod* by Donatello, its perspective construction is more easy and assured. In the meantime, Brunelleschi's discovery had been formulated in writing by Leone Battista Alberti, the author of the first Renaissance treatise on painting and later an important architect in his own right (see pages 434–37).

JACOPO DELLA QUERCIA. Outside Florence, the only major sculptor at that time was Jacopo della Quercia of Siena (c. 1374–1438). Like Ghiberti, he changed his style from Gothic to Early Renaissance in mid-career, mainly through contact with Donatello. Had he grown up in Florence, he might have been one of the great leaders of the new movement from the start, but his forcefully individual art remained outside the main trend. It had no effect on Florentine art until the very end of the century, when the young Michelangelo fell under its spell.

Michelangelo's admiration was aroused by the scenes from Genesis framing the main portal of the church of S. Petronio in Bologna, among them *The Creation of Adam* (fig. 540). The relief modeling of these panels is conservative—Jacopo had little interest in pictorial depth—but the figures are daring and profoundly impressive. Adam slowly rising from the ground,

as a statue brought to life might rise from its mold, recaptures the heroic beauty of a classical athlete. Here the nude body once again expresses the dignity and power of the individual as it did in classical antiquity. As he faces the Lord, Jacopo's *Adam* contains a hint of incipient conflict that will lead to Original Sin. He will surely fall, but in pride of spirit rather than as a hapless victim of the Evil One.

It is instructive to compare Jacopo's *Adam* with the work that probably inspired it, an *Adam in Paradise* from an Early Christian ivory diptych (fig. 541). The latter figure represents a classicizing trend around 400 A.D. (compare fig. 314), a final attempt to preserve the Greek ideal of physical beauty within a Christian context. Adam appears as the Perfect Man, divinely appointed to "have dominion . . . over every living thing," but the classic form has already become a formula, a mere shell. It was left to the fifteenth century to rediscover the sensuous beauty of the unclothed body. Jacopo's *Adam* is clearly nude, in the full classical sense.

Architecture

BRUNELLESCHI. Although Donatello was its greatest and most daring master, he did not create the Early Renaissance style in sculpture all by himself. The new architecture, on the other hand, owed its existence to one person, Filippo Brunelleschi (1377–1446). Ten years older than Donatello, he, too, had begun his career as a sculptor. After failing to win the competition of 1401–2 for the first Baptistery doors, Brunel-

542. Filippo Brunelleschi. S. Lorenzo, Florence. 1421–69

543. Plan of S. Lorenzo. Gray area indicates Michelangelo's later addition

leschi reportedly went to Rome with Donatello. He studied the architectural monuments of the ancients and seems to have been the first to take exact measurements of these structures. His discovery of scientific perspective (see page 414) may well have grown out of his search for an accurate method of recording their appearance on paper. What else he did during this long gestation period we do not know, but between 1417 and 1419 we again find him competing with Ghiberti, this time for the job of building the Florence Cathedral dome (see figs. 459 and 460). Its design had been established half a century earlier and could be altered only in details, but its vast size posed a difficult problem of construction. Brunelleschi's proposals, although contrary to all traditional practice, so impressed the authorities that this time he won out over his rival. Thus the dome deserves to be called the first work of post-medieval architecture, as an engineering feat if not for style.

Brunelleschi's main achievement was to build the dome in two separate shells which are ingeniously linked to reinforce each other, rather than in one solid mass. As the total weight of the structure was thereby lightened, he could dispense with the massive and costly wooden trusswork required by the older method of construction. Instead of having building materials carried up on ramps to the required level, he designed hoisting machines. His entire scheme reflects a bold, analytical mind, always discarding conventional solutions if better ones could be devised. This fresh approach distinguishes Brunelleschi from the Gothic stonemason-architects, with their time-honored procedures.

In 1419, while he was working out the final plans for the Cathedral dome, Brunelleschi received his first opportunity to create buildings entirely of his own design. It came from the head of the Medici family, one of the leading merchants and bankers of Florence, who commissioned him to add a sacristy to the Romanesque church of S. Lorenzo. His plans for this sacristy (which was to serve also as a burial chapel for the Medici) were so successful that he was immediately asked to develop a new design for the entire church. The construction, begun in 1421, was often interrupted, so that the interior was not completed until 1469, more than 20 years after the architect's death. The exterior itself remains unfinished to this day. Nevertheless, the building in its present form is essentially what Brunelleschi had envisioned about 1420, and thus represents the first full statement of his architectural aims (figs. 542 and 543).

The plan may not seem very novel, at first glance. Its general arrangement recalls Cistercian Gothic churches (see fig. 456), while the unvaulted nave and transept link it to Sta. Croce (see fig. 457). What distinguishes it is a new emphasis on symmetry and regularity. The entire design consists of square units. Four large squares form the choir, the crossing, and the arms of the transept. Four more are combined into the nave. Other squares, one-fourth the size of the large ones, make up the aisles and the chapels attached to the transept. (The oblong chapels outside the aisles were not part of the original design.) As we examine the plan, we realize that Brunelleschi must have first decided to make the floor area of the choir equal to four of the small square units. The nave and transept were thus to be twice as wide as the aisles or chapels. In other words, Brunelleschi conceived S. Lorenzo as a grouping of abstract "space blocks," the larger ones being simple multiples of the standard unit. Once we understand this, we realize how revolutionary he was, for his clearly defined, separate space compartments represent a radical departure from the Gothic architect's way of thinking. In fixing this system, he was not concerned with the thickness of the walls between these compartments, so that the transept arms are slightly longer than they are wide, and the length of the nave is not four but four and one-half times its width.

The interior bears out our expectations. Cool, static order has replaced the emotional warmth, the flowing spatial movement of Gothic church interiors. S. Lorenzo does not sweep us off our feet. It does not even draw us forward after we have entered it, and we are quite content to remain near the door. From that vantage point, our view seems to take in the entire structure, almost as if we were confronted with a particularly clear and convincing demonstration of scientific perspective (compare fig. 539). The total effect recalls the "old-fashioned" Tuscan Romanesque, such as Pisa Cathedral (see fig. 398), as well as Early Christian basilicas (compare fig. 299). These monuments, to Brunelleschi, exemplified the church architecture of classical antiquity. They inspired his return to the use of the round arch and of columns, rather than piers, in the nave arcade. Yet these earlier buildings lack the transparent lightness, the wonderfully precise articulation of S. Lorenzo. Unlike Brunelleschi's, their columns are larger and more closely spaced, tending to screen off the aisles from the nave. Only the arcade of the Florentine Baptistery is as gracefully proportioned as that of S. Lorenzo, but it is a *blind* arcade, without any supporting function (see fig. 399). The Baptistery, we will recall, was thought in Brunelleschi's day to have once been a classical temple. Hence, it was an appropriate source of inspiration for him.

Clearly, then, Brunelleschi did not revive the architectural vocabulary of the ancients out of mere antiquarian enthusiasm. The very quality that attracted him to the component parts of classical architecture must have seemed, from the medieval point of view, their chief drawback: inflexibility. A classical column, unlike a medieval column or pier, is strictly defined and self-sufficient, and its details and proportions can be varied only within narrow limits. (The ancients thought of it as an organic structure comparable to the human body.) The classical round arch, unlike any other arch (horseshoe, pointed, and so forth), has only one possible shape, a semicircle. The classical architrave and the classical repertory of profiles and ornaments are all subject to similarly strict rules. Not that the classical vocabulary is completely rigid. If it were, it could not have persisted from the seventh century B.C. to the fourth century A.D. in the ancient world. But the disciplined spirit of the Greek orders, which can be felt even in the most original Roman buildings, demands regularity and consistency and discourages sudden, arbitrary departures from the norm.

Without the aid of such a "standardized" vocabulary, Brunelleschi would have found it impossible to define the shape of his "space blocks" so convincingly. With remarkable logic, he emphasizes the edges or "seams" of the units without disrupting their rhythmic sequence. To single out a particu-

larly noteworthy example, consider the vaulting of the aisles. The transverse arches rest on pilasters attached to the outer wall (corresponding to the columns of the nave arcade), but a continuous architrave intervenes between arch and pilaster, linking all the bays. We would expect these bays to be covered by groin vaults of the classical, unribbed type. Instead, we find a novel kind of vault, the curved surface of which is formed from the upper part of a hemispherical dome. (Its radius equals half the diagonal of the square compartment.) Avoiding the ribs and even the groins, Brunelleschi has created a "one-piece" vault, strikingly simple and geometrically regular, that makes of each bay a distinct unit.

At this point we may well ask: if the new architecture consists essentially of separate elements added together, be they spaces, columns, or vaults, how did Brunelleschi relate these elements to each other? What makes the interior of S. Lorenzo seem so beautifully integrated? There is indeed a controlling principle that accounts for the harmonious, balanced character of his design. The secret of good architecture, Brunelleschi was convinced, lay in giving the "right" proportions—that is, proportional ratios expressed in simple whole numbers—to all the significant measurements of a building. The ancients had possessed this secret, he believed, and he tried to rediscover it by painstakingly surveying the remains of their monuments. What he found, and how he applied his theory to his own designs, we do not know for sure. He may have been the first to think out what would be explicitly stated a few decades later in Leone Battista Alberti's *Treatise on Architecture:* that the mathematical ratios determining musical harmony must also govern architecture, for they recur throughout the universe and are thus divine in origin.

Similar ideas, ultimately derived from the Greek philosopher Pythagoras, had been current during the Middle Ages, but they had not before been expressed so radically, directly, and simply. When Gothic architects "borrowed" the ratios of musical theory, they did so with the aid of the theologians and far less consistently than their Renaissance successors. But even Brunelleschi's faith in the universal validity of harmonious proportions did not tell him how to allot these ratios to the parts of any given building. It left him many alternatives, and his choice among them was necessarily subjective. We may say, in fact, that the main reason S. Lorenzo strikes us as the product of a single great mind is the very individual sense of proportion permeating every detail.

In the revival of classical forms, Renaissance architecture found a standard vocabulary. The theory of harmonious proportions provided it with the kind of syntax that had been mostly absent in medieval architecture. Lest this comparatively inflexible order be misinterpreted as an architectural impoverishment, we might carry our linguistic analogy a bit further. It is tempting to see a parallel between the "unclassical" flexibility of medieval architecture, proliferating in regional styles, and the equally "unclassical" attitude at that time toward language, as evidenced by its barbarized Latin and the rapid growth of regional vernaculars, the ancestors of our modern Western tongues. The revival of Latin and Greek in the Renaissance did not stunt these languages. On the contrary, the classical influence made them so much more stable, precise, and articulate that Latin before long lost the dominant

544. Filippo Brunelleschi and others. Pazzi Chapel, Sta. Croce, Florence. Begun 1430–33

545. Interior of the Pazzi Chapel

546. Plan of the Pazzi Chapel

547. Longitudinal section of the Pazzi Chapel

548. Filippo Brunelleschi. Plan of Sto. Spirito, Florence. Begun 1434–35

549. Filippo Brunelleschi. Plan of Sta. Maria degli Angeli, Florence. 1434–37

position it had maintained throughout the Middle Ages as the language of intellectual discourse. It is not by chance that today we can still read Renaissance literature in Italian, French, English, or German without much trouble, while texts of a century or two before can often be understood only by scholars. Similarly, the revival of classical forms and proportions enabled Brunelleschi to transform the architectural "vernacular" of his region into a stable, precise, and articulate system. The new rationale underlying his buildings soon spread to the rest of Italy and later to all of Northern Europe.

Among the surviving structures by Brunelleschi, not one exterior shows his original design unaltered by later hands, not even the facade of the Pazzi Chapel (fig. 544). The chapel was begun about 1430, but Brunelleschi (who died in 1446) could not have planned the front in its present form. It dates from about 1460, and the top story remains incomplete. Nevertheless, it is a most original creation, totally unlike any medieval facade. A porch, reminiscent of the narthex of Early Christian churches (see fig. 298), precedes the chapel, making the facade seem to screen the main body of the structure. The central arch linking two sections of a classical colonnade is a prime innovation. It frames the portal behind and draws attention to the dome. The plan (fig. 546) shows us that the interrupted architrave supports two barrel vaults, which in turn help to support a small dome above the central opening.

Inside the chapel, we find the same motif on a larger scale—two barrel vaults flanking the dome—and a third dome, like that over the entrance but twice its diameter, above the square compartment housing the altar (figs. 545 and 547). Interior surfaces are articulated much as in S. Lorenzo but their effect is richer and more festive. Here we also find some sculpture. On the four pendentives of the central dome are large roundels with reliefs of the evangelists, and on the walls 12 smaller ones of the apostles. These reliefs, however, are not essential to the design of the chapel. Brunelleschi provided the frames, but he need not have intended them to be filled with sculpture. Indeed, the medallions may very well have been planned "blind," like the recessed panels below them. In any case, the medieval interdependence of architecture and sculpture (never as strong in Italy as in Northern Europe) had ceased to exist. Donatello had liberated the statue from its setting, and Brunelleschi's conception of architecture as the visual counterpart of musical harmonies did not permit sculpture to play a more prominent role than the roundels in the Pazzi Chapel.

In the early 1430s, when the Cathedral dome was nearing completion, Brunelleschi's development as an architect entered a decisive new phase. His design for the church of Sto. Spirito (fig. 548) might be described as a perfected version of S. Lorenzo. All four arms of the cross are alike, with the nave being distinguished from the others only by its greater length, and the entire structure is now enveloped by an unbroken sequence of aisles and chapels. These chapels are the most surprising feature of Sto. Spirito. Brunelleschi had always shunned the apsidal shape before, but now he used it to express more dynamically the relation between interior space and its boundaries, for the wall seems to bulge under the outward pressure of the space. Unhappily, this novel feature was later walled over.

In the church of Sta. Maria degli Angeli, which Brunelleschi began about the same time as Sto. Spirito, this new direction reaches its ultimate conclusion (fig. 549): a domed, central-plan church—the first of the Renaissance—inspired by the round and polygonal structures of Roman and Early Christian times. Financial difficulties interfered with completing the project above the ground floor, so that we cannot be sure of the design of the upper part, or even of some details in the plan. It is nevertheless clear that Brunelleschi has recaptured here the ancient Roman principle of the "sculptured" wall. The dome was to rest on eight heavy piers of complex shape, which belong to the same mass of masonry from which the eight chapels have been "excavated." Wall and space are both charged with energy, and the plan records the precarious balance of their pressures and counterpressures. As a conception, Sta. Maria degli Angeli was so far in advance of Brunelleschi's previous work that it must have utterly bewildered his contemporaries. It had, in fact, no echoes until the end of the century.

550. Michelozzo. Palazzo Medici-Riccardi, Florence. Begun 1444

MICHELOZZO. The massive "Roman" style of the church of Sta. Maria degli Angeli may explain the great disappointment of Brunelleschi's final years: the rejection by his old patrons, the Medici, of his design for their new palace. The family had risen, since the 1420s, to such power that they were in practice, if not in theory, the rulers of Florence. For that very reason they thought it prudent to avoid any ostentation that might antagonize the public. If Brunelleschi's plan for their palace followed the style of Sta. Maria degli Angeli, it probably had such Imperial Roman magnificence that the Medici could not safely afford so grand an edifice. They awarded the commission to a younger and much less distinguished architect, Michelozzo (1396–1472); actual construction began in 1444, two years before Brunelleschi's death.

Michelozzo's design for the Palazzo Medici-Riccardi (fig. 550) still recalls the fortresslike Florentine palaces of old (the windows on the ground floor were added by Michelangelo 75 years later), but the type has been transformed by Brunelleschian principles (compare fig. 464). The three stories are in a graded sequence, each complete in itself. The lowest is built of rough-hewn, "rustic" masonry like the Palazzo Vecchio; the second has smooth-surfaced blocks with "rusticated" (indented) joints; and the third an unbroken surface. On top of the structure rests, like a lid, a strongly projecting cornice inspired by those of Roman temples, emphasizing the finality of the three stories.

Painting

MASACCIO. Although Early Renaissance painting did not appear until the early 1420s, a decade later than Donatello's *St. Mark* and some six years after Brunelleschi's first designs for S. Lorenzo, its inception was the most extraordinary of all. This new style was launched single-handedly by a young genius named Masaccio (1401–1428), who was only 21 years old at the time and who died just six years later. The Early Renaissance was already well established in sculpture and architecture by then, making Masaccio's task easier than it would have been otherwise. His achievement remains stupendous nevertheless.

His first fully mature work is a fresco of 1425 in Sta. Maria Novella (fig. 551) which shows the Holy Trinity accompanied by the Virgin, St. John the Evangelist, and two donors who kneel on either side. The lowest section of the fresco, linked with a tomb below, represents a skeleton lying on a sarcophagus, with the inscription (in Italian): "What you are, I once was; what I am, you will become." Here we seem to plunge into a new environment. But Masaccio's world is a realm of monumental grandeur rather than the lyrical grace of the International Gothic. It seems hard to believe that only two years before, in this city of Florence, Gentile da Fabriano had completed *The Adoration of the Magi* (see fig. 525). What the *Trinity* fresco brings to mind is not the style of the immediate past, but Giotto's art, with its sense of large scale, its compositional severity and sculptural volume. Masaccio's renewed allegiance to Giotto was only a starting point, however. For Giotto, body and drapery form a single unit, as if both had the same substance. In contrast, Masaccio's figures, like Donatello's, are "clothed nudes," whose drapery falls like real fabric. The Christ adheres to the example established by Duccio's *Maestà* altarpiece, but the nearly sculptural treatment suggests a knowledge of an early *Crucifixion* by Brunelleschi that translates the same model into three dimensions—no small feat, easy though it may seem. Like Donatello and Brunelleschi, Masaccio shows a thorough understanding of anatomy not seen since Roman art.

The fully up-to-date setting reveals an equally complete command of Brunelleschi's new architecture and of scientific perspective. For the first time in history, we are given all the data needed to measure the depth of this painted interior, to draw its plan, and to duplicate the structure in three dimensions. It is, in short, the earliest example of a *rational* picture space. For Masaccio, like Brunelleschi, it must have also been a symbol of the universe ruled by divine reason. This barrel-vaulted chamber is not a niche, but a deep space in which the figures could move freely if they so wished. As in Ghiberti's later relief panel *The Story of Jacob and Esau* (see fig. 539), the picture space is independent of the figures. They inhabit it but do not create it. Take away the architecture and you take away the figures' space. We could go even further and say that scientific perspective depends not just on architecture, but on this particular kind of architecture, so different from Gothic.

First we note that all the lines perpendicular to the picture plane converge upon a point below the foot of the Cross, on the platform that supports the kneeling donors. To see the fresco properly, we must face this point, which is at normal eye

551. Masaccio. *The Holy Trinity with the Virgin, St. John, and Two Donors.* 1425. Fresco. Sta. Maria Novella, Florence

552. Plan of *The Holy Trinity*

553. Left wall of Brancacci Chapel, with frescoes by Masaccio. Sta. Maria del Carmine, Florence

554. Right wall of Brancacci Chapel, with frescoes by Masolino and Filippino Lippi. Sta. Maria del Carmine, Florence

555. Masaccio. *The Tribute Money.* c. 1427. Fresco. Brancacci Chapel, Sta. Maria del Carmine, Florence

level, somewhat more than five feet above the floor of the church. The figures within the vaulted chamber are five feet tall, slightly less than lifesize, while the donors, who are closer to us, are fully lifesize. The exterior framework is therefore "lifesize," too, since it is directly behind the donors. The distance between the pilasters corresponds to the span of the barrel vault, and both are seven feet. The circumference of the arc over this span measures 11 feet. That arc is subdivided by eight square coffers and nine ridges, the coffers being one foot wide and the ridges four inches. Applying these measurements to the length of the barrel vault (it consists of seven coffers, the nearest one of which is invisible behind the entrance arch) we find that the vaulted area is nine feet deep.

We can now draw a complete floor plan (fig. 552). A puzzling feature may be the place of God the Father. His arms support the Cross, close to the front plane, while his feet rest on a ledge attached to a wall. How far back is this surface? If it is the rear wall of the chamber, God would appear to be exempt from the laws of perspective. But in a universe ruled by reason, this cannot be so. Hence Masaccio must have intended to locate the ledge directly behind the Cross. The strong shadow that St. John casts on the wall beneath the ledge bears this out.

The largest group of Masaccio's works to come down to us are frescoes in the Brancacci Chapel in Sta. Maria del Carmine (figs. 553 and 554), devoted to the life of St. Peter. *The Tribute Money,* in the upper tier (fig. 555), is the most famous of these. It illustrates the story in the Gospel of Matthew (17:24–27) by the age-old method known as "continuous narration" (see page 314). In the center, Christ instructs Peter to catch a fish, whose mouth will contain the tribute money for the tax collector. On the far left, in the distance, Peter takes the coin from the fish's mouth, and on the right, he gives it to the tax collector. Since the lower edge of the fresco is almost 14 feet above the floor of the chapel, Masaccio could not here coordinate his perspective with our actual eye level. Instead, he expects us to imagine that we are looking directly at the central vanishing point, which is located behind the head of Christ. Oddly enough, this feat is so easy that we take note of it only if we are in an analytical frame of mind. But then, pictorial illusion of any sort is always an imaginary experience. No matter how eager we are to believe in a picture, we never mistake it for reality itself, just as we are hardly in danger of confusing a statue with a living thing.

If we could see *The Tribute Money* from the top of a suitable ladder, the painted surface would be more visible, of course, but the illusion of reality would not improve markedly. This illusion depends to only a minor degree on Brunelleschian perspective. Masaccio controls the flow of light (which comes from the right, where the window of the chapel is actually located), and he uses atmospheric perspective in the subtly changing tones of the landscape. We now recall Donatello's preview of such a setting, a decade earlier, in his small relief of St. George (compare fig. 532).

The figures in *The Tribute Money,* even more than those in the *Trinity* fresco, display Masaccio's ability to merge the weight and volume of Giotto's figures with the new functional view of body and drapery. All stand in beautifully balanced contrapposto, and close inspection reveals fine vertical lines scratched in the plaster by the artist, establishing the gravitational axis of each figure from the head to the heel of the engaged leg. In accord with this dignified approach, the figures seem rather static. The narrative is conveyed to us by intense glances and a few emphatic gestures, rather than by physical movement. But in another fresco of the Brancacci

556. Masaccio.
The Expulsion from Paradise.
c. 1427. Fresco. Brancacci
Chapel, Sta. Maria del
Carmine, Florence

Chapel, *The Expulsion from Paradise* (fig. 556), Masaccio proves decisively his ability to display the human body in motion. The tall, narrow format leaves little room for a spatial setting. The gate of paradise is only indicated, and in the background are a few shadowy, barren slopes. Yet the soft, atmospheric modeling, and especially the forward-moving angel, boldly foreshortened, suffice to convey a free, unlimited space. In conception this scene is clearly akin to Jacopo della Quercia's Bolognese reliefs (see fig. 540). Masaccio's grief-stricken Adam and Eve, though less dependent on ancient models, are equally striking exemplars of the beauty and power of the nude human form.

Masaccio divided the work on the Brancacci Chapel with a much older artist, Masolino (documented 1423–died 1440), who had been decisively influenced by Gentile da Fabriano. Remarkably enough, the two cooperated well and even collaborated on several frescoes (the head of Christ in *The Tribute Money* is by Masolino, for instance), although the difference in their styles was great. Masaccio's impact notwithstanding, Masolino retained an allegiance to the International Style. Thus the figures in the upper tier of the right wall (fig. 554) are simply larger versions of those in Pietro Lorenzetti's *Birth of the Virgin* (see fig. 509). The setting, too, remains Gothic in character, despite the scientific perspective (compare fig. 511). Masolino constructs a self-consciously theatrical space that remains separate from his figures, whereas Masaccio's are fully integrated into their surroundings, both visually and dramatically.

Nowhere is the sharp contrast between their styles more striking than in *The Temptation* by Masolino (visible in the upper right of fig. 554), which forms an enchanting companion to the unprecedented anguish in Masaccio's *Expulsion from Paradise*. Regardless of their contrapposto, the figures of Adam and Eve are no more classical than Adam in our figure 541. Indeed, they may well derive from a similar source, for Masolino was utterly incapable of treating the nude in convincing organic terms. The comparison is telling: Masaccio's contribution, like Donatello's, was to recapture the substance of antiquity without relying on external forms. Masaccio left for Rome before he could finish the Brancacci Chapel, and Masolino's work, too, was interrupted for several years. It was finally completed toward the end of the century by Filippino Lippi (1457/8–1504), who was responsible for the lower tier to either side.

While he had a mural painter's temperament, Masaccio was skilled in panel painting. His large many-paneled altarpiece, or polyptych, made in 1426 for the Carmelite church in Pisa, has since been dispersed among various collections. Its center panel (fig. 557) is a more fully developed restatement of his earliest known work. The *Madonna Enthroned* is of the monumental Florentine type introduced by Cimabue and reshaped by Giotto (see figs. 499 and 507). The usual components, including the gold ground, are still present: a large, high-backed throne dominates the composition and on either side are adoring angels (here only two). Despite these traditional elements, the painting is revolutionary in several respects. The kneeling angels in Giotto's *Madonna* have become lute players, seated on the lowest step of the throne, and the Christ Child is no longer blessing us but eating a bunch of

557. Masaccio. *Madonna Enthroned*. 1426. Oil on panel, 56 x 29" (142 x 73.6 cm). The National Gallery, London
Reproduced by courtesy of the Trustees

grapes, a symbolic act that alludes to the Passion. (The grapes refer to wine, which represents the Saviour's blood in the sacrament of the Eucharist.) Above all, the figures have powerful proportions which make them infinitely more concrete and impressive than any that had preceded them, even Giotto's, although they are hardly beautiful by the elegant standards of the International Style.

It is no surprise, in light of the *Trinity* fresco, that Masaccio replaces Giotto's ornate but frail Gothic throne with a solid and austere stone seat in the style of Brunelleschi, or that he uses perspective expertly. (Note especially the two lutes.) We are perhaps less prepared by the murals to find such delicacy and precision in painting the light on the surfaces. Within the picture, sunlight enters from the left—not the brilliant glare of noontime but the softer glow of the setting sun. (Some of the shadows on the throne permit us to determine its exact angle.) There are consequently no harsh contrasts between

558. Fra Filippo Lippi. *Madonna Enthroned.* 1437. Oil on panel,
45 x 25¹/₂"(114.7 x 64.8 cm). Galleria Nazionale d'Arte Antica,
Rome

light and shade. Subtle half-shadows intervene, producing a
rich scale of transitional hues. The light retains its full descriptive function, while acting as an independent force that imposes a common tonality, as well as a common mood, on all
the forms it touches.

TEMPERA AND OIL. These new refinements were made
possible by oil painting. The basic medium of medieval panel
painting had been tempera, in which the finely ground pigments were mixed ("tempered") with diluted egg yolk. It produced a thin, tough, quick-drying coat admirably suited to the
medieval taste for high-keyed, flat color surfaces. However, in
tempera the different tones on the panel cannot be blended
smoothly, and the continuous progression of values necessary
for three-dimensional effects was difficult to achieve. Furthermore, the darks tended to look muddy and undifferentiated.
These were serious drawbacks that were overcome by substituting oil for the water-and-egg-yolk mixture. In a purely

material sense, oil was not unfamiliar to medieval artists, but
it had been used only for special purposes, such as the coating
of stone surfaces or painting on metal. Its artistic potential was
first discovered around the 1420s by the Master of Flémalle
and his contemporaries in the North (see page 506). Oil, a viscous, slow-drying medium, is capable of producing a wide
variety of effects, from thin, translucent films (called "glazes")
to the thickest impasto (that is, a thick layer of creamy, heavy-bodied paint). The hues can also yield a continuous scale
of tones, including rich, velvety dark shades previously
unknown. The medium offers a unique advantage over egg
tempera, encaustic, and fresco: oils give the artist the unprecedented ability to change his mind almost at will. Without oil,
the conquest of visible reality would have been much more
limited. The oil medium spread quickly to Italy, where it
became the foundation of modern painting. Although it continued to be mixed with tempera for some time, oil has been
the basic medium ever since.

FRA FILIPPO LIPPI. Masaccio's early death left a gap that
was not filled for some time. Among his younger contemporaries only Fra Filippo Lippi (c. 1406–1469) seems to have
had close contact with him ("fra" means "brother"; Lippi was
a friar). Fra Filippo's earliest dated work, the *Madonna Enthroned* of 1437 (fig. 558), evokes Masaccio's earlier *Madonna*
in several important ways: the lighting, the heavy throne, the
massive three-dimensional figures, the drapery folds over the
Virgin's legs. Nevertheless, the picture lacks Masaccio's monumentality and severity. In fact, it seems decidedly cluttered by
comparison, for Lippi reduces the divine to the mundane. The
background is a domestic interior (note the Virgin's bed on the
right), and the vividly patterned marble throne displays a
prayer book and a scroll inscribed with the date. Such a quantity of realistic detail, as well as the rather undisciplined perspective, indicates an artistic temperament very different from
Masaccio's. It also suggests that Fra Filippo must have seen
Flemish paintings (perhaps during his visit to northeastern
Italy in the mid–1430s).

Finally, we note the painter's interest in movement, which
is evident in the figures and, even more strikingly, in parts of
the drapery. The curly, fluid edge of the Virgin's headdress and
the curved folds of her mantle streaming to the left, which
accentuate her own turn to the right, show an interest in graceful decorative effects that will later become an end in itself.
Such effects are found earlier in the relief sculpture of Donatello and Ghiberti: compare the dancing Salome in *The Feast
of Herod* (fig. 534) and the maidens in the lower left-hand
corner of *The Story of Jacob and Esau* (fig. 539). It is not surprising that these two artists should have so strongly affected
Florentine painting in the decade after Masaccio's death. Age,
experience, and prestige gave them authority unmatched by
any painter then active in the city. Their influence, and that of
the Flemish masters, in modifying Fra Filippo's early Masacciesque outlook was particularly significant, because he lived
until 1469 and played a decisive role in setting the course of
Florentine painting during the second half of the century.

FRA ANGELICO. Fra Filippo's slightly older contemporary,
Fra Angelico (c. 1400–1455), was also a friar, but, unlike Fra

559. Fra Angelico. *Deposition.* Probably early 1440s. Oil on panel, 9'1¼" x 9'4¼" (275 x 285 cm). Museo di S. Marco, Florence

Filippo, he took his vows seriously and rose to a responsible position within his order. We sense this immediately in the large *Deposition* (fig. 559), which was painted in all likelihood for the same chapel as Gentile da Fabriano's *Adoration of the Magi* (see fig. 525). Fra Angelico took over the commission from Gentile's Florentine contemporary, Lorenzo Monaco, who was responsible for the Gothic shape of the frame and the triangular pinnacles but who died before he could complete the altar. It has been dated about 1435 by some scholars, to the early 1440s by others. Either date is plausible, for this artist, like Ghiberti, developed slowly, and his conservative style underwent no decisive changes upon reaching maturity. We are clearly in a different world from Fra Filippo's. This *Deposition* is an object of devotion. Fra Angelico preserves the very aspects of Masaccio that Fra Filippo had rejected: his dignity, directness, and spatial order. Thus Fra Angelico's dead Christ is the true heir of the monumental figure in Masaccio's *Trinity.*

Fra Angelico's art is something of a paradox. The deeply reverential attitude presents an admixture of traditional Gothic piety (compare fig. 515) and Renaissance grandeur bestilled by contemplative calm. The elaborate setting spreads behind the figures like a tapestry. The landscape, with the town in the distance, harks back to the *Allegory of Good Government* by Ambrogio Lorenzetti (see figs. 511 and 512). Our artist also shows a clear awareness of the achievements of Northerners such as the Limbourg brothers (compare fig. 522), for he evokes a brilliant sunlit day with striking success. Yet the scene does not strike us as Gothic in the least. It has the same quality of natural light that produces softly modeled, sculptural forms in Masaccio's *Madonna Enthroned* (fig. 557). This light suffuses the entire landscape with a sense of wonderment before God's creation that is wholly Renaissance in spirit. We shall meet it again in the work of Giovanni Bellini (see fig. 592). At the same time, the bright, enamellike hues, although remnants of the International Style, look forward to the colorism of Domenico Veneziano.

560. Domenico Veneziano. *Madonna and Child with Saints.* c. 1455. Oil on panel,
6'10" x 7' (2.08 x 2.13 m). Galleria degli Uffizi, Florence

DOMENICO VENEZIANO. In 1439 a gifted painter from Venice, Domenico Veneziano, settled in Florence. We can only guess at his age (he was probably born about 1410 and he died in 1461), training, and previous work. He must, however, have been in sympathy with the spirit of Early Renaissance art, for he quickly became a thoroughgoing Florentine-by-choice and a master of great importance in his new home. His *Madonna and Child with Saints,* shown in figure 560, is one of the earliest examples of a new kind of altar panel that was to prove popular from the mid-fifteenth century on, the so-called *sacra conversazione* ("sacred conversation"). The type includes an enthroned Madonna framed by architecture and flanked by saints, who may converse with her, with the beholder, or among themselves.

Looking at Domenico's panel, we can understand the wide appeal of the sacra conversazione. The architecture and the space it defines are supremely clear and tangible, yet elevated above the everyday world. The figures, while echoing the formal solemnity of their setting, are linked with each other and with us by a thoroughly human awareness. We are admitted to their presence, but they do not invite us to join them. Like spectators in a theater, we are not allowed "on stage." In Flemish painting, by way of contrast, the picture space seems a direct extension of the viewer's everyday environment (compare fig. 671).

The basic elements of our panel were already present in Masaccio's *Holy Trinity* fresco. Domenico must have studied it carefully, for his St. John looks at us while pointing toward the Madonna, repeating the glance and gesture of Masaccio's Virgin. Domenico's perspective setting is worthy of the earlier master, although the slender proportions and colored inlays of his architecture are less severely Brunelleschian. His figures, too, are balanced and dignified like Masaccio's, but without the same weight and bulk. The slim, sinewy bodies of the male saints, with their highly individualized, expressive faces, show Donatello's influence (fig. 533).

In his use of color, however, Domenico owes nothing to Masaccio. Unlike the great Florentine master, he treats color as an integral part of his work, and the sacra conversazione is as remarkable for its color scheme as for its composition. The blond tonality, its harmony of pink, light green, and white set off by strategically placed spots of red, blue, and yellow, reconciles the decorative brightness of Gothic panel painting with the demands of perspective space and natural light. Ordinarily, a sacra conversazione is an indoor scene, but this one takes place in a kind of loggia (a covered open-air arcade) flooded with sunlight streaming in from the right, as we can tell from the cast shadow behind the Madonna. The surfaces of the architecture reflect the light so strongly that even the shadowed areas glow with color. Masaccio had achieved a similar quality of light in his *Madonna* of 1426, which Domenico surely knew. In this sacra conversazione, the discovery has been applied to a far more complex set of forms and integrated with Domenico's exquisite color sense. The influence of its distinctive tonality can be felt throughout Florentine painting of the second half of the century.

PIERO DELLA FRANCESCA. When Domenico Veneziano settled in Florence, he had a young assistant from southeastern Tuscany named Piero della Francesca (c. 1420–1492), who became his most important disciple and one of the truly great artists of the Early Renaissance. Surprisingly, however, Piero left Florence after a few years, never to return. The Florentines seem to have regarded his work as somewhat provincial and old-fashioned, and from their point of view they were right. Piero's style, even more strongly than Domenico's, reflected the aims of Masaccio. He retained this allegiance to the founder of Italian Renaissance painting throughout his long career, whereas Florentine taste developed in a different direction after 1450.

Piero's most impressive achievement is the fresco cycle in the choir of S. Francesco in Arezzo, which he painted from about 1452 to 1459 (fig. 561). Its many scenes represent the legend of the True Cross (that is, the story of the Cross used for Christ's crucifixion). The section in figure 562 shows the empress Helena, the mother of Constantine the Great, discovering the True Cross and the two crosses of the thieves who died beside Christ (all three had been hidden by enemies of the Faith). On the left, they are being lifted out of the ground, and on the right, the True Cross is identified by its power to bring a dead youth back to life.

Piero's link with Domenico Veneziano is readily apparent from his colors. The tonality of this fresco, although less luminous than in Domenico's sacra conversazione, is similarly blond, evoking early morning sunlight in much the same way. Since the light enters the scene at a low angle, in a direction almost parallel to the picture plane, it serves both to define the

561. View into main chapel, with frescoes by Piero della Francesca. S. Francesco, Arezzo

562. Piero della Francesca. *The Discovery and Proving of the True Cross.* c. 1455. Fresco. S. Francesco, Arezzo

563. Paolo Uccello. *Battle of San Romano.* c. 1455.
Tempera and silver foil on wood panel, 6' x 10'5 3/4" (1.8 x 3.2 m). The National Gallery, London

three-dimensional character of every shape and to lend drama to the narrative. But Piero's figures have a harsh grandeur that recalls Masaccio, or even Giotto, more than Domenico. These men and women seem to belong to a lost heroic race, beautiful and strong—and silent. Their inner life is conveyed by glances and gestures, not by facial expressions. They have a gravity, both physical and emotional, that makes them seem kin to Greek sculpture of the Severe style (see fig. 187).

How did Piero arrive at these memorable images? Using his own testimony, we may say that they were born of his passion for perspective. More than any other artist of his day, Piero believed in scientific perspective as the basis of painting. In a rigorous mathematical treatise, the first of its kind, he demonstrated how it applied to stereometric bodies and architectural shapes, and to the human form. This mathematical outlook permeates all his work. When he drew a head, an arm, or a piece of drapery, he saw them as variations or compounds of spheres, cylinders, cones, cubes, and pyramids, thus endowing the visible world with some of the impersonal clarity and permanence of stereometric bodies. The medieval artist, in contrast, had used the opposite procedure, building natural forms on geometric scaffoldings (see fig. 495). We may regard Piero as the earliest ancestor of the abstract artists of our own time, for they, too, work with systematic simplifications of natural forms. It is not surprising that Piero's fame is greater today than ever before.

UCCELLO. In mid-fifteenth-century Florence there was only one painter who shared, and may have helped to inspire, Piero's devotion to perspective: Paolo Uccello (1397–1475), whose *Battle of San Romano* (fig. 563) perhaps influenced the battle scenes in Piero's frescoes at Arezzo (fig. 561). Uccello's

design shows an extreme preoccupation with stereometric shapes. The ground is covered with a gridlike design of discarded weapons and pieces of armor, forming a display of perspective studies neatly arranged to include one fallen soldier. The landscape, too, has been subjected to a process of stereometric abstraction, matching the foreground. Despite these strenuous efforts, however, the panel has none of the crystalline order and clarity of Piero della Francesca's work. In the hands of Uccello, perspective produces strangely disquieting, fantastic effects. What unites his picture is not its spatial construction but its surface pattern, decoratively reinforced by spots of brilliant color and the lavish use of gold.

Uccello had been trained in the Gothic International Style of painting. It was only in the 1430s that he was converted to the Early Renaissance outlook by the new science of perspective. This he superimposed on his earlier style like a straitjacket. The result is a fascinating and highly unstable mixture. As we study this panel we realize that surface and space are more at war than the mounted soldiers, who get entangled with each other in all sorts of implausible ways.

CASTAGNO. The third dimension held no difficulties for Andrea del Castagno (c. 1423–1457), the most gifted Florentine painter of Piero della Francesca's own generation. Less subtle but more forceful than Domenico Veneziano, Castagno recaptures something of Masaccio's monumentality in his *Last Supper* (fig. 564), one of the frescoes he painted in the refectory of the convent of S. Apollonia. The event is set in a richly paneled alcove designed as an extension of the real space of the refectory. As in medieval representations of the subject, Judas sits in isolation opposite Christ on the near side of the

564. Andrea del Castagno. *The Last Supper.* c. 1445–50. Fresco. S. Apollonia, Florence

table. The rigid symmetry of the architecture, emphasized by the colorful inlays, enforces a similar order among the figures and threatens to imprison them. There is so little communication among the apostles—only a glance here, a gesture there—that a brooding silence hovers over the scene.

Castagno, too, must have felt confined by a scheme imposed on him by the rigid demands of both tradition and perspective, for he used a daringly original device to break the symmetry and focus the drama of the scene. Five of the six panels on the wall behind the table are filled with subdued varieties of colored marble, but above the heads of St. Peter, Judas, and Christ, the marble panel has a veining so garish and explosive that a bolt of lightning seems to descend on Judas' head. When Giotto revived the ancient technique of illusionistic marble textures (see fig. 507), he hardly anticipated that it could hold such expressive significance.

Some five years after *The Last Supper,* between 1450 and 1457 (the year of his death), Castagno produced the remarkable *David* in figure 565. It is painted on a leather shield that was to be used for display, not protection. Its owner probably wanted to convey an analogy between himself and the biblical hero, since David is here defiant as well as victorious. This figure differs fundamentally from the apostles of *The Last Supper.* Solid volume and statuesque immobility have given way to graceful movement, conveyed by both the pose and the windblown hair and drapery. The modeling of the earlier figures has been minimized and the forms are now defined mainly by their outlines, so that the *David* seems to be in relief rather than in the round. This dynamic linear style has important virtues, but it is far removed from Masaccio's. During the 1450s, the artistic climate of Florence changed greatly. Castagno's *David* is early evidence of the outlook that was to dominate the second half of the century.

565. Andrea del Castagno. *David.* c. 1450–57. Leather, surface curved, height 45¹/₂" (115.8 cm). National Gallery of Art, Washington, D.C. Widener Collection

566. Leone Battista Alberti. Palazzo Rucellai, Florence. 1446–51

CENTRAL AND NORTHERN ITALY: 1450–1500

As the founders of Early Renaissance art and their immediate heirs disappeared one by one in the middle years of the fifteenth century, a younger generation began to assert itself. At the same time, the seeds planted by Florentine masters in other regions of Italy were beginning to flower. (We recall Donatello's stay in Padua.) When some of these regions, notably the northeast, produced distinctive versions of the new style, Tuscany ceased to have the privileged position it had previously enjoyed.

Architecture

ALBERTI. In architecture, the death of Brunelleschi in 1446 brought to the fore Leone Battista Alberti (1404–1472), whose career as a practicing architect, like Brunelleschi's own, had been long delayed. Until he was 40, Alberti seems to have been interested in the fine arts only as an antiquarian and theorist. He studied the monuments of ancient Rome, composed the earliest Renaissance treatises on sculpture and painting, and began a third treatise, far more exhaustive than the others, on architecture. [See Primary Sources, nos. 50 and 51, page 630.] After about 1430, he was close to the leading artists of his day: *On Painting* is dedicated to Brunelleschi and refers to "our dear friend" Donatello. Alberti began to practice art as a dilettante, eventually becoming a professional architect of outstanding

ability. Highly educated in classical literature and philosophy, he exemplifies both the humanist and the person of the world.

The design for the Palazzo Rucellai (fig. 566) may be Alberti's critique of the slightly earlier Medici Palace by Michelozzo (see fig. 550). Again we meet the heavy cornice and the three-story scheme, but the articulation of the facade is more strict and more self-consciously classical. It consists of three superimposed orders of pilasters, separated by wide architraves, in imitation of the Colosseum (see fig. 245). Yet Alberti's pilasters are so flat that they remain part of the wall, and the entire facade seems to be one surface on which the artist projects a linear diagram of the Colosseum exterior.

If we are to grasp the logic of this curiously abstract and theoretical design, we must understand that Alberti has met here an issue that became fundamental to Renaissance architecture: how to apply a classical system of articulation to the exterior of a nonclassical structure. Whether Brunelleschi ever coped with this problem is difficult to say. Only his exterior design for the Pazzi Chapel survives (fig. 544), but not unaltered, and it is too special a case to permit general conclusions. Be that as it may, Alberti's solution acknowledges the primacy of the wall, reducing the classical system to a network of incised lines. For his first church exterior, Alberti tried a radically different alternative. Sigismondo Malatesta, lord of the town of Rimini, engaged him toward 1450 to turn the Gothic church of S. Francesco into a "temple of fame" and a burial site for himself, his wife, and the humanists of his court. Alberti encased the older building in a Renaissance shell. The sides consist of austere, deeply recessed arched niches containing stone sarcophagi (figs. 567 and 568). The facade has three similar niches: the large one framing the central portal and the other two (now filled in) intended to receive the sarcophagi of Sigismondo and his wife.

The facade niches are flanked by columns, a scheme clearly derived from the triumphal arches of ancient Rome (see fig. 284). Unlike the pilasters of the Palazzo Rucellai, these columns are not part of the wall. Although partly embedded in it, they project so strongly that we see them as separate entities. We notice, too, that they are set on separate blocks, rather than on the platform supporting the walls, and that they would have nothing to support if the entablature had not been made to project above each capital. These projections make the vertical divisions of the facade more conspicuous than the horizontal ones, and we expect each column to support some important element of the upper story. Yet Alberti planned only one such feature: an arched niche (which remains incomplete) above the portal, with a window and framed by pilasters. Thus the second story fails to fulfill the promise of the first. Perhaps Alberti would have modified this aspect of his design in the end, but the whole enterprise was never finished, and the great dome, projected as its crowning feature, was never built.

Alberti's goal was to superimpose a classical temple front on the traditional basilican church facade. If the classical system of the Palazzo Rucellai is in danger of being devoured by the wall, that of S. Francesco retains too much of its ancient Roman character to fit the basilican shape. (For the medieval approach to this task, see the facade of Pisa Cathedral in fig. 397.) Only toward the end of his career did he succeed in accomplishing this seemingly impossible feat. In the majestic facade of S. Andrea at Mantua (fig. 569), his last work, designed in 1470,

567. Leone Battista Alberti. S. Francesco, Rimini. Facade designed 1450

568. Plan of S. Francesco

569. Leone Battista Alberti. S. Andrea, Mantua. Designed 1470

570. Leone Battista Alberti. Interior of S. Andrea

571. Plan of
S. Andrea (transept,
dome, and choir are
later additions)

572. Giuliano da Sangallo. Sta. Maria delle Carceri,
Prato. Begun 1485

573. Plan of Sta. Maria delle Carceri

he superimposed the triumphal-arch motif—now with a huge center niche—upon a classical temple front, and projected this combination onto the wall. He again uses flat pilasters that acknowledge the primacy of the wall surface, but these pilasters, unlike those of the Palazzo Rucellai, are clearly differentiated from their surroundings. They are of two sizes. The smaller ones sustain the arch over the huge center niche. The larger ones are linked with the unbroken architrave and the strongly outlined pediment and form what is known as a "colossal" order for all three stories of the facade wall, balancing exactly the horizontal and vertical impulses within the design.

So intent was Alberti on stressing the inner cohesion of the facade that he inscribed the entire design within a square, even though it is appreciably lower in height than the nave of the church. (The effect of the west wall protruding above the pediment is more disturbing in photographs than at street level, where it is nearly invisible.) While the facade is physically distinct from the main body of the structure, it offers a "preview" of the interior, where the same colossal order, the same proportions, and the same triumphal-arch motif reappear on the nave walls (fig. 570, page 435).

Comparing the plan (fig. 571) with that of Brunelleschi's Sto. Spirito (fig. 548), we are struck by its revolutionary compactness. Had the church been completed as planned, the difference would be even stronger, for Alberti's design had no transept, dome, or choir, only a nave terminating in an apse.

574. Interior of Sta. Maria delle Carceri

The aisles are replaced by chapels alternately large and small, and there is no clerestory. The colossal pilasters and the arches of the large chapels support a barrel vault of impressive span (the nave is as wide as the facade). Here Alberti has drawn upon his memories of the massive vaulted halls in ancient Roman baths and basilicas, yet he interprets his classical models as freely as in his facade design. They no longer embody an absolute authority that must be quoted literally, but serve as a valuable store of motifs to be utilized at will. With this sovereign attitude toward his sources, he was able to create a structure that truly deserves to be called a "Christian temple."

CENTRAL-PLAN CHURCHES. Because it occupies the site of an older basilican church (note the Gothic campanile next to the facade), with consequent limitations on the designer's freedom, S. Andrea does not conform to the ideal shape of sacred buildings as defined in Alberti's *Treatise on Architecture*. There he explains that the plan of such structures should be either circular, or of a shape derived from the circle (square, hexagon, octagon, and so forth), because the circle is the perfect, as well as the most natural, figure and therefore a direct image of divine reason. This argument rests, of course, on Alberti's faith in the God-given validity of mathematically determined proportions (discussed on page 420). How could he reconcile it with the historical evidence? After all, the standard form of both ancient temples and Christian churches was longitudinal. But, he reasoned, the basilican church plan became traditional only because the early Christians worshiped in private Roman basilicas. Since pagan basilicas were associated with the dispensing of justice (which originates from God), he admitted that their shape has some relationship to sacred architecture, but since they cannot rival the sublime beauty of the temple, their purpose is human rather than divine.

In speaking of temples, Alberti arbitrarily disregarded the standard form and relied instead on the Pantheon (see figs. 246–49), the round temple at Tivoli (see figs. 238 and 239), and the domed mausoleums, which he mistook for temples. Moreover, he asked, had not the early Christians themselves acknowledged the sacred character of these structures by converting them to their own use? Here he could point to such monuments as Sta. Costanza (see figs. 303–5), the Pantheon itself (which had been used as a church ever since the early Middle Ages), and the Baptistery in Florence (then thought to be a former temple of Mars).

Alberti's ideal church, then, demands a design so harmonious that it would be a revelation of divinity and would arouse pious contemplation in the worshiper. It should stand alone, elevated above the surrounding everyday life, and light should enter through openings placed high, for only the sky should be seen through them. That such an isolated, central-plan structure was ill-adapted to the requirements of Catholic ritual made no difference to Alberti. A church, he believed, must be a visible embodiment of "divine proportion," which the central plan alone could attain.

When Alberti formulated these ideas in his treatise, about 1450, he could have cited only Brunelleschi's revolutionary, but unfinished, Sta. Maria degli Angeli as a modern example of a central-plan church (fig. 549). Toward the end of the century, after his treatise became widely known, the central-plan church gained general acceptance. Between 1500 and 1525 it became a vogue reigning supreme in High Renaissance architecture.

GIULIANO DA SANGALLO. It is no coincidence that Sta. Maria delle Carceri in Prato (figs. 572–74), an early and distinguished example of this trend, was begun in 1485, the date of the first printed edition of Alberti's treatise. Its architect, Giuliano da Sangallo (c. 1443–1516), must have been an admirer of Brunelleschi. Many features of the interior and the plan recall the Pazzi Chapel (see figs. 545 and 546). The basic shape of his structure, however, conforms closely to Alberti's ideal. Except for the dome, the entire church would fit neatly inside a cube, since its height (up to the drum) equals its length and width. By cutting into the corners of this cube, as it were, Giuliano has formed a Greek cross (a plan he preferred for its symbolic value). The arms are barrel-vaulted, and the dome rests on these vaults. Yet the dark ring of the drum does not quite touch the supporting arches, making the dome seem to hover weightlessly, like the pendentive domes of Byzantine architecture (compare fig. 336). There can be no doubt that Giuliano wanted his dome to accord with the age-old tradition of the Dome of Heaven. The single round opening in the center and the 12 on the perimeter clearly refer to Christ and the apostles. Brunelleschi had anticipated this feature in the Pazzi Chapel, but Giuliano's dome, crowning a perfectly symmetrical structure, conveys its symbolic value far more strikingly.

Sculpture

Donatello left Florence for Padua in 1443. His ten-year absence had an effect similar to that of Brunelleschi's death, but whereas Alberti took Brunelleschi's place in architecture, there was no young sculptor of comparable stature to take Donatello's. As a consequence, the other sculptors remaining in the city gained greater prominence. The new talents who grew up under their influence brought about the changes between 1443 and 1453 that Donatello must have seen with dismay when he returned to Florence.

LUCA DELLA ROBBIA. Ghiberti aside, the only significant sculptor in Florence after Donatello left was Luca della Robbia (1400–1482). He had made his reputation in the 1430s with the marble reliefs of the *Cantoria* (singers' pulpit) in the Cathedral. The *Trumpet Players* panel reproduced here (fig. 575) shows the beguiling mixture of sweetness and gravity characteristic of all of Luca's work but leavened by an unusual note of exuberance. Its style has very little to do with Donatello. Instead, it recalls the classicism of Nanni di Banco (see fig. 527), with whom Luca may have worked as a youth. We also sense a touch of Ghiberti here and there, as well as the powerful influence of classicistic Roman reliefs (such as fig. 267). Unfortunately, Luca lacked a capacity for growth, despite his great gifts. So far as we know, he never did a free-standing statue, and the *Cantoria* remained his most ambitious achievement.

For the rest of his long career, he devoted himself almost exclusively to sculpture in terracotta, a cheaper and less demanding medium than marble, which he covered with enamellike glazes to mask its surface and make it impervious to weather. His finest works in this technique, which include *The*

575. Luca della Robbia. *Trumpet Players,* from the
Cantoria. c. 1435. Marble, 40⁵/8" x 36⁷/8" (103 x 93.5 cm).
Museo dell'Opera del Duomo, Florence

576. Luca della Robbia. *The Resurrection.*
1442–45. Glazed terracotta, 5'3" x 7'3¹/2" (1.6 x 2.22 m).
Museo Nazionale del Bargello, Florence

Resurrection in figure 576, have the dignity and charm of the *Cantoria* panels. The white glaze creates the impression of marble, with a deep blue for the background of the lunette. Other colors were confined almost entirely to the decorative framework of Luca's reliefs. This restraint, however, lasted only while he was in active charge of his workshop. Later, the quality of the modeling deteriorated and the simple harmony of white and blue often gave way to an assortment of more vivid hues. At the end of the century, the Della Robbia shop had become a factory, turning out small Madonna panels and garish altarpieces for village churches by the score.

Because of Luca's almost complete withdrawal from the domain of carving, there was a real shortage of capable marble sculptors in the Florence of the 1440s. By the time Donatello

returned, this gap had been filled by a group of men, most of them still in their twenties, from the little hill towns to the north and east of Florence that had long supplied the city with stonemasons and carvers. Now, because the exceptional circumstances gave them special opportunities, the most gifted of them developed into artists of considerable importance.

BERNARDO ROSSELLINO. The oldest of these, Bernardo Rossellino (1409–1464), seems to have begun as a sculptor and architect in Arezzo. He established himself in Florence about 1436, but received no commissions of real consequence until some eight years later, when he was entrusted with the Tomb of Leonardo Bruni (fig. 577). This great humanist and statesman had played a vital part in the city's affairs ever since the beginning of the century (see page 409). When he died in 1444, he received a grand funeral "in the manner of the ancients." His monument was probably ordered by the city government of Florence. Since Bruni had been born in Arezzo, his native town also wished to honor him and may have helped to secure the commission for Bernardo because of his earlier activity there. (One wonders, however, what chance Bernardo would have had if Donatello had been available.)

Although the Bruni monument is not the earliest Renaissance tomb, nor even the earliest large-scale tomb of a humanist, it can claim to be the first memorial that fully expresses the spirit of the new era. Echoes of Bruni's funeral *all'antica* are everywhere. The deceased reclines on a bier supported by Roman eagles, his head wreathed in laurel and his hands enfolding a volume (presumably his own *History of Florence,* rather than a prayer book). The monument is a fitting tribute to the man who, more than any other, had helped to establish the new historical perspective of the Florentine Early Renaissance. On the classically severe sarcophagus, two winged genii display an inscription very different from those on medieval tombs. Instead of recording the name, rank, and age of the deceased and the date of his death, it refers only to his timeless accomplishments: "At Leonardo's passing, history grieves, eloquence is mute, and it is said that the Muses, Greek and Latin alike, cannot hold back their tears." The religious aspect of the tomb is confined to the lunette, where the Madonna is adored by angels.

The entire monument may thus be viewed as an attempt to reconcile two contrasting attitudes toward death: the retrospective, commemorative outlook of the ancients (see page 155), and the Christian concern with afterlife and salvation. Bernardo's design, adapted from the Tomb of Guglielmo de Braye by Arnolfo di Cambio (fig. 490), is admirably suited to such a program, balancing architecture and sculpture within a compact, self-contained framework. Its dominant motif, the two pilasters supporting a round arch resting on a strongly accented architrave, suggests Alberti, who employed it repeatedly. It is derived from the doorway to the Pantheon (see fig. 249), which accounts for its use in church portals such as that of S. Andrea in Mantua (fig. 569). While Bernardo may have adopted it for the Bruni tomb on purely aesthetic grounds, it is possible that he also meant to convey a symbolic meaning: the deceased on his bier, pausing at the gateway between one life and the next. Perhaps he even wanted us to associate the motif with the Pantheon, the "temple of the immortals" for

577. Bernardo Rossellino. Tomb of Leonardo Bruni. c. 1445–50.
Marble, height 20' (6.1 m to top of arch). Sta. Croce, Florence

578. Desiderio da Settignano. *St. John the Baptist*. c. 1455–60.
Marble, height 63" (160 cm). Museo Nazionale del Bargello, Florence

pagans and Christians alike. (Once dedicated to all the gods of the Roman world, it had been rededicated to all the martyrs when it became a church, and in the High Renaissance it was to receive the remains of yet another breed of immortals: such famous artists as Raphael.)

All the tombs, tabernacles, and the reliefs of the Madonna produced in Florence between 1450 and 1480 have a common ancestor in the Bruni monument. Nevertheless its sculptural style is not easy to define, since its components vary a good deal in quality. Broadly speaking, it reflects the classicism of Ghiberti and Luca della Robbia; echoes of Donatello are few and

indirect. By the same token, we do not yet have a clear conception of Bernardo's style as a sculptor. He surely employed assistants here, as he did in his subsequent commissions. During the later 1440s, his workshop was the only training ground for ambitious young marble sculptors, such as his very gifted younger brother Antonio (1417–1470) and other members of the same generation. Their share in Bernardo's sculptural projects is hard to identify, however, for their personalities were not distinct until they began to work independently.

DESIDERIO DA SETTIGNANO. Of the many sculptors who passed through the Rossellino shop, the most gifted was Desiderio da Settignano (1429/30–1464), who came from a family of stonemasons. It was nevertheless the influence of Donatello, to whom he was probably apprenticed in the early 1440s, that proved decisive. Indeed, the *St. John the Baptist* in figure 578 was long considered to be by Donatello himself but

579. Antonio del Pollaiuolo. *Hercules and Antaeus.*
c. 1475. Bronze, height 18" (45.8 cm, with base).
Museo Nazionale del Bargello, Florence

widely practiced in ancient times, had ceased during the Middle Ages. The taste of kings, feudal lords, and others who could afford to collect for personal pleasure ran to gems, jewelry, goldsmith's work, illuminated manuscripts, and precious fabrics. The habit was reestablished in fifteenth-century Italy as part of the "revival of antiquity." Humanists and artists first collected ancient sculpture, especially small bronzes (such as fig. 217), which were numerous and of convenient size. Before long, contemporary artists began to cater to the spreading vogue, with portrait busts and small bronzes of their own "in the manner of the ancients."

A particularly fine piece of this kind is *Hercules and Antaeus* (fig. 579) by Antonio del Pollaiuolo (1431–1498), who represents a sculptural style very different from that of the marble carvers we discussed above. Trained as a goldsmith and metalworker, probably in the Ghiberti workshop, he was deeply impressed by the late styles of Donatello and Castagno, as well as by ancient art. From these sources, he evolved the distinctive manner that appears in our statuette. To create a freestanding group of two figures in violent struggle, even on a small scale, was a daring idea in itself. Even more astonishing is the way Pollaiuolo has endowed his composition with a centrifugal impulse. Limbs seem to radiate in every direction from a common center, and we see the full complexity of their movements only when we examine the statuette from all sides. Despite its strenuous action, the group is in perfect balance. To stress the central axis, Pollaiuolo in effect grafted the upper part of Antaeus onto the lower part of his adversary.

There is no precedent for this design among earlier statuary groups of any size, ancient or Renaissance. Pollaiuolo himself was a painter and engraver as well as a bronze sculptor, and we know that about 1465 he did a large picture of Hercules and Antaeus, which is now lost but whose design is preserved in a smaller replica, made for the Medici, who also owned the statuette. For the first time, a sculptural group has acquired the pictorial quality that had characterized reliefs since the early years of the Renaissance.

Few of his paintings have survived, and only a single engraving (see page 524), the *Battle of the Ten Naked Men* (fig. 580). This print, however, is of great importance, since it represents Pollaiuolo's most elaborate pictorial design. Its subject, undoubtedly a classical one, has not yet been convincingly identified, but that matter is not so significant. The primary purpose of the engraving obviously was to display Pollaiuolo's mastery of the nude body in action. About 1465–70, when the print must have been produced, this was still a novel problem, and Pollaiuolo contributed more than any other master to its solution. An interest in movement, coupled with slender proportions and an emphasis on outline rather than on modeling, had been seen in Castagno's *David* (fig. 565), which in these respects is clearly the progenitor of the *Ten Naked Men*. Pollaiuolo also drew upon the action poses he found in certain types of Greek vases (compare fig. 201). But he realized that a full understanding of bodily movement demands a detailed knowledge of anatomy, down to the last muscle and sinew. These ten naked men, in fact, have an oddly "flayed" appearance, as if their skin had been stripped off to reveal the play of muscles underneath, and so, to a somewhat lesser degree, do the two figures of our statuette.

is now recognized as the work of Desiderio. Although he is remembered for his beautiful Madonnas and enchanting children, no other sculptor of the day was so attuned to the ascetic side of Donatello's later sculpture. Desiderio's *Baptist* was manifestly inspired by Donatello's *Mary Magdalen* (fig. 537), but the differences are equally important, for Desiderio has magnified the visionary expressiveness by turning it inward. The young St. John has a disturbing, haunted look, as if lacerated by a spiritual experience of almost unbearable intensity. The effect is heightened by the subtlety of the carving, so refined that it is small wonder the statue passed as Donatello's.

POLLAIUOLO. By 1450 the great civic campaign of art patronage came to an end, and Florentine artists had to depend mainly on private commissions. This put the sculptors at a disadvantage because of the high costs involved in their work. Since the monumental tasks were few, they concentrated on works of moderate size and price for individual patrons, such as bronze statuettes. The collecting of sculpture,

580. Antonio del Pollaiuolo. *Battle of the Ten Naked Men.* c. 1465–70.
Engraving, 15¹/₈ x 23¹/₄" (38.3 x 59 cm). The Metropolitan Museum of Art, New York

Artists may have begun to study human anatomy from dissected cadavers as early as 1425, and the practice was almost certainly established during the 1450s by Andrea Mantegna, among others, but this is the clearest visual evidence we have of a custom that was to be followed by artists through the High Renaissance. Equally novel are the facial expressions, as strained as the bodily movements. We have already encountered contorted features in the work of Donatello and Masaccio (see figs. 534, 537, and 556). But the anguish they convey is inner and does not arise from or accompany the extreme physical action of Pollaiuolo's struggling nudes.

VERROCCHIO. Although Pollaiuolo did two monumental bronze tombs for St. Peter's in Rome during the late years of his career, he never had an opportunity to execute a large-scale freestanding statue. For such works we must turn to his slightly younger contemporary Andrea del Verrocchio (1435–1488), the greatest sculptor of his day and the only one to share some of Donatello's range and ambition. A modeler as well as a carver—we have works of his in marble, terracotta, silver, and bronze—he combined elements from Antonio Rossellino and Antonio del Pollaiuolo into a unique synthesis. He was also a respected painter and the teacher of Leonardo da Vinci, which is unfortunate, as he has been overshadowed ever since.

Like *Hercules and Antaeus* by Pollaiuolo, Verrocchio's *The Doubting of Thomas* (fig. 581) is closely related to a painting: a *Baptism of Christ,* painted with the assistance of the young Leonardo. The result is a pictorialism unique in monumental sculpture of the Early Renaissance, one surpassing even Donatello's efforts in this vein. In contrast to the *Quattro Coronati* of Nanni di Banco (fig. 527), the subject is a narrative. Moreover, Verrocchio's group does not quite fit its niche on Or San Michele, for it replaced a single figure by Donatello that had been moved; hence, the statues have no backs in order to accommodate them within the shallow tabernacle, which consequently acts as a foil rather than a container.

581. Andrea del Verrocchio. *The Doubting of Thomas.* 1465–83.
Bronze, lifesize. Or San Michele, Florence

582. Andrea del Verrocchio. *Equestrian Monument of Colleoni.*
c. 1483–88. Bronze, height 13' (3.9 m).
Campo SS. Giovanni e Paolo, Venice

Although the biblical text is inscribed on the drapery, the drama is conveyed by the eloquent poses and bold exchange of gestures between Christ and Thomas. It is heightened by the active drapery, with its deep folds, which echo the contrasting states of mind. *The Doubting of Thomas* is of extraordinary importance in the history of sculpture. The work was immediately admired for its great beauty, especially the head of Christ, which was to inspire Michelangelo. To the young Leonardo it served as a prototype of figures whose actions express the passions of the mind. And the sculpture of Bernini is virtually unthinkable without its example (compare fig. 753).

By a strange coincidence, the crowning achievement of Verrocchio's career, as of Donatello's, was a bronze equestrian statue: the monument of a Venetian army commander, Bartolommeo Colleoni (fig. 582). In his will, Colleoni had requested such a statue and, by way of encouragement, had left a sizable fortune to the Republic of Venice. He obviously knew the Gattamelata monument and wanted to ensure the same honor for himself. Verrocchio, too, must have regarded Donatello's work as the prototype of his own statue, yet he did not simply imitate his illustrious model. He reinterpreted the theme less subtly perhaps, but no less impressively. The horse, graceful and spirited rather than robust and placid, is modeled with the same sense of anatomy-in-action that we saw in the nudes of Pollaiuolo. Its thin hide reveals every vein, muscle, and sinew, in strong contrast to the rigid surfaces of the armored figure bestriding it. Since the horse is also smaller in relation to the rider than Gattamelata's, Colleoni looms in the saddle like the very embodiment of forceful dominance. Legs rigidly straight, one shoulder thrust forward, he surveys the scene before him with the utter concentration of Donatello's *St. George* (fig. 531), but his lip is now contemptuously curled.

Early Italian Renaissance Theater and Music

Medieval theater continued with little change until around 1500 (see "Medieval Music and Theater," page 326). Unlike other literary forms, theater was slow to show the influence of humanism, which dominated so much of Italian Renaissance intellectual life. This seems surprising, since the earliest humanist tragedy and comedy date from about 1390. (Both were written in Latin, and neither was actually performed.) Perhaps the main reason that new forms of drama were slow to develop in the Renaissance was that the works of the Greek and Roman dramatists were only gradually rediscovered in the West. Although the plays of Seneca (see page 209) were known in the Middle Ages, Plautus' second-century B.C. comedies were not rediscovered until 1429. Further, when Constantinople fell to the Turks in 1453, fleeing Greek scholars brought the manuscripts of many previously unknown classical dramas with them to Italy. Renaissance theater was further revolutionized when the printing press was introduced into Italy in 1465. As a result, between 1471 and 1518 all of the known Greek and Roman plays were published.

Italian humanists were always interested more in philosophy and theory than in actual practice. Plautus' *Menaechmi* was first staged only in 1486, then again five years later, but Seneca's *Hippolytus* had to wait until 1509. This emphasis on theory rather than practice also helped to inhibit the development of music, for Italy was slow to produce a composer of stature. Until the middle of the sixteenth century, the popes and the rulers of the Italian cities imported French and Flemish musicians to occupy all the important positions for composers in churches and at ducal courts. Since the goal of the humanists was to revive Latin and Greek, few of them were interested in writing poetry in Italian. Consequently, there were very few good writers for composers to work with, especially on secular motets and songs, which were fertile soil for experimentation. The first humanist to write extensively in Italian was Angelo Poliziano (1454–1494), a member of the Medici circle in Florence; his poetry inspired paintings by Botticelli and Raphael (see figs. 583 and 627). He also collaborated with the Flemish-born composer Heinrich Isaac (c. 1450–1517), and he wrote a play about the legendary Greek bard Orpheus with musical accompaniment in imitation of the antique; though the music is now lost, the stage design by the young Leonardo da Vinci still exists.

583. Sandro Botticelli. *The Birth of Venus.* c. 1480. Tempera on canvas, 5'8⁷/8" x 9'1⁷/8" (1.8 x 2.8 m). Galleria degli Uffizi, Florence

Neither *Gattamelata* nor *Colleoni* is a portrait in the specific sense of the term. Both project an idealization of the personality that each artist associated with successful leadership in war. If *Gattamelata* conveys steadfast purpose and nobility of character, *Colleoni* radiates an almost frightening sense of power. As an image of awesome self-assurance, it recalls the *Can Grande* (see fig. 489) rather than the *Gattamelata* monument. Perhaps Verrocchio visited the tomb of the Can Grande (who was well remembered in Florence as the patron of Dante) and decided to translate the wonderful arrogance of the statue into the style of his own day. In any case, Colleoni got a great deal more than he had bargained for in his will.

Painting

BOTTICELLI. In Florence, the trend forecast by Castagno's *David* substitutes energetic, graceful movement and agitated linear contours for the stable monumentality of Masaccio's style. Its climax comes in the final quarter of the century, in the art of Sandro Botticelli (1444/5–1510). He was trained by Fra Filippo Lippi, whose *Madonna Enthroned* (fig. 558) already had undercurrents of linear movement, and was strongly influenced by Pollaiuolo. Botticelli soon became the favorite painter of the so-called Medici circle: those patricians, literati, scholars, and poets surrounding Lorenzo the Magnificent, the head of the Medici family and, for all practical purposes, the real ruler of the city.

For one member of this group, Botticelli did *The Birth of Venus* (fig. 583), his most famous picture. Its kinship with Pollaiuolo's *Battle of the Ten Naked Men* (fig. 580) is unmistakable. The shallow modeling and the emphasis on outline produce an effect of low relief rather than of solid, three-dimensional shapes. In both we note a lack of concern with deep space. The ornamentalized thicket forms a screen behind the naked men much like the grove on the right-hand side of the Venus. But the differences are just as striking. Botticelli obviously does not share Pollaiuolo's passion for anatomy. His bodies are more attenuated and drained of all weight and muscular power. Indeed, they seem to float even when they touch the ground. All this seems to deny the basic values of the founders of Early Renaissance art, yet the picture does not look medieval. The bodies, ethereal though they be, retain their voluptuousness. They are genuine nudes (see the discussion on pages 415 and 418) enjoying full freedom of movement.

NEO-PLATONISM. Botticelli's *Venus* derives from a variant of the *Cnidian Aphrodite* of Praxiteles (fig. 206), but the subject itself was inspired by the Homeric *Hymn to Aphrodite,* which begins: "I shall sing of beautiful Aphrodite . . . who is obeyed by the flowery sea-girt land of Cyprus, whither soft Zephyr and the breeze wafted her in soft foam over the waves. Gently the golden-filleted Horae received her, and clad her in divine garments." Yet no single literary source accounts for the pictorial conception. It owes something as well to Ovid and the humanist poet Angelo Poliziano who was, like Botticelli, a member of the Medici circle and may well have advised him on the painting, as he undoubtedly did in other instances.

The subject of the picture is clearly meant to be serious, even solemn. How could such images be justified in a Christian civilization, without subjecting both artist and patron to the accusation of neo-paganism? To understand this paradox, we must consider the meaning of our picture, and the general use of classical subjects in Early Renaissance art. During the Middle Ages, classical form had become divorced from classical subject matter. Artists could only draw upon the ancient repertory of poses, gestures, expressions, and types by changing the identity of their sources. Philosophers became apostles, Orpheus turned into Adam, Herakles was now Samson. When medieval artists had occasion to represent the pagan gods, they based their pictures on literary descriptions rather than visual models. This was the situation, by and large, until the mid-fifteenth century. Only with Pollaiuolo—and Mantegna in northern Italy—does classical form begin to rejoin classical content. Pollaiuolo's lost paintings of the Labors of Herakles (about 1465) mark the earliest instance, so far as we know, of large-scale subjects from classical mythology depicted in a style inspired by ancient monuments.

In the Middle Ages, classical myths had at times been interpreted didactically, however remote the analogy, as allegories of Christian precepts. Europa abducted by the bull, for instance, could be declared to signify the soul redeemed by Christ. But such pallid constructions were hardly an adequate excuse for reinvesting the pagan gods with their ancient beauty and strength. To fuse the Christian faith with ancient mythology, rather than merely relate them, required a more sophisticated argument. This was provided by the Neo-Platonic philosophers, whose foremost representative, Marsilio Ficino, enjoyed tremendous prestige during the later years of the fifteenth century and after. Ficino, who was also an ordained priest, based his thought as much on the mysticism of Plotinus (see page 200) as on the authentic works of Plato. He believed that the life of the universe, including human life, was linked to God by a spiritual circuit continuously ascending and descending, so that all revelation, whether from the Bible, Plato, or classical myths, was one. Similarly, he proclaimed that beauty, love, and beatitude, being phases of this same circuit, were one. Thus, Neo-Platonists could invoke the "celestial Venus" (that is, the nude Venus born of the sea, as in our picture) interchangeably with the Virgin Mary, as the source of "divine love" (meaning the recognition of divine beauty).

This celestial Venus, according to Ficino, dwells purely in the sphere of Mind, while her twin, the ordinary Venus, engenders "human love." Of her Ficino wrote to a young Medici prince: "Venus . . . is a nymph of excellent comeliness, born of heaven and more than others beloved by God all highest. Her soul and mind are Love and Charity, her eyes Dignity and Magnanimity, the hands Liberality and Magnificence, the feet Comeliness and Modesty. The whole, then, is Temperance and Honesty, Charm and Splendor. Oh, what exquisite beauty! . . . a nymph of such nobility has been wholly given into your hands! If you were to unite with her in wedlock and claim her as yours she would make all your years sweet." In both form and content this passage follows odes to the Virgin by medieval church fathers.

Once we understand that Botticelli's picture has this quasi-religious meaning, it seems less astonishing that the wind god Zephyr and the breeze goddess Aura on the left look so much like angels and that the Hora personifying Spring on the right, who welcomes Venus ashore, recalls the traditional relation of St. John to the Saviour in the Baptism of Christ (compare fig. 411). As baptism is a "rebirth in God," so the birth of Venus evokes the hope for "rebirth" from which the Renaissance takes its name. Thanks to the fluidity of Neo-Platonic doctrine, the number of possible associations to be linked with our painting is almost limitless. All of them, however, like the celestial Venus herself, "dwell in the sphere of Mind," and Botticelli's deity would hardly be a fit vessel for them if she were less ethereal. Thus, rather than being merely decorative, it is the highly stylized treatment of the surface that elevates the picture to allegory.

Neo-Platonic philosophy and its expression in art were obviously too complex to become popular outside the select and highly educated circle of its devotees. In 1494, the suspicions of ordinary people were aroused by the friar Girolamo Savonarola, an ardent advocate of religious reform, who gained a huge following with his sermons attacking the "cult of paganism" in the city's ruling circle. [See Primary Sources, no. 52, pages 630–31.] Botticelli himself was perhaps a follower of Savonarola and reportedly burned a number of his "pagan" pictures. In his last works he returned to traditional religious themes but with no essential change in style. He seems to have given up painting entirely after 1500, even though the apocalyptic destruction of the world predicted by Savonarola at the millennium-and-a-half was not fulfilled.

PIERO DI COSIMO. *The Discovery of Honey* (fig. 584) by Botticelli's younger contemporary Piero di Cosimo (1462–1521) illustrates a view of pagan mythology diametrically opposed to that of the Neo-Platonists. Instead of "spiritualizing" the pagan gods, it brings them down to earth as beings of flesh and blood. In this alternate theory, humanity had slowly risen from a barbaric state through the discoveries and inventions of a few exceptionally gifted individuals. Gratefully remembered by posterity, they were finally accorded the status of gods. St. Augustine subscribed to such a view (which can be traced back to Hellenistic times) without facing all of the implications expressed by ancient authors. The complete theory, which was not revived until the late fifteenth century, postulates a gradual evolution from the animal level and so conflicts with the scriptural account of Creation. This could be glossed over, however, by making a happy idyll out of the achievements of these pagan "culture heroes" to avoid the impression of complete seriousness, which is exactly what Piero di Cosimo has done in our picture.

Its title refers to the central episode, a group of satyrs busying themselves about an old willow tree. They have discovered a swarm of bees, and are making as much noise as possible with their pots and pans to induce the bees to cluster on one of the branches. The satyrs will then collect the honey, from which they will produce mead. Behind them, to the right, some of their companions are about to discover the source of another fermented beverage: they are climbing trees to collect wild

584. Piero di Cosimo. *The Discovery of Honey.* c. 1499. Tempera on wood panel,
31¼ x 50⅝" (79.2 x 128.5 cm). Worcester Art Museum, Worcester, Massachusetts

grapes. Beyond is a barren rock, while on the left are gentle hills and a town. This contrast does not imply that the satyrs are city dwellers. It merely juxtaposes civilization, the goal of the future, with untamed nature. Here the "culture hero" is Bacchus, who appears in the lower right-hand corner with a tipsy grin on his face, next to his ladylove, Ariadne. Despite their classical appearance, Bacchus and his companions do not in the least resemble the frenzied revelers of ancient mythology. They have an oddly domestic air, suggesting a fun-loving family clan on a picnic. The brilliant sunlight, the rich colors, and the far-ranging landscape make the scene a still more plausible extension of everyday reality.

GHIRLANDAIO. The fresco cycles of Domenico Ghirlandaio (1449–1494), another contemporary of Botticelli, have so many portraits that they almost serve as family chronicles of the wealthy patricians who sponsored them. Among his most touching individual portraits is the panel *An Old Man and His Grandson* (fig. 585). The precise attention to surface texture and facial detail emphasizes the disfigurement of the old man's nose by rosacea. Ghirlandaio has rendered the tender relationship between the little boy and his grandfather with unprecedented human understanding. Psychologically, our panel plainly bespeaks its Italian origin.

PERUGINO. Rome, long neglected during the papal exile in Avignon (see page 370), once more became an important center of art patronage in the later fifteenth century. As the papacy regained its political power on Italian soil, the occupants of the Chair of St. Peter began to beautify both the Vatican and

585. Domenico Ghirlandaio. *An Old Man and His Grandson.*
c. 1480. Tempera and oil on wood panel, 24⅛ x 18"
(61.2 x 45.5 cm). Musée du Louvre, Paris

586. Pietro Perugino. *The Delivery of the Keys*. 1482. Fresco. Sistine Chapel, The Vatican, Rome

the city, in the conviction that the monuments of Christian Rome must outshine those of the pagan past. The most ambitious pictorial project of those years was the decoration of the walls of the Sistine Chapel beginning around 1482. Among the artists who carried out this large cycle of Old and New Testament scenes we encounter most of the important painters of central Italy, including Botticelli and Ghirlandaio, although these frescoes do not, on the whole, represent their best work.

There is, however, one notable exception: *The Delivery of the Keys* (fig. 586) by Pietro Perugino (c. 1450–1523) must rank as his finest achievement. Born near Perugia in Umbria (the region southeast of Tuscany), Perugino maintained close ties with Florence. His early development had been decisively influenced by Verrocchio, as the statuesque balance and solidity of the figures in *The Delivery of the Keys* suggest. The grave, symmetrical design conveys the special importance of the subject in this particular setting: the authority of St. Peter as the first pope, and that of all his successors, rests on his having received the keys to the Kingdom of Heaven from Christ himself. A number of contemporaries, with powerfully individualized features, witness the solemn event. Equally striking is the vast expanse of the background. Its two Roman triumphal arches (both modeled on the Arch of Constantine; fig. 284) flank a domed structure in which we recognize the ideal church of Alberti's *Treatise on Architecture*. The spatial clarity, achieved by the mathematically exact perspective of this view, is the heritage of Piero della Francesca, who spent much of his later life working for Umbrian clients, notably the duke of Urbino. Also from Urbino, shortly before 1500, Perugino received a pupil whose fame would soon outshine his own: Raphael, the most classic master of the High Renaissance.

SIGNORELLI. The Sistine frescoes were completed by Luca Signorelli (1445/50–1523), who was linked to Perugino by a similar background, although his personality was far more dramatic. Of provincial Tuscan origin, he had been a disciple of Piero della Francesca before coming to Florence in the 1470s. Like Perugino, Signorelli was strongly impressed by Verrocchio, but he also admired the energy, expressiveness, and anatomic precision of Pollaiuolo's nudes. Combining these influences with Piero's cubic solidity of form and mastery of perspective foreshortening, Signorelli achieved a style of epic grandeur that later made a lasting imprint on Michelangelo. He reached the climax of his career just before 1500 with a series of monumental frescoes on the walls of the S. Brizio Chapel in Orvieto Cathedral representing the end of the world.

The commission from Pope Alexander VI was an important one, rewarding the city for its faithfulness to the Vatican. The cycle conforms to the typology established by St. Augustine, but it is further rooted in St. Thomas Aquinas and Dante, as well as fifteenth-century Dominican theologians, especially St. Vincent Ferrer. The 1490s were a time of great hardship for Orvieto. It was beset by the plague, political upheaval, economic decline, and fear of the Turks, who crushed the Christian forces at Lepanto, Greece, in 1499—a defeat that was to be avenged in a second, more famous battle at the same site in 1571. This turmoil is vividly reflected in Signorelli's *The Rule of the Antichrist* (fig. 587), which is flanked by *The End of the World* and *The Coronation of the Elect*. Representing the chaos caused by political leaders and the "infidel" forces of Islam, the false Christ is Satan's chief ally, who rules the world before being defeated by St. Michael (seen in the upper left-hand

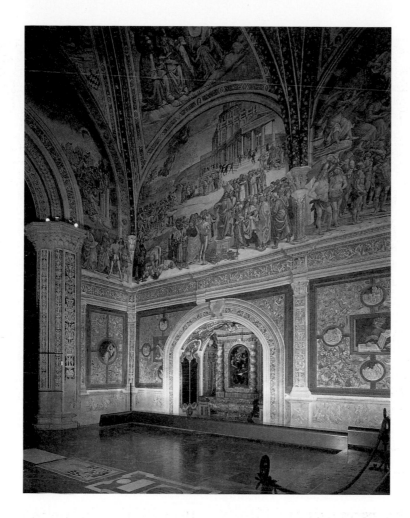

587. Luca Signorelli.
The Rule of the Antichrist.
1499–1500. Fresco.
S. Brizio Chapel, Orvieto
Cathedral

588. Luca Signorelli.
*The Damned Cast
into Hell.* 1499–1500.
Fresco. S. Brizio
Chapel, Orvieto
Cathedral

corner of the painting). He appears before the third Temple of Solomon, the center of his fiendish realm, which is presented in a skewed view that contrasts pointedly with the rational calm of Perugino's *The Delivery of the Keys* (fig. 586).

The most dynamic of the Orvieto frescoes is *The Damned Cast into Hell* (fig. 588). What most strikes us is not the harsh style, which is fully appropriate to the tumultuous scene, or Signorelli's use of the nude body as an expressive instrument, even though he far surpasses his predecessors in this respect, but the pervasive sense of tragedy. Signorelli's Hell, the exact opposite of Bosch's (compare fig. 684), is illuminated by the full light of day, without nightmarish machines of torture or grotesque monsters. The damned retain their dignity, and even the devils are less demonic. Even in Hell, it seems, the Renaissance faith in humanity does not lose its force.

VENICE AND PADUA. We must now consider the growth of Early Renaissance art in northern Italy. The International Style in painting and sculpture lingered there until mid-century, and architecture retained a strongly Gothic flavor long after the adoption of a classical vocabulary. As a result, there were hardly any achievements of major significance in these fields, but between 1450 and 1500 a great tradition was born in Venice and its dependent territories that was to flourish for the next three centuries. The Republic of Venice, although more oligarchic and unique in its eastward orientation, had many ties with Florence. It is therefore not surprising that Venice, rather than the duchy of Milan, should have become the leading center of Early Renaissance art in northern Italy.

MANTEGNA. Florentine masters had been carrying the new style to Venice and to the neighboring city of Padua since the 1420s. Fra Filippo Lippi, Uccello, and Castagno had worked there at one time or another. Still more important was Donatello's ten-year sojourn. Their presence, however, evoked only rather timid local responses until, shortly before 1450, the young Andrea Mantegna (1431–1506) emerged as an independent master. He was first trained by a minor Paduan painter, but his early development was decisively shaped by the impressions he received from locally available Florentine works and, we may assume, by personal contact with Donatello. Next to Masaccio, Mantegna was the most important painter of the Early Renaissance. He, too, was a precocious genius, fully capable at 17 of executing commissions of his own. Within the next decade, he reached artistic maturity, and during the next half-century (he died at the age of 75) he broadened the range of his art but never departed, in essence, from the style he had formulated in the 1450s.

The greatest achievement of Mantegna's early career, the frescoes in the Church of the Eremitani in Padua, was almost entirely destroyed by an accidental bomb explosion in 1944—a more grievous loss than the murals of the Pisa Camposanto (see fig. 513). *St. James Led to His Execution* (fig. 589) is the most dramatic scene of the cycle because of its daring "worm's-eye view" perspective, which is based on the beholder's actual eye level. (The central vanishing point is below the bottom of the picture, somewhat to the right of center.) The architectural setting consequently looms large, as in Masaccio's *Trinity* fresco (see fig. 551). Its main feature is a huge triumphal arch which, although not a copy of any known Roman monument, looks so authentic in every detail that it might as well be.

Here Mantegna's devotion to the visible remains of antiquity, almost like that of an archaeologist, shows his close association with the learned humanists at the University of Padua, who had the same reverence for every word of ancient literature. No Florentine painter or sculptor of the time could have transmitted such an attitude to him. The same desire for authenticity can be seen in the costumes of the Roman soldiers (compare fig. 264). It even extends to the use of "wet" drapery patterns, an invention of Classical Greek sculpture inher-

589. Andrea Mantegna. *St. James Led to His Execution.* c. 1455. Fresco. Ovetari Chapel, Church of the Eremitani, Padua. Destroyed 1944

590. Andrea Mantegna. *St. James Led to His Execution.* c. 1455. Pen drawing, 6¹/₈ x 9¹/₄" (15.7 x 23.5 cm). Collection G. M. Gathorne-Hardy, Donnington Priory, Newbury, Berkshire, England

ited by the Romans (see fig. 267). But the tense figures, lean and firmly constructed, and especially their dramatic interaction, clearly derive from Donatello. Mantegna's subject hardly demands this agitated staging. The saint, on the way to his execution, blesses a paralytic and commands him to walk. Many of the bystanders express by glance and gesture how deeply the miracle has stirred them. The large crowd generates an extraordinary emotional tension that erupts into real physical violence on the far right, as the great spiral curl of the banner echoes the turbulence below.

By rare good luck, a sketch for this fresco has survived (fig. 590), the earliest instance we know of a drawing that permits us to compare the preliminary and final versions of such a design. (Among the drawings by earlier masters, none, it seems, is related to a known picture in the same way.) This sketch differs from sinopie (full-scale drawings on the wall; see fig. 514) in its tentative, unsettled quality. The composition has not yet taken full shape. Still growing, as it were, the image in our drawing is "unfinished" both in the conception and the quick, shorthand style. We note, for example, that here the perspective is closer to normal, indicating that the artist worked out the exact scheme only on the wall. Our drawing also offers proof of what we suspected in the case of Masaccio: that Early Renaissance artists actually conceived their compositions in terms of nude figures. The group on the right is still in that first stage, and in the others the outlines of the body show clearly beneath the costume. But the drawing is more than a document. It is a work of art in its own right. The very quickness of its "handwriting" gives it an immediacy and rhythmic force that are necessarily lost in the fresco.

On the evidence of these works, we would hardly expect Mantegna to be much concerned with light and color. The *St. Sebastian* panel reproduced in figure 591, painted only a few years after the Paduan frescoes, shows that he was, however. In the foreground, to be sure, we find the familiar array of classical remains (including, this time, the artist's signature in Greek). The saint, too, looks more like a statue than a living body. But beyond we see a wonderfully atmospheric landscape and a deep blue sky dotted with the softest of white clouds. The entire scene is bathed in the warm radiance of late afternoon sunlight, which creates a gently melancholy mood, making the pathos of the dying saint doubly poignant. The background of our panel shows the influence, direct or indirect, of the Van Eycks (compare fig. 672, left).

Some works of the great Flemish masters had surely reached Florence as well as Venice between 1430 and 1450, and must have been equally admired in both cities. But in Venice they had more immediate effect, evoking the interest in lyrical, light-filled landscapes that became an ingrained part of Venetian Renaissance painting.

BELLINI. In the painting of Giovanni Bellini (c. 1431–1516), Mantegna's brother-in-law, we trace the further growth of the Flemish tradition. Bellini was slow to mature, and his finest pictures, such as *St. Francis in Ecstasy* (fig. 592), date from the last decades of the century or later. The subject is unique. The saint has left his wooden pattens behind and stands barefoot on holy ground, like Moses in the Lord's presence (see page 62). Despite the absence of the crucified seraph that appeared to him on Mount Alverna, the painting seemingly shows Francis receiving the stigmata (the wounds of Christ) on the Feast of the Holy Cross in 1224, although they are barely visible even in person. However, it also "illustrates" the Hymn of the Sun, which he composed the following year after his annual fast at a hermitage near his hometown of Assisi. During that time he could not bear the sight of light and was plagued as well by mice. The monk finally emerged from these torments after being assured by the Lord that he would enter the Kingdom of Heaven. We see him looking ecstatically up at the sun. (Note the direction of the shadows.) In the background is a magnificent expanse of Italian countryside. Yet this is no ordinary landscape. It represents the

591. Andrea Mantegna. *St. Sebastian.* c. 1455–60. Tempera on panel, 26³/₄ x 11⁷/₈" (68 x 30.6 cm). Kunsthistorisches Museum, Vienna

Heavenly Jerusalem, inspired by the Revelation of St. John the Divine. It lies across the river, separated from the everyday realm by the bridge to the left. Behind looms Mount Zion, where the Lord dwells. How, then, shall we enter the gate to paradise, shown as a large tower?

For Francis, the road to salvation lay in the ascetic life, signified by the cave, which also connects him symbolically to St. Jerome, the first great hermit saint. The donkey is a symbol of

592. Giovanni Bellini. *St. Francis in Ecstasy.* c. 1485. Oil and tempera on panel, 49 x 55⁷/8" (124 x 141.7 cm). The Frick Collection, New York

St. Francis himself, who referred to his body as Brother Ass, which must be disciplined. The other animals (difficult to discern in our illustration) are, like monks, solitary creatures in Christian lore: the heron, bittern, and rabbit.

The complex iconography is not sufficient in itself to explain the picture. Far more important is the treatment of the landscape. St. Francis is here so small in comparison to the setting that he seems almost incidental. Yet his mystic rapture before the beauty of the visible world sets our own response to the view that is spread out before us, ample and intimate at the same time. St. Francis revered nature as the Lord's handiwork, made for humanity's benefit. Our artist shares his tender lyricism, expressed in the Hymn of the Sun:

> Be praised, my Lord, with all Your creatures,
> Above all Brother Sun,
> Who gives the day and by whom You shed light on us.
> And he is beautiful and radiant with great splendor.
> Of Thee, Most High, he is a symbol.

Bellini's contours are less brittle than those of Mantegna, the colors softer and the light more glowing. He has as well the concern of the great Flemings for every detail and its symbolism. Unlike the Northerners, however, he can define the beholder's spatial relationship to the landscape. The rock formations of the foreground are structurally clear and firm, like architecture rendered by the rules of scientific perspective.

As the foremost painter of the city of Venice, Bellini pro-

duced a number of formal altar panels of the sacra conversazione type. The last and most monumental one of the series is the *Madonna and Saints* of 1505 in S. Zaccaria (fig. 593). Compared to Domenico Veneziano's sacra conversazione of 50 years earlier (fig. 560), the architectural setting is a good deal simpler but no less impressive. We stand in the nave of a church, near the crossing (which is partly visible), with the apse filling almost the entire panel. The figures appear in front of the apse, however, under the great vaulted canopy of the crossing. The structure is not a real church, for its sides are open and the entire scene is flooded with gentle sunlight, just as Domenico Veneziano had placed his figures in a semioutdoor setting. The Madonna's solid, high-backed throne and the music-making angel on its lowest step are derived (through many intermediaries, no doubt) from Masaccio's *Madonna Enthroned* of 1426 (see fig. 557).

What differentiates this altar immediately from its Florentine ancestors is not merely the ample spaciousness of the design but its wonderfully calm, meditative mood. Instead of "conversation," we sense the figures' deep communion, which makes all rhetorical gestures unnecessary. We shall encounter this quality again and again in Venetian painting. Here, we see it as through a diffusing filter of atmosphere, for the aged master has bathed the entire scene in a delicate aerial haze. All harsh contrasts are eliminated, light and shadow blend in almost imperceptible gradations, and colors glow with a new richness and depth. In this magical moment, Bellini unites Florentine grandeur with Venetian poetic intimacy.

593. Giovanni Bellini. *Madonna and Saints.* 1505. Oil on panel, 16'5¹/8" x 7'9" (5 x 2.4 m). S. Zaccaria, Venice

CHAPTER TWO

THE HIGH
RENAISSANCE
IN ITALY

It used to be taken for granted that the High Renaissance followed upon the Early Renaissance as naturally and inevitably
as night follows day. The great masters of the sixteenth century—Leonardo, Bramante, Michelangelo, Raphael, Giorgione,
Titian—were thought to have shared the ideals of their predecessors, but to have expressed them so completely that their
names became synonyms for perfection. They represented the
climax, the classic phase, of Renaissance art, just as Phidias had
brought the art of ancient Greece to its highest point. This
view could also explain why these two classic phases, though
2,000 years apart, were so short. If art is assumed to develop
along the pattern of a ballistic curve, its highest point cannot
be expected to last more than a moment.

Since the 1920s, art historians have come to realize the
shortcomings of this scheme. When we apply it literally, the
High Renaissance becomes so absurdly brief, for example, that
we wonder whether it happened at all. Moreover, we hardly
increase our understanding of the Early Renaissance if we
regard it as a "not-yet-perfect High Renaissance," any more
than an Archaic Greek statue can be satisfactorily viewed from
a Phidian standpoint. Nor is it very useful to insist that the
subsequent post-Classical phase, whether Hellenistic or "Late
Renaissance," must be decadent. The image of the ballistic
curve has now been abandoned, and we have gained a less
assured, but also less arbitrary, estimate of what, for lack of
another term, we still call the High Renaissance.

In some fundamental respects, we shall find that the High
Renaissance was indeed the culmination of the Early Renaissance, while in other respects it represented a significant departure. Certainly the tendency to view artists as sovereign
geniuses, rather than as devoted artisans, was never stronger
than during the first half of the sixteenth century. Plato's concept of genius—the spirit entering into poets that causes them
to compose in a "divine frenzy"—had been broadened by
Marsilio Ficino and his fellow Neo-Platonists to include architects, sculptors, and painters. For Giorgio Vasari, individuals

of genius were thought to be set apart from ordinary artists by
"grace," in the sense of both divine grace, a gift from God, and
gracefulness, which reflected it. To him, this concept had
moral and spiritual significance, inspired in good measure by
Dante's Inferno. Building further on Petrarch's scheme of history (see page 404), he saw the High Renaissance as superior
even to antiquity, for it belonged to the Christian era of grace
(*tempus gratia*), in contrast to the Old Testament of God's law
as received by Moses (*tempus legem*), which had not been
revealed to the pagans. Thus in his *Lives of the Painters*
(1550–68), Vasari extolls the "gracious," virtuous personalities of Michelangelo, Leonardo, and Raphael, as a way of
accounting for their universal talent. Grace served, moreover,
to justify his treatment of his close friend and idol Michelangelo as the greatest artist of all time, a view that remains with
us to this very day, although Michelangelo's character was far
from admirable in all respects.

What set these artists apart was the inspiration guiding
their efforts, which was worthy of being called "divine,"
"immortal," and "creative." (Before 1500 *creating,* as distinct
from *making,* was the privilege of God alone.) To Vasari, the
painters and sculptors of the Early Renaissance, like those of
the Late Gothic, had learned only to imitate coarse nature,
whereas the geniuses of the High Renaissance had conquered
nature by ennobling, transcending, or subjecting it to art. In
actual fact, the High Renaissance remained thoroughly
grounded in nature. Its achievement lay in the creation of a
new classicism through abstraction. It was an act of the imagination, not the intellect, for the result was a poetic ideal
informed by a spirit of ineffable harmony.

Faith in the divine origin of inspiration led artists to rely
on subjective, rather than objective, standards of truth and
beauty. If Early Renaissance artists felt bound by what they
believed to be universally valid rules, such as the numerical
ratios of musical harmony and the laws of linear perspective,
their High Renaissance successors were less concerned with

594. Leonardo da Vinci. *Adoration of the Magi.* 1481–82. Monochrome on panel, 8' x 8'1" (2.43 x 2.46 m). Galleria degli Uffizi, Florence

rational order than with visual effectiveness. They evolved a new drama and a new rhetoric to engage the emotions of the beholder, whether sanctioned or not by classical precedent. Indeed, the works of the great High Renaissance masters immediately became classics in their own right, their authority equal to that of the most renowned monuments of antiquity. At the same time, this cult of the genius had a profound effect on the artists of the High Renaissance. It spurred them to vast and ambitious goals, and prompted their awed patrons to support such enterprises. Since these ambitions often went beyond the humanly possible, they were apt to be frustrated by external as well as internal difficulties, leaving artists with a sense of having been defeated by a malevolent fate.

Here we encounter a contradiction: if the creations of genius are viewed as unique by definition, they cannot be successfully imitated by lesser artists, however worthy they may seem of such imitation. Unlike the founders of the Early Renaissance, the leading artists of the High Renaissance did not set the pace for a broadly based "period style" that could be practiced on every level of quality. The High Renaissance produced astonishingly few minor masters. It died with those who had created it, or even before. Of the six great personalities mentioned above, only Michelangelo and Titian lived beyond 1520.

External conditions after that date were undoubtedly less favorable to the High Renaissance style than those of the first two decades of the sixteenth century. Yet the High Renaissance might well have ended soon even without the pressure of circumstances. Its harmonious grandeur was inherently unstable, a balance of divergent qualities. Only these quali-

ties, not the balance itself, could be transmitted to the artists who reached maturity after 1520. In pointing out the limited and precarious nature of the High Renaissance we do not mean to deny its tremendous impact upon later art. For most of the next 300 years, the great personalities of the early sixteenth century loomed so large that the achievements of their predecessors seemed to belong to a forgotten era. Even when the art of the fourteenth and fifteenth centuries was finally rediscovered, people still acknowledged the High Renaissance as the turning point, and referred to all painters before Raphael as "the Primitives."

Leonardo da Vinci

One important reason why the High Renaissance rightfully deserves to be called a period is the fact that its key monuments were all produced between 1495 and 1520, despite the great differences in age of the artists who created them. Bramante, the oldest, was born in 1444, Raphael in 1483, and Titian about 1488–90. Yet the distinction of being the earliest High Renaissance master belongs to Leonardo da Vinci (1452–1519), not to Bramante. Born in the little Tuscan town of Vinci, Leonardo was trained in Florence by Verrocchio. Conditions there must not have suited him. At the age of 30 he went to work for the duke of Milan as a military engineer, and only secondarily as an architect, sculptor, and painter.

ADORATION OF THE MAGI. Leonardo left behind, unfinished, the most ambitious work he had then begun, a large *Adoration of the Magi* (fig. 594), for which he had made several preliminary studies. The design of the ruins shows a geometric order and a precisely constructed perspective that recall Florentine painting in the wake of Masaccio, rather than the style prevailing about 1480, which is reflected solely in the gracefulness of the Madonna and Child. Yet the structure is so peculiar as to heighten the contrast with the landscape. The result is a spatial disjunctiveness that is nearly hallucinatory. Without the trees to anchor it, the composition would consist of two wholly separate parts. The background is inexplicable in rational terms. What are we to make of the figures who inhabit the stairs of the wrecked building, or the combat of horsemen to either side? The foreground is no less visionary. The main figures are contained within a triangle surrounded by the sweeping arc of onlookers. The scene is framed by a philosopher lost in thought to the left and by a young soldier on the right looking outside the picture to something that has caught his attention. They undoubtedly represent ideal types—but what do they signify? The contemplative and active lives surely, youth and old age as well, perhaps moral and physical beauty, as one critic has suggested. Within these contrasts lies a duality of mind and body that Leonardo sought to resolve in his mature work. The inchoate assembly is as spellbinding as it is strange. The future is already writ within it, for it contains the germinal form of figures found in Leonardo's later paintings.

The most striking, and indeed revolutionary, aspect of the panel is the way it is executed, although Leonardo had not even completed the underpainting. The forms seem to materialize softly and gradually, never quite detaching themselves from a dusky realm. Leonardo, unlike Pollaiuolo or Botticelli, thinks not of outlines, but of three-dimensional bodies made visible in varying degrees by the incidence of light. In the shadows, these shapes remain incomplete. Their contours are only implied instead. In this method of modeling (called *chiaroscuro,* the Italian word for "light and dark"), the forms no longer stand abruptly side by side but partake of a new pictorial unity, for the barriers between them have been partially broken down. There is a comparable emotional continuity as well. The gestures and faces of the crowd convey with touching eloquence the reality of the miracle they have come to behold. We will recognize the influence of both Pollaiuolo and Verrocchio in the mobile expressiveness of these figures, but Leonardo may also have been impressed by the breathless shepherds in *The Portinari Altarpiece,* then newly installed in Florence (see fig. 682).

THE VIRGIN OF THE ROCKS. Soon after arriving in Milan, Leonardo did *The Virgin of the Rocks* (fig. 595), another altar panel, which suggests what the *Adoration* would have looked like had it been completed. Here the figures emerge from the semidarkness of the grotto, enveloped in a moisture-laden atmosphere that delicately veils their forms. This fine haze, called *sfumato,* is more pronounced than similar effects in Flemish and Venetian painting. It lends a peculiar warmth and intimacy to the scene. It also creates a remote, dreamlike quality, and makes the picture seem a poetic vision rather than an image of reality. The subject—the infant St. John adoring the Infant Christ in the presence of the Virgin and an angel— is without immediate precedent. The story of their meeting is

595. Leonardo da Vinci. *The Virgin of the Rocks.* c. 1485. Oil on panel transferred to canvas, 6'6" x 4' (1.9 x 1.2 m). Musée du Louvre, Paris

one of the many legends that arose to satisfy the abiding curiosity about the "hidden" early life of Christ, which is hardly mentioned in the Bible. (According to a similar legend, St. John, about whom equally little is known, spent his childhood in the wilderness; hence he is shown wearing a hair shirt.)

Leonardo was the first to depict this scene, but the treatment is mysterious in many ways: the secluded, rocky setting, the pool in front, and the plant life, carefully chosen and exquisitely rendered, all hint at levels of meaning that are somehow hard to define. How are we to interpret the relationships among the four figures, signified by the conjunction of gestures? Protective, pointing, blessing, they convey the wonderment of St. John's recognition of Christ as the Saviour, but with a tenderness that raises the scene above the merely doctrinal. The gap between these hands and St. John makes the exchange all the more telling. Although present in germinal form in *The Doubting of Thomas* by Leonardo's teacher, Verrocchio (fig. 581), the elegant gestures and the refined features are the first mature example of that High Renaissance "grace" signifying a spiritual state of being.

596. Leonardo da Vinci. *The Last Supper.* c. 1495–98. Tempera wall mural, 15'2" x 28'10" (4.6 x 8.8 m). Sta. Maria delle Grazie, Milan

THE LAST SUPPER. Despite their originality, the *Adoration* and the *Virgin of the Rocks* do not yet differ clearly in conception from the aims of the Early Renaissance. But Leonardo's *Last Supper,* later by a dozen years, has always been recognized as the first classic statement of the ideals of High Renaissance painting (fig. 596). Unfortunately, the famous mural began to deteriorate a few years after its completion. The artist, dissatisfied with the limitations of the traditional fresco technique, experimented in an oil-tempera medium that did not adhere well to the wall. We thus need some effort to imagine its original splendor. Yet what remains is more than sufficient to account for its tremendous impact. Viewing the composition as a whole, we are struck at once by its balanced stability. Only afterward do we discover that this balance has been achieved by the reconciliation of competing, even conflicting, aims such as no previous artist had attempted.

A comparison with Castagno's *Last Supper* (fig. 564), painted half a century before, is particularly instructive here. The spatial setting in both cases seems like an annex to the real interior of the refectory (dining hall), but Castagno's architecture has a strangely oppressive effect on the figures, unlike Leonardo's. The reason for this becomes clear when we realize that in the earlier work the space has been conceived autonomously. It was there before the figures entered and would equally suit another group of diners. Leonardo, in contrast, began with the figural composition, and the architecture had no more than a supporting role from the start. His perspective is an ideal one.

Leonardo's painting, high up on the refectory wall, assumes a vantage point some 15 feet above the floor and 30 feet back—an obvious impossibility, yet we readily accept it nonetheless. The central vanishing point, which governs our view of the interior, is located behind the head of Jesus in the exact middle of the picture and thus becomes charged with symbolic significance. Equally plain is the symbolic function of the main opening in the back wall: its projecting pediment acts as the architectural equivalent of a halo. We thus tend to see the perspective framework of the scene almost entirely in relation to the figures, rather than as a preexisting entity. How vital this relationship is we can easily test by covering the upper third of the picture. The composition then takes on the character of a frieze, the grouping of the apostles is less clear, and the calm triangular shape of Jesus becomes merely passive, instead of acting as a physical and spiritual force. At the same time, the perspective system helps to "lock" the composition in place, lending the scene an eternal quality without making it appear static in any way.

The Saviour, presumably, has just spoken the fateful words, "One of you shall betray me," and the disciples are asking, "Lord, is it I?" We actually see nothing that contradicts this interpretation, but to view the scene as one particular moment in a psychological drama hardly does justice to Leonardo's intentions. These went well beyond a literal rendering of the biblical narrative, for he crowded together all the disciples on the far side of the table, in a space quite inadequate for so many people. He clearly wanted to condense his subject

597. Peter Paul Rubens. Drawing after Leonardo's cartoon for *The Battle of Anghiari*. c. 1600. Cabinet des Dessins, Musée du Louvre, Paris

physically by the compact, monumental grouping of the figures, and spiritually by presenting many levels of meaning at one time. Thus the gesture of Jesus is one of submission to the divine will, and of offering. It is a hint at Jesus' main act at the Last Supper, the institution of the Eucharist, in which bread and wine become his body and blood through transubstantiation. The apostles do not simply react to these words. Each of them reveals his own personality, his own relationship to the Saviour. (Note that Judas is no longer segregated from the rest; his dark, defiant profile sets him apart well enough.) Leonardo has carefully calculated each pose and expression so that the drama unfolds across the picture plane. The figures exemplify what the artist wrote in one of his notebooks, that the highest and most difficult aim of painting is to depict "the intention of man's soul" through gestures and movements of the limbs—a dictum to be interpreted as referring not to momentary emotional states but to the inner life as a whole.

THE BATTLE OF ANGHIARI. In 1499, the duchy of Milan fell to the French, and Leonardo returned to Florence after brief trips to Mantua and Venice. He must have found the cultural climate very different from his recollections of it. The Medici had been expelled, and the city was briefly a republic again, until their return. For a while, Leonardo seems to have been active mainly as an engineer and surveyor, but in 1503 the city commissioned him to do a mural of some famous event from the history of Florence for the council chamber of the Palazzo Vecchio. Leonardo chose the Battle of Anghiari, where the Florentine forces had once defeated the Milanese army. He completed the cartoon (a full-scale drawing) and had just begun the mural itself when he returned once more to Milan in 1506 at the request of the French, abandoning the commission.

The cartoon for *The Battle of Anghiari* survived for more than a century and enjoyed enormous fame. Today we know it only through Leonardo's preliminary sketches and through copies of the cartoon by later artists, notably a splendid drawing by Peter Paul Rubens (fig. 597; see page 574). Leonardo had started with the historical accounts of the engagement. As his plans crystallized, however, he abandoned factual accuracy and created a monumental group of soldiers on horseback that

represents a condensed, timeless image of the spirit of battle, rather than any specific event. His concern with "the intention of man's soul" is even more evident here than in *The Last Supper*. In this case, a savage fury has seized not only the combatants but the animals as well, so that they become one with their riders. *The Battle of Anghiari* stands at the opposite end of the scale from Uccello's *Battle of San Romano* (fig. 563), where nothing has been omitted except the fighting itself; yet Leonardo's battle scene is not one of uncontrolled action. Its dynamism is held in check by the hexagonal outline that stabilizes this seething mass. Once again, balance has been achieved by the reconciliation of competing claims.

MONA LISA. While working on *The Battle of Anghiari*, Leonardo painted the *Mona Lisa* (fig. 598). The delicate sfumato of *The Virgin of the Rocks* is here so perfected that it seemed miraculous to the artist's contemporaries. The forms are built from layers of glazes so gossamer-thin that the entire panel seems to glow with a gentle light from within. But the fame of the *Mona Lisa* comes not from this pictorial subtlety alone. Even more intriguing is the psychological fascination of the sitter's personality. Why, among all the smiling faces ever painted, has this particular one been singled out as "mysterious"? Perhaps the reason is that, as a portrait, the picture does not fit our expectations. The features are too individual for Leonardo to have simply depicted an ideal type, yet the element of idealization is so strong that it blurs the sitter's character. Once again the artist has brought two opposites into harmonious balance. The smile, also, may be read in two ways: as the echo of a momentary mood, and as a timeless, symbolic expression, akin to the "Archaic smile" of the Greeks (see figs. 152 and 153). The *Mona Lisa* seemingly embodies a quality of maternal tenderness which was to Leonardo the essence of womanhood. Even the landscape in the background, composed mainly of rocks and water, suggests elemental generative forces. Who was the sitter for this, the most famous portrait in the world? Her identity remained a mystery until very recently. We now know that she was the wife of a Florentine merchant born in 1479 and dead before 1556. This is not the only painting of the Mona Lisa: Leonardo also painted a nude version that once belonged to the king of France.

DRAWINGS. In his later years, Leonardo devoted himself more and more to his scientific interests. Art and science, we recall, were first united in Brunelleschi's discovery of systematic perspective. Leonardo's work is the climax of this trend. The artist, he believed, must know not only the rules of perspective but all the laws of nature, and the eye was to him the perfect instrument for gaining such knowledge. The extraordinary scope of his own inquiries is attested in the hundreds of drawings and notes that he hoped to incorporate into an encyclopedic set of treatises. [See Primary Sources, no. 53, page 631.] How original he was as a scientist is still a matter of debate, but in one field his importance remains undisputed: he created the modern scientific illustration, an essential tool for anatomists and biologists. A drawing such as the *Embryo in the Womb* (fig. 599) combines his own vivid observation with the analytic clarity of a diagram—or, to paraphrase Leonardo's own words, sight and insight.

598. Leonardo da Vinci.
Mona Lisa. c. 1503–5.
Oil on panel, 30¼ x 21"
(77 x 53.5 cm).
Musée du Louvre, Paris

600. Leonardo da Vinci. *Project for a Church* (Ms. B).
c. 1490. Pen drawing. Bibliothèque de l'Arsenal, Paris

599. Leonardo da Vinci. *Embryo in the Womb.* c. 1510.
Detail of pen drawing, 11⅞ x 8⅜" (30.4 x 21.5 cm).
Windsor Castle, Royal Library
© 1991. Her Majesty Queen Elizabeth II

Contemporary sources show that Leonardo was esteemed as an architect. Actual building seems to have concerned him less, however, than problems of structure and design. The numerous architectural projects in his drawings were intended, for the most part, to remain on paper. Yet these sketches, especially those of his Milanese period, have great historic importance, for only in them can we trace the transition from the Early to the High Renaissance in architecture.

The domed, centrally planned churches of the type illustrated in figure 600 hold particular interest for us. The plan recalls Brunelleschi's Sta. Maria degli Angeli (see fig. 549), but the new relationship of the spatial units is more complex,

601. Donato Bramante. The Tempietto, S. Pietro in Montorio, Rome. 1502–11

602. Plan of the Tempietto (after Serlio, in *Regole generali di Architettura*). Gray indicates unbuilt sections

while the exterior, with its cluster of domes, is more monumental than any Early Renaissance structure. In conception, this design stands halfway between the dome of Florence Cathedral and the most ambitious structure of the sixteenth century, the new basilica of St. Peter's in Rome (compare figs. 459, 603, and 604). It gives evidence, too, of Leonardo's close contact, during the 1490s, with the architect Donato Bramante (1444–1514), who was then also working for the duke of Milan. Bramante went to Rome after Milan fell to the French, and it was in Rome, during the last 15 years of his life, that he became the creator of High Renaissance architecture.

Bramante

THE TEMPIETTO. The new style is shown fully formed in Bramante's Tempietto at S. Pietro in Montorio (figs. 601 and 602), designed soon after 1500. This chapel, which marks the site of St. Peter's crucifixion, was planned to be surrounded by a circular, colonnaded courtyard. The Tempietto would then have appeared less isolated from its environment than it does today, for Bramante intended it to be set within a "molded" exterior space, a conception as bold and novel as the design of the chapel itself. Its nickname, "little temple," is well deserved. In the three-step platform and the severe Doric order of the colonnade, Classical temple architecture is more directly recalled than in any fifteenth-century structure. Equally striking is Bramante's application of the "sculptured wall" in the Tempietto itself and the courtyard. Not since Brunelleschi's Sta. Maria degli Angeli have we seen such deeply recessed niches "excavated" from heavy masses of masonry. These cavities are counterbalanced by the convex shape of the dome and by strongly projecting moldings and cornices. As a result, the Tempietto has a monumentality that belies its modest size.

ST. PETER'S, ROME. The Tempietto is the earliest of the great achievements that made Rome the center of Italian art during the first quarter of the sixteenth century. Most of them belong to the decade 1503–13, the papacy of Julius II. It was he who decided to replace the old basilica of St. Peter's, which had been in precarious condition, with a church so magnificent as to overshadow all the monuments of ancient Imperial Rome. The task fell to Bramante, the foremost architect in the city. His original design of 1506 is known only from a plan (fig. 603) and from the medal commemorating the start of the building campaign (fig. 604), which shows the exterior in rather imprecise perspective. These are sufficient, however, to bear out the words Bramante reportedly used to define his aim: "I shall place the Pantheon on top of the Basilica of Constantine."

To surpass the two most famous structures of Roman antiquity by a Christian edifice of unexampled grandeur— nothing less would have satisfied Julius II, a pontiff of enormous ambition, who wanted to unite all Italy under his command and thus to gain a temporal power matching the spiritual authority of his office. Bramante's design is indeed of truly imperial magnificence. A huge hemispherical dome, similar to that of the Tempietto, crowns the crossing of the barrel-vaulted arms of a Greek cross, with four lesser domes and tall corner towers filling the angles. This plan fulfills all the demands laid down by Alberti for sacred architecture (see

603. Donato Bramante. Original plan for St. Peter's, Rome. 1506 (after Geymuller)

604. Caradosso. Bronze medal showing Bramante's design for St. Peter's. 1506. The British Museum, London

605. Plan of Brunelleschi's S. Lorenzo, Florence, reproduced at the same scale as figure 603

page 437). Based entirely on the circle and the square, it is so rigidly symmetrical that we cannot tell which apse was to hold the high altar. Bramante envisioned four identical facades like that on the medal of 1506, dominated by the same repertory of severely classical forms we saw in the Tempietto: domes, half-domes, colonnades, pediments.

These simple geometric shapes, however, do not prevail inside the church. Here the sculptured wall reigns supreme. The plan shows no continuous surfaces, only great, oddly shaped "islands" of masonry that have been well described by one critic as giant pieces of toast half-eaten by a voracious space. The actual size of these islands can be visualized only if we compare the measurements of Bramante's church with those of earlier buildings. S. Lorenzo in Florence, for instance, has a length of 268 feet, less than half that of the new St. Peter's (550 feet). Figure 605, which reproduces the plan of S. Lorenzo on the same scale as Bramante's plan (fig. 603), proves that Bramante's reference to the Pantheon and the Basilica of Constantine was no idle boast. His plan dwarfs these monuments, as well as every Early Renaissance church. (Each arm of the Greek cross has about the same dimensions as the Basilica of Constantine.)

How did he propose to build a structure of such overwhelming size? Cut stone and brick, the materials favored by medieval architects, would not do, for technical and economic reasons. Only construction in concrete, as used by the Romans but largely forgotten during the Middle Ages, was strong and cheap enough to fill Bramante's needs (see page 177). By reviving this ancient technique, he opened a new era in the history of architecture, for concrete permitted designs of far greater flexibility than the building methods of the medieval masons. The possibilities of the material, however, were not fully exploited for some time to come. The construction of St. Peter's progressed so slowly that in 1514, when Bramante died, only the four crossing piers had actually been built. For the next three decades the campaign was carried on hesitantly by architects trained under Bramante, who modified his design in a number of ways. A new and decisive phase in the history of St. Peter's began only in 1546, when Michelangelo took charge, and the present appearance of the church (fig. 622) is largely shaped by his ideas. But this must be considered in the context of Michelangelo's career as a whole.

Michelangelo

The concept of genius as divine inspiration, a superhuman power granted to a few rare individuals and acting through them, is nowhere exemplified more fully than in the life and work of Michelangelo (Michelangelo di Lodovico Buonarroti Simoni, 1475–1564). Not only his admirers viewed him in this light. He himself, steeped in Neo-Platonist tradition (see pages 443–44), accepted the idea of his genius as a living reality, although it seemed to him at times a curse rather than a blessing. The element that brings continuity to his long and stormy career is the sovereign power of his personality, his faith in the subjective rightness of everything he created. Conventions, standards, and traditions might be observed by lesser spirits, but he could acknowledge no authority higher than the dictates of his genius.

606. Michelangelo. *Pietà*. c. 1500. Marble, height 68 1/2" (173.9 cm). St. Peter's, Rome

Unlike Leonardo, for whom painting was the noblest of the arts because it embraced every visible aspect of the world, Michelangelo was a sculptor—more specifically, a carver of marble statues—to the core. Art, for him, was not a science but "the making of men," analogous (however imperfectly) to divine creation. Hence the limitations of sculpture that Leonardo decried were essential virtues in Michelangelo's eyes. Only the "liberation" of real, three-dimensional bodies from recalcitrant matter could satisfy his urge. (See his *Awakening Slave* fig. 3). Painting, for him, should imitate the roundness of sculptured forms, and architecture, too, must partake of the organic qualities of the human figure.

Michelangelo's faith in the human image as the supreme vehicle of expression gave him a sense of kinship with Classical sculpture closer than that of any Renaissance artist. Among recent masters, he admired Giotto, Masaccio, Donatello, and Della Quercia more than the men he knew as a youth in Florence. Yet his mind was decisively shaped by the

cultural climate of Florence during the 1480s and 1490s. Both the Neo-Platonism of Marsilio Ficino and the religious reforms of Savonarola affected him profoundly. These conflicting influences reinforced the tensions within Michelangelo's personality, his violent changes of mood, his sense of being at odds with himself and with the world. As he conceived his statues to be human bodies released from their marble prison, so the body was the earthly prison of the soul—noble, but a prison nevertheless. This dualism of body and spirit endows his figures with extraordinary pathos. Outwardly calm, they seem stirred by an overwhelming psychic energy that has no release in physical action.

PIETÀ. We sense none of these struggles in the *Pietà* commissioned in 1497 by a French cardinal for his tomb chapel in St. Peter's (fig. 606). The subject, of Northern origin (see page 351), is rare, though not unknown, in Italy before this time. One of the Seven Sorrows of the Virgin, it owed its sudden

607. Michelangelo. *David*. 1501–4. Marble, height 13'5" (4.08 m).
Galleria dell'Accademia, Florence

her dead son—a problem that evidently was of little interest to the German Gothic artist, who instead turned it to his expressive advantage. Michelangelo succeeded in his ambition of carving "the most beautiful work of marble in Rome, one that no living artist could better." To Vasari it "was a revelation of all the potentialities and force of the art of sculpture."

DAVID. The unique qualities of Michelangelo's art do not emerge fully until his *David* (fig. 607), the earliest monumental statue of the High Renaissance. Commissioned of the artist in 1501 as the symbol of the Florentine republic (see fig. 464), the huge figure was designed to be placed high above the ground, on one of the buttresses of Florence Cathedral. However, a committee of civic leaders and artists decided instead to put it in front of the Palazzo Vecchio. [See Primary Sources, no. 54, pages 631–32.]

We can well understand the decision. Because the head of Goliath has been omitted, Michelangelo's *David* looks challenging. Here is not a victorious hero but the champion of a just cause. To Michelangelo, he embodied Fortitude—the same virtue celebrated by the diminutive "Herakles" on Nicola Pisano's pulpit (fig. 484), which the *David* curiously resembles, but here the figure has a civic-patriotic rather than a moral significance. Vibrant with pent-up energy, he faces the world like Donatello's *St. George* (see fig. 531), although his nudity links him to the older master's bronze *David* as well. The style of the sculpture proclaims an ideal very different from the wiry slenderness of Donatello's youths. Michelangelo had just spent several years in Rome, where he had been deeply impressed with the emotion-charged, muscular bodies of Hellenistic sculpture. Their heroic scale, their superhuman beauty and power, and the swelling volume of their forms became part of Michelangelo's own style and, through him, of Renaissance art in general.

Whereas his earlier work could sometimes be taken for ancient statues, in the *David* Michelangelo competes with antiquity on equal terms and replaces its authority with his own. This resolute individualism is partly indebted to Leonardo da Vinci, who had recently returned to Florence. (As with all of Michelangelo's great peers, they soon became arch rivals.) So is the expressive attitude of the figure, which conveys the "intention of man's soul." In Hellenistic works (compare fig. 213) the body "acts out" the spirit's agony, while the *David*, at once calm and tense, shows the action-in-repose so characteristic of Michelangelo.

TOMB OF JULIUS II. This feature persists in the *Moses* (fig. 608) and the two *"Slaves"* (figs. 609 and 610) of about ten years later. They were part of the ambitious sculptural program for the Tomb of Julius II, which would have been Michelangelo's greatest achievement had he been able to carry it out as originally planned. (The unfinished *Awakening Slave* in fig. 3 is from a later plan for the tomb.) The majestic *Moses*, meant to be seen from below, has the awesome force which the artist's contemporaries called *terribilità*—a concept akin to the sublime. His pose, both watchful and meditative, suggests a man capable of wise leadership as well as towering wrath. The *"Slaves"* are more difficult to interpret. They seem to have belonged to a series representing the arts, now shackled by the

popularity at the end of the fifteenth century to the growing veneration of Mary. Seated on Golgatha, the extraordinarily lovely and youthful Madonna stands for the Church and serves as the gateway to Heaven. If this Lamentation lacks the pathos of the German *Andachtsbild* (compare fig. 479), it is because we are meant to contemplate the central mystery of Christian faith with the same serenity as Mary herself: Jesus as God in human form who sacrificed himself to redeem our sins.

Spiritually as well as aesthetically, this *Pietà* still belongs to the fifteenth century. It is indebted to two of Michelangelo's predecessors: Jacopo della Quercia, for the figure of the Virgin, and Andrea Verrocchio, for the nobility of the faces and the highly ornamental treatment of the drapery. The cloak flowing like a river over the Madonna enables Michelangelo to resolve her physically and visually awkward relationship with

608. Michelangelo. *Moses.* c. 1513–15. Marble, height 7'8¹/₂" (2.35 m). S. Pietro in Vincoli, Rome

609. Michelangelo. *"The Dying Slave."* 1513–16. Marble, height 7'6" (2.28 m). Musée du Louvre, Paris

610. Michelangelo. *"The Rebellious Slave."* 1513–16. Marble, height 7' (2.13 m). Musée du Louvre, Paris

death of their greatest patron. Later, apparently, they came to signify the territories conquered by Julius II. Be that as it may, Michelangelo has treated the two figures as a contrasting pair, the *"Dying Slave"* (fig. 609) yielding to his bonds, the *"Rebellious Slave"* (fig. 610) struggling to free himself. Perhaps their allegorical meaning mattered less to him than their expressive content, so evocative of the Neo-Platonic image of the body as the earthly prison of the soul. They represent humanity's spiritual condition, with all its inner conflicts. In them we may recognize the influence of *The Laocoön Group* (fig. 215), whose unearthing Michelangelo witnessed in 1506, although these figures were first conceived the previous year.

THE SISTINE CEILING. Julius II interrupted Michelangelo's labors on the tomb project at an early stage. He decided to enlarge St. Peter's, initially, it seems, to house his tomb, an idea that was soon abandoned. When the undertaking was turned over to Bramante (see page 458), Michelangelo left Rome in anger. Two years later, the pope half-forced, half-cajoled the reluctant artist to return to paint frescoes on the ceiling of the Sistine Chapel in the Vatican (fig. 611). Driven by his desire to resume work on the tomb, Michelangelo completed the entire ceiling in four years, between 1508 and 1512.

[See Primary Sources, no. 56, pages 632–33.] He produced a work of truly epochal importance. The ceiling is a huge organism with hundreds of figures rhythmically distributed within the painted architectural framework, dwarfing the earlier murals (fig. 586) by its size, and still more by its compelling inner unity. In the central area, subdivided by five pairs of girders, are nine scenes based on the Old Testament Book of Genesis, from the Creation of the World (at the far end of the chapel) to the Drunkenness of Noah.

The theological scheme of these scenes and the rich program accompanying them—the nude youths, the medallions, the prophets and sibyls, the scenes in the spandrels—have not been fully explained, but we know that they link early history and the coming of Jesus. What greater theme could Michelangelo wish than the creation, destruction, and salvation of humanity? We do not know how much responsibility he had for the program. The artist was not someone to submit to dictation, and the subject matter of the ceiling fits his cast of mind so perfectly that his own desires cannot, in any event, have conflicted strongly with those of his patron.

A detailed survey of the ceiling would fill a book, and we shall have to be content with two of the four major scenes in the center portion. Of these, the *Creation of Adam* (fig. 612)

611. Interior of the Sistine Chapel showing Michelangelo's ceiling fresco. The Vatican, Rome

must have stirred Michelangelo's imagination most deeply. It shows not the physical molding of Adam's body but the passage of the divine spark—the soul—and thus achieves a dramatic juxtaposition unrivaled by any other artist. Della Quercia had approximated it in his relief panel (see fig. 540), which Michelangelo is known to have admired. But Michelangelo's design has a dynamism that contrasts the earth-bound Adam, who has been likened to an awakening river-god (compare fig. 6), and the figure of God rushing through the sky. This relationship assumes even more meaning when we realize that Adam strains not only toward his Creator but toward Eve, whom he sees, yet unborn, in the shelter of the Lord's left arm.

Michelangelo has been regarded as a poor colorist—unjustly, as the recent cleaning of the frescoes has revealed. *The Fall of Man* and *The Expulsion from the Garden of Eden* (fig. 613) show the bold, intense hues typical of the whole ceiling. The range of his palette is astonishing. Contrary to what had been thought, the heroic figures have anything but the quality of painted sculpture. Full of life, they act out their epic roles in illusionistic "windows" that puncture the architectural setting. Michelangelo does not simply color the areas within the contours but builds up his forms from broad and vigorous brushstrokes in the tradition of Giotto and Masaccio. In fact, *The Expulsion* is particularly close to Masaccio's (see fig. 556) in its intense drama. *The Fall*, by contrast, has the astonishing elegance of the *Libyan Sibyl* (fig. 9), the last of her breed to be executed on the ceiling. This surely is not merely an expression of beauty but of a spiritual state as well.

Figure 613 also permits us to glimpse the garland-bearing nude youths that accompany the main sections of the ceiling. These wonderfully animated figures, recurring at regular intervals, play an important role in Michelangelo's design: they form a kind of chain linking the Genesis scenes. Yet their significance remains uncertain. Do they represent the world of pagan antiquity? Are they angels or images of human souls? They seem ideal beings, but ones who have not yet attained a state of grace and thus yearn for salvation. Whatever the answer, they clearly belong to the same category as the *"Slaves"* from the Tomb of Julius II, to which they are closely related visually and conceptually. Again the symbolic intent is overpowered by the wealth of expression Michelangelo has poured into these figures.

Theater and Music During the High Renaissance

Although the term applies specifically to art, the High Renaissance was intimately connected to literature, theater, and music. Indeed, these arts created the cultural climate that made the High Renaissance possible in the first place. The early sixteenth century ushered in the first great age of Italian literature since the time of Dante and Petrarch some 200 years earlier. It centered on the poet Ludovico Ariosto (1474–1533), whose masterpiece, *Orlando Furioso* (1532), used the story of the crusade knight Roland to glorify his patron, the d'Este family of Ferrara. As early as 1508, Ariosto had written the first comedy along classical lines in Italian: *The Chest,* which initiated the genre known as *commedia erudita* (learned or serious comedy). Even Niccolò Machiavelli (1469–1527), who is best known for his manual of power and courtly life, *The Prince* (published posthumously in 1532), wrote a comedy, *The Mandrake.* The first vernacular tragedy, *Sofonisba* (1515) by Giangiorgio Trissino (1478–1550), was written in the Greek style to combat the influence of Seneca, thus setting off a debate that was effectively won by partisans of Latin drama in 1541, when *Orbecche* by Giambattista Cinthio (1504–1573) became the first Italian tragedy actually to be produced.

The High Renaissance counterpart to Ariosto in music was the Fleming Josquin Des Prés (c. 1440–1521), who became the most celebrated composer of his time. Artistically he belonged to the same generation as Leonardo da Vinci, though he was even older. Despite his notorious artistic temperament, he was employed at one time or another by all the leading courts in Italy and France, and enjoyed the patronage of no fewer than three popes. (He was present at the Vatican when Perugino and Botticelli were decorating the walls of the Sistine Chapel.) Josquin was regarded with much the same awe as Michelangelo came to be by his peers. The first true musical genius we know of, Josquin was a virtuoso equally at ease in secular and religious music. His work represented the perfect marriage of Flemish composition and Italian humanism, which, inspired by Greek accounts, sought unity between text and music. He thus found his ideal outlet in song (*chanson*) and the motet, which made an entire realm of human action and feeling available to him that lay outside the scope of the traditional Mass. He cultivated a smooth, homogenous style that has aptly been compared to the art of Raphael as the embodiment of the classical ideal in its calm, balanced perfection. He was also important for beginning to lead music away from the system of modes used throughout the Middle Ages and Early Renaissance.

Josquin became famous throughout Europe, thanks not only to his travels but also to the invention of music publication using movable type by the Venetian Ottaviano Petrucci (1466–1539) in 1498, a development that proved as revolutionary as printing had been for books and printmaking. Petrucci enjoyed such success that during the 1520s and 1530s France, Germany, and the Netherlands emerged as rival centers of music publishing. The diffusion of music and ideas in print helped to elevate composers in humanist circles. Like artists, they now became "learned" and joined in debates over matters of theory with other intellectuals. Their status was further enhanced by the appearance of the first primers, which taught amateurs how to play instruments and set off a new wave of enthusiasm for music.

It is a sign of the growing importance of music that courts competed eagerly for the leading composers and musicians, who commanded high salaries. Moreover, the ideal prince or courtier was expected to cultivate some musical ability in addition to his other talents. That consummate courtier Leonardo da Vinci was himself an accomplished musician, as were Giorgione and Titian.

612. Michelangelo. *The Creation of Adam,* portion of the Sistine Ceiling. 1508–12. Fresco

613. Michelangelo. *The Fall of Man* and *The Expulsion from the Garden of Eden,* portion of the Sistine Ceiling. 1508–12. Fresco

614. Michelangelo. *The Last Judgment.* 1534–41. Fresco. Sistine Chapel, The Vatican, Rome

615. Michelangelo. *The Last Judgment* (detail, with self-portrait)

616. Michelangelo. Tomb of Giuliano de' Medici.
1524–34. Marble, height of central figure 71" (180.5 cm).
New Sacristy, S. Lorenzo, Florence

THE LAST JUDGMENT. When Michelangelo returned to the Sistine Chapel in 1534, more than 20 years after completing the ceiling fresco, the Western world was enduring the spiritual and political crisis of the Reformation (see page 539). Michelangelo's religious beliefs had changed as well. We see the new mood with shocking directness as we turn from the radiant vitality of Michelangelo's ceiling fresco to the somber vision of his *Last Judgment* (fig. 614; reproduced here freshly cleaned), which illustrates Matthew 24:29–31.

How unlike the well-ordered, majestic treatment of Giotto (compare fig. 505), whose conception of Hell in the lower right-hand corner is still closely related to that on the west tympanum at Autun (see fig. 404). Michelangelo must have looked partly to Luca Signorelli's frescoes for Orvieto Cathedral (fig. 587). In the Sistine Chapel, however, the agony has become essentially spiritual, as expressed through violent physical contortions within the turbulent atmosphere. The Blessed and Damned alike huddle together in tight clumps, pleading for mercy before a wrathful God. All traces of classicism have disappeared, save for the Apollolike figure of the Lord. Straddling a cloud just below him is the apostle Bartholomew (fig. 615), holding a human skin to represent his martyrdom (he had been flayed). The face on that skin, however, is not the saint's but Michelangelo's own. In this grimly sardonic self-portrait, so well hidden that it was recognized only in modern times, the artist has left his personal confession of guilt and unworthiness.

THE MEDICI CHAPEL. The interval between the Sistine Ceiling and *The Last Judgment* coincides with the papacies of Leo X (1513–21) and Clement VII (1523–34). Both were members of the Medici family and preferred to employ Michelangelo in Florence. His activities centered on the Medici church of S. Lorenzo. A century after Brunelleschi's revolutionary design for the sacristy (see pages 419–20), Leo X decided to build a matching structure, the New Sacristy, to house the tombs of Lorenzo the Magnificent, Lorenzo's brother Giuliano, and two younger members of the family, also named Lorenzo and Giuliano (see fig. 543). These tombs are nearly mirror-images of each other. Michelangelo took early charge of this project and worked on it for 14 years. He managed to complete the architecture and two of the tombs, those for the lesser Lorenzo and Giuliano (fig. 616). The New Sacristy was thus conceived as an architectural-sculptural ensemble. It is the only work of the artist where his statues remain in the setting planned specifically for them, although their exact placement is problematic.

Michelangelo's plans for the Medici tombs underwent many changes of program and form while the work was underway. Other figures and reliefs were planned, but never executed. The present state of the monuments can hardly be the final solution, but the dynamic process of design was halted when the artist left permanently for Rome in 1534.

The tomb of Giuliano remains a compelling visual unit,

although the niche is too narrow and too shallow to accommodate the seated figure comfortably. The great triangle of the statues is held in place by a network of verticals and horizontals whose slender, sharp-edged forms heighten the roundness and weight of the sculpture. The design still shows some kinship with such Early Renaissance tombs as that of Leonardo Bruni (see fig. 577), but the differences weigh more heavily. There is no inscription, and the effigy has been replaced by two allegorical figures—*Day* on the right and *Night* on the left in our illustration. What is the meaning of this triad? The question, put countless times, has never found a satisfactory answer. Some lines penned on one of Michelangelo's drawings suggest a possible answer: "Day and Night speak, and say: We with our swift course have brought the Duke Giuliano to death . . . It is only just that the Duke takes revenge [for] he has taken the light from us; and with his closed eyes has locked ours shut, which no longer shine on earth."

Giuliano, the ideal image of the prince, is a younger and more pensive counterpart of the *Moses*. The statue, in classical military garb, bears no resemblance to the deceased Medici. ("A thousand years from now, nobody will know what he looked like," Michelangelo is said to have remarked.) Originally the base of each tomb was to have included a pair of river-gods. The reclining figures, themselves derived from ancient river-gods (compare fig. 6), contrast in mood like the *"Slaves."* They embody the quality of action-in-repose more dramatically than any other works by Michelangelo. In the brooding menace of *Day,* whose face was left deliberately unfinished, and in the disturbed slumber of *Night,* the dualism of body and soul is expressed with unforgettable grandeur.

LAURENTIAN LIBRARY. The Tomb of Giuliano de' Medici is squeezed uncomfortably within an architectural framework that takes considerable liberties with the syntax of classicism. The New Sacristy inspired Vasari to write that "all artists are under a great and permanent obligation to Michelangelo, seeing that he broke the bonds and chains that had previously confined them to the creation of traditional forms." However, his full powers as a creator of new architectural forms are fully displayed for the first time only in the vestibule (fig. 617) to the Laurentian Library, adjoining S. Lorenzo. This library was built concurrently with the New Sacristy to house, for the public, the huge collection of books and manuscripts belonging to the Medici family.

By the standards of the 1520s, based on the classical ideal of Bramante, everything in the vestibule is wrong. The pediment above the door is broken, the pilasters of the niches taper downward, the columns belong to no recognizable order, and the scroll brackets sustain nothing. Most paradoxical of all from the point of view of established practice are the recessed columns. Though structurally logical—the columns support heavy piers, which in turn support the roof beams (fig. 618)— this feature upsets a hallowed rule of architectural propriety. In the classical post-and-lintel system the columns (or pilasters) and entablature must project from the wall on which they have been superimposed, to stress their separate identities. The system could be reduced to a linear pattern (as in the Palazzo Rucellai; fig. 566), but no one before Michelangelo had dared to defy it by incorporating columns into the wall.

617. Michelangelo. Vestibule of the Laurentian Library, Florence. Begun 1524; stairway designed 1558–59

618. Axonometric diagram of structural system, Vestibule of the Laurentian Library (after Ackerman)

The purpose of these innovations is, of course, expressive rather than functional. The walls push inward between the columns to make of the vestibule a kind of "compression chamber" where the beholder experiences an almost physical stress. Our unease is heightened by the blank stare of the empty niches and by the nightmarish stairway, whose solution came, appropriately enough, to Michelangelo in a dream many years later. The steps, constructed from his design by Bartolommeo Ammannati (see page 499), flow downward and outward so relentlessly that we wonder if we dare brave the current by mounting them.

619. Michelangelo. The Campidoglio
(engraving by Étienne Dupérac, 1569)

620. Plan of the Campidoglio, Rome

CAMPIDOGLIO. During the last 30 years of Michelangelo's life, architecture became his main preoccupation. In 1537–39, he received the most ambitious commission of his career: to reshape the Campidoglio, the top of Rome's Capitoline Hill, into a square with a monumental frame worthy of this venerable site, which once had been the symbolic center of ancient Rome. At last he could plan on a grand scale, and he took full advantage of the opportunity. Although not completed until long after his death, the project was carried out essentially as he had designed it. The Campidoglio remains the most imposing civic center ever built, and a model for countless others. Pope Paul III took the initiative by transferring the equestrian monument of Marcus Aurelius (see fig. 279) to the Campidoglio, and Michelangelo designed its base. The statue became the focal point of his entire scheme, placed at the apex of a gently rising oval mound that serves to integrate the space.

Three sides of the piazza are defined by palace facades, so that visitors, after ascending the flight of steps on the fourth side, find themselves enclosed in a huge "outdoor room." The effect of the ensemble cannot be rendered by photographs. Even the best view, an engraving based on Michelangelo's design (fig. 619), conveys it very imperfectly. The print shows the complete bilateral symmetry of the scheme and the energetic sense of progression along the main axis toward the Senators' Palace. However, it distorts the shape of the piazza, which is not a rectangle but a trapezoid (see fig. 620). This peculiarity was imposed on Michelangelo by the existing site. The Senators' Palace and the Conservators' Palace on the right were actually older buildings that had to be preserved behind newly designed exteriors, and they were placed at an angle of 80 instead of 90 degrees. But Michelangelo turned into an asset what would have hindered a less imaginative architect:

621. Michelangelo. Palazzo dei Conservatori, Campidoglio, Rome. Designed c. 1545

the divergence of the flanks makes the Senators' Palace look larger than it is, so that it dramatically dominates the piazza.

The whole conception has the visual effectiveness of a stage set: in the engraving the "New Palace" on the left is only a show front with nothing behind it. Yet this facade and its twin on the opposite side are not shallow screens, but vigorously three-dimensional structures (fig. 621) with the most muscular juxtaposition of voids and solids, of horizontals and verticals, to be found in any piece of architecture since Roman antiquity (compare fig. 257). They share the striking feature of an open portico which links the piazza and facades, just as a courtyard is related to the arcades of a cloister.

The columns and stone beams of the porticoes are inscribed within a colossal order of pilasters that supports a heavy cornice topped by a balustrade. We have encountered these elements on the facades of the Pazzi Chapel by Brunelleschi and Alberti's S. Andrea, and in the Tempietto of Bramante (see figs. 544, 569, and 601), but it was Michelangelo who welded them into a coherent system. For the Senators' Palace he employed the colossal order and balustrade above a tall basement, which emphasizes the massive quality of the building. The single entrance at the top of the huge double-ramped stairway seems to gather all the spatial forces set in motion by the oval mound and the divergent flanks, and thus provides a dramatic climax for the visitor traversing the piazza.

ST. PETER'S. With the Campidoglio, the colossal order became firmly established in the repertory of monumental architecture. Michelangelo himself used it again with even more impressive results on the exterior of St. Peter's (fig. 622). He took over the design of the church in 1546 upon the death of the previous architect, Antonio da Sangallo the Younger (the nephew of his close friend Giuliano da Sangallo but a rival nonetheless), whose work he completely recast. The system of the Conservators' Palace, with windows now replacing the open loggias and an attic instead of the balustrade, could be adapted perfectly here to the jagged contour of the plan. Unlike Bramante's many-layered elevation (see fig. 604), the colossal order emphasized the compact body of the structure, thus setting off the dome more dramatically. The same desire for compactness and organic unity led Michelangelo to simplify the interior, without changing its centralized character (figs. 623 and 624). He brought the complex spatial sequences of Bramante's plan (see fig. 602) into one cross-and-square, and defined its main axis by modifying the exterior of the eastern apse and projecting a portico for it. This part of his design was never carried out. The dome, however, reflects his ideas in every important respect, although it was largely built after his death and has a steeper pitch. (Compare the engraving after his original design, fig. 624.)

Bramante had planned his dome as a stepped hemisphere above a narrow drum, which would have seemed to press down on the church below. Michelangelo's plan conveys the opposite sensation, a powerful thrust that draws energy upward from the main body of the structure. The high drum, the strongly projecting buttresses accented by double columns, the ribs, the raised curve of the cupola, the tall lantern, all contribute to the insistent verticality. Michelangelo borrowed not only the double-shell construction but the Gothic profile from the Florence Cathedral dome (see fig. 459), yet the effects are

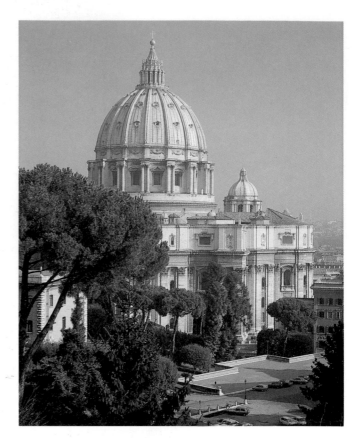

622. Michelangelo. St. Peter's, Rome, seen from the west. 1546–64 (dome completed by Giacomo della Porta, 1590)

623. Michelangelo. Plan for St. Peter's

624. Longitudinal section of St. Peter's (engraving by Étienne Dupérac, 1569)

625. Raphael. *La Belle Jardinière*. 1507. Oil on panel, 48 x 31½" (122 x 80 cm). Musée du Louvre, Paris

very different. The smooth planes of Brunelleschi's dome give no hint of the internal stresses. Michelangelo, in contrast, finds a sculptured shape for these contending forces and relates it to the rest of the building. The impulse of the paired colossal pilasters below is taken up by the double columns of the drum, continues in the ribs, and culminates in the lantern. The logic of this design is so persuasive that few domes built between 1600 and 1900 fail to acknowledge it in some way.

Michelangelo's magnificent assurance in handling such projects as the Campidoglio and St. Peter's seems to belie his portrayal of himself as a limp skin in *The Last Judgment*. It is indeed difficult to reconcile these contrasting aspects of his personality. Perhaps toward the end of his life he found greater fulfillment in architecture than in shaping human bodies, for we have no finished sculpture from his hand after 1545, when he at last completed the Tomb of Julius II. He devoted much of his final two decades to poetry and drawings of a religious and Neo-Platonic sort that are intensely personal in their content. [See Primary Sources. no. 55, page 632.] The statues undertaken for his own purposes, including a *Pietà* intended for his own tomb that was partly destroyed by his hand, show him groping for new forms, as if his earlier work had become meaningless to him.

Raphael

If Michelangelo exemplifies the solitary genius, Raphael (Raffaello Sanzio, 1483–1520) belongs just as surely to the opposite type: the artist as a person of the world. In consequence, they were natural antagonists. The contrast between the two was as clear to their contemporaries as it is to us. Although each had his defenders, they enjoyed equal fame. Twentieth-century sympathies have been less evenly divided, thanks to Vasari, Michelangelo's chief partisan, as well as to the authors of historical novels and fictionalized biographies. Michelangelo still fascinates people today, while Raphael is usually discussed only by historians of art, although his life was also the subject of a fanciful account. The younger artist's career seems too much a success story, his work too marked by effortless grace, to match the tragic heroism of Michelangelo. Raphael also appears to have been less of an innovator than Leonardo, Bramante, and Michelangelo, whose achievements were basic to his. Nevertheless, he is the central painter of the High Renaissance. Our conception of the entire style rests more on his work than on any other artist's.

The genius of Raphael was a unique power of synthesis that enabled him to merge the qualities of Leonardo and Michelangelo, creating an art at once lyric and dramatic, pictorially rich and sculpturally solid. This power is already present in the Madonnas he painted in Florence (1504–8), after he completed his apprenticeship with Perugino. The meditative calm of *La Belle Jardinière* (fig. 625) still reflects the style of his teacher (compare fig. 586), but the forms are ampler and enveloped in Leonardesque sfumato. The Virgin, grave and tender, makes us think of the *Mona Lisa* without engendering

626. Stanza della Segnatura, with frescoes by Raphael. Vatican Palace, Rome

any of her mystery. What is arcane in Leonardo becomes credibly human in Raphael, yet informed by a sensibility no less exquisite. At the same time, the insistent idealization of form already shows the grace and perfection that are the hallmarks of Raphael's style. The enigmatic gestures in *The Virgin of the Rocks* (fig. 595) are replaced by a gentle, rhythmic interplay, and the intricate grouping by a stable pyramid whose severity is relieved by Mary's billowing cape. Most striking is the beautiful landscape which, unlike any by Leonardo, is carefully observed. The human forms, too, have a firmness that further attests to his dedication to nature.

THE SCHOOL OF ATHENS. One of the reasons *La Belle Jardinière* looks different from *The Virgin of the Rocks,* to which it is otherwise so clearly indebted, is Michelangelo's influence. Its full force can be felt only in Raphael's Roman works, however. In 1508, at the time Michelangelo began to paint the Sistine ceiling, Julius II summoned the younger artist from Florence. At first Raphael mined ideas he had developed somewhat earlier, but the experience of Rome transformed him as an artist, and he underwent an astonishing growth. This metamorphosis is seen in the Stanza della Segnatura (Room of the Seal), the first in a series of private rooms he was called on to decorate at the Vatican Palace. The stanza housed the pope's library, but it was also where the tribunal of the seal (*segnatura*), presided over by the pope, dispensed canon and civil law.

Raphael's cycle of frescoes on its walls and ceiling refers to the four domains of learning: theology, philosophy, law, and the arts. The program, derived from St. Bonaventure, had no doubt already been provided by a Franciscan at the papal court, but the realization is Raphael's alone. To the right in our view (fig. 626) is the *Disputa,* or *Disputation over the Sacrament,* in which Jesus sits enthroned between the Virgin and St. John the Baptist, with God the Father behind him, saints and prophets to either side, and the Holy Spirit hovering over the Eucharist below. In the lunette over the door to the left are represented *The Three Legal Virtues;* beneath are *The Granting of Civil Law* (left) and *The Granting of Canon Law* (right). The opposite doorway depicts *Parnassus,* the sacred mountain of Apollo and the Muses.

Of these frescoes, *The School of Athens* (fig. 627), facing the *Disputa,* has long been acknowledged as Raphael's masterpiece and the perfect embodiment of the classical spirit of the High Renaissance. Its subject is "the Athenian school of thought," a group of famous Greek philosophers gathered around Plato and Aristotle, each in a characteristic pose or activity. Raphael must have already seen the Sistine ceiling, then nearing completion. He evidently owes to Michelangelo the expressive energy, the physical power, and the dramatic grouping of his figures. Yet Raphael has not simply borrowed Michelangelo's repertory of gestures and poses. He has absorbed it into his own style, and thereby given it different meaning.

Body and spirit, action and emotion, are now balanced harmoniously, and all members of this great assembly play their roles with magnificent, purposeful clarity. The total conception of *The School of Athens* suggests the spirit of Leonardo's *The Last Supper* (fig. 596) rather than the Sistine ceiling. This holds true of the way Raphael makes each philosopher reveal "the intention of his soul," distinguishes the relations among

627. Raphael. *The School of Athens*. 1510–11. Fresco. Stanza della Segnatura, Vatican Palace, Rome

individuals and groups, and links them in formal rhythm. The artist carefully worked out the poses in a series of drawings, many of them from life. Also Leonardesque is the centralized, symmetrical design, as well as the interdependence of the figures and their architectural setting. But Raphael's edifice shares far more of the compositional burden than the hall of *The Last Supper*. With its lofty dome, barrel vault, and colossal statuary, it is classical in spirit without being at all Greek in appearance. Inspired by Bramante, it seems like an advance view of the new St. Peter's. (Bramante was born in Urbino, the same birthplace as Raphael, and even posed for the figure of Pythagoras, seen holding a book in the foreground to the lower left. Michelangelo was added at the last minute, just to the right, as Heraclitus writing on the steps.) The geometric precision and spatial grandeur of this setting bring to a climax the tradition begun by Masaccio (see fig. 551) and transmitted to Raphael by his teacher Perugino, who had inherited it from Piero della Francesca. What is new is the active role played by the architecture in creating narrative space. This innovation was of such fundamental importance that it had a profound impact on the course of painting far beyond the sixteenth century.

GALATEA.   Raphael rarely set so splendid an architectural stage again. To create pictorial space, he relied increasingly on the movement of human figures, rather than perspective vistas.

628. Raphael. *Galatea*. 1513. Fresco, 9'8⅛" x 7'4" (3 x 2.2 m). Villa Farnesina, Rome

629. Raphael. *Pope Leo X with Giulio de' Medici and Luigi de' Rossi.*
c. 1518. Oil on panel, 60⁵/8 x 46⁷/8" (154 x 119 cm).
Galleria degli Uffizi, Florence

In the *Galatea* of 1513 (fig. 628), the subject is again classical: the beautiful nymph Galatea, vainly pursued by the giant Polyphemus, belongs to Greek mythology. Like the verse by Angelo Poliziano that inspired it, the painting celebrates the light-hearted, sensuous aspect of antiquity, in contrast to the austere idealism of *The School of Athens*. [See Primary Sources, no. 58, page 633.] If the latter presents an ideal concept of the antique past, *Galatea* captures its pagan spirit as if it were still a living force. The composition recalls Botticelli's *The Birth of Venus* (fig. 583), a picture Raphael knew from his Florentine days, which shares a debt to Poliziano (see page 443). Yet their very resemblance emphasizes their profound dissimilarity. Raphael's full-bodied, dynamic figures take on their expansive spiral movement from the vigorous *contrapposto* of Galatea. In Botticelli's picture, the movement is not generated by the figures but imposed on them from without by the decorative, linear design, so that it never detaches itself from the surface of the canvas.

PORTRAITS.   Given his adherence to nature, it is not surprising that Raphael had a special talent for portraiture. It is another tribute to his genius for synthesis that he combined the realism of fifteenth-century portraits (such as fig. 585)

with the human ideal of the High Renaissance, which in the *Mona Lisa* nearly overpowers the sitter's individuality. Raphael did not flatter or conventionalize his subjects. Surely Pope Leo X (fig. 629) looks here no handsomer than he did in reality. The sullen, heavy-jowled features of this most hedonistic pope have been recorded in concrete detail. Nevertheless, the pontiff has a commanding presence, his aura of power and dignity emanating more from his inner being than from his exalted office. Raphael, we feel, has not falsified the sitter's personality but ennobled and focused it, as if he had been fortunate enough to observe Leo X in his finest hour. The two cardinals, who lack this balanced strength although they are studied with equal care, enhance by contrast the sovereign quality of the main figure. Even the pictorial treatment shows a similar gradation: Leo X has been set off from his companions, his reality heightened by intensified light, color, and texture.

LATER WORKS.   When Michelangelo was dispatched to Florence by Leo X in 1516 to work on the Medici Chapel (see page 467), Raphael assumed undisputed leadership of art in Rome. He had already been named Bramante's successor at St. Peter's—Michelangelo was not put in charge of it until 30 years later—and appointed superintendent of antiquities in

630. Raphael. *The Sacrifice at Lystra*. 1514–15. Tempera on paper, 11'5 3/4" x 17'8 1/2" (3.5 x 5.4 m). Victoria & Albert Museum, London

Rome. Now he was flooded with commissions, and of necessity came to rely increasingly on his growing workshop. As a consequence, few of Raphael's later works, other than portraits such as that of Leo X, are entirely by his own hand. Thus, his achievement is partially obscured by the increasing participation of assistants, who adulterated his intent, as well as by the intervention of later restorers. The final phase of his brief career is nevertheless extraordinarily rich and complex.

Raphael elevated narrative painting to a new plane by greatly expanding its pictorial and expressive range. This unprecedented variety is marked by a creative tension between grandiose rhetoric and high theater that pushes classicism to its limits, and sometimes beyond. At times these forces coexist in an uneasy truce, but in *The Sacrifice at Lystra* (fig. 630), one of a series of tapestry cartoons for the Sistine Chapel that placed him in direct competition with Michelangelo, they are held in a state of dynamic equilibrium that is masterful. The scene, taken from Acts 14, shows Paul admonishing a crowd not to sacrifice animals in his honor after he had healed a cripple (to the far right in our illustration) and been mistaken for Mercury—hence, the statue of the god at upper center in the background. The architectural setting, reconstructed from the Antique with the passion of an archaeologist, is disposed

linearly across the picture plane, partly in imitation of Roman reliefs (compare fig. 273). In addition to framing the action, it plays an important expressive role by echoing the agitation of the surging crowd and the dignified strength of the saint and his companion, Barnabas.

Raphael has left a telling gap that serves not only to highlight the figure of Mercury but also to heighten the contrast between the two groups. The drama partakes of Leonardo's and Michelangelo's, but is of a different order, thanks to Raphael's unique power of concentration. In this work the artist has exhausted the possibilities that classicism had to offer him. What steps he might have taken next we shall never know, as his life was cut short at the critical juncture of the High Renaissance. Yet it is significant that some of the leading Mannerists of the next generation emerged from his atelier.

Giorgione

The distinction between Early and High Renaissance art, so marked in Florence and Rome, is far less sharp in Venice. Giorgione (Giorgione da Castelfranco, 1478–1510), the first Venetian painter to belong to the new era, left the orbit of Giovanni Bellini only during the final years of his short career.

631. Giorgione. *The Tempest.* c. 1505. Oil on canvas, 31¼ x 28¾" (79.5 x 73 cm).
Galleria dell'Accademia, Venice

THE TEMPEST. Among his few mature works, *The Tempest* (fig. 631) is both the most singular and the most enigmatic. There have been many attempts to explain this peculiar image. Perhaps the most persuasive one is that the painting represents Adam and Eve after the Fall. Their fate as decreed by God, whose awesome voice is represented by the lightning bolt, is that man shall till the ground from which he was taken, and that woman shall bring forth children in sorrow. Adam, dressed in contemporary Venetian costume, is seen resting from his labors, while Eve, whose draped nudity signifies shame and carnal knowledge, suckles Cain, her first-born son. In the distance is a bridge over the river surrounding the city of the earthly paradise, from which they have been expelled. Barely visible near the rock at river's edge is a snake, signifying the Temptation. The broken columns complete the tragic vision: they stand for death, the ultimate punishment of Original Sin.

The Tempest was probably commissioned by the wealthy merchant Gabriele Vendramin, one of Venice's greatest patrons of the arts, who owned the picture when it was first recorded in 1530. It certainly reflects the predilection for learned humanist allegories in Venetian painting, whose subjects are often obscured, as here, by static poses and alien settings. The iconography does not tell us the whole story of *The Tempest,* however. It is the landscape, rather than Giorgione's figures, that interprets the scene for us. Belonging themselves to nature, Adam and Eve are passive victims of the thunderstorm seemingly about to engulf them. The contrast to Bellini's *St. Francis in Ecstasy* (fig. 592) is striking. Bellini's landscape is meant to be seen through the eyes of the saint, as a piece of God's creation. Despite its biblical subject, the mood in *The Tempest* is subtly, pervasively pagan. The scene is like an enchanted idyll, a dream of pastoral beauty soon to be swept

632. Titian. *Bacchanal.* c. 1518. Oil on canvas, 5'8⅞" x 6'4" (1.7 x 1.9 m). Museo del Prado, Madrid

away. Only poets had hitherto captured this air of nostalgic reverie. Now, it entered the repertory of the painter. Indeed, the painting is very similar in its mood to the poem *Arcadia* by Jacopo Sannazaro, a pastoral poem about unrequited love that was popular in Giorgione's day. Thus, *The Tempest* initiates what was to become an important new tradition.

Titian

Giorgione died before he could explore in full the sensuous, lyrical world he had created in *The Tempest*. This task was taken up by Titian (Tiziano Vecellio, 1488/90–1576), an artist of comparable gifts who was decisively influenced by Giorgione and who dominated Venetian painting for the next half-century. [See Primary Sources, no. 57, page 633.]

BACCHANAL. Titian's *Bacchanal* of about 1518 (fig. 632) is frankly pagan, inspired by an ancient author's description of such a revel. The landscape, rich in contrasts of cool and warm tones, has all the poetry of Giorgione, but the figures are of another breed. Active and muscular, they move with a joyous freedom that recalls Raphael's *Galatea* (fig. 628). By this time, many of Raphael's compositions had been engraved (see fig. 5), and from these reproductions Titian became familiar with the Roman High Renaissance. A number of the celebrants in his *Bacchanal* also reflect the influence of classical art. Titian's approach to antiquity, however, is very different from Raphael's. He visualizes the realm of classical myths as part of the natural world, inhabited not by animated statues but by beings of flesh and blood. The figures of the *Bacchanal* are idealized just enough beyond everyday reality to persuade us that they belong to a long-lost golden age. They invite us to share

633. Titian. *Madonna with Members of the Pesaro Family.* 1526. Oil on canvas, 16' x 8'10" (4.9 x 2.7 m).
Sta. Maria del Gloriosa dei Frari, Venice

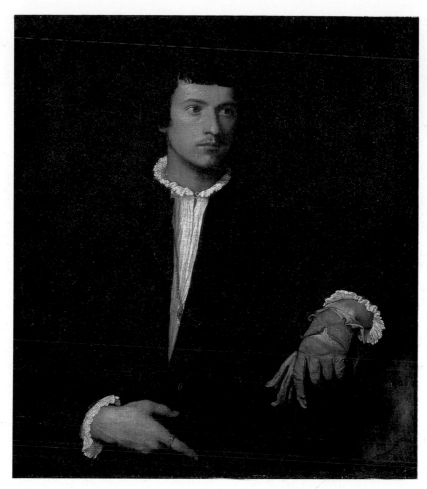

634. Titian. *Man with the Glove*. c. 1520. Oil on canvas,
39½ x 35" (100.3 x 89 cm). Musée du Louvre, Paris

their blissful state in a way that makes Raphael's *Galatea* seem cold and remote by comparison.

THE PESARO MADONNA. This quality of festive animation reappears in many of Titian's religious paintings, such as the *Madonna with Members of the Pesaro Family* (fig. 633). Although we recognize the subject as a variant of the sacra conversazione, Titian has thoroughly transformed it. For the first time, we feel that the participants are actually sharing in a dialogue. The Holy Family is no longer timeless and remote, as in Veneziano's prototype (compare fig. 560). The Infant Jesus is as natural as the child in the artist's *Bacchanal*, while the Virgin and St. Joseph now turn to the donor, Jacopo Pesaro, kneeling in devotion at the left. Joseph himself marks an innovation: instead of being the simple-minded old man of tradition, he is shown as a learned philosopher—an idea that had become current only a few years earlier.

Much of the picture's effectiveness is due to the composition, which replaces the familiar frontal view with an oblique one that is far more active. The Virgin is now enthroned in a great barrel-vaulted hall open on either side, a High Renaissance counterpart of the architectural setting in Bellini's *Madonna and Saints* in S. Zaccaria (fig. 593). The elevated columns, which are the key to the setting, represent the gateway to Heaven, identified with Mary herself; they are a sym-

bol of both eternal life and the Immaculate Conception (the belief that she was conceived without Original Sin). Because the view is diagonal, open sky and clouds now fill most of the background. Except for the kneeling donors, every figure is in motion—turning, leaning, gesturing—while the officer with the flag seems almost to lead a charge up the steps. (He is probably St. Maurice, namesake of the battle at Santa Mauro where the Venetian navy, which included the papal fleet commanded by Pesaro, prevailed against the Turks in 1502—note the turbaned figure beside him.) Yet the design remains harmoniously self-contained despite the strong element of drama. Brilliant sunlight makes every color and texture sparkle, in keeping with the joyous spirit of the altar. The only hint of tragedy is the cross of the Passion held by two angel-putti, hidden by clouds from the participants in the sacra conversazione but not from us, adding a note of poignancy to the scene.

PORTRAITS. After Raphael's death, Titian became the most sought-after portraitist of the age. His prodigious gifts, evident in the donors' portraits in the *Pesaro Madonna*, are even more striking in the *Man with the Glove* (fig. 634). The dreamy intimacy of this portrait, with its soft outline and deep shadows, still reflects the style of Giorgione. Lost in thought, the young man seems quite unaware of us. This slight melancholy

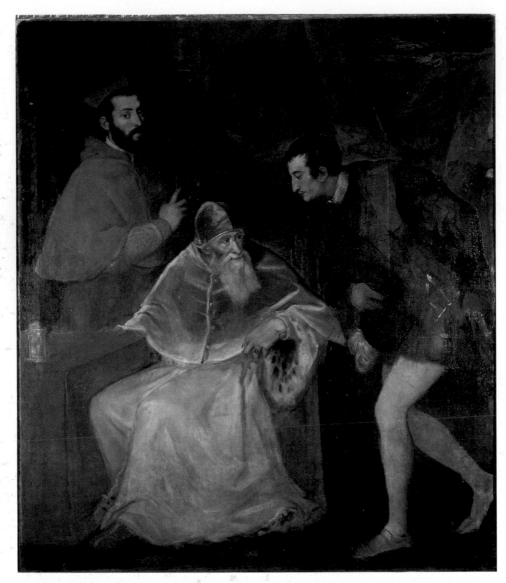

635. Titian. *Pope Paul III and His Grandsons.* 1546. Oil on canvas, 6'10" x 5'8" (2.1 x 1.7 m).
Museo di Capodimonte, Naples

in his features conjures up the poetic appeal of *The Tempest.* The breadth and power of form, however, go far beyond Giorgione's. In Titian's hands, the possibilities of the oil technique—rich, creamy highlights, deep dark tones that are transparent and delicately modulated—now are fully realized, and the separate brushstrokes, hardly visible before, become increasingly free.

We can see the rapid pace of Titian's development by turning from the *Man with the Glove* to the papal group portrait *Pope Paul III and His Grandsons* (fig. 635), painted a quarter-century later, whose formal composition is derived from Raphael's *Pope Leo X* (fig. 629). The quick, slashing strokes here endow the entire canvas with the spontaneity of a first sketch (some parts of it are, in fact, unfinished). In the freer technique, Titian's uncanny grasp of human character also comes out. The tiny figure of the pope, shriveled with age, dominates his tall attendants with awesome authority. Comparing these two portraits by Titian, we see that a change of pictorial technique is not a surface phenomenon. It reflects a change of the artist's aim.

LATE WORKS. This correspondence of form and technique, which we have already seen in Titian's *Danaë* (fig. 10), is even clearer in *Christ Crowned with Thorns* (fig. 636), the most awesome work of Titian's old age. To what does the canvas owe its power? Surely not to its large scale or dramatic composition, though these are contributing factors. (The painting is a variant of one he had made a quarter-century earlier that is considerably less successful.) The answer lies in the artist's technique. The shapes emerging from the semidarkness now consist wholly of light and color. Despite the heavy impasto, the shimmering surfaces have lost every trace of material solidity and seem translucent, as if aglow from within. The violent action has been miraculously suspended. What lingers in our minds is the strange mood of serenity engendered by deep religious feeling rather than the drama. As a result, we contemplate not Jesus' physical suffering but its purpose: the redemption and salvation of humanity. The painting's ethereality participates in a widespread visionary tendency that was shared by other late-sixteenth-century Venetian artists. We shall meet it again in the work of Tintoretto and El Greco.

636. Titian. *Christ Crowned with Thorns.* c. 1570. Oil on canvas,
9'2" x 6' (2.8 x 1.8 m). Alte Pinakothek, Munich

CHAPTER THREE

MANNERISM AND OTHER TRENDS

What happened after the High Renaissance? Eighty years ago the answer would have been simply that after the High Renaissance came the Late Renaissance, which lasted until the Baroque style emerged at the end of the sixteenth century. Today we take a far more positive view of the artists who reached maturity after 1520, and generally discard the term "Late Renaissance" as misleading. Yet we have still to agree on a name for the 75 years separating the High Renaissance from the Baroque. Any one label implies that the period has one style, but there is no single style in the years 1525 to 1600. Why, then, should this span be regarded as a period at all? This difficulty can be resolved by thinking of the period as a time of crisis that gave rise to several competing tendencies rather than one dominant ideal.

Although they had taken place during the High Renaissance, the great voyages of discovery—Columbus' landing in the New World in 1492, followed by Amerigo Vespucci's exploration of South America seven years later and Magellan's voyage to circumnavigate the globe beginning in 1519—had far-reaching consequences that were to reverberate until the end of the sixteenth century. The most immediate consequence was the rise of the great European colonial powers, which vied with each other for commercial supremacy around the world. The Spanish (as well as the Portuguese) quickly established themselves in the Americas: Mexico was conquered by Hernán Cortés in 1519–21, Peru by Francisco Pizarro during the following decade. By 1585, however, Sir Walter Raleigh had established the first English settlement in North America, and the French soon followed with outposts of their own. An unexpected effect was the explosion of knowledge as explorers brought back a host of natural and artistic wonders never before seen in Europe. Dazzled by these revelations, avid collectors formed Kunst- und Wunderkammern (literally, art and wonder rooms) to display exotic treasures from every corner of the earth. As Europeans struggled to assimilate this profusion of new discoveries into old categories of thought, the science inherited from ancient Greece and Rome by the Early Renaissance was largely discarded as inadequate by 1650 in favor of a new body of learning.

At almost the same time, the Protestant Reformation was launched by Martin Luther, a former Augustinian friar who had become professor of theology at the University of Wittenberg. At face value, the 95 theses he nailed to the Wittenberg Castle church door on All Saints' Eve in October 1517 were little more than a broadside against the sale of indulgences promising redemption of sins. More fundamentally they constituted a wholesale attack against Catholic dogma, for he claimed that the Bible and natural reason were the sole bases of religious authority. Freed from traditional doctrine, the Protestant movement rapidly developed splinter groups. Within a few years the Swiss pastor Huldreich Zwingli sought to reduce religion to its essentials by preaching an even more radical fundamentalism, denouncing the arts as distractions and denying the validity of even the Eucharist as a rite, which led to a split with Luther that was never healed. Even within Zwingli's camp there were rifts: the Anabaptists accepted only adult baptism.

What divided the reformers were the twin issues of grace and free will in attaining faith and salvation. These issues had been spelled out with the aid of the humanists, who initially counted Luther and Zwingli among their number; many of them, however, eventually turned against the Reformation because of its extremism. By the time of Zwingli's death at the hands of the Catholic forces at the Battle of Kappel in 1531, the essential corpus of Protestant theology had been defined. It was codified around mid-century by John Calvin of Geneva, who tried to mediate between Luther and Zwingli while adopting the puritanical beliefs of the Anabaptists.

The Catholic church soon inaugurated a reform movement of its own, generally known today as the Counter Reformation. It was spearheaded following the Council of Trent in 1545–47 by the Society of Jesus, the Jesuit order representing the Church militant, which had been founded by the Spanish St. Ignatius of Loyola in 1534. The internal reforms were carried out mainly by Pope Paul IV after he ascended the throne of St. Peter in 1555, and by St. Carlo Borromeo, who initiated the model reform as bishop of Milan five years later. The Reformation and Counter Reformation quickly became bound up in the political upheavals and social unrest sweeping Europe. Although they were sometimes passionate in their beliefs, rulers usually allied themselves with either movement depending on dynastic and economic self-interest. Thus Henry VIII of England established the Church of England in 1534 in order to make divorce easier so that he could produce a male heir. Later, Philip II of Spain made the Catholic cause part of the Hapsburg ambitions, cloaking his true motives in the mantle of a crusade for the true faith.

PAINTING

Mannerism in Florence and Rome

Among the various trends in art in the wake of the High Renaissance, Mannerism is the most significant, as well as the most problematic. In scope, the original meaning of the term was narrow and derogatory, designating a group of mid-sixteenth-century painters in Rome and Florence whose self-consciously "artificial" style (*maniera*) was derived from certain aspects of the work of Raphael and Michelangelo. This phase has since been recognized as part of a wider movement that had begun around 1520. Keyed to a sophisticated, even rarefied taste, early Mannerism had appealed to a small circle around aristocratic patrons such as Cosimo I, the grand duke of Tuscany. The style soon became international as a number of events—including the plague of 1522 and, above all, the Sack of Rome by Spanish forces in 1527—disrupted its development and displaced it abroad, where most of its next phase took place.

This new phase, High Mannerism, was the assertion of a purely aesthetic ideal. Through formulaic abstraction, it translated expression into a style of the utmost refinement, emphasizing grace, variety, and virtuoso display at the expense of content, clarity, and unity. This taste for mannered elegance and bizarre conceits appealed to a small but sophisticated audience, but in a larger sense Mannerism signified a major shift in Italian culture. In part, it resulted from the High Renaissance quest for originality as a projection of the individual's personality, which had given artists license to explore their imaginations freely. This investigation of new modes was ultimately healthy, but the Mannerist style itself came to be regarded by many as decadent, and no wonder: given such subjective freedom, it produced extreme personalities that today seem the most "modern" of all sixteenth-century painters.

The seemingly cold and barren formalism of High Mannerist work was part of a wider movement that placed inner vision, however private or fantastic, above the twin standards of nature and the ancients. Hence, some scholars have broadened the definition of Mannerism to include the later style of Michelangelo, who could himself acknowledge no artistic authority higher than his own genius. Mannerism is often considered a reaction against the normative ideal created by the High Renaissance as well. Save for a brief initial phase, however, Mannerism did not consciously reject the tradition from which it stemmed. Although the subjectivity inherent in this aesthetic was necessarily unclassical, it was not deliberately anticlassical, except in its more extreme manifestations. Even more conspicuous than Mannerism's anticlassicism is its insistent antinaturalism.

The relation of Mannerism to religious trends was equally paradoxical. Notwithstanding the intense religious feeling that informs many works by the first generation of artists, it has rightly been observed that Mannerism as a whole illustrates the spiritual bankruptcy of the age. In particular, the extreme worldliness of the next generation, the High Mannerists, was fundamentally antithetical to both the Reformation, with its stern morality, and the Counter Reformation, which demanded a strict adherence to doctrine. However, after mid-century there was a Counter Mannerist trend, which adapted the vocabulary of Mannerism for Counter Reformation ends. At the same time, the subjective latitude of Mannerism became valued for its visionary power as part of a larger shift in religious sensibility.

ROSSO. The first indications of disquiet in the High Renaissance appear shortly before 1520 in Florence. Art had been left in the hands of a younger generation that could refine but not further develop the styles of the great innovators who had spent their early careers there before leaving the city. Having absorbed the lessons of the leading artists at one remove, the first generation of Mannerists was free to apply High Renaissance formulas to a new aesthetic divorced from its previous content. By 1521, Rosso Fiorentino (1495–1540), the most eccentric member of this group, expressed the new attitude with full conviction in the *Descent from the Cross* (fig. 637). Nothing has prepared us for the shocking impact of this latticework of spidery forms spread out against the dark sky. The figures are agitated yet rigid, as if congealed by a sudden, icy blast. Even the draperies have brittle, sharp-edged planes. The acid colors and the light, brilliant but unreal, reinforce the nightmarish effect of the scene. Here is clearly a full-scale revolt against the classical balance of High Renaissance art: a profoundly disquieting, willful, visionary style that indicates a deep inner anxiety.

PONTORMO. Pontormo (1494–1556/7), a friend of Rosso's, had an equally strange personality. Introspective, willful, and shy, he worked only when and for whom he pleased, and he would shut himself up in his quarters for weeks on end, remaining inaccessible even to his closest friends. Pontormo's

637. Rosso Fiorentino. *Descent from the Cross.* 1521. Oil on panel,
11' x 6'5¹/₂" (3.4 x 2 m). Pinacoteca Communale, Volterra

638. Pontormo. *Deposition.* c. 1526–28.
Oil on panel, 10'3" x 6'4" (3.1 x 1.9 m). Sta. Felicita, Florence

Deposition (fig. 638) well reflects these facets of his character. The painting contrasts sharply with Rosso's *Descent from the Cross,* but is no less disturbing. Unlike Rosso's attenuated forms, Pontormo's have a nearly classical beauty and sculptural solidity inspired by Michelangelo, who in turned admired his art. Yet the figures are confined to a stage so claustrophobic as to cause acute discomfort in the viewer. The very implausibility of the image renders it convincing in spiritual terms. Indeed, this visionary quality is essential to its meaning, which is communicated by formal means alone. We have entered a world of innermost contemplation in which every pictorial element responds to a purely subjective impulse. Everything is subordinate to the play of graceful linear rhythms created by the tightly interlocking forms. These patterns unify the surface and impart a poignancy unlike any we have seen. Although they act in concert, the mourners are lost in a grief too personal to share with each other—or us. In this hushed atmosphere, anguish is transmuted into a lyrical expression of exquisite sensitivity. The entire scene is as haunted as Pontormo's self-portrait just to the right of the swooning Madonna. The artist, moodily gazing into space, seems to shrink from the outer

world, as if scarred by the trauma of some half-remembered experience, and into one of his own invention.

PARMIGIANINO. The first phase of Mannerism was soon replaced by one less overtly anticlassical, less laden with subjective emotion, but equally far removed from the confident, stable world of the High Renaissance. The *Self-Portrait* (fig. 639) by Parmigianino (Girolamo Francesco Maria Mazzuoli, 1503– 1540) suggests no psychological turmoil. The artist's appearance is bland and well groomed. The features, painted with Raphael's smooth perfection, are veiled by a delicate Leonardesque sfumato. The distortions, too, are objective, not arbitrary, for the picture records what Parmigianino saw as he gazed at his reflection in a convex mirror. Why was he so fascinated by this view "through the looking glass"? Earlier painters who used the mirror as an aid to observation had "filtered out" the distortions, except when the mirror image was contrasted with a direct view of the same scene (see fig. 677). But Parmigianino substitutes his painting for the mirror itself, even employing a specially prepared convex panel. Perhaps he wanted to demonstrate that there is no single "correct" reality, that distortion is as natural as the normal appearance of things. The painting bespeaks an interest in magic as well: the convex mirror was valued in the Renaissance for its visionary effects, which

639. Parmigianino. *Self-Portrait*. 1524. Oil on panel, diameter 9⅝" (24.7 cm). Kunsthistorisches Museum, Vienna

seemed to reveal the future, as well as hidden aspects of the past and present.

This may help to explain why Parmigianino's scientific detachment soon changed into its very opposite. Vasari tells us that Parmigianino, as he neared the end of his brief career (he died at 37), was obsessed with alchemy and became "a bearded, long-haired, neglected, and almost savage or wild man." Certainly his strange imagination is evident in his most famous work, *The Madonna with the Long Neck* (fig. 640), painted after he had returned to his native Parma following several years in Rome. He had been deeply impressed with the rhythmic grace of Raphael's art (compare fig. 628), but he has transformed the older artist's figures into a remarkable new breed. Their limbs, elongated and ivory-smooth, move with effortless languor, embodying an ideal of beauty as remote from nature as any Byzantine figure.

The pose of the Christ Child balanced precariously on the Madonna's lap echoes that of a *Pietà* (compare fig. 606). Although it has antecedents in Byzantine icons, this unusual device is of Parmigianino's own invention, and helps to explain the setting, which is not as arbitrary as it may seem. The gigantic column alludes to the flagellation of the Lord during the Passion, reminding us of his sacrifice, which the tiny figure of a prophet foretells on his scroll. But it also serves to disrupt our perception of space, which is strangely disjointed. Parmigianino seems determined to prevent us from measuring anything in this picture by the standards of ordinary experience. Here we have approached that "artificial" style for which the term *Mannerism* was originally coined. *The Madonna with the Long Neck* is a vision of unearthly perfection, its cold elegance no less arresting than the violence in Rosso's *Descent*.

Parmigianino is important as a printmaker as well as a painter. He was the first artist to explore the possibilities of etching seriously. Although the technique was introduced in the North shortly after 1510 (see page 524), it took the Italian Mannerists to appreciate the new medium. We can see why in Parmigianino's *The Entombment* (fig. 641): the print looks very much like his ink drawings in retaining a sketchlike immediacy that conveys the agitation of the scene. For that reason, etching

640. Parmigianino. *The Madonna with the Long Neck*. c. 1535. Oil on panel, 7'1" x 4'4" (2.2 x 1.3 m). Galleria degli Uffizi, Florence

641. Parmigianino. *The Entombment*. c. 1535. Etching printed in brown ink, 12¼ x 9⅜" (31.3 x 23.8 cm). Los Angeles County Museum of Art. Collection of Mary Stansburg Ruiz

The music and theater of Italy between 1530 and 1600 reflect the same rich variety found in art. The most characteristic musical form after about 1530 was the madrigal, which was an outgrowth of French and Italian popular songs. It was similar to the motet in that all the voices were equally important, but it was livelier and more expressive. The madrigal was also closely connected to the resurgence of Italian poetry in the work of Ludovico Ariosto (see page 464) and Torquato Tasso (1544–1595), Ariosto's successor as court poet to the ruling d'Este family of Ferrara. Tasso also treated the crusades in *Jerusalem Delivered* (1575), which remained the most popular poem of its kind through the seventeenth century. Although at first the best composers of madrigals were Flemish, after 1575 Italians dominated the form. Foremost among them was Carlo Gesualdo (c. 1560–1613), an aristocrat whose music was as bold and flamboyant as his personality. His madrigals, like those of Luca Marenzio (1553–1599), are full of complex verbal and musical conceits that make them counterparts to the paintings of the High Mannerists.

The church dignitaries at the Council of Trent (1545–63), which spearheaded the Counter Reformation in the Catholic church, objected to the growing use of secular melodies in sacred music, as well as to elaborate polyphony that obscured the words of the liturgy. In response, Giovanni Palestrina (c. 1525–1594) based his masses on traditional Gregorian chants. In many respects, however, his works are the successors of Josquin Des Prés' in their seamless texture and the perfect balance of melodic and harmonic values—that is, the beauty both of the principal melody and the other notes that accompany it, known as harmony. Palestrina, who held all the important musical posts in Rome during his lifetime, had special authority because of the backing of the papacy, and his style became "classic": it was held up as a model for imitation into the twentieth century.

Venice, unlike Rome, was ruled by secular authorities, so that Venetian music differed greatly from that composed for the pope. The vast spaces of St. Mark's church—which was the palace chapel of the Doges—encouraged the colorful music of Palestrina's contemporary, Andrea Gabrieli (1510–1586), who had studied under the Fleming Adrian Willaert (c. 1490–1562), and his nephew and pupil, Giovanni Gabrieli (1557–1612). The compositions of the Gabrielis emphasized sensuous effects of sound over counterpoint (different melodic lines moving independently, or "counter" to each other). Giovanni was also the first composer to specify which instruments should play which parts, to include dynamic markings in his music as indications of loudness and softness, and to make use of harmonies that sound "modern" to our ears, although Palestrina had effectively abandoned the modes except insofar as they were an inescapable part of church music. Much of Giovanni's music was purely instrumental. Instrument-only music in the late sixteenth century began to achieve its independence from vocal music by adapting popular dance tunes, often treated as a theme with variations. Such dances had been performed for centuries, although they were rarely written down. This development coincided with the creation of new families of instruments, such as viols and recorders, whose ranges—soprano, contralto, tenor, and bass—approximated those of human voices. These instruments lent Late Renaissance music a wonderfully diverse and distinctive sound.

The principal theatrical performances in sixteenth-century Italy were public spectacles paid for by the aristocracy. The most splendid were produced in Florence to glorify the Medici family in allegorical terms: *Masque of the Genealogy of the Gods* (1566), with sets and costumes designed by Giorgio Vasari, and *The Battle of the Argonauts,* mounted in 1608 on the Arno River. These displays spurred the development of more elaborate and sophisticated scenery design at the Medici court under Bernardo Buontalenti (1536–1608) and his pupil Giulio Parigi (c. 1570–1635), as well as in Ferrara, Mantua, Urbino, Milan, Parma, and Rome. Scenography initially relied on the accounts of Roman theater in the architectural treatise of Vitruvius, which was published in 1486, the same year that the humanist antiquarian Pomponius Laetus (1424–1498) began to produce ancient plays at the Roman Academy. Even more important was the influence of Leon Battista Alberti's linear perspective (see pages 459–62). Sebastiano Serlio (1475–1554) published an architectural treatise in 1545, which included a number of stage designs that made use of Alberti's perspective system to visualize Vitruvius' descriptions of Roman theaters. Serlio's designs proved so influential throughout Europe that they were often used to illustrate later editions of Vitruvius.

The occasional nature of dramatic presentations meant that few permanent theaters were built during the sixteenth century. The first court theater was erected by Buontalenti for the Medici in Florence. More important was the first

was ideally suited to capturing the artist's highly individual style and nervous temperament—traits prized above all others by the Mannerists.

BRONZINO. The second generation of Mannerists, with whom High Mannerism is identified, congealed the style they inherited from Rosso, Pontormo, and Parmigianino into a cool perfection that filtered out the last vestige of their intensely personal sensibility. As a consequence, they produced few masterpieces. In their best works, however, formal beauty becomes the aesthetic counterpart to recondite thought. Nowhere is this better seen than in the *Allegory of Venus* (fig. 642) painted by Agnolo Bronzino (1503–1572), Pontormo's favorite pupil, as a gift to Francis I of France from Cosimo I de' Medici. The central motif of Cupid embracing Venus was suggested by a lost *Triumph of Love* by Michelangelo that Pontormo and Bronzino are both known to have copied. However, as with so much else in Mannerism, it has been corrupted in content and treatment. Father Time tears back the curtain from Fraud in the upper left-hand corner to uncover Venus and Cupid in an incestuous embrace, to the delight of Folly, who is armed with roses, and the dismay of Jealousy, who tears her hair, as Pleasure, half-woman and half-snake, proffers a honeycomb. The moral is that folly blinds one to the jealousy and fraud of public theater, built in 1565 in Venice, which immediately established its leadership in theater writing and production. Twenty years later the architect Andrea Palladio (see pages 500–2) designed a theater for the Olympic Academy in Vicenza, which opened with a performance of Sophocles' *Oedipus Rex*. Although the theater was soon abandoned, its construction is a measure of sixteenth-century interest in serious classical theater.

After 1550, Renaissance theories of drama centered on Horace's *Art of Poetry* and Aristotle's *Poetics,* which had been published in a Latin translation in 1498. Drawing on these sources, Giulio Cesare Scaliger (1484–1558) and Lodovico Castelvetro (1505?–1571) insisted that both tragedy and comedy be presented in five acts and that they obey the "unities" of time, space, and action sanctioned as inviolable rules by Classical precedent: the events portrayed had to take place in roughly the same time as it took to present them (or at least within one day); in a space approximately the size of the actual stage; and with the story line revolving around a single incident or problem. The new body of theory also promoted the concept of verisimilitude, incorporating realism, morality, and universality (typical, normative traits). These ideas in turn led to an insistence on decorum: strict adherence to what was considered appropriate to the age, sex, temperament, and social status of each character. Drama was further divided into tragedy and comedy along class lines. Tragedy involved the actions of noble, that is, aristocratic, characters, while comedy was devoted to the buffooneries of the lower classes. However, the few plays written according to these rules met with a mixed reception in sixteenth-century Italy.

Among the most popular forms of theater were pastoral plays. These shared a common story line, in which a sophisticated young man or woman—in Torquato Tasso's *Aminta* (1573) this was actually the god Cupid—is forced by circumstance to spend some time among simple rural folk. The healthy manner of living and innocent goodness of the country people teach an important moral lesson and send the protagonist back to normal life refreshed in spirit. Also popular were comic interludes (*intermezzi*) between the acts of dramas, which featured such sensational scenery, costumes, music, dance, and special effects that they eventually became more important than the plays themselves.

642. Agnolo Bronzino. *Allegory of Venus.* c. 1546. Oil on panel, 57 1/2 x 45 1/4" (146.1 x 116.2 cm). The National Gallery, London

sensual love which time reveals. The literal unmasking of this deceit revels in the very lasciviousness it purports to condemn. The painting is thus a perversion of the elevated humanism that informs Botticelli's *Birth of Venus* (fig. 583). With its extreme stylization, Bronzino's subtle elegance proclaims an equally refined erotic ideal that reduces passion to a genteel exchange of serpentine gestures between figures as polished as marble.

VASARI. Bronzino's figures are indebted to Michelangelo in their sculptural quality (compare the Venus to *Night* in fig. 616). Those in *Perseus and Andromeda* (fig. 643) by Giorgio Vasari (1511–1574), the chronicler of the Italian Renaissance

643. Giorgio Vasari. *Perseus and Andromeda.* 1570–72. Oil on slate, 45 1/2 x 34" (115.6 x 86.4 cm). Palazzo Vecchio, Florence

644. Agnolo Bronzino. *Eleanora of Toledo and Her Son Giovanni de' Medici.* c. 1550. Oil on panel, 45 1/4 x 37 3/4" (115 x 96 cm). Galleria degli Uffizi, Florence

645. Sofonisba Anguissola. *Portrait of the Artist's Sister Minerva.* c. 1559. Oil on canvas, 33 1/2 x 26" (85 x 66 cm). Milwaukee Art Museum, Layton Art Collection
Gift of the Family of Mrs. Fred Vogel, Jr.

who worked in the same chill vein, owe more to Raphael, although he esteemed Michelangelo above all others. The painting, one of the artist's last works, is a play on the *Galatea* (see fig. 628). It forms part of the rich decorative scheme Vasari devised for the study of Francesco I de' Medici of Florence. The program, by the humanist Vincenzo Borghini, is devoted to the four elements. Vasari has chosen to represent water with the story of coral, which according to legend was formed by the blood of the monster slain by Perseus in rescuing the fair Andromeda. The subject provided an excuse to show voluptuous nudes, but in his hands the story has become an enchanting fantasy. In keeping with this lighthearted treatment, the Nereids, annealed versions of Raphael's mythological creatures, frolic with bits of coral they have discovered in the sea. Vasari's painting became a model in its own right: it spawned a host of imitations by minor artists in the waning years of Mannerism.

PORTRAITS. The Mannerists also produced splendid portraits in the same highly cultivated style, like Bronzino's painting of Eleanora of Toledo (fig. 644), the wife of Cosimo I de' Medici and Bronzino's main patron. The sitter here appears as a member of an exalted social caste, not as an individual personality. Frozen into immobility behind the barrier of her lavishly ornate costume, Eleanora seems more akin to Parmigianino's *Madonna* (compare the hands) than to ordinary flesh and blood.

ANGUISSOLA. So far, this book has not treated a named woman artist, although this does not mean that there were none. Pliny, for example, mentions in his *Natural History* (Book 35) the names and describes the work of women artists in Greece and Rome, and there are records of women manuscript illuminators during the Middle Ages. We must remember, however, that the vast majority of *all* artists remained anonymous until the late fourteenth century, so that all but a few works specifically by women have proved impossible to identify. Women began to emerge as distinct artistic personalities about 1550. The first of these to be widely recognized in her own lifetime was Sofonisba Anguissola (c. 1535–1625). The oldest of six artistic daughters from a prominent family in Cremona, she showed a precocious talent and at an early age exchanged drawings with Michelangelo. After establishing her reputation as a portraitist while still a young woman, she was called to Madrid, where she spent 20 years as a court painter until marriage brought her back to Italy. She became such a celebrity that her self-portraits, often showing her playing a spinet, were in considerable demand. Anguissola was highly regarded throughout her lifetime—Van Dyck drew her likeness shortly before her death—and her success was an important inspiration to other women artists. While her commissioned portraits follow the formal conventions of the day, she was at her best in more intimate paintings of her family, like the charming portrait she made of her sister Minerva shortly before leaving for Spain (fig. 645).

646. Jacopo Tintoretto. *Christ Before Pilate*. 1566–67. Wall painting, approx. 18'1" x 13'3½" (5.5 x 4.1 m). Scuola di San Rocco, Venice

Mannerism in Venice

TINTORETTO. Not until mid-century did Mannerism appear in Venice, where it became allied with the visionary tendencies already manifest in Titian's late work. Its leading exponent, Jacopo Tintoretto (1518–1594), was an artist of prodigious energy and inventiveness, who combined qualities of both its anticlassical and elegant phases in his work. He reportedly wanted "to paint like Titian and to design like Michelangelo," but his relationship to these two masters, though real enough, was as peculiar as Parmigianino's was to Raphael. *Christ Before Pilate* (fig. 646), one of his many huge

canvases for the Scuola di San Rocco, the home of the Confraternity of St. Roch, contrasts tellingly with Titian's *Christ Crowned with Thorns* (see fig. 636). The bold brushwork, the glowing colors, and the sudden lights and shadows show what Tintoretto owed to the older artist, and indeed the entire composition recalls the *Madonna with Members of the Pesaro Family* (see fig. 633). Yet the total effect is unmistakably Mannerist. The feverish emotionalism of the flickering, unreal light, and the ghostly Christ, pencil-slim and motionless among the agitated Michelangelesque figures, remind us of Rosso's *Descent*.

647. Jacopo Tintoretto. *The Last Supper*. 1592–94. Oil on canvas, 12' x 18'8" (3.7 x 5.7 m). S. Giorgio Maggiore, Venice

Tintoretto's final major work, *The Last Supper* (fig. 647), is also his most spectacular. At first, this canvas seems to deny in every possible way the classic values of Leonardo's version (see fig. 596), painted almost exactly a century before. Christ, to be sure, still occupies the center of the composition, but his small figure in the middle distance is distinguishable mainly by the brilliant halo, while the table is placed at a sharp angle to the picture plane in exaggerated perspective. In fact, this arrangement was designed to relate the scene to the space of the chancel of the church for which it was commissioned, and to be seen by the faithful as they knelt at the altar rail to receive Communion.

Tintoretto has gone to great lengths to give the event an everyday setting, cluttering the scene with attendants, containers of food and drink, and domestic animals. There are also celestial attendants who converge upon Christ just as he offers his body and blood, in the form of bread and wine, to the disciples. The smoke from the blazing oil lamp miraculously turns into clouds of angels, blurring the distinction between the natural and the supernatural and turning the scene into a magnificently orchestrated vision. Tintoretto barely hints at the human drama of Judas' betrayal, so important to Leonardo. Judas can be seen isolated on the near side of the table, but his role is so insignificant that he could almost be mistaken for an attendant. The artist's main concern has been to make visible the miracle of the Eucharist—the transubstantiation of earthly into divine food—the institution central to Catholic doctrine, which was reasserted during the Counter Reformation.

EL GRECO. The last, and today most famous, Mannerist painter was also trained in the Venetian School. Domenikos Theotocopoulos (1541–1614), called El Greco, came from Crete, which was then under Venetian rule. His earliest training must have been from a Cretan artist still working in the Byzantine tradition. Soon after 1560 El Greco arrived in Venice and quickly absorbed the lessons of Titian, Tintoretto, and other artists. A decade later, in Rome, he came to know the art of Raphael, Michelangelo, and the Central Italian Mannerists. In 1576/77 he went to Spain, settling in Toledo for the rest of his life. There he became established in the leading intellectual circles of the city, then a major center of learning as well as the seat of Catholic reform in Spain. Although it provides the content of his work, Counter Reformation theology does not account for the exalted emotionalism that informs his painting. [See Primary Sources, no. 59, pages 633–34.] The spiritual tenor of El Greco's mature work was primarily a response to mysticism, which was especially intense in Spain. Contemporary Spanish painting, however, was too provincial to affect him. His style had already been formed before he arrived in Toledo. Nor did he forget his Byzantine background. Until the very end of his career, he signed his pictures in Greek.

The largest and most resplendent of El Greco's major commissions, and the only one for a public chapel, is *The Burial of Count Orgaz* (figs. 648 and 649) in the church of Sto. Tomé. The program, which was given at the time of the commission, emphasizes the traditional role of good works in salvation and of the saints as intercessors with Heaven. This huge canvas honors a medieval benefactor so pious that St. Stephen and St.

648. Chapel with *The Burial of Count Orgaz.* 1586. Sto. Tomé, Toledo, Spain

649. El Greco. *The Burial of Count Orgaz.* 1586. Oil on canvas, 16' x 11'10" (4.9 x 3.6 m). Sto. Tomé, Toledo, Spain

650. El Greco. *Fray Felix Hortensio Paravicino.* c. 1605. Oil on canvas, 44 1/2 x 33 3/4" (112.5 x 85.5 cm). Museum of Fine Arts, Boston
Isaac Sweetser Fund

651. Girolamo Savoldo. *St. Matthew and the Angel.* c. 1535. Oil on canvas, 36 3/4 x 49" (93.3 x 124.5 cm). The Metropolitan Museum of Art, New York
Marquand Fund, 1912

Augustine miraculously appeared at his funeral and themselves lowered the body into its grave. The burial took place in 1323, but El Greco presents it as a contemporary event, portraying among the attendants many of the local nobility and clergy. The dazzling display of color and texture in the armor and vestments could hardly have been surpassed by Titian himself. Directly above, the count's soul (a small, cloudlike figure like the angels in Tintoretto's *Last Supper*) is carried to Heaven by an angel. The celestial assembly filling the upper half of the picture is painted very differently from the lower half: every form—clouds, limbs, draperies—takes part in the sweeping, flamelike movement toward the distant figure of Christ. Here, even more than in Tintoretto's art, the entire range of Mannerism fuses into a single ecstatic vision.

The full import of the work, however, becomes clear only when we see it in its original setting. Like an enormous window, it fills one entire wall of its chapel. The bottom of the canvas is 6 feet above the floor, and as the chapel is only about 18 feet deep, we must look sharply upward to see the upper half of the picture. El Greco's violent foreshortening is calculated to achieve an illusion of boundless space above, while the lower foreground figures appear as on a stage. (Their feet are cut off by the molding just below the picture.) The large stone plaque set into the wall also belongs to the ensemble, representing the front of the sarcophagus into which the two saints lower the body of the count; it thus explains the action within the picture. The beholder, then, perceives three levels of reality: the grave itself, supposedly set into the wall at eye level

and closed by an actual stone slab; the contemporary reenactment of the miraculous burial; and the vision of celestial glory witnessed by some of the participants. El Greco's task here was analogous to Masaccio's in his *Trinity* mural (see fig. 551). But whereas the Renaissance painter creates the illusion of reality through his command of rational pictorial space that appears continuous with ours, El Greco summons an apparition that remains essentially separate from its architectural surroundings. The contrast measures the dynamic evolution of Western art since the Early Renaissance.

El Greco has created a spiritual counterpart to his imagination, in contrast to Counter Reformation images, which were given a convincing physical presence to convey their doctrinal message as clearly as possible. Every passage is alive with his peculiar religiosity, which is felt as a nervous exaltation occurring as the dreamlike vision is conjured up. This kind of mysticism is very similar in character to the Spiritual Exercises of Ignatius of Loyola. St. Ignatius sought to make visions so real that they would seem to appear before the very eyes of the faithful. Such mysticism could be achieved only through strenuous devotion. That effort is mirrored in the intensity of El Greco's work, which fully retains a feeling of spiritual struggle.

From El Greco's Venetian training came his mastery of portraiture. We generally know little of his relationship to his sitters, but in his memorable portrait of Fray Felix Hortensio Paravicino (fig. 650), the sitter, an important scholar and poet, was also a friend who praised El Greco's genius in several son-

652. Jacopo Bassano. *The Adoration of the Shepherds.* 1542–47.
Oil on canvas, 4'7" x 7'2¹/₄" (1.39 x 2.19 m). The Royal Collection
© 1993 Her Majesty Queen Elizabeth II

nets. This portrait is an artistic descendant of Titian's *Man with the Glove* and the self-portrait in Pontormo's *Deposition* (see figs. 634 and 638). Yet the mood is one of neither reverie nor withdrawal. Paravicino's frail, expressive hands and the pallid face, with its sensitive mouth and burning eyes, convey a spiritual ardor of compelling intensity. Such, we like to think, were the saints of the Counter Reformation—mystics and intellectuals at the same time.

Realism

Although Mannerism spread to Venice and other cities, as a style it failed to establish dominance outside Florence and Rome. Elsewhere it competed with other tendencies. In towns along the northern edge of the Lombard plain, such as Brescia and Verona, there were a number of artists who worked in a style based on Giorgione and Titian, but with a stronger interest in everyday reality.

SAVOLDO. One of the earliest and most attractive of these North Italian realists was Girolamo Savoldo (c. 1480–1550) from Brescia, whose *St. Matthew and the Angel* (fig. 651) must be contemporary with Parmigianino's *Madonna with the Long Neck.* The broad, fluid manner of painting reflects the dominant influence of Titian, yet the great Venetian artist would never have placed the evangelist in so thoroughly domestic an environment. The humble scene in the background shows the saint's milieu to be lowly indeed and makes the presence of the angel doubly miraculous. This tendency to visualize sacred events among ramshackle buildings and simple people had been characteristic of Gothic painting, especially in the North, and Savoldo must have acquired it from that source. The nocturnal lighting, too, recalls such Gothic pictures as the *Nativity* by Gentile da Fabriano (see fig. 526). But whereas the main

illumination in Gentile's panel is the divine radiance of the child, Savoldo uses an ordinary oil lamp for his similarly magic and intimate effect.

BASSANO. A different form of realism is found in the paintings of Jacopo da Ponte (c. 1510–1592), called Bassano after the town 30 miles northwest of Venice where he passed virtually his entire career. He inevitably fell under the influence of Titian, but equally important to the formation of his style were prints by Germans such as Albrecht Dürer, who had twice visited Venice (see page 529), and by the Mannerists, notably Parmigianino. In *The Adoration of the Shepherds* (fig. 652), Bassano's most characteristic subject, the landscape will remind us of the setting in Titian's *Bacchanal,* but the figures show the impact of Parmigianino: their interlocking rhythms, the gentle grace of the Madonna, the gesture of the Infant Christ, the seemingly arbitrary column, all can be found in *The Madonna with the Long Neck.* The pose of the shepherd doffing his hat, too, has its specific source in Parmigianino's etching *The Entombment.* The high-pitched color is decidedly Mannerist as well.

The role of Northern art seems less immediately apparent, until we realize that the tender relationship between the Virgin and Child has an intimacy that can have come only from German prints (compare fig. 695), not Italian painting. The humble setting indicates that he must also have known a similar composition by Martin Schongauer (see page 525). And the mountains in the distance find their nearest counterpart in the watercolor *Italian Mountains* (see fig. 699) that Dürer sketched on his way back from Venice, rather than any work by Titian. Unlike Dürer's, Jacopo's landscape is a "portrait," showing Mount Grappa near Bassano. *The Adoration of the Shepherds* is more than a synthesis of diverse sources, however. What is novel in all this is the pastoral quality of the scene. The

653. Paolo Veronese. *Christ in the House of Levi*. 1573. Oil on canvas, 18'2" x 42' (5.5 x 12.8 m). Galleria dell'Accademia, Venice

654. Correggio. *The Assumption of the Virgin* (portion). c. 1525. Fresco. Dome, Parma Cathedral

artist includes peasants of the sort he must have encountered around his native town. Andrea Mantegna and the Fleming Hugo van der Goes had been among the few to show such coarse, simple people (see fig. 682). Yet for Bassano they were an essential feature of his work. His realism, then, is not one of specific details but of general type, which offsets the self-conscious artificiality of his style.

VERONESE. In the work of Paolo Veronese (Paolo Caliari, 1528–1588), North Italian realism takes on the splendor of a pageant. Born and trained in Verona, Veronese became, after Tintoretto, the most important painter in Venice. Both found favor with the public, although they were utterly unlike each other in style. The contrast is strikingly evident if we compare Tintoretto's *Last Supper* (fig. 647) and Veronese's *Christ in the House of Levi* (fig. 653), which have similar subjects. Veronese avoids all reference to the supernatural. His symmetrical composition harks back to paintings by Leonardo and Raphael, while the festive mood of the scene reflects examples by Titian of the 1520s, so that at first glance the picture looks like a High Renaissance work born 50 years too late. Missing, however, is one essential element: the elevated, ideal conception of humanity underlying the High Renaissance. Veronese paints a sumptuous banquet, a true feast for the eyes, but not "the intention of man's soul."

Significantly, we are not even sure which event from the life of Jesus he originally meant to depict, for he gave the canvas its present title only after he had been summoned by the religious tribunal of the Inquisition on the charge of filling his picture with "buffoons, drunkards, Germans, dwarfs, and similar vulgarities" unsuited to its sacred character. The account of this trial shows that the tribunal thought the painting represented the Last Supper, but Veronese's testimony never made clear whether it was the Last Supper or the Supper in the House of Simon. To him this distinction made little difference. In the end, he settled on a convenient third title, Christ in the House of Levi, which permitted him to leave the offending incidents in place. He argued that they were no more objectionable than the nudity of Jesus and the Heavenly Host in Michelangelo's *Last Judgment,* but the tribunal failed to see the analogy on the grounds that "in the Last Judgment it was not necessary to paint garments, and there is nothing in those figures that is not spiritual." [See Primary Sources, no. 60, pages 634–35.]

The Inquisition, of course, considered only the impropriety of Veronese's art, not its lack of concern with spiritual depth. His dogged refusal to admit the justice of the charge, his insistence on his right to introduce directly observed details, however "improper," and his indifference to the subject of the picture spring from an attitude so startlingly "extroverted" that it was not generally accepted until the nineteenth century. The painter's domain, Veronese seems to say, is the entire visible world, and here he acknowledges no authority other than his senses.

Proto-Baroque Painting

A third trend that emerged about 1520 in northern Italy has been labeled Proto-Baroque, as much because it eludes convenient categories as because it embodies so many features that would later characterize the Baroque style, although such a term hardly does justice to its highly individual qualities. This tendency centers largely on Correggio, although later in the century it has a counterpart in architecture (see pages 502–3).

CORREGGIO. Correggio (Antonio Allegri da Correggio, 1489/94–1534), a phenomenally gifted North Italian painter, spent most of his brief career in Parma, which lies to the west along the Lombard plain. Consequently, he absorbed a wide range of influences: first Leonardo and the Venetians, then Michelangelo and Raphael, but their ideal of classical balance did not attract him. Correggio's work partakes of North Italian realism but applies it with the imaginative freedom of the Mannerists, though we do not find any hint of his fellow resident Parmigianino in his style. His largest work, the fresco of *The Assumption of the Virgin* in the dome of Parma Cathedral (fig. 654), is a masterpiece of illusionistic perspective, a vast, luminous space filled with soaring figures. Although they move with such exhilarating ease that the force of gravity seems not to exist for them, these are healthy, energetic beings of flesh and blood, not disembodied spirits, and they frankly delight in their weightless condition.

There was little difference between spiritual and physical ecstasy for Correggio, who thereby established an important precedent for Baroque artists such as Gianlorenzo Bernini (see page 567). We can see this by comparing *The Assumption of the Virgin* with his *Jupiter and Io* (fig. 655), one canvas in a series illustrating the loves of the classical gods. The nymph,

655. Correggio. *Jupiter and Io.* c. 1532. Oil on canvas, 64 1/2 x 27 3/4" (163.8 x 70.5 cm). Kunsthistorisches Museum, Vienna

swooning in the embrace of a cloudlike Jupiter, is the direct kin of the jubilant angels in the fresco. Leonardesque sfumato, combined with a Venetian sense of color and texture, produces an effect of exquisite voluptuousness that far exceeds Titian's in his *Bacchanal* (see fig. 632). Correggio had no immediate successors, nor did he have any lasting influence on the art of his century, but toward 1600 his work began to be widely appreciated. For the next century and a half he was admired as the equal of Raphael and Michelangelo, while the Mannerists, so important before, were largely forgotten.

SCULPTURE

Italian sculptors of the later sixteenth century fail to match the achievements of the painters. Perhaps Michelangelo's overpowering personality discouraged new talent in this field, but the dearth of challenging new tasks is a more plausible reason. In any case, the most interesting sculpture of this period was produced outside of Italy, and in Florence—after the death of Michelangelo in 1564—the leading sculptor was a Northerner.

Mannerism, First and Second Phases

BERRUGUETE. If the anticlassical phase of Mannerism, represented by the style of Rosso and Pontormo, has no sculptural counterpart, the work of the Spaniard Alonso Berruguete (c. 1489–1561) most closely approaches it. Berruguete had been associated with the founders of the anticlassical trend in Florence about 1520; his *St. John the Baptist* (fig. 656), one of the reliefs carved 20 years later for the wood choir stalls of Toledo Cathedral, still reflects this experience. The angular, emaciated body, clawlike hands, and fixed, wide-eyed stare recall the otherworldly expressiveness of Rosso's *Descent from the Cross* (see fig. 637).

CELLINI. The second, elegant phase of Mannerism appears in countless sculptural examples in Italy and abroad. The best-known representative of the style is Benvenuto Cellini (1500–1571), the Florentine goldsmith and sculptor who owes much of his fame to his picaresque autobiography. The gold saltcellar for Francis I of France (fig. 657), Cellini's only major work in precious metal to escape destruction, displays the virtues and limitations of his art. To hold condiments is obviously the lesser function of this lavish conversation piece. Because salt comes from the sea and pepper from the land, Cellini placed the boat-shaped salt container under the guardianship of Neptune, while the pepper, in a tiny triumphal arch, is watched over by a personification of Earth. On the base are figures representing the four seasons and the four parts of the day.

The entire object thus reflects the cosmic significance of the Medici tombs (compare fig. 616), but on this miniature scale Cellini's program turns into playful fancy. We recognize it as a conceit on the same order as Vasari's *Perseus and Andromeda* (fig. 643). Cellini wants to impress us with his ingenuity and skill. Earth, he wrote, is "fashioned like a woman with all the beauty of form, the grace and charm, of which my art was capable." The allegorical significance of the design is simply a pretext for this display of virtuosity. When he tells us, for instance,

656. Alonso Berruguete. *St. John the Baptist.* c. 1540. Wood, 31¹/₂ x 19¹/₄" (80 x 49 cm). Toledo Cathedral, Spain

that Neptune and Earth each have a bent and a straight leg to signify mountains and plains, form is completely divorced from content. Despite his boundless admiration for Michelangelo, Cellini creates elegant figures that are as elongated, smooth, and languid as Parmigianino's (see fig. 640).

PRIMATICCIO. Parmigianino also strongly influenced Francesco Primaticcio (1504–1570), Rosso's assistant and successor at the royal château of Fontainebleau. A man of many talents, Primaticcio designed the interior decoration of some of the main rooms, which combine painted scenes and a richly sculptured stucco framework. The section shown in figure 658 caters to the same aristocratic taste that admired the *Saltcellar* of Cellini, who was Primaticcio's rival at the court of Francis I in 1540–45. The four maidens are not burdened with any specific allegorical significance—their role recalls the nudes of the Sistine ceiling—but perform a task for which they seem equally ill-fitted: they reinforce the piers that sustain the ceiling. These willowy caryatids epitomize the studied nonchalance of second-phase Mannerism. The painting is nearly lost in the luxurious ornamentation. Executed by assistants from Primaticcio's design, it shows Apelles painting the abduction of Campaspe by Alexander the Great, who presented his favorite concubine to the artist when he fell in love with her. Such a heady mixture of violence and eroticism appealed greatly to the Mannerists; yet the story was interpreted as a gesture of uncommon respect and magnanimity by the Roman historian Pliny, which justified the subject.

657. Benvenuto Cellini. *Saltcellar of Francis I.* 1539–43. Gold with enamel,
10$^{1}/_{4}$ x 13$^{1}/_{8}$" (26 x 33.3 cm). Kunsthistorisches Museum, Vienna

658. Francesco Primaticcio. *Stucco Figures.* c. 1541–45. Room of the Duchesse d'Estampes,
Château of Fontainebleau, France

659. Giovanni Bologna. *The Abduction of the Sabine Woman.* Completed 1583. Marble, height 13'6" (4.1 m). Loggia dei Lanzi, Florence

those critics who doubted his ability as a monumental sculptor in marble. He selected what seemed to him the most difficult feat, three figures of contrasting character united in a common action. Their identities were disputed among the learned connoisseurs of the day, who finally settled on *The Abduction of the Sabine Woman* as the most suitable title.

Here, then, is another artist who is noncommittal about subject matter, although his unconcern had a different motive from Veronese's. Like Cellini's, Bologna's purpose was virtuoso display. His self-imposed task was to carve in marble, on a massive scale, a sculptural composition that was to be seen not from one but from all sides; this had previously been attempted only in bronze and on a much smaller scale (see fig. 579). He has solved this purely formal problem, but at the cost of insulating his group from the world of human experience. These figures, spiraling upward as if confined inside a tall, narrow cylinder, perform their well-rehearsed choreographic exercise with ease; yet, like much Hellenistic sculpture (compare fig. 213), it is ultimately devoid of emotional meaning. We admire their discipline but we find no trace of genuine pathos.

ARCHITECTURE

Mannerism

The term *Mannerism* was first coined to describe painting of the period. We have not encountered any difficulty in applying it to sculpture. But can it be usefully extended to architecture as well? And if so, what qualities must we look for? These questions have proved surprisingly difficult to answer precisely. The reasons are all the more puzzling, because the important Mannerist architects were leading painters and sculptors. Reflecting our dilemma, only a few structures are generally acknowledged today as Mannerist. Such a building is the Palazzo del Te, Mantua, by Giulio Romano (c. 1499–1566), Raphael's chief assistant. The courtyard facade (fig. 660) features unusually squat proportions and coarse rustication. The massive and utterly useless keystones of the windows have been "squeezed" up by the force of the triangular lintels—an absurd impossibility, since there are no true arches except over the central doorway, which is surmounted by a pediment in violation of classical canon. Even more bizarre is how the metope midway between each pair of columns "slips" downward in defiance of all logic and accepted practice, creating the uneasy sense that the frieze might collapse before our eyes.

The reliance on idiosyncratic gestures that depart from Renaissance norms does not in itself provide a viable definition of Mannerism as an architectural period style. What, then, are the qualities we must look for? Above all, form is divorced from content for the sake of surface effect. The emphasis instead is on picturesque devices, especially encrusted decoration, with the occasional distortion of form and novel, even illogical, rearrangement of space. Thus Mannerist architecture lacks a consistent integration between elements.

GIOVANNI BOLOGNA.   Cellini, Primaticcio, and the other Italians employed by Francis I at Fontainebleau made Mannerism the dominant style in mid-sixteenth-century France. Their influence went far beyond the royal court. It reached Jean de Bologne (1529–1608), a gifted young sculptor from Douai in northern France, who went to Italy about 1555 for further training. He stayed and became, under the Italianized name of Giovanni Bologna, the most important sculptor in Florence during the last third of the century. His over-lifesize marble group, *The Abduction of the Sabine Woman* (fig. 659), won particular acclaim, and still has its place of honor near the Palazzo Vecchio.

The subject, drawn from the legends of ancient Rome, seems an odd choice for statuary. The city's founders, an adventurous band of men from across the sea, so the story goes, tried vainly to find wives among their neighbors, the Sabines, and resorted at last to a trick. Having invited the entire Sabine tribe into Rome for a peaceful festival, they fell upon them with arms, took the women away by force, and thus ensured the future of their race. Actually, the artist designed the group with no specific subject in mind, to silence

VASARI.   The Palazzo degli Uffizi in Florence, by Giorgio Vasari, whom we have already encountered as a painter and

660. Giulio Romano. Courtyard of the Palazzo del Te, Mantua. 1527–34

biographer, consists of two long wings—originally intended, as the name Uffizi suggests, for offices—facing each other across a narrow court and linked at one end by a loggia (fig. 661). Vasari's inspiration is not far to seek: the "tired" scroll brackets and the peculiar combination of column and wall have their source in the vestibule of the Laurentian Library. We will recall Vasari's praise for Michelangelo's unorthodox use of the classical vocabulary (see page 468). Does this mean that the Laurentian Library itself is Mannerist? The case can be argued both ways. On the one hand, Michelangelo's design is as willful a subversion of High Renaissance classicism as Rosso's *Descent from the Cross* (see fig. 637); on the other, these devices serve a powerful expressive purpose in the Laurentian Library that responds to the imperative of Michelangelo's genius, whereas in Vasari's paraphrase they have been reduced to empty gestures. Whichever side one takes (they are not mutually exclusive), the differences in the results are plain enough. The Uffizi loggia lacks the sculptural power and eloquence of its model; rather, it forms a screen as weightless as the facade of the Pazzi Chapel (see fig. 544). What is tense in Michelangelo's design becomes merely ambiguous. The architectural members seem as devoid of energy as the human figures in Vasari's *Perseus and Andromeda* (fig. 643), and their relationships as studiedly "artificial."

AMMANATI.   The same is true of the courtyard of the Palazzo Pitti (fig. 662) by Michelangelo's protégé, the sculptor Bartolommeo Ammanati (1511–1592), despite its display of muscularity. Here the three-story scheme of superimposed orders, derived from the Colosseum, has been overlaid with an extravagant pattern of rustication that "imprisons" the columns, reducing them to an oddly passive role. These welts disguise rather than enhance the massiveness of the masonry, the overall corrugated texture making us think of the fancies of a pastry cook.

Ammanati had worked under Jacopo Sansovino in Venice, and the Palazzo Pitti stands in the same relation to Sansovino's

661. Giorgio Vasari. Loggia of the Palazzo degli Uffizi, Florence (view from the Arno River). Begun 1560

662. Bartolommeo Ammanati. Courtyard of the Palazzo Pitti, Florence. 1558–70

663. Jacopo Sansovino. Mint (left) and Library of St. Mark's, Venice. Begun c. 1535/7

Mint (fig. 663) as Vasari's Palazzo degli Uffizi does to Michelangelo's Laurentian Library.

Other Trends

SANSOVINO. We have not encountered the architecture of Venice since the Ca' d'Oro (see fig. 465), for it remained outside the mainstream of the Renaissance. Its essential characteristics were defined by Jacopo Sansovino (1486–1570), a minor Florentine sculptor of incipient Mannerist persuasion from the circle of Raphael who settled there after the Sack of Rome in 1527 and established himself as the chief architect of the city. Not surprisingly, his buildings are remarkably sculptural in treatment. Indeed, his masterpiece, the Library of St. Mark's (fig. 663) facing the Piazzetta along the Grand Canal, looks like nothing so much as a huge wedding cake, so luxurious is the sculptural encrustation. The street-level arcade consists of the Roman Doric order, inspired by the Colosseum (see fig. 244), while the upper one shows an unusually elaborate treatment of the Ionic order (including triple engaged columns) surmounted by a garlanded entablature. The ensemble is capped off by a balustrade, with lifesize statues over every column cluster and obelisks at each corner. The facade, with its extravagant ornamentation, creates an effect of ponderous opulence that proclaims the Venetian republic as a new Rome. The Library set a new standard for lavish architecture. Sansovino's style was so authoritative that it enjoyed classic status and was followed in Venice for the remainder of the century. Nevertheless, we have left the commanding logic of the High Renaissance far behind.

Stranger still is the Mint to the left of the Library. Once again the facade has been penetrated wherever possible, but the results are yet more massive. Though of equal height, the rusticated arcade seems barely able to sustain the weight of the upper two stories (the top story was added belatedly around 1560), which feature unique corkscrew columns and support heavy cornices. We seem on the verge of Mannerism, but a glance at Ammanati's Pitti courtyard (see fig. 662) will con-

664. Plan of the Villa Rotonda

vince us of the differences. Art historians have yet to find a term adequate to Sansovino's grandiose style.

PALLADIO. Most later sixteenth-century architecture can hardly be called Mannerist at all. Although he, too, drew inspiration from Sansovino, Andrea Palladio (1518–1580), next to Michelangelo the most important architect of the century, belongs to the tradition of the humanist and theoretician Leone Battista Alberti (see page 434).

Although Palladio's career centered on Vicenza, his native town, his buildings and theoretical writings brought him international status. [See Primary Sources, no. 61, page 000.] Palladio insisted that architecture must be governed by reason and by certain rules that were perfectly exemplified by the buildings of the ancients. He thus shared Alberti's basic outlook and his faith in the cosmic significance of numerical ratios (see page 437). But the two differed in how each related theory and practice. With Alberti, this relationship had been loose and flexible, whereas Palladio believed quite literal-

665. Andrea Palladio.
Villa Rotonda,
Vicenza. c. 1567–70

666. Andrea Palladio. S. Giorgio Maggiore, Venice. Designed 1565

667. Plan of S. Giorgio Maggiore

ly in practicing what he preached. His architectural treatise *The Four Books of Architecture* (1570) is consequently more practical than Alberti's, which helps to explain its huge success, while his buildings are linked more directly with his theories. It has even been said that Palladio designed only what was, in his view, sanctioned by ancient precedent. Indeed, the usual term for both Palladio's work and theoretical attitude is "classicistic," to denote a conscious striving for classic qualities, though the results are not necessarily classical in style.

The Villa Rotonda (figs. 664 and 665), one of Palladio's finest buildings, perfectly illustrates the meaning of his classicism. An aristocratic country residence near Vicenza, it consists of a square block surmounted by a dome and is faced on all four sides with identical porches in the shape of temple fronts. Alberti had defined the ideal church as such a completely symmetrical, centralized design (see page 437), and it is evident that

Palladio found in the same principles the ideal country house. How could he justify a context so purely secular for the solemn motif of the temple front? Like Alberti, he sought support in a selective interpretation of the historical evidence. He was convinced, on the basis of ancient literary sources, that Roman private houses had porticoes like these (excavations have since proved him wrong; see page 186). But Palladio's use of the temple front here is not mere antiquarianism. He probably persuaded himself that it was legitimate because he regarded this feature as desirable for both beauty and utility. Beautifully correlated with the walls behind, the porches of the Villa Rotonda are an organic part of his design that lends the structure an air of serene dignity and festive grace.

The facade of S. Giorgio Maggiore in Venice (fig. 666), of about the same date as the Villa Rotonda, adds to the same effect a new sumptuousness and complexity. Palladio's problem here was how to create a classically integrated facade for a basilican church. He surely knew Alberti's solution at S. Andrea in Mantua (see fig. 569): a temple front enclosing a triumphal arch. But this design, although impressively logical and compact, did not fit the cross section of a basilica and really circumvented the problem. Palladio, again following what he believed to be ancient precedent, found a different answer. He superimposed a tall, narrow temple front on another low, wide one to reflect the different heights of nave and aisles. Theoretically, it was a perfect solution. In practice, however, he found that he could not keep the two systems as separate as his classicistic conscience demanded and still integrate them into a harmonious whole. This conflict, which makes ambiguous those parts of the design that have a dual allegiance, might be interpreted as a Mannerist quality. The plan (fig. 667), too, suggests a duality. The main body of the church is strongly centralized—the transept is as long as the nave—but the longitudinal axis reasserts itself in the separate compartments for the main altar and the chapel beyond.

Proto-Baroque Architecture

VIGNOLA AND DELLA PORTA.   Palladio's immense authority as a designer keeps the conflicting elements in the facade and plan of S. Giorgio from actually clashing. In less assured hands, such a precarious union would break apart. The most widely accepted solution was evolved just at that time in Rome by Giacomo Vignola (1507–1573) and Giacomo della Porta (c. 1540–1602), architects who had assisted Michelangelo at St. Peter's and were still using his architectural vocabulary. Il Gesù (Jesus) is a building whose importance for subsequent church architecture can hardly be exaggerated. Since Il Gesù was the mother church of the Jesuits, its design must have been closely supervised so as to conform to the aims of the militant new order, founded in 1534. We may thus view it as the architectural embodiment of the spirit of the Counter Reformation.

The planning stage of the structure began in 1550, only five years after the Council of Trent (see page 483). Michelangelo himself once promised a design, but apparently never furnished it. The present ground plan, by Vignola, was adopted in 1568 (fig. 668). Il Gesù contrasts in almost every possible respect with Palladio's S. Giorgio. It is a basilica, strikingly compact, dominated by its mighty nave. The aisles have been replaced by chapels, thus herding the congregation quite literally into one large, hall-like space directly in view of the altar. The attention of this audience is positively directed toward altar and pulpit, as our view of the interior shows (fig. 669). (The painting indicates how the church would look from the street if the center part of the facade were removed. For the later, High Baroque decoration of the nave vault, see fig. 737.) We also see here an unexpected feature that the ground plan cannot show: the dramatic contrast between the dim illumination in the nave and the abundant light beyond, in the eastern part of the church, supplied by the large windows in the drum of the dome. Light has been consciously exploited for its expressive possibilities—a novel device, "theatrical" in the best sense of the term—to give Il Gesù a stronger emotional focus than we have yet found in a church interior.

668. Giacomo Vignola. Plan of Il Gesù, Rome. 1568

669. Andrea Sacchi and Jan Miel. *Urban VIII Visiting Il Gesù.* 1639–41. Oil on canvas. Galleria Nazionale d'Arte Antica, Rome

Despite its great originality, the plan of Il Gesù is not entirely without precedent (see fig. 571). The facade by Giacomo della Porta (fig. 670) is as bold as the plan, although it, too, has its earlier sources. The paired pilasters and broken architrave on the lower story are clearly derived from the colossal order on the exterior of St. Peter's (compare fig. 622), and with good reason, for it was Della Porta who completed Michelangelo's dome. In the upper story the same pattern recurs on a somewhat smaller scale, with four instead of six pairs of supports. The difference in width is bridged by two scroll-shaped buttresses. This novel device, also taken from Michelangelo, forms a graceful transition to the large pediment crowning the facade, which retains

670. Giacomo della Porta. Facade of Il Gesù, Rome. c. 1575 – 84

the classic proportions of Renaissance architecture (the height equals the width).

What is fundamentally new here is the very element that was missing in the facade of S. Giorgio: the integration of all the parts into one whole. Della Porta, freed from classicistic scruples by his allegiance to Michelangelo, gave the same vertical rhythm to both stories of the facade. This rhythm is obeyed by all the horizontal members (note the broken entablature), but the horizontal divisions in turn determine the size of the vertical members (hence no colossal order). Equally important is the emphasis on the main portal: its double frame—two pediments resting on coupled pilasters and columns—projects beyond the rest of the facade and gives strong focus to the entire design. Not since Gothic architecture has the entrance to a church received such a dramatic con-

centration of features, attracting the attention of the beholder outside the building much as the concentrated light beneath the dome channels that of the worshiper inside.

What are we to call the style of Il Gesù? Obviously, it has little in common with Palladio, and it shares with Vasari's architecture only the influence of Michelangelo. But this influence reflects two very different phases of the great master's career: the contrast between the Uffizi and Il Gesù is hardly less great than that between the vestibule of the Laurentian Library and the exterior of St. Peter's. If we label the Uffizi Mannerist, the same term will not serve us for Il Gesù. As we shall see, the design of Il Gesù became basic to Baroque architecture. By calling it Proto-Baroque, we suggest both its germinal importance for the future and its special place in relation to the past.

CHAPTER FOUR

"LATE GOTHIC" PAINTING, SCULPTURE, AND THE GRAPHIC ARTS

RENAISSANCE VERSUS "LATE GOTHIC" PAINTING

Should we think of the Renaissance as one coherent style or as an attitude that might be embodied in more than one style? "Renaissance-consciousness," we know, was an Italian idea, and there can be no doubt that Italy played the leading role in the development of Renaissance art, at least until the early sixteenth century. This fact does not necessarily mean, however, that the Renaissance was confined to the South. When Boccaccio praised Giotto's imitation of nature, he was not in a position to know how many aspects of reality Giotto and his contemporaries had failed to investigate. These, we recall, were further explored by the painters of the International Style, albeit in somewhat tentative fashion. To advance beyond Gothic realism required a second revolution, which began simultaneously and independently in Italy and in the Netherlands about 1420. We must think of two events linked by a common aim—the conquest of the visible world—yet sharply divided in almost every other respect.

The Italian, or Southern, revolution, which originated in Florence and which we call the Early Renaissance, was the more systematic and, in the long run, the more fundamental, since it included architecture and sculpture as well as painting. Art historians are still of two minds about the scope and significance of the Northern focus of the revolution and its relation to the Renaissance as a whole. The new style emerged in Flanders around 1420, but we lack a satisfactory explanation why it took place at that particular time and in that particular area. This does not mean, however, that no explanation is possible. Unless we believe in sheer fate or chance, we find it difficult to place the entire burden of responsibility on the great masters who gave birth to it. There must, we feel, be some link between their accomplishment and the social, political, and cultural setting in which they worked, but it is not yet well understood.

Many scholars treat fifteenth-century Northern painting as the counterpart of the Early Renaissance in Italy. It is because the Flemish artists had an impact that went far beyond their own region. In Italy they were admired as greatly as the leading Italian artists of the period. Their intense realism had a conspicuous influence on Early Renaissance painting, for the Italians, as we have already noted, associated the exact imitation of nature in painting with a "return to the classics." To Italian eyes, then, "Late Gothic" painting appeared definitely post-medieval.

Nevertheless, Italian Renaissance art made very little impression north of the Alps during the fifteenth century. Not until the final decades did humanism begin to play an important role in Northern thought, which it changed decisively. Nor do we find an interest in the art of classical antiquity before that time. Rather, the artistic and cultural environment of Northern painters clearly remained "Late Gothic." The term suggests the continuity with the world view of the late Middle Ages. Moreover, the creators of the new style, unlike their Italian contemporaries, did not entirely reject the International Style. Instead, they took it as their point of departure, so that the break with the past was less abrupt in the North than in the South. Would it not be more reasonable to regard their work, despite its great importance, as the final phase of Gothic painting? "Late Gothic" also reminds us that fifteenth-century architecture and sculpture outside Italy remained firmly rooted in the Gothic tradition.

We have, in fact, no satisfactory name to designate the new Flemish painting. Whatever we choose to call the style, we shall find that it has some justification. For the sake of convenience, we shall use the customary label, "Late Gothic," but with quotation marks to indicate its doubtful status, as the

671. Master of Flémalle (Robert Campin?). *Mérode Altarpiece.* c. 1425–30. Oil on panel, center 25 3/16 x 24 7/8" (64.3 x 62.9 cm); each wing approx. 25 3/8 x 10 7/8" (64.5 x 27.4 cm). The Metropolitan Museum of Art, New York. The Cloisters Collection, 1956

term hardly does justice to the special character of Northern fifteenth-century art as a whole.

Netherlandish Painting

THE MASTER OF FLÉMALLE. The first, and perhaps most decisive, phase of the pictorial revolution in Flanders is represented by an artist whose name we do not know for certain. We call him the Master of Flémalle (after the fragments of a large altar from Flémalle), but he was probably Robert Campin, the foremost painter of Tournai, whose career we can trace in documents from 1406 to his death in 1444. His finest work is the *Mérode Altarpiece* (fig. 671), which he must have done soon after 1425. Comparing it with its nearest relatives, the Franco-Flemish pictures of the International Style (see figs. 519–22), we see that it falls within the same tradition. Yet we also recognize in it a new pictorial experience. Here, for the first time, we have the sensation of actually looking through the surface of the panel into a spatial world that has all the essential qualities of everyday reality: unlimited depth, stability, continuity, and completeness. The painters of the International Style, even at their most adventurous, had never aimed at such consistency, and their commitment to reality was far from absolute. The pictures they created have the enchanting quality of fairy tales, in which the scale and relationship of things can be shifted at will, and fact and fancy mingle without conflict. The Master of Flémalle, in contrast, has undertaken to tell the truth, the whole truth, and nothing but the truth. To be sure, he does not yet do it with total ease. His objects, overly foreshortened, tend to jostle each other in space. But with almost obsessive determination, he defines every last detail of every object to give it maximum concreteness: its individual shape and size; its color, material, surface textures; its degree of rigidity; and its way of responding to illu-

mination. The artist even distinguishes between the diffused light creating soft shadows and delicate gradations of brightness, and the direct light entering through the two round windows, which produces the twin shadows sharply outlined in the upper part of the center panel and the twin reflections on the brass vessel and candlestick.

The *Mérode Altarpiece* transports us from the aristocratic world of the International Style to the household of a Flemish burgher. The Master of Flémalle was no court painter, but a townsperson catering to the tastes of such well-to-do fellow citizens as the two donors piously kneeling outside the Virgin's chamber. This is the earliest Annunciation in panel painting that occurs in a fully equipped domestic interior, as well as the first to honor Joseph, the humble carpenter, by showing him at work next door.

This bold departure from tradition forced upon our artist a problem no one had faced before: how to transfer supernatural events from symbolic settings to an everyday environment, without making them look either trivial or incongruous. He has met this challenge by the method sometimes known as "disguised symbolism," which means that almost any detail within the picture, however casual, may carry a symbolic message. We saw its beginnings during the International Style in the *Annunciation* by Melchior Broederlam (see page 383), but his symbolism seems rudimentary in comparison with the profusion of hidden meanings in the *Mérode Altarpiece.* Thus, the flowers are associated with the Virgin: in the left wing the roses denote her charity and the violets her humility, while in the center panel the lilies symbolize her chastity. The shiny water basin and the towel on its rack are not ordinary household equipment either but further tributes to Mary as the "vessel most clean" and the "well of living waters." Perhaps the most intriguing symbol of this sort is the candle next to the vase of lilies. It was extinguished only moments before, as we can tell from the glowing wick and the curl of smoke. But why had it been lit in broad daylight, and what made the flame go out? Has the divine radiance of the Lord's presence overcome the material light? Or did the flame of the candle itself represent the divine light, now extinguished to show that God has become human, that in Jesus "the Word was made flesh"?

Clearly, the entire wealth of medieval symbolism survives in our picture, but it is so completely immersed in the world of everyday appearances that we are often left to doubt whether a given detail demands symbolic interpretation. Observers long wondered, for instance, about the boxlike object on Joseph's workbench (and a similar one on the ledge outside the open window), until one scholar identified them as mousetraps intended to convey a specific theological message. According to St. Augustine, God had to appear on earth in human form so as to fool Satan: "The Cross of the Lord was the devil's mousetrap."

Since iconographic explanations of this sort require much scholarly ingenuity, we tend to think of the *Mérode Altarpiece* and similar pictures as embodying a special kind of puzzle. And so they often do to the modern beholder, although they can be enjoyed apart from knowing all their symbolic content. But what about the patrons for whom these works were painted? Did they immediately grasp the meaning of every detail? They would have had no difficulty with such well-established symbols in our picture as the flowers, and they probably understood the significance of the water basin. The message of the extinguished candle and the mousetrap could not have been common knowledge even among the well-educated, however.

These two symbols—and from their incongruity we can hardly doubt that they are symbols—make their earliest appearance in the *Mérode Altarpiece*. They must be unusual, too, for St. Joseph with the mousetrap has been found in only one other picture, and the freshly extinguished candle does not recur elsewhere, so far as we know. Apparently, the Master of Flémalle introduced them into the visual arts, yet hardly any artists adopted them despite his great influence. If the candle and the mousetrap were difficult to understand even in the fifteenth century, why are they in our picture at all? Was the artist told to put them in by the patron, who may have been exceptionally erudite? This would be possible if it were the only case of its kind, but since there are countless instances of equally subtle or obscure symbolism in "Late Gothic" painting, it seems more likely that the initiative came from the artists, rather than from their patrons.

We have reason to believe, therefore, that the Master of Flémalle was either a man of unusual learning himself, or had contact with the theologians and other scholars who could supply him with the references that suggested the symbolic meanings of things such as the extinguished candle and the mousetrap. In other words, the artist did not simply continue the symbolic tradition of medieval art within the framework of the new realistic style. He expanded and enriched it by his own efforts. To him, even more than Broederlam (see pages 383–84), realism and symbolism were interdependent. We might say that the Master of Flémalle needed a growing symbolic repertory because it encouraged him to explore features

of the visible world never represented before, such as a candle immediately after it has been blown out or the interior of a carpenter's shop, which provided the setting for the mousetraps. For him to paint everyday reality, he had to "sanctify" it with a maximum of spiritual significance.

This deeply reverential attitude toward the physical universe as a mirror of divine truths helps us to understand why in the Mérode panels the smallest and least conspicuous details are rendered with the same concentrated attention as the sacred figures. Potentially, at least, everything is a symbol and thus merits an equally exacting scrutiny. The disguised symbolism of the Master of Flémalle and his successors was not an external device grafted onto the new realistic style, but ingrained in the creative process. Their Italian contemporaries must have sensed this, for they praised both the miraculous realism and the "piety" of the Flemish masters.

If we compare our illustration of the Mérode *Annunciation* with those of earlier panel paintings (figs. 508, 518, 519, and 525), we see vividly that, all other differences aside, its distinctive tonality makes the Master of Flémalle's picture stand out from the rest. The jewellike brightness of the older works, their patterns of brilliant hues and lavish use of gold, have given way to a color scheme far less decorative but much more flexible and differentiated. The subdued tints of muted greens, bluish- or brownish-grays show a new subtlety, and the scale of intermediate shades is smoother and has a wider range. All these effects are essential to the realistic style of the Master of Flémalle. They were made possible by the use of oil, the medium he was among the first to exploit.

JAN AND HUBERT VAN EYCK. Needless to say, the full range of effects made possible by oil was not discovered all at once, nor by any one individual. The Master of Flémalle contributed less than Jan van Eyck, a somewhat younger and much more famous artist who was long credited with the actual "invention" of oil painting. [See Primary Sources, no. 62, pages 635–36.] We know a good deal about Jan's life and career. Born about 1390, he worked in Holland from 1422 to 1424, in Lille from 1425 to 1429, and thereafter in Bruges, where he died in 1441. He was both a townsman and a court painter, highly esteemed by Duke Philip the Good of Burgundy, who occasionally sent him on confidential diplomatic errands. After 1432, we can follow Jan's career through a number of signed and dated pictures.

The inscription on the frame of the great *Ghent Altarpiece* (see figs. 673–75) tells us that Jan completed it in that year, after it had been begun by his older brother, Hubert, who had died in 1426. Jan's earlier development, however, remains disputed. There are several "Eyckian" works, obviously older than the *Ghent Altarpiece,* that may have been painted by either of the two brothers. The most fascinating of these is a pair of panels showing the *Crucifixion* and the *Last Judgment* (fig. 672). Scholars agree that their date is between 1420 and 1425, whichever brother, Jan or Hubert, was the author. The style of these paintings has many qualities in common with that of the *Mérode Altarpiece:* the all-embracing devotion to the visible world, the unlimited depth of space, and the angular drapery folds, less graceful but far more realistic than the unbroken loops of the International Style. At the same time, the indi-

672. Hubert and/or Jan van Eyck. *The Crucifixion; The Last Judgment.* c. 1420–25.
Tempera and oil on canvas, transferred from panel; each panel 22$\frac{1}{4}$ x 7$\frac{3}{4}$" (56.5 x 19.4 cm).
The Metropolitan Museum of Art, New York

Fletcher Fund, 1933

673. Hubert and Jan van Eyck. *Ghent Altarpiece* (open). Completed 1432.
Oil on panel, 11'3" x 14'5" (3.4 x 4.4 m). Church of St. Bavo, Ghent, Belgium

vidual forms are not starkly tangible, like those characteristic of the Master of Flémalle, and seem less isolated, less "sculptural." The sweeping sense of space is the result not so much of violent foreshortening as of subtle changes of light and color. If we inspect the *Crucifixion* panel closely, we see a gradual decrease in the intensity of local colors and in the contrast of light and dark, from the foreground figures to the far-off city of Jerusalem and the snow-capped peaks beyond. Everything tends toward a uniform tint of light bluish-gray, so that the farthest mountain range merges imperceptibly with the color of the sky.

This optical phenomenon is known as "atmospheric perspective." The Van Eycks were the first to utilize the effect fully and systematically, although the Boucicaut Master and the Limbourg brothers had already been aware of it. The atmosphere is never wholly transparent. Even on the clearest day, the air between us and what we are looking at acts as a hazy screen that interferes with our ability to see distant shapes clearly. As we approach the limit of visibility, it swallows them altogether. Atmospheric perspective is more fundamental to our perception of deep space than linear perspective, which records the diminution in the apparent size of objects as their distance from the observer increases. It is effective not only in faraway

vistas. In the *Crucifixion* panel, even the foreground seems enveloped in a delicate haze that softens contours, shadows, and colors. Thus the entire scene has a continuity and harmony quite beyond the pictorial range of the Master of Flémalle.

How did the Van Eycks achieve this effect? Their exact technical procedure is difficult to reconstruct, but there can be no question that they used the oil medium with extraordinary refinement. By alternating opaque and translucent layers of paint, they were able to impart to their pictures a soft, glowing radiance of tone that has never been equaled, probably because it depends fully as much on their individual sensibilities as it does on their skillful craftsmanship.

Seen as a whole, the *Crucifixion* seems singularly devoid of drama, as if the scene had been gently becalmed by some magic spell. Only when we concentrate on the details do we become aware of the violent emotions in the faces of the crowd beneath the Cross, and the restrained but profoundly touching grief of the Virgin Mary and her companions in the foreground. In the *Last Judgment* panel, this dual quality of the Eyckian style takes the form of two extremes. Above the horizon, all is order, symmetry, and calm; below it, on earth and in the subterranean realm of Satan, violent chaos prevails. The two states thus correspond to Heaven and Hell, contemplative

674. *Adam and Eve,* details of *Ghent Altarpiece,* left and right wings

675. *Ghent Altarpiece* (closed)

bliss as against physical and emotional turbulence. The lower half, clearly, was the greater challenge to the artist's imaginative powers. The dead rising from their graves with frantic gestures of fear and hope, the damned being torn apart by devilish monsters more frightful than any we have seen before (compare fig. 404), all have the awesome reality of a nightmare, but a nightmare "observed" with the same infinite care as the natural world of the *Crucifixion* panel.

The *Ghent Altarpiece* (figs. 673–75), the greatest monument of early Flemish painting, presents problems so complex that our discussion must be limited to bare essentials. We have already mentioned the inscription informing us that the work,

begun by Hubert, was completed by Jan in 1432. Since Hubert died in 1426, the altarpiece was presumably made in the seven-year span between 1425 and 1432. We may therefore expect it to introduce to us the next phase of the new style we have discussed so far. Its basic arrangement is a triptych—a central body with two hinged wings—the standard format of altarpieces. In addition, each of the three units consists of four separate panels. And since the wings are also painted on both sides, the altarpiece has a total of 20 components of assorted shapes and sizes. The ensemble makes what has rightly been called a "super-altar," overwhelming but far from harmonious, which could not have been planned this way from the start. Apparently Jan took over a number of panels left unfinished by Hubert, completed them, added some of his own, and assembled them at the behest of the wealthy donor whose portrait we see on one of the outer panels of the altar.

To reconstruct this train of events, and to determine each brother's share, is an interesting but difficult game. Suffice it to say that Hubert remains a somewhat shadowy figure. His style, overlaid with retouches by Jan, can probably be found in the four central panels inside, although they did not belong together originally. The upper three, whose huge figures in the final arrangement crush the multitude of small ones below, were intended, it seems, to form a self-contained triptych: the Lord between the Virgin Mary and St. John the Baptist. The lower panel and the four flanking it probably

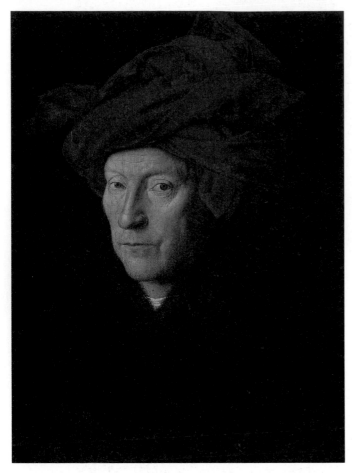

676. Jan van Eyck. *Man in a Red Turban (Self-Portrait?)*.
1433. Oil on panel, 10¼ x 7½" (26 x 19 cm). The National
Gallery, London

sculpture, like the scenes of Cain and Abel), the donor, and his wife, each in a separate niche, are the immediate kin of the *Adam* and *Eve* panels. The upper tier has two pairs of panels of different width. The artist has made a virtue of this awkward necessity by combining all four into one interior. Such an effect, we recall, had first been created by Pietro Lorenzetti almost a century earlier (compare fig. 509). Not content with perspective devices alone, Jan heightens the illusion by painting the shadows cast by the frames of the panels on the floor of the Virgin's chamber. Interestingly enough, this Annunciation resembles, in its homely detail, the *Mérode Altarpiece,* thus providing an important link between the two great pioneers of Flemish realism.

Donors' portraits of splendid individuality occupy conspicuous positions in both the Mérode and the Ghent altarpieces. A renewed interest in realistic portraiture had developed in the mid-fourteenth century, but until about 1420 its best achievements were in sculpture (see fig. 480). Painters usually confined themselves to silhouettelike profile views. Not until the Master of Flémalle, the first artist since antiquity to have real command of a close-up view of the human face from a three-quarter view, did the portrait play a major role in Northern painting.

In addition to donors' portraits, we now begin to encounter a growing number of small, independent likenesses whose intimacy suggests that they were treasured keepsakes, pictorial substitutes for the real presence of the sitter. One of the most compelling is Jan van Eyck's *Man in a Red Turban* of 1433 (fig. 676), which may well be a self-portrait. (The slight strain about the eyes seems to come from gazing into a mirror.) The sitter is bathed in the same gentle, clear light as Adam and Eve on the *Ghent Altarpiece.* Every detail of shape and texture has been recorded with almost microscopic precision. Jan does not suppress the sitter's personality, yet this face, like all of Jan's portraits, remains a psychological puzzle. It might be described as "even-tempered" in the most exact sense of the term: its character traits are balanced against each other so perfectly that none can assert itself at the expense of the rest. As Jan was fully capable of expressing emotion—we need only recall the faces of the crowd in the *Crucifixion,* or the scenes of Cain and Abel in the *Ghent Altarpiece*—the stoic calm of his portraits surely reflects his conscious ideal of human character rather than indifference or lack of insight.

The Flemish cities of Tournai, Ghent, and Bruges, where the new style of painting flourished, rivaled those of Italy as centers of international banking and trade. Their foreign residents included many Italian businessmen. Jan van Eyck probably painted his remarkable portrait in figure 677 to celebrate the alliance of two of these families that were active in Bruges and Paris. It represents in all likelihood the betrothal of Giovanni Arnolfini and Giovanna Cenami in the main room of the bride's house, rather than an exchange of marriage vows in the privacy of the bridal chamber, as commonly thought. The young couple touches hands in espousal as he raises his right hand in solemn oath. (In accordance with Northern custom, the actual wedding no doubt took place later in front of a church, when the young couple's right hands were literally joined in holy matrimony.) They seem to be quite alone, but in the mirror conspicuously placed behind them is the reflection

formed a separate altarpiece, the Adoration of the Lamb, symbolizing Jesus' sacrificial death. The two panels with music-making angels may have been planned by Hubert as a pair of organ shutters.

If this hypothesis is correct, the two tall, narrow panels showing Adam and Eve (fig. 674) are the only ones on the interior added by Jan to Hubert's stock. They certainly are the most daring of all: these, the earliest monumental nudes of Northern panel painting (hardly less than lifesize), are magnificently observed and caressed by the most delicate play of light and shade. Their quiet dignity and prominent place in the altar suggest that they should remind us not so much of Original Sin as of our creation in God's own image. Actual evil, by contrast, is represented in the small, violently expressive scenes above, which show the story of Cain and Abel. Even more extraordinary is the fact that the *Adam* and *Eve* were designed specifically for their present positions in the ensemble. Jan van Eyck has established a new, direct relationship between picture space and real space by depicting the two figures as they would really appear to the spectator, whose eye level is below the bottom of the panels.

The outer surfaces of the two wings (fig. 675) were evidently planned by Jan as one coherent unit. Here, as we would normally expect, the largest figures are not above, but in the lower tier. The two St. Johns (painted in grays to simulate

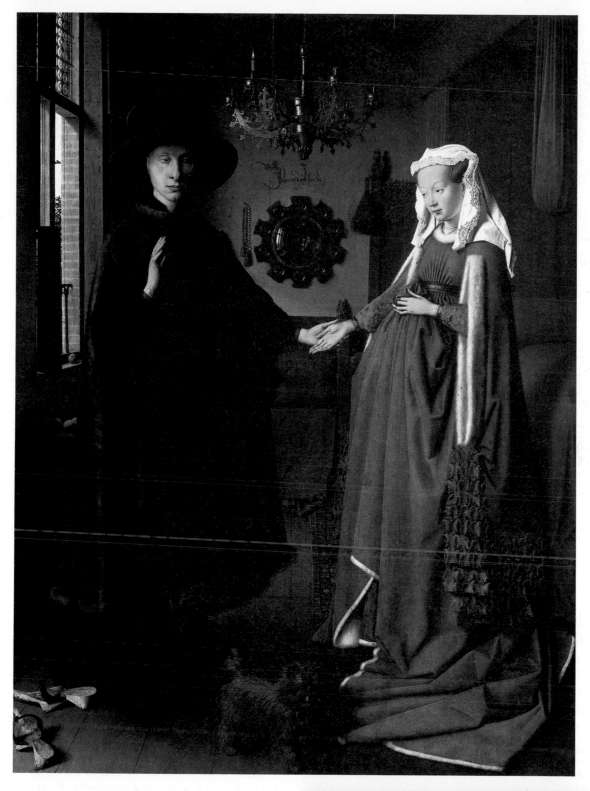

677. Jan van Eyck. *The Arnolfini Portrait*. 1434. Oil on panel,
33 x 22¹/2" (83.7 x 57 cm). The National Gallery, London

of two other people who have entered the room (fig. 678). One
of them is presumably the bride's father, who by tradition gives
her to the groom. The other must be the artist, since the words
above the mirror, in florid lettering, tell us that "Johannes de
eyck fuit hic" (Jan van Eyck was here) in the year 1434.

Jan's role, then, is that of a witness to the event, which also
entailed a legal and financial contract between the two families.

678. *(right)* Jan van Eyck. *The Arnolfini Portrait* (detail)

679. Rogier van der Weyden. *Descent from the Cross.* c. 1435. Oil on panel,
7'2⅝" x 8'7⅛" (2.2 x 2.6 m). Museo del Prado, Madrid

The picture claims to show exactly what he saw. Given its secular nature, we may wonder whether the picture is filled with the same sort of disguised symbolism as the *Mérode Altarpiece,* where the natural world contains the world of the spirit so completely that the two actually become one. Or does the pervasive realism serve simply as an accurate record of the domestic setting? The elaborate bed, the main piece of furniture in the well-appointed living room of the day, was used not for sleeping but for greeting new mothers and paying final respects to the deceased. May it not also contain a discreet allusion to the physical consummation that validated marriage? Has the couple taken off their shoes merely as a matter of custom, or to remind us that they are standing on "holy ground"? (For the origin of the theme, see page 62.) By the same token, is the little dog no more than a beloved pet or an emblem of fidelity? (The words *dog* and *fidelity* share the same root with *betrothal* in the Latin *fides.*) The other furnishings of the room pose similar problems of interpretation. What is the role of the single candle in the chandelier, burning in broad daylight (compare page 505)? And is the convex mirror, the frame of which is decorated with

scenes from the Passion, not a Vanitas symbol (see fig. 678, page 511)? Clearly Jan was so intrigued by its unusual visual effects that he incorporated it into two other paintings as well.

ROGIER VAN DER WEYDEN.   In the work of Jan van Eyck, the exploration of the reality made visible by light and color reached a level that was not to be surpassed for another two centuries. Rogier van der Weyden (1399/1400–1464), the third great master of early Flemish painting, set himself a different though equally important task: to recapture the emotional drama and the pathos of the Gothic past within the framework of the new style created by his predecessors. We see this greater expressive immediacy in his early masterpiece, *Descent from the Cross* (fig. 679), which dates from about 1435 when the artist was in his mid-thirties. Here the modeling is sculpturally precise, with brittle, angular drapery folds recalling those of his teacher, the Master of Flémalle. The soft half-shadows and rich, glowing colors show his knowledge of Jan van Eyck, with whom he may also have been in contact. Yet Rogier is far more than a follower of the two older artists.

680. Rogier van der Weyden. *The Miraflores Altarpiece*. c. 1440–44. Oil on panel, each panel 28 x 16⅞" (71.1 x 42.8 cm).
Staatliche Museen zu Berlin, Gemäldegalerie

Whatever he owes to them (and it is obviously a great deal) he uses for purposes that are not theirs but his. The external events (in this case, the lowering of Jesus' body from the Cross) concern him less than the world of human feeling: "the inner desires and emotions . . . whether sorrow, anger, or gladness," in the words of an early account. The visible world in turn becomes a means toward that same end.

Rogier's art has been well described as "at once physically barer and spiritually richer than Jan van Eyck's." This *Descent*, judged for its expressive content, could well be called a *Lamentation*. The Virgin's swoon echoes the pose and expression of her son. So intense is her pain and grief that it inspires in the viewer the same compassion. Rogier has staged his scene in a shallow architectural niche or shrine, and not against a landscape background. This bold device gives him a double advantage in heightening the effect of the tragic event. It focuses the viewer's entire attention on the foreground, and allows the artist to mold the figures into a coherent group. It seems uniquely fitting that Rogier treats his figures as if they were colored statues, for the artistic ancestry of these grief-stricken gestures and faces

is in sculpture rather than in painting. The panel descends from the Strasbourg *Death of the Virgin* (fig. 470), to which it bears a strong similarity in both composition and mood.

Truly "Late Gothic," Rogier's art never departs from the spirit of the Middle Ages. Yet visually it belongs just as clearly to the new era, so that the past is inevitably restated in contemporary terms. Thus, *The Miraflores Altarpiece* (fig. 680) is replete with self-conscious archaisms but looks thoroughly up to date. By now the artist was in great demand, and his work involved the participation of assistants: such is the case with our altar, named for the convent near Burgos that received it by 1445. (The composition is known in a second, equally fine version from his shop.) As the inscriptions on the scrolls tell us, the triptych celebrates the purity, faith, and perseverance of the Virgin, which are related in turn to the theme of her joys, sorrows, and glories.

A simulated portal provides the doorway into each scene, which is confined to the foreground of a small niche, despite the suggestion of space around it. This old-fashioned device once again creates the impression of figures as colored sculpture

681. Rogier van der Weyden. *Francesco d'Este.* c. 1455.
Tempera and oil on panel, 11³/4 x 8" (29.8 x 20.3 cm).
The Metropolitan Museum of Art, New York
The Friedsam Collection. Bequest of Michael Friedsam, 1931

in an architectural setting (see the Naumburg *Crucifixion,* fig. 476). The effect is heightened by the reliefs lining the archivolts, which carry much of the narrative and symbolic burden by depicting events from the life of Jesus related to the main subject below. The Virgin adoring the Christ Child in the left panel recalls a traditional Nativity (compare fig. 521) transferred to an indoor setting, which indicates that this Madonna of Humility is also the Queen of Heaven. The center panel similarly combines the Byzantine motif of the Last Kiss with the time-honored German *Pietà* (fig. 479). However, the Final Appearance of Jesus to his Mother, in the right panel, is unusu-

al in both subject and treatment. It is reminiscent of the more familiar *Noli me tangere,* where he appears to the Magdalen. Like *The Deposition, The Miraflores Altar* may be thought of as an enlarged Gothic *Andachtsbild* that is meant to be revered as an object of spiritual devotion. The figures bespeak the aristocratic ideal of the International Style. Attenuated and elegant, they represent Rogier's definitive type. He uses them to convey a remarkable range of emotion not simply through gesture and expression but also through purely formal means—the precise quality of line, form, and color—which communicate their intent with powerful conviction.

What is true of Rogier's religious works applies equally well to his portraits. The likeness of Francesco d'Este (fig. 681), an Italian nobleman resident at the Burgundian court, may strike us as less lifelike than Jan van Eyck's. Modeling is reduced to a minimum, and much descriptive detail has been simplified or omitted altogether. The gracefully elongated forms render an aristocratic ideal rather than the sitter's individual appearance. Yet this face, compared with that of the *Man in a Red Turban* (fig. 676), conveys a more vivid sense of character. Instead of striving for the psychologically "neutral" calm of Jan's portraits, Rogier interprets the human personality by suppressing some traits and emphasizing others through such features as the set of the eyes and mouth. As a result, he tells us more about the inner life of his sitters and less about their outward appearance. They are so self-contained as to remain enigmatic. Consequently, we are hard pressed to define their state of mind, witness the widely varying responses they evoke.

Nevertheless, Rogier was accessible to people still imbued with a medieval outlook. No wonder he set an example for countless other artists. When he died in 1464, after 30 years as the foremost painter of Brussels, his influence was supreme throughout Europe north of the Alps. Its impact continued to be felt almost everywhere outside Italy, in painting as well as sculpture, until the end of the fifteenth century, such was the authority of his style.

682. Hugo van der Goes. *The Portinari Altarpiece* (open). c. 1476. Tempera and oil on panel,
center 8'3¹/2" x 10' (2.5 x 3.1 m), wings each 8'3¹/2" x 4'7¹/2" (2.5 x 1.4 m). Galleria degli Uffizi, Florence

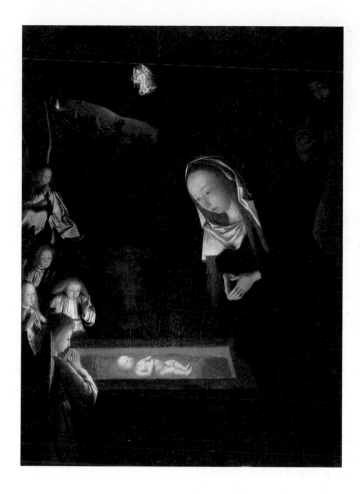

HUGO VAN DER GOES. Among the artists who followed Rogier van der Weyden, few succeeded in escaping from the great master's shadow. To them his paintings offered a choice between intense drama on the one hand and delicate restraint on the other. Most opted for the latter, and their work is marked by a fragile charm. The most dynamic of Rogier's disciples was Hugo van der Goes (c. 1440–1482), an unhappy genius whose tragic end suggests an unstable personality especially interesting to us today. After a spectacular rise to fame in the cosmopolitan atmosphere of Bruges, he decided in 1475, when he was nearly 35 years of age, to enter a monastery as a lay brother. [See Primary Sources, no. 63, pages 636–37.] He continued to paint for some time, but increasing fits of depression drove him to the verge of suicide, and four years later he was dead.

Van der Goes' most ambitious work, the huge altarpiece commissioned by Tommaso Portinari in 1475, is an awesome achievement (fig. 682). While we need not search here for hints of Hugo's future mental illness, it nonetheless evokes a nervous and restless personality. There is a tension between the artist's devotion to the natural world and his concern with the supernatural. Hugo has rendered a wonderfully spacious and atmospheric landscape setting, with a wealth of precise detail. Yet the disparity in the size of the figures seems to contradict this realism. In the wings, the kneeling members of the Portinari family are dwarfed by their patron saints, whose gigantic size characterizes them as being of a higher order. The latter figures are not meant to be "larger than life," however, for they share the same huge scale with Joseph, the Virgin Mary, and the shepherds of the Nativity in the center panel, whose height is normal in relation to the architecture and to the ox and ass. The angels are drawn to the same scale as the donors, and thus appear abnormally small.

This variation of scale stands outside the logic of everyday experience affirmed in the environment the artist has provided for his figures. Although it originated with Rogier van der Weyden and has a clear symbolic purpose, Hugo exploited the incongruity for expressive effect. There is another striking contrast between the hushed awe of the shepherds and the ritual solemnity of all the other figures. These field hands, gazing in breathless wonder at the newborn Child, react to the dramatic miracle of the Nativity with a wide-eyed directness new to Flemish art. They aroused particular admiration in the Italian painters who saw the work after it arrived in Florence in 1483.

GEERTGEN TOT SINT JANS. During the last quarter of the fifteenth century there were no painters in Flanders comparable to Hugo van der Goes, and the most original artists appeared farther north, in Holland. To one of these, Geertgen tot Sint Jans of Haarlem, who died at the age of 28, about 1495, we owe the enchanting *Nativity* reproduced in figure 683, a picture as daring in its quiet way as the center panel of the *Portinari Altarpiece*. The idea of a nocturnal Nativity, illuminated mainly by radiance from the Christ Child, goes back to the International Style (see fig. 526), but Geertgen, applying the pictorial discoveries of Jan van Eyck, gives new, intense

684. Hieronymus Bosch. *The Garden of Delights.* c. 1510–15. Oil on panel, center 7'2¹/₂" x 6'4³/₄" (2.19 x 1.95 m); wings, each 7'2¹/₂" x 3'2" (2.19 x .96 m). Museo del Prado, Madrid

reality to the theme. The magic effect of his little panel is greatly enhanced by the smooth, simplified shapes that record the play of light with striking clarity. The heads of the angels, the Infant, and the Virgin are all as round as objects turned on a lathe, while the manger is a rectangular trough.

BOSCH. If Geertgen's uncluttered forms seem surprisingly modern to us today, another Dutch artist, Hieronymus Bosch, appeals to our interest in the world of dreams. Little is known about Bosch except that he came from a family of painters named Van Aken, spent his life in the provincial town of 's Hertogenbosch, and died, an old man, in 1516. His work, full of weird and seemingly irrational imagery, has proved difficult to interpret.

We can readily see why when we study the triptych known as *The Garden of Delights* (fig. 684), the richest and most puzzling of Bosch's pictures. [See Primary Sources, no. 64, page 637.] Its peculiar qualities may be owing in part to the fact that this is not a traditional altarpiece but a secular work: it was probably commissioned by Henry III of Nassau for his palace in Brussels, where it was hanging immediately after Bosch's death. Henry would have been familiar with Bosch's work in 's Hertogenbosch, the royal summer residence. Many ingenious proposals have been put forward by scholars to explicate the enigmatic painting: for example, that it represents the days of Noah, or that it is a heretical allegory of redemption through

the acceptance of humanity's natural state before the Fall.

Much of the imagery in *The Garden of Delights* derives from treatises on astrology and alchemy, which Bosch would have known through his father-in-law, a well-to-do pharmacist. These unite the humors with the zodiac in a universal scheme of good and evil paralleling Neo-Platonism, which was itself interested in magic in this prescientific era. Yet, if the truth be told, none of these explanations is wholly satisfactory. In the end, we must take the character of the painting itself into account; moreover, any interpretation must be consistent with Bosch's work as a whole.

Of the three panels, only the left one has a clearly recognizable subject: the Garden of Eden, where the Lord introduces Adam to the newly created Eve. The landscape, almost Eyckian in its airy vastness, is filled with animals, among them such exotic creatures as an elephant and a giraffe, as well as hybrid monsters of odd and sinister kinds. The distant rock formations behind them are equally strange. They are perhaps a reference to the alchemical furnace, in which foul gases are purified. The right wing, a nightmarish scene of burning ruins and fantastic instruments of torture, surely represents Hell. But what of the center panel, a detail of which is seen in figure 685?

Here is a landscape much like that of the Garden of Eden, populated with countless nude men and women engaged in a variety of peculiar activities. In the center, they parade around a circular basin on the backs of all sorts of beasts. Many frolic

685. Hieronymus Bosch. *The Garden of Delights.*
Detail of center panel

The brilliance of the fifteenth-century Flemish painters had a close parallel in the field of music. After about 1420, The Netherlands produced a school of composers—Guillaume Dufay (c. 1400–1474), Johannes Ockeghem (c. 1420–1495), Josquin Des Prés (c. 1440–1521), and Adrian Willaert (c. 1490–1562)—so revolutionary as to dominate the development of music throughout Europe for the next 125 years. How much the new style was appreciated can be gathered from the words of the Flemish theorist Johannes Tinctoris (1446?–1511), who wrote of these composers in 1477: "Although it seems beyond belief, nothing worth listening to had been composed before their time." Except for the absence of any reference to the revival of antiquity, this remark, with its sweeping rejection of medieval music, shows a Flemish "Renaissance consciousness" much like that of the Italian humanists of the same period. In fact, Des Prés and Willaert held important positions in Italy, and Dufay had spent nearly a decade there early in his career. In Italy, during the High Renaissance, they were revered as the greatest composers of their day (see page 464). The main contribution of these Flemings was the invention of the fugue, the passing of a short theme from one voice to another of equal weight (think of "Three Blind Mice"), a technique that was to become highly developed in the sixteenth century.

Tinctoris credited the English composer John Dunstable (c. 1385–1453), active in France between 1422 and 1435, with beginning a revolution that replaced the complexities of Gothic polyphony with a simpler style. Dufay carried Dunstable's innovations further by placing the main melody, which earlier had been sung by the tenor, in the soprano voice. This simple change gave greater prominence to the melodic line and emphasized its beauty. Dufay also led a movement to replace plainsong in sacred music with themes from secular songs, which were more flexible than chant and more appealing to contemporary taste. In the sixteenth century, these innovations evolved into a form called the parody mass, in which most of the themes were taken from popular songs, freely modified, and connected with newly composed passages. Ockeghem completed the musical revolution toward a more mellifluous style. Though less well known today than Dufay, Ockeghem was highly honored in his own time. The humanist Erasmus wrote of him, "His golden voice caressed the ears of the angels, and swayed the hearts of men to their depths," and his passing was mourned by his pupil Josquin in the lament *Nymphs of the Woods.*

686. Conrad Witz. *The Miraculous Draught of Fishes*. 1444. Oil on panel, 51 x 61" (129.7 x 155 cm).
Musée d'Art et d'Histoire, Geneva, Switzerland

in pools of water. Most of them are closely linked with enormous birds, fruit, flowers, or marine animals. Only a few are openly engaged in lovemaking, but there can be no doubt that the delights in this "garden" are those of carnal desire, however oddly disguised. The birds, fruit, and the like are symbols or metaphors which Bosch uses to depict life on earth as an unending repetition of the Original Sin of Adam and Eve, which dooms us to be prisoners of our appetites. Nowhere does the artist even hint at the possibility of salvation. Corruption, on the animal level at least, had already asserted itself in the Garden of Eden before the Fall, and we are all destined for Hell, the Garden of Satan, with its grisly and refined instruments of torture.

Bosch conveys a profoundly pessimistic attitude about humanity. We nevertheless sense a fundamental ambiguity in the central panel. There is an innocence, even a haunting poetic beauty, in this panorama of human sinfulness. Consciously, Bosch was a stern moralist who intended his pictures to be visual sermons, every detail packed with didactic meaning. Unconsciously, however, he must have been so enraptured by the sensuous appeal of the world of the flesh that the images

he coined in such abundance tend to celebrate what they are meant to condemn. That, surely, is the reason why *The Garden of Delights* still evokes so strong a response today, even though we no longer understand every word of the sermon.

Swiss, German, and French Painting

We must now glance briefly at fifteenth-century art in the rest of Northern Europe. After about 1430, the new realism of the Flemish masters began to spread into France and Germany until, by the middle of the century, its influence prevailed everywhere from Spain to the Baltic. Among the countless artists (many of them still anonymous) who turned out provincial adaptations of Netherlandish painting, only a few were gifted enough to impress us with a distinctive personality.

WITZ. One of the earliest and most original of these masters was Conrad Witz of Basel (1400/10–1445/6), whose altarpiece for Geneva Cathedral, painted in 1444, includes the remarkable panel shown in figure 686. To judge from the drapery, with its tubular folds and sharp, angular breaks, he

687. Jean Fouquet. *Étienne Chevalier and St. Stephen*, left wing of the *Melun Diptych*. c. 1450. Oil on panel, 36½ x 33½" (92./ x 85 cm). Staatliche Museen zu Berlin, Gemäldegalerie

688. Jean Fouquet. *Madonna and Child*, right wing of the *Melun Diptych*. c. 1450. Oil on panel, 36⅝ x 33½" (93 x 85 cm). Musée Royal des Beaux-Arts, Antwerp, Belgium

must have had close contact with the Master of Flémalle. But the setting, rather than the figures, attracts our interest, and here the influence of the Van Eycks seems dominant. Witz, however, did not simply follow these great pioneers. An explorer himself, he knew more about the optical appearances of water than any other painter of his time, as we can see the bottom of the lake in the foreground. The landscape, too, is an original contribution. Representing a specific part of the shore of the Lake of Geneva, it is among the earliest landscape "portraits" that have come down to us.

FOUQUET. In France, the leading painter was Jean Fouquet (c. 1420–1481) of Tours, some 20 years younger than Witz. He had the exceptional fortune of a lengthy visit to Italy around 1445, soon after he had completed his training, so that his work represents a unique blend of Flemish and Early Renaissance elements, although it remains basically Northern. *Étienne Chevalier and St. Stephen*, the left wing of the *Melun Diptych* (fig. 687), his most famous work, shows his mastery as a portraitist. Remarkably, the head of the saint seems no less individual than that of the donor. Italian influence can be seen

in the style of the architecture and, less directly, in the statuesque solidity and weight of the two figures. According to an old tradition, the Madonna in the right wing (fig. 688) is also a portrait: that of Agnes Sorel, Charles VII's mistress, whose estate Chevalier represented as executor upon her death in 1450, when our diptych may have been painted. If so, it presents a highly idealized image of courtly beauty, as befits the Queen of Heaven, seen wearing a crown and robe amidst a choir of angels.

Here we see the beginnings of that tendency toward intellectual lucidity and abstraction which were to become distinctive to French art. This emphasis extends to the treatment of the background, which is very different in the two panels, not out of disregard for visual perspective but in order to distinguish clearly between the temporal and spiritual realms. Thus, each half of the diptych constitutes a separate, self-contained world. By the same token, pictorial space for Fouquet exists independently of the viewer's "real" space.

Manuscript painting continued to flourish on both sides of the Alps well into the sixteenth century, and Fouquet was justly the most famous illuminator of the day in the North. *The*

689. Jean Fouquet. *The Fall of Jerusalem*, from Josephus, *Les Antiquités Judaïques*. c. 1470–75. Illumination, 16 7/8 x 11 3/4" (42.8 x 29.8 cm). Bibliothèque Nationale, Paris

Fall of Jerusalem (fig. 689) shows him to be literally the inheritor of the Gothic: it comes from a copy of Josephus' *Les Antiquités Judaïques* that was started around 1410 for the duke of Berry and fell to our artist to complete some 60 years later. The scene, which closely follows Josephus' text, depicts the forces of the Babylonian king Nebuchadnezzar under general Nebuzar-Adar overrunning the city and destroying the Temple of Solomon in 586 B.C. Fouquet's mastery of outdoor space and atmospheric perspective is no less refined than in the *October* page of *Les Très Riches Heures du Duc du Berry* (fig. 522). Yet Fouquet was more than an imitator of the Limbourg brothers, no matter how great his admiration for them may have been.

The landscape is painted in the up-to-date style of Conrad Witz and presents a stunningly realistic evocation of a contemporary French town. It is hardly surprising that the page imitates effects found in panels, which had become the dominant vehicle for painting. Yet the quality of the narrative itself belongs to the tradition of manuscript illustration. Even here Fouquet reveals himself to be an innovator. The scene is not entirely without precedent among earlier illuminations, notably those by Jan van Eyck, who excelled in this sphere. Yet its closest relative is, surprisingly enough, *The Building of the* *Tower of Babel* at St.-Savin-sur-Gartempe (fig. 416), which presents a similar subject in reverse, so to speak. They share the same monumental spirit, despite the vast difference in size— truly a remarkable achievement!

AVIGNON PIETÀ. A Flemish style influenced by Italian art also characterizes the most famous of all fifteenth-century French pictures, the *Avignon Pietà* (fig. 690). As its name indicates, the panel comes from the extreme south of France and is attributed to an artist of that region, Enguerrand Quarton (c. 1410–c. 1466). He must have been thoroughly familiar with the art of Rogier van der Weyden, for the figure types and the expressive content of the *Avignon Pietà* could be derived from no other source. At the same time, the magnificently simple and stable design is Italian rather than Northern. These are qualities we first saw in the art of Giotto. Southern, too, is the bleak, featureless landscape emphasizing the monumental isolation of the figures. The distant buildings behind the donor on the left have an unmistakably Islamic flavor, suggesting that the artist meant to place the scene in an authentic Near Eastern setting. From these various features he has created an unforgettable image of heroic pathos.

690. Enguerrand Quarton. *Avignon Pietà*. c. 1470. Oil on panel, 5'3 ³/₄" x 7'1 ⁷/₈" (1.61 x 2.17 m). Musée du Louvre, Paris

"LATE GOTHIC" SCULPTURE

If we had to describe fifteenth-century art north of the Alps in a single phrase, we might label it "the first century of panel painting," which so dominated the art of the period between 1420 and 1500 that its standards apply to manuscript illumination, stained glass, and even, to a large extent, sculpture. After the later thirteenth century, we will recall, the emphasis had shifted from architectural sculpture to the more intimate scale of devotional images, tombs, pulpits, and the like. Claus Sluter, whose art is so impressive in weight and volume, had briefly recaptured the monumental spirit of the High Gothic. However, he had no real successors, although echoes of his style can be felt in French art for the next 50 years.

It was the influence of the Master of Flémalle and Rogier van der Weyden that ended the International Style in the sculpture of Northern Europe. The carvers, who quite often were also painters, began to reproduce in stone or wood the style of these artists, and continued to do so until about 1500.

PACHER. The most characteristic works of the "Late Gothic" carvers are wooden altar shrines, often large in size and incred-

ibly intricate in detail. Such shrines were especially popular in the Germanic countries. One of the richest examples is the *St. Wolfgang Altarpiece* (fig. 691) by the Tyrolean sculptor and painter Michael Pacher (c. 1435–1498). [See Primary Sources, no. 65, page 638.] Its lavishly gilt and colored forms make a dazzling spectacle as they emerge from the shadowy depth of the shrine under Flamboyant canopies. We enjoy it, but in pictorial rather than plastic terms. We have no experience of volume, either positive or negative. The figures and setting in the central panel, showing the *Coronation of the Virgin,* seem to melt into a single pattern of agitated, twisting lines that permits only the heads to stand out as separate entities.

Surprisingly, when we turn to the paintings of scenes from the life of the Virgin on the interior of the wings, we enter a different realm, one that already commands the vocabulary of the Northern Renaissance. Here the artist provides a deep space in scientific perspective that takes the viewer's vantage point into account, so that the upper panels are represented slightly from below. Paradoxically, the figures, powerfully modeled by the clear light, seem far more "sculptural" than the

691. Michael Pacher. *St. Wolfgang Altarpiece.* 1471–81. Carved wood, figures about lifesize. Church of St. Wolfgang, Austria

692. *St. Dorothy.* c. 1420. Woodcut, 10 5/8 x 7 1/2"
(27 x 19 cm). Staatliche Graphische Sammlung, Munich

693. *Woodcut of St. Christopher*, detail from an *Annunciation*
by Jacques Daret (?). c. 1435.
Musées Royaux d'Art et d'Histoire, Brussels, Belgium

694. Martin Schongauer. *The Temptation of St. Anthony.*
c. 1480–90. Engraving, 11 1/2 x 8 5/8" (29.2 x 21.8 cm).
The Metropolitan Museum of Art, New York
Rogers Fund, 1920

carved ones, despite the fact that they are a good deal smaller. It is as if Pacher, the "Late Gothic" sculptor, felt unable to compete with Pacher the painter in the rendering of three-dimensional bodies and therefore chose to treat the *Coronation of the Virgin* in pictorial terms, by extracting the maximum of drama from contrasts of light and shade.

THE GRAPHIC ARTS

WOODCUTS. We must now take note of another important event north of the Alps: the development of printmaking. (For the various techniques of printing, for pictures as well as books, see page 524.) The idea of printing pictorial designs from blocks of wood onto paper seems to have originated in Northern Europe at the very end of the fourteenth century. Many of the oldest surviving examples of such prints, called woodcuts,

are German, others are Flemish, and some may be French; but all show the familiar qualities of the International Style. The designs were probably furnished by painters or sculptors. The actual carving of the wood blocks, however, was done by specially trained artisans, who also produced wood blocks for textile prints. As a result, early woodcuts, such as the *St. Dorothy* in figure 692, have a flat, ornamental pattern. Forms are defined by simple, heavy lines, and there is little concern for three-dimensional effects, as indicated by the absence of hatching or shading. Since the outlined shapes were meant to be filled in with color, these prints often recall stained glass (compare fig. 494) more than the miniatures they replaced.

Despite their aesthetic appeal to modern eyes, we should remember that fifteenth-century woodcuts were popular art, on a level that did not attract artists of great ability until shortly before 1500. A single wood block yielded thousands of

The earliest printed books in the modern sense were produced in the Rhineland soon after 1450. (It is doubtful whether Johann Gutenberg deserves the priority long claimed for him.) The new technique quickly spread all over Europe and developed into an industry that had a profound effect on Western civilization, ushering in the era of increased literacy. Printed pictures had hardly less importance, for without them the printed book could not have replaced the work of the medieval scribe and illuminator so quickly and completely. The pictorial and literary aspects of printing were indeed closely linked from the start. But where is the start? When, and by whom, was printing invented?

The beginnings of the story lie in the ancient Near East 5,000 years ago. Mechanically speaking, the Sumerians were the earliest "printers," for their relief impressions on clay from stone seals were carved with both pictures and inscriptions. From Mesopotamia the use of seals spread to India and eventually to China. The Chinese applied ink to their seals in order to impress them on wood or silk, and, in the second century A.D., they invented paper. By the ninth century, they were printing pictures and books on paper from wooden blocks carved in relief, and 200 years later they developed movable type. Some of the products of Chinese printing surely reached the medieval West—through the Arabs, the Mongols, or travelers such as Marco Polo—although we lack direct evidence.

The technique of manufacturing paper, too, came to Europe from the East, and Chinese silk and porcelain were imported in small quantities from the fourteenth century on. Paper and printing from wood blocks were both known in the West during the later Middle Ages. However, paper gained ground very slowly as a cheap alternative to parchment, while printing was used only for ornamental patterns on cloth. All the more astonishing is the development, beginning about 1400, of a printing technology that within the century surpassed that of the Far East and proved of far wider cultural importance. After 1500, in fact, no basic changes were made in this field until the Industrial Revolution.

WOODCUT. In a woodcut, lines are ridges left by gouging out the block. The thinner they are, the more difficult they are to carve. Hence, the work was often left to specialists. Inscriptions are frequently found on early woodcuts, the letters having been either added by hand or printed from the same block as the picture. But to carve lines of text backward in relief on a wooden block was a wearisome and particularly risky task—a single slip could ruin an entire page. It is little wonder, then, that printers soon had the idea of putting each letter on its own small block. Wooden movable type carved by hand worked well for letters of large size but not for small ones. Moreover, it was too expensive to use for printing long texts such as the Bible. By 1450, this problem had been solved through the introduction of metal type cast from molds, and the stage was set for book production as we know it today.

ENGRAVING. Whoever first thought of metal type probably had the aid of goldsmiths and armorers to work out the technical production problems. This is all the more likely since many goldsmiths had already entered the field of printmaking as engravers. The technique of engraving—of embellishing metal surfaces with incised pictures—was developed in classical antiquity (see fig. 234) and continued to be practiced throughout the Middle Ages (see fig. 421, where the engraved lines are filled in with enamel). Thus, no new skill was required to engrave a plate that was to serve as the "matrix" for a paper print.

The idea of making an engraved print apparently came from the desire for an alternative, more refined and flexible, to woodcuts. In an engraving, lines are V-shaped grooves incised with a tool (called a burin) into a metal plate, usually copper, which is relatively soft and easy to work. The subsequent printing is done by rubbing ink into the grooves, wiping off the surface of the plate, covering it with a damp sheet of paper, and putting it through the press.

DRYPOINT. A variant of this technique is known as drypoint. It permitted artists to draw almost as freely as with a pen on a sheet of paper by scratching their designs into the copperplate with a fine steel needle. The needle, of course, did not cut grooves as deep as those made by the burin, so that a drypoint plate wore out after yielding a relative handful of impressions, whereas an engraved plate lasted through hundreds of printings. But the drypoint technique preserved the artist's personal "handwriting" and permitted soft, atmospheric effects—velvety shadows, delicate, luminous distances—unattainable with the burin.

ETCHING. Eventually the techniques of woodcut and engraving were employed mainly to reproduce other works. The creative printmakers came to prefer etching, often combined with drypoint. This technique, too, must have originated with goldsmiths and armorers in the North. An etching is made by coating a copperplate with resin to make an acid-resistant "ground," through which the design is scratched with a needle, laying bare the metal surface underneath. The plate is then bathed in an acid that etches (or "bites") the lines into the copper. The depth of these grooves varies with the strength and duration of the bath, and the biting is usually by stages. After a brief immersion in the acid bath the etcher will apply a protective coating to the plate in those areas where the lines should be faint. The plate is then immersed until it is time to protect the less delicate lines, and so on. To scratch a design into the resinous ground is, of course, an easier task than to scratch it into the copperplate itself. Hence, an etched line is smoother and more flexible than a drypoint line. An etched plate is also more durable; it yields a far greater number of prints than a drypoint plate. Its chief virtue is its wide tonal range, including velvety dark shades not possible in engraving or woodcut.

copies, to be sold for a few pennies apiece, bringing the individual ownership of pictures within everyone's reach for the first time in history. What people did with these prints is illustrated in figure 693, a detail from a Flemish *Annunciation* panel of about 1435, where a tattered woodcut of St. Christopher is pinned up above the mantel. Perhaps it is a hint at the Virgin's journey to Bethlehem (St. Christopher was the patron saint of travelers), but this charmingly incongruous feature must also be understood as a disguised symbol of her humility, for only the poor would have such an object on their walls. The *St. Christopher* woodcut has two lines of lettering—a short prayer, presumably—at the bottom. Such woodcuts combining image and text were sometimes assembled into popular picture books, called block books.

ENGRAVINGS.   Engravings appealed from the first to a smaller and more sophisticated public. The oldest examples we know, dating from about 1430, already show the influence of the great Flemish painters. Their forms are systematically modeled with fine hatched lines and often convincingly foreshortened. Nor do engravings share the anonymity of early woodcuts. Individual hands can be distinguished almost from the beginning, dates and initials appear shortly, and most of the important engravers of the last third of the fifteenth century are known to us by name. Even though the early engravers were usually goldsmiths by training, their prints are so closely linked to local painting styles that we may determine their geographic origin far more easily than for woodcuts. Especially in the Upper Rhine region, we can trace a continuous tradition of fine engravers from the time of Conrad Witz to the end of the century.

SCHONGAUER.   The most accomplished of the Upper Rhenish engravers was Martin Schongauer (c. 1430–1491), the first printmaker whom we also know as a painter, and the first to gain international fame. Schongauer might be called the Rogier van der Weyden of engraving. After learning the goldsmith's craft in his father's shop, he must have spent considerable time in Flanders, for he shows a thorough knowledge of Rogier's art. His prints are filled with Rogierian motifs and expressive devices, and they reveal a deep temperamental affinity to the great Fleming. Yet Schongauer had his own impressive powers of invention. His finest engravings have a complexity of design, spatial depth, and richness of texture that make them fully equivalent to panel paintings. In fact, lesser artists often found inspiration in them for large-scale pictures.

The Temptation of St. Anthony (fig. 694), one of Schongauer's most famous works, masterfully combines savage expressiveness and formal precision, violent movement and ornamental stability. The longer we look at it, the more we marvel at its range of tonal values, the rhythmic beauty of the engraved line, and the artist's ability to render every conceivable surface—spiky, scaly, leathery, furry—by varying the burin's attack upon the plate. He was not to be surpassed by any later engraver in this respect.

695. The Master of the Housebook. *Holy Family by the Rosebush.* c. 1480–90. Drypoint, 5 5/8 x 4 1/2" (14.2 x 11.5 cm). Rijksprentenkabinet, Rijksmuseum, Amsterdam

THE MASTER OF THE HOUSEBOOK. For originality of conception and technique, Schongauer had only one rival among the printmakers of his time, the Master of the Housebook (so called after a book of drawings attributed to him). Although he was probably of Dutch origin, he seems to have spent most of his career, from about 1475 to 1490, in the Rhineland. The very individual style of this artist is the opposite of Schongauer's. His prints—such as the *Holy Family by the Rosebush* (fig. 695)—are small, intimate in mood, and spontaneous, almost sketchy, in execution, which lends them a quaint charm that makes up for their naïveté. Even his tools were different from the standard engraver's equipment. Instead of submitting to the somewhat impersonal discipline demanded by the burin, the Master of the Housebook scratched his designs into the copperplate with a fine steel needle, a technique known as drypoint. The Master of the Housebook knew how to take full advantage of the medium. He was a pioneer in the use of a tool that was to become the supreme instrument of Rembrandt's graphic art a century and a half later.

CHAPTER FIVE

THE RENAISSANCE IN THE NORTH

North of the Alps, as we have seen, most fifteenth-century artists remained indifferent to Italian forms and ideas. Since the time of the Master of Flémalle and the Van Eycks they had looked to Flanders, rather than to Tuscany, for leadership. This relative isolation ended suddenly toward the year 1500. As if a dam had burst, Italian influence flowed northward in an ever wider stream, and Northern Renaissance art began to replace the "Late Gothic." That term, however, has a far less well-

defined meaning than "Late Gothic," which at least refers to a single, clearly recognizable stylistic tradition, however questionable the name may otherwise be. The diversity of trends north of the Alps is even greater than in Italy during the sixteenth century. Nor does Italian influence provide a common denominator, for this influence is itself diverse: Early Renaissance, High Renaissance, and Mannerist, all are to be found in regional variants from Lombardy, Venice, Florence, and Rome.

696. Matthias Grünewald. *St. Sebastian; The Crucifixion; St. Anthony Abbot*; predella: *Lamentation. Isenheim Altarpiece* (closed). c. 1510–15. Oil on panel, main body 9'9¹/2" x 10'9" (2.97 x 3.28 m), predella 2'5¹/2" x 11'2" (0.75 x 3.4 m). Musée Unterlinden, Colmar, France

Its effects, too, vary greatly. They may be superficial or profound, direct or indirect, specific or general. Nevertheless, we may speak for the first time of a Renaissance proper in the North. Like its cousin in Italy, it is distinguished by an interest in humanism, albeit with equally inconsistent results.

The "Late Gothic" tradition remained very much alive, if no longer dominant, and its encounter with Italian art resulted in a protracted conflict among styles that ended only when the Baroque emerged as an international movement in the early seventeenth century. The full history of this contest is yet to be written. Its course was decisively affected by the Reformation, which had a far more immediate impact on art north of the Alps than in Italy, but the major issues are nevertheless hard to trace. Our account, then, necessarily emphasizes the main phases.

GERMANY

Painting and the Graphic Arts

Let us begin with Germany, the home of the Reformation, where the first major stylistic developments took place during the first quarter of the century. Between 1475 and 1500, it had produced such important artists as Michael Pacher and Martin Schongauer (see figs. 691 and 694), but they hardly prepare us for the astonishing burst of creative energy that was to

follow. The range of achievements of this period, which was comparable in its brevity and brilliance to the Italian High Renaissance, is measured by the contrasting personalities of its greatest artists: Matthias Grünewald and Albrecht Dürer. Both died in 1528, probably at about the same age, although we know only Dürer's birth date (1471). Dürer quickly became internationally famous, while Grünewald, who was born about 1470–80, remained so obscure that his real name, Mathis Gothart Nithart, was discovered only at the end of the nineteenth century.

GRÜNEWALD. Grünewald's fame, like that of El Greco, has developed almost entirely within our own century. His main work, the *Isenheim Altarpiece,* is unique in the Northern art of his time in its ability to overwhelm us with something like the power of the Sistine ceiling. Long believed to be by Dürer, it was painted between 1509/10 and 1515 for the monastery church of the Order of St. Anthony at Isenheim, in Alsace, and is now in the museum of the nearby city of Colmar.

This extraordinary altarpiece is a carved shrine with two sets of movable wings, which give it three stages, or "views." The first of these views, formed when all the wings are closed, shows *The Crucifixion* in the center panel (fig. 696)—the most impressive ever painted. In one respect it is very medieval. Jesus' terrible agony and the desperate grief of the Virgin, St. John, and Mary Magdalen recall the older German

697. Matthias Grünewald. *The Annunciation; Madonna and Child with Angels; The Resurrection.* Second view of the
Isenheim Altarpiece. c. 1510–15. Oil on panel, each wing 8'10" x 4'8" (2.69 x 1.42 m); center panel 8'10" x 11'2¹/2" (2.69 x 3.41 m).
Musée Unterlinden, Colmar, France

698. Matthias Grünewald. *The Resurrection,* from second view of the *Isenheim Altarpiece*

Andachtsbild (see fig. 479). But the pitiful body on the Cross with its twisted limbs, its countless lacerations, its rivulets of blood, is on a heroic scale that raises it beyond the human and thus reveals the two natures of Jesus. The same message is conveyed by the flanking figures. The three historic witnesses on the left mourn Jesus' death as a man, while John the Baptist, on the right, points with calm emphasis to him as the Saviour. Even the background suggests this duality. Golgotha here is not a hill outside Jerusalem, but a mountain towering above lesser peaks. The Crucifixion, lifted from its familiar setting, thus becomes a lonely event silhouetted against a deserted, ghostly landscape and a blue-black sky. Darkness is over the land, in accordance with the Gospel, yet brilliant light bathes the foreground with the force of sudden revelation. This union of time and eternity, of reality and symbolism, gives Grünewald's *Crucifixion* its awesome grandeur.

When the outer wings are opened, the mood of the *Isenheim Altarpiece* changes dramatically (fig. 697). All three scenes in this second view—the Annunciation, the Angel Concert for the Madonna and Child, and the Resurrection (fig. 698)—celebrate events as jubilant in spirit as the Crucifixion is austere. Most striking in comparison with "Late Gothic" painting is the sense of movement pervading these panels. Everything twists and turns as though it had a life of its own. The angel of the Annunciation enters the room like a gust of wind that blows the Virgin backward, and the Risen Jesus leaps from his grave with explosive force. This vibrant energy is matched by the ecstatic vision of heavenly glory in celebration of Jesus' birth, seen behind the Madonna and Child, who are surely the most tender and lyrical in all of Northern art.

In contrast to the brittle, spiky contours and angular drapery patterns of "Late Gothic" art, Grünewald's forms are soft, elastic, fleshy. His light and color show a corresponding change. Commanding all the resources of his great Flemish predecessors, he employs them with extraordinary boldness and flexibility. His color scale is richly iridescent, its range matched only by the Venetians. Indeed, his exploitation of colored light is altogether without parallel at that time. Grünewald's genius has achieved miracles through light that were never to be surpassed in the luminescent angels of the Concert, the apparition of God the Father and the Heavenly Host above the Madonna, and, most spectacularly, the rainbow-hued radiance of the Risen Jesus.

How much did Grünewald owe to Italian art? Nothing at all, we are first tempted to say, yet he must have learned from the Renaissance in more ways than one. His knowledge of perspective (note the low horizons) and the physical vigor of some of his figures cannot be explained by the "Late Gothic" tradition alone, and occasionally his pictures show architectural details of Southern origin. Perhaps the most important effect of the Renaissance on him, however, was psychological. We know little about his career, but he apparently did not lead the settled life of an artisan-painter controlled by guild rules. He was also an architect, an engineer, something of a courtier, and an entrepreneur. Moreover, he worked for many different patrons and stayed nowhere for very long. He was in sympathy with Martin Luther even though as a painter he depended on Catholic patronage. [See Primary Sources, no. 66, page 638.]

In a word, Grünewald seems to have shared the free, indi-

699. Albrecht Dürer. *Italian Mountains.* c. 1495 or 1505–6. Brush drawing in watercolor, 8¼ x 12¼" (21 x 31.2 cm). Ashmolean Museum, Oxford, England

vidualistic spirit of Italian Renaissance artists. The daring of his pictorial vision likewise suggests a reliance on his own resources. The Renaissance, then, had a liberating influence on him but did not change the basic cast of his imagination. Instead, it helped him to epitomize the expressive aspects of the "Late Gothic" in a style of unique intensity and individuality.

DÜRER. For Albrecht Dürer (1471–1528), the Renaissance held a richer meaning. Attracted to Italian art while still a young journeyman, he visited Venice in 1494/5 and returned to his native Nuremberg with a new conception of the world and the artist's place in it. The unbridled fantasy of Grünewald's art was to him "a wild, unpruned tree" (a phrase he used for painters who worked by rules of thumb, without theoretical foundations) that needed the discipline of the objective, rational standards of the Renaissance. Taking the Italian view that the fine arts belong among the liberal arts, he also adopted the ideal of the artist as a gentleman and humanistic scholar. [See Primary Sources, no. 67, pages 638–39.] By steadily cultivating his intellectual interests he came to encompass in his lifetime an unprecedented variety of subjects and techniques. And since he was the greatest printmaker of the time, he had a wide influence on sixteenth-century art through his woodcuts and engravings, which circulated everywhere in Europe.

In Italy Dürer made copies after Mantegna and other Early Renaissance masters that display his eager and intuitive grasp of the essentials of their alien style. Equally astonishing are his watercolors painted on the way back from Venice, such as the one inscribed "Italian Mountains" (fig. 699). He was the first serious artist to work in watercolor, which acquired new importance as a sketching medium thanks to his experiments. Yet, significantly, Dürer did not record the name of the spot here or in his other sheets; the specific location had no interest for him. The title he jotted down seems exactly right, for this is not a "portrait," but a "study from the model" perceived in timeless freshness. The calm rhythm of this panorama of softly rounded slopes conveys a view of nature in its organic wholeness that was matched in those years only by Leonardo's landscapes (compare the background in the *Mona Lisa;* fig. 598).

700. Albrecht Dürer. *The Four Horsemen of the Apocalypse.*
c. 1497–98. Woodcut, 15¹/2 x 11¹/8" (39.3 x 28.3 cm).
The Metropolitan Museum of Art, New York
Gift of Junius S. Morgan, 1919

701. Albrecht Dürer. *Self-Portrait.* 1500. Oil on panel,
26¹/4 x 19¹/4" (66.3 x 49 cm). Alte Pinakothek, Munich

After the breadth and lyricism of the *Italian Mountains,* the expressive violence is doubly shocking in the woodcuts illustrating the Apocalypse, Dürer's most ambitious graphic work of the years following his return from Venice. The gruesome vision of *The Four Horsemen* (fig. 700) seems at first to return completely to the "Late Gothic" world of Martin Schongauer's *Temptation of St. Anthony* (see fig. 694). Yet the physical energy and solid, full-bodied volume of these figures would have been impossible without Dürer's earlier experience in copying the works of such artists as Mantegna (compare fig. 589). At this stage, Dürer's style has much in common with Grünewald's. The comparison with Schongauer, however, is instructive from another point of view. It shows how thoroughly Dürer has redefined his medium—the woodcut—by enriching it with the linear subtleties of engraving. In his hands, woodcuts lose their former charm as popular art (see fig. 692), but gain the precise articulation of a fully matured graphic style. He set a standard that soon transformed the technique of woodcuts all over Europe.

The first artist to be fascinated by his own image, Dürer was in this respect more of a Renaissance personality than any Italian artist. His earliest known work, a drawing made at 13, is a self-portrait, and he continued to produce self-portraits throughout his career. Most impressive, and uniquely revealing, is the panel of 1500 (fig. 701). Pictorially, it belongs to the

Flemish tradition (compare Jan van Eyck's *Man in a Red Turban;* fig. 676), but the solemn, frontal pose and the Christlike idealization of the features assert an authority quite beyond the range of ordinary portraits. The picture looks, in fact, like a secularized icon, reflecting not so much Dürer's vanity as the seriousness with which he regarded his mission as an artistic reformer. (One thinks of Martin Luther's "Here I stand; I cannot do otherwise.")

The didactic aspect of Dürer's art is clearest perhaps in the engraving *Adam and Eve* of 1504 (fig. 702), where the biblical subject serves as a pretext for the display of two ideal nudes: Apollo and Venus in a Northern forest (compare figs. 206 and 208). No wonder they look somewhat out of place. Unlike the picturesque setting and its animal inhabitants, Adam and Eve are not observed from life, but constructed according to what Dürer believed to be perfect proportions. Here, for the first time, both the form and the substance of the Italian Renaissance enter Northern art, but adapted to the unique cultural climate of Germany. That is why his ideal male and female figures, though very different from their classical exemplars, were to become models in their own right to countless Northern artists.

The same approach, now applied to the body of a horse, is evident in *Knight, Death, and Devil* (fig. 703), one of the artist's finest prints. This time, however, there is no incon-

702. Albrecht Dürer. *Adam and Eve.* 1504. Engraving,
9⁷/8 x 7⁵/8" (25.2 x 19.4 cm). Museum of Fine Arts, Boston
Centennial Gift of Landon T. Clay

703. Albrecht Dürer. *Knight, Death, and Devil.* 1513.
Engraving, 9⁷/8 x 7¹/2" (25.2 x 19.4 cm). Museum of Fine Arts, Boston
Gift of Mrs. Horatio Greenough Curtis in memory of her husband

gruity. The knight on his beautiful mount, poised and confident as an equestrian statue, embodies an ideal both aesthetic and moral. He is the Christian Soldier steadfast on the road of faith toward the Heavenly Jerusalem, undeterred by the hideous rider threatening to cut him off or the grotesque devil behind him. The dog, symbol of fidelity, loyally follows its master despite the lizards and skulls in their path. Italian Renaissance form, united with the heritage of "Late Gothic" symbolism (whether open or disguised), here takes on a new, characteristically Northern significance.

Dürer's convictions were essentially those of Christian humanism. He seems to have derived the subject of *Knight, Death, and Devil* from the *Manual of the Christian Soldier* by Erasmus of Rotterdam, the greatest of Northern humanists. It is the first of three engravings that were probably conceived as a unified program, as Dürer often sold them as a set. Taken together, they are an unusually personal statement. A *St. Jerome in His Study* complements the knight of action, who carries his faith into the world, with one who pursues it through private meditation.

The last of the trilogy, *Melencolia I* (fig. 704), is the very antithesis of the other two. One of the Four Temperaments, she holds the tools of geometry, yet is surrounded by chaos. She thinks but cannot act, while the infant scrawling on the slate, who symbolizes Practical Knowledge, can act but not

704. Albrecht Dürer. *Melencolia I.* 1514. Engraving, 9³/8 x 6⁵/8"
(23.8 x 16.8 cm). National Gallery of Art, Washington, D.C.
Rosenwald Collection

705. Albrecht Dürer. *The Four Apostles.* 1523–26. Oil on panel, each 7'1" x 2'6" (2.16 x .76 m).
Alte Pinakothek, Munich

think. This is, then, the melancholia of an artist, perhaps Dürer himself. He cannot achieve perfect beauty, which is known only to God, because he cannot extend his thinking beyond the limits of space and the physical world. The conception of this disturbing image comes from the humanist Marsilio Ficino, who esteemed melancholia (to which he was himself subject) as the source of divine inspiration. He tied it to Saturn, the Mind of the World, which, as the oldest and highest of the planets, he deemed superior even to Jupiter, the Soul of the World. It is evident, however, that in contrasting

the ineffectiveness of *Melencolia,* who derives her tools from Saturn, to the spiritual achievements of the knight and saint, Dürer asserts the superiority of faith over reason.

Not surprisingly, Dürer became an early and enthusiastic follower of Martin Luther, although, like Grünewald, he continued to work for Catholic patrons. His new faith can be sensed in the growing austerity of style and subject in his religious works after 1520. The climax of this trend is represented by *The Four Apostles* (fig. 705), paired panels containing what has rightly been termed Dürer's artistic testament.

706. Lucas Cranach
the Elder. *The Judgment of
Paris.* 1530. Oil on panel,
$13^{1}/2$ x $9^{1}/2$"
(34.3 x 24.2 cm).
Staatliche Kunsthalle,
Karlsruhe, Germany

Dürer presented the panels in 1526 to the city of Nuremberg, which had joined the Lutheran camp the year before. The chosen apostles are basic to Protestant doctrine: John and Paul face one another in the foreground, with Peter and Mark behind. Quotations from their writings, inscribed below in Luther's translation, warn the city government not to mistake human error and pretense for the will of God. They plead against Catholics and ultrazealous Protestant radicals alike. But in another, more universal sense, the figures represent the Four Temperaments and, by implication, the other cosmic quartets—the seasons, the elements, the times of day, and the ages of life—encircling, like the cardinal points of the compass, the Deity who is at the invisible center of this "triptych." In keeping with their role, the apostles have a cubic severity and grandeur such as we have not encountered since Masaccio and Piero della Francesca. That the style of *The Four Apostles* has evoked the names of these great Italians is no coincidence, for Dürer devoted a good part of his last years to the theory of art, including a treatise on geometry based on a thorough study of Piero della Francesca's discourse on perspective.

CRANACH THE ELDER. Dürer's hope for a monumental art embodying the Protestant faith remained unfulfilled.

Other German painters, notably Lucas Cranach the Elder (1472–1553), also tried to cast Luther's doctrines into visual form, but created no viable tradition. On his way to Vienna around 1500, Cranach had probably visited Dürer in Nuremberg. In any event, he fell early on under the influence of Dürer's work, which he turned to for inspiration throughout his career but invested with a highly individual expression. In 1504 Cranach left Vienna for Wittenberg, then a center of humanist learning. There he became court painter to Frederick the Wise of Saxony, as well as a close friend of Martin Luther, who even served as godfather to one of his children. Like Grünewald and Dürer, Cranach relied on Catholic patronage, but some of his altars have a Protestant content; ironically, they lack the fervor of those he painted before his conversion. Such efforts to embody Luther's doctrines in art were doomed, since the spiritual leaders of the Reformation looked upon religious images with indifference or, more often, outright hostility, even though Luther himself seems to have been relatively tolerant of them.

Cranach is best remembered today for his portraits and his delightfully incongruous mythological scenes. In *The Judgment of Paris* (fig. 706), nothing could be less classical than the three coquettish damsels, whose wriggly nakedness fits the

707. Albrecht Altdorfer. *The Battle of Issus*. 1529. Oil on panel, 62 x 47" (157.5 x 119.5 cm). Alte Pinakothek, Munich

Northern background better than does the nudity of Dürer's *Adam and Eve*. Paris is a German knight clad in fashionable armor, indistinguishable from the nobles at the court of Saxony who were the artist's patrons. The playful eroticism, small size, and precise, miniaturelike detail of the picture make it plainly a collector's item, attuned to the tastes of a provincial aristocracy.

Cranach's contribution lies above all in the handling of the landscape, which lends Dürer's naturalism a lively fantasy through the ornate treatment of forms, such as the crinkly veg-

etation. Cranach had formulated this manner soon after arriving in Vienna. It played a critical role in the formation of the Danube School, which culminated in the work of Albrecht Altdorfer (c. 1480–1538), a somewhat younger artist than Cranach who spent most of his career in Bavaria.

ALTDORFER. As remote from the classic ideal, but far more impressive, is Altdorfer's *Battle of Issus* (fig. 707). We could not possibly identify the subject, Alexander's victory over Darius, without the text on the tablet suspended in the sky and the inscriptions on the banners (they were probably written by the Regensburg court humanist Aventinus) or the label on Darius' fleeing chariot. The artist has tried to follow ancient descriptions of the actual number and kind of combatants in the battle. To accomplish this, he adopts a bird's-eye view, so that the two protagonists are lost in the antlike mass of their own armies. (Contrast the Hellenistic representation of the same subject in fig. 199.)

However, the soldiers' armor and the fortified town in the distance are unmistakably of the sixteenth century. The picture commemorates a major contemporary battle that took place in 1529, the year this panel was painted. At that time the Turks unsuccessfully invaded Vienna after gaining control over much of Eastern Europe. (They were to threaten the imperial city repeatedly for another 250 years.) Neither the Hapsburg emperor Charles V, the most powerful leader in Europe, nor Suleiman the Magnificent, the Turkish sultan, was present at this battle; yet, the painting proclaims Charles a new Alexander in his victory over Suleiman, the modern-day counterpart to Darius, who likewise became the ruler of a vast empire before his defeat at Issus.

To suggest its importance, Altdorfer treats the event as allegory: the sun triumphantly breaks through the clouds of the spectacular sky and "defeats" the moon, representing the Turkish Crescent. We have seen the same battle of good versus evil symbolized by the sun and moon in the Zoroastrian relief of *Mithras Slaying the Sacred Bull* (fig. 294). The celestial drama above a vast Alpine landscape, obviously correlated with the human contest below, raises the scene to the cosmic level. This is strikingly similar to the vision of the Heavenly Host above the Virgin and Child in the *Isenheim Altarpiece* (see fig. 697) by Grünewald, who influenced Altdorfer earlier in his career.

Music and Theater in the Northern Renaissance

The most significant musical development of the Reformation was the introduction of congregational singing in the services of the Protestant churches. The reformer Martin Luther, himself a singer and composer, admired the sophisticated polyphony of Josquin Des Prés, whose music he retained for use by choirs in the Latin Mass. Luther also believed strongly in the educational value of music, and he wanted every member of the church to participate in the service by singing. So in 1524 he wrote a German Mass with chorales—simple hymns to be sung by the congregation—based on traditional chants and secular songs for use especially in parishes without professional choirs. The Swiss reformer John Calvin, on the other hand, objected to hymns based on new poems, and insisted that only the Word of God be sung in church. The result was the Calvinist psalter: Old Testament psalms set to traditional melodies, generally sung in unison. Another form of Protestant music was the English anthem, a kind of motet that could be "full" (sung by the choir *a cappella*, "without accompaniment") or "verse" (for soloists with chorus and instruments).

In secular music, the most popular form throughout Northern Europe was the madrigal. Its chief exponent was Roland de Lassus (1532–1594), a Fleming who had lived in Italy as a youth, but spent most of his career in Munich. Widely regarded as the leading composer of his day, he was the equal of Giovanni Palestrina as a writer of religious music; but because his temperament was more secular, many of his religious compositions are parody masses (see page 517). In his later years he devoted himself chiefly to madrigals and motets. In its impulsive leaps, irregular rhythms, and dramatic harmonies, his style anticipates the bold brilliance of Carlo Gesualdo (see page 558). During the reign of Elizabeth I (1558–1603), the English developed a distinguished madrigal school under Thomas Morley (1557–c. 1602), Thomas Weelkes (c. 1575–1623), John Wilbye (1574–1638), and John Dowland (1563–1626), whose lute songs are sensitive settings of poems by Shakespeare and his contemporaries.

It is utterly remarkable that English theater developed into greatness during the late sixteenth century. Its tradition was deeply rooted in medieval religious drama, and secular theater reached back only to about 1520. When Queen Elizabeth suppressed religious theater in the 1570s, secular theater came to the fore under humanist influence at schools, universities, and inns—colleges where young men completed their education—despite the fact that theater was strictly regulated by the Master of the Revels. Yet neither the decline of religious theater nor the influence of the humanists can account satisfactorily for the enthusiastic support of theater throughout the realm—ten public outdoor theaters were built in London between 1567 and 1642, in addition to numerous private indoor theaters—or the sudden appearance of four very fine playwrights within just a few years. Thomas Kyd (1558–1594) inaugurated the theme of revenge with *The Spanish Tragedy* (c. 1587); Christopher Marlowe (1564–1593) presented the great morality play of the day in *Dr. Faustus* (c. 1588); John Lyly (c. 1553–1606) used classical mythology to flatter the queen in *Endimion* (c. 1588); and Robert Greene (c. 1558–1592) helped to introduce the history, or chronicle, drama with *James IV* (c. 1591). Shortly before, William Shakespeare (1564–1616) had written *Henry VI* (1590). Of these playwrights, Shakespeare was incomparably the finest. His plays featured bold plots (many of them drawn from English history and patterned after Roman dramas), and they refrained from conventional moralizing and traditional happy endings in favor of tragedy of unrelenting darkness. His greatness lies in his use of blank verse (unrhymed, although metrical composition), which he perfected into a poetic language of infinite richness and subtlety able to express any thought or mood on a transcendent, indeed universal, plane.

Shakespeare's only serious rival in popularity was Ben Jonson (1572–1637), the leading classicist of the 1590s, whose theories followed those of Giulio Scaliger and Lodovico Castelvetro (see page 607). It was Jonson who published the first integrated edition of Shakespeare's works upon his death in 1616, thereby establishing the primacy of the playwright as a literary figure. Nevertheless, Jonson primarily wrote tragi-comedies for reforming behavior based on Italian examples, which made him a great favorite at the court of James I, Elizabeth's successor.

708. Hans Baldung Grien. *Death and the Maiden*. c. 1510. Oil on panel, 15³/₄ x 12³/₄" (40 x 32.4 cm).
Kunsthistorisches Museum, Vienna

Altdorfer may indeed be viewed as a later, and lesser, Grünewald. Although Altdorfer, too, was an architect, well acquainted with perspective and the Italian stylistic vocabulary, his paintings show the unruly imagination already familiar from the work of the older painter. But Altdorfer is also unlike Grünewald. He treats the human figure with ironic intent by making it incidental to the spatial setting, whether natural or architectural. The tiny soldiers of *The Battle of Issus* have their counterpart in his other late pictures, and he painted at least one landscape with no figures at all—the earliest "pure" landscape we know of since antiquity. (Dürer's sketch, *Italian Mountains,* fig. 699, after all, is not a finished work of art.)

BALDUNG GRIEN. Altdorfer's fantastic landscape partakes of the imaginative qualities to be found in paintings by Hans Baldung Grien (1484/5–1545). This former apprentice of

Dürer spent much of his career in Strasbourg, which is not far from Isenheim and, like Nuremberg and Wittenberg, was a center of humanism. Yet he was fascinated above all with the magical and the demonic, which exemplify the dark side of the Renaissance. Humanism and the occult may be viewed as two sides of the same coin. Since the late thirteenth century, humanists had been nearly as interested in the treatises of the ancients on magic as in their literature and learning. In fact, the key text of Renaissance magic, the *Corpus Hermeticum,* was translated by the humanist Marsilio Ficino. But whereas the occult only rarely makes an appearance in Italian art, it was the object of continuing fascination in the North. Nowhere is this better seen than in Baldung Grien's *Death and the Maiden* (fig. 708). Clearly based on Dürer's *Eve* (see fig. 702), she is the personification of Vanitas, signifying the triumph of Death over Beauty. The three ages of life—infancy, adulthood, old age—are repeated in the mirror, where three heads stare out at the young woman, who nevertheless examines her features serenely.

The painting epitomizes the prophetic and demonic powers of the convex mirror. In antiquity, mirrors had often served as attributes of goddesses and sometimes of mortal women, such as brides. The motif of a woman contemplating her beauty reappeared in Gothic cycles of the Vices and Virtues. This moralizing tradition was revived after 1500 as part of a widespread renewal of Gothic piety and mysticism during the Reformation. It was closely linked in turn to resurgent occultism at a time when rationalism seemed inadequate to explain the world. Because of their association with light, mirrors have often had mystical connotations throughout history, and reflected images were widely valued for their revelatory power. At the same time, supernatural qualities were attributed to them in folklore as a means of effecting hexes and other forms of black magic.

Initially the convex mirror expressed the "Late Gothic" fascination with the visible world, as we have seen in Jan van Eyck's *Arnolfini Portrait* (fig. 677), which was painted within a few decades after mirrors began to be manufactured from polished metal. After 1500 the convex mirror came to be used almost exclusively as a Vanitas symbol, due to its extreme distortions, which heighten visionary reality; this, too, had its origin in another work by Jan. In Baldung Grien's painting, the characteristic image became a nude woman holding a convex mirror. It is used to convey a tragic vision of life to chilling effect through the striking contrast between the sensual nude and the grinning corpse, who holds an hourglass above her head as the horrified man vainly tries to stay Death's hand.

709. Hans Holbein the Younger. *Erasmus of Rotterdam.* c. 1523. Oil on panel, 16^1/2 x 12^1/2" (42 x 31.4 cm). Musée du Louvre, Paris

Portraiture

HOLBEIN. Gifted though they were, Cranach and Altdorfer both evaded the main challenge of the Renaissance so bravely faced, if not always mastered, by Dürer: the human image. Their style, antimonumental and miniaturelike, set the pace for dozens of lesser masters. Perhaps the rapid decline of German art after Dürer's death was due to a failure of ambition among artists and patrons alike. The career of Hans Holbein the Younger (1497–1543), the one painter of whom this is not true, confirms the general rule. The son of an important artist, he was born and raised in Augsburg, a center of international commerce in southern Germany particularly open to Renaissance ideas, but left at the age of 18 with his brother to seek work in Switzerland. Thanks in large part to the help of humanist patrons, he was firmly established in Basel by 1520 as a designer of woodcuts, a splendid decorator, and an incisive portraitist. Holbein took Dürer as his point of departure, but almost from the beginning his religious paintings and portraits show a keen interest in the Italian Renaissance, including the latest tendencies, especially from Venice and Rome.

Holbein's likeness of Erasmus of Rotterdam (fig. 709), painted soon after the famous author had settled in Basel, gives us a truly memorable image, at once intimate and monumental. This kind of profile view had been popular during the Early Renaissance. Here it has been reinterpreted with a characteristically Northern emphasis on tangible reality to convey the sitter's personality that is nevertheless thoroughly in keeping with High Renaissance ideas. The very ideal of the humanist scholar, this doctor of humane letters has a calm rationality that lends him an intellectual authority formerly reserved for the Doctors of the Church.

Holbein spent 1523–24 traveling in France, apparently with the intention of offering his services to Francis I. When he returned two years later, Basel was in the throes of the Reformation crisis, and he went to England, hoping for commissions at the court of Henry VIII. He bore with him the portrait of Erasmus in figure 709 as a gift to the humanist Thomas More, who became his first patron in London. (Erasmus, recommending him to More, wrote: "Here [in Basel] the arts are out in the cold.") On his return to Basel in 1528, he saw fanatical Protestant mobs destroying religious images as "idols," and reluctantly abandoned Catholicism. Despite the entreaties of the city council, Holbein departed for London four years later. He went back to Basel only once, in 1538, while traveling on the Continent as court painter to Henry VIII, who had More beheaded in 1525 for refusing to consent to the Act of Supremacy that made the king the head of the Church of England. The council made a last attempt to keep Holbein at home, but he had become an artist of international fame to whom Basel now seemed provincial indeed.

710. Hans Holbein the Younger. *Henry VIII.* 1540. Oil on panel, 32¹/₂ x 29" (82.6 x 74.5 cm). Galleria Nazionale d'Arte Antica, Rome

Holbein's style, too, had gained an international flavor. His portrait of Henry VIII (fig. 710) has the rigid frontality of Dürer's self-portrait (see fig. 701), but its purpose is to convey the almost divine authority of the absolute ruler. The monarch's physical bulk creates an overpowering sensation of his ruthless, commanding presence. The portrait of the king shares with Bronzino's *Eleanora of Toledo* (see fig. 644) the immobile pose, the air of unapproachability, and the precisely rendered costume and jewels. Holbein's picture, unlike Bronzino's, does not yet reflect the Mannerist ideal of elegance, but both clearly belong to the same species of court portrait. The link between the two may lie in such French works as Jean Clouet's *Francis I* (fig. 711), which Holbein could have seen on his travels. (For Francis I as a patron of Italian Mannerists, see page 496.) The type evidently was coined at the royal court of France, where its ancestry can be traced back as far as Jean Fouquet (see fig. 687). It gained international currency between 1525 and 1550 as reflecting a new aristocratic ideal.

Although Holbein's pictures molded British taste in aristocratic portraiture for decades, he had no English disciples of real talent. The Elizabethan genius was more literary and musical than visual, and the demand for portraits in the later sixteenth century continued to be filled largely by visiting foreign artists.

HILLIARD. The most notable English painter of the period was Nicholas Hilliard (1547–1619), a goldsmith who also

711. Jean Clouet. *Francis I.* c. 1525–30. Tempera and oil on panel, 37³/4 x 29" (96 x 74.5 cm). Musée du Louvre, Paris

712. Nicholas Hilliard. *A Young Man Among Roses.* c. 1588.
Oil on parchment, shown at actual size, 5³/8 x 2³/4" (13.7 x 7 cm).
Victoria & Albert Museum, London

specialized in miniature portraits on parchment, tiny keep-sakes often worn by their owners as jewelry. These "portable portraits" had been invented in antiquity and were revived in the fifteenth century. Holbein, too, produced miniature por-traits, which Hilliard acknowledged to be his model. We see this link with the older artist in the even lighting and meticu-lous detail of *A Young Man Among Roses* (fig. 712), but the elongated proportions and the pose of languorous grace come from Italian Mannerism, probably via Fontainebleau (com-pare fig. 658). Our lovesick youth also strikes us as the descen-dant of the fashionable attendants at the court of the duke of Berry. We can imagine him besieging his lady with sonnets and madrigals before presenting her with this exquisite token of devotion.

THE NETHERLANDS

Painting

The Netherlands in the sixteenth century had the most tur-bulent and painful history of any country north of the Alps.

When the Reformation began, they were part of the far-flung empire of the Hapsburgs under Charles V, who was also king of Spain. Protestantism quickly became powerful in The Netherlands, and the attempts of the crown to suppress it led to open revolt against foreign rule. After a bloody struggle, the northern provinces (today's Holland) emerged at the end of the century as an independent state, while the southern ones (roughly corresponding to modern Belgium) remained in Spanish hands.

The religious and political strife might have had cata-strophic effects on the arts, yet this, astonishingly, did not hap-pen. The art of the period, to be sure, does not equal that of the fifteenth century in brilliance, nor did it produce any pio-neers of the Northern Renaissance comparable to Dürer and Holbein. This region absorbed Italian elements more slowly than Germany, but more steadily and systematically, so that instead of a few isolated peaks of achievement we find a con-tinuous range. Between 1550 and 1600, their most troubled time, The Netherlands produced the major painters of North-ern Europe, who paved the way for the great Dutch and Flem-ish masters of the next century.

Two main concerns, sometimes separate, sometimes inter-woven, characterize Netherlandish sixteenth-century paint-ing: to assimilate Italian art from Raphael to Tintoretto (albeit in an often dry and didactic manner), and to develop a reper-tory supplementing, and eventually replacing, the traditional religious subjects.

"MANNERISM" AND ROMANISM. When Flanders passed from Burgundy to Spain in 1482, Antwerp, with its deep harbor, superseded Ghent and Bruges as the political, commercial, and artistic capital of The Netherlands. Flemish artists spent the next quarter-century largely imitating earlier Netherlandish painting. Then, around 1507, we find two im-portant new developments. "Antwerp Mannerism" is the mis-leading label applied to the largely anonymous school of painters which first arose in that city. Their preference for elongated forms, decorative surfaces, and arbitrary space seems to reassert Late Gothic tendencies, although the simi-larities are superficial at best. Actually, the style bore no direct relation to either the Renaissance or Mannerism in Italy. Still, the term is not without foundation. It suggests the peculiar fla-vor of their work, for it represented a "mannered" response to the "classics" by Jan van Eyck, Rogier van der Weyden, and their successors. Almost simultaneously, a second group of Netherlandish artists, the so-called Romanists, began to visit Italy in the wake of Albrecht Dürer and returned home with the latest tendencies. The preceding generation of Flemish painters had already shown a growing interest in Renaissance art and humanism, but none ventured below the Alps, so that they assimilated both at second hand.

GOSSAERT. The greatest of the Romanists, Jan Gossaert (c. 1478–1532; nicknamed Mabuse, for his hometown), was also the first to travel south. In 1508 he accompanied Philip of Burgundy to Italy, where the Renaissance and antiquity made a deep impression on him. He nevertheless viewed this experience through characteristically Northern eyes. Except for their greater monumentality, his religious subjects were

713. Jan Gossaert. *Danaë*. 1527. Oil on panel, 44^1/$_2$ x 37^3/$_8$" (113 x 95 cm).
Alte Pinakothek, Munich

based on fifteenth-century Netherlandish art, and he often found it easier to assimilate Italian classicism through the intermediary of Dürer's prints. *Danaë* (fig. 713), painted toward the end of Gossaert's career, is his most thoroughly Italianate work. In true humanist fashion, the subject of Jupiter's seduction of the mortal is treated as a pagan equivalent of the Annunciation, so that the picture may be seen as a chaste counterpart to Correggio's *Jupiter and Io* (fig. 655). The god enters Danaë's chambers, where she has been confined by her father against all suitors, disguised as a shower of gold comparable to the miraculous stream of light in the *Mérode Altarpiece* (fig. 671). Her partial nudity notwithstanding, she appears as modest as the Virgin in any Annunciation. Indeed, she hardly differs in type from Gossaert's paintings of the Madonna and Child, inspired equally by Van Eyck and Raphael. She even wears the blue robe traditional to Mary. The linear perspective of the architectural fantasy, compiled largely from Italian treatises, marks a revolution. Never before

have we encountered such a systematic treatment of space in The Netherlands.

STILL LIFE, LANDSCAPE, GENRE. Later religious art in The Netherlands presents a fusion of Antwerp Mannerism and Romanism, which produced a distinctive strain of Northern Mannerism that persisted until the end of the century. After 1550, however, narrative painting was largely supplanted by the secular themes that loom so large in Dutch and Flemish painting of the Baroque era: landscape, still life, and genre (scenes of everyday life). The process was gradual—it began around 1500 and was not complete until 1600—and was shaped less by the genius of individual artists than by the need to cater to popular taste as church commissions became steadily scarcer. (Protestant iconoclastic zeal was particularly widespread in The Netherlands.) Still life, landscape, and genre had been part of the Flemish tradition since the Master of Flémalle and the brothers Van Eyck. In the *Mérode Altar-*

714. Joachim Patinir. *Landscape with St. Jerome Removing the Thorn from the Lion's Paw.* c. 1520.
Oil on panel, 29¹/₈ x 35⁷/₈" (74 x 91 cm). Museo del Prado, Madrid

piece (fig. 671) we remember the objects grouped on the Virgin's table and the scene of Joseph in his workshop, or think of the setting of the Van Eyck *Crucifixion* (fig. 672). But these had remained ancillary elements, governed by the principle of disguised symbolism and subordinated to the devotional purpose of the whole. Now they acquired a new independence, until they became so dominant that the religious subject could be relegated to the background.

PATINIR. We see the beginnings of this approach in the paintings of Joachim Patinir (c. 1485–1524). *Landscape with St. Jerome Removing the Thorn from the Lion's Paw* (fig. 714) reveals him as the heir of Bosch in both his treatment of nature and choice of subject, but without the strange demonic overtones of *The Garden of Delights* (see fig. 684). Although the landscape dominates the scene, the figures, rather than being incidental, are central to it, both visually and iconographically. The landscape has been constructed around the hermit in

his cave, which could exist happily in another setting, whereas the picture would be incomplete without it. St. Jerome is an allegory of the pilgrimage of life, contrasting the way of the world with the road to salvation through ascetic withdrawal. (Note the two pilgrims wending their way up the hill to the right, past the lion hunt which takes place unnoticed by them.) The church on the mountain represents the Heavenly Jerusalem, which can be reached only by passing directly through the hermit's cave (compare fig. 592). Like Bosch, Patinir reveals a fundamental ambivalence toward his subject, for the vista in the background, with its well-kept fields and tidy villages, is enchanting in its own right. Yet, he seems to tell us, we should not be distracted from the path of righteousness by these temptations.

AERTSEN. Pieter Aertsen (1508/9–1575) is remembered today mainly as a pioneer of still lifes, but he seems to have first painted such pictures as a sideline, until he saw many of his

715. Pieter Aertsen. *The Meat Stall*. 1551. Oil on panel, 48$^{1}/_{2}$ x 59" (123.3 x 150 cm). University Art Collections, Uppsala University, Sweden

altarpieces destroyed by iconoclasts. *The Meat Stall* (fig. 715), done a few years before he moved from Antwerp to Amsterdam, seems at first glance to be an essentially secular picture. The tiny, distant figures are almost blotted out by the avalanche of edibles in the foreground. We see little interest here in selection or formal arrangement. The objects, piled in heaps or strung from poles, are meant to overwhelm us with their sensuous reality (the panel is nearly lifesize). Here the still life so dominates the picture that it seems independent of the religious subject. The latter, however, is not merely a pretext to justify the painting; it must be integral to the meaning of the scene. In the background to the left we see the Virgin on the Flight into Egypt giving bread to the poor, who are ignored by the faithful lined up for church, while to the right is a tavern scene with the prodigal son.

The Northern Mannerists often relegated subject matter to a minor position within their compositions. This "inverted" perspective was a favorite device of Aertsen's younger contemporary, Pieter Bruegel the Elder, who treated it with ironic intent in his landscapes. Aertsen belonged to the same tradition, whose greatest representative was the humanist Erasmus of Rotterdam (see page 531). *The Meat Stall* is, then, a moralizing sermon on charity and gluttony. Not until around 1600 was this vision replaced as part of a larger change in world view (see page 540). Only then did it no longer prove necessary to include religious or historical scenes in still lifes and landscapes.

BRUEGEL THE ELDER. The only genius among these Netherlandish painters, Pieter Bruegel the Elder (1525/30–1569), explored landscape and peasant life. Although his career was spent in Antwerp and Brussels, he may have been born near 's Hertogenbosch, the home of Hieronymus Bosch.

Certainly Bosch's work impressed him deeply, and he is in many ways as puzzling to us as the older master. What were his religious convictions, his political sympathies? We know little about him, but his preoccupation with folk customs and the daily life of humble people seems to have sprung from a complex philosophical attitude. Bruegel was highly educated, the friend of humanists, who, with wealthy merchants, were his main clients, though he was also patronized by the Hapsburg court. Yet he apparently never worked for the Church, and when he dealt with religious subjects he did so in a strangely ambiguous way.

His attitude toward Italian art is also hard to define. A trip to the South in 1552–53 took him to Rome, Naples, and the Strait of Messina, but the famous monuments admired by other Northerners seem not to have interested him. He returned instead with a sheaf of magnificent landscape drawings, especially Alpine views. He was probably much impressed by landscape painting in Venice, above all its integration of figures and scenery and the progression in space from foreground to background (see figs. 631 and 632).

Out of this experience came such sweeping landscapes in Bruegel's mature style as *The Return of the Hunters* (fig. 716), one of a set depicting the months. (He typically composed in series.) Such cycles, we recall, had begun with medieval calendar illustrations, and Bruegel's winter scene shows its descent from *Les Très Riches Heures du Duc de Berry*. Now, however, nature is more than a setting for human activities. It is the main subject of the picture. Men and women in their seasonal occupations are incidental to the majestic annual cycle of death and rebirth that is the breathing rhythm of the cosmos.

The *Peasant Wedding* (fig. 717) is Bruegel's most memo-

716. Pieter Bruegel the Elder. *The Return of the Hunters.* 1565. Oil on panel, 46¹/₂ x 63³/₄" (117 x 162 cm).
Kunsthistorisches Museum, Vienna

717. Pieter Bruegel the Elder. *Peasant Wedding.* c. 1565.
Oil on panel, 44⁷/₈ x 64" (114 x 162.5 cm). Kunsthistorisches Museum, Vienna

718. Pieter Bruegel the Elder. *The Blind Leading the Blind.* c. 1568. Oil on panel, 34¹/₂ x 60⁵/₈" (85 x 154 cm). Museo di Capodimonte, Naples

rable scene of peasant life. These are stolid, crude folk, heavy-bodied and slow, yet their very clumsiness gives them a strange gravity that commands our respect. Painted in flat colors with minimal modeling and no cast shadows, the figures nevertheless have a weight and solidity that remind us of Giotto. Space is created in assured perspective, and the entire composition is as monumental and balanced as that of any Italian master. Why, we wonder, did Bruegel endow this commonplace ceremony with the solemnity of a biblical event? It is because he saw in the life of these rural people the natural condition of humanity. We know from his biographer, Karel van Mander (the Netherlandish "Vasari"), that Bruegel and his patron Hans Franckert often disguised themselves as peasants and joined them in their revelries. There Bruegel would draw them from life. In his hands, they become types whose follies he knew at first hand, yet whose dignity remains intact. For him, Everyman occupies an important place in the scheme of things.

Bruegel's philosophical detachment, which was shared by his fellow humanists, also informs one of his last pictures, *The Blind Leading the Blind* (fig. 718). Its source is the Gospels (Matthew 15:12–19): Jesus, speaking of the Pharisees, says, "And if the blind lead the blind, both shall fall into the ditch." This parable of human folly recurs in humanistic as well as popular literature, and we know it in at least one earlier representation, but the tragic depth of Bruegel's forceful image gives new urgency to the theme. He has used continuous narrative to ingenious effect. Each succeeding pose becomes progressively more unstable along the downward diagonal, leaving us in little doubt that everyone will end up in the ditch with the leader. (The gap behind him is especially telling.) Perhaps he found the biblical context of the parable specially relevant to his time, which was marked by religious and political fanaticism, for Jesus continued: "Out of the heart proceed evil thoughts, murders . . . blasphemies." Could Bruegel have thought that this applied to the controversies then raging over details of religious ritual?

FRANCE

Architecture and Sculpture

It took the Northern countries longer to assimilate Italian forms in architecture and sculpture than in painting. France was more closely linked with Italy than the rest. We will recall that it had conquered Milan in 1499, and that King Francis I had shown his admiration for Italian art earlier by inviting first Leonardo and then several Mannerists to France (see page 483). As a consequence, France began to assimilate Italian art somewhat earlier than the other countries and was the first to achieve an integrated Renaissance style. We shall therefore confine our discussion to French monuments.

SOHIER. As we might expect, architects still trained in the Gothic tradition could not adopt the Italian style all at once. They readily used its classical vocabulary, but its syntax gave them trouble for many years. One glance at the choir of St.-Pierre at Caen (fig. 719), built by Hector Sohier, shows that he followed the basic pattern of French Gothic church choirs (compare fig. 430), simply translating flamboyant decoration

719. Hector Sohier. Choir of St.-Pierre, Caen, France. 1528–45

720. The Château of Chambord (north front), France. Begun 1519

721. Plan of center portion, Château of Chambord (after Du Cerceau)

into the vocabulary of the new language. Finials become candelabra, pier buttresses are shaped like pilasters, and the round-arched windows of the ambulatory chapels have geometric tracery.

CHÂTEAU OF CHAMBORD. The Château of Chambord (fig. 720) is stylistically more complicated. Its plan, and the turrets, high-pitched roofs, and tall chimneys, recall the Gothic Louvre. Yet the design, though greatly modified by later French builders, was originally by an Italian pupil of Giuliano da Sangallo, and his was surely the plan of the center portion (fig. 721), which is quite unlike its French predecessors. This square block, developed from the keep of medieval castles (see page 335), has a central staircase fed by four corridors. These

722. Pierre Lescot. Square Court of the Louvre, Paris. Begun 1546

form a Greek cross dividing the interior into four square sections. Each section is further subdivided into one large and two smaller rooms, and a closet, forming a suite, or apartment, in modern parlance. The functional grouping of these rooms, originally imported from Italy, was to become a standard pattern in France. It represents the starting point of all modern "designs for living."

LESCOT. Francis I, who built Chambord, decided in 1546 to replace the old Gothic royal castle, the Louvre, with a new palace on the old site. The project had barely begun at the time of his death, but his architect, Pierre Lescot (c. 1515–1578), continued it under Henry II, quadrupling the size of the court. This enlarged scheme was not completed for more than a century. Lescot built only the southern half of the court's west side (fig. 722), which represents its "classic" phase, so called to distinguish it from the style of such buildings as Chambord. This distinction is well warranted. The Italian vocabulary of Chambord and St.-Pierre at Caen is based on the Early Renaissance, whereas Lescot drew on the work of Bramante and his successors. Lescot's design is classic in another sense as well: it is the finest surviving example of Northern Renaissance architecture.

The details of Lescot's facade do indeed have an astonishing classical purity, yet we would not mistake it for an Italian structure. Its distinctive quality comes not from Italian forms superficially applied, but from a genuine synthesis of the traditional château with the Renaissance palazzo. Italian are the superimposed classical orders (see figs. 566 and 662), the pedimented window frames, and the arcade on the ground floor. But the continuity of the facade is interrupted by three projecting pavilions that have supplanted the château turrets, and the high-pitched roof is also traditionally French. The vertical accents thus overcome the horizonal ones (note the broken architraves), an effect reinforced by the tall, narrow windows.

723, 724. Jean Goujon. Reliefs from the Fontaine des Innocents,
Paris. 1548–49

GOUJON. Equally un-Italian is the rich sculptural decoration covering almost the entire wall surface of the third story. These reliefs, admirably adapted to the architecture, are by Jean Goujon (c. 1510–1565?), the finest French sculptor of the mid-sixteenth century. Unfortunately, they have been much restored. To get a more precise idea of Goujon's style we must turn to the relief panels from the Fontaine des Innocents (two are shown in figs. 723 and 724), which have survived intact, although their architectural framework by Lescot is lost. These graceful figures recall the Mannerism of Cellini (see fig. 657) and, even more, Primaticcio's decorations at Fontainebleau (see fig. 658). Like Lescot's architecture, their design combines classical details of remarkable purity with a delicate slenderness that gives them a uniquely French air.

CHAPTER SIX

THE BAROQUE IN ITALY AND SPAIN

What is Baroque? Like Mannerism, the term was originally coined to disparage the very style it designates. It meant "irregular, contorted, grotesque." Art historians otherwise remain divided over its definition. Should Baroque be used only for the dominant style of the seventeenth century, or should it include other tendencies, such as classicism, to which it bears a complex relationship? Should the time frame be extended to cover the period 1700–1750, known as the Rococo? More important, is the Baroque an era distinct from both Renaissance and modern, or the final phase of the Renaissance? Although a good case can be made for viewing the Baroque as the end of the Renaissance, we shall, for convenience, look at it here as a distinct era. Which of the alternatives is adopted is perhaps less important than an understanding of the factors that must enter into our decision.

The fact is that the Baroque eludes simple classification. Rather, it was a time full of inner contradictions, not unlike the present, and thus peculiarly fascinating to us. Hence, we run into a series of paradoxes typical of the conflicting nature of the Baroque. It has been claimed that the Baroque style expresses the spirit of the Counter Reformation, which, however, had already done its work by 1600. Catholicism had recaptured much of its former territory, and Protestantism was on the defensive, so that neither side any longer had the power to upset the new balance. As if to signify the triumph of the old faith, in 1622 the heroes of the Counter Reformation—Ignatius of Loyola, Francis Xavier (both Jesuits), Theresa of Avila, Filippo Neri, and Isidoro Agricola—were named saints (Carlo Borromeo had been made one in 1610), beginning a wave of canonizations that lasted through the mid-eighteenth century. In contrast to the piety and good deeds of these reformers, the new princes of the Church who

supported the growth of Baroque art were known primarily for worldly splendor.

Another reason why we should guard against overemphasizing the Baroque's ties to the Counter Reformation is that, unlike Mannerism, the new style was not specifically Italian, although historians generally agree that it was born in Rome during the final years of the sixteenth century. Nor was it confined to religious art. Baroque elements quickly penetrated the Protestant North, where they were applied primarily to other subjects.

Equally problematic is the assertion that Baroque is "the style of absolutism," reflecting the centralized state ruled by an autocrat of unlimited powers. Although absolutism reached its climax during the reign of Louis XIV in the later seventeenth century, it had been in the making since the 1520s (under Francis I in France and the Medici dukes in Tuscany). Moreover, Baroque art flourished in bourgeois Holland no less than in the absolutist monarchies, and the style officially sponsored under Louis XIV was a notably subdued, classicistic kind of Baroque.

It is nevertheless tempting to see the turbulent history of the era reflected in Baroque art, where the tensions of the era often seem to erupt into open conflict. The seventeenth century was one of almost continuous warfare, which involved virtually every nation in a complex web of shifting alliances. The Thirty Years' War (1618–1648) was fueled by the dynastic ambitions of the kings of France, who sought to exert their domination over Europe, and the Hapsburgs, who ruled Spain, The Netherlands, and Austria. Though fought largely in Germany, the war eventually engulfed nearly all of Europe, even absorbing the Dutch struggle for independence from Spain, which had been waged since 1581. After the Treaty of

Westphalia formally ended the war and granted their freedom, the United Provinces—as the independent Netherlands was known—entered into a series of battles with England and France for commercial and maritime supremacy that lasted until 1679. Yet, other than in Germany, which was left in ruins, there is little correlation between these rivalries and the art of the period. It is a remarkable fact that the seventeenth century has been called the Golden Age of painting in France, Holland, Flanders, and Spain. We look in vain, moreover, for the impact of these wars on Baroque imagery. Its chief manifestation is the etchings of Jacques Callot (see fig. 790), though we occasionally catch an indirect glimpse of it in Dutch militia scenes, such as Rembrandt's *Night Watch* (fig. 777).

We encounter similar difficulties when we try to relate Baroque art to the science and philosophy of the period. A direct link did exist in the Early and High Renaissance, when an artist then could also be a humanist and a scientist. During the seventeenth century, however, scientific and philosophical thought became too complex, abstract, and systematic for the artist to share. Gravitation and calculus could not stir the artist's imagination any more than Descartes' famous motto *Cogito, ergo sum* (I think, therefore I am).

There is nevertheless a relationship between Baroque art and science which, though subtle, is essential to an understanding of the entire age. The complex metaphysics of the humanists, which endowed everything with religious import, was replaced by a new physics, beginning with Copernicus, Kepler, and Galileo, and culminating in Descartes and Newton. They instituted a cosmology that severed the ties between sensory perception and science. By placing the sun, not the earth (and humanity), at the center of the universe, it contradicted what our eyes (and common sense) tell us: that the sun revolves around the earth. Scientists now defined underlying relationships in mathematical and geometrical terms as part of the simple, orderly system of mechanics. Not only was the seventeenth century's world view fundamentally different from what had preceded it, but its understanding of visual reality was forever altered by the new science, thanks to advances in optical physics and physiology. Thus we may say that the Baroque literally saw with new eyes.

The attack on Renaissance science and philosophy, which could trace their origins (and authority) back to antiquity, also had the effect of supplanting natural magic, a precursor of modern science that included both astrology and alchemy. The difference was that natural magic sought to exercise practical control of the world through prediction and manipulation, by uncovering nature's "secrets" instead of her laws. To be sure, traditional magic, linked as it was to religion and morality, continued to live on in popular literature and folklore long afterward.

In the end, Baroque art was not simply the result of religious, political, or intellectual developments. Let us therefore think of it as one among other basic features that distinguish the period from what had gone before: the refortified Catholic faith, the absolutist state, and the new role of science. These factors are combined in volatile mixtures that give Baroque its fascinating variety. Such diversity was perfectly suited to express the expanding view of life. What ultimately unites this refractory era is a reevaluation of humanity and its relation to the universe. Central to this image is the new psychology of the Baroque. A prominent role was now assigned by philosophers to human passion, which encompasses a wider range of emotions and social levels than ever before. The scientific revolution culminating in Newton's unified mechanics responded to the same impulses, for it assumes a more active role in our ability to understand and in turn affect the world around us. Remarkably, the Baroque remained an age of great religious faith, however divided it may have been in its loyalties. The counterpoint between the passions, intellect, and spirituality may be seen as forming a dialogue which has never been truly resolved.

PAINTING IN ITALY

Around 1600 Rome became the fountainhead of the Baroque, as it had of the High Renaissance a century before, by gathering artists from other regions to perform challenging new tasks. The papacy patronized art on a large scale with the aim of making Rome the most beautiful city of the Christian world "for the greater glory of God and the Church." This campaign had begun as early as 1585, but the artists then on hand were Late Mannerists of feeble distinction. Soon, however, it attracted ambitious young artists, especially from northern Italy, who created the new style.

CARAVAGGIO. Foremost among them was a painter of genius, Michelangelo Merisi, called Caravaggio after his birthplace near Milan (1571–1610). His first important religious commission was for a series of three monumental canvases devoted to St. Matthew that he painted for the Contarelli chapel in S. Luigi dei Francesi from 1599 to 1602 (fig. 725). As decorations they perform the same function that fresco cycles had in the Renaissance (compare fig. 561). Our view of the chapel includes *St. Matthew and the Angel,* in which the illiterate tax collector turns dramatically for inspiration to the angel who dictates the gospel. *The Calling of St. Matthew* (fig. 726), the most extraordinary picture of all, is remote from both Mannerism and the High Renaissance. Its only antecedent is the "North Italian realism" of artists like Savoldo (see fig. 651). But Caravaggio's realism is of a new and radical kind. According to contemporary accounts, Caravaggio painted directly on the canvas from the live model. He depicted the world he knew, so that his canvases are filled with ordinary people. Indeed, his pictures are often surprisingly autobiographical (see page 31).

Never have we seen a sacred subject depicted so entirely in terms of contemporary lowlife. Matthew, the tax gatherer, sits with some armed men (evidently his agents) in what is a common Roman tavern as two figures approach from the right. The arrivals are poor people, their bare feet and simple garments contrasting strongly with the colorful costumes of Matthew and his companions. For Caravaggio, however, naturalism is not an end in itself but a means of conveying profoundly religious content. Why do we sense a religious quality in this scene and do not mistake it for an everyday event? The answer is that Caravaggio's North Italian realism is wedded to elements derived from his study of Renaissance art in Rome, which lend the scene its surprising dignity. His style, in other

725. *(right)* Contarelli Chapel, S. Luigi dei Francesi, Rome

726. *(below)* Caravaggio. *The Calling of St. Matthew.* c. 1599–1602. Oil on canvas.11'1" x 11'5" (3.4 x 3.5 m). Contarelli Chapel, S. Luigi dei Francesi, Rome

727. Jusepe Ribera. St. *Jerome and the Angel of Judgment*. Oil on canvas, 8'7¹/8" x 5'4¹/2" (2.62 x 1.64 m). Museo e Gallerie Nazionali di Capodimonte, Naples

the mysteries of faith are revealed not by intellectual speculation but spontaneously, through an inward experience open to all people. What separates the Baroque from the later Counter Reformation is the externalization of the mystic vision, which appears to us complete, without any signs of the spiritual struggle in El Greco's art (see pages 490–93).

Caravaggio's paintings have a "lay Christianity" that appealed to Protestants no less than Catholics. This quality made possible his strong, though indirect, influence on Rembrandt, the greatest religious artist of the Protestant North. In Italy, Caravaggio fared less well. His work was acclaimed by artists and connoisseurs, but the ordinary people for whom it was intended resented meeting their own kind in these paintings; they preferred religious imagery of a more idealized and rhetorical sort. Conservative critics, moreover, regarded it as lacking decorum: the propriety and reverence demanded of religious subjects. For these reasons, Caravaggism largely ran its course by 1630, when it was assimilated into other Baroque tendencies.

RIBERA. Caravaggio's style lived on only in Naples, then under Spanish rule, where he fled from Rome after killing a man in a duel over a ball game. His main disciple in Naples was the Spaniard Jusepe Ribera (1591–1652), who settled there after having first absorbed Caravaggio's style in Rome and who in turn spawned a school of his own. Especially popular were his paintings of saints, prophets, and ancient beggar philosophers. The asceticism for which they were known appealed strongly to the otherworldliness of Spanish Catholicism. At the same time, such pictures reflected the learned humanism of the Spanish nobility who ruled Naples and were the artist's main patrons. Most of Ribera's figures are middle-aged or elderly men, who possess the unique blend of inner strength and intensity seen in St. *Jerome and the Angel of Judgment* (fig. 727), his masterpiece in this vein. The fervent characterization owes its expressive force to both the dramatic composition, inspired by Caravaggio (compare St. *Matthew and the Angel* in fig. 725), and the raking light, which lends the figure a powerful presence by heightening the realism and emphasizing the vigorous surface textures.

GENTILESCHI. It was in the Baroque era that women first began to play an important role in the arts. However, the obstacles they met in getting instruction in figure drawing and anatomy effectively barred them from painting narrative subjects. Hence, women artists were largely restricted to painting portraits, genre scenes, and still lifes until the middle of the nineteenth century. Many nevertheless carved out successful careers, often emerging as the equals or superiors of the men in whose styles they were trained (see page 488). The exceptions to this general rule were certain Italian women born into artistic families, for whom painting came naturally. The most significant contribution of all was made by Artemisia Gentileschi (1593–c. 1653). [See Primary Sources, no. 68, page 639.]

The daughter of Caravaggio's follower Orazio Gentileschi (1563–1639), she was born in Rome and became one of the leading painters and personalities of her day. Her characteristic subjects are Bathsheba, the tragic object of King David's passion, and Judith, who saved her people by beheading the

words, is classical, without being classicizing. The composition, for example, is disposed across the picture surface and its forms sharply highlighted, much as in a relief (see fig. 267). What identifies one of the figures as Christ? It is surely not the Saviour's halo, the only supernatural feature in the picture, which is an inconspicuous gold band that we might well overlook. Our eyes fasten instead upon his commanding gesture, borrowed from Michelangelo's *Creation of Adam* (fig. 612), which "bridges" the gap between the two groups and is echoed by Matthew, who points questioningly at himself.

Most decisive is the strong beam of sunlight above Jesus that illuminates his face and hand in the gloomy interior, thus carrying his call across to Matthew. Without this light, so natural yet so charged with symbolic meaning, the picture would lose its magic, its power to make us aware of the divine presence. Caravaggio here gives moving, direct form to an attitude shared by certain great saints of the Counter Reformation: that

728. Artemisia Gentileschi. *Judith and Maidservant with the Head of Holofernes.* c. 1625.
Oil on canvas, 6'1/2" x 4'7" (1.84 x 1.41 m). The Detroit Institute of Arts
Gift of Leslie H. Green

Assyrian general Holofernes. Both subjects were popular during the Baroque era, which delighted in erotic and violent scenes. Artemisia's frequent depictions of these biblical heroines throughout her restless career suggest a fundamental ambivalence toward men that was rooted in her life, which was as turbulent as Caravaggio's. While Gentileschi's early paintings of Judith take her father's and Caravaggio's work as their points of departure, our example (fig. 728) is a fully mature, independent work. The inner drama is uniquely hers, and no less powerful for its restraint in immortalizing Judith's courage.

Rather than the decapitation itself, the artist shows the instant after. Momentarily distracted, Judith gestures theatrically as her servant stuffs Holofernes' head into a sack. The object of their attention remains hidden from view, heightening the air of intrigue. The hushed, candlelit atmosphere in turn establishes a mood of exotic mystery that conveys Judith's complex emotions with unsurpassed understanding.

ANNIBALE CARRACCI. The conservative wishes of everyday people in Italy were met by artists less radical, and less tal-

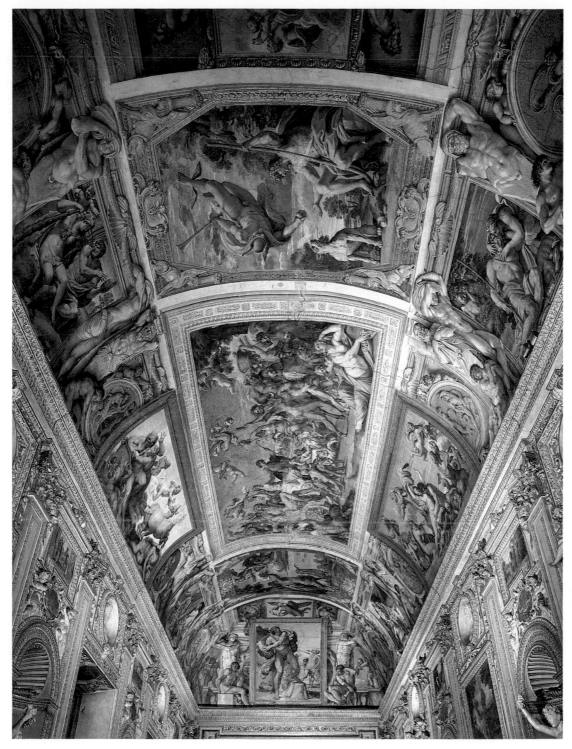

729. Annibale Carracci. Ceiling fresco. 1597–1601. Gallery, Palazzo Farnese, Rome

ented, than Caravaggio. They took their lead instead from Annibale Carracci (1560–1609), another recent arrival in Rome. Annibale came from Bologna where, since the 1580s, he and two other members of his family had evolved an anti-Mannerist style based on North Italian realism and Venetian art. He was a reformer rather than a revolutionary. Like Caravaggio, who apparently admired him, it was his experience of Roman classicism that transformed his art. He, too, felt that art must return to nature, but his approach emphasized a revival of the classics, which to him meant the art of antiquity,

and of Raphael, Michelangelo, Titian, and Correggio. At his best, he succeeded in fusing these diverse elements, although their union always remained somewhat precarious.

Between 1597 and 1604 Annibale produced the ceiling fresco in the gallery of the Farnese Palace (fig. 729), his most ambitious work, which soon became so famous that it ranked behind only the murals of Michelangelo and Raphael. [See Primary Sources, no. 69, pages 639–40.] Commissioned to celebrate a wedding in the family, it wears its humanist subject, the Loves of the Classical Gods, lightly. The historical significance

730. Annibale Carracci. Ceiling fresco (detail). Gallery,
Palazzo Farnese, Rome

731. Annibale Carracci. *Landscape with the Flight into Egypt.* c. 1603. Oil on canvas,
4'1/4" x 8'2 1/2" (1.22 x 2.50 m). Galleria Doria Pamphili, Rome

of the Farnese Gallery is great indeed. Our detail (fig. 730) shows Annibale's rich and intricate design. The narrative scenes, like those of the Sistine ceiling, are surrounded by painted architecture, simulated sculpture, and nude, garland-holding youths. The Farnese Gallery does not rely solely on Michelangelo's masterpiece. The style of the main panels is reminiscent of Raphael's *Galatea* (see fig. 628), and the whole is held together by an illusionistic scheme that reflects Annibale's knowledge of Correggio and the great Venetians. Carefully foreshortened and illuminated from below (as we can judge from the shadows), the nude youths and the simulated sculpture and architecture appear real. Against this background the mythologies are presented as simulated easel pictures, a solution adopted from Raphael. Each of these levels of reality

is handled with consummate skill, and the entire ceiling has an exuberance that sets it apart from both Mannerism and High Renaissance art.

The sculptured precision of the Farnese Gallery does not do justice to the important Venetian element in Annibale Carracci's style. This is most striking in his landscapes, such as the monumental *Landscape with the Flight into Egypt* (fig. 731). Its pastoral mood and the soft light and atmosphere hark back to Giorgione and Titian (see figs. 631 and 632). The figures, however, play a far less conspicuous role here. They are, indeed, as small and incidental as in any Northern landscape (compare fig. 716). Nor does the character of the panorama at all suggest the Flight into Egypt. It would be equally suitable for almost any story, sacred or profane. Still, we feel that the

732. Giovanni Lanfranco. *Annunciation*. c. 1616. Oil on canvas, 9'8¹/₂" x 6' (2.96 x 1.83 m). S. Carlo ai Catinari, Rome

733. Domenichino. *St. Cecilia*. c. 1617–18. Oil on canvas, 62⁵/₈ x 46¹/₈" (159 x 117 cm; enlarged). Musée du Louvre, Paris

figures could not be removed altogether (though we can imagine them replaced by others). This is not the untamed nature of Northern landscapes. The old castle, the roads and fields, the flock of sheep, the ferryman with his boat, all show that this "civilized," hospitable countryside has been inhabited for a long time. Hence the figures, however tiny, do not appear lost or dwarfed into insignificance, because their presence is implicit in the orderly, domesticated quality of the setting. This firmly constructed "ideal landscape" evokes a vision of nature that is gentle yet austere, grand but not awesome. We shall meet its descendants again and again in the next two centuries.

LANFRANCO; DOMENICHINO. The seeds of the reaction against Carracci's classicism were to be found within his own studio. The way was led by Giovanni Lanfranco (1582–1647), a native of Parma, whose *Annunciation* (fig. 732) unites Correggio's colorism with Caravaggio's drama. The result is an emotive style that announces the arrival of the High Baroque. Lanfranco's expressive intensity was the very opposite of the measured economy of Domenichino (1581–1641), Carracci's favorite pupil, who thought out every gesture and expression with impressive logic. Today, however, Domenichino is

remembered more for his paintings of sweetly lyrical female figures, such as *St. Cecilia* (fig. 733), the patron saint of music. Inspired by Raphael, the subject inaugurates a long line of successors through the Rococo.

RENI; GUERCINO. Lanfranco eventually vanquished his adversary Domenichino in fresco decoration, where the main development of Baroque painting was to take place through the 1630s. Their rivalry was repeated in this arena by two other pupils of the Carracci, Guido Reni (1575–1642) and Guercino (Giovanni Francesco Barbieri; 1591–1666). Reni exercised a widespread influence early on (Domenichino may have known Raphael's painting of St. Cecilia through a copy by Reni) and eventually assumed leadership of the Bolognese school. Guercino succeeded Reni upon his death, but only after making important concessions to his refined style.

To artists who were inspired by it, the Farnese Gallery seemed to offer two alternatives. Pursuing the Raphaelesque style of the mythological panels, they could arrive at a deliberate, "official" classicism; or they could take their cue from the sensuous illusionism present in the framework. The approach varied according to personal style and the conditions imposed by the actual site. Among the earliest responses to the first

734. Guido Reni. *Aurora.* 1613. Ceiling fresco. Casino Rospigliosi, Rome

735. Guercino. *Aurora.* 1621–23. Ceiling fresco. Villa Ludovisi, Rome

alternative is Reni's ceiling fresco *Aurora* (fig. 734), showing Apollo in his chariot (the Sun) led by Aurora (Dawn). Here grace becomes the pursuit of perfect beauty. Nevertheless, the relieflike design would seem like little more than a pallid reflection of High Renaissance art were it not for the glowing and dramatic light, which gives it an emotional force that the figures alone could never achieve. Hence, this style is called Baroque classicism to distinguish it from all earlier forms of classicism, no matter how much it may be indebted to them.

The *Aurora* ceiling (fig. 735) painted less than ten years later by Guercino is the very opposite of Reni's. Here archi-

tectural perspective, combined with the pictorial illusionism of Correggio and the intense light and color of Titian, converts the entire surface into one limitless space, in which the figures sweep past as if propelled by stratospheric winds. With this work, Guercino started what soon became a veritable flood of similar visions characteristic of the High Baroque after 1630.

DA CORTONA. The most overpowering of these is the ceiling fresco by Pietro da Cortona (1596–1669) in the great hall of the Barberini Palace in Rome, which presents a glorification of the reign of the Barberini pope, Urban VIII (fig. 736),

736. Pietro da Cortona. *Glorification of the Reign of Urban VIII.* 1633–39.
Portion of ceiling fresco. Palazzo Barberini, Rome

couched in the traditional terms of a complex humanist allegory. As in the Farnese Gallery, the ceiling area is subdivided
by a painted framework simulating architecture and sculpture,
but beyond it we now see the unbounded sky, as in Guercino's
Aurora. Clusters of figures, perched on clouds or soaring freely,
swirl above as well as below this framework, creating a dual
illusion: some figures appear to hover well inside the hall, perilously close to our heads, while others recede into a light-
filled, infinite distance. In the Barberini ceiling, the dynamism
of the High Baroque style reaches a resounding climax. The
effect is very similar to that of an illusionistic domed ceiling
painted by Lanfranco in Rome nearly a decade earlier, which
was based directly on Correggio's *The Assumption of the Virgin*
(fig. 654).

Cortona's frescoes provided the focal point for the rift
between the High Baroque and Baroque classicism that grew

out of the Farnese ceiling. The classicists asserted that art serves
a moral purpose and must observe the principles of clarity,
unity, and decorum. And supported by a long tradition reaching back to Horace's dictum *ut pictura poesis,* they further
maintained that painting should follow the example of tragic
poetry in conveying meaning through a minimum of figures
whose movements, gestures, and expressions can be easily
read. Cortona, though not anticlassical, presented the case for
art as epic poetry, with many actors and episodes that elaborate on the central theme and create a magnificent effect. He
was also the first to argue that art has a sensuous appeal which
exists as an end in itself.

Although it took place on a largely theoretical level, the
debate over illusionistic ceiling painting represented more
than fundamentally divergent approaches to telling a story
and expressing ideas in art. The issue lay at the very heart of

The most important contribution of the Baroque to music and theater was the invention of opera, which united all the theatrical elements of the period into a spectacular whole. It began modestly enough as a humanist exercise in Florence. Following the suggestion of Girolamo Mei of Rome, members of the Camerata of Florence, so called because it met *in camera* (behind closed doors) at the palace of Count Giorgio Bardi, set out to re-create ancient Greek drama, which they wrongly believed had been sung throughout a performance. Around 1590, Vincenzo Galilei (c. 1520–1591), the father of the astronomer Galileo, issued a polemic attacking the vocal counterpoint of madrigals as impersonal and artificial because it did not adhere to the Greek unity of text and music. Although Vincenzo experimented with monodies (short, dramatic monologues with continuo accompaniment), the first opera (short for *opera in musica,* "work in music") was *Dafne,* produced privately with a *libretto* (text) by Ottavio Rinuccini (1562–1621) and music mostly by Jacopo Peri (1561–1633). It was followed by *Euridice* from the same team, with arias by Giulio Caccini (c. 1546–1618), and was performed in 1600 in honor of the marriage of Henry IV and Marie de' Medici. That same year and in 1601, Caccini and Peri , who were singers and professional rivals, published separate versions of the opera. Despite its limitations, this new declamatory style, called representative or theatrical style, made an extraordinary impression on listeners.

Opera might nevertheless have remained of little more than antiquarian interest had it not been for Claudio Monteverdi (1567–1643). He has aptly been described as the "last great madrigalist and the first great opera composer." His *Orfeo,* produced in 1607 at Mantua with a libretto by Alessandro Striggio, enlarged the story of *Euridice* into the standard five acts demanded by the Roman poet Horace while increasing the variety of vocal music and giving a greater role to the instrumental accompaniment. This expansion required all the skills he had gained composing madrigals—the very kind of music attacked by Vincenzo Galilei! Monteverdi was openly experimental. He was acutely aware of the conflict between the earlier style of the Netherlanders and the later Italian madrigalists such as Carlo Gesualdo (see page 535), and he fended off attacks by saying that he was working in an entirely new vein so that none of the old rules applied.

From then on, music took precedence over words in opera, which often emphasized extreme emotional states of mind (*affetti*) through violent contrasts, as did Baroque art.

The future of the new form lay in Rome and Venice, which opened the first public opera house in 1637. Operas soon became wildly popular, not only in Italy but throughout Europe, and everyone vied for the services of the leading Italians. After 1650 the court in Vienna became the main center of theater and opera. Its zenith came with *The Golden Apple,* a huge spectacle staged there in 1668 to celebrate the wedding of Emperor Leopold I and the Infanta Margarita of Spain, with music by Pietro Antonio Cesti (1623–1669) and scenery by Ludovico Burnacini (1636–1707). The public wanted new operas as soon as they could be mounted, while star singers required virtuoso arias, solos to which they often added florid ornamentation to showcase their talents. Combined with the increasing emphasis on spectacle, these demands conspired to dilute opera as a dramatic form while the beauty of the music itself grew. The impact of opera was nevertheless pervasive. Even church music became operatic in the solo cantatas and oratorios of Giacomo Carissimi (1605–1674). These three vocal forms reached maturity in the compositions of Alessandro Scarlatti (1660–1725), who worked in Naples and Rome, so that he holds a position analogous to that of Francesco Solimena in painting. In addition to being the outstanding Italian opera composer of his time, Scarlatti wrote religious music of great beauty. He was the pivotal figure in late Italian Baroque music, comparable in importance to Jean-Baptiste Lully of France.

The Baroque was the first period in which instrumental music equaled vocal music in stature. While continuing the practice of imitating different dance types, it also began to mimic vocal style. The two approaches are exemplified in the trio sonatas of Arcangelo Corelli (1653–1713). His chamber sonatas use dance movements, while the church sonatas in principle do not, although they were often mixed. Both employ two violins and a continuo consisting of a lower viol and a keyboard instrument. When expanded to a full string orchestra, the trio sonata became the *concerto grosso* (grand concerto), the most characteristic type of Baroque instrumental music, which began as overtures to and during Mass. Corelli alternated sprightly, dancelike movements with slow ones that have a uniquely plaintive, bittersweet quality similar to the laments in Monteverdi's madrigals. Virtuoso touches of ornamentation are treated discretely so as not to disrupt the singing line, which is kept well within the range of the human voice. Each movement generally has one or two alternating melodies developed in clear progressions that became the basis for modern harmony.

the Baroque. Illusionism enabled artists to overcome the apparent contradictions of the era by fusing separate levels of reality into a pictorial unity of such overwhelming grandeur as to sweep aside any differences between them. Despite the intensity of the argument, in actual practice the two sides rarely came into conflict over easel paintings, where the differences between Cortona's and Carracci's followers were not always so clear-cut. Surprisingly, Cortona found inspiration in Classical art and Raphael throughout his career. Nevertheless, the leader of the reaction against what were regarded as the

excesses of the High Baroque was neither a fresco painter, nor was he an Italian, but a French artist living in Rome: Nicolas Poussin (see page 596), who, strangely enough, moved in the same antiquarian circle early on but drew very different lessons from it.

IL GESÙ. It is a peculiar fact that few ceiling frescoes were painted after Cortona finished his *Glorification of the Reign of Urban VIII,* ironically because the new style of architecture fostered by Francesco Borromini and Guarino Guarini (see

737. Giovanni Battista Gaulli. *Triumph of the Name of Jesus.* 1672–85. Ceiling fresco. Il Gesù, Rome

pages 560–63) provided so few opportunities for adornment. But after 1670 they enjoyed an astonishing revival in older buildings, which reached its culmination in the interior decoration of Il Gesù (fig. 737). Although his role in this case was only advisory, it is clear that the plan must be by Gianlorenzo Bernini (1598–1680), the greatest sculptor-architect of the century (see below). At Bernini's suggestion, the commission for the ceiling frescoes went to Giovanni Battista Gaulli (1639–1709), his young protégé known as Baciccia, while a talented assistant, Antonio Raggi (1624–1686), did the stucco sculpture. However, the program, which proved extraordinarily influential, is testimony to Bernini's imaginative daring. As in the Cornaro Chapel (fig. 754), the entire ceiling is treated as a single unit: the nave fresco, with its sharp contrasts of light and dark suggesting a mystical vision, spills dramatically over its frame, then turns into sculptured figures. Here Baroque illusionism achieves its ultimate expression.

GIORDANO. The Late Baroque found its greatest representative in Luca Giordano (1634–1705), a Neapolitan who began as an imitator of his teacher Ribera but became the principal heir to Pietro Cortona as the leading decorative painter in Italy. Legendary for his speed, Giordano was a virtuoso whose remarkable facility resulted in a prodigious and varied output. *The Abduction of Europa* (fig. 738) shows his spontaneous approach at its best. The composition is based on one by Veronese that also was to inspire François Boucher (see pages 614–15). The painting shares its graceful style with

738. Luca Giordano. *The Abduction of Europa.* 1686. Oil on canvas, 7'5 5/8" x 6'4 1/4" (2.27 x 1.93 m).
Wadsworth Atheneum, Hartford, Connecticut
Ella Gallup Sumner and Mary Catlin Sumner Collection

Cortona's, but instead of the latter's blond palette, it favors a rich tonalism. Although he never fully acceded to colorism, Giordano set the stage for the great Venetian painters of the eighteenth century, even in his peripatetic life-style: he became the first in a line of great Italian artists, culminating in Tiepolo (see page 626), to be called to the Spanish court.

Gaulli and Giordano mark the final flowering of Baroque exuberance. By this time, the pendulum had swung in the opposite direction. Italian painting during the third quarter of the seventeenth century was largely characterized by a conservative synthesis of the High Baroque and Baroque classicism. This yielded to an academic style that flourished in Rome and Naples, which were then closely linked. It was formulated chiefly by Carlo Maratta (1625–1713) of Rome, the most admired artist of his day, and Francesco Solimena (1657–1747), Giordano's successor in Naples. Maratta may be regarded as a less doctrinaire counterpart to Charles Lebrun in France (see page 600). In contrast to his rival Gaulli (see fig. 737), he sought to revive the grand manner of the Carracci by emphasizing individual figures through a clear, even light without entirely abandoning Cortona's color and drama. As might be expected, however, the results of such a compromise were generally unimpressive.

ARCHITECTURE IN ITALY

MADERNO. In architecture, the beginnings of the Baroque style cannot be defined as precisely as in painting. In the vast ecclesiastical building program that got under way in Rome toward the end of the sixteenth century, the most talented young architect to emerge was Carlo Maderno (1556–1629). In 1603 he was given the task of completing, at long last, the church of St. Peter's. The pope had decided to add a nave to Michelangelo's building (fig. 623), converting it into a basilica. The change of plan, which may have been prompted by the example of Il Gesù (see figs. 668 and 670), made it possible to link St. Peter's with the Vatican Palace to the right of the church (fig. 739). Maderno's design for the facade follows the pattern established by Michelangelo for the exterior of the church. It consists of a colossal order supporting an attic, but with a dramatic emphasis on the portals. The effect can only be described as a crescendo that builds from the corners toward the center. The spacing of the supports becomes closer, pilasters turn into columns, and the facade wall projects step by step.

This quickened rhythm had been hinted at a generation earlier in Giacomo della Porta's facade of Il Gesù (see fig. 670). Maderno made it the dominant principle of his facade designs, not only for St. Peter's but for smaller churches as well. In the process, he replaced the traditional concept of the church facade as one continuous wall surface, which was not yet challenged by the facade of Il Gesù, with the "facade-in-depth," dynamically related to the open space before it. The possibilities implicit in this new concept were not to be exhausted until 150 years later.

BERNINI. Maderno's work at St. Peter's was completed by Bernini, who molded the open space in front of the facade into a magnificent oval piazza. This "forecourt" acts as an immense

739. Aerial view of St. Peter's, Rome. Nave and facade by Carlo Maderno, 1607–15; colonnade by Gianlorenzo Bernini, designed 1657

atrium framed by colonnades which Bernini himself likened to the motherly, all-embracing arms of the Church. For sheer impressiveness, this integration of the building with such a grandiose setting of molded open space can be compared only with the ancient Roman sanctuary at Palestrina (see fig. 240).

The piazza can be thought of as a continuation on the exterior of the decoration program at St. Peter's that occupied Bernini at intervals during most of his long and prolific career. The enormous size of St. Peter's made the decoration of its interior a uniquely difficult task: how to relate its chill vastness to the human scale and imbue it with a measure of emotional warmth. He began by designing the huge bronze canopy for the main altar under the dome (fig. 740). The tabernacle is a splendid fusion of architecture and sculpture. Four ornate, spiral-shaped columns support an upper platform. At its corners are statues of angels and vigorously curved scrolls which raise high the symbol of the victory of Christianity over the pagan world, a cross above a golden orb. The entire structure is so alive with expressive energy that it strikes us as the very epitome of Baroque style. Yet its most impressive feature, the corkscrew columns, had been invented in late antiquity, and even employed, on a much smaller scale, in the old basilica of St. Peter's. Thus Bernini could claim the best possible precedent for his own use of the motif. This is not the only instance of an affinity between Baroque and ancient art. Several monuments of Roman architecture of the second and third centuries A.D. seem to anticipate the style of the seventeenth (see figs. 257–60).

BORROMINI. As a personality, Bernini represents a type we first met among the artists of the Early Renaissance, a self-assured, expansive person of the world. His great rival in architecture, Francesco Borromini (1599–1667), who also started out as an assistant to Maderno, was the very opposite: a secretive and emotionally unstable genius who died by suicide. The Baroque heightened the tension between the two types.

740. Carlo Maderno. Nave, with Bernini's Tabernacle (1624–33) at crossing, St. Peter's, Rome

741. Francesco Borromini. Facade of S. Carlo alle Quattro Fontane, Rome. 1665–67

742. Plan of S. Carlo alle Quattro Fontane. Begun 1638

The temperamental contrast between the two masters would be evident from their works alone, even without the testimony of contemporary witnesses. Both exemplify the climax of Baroque architecture in Rome, yet Bernini's design for the colonnade of St. Peter's is dramatically simple and unified, while Borromini's structures are extravagantly complex. Bernini himself agreed with those who denounced Borromini for flagrantly disregarding the classical tradition, enshrined in Renaissance theory and practice, that architecture must reflect the proportions of the human body.

In Borromini's first major project, the church of S. Carlo alle Quattro Fontane (figs. 741–43), it is the syntax, not the vocabulary, that is new and disquieting. The ceaseless play of concave and convex surfaces makes the entire structure seem elastic, "pulled out of shape" by pressures that no previous

743. *(above)* Dome of S. Carlo alle Quattro Fontane

744. *(right)* Francesco Borromini. Section, S. Ivo, Rome. Begun 1642

building could have withstood. The plan is a pinched oval suggesting a distended and half-melted Greek cross, as if it had been drawn on rubber. The inside of the dome, too, looks "stretched": if the tension were relaxed, it would snap back to normal. The facade was designed almost 30 years later, and the pressures and counterpressures here reach their maximum intensity. Borromini merges architecture and sculpture in a way that must have shocked Bernini. No such fusion had been ventured since Gothic art. S. Carlo alle Quattro Fontane established Borromini's local and international fame. "Nothing similar," wrote the head of the religious order for which the church was built, "can be found anywhere in the world. This is attested by the foreigners who . . . try to procure copies of the plan. We have been asked for them by Germans, Flemings, Frenchmen, Italians, Spaniards, and even Indians."

The design of Borromini's next church, S. Ivo (figs. 744 and 745), is more compact and equally daring. Its plan, a star-hexagon, belongs unequivocally to the central type. Here Borromini may have been thinking of octagonal structures, such as S. Vitale, Ravenna (compare figs. 317–20), but the result is

745. *(right)* Dome of S. Ivo

746. Francesco Borromini. S. Agnese in Piazza Navona, Rome.
1653–63

747. Guarino Guarini. Facade of Palazzo Carignano, Turin.
Begun 1679

748. Plan of Palazzo Carignano

completely novel. The space is not subdivided into a tall, domed "nave" ringed by an ambulatory or chapels. Instead Borromini covered all of it with one great dome, continuing the star-hexagon pattern up to the circular base of the lantern. Again the entire design is dominated by the concave-convex rhythm, which serves to focus our attention on the altar. The structure might almost be described as a larger version of the Temple of Venus at Baalbek, turned inside out (see figs. 258 and 259).

A third project by Borromini is of special interest as a High Baroque critique of St. Peter's. Maderno had found one problem insoluble: although his new facade forms an impressive unit with Michelangelo's dome when seen from a distance, the dome is gradually hidden by the facade as we approach the church. Borromini designed the facade of S. Agnese in Piazza Navona (fig. 746) with this conflict in mind. Its lower part is adapted from the facade of St. Peter's, but curves inward, so that the dome (a tall, slender version of Michelangelo's) functions as the upper part of the facade. The dramatic juxtaposition of concave and convex, always characteristic of Borromini, is further emphasized by the two towers, which form a monumental triad with the dome. (Such towers were also once planned for St. Peter's by Bernini but they would have been free-standing.) Once again Borromini joins Gothic and

Renaissance features—the two-tower facade and the dome—into a remarkably "elastic" compound.

GUARINI. The wealth of new ideas that Borromini introduced was to be exploited not in Rome but in Turin, the capital of Savoy, which became the creative center of Baroque architecture in Italy toward the end of the seventeenth century. In 1666 that city attracted Borromini's most brilliant successor, Guarino Guarini (1624–1683), a Theatine monk whose architectural genius was deeply grounded in philosophy and mathematics. His design for the facade of the Palazzo Carignano (figs. 747 and 748) repeats on a larger scale the undulating movement of S. Carlo alle Quattro Fontane (see fig. 741), using a highly individual vocabulary. Incredibly, the exterior of the building is entirely of brick, down to the last ornamental detail.

Still more extraordinary is Guarini's dome of the Chapel of the Holy Shroud, a round structure attached to Turin

749. Guarino Guarini. Dome of Chapel of the Holy Shroud,
Turin Cathedral. 1668–94

751. Wooden dome of the Ulu Mosque, Erzurum, Seljuk. c. 1150

750. Plan of the Chapel of the Holy Shroud and of the dome

Cathedral (figs. 749 and 750). The tall drum, with alternating windows and tabernacles, consists of familiar Borrominian motifs, but beyond it we enter a realm of pure illusion. The interior surface of the dome of S. Carlo alle Quattro Fontane, though dematerialized by light and the honeycomb of fanciful coffers, was still recognizable (see fig. 743). But here the surface has disappeared completely in a maze of segmental ribs, and we find ourselves staring into a huge kaleidoscope. Above this seemingly endless funnel of space hovers the dove of the Holy Spirit within a bright, 12-pointed star.

So far as we know, there is only one similar dome anywhere in the history of art: that of the Ulu Mosque at Erzurum in Turkish Armenia, built about 1150 (fig. 751). How could Guarini have known about it? Or did he recapture its effect entirely by coincidence? Guarini's dome retains the old symbolic meaning of the Dome of Heaven (see pages 436–37;

figs. 572–74), but the objective harmony of the Renaissance has here become subjective, a compelling experience of the infinite. If Borromini's style at times suggested a synthesis of Gothic and Renaissance, Guarini takes the next, decisive step. In his theoretical writings, he contrasts the "muscular" architecture of the ancients with the opposite effect of Gothic churches, which appear to stand only by means of some kind of miracle, and he expresses equal admiration for both. This attitude corresponds exactly to his own practice. By using the most advanced mathematical techniques of his day, he achieved architectural miracles even greater than those of the seemingly weightless Gothic structures.

SCULPTURE IN ITALY

We have already encountered Gianlorenzo Bernini as an architect. It is now time to consider him as a sculptor, although the two aspects are never far apart in his work. As in the tabernacle for St. Peter's (see fig. 740), a strong relationship can often be discovered between Bernini's and Hellenistic sculpture. If we compare Bernini's *David* (fig. 752) with Michelangelo's (see fig. 607) and ask which is closer to the Pergamum frieze or *The Laocoön Group* (see figs. 213 and 215), our vote must go to Bernini. His figure shares with Hellenistic works that unison of body and spirit, of motion and emotion, which Michelangelo so conspicuously avoids. This does not mean that Bernini is more classical than Michelangelo. It indicates, rather, that both the Baroque and the High Renaissance acknowledged the authority of ancient art, but each period drew inspiration from a different aspect of antiquity.

Bernini's *David*, obviously, is in no sense an echo of *The Laocoön Group.* What makes it Baroque is the implied pres-

752. Gianlorenzo Bernini. *David*. 1623. Marble, lifesize.
Galleria Borghese, Rome

ence of Goliath. Unlike earlier statues of David, Bernini's is conceived not as one self-contained figure but as half of a pair, his entire action focused on his adversary. Did Bernini, we wonder, plan a statue of Goliath to complete the group? He never did, for his *David* tells us clearly enough where *he* sees the enemy. Consequently, the space between David and his invisible opponent is charged with energy—it "belongs" to the statue.

Bernini's *David* shows us what distinguishes Baroque sculpture from the sculpture of the two preceding centuries: its new, active relationship with the space it inhabits. It rejects self-sufficiency for the illusion of presences or forces that are implied by the behavior of the statue. Because it so often presents an "invisible complement" (like the Goliath of Bernini's

David), Baroque sculpture is a tour de force, attempting essentially pictorial effects that were traditionally outside its province. Such a charging of space with active energy is, in fact, a key feature of all Baroque art. Caravaggio had achieved it in his *St. Matthew*, with the aid of a sharply focused beam of light. Indeed, Baroque art acknowledges no sharp distinction between sculpture and painting. And as we have seen, the two may even be combined with architecture to form a compound illusion, like that of the stage.

In fact, Bernini, who had a passionate interest in the theater, was at his best when he could merge architecture, sculpture, and painting in this fashion. His masterpiece in this vein is the Cornaro Chapel in the church of Sta. Maria della Vittoria, containing the famous group called *The Ecstasy of St.*

753. Gianlorenzo Bernini. *The Ecstasy of St. Theresa.* 1645–52. Marble, lifesize.
Cornaro Chapel, Sta. Maria della Vittoria, Rome

Theresa (fig. 753). Theresa of Avila, one of the great saints of the Counter Reformation (see page 548), had described how an angel pierced her heart with a flaming golden arrow: "The pain was so great that I screamed aloud; but at the same time I felt such infinite sweetness that I wished the pain to last forever. It was not physical but psychic pain, although it affected the body as well to some degree. It was the sweetest caressing of the soul by God."

Bernini has made this visionary experience as sensuously real as Correggio's *Jupiter and Io* (see fig. 655). In a different context, the angel would be indistinguishable from Cupid, and the saint's ecstasy is palpable. The two figures on their floating cloud are illuminated (from a hidden window above) in such a way as to seem almost dematerialized in their gleaming whiteness. The beholder experiences them as visionary. The "invisible complement" here, less specific than David's but equally important, is the force that carries the figures heavenward, causing the turbulence of their drapery. Its divine nature is suggested by the golden rays, which come from a source high above the altar. In an illusionistic fresco by Guidebaldo Abbatini on the vault of the chapel, the glory of the heavens is revealed as a dazzling burst of light from which tumble clouds of jubilant angels (fig. 754). This celestial "explosion" gives force to the thrusts of the angel's arrow and makes the ecstasy of the saint believable.

To complete the illusion, Bernini even provides a built-in audience for his "stage." On the sides of the chapel are balconies resembling theater boxes, where we see marble figures, depicting members of the Cornaro family, who also witness the ecstasy. Their space and ours are the same, and thus part of everyday reality, while the ecstasy, housed in a strongly framed niche, occupies a space that is real but beyond our reach. Finally, the ceiling fresco represents the infinite, unfathomable space of Heaven. We may recall that *The Burial of Count Orgaz* and its setting also form a whole embracing three levels of reality (see page 492). There is nevertheless a profound difference between the two chapels. El Greco's Mannerism evokes an ethereal vision in which only the stone slab of the sarcophagus is "real," in contrast to Bernini's Baroque theatricality, where the distinction nearly breaks down altogether. It would be all too easy to dismiss *The Ecstasy of St. Theresa* as a superficial, melodramatic display, but Bernini also was a devout Catholic who believed (as did Michelangelo) that he received his inspiration directly from God. Like the Spiritual Exercises of St. Ignatius, which Bernini practiced, his religious sculpture is intended to help the viewer achieve complete identification with miraculous events through a vivid appeal to the senses.

Bernini was steeped in Renaissance humanism and theory. Central to his sculpture is the role played by gesture and expression in arousing emotion. While no less important to the Renaissance (compare Leonardo), these devices have an apparent abandon that seems anticlassical in Bernini's hands. However, he essentially adhered to the concept of decorum, and calculated his effects very carefully, varying them in accordance with his subject. Unlike the Frenchman Nicolas Poussin (whom he respected), Bernini did this for the sake of expressive impact rather than conceptual clarity. Their approaches were diametrically opposed as well. For Bernini, antique art served

754. *The Cornaro Chapel.* 18th-century painting. Staatliches Museum, Schwerin, Germany

as no more than a point of departure for his own fertile inventiveness, whereas for classicists such as Poussin it provided a reference point that acted as a standard of comparison. It is nevertheless characteristic of the paradoxical Baroque that Bernini's theories should be far more orthodox than his art. An admirer of Annibale Carracci, he often sided with the classicists against his fellow High Baroque artists. Thus, he attacked Pietro da Cortona, despite the fact that their work has much in common. In this regard he was perhaps motivated by professional jealousy: Cortona, like Raphael before him, also made an important contribution to architecture and was a rival in that sphere.

ALGARDI. It is no less ironic that Cortona was the closest friend of the sculptor Alessandro Algardi (1596–1654), who is generally regarded as the leading classical sculptor of the Italian Baroque and the only serious rival to Bernini in ability. *The Meeting of Pope Leo I and Attila* (fig. 755), executed while he supplanted Bernini at the papal court, represents Algardi's main contribution, for it inaugurates a new kind of high relief that soon became widely popular. It depicts the defeat of the Huns in 452, a fateful event in the early history of Christianity when its very survival was at stake. The subject revives one familiar to us from antiquity: the victory over barbarian forces (compare fig. 210), but now it is the church, not civilization, that triumphs.

755. Alessandro Algardi. *The Meeting of Pope Leo I and Attila.* 1646. Marble, 28'1³/4" x 16'2¹/2" (8.5 x 4.9 m). St. Peter's, Vatican

The commission was given for a sculpture because the water condensation caused by the location in an old doorway of St. Peter's made a painting impossible. Never before had an Italian sculptor attempted such a large relief—it stands nearly 28 feet high. The problems posed by translating a pictorial conception (it had been treated by Raphael in one of the Vatican Stanze) into a relief on this gigantic scale were formidable, and if Algardi has not succeeded in resolving every detail, his achievement is stupendous nonetheless. By varying the depth of the carving, he nearly convinces us that the scene takes place in the same space as ours. The foreground figures are in such high relief as to appear detached from the background. To accentuate the effect, the stage on which they are standing projects several feet beyond its surrounding niche. Thus Attila seems to rush out toward us in fear and astonishment as he flees the heavenly vision of the two apostles defending the faith. The result is surprisingly persuasive, both visually and expressively.

Such illusionism is, of course, quintessentially Baroque. Baroque, too, is the intense drama, worthy of Bernini himself, which is heightened by the twisting poses and theatrical gestures of the protagonists. Algardi was obviously touched by Bernini's towering genius. Only in his observance of the three traditional levels of relief carving (low, middle, and high, instead of continuously variable depth), his preference for frontal poses wherever possible, and his degree of restraint in dealing with the violent action can he be called a classicist, and then purely in a relative sense. Clearly, then, we must not insist on drawing the distinction between the High Baroque and Baroque classicism too sharply in sculpture any more than in painting.

PAINTING IN SPAIN

During the sixteenth century, at the height of its political and economic power, Spain had produced great saints and writers, but no artists of the first rank. Nor did El Greco's presence prove a stimulus to native talent. The reason is that the Catholic church, the main source of patronage, was extremely conservative, while the Spanish court and most of the aristocracy preferred to employ foreign painters, above all Titian, so that native artists were held in low esteem. Thus the main impetus came from Italy and The Netherlands.

SANCHEZ COTÁN. Stimulated by the example of Aertsen and his contemporaries in The Netherlands, Spanish artists began to develop their own versions of still life in the 1590s. We see the distinctive character of this tradition in the example (fig. 756) by Juan Sanchez Cotán (1561–1627), a minor religious artist remembered today as one of the first and most remarkable members of the Toledo school of still-life painters. In contrast to the lavish display of food or luxury objects in Northern pictures, we here find an order and an austere simplicity that give a new context to these vegetables. They are so deliberately arranged that we cannot help wondering what symbolic significance the artist meant to convey. The juxtaposition of bright sunlight and impenetrable darkness, of painstaking realism and abstract form, creates a memorable image in which even these humble fruits and vegetables become sacred examples of God's work.

Although he probably used contemporary North Italian paintings as his point of departure, Sanchez Cotán's still lifes make one think of Caravaggio, whose effect on Spanish art, however, is not found until considerably later. We do not know exactly how Caravaggism was transmitted. The likeliest

756. Juan Sanchez Cotán. *Quince, Cabbage, Melon, and Cucumber.* c. 1602. Oil on canvas, 27 1/8 x 33 1/4" (68.8 x 84.4 cm). San Diego Museum of Art
Gift of Misses Anne R. and Amy Putnam

source was Naples, where Caravaggio had fled, which was then under Spanish rule. His principal follower there was Jusepe Ribera (see page 551), but too little is known of his activity before about 1625 for us to trace his influence on early Spanish Baroque art in detail. Be that as it may, the impact of Caravaggism was felt especially in Seville, the home of the most important Spanish Baroque painters before 1640.

VELÁZQUEZ. Diego Velázquez (1599–1660) painted in a Caravaggesque vein during his early years in Seville. His interests at that time centered on scenes of people eating and drinking rather than religious themes. Known as *bodegónes,* such

---

Baroque Theater in Italy and Spain

Besides the opera, the most popular form of Italian theater in the seventeenth century was the *commedia dell'arte,* which arose after 1570 as earlier sixteenth-century written farce declined. It then spread quickly throughout Europe, especially to France. The *commedia* actors improvised their dialogue on a rough plot outline, taking the roles of stock characters—the innocent young girl, the impoverished youth, the braggart captain, the pedantic doctor—in age-old scenarios of love and intrigue. The comedic characters were clever servants, often called *zanni* ("Johnny" in the Venetian dialect—from which the English word *zany* is derived), who delighted their audiences by outwitting their masters and other figures of authority. The best known of these *zanni* were Harlequin, Mezzetin, and Pulcinella, whose name and huge nose survived into the twentieth century in the character of Punch of Punch-and-Judy puppet shows. The Italian *commedia* was also the source of modern slapstick and burlesque comedy. Its success depended on the close identification of the actors with their roles, which they rarely changed except in advanced age, so that they became one and the same in life and in art. Although the *commedia dell'arte* remained popular for 200 years, its heyday was over by 1650, when its creativity began to wane.

Under Philip III and Philip IV the seventeenth century

in Spain was the golden age of theater, as it was of art. It began around 1580 with the plays of Juan de la Cueva (c. 1543–1610) and Miguel de Cervantes (1547–1616), the author of *Don Quixote,* but its greatest writer was Lope de Vega (1562–1635), who claimed to have scripted more than 1,200 dramas and comedies. In its combination of worldliness and religion, Vega's work reflects the character and social order of Spain, which centered on the often-conflicting demands of love, honor, church, and responsibility among the different social classes. The plots are lively and the writing fluid, but characters tend to be rather conventional because they conform to established codes. Tirso de Molina (1580– 1648), a member of the Mercedarian order, was likewise prolific: he professed to have written 300 plays by 1621, of which 80 survive, but he is known primarily for introducing the legend of Don Juan in *The Trickster of Seville.* Vega's successor, Pedro Calderón de la Barca (1600– 1681), wrote mainly cape-and-sword comedies for the court, which he served as Master of the Revels, as well as religious dramas (called *autos sacramentales*) after he was ordained a priest toward the end of his life. Throughout the century, both types were performed at court and in public theaters by professional actors employed by local municipalities.

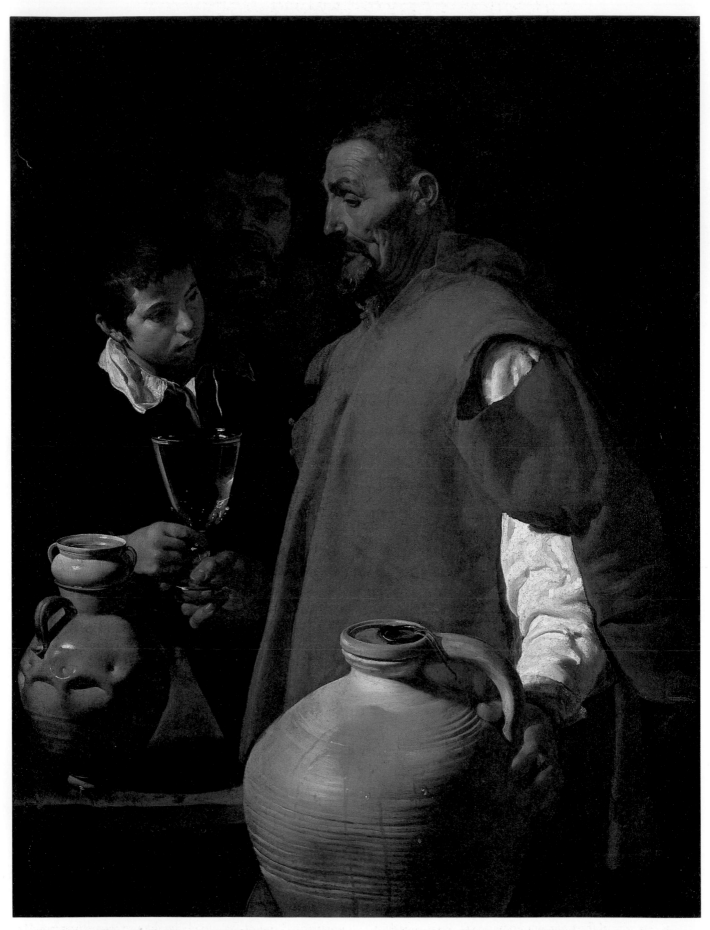

757. Diego Velázquez. *The Water Carrier of Seville.* c. 1619. Oil on canvas, 41¹/₂ x 31¹/₂" (105.3 x 80 cm). Wellington Museum, London

758. Diego Velázquez. *Pope Innocent X.* 1650. Oil on canvas, 55 x 45¼" (139.7 x 115 cm).
Galleria Doria Pamphili, Rome

paintings are the distinctive Spanish counterparts of Dutch breakfast pieces, for they evolved from the paintings of table-top displays brought to Spain by visiting Flemish artists in the early seventeenth century. *The Water Carrier of Seville* (fig. 757), which Velázquez did at the age of 20 under the apparent impress of Ribera, already shows his genius. His powerful grasp of individual character and dignity invests this everyday scene with the solemn spirit of a ritual—perhaps with good reason, for the scene is related to *Giving Drink to the Thirsty*, one of the Seven Acts of Mercy, a popular theme among Caravaggesque painters at the time.

A few years later, Velázquez was appointed court painter to Philip IV, whose reign from 1621 to 1665 represents the great age of painting in Spain. Much of the credit must go to the duke of Olivares, who largely restored Spain's fortunes and supported an ambitious program of artistic patronage to proclaim the monarchy's greatness. Upon moving to Madrid, Velázquez quickly displaced the mediocre Florentines who had enjoyed the favor of Philip III and his minister, the duke of Lerma. A consummate courtier, the artist quickly became a personal favorite of the king, whom he served as chamberlain. Velázquez spent the rest of his life in Madrid, doing mainly portraits of the royal family. The earlier of these still show the precise division of light and shade and the clear outlines of his

Seville period, but after the late 1620s his work acquired a new fluency and richness.

During his visit to the Spanish court on a diplomatic mission in 1628, the Flemish painter Peter Paul Rubens (see page 574) helped Velázquez to discover the beauty of the many Titians in the king's collection. The magnificent portrait of Pope Innocent X (fig. 758), painted in 1650 while Velázquez was visiting Italy, is meant to evoke the great tradition of the papal portraits of Raphael, but its fluid brushwork and glowing color derive from Titian (compare figs. 629 and 635). The sitter's gaze, sharply focused on the beholder, conveys a passionate and powerful personality so characteristic of the Baroque.

The Maids of Honor (fig. 759) displays Velázquez' mature style at its fullest. At once a group portrait and a genre scene, it might be subtitled "the artist in his studio," for Velázquez shows himself at work on a huge canvas. In the center is the little Princess Margarita, who has just posed for him, among her playmates and maids of honor. The faces of her parents, the king and queen, appear in the mirror on the back wall. They have just stepped into the room, to see the scene exactly as we do. Through their presence the canvas celebrates Velázquez' position as royal painter and his knighthood in the Order of Santiago, whose red cross he proudly wears on his tunic.

The painting shows Velázquez' fascination with light. The

759. Diego Velázquez. *The Maids of Honor.* 1656. Oil on canvas, 10'5" x 9' (3.2 x 2.7 m). Museo del Prado, Madrid

varieties of direct and reflected light in *The Maids of Honor* are almost limitless. The artist challenges us to match the mirror image against the paintings on the same wall, and against the "picture" of the man in the open doorway. Although the side lighting and strong contrasts of light and dark still suggest the influence of Caravaggio, Velázquez' technique is far more varied and subtle, with delicate glazes setting off the impasto of the highlights. The glowing colors have a Venetian richness, but the brushwork is even freer and sketchier than Titian's. Velázquez was concerned with the optical qualities of light rather than its metaphysical mysteries. These he penetrated more completely than any painter of his time. His aim is to show the movement of light itself and the infinite range of its effects on form and color. For Velázquez, as for Jan Vermeer

760. Francisco de Zurbarán. *St. Serapion*. 1628. Oil on canvas, 47¹/₂ x 41" (120.7 x 104.1 cm). Wadsworth Atheneum, Hartford, Connecticut

Ella Gallup Sumner and Mary Catlin Sumner Collection

761. Bartolomé Esteban Murillo. *Virgin and Child*. c. 1675–80. Oil on canvas, 65¹/₄ x 43" (165.7 x 109.2 cm). The Metropolitan Museum of Art, New York

Rogers Fund, 1943

in Holland (see page 592), light *creates* the visible world. Velázquez could not have known the work of Vermeer, then only 24, but he may have known scenes of domestic genre by older Dutch painters. Looking at the open, sketchy brushwork in *The Maids of Honor*, we wonder if he could also have seen works by Frans Hals (compare fig. 772). However, unlike Hals, Velázquez is not interested in capturing time on the wing, although the visual effects are fleeting. Rather, he suspends the moment for an eternity to make of the studio an ideal realm that conveys his elevated position as an artist.

ZURBARÁN. Francisco de Zurbarán (1598–1664) stands out among the painters of Seville for his quiet intensity. This artist's most important works were done for monastic orders, and consequently are filled with an ascetic piety that is uniquely Spanish. *St. Serapion* (fig. 760) shows an early member of the Mercedarians (Order of Mercy) who was brutally murdered by pirates in 1240 but canonized only a hundred years after this picture was painted. The canvas was appropriately placed as a devotional image in the funerary chapel of the order, which was originally dedicated to self-sacrifice.

The painting will remind us of Caravaggio's *David with the Head of Goliath* (see fig. 12). Each shows a single, three-quarter-length figure in lifesize. But Zurbarán's saint is both hero and martyr, and it is the viewer who now contemplates the slain monk with a mixture of compassion and awe. The sharp contrast between the white habit and dark background lends the motionless figure a heightened visual and expressive presence. Here pictorial and spiritual purity become one. The hushed stillness creates a reverential mood that counteracts the

stark realism, so that we identify with the strength of St. Serapion's faith rather than with his physical suffering. The very absence of rhetorical pathos makes this timeless image profoundly moving. [See Primary Sources, no. 70, page 640.]

MURILLO. The work of Bartolomé Esteban Murillo (1617–1682), Zurbarán's successor as the leading painter in Seville, is the most cosmopolitan, as well as the most accessible, of any Spanish artist. For that reason, he exerted a vast influence on innumerable followers, whose pale imitations have obscured his considerable achievement. He learned as much from Northern artists, including Rubens and Rembrandt, as he did from Italians such as Reni and Guercino. The *Virgin and Child* in figure 761 unites these influences in an image that nevertheless retains an unmistakably Spanish character. The haunting expressiveness of the faces achieves a gentle pathos that lends a more overt appeal to Zurbarán's pietism. In addition to reflecting changes in religious practice, this must be seen as part of an attempt to inject new life into standard devotional images that had been reduced to formulaic repetition in the hands of lesser artists. The extraordinary sophistication of Murillo's brushwork and the subtlety of his color show the influence of Velázquez. There is a debt as well to the great Flemish Baroque painters Peter Paul Rubens and Anthony van Dyck (see fig. 766).

CHAPTER SEVEN

THE BAROQUE IN FLANDERS AND HOLLAND

In 1581, the six northern provinces of The Netherlands, led by William the Silent of Nassau, declared their independence from Spain, capping a rebellion that had begun 15 years earlier against Catholicism and the attempt by Philip II to curtail local power. The southern Netherlands, called Flanders (now divided between France and Belgium), were soon recovered; but after a long struggle the United Provinces (today's Holland) gained their autonomy, which was recognized by the truce declared in 1609. Although hostilities broke out again in 1621, the freedom of the Dutch was ratified by the Treaty of Münster, which ended the Thirty Years' War in 1648.

The division of The Netherlands had very different consequences for the economy, social structure, culture, and religion of the north and the south. After being sacked by marauding Spanish troops in 1576, Antwerp, its leading port, lost half its population. Although Brussels was the seat of government, Antwerp gradually regained its position as Flanders' commercial and artistic capital, until the Scheldt River leading to its harbor, which had been periodically shut down during the war, was closed permanently to shipping as part of the Treaty of Münster, thereby crippling trade for the next two centuries. Because Flanders continued to be ruled by Spanish regents, who were staunchly Catholic and viewed themselves as the defenders of the true faith, its artists relied heavily on commissions from Church and State, although the patronage of the aristocracy and wealthy merchants was also of considerable importance.

Holland, in contrast, was proud of its hard-won freedom. While the cultural links with Flanders remained strong, several factors encouraged the quick development of Dutch artistic traditions. Unlike Flanders, where all artistic activity radiated from Antwerp, Holland had a number of flourishing local schools. Besides Amsterdam, the commercial capital, we find important groups of painters in Haarlem, Utrecht, Leyden, Delft, and other towns. Thus Holland produced an almost bewildering variety of masters and styles.

The new nation was one of merchants, farmers, and seafarers, and its religion was Reformed Protestant, which was iconoclastic. Hence, Dutch artists did not have the large-scale commissions sponsored by State and Church that were available throughout the Catholic world. While municipal authorities and civic bodies provided a certain amount of art patronage, their demands were limited, so that the private collector now became the painter's chief source of support. This condition had already existed to some extent before (see page 540), but its full effect can be seen only after 1600. There was no shrinkage of output. On the contrary, the general public developed so insatiable an appetite for pictures that the whole country became gripped by a kind of collector's mania. John Evelyn, during a visit to Holland in 1641, noted in his diary that "it is an ordinary thing to find a common farmer lay out two or three thousand pounds in this commodity. Their houses are full of them, and they vend them at their fairs to very great gain." The collectors' mania in seventeenth-century Holland caused an outpouring of artistic talent comparable only to Early Renaissance Florence. Pictures became a commodity, and their trade followed the law of supply and demand. Many artists produced for the market rather than for individual patrons. They were lured into becoming painters by hopes of success that often failed to materialize, and even the greatest masters were sometimes hard-pressed. (It was not unusual for an artist to keep an inn, or run a small business on the side.) Yet they survived—less secure, but freer.

FLANDERS

RUBENS. Although Rome was its birthplace, the Baroque style soon became international. The great Flemish painter Peter Paul Rubens (1577–1640) holds a place of unique importance in this process. It might be said that he finished what Dürer had started a hundred years earlier: the breakdown of the artistic barriers between north and south. Rubens' father

762. Peter Paul Rubens. *The Raising of the Cross.* 1609–10. Center panel of a triptych, 15'1" x 11'9 5/8" (4.6 x 3.4 m). Antwerp Cathedral, Belgium

was a prominent Antwerp Protestant who fled to Germany to escape Spanish persecution during the war of independence (see page 539). The family returned to Antwerp after his death, when Peter Paul was ten years old, and the boy grew up a devout Catholic. Trained by local painters, Rubens became a master in 1598, but developed a personal style only when, two years later, he went to Italy.

During his eight years in the south, he absorbed the Italian tradition far more thoroughly than had any Northerner before him. He eagerly studied ancient sculpture, the masterpieces of the High Renaissance (see his splendid drawing after Leonardo's *Battle of Anghiari,* fig. 597), and the work of Caravaggio and Annibale Carracci. Rubens competed, in fact, with the best Italians of his day on even terms, and could well have made his career in Italy. When his mother's illness in 1608 brought him back to Flanders, he meant the visit to be brief, but he received a special appointment as court painter to the Spanish regent, which permitted him to establish a workshop in Antwerp, exempt from local taxes and guild regulations. Rubens had the best of both worlds. Like Jan van Eyck before him (see page 506), he was valued at court not only as an artist, but as a confidential adviser and emissary. Diplomatic errands gave him entrée to the royal households of the major powers, where he procured sales and commissions. Aided by a growing number of assistants, he was also free to carry out a huge volume of work for the city of Antwerp, for the Church, and for private patrons.

In his life, Rubens epitomized the extroverted Baroque ideal of the virtuoso for whom the entire universe is a stage. He was, on the one hand, a devoutly religious person and, on the other, a person of the world who succeeded in every arena by virtue of his character and ability. Rubens resolved the contradictions of the era through humanism, that union of faith and learning attacked by the Reformation and Counter Reformation alike. In his paintings as well, Rubens reconciled seemingly incompatible opposites. His enormous intellect and vitality enabled him to synthesize his sources into a unique style that unites the natural and supernatural, reality and fantasy, learning and spirituality. Thus his epic canvases defined the scope and the style of High Baroque painting. They possess a seemingly boundless energy and inventiveness, which, like his heroic nudes, express life at its fullest. The presentation of this heightened existence required the expanded arena that only Baroque theatricality, in the best sense of the term, could provide, and Rubens' sense of drama was as highly developed as Bernini's. At the same time, he could be the most human of artists.

The Raising of the Cross (fig. 762), the first major altarpiece Rubens produced after his return to Antwerp, shows strikingly how much he was indebted to Italian art. The muscular figures, modeled to display their physical power and passionate feeling, recall those of the Sistine ceiling and the Farnese Gallery, while the lighting suggests Caravaggio's. The panel nevertheless owes much of its success to Rubens' remarkable

763. Peter Paul Rubens. *Marie de' Medici, Queen of France, Landing in Marseilles.* 1622–23. Oil on panel, 25 x 19 3/4" (63.5 x 50.3 cm). Alte Pinakothek, Munich

ability to unite Italian influences with Netherlandish ideas, updating them in the process. The painting is more heroic in scale and conception than any previous Northern work, yet it is unthinkable without Rogier van der Weyden's *Descent from the Cross* (see fig. 679). Rubens is also a Flemish realist in such details as the foliage, the armor of the soldier, and the curly-haired dog in the foreground. These varied elements, integrated with sovereign mastery, form a composition of tremendous dramatic force. The unstable pyramid of bodies, swaying precariously, bursts the limits of the frame in a characteristically Baroque way, making the beholder feel like a participant in the action.

In the decade of the 1620s, Rubens' dynamic style reached its climax in his huge decorative schemes for churches and palaces. The most famous is the cycle in the Luxembourg Palace in Paris glorifying the career of Marie de' Medici, the widow of Henri IV and mother of Louis XIII. Our illustration shows the artist's oil sketch for one episode, the young queen landing in Marseilles (fig. 763). This is hardly an exciting subject in itself, yet Rubens has turned it into a spectacle of unprecedented splendor. As Marie de' Medici walks down the gangplank, Fame flies overhead sounding a triumphant blast on two trumpets, and Neptune rises from the sea with his fish-tailed crew. Having guarded the queen's journey, they rejoice at her arrival. Everything flows together here in swirling movement: heaven and earth, history and allegory—even drawing and painting, for Rubens used oil sketches like this one to prepare his compositions. Unlike earlier artists, he preferred to

design his pictures in terms of light and color from the very start. (Most of his drawings are figure studies or portrait sketches.) This unified vision, explored but never fully achieved by the great Venetians, was Rubens' most precious legacy to subsequent painters.

Around 1630, the turbulent drama of Rubens' preceding work changes to a late style of lyrical tenderness inspired by Titian, whose work Rubens discovered anew in the royal palace while he visited Madrid. *The Garden of Love* (fig. 764), one result of this encounter, is as glowing a tribute to life's pleasures as Titian's *Bacchanal* (see fig. 632). But these celebrants belong to the present, not to a golden age of the past, though they are playfully assaulted by swarms of cupids. To understand the artist's purpose, we must first realize that this subject, the Garden of Love, had been a feature of Northern painting ever since the courtly style of the International Gothic. The early versions, however, were genre scenes showing groups of fashionable young lovers in a garden. By combining this tradition with Titian's classical mythologies, Rubens has created an enchanted realm where myth and reality become one.

The picture must have had special meaning for him, since he had just married a beautiful girl of 16. (His first wife died in 1626.) He also bought a country house, Château Steen, and led the leisurely life of a squire. This change induced a renewed interest in landscape painting, which he had practiced only intermittenly before. Here, too, the power of his genius is undiminished. In *Landscape with the Château Steen* (fig. 765), a magnificent open space sweeps from the hunter and his prey

764. Peter Paul Rubens. *The Garden of Love.* c. 1638. Oil on canvas, 6'6" x 9'3 1/2" (2 x 2.8 m). Museo del Prado, Madrid

765. Peter Paul Rubens. *Landscape with the Château Steen.* 1636.
Oil on panel, 4'5" x 7'9" (1.34 x 2.36 m). The National Gallery, London
Reproduced by courtesy of the Trustees

766 . Anthony van Dyck. *Rinaldo and Armida*. 1629. Oil on canvas, 7'9" x 7'6" (2.36 x 2.24 m). The Baltimore Museum of Art
The Jacob Epstein Collection

767. Anthony van Dyck. *Portrait of Charles I Hunting*. c. 1635. Oil on canvas, 8'11" x 6'11¹/2" (2.7 x 2.1 m). Musée du Louvre, Paris

in the foreground to the mist-veiled hills along the horizon. As a landscapist, Rubens again creates a synthesis from his Northern and Southern sources, for he is the heir of both Pieter Bruegel and Annibale Carracci (compare figs. 716 and 731).

VAN DYCK. Besides Rubens, only one Flemish Baroque artist won international stature. Anthony van Dyck (1599– 1641) was that rarity among painters, a child prodigy. Before he was 20, he had become Rubens' most valued assistant. But like Rubens, he developed his mature style only after a formative stay in Italy.

Van Dyck's achievement as a history painter has been overshadowed by Rubens', yet it was of considerable importance in its own right. He was at his best in lyrical scenes of mythological love. *Rinaldo and Armida* (fig. 766), taken from Torquato Tasso's immensely popular poem *Jerusalem Freed* (1581) about the crusades, which gave rise to a new courtly ideal throughout Europe and inspired numerous operas as well as paintings, shows the sorceress falling in love with the Christian knight she intended to kill. The painting reflects the conception of the English monarchy, for whom it was painted. Charles I, a Protestant, had married the Catholic Henrietta Maria, sister of his rival, the king of France. Charles found parallels in Tasso's epic. He saw himself as the virtuous ruler of a peaceful realm much like the Fortunate Isle where Armida brought Rinaldo. (Ironically, Charles' reign ended in civil war and his beheading in 1649.) Van Dyck tells his story of ideal love in the pictorial language of Titian and Veronese, but with a lyrical tenderness and visual opulence that would have been the envy of any Venetian artist. The picture was so successful that it helped gain Van Dyck appointment to the English court two years later.

Van Dyck's fame rests mainly on the portraits he painted in London between 1632 and 1641. *Charles I Hunting* (fig. 767) shows the king standing near a horse and two grooms against a landscape backdrop. Representing the sovereign at ease, it might be called a "dismounted equestrian portrait"— less rigid than a formal state portrait, but hardly less grand, for the king remains fully in command of the state, symbolized by the horse. The fluid Baroque movement of the setting complements the self-conscious elegance of the king's pose, which continues the stylized grace of Hilliard's portraits (compare fig. 712). Van Dyck has brought the Mannerist court portrait up to date, using Rubens and Titian as his points of departure. In the process, he created a new aristocratic portrait tradition that continued in England until the late eighteenth century, and had considerable influence on the Continent as well.

JORDAENS. Jacob Jordaens (1593—1678) was the successor to Rubens and Van Dyck as the leading artist in Flanders. Although he was never a member of Rubens' studio, he turned to Rubens for inspiration throughout his career. His most characteristic subjects are mythological themes depicting the revels of nymphs and satyrs. Like his eating and drinking scenes, which illustrate popular parables of an edifying and moralizing sort, they reveal him to be a close observer of people. These denizens of the woods, however, inhabit an idyllic realm, untouched by the cares of human affairs. The painterly execution in *Homage to Pomona (Allegory of Fruitfulness)* (fig. 768)

768. Jacob Jordaens. *Homage to Pomona (Allegory of Fruitfulness)*.
c. 1623. Oil on canvas, 5'10⁷/8" x 7'10⁷/8" (1.8 x 2.4 m).
Musée Royaux d'Art et d'Histoire, Brussels

ing Jan Brueghel the Elder (1568–1625), the leader of the preceding generation, with whom he frequently collaborated. Although he was the principal heir to the tradition of his illustrious father, Pieter Bruegel the Elder (see page 542), Jan was an innovator who occupied a position of central importance in the transition from Mannerism to the Baroque in the North. *Allegory of Earth* (fig. 769) shows one of his major contributions to Flemish art: the "paradise" landscape. It originally belonged to a series devoted to the four elements, a common theme in Northern seventeenth-century painting, each with an appropriate biblical or mythological subject. Barely visible in the background is the expulsion of Adam and Eve from the Garden of Eden, a remnant of the Mannerist inverted perspective (see pages 540–41). Jan's enchanting vision of this innocent realm is made convincing by his meticulous realism. The small copperplate, which he, like many older artists, preferred, offered a smooth, hard surface ideally suited to his jewellike style.

acknowledges a strong debt to Rubens, yet the monumental figures dispense with Rubens' rhetoric and possess a calm dignity all their own.

JAN BRUEGHEL. Rubens' towering genius dominated Flemish painting. It touched every artist around him, includ-

SNYDERS. Brueghel also made an important contribution to flower painting. However, the development of the Baroque still life in Flanders was largely the responsibility of Frans Snyders (1579–1657), who studied with Jan's brother, Pieter Brueghel the Younger (1564–1638). Snyders concentrated on elaborate table still lifes piled high with food that epitomize the Flemish gusto for life during the Baroque era. His

769. Jan Brueghel the Elder. *Allegory of Earth*. c. 1618. Oil on copper, 18¹/8 x 26³/8" (46 x 67 cm). Musée du Louvre, Paris

770. Frans Snyders. *Market Stall.* 1614. Oil on canvas, 6'11⁷/8" x 10'3⁵/8" (2.1 x 3 m). © 1991 The Art Institute of Chicago
Charles H. and Mary F. S. Worcester Fund, 1981

771. Hendrick Terbrugghen.
The Calling of St. Matthew. 1621.
Oil on canvas, 40 x 54"
(101.5 x 137.2 cm).
Centraal Museum, Utrecht,
The Netherlands

splendid *Market Stall* (fig. 770) is a masterpiece of its kind. This early picture appeals frankly to the senses. The artist revels in the bravura application of paint, as seen in the varied textures of the game. The scene is further enlivened by the little drama of the youth picking the old man's pocket and the hens fighting in the foreground as a cat looks on from its safe retreat beneath the low bench.

Even here Rubens' influence can be felt: the composition descends from one Snyders painted with Rubens based on the latter's design shortly after both returned from Italy around

1609. *Market Stall* updates *The Meat Stall* of Pieter Aertsen (fig. 715) into a Baroque idiom. Unlike Aertsen, Snyders subordinates everything to the ensemble, which has a characteristically Baroque ebullience and immediacy. There is a fundamental difference in content as well. No longer is it necessary to include a religious subject in the background of this scene of plenty. Although an emblematic meaning has been suggested, the painting also celebrates a time of peace and prosperity after the truce of 1609, when hunting was resumed in the replenished game preserves.

772. Frans Hals. *The Jolly Toper*. c. 1628–30. Oil on canvas, 31 7/8 x 26 1/4" (81 x 66.6 cm). Rijksmuseum, Amsterdam

773. Frans Hals. *Malle Babbe*. c. 1650. Oil on canvas, 29 1/2 x 25" (75 x 63.5 cm). Gemäldegalerie, Berlin

HOLLAND

UTRECHT SCHOOL. The Baroque style came to Holland from Antwerp through the work of Rubens, and from Rome through direct contact with Caravaggio and his followers. Although most Dutch painters did not go to Italy, most of those who went in the early years of the century were from Utrecht, a town with strong Catholic traditions. It is not surprising that these artists were more attracted by Caravaggio's realism and "lay Christianity" than by Annibale Carracci's classicism. *The Calling of St. Matthew* by Hendrick Terbrugghen (1588–1629), the oldest and ablest of this group (fig. 771), directly reflects Caravaggio's earlier version (fig. 726) in the sharp light, the dramatic timing, and the everyday detail. Missing, however, is the element of grandeur and simplicity. While it produced few other major artists, the Utrecht School was important for transmitting the style of Caravaggio to other Dutch masters, who then made better use of these new Italian ideas.

HALS. One of the first to profit from this experience was Frans Hals (1580/85–1666), the great portrait painter of Haarlem. He was born in Antwerp, and what little is known of his early work suggests the influence of Rubens. His developed style, however, seen in *The Jolly Toper* (fig. 772), combines Rubens' robustness and breadth with a concentration on

the "dramatic moment" that must be derived from Caravaggio via Utrecht. Everything here conveys complete spontaneity: the twinkling eyes and half-open mouth, the raised hand, the teetering wineglass, and—most important of all—the quick way of setting down the forms. Hals works in dashing brushstrokes, each so clearly visible as a separate entity that we can almost count the total number of "touches." With this open, split-second technique, the completed picture has the immediacy of a sketch (compare our example by Rubens, fig. 763). The impression of a race against time is, of course, deceptive. Hals spent hours, not minutes, on this lifesize canvas, but he maintains the illusion of having done it all in the wink of an eye.

These qualities are even more forceful in the *Malle Babbe* (fig. 773), one of the artist's genre pictures. A lower-class counterpart of *The Jolly Toper,* this folk character, half-witch (note the owl), half-village idiot, screams invectives at other guests in a tavern. Hals seems to share their attitude toward this benighted creature, one of cruel amusement rather than sympathy, but his characterization is masterfully sharp and his lightninglike brushwork has the bravura of incredible skill.

In the artist's last canvases these pictorial fireworks are transmuted into an austere style of great emotional depth. His group portrait, *The Women Regents of the Old Men's Home at*

774. Frans Hals. *The Women Regents of the Old Men's Home at Haarlem.* 1664. Oil on canvas, 5'7" x 8'2" (1.70 x 2.49 m).
Frans Halsmuseum, Haarlem, The Netherlands

775. Judith Leyster. *Boy Playing a Flute.* 1630–35. Oil on canvas,
28 1/8 x 24 1/8" (73 x 62 cm). Nationalmuseum, Stockholm

Haarlem (fig. 774), has an insight into human character matched only in Rembrandt's late style (compare figs. 779 and 780). The daily experience of suffering and death has so etched the faces of these women that they seem themselves to have become images of death—gentle, inexorable, and timeless.

LEYSTER. Hals' virtuosity was such that it could not be imitated readily, and his followers were necessarily few. The most important among them was Judith Leyster (1609–1660). Like many women artists before modern times, her career was partially curtailed by motherhood. Leyster's enchanting *Boy Playing a Flute* (fig. 775) is her masterpiece. Significantly, its style is closer to Terbrugghen's than to Hals'. The rapt musician is a memorable expression of lyrical mood. To convey this spirit, Leyster investigated the poetic quality of light with a quiet intensity that anticipates the work of Jan Vermeer a generation later (see pages 592–93).

REMBRANDT. Like Hals, Rembrandt (1606–1669), the greatest genius of Dutch art, was stimulated at the beginning of his career by indirect contact with Caravaggio through the Utrecht School. His earliest pictures, painted in his native Leyden, are small, sharply lit, and intensely realistic. Many deal with Old Testament subjects, a lifelong preference. They show both his greater realism and his new emotional attitude. Since

776. Rembrandt. *The Blinding of Samson*. 1636. Oil on canvas, 7'9" x 9'11" (2.4 x 3 m).
Städelsches Kunstinstitut, Frankfurt

the beginning of Christian art, episodes from the Old Testament had often been represented for the light they shed on Christian doctrine, rather than for their own sake. (The Sacrifice of Isaac, for example, "prefigured" the sacrificial death of Christ.) This perspective not only limited the choice of subjects, it also colored their interpretation. Rembrandt, by contrast, viewed the stories of the Old Testament in much the same lay Christian spirit that governed Caravaggio's approach to the New Testament: as direct accounts of God's ways with his human creations.

How strongly these stories affected him is evident from *The Blinding of Samson* (fig. 776). Painted in the High Baroque style he developed in the 1630s after moving to Amsterdam, it shows Rembrandt as master storyteller. The artist depicts the Old Testament world as full of Oriental splendor and violence, cruel yet seductive. The flood of brilliant light pouring into the dark tent is unabashedly theatrical, heightening the drama to the pitch of *The Raising of the Cross* (fig. 762) by Rubens, whose work Rembrandt attempted to rival.

Rembrandt was at this time an avid collector of Near Eastern paraphernalia, which serve as props in these pictures. He was now Amsterdam's most sought-after portrait painter, as well as a man of considerable wealth. His famous group portrait known as *The Night Watch* (fig. 777), painted in 1642, shows a military company assembling for the visit of Marie de'

Medici to Amsterdam. Although its members had each contributed toward the cost of the huge canvas (originally it was even larger), Rembrandt did not give them equal weight. He was anxious to avoid the mechanically regular designs that afflicted earlier group portraits—a problem only Frans Hals had overcome successfully. Instead, he made the picture a virtuoso performance of Baroque movement and lighting, which captures the excitement of the moment and lends the scene unprecedented drama. Thus some of the figures were plunged into shadow, while others were hidden by overlapping. Legend has it that the people whose portraits he had obscured were dissatisfied. There is no evidence that they were. On the contrary, we know that the painting was much admired in its time.

Like Michelangelo and, later, Van Gogh, Rembrandt has been the subject (one might say, the victim) of many fictionalized biographies. In these, the artist's fall from public favor is usually explained by the "catastrophe" of *The Night Watch*. It is undeniable that his prosperity petered out in the 1640s, as he was replaced by other artists, including some of his own pupils. Nevertheless, his fortunes declined less suddenly and completely than his romantic admirers would have us believe. Certain important people in Amsterdam continued to be his steadfast friends and supporters, and he received some major public commissions in the 1650s and 1660s. Actually, his financial difficulties resulted largely from poor management

777. Rembrandt. *The Night Watch (The Company of Captain Frans Banning Cocq)*. 1642.
Oil on canvas, 12'2" x 14'7" (3.8 x 4.4 m). Rijksmuseum, Amsterdam

and his own stubbornness, which alienated his patrons. [See Primary Sources, no 71, pages 640–41.]

Still, the 1640s were a period of crisis, of inner uncertainty and external troubles, especially his wife's death. Rembrandt's outlook changed profoundly: after about 1650, his style eschews the rhetoric of the High Baroque for lyric subtlety and pictorial breadth. Some exotic trappings from the earlier years remain, but they no longer create an alien, barbarous world. Rembrandt's etchings from these years, such as *Christ Preaching* (fig. 778), show this new depth of feeling. The sensuous beauty seen in *The Blinding of Samson* has now yielded to a humble world of bare feet and ragged clothes. The scene is full of the artist's deep feeling of compassion for the poor and outcast who make up Christ's audience. Rembrandt had a special sympathy for the Jews, as the heirs of the biblical past and as the patient victims of persecution; they were often his models. This print, like the sketch in figure 7, strongly suggests some corner in the Amsterdam ghetto, and surely incorporates observations of life from the drawings he habitually made throughout his

career. Here it is the magic of light that endows *Christ Preaching* with spiritual significance. Rembrandt's importance as a graphic artist is second only to Dürer's, although we get no more than a hint from this single example.

In the many self-portraits Rembrandt painted over his long career, his view of himself reflects every stage of his inner development: experimental in the early Leyden years, theatrically disguised in the 1630s, frank toward the end of his life. While our late example (fig. 779) is partially indebted to Titian's sumptuous portraits (compare fig. 634), Rembrandt scrutinizes himself with the same typically Northern candor found in Jan van Eyck's *Man in a Red Turban* (see fig. 676). The bold pose and penetrating look bespeak a resigned but firm resolve in the face of adversity.

This self-analytical approach helps to account for the plain dignity we see in the religious scenes that play so large a part in Rembrandt's work toward the end of his life. *The Return of the Prodigal Son* (fig. 780), created a few years before his death, is perhaps Rembrandt's most moving painting. It is also his

778. Rembrandt. *Christ Preaching*. c. 1652. Etching, 6¹/₈ x 8¹/₈" (15.6 x 20.6 cm). The Metropolitan Museum of Art, New York

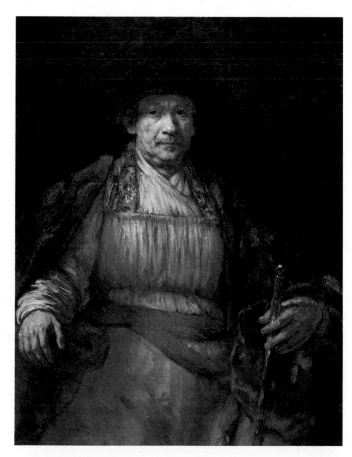

779. Rembrandt. *Self-Portrait*. 1658. Oil on canvas, 52⁵/₈ x 40⁷/₈"
(133.6 x 103.8 cm). The Frick Collection, New York

780. Rembrandt. *The Return of the Prodigal Son*.
c. 1665. Oil on canvas, 8'8" x 6'7³/₄" (2.6 x 2.1 m).
Hermitage Museum, St. Petersburg

quietest—a moment stretching into eternity. So pervasive is the mood of tender silence that the beholder senses a spontaneous kinship with this group. Our bond of shared experience is perhaps stronger and more intimate in this picture than in any earlier work of art. Here the wealth of human understanding accumulated over a lifetime of experience achieves a universal expression of sorrow and forgiveness.

LANDSCAPES. Rembrandt's religious pictures demand an insight that was beyond the capacity of all but a few collectors. Most art buyers in Holland preferred subjects within their own experience: landscapes, architectural views, still lifes, everyday scenes. These various types, we recall, originated in the latter half of the sixteenth century (see page 540). As they became fully defined, an unheard-of specialization began. The trend was not confined to Holland. We find it everywhere to some degree, but Dutch painting was its fountainhead, in both volume and variety.

VAN GOYEN. *Pelkus-Poort* (fig. 781) by Jan van Goyen (1596–1656) is the kind of landscape that enjoyed great popularity because its elements were so familiar: the distant town under a looming overcast sky, seen through a moisture-laden atmosphere across an expanse of water. Such a view remains characteristic of the Dutch countryside to this day, and no one knew better than Van Goyen how to evoke the special mood of these "nether lands," ever threatened by the sea.

Like other early Dutch Baroque landscapists, Van Goyen restricted his palette to grays and browns highlighted by green accents, but within this narrow range he achieved an almost infinite variety of effects. The tonal landscape style in Holland was allied to a drastic simplification of composition, which reduced the complex constructions of Northern Mannerism to orderly arrangements. Van Goyen's scene is based on a lucid scheme of parallel bands surmounted by a triangle. He discovered what Annibale Carracci had already learned from Giorgione and the Venetians: that the secret to depicting landscape lay in geometry, which enabled the artist to gain visual control over nature as it did architecture.

781. Jan van Goyen. *Pelkus-Poort.* 1646. Oil on panel, 14 1/2 x 22 1/2" (36.8 x 57.2 cm). The Metropolitan Museum of Art, New York
Gift of Francis Neilson, 1954

CUYP. Other Northern artists absorbed this lesson directly in Rome, where they congregated in growing numbers. The Dutch Italianates who returned home in the 1640s brought with them new ideas that were to have an invigorating effect on landscape painting. Their impact can be seen in the work of Aelbert Cuyp (1620–1691), who never left his native soil. A follower of Van Goyen, he quickly abandoned tonalism in favor of the radiant light found in their views of the Roman Campagna, which parallel the work of Claude Lorraine (see fig. 796). The golden sunlight of late afternoon imbues Cuyp's *View of the Valkhof at Nijmegen* (fig. 782) with a poetic mood that suspends the scene in time and space. The nearly classical structure of the composition and cubic handling of the architecture heighten the sense of repose created by Cuyp's grasp of even the subtlest atmospheric effects.

RUISDAEL. Although nature was enjoyed for its own sake, it could also serve as a means of divine revelation through contemplation of God's work. Such is the case with *The Jewish Cemetery* (fig. 783) by Jacob van Ruisdael (1628/9–1682), the

---

782. Aelbert Cuyp. *View of the Valkhof at Nijmegen.* c. 1655–65. Oil on panel, 19¹/₄ x 29" (48.9 x 73.7 cm).
Gift of Mrs. James W. Fesler. © 1993 Indianapolis Museum of Art

783. Jacob van Ruisdael. *The Jewish Cemetery.* 1655–60. Oil on canvas, 4'6" x 6'2¹/₂" (1.42 x 1.89 m).
The Detroit Institute of Arts
Gift of Julius H. Haass in memory of his brother, Dr. Ernest W. Haass

784. Pieter Saenredam. *Interior of the Choir of St. Bavo's Church at Haarlem.* 1660. Oil on panel, 27 7/8 x 21 5/8" (70.4 x 54.8 cm). Worcester Art Museum, Worcester, Massachusetts

Charlotte E. W. Buffington Fund

greatest Dutch landscape painter. Natural forces dominate this wild scene, which is frankly imaginary, except for the tombs, which depict the Jewish cemetery in Amsterdam. The thunderclouds passing over a deserted mountain valley, the medieval ruin, the torrent that has forced its way between ancient graves, all create a mood of deep melancholy. Nothing endures on this earth, the artist tells us: time, wind, and water grind all to dust, the trees and rocks, as well as the feeble works of human hands. Even the elaborate tombs offer no protection from the same forces that destroy the church built in God's glory. Within the context of this extended allegory, the rainbow may be understood as a sign of the promise of redemption through faith. Ruisdael's view of nature is thus the exact opposite of Annibale Carracci's "civilized" landscape (compare fig. 731). It harks back instead to Giorgione's tragic vision (see fig. 631). *The Jewish Cemetery* inspires that awe on which the Romantics, 150 years later, based their concept of the Sublime. The difference is that for Ruisdael, God ultimately remains separate from his creation, instead of a part of it.

SAENREDAM. Nothing at first seems further removed from *The Jewish Cemetery* than the painstakingly precise *Interior of the Choir of St. Bavo's Church at Haarlem* (fig. 784), painted by Pieter Saenredam at almost the same time. Yet it, too, is meant to serve as more than a mere topographic record. (These architectural views were often freely invented as well.) The medieval structure, stripped of all furnishings and whitewashed under Protestant auspices, has acquired a crystalline spaciousness that invites meditation.

STILL LIFES. Still lifes exist above all to delight the senses, but even they can be tinged with a melancholy air. As a result of Holland's conversion to Calvinism, these visual feasts

785. Willem Claesz. Heda. *Still Life.* 1634. Oil on panel, 16 7/8 x 22 7/8" (43 x 57 cm). Museum Boymans-van Beuningen, Rotterdam, The Netherlands

became vehicles for teaching moral lessons. Most Dutch Baroque still lifes treat the theme of Vanitas (the vanity of all earthly things). Overtly or implicitly, they preach the virtue of temperance, frugality, and hard work by admonishing the viewer to contemplate the brevity of life, the inevitability of death, and the passing of all earthly pleasures. The medieval tradition of imbuing everyday objects with religious significance was absorbed into vernacular culture though emblem books which, together with other forms of popular literature and prints, encompassed the prevailing ethic in words and pictures. The stern Calvinist sensibility is exemplified by such homilies as, "A fool and his money are soon parted" (a saying

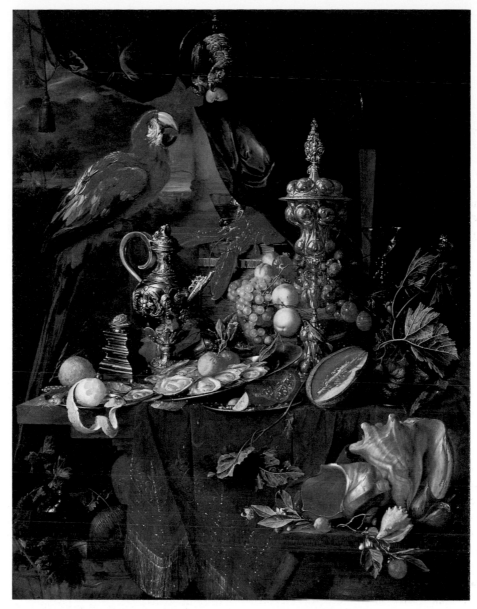

786. Jan de Heem. *Still Life with Parrots.* Late 1640s. Oil on canvas, 59¼ x 45½" (150.5 x 115.5 cm).
John and Mable Ringling Museum of Art, Sarasota, Florida

that goes all the way back to ancient Rome), and illustrated by flowers, shells, and other exotic luxuries. The very presence in Vanitas still lifes of precious goods, scholarly books, and objects appealing to the senses suggests an ambivalent attitude toward their subject. Such symbols usually take on multiple meanings which, though no longer comprehensible to us, were readily understood at the time. In their most elaborate form, these moral allegories become visual riddles that rely on the very learning they sometimes ridicule.

HEDA. The banquet (or breakfast) piece, showing the remnants of a meal, had Vanitas connotations almost from the beginning. The message may lie in such established symbols as death's-heads and extinguished candles, or be conveyed by less direct means. *Still Life* (fig. 785) by Willem Claesz. Heda (1594–1680) belongs to this widespread type. Food and drink are less emphasized here than luxury objects, such as crystal goblets and silver dishes, which are carefully juxtaposed for their contrasting shape, color, and texture. How different this seems from the piled-up edibles of Aertsen's *Meat Stall* (see fig. 715)! But virtuosity was not Heda's only aim. He reminds us

that all is Vanity. His "story," the human context of these grouped objects, is suggested by the broken glass, the half-peeled lemon, the overturned silver dish. The unstable composition, with its signs of a hasty departure, is itself a reference to transience. Whoever sat at this table has been suddenly forced to abandon the meal. The curtain that time has lowered on the scene, as it were, invests the objects with a strange pathos. The disguised symbolism of "Late Gothic" painting lives on here in a new form.

DE HEEM. The breakfast piece soon evolved into an even more lavish display, known appropriately as the "fancy" still life for its visual splendor, which culminated in the work of Jan de Heem (1606–1684). De Heem began his career in Protestant Holland, but he soon moved to Catholic Flanders. However, he traveled back and forth between the two countries and eventually returned to his native land. His achievement was to synthesize the sober Dutch tradition with the flamboyant manner of Frans Snyders into a unique style that proved equally influential on both sides of the border. In *Still Life with Parrots* (fig. 786), De Heem has compiled delicious food,

787. Rachel Ruysch. *Flower Still Life*. After 1700. Oil on canvas, 29³/4 x 23⁷/8" (75.5 x 60.7 cm).
The Toledo Museum of Art, Ohio
Purchased with funds from the Libbey Endowment, Gift of Edward Drummond Libbey

exotic birds, and luxurious goods from around the world. The result is a stunning tour de force. Despite its profusion, the painting is unified by the balanced composition and colorful palette. In keeping with the appetitive theme, the viewer is meant to enjoy the visual abundance, which celebrates the work of the Lord and humanity. At the same time, the picture has a covert meaning. Many of these objects, including the oysters, melon, and shells (which commanded high prices), are also standard Vanitas symbols conveying an admonition to be temperate. The extravagant display further incorporates the time-honored theme of the four elements, as well as traditional Christian imagery: the parrot is identified with the Madonna as the mother of Christ, while the grapes are a reference to the Eucharistic wine and, hence, resurrection, as is the pomegranate, which stands for the Virgin's purity as well.

RUYSCH. De Heem also formulated the High Baroque floral still life so definitively that flower painters were to feel his impact for the next 200 years. Many of them were women, including his pupil Maria van Oosterwijck (1630–1693), who became a celebrated artist in her own right. Her achievements were soon outstripped by those of Rachel Ruysch (1664–1750), who shared honors with Jan van Huysum

(1682–1749) as the leading Dutch flower painters of the day. Was she aware of the significance of every blossom, and of the butterflies, moths, and snails she put into the beautiful piece in figure 787, each of which has a complex symbolic meaning? By this time it is doubtful that she assembled her bouquet to a moralizing end. Instead, the main purpose of Ruysch's painting was surely to please the eye. She imparts such a sweeping vitality to the swirling profusion of buds that they fairly leap from their vase.

STEEN. The large class of pictures termed genre is as varied as that of landscapes and still lifes. It ranges from tavern brawls to refined domestic interiors. *The Feast of St. Nicholas* (fig. 788) by Jan Steen (1625/6–1679) is midway between. St. Nicholas has just paid his pre-Christmas visit to the household, leaving toys, candy, and cake for the children. The little girl and boy are delighted with their presents. She clutches a doll of St. John the Baptist and a bucket filled with sweets, while he plays with a golf club and ball. Everybody is jolly except their brother, on the left, who has received only a birch rod (held by the young maidservant) for caning naughty children. Soon his tears will turn to joy, however: his grandmother, in the background, beckons to the bed, where a toy is hidden.

788. Jan Steen. *The Feast of St. Nicholas.* c. 1660–65. Oil on canvas, 32 1/4 x 27 3/4" (82 x 70.5 cm).
Rijksmuseum, Amsterdam

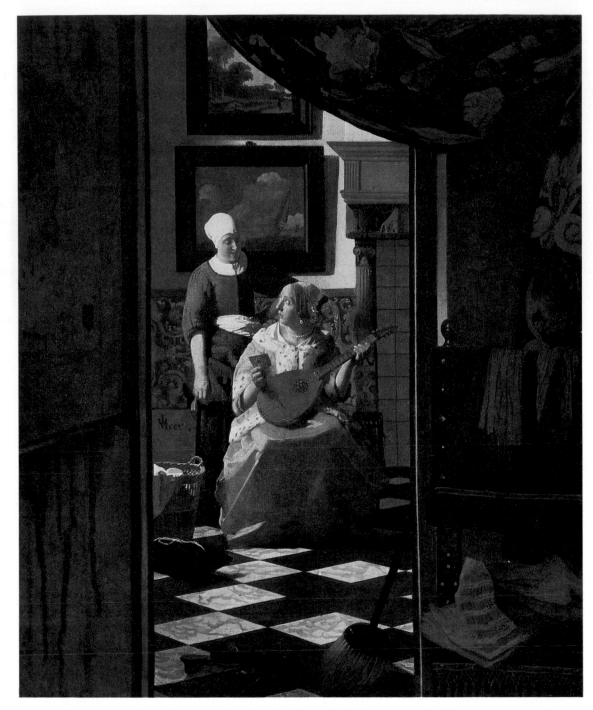

789. Jan Vermeer. *The Letter*. 1666. Oil on canvas, 17 1/4 x 15 1/4" (43.3 x 38.3 cm). Rijksmuseum, Amsterdam

Steen tells this story with relish, embroidering it with many delightful details. Of all the Dutch painters of daily life, he was the sharpest and the most good-humored observer. To supplement his earnings he kept an inn, which perhaps explains his keen insight into human behavior. His sense of timing and his characterization often remind us of Frans Hals (compare fig. 773), while his story-telling stems from the tradition of Pieter Bruegel the Elder (compare fig. 717). At the same time, Steen was a gifted history painter, and although his pictures often contain parodies of well-known works by Italian artists, they usually convey a serious message as well. Thus the doll of the hermit saint John is meant to remind the viewer about the

importance of spiritual matters over worldly possessions, no matter how delightful or innocent the latter may be.

VERMEER. In the genre scenes of Jan Vermeer (1632–1675), by contrast, there is hardly any narrative. Single figures, usually women, are seemingly engaged in simple, everyday tasks (see fig. 23). They exist in a timeless "still life" world, as if calmed by some magic spell. When there are two, as in *The Letter* (fig. 789), they do no more than exchange glances. The painting nonetheless does tell a story, but with unmatched subtlety. The carefully "staged" entrance serves to establish our relation to the scene. We are more than privileged bystanders:

we become the bearer of the letter that has just been delivered to the young woman. Dressed in sumptuous clothing, she has been playing the lute, as if awaiting our visit. This instrument, laden with erotic meaning, traditionally signifies the harmony between lovers, who play each other's heart strings. Are we, then, her lover? The amused expression of the maid suggests just such an anecdotal interest. Moreover, the lover in Dutch art and literature is often compared to a ship at sea, whose calm waters depicted in the painting here indicate smooth sailing. As usual with Vermeer, however, the picture refuses to yield a final answer, since the artist has concentrated on the moment before the letter is opened.

Vermeer's real interest centers on the role of light in creating the visible world. The cool, clear daylight that filters in from the left is the only active element, working its miracles upon all the objects in its path. As we look at *The Letter*, we feel as if a veil had been pulled from our eyes, for the everyday world shines with jewellike freshness, beautiful as we have never seen it before. No painter since Jan van Eyck *saw* as in-

tensely as this. But Vermeer, unlike his predecessors, perceives reality as a mosaic of colored surfaces—or perhaps more accurately, he translates reality into a mosaic as he puts it on canvas. We see *The Letter* not only as a perspective "window," but as a plane, a "field" composed of smaller fields. Rectangles predominate, carefully aligned with the picture surface, and there are no "holes," no undefined empty spaces. Only Pieter de Hooch (1629–1684), his contemporary in Delft, had such a feel for visual order (see fig. 14).

The interlocking shapes give to Vermeer's work a uniquely modern quality within seventeenth-century art. How did he acquire it? Despite the discovery of considerable documentary evidence relating to his life, we still know very little about his training. Some of his works show the influence of Carel Fabritius (1622–1654), the most brilliant of Rembrandt's pupils; other pictures suggest his contact with the Utrecht School. But none of these sources really explains the genesis of his style, so daringly original that his genius was not recognized until about a century ago.

CHAPTER EIGHT

THE BAROQUE
IN FRANCE AND
ENGLAND

FRANCE: THE AGE OF VERSAILLES

Under Henry IV (1553–1610), Louis XIII (1601–1643), and Louis XIV (1638–1715), France became the most powerful nation of Europe, militarily and culturally. In this they were aided by a succession of extremely able ministers and advisers: the Duc de Sully, Cardinal Richelieu, Cardinal Mazarin, and Jean-Baptiste Colbert. By the late seventeenth century, Paris was vying with Rome as the world capital of the major and minor arts, a position the Holy City had held for centuries. How did this change come about? Because of the Palace of Versailles and other vast projects glorifying the king of France, we are tempted to think of French art in the age of Louis XIV as the expression—and one of the products—of absolutism. This is true of the climactic phase of Louis' reign, 1660–85, but by that time seventeenth-century French art had already attained its distinctive style.

The French are reluctant to call this manner Baroque. To them, it is the Style of Louis XIV. Often they also describe the art and literature of the period as "classic." In this context, the word has three meanings. It is first of all a synonym for "highest achievement," which implies that the Style of Louis XIV corresponds to the High Renaissance in Italy or the age of Pericles in ancient Greece. The term also refers to the emulation of the form and subject matter of classical antiquity. Finally, "classic" suggests qualities of balance and restraint, shared by ancient art and the Renaissance. The second and third of these meanings describe what could more accurately be called "classicism." Since the Style of Louis XIV reflects Italian Baroque art, however modified, we may label it "Baroque classicism."

This classicism was the official court style between 1660 and 1685, but its origin was primarily artistic, not political. Sixteenth-century architecture in France, and to a lesser extent sculpture, were more intimately linked with the Italian Renaissance than in any other Northern country, although painting

continued to be governed by the Mannerist style of the later school of Fontainebleau until after 1600 (see page 496). Classicism was also nourished by French humanism, with its intellectual heritage of reason and Stoic virtue, which reflected the values of the middle-class who dominated cultural and political life. These factors retarded the spread of the Baroque in France and modified its interpretation. Rubens' Medici cycle (see fig. 763), for example, had no effect on French art until the very end of the century. In the 1620s, when he painted it, the young artists in France were still assimilating the Early Baroque.

Printmaking

CALLOT. An important transitional figure among these neglected masters was Jacques Callot (1592/3–1635), an etcher and engraver whose work was of importance for both Georges de La Tour and the young Rembrandt. Much of his early career was spent at the court of Cosimo II de' Medici in Florence, where he mainly executed prints dealing with the theater, especially the *commedia dell'arte* (see box page 569). After he returned in 1621 to his native town of Nancy, his work underwent a profound change. His prints now alternate between apocalyptic intensity, which allies him directly with Hieronymus Bosch, and astonishing directness, which draws close to the spirit of Pieter Bruegel the Elder, yet he belongs fully to his own time. Thus, Callot's work looks as much to past tradition as it does to the art of the present. These qualities merge in *Great Miseries of War,* which appeared in 1633, the year Richelieu conquered Nancy. This series of etchings represents a distillation of Callot's experience of the Thirty Years' War, but it also has a moralizing purpose. *Hangman's Tree* (fig. 790) depicts soldiers paying for their crimes. "Finally

790. Jacques Callot. *Hangman's Tree*, from *Great Miseries of War.* 1633. Etching, 3¹/2 x 9" (9 x 23 cm). The British Museum, London

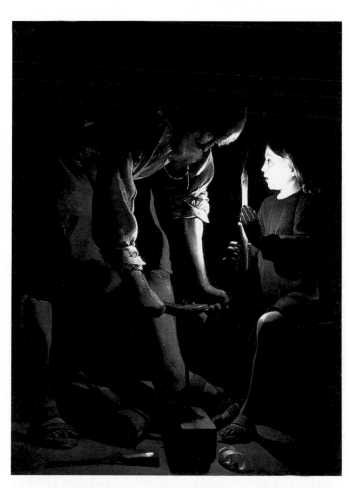

791. Georges de La Tour. *Joseph the Carpenter.* c. 1645. Oil on canvas, 51¹/8 x 39³/4" (130 x 100 cm). Musée du Louvre, Paris

these thieves, sordid and forlorn, hanging like unfortunate pieces of fruit from this tree," so the inscription tells us, "experience the justice of Heaven sooner or later." The style remains Mannerist, except in the group to the right, which participates in the same naturalism as the Le Nains'. Callot's unflinching portrayal makes this stark scene far grimmer than Bosch's vision of Hell in *The Garden of Delights* (see fig. 684). The plate has a striking immediacy, gained from the artist's experience of the theater, that in turn anticipates the vividness of Goya's imagery (see fig. 864).

Painting

DE LA TOUR. Many early French Baroque painters were influenced by Caravaggio, although how they absorbed his style is far from clear. They were for the most part minor artists toiling in the provinces, but a few developed highly original styles. The finest of them was Georges de La Tour (1593–1652), whose importance was recognized only 200 years later. Although he spent his career in Lorraine in northeast France, he was by no means a simple provincial artist. In addition to being named a painter to the king, De La Tour received important commissions from the governor of Lorraine. He began his career painting picturesque figures in the tradition of Callot, then turned to elaborate stock scenes from contemporary theater derived largely from Caravaggio's Northern followers.

Although the latter are well painted, De La Tour would arouse no more than passing interest were it not for his mature religious pictures, which possess both seriousness and grandeur. *Joseph the Carpenter* (fig. 791) might be mistaken for a genre scene, but its devotional spirit has the power of Caravaggio's *Calling of St. Matthew* (see fig. 726). De La Tour's

792. Louis Le Nain. *Peasant Family.* c. 1640. Oil on canvas, 44 1/2 x 62 1/2" (113 x 158.7 cm). Musée du Louvre, Paris

intensity of vision lends each gesture, each expression, its maximum significance within this spellbinding composition. The boy Jesus holds a candle, a favorite device with this artist, which lights the scene with an intimacy and tenderness reminiscent of the *Nativity* by Geertgen tot Sint Jans (fig. 683). De La Tour also shares Geertgen's tendency to reduce forms to a geometric simplicity that elevates them above the everyday world, despite their apparent realism.

THE LE NAINS. Like Georges de La Tour, the three Le Nain brothers—Antoine, Louis, and Mathieu—were rediscovered in modern times, but they did not have to wait quite so long. Although their birth dates are not known, all must have been born in Laon during the first decade of the century. By 1629 they were in Paris, where the eldest two died of the plague in 1648. Despite the fact that they shared the same style, signed their pictures simply "Le Nain," and worked on paintings together, each had a distinctive personality. Antoine was a miniaturist at heart, Louis the most severe, and Mathieu the most robust. Louis' *Peasant Family* (fig. 792) nevertheless exemplifies their "family" style and its virtues. Like the peasant scenes of seventeenth-century Holland and Flanders, with which it has much in common, the picture stems from a tradition going back to Pieter Bruegel the Elder (see fig. 717). But whereas the Netherlandish scenes of lowlife are often humorous or satirical (see fig. 773), Le Nain endows them with a human dignity and monumental weight that recall Velázquez' *Water Carrier of Seville* (see fig. 757).

POUSSIN. Why were these artists forgotten so quickly? The reason is simply that after the 1640s, classicism was supreme

in France. The clarity, balance, and restraint of their art, when measured against other Caravaggesque painters, might be termed "classical," but neither was a "classicist." The artist who did the most to bring the rise of classicism about was Nicolas Poussin (1593/4–1665). The greatest French painter of the century and the first French painter in history to win international fame, Poussin nevertheless spent almost his entire career in Rome. There, under the influence of Raphael, he formulated the style that was to become the ideal model for French painters of the second half of the century.

Poussin was initially inspired by Titian's warm, rich colors and by his approach to classical mythology. In *Cephalus and Aurora* (fig. 793) Poussin visualizes the ancient past as a poetic dream world, although the unalloyed bliss of Titian's *Bacchanal* (fig. 632) is now overcast with melancholy. Like many other early subjects by Poussin, this is a tale of frustrated love drawn from the Roman poet Ovid's *Metamorphoses,* a favorite source for Baroque artists (see also fig. 20), although the picture characteristically departs from the text. Aurora, the goddess of dawn, tries to embrace the mortal Cephalus, who spurns her love out of faithfulness to his wife, Procris. Cephalus' fidelity is shown by the charming device of a putto holding up a portrait of Procris to his gaze. The sleeping river-god to the left signifies night, as the sun-god Apollo waits by his chariot in the background for daybreak (see also fig. 734).

By contrast, *The Abduction of the Sabine Women* (fig. 794) must be seen altogether differently. It, too, shows his profound allegiance to antiquity, but in style and attitude the two works are much farther apart than the seven years' difference in date would suggest. *The Abduction of the Sabine Women* epitomizes the severe discipline of Poussin's intellectual style, which

793. Nicolas Poussin. *Cephalus and Aurora*. c. 1630. Oil on canvas, 38 x 51" (96.7 x 129.7 cm). The National Gallery, London

794. Nicolas Poussin. *The Abduction of the Sabine Women*. c. 1636–37.
Oil on canvas, 5'7/8" x 6'10⁵/8" (1.54 x 2.09 m). The Metropolitan Museum of Art, New York

795. Nicolas Poussin. *The Birth of Bacchus*. c. 1657. Oil on canvas,
48¼ x 70½" (122.6 x 179.1 cm). Fogg Art Museum,
Harvard University Art Museums, Cambridge, Massachusetts
Gift of Mrs. Samuel Sachs in memory of her husband

developed in response to what he regarded as the excesses of the High Baroque (see page 558). The strongly modeled figures are "frozen in action" like statues; many are, in fact, derived from Hellenistic sculpture. Poussin has placed them before reconstructions of Roman architecture that he believed to be archaeologically correct. The composition has an air of theatricality, and with good reason. It was worked out by moving clay figurines around a miniature stagelike setting until it looked right to the artist. Emotion is abundantly displayed, but it is so lacking in spontaneity that it fails to touch us. The attitude reflected here is clearly Raphael's (see figs. 626 and 627). More precisely, it is Raphael as filtered through Annibale Carracci and his school (compare figs. 729 and 734). The Venetian qualities that asserted themselves early in his career have been consciously suppressed.

Poussin now strikes us as an artist who knew his own mind only too well, an impression confirmed by the numerous letters in which he expounded his views to friends and patrons. The highest aim of painting, he believed, is to represent noble and serious human actions. This is true even in *The Abduction of the Sabine Women,* which, ironically, was admired as an act of patriotism that insured the future of Rome. (According to the accounts of Livy and Plutarch, the Sabines otherwise escaped unharmed, and the young women abducted as wives by the Romans later became peacemakers between the two sides.) Be that as it may, such actions must be shown in a logical and orderly way—not as they really happened, but as they would have happened if nature were perfect. To this end, art must strive for the general and typical. In appealing to the mind rather than the senses, the painter should suppress such incidentals as color, and stress form and composition. In a good picture, the beholder must be able to "read" the exact emotions of each figure and relate them to the story. [See Primary Sources, no. 72, page 641.] These ideas were not new. We recall Horace's dictum *ut pictura poesis* and Leonardo's statement that the highest aim of painting is to depict "the intention of man's soul" (see pages 408 and 456). Before

Poussin, however, no one made the analogy between painting and literature so close, nor put it into practice so single-mindedly. His method accounts for the cold and over-explicit rhetoric in *The Abduction of the Sabine Women,* which makes the picture seem so remote, much as we may admire its rigor.

Poussin also painted "ideal" landscapes according to this theoretical view, with surprisingly impressive results, for they have an austere beauty and somber calm. This severe rationalism lasted until about 1650, when he began to paint a series of landscapes that return to the realm of mythology he had abandoned in middle age. They unite the Titianesque style of his early work with his later, Raphaelesque classicism to produce a new kind of mythological landscape, close in spirit to Claude Lorraine's (see below) but rich in personal associations that lend them multiple levels of meaning. Indeed, the artist's late ruminations have rightly been called transcendental meditations, for they contain archetypal imagery of universal significance. *The Birth of Bacchus* (fig. 795), among his most profound statements, takes up the great Stoic theme (which Poussin had treated twice already as a young man) that death is to be found even in the happiest realm. The painting shows the moment when the infant, created by Jupiter's union with Semele, the moon-goddess, and born from his thigh, is delivered for safe-keeping by Mercury to the river-goddess Dirce, while the satyr Pan plays the flute in rapt inspiration. (Jupiter himself had been raised by sylvan deities.)

The picture is not beautifully executed. The act of painting became difficult for the artist in old age, so that the brushwork is shaky. He nevertheless turned this liability to his advantage, and *The Birth of Bacchus* represents the purest realization of expressive intent in painted form. It is full of serene lyricism conveying the joy of life on the one hand, and dark forebodings of death on the other: to the right, the nymph Echo weeps over the dead Narcissus, the beautiful youth who spurned her love and instead drowned kissing his reflection. Like Cephalus and Aurora, the story of Echo and Narcissus is taken from Ovid, but now it is the meaning, not the narrative, that interests Poussin. He treats it as part of the eternal cycle of nature, in which the gods embody natural forces and the myths contain fundamental truths. Although he certainly drew on the pantheistic writings of Tommaso Campanella and the learned commentaries of the Stoic Natale Conti, it is the artist's personal synthesis that brings these ideas to life.

CLAUDE LORRAINE. If Poussin developed the heroic qualities of the ideal landscape, the great French landscapist Claude Lorraine (1600–1682) brought out its idyllic aspects. He, too, spent almost his entire career in Rome. Like many Northerners, Claude explored the surrounding countryside, the Campagna, more thoroughly and affectionately than any Italian. Countless drawings made on the spot bear witness to his extraordinary powers of observation. He is also documented as having sketched in oils outdoors, the first artist known to have done so. Sketches, however, were only the raw material for his paintings, which do not aim at topographic exactitude but evoke the poetic essence of a countryside filled with echoes of antiquity. Often, as in *A Pastoral Landscape* (fig. 796), the compositions are suffused with the hazy, luminous atmosphere of early morning or late afternoon. The space

796. Claude Lorraine. *A Pastoral Landscape.* c. 1650. Oil on copper, 15¹/₂ x 21" (39.3 x 53.3 cm).
Yale University Art Gallery, New Haven, Connecticut
Leo C. Hanna, Jr., Fund

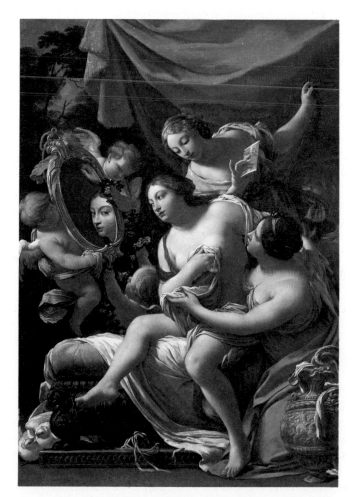

797. Simon Vouet. *The Toilet of Venus.* c. 1640. Oil on canvas, 65¹/₄ x
45" (165.7 x 114.3 cm). The Carnegie Museum of Art, Pittsburgh
Gift of Mrs. Horace Binney Hare

expands serenely, rather than receding step-by-step as in Poussin's landscapes. An air of nostalgia hangs over such vistas, of past experience gilded by memory. Hence they appealed especially to the English who had seen Italy only briefly or even not at all.

VOUET. At an early age Simon Vouet (1590–1649), too, went to Rome, where he became the leader of the French Caravaggesque painters; but unlike Poussin and Claude, he returned to France. Upon settling in Paris, he quickly shed all vestiges of Caravaggio's manner and formulated a colorful style based on Carracci's which won such acclaim that Vouet was named First Painter to the king. He also brought with him memories of the great North Italian precursors of the Baroque. *The Toilet of Venus* (fig. 797) depicts a subject popular in Venice from Titian to Veronese. Vouet's figure looks back as well to Correggio's Io (see fig. 655), but without her frank eroticism. Instead, she has been given an elegant sensuousness that could hardly be further removed from Poussin's disciplined art.

Ironically, *The Toilet of Venus* was painted about 1640, toward the beginning of Poussin's ill-fated sojourn in Paris, where he had gone at the invitation of Louis XIII. He met with no more success than Bernini was to have 20 years later (see page 606). After several years Poussin left, deeply disillusioned by his experience at the court, whose taste and politics Vouet understood far better. In one sense, their rivalry was to continue long afterward. Vouet's decorative manner provided the foundation for the Rococo, but it was Poussin's classicism that soon dominated art in France. The two traditions vied with each other through the Romantic era, alternating in succession without gaining the upper hand for long.

The central fact of French culture in the seventeenth century was the taste for classicism, which had been established 50 years earlier. The Pléiade, a group of poets led by Pierre de Ronsard (1524–1585), was founded in 1550 to develop French literature along the lines of Greek and Roman poetry and plays, which had been published and studied since early in the century. Around the same time, court festivals became popular, as did *intermezzi* (also called *ballets de cour*), which combined song, dance, drama, and spectacle in the "antique" manner. Public theater was monopolized by the Confrérie de la Passion (Confraternity of the Passion), which was given control over secular drama. (Religious plays were banned in 1548.) These three factors—classical taste, antiquarianism, and court patronage—decisively shaped French theater and music. The preference for classicism and humanism was reinforced during the regency of Henry II's Italian queen, Catherine de' Medici (1560–74). However, the development of the arts was disrupted by the Wars of Religion between Catholics and Protestants that broke out in 1562. Hostilities continued until the Protestants were defeated in 1629 by the soldiers of Louis XIII under the direction of prime minister Cardinal Richelieu (1585–1642).

The end of the Wars of Religion placed Richelieu in a position of immense power. A highly cultivated man, he now turned his attention not only to governing France, but also to patronage of the arts. In 1629, the same year that the Protestants were defeated, the French Academy, a small group of intellectuals, began to meet informally to discuss literature. At Cardinal Richelieu's behest, it became a state institution based on Italian models in 1636. The Academy required that theater teach moral lessons and adhere to the Italian concept of verisimilitude (see page 487). This was the first of a number of French academies that would be founded during the course of the seventeenth century to foster painting and sculpture, music, architecture, and even dance. These state-controlled academies oversaw the training of young artists and were responsible for awarding royal commissions. As time went on, the academies became increasingly authoritarian, eventually exercising rigid control over all of the arts.

The first important French dramatist was Alexandre Hardy (c. 1572–1632), a prolific playwright who wrote some 700 tragicomedies (plays of serious subject that end happily) and pastoral plays for the Hôtel de Bourgogne, the only permanent playhouse in Paris before the end of the wars in 1629. Otherwise, plays were performed on tennis courts (*jeux de paume*), with a platform erected as a stage. In 1640 Cardinal Richelieu had a theater erected at his palace, the first in France to feature a proscenium (the arch separating the stage from the auditorium), an innovation from Italy that was soon to become standard throughout Europe. Richelieu took a particular interest in drama and personally employed five playwrights to work under his supervision. The only one to achieve lasting fame was Pierre Corneille (1606–1684), whose tragedies, drawn from ancient history and mythology, center on the hero who chooses death over dishonor. They are written in the ornate, emotional language that defined French classical drama before 1650. Yet when Corneille submitted *Le Cid* to the Academy for review the year it was founded, the play met with such harsh criticism that he stopped writing for four years. Corneille's younger brother, Thomas (1625–1709), was also a noted playwright whose finest works date from the 1670s.

French drama reached its zenith in the plays of Jean Racine (1639–1699), whose tragedies in the Greek manner revolved around the conflict of desire and duty, expressed in direct, simple language that quickly replaced the elaborate language of Pierre Corneille. Racine's plays embody the theories of Nicolas Boileau-Despréaux (1636–1711), who championed the three unities of action, time, and place, and decorum in speech, manner, and moral behavior. Early in his career Racine had been befriended by Molière (Jean-Baptiste Poquelin, 1622–1673), whose plays marked the high tide of French comedy. *The Misanthrope* (1666) and *Tartuffe* (1664), influenced by the *commedia dell'arte* which enjoyed great success in France, are masterpieces of cynical wit written in the twelve-syllable Alexandrine couplets that had become the standard verse form of French theater. The Comédie Français, formed by royal decree in 1680 from Molière's troupe and that of the rival Hôtel Bourgogne, was granted a monopoly on all dramas in French, with the sole exception of the *commedia dell'arte* (see page 569), which was eventually banned in 1697 for an imagined slight of the king's mistress.

Cardinal Mazarin, Richelieu's successor who was an Italian by birth, had an abiding love of opera, which he actively promoted. Soon after taking the reins of full power upon Mazarin's death in 1661, Louis XIV began construction of a new palace at Versailles, outside Paris, where the aristocracy would be forced to live following the disastrous Fronde rebellion of 1648–52. Even before the palace was completed in 1682 Louis staged huge spectacles, such as *The Pleasure of the Enchanted Land* (1664), an allegory of his reign. The arts during the age of Louis XIV were meant to glorify the king, and classicism had an essential role to play. Classicism was favored not only because of its learned humanism and

THE ROYAL ACADEMY. When young Louis XIV took over the reins of government in 1661, Jean-Baptiste Colbert, his chief adviser, built the administrative apparatus to support the power of the absolute monarch. In this system, aimed at subjecting the thoughts and actions of the entire nation to strict control from above, the visual arts had the task of glorifying the king. As in music and theater, which shared the same task, the official "royal style" was classicism in both theory and practice. Centralized control over the visual arts was exerted by Colbert and the artist Charles Lebrun (1619–1690), who became supervisor of all the king's artistic projects. As chief dispenser of royal art patronage, Lebrun commanded so much power that for all practical purposes he was the dictator of the arts in France. This authority extended beyond the power of the purse. It also included a new system of educating artists in the officially approved style.

elevated moral tone, but also because it suggested that France was the successor to Greece and Rome. In the debates after 1688 known as the Battle of the Ancients and the Moderns, French academicians even sought to show the supremacy of French culture by using it to replace antiquity as the new standard.

Louis XIV appeared regularly in ballets during the 1650s, when they became great spectacles. Thereafter he continued to enjoy ballets and operas by his court composer and dancing master, Jean-Baptiste Lully (1632–1687). Lully had initially collaborated with Molière on comic ballets for the court, but the two ceased to work together in 1672 because of Lully's unscrupulous practices. Lully then forged a partnership with the playwright Philippe Quinault (1635–1688) that lasted a decade, from *Atys* (1676) through *Armide* (1686), based on Torquato Tasso's *Jerusalem Freed.* Their work, which emphasized the unity between text and music, was comparable in character to the tragedies of Corneille and Racine. Because he clung to the Florence *camerata*'s ideal of emphatic declamation (see page 558), Lully composed music of measured and stately simplicity. He also introduced additional choruses and ballets to the opera, which lent the performances a greater pageantry that benefited greatly from the costumes designed by Jean Bérain (1637–1711). The results were sober and pompous, but also colorful—perfectly suited to life at Versailles. Lully occupied a position in French music comparable to that of Charles Lebrun in the arts. He was instrumental in founding the Royal Academy of Dancing upon the king's retirement from active participation in ballets in 1661. In 1672, Lully merged the academies of music and dance to create the forerunner of the Opéra, the national opera company of France.

Lully was by far the most powerful force in French Baroque music. His only rival was Marc-Antoine Charpentier (1634–1704), a student of Carissimi, who as music director to the Jesuit order in Paris became the greatest French composer of religious music. Charpentier's secular music was also of high quality, particularly the opera *The Imaginary Illness* (1673), written with Molière after the latter had broken with Lully. The other major figure was the much younger François Couperin (1668–1733), organist to the king at Versailles, whose harpsichord and orchestral suites are notable for their lively invention. As a composer he straddled two eras: his most important compositions were written during the reign of Louis XV, although his music remained Late Baroque in style.

Throughout antiquity and the Middle Ages, artists had been trained by apprenticeship, and this time-honored practice still prevailed in the Renaissance. As painting, sculpture, and architecture gained the status of liberal arts, artists wished to supplement their "mechanical" training with theoretical knowledge. For this purpose, "art academies" were founded, patterned on the academies of the humanists. (The name *academy* is derived from the Athenian grove where Plato met

798. François Mansart. Vestibule of the Château of Maisons. 1642–50

with his disciples.) Art academies appeared first in Italy in the later sixteenth century as an outgrowth of literary academies. They seem to have been private associations of artists who met periodically to draw from the model and discuss questions of art theory. These academies later became formal institutions that took over some functions from the guilds, but their teaching was limited and far from systematic.

This was the case as well with the Royal Academy of Painting and Sculpture in Paris, founded in 1648. But when Lebrun became its director in 1663, he established a rigid curriculum of compulsory instruction in practice and theory, based on a system of "rules." This set the pattern for all later academies, including their successors, the art schools of today. Much of this doctrine was derived from Poussin, under whom Lebrun had spent several years studying in Rome, but it was carried to rationalistic extremes. The Academy even devised a method for tabulating, in numerical grades, the merits of artists past and present in such categories as drawing, expression, and proportion. The ancients received the highest marks, needless to say, then came Raphael and his school, and Poussin. The Venetians, who "overemphasized" color, ranked low, the Flemish and Dutch even lower. Subjects were similarly classified, from "history" (that is, narrative subjects, be they classical, biblical, or mythological) at the top to still life at the bottom.

Architecture

MANSART. Meanwhile, the foundations of Baroque classicism in architecture were laid by a group of designers whose most distinguished member was François Mansart (1598–1666). Apparently he never visited Italy, but other French architects had already imported and acclimatized some aspects of the Roman Early Baroque, especially in church design, so that Mansart was not unfamiliar with the new Italian style. What he owed to it, however, is hard to determine. His most important buildings are châteaux, and in this field the French Renaissance tradition outweighed any direct Italian Baroque influences. The Château of Maisons near Paris, built for a newly risen administrative official, shows Mansart's mature style at its best. The vestibule leading to the grand staircase (fig. 798) has a particularly beautiful effect, severe yet festive.

799. Claude Perrault. East Front of the Louvre, Paris. 1667–70

On seeing the classically pure articulation of the walls, one first thinks of Palladio (see page 501), whose treatise Mansart certainly knew and admired. But sculpture is used here in the characteristically French way as an integral part of architectural design. The complex curves of the vaulting further inform us that this structure, for all its classicism, belongs to the Baroque.

LOUIS XIV, COLBERT, AND THE LOUVRE. Mansart died too soon to have a share in the climactic phase of Baroque classicism. It began with the first great project Colbert directed, the completion of the Louvre. Work on the palace had proceeded intermittently for over a century, along the lines of Lescot's design (see fig. 722). What remained to be done was to close the square court on the east side with an impressive facade. Colbert, dissatisfied with the proposals of French architects, invited Bernini to Paris in the hope that the most famous master of the Roman Baroque would do for the French king what he had already done so magnificently for the Church. Bernini spent several months in Paris in 1665 and submitted three designs, all of them on a scale that would have completely engulfed the existing palace. After much argument and intrigue, Louis XIV rejected these plans and turned over the problem of a final solution to a committee of three: Charles Lebrun, his court painter; Louis Le Vau (1612–1670), his court architect, who had worked on the project before; and Claude Perrault (1613–1688), who was a student of ancient architecture, not a professional architect. All three were responsible for the structure that was actually built (fig. 799), although Perrault is usually credited with the major share. [See Primary Sources, no. 73, page 641.]

The design in some ways suggests the mind of an archaeologist, but one who knew how to select those features of classical architecture that would link Louis XIV with the glory of the Caesars and still be compatible with the older parts of the palace. The center pavilion is a Roman temple front, and the wings look like the flanks of that temple folded outward. The temple theme demanded a single order of free-standing columns, but the Louvre had three stories. This difficulty was skillfully resolved by treating the ground story as the podium of the temple and recessing the upper two behind the screen of the colonnade. The entire design combines grandeur and elegance in a way that fully justifies its fame. The East Front of the Louvre signaled the victory of French classicism over Italian Baroque as the royal style. Ironically, this great example proved too pure, and Perrault soon faded from favor.

PALACE OF VERSAILLES. The king's largest enterprise was the Palace of Versailles, located 11 miles from the center of Paris. It was begun in 1669 by Le Vau, who designed the elevation of the Garden Front (fig. 800) but died within a year. Under Jules Hardouin-Mansart (1646–1708), a great-nephew of François Mansart, the entire project was greatly expanded to accommodate the ever-growing royal household. The Garden Front, intended by Le Vau to be the main view of the palace, was stretched to an enormous length with no modification of the architectural membering, so that his original facade design, a less severe variant of the East Front of the Louvre, now looks repetitious and out of scale. The whole center block contains a single room, the famous Galerie des Glaces (Hall of Mirrors, fig. 801), with the Salon de la Guerre (War) and its counterpart, the Salon de la Paix (Peace), at either end.

800. Louis Le Vau and Jules Hardouin-Mansart. Garden Front of the center block of the Palace of Versailles. 1669–85

801. Hardouin-Mansart, Lebrun, and Coysevox. Galerie des Glaces (Hall of Mirrors), Palace of Versailles

802. Hardouin-Mansart, Lebrun, and Coysevox. Salon de la Guerre,
Palace of Versailles. Begun 1678

Baroque features, although not officially acknowledged, reappeared inside the Palace of Versailles. This shift corresponded to the king's own taste. Louis XIV was interested less in architectural theory and monumental exteriors than in the lavish interiors that would make suitable settings for himself and his court. Thus the man to whom he really listened was not an architect, but the painter Lebrun. Lebrun's goal was in itself Baroque: to subordinate all the arts to the glorification of Louis XIV. To accomplish it, he drew freely on his memories of Rome; the great decorative schemes of the Baroque that he saw there must also have impressed him, for they stood him in good stead 20 years later, both in the Louvre and at Versailles. Although a disciple of Poussin, he had studied first with Vouet, and became a superb decorator, utilizing the combined labors of architects, sculptors, painters, and artisans for ensembles of unheard-of splendor. The Salon de la Guerre at Versailles (fig. 802) is closer in many ways to the Cornaro Chapel than to the vestibule at Maisons (compare figs. 754 and 798). If Lebrun's ensemble is less adventurous than Bernini's, he has emphasized surface decoration just as much. And, as in so many Italian Baroque interiors, the separate ingredients are less impressive than the effect of the whole.

GARDENS OF VERSAILLES. Apart from the magnificent interior, the most impressive aspect of Versailles is the park extending west of the Garden Front for several miles (fig. 803). Its design, by André Le Nôtre (1613–1700), is so strictly correlated with the plan of the palace that it becomes a continuation of the architectural space. Like the interiors, these formal gardens, with their terraces, basins, clipped hedges, and statuary, were meant to provide an appropriate setting for the king's appearances in public. They form a series of "outdoor rooms" for the splendid fêtes and spectacles that Louis XIV so

enjoyed. The spirit of absolutism is even more striking in this geometric regularity imposed upon an entire countryside than it is in the palace itself.

HARDOUIN-MANSART. At Versailles, Jules Hardouin-Mansart worked as a member of a team, constrained by the design of Le Vau. His own architectural style can be better seen in the Church of the Invalides (figs. 804 and 805), named after the institution for disabled soldiers of which it formed one part. The building presents a combination of Italian Renaissance and Baroque features, but reinterpreted in a distinctly French manner. The plan, consisting of a Greek cross with four corner chapels, is based ultimately (with various French intermediaries) on Michelangelo's plan for St. Peter's (see fig. 623); its only Baroque element is the oval choir. The dome, too, reflects the influence of Michelangelo (figs. 622 and 624), and the classicistic vocabulary of the facade is reminiscent of the East Front of the Louvre, but the exterior as a whole is unmistakably Baroque. It breaks forward repeatedly in the crescendo effect introduced by Maderno (see fig. 739). And, as in Borromini's S. Agnese in Piazza Navona (see fig. 746), the facade and dome are closely correlated. The dome itself is the most original, and the most Baroque, feature of Hardouin-Mansart's design. Tall and slender, it rises in one continuous curve from the base of the drum to the spire atop the lantern. On the first drum rests, surprisingly, a second, narrower drum. Its windows provide light for the painted vision of heavenly glory inside the dome, but they themselves are hidden behind a "pseudo-shell" with a large opening at the top, so that the heavenly glory seems mysteriously illuminated and suspended in space. "Theatrical" lighting so boldly directed would do honor to any Italian Baroque architect.

803. Charles Rivière. *Perspective View of the Château and Gardens of Versailles.* Lithograph after an 1860 photograph

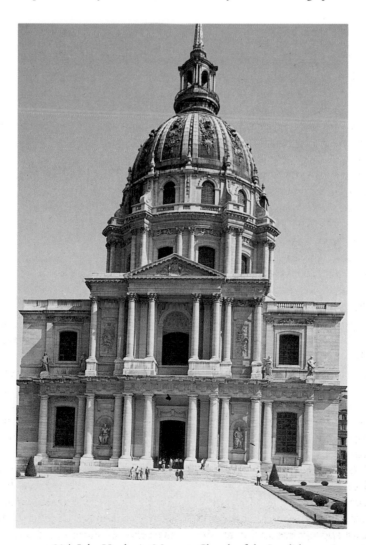

804. Jules Hardouin-Mansart. Church of the Invalides,
Paris. 1680–91

805. Plan of the Church
of the Invalides

806. Gianlorenzo Bernini. *Model for Equestrian Statue of Louis XIV.* 1670. Terracotta, height 30" (76.3 cm). Galleria Borghese, Rome

807. Antoine Coysevox. *Charles Lebrun.* 1676. Terracotta, height 26" (66 cm). The Wallace Collection, London

Sculpture

Sculpture arrived at the official royal style in much the same way as architecture. While in Paris, Bernini carved a marble bust of Louis XIV and was commissioned to do an equestrian statue of him. [See Primary Sources, no. 74, pages 641–42.] The latter project, for which he made a splendid terracotta model (fig. 806), shared the fate of Bernini's Louvre designs. Although he portrayed the king in classical military garb, the statue was rejected. Apparently it was too dynamic to safeguard the dignity of Louis XIV. This decision was far-reaching: equestrian statues of the king were later erected throughout France as symbols of royal authority, and Bernini's design, had it succeeded, might have set the pattern for these monuments.

COYSEVOX. Bernini's influence can nevertheless be felt in the work of Antoine Coysevox (1640–1720), one of the sculptors Lebrun employed at Versailles. The victorious Louis XIV in Coysevox's large stucco relief for the Salon de la Guerre (see fig. 802) retains the pose of Bernini's equestrian statue, albeit with a certain restraint. Coysevox is the first of a long line of distinguished French portrait sculptors. His bust of Lebrun (fig. 807) likewise repeats the general outlines of Bernini's model of Louis XIV. The face, however, shows a realism and a subtlety of characterization that are Coysevox's own.

PUGET. Coysevox approached the Baroque in sculpture as closely as Lebrun would permit. Pierre-Paul Puget (1620–1694), the most talented and most Baroque of seventeenth-century French sculptors, had no success at court until after Colbert's death, when the power of Lebrun was on the decline. *Milo of Crotona* (fig. 808), Puget's finest statue, bears comparison to Bernini's *David* (see fig. 752). Puget's composition is

808. Pierre-Paul Puget. *Milo of Crotona.* 1671–83. Marble, height 8'10¹/₂" (2.7 m). Musée du Louvre, Paris

more contained than Bernini's, but the agony of the hero has such force that its impact on the beholder is almost physical. The internal tension fills every particle of marble with an intense life that also recalls *The Laocoön Group* (see fig. 215). That, one suspects, is what made it acceptable to Louis XIV.

ENGLAND

The English made no significant contribution to Baroque painting and sculpture. They were content instead with feeble offshoots of Van Dyck's portraiture by imported artists like the Dutch-born Peter Lely (1618–1680) and his German successor, Godfrey Kneller (1646–1723). The English achievement in architecture, however, was of genuine importance. This is all the more surprising in light of the fact that the insular form of "Late Gothic" known as the Perpendicular style (see fig. 451) proved extraordinarily persistent.

JONES. The first English architect of genius was Inigo Jones (1573–1652), who was also the leading theatrical designer of the day. When he went to Italy about 1600 and again in 1613, he was influenced by the Baroque stage designs of Giulio Parigi; yet, surprisingly he returned a thoroughgoing disciple of Palladio (who, after all, had designed the theater of the Olympic Academy in Vicenza, one of the earliest of its kind). The Banqueting House Jones built at Whitehall Palace in London (fig. 809) to hold the masques and other entertainment he presented at the court conforms in every respect to

809. Inigo Jones. West front of the Banqueting House, Whitehall Palace, London. 1619–22

the principles in Palladio's treatise, yet does not copy any specific building by Palladio. Symmetrical and self-sufficient, it is, for its date, more like a Renaissance palazzo than any other building north of the Alps. Jones' spare style, supported by Palladio's authority as a theorist, stood as a beacon of classicist orthodoxy in England for 200 years.

Baroque Theater and Music in England

In England, court masques adapted from Italian court pageants played a similar role to the French *ballets de cour* in that they promoted an idealized vision of monarchy presented through allegory and myth expressed in elegant speeches, music, and dance. Many of these masques were created for James I by the playwright Ben Jonson (1572–1637) and staged by Inigo Jones, who became surveyor of the king's works in 1615. Upon the overthrow in 1642 of Charles I by the Puritans—whose religious views demanded the most austere social standards—all theaters were closed, and remained so during the Commonwealth, the Puritan period of rule led by Oliver Cromwell. Theaters were reopened only when the monarchy was restored in 1660. The Restoration, as the reign of the new king, Charles II, came to be known, was a great period of creativity for theater and music. There was an almost immediate demand for new plays, which were supplied by John Dryden (1631–1700), whose work was influenced by Shakespeare and the classical Roman authors. The later plays by Dryden and William D'Avenant (1606–1668), Jonson's successor at court, are rather stilted, moralizing tragedies about people of noble birth. Comedy fared better, while adhering to the same goal of moral instruction. *The Rover: or the Banished Cavalier* (1677) by Mrs. Aphra Behn (1640–1689) and *The Way of the World* (1700) by William Congreve (1670–1729) and John Vanbrugh (best known as the architect of Blenheim Palace; see fig. 813) are uproarious comedies of manners that reflect the cynicism—and what later critics would call the licentiousness—of the age. The Restoration marked a revolution in English theater: not only did women begin to write plays, but they also appeared on the legitimate stage for the first time. Some became sensationally successful: one, Nell Gwynn, soon retired from the stage to become Charles II's mistress.

Theater gave rise to a new class of stage music by the leading composer of the Restoration, Henry Purcell (1659–1695). During the Commonwealth, English operas were plays set to music, which managed to avoid the ban against theater because they were considered concerts. This practice continued even during the Restoration. Thus *Venus and Adonis*, by Henry Purcell's teacher John Blow (1649–1708), is essentially a masque in disguise. A large part of Purcell's output is theater music, such at *The Fairy Queen* (1692), which is a free adaptation of Shakespeare's *A Midsummer Night's Dream*. The closest Purcell came to opera was *Dido and Aeneas* (1689), which is basically a concert opera reputedly composed for a girls' boarding school but perhaps given as a court entertainment instead. Blow and Purcell also wrote numerous odes for the royal family and to celebrate other occasions, as well as many church anthems and a considerable body of chamber music and keyboard works.

810. Sir Christopher Wren. Facade of St. Paul's Cathedral, London. 1675–1710

811. Plan of St. Paul's Cathedral

WREN. This classicism can be seen in some parts of St. Paul's Cathedral (figs. 810–12) by Sir Christopher Wren (1632–1723), the great English architect of the late seventeenth century: note the second-story windows and especially the dome, which looks like Bramante's Tempietto much enlarged (see fig. 601). St. Paul's is otherwise an up-to-date Baroque design reflecting a thorough acquaintance with contemporary architecture in Italy and France. Sir Christopher came close to being a Baroque counterpart of the Renaissance artist-scientist. An intellectual prodigy, he first studied anatomy, then physics, mathematics, and astronomy, and was highly esteemed by Sir Isaac Newton. His serious interest in architecture did not begin until he was about 30. However, it is characteristic of the Baroque as opposed to the Renaissance that there is apparently no direct link between his scientific and artistic ideas. It is hard to determine whether his technological knowledge significantly affected the shape of his buildings.

Had not the great London fire of 1666 destroyed the Gothic cathedral of St. Paul and many lesser churches, Sir Christopher might have remained an amateur architect. But following that catastrophe, he was named to the royal commission for rebuilding the city, and a few years later he began his designs for St. Paul's. [See Primary Sources, no. 75, page 642.] The tradition of Inigo Jones did not suffice for this task, beyond providing a starting point. On his only trip abroad, Sir Christopher had visited Paris at the time of the dispute over the completion of the Louvre, and he must have sided with Perrault, whose design for the East Front is clearly reflected in the facade of St. Paul's. Yet, despite his belief that Paris provided "the best school of architecture in Europe," Sir Christopher was not indifferent to the achievements of the Roman Baroque. He must have wanted the new St. Paul's to be the St. Peter's of the Church of England: soberer and not so large, but equally impressive. His dome, like that of St. Peter's, has a

812. Interior of St. Paul's Cathedral

diameter as wide as nave and aisles combined, but it rises high above the rest of the structure and dominates even our close view of the facade. The lantern and the upper part of the clock towers also suggest that he knew Borromini's S. Agnese in Piazza Navona (see fig. 746), probably from drawings or engravings.

VANBRUGH. Italian Baroque elements are still more conspicuous in Blenheim Palace (fig. 813), the grandiose structure designed by Sir John Vanbrugh (1664–1726), a gifted amateur, with the aid of Nicholas Hawksmoore (1661–1719), Wren's most talented pupil. Vanbrugh, like Jones, had a strong interest in the theater. (He was a popular playwright.) That his kinship was even closer to Bernini can be seen when we compare the facade of Blenheim and its framing colonnade with the piazza of St. Peter's (see fig. 739). The main block uses a colossal Corinthian order to wed a temple portico with a Renaissance palace (compare fig. 621), whereas the wings rely on a low-slung Doric. Such eclecticism, extreme even by the relaxed standards of the period, is maintained throughout the welter of details. Compared to Versailles (fig. 800), the effect has a massiveness that makes Blenheim a fitting symbol of English power: it was presented by a grateful nation to the duke of Marlborough for his great victories over French and German forces in the War of Spanish Secession.

813. Sir John Vanbrugh. Blenheim Palace, Woodstock, England. Begun 1705

THE ROCOCO

Much as the Baroque is often considered the final phase of the Renaissance, so the Rococo has been treated as the end of the Baroque: a long twilight, delicious but decadent, that was cleaned away by the Enlightenment and Neoclassicism. In France, the Rococo is linked with Louis XV, to whose lifespan (1710–1774) it corresponds roughly in date. However, it cannot be identified with the absolutist State or the Church any more than can the Baroque, even though these continued to provide the main patronage. Moreover, the essential characteristics of Rococo style were created before the king was born. Its first symptoms begin as much as 50 years earlier, during the lengthy transition that constitutes the Late Baroque. Hence, the view of the Rococo as the final phase of the Baroque is not without basis: as the philosopher François-Marie Voltaire acknowledged, the eighteenth century lived in the debt of the past. In art, Poussin and Rubens cast their long shadows over the Rococo. The controversy between their partisans, in turn, goes back much further to the debate between the supporters of Michelangelo and of Titian over the merits of design versus color. In this sense, the Rococo, like the Baroque, still belongs to the Renaissance world.

To overemphasize the similarities and stylistic debt of the Rococo to the Baroque, however, risks ignoring a fundamental difference between them. What is it? In a word, it is fantasy. If the Baroque presents theater on a grand scale, the Rococo stage is smaller and more intimate. At the same time, the Rococo is both more lighthearted and tender-minded, marked equally by playful whimsy and wistful nostalgia. Its artifice evokes an enchanted realm that presents a temporary diversion from real life. Because the modern age is the product of the Enlightenment that followed, it is still fashionable to denigrate the Rococo for its unabashed escapism and eroticism. To its credit, however, the Rococo discovered the world of love and broadened the range of human emotion in art to include, for the first time, the family as a major theme.

FRANCE

THE RISE OF THE ROCOCO. After the death of Louis XIV in 1715, the centralized administrative machine that Colbert (see page 600) had created ground to a stop. The nobility, formerly attached to the court at Versailles, were now freer of royal surveillance. Many of them chose not to return to their ancestral châteaux in the provinces, but to live in Paris, where they built elegant town houses, known as *hôtels*. As state-sponsored building activity was declining, the field of "design for private living" took on new importance. These city sites were usually cramped and irregular, so that they offered scant opportunity for impressive exteriors. Hence, the layout and décor of the rooms became the architects' main concern. The hôtels demanded a style of interior decoration less grandiloquent and cumbersome than Lebrun's. They required instead an intimate, flexible style that would give greater scope to individual fancy uninhibited by classicistic dogma. French designers created the Rococo ("The Style of Louis XV," as it is often called in France) from Italian gardens and interiors to fulfill this need. The name fits well: it was coined as a caricature of *coquillage* and *rocaille* (echoing the Italian *barocco*), which meant the playful decoration of grottoes with irregular shells and stones.

The Decorative Arts

It was in the decorative arts that the Rococo flourished first and foremost. We have not considered the decorative arts until now, because the conservative nature of the crafts permitted only limited creativity except to a few individuals of outstanding ability. But the latter half of the seventeenth century ushered in a period of unprecedented change in French design. A central role was played by Colbert, who in the 1660s acquired the Gobelins (named after the brothers who founded them) for the crown and turned them into royal works supplying luxurious furnishings, including tapestries, to the court under the direction of the king's chief artistic adviser, Charles

Lebrun. After 1688 the War of the League of Augsburg forced major economies on the crown, including reductions at the Gobelins that gradually loosened central control of the decorative arts and opened the way to new stylistic developments. Thus the situation paralleled the decline of the Academy's tyrannical influence over the fine arts, which gave rise to the Rococo in painting (see page 600).

This does not explain the excellence of French décor, however. Critical to its development was the importance assigned to designers: their engravings established new standards of design that were expected to be followed by artisans, who thereby lost much of their independence. Let us note, too, the collaboration of architects, who became increasingly involved in the decoration of the rooms they designed. Together with sculptors, who often designed the ornamentation, they helped to elevate the decorative arts virtually to the level of the fine arts, thus establishing a tradition that continued into modern times. The decorative and fine arts intersected most clearly in major furniture. French cabinetmakers known as *ébénistes* (after ebony, their preferred wood veneer) helped to bring about the revolution in interior décor by introducing new materials and techniques. Many of these upstarts hailed originally from Holland, Flanders, Germany, and even Italy.

The decorative arts played a unique role during the Rococo. Hôtel interiors were more than assemblages of objects. They were total environments put together with fastidious care by discerning collectors and the talented architects, sculptors, decorators, and dealers who catered to their taste. A room, like a single item of furniture, could involve the services of a wide variety of artisans—cabinetmakers, wood carvers, gold- and silversmiths, upholsterers, porcelain makers—all dedicated to producing the ensemble, even though each craft was, by tradition, a separate specialty subject to strict regulations. Together they fueled the insatiable hunger for novelty that swept Europe.

PINEAU. Virtually none of these rooms has survived intact. Like the furniture they housed, most have been destroyed, heavily altered, or dispersed. We can nevertheless get a good idea of their appearance by the reconstruction of one such room from the Hôtel de Varengeville, Paris, designed about 1735 by Nicolas Pineau (1684–1754) for the Duchesse de Villars (fig. 814). To create a sumptuous effect, the walls and ceiling are encrusted with ornamentation, and the elaborately carved furniture is adorned with gilt bronze. Everything swims in a sea of swirling patterns united by the most sophisticated sense of design and materials the world has ever known. Here there is no clear distinction between decoration and function, for example in the clock on the mantel and the statuette in the corner of our illustration. Note, too, how the painting has been thoroughly integrated into the room.

Sculpture

CLODION. Because so much of it was done to adorn interiors, French Rococo sculpture generally took the form of small groups in a "miniature Baroque" style, which were designed to be viewed at close range. A typical example is *Satyr and Bacchante* (fig. 815) by Claude Michel (1738–1814),

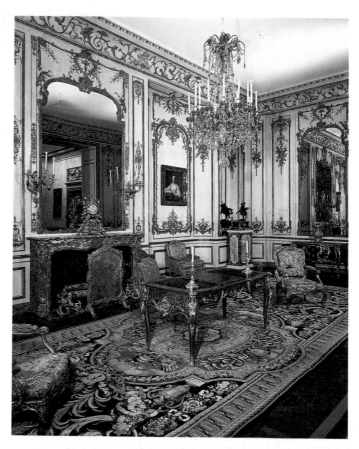

814. Nicolas Pineau. Room from the Hôtel de Varengeville, Paris. c. 1735. The Metropolitan Museum of Art, New York, Wrightsman Collection

815. Claude Michel, known as Clodion. *Satyr and Bacchante.* c. 1775. Terracotta, height 23¹/₄" (59 cm). The Metropolitan Museum of Art, New York
Bequest of Benjamin Altman, 1913

known as Clodion. Its coquettish eroticism is a playful echo of the ecstasies of Bernini, whose work he studied during a nine-year stay in Italy (compare fig. 753). Despite the fact that he undertook several large decorative cycles, Clodion was by nature a modeler who was at his best working on a small scale. Able to work miracles with terracotta, he reigned supreme in this intimate realm.

PIGALLE.   Monumental commissions for French Rococo sculptors were few. Lifesize statues were confined largely to decorative figures of nymphs, goddesses, and the like who are the counterparts to the mythological creatures in the paintings of Boucher and his followers (see below). The Tomb of the Maréchal de Saxe (fig. 816) by Jean-Baptiste Pigalle (1714–1785), Clodion's teacher and the most gifted sculptor of the era, shows that they could recapture something of Baroque grandeur when given the opportunity. The Maréchal steps unafraid from a pyramid denoting immortality toward a casket held open for him by the beckoning figure of Death, as France tries vainly to intervene. He is mourned by the grief-stricken Herakles to the left, representing the French army, and, to the right, the weeping infant personifying the Genius of War, who extinguishes his torch before the fallen military standards. The strange menagerie to the left stands for the nations defeated by the Maréchal in combat: Holland, England, and the Holy Roman Empire. If the allegory strikes us as heavy-handed, there can be no denying the effectiveness of the presentation, which is among the most astonishing in all of sculpture. The poses show the classicism requisite for official French art, but the spirit of the whole is unmistakably Baroque. Pigalle has mounted a tableau worthy of Bernini, whose works he studied during several years in Rome as a young man, although the relative restraint also suggests the example of Algardi (see pages 564–68). The pyramid is not a three-dimensional structure but a low relief built against the wall of the church, while the steps leading up to it and the figures occupying them are "real," like actors performing before a backdrop. We must therefore view the monument as a kind of theatrical performance in marble. The artist has even set it apart from its surroundings by creating an elevated "stage space" that projects outward.

Painting

"POUSSINISTES" VERSUS "RUBÉNISTES."   It is hardly surprising that the straitjacket system of the French Academy (see page 600) produced no significant artists. Even Charles Lebrun, as we have seen, was far more Baroque in his practice than we would expect from his classicistic theory. The absurd rigidity of the official doctrine generated, moreover, a counter-pressure that vented itself as soon as Lebrun's authority began to decline. Toward the end of the century, the members of the Academy formed two warring factions over the issue of drawing versus color: the "Poussinistes" (or conservatives) against the "Rubénistes." The conservatives defended Poussin's view that drawing, which appealed to the mind, was superior to color, which appealed to the senses. The Rubénistes advocated color, rather than drawing, as being more true to nature. They also pointed out that drawing, admittedly based on reason, appeals

816. Jean-Baptiste Pigalle. Tomb of the Maréchal de Saxe. 1753–76. Marble. St. Thomas, Strasbourg, France

only to the expert few, whereas color appeals to everyone. This argument had revolutionary implications, for it proclaimed the lay person to be the ultimate judge of artistic values and challenged the Renaissance notion that painting, as a liberal art, could be appreciated only by the educated mind.

WATTEAU.   By the time Louis XIV died in 1715, the dictatorial powers of the Academy had long been overcome, and the influence of Rubens and the great Venetians was everywhere. The greatest of the Rubénistes was the painter Jean-Antoine Watteau (1684–1721). Watteau's pictures violated all academic canons, and his subjects did not conform to any established category. To accommodate Watteau, the Academy invented the new category of *fêtes galantes* (elegant fêtes or entertainments). The term refers to the fact that the artist's work mainly shows scenes of elegant society or comedy actors in parklike settings. Watteau characteristically interweaves theater and real life so that no clear distinction can be made between the two. *A Pilgrimage to Cythera* (fig. 817), painted as his reception piece for the Academy, is an evocation of love that includes yet another element: classical mythology. Accompanied by swarms of cupids, these young couples have come to Cythera, the island of love, to pay homage to Venus, whose garlanded image appears on the far right. The action unfolds in the foreground, like a continuous narrative, from right to left, which informs us that they are about to board the boat: two lovers are still engaged in their amorous tryst; behind

817. Jean-Antoine Watteau. *A Pilgrimage to Cythera.* 1717. Oil on canvas, 4'3" x 6'4½" (1.3 x 1.9 m). Musée du Louvre, Paris

them, another couple rises to follow a third pair down the hill as the reluctant young woman casts a wistful look back at the goddess' sacred grove.

As a fashionable conversation piece, the scene at once recalls Rubens' *Garden of Love* (compare fig. 764), but Watteau has added a touch of poignancy, lending it a poetic subtlety reminiscent of Giorgione and Titian (see figs. 631 and 10). His figures, too, lack the robust vitality of Rubens'. Slim and graceful, they move with the studied assurance of actors who play their roles so superbly that they touch us more than reality ever could. They recapture an earlier ideal of "mannered" elegance.

Many of Watteau's paintings center on the *commedia dell'-arte.* His treatment of this Italian theme is all the more remarkable because the *commedia dell'arte* was officially banned in France from 1697 until 1716, despite the fact that it had been far more popular with the middle class than the classical tragedies of the official Comédie Français (see page 628), which were favored by the court. Shortly before his death, Watteau painted perhaps his most moving work: *Pierrot* (fig. 818), known traditionally as *Gilles* after a similar stock character in

818. *(right)* Jean-Antoine Watteau. *Gilles and Four Other Characters from the Commedia dell'Arte (Pierrot).* c. 1719.
Oil on canvas, 72½ x 58⅜" (184 x 149 cm). Musée du Louvre, Paris

the *commedia dell'arte*. It was probably done as a sign for a café owned by a friend of the artist who retired from the stage after achieving fame in the racy role of the clown. The troupe's performance having ended, the actor has stepped forward to face the audience. The other characters all bear highly individualized likenesses, no doubt belonging to friends from the same circle. Yet the painting transcends portraiture and its purpose as an advertisement. Watteau approaches his subject with incomparable human understanding and artistic ability. Pierrot is life-size, so that he confronts us as a full human being, not simply as a stock character. In the process, Watteau transforms Pierrot into Everyman, with whom he evidently identified himself—a merger of identity basic to the *commedia dell'arte* as a whole. The face and pose have a poignancy that suggests a subtle sense of alienation. Like the rest of the actors, except the doctor on the donkey who looks mischievously at us, he seems lost in his own thoughts. Still, it is difficult to define his mood, for the expression remains as elusive as it is eloquent.

BOUCHER.   The work of Watteau signals a shift in French art as a whole to the Rococo. The term originally applied to the decorative arts (see page 610), but it suits the playful character of French painting before 1765 equally well. By about 1720 even history painting becomes intimate in scale and delightfully ebullient in style and subject. The finest painter in this vein was François Boucher (1703–1770), who epitomizes the age of Madame de Pompadour, the mistress of Louis XV. *The Toilet of Venus* (fig. 819), painted for her private retreat, is full of silk and perfume. Compared to Vouet's sensuous goddess (see fig. 797), from which she is descended, Boucher's Venus has been transformed into a coquette of enchanting beauty. In this cosmetic land, she is an eternally youthful

819. François Boucher. *The Toilet of Venus.* 1751.
Oil on canvas, 43 x 33¹/2" (109.2 x 85.1 cm).
The Metropolitan Museum of Art, New York
Bequest of William K. Vanderbilt

820. Jean-Honoré Fragonard. *Bathers.* c. 1765.
Oil on canvas, 25¹/4 x 31¹/2" (64 x 80 cm). Musée du Louvre, Paris

Venus with the same soft, rosy skin as the cherubs who attend her. If Watteau elevated human love to the level of mythology, Boucher raised playful eroticism to the realm of the divine. What Boucher lacks in the emotional depth that distinguishes Watteau's art, he makes up for in unsurpassed understanding of the world of fantasies that enrich people's lives.

FRAGONARD. *Bathers* (fig. 820), by Jean-Honoré Fragonard (1732–1806), Boucher's star pupil, shows him to be an even franker Rubéniste than Boucher. He paints with a fluid breadth and spontaneity reminiscent of Rubens' oil sketches and even paraphrases the Flemish master's figures (see fig. 763). They move with a floating grace that also links him with Tiepolo, whose work he had admired on an extended stay in Italy (compare fig. 838). Fragonard had the misfortune to outlive his era; his pictures became outmoded as the French Revolution approached. After 1789 he was reduced to poverty, supported, ironically, only by a curatorship to which he was appointed in 1793 by Jacques-Louis David (see page 639), who recognized his achievement, although their styles were antithetical. He died, virtually forgotten, in the heyday of the Napoleonic era.

CHARDIN. The style Fragonard practiced with such mastery was not the only alternative open to him and the other French painters of his generation. His art might have been different had he followed that of his first teacher, Jean-Baptiste-Siméon Chardin (1699–1779), whose style can be called Rococo only with reservations. The Rubénistes had cleared the way for a renewed interest in still-life and genre paintings by Dutch and Flemish masters. This revival was facilitated by the presence of numerous artists from The Netherlands, especially Flanders, who settled in France in growing numbers after about 1550 while maintaining artistic ties to their native lands. Chardin is the finest French painter in this vein. He is nevertheless far removed in spirit and style, if not in subject matter, from any Dutch or Flemish painter. Indeed, he is more akin to Le Nain and Sanchez Cotán (see pages 596 and 569). His paintings act as moral exemplars, not by conveying symbolic messages as Baroque art often does (see page 588), but by affirming the rightness of the existing social order and its values. To the rising middle class who were the artist's patrons, his genre scenes and kitchen still lifes proclaimed the virtues of hard work, frugality, honesty, and devotion to family.

Back from the Market (fig. 821) shows life in a Parisian middle-class household with such feeling for the beauty hidden in the commonplace, and so clear a sense of spatial order, that we can compare him only to Vermeer and De Hooch (see figs. 789 and 14), but his remarkable technique is quite unlike any Dutch artist's. Devoid of bravura, his brushwork renders the light on colored surfaces with a creamy touch that is both analytical and subtly lyrical. To reveal the inner nature of things, he summarizes forms, subtly altering their appearance and texture, rather than describing them in detail.

Chardin's genius discovered a hidden poetry in even the most humble objects and endowed them with timeless dignity. His still lifes usually depict the same modest environment, eschewing the "object appeal" of their Dutch predecessors. In *Kitchen Still Life* (fig. 822), we see only the common objects

821. Jean-Baptiste-Siméon Chardin. *Back from the Market.* 1739. Oil on canvas, 18 1/2 x 14 3/4" (47 x 37.5 cm). Musée du Louvre, Paris

822. Jean-Baptiste-Siméon Chardin. *Kitchen Still Life.* c. 1731. Oil on canvas, 12 1/2 x 15 3/8" (32 x 39 cm). Ashmolean Museum, Oxford
Bequeathed by Mrs. W. F. R. Weldon

that belong in any kitchen: earthenware jugs, a casserole, a copper pot, a piece of raw meat, smoked herring, two eggs. But how important they seem, each so firmly placed in relation to the rest, each so worthy of the artist's—and our—scrutiny! Despite his concern with formal problems, evident in the beautifully balanced design, Chardin treats these objects with a respect close to reverence. Beyond their shapes, colors, and textures, they are to him symbols of the life of common people.

823. Marie-Louise-Elisabeth Vigée-Lebrun.
The Duchesse de Polignac. 1783. Oil on canvas, 38³/4 x 28" (98.3 x 71 cm)
© The National Trust Waddesdon Manor

VIGÉE-LEBRUN. It is from portraits that we can gain the clearest understanding of the French Rococo, for the transformation of the human image lies at the heart of the age. In portraits of the aristocracy, men were endowed with the illusion of character as a natural attribute of their station in life, stemming from their noble birth. But the finest achievements of Rococo portraiture were reserved for depictions of women, hardly a surprising fact in a society that idolized the cult of love and feminine beauty. Indeed, one of the finest practitioners in this vein was herself a beautiful woman: Marie-Louise-Elisabeth Vigée-Lebrun (1755–1842). [See Primary Sources, no. 76, pages 642–43.]

Throughout Vigée's long life she enjoyed great fame, which took her to every corner of Europe, including Russia, when she fled the French Revolution. *The Duchesse de Polignac* (fig. 823) was painted a few years after Vigée had become the portraitist for Queen Marie Antoinette, and it amply demonstrates her ability. We will recognize the duchesse as the descendant of Domenichino's *St. Cecilia* (fig. 733). She has the eternally youthful loveliness of Boucher's *Venus* (fig. 819), made all the more persuasive by the artist's ravishing treatment of her clothing. At the same time, there is a sense of transience in the engaging mood that exemplifies the Rococo's whimsical theatricality. Interrupted in her singing, the lyrical duchesse becomes a real-life counterpart to the poetic creatures in

Watteau's *A Pilgrimage to Cythera* (fig. 817) by way of the delicate sentiment she shares with the girl in Chardin's *Back from the Market* (fig. 821).

ENGLAND

Painting

Across the English Channel the Venetians were the predominant artists for more than a half-century (see page 628), but the French Rococo had an important, though unacknowledged, effect and, in fact, helped to bring about the first school of English painting since the Middle Ages that had more than local importance.

HOGARTH. The earliest of these painters, William Hogarth (1697–1764), was the first English artist of genius since Nicholas Hilliard (see fig. 712). A natural-born satirist, he began as an engraver and soon took up painting. Although he certainly learned something about color and brushwork from Venetian and French examples, as well as Van Dyck, his work is of such originality as to be essentially without precedence. He made his mark in the 1730s with a new kind of picture, which he described as "modern moral subjects . . . similar to representations on the stage." It follows the vogue for senti-

824. William Hogarth. *The Orgy*, Scene III of *The Rake's Progress*. c. 1734.
Oil on canvas, 24¹/₂ x 29¹/₂" (62.2 x 74.9 cm). Sir John Soane's Museum, London

mental comedies, such as those by Richard Steele, that sought to teach moral lessons through satires of the protagonist's dissolute life. In the same vein is John Gay's *The Beggar's Opera* of 1728, a social and political satire which Hogarth illustrated in one of his paintings. Hogarth wished to be judged as a dramatist, he said, even though his "actors" could only "exhibit a dumb show." These pictures, and the prints he made from them for popular sale, came in sets, with details recurring in each scene to unify the sequence. Hogarth's "morality plays" teach, by horrid example, the solid middle-class virtues. They show a country girl who succumbs to the temptations of fashionable London; the evils of corrupt elections; and aristocratic rakes who live only for ruinous pleasure, marrying wealthy women of lower status for their fortunes, which they soon dissipate. Hogarth is probably the first artist in history to become a social critic in his own right.

In *The Orgy* (figs. 824 and 825), from *The Rake's Progress*, the young wastrel is overindulging in wine and women. The scene is so full of visual clues that a full account would take pages, and also constant references to the adjoining episodes. However literal-minded, the picture has great appeal. Hogarth combines some of Watteau's sparkle with Jan Steen's narrative gusto (compare figs. 817 and 788), and entertains us so well that we enjoy his sermon without being overwhelmed by its message.

825. William Hogarth. *He Revels (The Orgy)*, Scene III of *The Rake's Progress*. 1735. Engraving.
The Metropolitan Museum of Art, New York
Harris Brisbane Dick Fund, 1932

826. Thomas Gainsborough. *Robert Andrews and His Wife.* c. 1748–50.
Oil on canvas, 27$^{1}/_{2}$ x 47" (69.7 x 119.3 cm). The National Gallery, London

GAINSBOROUGH. Portraiture remained the only constant source of income for English painters. Here, too, eighteenth-century England produced a style that differed from Continental traditions. Hogarth was a pioneer in this field as well. Its greatest master, Thomas Gainsborough (1727–1788), began by painting landscapes, but ended as the favorite portraitist of British high society. His early portraits, such as *Robert Andrews and His Wife* (fig. 826), have a lyrical charm that is not always found in his later pictures. Compared to Van Dyck's artifice in *Charles I Hunting* (see fig. 767), this country squire and his wife are unpretentiously at home in their setting. The landscape, although derived from Ruisdael and his school, has a sunlit, hospitable air never achieved (or desired) by the Dutch masters, while the casual grace of the two figures, which affects an air of naturalness, indirectly recalls Watteau's style. The newlywed couple—she dressed in the fashionable attire of the day, he armed with a rifle to denote his status as a country squire (hunting was a privilege of wealthy landowners)—do not till the soil themselves. The painting nevertheless conveys the gentry's closeness to the land, from which the English derived much of their sense of national identity. (Many private estates had been created in 1535, when Henry VIII broke with the Catholic church and redistributed its property to his supporters.) Out of this attachment to place was to develop a feeling for nature that became the basis for English landscape painting, to which Gainsborough himself made an important early contribution.

Gainsborough spent most of his career working in the provinces, first in his native Suffolk, then in the fashionable resort town of Bath. Toward the end of his career, he moved to London, where his work underwent a pronounced change. The very fine portrait of the famous actress Mrs. Siddons (fig. 827) has the virtues of Gainsborough's late style: a cool ele-

827. Thomas Gainsborough. *Mrs. Siddons.* 1785. Oil on canvas,
49$^{1}/_{2}$ x 39" (125.7 x 99.1 cm). The National Gallery, London

828. Sir Joshua Reynolds. *Mrs. Siddons as the Tragic Muse.* 1784.
Oil on canvas, 7'9" x 4'9 1/2" (2.36 x 1.46 m). Henry E. Huntington
Library and Art Gallery, San Marino, California

gance that translates Van Dyck's aristocratic poses into late-eighteenth-century terms, and a fluid, translucent technique reminiscent of Rubens' that renders the glamorous sitter, with her fashionable attire and coiffure, to ravishing effect.

REYNOLDS. Gainsborough painted Mrs. Siddons in conscious opposition to his great rival on the London scene, Sir Joshua Reynolds (1723–1792), who had portrayed the same sitter as the Tragic Muse (fig. 828). Reynolds, president of the Royal Academy since its founding in 1768, was the champion of the academic approach to art, which he had acquired during two years in Rome. In his famous *Discourses* he formulated what he felt were necessary rules and theories. [See Primary Sources, no. 77, page 643.] His views were essentially those of Lebrun, tempered by British common sense. Like Lebrun, he found it difficult to live up to his theories in actual practice. Although he preferred history painting in the grand style, most of his works are portraits "enabled," whenever possible, by allegorical additions or disguises like those in his picture of Mrs. Siddons. His style owed a good deal more to the Venetians, the Flemish Baroque, and even to

Rembrandt (note the lighting in Mrs. Siddons) than he conceded in theory, though he often recommended following the example of earlier masters.

Reynolds was generous enough to give praise to Gainsborough, whom he outlived by a few years, and whose instinctive talent he must have envied. He eulogized him as one who saw with the eye of a painter rather than a poet. There is more truth to this statement than it might seem. Gainsborough's paintings epitomized the Enlightenment philosopher David Hume's idea that painting must incorporate both nature and art. Gainsborough himself was a simple and unpretentious person who exemplified Hume's "natural man," free of excessive pride or humility. Reynolds' approach, on the other hand, as enunciated in his *Discourses,* was based on the Roman poet Horace's dictum *ut pictura poesis.* His frequent borrowing of poses from the antique was intended to elevate the sitter from an individual to a universal type through association with the great art of the past and the noble ideals it embodied. This heroic model was closely related to the writings of the playwright Samuel Johnson and the practices of the actor David Garrick, both of whom were friends of Reynolds. In this,

829. Louis-François Roubiliac. *George Frideric Handel.* 1738. Marble, lifesize. Victoria & Albert Museum, London

Reynolds was the very opposite of Gainsborough. Yet, for all of the differences between them, the two artists had more in common, artistically and philosophically, than they cared to admit.

Reynolds and Gainsborough looked back to Van Dyck, drawing different lessons from his example. Both emphasized, albeit in varying degrees, the visual appeal and technical proficiency of their paintings. Moreover, their portraits of Mrs. Siddons bear an unmistakable relationship to the Rococo style of France—note their resemblance to Vigée's *Duchesse* (fig. 823)—yet remain distinctly English in character. Hume and Johnson were similarly linked by an abiding skepticism. If anything, Johnson's writings, which inspired Reynolds, were more bitterly pessimistic than Hume's, which generally advocated a tolerant and humane ethical system.

Sculpture

English sculpture has not been discussed in these pages since that of the thirteenth century (see fig. 475). During the Reformation, we will recall, there was a wholesale destruction of sculpture in England. This had so chilling an effect that for 200 years the demand for statuary of any kind was too low to sustain more than the most modest local production. With the rise of a vigorous English school of painting, however, sculp-

tural patronage grew as well, and during the eighteenth century England set an example for the rest of Europe in creating the "monument to genius": statues in public places honoring culture heroes such as Shakespeare, a privilege hitherto reserved for heads of state.

ROUBILIAC. One of the earliest and most ingratiating of these statues is the monument to the great composer George Frideric Handel (fig. 829) by the French-born Louis-François Roubiliac (1702–1762). It was also the first to be made of a culture hero within his lifetime. (The next to achieve this distinction would be Voltaire in France, a full generation later; see fig. 851). Roubiliac (who is portrayed in fig. 27) carved the figure in 1738 for the owner of Vauxhall Gardens in London, a pleasure park with dining facilities and an orchestra stand where Handel's music was often performed, so that the statue served two purposes: homage and advertising. Handel is in the guise of Apollo, the god of music, playing a classical lyre, while a putto at his feet writes down the divine music. But Handel is a most domestic Apollo, in slippers and a worn dressing gown, a soft beret on his head instead of the then-customary wig. These attributes distinguish him as a man of arts and letters. Although Roubiliac shows himself in full command of the Baroque sculptural tradition, the studied informality of his deified *Handel* seems peculiarly English. Touches such as the right foot resting

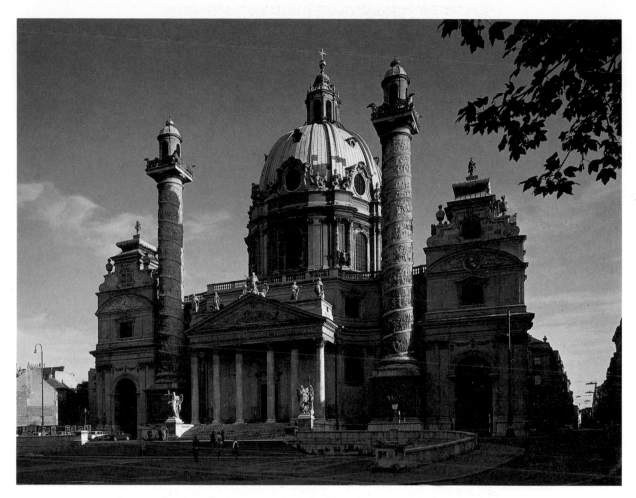

830. Johann Fischer von Erlach. Facade of St. Charles Borromaeus (Karlskirche), Vienna. 1716–37

upon rather than inside the slipper (a hint at the composer's gouty big toe?) suggest that he sought advice from William Hogarth, with whom he was on excellent terms (see page 616). Be that as it may, *Handel* was Roubiliac's first big success in his adopted homeland, and it became the forebear of countless monuments to culture heroes everywhere (see fig. 957).

GERMANY AND AUSTRIA

Rococo was a refinement in miniature of the curvilinear, "elastic" Baroque of Borromini and Guarini, and thus could be happily united with architecture in Central Europe, where the Italian style had taken firm root. It is not surprising that the Italian style received such a warm response there. In Austria and southern Germany, ravaged by the Thirty Years' War, the number of new buildings remained small until near the end of the seventeenth century. Baroque was an imported style, practiced mainly by visiting Italians. Not until the 1690s did native designers come to the fore. There followed a period of intense activity that lasted more than 50 years and gave rise to some of the most imaginative creations in the history of architecture. These monuments were erected for the glorification of princes and prelates who, generally speaking, deserve to be remembered only as lavish patrons of the arts. Rococo architecture in Central Europe is larger in scale and more exuberant than in France. Moreover, painting and sculpture are more closely linked with their settings. Palaces and churches are dec-

831. Plan of St. Charles Borromaeus

orated with ceiling frescoes and decorative sculpture unsuited to domestic interiors, however lavish, although they reflect the same taste that produced the Hôtel de Varengeville.

FISCHER VON ERLACH. The Austrian Johann Fischer von Erlach (1656–1723), the first great architect of the Rococo in Central Europe, is a transitional figure linked most directly to the Italian tradition. His design for the church of St. Charles Borromaeus in Vienna (figs. 830 and 831) combines the facade of Borromini's S. Agnese and the Pantheon portico (figs. 746 and 249). Here a pair of huge columns derived from the Column of Trajan (see fig. 273) substitutes for facade towers, which have become corner pavilions reminiscent of those on the Louvre court (compare fig. 722). With these inflexible elements of Roman Imperial art embedded into the elastic curvatures of his church, Fischer von Erlach expresses, more boldly than any Italian Baroque architect, the power of the Christian faith to absorb and transfigure the splendors of antiquity.

PRANDTAUER. Even more monumental, thanks to its superb site, is the Monastery of Melk (fig. 832) by Jakob Prandtauer (1660–1726). The buildings form a tightly knit unit that centers on the church. It occupies the crest of a promontory above the Danube, rising from the rock, not like a fortress but like a vision of heavenly glory. The interior of the church (fig. 833) still reflects the plan of Il Gesù, but the abundant illumination, the play of curves and countercurves, and the weightless grace of the stucco sculpture give it an airy lightness far removed from the Roman Baroque. The vaults and wall surfaces seem thin and pliable, like membranes easily punctured by the expansive power of space.

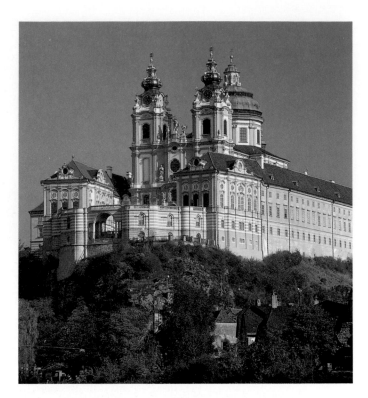

832. Jakob Prandtauer. Monastery Church, Melk, Austria. Begun 1702

Rococo Music

Although music after 1700 was the direct outgrowth of the previous century, it had not only a different sound but also was dominated by a handful of great composers—or so it seems to us today. They were nevertheless surrounded by many others of equal ability who began to form recognizable schools. These phenomena were interrelated. They were made possible by the international circulation of printed scores and musical treatises and the codification of the modern major-minor harmonic system (see "Modern Harmony," page 624). Of course, we have encountered great composers before; yet, when we listen to their music, it does not sound "modern" to our ears, no matter how beautiful or intricate it may be on its own terms.

The earliest of these eighteenth-century giants was Antonio Vivaldi (1678–1741). The son of a violinist at St. Mark's in Venice, he trained for the priesthood but was allowed to leave after one year for health reasons. From then on, he was employed chiefly as head of the Conservatory of the Pietà orphanage for girls. His vast body of work in virtually every instrumental and vocal form shows enormous versatility, one of the chief characteristics of the Rococo. Like the other great composers of the time, he was under constant pressure, due to his responsibilities and popularity, to write new music. He was, for example, the most successful composer of operas in Venice. He claimed to have written 90 in all; of the 20 that survive relatively intact, some show signs of haste (one of them was composed in only five days!). Nevertheless, *Orlando Furioso* (1727), inspired by Ariosto's epic poem, is unquestionably a masterpiece that is much superior to Handel's better-known *Alcina* (1735), based on the same story. Today Vivaldi is known almost exclusively for his concertos, which number nearly 500, the large majority of them for the violin, of which *The Four Seasons,* set to verses probably written by Vivaldi himself, is justly the most famous.

Johann Sebastian Bach (1685–1750), trained as organist and violinist, spent part of his early career as a court composer, then settled down as music director at the church of St. Thomas in Leipzig, a position that made huge demands on him for new music. As an organist, he was indebted to a virtuoso tradition that began in Italy with Girolamo Frescobaldi (1583–1643) and continued in Germany with Dietrich Buxtehude (1637–1707), whom he went out of his way to hear in Lübeck. Bach was influenced early on by Italian music, which helped to shape his sense of melody and harmony. His keyboard compositions show the impact of François Couperin as well. Bach's music balances melody and polyphony, harmony and counterpoint, expressive power and supreme rationality. The instrumental works are built largely on fugues and variations, for he believed completely in his system of counterpoint, even when it forced unsatisfactory results. He is remembered chiefly for choral music, including the justly celebrated *Mass in B Minor,* several oratorios, which are nearly miniature operas, and voluminous cantatas. They owe their character to the revolution brought about in 1700 by Erdmann Neumeister (1671–1756) of Hamburg, a theologian and poet who introduced a new kind of sacred poetry, which he called "cantata." It effectively reconciled the difference between the Lutheran chorale and Calvinist Psalm by alternating biblical passages with original texts that expand on the scripture's meaning by offering personal responses and meditations.

Bach was hardly the most famous or prolific German composer of his time. That honor belonged to his friend Georg Philipp Telemann (1681–1767), who worked for a while in Leipzig but spent most of his life in Hamburg. New issues of his compositions were eagerly sought after, for they show the fertile imagination of Vivaldi, the technical mastery of Bach, and the cosmopolitan flair of Rameau. This is especially true of his overtures (which are really dance suites), chamber suites for entertainment, and concertos.

George Frideric Handel (1685–1759), too, was famous throughout almost his entire career. Born at Halle in Saxony, he first worked in Hamburg, then visited Italy between 1706 and 1710, when he met Arcangelo Corelli, Alessandro Scarlatti, and his son Domenico Scarlatti (1685–1757), a brilliant composer of harpsichord sonatas. The stay in Italy was decisive to Handel's formation, for it was there that he learned to compose operas and adopted the lyrical manner that distinguishes his work. Upon his return to Germany, he was appointed music director at Hannover, but soon went to London on a leave of absence and never really returned. As fate would have it, the elector of Hannover then became King George I of England, and he continued to support Handel in London. Handel was both composer and impresario who made and lost fortunes in Italian opera. Italian opera flourished until John Gay's *The Beggar's Opera* (1728), a social and political satire written in English at the suggestion of the author Jonathan Swift (1667–1745), took England by storm. *The Beggar's Opera* used familiar songs culled from a variety of sources (including Purcell) and arranged by the German-born

Johann Christoph Pepusch (1667–1752), who had settled in London in 1700 and no doubt enjoyed creating this spoof of his rival's music. Handel, who by this time had become an English citizen, turned to oratorios in his adopted tongue. They have a drama that makes them virtually concert operas, not church music, although many are based on biblical subjects. Their extroverted character expresses the confidence of the English as the new chosen people. His instrumental music is extremely appealing in its poetry and stateliness.

After failing to achieve success in Paris early in his career, Jean-Philippe Rameau (1683–1764) made his mark as a theorist in 1722 with the *Treatise on Harmony,* then returned the following year to Paris, where he gained the backing of a major patron and began to write operas, which established his reputation and earned him the support of the court. His style has the clarity and grace of Watteau and the intelligence of Voltaire. Despite the fact that Rameau's operas, such as *The Gallant Indes* (1735, a "heroic ballet" in several episodes) and *Castor and Pollux* (1737), are the direct descendants of Jean-Baptiste Lully's, they were attacked by the latter's supporters for their variety and drama. Ironically, the Lullyists later championed him against Italian opera, whose cause was being promoted by the Enlightenment philosopher Jean-Jacques Rousseau (1712–1778) on the grounds that French was not fit for singing! Nevertheless, the revival of *Castor and Pollux* in 1754, after it had been heavily reworked by the composer, was an outstanding success that marked the defeat of Italian opera. The declamatory style satisfied the Lullyists, while the brilliant inventiveness, especially of the instrumental writing, pleased Rameau's partisans, who proclaimed the opera his masterpiece.

Modern Harmony

The development of eighteenth-century music was made possible by the codification of the modern system of harmony, which, after a gradual development over approximately 300 years, was spelled out in its final form in the *Treatise on Harmony* (1722) by the French composer Jean-Philippe Rameau (1683–1764). This system was based on the "tempered" diatonic scale, a progression of notes derived by equally spacing ("tempering") 12 tones within an octave (in essence, the black and white keys of a piano). The tonal distance, or interval, between any two of these one-twelfth-octave tones is called a semitone or "half step." Twice that interval is called a whole tone or "whole step." The diatonic system includes two principal scales, the major scale—the familiar "do-re-mi" that music students practice—and a modification of it called the minor scale. Both major and minor scales include a specific progression of five whole tones and two semitones, which start from the tonic, the note on which the scale is based, to the same note an octave above it. Like Greek modes, the major and minor scales communicate emotional qualities. Generally, a listener experiences the major scale as positive and optimistic, and the minor scale as somber or plaintive.

The tempered scale allowed a keyboard to include a number of octaves, which in turn increased the range of music that could be written for keyboard instruments. The 48 pieces that Johann Sebastian Bach (1685–1750) wrote in his *Well-Tempered Clavier* (1722, 1744) were one of the first series of compositions that exploited the possibilities of the newly expanded keyboard.

Another feature of the system as defined by Rameau were chords, sets of notes based on specific tones of the scale, sounded together in accompaniment to the melody. The major chord, for example, is derived from the major scale. It is made up of the tonic, the third note of the scale, and the fifth note of the scale. The chords for each scale were intended to create a full multivoice sound that is pleasing to the ear. Rameau's rules defined which chords were to be used in which musical circumstances; however, it was also understood that a composer might "break" the rules to create a deliberately discordant effect, or dissonance, for expressive purposes. Such dissonances were almost always "resolved" back to the notes of the scale in which the work was being played.

We need not be schooled in music theory to appreciate the virtues of the new system, which are readily apparent to the ear: its orderliness and flexibility, which not only permitted the fullest development of counterpoint, but created new melodic possibilities as well. Modern harmony was an essential precondition for the work of the great composers of the eighteenth and nineteenth centuries, and it remained the basis of Western music composition until the end of World War I, when avant-garde composers began to seek other modes of musical expression.

834. Balthasar Neumann. The Kaisersaal, Residenz, Würzburg, Germany. 1719–44. Frescoes by Giovanni Battista Tiepolo, 1751

NEUMANN. The architects of the next generation favored a tendency toward lightness and elegance. The Episcopal Palace in Würzburg by Balthasar Neumann (1687–1753) includes the breathtaking Kaisersaal (fig. 834), a great oval hall decorated in the favorite color scheme of the mid-eighteenth century: white, gold, and pastel shades. The number and aesthetic role of structural members such as columns, pilasters, and architraves are now minimized. Windows and vault segments are framed by continuous, ribbonlike moldings, and the white surfaces are spun over with irregular ornamental designs. This repertory of lacy, curling motifs, the hallmark of the French style (see fig. 814), is happily combined with German Rococo architecture.

ZIMMERMANN. A contemporary of Balthasar Neumann, Dominikus Zimmermann (1685–1766), created what may be the finest spatial design of the mid-eighteenth century, the Bavarian pilgrimage church nicknamed "Die Wies" (figs. 835 and 836). The exterior is so plain that its interior richness seems truly overwhelming. Like the Kaisersaal, its shape is oval, but since the ceiling rests on paired, free-standing supports, the spatial configuration is more fluid and complex. As a result, we are reminded of a German Gothic Hallenkirche (see fig. 454),

835. Dominikus Zimmermann. Interior of Die Wies,
Upper Bavaria, Germany. 1745–54

despite the playful Rococo décor. Guarini's prophetic revaluation of Gothic architecture has here become reality.

ITALY

Just as the style of architecture invented in Italy achieved its climax north of the Alps, much of the Italian Rococo took place in other countries. The timid style of the Late Baroque in Italy was suddenly transformed during the first decade of the eighteenth century by the rise of the Rococo in Venice, which had been relegated to a minor outpost for a hundred years. The Italian Rococo is distinguished from the Baroque by a renewed appreciation of Veronese's colorism and pageantry, but with a light and airy sensibility that is new. The first to formulate this style was Sebastiano Ricci (1659–1734), who began his career as a stage painter and emerged as an important artist only in mid-career. Their skill at blending this painterly manner with High Baroque illusionism made Ricci and the Venetians the leading decorative painters in Europe between 1710 and 1760, and they were active in every major center throughout Europe, particularly London and Madrid. They were not alone: artists from Rome and other parts of Italy also worked abroad in large numbers.

836. Plan of Die Wies

837. Giovanni Battista Tiepolo. Ceiling fresco (detail). 1751. The Kaisersaal, Residenz, Würzburg

TIEPOLO. The last and most refined stage of Italian illusionistic ceiling decoration is represented in Würzburg by its greatest master, Giovanni Battista Tiepolo (1696–1770). In his mastery of light and color, his grace and felicity of touch, and his power of invention, Tiepolo far surpassed his fellow Venetians, and these qualities made him famous far beyond his home territory. When Tiepolo painted the Würzburg frescoes (figs. 834, 837, and 838), his powers were at their height. The tissuelike ceiling so often gives way to illusionistic openings of every sort that we no longer feel it to be a spatial boundary. These openings do not, however, reveal avalanches of figures propelled by dramatic bursts of light, like those of Roman ceilings (compare fig. 737), but rather blue sky and sunlit clouds, and an occasional winged creature soaring in this limitless expanse. Only along the edges of the ceiling are there solid clusters of figures (fig. 837).

At one end, replacing a window (see fig. 834), is *The Marriage of Frederick Barbarossa* (fig. 838). As a public spectacle, it is as festive as *Christ in the House of Levi* (fig. 653) by Veronese, whose example the artist has followed by placing the event (which took place in the twelfth century) in a contemporary setting. Its allegorical fantasy is literally revealed by the carved putti opening a curtain onto the wedding ceremony in a display of theatrical illusionism worthy of Bernini. Unexpected

in this lively procession is the element of classicism, which lends an air of noble restraint to many of the figures.

Tiepolo afterward became the last in the line of Italian artists, beginning with Luca Giordano (see page 560), invited to work at the Royal Palace in Madrid. There he encountered the German painter Anton Raphael Mengs, a proponent of the classical revival whose presence signaled the effective end of the Rococo (see page 638).

GIAQUINTO. The artist replaced by Mengs was Corrado Giaquinto (1703–1765), who departed because of ill health. The only serious rival in ability to Tiepolo, he can be claimed with equal justice as the last great representative of painting in both Naples, where he trained under Francesco Solimena, and Rome, where he passed most of his career, for the two schools were intimately related (see page 560). At the Spanish court, where he exercised powers comparable to Lebrun's (see page 600), Giaquinto was hailed as the successor to Giordano, whose work in turn had a decisive impact on his art. *Justice and Peace* (fig. 839) bears an obvious resemblance to Giordano's *Abduction of Europa* (fig. 738), but with overtones of the work of Boucher that suggest an awareness of his style (see fig. 819). The painting happily unites the best of both worlds: the monumentality of Italy and the charm of France. What sets it apart

838. Giovanni Battista Tiepolo. *The Marriage of Frederick Barbarossa* (partial view). 1752. Fresco. Kaisersaal, Residenz, Würzburg

839. Corrado Giaquinto. *Justice and Peace.* c. 1753–54.
Oil on canvas, 7'1" x 13'11¹/4" (2.16 x 4.25 m). Museo del Prado, Madrid

Theater throughout the Rococo period was marked by sentimentality, usually with a moralizing theme. In England this trend began with *Love's Last Shift* by Colley Cibber (1671–1757), which was presented even before the attacks of Jeremy Collier (1650–1726) in 1698 on the morality of the theater. The net result was a more conservative kind of domestic drama for the middle class, exemplified by *The Conscious Lovers* (1722) by Richard Steele (1672–1729), in which people recant the folly of their ways. As a result of the political satires by Henry Fielding (1707–1754), which offended the Prime Minister, Sir Robert Walpole, theater was further constrained by the Licensing Act of 1737, which imposed strict censorship. England, which had been influenced by Molière and Racine during the seventeenth century, now made an important contribution to French theater. The counterpart to Steele's plays in France were the "tearful comedies" of Philippe Destouches (1680–1754), who served as a diplomat in London in 1716, Pierre-Claude Nivelle de La Chaussée (1692–1754), and Pierre Marivaux (1688–1763). Tragedy enjoyed a final resurgence in the plays of the writer and philosopher Voltaire (François-Marie Arouet, 1694–1778), who sought to liberalize classical drama after living as a refugee in 1726–29 in England, where he came to know all the leading intellectuals and developed a superficial admiration for Shakespeare. His later plays are no less sentimental than those of his peers, but the growing emphasis on spectacle led him in 1759 to banish spectators from the stage for the first time. Comedy was left in the hands of Comédie Italienne, created in 1716 when the *commedia dell'arte* was invited back to France by the Duc d'Orléans upon the death of his brother, Louis XIV. In Italy, by contrast, the energies of the playwrights were absorbed by the mania for opera. The main exception was Carlo Goldoni (1707–1793), a Venetian dramatist whose vivid comedies deliberately imitated those of Molière.

The major contributions of Rococo theater thus lay not in writing but in stagecraft: scenic design and acting. With the increased demand for spectacle, many artists were trained or employed as scenographers, including François Boucher and Canaletto. The affinity was natural, since the backgrounds in many paintings came to look increasingly like set designs after 1700.

Boucher's pupil Philippe-Jacques de Loutherbourg (1740–1812), who also trained under the scene designer Louis-René Boquet (1717–1814), brought French practices with him to England, where many painters, including Hogarth's father-in-law James Thornhill (1676–1734), George Lambert (c. 1699–1765), and Francis Hayman (1708–1776), regularly worked for the theater.

De Loutherbourg, who became a friend of Thomas Gainsborough, had been invited to England by the actor David Garrick (1717–1779) to supervise scene painting at his Drury Lane Theater, and both men introduced a number of innovations in the theater, especially in improved lighting. Garrick, whose portrait was painted by all the leading artists of the day, including Hogarth, Reynolds, and Gainsborough, dominated the English stage after his debut in 1741, and played a major role in theatrical reform on the Continent following his visits to France in 1763 and Italy and Germany two years later. Like Voltaire, he removed spectators from the stage. Nevertheless, Garrick had several rivals, chief among them Charles Macklin (1697?–1797) and Samuel Foote (1720–1777), who established The Haymarket as a rival to Drury Lane and Covent Garden, the two legitimate theaters in London. These three men were among the first English actors to show an awareness of period dress, which was also taken up by the French theater. Voltaire's main actor, Henri-Louis Lekain (1729–1778), and his leading lady, Mademoiselle Clairon (1723–1803), became the first French actors to use authentic costumes, as part of the trend toward greater realism in theater.

Women had been acting in the Comédie Français since the 1690s, but they never achieved the status of English actresses. Thus, Adrienne Lecouvreur (1692–1730), who was the first to adopt formal court costumes for tragic heroines, was buried anonymously the same year that Anne Oldfield (1683–1730) was interred in Westminster Abbey. After 1780 the reigning actress was Sarah Siddons (1755–1831), the sister of the great impresario John Philip Kemble (1757–1823); like Garrick, she sat for both Gainsborough and Reynolds (see figs. 827 and 828). During the early decades of the eighteenth century, a number of women in England also became successful playwrights.

is its ravishing beauty. The seemingly effortless brushwork and bold palette are unique to Giaquinto. No other painter of the Rococo could apply such a daring array of hues with such creamy consistency.

CANALETTO. During the eighteenth century, landscape in Italy evolved a new form in keeping with the character of the Rococo: *veduta* (view) painting. Its beginnings can be traced back to the seventeenth century with the many foreigners, such as Claude Lorraine (see fig. 796), who specialized in depicting Rome's environs, but after 1720 it acquired a specifically urban identity. The most renowned of the vedutists was Canaletto (1697–1768) of Venice. His pictures were great favorites with the British, who purchased them as souvenirs of the grand tours of Italy, then so popular. Indeed, he enjoyed such success with clients from England that he later became one of several prominent Venetian artists to spend lengthy sojourns in London. *The Bucintoro at the Molo* (fig. 840) was one of a series of paintings commissioned by Joseph Smith, an English entrepreneur living in Venice. These served both to decorate Smith's house and to introduce Canaletto's work to prospective buyers. Smith subsequently issued them as a suite of etchings to meet the demand for remembrances of Venice by those who could not afford an original canvas by the artist.

Canaletto's landscapes are, for the most part, topographically accurate. However, he was not above tampering with the truth, and while he usually made only slight adjustments for the sake of compositional effectiveness, he would sometimes

840. Canaletto. *The Bucintoro at the Molo*. c. 1732. Oil on canvas, 30¼ x 49½" (77 x 126 cm). The Royal Collection
© 1993 Her Majesty Queen Elizabeth II

841. Giovanni Battista Piranesi. *Tower with Bridges,* from
Prison Caprices. 1760–61. Etching, 21¾ x 16⅜" (55.2 x 41.6 cm).
The Metropolitan Museum of Art, New York
Rogers Fund

treat scenes with considerable license or create composite views. He may have used a mechanical or optical device (perhaps a camera obscura, a forerunner of the photographic camera) to render some of his views, although he was a consummate draftsman who hardly needed such aids. In any event, they fail to account for the visual sparkle of his pictures and his sure sense of composition. These features sprang in part from Canaletto's training as a scenographer. This experience in the theater also helps to explain the liveliness of his paintings. He often included vignettes of daily life in Venice that lend a human interest to his scenes and make them fascinating cultural documents as well. *The Bucintoro at the Molo* shows a favorite theme: the Doge returning on his magnificent barge to the Piazza San Marco from the Lido (the city's island beach) on Ascension Day after celebrating the Marriage of the Sea. Canaletto has captured to perfection the festive air surrounding this great public celebration, which is presented as a theatrical display of spectacular brilliance.

PIRANESI. Canaletto shared his background as a designer of stage sets with Ricci (see above) and also with Giovanni Panini (1691–1765), his fellow vedutist in Rome who had a passion for classical antiquity (see fig. 246). They, in turn, are the forerunners of another Roman artist, Giovanni Battista Piranesi (1720–1778), whose *Prison Caprices* (fig. 841) are rooted in contemporary designs for theater and opera. Unlike the prints after Canaletto's paintings, these masterful etchings were intended as original works of art from the beginning, so that they have a gripping power. In Piranesi's imagery, the play between reality and fantasy, so fundamental to the theatrical Rococo, has been transformed into a romanticized vision of despair as terrifying as any nightmare. His bold imagination appealed greatly to many artists of the next generation, on whom he exercised a decisive influence.

Primary Sources for Part Three

The following is a selection of excerpts, in modern translations, from original texts by artists, architects, religious figures, and historians from the Renaissance through the Rococo periods. These readings supplement the main text and are keyed to it. Their full citations are given in the Credits section at the end of the book.

50
Leone Battista Alberti (1404–1472)
From *On Painting*

Alberti's On Painting, *published in 1435, and his* On Sculpture, *which appeared in 1464, are among the most influential and revealing documents of the Early Renaissance.*

The fundamental principle will be that all the steps of learning should be sought from Nature: the means of perfecting our art will be found in diligence, study and application. I would have those who begin to learn the art of painting do what I see practised by teachers of writing. They first teach all the signs of the alphabet separately, and then how to put syllables together, and then whole words. Our students should follow this method with painting. First they should learn the outlines of surfaces, then the way in which surfaces are joined together, and after that the forms of all the members individually; and they should commit to memory all the differences that can exist in those members, for they are neither few nor insignificant. Some people will have a crook-backed nose; others will have flat, turned-back, open nostrils; some are full around the mouth, while others are graced with slender lips, and so on. . . . But, considering all these parts, he should be attentive not only to the likeness of things but also and especially to beauty, for in painting beauty is as pleasing as it is necessary. The early painter Demetrius failed to obtain the highest praise because he was more devoted to representing the likeness of things than to beauty. Therefore, excellent parts should all be selected from the most beautiful bodies.

51
Leone Battista Alberti
From *On Architecture*

Modeled on Vitruvius' treatise on architecture (1st century B.C.), On Architecture *was completed in 1452 but not published until 1485, after Alberti's death.*

The most expert Artists among the Ancients . . . were of [the] opinion that an Edifice was like an Animal, so that in the formation of it we ought to imitate Nature. . . . It is manifest that in those [animals] which are esteemed beautiful, the parts or members are not constantly all the same, . . . but we find that even in those parts wherein they vary most, there is something inherent and implanted which tho' they differ extremely from each other, makes each of them be beautiful. . . . But the judgment which you make that a thing is beautiful, does not proceed from mere opinion, but from a secret argument and discourse implanted in the mind itself. . . . There is a certain excellence and natural beauty in the figures and forms of buildings, which immediately strike the mind with pleasure and admiration. It is my opinion that beauty, majesty, gracefulness and the like charms, consist in those particulars which if you alter or take away, the whole wou'd be made homely and disagreeable. . . . There is . . . something . . . which arises from the conjunction and connection of these other parts, and gives the beauty and grace to the whole: which we will call Congruity, which we may consider as the original, of all that is graceful and handsome. . . . Wherever such a composition offers itself to the mind either by the conveyance of the sight, hearing, or any of the other senses, we immediately perceive this congruity: for by Nature we desire things perfect, and adhere to them with pleasure when they are offered to us; nor does this Congruity arise so much from the body in which it is found, or any of its members, as from itself and from Nature, so that its true Seat is in the mind and in reason. . . . This is what Architecture chiefly aims at, and by this she obtains her beauty, dignity and value.

52
Girolamo Savonarola (1452–1498)
From a sermon delivered in Florence in 1493

The monk and religious reformer Savonarola preached against the growing worldliness of Florentine culture and was highly influential in that city for a time. As a result of his unwillingness to curb his outspoken criticisms of the papacy, he was excommunicated in 1497 and burned at the stake in 1498.

The primitive Church was constructed of living stones, Jesus Christ himself being the chief corner-stone. The Church was then a garden of delights, a very heaven upon earth. How holy was the zeal which animated its pastors for the good of souls! How anxiously did they employ themselves in things divine!

. . . Alas, how changed the scene! The devil, through the instrumentality of wicked prelates, has destroyed the temple of God. . . .

The holiest festivals are devoted to worldly amusements, to indecent spectacles, and to games suited to a heathen taste. On Christmas Eve, instead of filling our churches and sharing in their sacred offices, and proffering to God their thanksgivings for his inestimable love in the redemption of the world, Christians, so called, go off to taverns, to gratify their appetites, and to practise all sorts of evil. This very day I beheld in the streets females, who know better, exercising seductive arts, and clothed with meretricious ornaments. Such are not the insignia of female purity. Priests appear in public, arrayed more pompously than laymen. They are to be found in gambling houses and taverns. . . . Go to Rome,—go through all Christendom; study what is passing in the houses of great prelates and grand masters. Poetry and oratory chiefly occupy their thoughts. They prepare themselves by the study of Virgil, and Horace, and Cicero, for the cure of souls. Will you believe it? . . . The primitive bishops . . . were poor and humble men; they could not boast of great revenues and rich abbeys like the modern. They had neither mitres nor chalices of gold; or, if they had them, they were ready to sacrifice them for the necessities of the poor. . . . In the primitive Church, the chalices were of wood, and the prelates of gold. Now-a-days the Church has prelates of wood, and chalices of gold.

53

Leonardo da Vinci (1452–1519)
From his undated manuscripts

Leonardo, the consummate High Renaissance man, wrote on a variety of intellectual topics. The comparison of the arts, or Paragone, *was a common subject in High Renaissance scholarship.*

HE WHO DEPRECIATES PAINTING LOVES NEITHER PHILOSOPHY NOR NATURE

If you despise painting, which is the sole imitator of all visible works of nature, you certainly will be despising a subtle invention which brings philosophy and subtle speculation to bear on the nature of all forms—sea and land, plants and animals, grasses and flowers—which are enveloped in shade and light. Truly painting is a science, the true-born child of nature. For painting is born of nature; to be more correct we should call it the grandchild of nature, since all visible things were brought forth by nature and these, her children, have given birth to painting. Therefore we may justly speak of it as the grandchild of nature and as related to God.

A COMPARISON BETWEEN POETRY AND PAINTING

The imagination cannot visualize such beauty as is seen by the eye, because the eye receives the actual semblances or images of objects and transmits them through the sense organ to the understanding where they are judged. But the imagination never gets outside the understanding; . . . it reaches the memory and stops and dies there if the imagined object is not of great beauty; thus poetry is born in the mind or rather in the imagination of the poet who, because he describes the same things as the painter, claims to be the painter's equal! . . . The object of the imagination does not come from without but is born in the darkness of the mind's eye. What a difference between forming a mental image of such light in the darkness of the mind's eye and actually perceiving it outside the darkness!

If you, poet, had to represent a murderous battle you would have to describe the air obscured and darkened by fumes from frightful and deadly engines mixed with thick clouds of dust polluting the atmosphere, and the panicky flight of wretches fearful of horrible death. In that case the painter will be your superior, because your pen will be worn out before you can fully describe what the painter can demonstrate forthwith by the aid of his science, and your tongue will be parched with thirst and your body overcome by sleep and hunger before you can describe with words what a painter is able to show you in an instant.

ON PAINTING AND POETRY

Poetry is superior to painting in the presentation of words, and painting is superior to poetry in the presentation of facts. . . . For this reason I judge painting to be superior to poetry. But as painters did not know how to plead for their own art she was left without advocates for a long time. For painting does not talk; but reveals herself as she is, ending in reality; and Poetry ends in words in which she eloquently sings her own praises.

54

From the *Journal* of Luca Landucci

Landucci's journal entry for January 25, 1503, records varied opinions on the placement of Michelangelo's David *(fig. 607).*

Considering that the statue of David is almost finished, and desiring to install it and to give it an appropriate and acceptable location, with the installation at a suitable time, and since the installation must be solid and structurally trustworthy according to the instructions of Michelangelo, master of the said Giant, and of the consuls of the [wool guild], and desiring such advice as may be useful for choosing the aforesaid suitable and sound installation, etc., they decided to call together and assemble, to decide on this, competent masters, citizens, and architects, . . . and to record their opinions, word for word. . . .

All of these [28] men . . . gave advice as to where, and in what place, the said statue was to go; their statements are recorded below verbatim in their own words.

MESSER FRANCESCO, FIRST HERALD OF THE SIGNORIA
There are two places where such a statue might be erected. The first is where the Judith is [Donatello's *Judith and Holofernes,* then located outside the Palazzo Vecchio] and the second the center of the courtyard of the Palace, where the David is [Donatello's *David,* see fig. 535, then located in the courtyard of the Palazzo Vecchio]. The reason for the first is because the Judith is an emblem of death, and it is not fitting for the Republic and I say it is not fitting that the woman should kill the man. And even more important, it . . . was erected under an evil star, for . . . then we lost Pisa. The David of the courtyard is a figure that is not perfect, because the leg that is thrust backwards is faulty. For these reasons I would advise putting this statue in one of the two places . . . but with my preference for where the Judith now is.

SANDRO BOTTICELLI
Cosimo [Rosselli] has hit upon the place where I think it can best be seen by passers-by [steps of the cathedral], with a Judith at the other corner. Perhaps also in the Loggia of the Signoria [a covered, open-air assembly hall used for state ceremonies]—but preferably at the corner of [the cathedral].

GIULIANO DA SAN GALLO
My judgment too was much inclined in favor of the corner of the Duomo that Cosimo mentioned, where it would be seen by the people. But, consider that this is a public thing, and consider the weakness of the marble, which is delicate and fragile. Then, if it is placed outside and exposed to the weather, I think that it will not endure. For this reason as much as any, I thought that it would be better underneath the central arch of the Loggia of the Signoria.

LEONARDO DA VINCI
I agree that it should be in the Loggia, where Giuliano said, but on the parapet where they hang the tapestries on the side of the wall, and with decency and decorum, and so displayed that it does not spoil the ceremonies of the officials.

SALVESTRO, WORKER IN PRECIOUS STONES
Almost all the places have been talked about, and much has been said one way or the other. But I believe that the man who made it did so to be worthy of giving it the best possible location. Though for my part I favor the place outside the palace [Palazzo Vecchio].

55

Michelangelo Buonarroti (1475–1564)
Sonnet

In addition to being a painter, a sculptor, and an architect, Michelangelo was also a prolific, although unpublished, poet. This sonnet was written in 1554.

My course of life already has attained,
Through stormy seas, and in a flimsy vessel,
The common port, at which we land to tell
All conduct's cause and warrant, good or bad,

So that the passionate fantasy, which made
Of art a monarch for me and an idol,
Was laden down with sin, now I know well,
Like what all men against their will desired.

What will become, now, of my amorous thoughts,
Once gay and vain, as toward two deaths I move,
One known for sure, the other ominous?

There's no painting or sculpture now that quiets
The soul that's pointed toward that holy Love
That on the cross opened Its arms to take us.

56

Giorgio Vasari (1511–1574)
From *The Lives of the Most Excellent Italian Architects, Painters, and Sculptors from Cimabue to Our Times*

Vasari was inspired to write the Lives *by his patron, Cardinal Farnese, later Pope Paul III. The book, first published in 1550 and expanded in 1568, was based on interviews conducted throughout Italy. Vasari personally knew many of the artists about whom he wrote, including Michelangelo.*

When Michelangelo had finished the statue [a portrait of Pope Julius II, later destroyed], Bramante, the friend and relation of Raphael and therefore ill-disposed to Michelangelo, seeing the Pope's preference for sculpture, schemed to divert his attention, and told the Pope that it would be a bad omen to get Michelangelo to go on with his tomb, as it would seem to be an invitation to death. He persuaded the Pope to get Michelangelo, on his return, to paint the vaulting of the Sixtine Chapel. In this way Bramante and his other rivals hoped to confound him, for by taking him from sculpture, in which he was perfect, and putting him to colouring in fresco, in which he had had no experience, they thought he would produce less admirable work than Raphael. . . . Thus, when Michelangelo returned to Rome, the Pope was disposed not to have the tomb finished for the time being, and asked him to paint the vaulting of the chapel. Michelangelo tried every means to avoid it, and recommended Raphael. . . . At length, seeing that the Pope was resolute, [he] decided to do it. . . . Michelangelo then made arrangements to do the whole work singlehanded. . . . When he had finished half, the Pope . . . daily became more convinced of Michelangelo's genius, and wished him to complete the work, judging that he would do the other half even better. Thus, singlehanded, he completed the work in twenty months, aided only by his mixer of colours. He sometimes complained that owing to the impatience of the Pope he had not been able to finish it as he would have desired, as the Pope was always asking him when he would be done. On one occasion Michelangelo replied that he would be finished when he had satisfied his own artistic sense. "And we require you to satisfy us in getting it done quickly," replied the Pope, adding that if it was not done soon he would have the scaffolding down. . . . The work was executed in great discomfort, as Michelangelo had to stand with his head thrown back, and he so injured his eyesight that for several months he could only read and look at designs in that posture. . . . I marvel that Michelangelo supported the discomfort. However, he became more eager every day to be doing and making progress, and so he felt no fatigue, and despised the discomfort.

57

Giorgio Vasari
From *The Lives of the Most Excellent Italian Architects, Painters, and Sculptors from Cimabue to Our Times*

Gian. Bellini and other painters of [Venice], through not having studied antiquities, employed a hard, dry and laboured style, which Titian acquired. But in 1507 arose Giorgione, who began to give his works more tone and relief, with better style, though he imitated natural things as best he could, colouring them like life, without making drawings previously, believing this to be the true method of procedure. He did not perceive that for good composition it is necessary to try several various methods on sheets, for invention is quickened by showing these things to the eye, while it is also necessary to a thorough knowledge of the nude. . . .

On seeing Giorgione's style Titian abandoned that of Bellini, although he had long practised it, and imitated Giorgione so well that in a short time his works were taken for Giorgione's. . . . He also did a marvellous Venus and Adonis. . . . In a panel of the same size he did Perseus freeing Andromeda from the marine monster, a work of unsurpassable charm. . . .

Titian's methods in these paintings differ widely from those he adopted in his youth. His first works are executed with a certain fineness and diligence, so that they may be examined closely, but these are done roughly in an impressionist manner, with bold strokes and blobs, to obtain the effect at a distance. This is why many in trying to imitate him have made clumsy pictures, for if people think that such work can be done without labour they are deceived, as it is necessary to retouch and recolour them incessantly, so that the labour is evident. The method is admirable and beautiful if done judiciously, making paintings appear alive and achieved without labour.

58

Raphael Sanzio (1485–1520)
Letter to Baldassare Castiglione

Castiglione was the author of the famous book of Renaissance manners, The Courtier. *This letter, probably written in 1514, suggests Raphael's familiarity with the Platonic notion that individual creatures and things are imperfect expressions of an original "ideal." The individual who wishes to glimpse that ideal can do so only through the higher powers of the mind. The concept became central to the classical idealism of Renaissance and post-Renaissance art.*

I have made drawings of various types based on Your Lordship's indications, and unless everybody is flattering me, I have satisfied everybody; but I do not satisfy my own judgment, because I am afraid of not satisfying yours. I am sending these drawings to you. Your Lordship may choose any of them, if you think any worthy of your choice.

The Holy Father, in honoring me, has laid a heavy burden upon my shoulders: the direction of the work at St. Peter's. I hope, indeed, I shall not sink under it; the more so, as the model I have made for it pleases His Holiness and has been praised by many connoisseurs. But my thoughts rise still higher. I should like to revive the handsome forms of the buildings of the ancients. Nor do I know whether my flight will be a flight of Icarus. Vitruvius affords me much light, but not sufficient.

As for the Galatea, I should consider myself a great master if it had half the merits you mention in your letter. However, I perceive in your words the love you bear me; and I add that in order to paint a fair one, I should need to see several fair ones, with the proviso that Your Lordship will be with me to select the best. But as there is a shortage both of good judges and of beautiful women, I am making use of some sort of idea which comes into my mind. Whether this idea has any artistic excellence in itself, I do not know. But I do strive to attain it.

59

From the Canons and Decrees of the Council of Trent

The Catholic church responded to the growth in Northern Europe of independent "Reformed" churches (inaugurated by Martin Luther's 1517 critique of the Church) by attempting to stop the

Reformation and win back the territories and peoples lost to the Roman Church. These various measures of the sixteenth and early seventeenth centuries are collectively called the Counter Reformation. One agency of this development was the Council of Trent, a series of three meetings of church leaders in 1545–47, 1551–52, and 1562–63. The following is from one of the council's last edicts, dated December 3–4, 1563, a response to ongoing Protestant attacks against religious images.

The holy council commands all bishops and others who hold the office of teaching and have charge of the *cura animarum,* that in accordance with the usage of the Catholic and Apostolic Church, received from the primitive times of the Christian religion, and with the unanimous teaching of the holy Fathers and the decrees of sacred councils, they above all instruct the faithful diligently in matters relating to intercession and invocation of the saints, the veneration of relics, and the legitimate use of images. . . . Moreover, that the images of Christ, of the Virgin Mother of God, and of the other saints are to be placed and retained especially in the churches, and that due honor and veneration is to be given them; not, however, that any divinity or virtue is believed to be in them by reason of which they are to be venerated, or that something is to be asked of them, or that trust is to be placed in images, as was done of old by the Gentiles who placed their hope in idols; but because the honor which is shown them is referred to the prototypes which they represent, so that by means of the images which we kiss and before which we uncover the head and prostrate ourselves, we adore Christ and venerate the saints whose likeness they bear. That is what was defined by the decrees of the councils, especially of the Second Council of Nicaea, against the opponents of images.

Moreover, let the bishops diligently teach that by means of the stories of the mysteries of our redemption portrayed in paintings and other representations the people are instructed and confirmed in the articles of faith, which ought to be borne in mind and constantly reflected upon; also that great profit is derived from all holy images, not only because the people are thereby reminded of the benefits and gifts bestowed on them by Christ, but also because through the saints the miracles of God and salutary examples are set before the eyes of the faithful, so that they may give God thanks for those things, may fashion their own life and conduct in imitation of the saints and be moved to adore and love God and cultivate piety. But if anyone should teach or maintain anything contrary to these decrees, let him be anathema.

If any abuses shall have found their way into these holy and salutary observances, the holy council desires earnestly that they be completely removed, so that no representation of false doctrines and such as might be the occasion of grave error to the uneducated be exhibited. . . . Finally, such zeal and care should be exhibited by the bishops with regard to these things that nothing may appear that is disorderly or unbecoming and confusedly arranged, nothing that is profane, nothing disrespectful, since holiness becometh the house of God.

60

From a session of the Inquisition Tribunal in Venice of Paolo Veronese

Because of the liberal religious atmosphere of Venice, Veronese was never required to make the various changes to his painting of the Last Supper (fig. 653) asked for by the tribunal of the Inquisition in this interrogation. All parties seem to have been satisfied with a mere change of title, to Supper in the House of Levi (now Christ in the House of Levi).

Today, Saturday, the 18th of the month of July, 1573, having been asked by the Holy Office to appear before the Holy Tribunal, Paolo Caliari of Verona, . . . Questioned about his profession:

Answer: I paint and compose figures.

Q: Do you know the reason why you have been summoned?

A: No, sir.

Q: Can you imagine it?

A: I can well imagine.

Q: Say what you think the reason is.

A: According to what the Reverend Father, the Prior of the Convent of SS. Giovanni e Paolo, . . . told me, he had been here and Your Lordships had ordered him to have painted [in the picture] a Magdalen in place of a dog. I answered him by saying I would gladly do everything necessary for my honor and for that of my painting, but that I did not understand how a figure of Magdalen would be suitable there. . . .

Q: What picture is this of which you have spoken?

A: This is a picture of the Last Supper that Jesus Christ took with His Apostles in the house of Simon. . . .

Q: At this Supper of Our Lord have you painted other figures?

A: Yes, milords.

Q: Tell us how many people and describe the gestures of each.

A: There is the owner of the inn, Simon; besides this figure I have made a steward, who, I imagined, had come there for his own pleasure to see how the things were going at the table. There are many figures there which I cannot recall, as I painted the picture some time ago. . . .

Q: In this Supper which you made for SS. Giovanni e Paolo what is the significance of the man whose nose is bleeding?

A: I intended to represent a servant whose nose was bleeding because of some accident.

Q: What is the significance of those armed men dressed as Germans, each with a halberd in his hand? . . .

A: We painters take the same license the poets and the jesters take and I have represented these two halberdiers, one drinking and the other eating nearby on the stairs. They are placed there so that they might be of service because it seemed to me fitting, according to what I have been told, that the master of the house, who was great and rich, should have such servants.

Q: And that man dressed as a buffoon with a parrot on his wrist, for what purpose did you paint him on that canvas?

A: For ornament, as is customary.

Q: Who are at the table of Our Lord?

A: The Twelve Apostles.

Q: What is St. Peter, the first one, doing?

A: Carving the lamb in order to pass it to the other end of the table.

Q: What is the Apostle next to him doing?

A: He is holding a dish in order to receive what St. Peter will give him.

Q: Tell us what the one next to this one is doing.

A: He has a toothpick and cleans his teeth. . . .

Q: Did any one commission you to paint Germans, buffoons, and similar things in that picture?

A: No, milords, but I received the commission to decorate the picture as I saw fit. It is large and, it seemed to me, it could hold many figures.

Q: Are not the decorations which you painters are accustomed to add to paintings or pictures supposed to be suitable and proper to the subject and the principal figures or are they for pleasure—simply what comes to your imagination without any discretion or judiciousness?

A: I paint pictures as I see fit and as well as my talent permits.

Q: Does it seem fitting at the Last Supper of the Lord to paint buffoons, drunkards, Germans, dwarfs and similar vulgarities?

A: No, milords.

Q: Do you not know that in Germany and in other places infected with heresy it is customary with various pictures full of scurrilousness and similar inventions to mock, vituperate, and scorn the things of the Holy Catholic Church in order to teach bad doctrines to foolish and ignorant people?

A: Yes that is wrong. . . .

After these things had been said, the judges announced that the above named Paolo would be obliged to improve and change his painting within a period of three months from the day of this admonition and that according to the opinion and decision of the Holy Tribunal all the corrections should be made at the expense of the painter and that if he did not correct the picture he would be liable to the penalties imposed by the Holy Tribunal. Thus they decreed in the best manner possible.

61
Andrea Palladio (1518–1580)
From *The Four Books of Architecture*

Published in 1570, Palladio's Four Books of Architecture *made an enormous impression on his European contemporaries.*

His book provided the basis for much French and English architecture of the seventeenth and eighteenth centuries.

Guided by a natural inclination, I gave myself up in my most early years to the study of architecture: and as it was always my opinion, that the ancient Romans, as in many other things, so in building well, vastly excelled all those who have been since their time, I proposed to myself Vitruvius for my master and guide, who is the only ancient writer of this art, and set myself to search into the reliques of all the ancient edifices, that, in spight of time and the cruelty of the Barbarians, yet remain; and finding them much more worthy of observation, than at first I had imagined, I began very minutely with the utmost diligence to measure every one of their parts; of which I grew at last so sollicitous an examiner, (not finding any thing which was not done with reason and beautiful proportion) that I have very frequently not only travelled in different parts of Italy, but also out of it. . . .

Whereupon perceiving how much this common use of building was different from the observations I had made upon the said edifices, and from what I had read in Vitruvius, Leon Battista Alberti, and in other excellent writers . . . it seemed to me a thing worthy of a man, who ought not to be born for himself only, but also for the utility of others, to publish the de-signs of those edifices, (in collecting which, I have employed so much time, and exposed myself to so many dangers) and concisely to set down whatever in them appeared to me more worthy of consideration; and moreover, those rules which I have observed, and now observe, in building; that they who shall read these my books, may be able to make use of whatever will be good therein, and supply those things in which . . . I shall have failed; that one may learn, by little and little, to lay aside the strange abuses, the barbarous inventions, the superfluous expence, and (what is of greater consequence) avoid the various and continual ruins that have been seen in many fabricks. . . .

The first part shall be divided into two books; in the first shall be treated of the preparation of the materials, and when prepared, how, and in what manner, they ought to be put to use, from the foundation up to the roof: where those precepts shall be, that are universal, and ought to be observed in all edifices, as well private as publick.

In the second I shall treat of the quality of the fabricks that are suitable to the different ranks of men: first of those of a city; and then of the most convenient situation for villas, and in what manner they are to be disposed.

62
Carel van Mander (1548–1606)
From *The Painter's Treatise*

Van Mander's biographies of distinguished Dutch and Flemish painters, published in 1604, are a counterpart to the lives of

Italian artists by Giorgio Vasari, which first appeared in 1550. Van Mander, a painter himself, begins his biographies with Jan van Eyck because he was considered the inventor of oil painting and consequently the originator, with his brother Hubert, of the Netherlandish tradition of painting. Among the works described by Van Mander are the Ghent Altarpiece *(see figs. 673–75) and a painting that is probably the* Arnolfini Portrait *(see figs. 677 and 678).*

It is supposed that the art of painting with a glue and egg medium [tempera painting] was imported into the Netherlands from Italy, because, as we have noted in the biography of Giovanni of Cimabue, this method was first used in Florence, in 1250. . . .

According to the people of Bruges, Joannes [Jan] was a learned man, clever and inventive, who studied many subjects related to painting: He examined many kinds of pigment; he studied alchemy and distillation. At length, he worked out a method of varnishing his egg and glue paintings with oil, so that these shining and lustrous pictures exceedingly delighted all who saw them. . . .

Joannes had painted a panel on which he had spent much time. . . . He varnished the finished panel according to his new invention and placed it in the sunlight to dry. . . . The panel burst at the joints and fell apart. Joannes . . . took a resolve that the sun should not damage his work ever again.

Accordingly, . . . he set himself to discover or invent some kind of varnish which would dry within the house, away from the sunlight. He had already examined many oils and other similar materials supplied by nature, and had found that linseed oil and nut oil had the best drying ability of them all. . . .

Joannes found, after many experiments, that colors mixed with these oils could be handled easily, that they dried well, became hard, and, once dry, could resist water. The oil made the color appear more alive, owing to a lustre of its own, without varnish. And what surprised and pleased him most was that paint made with oil could be applied more easily and mixed more thoroughly than paint made with egg and glue. . . .

Joannes . . . had created a new type of painting, to the amazement of the world. . . . This noble discovery, of painting with oil, was the only thing the art of painting still needed to achieve naturalistic rendition.

If the ancient Greeks, Apelles and Zeus [Zeuxis] had come to life again in this country and had seen this new method of painting, they would not have been any less surprised than if war-like Achilles [had] witnessed the thunder of cannon fire. . . .

The most striking work which the Van Eyck brothers did together is the altar-piece in the church of St John, in Ghent. . . .

The central panel of the altar-piece represents a scene from the Revelation of St John, in which the elders worship the Lamb. . . . In the upper part, Mary is represented; she is being crowned by the Father and the Son. . . .

Next to the figure of Mary are little angels singing from sheets of music. They are painted so exquisitely and so well that one can detect readily, from their facial expressions, who is singing the higher part, the high counter part, the tenor part, and the bass. . . .

Adam and Eve are represented. One may observe that Adam has a certain fear of breaking the command of the Lord, for he has a worried expression. . . .

The altar painting of the Van Eyck brothers was shown only to a few personages of high standing or to someone who would reward the keeper very well. Sometimes it was shown on important holidays, but then there was usually such a crowd that it was difficult to come near it. Then the chapel containing the altar-piece would be filled with all kinds of people—painters young and old, every kind of art lover, swarming like bees and flies around a basket of figs or raisins. . . .

Some Florentine merchants sent a splendid painting, made in Flanders, by Joannes to King Alphonso I of Naples. . . . A huge throng of artists came to see this marvelous painting, when it reached Italy. But although the Italians examined the picture very carefully, touching it, smelling at it, scenting the strong odor produced by the mixture of the colors with oil, and drawing all kinds of conclusions, the secret held until Antonello of Messina, in Sicily, went to Bruges to learn the process of oil-painting. Having mastered the technique, he introduced the art into Italy, as I have described in his biography. . . .

Joannes had once painted in oil two portraits in a single scene, a man and a woman, who give the right hand to each other, as if they had been united in wedlock by *Fides*. This little picture came through inheritance into the hands of a barber in Bruges. Mary, aunt of King Philip of Spain and widow of King Louis of Hungary, . . . happened to see this painting. The art loving princess was so pleased with this picture that she gave a certain office to the barber which brought him a yearly income of a hundred guilders.

63

Gaspar Ofhuys (c. 1456–1523)
From an account of the illness of Hugo van der Goes

Gaspar Ofhuys entered the "Red Cloister" monastery near Brussels together with Hugo van der Goes in 1475. Ofhuys was perhaps jealous of the special privileges Van der Goes enjoyed because of his status as a painter, and intimates that his mental illness was an affliction brought on by the sin of pride. This sin was often attributed to artists in the Middle Ages.

About five or six years after he had taken the vows it fell to our brother [Hugo van der Goes] to make a journey which—if I remember right—took him to Cologne. . . . Hugo, during one night of his journey home, was seized by a strange illness of his mind; he uttered unceasing laments about being doomed and sentenced to eternal damnation. He even wanted to lay murderous hands on himself and had to be prevented by force from doing so. Because of this strange illness that journey came to an extremely sad end. However, thanks to efficient help, Brussels was safely reached, and prior Thomas was immediately summoned. When he saw and heard all that had happened he suspected that Hugo was vexed by the same illness which had befallen King Saul; and remembering that Saul was relieved when David played the harp he at once permitted plenty of music to be made in the presence of Hugo and also other soothing performances to be arranged in order to chase away those fantasies. But with all this, Hugo's health did not improve; he continued to rave and to pronounce himself a child of perdition. In this sad state he came home to the monastery. . . .

We can speak of two possible assumptions concerning the illness of our painter-brother converse. The first is that it was a natural one, a kind of frenzy. There exist various natural species of this disease: sometimes it is caused by "melancholy" victuals, sometimes by imbibing strong wine; then again by passions of the soul such as anxiety, sadness, overwork, or fear. . . . As regards those passions of the soul, I know for certain that this converse brother was much afflicted by them. For he was deeply troubled by the thought of how he could ever finish the works of art he wanted to paint, and it was said at that time that nine years would hardly suffice for it. . . .

The second possibility of explaining this disease is that it was sent by Divine Providence which, as it is written in the second Epistle of St. Peter, ch. 3, "is long-suffering to us-ward, not willing that any should perish, but that all should come to repentance." For this converse brother was highly praised in our order because of his special artistic achievements—in fact, he thus became more famous than he would have been outside our walls; and since he was only human—as are all of us—the various honors, visits, and accolades that came to him made him feel very important. Thus, since God did not want him to perish, He in His compassion sent him this humiliating disease which indeed made him very contrite. This our brother understood very well, and as soon as he had recovered he became most humble.

64

Fray José de Sigüenza (1544?–1606)
From the *History of the Order of St. Jerome*

The works of Hieronymus Bosch were collected by the Spanish king Philip II (reigned 1556–98) and were displayed in his Escorial Palace near Madrid, where Sigüenza was the librarian. The interpretation of Bosch's work was as difficult then as it is today and caused just as much disagreement. This passage is Sigüenza's attempt to interpret the painting that we call The Garden of Delights *(figs. 684 and 685).*

Among these German and Flemish pictures . . . there are distributed throughout the house many by a certain Geronimo Bosch. Of him I want to speak at somewhat greater length for various reasons: first, because his great inventiveness merits it; second, because they are commonly called the absurdities of Geronimo Bosque by people who observe little in what they look at; and third, because I think that these people consider them without reason as being tainted by heresy. . . .

The difference that, to my mind, exists between the pictures of this man and those of all others is that the others try to paint man as he appears on the outside, while he alone had the audacity to paint him as he is on the inside. . . .

The . . . painting has as its basic theme and subject a flower and the fruit of [a] type that we call strawberries. . . . In order for one to understand his idea, I will expound upon it in the same order in which he has organized it. Between two pictures is one large painting, with two doors that close over it. In the first of the panels he painted the Creation of Man, showing how God put him in paradise, a delightful place . . . and how He commands him as a test of his obedience and faith not to eat from the tree, and how later the devil deceived him in the form of a serpent. He eats and, trespassing God's rule, is exiled from that wondrous place and deprived of the high dignity for which he was created. . . . This is [shown] with a thousand fantasies and observations that serve as warnings. . . .

In the large painting that follows he painted the pursuits of man after he was exiled from paradise and placed in this world, and he shows him searching after the glory that is like hay or straw, like a plant without fruit, which one knows will be cast into the oven the next day, . . . and thus uncovers the life, the activities, and the thoughts of these sons of sin and wrath, who, having forgotten the commands of God . . . strive for and undertake the glory of the flesh. . . .

In this painting we find, as if alive and vivid, an infinite number of passages from the scriptures that touch upon the evil ways of man, . . . many allegories or metaphors that present them in the guise of tame, wild, fierce, lazy, sagacious, cruel, and bloodthirsty beasts of burden and riding animals. . . . Here is also demonstrated the transmigration of souls that Pythagoras, Plato, and other poets . . . displayed in the attempt to show us the bad customs, habits, dress, disposition, or sinister shades with which the souls of miserable men clothe themselves—that through pride they are transformed into lions; by vengefulness into tigers; through lust into mules, horses, and pigs; by tyranny into fish; by vanity into peacocks; by slyness and craft into foxes; by gluttony into apes and wolves; by callousness and evil into asses; by stupidity into sheep; because of rashness into goats. . . .

One can reap great profit by observing himself thus portrayed true to life from the inside. . . . And he would also see in the last panel the miserable end and goal of his pains, efforts, and preoccupations, and how . . . the brief joys are transformed into eternal wrath, with no hope or grace.

65

From the contract for the
St. Wolfgang Altarpiece

It took Michael Pacher ten years (1471–81) to complete this elaborate altarpiece for the pilgrimage church of St. Wolfgang. The altarpiece is still in its original location (fig. 691).

Here is recorded the pact and contract concerning the altar at St. Wolfgang, concluded between the very Reverend, Reverend Benedict, Abbot of Mondsee and of his monastery there, and Master Michael, painter of Bruneck, on St. Lucy's day of the year 1471.

Item, it is first to be recorded that the altar shall be made conforming to the elevation and design which the painter has brought to us at Mondsee, and to its exact measurements.

Item, the predella shrine shall be guilded on the inside and it shall show Mary seated with the Christ Child, Joseph, and the Three Kings with their gifts; and if these should not completely fill the predella shrine he shall make more figures or armored men, all gilt.

Item, the main shrine shall show the Coronation of Mary with angels and gilt drapery—the most precious and the best he can make.

Item, on one side St. Wolfgang with mitre, crozier, church, and hatchet; on the other St. Benedict with cap, crozier, and a tumbler, entirely gilded and silvered where needed.

Item, to the sides of the altar shall stand St. Florian and St. George, fine armored men, silvered and gilded where needed.

Item, the inner wings of the altar shall be provided with good paintings, the panels gilded and equipped with gables and pinnacles, representing four subjects, one each. . . .

Item, the outer wings—when the altar is closed—shall be done with good pigments and with gold added to the colors; the subject from the life of St. Wolfgang. . . .

Item, at St. Wolfgang, while he completes and sets up the altar, we shall provide his meals and drink, and also the iron work necessary for setting up the altar, as well as help with loading wherever necessary.

Item, the contract is made for the sum of one thousand two hundred Hungarian guilders or ducats. . . .

Item, if the altar is either not worth this sum or of higher value, and there should be some difference of opinion be-tween us, both parties shall appoint equal numbers of experts to decide the matter.

66

Martin Luther (1483–1546)
From *Against the Heavenly Prophets in the Matter of Images and Sacraments*

Luther inaugurated the Protestant Reformation movement in 1517 with a public critique of certain church practices, especially the sale of indulgences. His actions soon inspired a number of similar reformers in the North, some of whom were more extreme in their denunciations of the conventional artistic and musical trappings of the Church. The ideas of one of these, Andreas Bodenstein, inspired this writing of 1525.

I approached the task of destroying images by first tearing them out of the heart through God's Word and making them worthless and despised. . . . For when they are no longer in the heart, they can do no harm when seen with the eyes. But Dr. Karlstadt [Andreas Bodenstein], who pays no attention to matters of the heart, has reversed the order by removing them from sight and leaving them in the heart. . . .

I have allowed and not forbidden the outward removal of images, so long as this takes place without rioting and uproar and is done by the proper authorities. . . . And I say at the outset that according to the law of Moses no other images are forbidden than an image of God which one worships. A crucifix, on the other hand, or any other holy image is not forbidden. Heigh now! you breakers of images, I defy you to prove the opposite! . . .

Thus we read that Moses' Brazen Serpent remained (Num. 21:8) until Hezekiah destroyed it solely because it had been worshiped (II Kings 18:4). . . .

However, to speak evangelically of images, I say and declare that no one is obligated to break violently images even of God, but everything is free, and one does not sin if he does not break them with violence. . . .

Nor would I condemn those who have destroyed them, especially those who destroy divine and idolatrous images. But images for memorial and witness, such as crucifixes and images of saints, are to be tolerated. This is shown above to be the case even in the Mosaic law. And they are not only to be tolerated, but for the sake of the memorial and the witness they are praiseworthy and honorable, as the witness stones of Joshua (Josh. 24:26) and of Samuel (I Sam. 7:12).

67

Albrecht Dürer (1471–1528)
From the draft manuscript for
The Book on Human Proportions

Dürer made two trips to Italy and was exposed to the new art theories being discussed there, which impressed him greatly. He did not accept them uncritically, however. His rethinking of Italian ideas often appears only in preliminary form, in drafts such as this one, written in 1512–13.

How beauty is to be judged is a matter of deliberation. . . . In some things we consider that as beautiful which elsewhere would lack beauty. "Good" and "better" in respect of beauty are not easy to discern, for it would be quite possible to make two different figures, neither of them conforming to the other, one stouter and the other thinner, and yet we scarce might be able to judge which of the two may excel in beauty. What beauty is I know not, though it adheres to many things. When we wish to bring it into our work we find it very hard. We must gather it together from far and wide, and especially in the case of the human figure. . . . One may often search through two or three hundred men without finding amongst them more than one or two points of beauty which can be made use of. You therefore, if you desire to compose a fine figure, must take the head from some and the chest, arm, leg, hand, and foot from others. . . .

Many follow their taste alone; these are in error. Therefore let each take care that his inclination blind not his judgment. For every mother is well pleased with her own child. . . .

Men deliberate and hold numberless differing opinions about these things and they seek after them in many different ways, although the ugly is more easily attained than the beautiful. Being then, as we are, in such a state of error, I know not how to set down firmly and with finality what measure approaches absolute beauty. . . .

It seems to me impossible for a man to say that he can point out the best proportions for the human figure; for the lie is in our perception, and darkness abides so heavily within us that even our gropings fail. . . .

However, because we cannot altogether attain perfection, shall we therefore wholly cease from our learning? This bestial thought we do not accept. For evil and good lie before men, wherefore it behooves a rational man to choose the better.

Artemisia Gentileschi (1593–c. 1653)
From a letter to Don Antonio Ruffo

Being a woman in what was considered until very recently a man's field was not easy, as this letter of November 13, 1649, only begins to suggest. Ruffo was one of Artemisia's patrons.

I have received a letter of October 26th, which I deeply appreciated, particularly noting how my master always concerns himself with favoring me, contrary to my merit. In it, you tell me about that gentleman who wishes to have some paintings by me, that he would like a Galatea and a Judgment of Paris, and that the Galatea should be different from the one that Your Most Illustrious Lordship owns. There was no need for you to urge me to do this, since by the grace of God and the Most Holy Virgin, they [clients] come to a woman with this kind of talent, that is, to vary the subjects in my painting; never has anyone found in my pictures any repetition of invention, not even of one hand.

As for the fact that this gentleman wishes to know the price before the work is done, . . . I do it most unwillingly. . . . I never quote a price for my works until they are done. However, since Your Most Illustrious Lordship wants me to do this, I will do what you command. Tell this gentleman that I want five hundred ducats for both; he can show them to the whole world and, should he find anyone who does not think the paintings are worth two hundred *scudi* more, I won't ask him to pay me the agreed price. I assure Your Most Illustrious Lordship that these are paintings with nude figures requiring very expensive female models, which is a big headache. When I find good ones they fleece me, and at other times, one must suffer [their] pettiness with the patience of Job.

As for my doing a drawing and sending it, I have made a solemn vow never to send my drawings because people have cheated me. In particular, just today I found . . . that, having done a drawing of souls in Purgatory for the Bishop of St. Gata, he, in order to spend less, commissioned another painter to do the painting using my work. If I were a man, I can't imagine it would have turned out this way. . . .

I must caution Your Most Illustrious Lordship that when I ask a price, I don't follow the custom in Naples, where they ask thirty and then give it for four. I am Roman, and therefore I shall act always in the Roman manner.

Giovanni Pietro Bellori (1613–1696)
From *Lives of the Modern Painters, Sculptors, and Architects*

Unlike Vasari's Lives, *Bellori's book is more selective and critical. He often ignores or gives minimal treatment to those artists and architects who offended his classical taste. Bellori's account was published in Rome in 1672.*

When the divine Raphael with the ultimate outlines of his art used its beauty to the summit, restoring it to the ancient majesty of all those graces and enriching the merits that once made it most glorious in the presence of the Greeks and the Romans, painting was most admired by men and seemed descended from Heaven. But since things of the earth never stay the same, and whatever gains the heights inevitably must with perpetual vicissitude fall back again, so art, which from Cimabue and Giotto had slowly advanced over the long period of two hundred and fifty years, was seen to decline rapidly and from a queen become humble and common. Thus, with the passing of that happy century, all of its beauties quickly vanished. The artists, abandoning the study of nature, corrupted art with the *maniera*, that is to say, with the fantastic idea based on practice and not on imitation. This vice, the destroyer of painting, first began to appear in masters of honored acclaim. It rooted itself in the schools that later followed. . . .

Thus, when painting was drawing to its end, . . . It pleased God that in the city of Bologna, the mistress of sciences and studies, a most noble mind was forged and through it the declining and extinguished art was reforged. He was that Annibale Carracci, of whom I now mean to write. . . .

Annibale continued in the [Farnese] gallery [fig. 729] . . . ordering various myths toward an end: the theme . . . is human love governed by Heaven. Thus the theme of love . . . displays its power, subjecting the breasts of the strong, the chaste, and the savage: the loves, that is to say, of Hercules, Diana, and of Polyphemus. . . . The amours of Jupiter, Juno, Aurora, and Galatea reveal its power in the universe. The white wool that Diana receives from the god Pan and the golden apples given to Paris by Mercury are the gifts by which Amor sways human minds, and the discords provoked by beauty. The Bacchanal is the symbol of drunkenness, the source of impure desires. And since the end of all irrational pleasures is sorrow and punishment, . . . he painted Andromeda bound to the rock to be devoured by the sea monster, symbolizing that the soul bound to emotion becomes the food of vice if Perseus—that is to say, reason and the love of the worthy—does not come to her assistance.

70
Francisco Pacheco (1564–1654)
From *The Art of Painting*

Pacheco, a painter, was the most influential Spanish writer on art in the seventeenth century. For his conception of the aim of painting he relied heavily on the ideas stated by the Council of Trent. This book, which Pacheco worked on for 40 years, was published in Seville in 1649.

When dealing with the aim of painting . . . it is necessary to . . . distinguish between the aim of the work and the aim of the worker . . . [and] between the aim of the painting and the aim of the painter. The aim of the painter . . . will be by means of his art to earn a living, achieve fame or renown, to afford pleasure or service to another or to work for his own enjoyment. . . .

But considering the aim of the painter as a Christian [his] . . . principal goal will be to achieve a state of grace through the study and practice of this profession; because the Christian, born to achieve high things, is not content to restrict his activities to lower things, attending only to human rewards and earthly comfort. . . .

It would be hard to overstate the good that holy images do: they perfect our understanding, move our will, refresh our memory of divine things. They heighten our spirits . . . and show to our eyes and hearts the heroic and magnanimous acts of patience, of justice, chastity, meekness, charity and contempt for worldly things in such a way that they instantly cause us to seek virtue and to shun vice, and thus put us on the roads that lead to blessedness. . . .

Would that our painters nowadays realized these obligations; but how many of them are capable of understanding these words of mine? Oh, what a shame it is, what a terrible shame! . . .

I say that the principal goal of Christian images will always be to persuade men to be pious and to lead them to God . . . even though other specific goals may also be involved, such as leading men to penitence, to suffering with pleasure, charity, contempt of the world, or to other virtues, which are all ways of uniting men with God, which is indeed the highest end that the painting of sacred images can aspire to.

71
From the "Inventory of the Paintings, Furniture and Other Effects Contained in the House of Rembrandt van Rijn Living in the Breestreet by the St. Anthony Water-Gate"

This list, dated July 25–26, 1656, was prepared for the liquidation sale of all Rembrandt's properties, which was forced by his numerous creditors. The list provides invaluable information on Rembrandt's diverse tastes and interests.

1. One small picture of Adrian Brouwer, representing a pastrycook. . . .
13. One Nativity by Jan Lievens. . . .
57. One perspective by Lucas van Leyden. . . .
67. One head by Raphael of Urbino. . . .
81. One copy after Anibale Carracci. . . .
85. One head of an old man by van Eyck. . . .
93. Two small landscapes by Hercules Seghers. . . .
196. One ditto [book] with copper-plate engravings by [after] Raphael of Urbino. . . .
200. The precious book of Andrea Mantegna. . . .
204. One ditto containing prints of Breughel the elder. . . .
208. One ditto containing prints by Lucas Cranach. . . .
216. One ditto, very large with almost all the work of Titian. . . .
230. One ditto full of the work of Michelangelo Buonarotti. . . .
232. One book with erotica by Raphael, Rosso, Anibale Carracci and Giulio Bonasone. . . .
234. One ditto containing Turkish buildings by Melchior Lorch, Hendrick van Aelst and others, illustrating Turkish life. . . .
245. One ditto with trial proofs [after pictures] by Rubens and Jordaens. . . .
273. Albrecht Dürer's book on proportion with woodcuts. . . .
312. Thirty-three pieces of ancient weapons and wind instruments. . . .
313. Thirty-three pieces of ancient hand weapons, arrows,

staffs, assegais and bows. . . .

317. Seventeen hands and arms, cast from life. . . .

329. One antique Laocoön. . . .

333. Three or four antique heads of women. . . .

340. One [pair of] costumes for an Indian man and woman.

72

Nicolas Poussin (c. 1593–1665)
From an undated manuscript

Poussin's ideas on art were central to the formation of the French Academy in 1648 and, because of the preeminence of that academy, therefore to the entire European academic movement of the seventeenth through the nineteenth centuries.

The magnificent manner consists of four things: subject, or topic, concept, structure and style. The first requirement, which is the basis for all the others, is that the subject or topic should be great, such as battles, heroic actions and divine matters. However, given the subject upon which the painter is engaged is great, he must first of all make every effort to avoid getting lost in minute detail, so as not to detract from the dignity of the story. He should describe the magnificent and great details with a bold brush and disregard anything that is vulgar and of little substance. Thus the painter should not only be skilled in formulating his subject matter, but wise enough to know it well and to choose something that lends itself naturally to embellishment and perfection. Those who choose vile topics take refuge in them on account of their own lack of ingenuity. Faintheartedness is therefore to be despised, as is baseness of subject matter for which any amount of artifice is useless. As for the concept, it is simply part of the spirit, which concentrates on things, like the concept realized by Homer and Phidias of Olympian Zeus who could make the Universe tremble with a nod of his head. The drawing of things should be such that it expresses the concept of the things themselves. The structure, or composition of the parts, should not be studiously researched, and not sought after or contrived with effort but should be as natural as possible. Style is a particular method of painting and drawing, carried out in an individual way, born of the singular talent at work in its application and in the use of ideas. This style, and the manner and taste emanate from nature and from the mind.

73

Charles Perrault (1628–1703)
From *Memoirs of My Life*

Charles Perrault, a poet, critic, and adviser to Colbert on arts and letters, helped his brother, Claude, get the assignment to

design the East Front of the Louvre (fig. 799).

Since the Cavaliere Bernini's design was not very well conceived, and could only be carried out to the shame of France, I made a listing of only a few of the incongruities with which it was ridden, because I thought it inappropriate to point out too many of them the first time. I sent this memorandum to Monsieur Colbert, who was then at Saint-Germain. The first time he came to Paris, after having received my list, he had me step into the garden with him, and even cut short the audience he was granting to someone else, in order to talk to me. . . .

"You did well," he told me; "continue doing so, because one cannot be too well informed on a matter of this importance. I don't understand," he added, "how this man believes he can give us a design in which so many things are misunderstood."

From that moment on, Monsieur Colbert undoubtedly saw that he had approached the wrong party, but he believed he had to follow through on his gamble. Perhaps he thought also that with good advice, he could redirect the Cavaliere to the right way of doing things, and that by showing him his mistakes, he would have him produce something excellent; but he still did not know the Cavaliere. . . .

I am persuaded that as an architect he hardly excelled at all, except with the decor and machinery of the theater. . . .

Monsieur Colbert, in contrast, wanted precision, and wanted to see where and how the King would be lodged, and how he could be most easily served. He was persuaded, and with reason, that one must manage not only to accommodate the person of the King and all other royalty, but also give convenient lodging to all the household officials. . . . He was killing himself to produce and to have others produce memoranda of everything which had to be observed in the construction of all these apartments.

The Cavaliere was extremely bored with all these lists of which he understood nothing and wished to understand nothing, imagining erroneously that it was beneath the dignity of a great architect like himself to descend to the level of these *minutiae*. He complained to Monsieur de Chantelou, even doing so in a disrespectful manner. "Monsieur Colbert," he said, "treats me like a little boy" (these are the words of Monsieur de Chantelou's diary, which was shown to me after his death); "with his useless speeches about privies and underground passages, he fills up entire meetings; he wants to be the clever one and understands nothing; he's a real boaster." . . .

If the Cavaliere was unhappy with Monsieur Colbert, Monsieur Colbert for his part was no less dissatisfied with the Cavaliere, although he revealed nothing outwardly, and on the contrary, he always spoke of Bernini with remarkable respect.

74

Paul de Fréart (1609–1694)
From his unpublished diary

Fréart, Sieur de Chantelou, was an art collector and student of artistic theory. Louis XIV appointed him to assist Bernini during his stay in Paris, and Chantelou became one of Bernini's few French friends and admirers. The following passage is taken from Chantelou's diary, dated June 6, 1665.

He [M. Colbert] went into the room where the bust stood [Bernini's unfinished portrait bust of Louis XIV]. Having looked at it for a long time, he expressed astonishment . . . at the progress of the work. . . . The Cavalier replied that there was always something to do for those who want to do well. Up until now he had almost always worked from his imagination and had looked only rarely at his drawings. He had looked principally at what was inside (pointing at his forehead) where, he said, he had his image of His Majesty (otherwise he would only have made a copy in place of an original), but this was giving him a great deal of trouble. The King, in asking him for a portrait, could not have asked him for anything more difficult. He would strive to see to it that the portrait would turn out to be the least bad of all. In this type of portrait beyond the likeness, it is necessary to render what ought to be in the face of heroes.

75
Sir Christopher Wren (1632–1723)
From *Proposals for Rebuilding the City of London After the Great Fire*

The manner of building in the city of London, practised in the former ages, was commonly with timber, a material easily procured, and at little expense. . . . This often subjected the town to great and destructive fires, sometimes to the ruin of the whole. . . . This mode continued until the two fatal years 1665 and [166]6; but then the successive calamities of plague and fire gave all people occasion seriously to reflect on the causes of the increase of both to that excessive . . . closeness of buildings, and combustible materials; and hence the wishes for the necessary amendment of both, by widening the streets, and building with stone and brick, became universal.

Some intelligent persons went farther, and thought it highly requisite the city in the restoration should rise with beauty, by the straightness and regularity of buildings, and convenience for commerce, by the well disposing of streets and public places, and the opening of wharfs. . . . In order therefore to a proper reformation, Dr. Wren (pursuant to the royal commands) immediately after the fire, took an exact survey of the whole area . . . and designed a plan or model of a new city. . . .

The observations of a late critic (allowing for some mistakes in his description of [my] scheme for rebuilding the city) are judicious and right.

"Towards the end of King James the First's reign, . . . taste in architecture made a bold step from Italy to England at once, and scarce staid a moment to visit France by the way. From the most profound ignorance in architecture, the most consummate night of knowledge, Inigo Jones started up, a prodigy of art, and vied even with his master, Palladio himself. From so glorious an outset there was not any excellency that we might not have hoped to attain; Britain had a reasonable prospect to rival Italy. . . . But in the midst of these sanguine expectations, the fatal civil war commenced. . . .

"Wren was the next genius that arose. . . .

"The fire of London furnished the most perfect occasion that can ever happen in any city, to rebuild it with pomp and regularity. This Wren foresaw, and . . . offered a scheme for that purpose, which would have made it the wonder of the world. He proposed to have laid out one large street from Aldgate to Temple Bar, in the middle of which was to have been a large square, capable of containing the new church of St. Paul [figs. 810–12], with a proper distance for the view all round it; whereby that huge building would not have been cooped up, as it is at present, in such a manner as nowhere to be seen to advantage at all; but would have had a long and ample vista at each end. . . . He further proposed to rebuild all the parish churches in such a manner as to be seen at the end of every vista of houses. . . . Lastly, he proposed to build the houses uniform, and supported on a piazza, . . . and by the waterside . . . he had planned a long and broad wharf . . . with proper warehouses for merchants between, to vary the edifices, and make it at once one of the most beautiful and most useful ranges of structure in the world. But the hurry of rebuilding, and the disputes about property, prevented this glorious scheme from taking place."

76
Marie-Louise-Elisabeth Vigée-Lebrun (1755–1842)
From the *Memoirs of Vigée-Lebrun*

Vigée-Lebrun published three volumes of memoirs (1835 and 1837) when she was in her eighties. Female portraits and the painting of flowers were considered the most appropriate subjects for women artists in the eighteenth and nineteenth centuries.

M. Le Brun asked for my hand in marriage. Nothing could have been further from my thoughts than my marrying Le

Brun. . . . I was then twenty years old; I had few worries about my future since I was already earning a substantial amount of money. In short, I had no inclination to wed at all. . . . Finally, I accepted, goaded on by the desire to escape the torment of living with my stepfather. . . . So little inclined was I to sacrifice my freedom, that even as I approached the church on my wedding day, I was still asking myself, "Shall I say yes or no?" Alas, I said yes and merely exchanged my old problems for new ones. . . . His overwhelming passion for extravagant women, combined with a love of gambling, decimated both his fortune and my own, of which he made very free use. So, by the time I left France in 1789 I had less than twenty francs to my name, in spite of the fact that I had earned more than a million from my work: he had squandered the lot! . . .

When I finally announced my marriage officially . . . I was not as downcast as I might have been, for I still had my beloved painting. I was overwhelmed with commissions from every quarter and although Le Brun took it upon himself to appropriate my earnings, this did not prevent him from insisting that I take pupils in order to increase our income even further. I consented to this demand without really taking time to consider the consequences and soon the house was full of young ladies learning how to paint "eyes, noses and faces." I was constantly correcting their efforts and was thus distracted from my own work, which I found very irritating indeed. . . .

I believe the strain of having to leave my precious brushes for several hours each day only increased my eagerness to paint. I refused to leave my easel until nightfall and the number of portraits I painted at this period is quite astonishing. As I had a horror of the current fashion, I did my best to make my models a little more picturesque. I was delighted when, having gained their trust, they allowed me to dress them after my fancy. No-one wore shawls then, but I liked to drape my models with large scarves, interlacing them around the body and through the arms, which was an attempt to imitate the beautiful style of draperies seen in the paintings of Raphael and Dominichino. . . . Above all I detested the powdering of hair and succeeded in persuading the beautiful Duchesse de Grammont-Caderousse not to wear any when she sat for me. Her hair was as black as ebony and I parted it on the forehead, arranging it in irregular curls. After the sitting, which ended around dinner time, the Duchess did not alter her hair at all and left directly for the theatre; being such a pretty woman, she was quite influential and her hair style gradually insinu-ated itself into fashionable society and eventually became universal. . . .

Happy as I was at the idea of becoming a mother, after nine months of pregnancy, I was not in the least prepared for the birth of my baby. The day my daughter was born, I was still in the studio, trying to work on my *Venus Binding the Wings of Cupid* in the intervals between labour pains.

77
Sir Joshua Reynolds (1723–1792) From "A Discourse, Delivered at the Opening of the Royal Academy, January 2, 1769"

An Academy, in which the Polite Arts may be regularly cultivated, is at last opened among us by Royal Munificence. This must appear an event in the highest degree interesting, not only to the Artists, but to the whole nation.

It is indeed difficult to give any other reason, why an empire like that of Britain, should so long have wanted an ornament so suitable to its greatness, than that slow progression of things, which naturally makes elegance and refinement the last effect of opulence and power. . . .

The principal advantage of an Academy is, that . . . it will be a repository for the great examples of the Art. These are the materials on which Genius is to work, and without which the strongest intellect may be fruitlessly or deviously employed. By studying these authentick models, that idea of excellence which is the result of the accumulated experience of past ages may be at once acquired, and the tardy and obstructed progress of our predecessors, may teach us a shorter and easier way. The Student receives, at one glance, the principles which many Artists have spent their whole lives in ascertaining. . . . How many men of great natural abilities have been lost to this nation, for want of these advantages? . . .

Raffaelle, it is true, had not the advantage of studying in an Academy; but all *Rome*, and the works of Michael Angelo in particular, were to him an Academy. . . .

One advantage, I will venture to affirm, we shall have in our Academy, which no other nation can boast. We shall have nothing to unlearn. . . .

But as these Institutions have so often failed in other nations . . . I must take leave to offer a few hints, by which those errors may be rectified. . . .

I would chiefly recommend, that an implicit obedience to the *Rules of Art,* as established by the practice of the great Masters, should be exacted from the *young* Students. That those models, which have passed through the appro-bation of ages, should be considered by them as perfect and infallible Guides; as subjects for their imitation, not their criticism.

I am confident, that this is the only efficacious method of making a progress in the Arts; and that he who sets out with doubting, will find life finished before he becomes master of the rudiments. For it may be laid down as a maxim, that he who begins by presuming on his own sense, has ended his studies as soon as he has commenced them. Every opportunity, therefore, should be taken to discountenance that false and vulgar opinion, that rules are the fetters of Genius.

	1350–1375	1375–1400	1400–1425
HISTORY AND POLITICS	**1356** Edward, the "Black Prince," son of Edward III of England, defeats the French at Poitiers and takes prisoner Jean le Bon, king of France **c. 1358** Foundation of the powerful Hanseatic League of Baltic mercantile cities Peasant uprisings: 1358, Jacquerie revolt in France; 1381, Wat Tyler's rebellion in England, London sacked **1368** In China, the Buddhist monk Chu Yüan-chang leads a peasants' revolt, driving the Mongols out of Beijing and founding the Ming dynasty, taking the title Hungwu Timur (Tamerlane, c. 1369–1405), Mongol leader with capital at Samarkand, establishes the Timurid empire, conquering much of the Mideast and Persia and invading India		**1410** Teutonic Knights defeated by Poles and Lithuanians at battle of Tennenberg, ending their sole jurisdiction over Prussia Philip the Good of Burgundy (r. 1419–67) inherits the Northern Provinces; including Holland, Flanders, and Luxembourg, it is one of the largest and richest holdings in Europe and a threat to France

Sources of Renaissance Neo-Platonism Neo-Platonic ideas of harmony, balance, proportion, and spirituality appeared in Western thought throughout the Middle Ages, but the source texts of Plato, Plotinus, and their followers were little known. In 1394 the Greek scholar Manuel Chrysoloras visited Italy from Constantinople and remained to teach Greek in Florence. In 1439 other Greek scholars from the Byzantine Empire attended the ecclesiastical Council of Florence, which attempted to unite the Eastern and Western churches, and they further exposed local writers and artists to the intellectual heritage of classical Greece, especially its idealism. The work of the Early Renaissance architects

	1350–1375	1375–1400	1400–1425
RELIGION		**1378** Papal court returns to Rome from Avignon. Great Papal Schism begins, in which several candidates compete for the papacy **c. 1382** John Wycliffe, English theologian and religious reformer, initiates first complete translation of the Bible into English	**1405–15** Jan Hus, influenced by Wycliffe, leads the Hussite movement to reform the church in Bohemia and denounces sale of indulgences; 1415, burned at the stake as a heretic at the Council of Constance **1417** Pope Martin V ends Great Schism

(left) BOHEMIAN MASTER
Death of the Virgin, Prague, 1350–60
(right) Florence Cathedral, begun by ARNOLFO DI CAMBIO, 1296; dome by FILIPPO BRUNELLESCHI, 1420–36

CLAUS SLUTER
The Moses Well, Dijon, 1395–1406

(left) DONATELLO, *St. Mark,* 1411–13

(right) GENTILE DA FABRIANO
The Adoration of the Magi, Italy, 1423

	1350–1375	1375–1400	1400–1425
MUSIC, LITERATURE, AND PHILOSOPHY	**1361** Foundation of the University of Pavia, in northern Italy Christine de Pisan (c. 1363–c. 1430), French writer of poems on courtly love, best known for her spirited defense of women in *The Book of the City of Ladies,* c. 1404–5 Leonardo Bruni (1370–1444), prominent humanist and classical scholar in Florence, author of *Praise of the City of Florence,* 1402–3	**1395–98** Manuel Chrysoloras, a Byzantine Greek scholar, teaches Greek in Florence; translates Plato's *Republic* into Latin; author of first Greek grammar used in Western Europe	Leone Battista Alberti (1404–72) writes influential treatises *On Painting,* 1435, *On Architecture,* 1452, and *On Sculpture,* 1464
SCIENCE, TECHNOLOGY, AND EXPLORATION	**1355** Death of Jacopo Dondi (b. 1298), creator of an early clock run by weights	**1375** Charles V of France commissions the *Carta catalana,* an accurate map of Europe, North Africa, and Western Asia Prince Henry the Navigator of Portugal (1394–1460) sponsors exploration, especially of the African coasts, an observatory, a school of navigation, and improvements in ship design, the compass, and cartography **1398** Cennino Cennini writes the *Libro dell' arte,* a technical manual for painters	**1406** King Edward IV of England founds the Society of Merchant Adventurers to encourage trade and commerce **1407** Establishment of Bank of St. George, first public bank, in Genoa **1410** Ptolemy's *Geography* translated into Latin **c. 1413** Pictorial perspective invented in Italy, by Filippo Brunelleschi

1425–1450	1450–1475	1475–1500
1438 Hapsburg rule of the Holy Roman Empire (later Germany and Austria) begins (until 1806) **By 1450** Medici family, founded by Cosimo the Elder (1389–1464), gains power in Florence; 1469–92, Lorenzo the Magnificent virtually rules the city	**1453** Constantinople falls to the Turkish army of Mohammed II; Ottoman Empire founded Matthias the Just (r. 1458–90) establishes Hungary as dominant power in central Europe **1469** Marriage of Ferdinand of Aragon and Isabella of Castile unites Spain	**1477** French army defeats Charles the Bold of Burgundy at Nancy. Northern Provinces pass to Maximilian, Hapsburg emperor; 1488, Flemish cities revolt against his rule **1478** Pazzi Conspiracy in Florence; Giuliano de' Medici assassinated during Easter mass, and Pazzi family decimated in revenge; 1480, turmoil among Tuscan city-states quelled by Lorenzo's leadership **1492** Defeat of Moslem Grenada by the Spanish Christian powers; 1502, expulsion of Jews and Moors **1493–94** Territories of South America divided between Spain and Portugal by the pope **1494** Medici rulers expelled for the first time from Florence; a republic declared **1495–96** Charles VIII of France invades Italian peninsula and claims the kingdom of Naples; repulsed by the Holy League (the Papacy, Spain, and Holy Roman Empire)

Leone Battista Alberti (1404–72) and Filarete (c. 1400– c. 1469) reflects this influence to a certain degree.

After the fall of Constantinople to the Turks in 1453, many scholars fled permanently to the West. Their ideas, and the precious manuscripts they brought, stimulated interest in humanist studies. Neo-Platonism was particularly influential at the erudite Florentine court of Lorenzo de' Medici, known as the Platonic Academy. The philosopher Marsilio Ficino (1433–99) and the artists Sandro Botticelli (1444/5–1510) and Michelangelo (1475–1564) were prominent members of this circle.

1425–1450	1450–1475	1475–1500
1431 Joan of Arc burned at the stake in Rouen, accused of heresy and witchcraft **1439** Council of Florence attempts to reunite the Eastern Orthodox church with the Western Catholics; its success is short-lived	**1464** Pope Pius II, humanist and patron of learning, dies during a failed crusade against the Turks Pope Sixtus IV (r. 1471–84) condemns the excesses of the Spanish Inquisition and tries to reunite Russian church with Rome	**1494** Rise in Florence of Fra Girolamo Savonarola (1452–98), monk and religious radical advocating moral and governmental reform; 1498, he is burned at the stake for heresy

(left) JAN VAN EYCK
Arnolfini Portrait, detail, 1434

(right) LORENZO GHIBERTI
Panel of the *"Gates of Paradise,"* c. 1435

(right) HUGO VAN DER GOES
The Portinari Altarpiece, center panel, c. 1476

(right) SANDRO BOTTICELLI
The Birth of Venus, c. 1480

1425–1450	1450–1475	1475–1500
François Villon (born c. 1431), French poet Marsilio Ficino (1433–99), humanist and philosopher, undertakes a translation of Plato, under the patronage of the Medici in Florence Josquin Des Prés (c. 1440–1521), Flemish composer of madrigals Pope Nicholas V (r. 1447–55) founds Vatican Library	Desiderius Erasmus of Rotterdam (c. 1466–1536), scholar and satirical author (*Praise of Folly,* 1509), epitomizes the humanist intellectual concerns of the Northern Reformation	**1481** A commentary on Dante's *Divine Comedy* is published, with illustrations by Botticelli and a preface by Marsilio Ficino **1494** Sebastian Brant (1458?–1521), German humanist, writes *The Ship of Fools,* a satirical poem
c. 1425 Discovery and proliferation in Northern Europe of the technique of painting with oil **c. 1440** Earliest record of a suction pump	**c. 1450** Movable type for printing invented in Germany (by Johann Gutenberg?); books become more readily available; literacy gradually spreads Leonardo da Vinci (1452–1519) performs dissections of human cadavers; his experiments in hydraulics, mechanics, engineering, flight, and optics, recorded in coded manuscripts, address a dazzling range of intellectual and scientific problems	**1487–88** Bartholomew Diaz of Portugal rounds Cape of Good Hope and circumnavigates African continent **1490** First Latin edition of Galen's works on medicine published in Venice **1492** Columbus lands in the Bahamas **1497–1501** Voyages of Vasco da Gama and Pedro Cabral establish Portuguese dominance of trade with India, utilizing both Atlantic and Pacific sea passages

	1500–1525	**1525–1550**	**1550–1575**
HISTORY AND POLITICS	Francis I of France (r. 1515–47), a popular king. His rich and cultured court introduces Italian ideas and art to the North **1519–21** The Spaniard Hernán Cortés defeats Aztecs in Mexico; 1532, Francisco Pizarro conquers Peru Charles V of Spain elected Holy Roman Emperor (r. 1519–56); founder of Hapsburg dynasty Suleiman I, Turkish sultan (r. 1520–66), raids the European continent, threatening Hungary, Austria, and Italy; begins a gradual Turkish conquest of the eastern Mediterranean islands over the next century **1524–25** Peasants' War in Germany, inspired by Martin Luther	**1527** Henry VIII of England, seeking a divorce from his first wife, Catherine of Aragon, breaks with the Catholic church. 1534, his Act of Supremacy establishes the Church of England and confiscates Catholic church property **1527** Charles V of Spain sacks Rome, demoralizing the Italian states and signaling the end of Roman dominance **1533–84** Ivan the Terrible rules in Russia	Wars of Lutheran against Catholic princes in Germany; 1555, Peace of Augsburg lets each sovereign decide the religion of his subjects **1556** Philip II reigns in Spain; territories include lands in the Americas, Italy, France, and The Netherlands as well as the Iberian Peninsula Elizabeth I (r. 1558–1603) succeeds to the English throne, fostering a period of prosperity, international trade, and exploration **1562–98** Henry IV's persecution of Protestants in France leads to religious wars **1568–1648** Netherlands revolt against Spain. 1579, Union of Utrecht affirms the unification of the Northern Netherlands; 1581, they declare independence from Spain **1571** Battle of Lepanto, off the Greek coast. Spanish and Venetian fleets defeat the Turks, beginning the decline of Turkish naval power
RELIGION	**1517** Martin Luther (1483–1546) posts "95 Theses," against Catholic practice of selling indulgences, on door of Wittenberg church, signaling the beginning of the Protestant Reformation	**1534** Ignatius of Loyola (1491–1556) founds Society of Jesus (Jesuits) **1541** John Calvin (1509–64) brings Reformation to the Swiss city of Geneva. His writings establish the rigorous Calvinist branch of Protestantism **1545** Pope Paul III (r. 1534–49), in response to the threat of Protestantism, calls the Council of Trent, first major conference on church reform. Its tenets provide the basis for the Catholic Counter Reformation, including a number of rules for artists depicting religious subjects. The council meets periodically until 1563	**1560** John Knox, Scottish minister, founds Presbyterian branch of Protestant church
	 (left) MICHELANGELO *David*, 1501–4 (right) HIERONYMUS BOSCH *The Garden of Delights*, center panel, c. 1510–15	 PONTORMO *Deposition*, c. 1526–28	 TITIAN *Christ Crowned with Thorns*, c. 1570
MUSIC, LITERATURE, AND PHILOSOPHY	Sir Thomas Wyatt (1503–42), English poet and courtier under Henry VIII, translates Petrarch's sonnets and creates the English sonnet form **1516** Ludovico Ariosto (1474–1533), Italian poet and diplomat, publishes *Orlando Furioso*, an epic poem	**1528** Baldassare Castiglione (1478–1529) writes *The Book of the Courtier* **1532** Niccolò Machiavelli (1469–1527) writes *The Prince*, examining Renaissance political practice and thought **1534** François Rabelais (1483–1553) authors the satires *Gargantua and Pantagruel* **1547** Henry Howard translates Vergil's *Aeneid* into English blank verse	**1550** Giorgio Vasari (1511–74), Italian painter, publishes *The Lives of the Artists* Felix Lope de Vega (1562–1635), Spanish poet and playwright William Shakespeare (1564–1616), English dramatist and poet Ben Jonson (1572–1637); John Donne (1573–1631), English master of metaphysical poetry and prose
SCIENCE, TECHNOLOGY, AND EXPLORATION	**1501** Amerigo Vespucci, a Florentine navigator in the service of Portugal, explores coast of Brazil **1511** First road map of Europe **1513** The Spaniard Vasco Nuñez de Balboa crosses Panama and finds the Pacific Ocean **1516** Portuguese sailors reach China; 1543, Japan **1519–22** Ferdinand Magellan of Portugal circumnavigates the globe	**1543** Nicolaus Copernicus (1473–1543), Polish astronomer, publishes theory of the solar system in which the planets revolve around the sun; beginning of modern astronomy **1543** Andreas Vesalius (1514–64), court physician to Emperor Charles V, publishes first scientific study of human anatomy based on dissections	**1556** Georgius Agricola (1494–1555) publishes *De re metallica*, on metallurgy **1569** Gerhard Mercator (1512–94) designs correct projection of the earth onto a flat map, for accurate navigation charts **c. 1572** Tycho Brahe (1546–1601), Danish astronomer, produces a catalogue of stars; Johannes Kepler (1571–1630), German astronomer, discovers the elliptical orbits of the planets

1575–1600	1600–1625	1625–1650
1588 Spanish Armada, aiming to attack England, defeated by English navy	**1607** Colony of Jamestown, Virginia, first permanent settlement in North America, founded by English; 1620, Pilgrims arrive at Plymouth, in New England **1613** Romanov dynasty comes to power in Russia (deposed 1917) **1618–48** Thirty Years' War; much of Protestant Europe erupts in political and religious struggles against Catholic regimes	**1625** Charles I rules England. Disputes with Parliament and autocratic measures lead, in 1642, to Civil War. 1649, Charles beheaded, ending the war and founding the Commonwealth (1649–53), under Oliver Cromwell **1630–42** Large-scale emigration of English settlers to North American colonies: 16,000 arrive in Massachusetts **1639** Japanese enforce policy of isolation from all Europeans, except a token Dutch trading post **1648** Treaty of Westphalia ends Thirty Years' War; Spain acknowledges the sovereignty of the Northern Netherlands

The Protestant Reformation The history of European Christianity before the Renaissance was punctuated by periodic movements to reform corrupt practices within the Catholic church. In the Middle Ages these were usually local and short-lived. But the fifteenth century saw the spread of literacy and education, growing economic power, a much-envied rise in the wealth of the papacy, and persistent quarrels between the pope and secular princes; these forces made criticism of the Church especially fierce. In 1517, the German cleric Martin Luther proclaimed his "95 Theses" condemning abuses of the Church and sparked a popular revolt, soon joined by rulers who saw the pope as a rival and who coveted the vast territories held by the papacy. The movement grew dramatically, especially in Northern Europe. What had begun as a protest with mixed political, pious, and social aims developed into a detailed reformulation of the Christian religion itself; this restructuring is generally called Protestantism.

Protestantism focused on the relationship of the individual believer to God and was characterized by an austerity of taste that signified a rejection of the corrupt and worldly opulence of Rome. Use of images in churches was strictly prohibited. Renaissance taste for the personal, the contemporary, and the material was to some degree a product of Protestant culture, which patronized secular arts. For this new market, artists began to create small images for personal use. A new vocabulary of subject matter developed: landscape, still life, and scenes of daily life. In the North such paintings were sold directly to the public in a free-market system, rather than solely by patronage or commission.

Publications of Cornelius Jansenius (*Augustinus*, 1640) lead to conflict with Jesuits. Preoccupied with internal strife, the papacy loses its dominant position in European politics

(left) ARTEMISIA GENTILESCHI, *Judith and Maidservant with the Head of Holofernes,* c. 1625

(right) JACQUES CALLOT, detail of *Hangman's Tree,* from *Great Miseries of War,* 1633

1588 St. Theresa of Avila writes *Interior Castle,* a visionary text; Michel de Montaigne, French thinker, writes *Essays* **1590** Edmund Spenser, English poet, publishes *The Faerie Queene*	**1604** Carel van Mander publishes biographical history of Dutch and Flemish painting **1605** Miguel de Cervantes Saavedra (1547–1616) writes *Don Quixote* **1607** Claudio Monteverdi's *Orpheus* is performed in Mantua, one of the first operas Baruch Spinoza (1632–77), Dutch philosopher	**1636** Pierre Corneille (1606–84), French dramatist, writes *Le Cid* **1637** René Descartes (1596–1650), French philosopher and scientist, writes *Discourse on Method* Molière (1622–73) and Jean Racine (1639–99), French playwrights **1649** Francisco Pacheco (1564–1654), Spanish historian, publishes *The Art of Painting*
c. 1575 Potatoes, maize, tobacco, cocoa, coffee imported from the Americas to Europe **1578** Li Shih-chen, Chinese physician, publishes an illustrated compendium of medicines **1582** Pope Gregory XIII reforms the calendar, aligning it more accurately with astronomy; in order to do so, he decrees that Thursday, October 4, be followed by Friday, October 15	**c. 1600** Invention of the telescope and microscope, based on new lens-grinding techniques developed in Holland **1610** Galileo Galilei (1564–1642), in Italy, first uses the telescope to view the stars and planets; his conclusions support the Copernican system and are banned by the Catholic church in 1633	**1628** William Harvey, English physician (1575–1657), describes the circulation of blood **1636** Founding of Harvard College, Boston **1642** Blaise Pascal (1623–62) invents first adding machine Antonio Stradivari (1644–1737), Italian designer of fine stringed instruments **1648** Royal Academy of Painting and Sculpture founded in Paris

	1650–1675	1675–1700	1700–1725
HISTORY AND POLITICS	**1652–54** Naval and mercantile competition between English and Dutch leads to war **1659** Louis XIV of France marries Maria Teresa, daughter of Philip IV of Spain; 1661, establishes autocratic regime (r. 1661–1715) with his influential adviser Jean-Baptiste Colbert **1660** Parliament proclaims Charles II king, restoring English monarchy **1666** Great Fire in London destroys over 450 acres of the city **1672–78** France and England wage war against Netherlands. William III of Orange beats back invasion of French forces	**1679** English Parliament passes Habeas Corpus Act, which sets foundation for fair judicial procedure and prisoners' rights **1685** Louis XIV revokes Edict of Nantes (1598), which had granted Protestants some religious freedom. Mass emigration of educated Protestants ensues, a blow to French industry and commerce. In England, James II, a Catholic, succeeds to the throne and attempts to restore Catholicism **1688** The so-called Glorious Revolution in England: James II flees; Parliament passes Declaration of Rights, limiting the power of the monarchy **1689** Protestants William III of Orange and Mary rule England; new laws protect freedom of religion, establish annual parliaments, and guarantee individual liberty Peter the Great (r. 1689–1725) rules Russia, with a program of westernization **1692** Witchcraft trials in Salem, Massachusetts	**1701** Frederick III crowns himself king of Prussia. Prussia gains international power through military strength **1702–13** War of Spanish Succession: extinction of the Hapsburg line in Spain leads to war among major European powers. At conclusion, Philip of Anjou, grandson of Louis XIV, takes the Spanish throne as Philip V; beginning of Bourbon rule in Spain **1704** Defeat of French at Blenheim by English and allies, led by John Churchill, Duke of Marlborough **1707** Union of England and Scotland as the United Kingdom of Great Britain Louis XV (r. 1715–74), king of France, consolidates absolute power of the monarchy
RELIGION	**c. 1667** Russian church changes liturgy and ritual to conform to Greek practice. Secession from the church of the conservative "Old Believers" **1668** Society of Friends (Quakers) officially established in England	**1682** Louis XIV's Four Articles are adopted in France, placing secular power over religious authority. Vehemently opposed by Pope Innocent XI (r. 1676–89)	**1721** Peter the Great reforms Russian church government John Wesley (1703–91), with his brother, Charles, founds the Methodist branch of Protestantism in England

(*left*) DIEGO VELÁZQUEZ, *The Maids of Honor*, 1656

(*right*) FRANS HALS, *The Women Regents of the Old Men's Home at Haarlem*, 1664

(*left*) BARTOLOMÉ ESTEBAN MURILLO *Virgin and Child*, c. 1675–80

(*right*) SIR CHRISTOPHER WREN Facade of St. Paul's Cathedral, London, 1675–1710

RACHEL RUYSCH *Flower Still Life*, after 1700

MUSIC, LITERATURE, AND PHILOSOPHY	**1667** John Milton (1608–74), English poet, writes *Paradise Lost* Joseph Addison (1672–1719), English essayist, editor with the writer and statesman Sir Richard Steele (1672–1729) of the *Spectator*, a literary and satirical periodical **1672** Giovanni Pietro Bellori (1613–96), Italian commentator on Baroque art, publishes *Lives of the Modern Painters*	John Locke (1632–1704), founder of English school of empirical philosophy Baroque composers: Alessandro Scarlatti (1659–1725) and Antonio Vivaldi (1678–1741), Italian; Johann Sebastian Bach (1685–1750), George Frideric Handel (1685–1759), German François-Marie Voltaire (1694–1778), French critical writer	**1711** Alexander Pope (1688–1744), English poet, writes *The Rape of the Lock* David Hume (1711–76), Scottish philosopher Jean-Jacques Rousseau (1712–78), French philosopher and novelist Denis Diderot (1713–84), editor of first *Encyclopedia*, in France Johann Joachim Winckelmann (1717–68), German art theorist and antiquarian
SCIENCE, TECHNOLOGY, AND EXPLORATION	**1662** Royal Society of London founded by Charles II, a forum for scientific activity for two centuries; 1662, Boyle's Law describes the properties of gas pressure **1663** Charles Lebrun, at Royal Academy in Paris, institutes strict guidelines for art **1665** In England Robert Hooke publishes his discovery of cells and microorganisms **1673** Pendulum clock invented by the Dutchman Christiaan Huygens	**1687** Isaac Newton (1642–1727) publishes theory of the laws of motion, including the principle of gravity, in England; 1704, his *Optics* investigates the nature and behavior of light **1698** Steam engine invented in England by Thomas Savery	**1705** Edmund Halley (1656–1742), in England, discovers similarities in the paths of comets Benjamin Franklin (1706–1790), American statesman and inventor, invents bifocal lens, lightning rod, and Franklin stove, and publishes observations on electricity in Philadelphia **1717** Temperature gradation system proposed by Gabriel Fahrenheit, in Holland

1725–1750	1750–1775	1775–1800
	1756–66 Seven Years' War: England and Prussia fight Austria and France on land and sea and throughout the colonies; called the French and Indian Wars in North America; 1769, French defeated at Quebec Catherine the Great (r. 1762–96) increases the power, territory, and influence of Russia	**1775–83** American Revolution: 1776, Declaration of Independence; 1787–88, United States Constitution ratified
1789 French Revolution begins. Declaration of a National Assembly dedicated to producing a constitution. Mobs storm Bastille prison and riot in Paris; 1792, French monarchy is abolished; 1793, Louis XVI is beheaded. European states declare war against the French Republic, whose radical ideas are feared to encourage unrest
1793–95 Reign of Terror in France, dominated by Maximilien Robespierre, with as many as 350 executions per month
1793–95 Partition of Poland by Russia, Prussia, and Austria completely erases the country
1796–97 Napoleon Bonaparte's Italian campaign conquers most of Italy; after his Egyptian campaign (1798–99), his reputation as soldier and diplomat is established; 1799, he controls France

The Enlightenment The European eighteenth century was a time of colonial expansion and development of new methods in industry, farming, financial markets, and government. Constitutions and parliamentary systems weakened monarchs and the church and offered the vote to broader populations. English parliamentary monarchy, American representative democracy, and the various forms of the French government after the Revolution were all attempts to remake the political system more inclusively, while radical discoveries in the sciences and technology encouraged a new definition of society itself. Thinkers such as Rousseau, Hume, Voltaire, Diderot, Kant, and Swift sought to use reason and scientific method in their inquiries, and took experience as the measure of knowledge. Coupled with this skeptical, modernist attitude was a taste for sentimentality and idealism, expressed as a commitment to the perfectibility of humanity. This led, in public life, to reforms in education, medicine, taxation, and religious tolerance, as well as movements to abolish slavery. The Neoclassical and Romantic movements in art are both a reflection of and reaction to this impulse.

1793 French government, under Robespierre, outlaws the worship of God; Cult of Reason established
1798 Napoleon abolishes papal rule and establishes a French-dominated Roman Republic in the Papal States

CANALETTO
The Bucintoro at the Molo, c. 1732

(left) FRANÇOIS BOUCHER, *The Toilet of Venus,* 1751

(right) GIOVANNI BATTISTA TIEPOLO
The Marriage of Frederick Barbarossa, 1752

 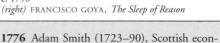

(left) MARIE-LOUISE-ELISABETH VIGÉE-LEBRUN
The Duchesse de Polignac, 1783
(center) JOHN HENRY FUSELI, *The Nightmare,* c. 1790
(right) FRANCISCO GOYA, *The Sleep of Reason*

1725–1750	1750–1775	1775–1800
1726 Jonathan Swift (1667–1745), Irish political satirist, writes *Gulliver's Travels*	**1755** Samuel Johnson (1709–1784) compiles a *Dictionary of the English Language*
1774 Johann von Goethe (1749–1832) publishes *The Sorrows of Young Werther* in Germany, extolling naturalism and sentimentality; it inspires numerous suicides
Wolfgang Amadeus Mozart (1756–91), innovative Austrian composer of symphonies, operas, and church music	**1776** Adam Smith (1723–90), Scottish economist, writes *The Wealth of Nations*
1781 Immanuel Kant (1724–1804), German critical philosopher, writes the *Critique of Pure Reason*
1792 Mary Wollstonecraft (1759–1836) writes *Vindication of the Rights of Women,* first English feminist treatise
1744 Geographical survey of France begun, the first such topographical survey
1745 Discovery of Pompeii and Herculaneum
1749 George Leclerc (1707–88) writes a treatise on natural history in England	**1753** Carl Linnaeus, Swedish botanist (1707–78), writes the *Species Plantarum,* the definitive modern classification system for plants
1764 Invention of the spinning jenny and cotton gin (1793) hastens mechanization of textile production
1768–79 Captain James Cook (1728–79) explores the islands of the Pacific
1774 Joseph Priestly (1733–1804), English chemist, isolates oxygen	**1783** First flight in a hot-air balloon, France
1789 Antoine Lavoisier (1743–94) publishes his systematic study of chemistry in France
1790–1801 Revolutionary government of France institutes metric system
1798 Edward Jenner (1749–1823) demonstrates first vaccination against smallpox
1798 Alois Senefelder (1771–1834), Hungarian inventor, develops lithography

PART FOUR

THE MODERN WORLD

Art history, according to the classical model of Johann Winckelmann, unfolds in an orderly progression in which one phase follows another as inevitably as night follows day. In addition, the concept of period style implies that the arts march in lockstep, sharing the same characteristics and developing according to the same inner necessity. The thoughtful reader will already suspect, however, that any attempt to synthesize the history of art and place it into a broader context must inevitably mask a welter of facts that do not conform to such a systematic model and may, indeed, call it into question. So far as the art of the distant past is concerned, we may indeed have little choice but to see it in larger terms, since so many facts have been erased that we cannot possibly hope to reconstruct a full and accurate historical record. Hence it is arguably the case that any reading is an artificial construct inherently open to question. As we approach the art of our times, these become more than theoretical issues. They take on a new urgency as we try, perhaps vainly, to understand modern civilization and how it came to be this way.

It is suggestive of the difficulties facing the historian that the period which began 250 years ago has not acquired a name of its own. Perhaps this does not strike us as peculiar at first. We are, after all, still in its midst. Considering how promptly the Renaissance coined a name for itself, however, we may well wonder why no key concept comparable to the "rebirth of antiquity" has yet emerged. It is tempting to call this "The Age of Revolution," for it has been characterized by rapid and violent change. It began with revolutions of two kinds: the Industrial Revolution, symbolized by the invention of the steam engine; and the political revolution, under the banner of democracy, inaugurated in America and France.

Both of these revolutions are still going on. Industrialization and democracy are sought over much of the world. Western science and Western political thought (and, in their wake, all the other products of modern civilization: food, dress, art, music, literature) will eventually belong to all peoples, although they have been challenged by other ideologies that command allegiance—nationalism, religion, even tribalism. These two movements are so closely linked today that we tend to think of them as different aspects of one process, with effects more far-reaching than any basic shift since the Neolithic Revolution 10,000 years ago. Still, the twin revolutions are not the same. Indeed, we cannot discern a common impulse behind these developments, despite attempts to relate them to the rise of capitalism. The more we try to explain their relationship and trace their historic roots, the more paradoxical they seem. Both are founded on the idea of progress. But whereas progress in science and technology during the past two centuries has been more or less continuous and measurable, we can hardly make this claim for our pursuit of happiness, however we choose to define it. Here, then, is a fundamental conflict that continues to this very day.

If we nevertheless accept "The Age of Revolution" as a convenient name for the era as a whole, we must still make a distinction for the century to which we belong. For lack of a better word, we shall call it *modernity*. It is a problematic term, modernity. What is it? When did it begin? These questions are not unlike those posed by the Renaissance, and so perhaps is the answer. No matter how many different opinions there may be about the nature of the beast—and scholars remain deeply divided over the issues—the modern era clearly began when people acquired "modern consciousness." Around 1900 men and women in the Western world became aware that the character of the new age in which they were living was defined by the machine, which brought with it a different sense of time and space, as well as the promise of a new kind of humanity and society.

It is difficult for us to appreciate from our vantage point just how radical the technological revolution seemed to people of the time, for it has since become commonplace and been outstripped by even more far-reaching changes. The advances that took place in science, mathematics, engineering, and psychology during the 1880s and 1890s laid the foundation for the Machine Age. The diesel and turbine engines, electric motor, tire, automobile, light bulb, phonograph, radio, box camera: all these were invented before 1900, and the airplane shortly thereafter. They forever transformed the quality of life—its very feel—but it was not until these changes reached a "critical mass" in the opening years of this century that the sweeping magnitude of these changes was fully realized. Of course, this was by no means the first time that people have felt modern, which simply means contemporary. Yet modern consciousness has been so fundamental to our identity that we can hardly hope to understand civilization for the past 100 years without it.

The word *modern* has its origins in the early medieval *modernus,* meaning that which is present, of our time, and, by extension, new, novel—in contrast to antiquity, which, surprisingly, lacked a comparable expression, even though modern derives ultimately from the Latin *modo* (now). As this odd and unusual fact suggests, modernity is based on the Christian view of history as a break in time (before and after Christ), instead of the concept of recurring cycles that had prevailed in Greece and Rome. It is to Petrarch that we owe the idea of history as a succession of periods, which he separated into eras of light, dark, and rebirth. For him history was linear and progressive, permitting humanity to play an active part in shaping its outcome. Petrarch's veneration for antiquity was indebted partly to Bernard of Chartres, who in the early twelfth century argued that we are puny dwarfs who see farther than our predecessors because we are standing on the shoulders of giants. However, such a position did not allow the authority of the past, no matter how great, to go unchallenged. The end of the twelfth century witnessed the first dispute between disciples of ancient versus modern poetry; ever since, literature and criticism have taken the lead in framing the central issues of modernity. The controversy was revived in late-seventeenth-century France as the Quarrel of Ancients and Moderns (satirized by the English writer Jonathan Swift in *The Battle of the Books*). Throughout the debate, modern generally held negative connotations, for it was taken as the opposite of classic, whose original antonym in Latin was "vulgar." Yet not even the most conservative voices recommended the slavish imitation of antiquity. Moreover, the moderns saw themselves as adhering to eternal values even more faithfully than had the ancients themselves! As Christians, they held the advantage over the ancients on another count as well, since religious truth was deemed superior to scientific truth or aesthetic beauty, the only area where the pagans had excelled.

The nineteenth century gave birth to two conflicting views of modernity that have continued to compete with each other to this day: one based on scientific and material progress, which arose out of the Enlightenment, with its belief in reason and freedom, and is identified with the middle class; and a radical alternative regarding the bourgeoisie as the enemy of culture—in a word, philistines. Although its roots lie in eighteenth-century German thought, the second of these is a peculiarly Romantic notion first formulated by the French writer Stendhal (Marie-Henri Beyle). Not only did he relate modernity specifically to Romanticism as a reaction against classicism, he regarded the Romantic as a warrior in the service of modernity. But why should modernity need such a warrior in the first place? Because the times were slow to accept the new, which could therefore only be validated by the future, not the present. We will recognize in Stendhal's warrior the forerunner of the avant-garde.

It was, nevertheless, Charles Baudelaire who gave modernity its current meaning. "Modernity," he wrote, "is the transitory, the fugitive, the contingent, the half of art, of which the other half is the eternal and the immutable. . . ." And "since all centuries and all peoples have had their own form of beauty, so inevitably we have ours. The particular element in each manifestation comes from the emotions; and just as we have our own particular emotions, so we have our own beauty." Perceptively, he located the source of that beauty in urban existence: "The life of our city is rich in poetic and marvellous subjects. We are enveloped and steeped as though in an atmosphere of the marvellous; but we do not notice it." In this he relied partly on his fellow critic Théophile Gautier, who said that modern beauty is based on accepting modern civilization as it is. To do so, however, artists must go against tradition and rely on their own imaginations, which requires taking enormous risks.

Baudelaire had the distinction of being the first to use mechanical metaphors for beauty in place of the organic ones favored by the Romantics. He further denounced the material progress of modern civilization, thereby helping to create the schism between modernity and modernism. What is the difference between them? Paradoxically, modernism looks to the future, whereas modernity is concerned with the present, which can stand in the way of progress. To artists, modernism is a trumpet call that both asserts their freedom to create in a new style and provides them with the mission to define the meaning of their times—and even to reshape society through their art. To be sure, artists have always responded to the changing world around them, but rarely have they risen to the challenge as they have under the banner of modernism, or with so fervent a sense of personal cause.

This is a role for which the "avant-garde" (literally, vanguard) is hardly sufficient. Although both arose as part of the decadent movement toward the end of the nineteenth century, the term *avant-garde,* like modernism, has a long history reaching back to the Middle Ages. The term originated in French warfare and was first applied to the arts in the sixteenth century, but began to acquire its modern definition only under the Romantics. The Socialist reformer Comte de Saint-Simon included artists with scientists and industrialists in the elite group that would rule the ideal state, because as people of imagination they can foresee the future and therefore help to create it. As Baudelaire realized, however, there is an inherent contradiction between Romantic individualism and the discipline necessary for political action. Although its scope was subsequently limited mainly to culture, the avant-garde has sometimes played an active part in politics. Despite the fact that they are closely linked, the avant-garde is by no means synonymous with—and is even antithetical to—modernism. We shall find that the two have held very different meanings for different artists—and produced surprisingly different results in each of the visual arts. Both run counter to their times. But whereas modernism remains dedicated to a utopian vision of the future that stems from the Enlightenment, the avant-garde is bent solely on the destruction of bourgeois modernity. Judged by this standard, few of the twentieth-century's leading artists have been members of a self-styled avant-garde.

Today, having cast off the framework of traditional authority which confined and sustained us before, we can act with a latitude both frightening and exhilarating. The consequences of this freedom to question all values are everywhere around us. Our knowledge about ourselves is now vastly greater, but this has not reassured us as we had hoped. In a world without fixed reference points, we search constantly for our own identity and for the meaning of human existence, individual and collective.

Because modern civilization lacks the cohesiveness of the past, it no longer proceeds by readily identifiable periods; nor are there clear period styles to be discerned in art or in any other form of culture. Instead, we find a continuity of another kind: movements and countermovements. Spreading like waves, these "isms" defy national, ethnic, and chronological boundaries. Never dominant anywhere for long, they compete or merge with each other in endlessly shifting patterns. Hence our account of modern art is guided more by movements than by countries. Only in this way can we hope to do justice to the fact that modern art, all regional differences notwithstanding, is as international as modern science.

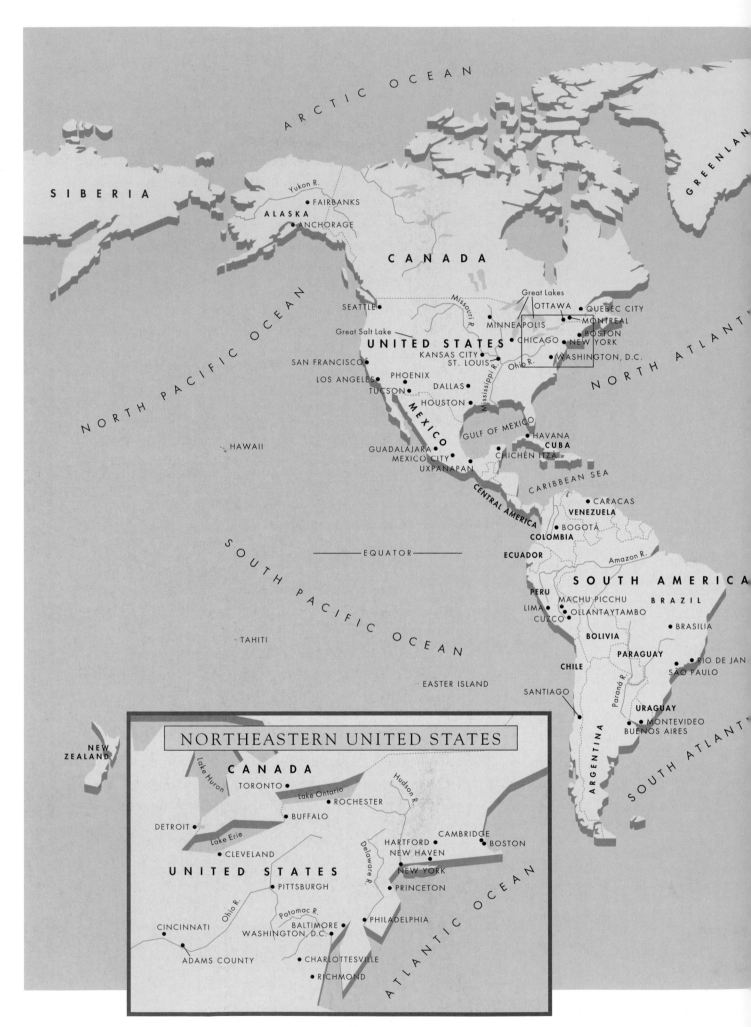

ARCTIC OCEAN

SIBERIA

Yukon R.

• FAIRBANKS

ALASKA

• ANCHORAGE

CANADA

GREENLAND

Great Lakes

SEATTLE •

Missouri R.

OTTAWA •   • QUEBEC CITY

MINNEAPOLIS   • MONTREAL

Great Salt Lake

UNITED STATES

• CHICAGO   • BOSTON

NEW YORK

NORTH PACIFIC OCEAN

KANSAS CITY

ST. LOUIS

Ohio R.

• WASHINGTON, D.C.

SAN FRANCISCO •

PHOENIX •

Mississippi R.

LOS ANGELES •

NORTH ATLANTIC

TUCSON •

DALLAS •

HOUSTON •

MEXICO

HAWAII •

GULF OF MEXICO

• HAVANA

CUBA

GUADALAJARA •

CHICHÉN ITZÁ •

MEXICO CITY •

UXPANAPAN •

CARIBBEAN SEA

CENTRAL AMERICA

• CARACAS

VENEZUELA

• BOGOTÁ

COLOMBIA

EQUATOR

ECUADOR

Amazon R.

SOUTH AMERICA

SOUTH PACIFIC OCEAN

PERU

MACHU PICCHU

BRAZIL

LIMA •

• BRASILIA

CUZCO •

OLLANTAYTAMBO •

TAHITI •

BOLIVIA

PARAGUAY

• RIO DE JAN

SÃO PAULO

EASTER ISLAND

CHILE

Paraná R.

SANTIAGO •

NEW
ZEALAND

URAGUAY

• MONTEVIDEO

BUENOS AIRES

ARGENTINA

SOUTH ATLANTIC

NORTHEASTERN UNITED STATES

CANADA

Lake Huron

TORONTO •

Hudson R.

Lake Ontario

• ROCHESTER

DETROIT •

• BUFFALO

Lake Erie

CAMBRIDGE

HARTFORD •   • BOSTON

• CLEVELAND

Delaware R.

NEW HAVEN

UNITED STATES

NEW YORK

• PITTSBURGH

• PRINCETON

Ohio R.

Potomac R.

• PHILADELPHIA

CINCINNATI •

BALTIMORE •

WASHINGTON, D.C. •

ADAMS COUNTY •

• CHARLOTTESVILLE

ATLANTIC OCEAN

• RICHMOND

THE MODERN WORLD

IRELAND • ENGLAND
SCOTLAND
GLASGOW •
EDINBURGH •
LIVERPOOL
MANCHESTER •
CAMBRIDGE •
BIRMINGHAM •
LONDON •
TWICKENHAM •
BRIGHTON •

ATLANTIC OCEAN

EUROPE

DENMARK • HUMLEBAEK

ARNHEM
UTRECHT
AMSTERDAM •
THE HAGUE •
ANTWERP •
GHENT •
BRUSSELS •
COLOGNE •

NEUKIRCHEN •

HAMBURG •
HANOVER •
BERLIN •
DESSAU •
DRESDEN •

GERMANY

WEIMAR •
Elbe R.

POLAND

KIEV •

UKRAINE

LATVIA
LITHUANIA

BYELARUS

FRANKFURT •
POISSY-SUR-SEINE •
PARIS •
BARBIZON •
ORMANS •
BASEL •
RONCHAMP •

HANAU
AM-MAIN
MUNICH •
ZURICH •
BERN • LUCERNE •
SWITZERLAND

CZECH REPUBLIC
SLOVAKIA
VIENNA •
AUSTRIA

HUNGARY

SLOVENIA
Danube R.

ROMANIA

FRANCE

BORDEAUX •

AIX-EN-PROVENCE
MONTPELIER •

GUERNICA •

MILAN •
ARCOLE •

CROATIA

BOSNIA-
HERZEGOVINA

SERBIA

BULGARIA

BAY OF BISCAY

MARSEILLES •
ARLES •
ITALY

SPAIN

ROME •
HERCULANEUM
POMPEII •
PAESTUM •

ALBANIA

GREECE

PORTUGAL

MEDITERRANEAN SEA

CORFU •
MISSOLONGHI •
ATHENS •
CHIOS •

CHAPTER ONE

NEOCLASSICISM AND ROMANTICISM

The history of the two movements to be dealt with in this chapter covers roughly a century, from about 1750 to 1850. Paradoxically, Neoclassicism has been seen as the opposite of Romanticism on the one hand and as no more than one aspect of it on the other. The difficulty is that the two terms are not evenly matched, any more than are "quadruped" and "carnivore." Neoclassicism is a new revival of classical antiquity, more consistent than earlier classicisms, and one that was linked, at least initially, to Enlightenment thought. Romanticism, in contrast, refers not to a specific style but to an attitude of mind that may reveal itself in any number of ways, including classicism. Romanticism, therefore, is a far broader concept and is correspondingly harder to define. To compound the difficulty, the Neoclassicists and early Romantics were exact contemporaries, who in turn overlapped the preceding generation of Rococo artists. David and Goya, for example, were born within a few years of each other. And in England the leading representatives of the Rococo, Neoclassicism, and Romanticism—Reynolds, West, and Fuseli—shared many of the same ideas, although they were otherwise separated by clear differences in style and approach.

NEOCLASSICISM

The Enlightenment

If the modern era was born during the American Revolution of 1776 and the French Revolution of 1789, these cataclysmic events were preceded by a revolution of the mind that had begun half a century earlier. Its standard-bearers were those thinkers of the Enlightenment in England, France, and Germany—David Hume, François-Marie Voltaire, Jean-Jacques Rousseau, Heinrich Heine, and others—who proclaimed that all human affairs ought to be ruled by reason and the common good, rather than by tradition and established authority. In the arts, as in economics, politics, and religion, this rationalist movement turned against the prevailing practice: the ornate and aristocratic Rococo. In the mid-eighteenth century, the call for a return to reason, nature, and morality in art meant a return to the ancients. After all, had not the classical philosophers been the original "apostles of reason"? The first to formulate this view was Johann Joachim Winckelmann, the German art historian and theorist who popularized the famous concept of the "noble simplicity and calm grandeur" of Greek art (in *Thoughts on the Imitation of Greek Works . . . ,* published in 1755). [See Primary Sources, no. 78, page 934.] His ideas deeply impressed two painters then living in Rome, the German Anton Raphael Mengs (1728–1779) and the Scotsman Gavin Hamilton (1723–1798). Both had strong antiquarian leanings but otherwise limited artistic powers. This may explain why they accepted Winckelmann's doctrine so readily. Mengs' importance lies principally in his role as a propagator of the "Winckelmann program," since his paintings amount to little more than weak paraphrases of Italian art. He left Rome in 1761 after executing his major work, a ceiling fresco of Parnassus inspired by Raphael, and went to Spain, where he vied with the aging Tiepolo (see page 626).

It is a measure of Italy's decline that leadership should pass

842. Jean-Baptiste Greuze. *The Village Bride*. 1761. Oil on canvas, 36 x 46½" (91.4 x 118.1 cm). Musée du Louvre, Paris

to the Northerners who gathered in Rome, which remained a magnet for artists from all over Europe. The only Roman painter who could compete on even terms with the foreigners was Pompeo Batoni (1708–1787), a splendid technician who continued the eclectic classicism of Carlo Maratta (see page 560) but is remembered today chiefly for portraits of his English patrons. This vacuum helps to account for the astonishing success of Mengs and Hamilton. Toward the end of Batoni's career the Italian school was eclipsed once and for all by the French Academy in Rome under Joseph-Marie Vien (1716–1809), its head from 1775 to 1781. To French artists, a return to the classics meant, of course, the style and "academic" theory of Poussin, combined with a maximum of archaeological detail newly gleaned from ancient sculpture and the excavations of Pompeii. Vien himself was a minor artist, who reduced history painting to genre scenes of ancient life, but he was a gifted teacher, and it was his pupils who were to establish French painting as the inheritor and self-proclaimed guardian of the great tradition of Western art.

PAINTING

France

GREUZE. In France, the anti-Rococo trend in painting was at first a matter of content rather than style, which accounts for the sudden fame around 1760 of Jean-Baptiste Greuze (1725–1805). *The Village Bride* (fig. 842), like his other pictures of those years, is a scene of lower-class family life. What distinguishes it from earlier genre paintings (compare fig. 788) is its contrived, stagelike character, borrowed from Hogarth's "dumb show" narratives (see figs. 824 and 825). But Greuze had neither wit nor satire. His pictorial sermon illustrates the social gospel of Jean-Jacques Rousseau that the poor, in contrast to the immoral aristocracy, are full of "natural" virtue and honest sentiment. Everything is intended to remind us of this, from the declamatory gestures and expressions of the actors to the smallest detail, such as the hen with her chicks in the foreground: one chick has left the brood and sits alone on a saucer, like the bride who is about to leave her "brood." *The Village Bride* was acclaimed a masterpiece; the loudest praise came from Denis Diderot, that apostle of Reason and Nature. Here at last was a painter with a social mission who appealed to the beholder's moral sense, instead of merely giving pleasure like the frivolous artists of the Rococo! In his first flush of enthusiasm, Diderot accepted the narrative of Greuze's pictures as "noble and serious human action" in Poussin's sense. Diderot's extravagant praise of Greuze is understandable. *The Village Bride* is a pictorial counterpart to Diderot's own melodramas.

DAVID. Diderot modified his views later, when a far more gifted and rigorous "Neo-Poussinist" appeared on the scene: Jacques-Louis David (1748–1825). A disciple of Vien, David had developed his Neoclassical style in Rome during the years 1775–81. Upon his return to France, he quickly established himself as the leading Neoclassical painter, overshadowing all others by far, so that our conception of the movement is largely based on his accomplishments. In *The Death of Socrates*

843. Jacques-Louis David. *The Death of Socrates.* 1787. Oil on canvas, 4'3" x 6'5¼" (1.3 x 1.96 m). The Metropolitan Museum of Art, New York. Wolfe Fund, 1931

Catherine Lorillard Wolfe Collection

(fig. 843) of 1787, he seems more "Poussiniste" than Poussin himself (compare fig. 794). The composition unfolds parallel to the picture plane like a relief, and the figures are as solid and immobile as statues. David has added one unexpected element: the lighting, sharply focused and casting precise shadows. It is derived from Caravaggio, as is the firmly realistic detail. (Note the hands and feet, the furniture, the texture of the stone surfaces.) Consequently, the picture has a quality of life rather astonishing in so doctrinaire a statement of the new ideal style. The very harshness of the design suggests that its creator was passionately engaged in the issues of his age, artistic as well as political. Socrates, refusing to compromise his principles, was convicted of a trumped-up charge and sentenced to death. About to drink poison from the cup, he is shown not only as an example of Ancient Virtue, but also as the founder of the "religion of Reason." Here he is a Christ-like figure amid his 12 disciples.

David took an active part in the French Revolution, and for some years he had controlling power over the artistic affairs of the nation comparable only to Lebrun's a century before (see pages 600–1). During this time he painted his greatest picture, *The Death of Marat* (fig. 844). David's deep emotion has made a masterpiece from a subject that would have embarrassed any lesser artist, for Marat, one of the political leaders of the Revolution, had been murdered in his bathtub. A painful skin condition required immersion, and he did his work there, with a wooden board serving as his desk. One day a young woman named Charlotte Corday burst in with a personal petition, and plunged a knife into his chest while he read it. David has composed the scene with a stark directness that is awe-inspiring. In this canvas, which was planned as a public memorial to the martyred hero, classical art coincides with devotional image and historical account. However, classical art could offer little specific guidance here, even though the slain figure probably derives from an antique source, and the artist has drawn on the Caravaggesque tradition of religious art far more than in *The*

Death of Socrates. It is no accident that his Marat reminds us so strongly of Zurbarán's *St. Serapion* (see fig. 760).

England

WEST. The martyrdom of a secular hero was first immortalized by Benjamin West (1738–1820) in *The Death of General Wolfe* (fig. 845). West traveled to Rome from Pennsylvania in 1760 and caused something of a sensation, since no American painter had appeared in Europe before. He relished his role of frontiersman. On being shown the *Apollo Belvedere* (see fig. 208) he reportedly exclaimed, "How like a Mohawk warrior!" He also quickly assimilated the lessons of Neoclassicism, so that when he left a few years later, he was in command of the most up-to-date style. West stopped in London for what was intended to be a brief stay on his way home, but stayed on to became first a founding member of the Royal Academy, then, after the death of Reynolds, its president. His career was thus European rather than American, but he always took pride in his New World background.

We can sense this in *The Death of General Wolfe,* his most famous work. Wolfe's death in 1759, which occurred in the siege of Quebec during the French and Indian War, had aroused considerable feeling in London. When West, among others, decided to represent this event, two methods were open to him. He could give a factual account with the maximum of historic accuracy, or he could use "the grand manner," Poussin's ideal conception of history painting (see pages 557–58), with figures in "timeless" classical costume. Although he had absorbed the influence of Mengs and Hamilton, he did not follow them in this painting—he knew the American scene too well for that. Instead, he merged the two approaches. His figures wear contemporary dress, and the conspicuous figure of the Indian places the event in the New World for those unfamiliar with the subject. Yet all the attitudes and expressions are "heroic." The composition, in fact,

844. Jacques-Louis David. *The Death of Marat*. 1793.
Oil on canvas, 65 x 50^1/2" (165 x 128.3 cm). Musées Royaux des Beaux-Arts de Belgique, Brussels

845. Benjamin West. *The Death of General Wolfe.* 1770. Oil on canvas, 4'11½" x 7' (1.51 x 2.13 m). National Gallery of Canada, Ottawa

Gift of the Duke of Westminster

846. John Singleton Copley. *Watson and the Shark.* 1778. Oil on canvas, 7'6¼" x 6'1½" (2.29 x 1.84 m). Museum of Fine Arts, Boston

Gift of Mrs. George von Lengerke Meyer

recalls an old and hallowed theme, the lamentation over the dead Christ (see fig. 506), dramatized by Baroque lighting (see fig. 762). West thus endowed the death of a modern military hero with both the rhetorical pathos of "noble and serious human actions," as defined by academic theory, and the trappings of a real event. He created an image that expresses a phe-

nomenon basic to modern times: the shift of emotional allegiance from religion to nationalism. No wonder his picture had countless successors during the nineteenth century.

COPLEY. West's gifted compatriot, John Singleton Copley of Boston (1738–1815), moved to London just two years before the American Revolution. As New England's outstanding portrait painter, he had adapted the formulas of the British portrait tradition to the cultural climate of his hometown. In Europe, Copley was at last able to attain his ideal of history painting in the manner of West. His most memorable work is *Watson and the Shark* (fig. 846). As a young man, Watson had been dramatically rescued from a shark attack while swimming in Havana harbor, but not until he met Copley did he decide to have this gruesome experience memorialized. Perhaps he thought that only a painter newly arrived from America would do full justice to the exotic flavor of the incident. Copley, in turn, must have been fascinated by the task of translating the story into pictorial terms. Following West's example, he made every detail as authentic as possible (here the black man has the purpose of the Indian in *The Death of General Wolfe*) and utilized all the expressive resources of Baroque painting to invite the beholder's participation. Copley may have remembered representations of Jonah and the Whale, which include the elements of his scene, except that the action is reversed: the prophet is thrown overboard into the jaws of the sea monster. The shark becomes a monstrous embodiment of evil; the man with the boat hook recalls an Archangel Michael fighting Satan; and the nude youth, resembling a fallen gladiator, flounders helplessly between the forces of doom and salvation. This kind of moral allegory is typical of Neoclassicism as a whole, and despite its charged emotion, the picture has the same logic and clarity found in David's *Death of Socrates*.

KAUFFMANN. One of the leading Neoclassicists in England was the Swiss-born painter Angelica Kauffmann (1741–1807). A founding member of the Royal Academy, she spent 15 years in London among the group that included Reynolds and West, whom she had met in Winckelmann's circle in Rome (see page 658). From the antique this disciple of Mengs developed a delicate style admirably suited to the interiors of Robert Adam (see page 651), which she was often commissioned to adorn. Nevertheless, Kauffmann's most ambitious works are narrative paintings, of which the artist John Henry Fuseli (see page 666) observed, "Her heroines are herself." *The Artist in the Character*

847. Angelica Kauffmann. *The Artist in the Character of Design Listening to the Inspiration of Poetry.* 1782. Oil on canvas, diameter 24" (61 cm). The Iveagh Bequest, Kenwood, London

of Design Listening to the Inspiration of Poetry (fig. 847), one of her finest paintings, combines both aspects of her art. The subject must have held particular meaning for her. The prototype of the allegorical "friendship" pictures showing two female figures that remained popular into the Romantic era (see fig. 896), it is eloquent testimony to women's struggle to gain recognition in the arts. The artist has assumed the guise of Design, attesting to her strong sense of identification with the muse.

STUBBS. George Stubbs (1724–1806), who painted portraits of racehorses (and sometimes their owners) for a living, developed a new type of animal picture full of feeling for the grandeur and violence of nature. On a visit to North Africa, he is said to have seen a horse killed by a lion. Certainly this image haunted his imagination. *Lion Attacking a Horse* (fig. 848) can

848. George Stubbs. *Lion Attacking a Horse.* 1770. Oil on canvas, 40 1/8 x 50 1/4" (102 x 127.6 cm). Yale University Art Gallery, New Haven, Connecticut

Gift of the Yale University Art Gallery Associates

849. Alexander Cozens. *Landscape,* from *A New Method of Assisting the Invention in Drawing Original Compositions of Landscape.* 1784–86. Aquatint. The Metropolitan Museum of Art, New York
Rogers Fund, 1906

be seen as an animal counterpart to Copley's *Watson and the Shark,* and it has similar allegorical overtones as well. People have no place in this realm, and the artist identifies himself emotionally with the horse, whose pure whiteness contrasts so dramatically—and symbolically—with the sinister rocks of the lion's domain. Thunderclouds racing across the sky reinforce the mood of doom. The poor horse, frightened also by the approaching storm, seems doubly defenseless against these forces of destruction. We respond to the horse in the same way as to the unfortunate Watson: with mixed fascination and horror.

Although it looks forward to Romanticism, Stubbs' effort at endowing his animals with nearly human action and emotion was the beginning of a larger investigation that was characteristic of the Enlightenment. He later made a series of drawings for a book of comparative anatomy—including one that could well be used to illustrate Plato's dictum of human beings as featherless bipeds—which emphasizes the similarities in physiology and psychology between people and animals. His scientific curiosity and comprehensive approach relate him to the attempt by Diderot in his massive *Encyclopédie* to unite knowledge and philosophy into a single, coherent system.

THE PICTURESQUE AND THE SUBLIME. Picturesque landscape painting was as distinctive to the Enlightenment as the English garden (see pages 668–69), to which it was closely related. As the term implies, the picturesque was a way of looking at nature through the eyes of landscape painters. The scenery of Italy and the idyllic landscapes of Claude contributed to the English appreciation of nature. In articulating sentiments inspired by these examples, English nature poets such as James Thomson further validated the aesthetic response to nature, often through references to mythology. The picturesque was soon joined by wilder scenes reflecting a taste for the sublime—that delicious sense of awe experienced before grandiose nature, as defined by Edmund Burke in *Inquiry into the Origin of Our Ideas of the Sublime and the Beautiful* of 1756. After touring the rugged lake region of England in 1780, William Gilpin claimed, however, that the picturesque lay somewhere between Burke's extremes, since it is neither vast nor smooth but finite and rough. The picturesque later came to include a topographical mode and a rustic mode, but remained fundamentally a way of manipulating nature to conform to artistic examples.

COZENS. Alexander Cozens (c. 1717–1786), who helped to originate the picturesque, soon tired of these models, which he felt could produce only stereotyped variations on an established theme. The direct study of nature, important though it was, could not be the new starting point either, for it did not supply the imaginative, poetic quality that for him constituted the essence of landscape painting. As a teacher, Cozens developed what he called "a new method of assisting the invention in drawing original compositions of landscapes," which he published, with illustrations such as figure 849, shortly before his death. What was this method? Leonardo da Vinci, Cozens noted, had observed that an artist could stimulate his imagination by trying to find recognizable shapes in the stains on old walls. Why not then produce such chance effects on purpose, to be used in the same way? Crumple a sheet of paper, smooth it; then, while thinking generally of landscape, blot it with ink, using as little conscious control as possible. (Our example is such an "ink-blot landscape.") With this as the point of departure, representational elements may be picked out in the configuration of blots, and then elaborated into a finished picture. Cozens' blotscape, then, is not a work of nature but a work of art. Even though only half-born, it shows, if nothing else, a highly individual graphic rhythm.

Because it relies on art, the Cozens method still falls within the picturesque, while the sweeping nature of his attempt places it within the Enlightenment, with its love of systems. Needless to say, however, it has far-reaching implications, theoretical as well as practical, but these could hardly have been understood by his contemporaries, who regarded the "blotmaster" as ridiculous. Nevertheless, the "method" was not forgotten, its memory kept alive partly by its very notoriety. The two great masters of Romantic landscape in England, John Constable and William Turner, both profited from it, although they differed in almost every other way.

SCULPTURE

The history of Neoclassical sculpture does not simply follow that of painting. The phenomenon of Neoclassicism, which in painting is sometimes hard to distinguish from Romanticism, stands out far more clearly in sculpture. Unlike painters, Neoclassical sculptors were overwhelmed by the authority accorded since Winckelmann to ancient statues such as the *Apollo Belvedere* (see fig. 208), praised as being supreme manifestations of the Greek genius, although in fact most of them were mechanical Roman copies of no great distinction after Hellenistic pieces. (Goethe, upon seeing the newly discovered late Archaic sculpture from Aegina, pronounced it clumsy and inferior; see figs. 160 and 161.)

When Winckelmann published his essay advocating the imitation of Greek works, enthusiasm for the virtues of classical antiquity was already well established among the intellectuals of the Enlightenment. In Rome from 1760 on, the restoring of ancient sculpture and its sale, especially to wealthy visitors from abroad, was a flourishing business. To these patrons, "classics" such as the *Apollo Belvedere* or *The Laocoön Group* (fig. 215), to cite only two of the most famous, belonged to a different world. They were venerated as embodiments of an aesthetic ideal, undisturbed by the demands of time and place. To enter this world, the modern sculptor set himself the goal of creating "modern classics," that is, sculpture demanding to be judged on a basis of equality with its ancient predecessors. This was not merely a matter of style and subject matter. It meant that the sculptor had to find a way of creating monumental sculpture in the hope that critical acclaim would establish such works as modern classics and attract buyers. The solution to this problem was the original plaster, which permitted him to present major works to the public without a ruinous investment in expensive materials. We first encounter it at the Salons, the exhibitions sponsored by the French Academy, where success was crucial for young artists. Without the original plaster, the Neoclassic revolution in sculpture would have been impossible to accomplish.

If Paris was the artistic capital of the Western world, Rome during the second half of the eighteenth century became the birthplace and spiritual home of Neoclassicism. However, as we have seen, the new style was pioneered by the resident foreigners from north of the Alps, rather than Italians. That Rome should have been an even stronger magnet for sculptors than for painters is hardly surprising. After all, it was in ancient sculpture that the "noble simplicity and calm grandeur" praised by Winckelmann were most strikingly evident, and Rome offered an abundance of sculptural monuments but only a meager choice of ancient painting. (The city also had many skilled artisans in both marble and bronze.) In the shadow of these monuments, Northern sculptors trained in the Baroque tradition awakened to a new conception of what sculpture ought to be and thus paved the way for Antonio Canova, whose success as the creator of modern classics was the ultimate fulfillment of their aspirations (see pages 699–700).

England

The leading role of Anglo-Roman artists prior to 1780 in the formulation of Neoclassicism was a result of England's enthusiasm for classical antiquity since the early years of the century. This precocious appreciation was political, philosophic, and literary, with a new nationalism as its common denominator, but this soon turned into a demand that England become "the principal seat of the arts" as well.

BANKS. Thomas Banks (1735–1805) came closest to establishing the creation of modern classics as the sculptor's true goal. Little is known of Banks' career before he went to Rome in 1772 for seven years on a traveling fellowship from the Royal Academy. *The Death of Germanicus* (fig. 850) of 1774, a large relief, shows his close study of classical sources, yet it is not in the least archaeological in flavor. While the facial types and drapery treatment derive from classical sources, the strained poses, the pronounced linear rhythms, and the emo-

850. Thomas Banks. *The Death of Germanicus.* 1774. Marble, height 30" (76.2 cm). Holkham Hall, Norfolk, England
By kind permission of The Earl of Leicester and the Trustees of the Holkham Estate

tional intensity of the scene have no counterpart in ancient sculpture. They reflect, rather, Banks' admiration for the two chief Anglo-Roman painters, Gavin Hamilton (who had treated the same subject, but with much less originality) and Henry Fuseli (see page 686).

On his return to England, Banks found little demand for his "new classics," although they were enthusiastically received by the recently established Royal Academy. Devoted to the nude and to heroic drama, he nevertheless sought commissions for funerary monuments, which were the main source of steady employment for sculptors in England.

France

HOUDON. Jean-Antoine Houdon (1741–1828), unlike most of his contemporaries, built his career on portrait sculpture. He would have been glad to accept state commissions had they been available. However, he discovered quite soon his special gift for portraits, for which there was a growing demand. Portraiture proved the most viable field for Neoclassic sculpture. How else could modern artists rise above the quality of the Greek and Roman classics, which they were everywhere assured were the acme of sculptural achievement?

Houdon's portraits still retain the acute sense of individual character introduced by Coysevox (see fig. 807). Indeed, they established entirely new standards of physical and psychological verisimilitude that reflect Enlightenment ideals. Houdon, more than any other artist of his time, knew how to give them visible form. His portraits have an apparent lack of style that is deceptive: his style consists of the uncanny ability to make all his sitters into Enlightenment personalities while remaining conscientiously faithful to their individual physiognomies. He even managed this on the rare occasions when he had to make portrait busts of figures long dead, or when he had to work from a death mask only.

With Voltaire, he was more fortunate, modeling him from life a few weeks before the famous author's death in May 1778, and then making a death mask as well. From these he created

851. Jean-Antoine Houdon. *Voltaire Seated.* 1781.
Terracotta model for marble original, height 47" (119.3 cm).
Musée Fabre, Montpellier, France

852. Jean-Antoine Houdon. *George Washington.* 1788–92.
Marble, height 6'2" (1.88 m). State Capitol, Richmond, Virginia

Voltaire Seated (fig. 851), which was immediately acclaimed as towering above all others of its kind. The original plaster has not survived, but a terracotta cast from it, retouched by Houdon, offers a close approximation. As contemporary critics quickly pointed out, the *Voltaire Seated* was a "heroicized" likeness, enveloping the frail old man in a Roman toga and even endowing him with some hair he no longer had so as to justify the classical headband. Yet the effect is not disturbing, for Voltaire wears the toga as casually as a dressing gown, and his facial expression and the turn of his head suggest the atmosphere of an intimate conversation. Thus Voltaire is not cast in the role of classical philosopher—he becomes the modern counterpart of one, a modern classic in his own right! In him, we recognize ourselves. Voltaire is the image of modern man: unheroic, skeptical, with his own idiosyncratic mixture of rationality and emotion. That is surely why Voltaire strikes us as so "natural." We are, after all, the heirs of the Enlightenment, which coined this ideal type.

Aside from his *Voltaire Seated,* the Virginia *George Washington* (fig. 852) is Houdon's finest effort. In 1778, the year he

portrayed Voltaire, Houdon became a Freemason and modeled Benjamin Franklin. Replicas of the Franklin bust spread the artist's fame in the New World. American colonial sculpture hardly existed aside from weathervanes, tombstone carvings, and cigar-store Indians. Public monuments were few, and imported from England rather than produced at home. Thus the newborn republic had to look to France for a sculptor to immortalize its Founding Father (see pages 699–704). It could not be entrusted to an Englishman, for obvious reasons, and there was, it seems, no contact with British sculpture from 1776 until after the fall of Napoleon. Thus when the Virginia legislature decided to commission a marble statue of George Washington, the natural choice was Houdon. Houdon insisted on coming over to model his sitter directly, and in October 1785, he spent two weeks at Mount Vernon as Washington's guest. The figure was finally erected in the rotunda of the State Capitol 11 years later.

Houdon initially made two versions, one in classical and one in modern costume, the final form of the statue. Even the latter, though meticulously up-to-date in detail, has a classi-

In France, around the middle of the eighteenth century, the philosopher and encyclopedist Denis Diderot (1713–1784) attempted to add domestic tragedy and the comedy of virtue (the so-called middle genres) to the accepted classifications of theater through his sentimental plays *The Illegitimate Son* (1757) and *The Father of a Family* (1758). They were quickly forgotten, with good reason. The only important French playwright of the later Enlightenment was Pierre-Augustin Caron de Beaumarchais (1732– 1799), whose comedies *The Barber of Seville* (1775) and *The Marriage of Figaro* (1783) became the basis for operas by Rossini and Mozart. While the *Barber* is a lighthearted farce about the triumph of young lovers over lecherous old men, *Figaro* was a critique of the aristocracy, whose ranks Beaumarchais joined, thanks to the wealth he amassed through his inventions and business ventures.

Neoclassicism in German theater was represented chiefly by the playwright, critic, and university professor Johann Christoph Gottsched (1700–1766), who modeled his plays on French examples and who based his ideas on those of Nicolas Boileau (1636–1711); however, their success depended heavily on his close association with the actress Caroline Neuber (1697–1760). His theories were attacked by Gotthold Ephraim Lessing (1729–1781) in *Laokoon* (1766) and in the journal *Hamburgische Dramaturgie* (1767–68) by arguing that the goal of drama is to arouse compassion, thereby fulfilling an important moral and social function. Although he belittled his own work, Lessing's plays, such as *Minna von Barnhelm* (1767), embody his principles very capably.

Lessing helped pave the way for the *Sturm und Drang* (Storm and Stress) period (1770–87), which constituted a rebellion against the restrictions of the Neoclassical drama and Enlightenment philosophy and were the first attempt to create a distinctive German form of theater. Although this literary movement took its name from a play of that title (1776) by F. M. Klinger, it centered on the young poet Johann Wolfgang von Goethe (1749–1832), whose drama *Goetz van Berlichingen* (1773), inspired by the memoirs of a famous sixteenth-century German knight, launched the movement in theater. Its extreme subjectivity was epitomized by his novel *The Sorrows of Young Werther,* published the following year. *Sturm und Drang* in theater was poorly received but widely discussed; it was finally legitimized by August von Kotzebue (1761–1819), who became the most popular playwright in Europe. The late eighteenth century was notable for the establishment of national theaters throughout Germany, as well as Austria: the Hamburg National Theater, which employed Lessing as its artistic adviser (dramaturge) when it opened in 1767, and the Burgtheater in Vienna in 1776.

After the publication of *The Sorrows of Young Werther,* which established his reputation, Goethe was invited to the court in Weimar, where he spent the rest of his career and even served as minister of state for ten years. During a sojourn to Italy in 1786–88 he became a convert to classicism and rejected *Sturm und Drang.* In 1791 he was appointed director of the theater at Weimar, in which he showed little interest until his friendship with the poet Friedrich von Schiller (1759–1805). Schiller had written some early dramas before turning to the study of history, which led to a professorship at the university in Jena, not far from Weimar. The two men became such close friends that Schiller moved to Weimar in 1799. From then until his death Schiller wrote his great dramas, which were a direct outgrowth of his abiding interest in history. They center on the Thirty Years' War, about which he wrote the first major treatise, particularly General Albrecht Wallenstein (1583– 1634). His other plays concern William Tell, Mary Stuart, and Joan of Arc. Under Goethe and Schiller, Weimar became home to the leading theater on the Continent. They argued that theater should transform experience through harmony and grace rather than create an illusion of real life; hence, they instituted stylized conventions designed to lead the viewer to ideal truth. After Schiller's death, however, Goethe lost interest in the theater.

cal pose, and we can feel the chill breath of the *Apollo Belvedere* (fig. 208), as it were, on the becalmed, smooth surfaces. By this time, Washington no longer held public office; he was simply a gentleman farmer. Houdon has given him a general's uniform, but the sword, no longer needed in peacetime, is suspended from a bundle of 13 rods (the fasces, representing the original states of the Union) and his right hand rests on a cane. Behind his feet is a plow, the symbol of peace. These attributes, with their classical allusions, blend easily with the contemporary dress, and the contrapposto stance of the figure is so well motivated that the beholder is hardly aware of its antique origin. Above all, Houdon has created a powerful impression of Washington's character along with a meticulous record of his physical appearance, in the framework of the personality type of the Enlightenment. Far more than any other portrait, Houdon's statue, and the busts associated with it, determined how the nation visualized the Father of His Country.

ARCHITECTURE

England

THE PALLADIAN REVIVAL. England was the birthplace of Neoclassicism in architecture, as it had been in the forefront of painting and sculpture. The earliest sign of this attitude was the Palladian revival in the 1720s, sponsored by the wealthy amateur Richard Boyle, Lord Burlington (1694–1753). Chiswick House (figs. 853 and 854), adapted from the Villa Rotonda (see figs. 664 and 665), is compact, simple, and geometric—the antithesis of the Baroque pomp of Blenheim Palace (see fig. 813). What distinguishes this style from earlier

853. Lord Burlington and William Kent. Chiswick House, near London. Begun 1725

854. Plan of Chiswick House

classicisms is less its external appearance than its motivation. Instead of merely reasserting the superior authority of the ancients, it claimed to satisfy the demands of reason, and thus to be more "natural" than the Baroque, which at the time was identified with Tory policies by the Whig opposition, thus beginning an association between Neoclassicism and liberal politics that was to continue through the French Revolution. This rationalism helps to explain the abstract, segmented look of Chiswick House. The surfaces are flat and unbroken, the ornament is meager, and the temple portico juts out abruptly from the blocklike body of the structure.

THE ENGLISH GARDEN. Should such a villa be set in a geometric, formal garden, like Le Nôtre's at Versailles (see fig. 800)? Indeed not, Lord Burlington and his circle maintained. That would be unnatural, hence contrary to reason, so they invented what became known all over Europe as "the English landscape garden." Carefully planned to look unplanned, with winding paths, irregularly spaced clumps of trees, and little lakes and rivers instead of symmetrical basins and canals, the "reasonable" garden must seem as unbounded, as full of surprise and variety, as nature itself. It must, in a word, be "picturesque," like the landscapes of Claude Lorraine (fig. 796), which English landscape architects now took as their source of inspiration. A standard feature was the inclusion of little temples half concealed by the shrubbery, or artificial ruins, "to draw sorrowful reflections from the soul."

Such sentiments were not new. They had often been expressed before in poetry and painting. But to project them onto nature itself, through planned irregularity, was a new idea. The landscape garden, a work of art intended not to look like a work of art, blurred the long-established demarcation between artifice and reality, and thus set an important precedent for the revival styles to come. After all, the landscape garden stands in the same relation to nature as a synthetic ruin to an authentic one, or a Neoclassic or Neo-Gothic building to

855. Henry Flitcroft and Henry Hoare. Landscape garden with Temple of Apollo, Stourhead, England. 1744–65

its ancient or medieval model. When the fashion spread to the other side of the Channel, it was welcomed not only as a new way to lay out gardens but as a vehicle of Romantic emotion.

STOURHEAD. Of all the landscape gardens laid out in England in the mid-eighteenth century, the one at Stourhead most nearly retains its original appearance. Its creators, the banker Henry Hoare and the designer Henry Flitcroft (1697–1769), were both enthusiastic followers of Lord Burlington and William Kent. Stourhead is unique not only for its fine preservation but also for the owner's active role in planning every detail of its development. Our view (fig. 855) is across a small lake made by damming the river Stour. High on the far shore is the Temple of Apollo modeled on the Temple of Venus at Baalbek (see fig. 258), which became known in the West only

856. Jacques-Germain Soufflot. The Panthéon (Ste.-Geneviève), Paris. 1755–92

857. Étienne-Louis Boullée. Project for a Memorial to Isaac Newton. 1784. Ink and wash drawing, 15½ x 25½" (39.3 x 64.7 cm). Bibliothèque Nationale, Paris

858. Claude-Nicolas Ledoux. Barrière de Villette (after restoration), Paris. 1785–89

after 1757. Occupying other focal points at Stourhead are a grotto, a Temple of Venus, a Pantheon, a genuine Gothic cross, and a neo-medieval tower built to commemorate King Alfred the Great, the "Father of His People."

France

SOUFFLOT. The rationalist movement came somewhat later in France. Its first great monument, the Panthéon in Paris (fig. 856), by Jacques-Germain Soufflot (1713–1780), was built as the church of Ste.-Geneviève, but secularized during the Revolution. As with so much else in eighteenth-century France, the building looks back to the preceding century, in this case Hardouin-Mansart's Church of the Invalides (fig. 804). Its dome, interestingly enough, is derived from St. Paul's Cathedral in London (see fig. 810), indicating England's new importance for Continental architects. The smooth, sparsely decorated surfaces are abstractly severe, akin to those of Chiswick House (an effect further emphasized by having to wall in the windows later because the architect miscalculated the stresses), while the huge portico is modeled directly on ancient Roman temples. From this coolly precise exterior we would never suspect that Soufflot also had a strong interest in Gothic churches. He admired them, not for the seeming miracles they perform but for their structural elegance—a rationalist version of Guarini's point of view (see fig. 749). His ideal, in fact, was "to combine the classic orders with the lightness so admirably displayed by certain Gothic buildings," although he did not study them in detail.

BOULLÉE. Étienne-Louis Boullée (1728–1799) was half a generation younger than Soufflot and far more daring. He began as a painter and retired early, but though he built little, his teaching at the Royal Academy helped to create a tradition of visionary architecture that flourished during the last third of the century and the early years of the next. [See Primary Sources, no. 79, pages 934–35.] Boullée's ideal was an architecture of "majestic nobility," an effect he sought to achieve by combining huge, simple masses. Most of his designs were for structures on a scale so enormous that they could hardly be built even today.

He hailed the sphere as the perfect form, since no trick of perspective can alter its appearance (except, of course, its apparent size). Thus he projected a memorial to Isaac Newton as a gigantic hollow sphere, mirroring the universe (fig. 857). "O Newton!" he exclaimed, "I conceived the idea of surrounding you with your discovery, and thus, somehow, of surrounding you with yourself." The interior was to be bare, apart from an empty sarcophagus symbolizing the mortal remains of the great man, but the surface of its upper half was pierced by countless small holes, points of light meant to give the illusion of stars. Bathed in deep shadow, Boullée's plan for the memorial to Newton has a striking pictorialism inspired in part by the *Prison Caprices* of Piranesi (see fig. 841). Plans such as this have a utopian grandeur that dwarfs the boldest ambitions of earlier architects. Largely forgotten during most of the nineteenth century, Boullée was rediscovered in the early twentieth, when architects again dared to "think the unthinkable."

LEDOUX. Claude-Nicolas Ledoux (1736–1806) was the opposite of Boullée: an architect who built much and turned to theory only late in his career. Yet his work quickly developed visionary qualities that are readily apparent in his most important achievement, the 50 tollgates he designed for the new walls around Paris in 1785–89, of which only four still exist. (The rest were dismantled during the French Revolution.) Our example (fig. 858) shows a remarkable sense of geometry placed at the

Neoclassicism and *Sturm und Drang* (see box page 667) were also important to music. The leading representative of the former was Christoph Willibald Glück (1714–1787). Gluck wrote two operas, *Orfeo ed Euridice* (1762) and *Alceste* (1767) with the poet Raniero Calzabigi (1714–1795), who was influenced by Rameau's operas during a sojourn in Paris. They sought to correct the excesses of Italian opera through "a beautiful simplicity" and to "confine music to its proper function of serving the poetry for the expression and the situation of the plot." Though originally produced in Vienna, which had become the opera capital of Europe, the two operas enjoyed greater success in Paris, where classicism was an uninterrupted tradition. Glück's operas have a nobility and depth of feeling that hark back to Monteverdi but with a classicism and pageantry worthy of Lully and Rameau. The subject of both works is the immortality of love, which conquers even death. Alceste, who was willing to die so that her husband, King Admetes, could live, was seen as a paradigm of conjugal love. Thanks in good measure to the opera's popularity, Jean-François Peyron (1744–1814), the only serious rival of Jacques-Louis David (see pages 559–60), made it the subject of his first important commission from Louis XVI in 1785. (The painting is now in the Louvre.)

Carl Philipp Emanuel Bach (1714–1788), a son of Johann Sebastian Bach, served for nearly 30 years at the Berlin court of Frederick the Great (1712–1786), himself a very able composer. Unlike his illustrious father, he loathed counterpoint. The widespread reaction against counterpoint, with its complexities, may be likened to the call for natural morality by Bach's exact contemporary, the philosopher Jean-Jacques Rousseau (1712–1778). Bach nevertheless adopted a conservative style that suited his patron's taste. Upon being appointed music director of Hamburg, one of the most important posts in Germany, he felt free to pursue a direct, expressive style that sometimes shows a debt to his predecessor there, Georg Philipp Telemann. His first Hamburg symphonies exemplify the *Sturm und Drang* in music: they are full of extremes, with brooding, sighing, slow movements sandwiched between dynamic fast ones characterized by irregular rhythms and emotional outbursts that startle the listener. Their limitation, and it is a significant one, is the composer's disregard for form, which prevented him from developing them further.

Sturm und Drang influenced the middle symphonies written by Franz Joseph Haydn (1732–1809) in 1771–74. He spent almost his entire career at the estate of the Esterházys south of Vienna, where he had a small but excellent ensemble of instrumentalists and singers in the service of an enlightened if demanding patron. Haydn became the most famous composer of his era and was called to Paris (1785–86) and London (1790, 1794), where he created symphonies of unrivaled sophistication and richness. He was no less a master of the string quartet, which he wrote in large numbers, all of them marked by unprecedented variety, formal mastery, and refined feeling. Haydn remained a person of his times: the late oratorios—*The Creation* (1798), based on Milton's *Paradise Lost,* and *The Seasons* (1801), adapted from James Thomson's poem (1726–30) of the same name—maintain the late-eighteenth-century view of an orderly cosmos created by a benevolent god.

Haydn became a close friend of Wolfgang Amadeus Mozart (1756–1791), despite their great differences in age, temperament, and outlook. A child prodigy, Mozart received a rigorous training from his father, Leopold (1719–1787), who paraded him around the great courts of Europe, where he was exposed to the full range of contemporary music. Mozart failed in his efforts to gain a major court appointment; deprived of this measure of security, he became a prolific composer for the open market who put the stamp of his individual genius on everything he wrote. His finest quartets are the six dedicated to Haydn, who declared him the greatest composer alive, while the late symphonies blaze new territory that foreshadow those of the young Beethoven. His numerous concertos for piano, of which he was a virtuoso, combine enchanting lyricism with brilliant technical display. Mozart was a supreme vocal composer, and it is the singing quality of the human voice that underlies his mature work, regardless of instrument. He was also a master of compositional technique, including counterpoint (he had discussed Bach's music with his successor at Leipzig), and his compositions depend for much of their success on their formal perfection. Indeed, for Mozart form was the vehicle of expression, which it served to contain, so that there was an ideal, "classical" balance between the two. He was fully sympathetic to the Enlightenment. Its philosophy both informs and burdens his operas, including his acknowledged masterpieces *The Marriage of Figaro* (1787), based on the play by Beaumarchais, and *Don Giovanni* (1787). Both are a new type of comic opera, called *opera buffo* to distinguish it from traditional serious operas (*opera seria*), but unlike others of their kind, they have a wonderful humanity and substantial content, thanks in part to the librettos by Mozart's collaborator, Lorenzo Da Ponte (1749–1838).

service of a singular imagination. Ledoux has mounted a huge rotunda on a square base, which is entered through a Greek portico supported by pillars instead of columns. (All four sides are identical in appearance.) Although the structure derives from antiquity, the effect is anything but classical. Visually the portico seems almost crushed by the burden of the rotunda, whose massiveness is barely relieved by the strangely medieval-looking screen of arches over paired columns (compare fig. 397). Implicit in the radically simplified forms and decidedly odd proportions is a critique of all earlier examples of the same type, from the Pantheon (fig. 249) through Soufflot's Ste.-Geneviève (fig. 856). (See also figs. 544, 665, 804, and 853.) The building, nearly Mannerist in its gestures, is among the most peculiar of any before Wright's Guggenheim Museum (fig. 21), which may be regarded as its descendant.

Neoclassicism and the Antique

The mid-eighteenth century was greatly stirred by two experiences: the rediscovery of Greek art as the original source of

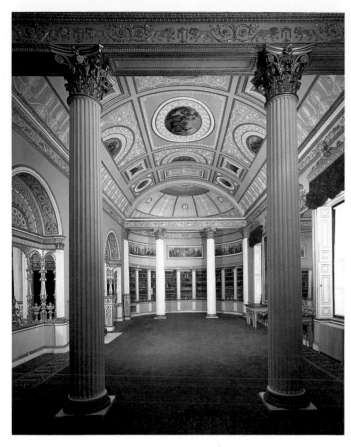

859. Robert Adam. The Library, Kenwood, London. 1767–69

860. Thomas Jefferson. Monticello, Charlottesville, Virginia. 1770–84; 1796–1806

861. Plan of Monticello

classic style, and the excavations at Herculaneum and Pompeii, which for the first time revealed the daily life of the ancients and the full range of their arts and crafts. Richly illustrated books about the Acropolis at Athens, the temples at Paestum, and the finds at Herculaneum and Pompeii were published in England and France. Archaeology caught everyone's imagination. From this came a new style of interior decoration. The Greek phase of this revival proved necessarily limited, as only a narrow range of household furnishings was known at second hand from paintings and sculpture, such as our *Grave Stele of Hegeso* (fig. 197). When they wanted to work in a Greek style, designers turned chiefly to architecture, whose vocabulary could be readily adapted to large pieces of furniture where it was commingled with Roman elements. Thus it was, for the most part, a classicism of particulars.

ADAM.   The Neoclassical style was epitomized by the work of the Englishman Robert Adam (1728–1792). His friendship with Piranesi in Rome reinforced Adam's goal of arriving at a personal style based on the antique without slavishly imitating it. His genius is seen most fully in the interiors he designed in the 1760s for palatial homes. Because he commanded an extraordinarily wide vocabulary, each room is different; yet the syntax remains distinctive to him. The library wing he added to Kenwood (fig. 859) shows Adam at his finest. Clearly Roman in inspiration (compare fig. 255), it is covered with a barrel vault connected at either end to an apse that is separated by a screen of Corinthian columns. (The basic scheme had been anticipated more than 40 years earlier by Johann Fischer von Erlach; see pages 621–22.) Adam was concerned above all with movement, but this must be understood

not in terms of Baroque dynamism or Rococo ornamentation but the careful balance of varied shapes and proportions. The play of semicircles, half-domes, and arches lends an air of festive grace. The library thus provides an apt setting for "the parade, the convenience, and the social pleasures of life," since it was also a room "for receiving company." This intention was in keeping with Adam's personality, which was at ease with the aristocratic milieu in which he moved. The room owes much of its charm to the paintings by Antonio Zucchi (1762–1795), later the husband of Angelica Kauffmann, who also worked for Adam, and the stucco ornament by Adam's plasterer Joseph Rose, which was adapted from Roman examples (compare fig. 270). The color, too, was in daring contrast to the stark white that was widely preferred for interiors at the time. The effect, stately yet intimate, echoes the delicacy of Rococo interiors (Adam had stayed in Paris in 1754 before going to Rome) but with a characteristically Neoclassic insistence on planar surfaces, symmetry, and geometric precision.

JEFFERSON.   Meanwhile, the Palladianism launched by Lord Burlington had spread overseas to the American Colonies, where it became known as the Georgian style. An example of great distinction is Thomas Jefferson's house, Monticello (figs. 860 and 861). Built of brick with wood trim, it is not so doctrinaire in design as Chiswick House. (Note the less compact plan and the numerous windows.) Instead of using the Corinthian order, Jefferson (1743–1826) chose the Roman Doric, which Adam had helped to legitimize as an alternative to the stark simplicity favored by Lord Burlington, although the late eighteenth century came to favor the heavier and more austere Greek Doric.

THE ROMANTIC MOVEMENT

Of all the "isms" that populate Western art of the past two centuries, Romanticism has always been the most difficult to define. It deserves to be termed an "ism" only because its practitioners (or at least some of them) thought of themselves as being part of a movement. But none has left us anything approaching a definition. Romanticism, it seems, was a certain state of mind rather than the conscious pursuit of a goal. If we try to analyze this state of mind, it breaks down into a series of attitudes, none of which, considered individually, is unique to Romanticism. It is only their peculiar combination that seems characteristic of the Romantic movement.

How did Romanticism come about? The Enlightenment, paradoxically, liberated not only reason but also its opposite: it helped to create a new wave of emotionalism that was to last for the better part of a half-century, and came to be known as Romanticism. The word derives from the late-eighteenth-century vogue for medieval tales of adventure (such as the legends of King Arthur or the Holy Grail), called "romances" because they were written in a Romance language, not in Latin. This interest in the long-neglected "Gothick" past was symptomatic of a general trend. Those who shared a revulsion against the established social order and religion—against established values of any sort—could either try to found a new order based on their faith in the power of reason, or they could seek release in a craving for emotional experience. Their common denominator was a desire to "return to Nature." The rationalist acclaimed nature as the ultimate source of reason, while the Romantic worshiped it as unbounded, wild, and ever-changing. The Romantic believed that evil would disappear if people were only to behave "naturally," giving their impulses free rein. In the name of nature, the Romantics acclaimed liberty, power, love, violence, the Greeks, the Middle Ages, or anything else that aroused them, although actually they exalted emotion as an end in itself. This attitude has motivated some of the noblest, as well as vilest, acts of our era. In its most extreme form, Romanticism could be expressed only through direct action, not through works of art. No artist, then, can be a wholehearted Romantic, for the creation of a work of art demands some detachment, self-awareness, and discipline. What William Wordsworth, the great Romantic poet, said of poetry in 1798—that it is "emotion recollected in tranquility"—applies also to the visual arts.

To cast fleeting experience into permanent form, Romantic artists needed a style. But since they were in revolt against the old order, this could not be the established style of the time. It had to come from some phase of the past to which they felt linked by "elective affinity" (another Romantic concept). Romanticism thus favored the revival not of one style,

but of a potentially unlimited number of styles. In fact, the rediscovery and utilization of forms hitherto neglected or scorned evolved into a stylistic principle in itself, so that revivals became the "style" of Romanticism in art, as it did, to a degree, in literature and music.

Seen in this context, Neoclassicism was simply the first phase of Romanticism, a revival that continued all the way through the nineteenth century, although it came to represent conservative taste. Perhaps it is best, then, to think of them as two sides of the same modern coin. If we maintain the distinction between them, it is because, until about 1800, Neoclassicism loomed larger than the other Romantic revivals, and because of the Enlightenment's dedication to the cause of liberty as against the cult of the individual represented by the Romantic hero.

PAINTING

It is one of the many apparent contradictions of Romanticism that it became, despite the desire for untrammeled freedom of individual creativity, art for the rising professional and commercial class, which effectively dominated nineteenth-century society and which replaced state commissions and aristocratic patronage as the most important source of support for artists. Painting remains the greatest creative achievement of Romanticism in the visual arts precisely because, being less expensive, it was less dependent than architecture or sculpture on public approval. It held a correspondingly greater appeal for the individualism of the Romantic artist. Moreover, it could better accommodate the themes and ideas of Romantic literature. Romantic painting was not essentially illustrative; but literature, past and present, now became a more important source of inspiration for painters than ever before, and provided them with a new range of subjects, emotions, and attitudes. Romantic poets, in turn, often saw nature with a painter's eye. Many had a strong interest in art criticism and theory. Some, notably Johann Wolfgang von Goethe and Victor Hugo, were capable draftsmen; and William Blake cast his visions in both pictorial and literary form (see page 687). Art and literature thus have a complex, subtle, and by no means one-sided relationship within the Romantic movement.

Spain

GOYA. We must begin with the great Spanish painter Francisco Goya (1746–1828), David's contemporary and the only artist of the age who may unreservedly be called a genius. When Goya first arrived in Madrid in 1766, he found both Mengs and Tiepolo working there. He was much impressed with the latter (see page 626), whom he must have recognized immediately as the greater of the two. Goya's early works, in a delightful late Rococo vein, reflect the influence of Tiepolo, as well as the French masters of the Rococo. (Spain had produced no painters of significance for over a century.) Nor did he respond to the growing Neoclassic trend during his brief visit to Rome five years later.

In the 1780s, however, Goya became more of a libertarian. His involvement with Enlightenment thought is best seen in his etchings, which made him the most important printmaker since Rembrandt. Published in series at intervals throughout his career, they ridicule human folly from the same moral viewpoint as Hogarth. But what a vast difference separates the two artists! Although suggested by proverbs and popular superstitions, many of Goya's prints defy exact analysis. He creates terrifying scenes such as *The Sleep of Reason Produces Monsters* from the series *Los Caprichos* of the late 1790s (fig. 862). The subtitle, added later, elaborates its meaning: "Imagination abandoned by reason produces impossible monsters; united with her, she is the mother of the arts." The artist, shrinking from the assault of his visions, suffers from the same affliction as Dürer's *Melencolia I* (see fig. 704), but his paralysis is psychological rather than conceptual. The image belongs to that realm of subjectively experienced horror which we will meet in Fuseli's *The Nightmare* (see fig. 884), but is infinitely more compelling. Goya's etching owes part of its success to the technique of aquatint, whose potential he was the first to exploit fully, although he did not invent it (see box page 674).

Goya surely sympathized with the French Revolution, and not with the king of Spain, who had joined other monarchs in war against the young Republic. Yet he was much esteemed at court, where he was appointed painter to the king in 1799. Goya now abandoned the Rococo for a Neo-Baroque style based on Velázquez and Rembrandt, the masters he had come to admire most. It is this Neo-Baroque style that announces the arrival of Romanticism.

The Family of Charles IV (fig. 863), Goya's largest royal portrait, deliberately echoes Velázquez' *The Maids of Honor* (see fig. 759). The entire clan has come to visit the artist, who is painting in one of the picture galleries of the palace. As in the earlier work, shadowy canvases hang behind the group and the light pours in from the side, although its subtle gradations owe as much to Rembrandt as to Velázquez. The brushwork, too, has an incandescent sparkle rivaling that of *The Maids of*

862. Francisco Goya. *The Sleep of Reason Produces Monsters,* from *Los Caprichos.* c. 1798. Etching and aquatint, 8¹⁄₂ x 6" (21.6 x 15.2 cm). The Metropolitan Museum of Art, New York
Gift of M. Knoedler & Co., 1918

863. Francisco Goya. *The Family of Charles IV.* 1800. Oil on canvas, 9'2" x 11' (2.79 x 3.35 m). Museo del Prado, Madrid

864. Francisco Goya. *The Third of May, 1808.* 1814–15. Oil on canvas, 8'9" x 13'4" (2.67 x 4.06 m). Museo del Prado, Madrid

Honor. Goya does not utilize the Caravaggesque Neoclassicism of David, yet his painting has more in common with David's work than we might think. Like David, he practices a revival style and, in his way, is equally devoted to the unvarnished truth: he uses the Neo-Baroque of Romanticism to unmask the royal family.

Psychologically, *The Family of Charles IV* is almost shockingly modern. No longer shielded by the polite conventions of Baroque court portraiture, the inner being of these individuals has been laid bare with pitiless candor. They are like a collection of ghosts: the frightened children, the bloated king, and—in a master stroke of sardonic humor—the grotesquely vulgar queen, posed like Velázquez' Princess Margarita. (Note the left arm and the turn of the head.) How could Goya get away with this? Was the royal family so dazzled by the splendid painting of their costumes that they failed to realize what

New Printmaking Techniques

During the eighteenth century, the range of printmaking was enlarged by the addition of two techniques on copperplates. The first, aquatint, is an extension of etching. It involves melting resin powder on the plate, which leaves a fine crackle pattern exposed to the acid bath. The result is an even, medium tone similar to that of a wash drawing. The other, called mezzotint, is found almost exclusively in portrait and other reproductive engravings. It utilizes a cylindrical rocker covered with tiny teeth to pit the surface, providing velvety grays and rich blacks.

The first completely new print medium, however, was lithography. Invented in Germany shortly before 1800 by Alois Senefelder, it is the most important of the plano-graphic processes, meaning that the print is made on a flat surface. Using a greasy crayon or ink, called tusche, the artist draws or brushes the design onto a special lithographic stone; alternatively, it can be transferred from paper. (Metals such as zinc and aluminum have also been used as plates.) Once the design is fixed by an acid wash, the surface is dampened, then rolled with oily ink, which adheres to the greasy design but is repelled by water. The print is made by rubbing moistened paper under light pressure against the stone. Because a limitless number of prints can be pulled relatively cheaply, lithography has been closely associated from the beginning with commercial printing and the popular press.

865. Anne-Louis Girodet-Trioson. *The Funeral of Atala*. 1808. Oil on canvas, 5'5³/4" x 6'10⁵/8" (1.67 x 2.10 m). Musée du Louvre, Paris

he had done to them? Goya, we realize, must have painted them as they saw themselves, while unveiling the truth for all the world to see.

When Napoleon's armies occupied Spain in 1808, Goya and many other Spaniards hoped that the conquerors would bring the liberal reforms so badly needed. The barbaric behavior of the French troops crushed these hopes and generated a popular resistance of equal savagery. Many of Goya's works from 1810 to 1815 reflect this bitter experience. The greatest is *The Third of May, 1808* (fig. 864), commemorating the execution of a group of Madrid citizens. Here the blazing color, broad, fluid brushwork, and dramatic nocturnal light are more emphatically Neo-Baroque than ever. The picture has all the emotional intensity of religious art, but these martyrs are dying for Liberty, not the Kingdom of Heaven. Nor are their executioners the agents of Satan but of political tyranny: a formation of faceless automatons, impervious to their victims' despair and defiance. The same scene was to be reenacted countless times in modern history. With the clairvoyance of genius, Goya created an image that has become a terrifying symbol of our era.

After the defeat of Napoleon, the restored Spanish monarchy brought a new wave of repression, and Goya withdrew more and more into a private world. Finally, in 1824, he went into voluntary exile. After a brief stay in Paris, Goya settled in Bordeaux, where he died. His importance for the Neo-Baroque Romantic painters of France is well attested by the greatest of them, Eugène Delacroix (see pages 678–81), who said that the ideal style would be a combination of Michelangelo's and Goya's art.

France

GIRODET. By 1795 Neoclassicism had largely run its course, and rapidly lost its purity and rigor. Thus within a few years French Romantic painting began to emerge among the Primitif faction of Jacques Louis David's studio. These rebellious students simplified his stringent Neoclassicism still further by reverting to the linear designs of Greek and Etruscan vase painting, and the unadorned manner of the Italian Early Renaissance. At the same time, they subverted its content by preferring subjects whose appeal was primarily emotional rather than intellectual. Their sources were not the classical authors such as Horace or Ovid but the Bible, Homer, Ossian (the legendary Gaelic bard whose poems were forged by James Macpherson in the eighteenth century), and Romantic literature—anything that excited the imagination. The ablest, as well as most radical, member of the group was Anne-Louis Girodet-Trioson (1767–1824), whose *Funeral of Atala* (fig. 865) has all the hallmarks of the Primitif style. Without abandoning his teacher's exacting technique, he reduces the composition to a rhythmic play of lines across the picture plane by emphasizing simple shapes with strong contours, which are further accentuated by the selective highlighting. The scene is taken from the wildly popular *Atala, or The Love of Two Savages in the Desert* by François-René de Chateaubriand, one of the first Romantic authors and later foreign minister of France. The unfinished novel, published as excerpts in 1801, unites the character of a classical idyll and the taste for the exotic with a religious theme at a time of resurgent Catholicism. These elements are conspicuously present in Girodet's canvas, which treats the burial

866. Antoine-Jean Gros. *Napoleon at Arcole.* 1796. Oil on canvas, 29¹/₂ x 23" (74.9 x 58.4 cm). Musée du Louvre, Paris

867. Théodore Géricault. *Mounted Officer of the Imperial Guard.* 1812. Oil on canvas, 9'7" x 6'4¹/₂" (2.9 x 1.9 m). Musée du Louvre, Paris

of the virtuous young woman in the cave as the entombment of a Christian martyr. (Note the cross on the hillside.) Yet unlike the secular martyrdom memorialized by David in *The Death of Marat,* the painting is a celebration of sentiment. Girodet uses an eerie light to evoke an elegiac mood that is his real aim.

GROS. With its glamour and its adventurous conquests in remote parts of the world, the reign of Napoleon (which lasted from 1799 to 1815, with one interruption) gave rise to French Romanticism. David became an ardent admirer of Napoleon and executed several large pictures glorifying the emperor. As a portrayer of the Napoleonic myth, however, he was partially eclipsed by artists who had been his students. They felt the style of David too confining and fostered a Baroque revival to capture the excitement of the age. Antoine-Jean Gros (1771–1835), David's favorite pupil, shows us Napoleon as a 27-year-old general leading his troops at the Battle of Arcole in northern Italy (fig. 866). Painted in Milan, soon after the series of victories that gave the French the Lombard plain, it conveys Napoleon's magic as an irresistible "man of destiny," with a Romantic enthusiasm David could never match.

After Napoleon's empire collapsed, David spent his last years in exile in Brussels, where his major works were playfully amorous subjects drawn from ancient myths or legends and painted in a coolly sensuous Neo-Mannerist style he had initiated in Paris. He turned his pupils over to Gros, urging him to return to Neoclassic orthodoxy. Much as Gros respected his teacher's doctrines, his emotional nature impelled him toward the color and drama of the Baroque. He remained torn between his pic-

torial instincts and these academic principles. Consequently, he never achieved David's authority and ended his life by suicide.

GÉRICAULT. The Neo-Baroque trend initiated in France by Gros aroused the imagination of many talented younger artists. The chief heroes of Théodore Géricault (1791–1824), apart from Gros, were Michelangelo and the great Baroque masters. *Mounted Officer of the Imperial Guard* (fig. 867), painted by Géricault at the astonishing age of 21, offers the same conception of the Romantic hero as Gros' *Napoleon at Arcole* (see fig. 866), but on a large scale and with a Rubens-like energy. For Géricault, politics no longer had the force of a faith. All he saw in Napoleon's campaigns was the thrill—irresistible to the Romantic—of violent action. Ultimately, the ancestors of this splendid figure are the equestrian soldiers in Leonardo's *Battle of Anghiari* (see fig. 597); as in Leonardo's equestrian image, the rider becomes one with his animal, whose frenzy he shares. Géricault, himself an enthusiastic horseman, later became interested in the British animal painters such as George Stubbs (see pages 663–64).

Géricault painted his most ambitious work, *The Raft of the "Medusa"* (fig. 868), in response to a political scandal and a modern tragedy of epic proportions. The *Medusa,* a government vessel, had foundered off the West African coast with hundreds of men on board. Only a handful were rescued, after many days on a makeshift raft which had been set adrift by the ship's heartless captain and officers. The event attracted Géricault's attention because, like many French liberals, he opposed the monarchy that was restored after Napoleon. He went to extra-

868. Théodore Géricault. *The Raft of the "Medusa."* 1818–19. Oil on canvas, 16'1" x 23'6" (4.9 x 7.16 m). Musée du Louvre, Paris

ordinary lengths in trying to achieve a maximum of authenticity. He interviewed survivors, had a model of the raft built, even studied corpses in the morgue. This search for uncompromising truth is like David's, and *The Raft* is indeed remarkable for its powerfully realistic detail. Yet these preparations were subordinate in the end to the spirit of heroic drama that dominates the canvas. Géricault depicts the exciting moment when the rescue ship is first sighted. From the prostrate bodies of the dead and dying in the foreground, the composition is built up to a climax in the group that supports the frantically waving black man, so that the forward surge of the survivors parallels the movement of the raft itself. Sensing, perhaps, that this theme of "man against the elements" would have strong appeal across the Channel, where Copley had painted *Watson and the Shark* 40 years before (fig. 846), Géricault took the monumental canvas to England on a traveling exhibit in 1820.

His numerous studies for *The Raft of the "Medusa"* had taught him how to explore extremes of the human condition scarcely touched by earlier artists. He went now not only to the morgue, but to the insane asylum of Paris. There he became a friend of Dr. Georget, a pioneer in modern psychiatry, and painted for him a series of portraits of individual patients to illustrate various types of derangement, such as that in figure 869. The conception and execution of this oil sketch has an immediacy that recalls Frans Hals, but Géricault's sympathy toward his subject makes his work contrast tellingly with *Malle Babbe* (see fig. 773). This ability to see the victims of mental disease as fellow human beings, not as accursed or bewitched outcasts, is one of the noblest fruits of the Romantic movement.

869. Théodore Géricault. *The Madman.* 1821–24.
Oil on canvas, 24 x 20" (61 x 50.8 cm). Museum voor
Schone Kunsten, Ghent, Belgium

870. Jean-Auguste-Dominique Ingres. *Odalisque.* 1814. Oil on canvas, 35¼ x 63¾" (89.7 x 162 cm). Musée du Louvre, Paris

INGRES. The mantle of David finally descended upon his pupil Jean-Auguste-Dominique Ingres (1780–1867). Too young to share in the political passions of the Revolution, Ingres never was an enthusiastic Bonapartist. In 1806 he went to Italy and remained for 18 years, so that he largely missed out on the formation of Romantic painting in France. Thus after his return he became the high priest of the Davidian tradition, defending it from the onslaughts of younger artists. [See Primary Sources, no. 80, page 935.] What had been a revolutionary style only half a century before now congealed into rigid dogma, endorsed by the government and backed by the weight of conservative opinion.

Ingres is usually called a Neoclassicist, and his opponents Romantics. Actually, both factions stood for aspects of Romanticism after 1800: the Neoclassic phase, with Ingres as the last important survivor, and the Neo-Baroque, first announced in France by Gros' *Napoleon at Arcole.* Indeed, the two seem so interdependent that we should prefer a single name for both if we could find a suitable one. ("Romantic Classicism," which is appropriate only to the classical camp, has not won wide acceptance.) The two sides seemed to revive the old quarrel between Poussinistes and Rubénistes (see page 612). The original Poussinistes had never quite practiced what they preached, and Ingres' views, too, were far more doctrinaire than his pictures. He always held that drawing was superior to painting, yet a canvas such as his *Odalisque* (fig. 870) reveals an exquisite sense of color. Instead of merely tinting his design, he sets off the petal-smooth limbs of this Oriental Venus (*odalisque* is a Turkish word for a harem slave girl) with a dazzling array of rich tones and textures. The exotic subject, redolent with the enchantment of the *Thousand and One Nights,* is characteristic of the Romantic movement. (It would be perfectly at home in the Royal Pavilion at Brighton; see fig. 912.) Despite Ingres' professed worship of Raphael, this nude embodies no classical ideal of beauty. Her elongated proportions, languid grace, and strange mixture of coolness and voluptuousness

remind us, rather, of Parmigianino's figures (compare fig. 640).

History painting as defined by Poussin remained Ingres' lifelong ambition, but he had great difficulty with it, while portraiture, which he pretended to dislike, was his strongest gift and his steadiest source of income. He was, in fact, the last great professional in a field soon to be dominated by the camera. Ingres' *Louis Bertin* (fig. 871) at first glance looks like a kind of "super-photograph," but this impression is deceptive. Comparing it with the preliminary pencil drawing (fig. 872), we realize how much interpretation the portrait contains. The drawing, quick, sure, and precise, is a masterpiece of detached observation, but the painting endows the sitter with a massive force of personality. Bertin's pose is shifted slightly to the left, his jacket open to lend the figure greater weight. The position of his powerful hands, which are barely indicated in the drawing, has been adjusted to convey an almost leonine strength. Ingres further applies the Caravaggesque Neoclassicism he had inherited from David to introduce slight changes of light and emphasis in the face, subtly altering its expression, which now manifests a frightening intensity.

Among the Romantics, only Ingres could so unify psychological depth and physical accuracy. His followers focused on physical accuracy alone, competing vainly with the camera. The Neo-Baroque Romantics, in contrast, emphasized the psychological aspect to such a degree that their portraits tended to become records of the artist's private emotional relationship with the sitter. Often these are interesting and moving, but they are no longer portraits in the proper sense of the term.

DELACROIX. The year 1824 was crucial for French painting. Géricault died after a riding accident. Ingres returned to France from Italy and had his first public success. The first showing in Paris of works by the English Romantic painter John Constable was a revelation to many French artists (see pages 667–70). *The Massacre at Chios* (fig. 873) established

871. Jean-Auguste-Dominique Ingres. *Louis Bertin*. 1832. Oil on canvas, 46 x 37¹/₂" (116.8 x 95.3 cm). Musée du Louvre, Paris

872. Jean-Auguste-Dominique Ingres. *Louis Bertin*. 1832. Pencil drawing. Musée du Louvre, Paris

873. Eugène Delacroix. *The Massacre at Chios*. 1822–24. Oil on canvas, 13'10" x 11'7" (4.2 x 3.5 m). Musée du Louvre, Paris

874. Eugène Delacroix. *Odalisque*. 1845–50.
Oil on canvas, 14⁷/8 x 18¹/4" (37.3 x 46.5 cm). Fitzwilliam Museum, Cambridge, England

Eugène Delacroix as the foremost Neo-Baroque Romantic painter. An admirer of both Gros and Géricault, Delacroix (1798–1863) had been exhibiting for some years, but *The Massacre* made his reputation. Conservatives called it "the massacre of painting," others acclaimed it enthusiastically. For the next quarter-century, he and Ingres were acknowledged rivals, and their polarity, fostered by partisans, dominated the artistic scene in Paris. [See Primary Sources, no. 81, page 935.]

Like *The Raft of the "Medusa," The Massacre at Chios* was inspired by a contemporary event: the Greek war of independence against the Turks, which stirred a wave of sympathy throughout western Europe. (The full title of the painting is *Scenes of the Massacre at Chios: Greek Families Awaiting Death or Slavery.*) Delacroix, however, aimed at "poetic truth" rather than at recapturing a specific, actual event. In this, he relied on tradition to a surprising degree, for he has conjured up a scene as brutal as *The Abduction of the Sabine Women* by Nicolas Poussin (compare fig. 794). The picture is treated as the kind of secular martyrdom already familiar to us from Benjamin West's *The Death of General Wolfe* (fig. 845). Now, however, the victims are as nameless as those in *The Raft of the "Medusa."*

Such sources have been combined into an intoxicating mixture of sensuousness and cruelty. Delacroix does not entirely succeed, however, in forcing us to suspend our disbelief. While we revel in the sheer splendor of the painting, we do not quite accept the human experience as authentic. We react instead much as we do to J. M. W. Turner's *Slave Ship* (see fig. 890). One reason may be the discontinuity of the fore-

875. Eugène Delacroix. *The Entombment of Christ*. 1848.
Oil on canvas, 64 x 52" (162.6 x 132.1 cm).
Museum of Fine Arts, Boston

ground, with its dramatic contrasts of light and shade, and the luminous sweep of the landscape behind. Delacroix is said to have hastily repainted part of the background after seeing Constable's *The Haywain* (see fig. 888). Originally, the background of *The Massacre* was probably like that in Géricault's *Mounted Officer* (fig. 867), and the Turkish horseman, too, directly recalls the rider in the earlier picture.

Delacroix's sympathy with the Greeks did not prevent him from sharing the enthusiasm of fellow Romantics for the Near East. He was enchanted by a visit to North Africa in 1832, finding there a living counterpart of the violent, chivalric, and picturesque past evoked in Romantic literature. His sketches from this trip supplied him with a large repertory of subjects for the rest of his life: harem interiors, street scenes, lion hunts. It is fascinating to compare his *Odalisque* (fig. 874) with Ingres' (fig. 870). Sonorous color and the energetically fluid brushwork show Delacroix to be a Rubéniste of the first order. In his version, Ingres also celebrates the exotic world of the Near East—alien, seductive, and violent—but how different the result! Reclining in ecstatic repose, Delacroix's *Odalisque* exudes passionate abandon and animal vitality—the exact opposite of Ingres' ideal.

The Entombment of Christ (fig. 875), painted in 1848, marks a shift in Delacroix's art. The painting has a new grandeur and an air of almost classical restraint. This change was perhaps an outgrowth of a decorative cycle Delacroix did over the previous several years in the Bourbon Palace, which brought him into renewed contact with the tradition of Western art: his work shows a preference for literary and biblical themes, without abandoning his earlier subjects. This may be seen as part of a larger crisis of tradition that gripped French art beginning in 1848, when revolution was in the air everywhere. Delacroix was now seen, with Ingres, as the last great representative of the mainstream of European painting. As the critic Charles Baudelaire wrote in his Salon of 1846: "Delacroix is . . . heir to the great tradition. . . . But take away Delacroix, and the great chain of history is broken and slips to the ground. It is true that the great tradition has been lost, and that the new one is not yet established." *The Entombment* suggests Delacroix's awareness of his new status. The painting combines overtones of Titian and Rubens with Poussinesque nobility to make it that rarity in nineteenth-century art—a truly moving religious image.

DAUMIER. The later work of Delacroix reflects the attitude that eventually doomed the Romantic movement: its growing detachment from contemporary life. History, literature, the Bible, and the Near East were the domains of the imagination where he sought refuge from the turmoil of the Industrial Revolution. It is ironic that Honoré Daumier (1808–1879), one of the few Romantic artists who did not shrink from reality, remained in his day practically unknown as a painter. He turned to painting in the 1840s but found no public for his work. Only a few friends encouraged him and, a year before his death, arranged his first solo exhibition. Thus his pictures had little impact during his lifetime. A biting political cartoonist, Daumier contributed satirical drawings to various Paris weeklies for most of his career. Nearly all of Daumier's cartoons were done with lithography (see box page 674).

876. Honoré Daumier. *It's Safe to Release This One!* 1834. Lithograph

Although Daumier is sometimes called a realist, his work falls entirely within the range of Romanticism. The neat outlines and systematic crosshatching in Daumier's early cartoons (fig. 876) show his conservative training. He quickly developed a bolder and more personal style of draftsmanship, however, and his paintings of the 1850s and 1860s have the full pictorial range of the Neo-Baroque. Their subjects vary widely. Many show aspects of everyday urban life that also occur in his cartoons, now viewed with a painter's eye rather than from a satirist's angle. In *The Third-Class Carriage* (fig. 877), Daumier's forms reflect the compactness of Millet's (compare fig. 882), but are painted so freely that they must have seemed raw and "unfinished" even by Delacroix's standards. Yet its power derives from this very freedom. Daumier's concern is not for the tangible surface of reality but for the emotional meaning behind it. In *The Third-Class Carriage*, he has captured a peculiarly modern human condition: "the lonely crowd." These people have in common only that they are traveling together in a railway car. Though they are physically crowded, they take no notice of one another, for each is alone with his or her own thoughts. Daumier explores this state with an insight into character and a breadth of human sympathy worthy of Rembrandt, whose work he revered. His feeling for the dignity of the poor also suggests the Le Nains, who had recently been rediscovered by French critics. Indeed, the old woman on the left in Louis Le Nain's *Peasant Family* (fig. 792) seems the direct ancestor of the central figure in *The Third-Class Carriage*.

Other paintings by Daumier have subjects more characteristic of Romanticism. The numerous canvases and drawings of the adventures of Don Quixote, from Cervantes' sixteenth-century novel, show the fascination this theme had for him. The lanky knight-errant, vainly trying to live his dream of noble deeds, and Sancho Panza, the dumpy materialist, seemed to embody for Daumier a tragic conflict within human nature that forever pits the soul against the body, ideal

877. Honoré Daumier. *The Third-Class Carriage.* c. 1862.
Oil on canvas, 25³/4 x 35¹/2"(65.4 x 90.2 cm). The Metropolitan Museum of Art, New York
Bequest of Mrs. H. O. Havemeyer, 1929. The H. O. Havemeyer Collection

878. Honoré Daumier. *Don Quixote Attacking the Windmills.*
c. 1866. Oil on canvas, 22¹/4 x 33" (56.5 x 83.7 cm).
Collection Mr. Charles S. Payson, New York

aspirations against harsh reality. In *Don Quixote Attacking the Windmills* (fig. 878), this polarity is forcefully realized. The mock hero dashes off in the noonday heat toward an invisible, distant goal, while Panza helplessly wrings his hands, a monument of despair. The sculptured simplicity of Daumier's shapes, and the expressive freedom of his brushwork, make Delacroix's art seem almost conventional by comparison.

French Landscape Painting

Thanks to the cult of nature, landscape painting became the most characteristic form of Romantic art. The Romantics believed that God's laws could be seen written in nature. While it arose out of the Enlightenment, their faith, known as pantheism, was based not on rational thought but on subjective experience, and the appeal to the emotions rather than the intellect made those lessons all the more compelling. In order to express the feelings inspired by nature, the Romantics sought to transcribe landscape as faithfully as possible, in contrast to the Neoclassicists, who subjected landscape to prescribed ideas of beauty and linked it to historical subjects. At the same time, the Romantics felt equally free to modify nature's appearance as a means of evoking heightened states of mind in accordance with dictates of the imagination, the only standard they ultimately recognized. Landscape inspired the Romantics with passions so exalted that only in the hands of the greatest history painters could humans equal nature in power as protagonists. Hence, the Romantic landscape lies outside the descriptive and emotional range of the eighteenth century.

COROT. The first and undeniably greatest French Romantic landscape painter was Camille Corot (1796–1875). In 1825 he went to Italy for two years and explored the countryside around Rome, like a latter-day Claude Lorraine. What Claude recorded in his drawings—the quality of a particular place at a particular time—Corot made into paintings, small canvases done on the spot in an hour or so (fig. 879). In size and immediacy, these quickly executed pictures are analogous to Constable's oil sketches (see fig. 887), yet they stem from different traditions. If Constable's view of nature, which emphasizes the sky as "the chief organ of sentiment," is derived from Dutch seventeenth-century landscapes, Corot's instinct for architectural clarity and stability recalls Poussin and

879. Camille Corot. *View of Rome: The Bridge and Castel Sant'Angelo with the Cupola of St. Peter's.*
1826–27. Oil on paper mounted on canvas, 10^1/$_2$ x 17" (22 x 38 cm). Fine Arts Museums of San Francisco
Museum Purchase, Archer M. Huntington Fund

880. Camille Corot. *Morning: Dance of the Nymphs.* 1850. Oil on canvas, 38^5/$_8$ x 51^5/$_8$" (97.1 x 130 cm). Musée d'Orsay, Paris

Claude. But he, too, insists on "the truth of the moment." His exact observation and his readiness to seize upon any view that attracted him during his excursions show the same commitment to direct visual experience that we find in Constable. The Neoclassicists had also painted oil sketches out-of-doors. Unlike them, Corot did not transform his sketches into idealized pastoral visions. His willingness to accept them as inde-

pendent works of art marks him unmistakably as a Romantic.

After returning from his second visit to Italy in 1834, Corot began to paint historical landscapes which combine stylistic and topographical features from Italy and the North in eclectic fashion. But during the 1840s he gradually developed a unique style that appears in its definitive form in *Morning: Dance of the Nymphs* (fig. 880). The painting has rightly

881. Théodore Rousseau. *A Meadow Bordered by Trees.* c. 1840–45.
Oil on panel, 16³/8 x 24³/8" (41.6 x 61.9 cm). The Metropolitan Museum of Art, New York
Bequest of Robert Graham Dun, 1911

been called a souvenir of the opera, especially the ballets traditional in Parisian productions which he habitually sketched. He found in them a common bond of feeling with painting that provided inspiration for his work. The landscape shows a new unity between the figures and their setting. The silvery light creates a veiled atmosphere that envelops the forms and lends the painting an elusive mood reminiscent of that in Poussin's late works (see fig. 795). In this way, Corot reconciles romantic sentiment and classical content.

Morning: Dance of the Nymphs was the outgrowth of the crisis of tradition in French art and of a personal crisis: when he painted it, Corot was approaching old age with considerable anxiety, and in Poussin he discovered a kindred spirit burdened with similar fears. Thus it was Corot's own development that enabled him to unlock the secret of late Poussin and learn how to interpret nature in a deeply poetic way.

ROUSSEAU. Corot's early fidelity to nature was an important model for the Barbizon School, though he was not actually a member. This group of younger painters, centering on Théodore Rousseau (1812–1867), settled in the village of Barbizon on the edge of the forest of Fontainebleau near Paris to paint landscapes and scenes of rural life. Enthused, however, by Constable, whose work had been exhibited in Paris in 1824, they turned to the Northern Baroque landscape as an alternative to the Neoclassical tradition. From Ruisdael's

example (fig. 783), Rousseau learned how to imbue his encrusted forms and gnarled trees with a sense of inner life, but it was the hours of solitary contemplation in the forest of Fontainebleau that enabled him to penetrate nature's secrets. *A Meadow Bordered by Trees* (fig. 881) is a splendid representative of his landscapes, which are filled with a simple veneration that admirably reflects the rallying cry of the Romantics—sincerity.

MILLET. Jean-François Millet (1814–1875) became a member of the Barbizon School in 1848, the year revolution swept France and the rest of Europe. Although he was no radical, *The Sower* (fig. 882) was championed by liberal critics, because it was the very opposite of the Neoclassical history paintings sanctioned by the establishment. Millet's archetypal image nonetheless has a self-consciously classical flavor that reflects his admiration for Poussin. Blurred in the hazy atmosphere, this "hero of the soil" is a timeless symbol of the ceaseless labor that the artist viewed as the peasant's inexorable fate. (Could Millet have known the pathetic sower from the October page of *Les Très Riches Heures du Duc de Berry?* Compare fig. 522.) Ironically, the painting monumentalizes a rural way of life that was rapidly disappearing under the pressure of the Industrial Revolution. For that very reason, however, the peasant was seen as the quintessential victim of the evils arising from the Machine Age.

882. Jean-François Millet. *The Sower.* c. 1850. Oil on canvas, 40 x 32½" (101.6 x 82.6 cm). Museum of Fine Arts, Boston
Gift of Quincy Adams Shaw through Quincy A. Shaw, Jr., and Mrs. Marion Shaw Haughton

883. Rosa Bonheur. *Plowing in the Nivernais.* 1849. Oil on canvas, 5'9" x 8'8" (1.75 x 2.64 m). Musée d'Orsay, Paris

BONHEUR. The Barbizon School generally advocated a return to nature as a way of fleeing the social ills attendant to industrialization and urbanization. Despite their conservative outlook, these artists were elevated to a new prominence in French art by the popular revolution of 1848. That same year Rosa Bonheur (1822–1899), also an artist who worked out-of-doors, received a French government commission that led to her first great success and helped to establish her as a leading painter of animals—and eventually as the most famous woman artist of her time. [See Primary Sources, no. 82, page 936.] Her painting *Plowing in the Nivernais* (fig. 883) was exhibited the following year, after a winter spent making studies from life. The theme of humanity's union with nature had already been popularized in the country romances of George Sand, among others. Bonheur's picture shares Millet's reverence for peasant life, but the real subject here, as in all her work, is the animals within the landscape. These she depicts with a convincing naturalism that later placed her among the most influential realists.

England

FUSELI. England was as precocious in nurturing Romanticism as it had been in promoting Neoclassicism. In fact, one of its first representatives, John Henry Fuseli (1741–1825), was a contemporary of West and Copley. This Swiss-born painter (originally named Füssli) had an extraordinary impact on his time, more perhaps because of his adventurous and forceful personality than the merits of his work. Ordained a minister at 20, he had left the Church by 1764 and gone to London in search of freedom. Encouraged by Reynolds, he spent the 1770s in Rome. There he encountered Gavin Hamilton, but Fuseli based his style on Michelangelo and the Mannerists, not on Poussin and the antique. A German acquaintance of those years described him as "extreme in everything, Shakespeare's painter." Shakespeare and Michelangelo were indeed his twin

884. John Henry Fuseli. *The Nightmare.* c. 1790. Oil on canvas, 29½ x 25¼" (74.9 x 64.1 cm). Freies Deutsches Hochstift-Frankfurter Goethe-Museum, Frankfurt

gods. He even visualized a Sistine Chapel with Michelangelo's figures transformed into Shakespearean characters where the sublime would be the common denominator for "classic" and "Gothic" Romanticism. Such fusion marks Fuseli as a transitional figure. He espoused many of the same Neoclassical theories as Reynolds, West, and Kauffmann, but bent their rules virtually to the breaking point.

885. William Blake. *The Ancient of Days,* frontispiece of *Europe, A Prophesy.* 1794. Metal relief etching, hand-colored illustration, 9¹/8 x 6⁵/8" (23.2 x 16.8 cm). Library of Congress, Washington, D.C.
Lessing J. Rosenwald Collection

886. Taddeo Zuccaro. *The Conversion of St. Paul* (detail). c. 1555. Oil on canvas. Galleria Doria Pamphili, Rome

We see this in *The Nightmare* (fig. 884). The sleeping woman, more Mannerist than Michelangelesque, is Neoclassical. The grinning devil and the luminescent horse, however, come from the demon-ridden world of medieval folklore, while the Rembrandtesque lighting reminds us of Reynolds (compare fig. 828). Here the Romantic quest for terrifying experiences leads not to physical violence but to the dark recesses of the mind. What was the genesis of *The Nightmare*? Nightmares often have a strongly sexual connotation, sometimes quite openly expressed, at other times concealed behind a variety of disguises. We know that Fuseli originally conceived the subject not long after his return from Italy, when he had fallen violently in love with a friend's niece who soon married a merchant, much to the artist's distress. We can see in the picture a projection of his "dream girl," with the demon taking the artist's place while the horse, a well-known erotic symbol, looks on.

BLAKE. Later, in London, Fuseli befriended the poet-painter William Blake (1757–1827), who possessed an even greater creativity and stranger personality than his own. A recluse and visionary, Blake produced and published his own books of poems with engraved text and hand-colored illustrations. Though he never left England, he acquired a large repertory of Michelangelesque and Mannerist motifs from engravings, as well as through the influence of Fuseli. He also conceived a

tremendous admiration for the Middle Ages, and came closer than any other Romantic artist to reviving pre-Renaissance forms. (His books were meant to be the successors of illuminated manuscripts.)

These elements are all present in Blake's memorable image *The Ancient of Days* (fig. 885). The muscular figure, radically foreshortened and fitted into a circle of light, is derived from Mannerist sources (see fig. 886), while the symbolic compasses come from medieval representations of the Lord as Architect of the Universe. With these precedents, we would expect the Ancient of Days to signify Almighty God, but in Blake's esoteric mythology, he stands rather for the power of reason, which the poet regarded as ultimately destructive, since it stifles vision and inspiration. To Blake, the "inner eye" was all-important; he felt no need to observe the visible world around him.

English Landscape Painting

CONSTABLE. It was nevertheless in landscape rather than in narrative scenes that English painting reached its fullest expression. During the eighteenth century, landscape paintings had been, for the most part, imaginative exercises conforming to Northern and Italian examples. John Constable (1776–1837) admired both Ruisdael and Claude, yet he strenuously opposed all flights of fancy. Landscape painting, he believed, must be based on observable facts. It should aim

887. John Constable. *Hampstead Heath.* 1821. Oil sketch on paper, mounted on canvas, 10 x 12" (25.3 x 30.5 cm). City Art Galleries, Manchester, England

888. John Constable. *The Haywain.* 1821. Oil on canvas, 4'3¹/₄" x 6'1" (1.3 x 1.85 m). The National Gallery, London

at "embodying a pure apprehension of natural effect." Toward that end, he painted countless oil sketches outdoors. These were not the first such studies, but, more than his predecessors, he was concerned with the intangible qualities—conditions of sky, light, and atmosphere—rather than the concrete details of the scene. Often, as in *Hampstead Heath* (fig. 887), the land serves as no more than a foil for the ever-changing drama over-head, which he studied with a meteorologist's accuracy, the bet-ter to grasp its infinite variety. In endeavoring to record these fleeting effects, he arrived at a painting technique as broad, free, and personal as that of Cozens' "ink-blot landscapes," even though his point of departure was the exact opposite.

All of Constable's pictures show familiar views of the Eng-lish countryside. It was, he later claimed, the scenery around

889. John Constable. *Salisbury Cathedral from the Meadows.* 1829–34. Oil on canvas, 59³/4 x 74³/4" (151.8 x 189.9 cm). Private collection, on loan to the National Gallery, London

his native Stour Valley that made him a painter. [See Primary Sources, no. 83, page 936.] Although he painted the final versions in his studio, he prepared them by making oil studies based on sketches from nature. The sky, to him, remained "the key note, standard scale, and the chief organ of sentiment," as a mirror of those sweeping forces so dear to the Romantic view of nature. In *The Haywain* (fig. 888), painted the same year as *Hampstead Heath,* he has caught a particularly splendid moment: a great expanse of wind, sunlight, and clouds over the spacious landscape. The earth and sky have both become organs of sentiment informed with the artist's poetic sensibility. At the same time, there is an intimacy in this monumental composition that reveals Constable's deep love of the countryside. This new, personal note is characteristically Romantic. Since Constable has painted the landscape with such conviction, we see the scene through his eyes and believe him, even though it perhaps did not look quite this way in reality.

In 1829 a marked change came over Constable's work. Deeply affected by his wife's death a year earlier, he was subject to darkened moods. *Salisbury Cathedral from the Meadows* (fig. 889), begun that summer, stands as his most personal state-

ment. When the canvas was exhibited two years later, he appended nine lines from *The Seasons* by the eighteenth-century poet James Thomson that reveal its meaning: the rainbow is a symbol of hope after a storm that follows on the death of the young Amelia in the arms of her lover Celadon. Although a political intent has sometimes been seen in the landscape, there can be little doubt of its autobiographical significance. To the left of the huge ash tree, a symbol of life, is a cenotaph; to the right the great church, one of his major themes, a symbol of faith and resurrection. The rainbow, added late in the composition's development, suggests the artist's renewed optimism. Thus the painting reflects his changing frame of mind.

Constable continued to work on *The Rainbow,* as he called it, on and off for several more years. He attached great importance to the painting, which he regarded as the fullest expression of his art and felt would be considered his finest work by future generations. It is indeed an astonishing achievement. The amazingly free application of paint (much of it done with a palette knife) and rich, somber color evoke an agitation not seen before in his landscapes. All nature is caught up in the fury of a cataclysmic event beyond human comprehension.

890. Joseph Mallord William Turner. *The Slave Ship*. 1840.
Oil on canvas, 35³/4 x 48" (90.8 x 121.9 cm). Museum of Fine Arts, Boston
Henry Lillie Pierce Fund (Purchase)

Every leaf, every branch acts as an index of feeling, expressing the artist's turbulent emotions. Once again it is the sky that provides the keynote: now the storm has clearly passed. No other painter before or since was able to capture the play of the elements with such power. Even paintings by his great rival Joseph Mallord William Turner seem tame by comparison.

TURNER. Joseph Mallord William Turner (1775–1851) arrived at a style that Constable deprecatingly but accurately described as "airy visions, painted with tinted steam." Turner began as a watercolorist; the use of translucent tints on white paper may help to explain his preoccupation with colored light. Like Constable, he made copious studies from nature (though not in oils), but the scenery he selected satisfied the Romantic taste for the picturesque and the sublime—mountains, the sea, or sites linked with historic events. In his full-scale pictures he often changed these views so freely that they became quite unrecognizable.

Many of Turner's landscapes are linked with literary themes and bear such titles as *The Destruction of Sodom,* or *Snowstorm: Hannibal Crossing the Alps,* or *Childe Harold's Pilgrimage: Italy.* When they were exhibited, he would add appropriate quotations from ancient or modern authors to the catalogue, or he would make up some lines himself and claim to be "citing" his own unpublished poem, "Fallacies of Hope." Yet these canvases are the opposite of history painting as defined by Poussin: the titles indeed indicate "noble and seri-

ous human actions," but the tiny figures, who are lost in the seething violence of nature, suggest the ultimate defeat of all endeavor—"the fallacies of hope."

The Slave Ship (fig. 890) is one of Turner's most spectacular visions and illustrates how he transmuted his literary sources into "tinted steam." First entitled *Slavers Throwing Overboard the Dead and Dying—Typhoon Coming On,* the painting compounds several levels of meaning. Like Géricault's *The Raft of the "Medusa"* (see fig. 868), which had been exhibited in England in 1820, it has to do, in part, with a specific incident that Turner had recently read about.

When an epidemic broke out on a slave ship, the captain jettisoned his human cargo because he was insured against the loss of slaves at sea, but not by disease. Turner also thought of a relevant passage from James Thomson's poem *The Seasons* that describes how sharks follow a slave ship during a typhoon, "lured by the scent of steaming crowds, or rank disease, and death." But what is the relation between the slaver's action and the typhoon? Are the dead and dying slaves being cast into the sea against the threat of the storm, perhaps to lighten the ship? Is the typhoon nature's retribution for the captain's greed and cruelty? Of the many storms at sea that Turner painted, none has quite this apocalyptic quality. A cosmic catastrophe seems about to engulf everything, not merely the "guilty" slaver but the sea itself, with its crowds of fantastic and oddly harmless-looking fish.

While we still feel the force of Turner's imagination, most

891. Joseph Mallord William Turner. *Rain, Steam and Speed—The Great Western Railway.* 1844.
Oil on canvas, 35³/4 x 48" (90.8 x 122 cm). The National Gallery, London

of us enjoy, perhaps with a twinge of guilt, the tinted steam for its own sake rather than as a vehicle of the awesome emotions the artist meant to evoke. Even in terms of the values he himself acknowledged, Turner strikes us as "a virtuoso of the Sublime," led astray by his very exuberance. He must have been pleased by praise from the theorist John Ruskin, that protagonist of the moral superiority of Gothic style, who saw in *The Slave Ship,* which he owned, "the true, the beautiful, and the intellectual"—all qualities that raised Turner above older landscape painters. Still, Turner may have come to wonder if his tinted steam had its intended effect on all beholders. Soon after finishing *The Slave Ship,* he read in his copy of Goethe's *Color Theory,* recently translated into English, that yellow has a "gay, softly exciting character," while orange-red suggests "warmth and gladness." Surely these would not be the emotions aroused by *The Slave Ship* in a viewer who did not know its title. Interestingly enough, Turner soon modified his approach to take Goethe's ideas into account. He even painted a pair of canvases about the Deluge that were meant to illustrate Goethe's theory of positive (light and warm) and minus (dark and cold) colors; yet they hardly differ in appearance from the rest of his work.

Many of Turner's paintings had their origin in watercolors called "color beginnings" that are as abstract as American Color Field Painting (see pages 826–27). Nevertheless, they always retained a basis in the artist's actual experiences. Indeed, Turner seems to have sought them out. *Rain, Steam and*

Speed—The Great Western Railway (fig. 891) shows the recently completed Maidenhead railway bridge looking across the Thames River toward London. It was painted after Turner stuck his head out of a window on the Exeter express for some nine minutes during a rainstorm. One could hardly ask for a more vivid impression of speed and atmospheric turbulence! Yet, in a touch of delicious irony, he has added a hare (hardly visible in our illustration) racing ahead of the oncoming train.

WATERCOLORS. Turner was the preeminent watercolorist of his time. Watercolors were first introduced into Britain by visiting Northerners, who had used them as a means of recording on-the-spot observations since the time of Dürer (see fig. 699), but the English made the medium their own. Because they became an indispensable part of the genteel person's education, watercolors are often thought of as an amateur's medium. After the middle of the eighteenth century, however, they emerged as a vehicle of serious artistic expression in the hands of gifted painters like Thomas Gainsborough (see page 618). There was a direct lineage from them to Turner and Constable, who turned to them late in his career. It descended through Cozens' equally talented son, John Robert Cozens (1752–1797), the first to introduce poetic melancholy into watercolors, and Thomas Girtin (1752–1802), Turner's brilliant contemporary, who during his brief career revolutionized the English landscape by investing it with a Romantic mood. The full potential of watercolors was realized only in the

892. John Cotman. *Durham Cathedral*. 1805. Watercolor on paper, 17¼ x 13" (43.8 x 33 cm). The British Museum, London

tern. The result is an expressiveness of astonishing intensity. Cotman emphasizes the sheer massiveness of the great church, which looms over the house below, as if threatening to crush it. The landscape bespeaks the English Romantic fascination with the Gothic. It inspired him with much the same sentiment found in Ruisdael's *The Jewish Cemetery* (fig. 783), while the picture has the elemental power of Constable's *Salisbury Cathedral from the Meadows* (fig. 889). Did Cotman intend it as a testimony of his personal faith? Of man's works, he seems to say, only the cathedral, a house of worship, will endure. Yet we know surprisingly little about his beliefs.

Germany

FRIEDRICH. In Germany, as in England, landscape was the finest achievement of Romantic painting, and the underlying ideas, too, were often strikingly similar. About 1800 German artists rediscovered the Gothic, which they regarded as their native heritage. For the most part, this "Gothic Revival" remained limited in subject matter and scope, but in the hands of Caspar David Friedrich (1774–1840), the most important German Romantic artist, it acquired a haunting mystery. A devout Protestant, he had a pantheistic love of nature that became a vehicle of profound religious sentiment. In *Abbey in an Oak Forest* (fig. 893) all is death—the ancient graves, the barren trees, and ruined church silhouetted against the somber winter sky at twilight. Yet we contemplate the forlorn scene with the same hushed reverence as the solemn procession of monks. Hardly distinguishable from the tombstones, they seek the crucifix enshrined in the arched portal, which offers eternal life to the faithful. The frozen stillness is in marked contrast to the painting by Ruisdael that probably inspired it (similar to fig. 783). Infinitely lonely, the bleak landscape is a reflection of the artist's own melancholy.

When Friedrich painted *The Polar Sea* (fig. 894), he may have known of Turner's "Fallacies of Hope," for in an earlier picture on the same theme (now lost) he had inscribed the name "Hope" on the crushed vessel. In any case, he shared Turner's attitude toward human fate. The painting, as so often before, was inspired by a specific event which the artist endowed with symbolic significance: a dangerous moment in William Parry's Arctic expedition of 1819–20.

One wonders how Turner might have depicted this scene. Perhaps it would have been too static for him, but Friedrich was attracted by this very immobility. He has visualized the piled-up slabs of ice as a kind of megalithic monument to human defeat built by nature itself. There is no hint of tinted steam—the very air seems frozen—nor any subjective handwriting. We look right through the paint-covered surface at a reality that seems created without the painter's intervention.

This technique, impersonal and meticulous, is peculiar to German Romantic painting. It stems from the early Neoclassicists, but the Germans, whose tradition of Baroque painting was weak, adopted it more wholeheartedly than the English or the French. Friedrich absorbed this approach at the Royal Academy in Copenhagen, and although in his hands it yielded extraordinary effects, the results proved disappointing for most German artists, who lacked his compelling imagination.

nineteenth century, when artists like Turner greatly extended the range of subjects, techniques, and expression. Many of its most famous practitioners are all but forgotten today, while others, such as John Sell Cotman (1782–1842), who were largely ignored, are now seen as having made important contributions.

COTMAN. Cotman started out in London, where he moved in the same circles as Turner, but spent most of his career as a drawing master in the north of England, as much out of a weakness in his character as the force of circumstances. Although he achieved modest local recognition as a leader of the Norwich landscape school, he died in obscurity and was only rediscovered in the 1920s, when his highly unusual style suddenly seemed remarkably modern. Cotman's watercolors are distinguished by an economy of means that endows even the simplest subject with monumentality and dignity. His formalism grew out of the landscape tradition of Nicolas Poussin and Claude Lorraine, yet he was no classicist. And although he was affected by the Dutch and Flemish Baroque artists who so influenced Constable, Cotman's watercolors are among the most original creations of the English Romantic landscape school during its formative phase.

Durham Cathedral (fig. 892), a finished watercolor painted in the studio from nature studies, bears the individual stamp of his genius. The artist has concentrated on the essential elements, reducing the scene to a flat, nearly abstract pat-

893. Caspar David Friedrich. *Abbey in an Oak Forest.* 1809–10.
Oil on canvas, 44 x 68$^{1}/_{2}$" (111.8 x 174 cm). Schloss Charlottenburg, Berlin

894. Caspar David Friedrich. *The Polar Sea.* 1824.
Oil on canvas, 38$^{1}/_{2}$ x 50$^{1}/_{2}$" (97.8 x 128.3 cm). Kunsthalle, Hamburg, Germany

Romanticism in art had an exact counterpart in literature and the theater. It was inextricably entwined with Johann Wolfgang von Goethe, whose dramatic poem *Faust* (Part 1, 1808; Part 2, 1832) remains the greatest monument of the Romantic movement. Goethe was interested in a vast range of subjects, including botany and architecture. His book on color theory (1810), which constituted an attack on Newtonian optics, exercised widespread influence on painters. He was also a gifted amateur musician who conducted operas and wrote librettos, as well as lyrical poems that inspired some of the finest songs by Beethoven and Schubert.

Romanticism in the theater began in Germany just before the turn of the nineteenth century as an outgrowth of Friedrich von Schiller and Goethe. It centered on August Wilhelm von Schlegel (1767–1845), the editor of the literary journal *Athenäum* from 1798–1800, and his brother Friedrich (1772–1829), a noted philosopher. Together they promoted Romanticism as an all-embracing vision. An early admirer of Shakespeare, whose plays he began to translate, August Schlegel emphasized mood and character over plot in literature, and championed the revival of such medieval works as the twelfth-century German epic *Nibelungenlied (The Song of the Niebelungs)*. The Schlegels were part of a small, tightly knit group that included Ludwig Tieck (1773–1853), who completed the job of translating Shakespeare after August's death. Tieck, who wrote both comedies and tragedies, was also an important theorist, especially later in life, and exercised considerable influence on German Romantic painting through his friendship with Philipp Otto Runge. In the heady early days of Romanticism he collaborated with Wilhelm Heinrich Wackenroder (1773–1798), who stated that "the Gothic church and the Greek temple are equally pleasurable in the sight of God." Medievalism, with its reverence for Christian ideals, was also taken up in 1799 by the writer Novalis (Friedrich von Hardenberg, 1772–1801). The writings of the Schlegel circle inspired not only the landscape painter Caspar David Friedrich but also the Nazarenes, who were to establish the mainstream of German Romantic art. Though he was generally overlooked during his lifetime, the finest playwright of the early nineteenth century in Germany was Heinrich von Kleist (1777–1811), a poet and novelist, whose tragedies and comedies are filled with the conflict of extreme emotions typical of Romanticism.

German ideas were first introduced into France by Madame de Staël (Germain Necker, 1760–1817), the daughter of Louis XVI's finance minister and the wife of the Swedish ambassador to France, who detested Napoleon. She went into exile in Germany, where she wrote *Of Germany*, which presented many of the Schlegels' theories. The book, initially suppressed upon its publication in 1810, was reissued after Napoleon's exile to Elba in 1813. Even more important for French Romanticism was the enthusiasm for all things English, which reached its height during the following decade. The novels of Sir Walter Scott sparked the taste for medieval legends, while an English troupe caused a sensation in Paris with its performances of Shakespeare four years after his plays had been declared superior to Racine's by Marie-Henri Beyle, known as Stendhal (1783–1842), in 1823.

The central figure among the French Romantics was the novelist Victor Hugo (1802–1885). The introduction to his play about Oliver Cromwell (1827), the puritan who ruled England after the execution of King Charles II, was a broadside attack on classical drama. In 1830 his drama *Hernani* announced the triumph of Romanticism. It reversed the shopworn triumph of young lovers (so dear to classical French theater) by ending in tragedy, and broke from the stilted literary conventions of French drama by altering the length of the poetic line. Perhaps fittingly, it was the failure of Hugo's *The Burgraves* in 1843 that signaled the end of Romantic theater. The other leading dramatist of the 1830s was Alexandre Dumas the Elder (1802–1870), who wrote a number of successful historical and domestic plays before turning to the novels for which he is best known today: *The Three Musketeers* (1844) and *The Count of Monte Cristo* (1845). George Sand (Amandine-Aurore-Lucile Dupin Dudevant, 1804–1876), who adopted a male pen name to help gain acceptance of her work, was a favorite novelist as well as a prolific playwright.

It was popular theater that enjoyed the greatest success, fueled by the huge growth of cities spawned by the Industrial Revolution. Much of it took the form of bourgeoise melodramas, which owed their appeal to their simple plots and morality. New kinds of spectacle were made possible by the same technology that gave rise to the Industrial Revolution itself, for example, the invention in 1816 of gaslight and limelight, which involved heating lime with compressed oxygen and compressed hydrogen. They were superseded by Thomas Edison's invention of the electric light in 1879, which made possible the improved carbon arc lamp a year

RUNGE. Philipp Otto Runge (1777–1810), who attended the Copenhagen academy soon after Friedrich, shared many of the same ideas but expressed them very differently. His most important work was a series of four allegorical landscapes devoted to the times of day that occupied him throughout his brief career and was left incomplete at his death. The paintings incorporate an ambitious program having several levels of meaning. They stand for, among other things, the seasons and the ages of life. The set was intended for a Gothic chapel of Runge's own design, where poetry and music by his friends would be heard.

Morning, the only picture to be finished, was later cut up and survives only in fragments, but a slightly earlier, smaller version (fig. 895) gives a good idea of its appearance. The landscape represents spring and childhood. Within Runge's program, it also signifies "the boundless illumination of the later. Among the favorite spectacles were large paintings of panoramas and dioramas, which created special effects through changes of light and color. The leader in this field was Louis Daguerre, who was also an important scene designer before he turned to the invention of photography (see pages 713–14).

In England, all the important Romantic poets tried their hand at plays but with little success: Samuel Taylor Coleridge (1772–1834), William Wordsworth (1770–1850), John Keats (1795–1821), Percy Bysshe Shelley (1792–1822), and even Robert Browning (1812–1889). The most important among them was Lord Byron (George Gordon, 1788–1824), the very prototype of the Romantic writer. His impact was immediate—Delacroix painted canvases inspired by Byron's dramas *Marino Faliero* and *Sardanapalus*—and lasted well beyond his own brief lifetime. The novelist Sir Walter Scott (1771–1832) also wrote plays, but mainly his novels were adapted to the stage by others to great acclaim. The most popular productions in England were translations of middle-class plays by the German Kotzebue; these were superseded by the works of George Bulwer-Lytton (1803–1873)—famous for "It was a dark and stormy night"—who invented the "gentlemanly" melodrama that gave an air of Victorian respectability to the theater.

Philadelphia was the theater capital in the United States, as it was of art, before 1815. The most important house, the Chestnut Street Theater, was designed by the great English architect Inigo Jones. New York City soon superseded Philadelphia. The close ties between art and theater in America are illustrated by William Dunlap (1766–1839), who was the nation's leading playwright before turning to painting in 1812; toward the end of his long life he also wrote the first histories of American theater and art. Many artists, especially aspiring younger ones along the frontier, found their first employment painting stage scenery. As in Europe, the growth of cities in America created a demand for larger and more numerous theaters around the country. Especially popular were Native American and Yankee plays as symbols of the young nation. They were soon joined by African-American minstrel shows (the term *Jim Crow* comes from a song introduced by Thomas D. Rice in 1829), which featured the "end men" Tambo and Bones, and a "middle" man who functioned as a master of ceremonies. The 1840s saw the rise of a new type, the city boy, who was often pitted against his country cousin.

universe." Aurora-Venus (compounding the rising sun and the morning star) hovers over the Christlike infant as child genii sprout from a lily above. (Flowers in Runge's highly personal system become symbols of universal life through emotional identification with their forms.) The decorated frame, inspired by medieval manuscripts (compare fig. 418), expands on the meaning of the central image. The light of revelation, eclipsed by darkness below, liberates the soul trapped beneath

895. Philipp Otto Runge. *Morning.* 1808. Oil on canvas, 42⅞ x 33⅝" (109 x 85.4 cm). Kunsthalle, Hamburg

the earth within the roots of the bulb. Above, the soul rises transcendent as a genius from the lily to the heavens and is transformed into an angel.

Morning is an extraordinary synthesis of Classical mythology and Christian faith, Romantic attitudes and Neoclassical technique. Painting for Runge was a deeply spiritual act revealing the divinity of nature. To him, this elevated conception required abstraction to express the poetic idea. Thus the artist communicates his intent through the stylized forms and symmetrical composition. More generally, *Morning* represents the mystical yearning of the soul for the infinite so dear to the German Romantic. This ecstatic vision, the "chord" of harmony as he put it, is depicted using the same method as Friedrich's. Every detail has been precisely observed. The picture surface, transparent as glass, makes us look at nature with the same innocence as the newborn child. As a result, the landscape has a disarming simplicity, despite the complexity of its program. In the end, it is the painting technique that validates Runge's ideas and makes them convincing.

THE NAZARENES. In 1808 a group of young German painters at the Vienna Academy banded together to form the Guild of St. Luke, after the artists' guilds of old. They equated

896. Friedrich Overbeck. *Italia and Germania*. 1811–28.
Oil on canvas, 37³/4 x 41⁷/8" (96 x 106.4 cm). Bayerische Staatsgemäldesammlungen, Neue Pinakothek, Munich

897. William Sidney Mount. *Dancing on the Barn Floor*. 1831.
Oil on canvas, 25 x 30" (63.5 x 76.2 cm).
Collection of The Museums at Stony Brook
Gift of Mr. and Mrs. Ward Melville

simplicity with pious virtue, as against virtuosity, which precluded the heartfelt sincerity that was their goal. Two years
later they decided to lead the life of artists-monks at an abandoned monastery near Rome, where they became known as
the Nazarenes. Although their work at first had a striking
purity, the painstaking precision of the old German masters
and the style of the Early Renaissance they also affected reinforced the Neoclassic emphasis on form at the expense of
color, which was put to the service of an increasingly inflated
rhetoric. The Nazarene movement gradually petered out as its
members died or returned to Germany, where they established
the mainstream of German Romanticism.

OVERBECK. The Nazarenes were at their best in intimate
subjects, such as *Italia and Germania* (fig. 896) by Friedrich
Overbeck (1789–1869). This manifesto by the movement's
"priest" expresses the North's long-standing love-hate relationship with the South. It shows personifications of the two
countries, so different in every respect, reconciled in tender
friendship. The painting is at once a nostalgic reminiscence of
the artist's homeland and a celebration of the beauty he found
around him in Rome, both united in harmony and mutual
respect. Its source, we recognize, is Angelica Kauffmann's self-
portrait (fig. 847), by way of German portraiture.

United States

Painting following the American Revolution was dominated by
protégés of Benjamin West, who took every young artist arriving in London from the New World under his wing. Strangely
enough, the only ones to enjoy much success were portraitists
such as Gilbert Stuart (1755–1828). Using the fashionable conventions of Joshua Reynolds, they conferred the aura of established aristocracy on the Federalists, who were only too eager to
forget the recent revolutionary past enshrined by the history
painters. What Americans wanted was an art based not on the
past but on the present. Romantic painting in the United States
rode the tidal wave of cultural nationalism fostered by Jackson-
ian democracy. Collectors now began to support artists who
could articulate their vision of the United States. For perhaps the
only time in the country's history, artists, patrons, and intellectuals came to share a common point of view.

MOUNT. During the 1820s, America found its history painting in genre scenes descended from Dutch and English examples. The first native genre painter of real talent, William
Sidney Mount (1808–1868), spent his career on rural Long
Island, which provided him with a rich vein of subjects. Although he began as a history painter and was associated with
the leading ones in New York City, Mount quickly turned to
subjects of everyday life, which he imbued with the humor of

898. Thomas Cole. *View of Schroon Mountain, Essex County, New York, After a Storm*. 1838.
Oil on canvas, 39³/8 x 63" (100 x 160 cm). The Cleveland Museum of Art
Hinman B. Hurlbut Collection

Jan Steen. *Dancing on the Barn Floor* (fig. 897), one of his first efforts, projects the ideal of America as a land of contentment in which its fun-loving people enjoy a simple, happy life as the fruit of their honest labor. The carefully observed violinist testifies to the artist's love of music, his favorite theme. Indeed, this ingenious inventor and theoretician wrote considerable "fiddle" music himself, and later patented a violin of unusual design.

THE HUDSON RIVER SCHOOL. At about the same time, Americans began to discover landscape painting. Before then, settlers were far too busy carving out homesteads to pay much attention to the poetry of nature's moods. The attitude toward landscape began to change only as the surrounding wilderness was gradually tamed, allowing Americans for the first time to see nature as the escape from civilization that inspired European painters. As in England, the contribution of the poets proved essential to shaping American ideas about nature. By 1825, they were calling on artists to depict the wilderness as the most conspicuous feature of the New World and its emerging civilization. Pantheism virtually became a national religion during the Romantic era. While it could be frightening, nature was everywhere, and was believed to play a special role in determining the American character. Led by Thomas Cole (1801–1848), the founder of the Hudson River School, which flourished from 1825 until the Centennial celebration in 1876, American painters elevated the forests and mountains to symbols of the United States.

COLE. Like many early American landscapists, Cole came from England, where he was trained as an engraver, but learned the rudiments of painting from an itinerant artist in the Midwest. Following a summer sketching tour up the Hudson River, he invented the means of expressing the elemental power of the country's primitive landscape by transforming the formulas of the English picturesque into Romantic hymns based on the direct observation of nature. Because he also wrote poetry, Cole was able to create a visual counterpart to the literary rhetoric of the day. His painting *View of Schroon Mountain, Essex County, New York, After a Storm* (fig. 898) shows the peak rising majestically, like a pyramid, from the forest below. It is treated as a symbol of permanence surrounded by death and decay, signified by the autumnal foliage, passing storm, and lightning blasted trees. Stirred by sublime emotion, the artist has heightened the dramatic lighting, so that the broad landscape becomes a revelation of God's eternal laws.

BINGHAM. *Fur Traders Descending the Missouri* (fig. 899) by George Caleb Bingham (1811–1879) shows this close identification with the land in a different way. The picture, both a landscape and a genre scene, is full of the vastness and silence of the wide-open spaces. The two trappers in their dugout canoe, gliding downstream in the misty sunlight, are entirely at home in this idyllic setting. The assertion of a human presence portrays the United States as a benevolent Eden in which settlers assume their rightful place. Rather than being

899. George Caleb Bingham. *Fur Traders Descending the Missouri.* c. 1845.
Oil on canvas, 29 x 36¹/2" (73.7 x 92.7 cm). The Metropolitan Museum of Art, New York
Morris K. Jesup Fund, 1933

dwarfed by a vast and often hostile continent, these hardy pioneers live in an ideal state of harmony with nature, symbolized by the waning daylight. The picture reminds us of how much Romantic adventurousness went into the westward expansion of the United States. The scene owes much of its haunting charm to the silhouette of the black cub chained to the prow and its reflection in the water. This masterstroke adds a note of primitive mystery that we shall not meet again until the work of Henri Rousseau (see pages 764–65).

SCULPTURE

In attempting to define Romanticism in sculpture, we are immediately struck by one rather extraordinary fact: in contrast to the abundance of theoretical writings that accompanied Neoclassical sculpture from Winckelmann on, there exists only one piece of writing that sets forth a general theory of sculpture from the Romantic point of view: Baudelaire's essay of 1846, "Why Sculpture is Boring," which occupies only a few pages of his long review of the Salon of that year. Actually, Baudelaire is less concerned with the state of French

sculpture at that moment, which strikes him as deplorable, than he is with the limitations of sculpture as a medium. To him, there can be no such thing as Romantic sculpture, because every piece of sculpture is to him a "fetish" whose objective existence prevents the artist from making it a vehicle of his subjective view of the world, his personal sensibility. It can transcend this limitation only if it is placed in the service of architecture, enhancing a larger whole such as a Gothic cathedral, but as soon as it detaches itself from this context, sculpture reverts to its primitive status. Fortunately, Baudelaire's theory was not taken at face value by either artists or patrons, but it does suggest the difficulty Romantic sculptors (or at least those who thought of themselves as part of the Romantic movement) had in establishing a self-image they could live with. Indeed, the unique virtue of sculpture—its solid, space-filling reality (its "idol" quality)—was not congenial to the Romantic temperament. The rebellious and individualistic urges of Romanticism could find expression in rough, small-scale sketches but rarely survived the laborious process of translating the sketch into a permanent, finished monument.

900. Antonio Canova. Tomb of the Archduchess Maria Christina. 1798–1805
Marble, lifesize. Augustinerkirche, Vienna

Italy

CANOVA. At the beginning of the Romantic era, we find an adaptation of the Neoclassical style to new ends by sculptors, led by Antonio Canova (1757–1822). He was not only the greatest sculptor of his generation, he was the most famous artist of the Western world from the 1790s until long after his death. Both his work and his personality became a model for every sculptor during those years. Canova's meteoric rise is well attested by his numerous commissions. The Tomb of Maria Christina, archduchess of Austria, in the Church of the Augustinians in Vienna (fig. 900) is remarkable as much for its "timeless" beauty as for its gently melancholy sentiment. It was commissioned by her husband soon after her death in 1798, although its framework had been anticipated in a monument to Titian planned by Canova several years before. This ensemble, in contrast to the tombs of earlier times (such as fig. 577), does not include the real burial place. Moreover, the deceased appears only in a portrait medallion framed by a snake biting its own tail, a symbol of eternity, and sustained by two floating genii. Presumably, but not actually, the urn carried by the

woman in the center contains her ashes. This is an ideal burial service performed by classical figures, mostly allegorical: a mourning winged genius on the right, and the group about to enter the tomb on the left, who represent the Three Ages of Life. The slow procession, directed away from the beholder, stands for "eternal remembrance." All references to Christianity are conspicuously absent.

It is readily apparent that Canova must have known of Pigalle's tomb for the Maréchal de Saxe (fig. 816), which looks forward to it in so many respects. The differences are equally striking, however. Canova's design looks surprisingly like a very high relief, for most of the figures are seen in strict profile, so that they seem to hug the wall plane despite the deep space. Gestures are kept to a minimum, and the allegorical trappings that clutter Pigalle's monument have been swept away, so that nothing distracts us from the solemn ritual being acted out before us. It is this intense concentration that distinguishes Canova's classicism from the Rococo of Pigalle.

Canova's friends included Jacques-Louis David (see pages 659–60), who helped to spread his fame in France. In 1802, Canova was invited to Paris by Napoleon, who wanted his

901. Antonio Canova. *Napoleon.*
1806. Marble, over-lifesize.
Apsley House, London

902. Antonio Canova. *Pauline Borghese as Venus.* 1808. Marble, lifesize.
Galleria Borghese, Rome

portrait done by the greatest sculptor of the age. With Napoleon's approval, he made a colossal nude figure in marble showing the conqueror as a victorious and peace-giving Mars (fig. 901). The head is an idealized but thoroughly recognizable portrait of Napoleon, while the figure is based on statues of ancient rulers in the guise of nude classical deities. The elevation of the emperor to a god marks a decisive shift away from the noble ideals of the Enlightenment that had given rise to Neoclassicism. The glorification of the hero as a noble example, seen in Houdon's statue of George Washington (fig. 852), is abandoned in favor of the Romantic cult of the individual. There is no longer any higher authority—neither religion, nor reason is invoked—only the imperative of Greek art remains unquestioned as a style divorced from content. Fittingly enough, the statue was given to the Duke of Wellington after he defeated Napoleon at Waterloo.

Not to be outdone, Napoleon's sister Pauline Borghese permitted Canova to sculpt her as a reclining Venus (fig. 902). The statue is so obviously idealized as to still any gossip. We recognize it as a precursor, more classically proportioned, of Ingres' *Odalisque* (see fig. 870). She is equally typical of early Romanticism, which incorporated Rococo eroticism but in a less sensuous form. Strangely enough, Pauline Borghese seems less three-dimensional than the painting. She is designed like a "relief in the round," for front and back view only, and her very considerable charm radiates almost entirely from the fluid grace of her contours.

THORVALDSEN. Canova remained the model for every sculptor of ambition for most of the nineteenth century. Yet the Napoleonic era was not a propitious one for sculptors who wanted to be like him: independent, beholden to no single patron, free to create "modern classics." The only one who

succeeded, and the sculptor on whom Canova's mantle ultimately descended, was Bertel Thorvaldsen (1770–1844), a Dane who came to Rome in 1797 on a scholarship from the Royal Academy in Copenhagen. Although he established his reputation early, he had to live through some difficult years before he could feel artistically and financially secure.

Thorvaldsen became the first to revive the most heroic phase of Greek art, but soon underwent a basic change not only of style but of outlook. His *Venus* (fig. 903) is closer to a living model than to any ancient source, though its immediate precedent is a statue by Houdon. Thorvaldsen shows her in a moment of triumph, holding the golden apple awarded by Paris in the beauty contest that started the Trojan War, yet she contemplates the apple in a way that might lead us to mistake her for an Eve tempted, were it not for the garment in her left hand. The statue shows Thorvaldsen's new emphasis on poetic sentiment, as well as his reawakened religious feeling, which he shared with the young German painters in Rome known as the Nazarenes, many of whom were his friends (see page 696). Thus his *Venus* is far more Romantic than Neoclassic, despite its style.

For all of Europe except France and Spain, Thorvaldsen remained the model of sculptural perfection until the 1850s. Germans, Scandinavians, and many Italians viewed him as more "truly Greek" than Canova, and for the English he became the heir of John Flaxman as well.

France

It was in France that the main development of Romantic sculpture took place. Although the doctrine of the Academy came to be broadened and modified in the course of time, its core lasted until Rodin. This core might be defined as the

903. Bertel Thorvaldsen. *Venus.* 1813–16. Marble, lifesize. Thorvaldsens Museum, Copenhagen

904. François Rude. *La Marseillaise.* 1833–36. Stone, approx. 42 x 26' (12.8 x 7.9 m). Arc de Triomphe, Paris

belief that the human body is nature's noblest creation and, hence, the sculptor's noblest subject. Translated into practice, this meant that every student of sculpture at such academies as the Paris École des Beaux-Arts received a rigorous training. Since the level of teaching was far higher than it was in painting, the limitations of the academic sculptural tradition became apparent much later. The Romantic reaction against the ideal of the "modern classic" asserted itself in the sculpture sections of the French Salons right after the Revolution of 1830, which brought the fall of the ancient regime of the Bourbons, but the antiacademic tradition did not become dominant until the last two decades of the century, when Michelangelo, Rodin's ideal, at last won out over Canova. What ultimately destroyed it was the cult of the fragmentary and the unfinished.

That the Romantic "rebellion" started so much later than in painting also attests to how closely sculpture and politics were linked in nineteenth-century France. Artists were often passionately involved in politics during an era when political feelings were especially intense, but because the state remained the largest single source of commissions, the fortunes of the sculptors were more directly affected than those of the painters by changes in regime. This is not meant to suggest that French

sculpture was dominated by its social and political environment. Yet, to the extent that it was a public art, sculpture responded to the pressure of these forces, directly or indirectly, far more than did painting, and was shaped by them in varying degrees, depending on local circumstances. Thus we cannot understand its development without reference to the changing politics around it.

RUDE. François Rude (1784–1855), who enthusiastically took Napoleon's side after the emperor's return from Elba, sought refuge in Brussels from Bourbon rule, as had Jacques-Louis David, whom he knew and revered. Following his return to Paris, Rude must have felt that artistically he had reached a dead end and decided to strike out in new directions. He conceived a new interest in the French Renaissance tradition of the School of Fontainebleau and Giovanni Bologna (see pages 496–98), which would eventually lead him back to Claus Sluter. This rediscovery of national sculptural traditions, so characteristic of Romantic revivalism, was part of a new nationalism, which was also exemplified by a passion for historic portraits as "morally elevating for the public."

These concerns are manifest in Rude's masterpiece, *The Departure of the Volunteers of 1792,* commonly called *La*

Music became the ideal Romantic art form because it was widely believed to allow the fullest expression of pure feeling, without the hindrance of literal meaning or the reality of appearance. The archetype of the early Romantic composer was Ludwig van Beethoven (1770–1827). He sympathized strongly with the American and French Revolutions, which fed his restless Romantic spirit, and in his personal relations he bowed to no one, least of all to his aristocratic patrons. Nevertheless, he was closest spiritually to Goethe, a member of the previous generation. His early works properly belong to the Neoclassical period of music (see box page 670), but his style has greater affinities with that of C. P. E. Bach than of Mozart or Haydn, with whom he studied for four years. Beethoven greatly expanded the expressive range of the forms he inherited. His works are more explosive and dynamic, louder and more grandiose. Like Mozart, Beethoven was a universal genius. By emphasizing content over form, he pushed the boundaries of classical music to their limits, and sometimes beyond. Mercilessly self-critical, he composed far fewer works than his predecessors, but with few exceptions they are substantial contributions to the literature. In addition to the famous nine symphonies, on which his public reputation rests, there are 31 sonatas for piano, an instrument that was at once personal and symphonic, and 17 quartets that are the most profound utterances in all of chamber music. The most striking aspect of Beethoven's music is its novelty, which made it controversial to many of his contemporaries. It features heroic expression counterbalanced by melting lyricism. No other composer could scale the heights or plumb the depths of the soul to such stirring effect. Extremely public during his youth and early maturity, his music became increasingly private over time, perhaps as the result of his growing deafness, which was largely complete by 1816, as well as his troubled personal life. Yet its complexity was a consistent outgrowth of the composer's personality, and makes the late works demanding for interpreter and listener alike.

Beethoven was the essential point of departure for most Romantic composers of the next generation. Yet, no matter how awed they were by his commanding presence, they remained independent personalities determined to make their own contributions.

Franz Schubert (1797–1828), in contrast to Beethoven, was a man of gentle temperament. His dreamy sensibility found its ideal outlet in German art songs (*Lieder;* singular, *Lied*), inspired by the poetry of Goethe and Schiller among others, which he wrote in great quantity and variety. Although he had some difficulty handling extended symphonic form, Schubert's piano sonatas present an ideal combination of intimate lyricism and large scale.

Orchestral writing presented no difficulties to Felix Mendelssohn-Bartholdy (1809–1847). Like Mozart, he was a child prodigy who was writing significant music by late adolescence. (His sister, Fanny, was also gifted and remains unjustly neglected.) His five symphonies and numerous overtures are notable for their vitality and colorism, which "paint" vivid images in sound. Mendelssohn, too, was stirred by literature, above all by the plays of Shakespeare. For an 1843 production by Ludwig Tieck he set Shakespeare's *A Midsummer Night's Dream* to music that perfectly captures its impish spirit. Mendelssohn, like Schubert, succumbed early to syphilis (the AIDS of the time), which also claimed the lives of numerous other people in the arts.

The most characteristic music of Robert Schumann (1810–1856) was piano and vocal music. But although he lacked the facility for orchestration of his friend Mendelssohn, his four symphonies were of major importance for the next generation of German composers. They breathe an innocence and love of nature that make them the musical counterparts of Romantic landscape paintings. Schumann was also inspired by Romantic writers, and undertook a series of large-scale vocal works: incidental music for *Manfred* (1849), incorporating the poem by Lord Byron; the opera *Genoveva* (1850), taken from Ludwig Tieck's drama; and *Scenes from Faust* (1853), based on Goethe's poetry. Schumann's wife, Clara Wieck (1819–1896), was also an excellent pianist and composer, but she put her career second to her husband's, so that only recently has her music come to the fore. Schumann died young after suffering from two years of madness, perhaps brought on by syphilis.

The only composer to equal Beethoven's heroic stature was the Frenchman Hector Berlioz (1803–1869), whose music employs the full force of a very large orchestra. Despite being mainly self-taught, Berlioz was a masterful composer in command of orchestration—the technique of specifying which instruments should play which parts of a musical composition. Berlioz's music is programmatic, that is, it tells a story, or at least suggests a sequence of incidents, and this emphasis on story line over pure form is one of his most Romantic qualities. Berlioz's *Symphonie fantastique* (*Fantastic Symphony,* 1830) is a morbid account of unrequited love. Shakespeare made a deep impression on him, and his most successful work is a dramatic realization of *Romeo and Juliet* (1839). No one, not even Verdi and Tchaikovsky later in the century, understood better the magic of love or the power of tragedy in Shakespeare. Although they were little performed during his lifetime, Berlioz's operas were of great importance for successfully reviving the grand tradition of Lully and Rameau.

Marseillaise (fig. 904), for Napoleon's unfinished triumphal arch on the Place de l'Étoile. Louis-Philippe and his energetic minister of the interior Adolphe Thiers saw its completion as an opportunity to demonstrate that the new government was one of national reconciliation. Hence, the sculptural program had to offer something to every segment of the French political spectrum. Rude was fortunate in getting a commission for one of the four groups that flank the opening. He raised his subject—the French people rallying to defend the Republic against attack from abroad—to the level of mythic splendor. The volunteers surge forth, some nude, others in classic armor, inspired by the great forward movement of the winged genius of Liberty above them. No wonder the work engendered an emotional response that made people identify the group with

Paris was the opera capital of Europe during the first half of the nineteenth century. The most prolific and popular composer of opera was Giacchino Rossini (1792–1868), who adapted his Italian style to suit the French taste. While his operas generally have ridiculous plots, the music itself is glorious and, given a libretto of quality, the result is a masterpiece: *The Barber of Seville* (1816), based on Beaumarchais' play, and *William Tell* (1829), his last opera, inspired by Schiller's drama of 1804. The classical antithesis of Rossini's unabashed Romanticism was another Italian, Luigi Cherubini (1760–1842), who settled in Paris in 1788. A later academic counterpart to Glück, he was regarded as the equal of Beethoven, whose lone opera was influenced by Cherubini's *Medea* (1797), taken from the Greek tragedy by Euripides.

When Rossini departed for Paris in 1824, Italian opera was left in the capable hands of Gaetano Donizetti (1797–1848). Most of his 70 operas are potboilers, but the finest ones, notably *Lucia di Lammermoor* (1835), have spirited drama and appealing music. Donizetti's style largely determined the character of Italian opera before Giuseppe Verdi. His chief rival, Vincenzo Bellini (1801–1835), died too young to achieve his full potential a few years after writing *Norma* and *La Somnambula* in 1831.

Among the most unusual musical personalities of the Romantic movement was the Polish composer Frédéric Chopin (1810–1849), who was drawn to Paris. A great virtuoso of the piano, Chopin introduced a wide range of new types of composition for the keyboard, most of them—such as the *polonaise* and the *mazurka*—based on the national music of Poland, although John Field (1782–1837) helped to pave the way for his nocturnes. These compositions are so free and inventive that they seem to be entirely new forms spun as if by magic from Chopin's endlessly fertile imagination. Though mostly small in scale, they yielded not only poetic intimacy, at which he excelled, but also heroic grandeur. Chopin and his companion, the novelist George Sand, sat for a famous portrait by Delacroix.

For Chopin, music remained an expressive vehicle first, a technical display second. With the Italian violinist Niccolò Paganini (1782–1840), who also spent much of his life in Paris, virtuosity became an end in itself, which greatly enlarged the scope of violin playing. He was one of the first great music stars to be idolized by an adoring public. Paganini became the model in turn for the Hungarian pianist Ferenc Liszt (1811–1886), a friend of Chopin who came to Paris for a while, but later traveled widely.

905. Antoine-Louis Barye. *Tiger Devouring a Gavial of the Ganges.* 1831–32. Bronze, length 39¹/₂" (100.3 cm). Musée du Louvre, Paris

in opposition to the regime, and his most important works between 1836 and 1848 were direct expressions of his Bonapartist political beliefs.

BARYE. The ultimate source of *La Marseillaise* is pictorial. In a similar way, Stubbs' *Lion Attacking a Horse* (see fig. 848) is the sire of animal groups by Antoine-Louis Barye (1795–1875). Barye followed in his father's footsteps as a goldsmith, but spent all his free hours at the Paris zoo, sketching live animals and studying their anatomy. He also became a friend of Delacroix, who shared these interests and sometimes treated the same themes. Barye scored his first public success at the Salon of 1831 with the plaster model of *Tiger Devouring a Gavial of the Ganges* (see fig. 905). His group displays a realism based on thorough zoological knowledge, but what really impressed critics and public alike was the ferocity of the tiger, the pitiless display of "nature red in tooth and claw" so exciting to the Romantic imagination. Animal combats had a long tradition in Western art going all the way back to classical antiquity, but these followed well-established formal conventions that governed both the choice of animals and their compositional relationship. Barye disregarded all such precedents. Not only did he study his animals directly from nature, he chose exotic species and combinations. What mattered was not the zoological implausibility of the group (gavials are unlikely prey for tigers) but its expressive power, intensified by the monumental compactness of design.

PRÉAULT. The Salons of the early 1830s, besides bringing Rude and Barye into prominence, served as showcases for sculptors then still in their twenties. What separated them from the generation of their teachers was that none was old enough to have experienced the Napoleonic era. As it happened, there was not a single first-rate artist in this group. Auguste Préault (1809–1879), the most interesting of them, may have been the first to earn the epithet "a genius without talent," as he was termed by one of his contemporaries. His ambitious relief titled *Tuerie (Slaughter)* (fig. 906), sent to the Salon of 1834, indicates that his interest centered on extreme physical and emotional states. He submitted the panel as the fragment of a larger composition, but this, one suspects, was merely for the purpose of easing it past the jury. The design is actually quite self-contained, even though every figure in it is a fragment, except for the baby. The style of *Tuerie* must be termed Neo-Baroque, yet it is brimming with a physical and

the national anthem itself. For Rude, the group had a deeply felt personal meaning: his father had been among those volunteers. When the arch was officially unveiled in 1836, there was almost unanimous agreement that Rude's group made the other three pale into insignificance. Despite its great public acclaim, *The Departure* failed to gain Rude the official honors he so clearly deserved. He found himself more and more

906. Auguste Préault. *Tuerie (Slaughter).* 1834. Bronze, 43 x 55" (109.2 x 139.7 cm). Musée des Beaux-Arts, Chartres, France

emotional violence far beyond anything found in Baroque art, and its expressive distortions, its irrational space filled to the bursting point with writhing shapes, evoke memories of Gothic sculpture (compare fig. 488). In fact, the helmeted knight's face next to that of the screaming mother hints that the subject itself—some dread apocalyptic event beyond human control—is medieval. But in true Romantic fashion, Préault does not define this event.

Tuerie established Préault's reputation as the archetypal Romantic sculptor. As a radical attack on the rules of classical relief, it was acclaimed by avant-garde critics. (What the other side thought of it can easily be imagined.) Its very extremism, however, condemned *Tuerie* to being a dead end. Neither Préault nor anyone else could make it the starting point of a new development.

CARPEAUX. If the high tide of Romanticism is to be found among the French sculptors born during the first decade of the century, those born during the second may, with some hesitation, be designated late (or belated) Romantics, but we again look in vain for a major talent among them. The third decade,

in contrast, saw the birth of several important sculptors. Of these, the greatest and best known was Jean-Baptiste Carpeaux (1827–1875). Carpeaux's masterpiece came at the end of the Second Empire, which succeeded the short-lived Second Republic in 1852. In 1861 his old friend the architect Charles Garnier began the Paris Opéra (see pages 710–12) and entrusted him with one of the four sculptural groups across the facade. *The Dance* (fig. 907) perfectly matches Garnier's Neo-Baroque architecture. (The plaster model in our illustration is both livelier and more precise than the final stone group, visible in fig. 920, lower right). The group created a scandal after the unveiling in 1869. The nude dancing bacchantes around the winged male genius in the center were denounced as drunk, vulgar, and indecent—and small wonder, for their coquettish gaiety derives from small Rococo groups such as Clodion's (see fig. 815). But unlike Clodion's, Carpeaux's enormous figures (they are 15 feet tall) look undressed rather than nude, so that we do not accept them as legitimate denizens of the realm of mythology. Public opinion insisted that it be replaced, but after the war with Germany ended in 1871 the old complaints were forgotten and *The Dance* was

907. Jean-Baptiste Carpeaux. *The Dance.* 1867–69. Plaster model, approx. 15' x 8'6"
(4.6 x 2.6 m). Musée de l'Opéra, Paris

acclaimed as a masterpiece. It is as obviously superior to the other three Opéra groups by more conservative authors as Rude's *Marseillaise* is to its neighbors on the Arc de Triomphe.

BARTHOLDI. To defy established society, its values and institutions, was easier for writer and painters than for sculptors. To the latter, the late nineteenth century offered vast opportunities for official commissions. Of the total of such monuments in the Western world, it is a safe guess that the great majority were erected, or at least begun, between 1872 and 1905. The most ambitious of these was the *Statue of Liberty* (or, to use its official title, *Liberty Enlightening the World;* fig. 908) by Auguste Bartholdi (1834–1904).

This monument in memory of French assistance to America during the War of Independence was a gift of the French people, not of the government. Hence, its enormous cost was raised by public subscription, which took ten years. Bartholdi conceived the *Statue of Liberty* out of a previous one for a gigantic lighthouse in the form of a woman holding a lamp to be erected at the northern entry to the Suez Canal. All he had to do was exchange the Egyptian headdress for a radiant crown and the lantern for a torch. The final model shows an austere, classically draped young woman holding the torch in her raised right hand and a tablet in her left. With her left foot, on which her weight rests, she steps on the broken shackles of tyranny. The right leg (the "free" one in accordance with the rules of classical contrapposto) is set back, so that the figure seems to be advancing when viewed from the side but looks stationary in the frontal view. As a piece of sculpture, the *Statue of Liberty* is less original than one might think. Formally and iconographically, it derives from a well-established ancestry reaching back to Canova and beyond. Its conservatism is, however, Bartholdi's conscious choice. He sensed that only a "timeless" statue could embody the ideal he wanted to glorify.

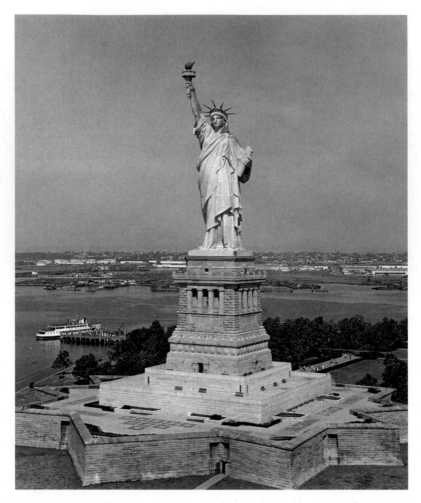

908. Auguste Bartholdi. *Statue of Liberty (Liberty Enlightening the World).* 1875–84.
Copper sheeting over metal armature, height of figure 151'6" (46 m). Liberty Island, New York Harbor

The figure, which stands over 150 feet tall, presented severe structural problems that called for the skills of an architectural engineer. Bartholdi found the ideal collaborator in Gustave Eiffel, the future builder of the Eiffel Tower (see pages 742–43 and fig. 964). The project took more than a decade to complete. The *Statue of Liberty* was inaugurated at last in the fall of 1886, having been placed on a tall pedestal built with funds raised by the American public. Its fame as the symbol—one is tempted to say "trademark"—of the United States has been worldwide ever since.

ARCHITECTURE

Given the individualistic nature of Romanticism, we might expect the range of revival styles to be widest in painting, the most personal and private of the visual arts, and narrowest in architecture, the most communal and public. Yet the opposite is true. Painters and sculptors were unable to abandon Renaissance habits of representation, and never really revived medieval art or ancient art before the Classical Greek era. Architects were not subject to this limitation, however, and the revival styles persisted longer in architecture than in the other arts.

The Classic and Gothic Revivals

The late eighteenth century, as we noted before, had come to favor the heavier and more austere Greek Doric over the Roman. This "Greek revival" phase of Neoclassicism was pioneered on a small scale in England, but was quickly taken up everywhere, since it was believed to embody more of the "noble simplicity and calm grandeur" of classical Greece than did the later, less "masculine" orders. Greek Doric was also the least flexible order, hence particularly difficult to adapt to modern tasks even when combined with Roman or Renaissance elements. Only rarely could Greek Doric architecture furnish a direct model for Neoclassic structures. We instead find adaptations of it combined with elements derived from the other Greek orders.

SCHINKEL. The Altes Museum (Old Museum; fig. 909) by Karl Friedrich Schinkel (1781–1841) is a spectacular example of the Greek revival. The main entrance looks like a Doric temple seen from the side (see fig. 166), but with Ionic columns strung across a Corinthian order (compare figs. 162 and 177). The building is notable for its bold design and

909. Karl Friedrich Schinkel. Altes Museum, Berlin. 1824–28

refined proportions. Schinkel, an architect of great ability, began as a painter in the style of Caspar David Friedrich (see pages 692–93) and also worked as a stage designer before joining the Berlin public works office, which he later headed. Hence, he knew well how to infuse architecture with Romantic associations and a theatrical flair worthy of Piranesi. Schinkel's first love was the Gothic, and although most of his public buildings are in a Greek style, they retain a strong element of the picturesque. Here the measured cadence of the monumental facade is intended to establish a contemplative mood appropriate to viewing art in a repository of antiquities.

Schinkel set a precedent that was soon taken up everywhere. He was the first to treat a museum as a temple of the arts. Such an association could find sanction in the classical past: the small *pinakotheke* (picture gallery) at the entrance to the Acropolis (fig. 173). The Altes Museum expresses the veneration of ancient Greece in the land of Winckelmann and Mengs. To the poet Goethe, it remained the pinnacle of civilization. The Altes Museum is, furthermore, testament to the Enlightenment attitude that gave rise to art museums, galleries, and academies on both sides of the Atlantic after 1760. At the same time, the Greek style served the imperial ambitions of Prussia, which emerged as a major power at the Congress of Vienna in 1815. The imposing grandeur of the Altes Museum proclaims Berlin as the new Athens, with Kaiser Wilhelm III as a modern Pericles.

It is characteristic of Romanticism that at the time architects launched the classical revival, they also started a Gothic revival. England was far in advance here, as it was in the development of Romantic literature and painting. Gothic forms had never wholly disappeared in England. They were used on occasion for special purposes, even by Sir Christopher Wren and Sir John Vanbrugh (see pages 608–9), but these were survivals of an authentic, if outmoded, tradition. The conscious revival, by contrast, was linked with the cult of the picturesque, and with the vogue for medieval (and pseudo-medieval) romances.

WALPOLE. In this spirit Horace Walpole (1717–1797), midway in the eighteenth century, enlarged and "gothicized" his country house, Strawberry Hill (figs. 910 and 911), a process that took some two decades and involved his circle of friends (including Robert Adam, who was responsible for the round tower). On the exterior, the rambling structure has a

910. Horace Walpole, with William Robinson and others. Strawberry Hill, Twickenham, England. 1749–77

911. Interior of Strawberry Hill

studied irregularity that is decidedly picturesque. Inside, most of the elements were copied or faithfully adapted from authentic Gothic sources. The interior in figure 911 is a splendid imitation of the English Perpendicular style found in the chapel of Henry VII at Westminster Abbey (compare fig. 452), with its conical vaults. The richly brocaded, yet dainty wall surfaces look almost as if they were decorated with lace-paper doilies. Although Walpole associated the Gothic with the pathos of

912. John Nash. The Royal Pavilion, Brighton. 1815–18

the Sublime, he acknowledged that the house is "pretty and gay." This playfulness, so free of dogma, gives Strawberry Hill its special charm. Gothic here is still an "exotic" style. It appeals because it is strange, but for that very reason it must be "translated," like a medieval romance, or like the Chinese motifs that crop up in Rococo decoration.

NASH. The Romantic imagination saw the Gothic and the mysterious East in much the same light. The masterpiece in this vein is the Royal Pavilion at Brighton (fig. 912), created half a century later by John Nash (1752–1835). The greatest architect of the English picturesque, he commanded the full range of revival styles, which here have been combined to brilliant effect. The style of this "stately pleasure dome" is a cream-puff version of the Taj Mahal. Over a Neo-Palladian building Nash imposed a facade of cast-iron domes, minarets, and lacy screens, with Chinese and even Gothic motifs thrown in for good measure; hence, it was known as Indian Gothic.

LATROBE. By 1800 the Gothic was a fully acceptable alternative to the Greek revival as a style for major churches. Benjamin Latrobe (1764–1820), an Anglo-American who under Jefferson became the most influential architect of "Federal" Neoclassicism, submitted a design in each style for the Cathedral in Baltimore. In this he may be called a disciple of the English architect John Soane (1753–1837), who also worked in a variety of revival styles. The Neoclassic one was chosen, but it might well have been the Neo-Gothic. The exterior of the present building (fig. 913) has walls that resemble Soufflot's Panthéon (see fig. 856), a dome of more severe design, a

temple front, and bell towers of disguised Gothic-Baroque ancestry. (The bulbous crowns are not his work.)

Far more distinguished is the interior (fig. 914). Although inspired by the domed and vaulted spaces of ancient Rome, especially the Pantheon (see fig. 246), Latrobe was not interested in archaeological correctness. The "muscularity" of Roman structures has been suppressed. The delicate moldings, profiles, and coffers are derived straight from Robert Adam (compare fig. 859); they are no more than linear accents that do not disturb the continuous, abstract surfaces. Here Latrobe shows how much he had learned from Soane's masterpiece, the Bank of England in London, before his departure from that city in 1796. Unfortunately, the bank was largely destroyed in 1927, but it is still known from photographs (see fig. 916). Like Adam, Soane was enthused by Piranesi's epic architectural fantasies, which he joined with the latest French theories. In Latrobe's Romantic interpretation, the spatial qualities of ancient architecture have acquired the visionary quality of Boullée's memorial to Isaac Newton (see fig. 857)—vast, pure, sublime. The strangely weightless interior presents almost that combination of classic form and Gothic lightness first postulated by Soufflot. It also shows the free and imaginative look of the mature Neoclassic style, when handled by a gifted architect. Had the Gothic design (fig. 915) been chosen, the exterior might have been more striking, but the interior probably less impressive. Like most Romantic architects seeking the sublime, Latrobe viewed Gothic churches "from the outside in"—as mysterious, looming structures silhouetted against the sky—but nourished his spatial fantasy on Roman monuments.

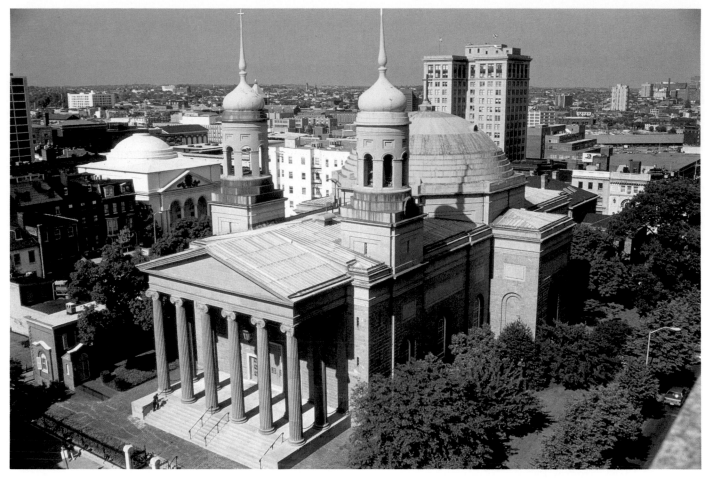

913. Benjamin Latrobe. Baltimore Cathedral (Basilica of the Assumption), Baltimore, Maryland. Begun 1805

914. Interior of Baltimore Cathedral

915. Benjamin Latrobe
Alternative design for Baltimore Cathedral

After 1800, the choice between classical and Gothic modes was more often resolved in favor of Gothic. Nationalist sentiments, strengthened in the Napoleonic wars, became important factors. England, France, and Germany each tended to think that Gothic expressed its particular national genius. Certain theorists (notably John Ruskin) also regarded Gothic as superior for ethical or religious reasons on the grounds that it was "honest" and "Christian." [See Primary Sources, no. 84, pages 936–37.]

BARRY AND PUGIN. All these considerations lie behind the design by Sir Charles Barry (1785–1860) and A. N. Welby

916. Sir John Soane. Consols' Office, Bank of England, London. 1794. Destroyed

Pugin (1812–1852) for the Houses of Parliament in London, the largest monument of the Gothic revival (fig. 917). As the seat of a large and complex governmental apparatus, but at the same time as a focus of patriotic feeling, it presents a curious mixture: repetitious symmetry governs the main body of the structure and picturesque irregularity its silhouette. The building is indeed a contradiction in terms, for it imposes Pugin's Gothic vocabulary, inspired by the later English Perpendicu-

lar (compare fig. 452), onto the classically conceived structure by Barry, with results that satisfied neither. Nevertheless the Houses of Parliament admirably convey the grandeur of Victorian England at the height of its power.

Neo-Renaissance and Neo-Baroque Architecture

GARNIER. Meanwhile the stylistic alternatives were continually increased for architects by other revivals. When, by mid-century, the Renaissance, and then the Baroque, returned to favor, the revival movement had come full circle: Neo-Renaissance and Neo-Baroque replaced the Neoclassical. This final phase of Romantic architecture, which dominated the years 1850–75 and lingered through 1900, is epitomized in the Paris Opéra (figs. 918–20), designed by Charles Garnier (1825–1898). The Opéra was the culmination of Baron Georges-Eugène Haussmann's plan to modernize Paris under Napoleon III, for it is the focal point for a series of main avenues that converge on it from all sides. Although the building was not completed until after the fall of the Second Empire, the opulence of its Beaux-Arts style typified the new Paris. The building is a masterpiece of eclecticism. The fluid curves of the Grand Staircase, for example, recall the Vestibule of the Laurentian Library (see fig. 617). The massing of the main entrance is reminiscent of Lescot's Square Court of the Louvre (see fig. 722). But the paired columns of the facade, "quoted" from Perrault's East Front of the Louvre (see fig. 799), are combined with a smaller order, in a fashion suggested by Michelangelo's Palazzo dei Conservatori (see fig. 621). The other entrance consists of a temple front.

The totality consciously suggests a palace of the arts combined with a temple of the arts. The theatrical effect projects the festive air of a crowd gathering before the opening curtain. Its Neo-Baroque quality derives more from the profusion of

917. Sir Charles Barry and A. N. Welby Pugin. The Houses of Parliament, London. Begun 1836

918. *(left)* Charles Garnier. Grand Staircase, the Opéra, Paris. 1861–74

919. *(below)* Plan of the Opéra

920. The Opéra

921. François-Honoré Jacob-Desmalter (after a design by Charles Percier and Pierre-François Fontaine). Bedroom of Empress Joséphine Bonaparte. c. 1810. Château de Malmaison, Rueil-Malmaison, France

sculpture—including Carpeaux's *The Dance* (see fig. 907)—and ornament than from its architectural vocabulary. The whole building looks "overdressed," its luxurious vulgarity so naïve as to be disarming. It reflects the taste of the beneficiaries of the Industrial Revolution, newly rich and powerful, who saw themselves as the heirs of the old aristocracy. For a comparably extravagant display, we must turn to Sansovino's Library of St. Mark's (fig. 663), which celebrates the wealth of Venice. Small wonder, then, that magnates found the styles predating the French Revolution more appealing than Neoclassical or Neo-Gothic.

DECORATIVE ARTS

THE EMPIRE STYLE. The decorative arts followed much the same course as architecture during the Romantic era, but they were, if anything, more eclectic still. The revival sparked by the discoveries at Pompeii and Herculaneum reached its climax during the early nineteenth century with the Empire style, that late form of Neoclassicism which spread throughout Europe in the wake of Napoleon's conquests. As the term suggests, the style drew heavily on Roman art, which associated Napoleon with the Caesars by borrowing imperial attributes. Initially Roman prototypes had been copied more or less faithfully, but such imitations are among the least interesting products of the Empire style. Far more significant are the free adaptations of these sources to glorify the Bonapartes. These often incorporate Egyptian motifs to commemorate Napoleon's invasion in 1798 which opened up the Middle East.

PERCIER AND FONTAINE. We have already caught a glimpse of the Empire style in the bed of Canova's Pauline Borghese as Venus (fig. 902). We see it at its fullest in the Château de Malmaison, Napoleon's private residence near Paris, which was remodeled after 1798 by the architects Charles Percier (1764–1838) and Pierre-François Fontaine (1762–1853). They were also entrusted with its furnishings, and their book on interior decoration, printed in 1812, set the

standard for the Empire style. The bedroom of Napoleon's wife, Joséphine, reveals her taste for the ostentatious, which was so characteristic of the Empire style as a whole (fig. 921). Thus its lavish splendor tells us a great deal about the First Empire and its ambitions. The décor here serves the same propagandistic purpose as at Versailles (see fig. 802), for this is a state bedroom. (She usually slept in an ordinary one nearby.) Although ordered previously, the remarkable bed—made by François-Honoré Jacob-Desmalter (1770–1841), the preeminent furniture manufacturer under Napoleon, after a design by Percier and Fontaine—became the centerpiece of a total redecoration in 1810 that continues to proclaim Joséphine as empress after their marriage was annulled earlier that year. It incorporates swans and cornucopias, standard Napoleonic devices, with a traditional canopy that evokes a military tent surmounted by an imperial eagle. Nearby is a tripod washstand, with basin and jug, based on Pompeiian examples. Like everything else about the bedroom, it adheres to archaeological fact in details. Yet nothing in antiquity looked like this, and the effect is surprisingly close to the style of Louis XVI on the eve of the French Revolution.

THE INDUSTRIAL REVOLUTION. The rise of the Industrial Revolution led to the debasement of the decorative arts as everything from porcelain and silverware to drapery and furniture became mass-produced to meet the needs of the rapidly expanding middle class. Despite attempts to preserve the craftsmanship of the past, the machine won out after the Revolution of 1848. This was accompanied by a corresponding decline in the standards of design, which catered to the largest possible clientele. During the Restoration and Second Empire, the decorative arts were intended to evoke the earlier glory of France through indiscriminate imitation. There were even revivals of revival styles! By 1840 furnishings began to disappear in a welter of eclectic bric-a-brac that provided an opulent setting for the new captains of industry. In consequence, only rarely did the decorative arts manage to rise above the pedestrian. Among the few exceptions are the enormous torchères for the Grand Staircase of the Paris Opéra (see fig. 918) by the gifted sculptor Albert-Ernest Carrier-Belleuse (1824–1887). In the end, however, the only thing that could reverse the trend was another revolution in the decorative arts: the Arts and Crafts Movement (see pages 744–45).

PHOTOGRAPHY

Is photography art? The fact that we still pose the question testifies to the continuing debate. The answers have varied with the changing definition and understanding of art. In itself, of course, photography is simply a medium, like oil paint or pastel, used to make art but having no inherent claim to being art. After all, what distinguishes an art from a craft is why, not how, it is done. But photography shares creativity with art because, by its very nature, its performance necessarily involves the imagination. Any photograph, even a casual snapshot, represents both an organization of experience and the record of a mental image. The subject and style of a photograph thus tell us about the photographer's inner and outer worlds. Furthermore, like painting and sculpture, photography participates in

922. Joseph Nicéphore Niépce. *View from His Window at Le Gras.* 1826.
Heliograph, 6¹/₂ x 7⁷/₈" (16.5 x 20 cm). Gernsheim Collection,
Harry Ransom Research Center, University of Texas at Austin

aspects of the same process of seek-and-find. Photographers may not realize what they respond to until after they see the image that has been printed.

Like woodcut, etching, engraving, and lithography, photography is a form of printmaking that is dependent on mechanical processes. But in contrast to the other graphic mediums, photography has always been tainted as the product of a new technology. Apart from pushing a button or lever, or setting up special effects, no active intervention is required of the artist's hand to guide an idea. For this reason, the camera has usually been considered to be little more than a recording device. Photography, however, is by no means a neutral medium; its reproduction of reality is never completely faithful. Whether we realize it or not, the camera alters appearances. Photographs reinterpret the world around us, making us literally see it in new terms.

Photography and painting represent parallel responses to their times and have generally expressed the same world view. Sometimes the camera's power to extend our way of seeing has been realized first by the painter's creative vision. The two mediums nevertheless differ fundamentally in their approach and temperament. Painters communicate their understanding through techniques that represent their cumulative response over time, whereas photographers recognize the moment when the subject before them corresponds to the mental image they have formed of it.

It is hardly surprising that photography and art have enjoyed an uneasy relationship from the start. Artists have generally treated the photograph as something like a preliminary sketch, as a convenient source of ideas or record of motifs to be fleshed out and incorporated into a finished work. Academic painters found the detail provided by photographs to be in keeping with their own precise naturalism. Many other kinds of artists resorted to photographs, though not always admitting it. Photography has in turn been heavily influenced throughout its history by the painter's mediums, and photographs may still be judged according to how well they imitate paintings and drawings. To understand photography's place in the history of art, we must recognize the medium's particular strengths and inherent limitations.

The Founders of Photography

In 1822 a French inventor named Joseph Nicéphore Niépce (1765–1833) succeeded, at the age of 57, in making the first permanent photographic image, although his earliest surviving example (fig. 922) dates from four years later. He then joined forces with a younger man, Louis-Jacques-Mandé Daguerre (1789–1851), who had devised an improved camera. After ten more years of chemical and mechanical research, the daguerreotype, using positive exposures, was unveiled publicly in 1839, and the age of photography was born. The announcement spurred the Englishman William Henry Fox Talbot (1800–1877) to complete his own photographic process, involving a paper negative from which positives could be made, that he had been pursuing independently since 1833.

What motivated the earliest photographers? They were searching for an artistic medium, not for a device of practical utility. Though Niépce was a research chemist rather than an artist, his achievement was an outgrowth of his efforts to improve the lithographic process. Daguerre was a skilled painter, and he probably turned to the camera to heighten the illusionism in his huge painted dioramas, which were the sensation of Paris during the 1820s and 1830s. Fox Talbot saw in photography a substitute for drawing, as well as a means of reproduction, after using a camera obscura as a tool to sketch landscapes while on a vacation. The interest that all of the founders had in the artistic potential of the medium they had created is reflected in their photographs. Daguerre's first

923. Louis-Jacques-Mandé Daguerre. *Still Life*. 1837.
Daguerreotype, 6¹/₂ x 8¹/₂"(16.5 x 21.7 cm). Société Française de
Photographie, Paris

924. William Henry Fox Talbot. *Sailing Craft.*
c. 1845. Calotype. Science Museum, London

picture (fig. 923) imitates a type of still life originated by Chardin while Fox Talbot's *Sailing Craft* (fig. 924) looks like the English marine paintings of his day.

That the new medium should have a mechanical aspect was particularly appropriate. It was as if the Industrial Revolution, having forever altered civilization's way of life, now had to invent its own method for recording itself, although the transience of modern existence was not captured by "stopping the action" until the 1870s. Photography underwent a rapid series of improvements, including inventions for better lenses, glass-plate negatives, and new chemical processes, which provided faster emulsions and more stable images. Since many of the initial limitations of photography were overcome around mid-century, it would be misleading to tell the early history of the medium in terms of technological developments, important though they were.

The basic mechanics and chemistry of photography, moreover, had been known for a long time. The camera obscura, a box with a small hole in one end, dates back to antiquity. In the sixteenth century it was widely used for visual demonstrations. The camera was fitted with a mirror and then a lens in the Baroque period, which saw major advances in optical science culminating in Newtonian physics. By the 1720s it had become an aid in drawing architectural scenes. At the same time, silver salts were discovered to be light-sensitive.

Why, then, did it take another hundred years for someone to put this knowledge together? Much of the answer lies in the nature of scientific revolutions, which as a rule combine old technologies and concepts with new ones. (They do this in response to changing world views that they, in turn, influence.) Photography was neither inevitable in the history of technology, nor necessary to the history of art; yet it was an idea whose time had clearly come. If we try for a moment to imagine that photography was invented a hundred years earlier, we will find this to be impossible simply on artistic, apart from technological, grounds: the eighteenth century was too devoted to fantasy to be interested in the literalness of photography. Rococo portraiture, for example, was more concerned with providing a flattering image than an accurate likeness, so that the camera's straightforward record would have been totally out of place. Even in architectural painting, extreme liberties were willingly taken with topographical truth (see pages 628–29).

The invention of photography was a response to the artistic urges and historical forces that underlie Romanticism. Much of the impulse came from a quest for the True and the Natural. The desire for "images made by Nature" can already be seen, on the one hand, in Cozens' ink-blot compositions (see fig. 849), which were "natural" because they were made by chance; and, on the other, in the late-eighteenth-century vogue for silhouette portraits (traced from the shadow of the sitter's profile), which led to attempts to record such shadows on light-sensitive materials. David's harsh realism in *The Death of Marat* (fig. 844) had already proclaimed the cause of unvarnished truth. So did Ingres' *Louis Bertin* (fig. 871), which established the standards of physical reality and character portrayal that photographers would follow. [See Primary Sources, no. 85, page 937.]

925. Nadar. *Sarah Bernhardt.* 1859. George Eastman House, Rochester, New York

926. Honoré Daumier. *Nadar Elevating Photography to the Height of Art.* 1862. Lithograph. George Eastman House, Rochester, New York

Portraiture

Like lithography, which was invented in 1797, photography met the growing middle-class demand for images of all kinds. By 1850, large numbers of the bourgeoisie were having their likenesses painted, and it was in portraiture that photography found its readiest acceptance. Soon after the daguerreotype was introduced, photographic studios sprang up everywhere, especially in America, and multi-image *cartes de visites,* invented in 1854 by Adolphe-Eugène Disdéri, became ubiquitous. Anyone could have a portrait taken cheaply and easily. In the process, the average person became memorable. Photography thus became an outgrowth of the democratic values fostered by the American and French revolutions. There was also keen competition among photographers to get the famous to pose for portraits.

NADAR. Gaspard Félix Tournachon (1820–1910), better known as Nadar, managed to attract most of France's leading personalities to his studio. Like many early photographers, he started out as an artist but came to prefer the lens to the brush. He initially used the camera to capture the likenesses of the 280 sitters whom he caricatured in an enormous lithograph, *Le Panthéon Nadar.* The actress Sarah Bernhardt posed for him several times, and his photographs of her (fig. 925) are the direct ancestors of modern glamour photography (compare fig. 1210). With her romantic pose and expression, she is a counterpart to the soulful maidens who inhabit much of nineteenth-century painting. Nadar has treated her in remarkably

sculptural terms. Indeed, the play of light and sweep of drapery are reminiscent of the sculptured portrait busts that were so popular with collectors at the time.

The Restless Spirit

Early photography reflected the outlook and temperament of Romanticism, and indeed the entire nineteenth century had a pervasive curiosity and an abiding belief that everything could be discovered. While this fascination sometimes manifested a serious interest in science—witness Darwin's voyage on the *Beagle* from 1831 to 1836—it more typically took the form of a restless quest for new experiences and places. Photography had a remarkable impact on the imagination of the period by making the rest of the world widely available, or by simply revealing it in a new way. Sometimes the search for new subjects was close to home. Nadar, for example, took aerial photographs of Paris from a hot-air balloon. This feat was wittily parodied by Daumier (fig. 926), whose caption, "Nadar Elevating Photography to the Height of Art," expresses the prevailing skepticism about the aesthetics of the new medium.

A love of the exotic was fundamental to Romantic escapism, and by 1850 photographers had begun to cart their equipment to faraway places. The same restless spirit that we saw in George Caleb Bingham's *Fur Traders Descending the Missouri* (see fig. 899) also drew photographers to the frontier, where they documented the westward expansion of the United States, often for the U.S. Geological Survey, with pictures that have primarily historical interest today.

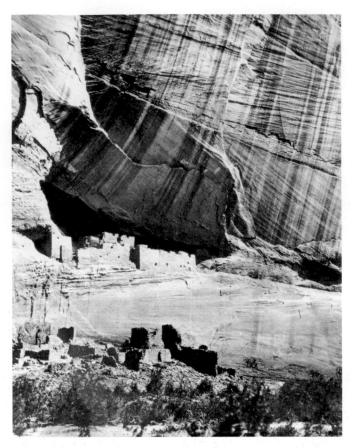

927. Timothy O'Sullivan. *Ancient Ruins in the Cañon de Chelle, N.M.,
in a Niche 50 Feet Above the Present Cañon Bed*
(now Canyon de Chelly National Monument, Arizona). 1873.
Albumen print. George Eastman House, Rochester, New York

O'SULLIVAN. An exception is the landscape photography of Timothy O'Sullivan (c. 1841–1882), who often preferred scenery that contemporary painters had overlooked. He practically invented his own aesthetic in photographing the *Cañon de Chelle* (fig. 927), for it conforms to no established pictorial type. The view fills the entire photograph, allowing no visual relief and lending it awesome force. The composition is held together by the play of lines of the displaced strata of the rock, which creates a striking abstract design. O'Sullivan's control of tonal relations is so masterful that even color photographs taken since then of the same site have far less impact.

Stereophotography

The unquenchable thirst for vicarious experiences accounts for the expanding popularity of stereoscopic daguerreotypes. Invented in 1849, the two-lens camera produced two photographs that correspond to the slightly different images perceived by our two eyes. When seen through a special viewer called a stereoscope, the stereoptic photographs fuse to create a remarkable illusion of three-dimensional depth. Two years later, stereoscopes became the rage at the Crystal Palace exposition in London (see fig. 962). Countless thousands of double views were taken, such as that in figure 928. Virtually every corner of the earth became accessible to practically any household, with a vividness second only to being there.

Stereophotography was an important breakthrough, for its binocular vision marked a distinct departure from perspective in the pictorial tradition and demonstrated for the first time photography's potential to enlarge vision. Curiously enough, this success waned, except for special uses. People were simply too habituated to viewing pictures as if with one eye. Later on, when the halftone plate was invented in the 1880s for reproducing pictures on a printed page, stereophotographs revealed another drawback. As our illustration shows, they were unsuitable for this process of reproduction. From then on, single-lens photography was inextricably linked with the mass media of the day.

Photojournalism

Fundamental to the rise of photography was the pervasive nineteenth-century sense that the present was already history in the making. Only with the advent of the Romantic hero did great acts other than martyrdom become popular subjects for contemporary painters and sculptors, and it can hardly be surprising that photography was invented a year after the death of Napoleon, who had been the subject of more paintings than any secular leader ever before. At about the same time, Géricault's *The Raft of the "Medusa"* (fig. 868) and Delacroix's *The Massacre at Chios* (fig. 873) signaled a decisive

928. *Tsar Cannon Outside the Spassky Gate, Moscow* (cast 1586; presently inside the Kremlin). Second half of 19th century. Stereophotograph

929. Alexander Gardner. *Home of a Rebel Sharpshooter, Gettysburg.* July 1863. Wet-plate photograph. Chicago Historical Society

shift in the Romantic attitude toward representing contemporary events. This outlook brought with it a new kind of photography: photojournalism.

BRADY. Its first great representative was Mathew Brady (1823–1896), who covered the Civil War in the United States. Other wars had already been photographed, but Brady and his 20 assistants (including Timothy O'Sullivan), using cameras too slow and cumbersome to show actual combat, nevertheless were able to bring home the horrors of that war with unprecedented directness.

GARDNER. *Home of a Rebel Sharpshooter, Gettysburg* (fig. 929) by Alexander Gardner (1821–1882), who left Brady to form his own photographic team in 1863, is a landmark in the history of art. Never before had both the grim reality and the significance of death on the battlefield been conveyed so inexorably in a single image. Compared with the heroic act celebrated by Benjamin West (see fig. 845), this tragedy is as anonymous as the slain soldier himself. The photograph is all the more persuasive for having the same harsh realism found in David's *The Death of Marat* (see fig. 844), and the limp figure, hardly visible between the rocks framing the scene, is no less poignant. In contrast, the paintings and engravings by the artists—notably Winslow Homer (see pages 732–33)—who illustrated the Civil War for magazines and newspapers were mostly genre scenes that kept the reality of combat safely at arm's length.

CHAPTER TWO

REALISM AND IMPRESSIONISM

PAINTING

France

"Can Jupiter survive the lightning rod?" asked Karl Marx, not long after the middle of the century. The question, implying that the ancient god of thunder and lightning was now in jeopardy through science, sums up the dilemma we felt in the sculptor Carpeaux's *The Dance* (fig. 907). The French poet and art critic Charles Baudelaire was addressing himself to the same problem when, in 1846, he called for paintings that expressed "the heroism of modern life." [See Primary Sources, no. 86, page 937.] At that time only one painter was willing to make an artistic creed of this demand: Baudelaire's friend Gustave Courbet (1819–1877).

COURBET AND REALISM. Courbet was born in Ornans, a village near the French-Swiss border, and remained proud of his rural background. He had begun as a Neo-Baroque Romantic in the early 1840s. But by 1848, under the impact of the revolutionary upheavals then sweeping over Europe, he had come to believe that the Romantic emphasis on feeling and imagination was merely an escape from the realities of the time. The modern artist must rely on direct experience—"I cannot paint an angel because I have never seen one," he said—they must be Realists. [See Primary Sources, no. 87, page 938.] As a descriptive term, "realism" is not very precise. For Courbet, it meant something akin to the "naturalism" of Caravaggio (fig. 726). As an admirer of Louis Le Nain and Rembrandt he had, in fact, strong links with the Caravaggesque tradition, and his work, like Caravaggio's, was denounced for its supposed vulgarity and lack of spiritual content. What ultimately defines Courbet's Realism, however, and distinguishes it from Romanticism is his allegiance to radical politics. His Socialist views colored his entire outlook, and although it did not determine the specific content or appearance of his pictures, it does help to account for his choice of subject matter and style, which went against the grain of tradition.

The storm broke in 1849, when Courbet exhibited *The Stone Breakers* (fig. 930), the first canvas fully embodying his programmatic Realism. Here, for the first time, was a picture that treated an apparent genre scene with the same seriousness and monumentality as a history painting, in disregard of the academic hierarchy, and with a heavy impasto that violated accepted standards of finish. Courbet had seen two men working on a road, and had asked them to pose for him in his studio. He painted them lifesize, solidly and matter-of-factly. The picture is very much larger than anything by Millet, and with none of his overt pathos or sentiment (compare fig. 882). The young man's face is averted, the old one's half hidden by a hat. Yet he cannot have picked them casually. Their contrast in age is significant: one is too old for such heavy work, the other too young. Endowed with the dignity of their symbolic status, they do not turn to us for sympathy. Courbet's friend, the Socialist Pierre-Joseph Proudhon, likened them to a parable from the Gospels.

During the 1855 Paris Exposition, where works by Ingres and Delacroix were prominently displayed, Courbet brought his pictures to attention by organizing a private exhibition in a large shed and by distributing a "manifesto of Realism." The show centered on a huge canvas, the most ambitious of his career, entitled *Studio of a Painter: A Real Allegory Summarizing My Seven Years of Life as an Artist* (fig. 931). "Real allegory" is something of a teaser. Allegories, after all, are unreal by definition. Courbet meant either an allegory couched in the terms of his particular Realism, or one that did not conflict with the "real" identity of the figures or objects embodying it.

The framework is familiar: Courbet's composition clearly belongs to the type of Velázquez' *The Maids of Honor* and Goya's *The Family of Charles IV* (see figs. 759 and 863). But now the artist has moved to the center, and the visitors here are his guests, not royal patrons who enter whenever they wish.

930. Gustave Courbet. *The Stone Breakers.* 1849. Oil on canvas, 5'3" x 8'6" (1.6 x 2.6 m).
Formerly Gemäldegalerie, Dresden. Destroyed 1945

931. Gustave Courbet. *Studio of a Painter: A Real Allegory Summarizing My Seven Years of Life as an Artist.* 1854–55.
Oil on canvas, 11'10" x 19'7" (3.6 x 6 m). Musée d'Orsay, Paris

He has invited them specially for a purpose that becomes evident only upon thoughtful reflection. The picture does not yield its full meaning unless we take the title seriously and inquire into Courbet's relation to this assembly.

There are two main groups. On the left are "the people." They are types rather than individuals, drawn largely from the artist's home environment at Ornans: hunters, peasants, workers, a Jew, a priest, a young mother with her baby. On the right, in contrast, we see groups of portraits representing the Parisian side of Courbet's life: clients, critics, intellectuals. (The man reading is Baudelaire.) All of these people are strangely passive, as if they were waiting for we know not what. Some are quietly conversing among themselves, others seem immersed in thought. Yet hardly anybody looks at Courbet. They are not his audience, but a representative sampling of his social environment.

Only two people watch the artist at work: a small boy, intended to suggest "the innocent eye," and the nude model. What is her role? In a more conventional picture, we would identify her as Inspiration, or Courbet's Muse, but she is no less "real" than the others here. Courbet probably meant her to be Nature, or that undisguised Truth which he proclaimed to be the guiding principle of his art. (Note the emphasis on the clothing she has just taken off.) Significantly enough, the center group is illuminated by clear, sharp daylight, but the background and the lateral figures are veiled in semidarkness, to underline the contrast between the artist—the active creator—and the world around him that waits to be brought to life.

MANET AND THE "REVOLUTION OF THE COLOR PATCH." Courbet's *Studio* helps us to understand a picture that shocked the public even more: *Luncheon on the Grass* (see fig. 4), showing a nude model accompanied by two gentlemen in frock coats, by Édouard Manet (1832–1883). Manet was the first to grasp Courbet's full importance; his *Luncheon,* among other things, is a tribute to the older artist. He particularly offended contemporary morality by juxtaposing the nude and nattily attired figures in an outdoor setting, the more so since the noncommittal title offered no "higher" significance. Yet the group has so formal a pose that Manet certainly did not intend to depict an actual event. (For its classical source, see figs. 5 and 6.) Perhaps the meaning of the canvas lies in this denial of plausibility, for the scene fits neither the plane of everyday experience nor that of allegory.

The *Luncheon,* as a visual manifesto of artistic freedom, is much more revolutionary than Courbet's. It asserts the painter's privilege to combine whatever elements he pleases for aesthetic effect alone. The nudity of the model is "explained" by the contrast between her warm, creamy flesh tones and the cool black-and-gray of the men's attire. Or, to put it another way, the world of painting has "natural laws" that are distinct from those of familiar reality, and the painter's first loyalty is to his canvas, not to the outside world. Here begins an attitude that was later summed up in the doctrine of Art for Art's Sake and became a bone of contention between progressives and conservatives for the rest of the century (see page 731). Manet himself disdained such controversies, but his work attests to his lifelong devotion to "pure painting": to the belief that brushstrokes and color patches themselves—not what they stand for—are the artist's

932. Édouard Manet. *The Fifer.* 1866. Oil on canvas, 63 x 38¼" (160 x 97.5 cm). Musée d'Orsay, Paris

primary reality. Among painters of the past, he found that Hals, Velázquez, and Goya had come closest to this ideal. He admired their broad, open technique, their preoccupation with light and color values. Many of his canvases are, in fact, "pictures of pictures": they translate into modern terms those older works that particularly challenged him. Yet he always took care to filter out the expressive or symbolic content of his models, lest the beholder's attention be distracted from the pictorial structure itself. His paintings, regardless of subject, have an emotional reticence that can easily be mistaken for emptiness unless we understand its purpose.

Courbet is said to have remarked that Manet's pictures were as flat as playing cards. Looking at *The Fifer* (fig. 932), we can see what he meant. Done three years after the *Luncheon,* it is a painting with very little modeling, no depth, and hardly any shadows. (There are a few, actually, but it takes a real effort to find them.) The figure looks three-dimensional only because its contour renders the forms in realistic fore-

933. Claude Monet. *On the Bank of the Seine, Bennecourt.* 1868.
Oil on canvas, 32¹/₈ x 39⁵/₈" (81.5 x 100.7 cm). The Art Institute of Chicago
Mr. and Mrs. Potter Palmer Collection

shortening. Otherwise, Manet eschews all the methods devised since Giotto's time for transforming a flat surface into a pictorial space. The undifferentiated light-gray background seems as near to us as the figure, and just as solid. If the fifer stepped out of the picture, he would leave a hole, like the cutout shape of a stencil.

Here, then, the canvas itself has been redefined. It is no longer a "window," but a screen made up of flat patches of color. How radical a step this was can be readily seen if we match *The Fifer* against Delacroix's *The Massacre at Chios* (fig. 873), and a Cubist work such as Picasso's *Three Dancers* of 1925 (fig. 1049). The structure of Manet's painting obviously resembles that of Picasso's, whereas Delacroix's—or even Courbet's—still follows the "window" tradition of the Renaissance. In retrospect, we realize that the revolutionary qualities of Manet's art could already be seen in the *Luncheon,* even if they were not yet so obvious. The three figures lifted from Raphael's group of river-gods form a unit nearly as shadowless and stencillike as *The Fifer.* They would be more at home on a flat screen, for the chiaroscuro of their present setting, which is inspired by the landscapes of Courbet, no longer fits them.

MONET AND IMPRESSIONISM. What brought about this "revolution of the color patch"? We do not know, and Manet himself surely did not reason it out beforehand. It is tempting to think that he was impelled to create the new style by the challenge of photography. The "pencil of nature," then known for a quarter-century, had demonstrated the objective truth of Renaissance perspective, but it established a standard of representational accuracy that no handmade image could hope to rival. Painting needed to be rescued from competition with the camera. This Manet accomplished by insisting

that a painted canvas is, above all, a material surface covered with pigments—that we must look at it, not through it. Unlike Courbet, he gave no name to the style he had created. When his followers began calling themselves Impressionists, he refused to adopt the term for his own work. His aim was to be accepted as a Salon painter, a goal that eluded him until late in life.

The word *Impressionism* had been coined in 1874, after a hostile critic had looked at a picture entitled *Impression: Sunrise* by Claude Monet (1840–1926), and it certainly fits Monet better than it does Manet. Monet had adopted Manet's concept of painting and applied it to landscapes done outdoors. Monet's *On the Bank of the Seine, Bennecourt* of 1868 (fig. 933) is flooded with sunlight so bright that conservative critics claimed it made their eyes smart. In this flickering network of color patches, shaped like mosaic tesserae, the reflections on the water are as "real" as the banks of the Seine. [See Primary Sources, no. 88, page 938.] Even more than *The Fifer,* Monet's painting is a "playing card." Were it not for the woman and the boat in the foreground, the picture would be just as effective upside-down. The mirror image here serves a purpose contrary to that of earlier mirror images (compare fig. 686). Instead of adding to the illusion of real space, it strengthens the unity of the actual painted surface. This inner coherence sets *On the Bank of the Seine, Bennecourt* apart from Romantic "impressions" such as Constable's *Hampstead Heath* (see fig. 887) or Corot's *View of Rome* (see fig. 879), even though all three share the same on-the-spot immediacy and fresh perception.

In the late 1860s and early 1870s Monet and his friend Auguste Renoir (1841–1919) worked together to develop Impressionism into a fully mature style, one that proved ideally

934. Claude Monet. *Red Boats, Argenteuil.* 1875.
Oil on canvas, 23¹/2 x 31⁵/8" (59.7 x 80.3 cm). Fogg Art Museum,
Harvard University Art Museums, Cambridge, Massachusetts

935. Camille Pissarro. *The Côte des Boeufs at l'Hermitage, near Pontoise.*
1877. Oil on canvas, 45¹/4 x 34¹/2" (114.9 x 87.6 cm).
The National Gallery, London

suited to painting outdoors. Monet's *Red Boats, Argenteuil* (fig. 934) captures to perfection the intense sunlight of Argenteuil along the Seine near Paris, where the artist was spending his summers. Now the flat brushstrokes have become flecks of paint, which convey an extraordinary range of visual effects.

The amazingly free brush weaves a tapestry of rich color inspired by the late paintings of Delacroix. Despite its spontaneity, Monet's technique retains an underlying logic in which each color and brushstroke has its place. As an aesthetic, then, Impressionism was hardly the straightforward realism it first seems. It nevertheless remained an intuitive approach, even in its color, although the Impressionists were familiar with many of the optical theories that were to provide the basis for Seurat's Divisionism (see pages 750–51).

PISSARRO. The method that Monet and Renoir evolved was soon adopted by other members of the group. The landscapes of Camille Pissarro (1830–1903) have an unaffected naturalism that places him close to the Barbizon School, and a firm, almost classical structure that was shared only by his friend Paul Cézanne (see pages 746–49). We see these qualities in *The Côte des Boeufs at l'Hermitage, near Pontoise* (fig. 935). The painting has a real feel for rural life and scenery, which concerned Pissarro more than any other Impressionist. The artist makes no attempt to beautify the overgrown landscape, yet the stately procession of trees and blocklike buildings lend the picture a timeless dignity. The surprisingly abstract composition establishes a complex rhythm across the picture plane. This structure lends order to the tangled network of forms embedded in the dense surface texture, which evokes the rebirth of life in early springtime.

RENOIR. The Impressionist painters answered Baudelaire's call to artists to capture the "heroism of modern life" by depicting its dress and its pastimes. Scenes from the world of entertainment—dance halls, cafés, concerts, the theater—were favorite subjects for them. These carefree vignettes of bourgeois pleasure are flights from the cares of daily life. Renoir filled his work with the *joie de vivre* of a singularly happy temperament. The flirting couples in *Le Moulin de la Galette* (fig. 936), dappled with sunlight and shadow, radiate a human warmth that is utterly entrancing, even though the artist permits us no more than a fleeting glance at any of them. Our role is that of the casual stroller, who takes in this slice of life in passing.

MANET AND IMPRESSIONISM. Such spontaneity came less easily to the austere, deliberate Manet; it appears in his work only after about 1870, under Monet's influence. Manet nevertheless remained the finest painter of all the Impressionists. His last major picture, *A Bar at the Folies-Bergère,* of 1881–82 (fig. 937), is an unequaled tour de force. The canvas shows a single figure as calm and as firmly set within the rectangle of the canvas as the fifer, but the background is no longer neutral. A huge shimmering mirror image now fills four-fifths of the picture. The mirror, close behind the barmaid, shows the whole interior of the nightclub, but deprives it of three-dimensionality, in part by taking liberties with the scene. (Note how the barmaid's reflection is shown off to one side, something that is impossible in reality.) The serving girl's attitude, detached and touched with melancholy, contrasts poignantly with the gaiety of her setting, which she is not permitted to share. For all its urbanity, the mood of the canvas reminds us oddly of Daumier's *The Third-Class Carriage* (see fig. 877).

936. Auguste Renoir. *Le Moulin de la Galette.* 1876.
Oil on canvas, 51$\frac{1}{2}$ x 69" (130.7 x 175.3 cm). Musée d'Orsay, Paris

937. Édouard Manet. *A Bar at the Folies-Bergère.* 1881–82.
Oil on canvas, 37$\frac{1}{2}$ x 51" (95.3 x 129.7 cm). Courtauld Institute Galleries, Home House Trustees, London

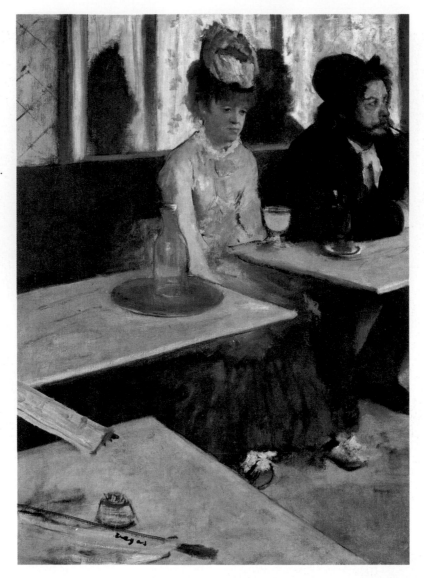

938. Edgar Degas.
The Glass of Absinthe. 1876.
Oil on canvas, 36 x 27"
(91.3 x 68.7 cm).
Musée d'Orsay, Paris

939. *(opposite):*
Edgar Degas. *Prima
Ballerina*. c. 1876.
Pastel, 23 x 16¹/2"
(58.3 x 42 cm).
Musée d'Orsay, Paris

DEGAS.   Edgar Degas (1834–1917), too, had a profound sense of human character that lends weight even to seemingly casual scenes such as that in *The Glass of Absinthe* (fig. 938). He makes us look steadily at the disenchanted pair in his café scene, but out of the corner of our eye, so to speak. The design of this picture at first seems as unstudied as a snapshot—Degas practiced photography—yet a longer look shows us that everything here dovetails precisely. The zigzag of empty tables between us and the luckless couple reinforces their brooding loneliness, for example. Compositions as boldly calculated as this set Degas apart from other Impressionists.

A wealthy aristocrat by birth, he had been trained in the tradition of Ingres, whom he greatly admired. When he joined the Impressionists, Degas did not abandon his early allegiance to draftsmanship. His finest works were often done in pastels (powdered pigments molded into sticks), which had a strong appeal for him since they yielded effects of line, tone, and color simultaneously. *Prima Ballerina* (fig. 939) well demonstrates this flexible medium. The oblique view of the stage, from a box near the proscenium arch, has been shaped into another deliberately off-center composition. The dancer floats above the steeply tilted floor like a butterfly caught in the glare of the footlights.

940. Edgar Degas. *The Tub*. 1886. Pastel,
23¹/2 x 32³/8"(59.7 x 82.3 cm). Musée d'Orsay, Paris

A decade later, *The Tub* (fig. 940) is again an oblique view, but now severe, almost geometric, in design. The tub and the crouching woman, both vigorously outlined, form a circle within a square, and the rest of the rectangular format is filled by a shelf so sharply tilted that it almost shares the plane of the picture. Yet on this shelf Degas has placed two pitchers that are

941. Berthe Morisot. *La Lecture (Reading)*. 1888.
Oil on canvas, 29¼ x 36½" (74.3 x 92.7 cm).
Museum of Fine Arts, St. Petersburg, Florida
Gift of Friends of Art in Memory of Margaret Acheson Stuart

942. Mary Cassatt. *The Bath*. 1891–92. Oil on canvas,
39½ x 26" (100.3 x 66 cm). The Art Institute of Chicago
Robert A. Waller Collection

hardly foreshortened at all. (Note how the curve of the small one fits the handle of the other.) Here the tension between "two-D" and "three-D" surface and depth comes close to the breaking point. *The Tub* is Impressionist only in its shimmering, luminous colors. Its other qualities are more characteristic of the 1880s, the first Post-Impressionist decade, when many artists showed a renewed concern with problems of form (see Chapter 3).

MORISOT. The Impressionists' ranks included several women of great ability. The subject matter of Berthe Morisot (1841–1895), a member of the group from its inception, was the world she knew: the domestic life of the French upper middle class, which she depicted with authentic understanding. Morisot's early paintings, centering on her mother and her sister Edma, were influenced at first by Manet, whose brother she later married, but they have a subtle sense of alienation distinctive to her. Her mature work is altogether different in character. The birth of her daughter Julie in 1878 signaled a change in her art, which reached its height during the following decade. Her painting of a little girl reading in a room overlooking the artist's garden (fig. 941) shows a light-filled style

of her own making. Morisot applied her virtuoso brushwork with a sketchlike brevity that omits nonessential details yet conveys a complete impression of the scene. The figure is fully integrated within the formal design, whose appeal is enhanced by the pastel hues she favored. Morisot's painting radiates an air of contentment free of the sentimentality that often affects genre paintings of the period.

CASSATT. Surprisingly, Americans were the first patrons of the Impressionists, responding to the new style sooner than Europeans did. At a time when no French museum would have them, Impressionist works entered public collections in the United States, and American painters such as Whistler and Mary Cassatt (1845–1926) were among the earliest followers of Manet and his circle. Cassatt joined the Impressionists in 1877, becoming a tireless champion of their work. [See Primary Sources, no. 89, page 938.] She had received a standard academic training in her native Philadelphia, but had to struggle to overcome traditional barriers. Like Morisot, she was able to pursue her career as an artist, an occupation regarded as unsuitable for women, because she was independently wealthy. Cassatt was instrumental in gaining early acceptance of Impres-

943. Claude Monet. *Water Lilies*. 1907. Oil on canvas,
36¹/2 x 29" (92.7 x 73.7 cm). Kawamura Memorial Museum of Art,
Sakura City, Chiba Prefecture, Japan

sionist paintings in the United States through her social contacts with wealthy private collectors. Although she never married, maternity provided the thematic and formal focus of most
of her work. Cassatt developed a highly accomplished individual style, seen at its best in *The Bath* (fig. 942), which is characteristic of her mature work around 1890. The oblique view,
simplified color forms, and flat composition show the impact
of her mentor Degas, as well as her study of Japanese prints.
Despite the complexity of its design, the painting has a directness that lends simple dignity to motherhood.

MONET'S LATER WORKS. By the mid-1880s Impressionism became widely accepted, its technique imitated by
conservative painters and practiced as a fusion style by a growing number of artists worldwide. Ironically, the movement
now underwent a deep crisis. Manet died in 1883. Renoir,
already beset by doubts, moved toward a more classical style.
Racked by internal dissension, the group held its last show in
1886. At that time Pissarro abandoned Impressionism altogether in favor of Seurat's Divisionism for several years (see
pages 750–51). Among the major figures of the movement,
Monet alone remained faithful to the Impressionist view of

nature. Nevertheless, his work became more subjective over
time, although he never ventured into fantasy, nor did he forsake the basic approach of his earlier landscapes.

About 1890, Monet began to paint pictures in series,
showing the same subject under various conditions of light
and atmosphere. These tended increasingly to resemble Turner's "airy visions, painted with tinted steam" as Monet concentrated on effects of colored light. (He had visited London
and knew Turner's work; see pages 690–91.) His *Water Lilies*
(fig. 943) is a fascinating sequel to *On the Bank of the Seine* (fig.
933) across a span of almost 40 years. The surface of the pond
now takes up the entire canvas, so that the effect of a weightless screen is stronger than ever. The artist's brushwork, too,
has greater variety and a more individual rhythm. While the
scene is still based on nature, this is no ordinary landscape but
one entirely of his making. On the estate at Giverny given to
him late in life by the French government, the artist created a
self-contained world for purely personal and artistic purposes.
The subjects he painted there are as much reflections of his
imagination as they are of reality. They convey a very different
sense of time as well. Instead of the single moment captured
in *On the Bank of the Seine*, his *Water Lilies*, painted at Giverny,

944. Ford Madox Brown. *The Last of England.* 1852–55.
Oil on panel, 32¹/2 x 29¹/2" (82.5 x 74.9 cm). City Museum and Art
Gallery, Birmingham, England
By permission Birmingham Museum and Art Gallery

945. William Holman Hunt. *The Awakening Conscience.* 1853.
Oil on canvas, 30 x 20" (76.2 x 50.8 cm).
The Tate Gallery, London

summarizes a shifting impression of the pond in response to the changing water as the breezes play across it.

England

REALISM. By the time Monet came to admire his work, Turner's reputation was at a low ebb in his own country. In 1848, when Courbet launched his revolutionary doctrine of Realism, a concern with "the heroism of modern life" asserted itself quite independently in English painting as well, although the movement lacked a leader of Courbet's stature and assertiveness.

Perhaps the best-known example of English Realism is *The Last of England* (fig. 944) by Ford Madox Brown (1821–1893), a picture that enjoyed enormous popularity throughout the latter half of the century in the English-speaking world. The subject—a group of emigrants as they set out on their long overseas journey—may be less obvious today than it once was; nor does it carry the same emotional charge. Nonetheless, there can be no question that the artist has treated an important theme taken from modern experience, and that he has done so with touching seriousness.

The painting is intended to dramatize the conditions that made the emigrants decide to leave England. The pathos of the scene may strike us as a bit theatrical: note the contrast between the brooding young family in the foreground (Brown used himself, his wife, and daughter as the models) and the "good riddance" gesture of the man at the upper left. We rec-

ognize its source in the "dumb shows" of Hogarth, whom Brown revered (see fig. 824). Brown's style, however, has nothing in common with Hogarth's. Its extreme precision of detail strikes us as almost photographic. No hint of subjective "handwriting" is permitted to intervene between us and the scene depicted. Brown had acquired this painstaking technique some years earlier, after he met the Nazarenes, the group of German painters in Rome who practiced what they regarded as a "medieval" style (see page 696). He in turn transmitted it to his three pupils who together in 1848 helped to found an artists' society called the Pre-Raphaelite Brotherhood: William Holman Hunt (1827–1910), John Everett Millais (1829–1896), and Dante Gabriel Rossetti (1828–1882).

THE PRE-RAPHAELITES. Brown himself never actually joined the Pre-Raphaelites, but he shared their basic aims: to do battle against the frivolous art of the day by having "genuine ideas to express" and by producing "pure transcripts . . . from nature," an objective inspired by the writings of John Ruskin. As the name of the Brotherhood proclaims, its members took their inspiration from the "primitive" masters of the fifteenth century. To that extent, they belong to the Gothic revival, which had long been an important aspect of the Romantic movement. What set the Pre-Raphaelites apart from Romantics like the Nazarenes was an urge to reform the ills of modern civilization through their art. In this they were aroused by Chartism, the democratic working-class movement that reached its peak in the revolutionary year 1848.

946. Dante Gabriel Rossetti. *Beata Beatrix.* 1872.
Oil on canvas, 34¹/₂" x 27¹/₄" (87.5 x 69.3 cm);
predella 10¹/₂ x 27¹/₄" (26.5 x 69.3 cm). The Art Institute of Chicago
Charles L. Hutchinson Collection

The Awakening Conscience (fig. 945) by William Holman
Hunt, the artist who remained truest to the Brotherhood's
ideals, stands as perhaps the quintessential Pre-Raphaelite
statement. It, too, is a morality play in the tradition of
Hogarth. Inspired by an episode in Charles Dickens' *David
Copperfield,* the picture shows a young woman stirred to the
realization by the music she sings that she has been living in
sin. The scene is presented in obsessive detail, which is laden
with symbolic meaning: the print above the piano, for example, shows Christ and the Woman Taken into Adultery, while
the light reflected in the mirror is that of religious revelation.
Here the artist looked to the example of Jan van Eyck's *Arnolfini Portrait* (fig. 677), which had recently been acquired by the
National Gallery in London. Although he treated it as a personal moral crisis, *The Awakening Conscience* addresses a very
real social problem of the time.

Rossetti, unlike Hunt, was not concerned with social
issues. He thought of himself, rather, as a reformer of aesthetic sensibility. The vast majority of his work consists of watercolors or pastels showing women taken from literary sources
who bear a striking resemblance to his wife, Elizabeth Siddal.
Beata Beatrix (fig. 946), created as a memorial to Siddal,
imposes her features on the wife of his namesake, the Italian
poet Dante, whose account of her death inspired the painting.
Rossetti explained the program in considerable detail: "The
picture illustrates the 'Vita Nuova,' embodying symbolically
the death of Beatrice as treated in that work. The picture is not
intended at all to represent death, but to render it under the

947. Edward Burne-Jones. *The Wheel of Fortune.* 1877–83.
Oil on canvas, 6'6³/₄" x 3'3³/₈" (2 x 1 m). Musée d'Orsay, Paris

semblance of a trance. . . . I have introduced . . . the figures of
Dante and Love passing through the street and gazing omi-
nously on one another, conscious of the event; while the bird,
a messenger of death, drops the poppy between the hands of
Beatrice. She, through her shut lids, is conscious of a new
world." In this version, the artist has expressed the hope of seeing his beloved Elizabeth again by adding a second panel
showing Dante and Beatrice meeting in Paradise and inscribing the dates of their deaths on the frame. For all its apparent
spirituality, the painting radiates an aura of repressed eroticism
that is the hallmark of Rossetti's work and exerted a powerful
influence on other Pre-Raphaelites.

BURNE-JONES. We can sense it again in the work of
Rossetti's pupil Edward Burne-Jones (1833–1898), who, although he was too young to have been a member, came to be
identified most completely with the Brotherhood in the public's mind. *The Wheel of Fortune* (fig. 947) was initially planned
as part of a large pseudo-triptych devoted to the story of Troy.
Although the project was never realized, its content was allegorical, rather than illustrative, in character. Based on a poem
by William Morris that likewise remained unfinished, it

Instead of Realism, composers turned for inspiration to their native heritages. The fascination with folk music, as well as folklore, was an outgrowth of nationalism, an intrinsic part of Romanticism that became nearly universal after the mid-nineteenth century. Among the first to take up this interest was Johannes Brahms (1833–1897), a pupil of Robert Schumann, for whose widow, Clara, he developed an abiding but unrequited love. Brahms' development was slow: his first symphony was not completed until 1876, but it is cast in the heroic mold of Beethoven. No other composer of his generation wrote masterpieces in such a wide range of music. The works are characteristically intense, with writing high in the string sections, but the slow movements are of astonishingly tender lyricism. They are nevertheless without the bombast found in that of other composers from the same time, and are held together by a thorough command of composition and strong, classical structure.

Brahms was one of the first to appreciate the Czech composer Antonin Dvořák (1841–1904), whose career he encouraged. Whereas Brahms' music is alternately brooding and rapturous, Dvořák's is almost uniformly sunny and uniquely Czech in flavor—he called himself proudly "a happy Bohemian." Love of nature and homeland fill his music. Dvořák was proud of his national music, but he was affected by the music of other cultures, especially during his sojourn in New York as head of the National Conservatory of Music (1892–95), when he produced his celebrated *New World Symphony* and *American Quartet.* He left behind a body of chamber music even more substantial than Brahms', and a splendid cello concerto that is the greatest of its kind. The late tone poems, inspired mostly by folk tales, became important models for the next generation of Czech composers centering on Leoš Janáček (1854–1928).

Perhaps the most distinctive national school was to be found in Russia. The group known as "The Five" sought to infuse their music with the sound of their country and often took folk melodies as the basis for their work. They also revived the system of modes, which had remained intact in Orthodox music and was indigenous to large parts of Russia. The most original member of the Russian school was Modest Moussorgsky (1839–1881), despite being the least trained. His opera *Boris Godunov* (1868–72), written about the same time as Aleksei Tolstoy's drama but taken from an earlier play by Aleksandr Pushkin (1799–1837) and the history of Russia by Nikolai Karamzin, is the undisputed masterpiece of the entire movement.

The greatest Russian composer remains Peter Ilyich Tchaikovsky (1840–1893), who began as a student of the traditionalist Anton Rubinstein (1829–1894) but was decisively influenced early in his career by "The Five." The tone poems, all based on literature, pulsate with Romantic yearning and adventure, while the six symphonies, several of which incorporate Russian themes, are programmatic—especially the last three, which are virtually autobiographical. Indeed, the final one (the *Pathétique*) is a valedictory statement of the composer's life, with its struggles and triumphs. Its undeniable Russian elements notwithstanding, Tchaikovsky's music owes its enduring appeal to its internationalism. Despite its physical isolation, Russia was closely linked to the musical capitals of western Europe. Thus, Tchaikovsky's three great ballets build on the French tradition and possess a sophistication that is extraordinarily cosmopolitan. Two of them are based on folk tales retold by the brothers Grimm, and were written for Marius Petipa (1819–1910), under whom Russian ballet reached its zenith.

With Richard Wagner (1813–1883), nationalist rhetoric came to express the growing expansionist mood of Germany that led ultimately to the rise of Nazism during the 1930s. He manned the barricades in Dresden during the revolutionary upheavals that struck Europe throughout 1848–49, and was forced into exile for 13 years, until he won the support of Ludwig II of Bavaria. His operas, such as *Tristan and Isolde* (1859), written under the influence of the philosophy of Arthur Schopenhauer (1788–1860), and the enormous four-part cycle *The Ring of the Niebelungen* (1853–74), which dates from about the same time as Christian Hebbel's plays, expand greatly on medieval Germanic legends. Wagner's goal was a total work of art that united music, literature, and theater. His texts reflect the influence of Goethe in their literary, declamatory style. One of Wagner's characteristic devices is the leitmotif (pronounced "light moteef," from German, "leading motif"), a melodic line that represents a person, idea, or situation. If, for example, the music brings together the leitmotif for Tristan with one that signifies Fate, the informed listener understands that Tristan is being drawn toward his destiny. Add the motif for Isolde, and we know that his fate is intertwined with hers. Music of such sophistication demanded a highly educated audience, which the prosperous cities of nineteenth-century Europe could readily supply.

Despite the enormous demands Wagner placed on singers, it was the orchestra that carried the largest part of the musical burden. His highly unconventional orchestration techniques and integrated drama set an important example for the Italian composer Giuseppe Verdi (1813–1901), who nevertheless denied their influence. His early operas often have patriotic subjects espousing the cause of Italian independence (the *risorgimento*). Although Verdi's arias remained vehicles of virtuoso singing, the last five operas broke decisively with the style of Donizetti and Bellini. Dating from 1862 to 1893, they are the finest in the entire Italian tradition stretching back to Monteverdi. Like Berlioz and Tchaikovsky, Verdi was attracted above all to the plays of Shakespeare—*Macbeth, Othello,* and *The Merry Wives of Windsor*—which brought out the best in him.

As in art and architecture, revivalism was an important factor in music, although it never became a guiding principle. Mendelssohn resuscitated Bach's *St. Matthew Passion,* Wagner rediscovered Palestrina and Glück (his very antitheses as composers), while Brahms helped to prepare complete editions of the works of Handel, C. P. E. Bach, and Mozart that mark the beginning of modern musicology.

948. James Abbott McNeill Whistler.
Arrangement in Black and Gray:
The Artist's Mother. 1871.
Oil on canvas, 57 x 64½"
(144.6 x 163.8 cm).
Musée d'Orsay, Paris

was divided into four sections representing Fortune, Fame, Oblivion, and Love. The figures chained to the wheel of fortune, from which they cannot escape, include a slave, a king, and a poet. The composition was inspired by an altarpiece by Mantegna, while the figures show the impact of the sibyls and nudes that populate the ceiling of the Sistine Chapel (see figs. 9 and 613), which the artist studied in detail during a visit to Rome, as well as Michelangelo's "Captives" (compare figs. 609 and 610). Dame Fortune also reflects his admiration for Botticelli's figures, such as those in figure 583. The artist's principal interest lies in the decorative design, inspired by Early Renaissance paintings, which has the flatness and luxuriance of a tapestry. Even more than Whistler's, Burne-Jones' work represents an escape from reality into a dreamlike world of heightened beauty and attenuated feeling.

WHISTLER. James Abbott McNeill Whistler (1834–1903) came to Paris from America in 1855 to study painting; four years later he moved to London, where he spent the rest of his life, but he visited France during the 1860s and was in close touch with the rising Impressionist movement. His best-known picture, *Arrangement in Black and Gray: The Artist's Mother* (fig. 948), reflects the influence of Manet in its emphasis on flat areas, and the likeness has the austere precision of Degas. Its fame as a symbol of our latter-day "mother cult" is a paradox of popular psychology that would have dismayed Whistler, who wanted the canvas to be appreciated for its formal qualities alone.

A witty, sharp-tongued advocate of Art for Art's Sake, he thought of his pictures as analogous to pieces of music, calling them "symphonies" or "nocturnes." [See Primary Sources, no. 90, page 939.] The boldest example, painted about 1874, is *Nocturne in Black and Gold: The Falling Rocket* (fig. 949). Without an explanatory subtitle, we would have real difficulty making it out. No French painter had yet dared to produce a picture so "nonrepresentational," so reminiscent of Cozens' "blotscapes" and Turner's "tinted steam" (see figs. 849 and 890). It was this canvas, more than any other, that prompted John Ruskin to accuse Whistler of "flinging a pot of paint in the

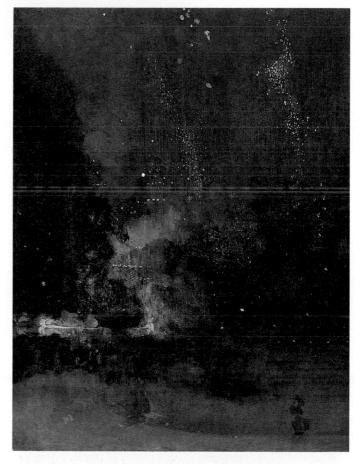

949. James Abbott McNeill Whistler. *Nocturne in Black and Gold:*
The Falling Rocket. c. 1874. Oil on panel,
23¾ x 18⅜" (60.2 x 46.8 cm). The Detroit Institute of Arts
Gift of Dexter M. Ferry, Jr.

public's face." (Since the same critic had highly praised Turner's *The Slave Ship,* we must conclude that what Ruskin admired was not the tinted steam itself but the Romantic sentiment behind it.)

During Whistler's subsequent suit for libel, he offered a definition of his aims that seems to be particularly applicable

950. George Inness.
The Rainbow.
c. 1878–79.
Oil on canvas,
30¼ x 45¼"
(76.8 x 114.9 cm).
© 1993 Indianapolis
Museum of Art
Gift of George E. Hume

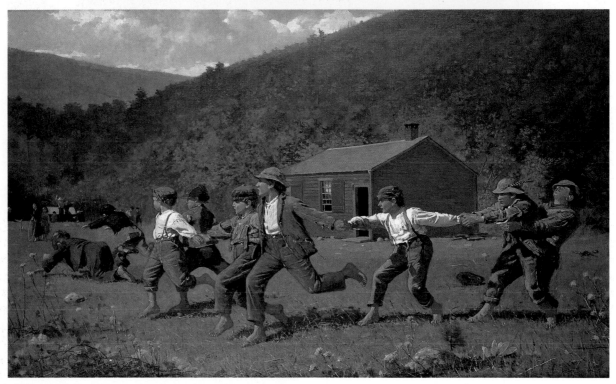

951. Winslow Homer. *Snap the Whip.* 1872. Oil on canvas, 22¼ x 36½" (56.5 x 92.7 cm). The Butler Institute of Art, Youngstown, Ohio

to *The Falling Rocket:* "I have perhaps meant rather to indicate an artistic interest alone in my work, divesting the picture from any outside sort of interest. . . . It is an arrangement of line, form, and color, first, and I make use of any incident of it which shall bring about a symmetrical result." The last phrase has special significance, since Whistler acknowledges that in utilizing chance effects, he does not look for resemblances but for a purely formal harmony. While he rarely practiced what he preached to quite the same extent as he did in *The Falling Rocket,* his statement reads like a prophecy of American abstract painting (see fig. 1079).

United States

THE AMERICAN BARBIZON SCHOOL. After the Civil War, the United States underwent unprecedented industrial growth, immigration, and westward expansion. These changes led to not only a new range of social and economic problems but a different outlook and taste. As the United States became more like the Old World, Americans traveled abroad in growing numbers, seeking their cultural models in Europe, particularly France, which promoted a new cosmopolitanism in art. There was an equally dramatic shift in the attitude toward nature. The uneasy balance between civilization and nature shifted irrevocably in favor of progress by the end of the Centennial Celebration in 1876. The loss of the twin Romantic visions of the virgin wilderness and a pastoral Eden left nature as little more than a sentimental vestige to be preserved in parks. Since landscape ceased to be a teacher of moral truths as well, the viewer was left only with a personal reaction to a total impression of the scenery at hand. Through this resonance, the mystery of nature retained its spiritual

952. Thomas Eakins. *William Rush Carving His Allegorical Figure of the Schuylkill River.* 1877.
Oil on canvas, 20^1/8 x 26^1/2" (51.1 x 67.3 cm). Philadelphia Museum of Art
Given by Mrs. Thomas Eakins and Miss Mary A. Williams

significance but required an alternative mode of expression. The American Barbizon painters answered the need for a new form of landscape: they responded to the transformation of America by turning inward. Their canvases embody the altered mentality of the United States by evoking a poetic state of mind with ever-increasing freedom.

INNESS. The leader of the American Barbizon School was George Inness (1825–1894), who had been deeply impressed by the work of Théodore Rousseau and his followers during a visit to France. *The Rainbow* (fig. 950) shows one of the storm scenes so characteristic of this artist. The contrast of nature's beneficence with the tumultuous sweep of cosmic forces is reminiscent of Cole's *View of Schroon Mountain* (see fig. 898), but instead of depicting the wilderness, this former member of the Hudson River School has followed a rustic scene by Millet. Inness imbued his landscape with a sense of divine presence by freely rearranging nature according to formulas that act as indexes of personal feelings. Deeply religious, he had converted to the spiritualism of Emanuel Swedenborg, who believed in an immaterial but light-filled realm inhabited by departed souls that is visually similar and parallel to our own. Although only a few of his landscapes have a specific symbolic content, rainbows had spiritual significance for Inness. Swedenborg's ideas confirmed and intensified his approach, which relied increasingly on light and color to impart his vision of a deeper reality lying hidden from people's eyes but not their souls.

HOMER. The far more gifted Winslow Homer (1836–1910) was a pictorial reporter throughout the Civil War and continued as a magazine illustrator until 1875. He went to Paris in 1866, but though he left too soon to receive its full impact, French art did have an important effect on his work. *Snap the Whip* (fig. 951) conveys a nostalgia for the simpler era of America before the Civil War (see fig. 899). The picture carries us back to the innocent era of Mark Twain's Tom Sawyer and Huckleberry Finn. The sunlit scene might be called "pre-Impressionist." Its fresh delicacy lies halfway between Corot and Monet (compare figs. 879 and 933). The air of youthful innocence relies equally on the composition, which was undoubtedly inspired by the bacchanals then popular in French art (compare fig. 907). The sophisticated design shows the same subtle understanding of motion as Bruegel's *The Blind Leading the Blind* (see fig. 718), which also terminates in a fallen figure.

EAKINS. Thomas Eakins (1844–1916) arrived in Paris from Philadelphia about the same time as Homer. He went home four years later, after receiving a conventional academic training but with decisive impressions of Velázquez and Courbet. Elements from both these artists are combined in *William Rush Carving His Allegorical Figure of the Schuylkill River* (fig. 952; compare figs. 759 and 931). Eakins had encountered stiff opposition for advocating traditional life studies at the Pennsylvania Academy of the Fine Arts. To him, Rush was a hero for basing his 1809 statue for the Philadelphia Water Works on the nude

953. Henry O. Tanner. *The Banjo Lesson*. c. 1893. Oil on canvas, 48 x 35" (121.9 x 88.9 cm). Hampton University Museum, Hampton, Virginia

model, though the figure itself was draped in a classical robe. Eakins no doubt knew contemporary European paintings of sculptors carving from the nude; these were related to the theme of Pygmalion and Galatea popular at the time among academic artists. Conservative critics nevertheless denounced *William Rush Carving His Allegorical Figure of the Schuylkill River* for its nudity, despite the presence of the chaperon knitting quietly to the right. To us the painting's declaration of unvarnished truth seems a courageous fulfillment of Baudelaire's demand for pictures that express the heroism of modern life.

TANNER. Thanks in large part to Eakins' enlightened attitude, Philadelphia became the leading center of minority artists in the United States. Eakins encouraged women and blacks to study art seriously at a time when professional careers were closed to them. African-Americans had no chance to enter the arts before Emancipation, and after the Civil War the situation improved only gradually. Henry O. Tanner (1859–1937), the first important black painter, studied with Eakins in the early 1880s. Tanner's masterpiece, *The Banjo Lesson* (fig. 953), painted after he moved permanently to Paris, bears Eakins' unmistakable impress. Avoiding the mawkishness of similar subjects by other American painters, the scene is rendered with the same direct realism as *William Rush Carving His Allegorical Figure of the Schuylkill River.*

SCULPTURE

Impressionism, it is often said, revitalized sculpture no less than painting. The statement is at once true and misleading. Auguste Rodin (1840–1917), the first sculptor of genius since Bernini, redefined sculpture during the same years that Manet and Monet redefined painting. In so doing, however, he did not follow these artists' lead. How indeed could the effect of such pictures as *The Fifer* or *On the Bank of the Seine* be reproduced in three dimensions and without color?

RODIN. What Rodin did accomplish is already visible in the first piece he tried to exhibit at the Salon, *The Man with the Broken Nose* of 1864 (fig. 954). (It was rejected, as we might expect, on the grounds that it conformed to no established category of sculpture.) Earlier, he had worked briefly under Carrier-Belleuse and Barye, whose influence may help to explain the vigorously creased surface (compare fig. 905). These welts and wrinkles produce, in polished bronze, an ever-changing pattern of reflections. But is this effect borrowed from Impressionist painting? Does Rodin actually dissolve three-dimensional form into flickering patches of light and dark? These fiercely exaggerated shapes pulsate with sculptural energy, and they retain this quality under whatever conditions the piece is viewed. Rodin did not work directly in bronze; he modeled in wax or clay. How, then, could he calculate in advance the reflections on the bronze surfaces of the casts that would ultimately be made from these models?

He worked as he did, we must assume, for an altogether different reason: not to capture elusive optical effects, but to emphasize the process of "growth"—the miracle of dead matter coming to life in the artist's hands. As the color patch for Manet and Monet is the primary reality, so are the malleable lumps from which Rodin builds his forms. Conservative critics rejected *The Man with the Broken Nose* and Impressionist painting on the same grounds: it was "unfinished," a mere sketch.

The Man with the Broken Nose was Rodin's confession of aesthetic faith. Later on, he said of it: "That mask determined all my future work." The head, on which he had worked for about a year, represented a revolutionary insight. What matters in sculpture is not whether it is "finished" or "complete" but whether it conveys to the beholder the way it grew. *The Man with the Broken Nose* certainly does, and that is why Rodin thought of it as the cornerstone of his entire future oeuvre. He was the first to make of unfinishedness an aesthetic principle that governed both his handling of surfaces and the whole shape of the work. (*The Man with the Broken Nose* is not a bust, but a head "broken off" at the neck.) By discovering what might be called the autonomy of the fragment, he rescued sculpture from mechanical verisimilitude just as Manet rescued painting from photographic realism.

Despite the sculptural revolution proclaimed with such daring by Rodin at 24, he still believed that the sculptor's noblest task is to show the nude human form, although it could now be done in fragmentary form, and he persisted in the claim that the sculptor's vocation is to create "new classics"—that is, works free from the dictates of the patron and demanding to be judged on their own terms. [See Primary Sources, no. 91, page 939.] When in 1880 he was at last entrusted with a major

954. Auguste Rodin. *The Man with the Broken Nose.* 1864. Bronze, height 9¹/2" (24 cm). Rodin Museum, Philadelphia Museum of Art

955. Auguste Rodin. *The Thinker.* 1879–89. Bronze, height 27¹/2" (69.8 cm). The Metropolitan Museum of Art, New York
Gift of Thomas F. Ryan, 1910

task, the entrance of the École des Arts Décoratifs in Paris, Rodin elaborated the commission into an ambitious ensemble called *The Gates of Hell,* which, characteristically, he never finished. The symbolic program was inspired by Dante's *Inferno,* but it was equally indebted to Baudelaire's *The Flowers of Evil.* Its common denominator is a tragic view of the human condition— guilty passions, desire forever unfulfilled here and in the beyond, the vain hope of happiness. The perceptive critic Gustave Geffroy, writing of *The Gates of Hell* in 1889, defined their subject as the endless reenactment of the sufferings of Adam and Eve. Indeed, Rodin had tried in 1881 to persuade the government to let him flank *The Gates* with statues of the two.

The Gates served as a matrix for countless smaller pieces that he eventually made into independent works. The most famous of these autonomous fragments is *The Thinker* (fig. 955), intended for the lintel of the *Gates,* whence the figure was to contemplate the panorama of despair below him. It descends partly from a statue by Carpeaux of another subject from *The Inferno,* Ugolino and his sons. The ancestry of *The Thinker* can be traced back much further, however. It goes back, indirectly, to the first phase of Christian art. (The pen-

sive man seated at the left in the Byzantine ivory in figure 346 reflects an Early Christian source.) It also includes the action-in-repose of Michelangelo's superhuman bodies (see figs. 610, 613, and 616), the tension in Puget's *Milo of Crotona* (see fig. 808, especially the feet), and the expressive dynamism of *The Man with the Broken Nose.*

Who is *The Thinker*? In the context of *The Gates of Hell,* he was originally conceived as a generalized image of Dante, the poet who in his mind's eye sees what goes on all around him. Once Rodin decided to detach him from *The Gates,* he became *The Poet-Thinker,* and finally just *The Thinker.* But what kind of thinker? Partly Adam, no doubt (though there is also a different Adam by Rodin, another "outgrowth" of the Gates), partly Prometheus, and partly the brute imprisoned by the passions of the flesh. Rodin wisely refrained from giving him a specific name, for the statue fits no preconceived identity. In this new image of a man, form and meaning are one, instead of cleaving apart as in Carpeaux's *The Dance* (see fig. 907). Carpeaux's naked figures pretend to be nude, while *The Thinker,* like the nudes of Michelangelo, is free from subservience to the undressed model.

956. Auguste Rodin. *The Kiss.* 1886–98.
Marble, over-lifesize. Rodin Museum, Paris

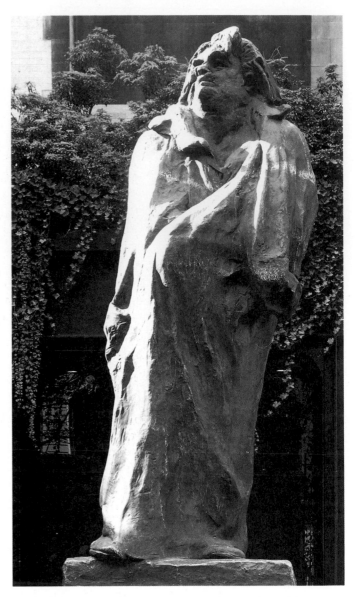

957. Auguste Rodin. *Monument to Balzac.* 1897–98. Bronze
(cast 1954), height 9'3" (2.82 m). The Museum of Modern Art,
New York
Presented in memory of Curt Valentin by his friends

The Kiss (fig. 956), an over-lifesize group in marble, also derives from *The Gates.* It was meant to be Dante's Paolo and Francesca, but Rodin rejected it as unsuitable. Evidently he realized that *The Kiss* shows the ill-fated pair succumbing to their illicit desire for each other here on earth, not as tortured souls in Hell. Knowing its original title helps us to understand a salient aspect of the group: passion reigned in by hesitancy, for the embrace is not yet complete. Less powerful than *The Thinker,* it exploits another kind of artful unfinishedness. Rodin had been impressed by the struggle of Michelangelo's *"Slaves"* against the remnants of the blocks that imprison them. *The Kiss* was planned from the start to include the mass of roughhewn marble to which the lovers are attached, and which thus becomes symbolic of their earthbound passion. The contrast of textures emphasizes the veiled, sensuous softness of the bodies.

But Rodin was by instinct a modeler, not a carver like Michelangelo. His greatest works were intended to be cast in bronze. Even these, however, reveal their full strength only when we see them in plaster casts made directly from Rodin's clay originals. The *Monument to Balzac,* his last, as well as most daring and controversial creation (fig. 957), remained in plaster for many years, rejected by the writers' association that had commissioned it. He had been asked at the insistence of the author Émile Zola to take over the project when the first sculptor died after producing only a sketch. He declared it to be "the sum of my whole life. . . . From the day of its conception, I

was a changed man." Outward appearance did not pose a problem (Balzac's features were well known). But Rodin desired far more than that. He was searching for a way to cast Balzac's whole personality into visible form, without the addition of allegorical figures, the habitual props of monuments to genius. The final version gives no hint of the many alternative solutions he tried. (More than 40 have survived.) The element common to them all is that Balzac is standing, in order to express the virile energy Rodin saw in his subject.

The final sculpture shows the writer clothed in a long dressing gown—described by his contemporaries as a "monk's robe"—which he liked to wear while working at night. Here was a "timeless" costume that permitted Rodin to conceal and simplify the contours of the body. Balzac awakens in the middle of the night, seized by a sudden creative impulse, and hastily throws the robe over his shoulders without putting his arms through the sleeves, before he settles down to record his thoughts on paper. But, of course, Balzac is not about to write.

958. Camille Claudel. *Ripe Age*. c. 1907. Bronze, 34¹/₂ x 20¹/₂"
(87.6 x 21.9 cm). Musée d'Orsay, Paris

He looms before us with the frightening insistence of a specter, utterly unaware of his surroundings—the entire figure leans backward to stress its isolation from the beholder.

The statue is larger than life, physically and spiritually: it has an overpowering presence. Like a huge monolith, the man of genius towers above the crowd. He shares "the sublime egotism of the gods" (as the Romantics put it). From a distance we see only the great bulk of the figure. From the mass formed by the shroudlike cloak, the head thrusts upward—one is tempted to say, erupts—with elemental force. When we are close enough to make out the features clearly, we sense beneath the disdain an inner agony that stamps *Balzac* as the kin of *The Man with the Broken Nose*.

To this day, the *Balzac* remains a startling sight. Rodin had indeed reached the outer limits of his art, as he himself realized. The question remains, Why did he never have it cast in bronze, even though a wealthy private collector offered to pay for it? Its compact shape certainly lent itself to a marble statue, and it may be that he visualized the monument as one all along.

CLAUDEL. Rodin employed various assistants throughout his career. One of them, Camille Claudel (1864–1943), has emerged as an important artist. Claudel entered Rodin's studio as a 19-year-old, and for the next decade she was his artistic collaborator and his mistress. Her work is strongly in her mentor's mode, and her best sculptures might be mistaken for his. Much of her work is autobiographical. *Ripe Age* (fig. 958) depicts a grisly Rodin, whose features are clearly recognizable,

being led away with apparent reluctance by his longtime companion, Rose Beuret, whom Claudel sought to replace in his affections. Beuret is shown as a sinister, shrouded figure who first appears in Claudel's work as Clotho, one of the three Fates, ironically caught in the web of life she has woven. The nude figure is a self-portrait of Claudel, likewise evolved from an earlier work, *Entreaty*.

DEGAS. It is significant of the fundamental difference between painting and modeling that only Degas among the Impressionists tried his hand at sculpture, producing dozens of small-scale wax figurines that explore the same themes as his paintings and drawings. These are private works made for his own interest; few of them were exhibited during the artist's lifetime, and none were cast until after his death in this century. During the 1870s, there was a growing taste for casts made from artists' working models, reflecting the same appreciation for the qualities of spontaneity and inspiration found in drawings and oil sketches, which had long appealed to collectors. For the first time sculptors felt emboldened to violate time-honored standards of naturalism and craftsmanship for statuettes, and to leave the impress of their fingers on the soft material as they molded it. Nevertheless, when Degas showed the wax original of *The Little Fourteen-Year-Old Dancer* at the Impressionist exhibitions of 1880 and 1881, the public was scandalized by its lack of traditional finish and uncompromising adherence to unvarnished truth, although the response from critics was less harsh. The sculpture, reproduced here in

959. Edgar Degas. *The Little Fourteen-Year-Old Dancer.* 1878–80.
Bronze with gauze tutu and satin hair ribbon, height 38" (96.5 cm).
Norton Simon Art Foundation, Pasadena, California

a posthumous cast (fig. 959), is nearly as rough in texture as the slightly smaller nude study from life on which it is based.

Instead of sculpting her costume, Degas used real cotton and silk, a revolutionary idea for the time but something the Romantics, with their emphatic naturalism, must often have felt tempted to do. Degas was intrigued by the tension between the concrete surface and the abstract but powerfully directional forces beneath it. The ungainliness of the young adolescent's body is subtly emphasized by her pose, that of a dancer at "stage rest," which becomes in his hands an extremely stressful one, so full of sharply contrasting angles that no dancer could maintain it for more than a few moments. Yet, rather than awkwardness, the statuette conveys a simple dignity and grace that are irresistible. The openness of the stance, with hands clasped behind the back and legs pointing in opposite directions, demands that we walk around the dancer to arrive at a complete image of it. As we view the sculpture from different angles, the surface provides a constantly shifting impression of light comparable to that in Degas' numerous paintings and pastels of the ballet (compare fig. 939).

ARCHITECTURE

For more than a century, from the mid-eighteenth to the late nineteenth, architecture had been dominated by a succession of "revival styles" (see pages 706–12). This term, we will recall, does not imply that earlier forms were slavish copies; the best work of the time has both individuality and high distinction. Yet the architectural wisdom of the past, however freely interpreted, proved in the long run to be inadequate for the practical demands of the Industrial Age: the factories, warehouses, stores, and city apartments that formed the bulk of building construction. After about 1800, in the world of commercial architecture, we find the gradual introduction of new materials and techniques that were to have a profound effect on architectural style by the end of the century. The most important was iron, never before used as an actual structural member. Within a few decades of their first appearance, cast-iron columns and arches had become the standard means of supporting roofs over the large spaces required by railroad stations, exhibition halls, and public libraries.

LABROUSTE. A famous early example is the Bibliothèque Ste.-Geneviève in Paris by Henri Labrouste (1801–1875).

960. Henri Labrouste. Bibliothèque Ste.-Geneviève, Paris. 1843–50

961. Henri Labrouste. Reading Room, Bibliothèque Ste.-Geneviève

The exterior (fig. 960) represents the historicism prevailing at mid-century. It is drawn chiefly from Italian Renaissance banks, libraries, and churches. To identify the building as a library, Labrouste used the simple but ingenious device of inscribing the names of great writers around the facade. The reading room (fig. 961), on the other hand, recalls the nave of a French Gothic cathedral (compare fig. 439). But why did Labrouste choose cast-iron columns and arches, hitherto used exclusively for railroad stations? Cast iron was necessary not to provide structural support for the two barrel roofs—this could have been done using other materials—but to complete the building's symbolic program. The library, Labrouste suggests to us, is a storehouse of something even more valuable and sacred than material wealth: the world's literature, which takes us on a journey not to faraway places but of the mind.

Labrouste chose to leave the interior iron skeleton uncovered, and to face the difficulty of relating it to the massive Renaissance revival style of the exterior of his building. If his

Realism was the dominant style in mid-nineteenth-century theater, as it was in painting. In part, theatrical realism was a reflection of the pragmatic character of the Industrial Revolution. Its principal theorist was the French philosopher Auguste Comte (1798–1857), the founder of a system of thought known as Positivism, which called for a material explanation of truth based on objective observation and scientific analysis. As in art, Realism in drama covered a wide range of tendencies, from simple adherence to historic fact, social reality, or physical appearance, to highly emotional treatments that have much in common with Romanticism.

The Realist playwright best known today is Alexandre Dumas the Younger (1824–1895), whose drama *Camille* (1852) was the first to treat the now-familiar theme of the prostitute with a heart of gold. While a modern audience might find *Camille* somewhat melodramatic, in its own time the play was considered an unflinching depiction of life at the fringes of Parisian society. In response to the criticism of *Camille* contained in *Olympe's Marriage* by Émile Augier (1820–1889), Dumas abandoned Realism three years later in *The Demi-Monde,* his first attempt at social and moral criticism. The most popular playwright of the period was Victorien Sardou (1831–1908), whose drama *La Tosca* (1887) was later turned into a well-known opera by the Italian composer, Giacomo Puccini (see box page 758). This story of love, treachery, and revenge during the Italian struggle for independence was an important starring role for the great British tragic actress, Sarah Bernhardt (1844–1923; see fig. 925). A gifted sculptor as well, Bernhardt specialized in tragic heroines such as Camille and Adrienne Lecouvreur. Her only rival was Ellen Terry (1847–1928), who came from a long line of actors. She was the leading lady to Henry Irving (1838–1905), by far the most important actor and manager in England during the later nineteenth century, who commissioned Edward Burne-Jones and other prominent artists to design stage sets for him. Irving was knighted in 1895, while Terry was made a Dame Commander of the British Empire only in 1925.

Germany produced few major dramatists during the third quarter of the century. Instead, it was content to rely on the plays of Shakespeare, Goethe, and Schiller, and on translations of Sardou and the younger Dumas. Vienna became the main theater center under Heinrich Laube (1806–1884), a former member of Young Germany, and Franz Dingelstedt (1814–1881), who had produced Chris-

tian Friedrich Hebbel's (1813–1863) trilogy *The Niebelungen* in 1861 at Weimar. A fascination with old Germanic legends that was fueled by growing nationalism helped to make historical accuracy the goal of German theater. The chief contributors to theater in Germany at this time were Duke George II of Saxe-Meiningen (1826–1914) and his wife, the actress Helene Franz (1839–1923), who elevated the quality of acting through careful preparation and emphasis on ensemble. Attention was also paid to costumes and scenery.

Russian authors of the time had a particular affinity for psychological Realism. The first Russian professional playwright, Aleksandr Ostrovsky (1823–1886), had an abiding interest in characters and their relationships. However, the major plays were written by the great novelists of the era. Ivan Turgenev (1818–1883) wrote a number of dramas that are remarkable for their portrayal of their characters' inner lives and complex relationships. Leo Tolstoy (1828–1910) also tried his hand at plays, notably *The Power of Darkness,* which was produced in 1895, some 30 years after it was written. Aleksei Tolstoy (1817–1875), a distant relative, established himself as the leading Realist with a strong interest in the history of Russia. *The Death of Ivan the Terrible* and *Tsar Boris,* both of 1870, were based on the historical research of Nikolai Karamzin (1766–1826), which did much to stimulate Russian nationalism.

In the United States, the favorite dramas before the Civil War were various adaptations of the novel *Uncle Tom's Cabin* by Harriet Beecher Stowe (1811–1896). This portrayal of the life of slaves on southern plantations helped fuel abolitionist sentiment. It was also a time of great actors. The Englishman William Burton (1804–1860) headed the finest company in New York, the undisputed theater capital of America, although the Boston Museum also staged many plays after 1850. Burton had been preceded by another English performer, Junius Booth (1796–1852), whose son Edwin Booth (1833–1893) became the greatest actor America has ever produced. Unfortunately, the family remains notorious for another son, John Wilkes Booth (1838–1865), the assassin of President Abraham Lincoln. The most popular form of theater was the burlesque extravaganza. Over time it came to appeal mainly to men by featuring beautiful women, although striptease was added only in 1929. Vaudeville, a more genteel form of family entertainment that reached its height between 1890 and 1930, was defined largely by Tony Pastor (1837–1908).

---

solution does not fully integrate the two systems, it at least lets them coexist. The iron supports, shaped like Corinthian columns, are as slender as the new material permits. Their collective effect is that of a space-dividing screen, belying their structural importance. To make them weightier, Labrouste has placed them on tall pedestals of solid masonry, instead of directly on the floor. Aesthetically, the arches presented greater difficulty, since there was no way to make them look as powerful as their masonry ancestors. Here Labrouste has gone to the other

extreme, perforating them with lacy scrolls as if they were pure ornament. This architectural (as against merely technical) use of exposed iron members has a fanciful and delicate quality that links it, indirectly, to the Gothic revival. Later superseded by structural steel and ferroconcrete, it is a peculiarly appealing final chapter in the history of Romantic architecture.

The authority of historic modes had to be broken if the industrial era was to produce a truly contemporary style. It nevertheless proved extraordinarily persistent. Labrouste, pio-

962. Sir Joseph Paxton. The Crystal Palace, London. 1851;
recreated in Sydenham 1852; destroyed 1936

neer though he was of cast-iron construction, could not think of architectural supports as anything but columns having proper capitals and bases, rather than as metal rods or pipes (see pages 768–70). The "architecture of conspicuous display" espoused by Garnier (see pages 710–11) was divorced, even more than were the previous revival styles, from the needs of the present. It was only in structures that were not considered "architecture" at all that new building materials and techniques could be explored without these inhibitions.

PAXTON. Within a year of the completion of the Bibliothèque Ste.-Geneviève, the Crystal Palace (fig. 962) was built in London. A pioneering achievement far bolder in conception than Labrouste's library, the Crystal Palace was designed to house the first of the great international expositions that continue in our day. Its designer, Sir Joseph Paxton (1801–1865), was an engineer and builder of greenhouses. The Crystal Palace was, in fact, a gigantic greenhouse—so large that it enclosed

some old trees growing on the site—with its iron skeleton freely on display. Paxton's design was such a success that it set off a wave of similar buildings for commercial purposes, such as public markets. Still, the notion that there might be beauty, and not merely utility, in the products of engineering made headway very slowly, even though the doctrine "form follows function" found advocates from the mid-nineteenth century on. Hence most such edifices were adorned with decorations that follow the eclectic taste of the period.

ROEBLING. Only rarely could an engineering feat express the spirit of the times. One of the few to do so was the Brooklyn Bridge, built by John and Washington Roebling (fig. 963), which was referred to, appropriately enough, as America's Arch of Triumph. It remains one of the outstanding achievements of the Industrial Revolution. The massive towers nevertheless incorporate aspects of Egyptian, Roman, and Gothic architecture (note the pointed arches) to express a

963. John and Washington Roebling. The Brooklyn Bridge, New York. 1867–83

combination of eternal strength, civic pride, and soaring spirituality. Small wonder it was celebrated by poets and artists alike (see fig. 1056).

EIFFEL. What was needed for products of engineering to be accepted as architecture was a structure that would capture the world's imagination through its bold conception. The breakthrough came with the Eiffel Tower, named after its designer, Gustave Eiffel (1832–1923). As shown in a contemporary photograph (fig. 964), it was erected at the entrance to the Paris World's Fair of 1889, where it, too, served as a triumphal arch of science and industry. It has become such a visual cliché beloved of tourists—much like the *Statue of Liberty*, which also involved Eiffel (see fig. 908)—that we can hardly realize what a revolutionary impact it had at the time. [See Primary Sources, no. 92, pages 939–40.] The tower, with its frankly technological aesthetic, so dominates

the city's skyline even now that it provoked a storm of protest by the leading intellectuals of the day. Eiffel used the same principles of structural engineering that he had already applied successfully to bridges. Yet it is so novel in appearance and so daring in construction that nothing like it has ever been built, before or since.

The Eiffel Tower owed a good measure of its success to the fact that for a small sum anyone could ascend its elevators to see a view of Paris previously reserved for the privileged few able to afford hot-air balloon rides (see fig. 926). It thus helped to define a distinctive feature of modern architecture, one that it shares with modern technology as a whole: it acts on large masses of people, without regard to social or economic class. Although this capacity, shared only by the largest churches and public buildings of the past, has also served the aims of political extremists at both ends of the spectrum, modern architecture has tended by its very nature to function as a vehicle of democracy. We can

964. Gustave Eiffel. The Eiffel Tower, Paris. 1887–89

readily understand, then, why the Eiffel Tower quickly became a popular symbol of Paris itself. It could do so, however, precisely because it serves no practical purpose whatsoever.

OTHER FIELDS

MORRIS. We must take note of the unusually important role played by the decorative arts in England during the second half of the nineteenth century. William Morris (1834–1896), the early leader in what came to be known as the Arts and Crafts Movement, started out with William Holman Hunt as a student of the Pre-Raphaelite painter Rossetti but soon shifted his interest to "art for use"—domestic architecture and interior decoration such as furniture, tapestries, and wallpapers. He wanted to displace the shoddy products of the Machine Age by reviving the handicrafts of the preindustrial

965. William Morris (Morris & Co.). Green Dining Room. 1867.
Victoria & Albert Museum, London

past, an art "made by the people, and for the people, as a happiness to the maker and the user."

Morris was an apostle of simplicity. Architecture and furniture ought to be designed in accordance with the nature of their materials and working processes; surface decoration must be flat rather than illusionistic. His interiors (fig. 965) are total environments that create an effect of quiet intimacy. Despite Morris' self-proclaimed championship of the medieval tradition, he never imitated its forms directly but sought to capture its spirit. His achievement was to invent the first original system of ornament since the Rococo.

Through the many enterprises he sponsored, as well as his skill as a writer and publicist, Morris became a tastemaker without peer in his day. Toward the end of the century, his influence had spread throughout Europe and America. Nor was he content to reform the arts of design alone. He saw them, rather, as a lever by which to reform modern society as a whole. As a consequence, he played an important part in the early history of Fabian socialism (the gradualist variety invented in England as an alternative to the revolutionary socialism of the Continent).

CRANE. Many of Morris' artist friends came to share his convictions, and some contributed their artistic talents to the cause. A political cartoon (fig. 966) by the illustrator and book designer Walter Crane (1845–1915) shows the genius of Liberty, strongly reminiscent of the style of Botticelli (see fig. 583), bringing the glad tidings of socialism to a sleeping

966. Walter Crane. Political cartoon from *Cartoons for the Cause*.
1886. Woodcut

967. James Abbott McNeill Whistler. *Harmony in Blue and Gold: The Peacock Room.*
1876–77. Oil color and gold on leather and wood. Courtesy of the Freer Gallery of Art,
Smithsonian Institution, Washington, D.C.

worker who is being oppressed by capitalism in the shape of a nightmarish vampire. Shades of Henry Fuseli!

WHISTLER. In the 1860s the reform ideas of William Morris began to bear fruit in domestic architecture and decoration. The boldest innovations, however, came not from members of his immediate circle but from Whistler and his entourage. Whistler himself created one of the masterpieces of nineteenth-century design: the Peacock Room (fig. 967), which housed the blue-and-white porcelain collection of his patron Frederick Leyland. What began as a modest project to remedy the previous decorations soon escalated into an ambitious overhaul by Whistler, who spared no expense to realize his lavish scheme while the unwitting Leyland was away. The results were inevitably mixed, as the preexisting room embodies fundamentally the same sensibility as Morris' Green Dining Room (see fig. 965). The fanciful decorations, with gilt everywhere, nevertheless epitomize the Aesthetic Movement, which sought refuge from the tawdry reality of the Industrial Revolution by retreating into a realm of pure beauty. The peacock motif, which reflects Whistler's fascination with Japanese art, seems a singularly apt symbol of his aestheticism, which regarded beauty as an end in itself, without regard to social responsibility.

CHAPTER THREE

POST-IMPRESSIONISM, SYMBOLISM, AND ART NOUVEAU

PAINTING

Post-Impressionism

In 1882, just before his death, Manet was made a chevalier of the Legion of Honor by the French government. This event marks the turn of the tide: Impressionism had gained wide acceptance among artists and the public—but by the same token it was no longer a pioneering movement. When the Impressionists held their last group show four years later, the future already belonged to the "Post-Impressionists." Taken literally, this colorless label applies to all painters of significance in the 1880s and 1890s. In a more specific sense, it designates a group of artists who passed through an Impressionist phase but became dissatisfied with the limitations of the style and pursued a variety of directions. Because they did not share one common goal, we have no more descriptive term for them than Post-Impressionists. In any event, they were not "anti-Impressionists." Far from trying to undo the effects of the "Manet Revolution," they wanted to carry it further. Thus Post-Impressionism is in essence just a later stage, though a very important one, of the development that had begun in the 1860s with such pictures as Manet's *Luncheon on the Grass*.

CÉZANNE. Paul Cézanne (1839–1906), the oldest of the Post-Impressionists, was born in Aix-en-Provence, near the Mediterranean coast, where he formed a close friendship with the writer Émile Zola, later a champion of the Impressionists. A man of intensely emotional temperament, he came to Paris in 1861 imbued with enthusiasm for the Romantics. Delacroix was his first love among painters, and he never lost his admiration for him. Cézanne, however, quickly grasped the nature of the "Manet Revolution," but utterly transformed it. *A Modern Olympia* (fig. 968) was painted in response to an *Olympia* by Manet featuring a prostitute whose frank naked-ness scandalized the art world. As in *Luncheon on the Grass* (fig. 4), executed by Manet the same year as the *Olympia*, Cézanne's nude is in the company of a man wearing contemporary garb; his features are plainly those of Cézanne himself (see fig. 969). Like many of his early works, *A Modern Olympia* is sexually charged, albeit in a curiously ambivalent way that suggests why he never formed a durable relationship. While the setting is a boudoir, the picture is one of the first to treat what was to become one of the recurring themes in modern art: the artist and his model, a subject often fraught with erotic overtones. He sits in mute adoration of the young woman, whose sumptuous surroundings suggest that she is indeed a modern goddess. Yet the juxtaposition of the two figures is strange indeed. Although separated in space, they are placed so near each other on the picture plane that she seems almost to recoil from his dark presence! Equally disturbing is the brushwork, which communicates the turbulent passion repressed by the seemingly impassive artist. Never before have we seen such brusqueness, not even in Cézanne's ideal, Delacroix. The subtitle *The Pasha* pays homage to the Orientalism of Delacroix, whose *Odalisque* (fig. 874) nevertheless has a sensuousness absent from Cézanne's *Olympia*. This artist-as-potentate can admire, but not possess, his "harem girl."

After passing through this Neo-Baroque phase, Cézanne began to paint bright outdoor scenes with Pissarro, but he never shared his fellow Impressionists' interest in "slice-of-life" subjects, in movement and change. About 1879, when he painted the *Self-Portrait* in figure 969, he had decided "to make of Impressionism something solid and durable, like the art of the museums." His Romantic impulsiveness of the 1860s has now given way to a patient, disciplined search for

968. Paul Cézanne. *A Modern Olympia (The Pasha)*. Early 1870s. Oil on canvas,
22 x 21⁵/8" (56 x 55 cm). Private collection

harmony of form and color. Every brushstroke is like a building block, firmly placed within the pictorial architecture, which creates a subtle balance of "two-D" and "three-D." (Note how the pattern of wallpaper in the background frames the rounded shape of the head.) The colors, too, are deliberately controlled so as to produce "chords" of warm and cool tones that reverberate throughout the canvas.

In Cézanne's still lifes, such as *Still Life with Apples in a Bowl* (fig. 970), this quest for the "solid and durable" can be seen even more clearly. Not since Chardin have simple everyday objects assumed such importance in a painter's eye. Again the ornamental backdrop is integrated with the three-dimensional shapes, and the brushstrokes have a rhythmic pattern that gives the canvas its shimmering texture. We also notice aspects of Cézanne's mature style that are more conspicuous here than in the *Self-Portrait* and may puzzle us at first. The forms are deliberately simplified and outlined with dark contours, and the perspective is "incorrect" for both the fruit bowl and the horizontal surfaces, which seem to tilt upward. The longer we study the picture, the more we realize the rightness of these apparently arbitrary distortions. When Cézanne took these liberties with reality, his purpose was to uncover the permanent qualities beneath the accidents of appearance. All

forms in nature, he believed, are based on the cone, the sphere, and the cylinder. This order underlying the external world was the true subject of his pictures, but he had to interpret it to fit the separate, closed world of the canvas.

To apply this method to landscape became the greatest challenge of Cézanne's career. From 1882 on, he lived in isolation near his hometown of Aix-en-Provence, exploring its environs as Claude Lorraine and Corot had explored the Roman countryside. One feature, the distinctive shape of a mountain called Mont Ste.-Victoire, seemed almost to obsess him. Its craggy profile looming against the blue Mediterranean sky appears in a long series of compositions, such as the monumental late work in figure 971. There are no hints of human presence here—houses and roads would only disturb the lonely grandeur of this view. Above the wall of rocky cliffs that bar our way like a chain of fortifications, the mountain rises in triumphant clarity, infinitely remote yet as solid and palpable as the shapes in the foreground. For all its architectural stability, the scene is alive with movement; but the forces at work here have been brought into equilibrium, subdued by the greater power of the artist's will. This disciplined energy, distilled from the trials of a stormy youth, gives the mature style of Cézanne its enduring strength.

969. Paul Cézanne. *Self-Portrait.* c. 1879. Oil on canvas, 13³/4 x 10⁵/8" (35 x 27 cm). The Tate Gallery, London

970. Paul Cézanne. *Still Life with Apples in a Bowl.* 1879–82. Oil on canvas,
17¹/8 x 21¹/4" (43.5 x 54 cm). Ny Carlsberg Glyptotek, Copenhagen, Denmark

971. Paul Cézanne. *Mont Ste.-Victoire seen from Bibemus Quarry.*
c. 1897–1900. Oil on canvas, 25¹/2 x 31¹/2" (65.1 x 80 cm). The Baltimore Museum of Art
The Cone Collection, formed by Dr. Claribel Cone and Miss Etta Cone of Baltimore, Maryland

972. Georges Seurat. *A Sunday Afternoon on the Island of La Grande Jatte.* 1884–86.
Oil on canvas, 6'10" x 10'1¹/₄" (2.08 x 3.08 m). The Art Institute of Chicago
Helen Birch Bartlett Memorial Collection

SEURAT. Georges Seurat (1859–1891) shared Cézanne's aim to make Impressionism "solid and durable," but he went about it very differently. His goal, he once stated, was to make "modern people, in their essential traits, move about as if on friezes, and place them on canvases organized by harmonies of color, by directions of the tones in harmony with the lines, and by the directions of the lines." Seurat's career was as brief as those of Masaccio, Giorgione, and Géricault, and his achievement just as astonishing. Although he participated in the last Impressionist show, it is an indication of the Post-Impressionist revolution that thereafter he exhibited with an entirely new group, the Society of Independents.

Seurat devoted his main efforts to a few very large paintings, spending a year or more on each of them and making endless series of preliminary studies before he felt sure enough to tackle the definitive version. *A Sunday Afternoon on the Island of La Grande Jatte* (fig. 972), his greatest masterpiece, had its genesis in this painstaking method. The subject is of the sort that had long been popular among Impressionist painters. Impressionist, too, are the brilliant colors and the effect of intense sunlight. Otherwise, however, the picture is the very opposite of a quick "impression." The firm, simple

contours and the relaxed, immobile figures give the scene a stability that recalls Piero della Francesca (see fig. 562) and shows a clear awareness of Puvis de Chavannes (see pages 579–60).

In the *Grande Jatte,* modeling and foreshortening are reduced to a minimum, and the figures appear mostly in either strict profile or frontal views, as if Seurat had adopted the rules of ancient Egyptian art. Moreover, he has fitted them within the composition as tightly as the pieces of a jigsaw puzzle. So exactly are they fixed in relation to each other that not a single one could be moved by even a millimeter. Frozen in time and space, they act out their roles with ritualized gravity, in contrast to the joyous abandon of the relaxed crowd in Renoir's *Le Moulin de la Galette* (fig. 936), who are free to move about in the open air. Thus despite the period costumes, we read this cross section of Parisian society as timeless. Small wonder the picture remains so spellbinding more than a century after it was painted.

Even the brushwork demonstrates Seurat's passion for order and permanence. The canvas surface is covered with systematic, impersonal "flicks" that make Cézanne's architectural brushstrokes seem temperamental and dynamic by comparison. These tiny dots of brilliant color were supposed to

973. Georges Seurat. *The Couple*. c. 1884–85. Conté crayon on paper, 11¹/₂ x 9" (29.2 x 22.8 cm). Private collection, Paris

974. Georges Seurat. *Chahut*. 1889–90. Oil on canvas, 66¹/₂ x 54³/₄" (169 x 139 cm). Rijksmuseum Kröller-Müller, Otterlo, Holland

merge in the beholder's eye and produce intermediary tints more luminous than those obtainable from pigments mixed on the palette. This procedure was variously known as Neo-Impressionism, Pointillism, or Divisionism (the term preferred by Seurat). The actual result, however, did not conform to the theory. Looking at the *Grande Jatte* from a comfortable distance (seven to ten feet from the original), we find that the mixing of colors in the eye remains incomplete; the dots do not disappear, but are as clearly visible as the tesserae of a mosaic (compare figs. 321 and 322). Seurat himself must have liked this unexpected effect, which gives the canvas the quality of a shimmering, translucent screen. Otherwise he would have reduced the size of the dots.

The painting has a dignity and simplicity suggesting a new classicism, but it is a distinctly modern classicism based on scientific theory. Seurat adapted the laws of color discovered by Eugène Chevreul, O. N. Rood, and David Sutter, as part of a comprehensive approach to art. Like Degas, he had studied with a follower of Ingres, and his theoretical interests grew out of this experience. He came to believe that art must be based on a system. With the help of his friend Charles Henry (who was, like Rood and Sutter, an American), he formulated a series of artistic "laws" based on early experiments in the psychology of visual perception. These principles helped him to control every aesthetic and expressive aspect of his paintings. But, as with all artists of genius, Seurat's theories do not really explain his pictures. It is the pictures, rather, that explain the theories.

Strange as it may seem, color was an adjunct to form in Seurat's work—the very opposite of the Impressionists' technique. Most of his output consists of drawings done in conté crayon, made of graphite and clay, which provides rich, velvety blacks (fig. 973). These have a haunting mystery all their own, in contrast to the festive colors of his paintings. In sheets such as ours, Seurat's forms achieve a machinelike quality through rigorous abstraction. This is the first expression of a peculiarly modern outlook leading to Futurism (see page 794). Seurat's systematic approach to art has the internal logic of modern engineering, which he and his followers hoped would transform society for the better. This social consciousness was allied to a form of anarchism descended from Courbet's friend Proudhon, and contrasts with the general political indifference of the Impressionists. The fact that Seurat shares the same subject matter as the Impressionists serves only to emphasize further the fundamental difference in attitude.

Toward the end of his brief career, Seurat's paintings acquired a new liveliness, seen in *Chahut* (fig. 974). True, everything is held very precisely in place by a system of vertical and horizontal coordinates that defines the canvas as a self-contained rectilinear field. Only in the work of Vermeer have we encountered a similar "area-consciousness" (compare fig. 789). But while these dancers move in lockstep, the decorative arabesques within the flat design possess an unexpected energy. Consciously or unconsciously, Seurat here moves close to the world of commercial art. The speckled surface resembles the cheap offset printing then coming into use. The subject and composition, too, directly anticipate the posters of Henri de Toulouse-Lautrec—even in the marvelous wit and insight with which the facial expressions are observed.

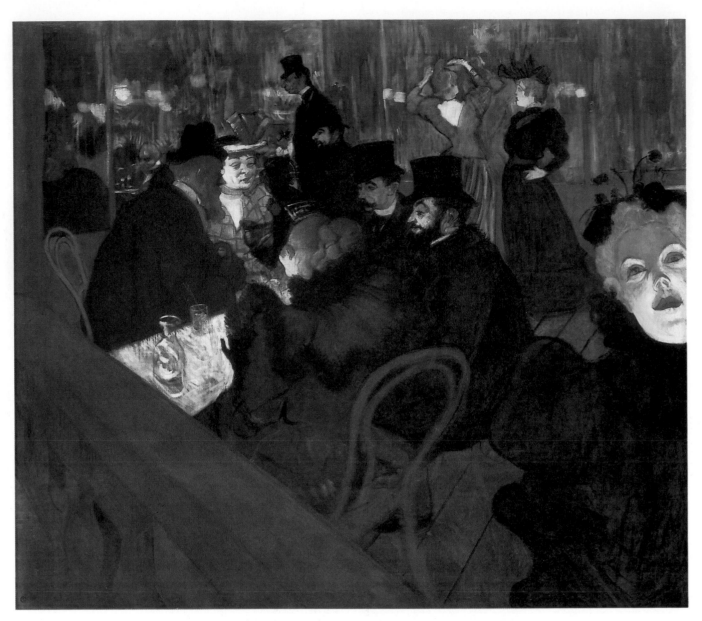

975. Henri de Toulouse-Lautrec. *At the Moulin Rouge.* 1893–95.
Oil on canvas, 48³/₈ x 55¹/₂" (123 x 141 cm). The Art Institute of Chicago
Helen Birch Bartlett Memorial Collection

TOULOUSE-LAUTREC. Physically a dwarf, Henri de Toulouse-Lautrec (1864–1901) was an artist of superb talent who led a dissolute life in the night spots and brothels of Paris and died of alcoholism. He was a great admirer of Degas, and his *At the Moulin Rouge* (fig. 975) recalls the zigzag pattern of Degas' *The Glass of Absinthe* (see fig. 938). Yet this view of the well-known nightclub is no Impressionist "slice of life." Toulouse-Lautrec sees through the gay surface of the scene, viewing performers and customers with a pitilessly sharp eye for their character—including his own: he is the tiny bearded man next to the very tall one in the back of the room. The large areas of flat color, however, and the emphatic, smoothly curving outlines, reflect the influence of Gauguin (compare fig. 980). The Moulin Rouge that Toulouse-Lautrec shows here has an atmosphere so joyless and oppressive that we have to wonder if the artist did not regard it as a place of evil.

If his paintings inevitably bring to mind Degas and Gauguin, Toulouse-Lautrec is without precedent as a graphic artist. His posters, done in a distinctive style of his own invention, are ideally suited to inexpensive lithography, which enforces an equal economy of form and color. His first poster, *La Goulue* (fig. 976), which established his fame, lends this seedy demimonde an air of glamour that is at once captivating and mysterious. As advertising it sets a standard that has rarely been matched. The design is wed to the text so seamlessly that they cannot live without each other.

VAN GOGH. While Cézanne and Seurat were converting Impressionism into a more severe, classical style, Vincent van Gogh (1853–1890) pursued the opposite direction. He believed that Impressionism did not provide the artist with enough freedom to express his emotions. Since this was his main

976. Henri de Toulouse-Lautrec. *La Goulue.* 1891.
Colored lithographic poster, 6'3" x 3'10" (1.90 x 1.16 m)

concern, he is sometimes called an Expressionist, although the term ought to be reserved for certain later painters (see page 780). Van Gogh, the first great Dutch master since the seventeenth century, did not become an artist until 1880; as he died only ten years later, his career was even briefer than Seurat's. His early interests were in literature and religion. Profoundly dissatisfied with the values of industrial society and imbued with a strong sense of mission, he worked for a while as a lay preacher among poverty-stricken coal miners in Belgium. This same intense feeling for the poor dominates the paintings of his pre-Impressionist period, 1880–85. In *The Potato Eaters* (fig. 977), the last and most ambitious work of those years, there remains a naïve clumsiness that comes from his lack of conventional training, but this only adds to the expressive power of his style. [See Primary Sources, no. 93, page 940.] We are reminded of Daumier and Millet (see figs. 877 and 882), and of Rembrandt and Le Nain (see figs. 780 and 792). For this peasant family, the evening meal has the solemn importance of a rite.

When he painted *The Potato Eaters,* Van Gogh had not yet discovered the importance of color. A year later in Paris, where his brother Theo had a gallery devoted to modern art, he met

977. Vincent van Gogh. *The Potato Eaters.* 1885. Oil on canvas, 32¼ x 45" (82 x 114.3 cm). Vincent van Gogh Foundation/ Van Gogh Museum, Amsterdam

978. Vincent van Gogh. *Wheat Field and Cypress Trees.* 1889.
Oil on canvas, 28¹/2 x 36" (72.4 x 91.4 cm). The National Gallery, London
Reproduced by courtesy of the Trustees

979. Vincent van Gogh. *Self-Portrait.* 1889. Oil on canvas,
22¹/2 x 17" (57.2 x 43.2 cm). Collection Mrs. John Hay Whitney,
New York

Degas, Seurat, and other leading French artists. Their effect on him was electrifying. His pictures now blazed with color, and he even experimented briefly with the Divisionist technique of Seurat. This Impressionist phase, however, lasted less than two years. Although it was vitally important for his development, he had to integrate it with the style of his earlier years before his genius could fully unfold. Paris had opened his eyes to the sensuous beauty of the visible world and had taught him the pictorial language of the color patch, but painting continued to be nevertheless a vessel for his personal emotions. To investigate this spiritual reality with the new means at his command, he went to Arles, in the south of France. It was there, between 1888 and 1890, that he produced his greatest pictures.

Like Cézanne, Van Gogh now devoted his main energies to landscape painting, but the sun-drenched Mediterranean countryside evoked a very different response in him: he saw it filled with ecstatic movement, not architectural stability and permanence. In *Wheat Field and Cypress Trees* (fig. 978), both earth and sky pulsate with an overpowering turbulence. The wheat field resembles a stormy sea, the trees spring flamelike from the ground, and the hills and clouds heave with the same undulant motion. The dynamism contained in every brushstroke makes of each one not merely a deposit of color, but an incisive graphic gesture. The artist's personal "handwriting" is here an even more dominant factor than in the canvases of Daumier (compare figs. 877 and 878). Yet to Van Gogh himself it was the color, not the form, that determined the expressive content of his pictures. The letters he wrote to his brother include many eloquent descriptions of his choice of hues and the emotional meanings he attached to them. He

980. Paul Gauguin. *The Vision After the Sermon (Jacob Wrestling with the Angel)*. 1888.
Oil on canvas, 28³/4 x 36¹/2" (73 x 92.7 cm). The National Galleries of Scotland, Edinburgh

had learned about Impressionist color from Pissarro, but his personal color symbolism probably stemmed from discussions with Paul Gauguin (see below), who stayed with Van Gogh at Arles for several months. (Yellow, for example, meant faith or triumph or love to Van Gogh, while carmine was a spiritual color, cobalt a divine one; red and green, on the other hand, stood for the terrible human passions.) Although he acknowledged that his desire "to exaggerate the essential and to leave the obvious vague" made his colors look arbitrary by Impressionist standards, he nevertheless remained deeply committed to the visible world. [See Primary Sources, no. 94, page 940.]

Compared to Monet's *On the Bank of the Seine* (see fig. 933), the colors of *Wheat Field and Cypress Trees* are stronger, simpler, and more vibrant, but in no sense "unnatural." They speak to us of that "kingdom of light" Van Gogh had found in the South, and of his mystic faith in a creative force animating all forms of life—a faith no less ardent than the sectarian Christianity of his early years. His *Self-Portrait* (fig. 979) will remind us of Dürer's (fig. 701), and with good reason: the missionary had now become a prophet. His emaciated, luminous head with its burning eyes is set off against a whirlpool of darkness. "I want to paint men and women with that something of the eternal which the halo used to symbolize," Van Gogh had written, groping to define for his brother the human essence that was his aim in pictures such as this. At the time of the *Self-Portrait,* he had already begun to suffer fits of a mental illness that made painting increasingly difficult for him. Despairing of a cure, he committed suicide a year later, for he felt very deeply that art alone made his life worth living.

GAUGUIN. The quest for religious experience also played an important part in the work, if not in the life, of another great

Post-Impressionist, Paul Gauguin (1848–1903). He began as a prosperous stockbroker in Paris and an amateur painter and collector of modern pictures. At the age of 35, however, he became convinced that he must devote himself entirely to art. He abandoned his business career, separated from his family, and by 1889 was the central figure of a new movement called Synthetism or Symbolism.

Gauguin started out as a follower of Cézanne and once owned one of his still lifes. He then developed a style that, though less intensely personal than Van Gogh's, was in some ways an even bolder advance beyond Impressionism. Gauguin believed that Western civilization was "out of joint," that industrial society had forced people into an incomplete life dedicated to material gain, while their emotions lay neglected. To rediscover for himself this hidden world of feeling, Gauguin left Paris in 1886 to live among the peasants of Brittany at Pont Aven in western France. There two years later he met the painters Émile Bernard (1868–1941) and Louis Anquetin (1861–1932), who had rejected Impressionism and began to evolve a new style which they called Cloissonism (after an enamel technique), for its strong outlines. Gauguin incorporated their approach into his own, and emerged as the most forceful member of the Pont-Aven group, which quickly came to center on him.

The Pont-Aven style was first developed fully in the works Gauguin and Bernard painted at Pont Aven during the summer of 1888. Gauguin noticed particularly that religion was still part of the everyday life of the country people, and in pictures such as *The Vision After the Sermon (Jacob Wrestling with the Angel)* (fig. 980), he tried to depict their simple, direct faith. Here at last is what no Romantic artist had achieved: a style based on pre-Renaissance sources. Modeling and

981. Paul Gauguin. *Where Do We Come From? What Are We? Where Are We Going?* 1897.
Oil on canvas, 4'6³/4" x 12'3¹/2"(1.3 x 3.7 m). Museum of Fine Arts, Boston
Arthur Gordon Tompkins Residuary Fund

perspective have given way to flat, simplified shapes outlined heavily in black, and the brilliant colors are equally "unnatural." This style, inspired by folk art and medieval stained glass, is meant to re-create both the imagined reality of the vision and the trancelike rapture of the peasant women. The painting fulfills the goal of Synthetism: by treating the canvas in this decorative manner, the artist has turned it from a representation of the external world into an aesthetic object that projects an internal idea without using narrative or literal symbols. Yet we sense that although he tried to share this experience, Gauguin remains an outsider. He could paint pictures about faith, but not from faith.

Two years later, Gauguin's search for the unspoiled life led him even farther afield. He went to Tahiti—he had already visited Martinique in 1887—as a sort of "missionary in reverse," to learn from the natives instead of teaching them. [See Primary Sources, no. 95, page 940.] Although he spent the rest of his life in the South Pacific (he returned home only once, from 1893 to 1895), he never found the virgin Eden he was seeking. Indeed, he often had to rely on the writings and photographs of those who had recorded its culture before him. Nonetheless his Tahitian canvases conjure up an ideal world filled with the beauty and meaning he sought so futilely in real life.

His masterpiece in this vein is *Where Do We Come From? What Are We? Where Are We Going?* (fig. 981), painted as a summation of his art shortly before he was driven by despair to attempt suicide. Even without the suggestive title, we would recognize the painting's allegorical purpose from its monumental scale, the carefully thought out poses and placement of the figures within the tapestrylike landscape, and their pensive air. Although Gauguin intended the surface to be the sole conveyer of meaning, we know from his letters that the huge canvas represents an epic cycle of life. The scene unfolds from right to left, beginning with the sleeping girl, continuing with the beautiful young woman (a Tahitian Eve) in the center picking fruit, and ending with "an old woman approaching death who seems reconciled and resigned to her thoughts." In effect, the picture constitutes a variation on the three ages of life found in *Death and the Maiden* by Hans Baldung Grien (see fig. 708). The enigmatic Maori god overseeing everything acts as a counterpart to the figure of Death in Baldung Grien's painting. Gauguin has cast the answer to his title in distinctly Western terms. Moreover, he painted the composition in response to Puvis de Chavannes' classical allegories, such as those in the Lyons museum—especially *The Sacred Grove* (fig. 984, left). In this primitive Eden, Gauguin tell us, lies the real secret to the central mystery of life, not in some mythical past.

The works that come closest in flavor to Tahitian culture are Gauguin's woodcuts. *Offerings of Gratitude* (fig. 982), like the *Vision,* presents the theme of religious worship, but the image of a local god replaces the biblical subject. In its frankly "carved" look and its bold white-on-black pattern, we can feel the influences of the native art of the South Seas and of other non-European styles. The renewal of Western art and civilization as a whole, Gauguin believed, must come from "the Primitives." He advised other Symbolists to shun the Greek tradition and to turn instead to Persia, the Far East, and ancient Egypt.

The idea of primitivism itself was not new. It stems from the Romantic myth of the Noble Savage, propagated by the thinkers of the Enlightenment more than a century before, and its ultimate source is the age-old tradition of an earthly paradise where human societies once dwelled—and might perhaps live again—in a state of nature and innocence. But no one before Gauguin had gone as far to put the doctrine of

982. Paul Gauguin. *Offerings of Gratitude.* 1893–94.
Wood engraving, 8¹/16 x 14" (20.4 x 35.5 cm). The Museum of Modern Art, New York
Lillie P. Bliss Collection

primitivism into practice. His pilgrimage to the South Pacific had more than a purely private meaning. It symbolizes the end of the 400 years of colonial expansion which had brought almost the entire globe under Western domination. The "white man's burden," once so cheerfully and ruthlessly shouldered by the empire builders, was becoming unbearable.

Symbolism

Van Gogh's and Gauguin's discontent with the spiritual ills of Western civilization was part of a sentiment widely shared at the end of the nineteenth century. It reflected an intellectual and moral upheaval that rejected the modern world and its materialism in favor of irrational states of mind. A self-conscious preoccupation with decadence, evil, and darkness pervaded the artistic and literary climate. Even those who saw no escape analyzed their predicament in fascinated horror. Yet, somewhat paradoxically, this very awareness proved to be a source of strength, for it gave rise to the remarkable movement known as Symbolism. (The truly decadent, we may assume, are unable to realize their plight.)

Symbolism in art was at first an outgrowth of the literary movement that arose in 1885–86, with Jean Moréas and Gustave Kahn at its helm. Reacting against the Naturalism of the novelist Émile Zola, they reasserted the primacy of subjective ideas and championed the *poètes maudits* (the doomed poets) Stéphane Mallarmé and Paul Verlaine. There was a natural sympathy between the Pont-Aven painters and the Symbolist poets, and in a long article defining Symbolism published in April 1892, the writer G. Albert Aurier insisted on Gauguin's leadership. Nevertheless, unlike Post-Impressionism, which

was a stylistic tendency, Symbolism was a general outlook, one that allowed for a wide variety of styles—whatever would embody its peculiar frame of mind.

THE NABIS. Gauguin's Symbolist followers, who called themselves Nabis (from the Hebrew word for "prophet"), were less remarkable for creative talent than for their ability to spell out and justify the aims of Post-Impressionism in theoretical form. One of them, Maurice Denis, coined the statement that was to become the first article of faith for modernist painters of the twentieth century: "A picture—before being a war horse, a female nude, or some anecdote—is essentially a flat surface covered with colors in a particular order." He added that "every work of art is a transposition, a caricature, the passionate equivalent of a received sensation." The theory of equivalents gave the Nabis their independence from Gauguin. "We supplemented the rudimentary teaching of Gauguin by substituting for his over-simplified idea of pure colors the idea of beautiful harmonies, infinitely varied like nature; we adapted all the resources of the palette to all the states of our sensibility; and the sights which caused them became to us so many signs of our own subjectivity. We sought equivalents, but equivalents in beauty!"

VUILLARD. We can now understand why paintings by the Nabis soon came to look so different from Gauguin's. They became involved with decorative projects which, like Whistler's Peacock Room (see fig. 967), participate in the late-nineteenth-century's retreat into a world of beauty. The pictures of the 1890s by Édouard Vuillard (1868–1940), the most gifted member of the Nabis, share this quality. They consist mainly of domestic scenes, small in scale and intimate in effect, like

The late nineteenth century presents a welter of musical tendencies no less perplexing than the diversity found in Post-Impressionism. Strictly speaking, the term *Impressionism* cannot be applied to music, because music, by its very nature, cannot describe, it can only evoke. The term has nevertheless often been used to characterize the works of the Frenchman Claude Debussy (1862–1918), such as *La Mer* (1905), which successfully conveys the contrasting moods of the sea. In reality, however, his compositions are much closer in spirit to Symbolist poetry. (His closest friends, such as Pierre Louÿs, were writers.) This is especially evident in his lone opera, *Pelléas et Mélisande* (1893–1902), which was derived from a play by the Franco-Belgian Symbolist Maurice Maeterlinck (1862–1949); despite the vast difference between them, the opera reveals a debt to Wagner's music, which Debussy first heard at Bayreuth in 1888. Early in his career, Debussy summered in Russia as the guest of Tchaikovsky's patron, Madame von Meck, and it must have been at that time that he first became interested in modes, as well as other "lost" and exotic musical forms. This interest was reinforced by hearing Javanese music at the Universal Exposition in Paris in 1889. As a consequence, he began to employ such unusual devices as the pentatonic scale (the five black notes on the piano), which in his later years push conventional tonalism virtually to its breaking point.

Symbolism also touched Debussy's fellow "Impressionist," Maurice Ravel (1875–1937), particularly in such early works as *Gaspard de la nuit* (1908) for piano, which was inspired by a poem by Aloysius Bertrand (1807–1841). It also underlies the enchanting *Mother Goose,* originally composed that same year as a piano duet for the daughters of a close friend and later orchestrated as a ballet: the choice of stories and their musical treatment revels in the realm of dreams and other emanations of the subconscious, despite the air of childlike innocence.

The music of Debussy and Ravel was in many respects the conscious antithesis of Neo-Romanticism, that late phase of Romanticism which is identified particularly with the German composers Gustav Mahler (1866–1911) and Richard Strauss (1864–1949). Strauss started out as a classicist but through his friendship with the poet Alexander Ritter (1833–1896) became a disciple of Wagner and Liszt. While pursuing a career as a conductor, he first gained fame for his tone poems, such as *Death and Transfiguration* (1889). From 1905 on, however, Strauss devoted himself primarily to operas, notably *Der Rosenkavalier (The Cavalier of the Rose;* 1911), which, like all his finest efforts, was the result of his collaboration with the Austrian Neo-Romantic poet and dramatist Hugo von Hofmannsthal (1874–1929). The composer later supported the Nazis and served for a while as head of musical affairs under Hitler, although he was officially exonerated of collaboration shortly before his death.

If Strauss represents the final glory of German Romanticism, the symphonies and orchestrated song cycles by his friend and fellow conductor Gustav Mahler of Vienna can be seen as the musical counterpart to the morbid sensitivity of Gustav Klimt and the Vienna Secession movement. Their enormous scale makes huge demands on orchestra and chorus alike, while the extremes of hypersensitive introspection and almost hysterical bombast go beyond the expressive limits of Romanticism. Mahler's late works, sparser in character, were the point of departure for the next generation of Viennese composers, whose work he encouraged: Arnold Schoenberg, Anton Webern, and Alban Berg, who were to revolutionize twentieth-century music.

This fact points to an anomaly, namely, that a number of late Romantics had the unfortunate fate of living well beyond the advent of modern music. Both Ravel and the Finnish composer Jean Sibelius (1865–1957) responded by virtually ceasing to write music after 1925. Sibelius was a throwback to the nationalist composers of the mid-nineteenth century. His early works are tone poems, based on Nordic legends, that are filled with a brooding melancholy. His major contribution, however, lies in the seven symphonies, which build short motifs into large structures of decidedly unconventional form that nearly stand Romanticism on its ear. Although passionate at times, his compositions lack the lush, sentimental appeal of those by the other great nationalist composer of the era, the Russian Sergei Rachmaninov (1873–1943), who wrote piano concertos as showcases for his virtuosity, in addition to three symphonies that follow in a direct line of descent from Tchaikovsky's.

Just as there was no true Impressionism in music, so the term *realism* in late-nineteenth-century opera is something of a misnomer. It was applied to a small group of operas—including *Carmen* (1875) by Georges Bizet (1838–1875) and *Pagliacci* (1892) by Ruggiero Leoncavallo (1858–1919), which is often produced on the same bill with *Cavalleria Rusticana* (1889) by Pietro Mascagni (1863–1945)—set in contemporary Europe that are nonetheless sentimental melodramas. *La Bohème* (1896) and *Tosca* (1900) by Giacomo Puccini (1858–1924), Verdi's successor as the leading composer of this genre in Italy, partake of this *verismo,* as it was called, although they are set earlier in the century; however, they owe their success much more to their combination of melting lyricism and pungent drama. The later operas, such as *Madame Butterfly* (1904) and *Girl of the Golden West* (1910), based on successful melodramas by the American playwright David Belasco (c. 1853–1931), exploit the European taste for the exotic, although they were failures initially. Belasco's plays, however, were considered examples of realism by audiences in the United States, to whom their setting and moral meaning were instantly recognizable. Their realism was heightened by spectacular staging and special effects.

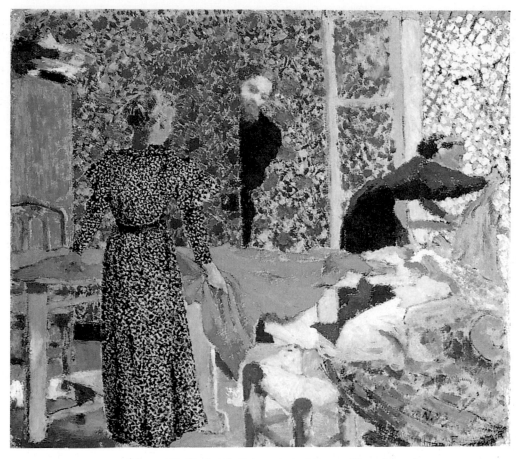

983. Édouard Vuillard. *The Suitor*. 1893. Oil on millboard panel,
12¹/₂ x 14" (31.8 x 35.6 cm). Smith College Museum of Art, Northampton, Massachusetts
Purchased, Drayton Hillyer Fund, 1938

The Suitor (fig. 983). These combine into a remarkable new entity the flat planes and emphatic contours of Gauguin (fig. 980) with the shimmering Divisionist "color mosaic" and the geometric surface organization of Seurat (see fig. 974). This seemingly casual view of his mother's corset-shop workroom has a delicate balance of "two-D" and "three-D" effects. Indeed, Vuillard probably derived his flat patterns from the fabrics themselves. The picture's quiet magic makes us think of Vermeer and Chardin (compare figs. 789 and 821), whose subject matter, too, was the snug life of the middle class.

In both subject and treatment, the painting has counterparts as well in Symbolist literature and theater: the poetry of Paul Verlaine, the novels of Stéphane Mallarmé, and the productions of Aurélian-Marie Lugné-Poë, for whom Vuillard designed stage sets. It evokes a host of feelings through purely formal means that could never be conveyed by naturalism alone. The Nabis established an important precedent for Matisse a decade later (see fig. 1022). By then, however, the movement had disintegrated as its members became more conservative. Vuillard himself turned more to naturalism, and he never recaptured the delicacy and daring of his early canvases.

PUVIS DE CHAVANNES. The Symbolists discovered that there were some older artists, descendants of the Romantics, whose work, like their own, placed inner vision above the observation of nature. Many of them, as well as other Post-Impressionists, took their inspiration from the classicism of Pierre-Cécile Puvis de Chavannes (1824–1898), a follower of Ingres who succeeded in becoming the leading muralist of his day. Rejecting academic conventions, he sought a radical simplification of style, which at first seemed anachronistic but was soon hailed by the critics and artists of all persuasions. The effectiveness of the murals he executed in the 1880s for the museum at Lyons (fig. 984) depends in large part on Puvis' formal devices—the compressed space, schematic forms, and restricted palette, which imitates in oil the chalky surface of old frescoes. The antinaturalism of his style emphasizes the allegorical character of the scene, lending it a gravity and mystery absent from other decorative paintings by his contemporaries. Anecdotal interest is replaced by nostalgia for an idealized, mythical past. The stiff, ritualistic poses serve both to freeze time and to convey a poetry that is at once elegiac and serene. Puvis' economy of means was intended to present his ideas with maximum clarity, but it has just the opposite effect: it heightens their suggestiveness. His popularity resulted precisely from this ambiguity, which permitted a wide variety of interpretation. Symbolists from Gauguin through the young Picasso could thus claim him as one of their own; nevertheless, he vehemently protested any association with the Symbolist movement, although he reciprocated an admiration with the English Pre-Raphaelite Burne-Jones (see pages 728–29).

984. Pierre-Cécile Puvis de Chavannes. *The Sacred Grove.* c. 1883–84;
Vision of Antiquity. c. 1888–89; and *Christian Inspiration.* c. 1888–89. Painting cycle,
grand staircase, Musée des Beaux-Arts, Lyons, France

985. Gustave Moreau. *The
Apparition (Dance of Salome).*
c. 1876. Watercolor,
41³/4 x 28³/8" (106 x 72 cm).
Musée du Louvre, Paris

987. Odilon Redon. *The Eye Like a Strange Balloon Mounts Toward Infinity,* from the series *Edgar A. Poe.* 1882. Lithograph, 10¼ x 7¹¹/₁₆" (25.9 x 19.6 cm). The Museum of Modern Art, New York

Gift of Peter H. Deitsch

986. Aubrey Beardsley. *Salome.* 1892. Pen drawing, 10¹⁵/₁₆ x 5¹³/₁₆" (27.8 x 14.8 cm). Aubrey Beardsley Collection. Manuscripts Division, Department of Rare Books and Special Collections, Princeton University Library, New Jersey

MOREAU. One of the Symbolists, Gustave Moreau (1826–1898), a recluse who admired Delacroix, created a world of personal fantasy that has much in common with the medieval reveries of some of the English Pre-Raphaelites. *The Apparition* (fig. 985) shows one of his favorite themes: the head of John the Baptist, in a blinding radiance of light, appears to the dancing Salome. Her odalisquelike sensuousness, the stream of blood pouring from the severed head, the vast, mysterious space of the setting suggestive of an exotic temple rather than of Herod's palace, all these summon up the dreams of Oriental splendor and cruelty so dear to the Romantic imagination, combined with an insistence on the reality of the supernatural. Only late in life did Moreau achieve a measure of recognition. Suddenly, his art was in tune with the times. During his last six years, he even held a professorship at the conservative École des Beaux-Arts, the successor of the official art academy that had been founded under Louis XIV (see page 600). There he attracted the most gifted students, among them such future modernists as Matisse and Rouault.

BEARDSLEY. How prophetic Moreau's work was of the taste prevailing at the end of the century is evident from a comparison with Aubrey Beardsley (1872–1898), a gifted young Englishman whose elegantly "decadent" black-and-white drawings were the very epitome of that taste. They include a *Salome* illustration (fig. 986) that might well be the final scene of the drama depicted by Moreau: Salome has taken up John's severed head and triumphantly kissed it. Whereas Beardsley's erotic meaning is plain—Salome is passionately in love with John and has asked for his head because she could not have him in any other way—Moreau's remains ambiguous. Nevertheless, the parallel is striking, and there are formal similarities as well, such as the "stem" of trickling blood from which John's head rises like a flower. Yet Beardsley's *Salome* cannot be said to derive from Moreau's. The sources of his style are English—the graphic art of the Pre-Raphaelites (see fig. 966)—with a strong mixture of Japanese influence.

REDON. Another solitary artist whom the Symbolists discovered and claimed as one of their own was Odilon Redon (1840–1916). Like Moreau, he had a haunted imagination, but his imagery was even more personal and disturbing. A master of etching and lithography, he drew inspiration from the fantastic visions of Goya (see fig. 862) as well as Romantic literature. The lithograph shown in figure 987 is one of a

988. James Ensor. *Christ's Entry into Brussels in 1889*. 1888. Oil on canvas, 8'6¹/₂" x 14'1¹/₂" (2.6 x 4.3 m).
Collection of the J. Paul Getty Museum, Malibu, California

set he issued in 1882 and dedicated to Edgar Allan Poe. The American poet had been dead for 33 years; but his tormented life and his equally tortured imagination made him the very model of the *poète maudit,* and his works, excellently translated by Baudelaire and Mallarmé, were greatly admired in France. Redon's lithographs do not illustrate Poe. They are, rather, "visual poems" in their own right, evoking the macabre, hallucinatory world of Poe's imagination. In our example, the artist has revived an ancient device, the single eye representing the all-seeing mind of God. But, in contrast to the traditional form of the symbol, Redon shows the whole eyeball removed from its socket and converted into a balloon that drifts aimlessly in the sky.

ENSOR. The disquieting visual paradoxes in Redon's lithographs express the pessimism of a troubled mind struggling to find itself; only after 1900 did his outlook give way to a new serenity laden with spiritual overtones. In the art of the Belgian painter James Ensor (1860–1949), a cynical view of the human condition reaches obsessive intensity, and for much the same reason. In *Christ's Entry into Brussels in 1889* (fig. 988) the demon-ridden world of Bosch and Schongauer has come to life again in modern guise (compare figs. 685 and 694). The painting, showing the Second Coming of Christ in contem-

porary Belgium, is a grotesque parody of a subject familiar to us since the Late Gothic (compare figs. 502 and 504). Here Christ is virtually lost in a sea of leering faces, which are treated as the epitome of evil. As we scrutinize these masks we become aware that they are the crowd's true faces, revealing the depravity ordinarily hidden behind the facade of everyday appearances. At the time, Ensor identified with Christ, whose suffering he felt paralleled his own at the hands of hostile critics and an indifferent public. Later, when his art began to gain wide acceptance, he abandoned this bitter attitude.

MUNCH. Something of the same macabre quality pervades the early work of Edvard Munch (1863–1944), a far more gifted artist who came to Paris from Norway in 1889 and based his starkly expressive style on Toulouse-Lautrec, Van Gogh, and Gauguin. *The Scream* (fig. 989) shows the influences of all three. It is an image of fear, the terrifying, unreasoned fear we feel in a nightmare. Unlike Goya and Fuseli (see figs. 862 and 884), Munch visualizes this experience without the aid of frightening apparitions, and his achievement is the more persuasive for that very reason. The rhythm of the long, wavy lines seems to carry the echo of the scream into every corner of the picture, making of earth and sky one great sounding board of fear.

989. Edvard Munch. *The Scream*. 1893. Tempera and casein on cardboard, 36 x 29" (91.4 x 73.7 cm). Nasjonalgalleriet, Oslo, Norway

KLIMT. Munch's works generated such controversy when they were exhibited in Berlin in 1892 that a number of young radicals broke from the artists association and formed the Berlin Secession, which took its name from a similar group that had been founded in Munich earlier that year. The Secession quickly became a loosely allied international movement. In 1897 it spread to Austria, where Gustav Klimt (1862–1918) established the Vienna Secession with the purpose of raising the level of the arts and crafts in Austria through close ties to Art Nouveau (see pages 768–69). *The Kiss* (fig. 990) by Klimt expresses a different kind of anxiety from Munch's *The Scream*. The image will remind us of Beardsley's *Salome* (fig. 986), but here the barely suppressed eroticism has burst into desire. Engulfed in mosaiclike robes that create an illusion of rich beauty, the angular figures steal a moment of passion whose brevity emphasizes their joyless existence.

PICASSO'S BLUE PERIOD. When he came to Paris from his native Spain in 1900, Pablo Picasso (1881–1973) felt the spell of the same artistic atmosphere that had generated the style of Munch. His so-called Blue Period (the term refers to the prevailing color of his canvases as well as to their mood) consists almost exclusively of pictures of beggars and derelicts,

990. Gustav Klimt. *The Kiss*. 1907–8. Oil on canvas, 70⅞ x 70⅞" (180 x 180 cm). Österreichische Galerie, Vienna

991. Pablo Picasso. *The Old Guitarist.* 1903. Oil on panel, 48³/8 x 32¹/2" (122.9 x 82.6 cm). The Art Institute of Chicago
Helen Birch Bartlett Memorial Collection

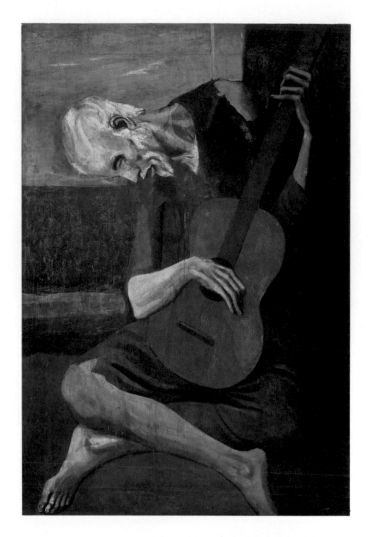

such as *The Old Guitarist* (fig. 991). These outcasts or victims of society have a pathos that reflects the artist's own sense of isolation. Yet they convey poetic melancholy more than outright despair. The aged musician accepts his fate with a resignation that seems almost saintly, and the attenuated grace of his limbs reminds us of El Greco (compare fig. 649). *The Old Guitarist* is a strange amalgam of Mannerism and of the art of Gauguin and Toulouse-Lautrec (note the smoothly curved contours), imbued with the personal gloom of a 22-year-old genius.

ROUSSEAU. A few years later, Picasso and his friends discovered a painter who until then had attracted no attention, although he had been exhibiting his work since 1886. He was Henri Rousseau (1844–1910), a retired customs collector who had started to paint in his middle age without training of any sort. His ideal—which, fortunately, he never achieved—was the arid academic style of the followers of Ingres. Rousseau is that paradox, a folk artist of genius. How else could he have done a picture like *The Dream* (fig. 992)? What goes on in the enchanted world of this canvas needs no explanation, because none is possible. Perhaps for that very reason its magic becomes believably real to us. Rousseau himself described the scene in a little poem:

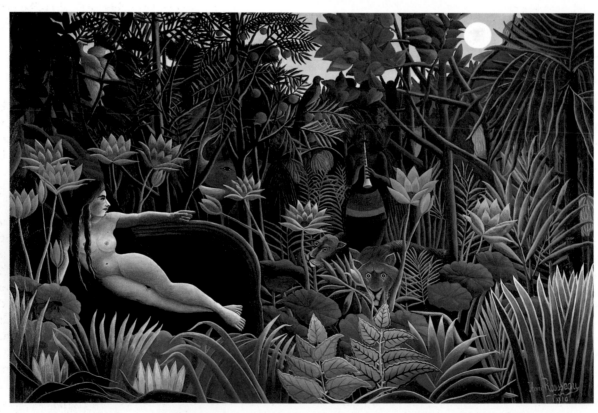

992. Henri Rousseau. *The Dream.* 1910. Oil on canvas, 6'8¹/2" x 9'9¹/2" (2.05 x 2.96 m). The Museum of Modern Art, New York
Gift of Nelson A. Rockefeller

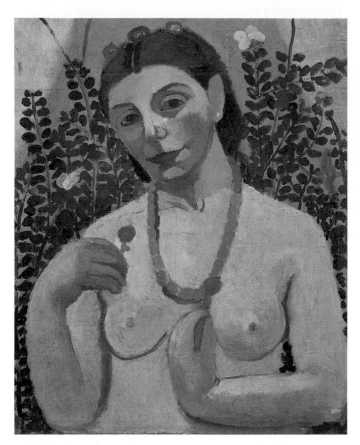

993. Paula Modersohn-Becker. *Self-Portrait*. 1906. Oil on canvas, 24 x 19³/4" (61 x 50.2 cm). Öffentliche Kunstsammlung Basel, Kunstmuseum, Switzerland

994. Aristide Maillol. *Seated Woman* (*La Méditerranée*). c. 1901. Stone, height 41" (104.1 cm). Collection Oskar Reinhart, Winterthur, Switzerland

Yadwigha, peacefully asleep
Enjoys a lovely dream:
She hears a kind snake charmer
Playing upon his reed.
On stream and foliage glisten
The silvery beams of the moon.
And savage serpents listen
To the gay, entrancing tune.

Here at last was an innocent directness of feeling that Gauguin thought was so necessary for the age. Picasso and his friends were the first to recognize this quality in Rousseau's work. They revered him as the godfather of twentieth-century painting.

MODERSOHN-BECKER. The inspiration of primitivism that Gauguin had traveled so far to find was discovered by Paula Modersohn-Becker (1876–1907) in the village of Worpswede, near her family home in Bremen, Germany. Among the artists and writers who congregated there was the Symbolist lyric poet Rainer Maria Rilke, Rodin's friend and briefly his personal secretary. Rilke had visited Russia and been deeply impressed with what he viewed as the purity of Russian peasant life. His influence on the colony at Worpswede affected Modersohn-Becker, whose last works are direct precursors of modern art. Her gentle but powerful *Self-Portrait* (fig. 993), painted the year before her early death, presents a transition from the Symbolism of Gauguin and his followers, which she absorbed during several stays in Paris, to Expressionism. The

color has the intensity of Matisse and the Fauves (see page 781). At the same time, her deliberately simplified treatment of forms parallels the experiments of Picasso, which were to culminate in *Les Demoiselles d'Avignon* (fig. 1033).

SCULPTURE

MAILLOL. In sculpture, there are no tendencies to be equated with Post-Impressionism, but a form of Symbolism makes its appearance about 1900. Sculptors in France of a younger generation had by then been trained under the dominant influence of Rodin and were ready to go their own ways. The finest of these, Aristide Maillol (1861–1944), began as a Symbolist painter, although he did not share Gauguin's anti-Greek attitude. Maillol might be called a "classic primitivist": admiring the simplified strength of early Greek sculpture, he rejected its later phases. The *Seated Woman* (fig. 994) evokes memories of the Archaic and Severe styles rather than of Phidias and Praxiteles. The solid forms and clearly defined volumes also recall Cézanne's statement that all natural forms are based on the cone, the sphere, and the cylinder. But the most notable quality of the figure is its harmonious, self-sufficient repose, which the outside world cannot disturb. A statue, Maillol thought, must above all be "static," structurally balanced like a piece of architecture. It must represent a state of being that is detached from the stress of circumstance, with none of the restless, thrusting energy of Rodin's work. In this respect, the *Seated Woman* is the exact opposite of *The Thinker* (see fig. 955). Maillol later gave it the

The major competing tendencies of the late nineteenth century were Realism and Symbolism, which were sometimes found in the work of the same author. The most important Realist was the French novelist Émile Zola (1840–1902). Inspired by Charles Darwin's theory of evolution and Auguste Comte's socialism, he argued that the dramatist should observe the human condition with the detachment of the scientist and illustrate the "inevitable laws of heredity and environment." However, his plays, like those of the Goncourt brothers, were more important in theory than in practice, and Realism found its main expression in the plays of Henri Becque (1837–1899), which are pessimistic to the point of cynicism. Even so, Realism's success depended in the end on the determination of André Antoine (1858–1943), who established the Théâtre Libre (Free Theater) in 1887 and then the Théâtre Antoine a decade later, which became proving grounds for Realist drama and experimental staging techniques until Antoine was appointed head of the state-supported Odéon in 1906.

Antoine also mounted productions of foreign playwrights, notably the Norwegian Henrik Ibsen (1828–1906), who first established his reputation with verse-dramas about the legendary past, notably *Peer Gynt* (1867), which is still considered the great national saga of Norway. In the 1870s, however, he turned to Realism in such plays as *The Doll's House* (1879), then began making greater use of Symbolism beginning with *The Wild Duck* (1884). The basic theme of his mature works nevertheless remained the same: the conflict between duty and self, which finally sees the consequences of its actions in a moment of revelation. However, Ibsen's treatment of this theme changed considerably over time, almost reversing itself, whereas at first he condemned excessive devotion to duty, in the end he came to criticize unbridled self-interest.

Like the Norwegian painter Edvard Munch, Ibsen enjoyed considerable influence in Germany, thanks in part to the productions mounted by Otto Brahm (1856–1912), who was president of the Freie Bühne (Free Theater) in Berlin in 1889–94 and then director of the Deutsches Theater (German Theater) for a decade before taking over the Lessing Theater until his death. The most important Germany playwright associated with the Freie Bühne was Gerhart Hauptmann (1862–1946), whose drama *The Weavers* (1892) shows the same social conscience as the early paintings of Van Gogh and the sculpture of Constantin Meunier.

Psychological, not social, realism was the particular interest of Arthur Schnitzler (1862–1931), whose major play, *Anatol* (1893), follows the ideas of his friend Sigmund Freud, the founder of modern psychiatry, in treating human sexuality through a series of affairs that inevitably give way to boredom because ego gratification cannot give rise to enduring love. Thanks in good measure to heavy government funding, it was in Germany where most of the major technical innovations in stagecraft were devised, including the revolving stage, the elevator stage, the rolling platform, and the sliding platform.

In England, the counterpart of the Théâtre Libre and the Freie Bühne was the Independent Theater, where George Bernard Shaw (1856–1950) first achieved critical acclaim in 1892. Shaw used sharp wit to illustrate philosophical propositions in the guise of national and social issues. His belief in human progress through moral persuasion and exercise of free choice found its highest expression in *Man and Superman* (1901), in which a socialist intellectual representing man as spiritual creator outwits his rivals but succumbs to a woman who exemplifies the life force.

The leading Realist in Russia at the turn of the century was Anton Chekhov (1860–1904), whose fame rests on the four plays about ennui in the upper class he wrote for the Moscow Art Theater during the last five years of his life, especially *The Three Sisters* (1901). Like Chekhov, who befriended him, Maxim Gorky (1868–1936) was at first better known as a writer of short stories; his plays, likewise written mainly for the Moscow Art Theater and centering on class conflict, reflect his political activism.

The antithesis of Zola's Realism was the Symbolism of Stéphane Mallarmé (1842–1898), a poet who was inspired by Edgar Allan Poe's macabre writings, Charles Baudelaire's art criticism, and Richard Wagner's operas. He proposed theater that evoked the mystery of life through poetic metaphor. Symbolism was championed first by the short-lived Théâtre d'Art of Paul Fort (1872–1962), and then by the Théâtre de l'Oeuvre under Aurélian-Marie Lugné-Poë (1869–1940). Lugné-Poë drew many of his ideas about scenery from his friends Édouard Vuillard, Maurice Denis, and Pierre Bonnard, whom he also employed to create sets, along with Odilon Redon and Henri de Toulouse-Lautrec. The most important French dramatist associated with Lugné-Poë was the Belgian-born Maurice Maeterlinck (1862–1949), whose masterpiece, *Pelléas and Mélisande* (1892), which was to

---

title *La Méditerranée*—The Mediterranean—to suggest the source from which he drew the timeless serenity of his figure.

MEUNIER. If Maillol sought to transcend his epoch, the Belgian Constantin Meunier (1831–1905) was thoroughly immersed in it. Politically and socially, Belgium exemplified all the tensions of the later nineteenth century: a conservative government, insensitive to the extremes of wealth and poverty in the country, seemed determined to suppress all protest or attempts at reform. The workers' movement had a late start in such a setting; it was not until 1885 that labor unions were strong enough to found the Belgian Workers' Party. By that

time, many writers and artists had become partisans of social reform. Meunier began as a painter but soon began to model in clay. From 1885 until the end of his life, his output consisted almost entirely of sculpture. The change was motivated by his search for a more "heroic" medium. The heroism of labor, its pride and its pathos, was to be his theme as a sculptor. He treated it with a solemnity carried over from his earlier religious subjects—a concern that he shared with Vincent van Gogh, who had an unforgettable experience of human misery in the mining district of Belgium (see page 753). His lifesize *Bust of a Puddler* (fig. 995) has an air of pathos, of noble suffering such as befits a "martyr of labor." It also betrays inspire Debussy's opera 10 years later, relies heavily on symbolic devices to create an air of mystery. Lugné-Poë also staged *Ubu Roi* by Alfred Jarry (1873– 1907), which sparked a riot on opening night in 1896. Originally written as a schoolboy satire of a chemistry teacher, this play about an unscrupulous bourgeois king and his wife who give in to every appetitive and depraved whim later exercised great influence on the absurdist theater of the Surrealists. A year later Lugné-Poë abandoned Symbolism out of admiration for Ibsen, whose dramas offered far richer content.

After establishing his reputation as a Realist in the late 1880s with *Miss Julie,* the Swedish playwright August Strindberg (1849–1912) began to write "dream plays" in which he tried, as he put it, "to imitate the disconnected but seemingly logical form of the dream. Anything may happen; everything is possible and probable. Time and space do not exist. But one consciousness reigns above them all—that of the dreamer." Unlike Schnitzler's plays, they arose not from Freudian theory but from the dramatist's own bout with madness during the 1890s, when he was living in Berlin, from which he recovered with the aid of Emanuel Swedenborg's spiritualist belief in a higher reality.

Closely related to Strindberg as a dramatist was the German Benjamin Franklin Wedekind (1864–1918), whose two major plays, *Earth Spirit* and *Pandora's Box* (both 1895), deal with frankly sexual themes through the prostitute Lulu, who inspired Alban Berg's unfinished opera. After becoming disillusioned with the power of words, Hugo von Hofmannsthal (1874–1929) actually gave up theater almost entirely to write librettos for Richard Strauss' operas. Another leader in the reaction against Realism was the Swiss-born Adolphe Appia (1861–1928), who emphasized the staging of Wagner's operas through three-dimensional scenery and carefully calculated light effects that made full use of the recent advantages in lighting technology.

The only serious experiment with Symbolism by an English dramatist was *Salomé* (1892) by Oscar Wilde (1856–1900), but it can hardly be called an English play. It had been written in French during the previous decade and was published in Paris with illustrations by Aubrey Beardsley. Moreover, the work, which was banned in England until 1931, was first produced in Paris by Lugné-Poë in 1896 with Sarah Bernhardt in the lead role. Wilde was otherwise a writer of extremely clever, albeit conventional, comedies, whose main connection to Symbolism was his involvement with the Aesthetic Movement, whose dandyism he personified.

995. Constantin Meunier. *Bust of a Puddler.* c. 1885–90. Bronze, lifesize. Private collection

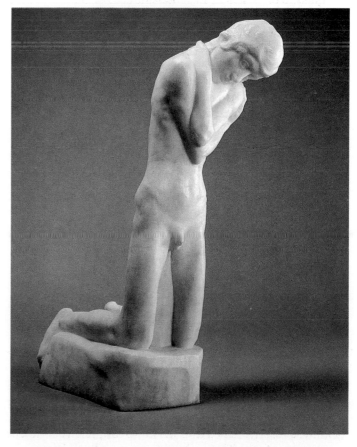

996. George Minne. *Kneeling Boy.* 1898. Marble, height 31" (78.7 cm). Museum voor Schone Kunsten, Ghent, Belgium

Meunier's considerable debt to Rodin, for whom he always expressed the greatest admiration.

MINNE. The youngest of Belgian nineteenth-century sculptors and, during the first dozen years of his career, the most original was George Minne (1866–1941). Minne contributed woodcut illustrations to books by his friends the Belgian Symbolist writers Maurice Maeterlinck and Émile Verhaeren, who introduced him to Les Vingt (The Twenty), a group of Belgian avant-garde artists, and it was at their annual exhibition in 1890 that Minne first presented his sculpture. *Kneeling Boy* (fig. 996), on which his fame rests, shows a state of brooding

997. Wilhelm Lehmbruck. *Standing Youth.* 1913.
Cast stone, height 7'8" (2.33 m); base 33¹/2 x 26³/4" (85.1 x 68 cm).
The Museum of Modern Art, New York
Gift of Abby Aldrich Rockefeller

998. Ernst Barlach. *Man Drawing a Sword.* 1911. Wood,
height 31" (78.7 cm). Private collection

calm, but the haggard, angular limbs reflect Gothic, not classical, influence, and the trancelike rigidity of the pose suggests religious meditation. The statue became the basis for a fountain design with five kneeling boys grouped around a circular basin as if engaged in a solemn ritual. By treating the figure as an anonymous member of a rhythmically repeated sequence, Minne heightened its mood of ascetic withdrawal.

LEHMBRUCK. Minne's art attracted little notice in France, but was admired in Germany. His influence is apparent in *Standing Youth* (fig. 997) by Wilhelm Lehmbruck (1881–1919). Here a Gothic elongation and angularity are combined with a fine balance derived from Maillol's art, as well as with some of Rodin's expressive energy. The total effect is a looming monumental figure well anchored in space, yet partaking of that poetic melancholy we observed in Picasso's Blue Period.

BARLACH. Ernst Barlach (1870–1938), another important German sculptor who reached maturity in the years before World War I, seems the very opposite of Lehmbruck. He is a "Gothic primitivist," and more akin to Munch than to the Western Symbolist tradition. What Gauguin had experienced in Brittany and the tropics, Barlach found by going to Russia: the simple humanity of a preindustrial age. His figures, such

as *Man Drawing a Sword* (fig. 998), embody elementary emotions—wrath, fear, grief—that seem imposed upon them by invisible presences. When they act, they are like somnambulists, unaware of their own impulses. Human beings, to Barlach, are humble creatures at the mercy of forces beyond their control; they are never masters of their fate. Characteristically, these figures do not fully emerge from the material substance (often, as here, a massive block of wood) of which they are made. Their clothing is like a hard chrysalis that hides the body, as in medieval sculpture. Barlach's art has a range that is severely restricted in both form and emotion, yet its mute intensity within these limits is not easily forgotten.

ARCHITECTURE

Art Nouveau

During the 1890s and early 1900s a movement now usually known as *Art Nouveau* arose throughout Europe and America. It takes its name from the shop opened in Paris in 1895 by the entrepreneur Siegfried Bing, who employed most of the leading designers of the day and helped to spread their work everywhere. By that time, however, the movement had already been in full force for several years. Art Nouveau has various other names as well: it is called *Jugendstil* (literally Youth Style) in Germany and Austria, *Stile Liberty* (after the well-known London store that helped to launch it) in Italy, and *Modernista* in Spain. Like Post-Impressionism and Symbolism, Art Nouveau is not easy to characterize. It was primarily a new style of decoration based on sinuous curves, nominally inspired by Rococo forms, that often suggest organic shapes. Its favorite pattern was the whiplash line, its typical shape the lily. Yet there was a severely geometric side as well that in the long run proved of even greater significance. The ancestor of Art Nouveau was the ornament of William Morris and the Japonist enthusiasm of Whistler. It was also related to the styles of Gauguin, Beardsley, Munch, and Klimt, among others. In turn it was allied to such diverse outlooks as aestheticism, socialism, and symbolism.

The avowed goal of Art Nouveau was to raise the crafts to the level of the fine arts, thereby abolishing the distinction between them. In this respect, it was meant to be a "popular" art, available to everyone. Yet it often became so extravagant as to be affordable only by the wealthy few. Art Nouveau had a profound impact on public taste, and its pervasive influence on the applied arts can be seen in wrought-iron work, furniture, jewelry, glass, typography, and even women's fashions. Historically Art Nouveau may be regarded as a prelude to modernism, but its preciousness was perhaps the most conspicuous symptom of the malaise that afflicted the Western world at the end of the nineteenth century. Hence it is uniquely worthy of our attention as our own culture passes through a similar transition.

Although it is usually thought of in terms of the decorative arts, Art Nouveau had perhaps its most important impact on architecture. As a style of decoration it did not lend itself easily to translation on a large scale. Indeed, it was aptly called book-decoration architecture by wags, for the origin of its designs, which were best suited to two-dimensional surface effects. But in the hands of architects of greatness, Art Nouveau yielded impressive results. Thus the authority of the "revival styles" was undermined once and for all in Europe.

HORTA. The first architect to explore the full potential of Art Nouveau was Victor Horta (1861–1947), the founder of the movement in Brussels. The stairwell in Tassel House (fig. 999), built in 1892–93, has a fluid grace that is truly amazing. Horta has made maximum use of wrought iron, which could be drawn out into almost any shape. The supporting role of the column is frankly acknowledged, although it has been made as slender as possible. But in a charming play on the Corinthian capital (compare fig. 176), it sprouts ribbonlike tendrils that dissolve the conjoining arches—an effect amplified by continuing the vegetable motif in the vault above. Similarly the bannister, which is light and supple, uncoils with taut springiness. This extends to the linear patterns on the floor and walls, which serve to integrate the space visually. The entire ensemble has a litheness and airiness that make the grand staircase of Garnier's Opéra seem utterly ponderous and vulgar by comparison (see fig. 918).

GUIMARD. Despite the use of iron, Horta's interior presents no structural advance. And although they lie largely on the

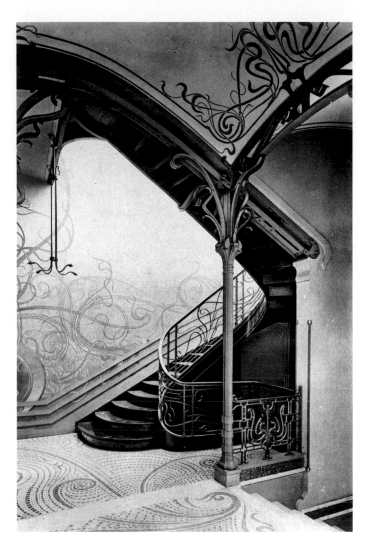

999. Victor Horta. Interior Stairwell of the Tassel House, Brussels. 1892–93

1000. Hector Guimard. Métro Station, Paris. 1900

surface, the same devices could be translated readily into independent three-dimensional forms whose role was essentially sculptural. The entrances for the Métro (the Paris subway) designed in 1900 by Hector Guimard (1867–1942) present just such a case (see fig. 1000). Like Horta, whose work he clearly admired, Guimard was a designer of universal scope,

1002. Floor plan of typical floor,
Casa Milá

1001. Antoní Gaudí. Casa Milá apartments, Barcelona. 1905–7

rather than an engineer, and it is this background in the applied arts that renders these stations appealing even today. The functional purpose is so thoroughly disguised by the fanciful forms that we readily overlook their role in providing safety and light, which comes from the plantlike posts springing like strange hybrids from the sidewalk.

GAUDÍ. The most remarkable instance of Art Nouveau in architecture is the Casa Milá in Barcelona (figs. 1001 and 1002), a large apartment house by Antoní Gaudí (1852–1926). It shows an almost maniacal avoidance of all flat surfaces, straight lines, and symmetry of any kind, so that the building looks as if it had been freely modeled of some malleable substance. (The material is not stucco or cement, as we might suppose, but cut stone.) The softly rounded openings anticipate the "eroded" shapes of Henry Moore's sculpture (see fig. 1127), the roof has the rhythmic motion of a wave, and the chimneys seem to have been squeezed from a pastry tube. The Casa Milá expresses one man's fanatical devotion to the ideal of "natural" form. It could never be repeated, let alone developed further. Structurally, it is a tour de force of old-fashioned craftsmanship, an attempt at architectural reform from the periphery, rather than from the center.

MACKINTOSH. Gaudí represents one extreme of Art Nouveau architecture. The Scot Charles Rennie Mackintosh (1868–1928) represents another. Although they stood at opposite poles, both strove for the same goal—a contemporary style independent of the past. Mackintosh's basic outlook is so close to the functionalism of Louis Sullivan (see below) that at first glance his work hardly seems to belong to Art Nouveau at all. The north facade of the Glasgow School of Art (fig. 1003) was designed as early as 1896, but might be mistaken for a building done 30 years later. Huge, deeply recessed studio windows have replaced the walls, leaving only a framework of massive, unadorned cut-stone surfaces except in the center

1003. Charles Rennie Mackintosh. North facade of the Glasgow
School of Art, Glasgow, Scotland. 1896–1910

bay. This bay, however, is "sculptured" in a style not unrelated to Gaudí's, despite its preference for angles over curves. Another Art Nouveau feature is the wrought-iron grillwork (here with a minimum of ornament). Even more surprising than the exterior is the two-story library (fig. 1004), with its rectangular wooden posts and lintels supporting the balcony.

VAN DE VELDE. Through architectural magazines and exhibitions, Mackintosh's work came to be widely known abroad. Its structural clarity and force had a profound effect on one of the leaders of Art Nouveau in Belgium, Henry van de Velde (1863–1957). He began as a Divisionist painter but, under the influence of William Morris, became a designer of posters, furniture, silverware, and glass. Then, after 1900, he worked mainly as an architect. Van de Velde founded the

1004. Interior of the Library, Glasgow School of Art

1005. Henry van de Velde. Theater, Werkbund Exhibition, Cologne. 1914. Destroyed

1006. Plan of the Theater, Werkbund Exhibition

Weimar School of Arts and Crafts in Germany, which became famous after World War I as the Bauhaus (see page 876). His most ambitious building (figs. 1005 and 1006), the theater he designed in Cologne for an exhibition sponsored by the Werkbund (arts and crafts association) in 1914, makes a telling contrast with the Paris Opéra (figs. 919 and 920). Whereas the older building tries to evoke the splendors of the Louvre Palace, Van de Velde's exterior is a tightly stretched, unadorned "skin" that covers—and reveals—the individual units of which the internal space is composed. So vast is the difference that it seems almost incredible that the Opéra should have been completed only 40 years before.

United States

The search for a modern architecture first began in earnest around 1880. It required wedding the ideas of William Morris and a new machine aesthetic, tentatively explored some 15 years earlier in the decorative arts, to new construction materials and techniques. The process itself took several decades, during which architects experimented with a variety of styles. It is significant that the symbol was the skyscraper, and that its first home was Chicago, then a burgeoning metropolis not yet encumbered by allegiance to the styles of the past.

RICHARDSON. The Chicago fire of 1871 had opened enormous opportunities to architects from older cities such as Boston and New York. Among them was Henry Hobson Richardson (1838–1886), who profited as a young man from contact with Labrouste in Paris (see fig. 961). Most of his work along the eastern seaboard shows a massive Neo-Romanesque style. There are still echoes of this in his last major project for Chicago, the Marshall Field Wholesale Store designed in 1885 (fig. 1007). The huge structure filled an entire city block. In its symmetry and the treatment of masonry, it may remind us of Italian Early Renaissance palaces (see fig. 550). Yet the complete lack of ornament proclaims its utilitarian purpose.

Warehouses and factories as commercial building types had a history of their own dating to the later eighteenth century. Richardson must have been familiar with this tradition, which

1007. Henry Hobson Richardson. Marshall Field Wholesale Store, Chicago. 1885–87. Demolished 1930

on occasion had produced remarkably impressive "stripped-down" designs (see fig. 1008). In contrast to these earlier structures, however, the walls of the Marshall Field Wholesale Store do not present a continuous surface pierced by windows. Except for the corners, which have the effect of heavy piers, they show a series of superimposed arcades, like a Roman aqueduct (see fig. 243), an impression strengthened by the absence of ornament and the thickness of the masonry. (Note how deeply the windows are recessed.) These arcaded walls are as functional and self-sustaining as their ancient predecessors. They invest the building with a strength and dignity unrivaled in any earlier commercial structure. Behind them is an iron skeleton that actually supports the seven floors, but the exterior does not depend on it, either structurally or aesthetically.

1008. Warehouses on New Quay, Liverpool. 1835–40

1009. Louis Sullivan. Wainwright Building, St. Louis, Missouri. 1890–91. Destroyed

SULLIVAN. Richardson's Marshall Field building thus stands midway between the old and the new. It embodies, with utmost severity and logic, a concept of monumentality derived from the past, but its opened-up walls, divided into vertical "bays," look forward to the work of Louis Sullivan (1856–1924). The Wainwright Building in St. Louis (fig. 1009), his first skyscraper, is only five years after the Marshall Field Store. It, too, is monumental, but in a very untraditional way. The organization of the exterior reflects and expresses the internal steel skeleton, in the slender, continuous brick piers that rise between the windows from the base to the attic. Their collective effect is that of a vertical grating encased by the corner piers and by the emphatic horizontals of attic and mezzanine.

This is, of course, only one of the many possible "skins" that could be stretched over the structural framework. What counts is that we immediately feel this wall is derived from the skeleton underneath, that it is not self-sustaining. "Skin" is perhaps too weak a term to describe this brick sheathing. To Sullivan, who often thought of buildings as analogous to the human body, it was more like the "flesh" and "muscle" that are attached to the "bone" yet are capable of an infinite variety of expressive effects. When he insisted that "form ever follows function," he meant a flexible relationship between the two, not rigid dependence. [See Primary Sources, no. 96, pages 940–41.]

The range of Sullivan's invention becomes evident if we compare the Wainwright Building with his last building, the department store of Carson Pirie Scott & Company in Chicago, begun nine years later (fig. 1010). The sheathing of white

1010. Louis Sullivan. Carson Pirie Scott & Company Department Store, Chicago. 1899–1904

1011. Detail of facade, showing window, Carson Pirie
Scott & Company Department Store

1012. Jacob Riis. *Bandits' Roost*. c. 1888. Gelatin-silver print.
Museum of the City of New York

terracotta here follows the grid of the steel frame far more closely, and the overall effect, enhanced by the simple molding around the windows (fig. 1011), is one of lightness and crispness rather than of harnessed energy. The contrast between the horizontal continuity of the flanks and the vertical accent at the corner has been subtly calculated to provide a clear terminus to the facade.

Paradoxically, Sullivan's buildings are based on a lofty idealism and adorned with a type of ornamentation that remain firmly rooted in the nineteenth century, even as they point the way to the architecture of our own era. From the beginning his geometry carried a spiritual meaning, inspired partly by Emanuel Swedenborg, that centered on birth, flowering, decay, and regeneration. It was tied to a highly original style of decoration in accordance with Sullivan's theory that ornament must give expression to structure—not by reflecting it literally but by interpreting the same concepts through organic abstraction. The soaring verticality of the Wainwright Building, for example, stands for growth, which is elaborated by the vegetative motifs of the moldings along the cornice and between the windows. Likewise the clean articulation of the windows on the upper stories of the Carson Pirie Scott building gives way on the ground floor and mezzanine to a lavish display of ironwork (designed largely by George G. Elmslie using Sullivan's system), enhancing the store-front's appeal to shoppers.

PHOTOGRAPHY

Documentary Photography

During the second half of the nineteenth century, the press played a leading role in the social movement that brought the harsh realities of poverty to the public's attention. The camera became an important instrument of reform through the photodocumentary, which tells the story of people's lives in a pictorial essay. It responded to the same conditions that had stirred Courbet (see pages 718–20), and its factual reportage likewise fell within the Realist tradition. Before then, photographers had been content to present the romanticized image of the poor like those in genre paintings of the day. The first photodocumentary was John Thomson's illustrated sociological study *Street Life in London,* published in 1877. To get his pictures, he had to pose his figures.

RIIS. The invention of gunpowder flash ten years later allowed Jacob Riis (1849–1914) to rely for the most part on the element of surprise. Riis was a police reporter in New York City, where he learned at first hand about the crime-infested slums and their appalling living conditions. He kept up a steady campaign of illustrated newspaper exposés, books, and lectures which in some cases led to major revisions of the city's housing codes and labor laws. His photographs' unflinching realism has lost none of its force. Certainly it would be difficult to imagine a more nightmarish scene than *Bandits' Roost* (fig. 1012). With good reason we sense a pervasive air of

1013. Oscar Rejlander. *The Two Paths of Life.* 1857. Combination albumen print, 16 x 31" (40.6 x 78.7 cm). George Eastman House, Rochester, New York

danger in the eerie light. The notorious gangs of New York City's Lower East Side sought their victims by night, killing them without hesitation. The motionless figures seem to look us over with the practiced casualness of hunters coldly sizing up potential prey.

Pictorialism

The raw subject matter and realism of documentary photography had little impact on art and were shunned by most other photographers as well. England, through such organizations as the Photographic Society of London, founded in 1853, became the leader of the movement to convince doubting critics that photography, by imitating painting and printmaking, could indeed be art. To Victorian England, beauty above all meant art with a high moral purpose or noble sentiment, preferably in a classical style.

REJLANDER. *The Two Paths of Life* (fig. 1013) by Oscar Rejlander (1818–1875) fulfills these ends by presenting an allegory clearly descended from Hogarth's *Rake's Progress* series (figs. 824 and 825). This tour de force, almost three feet wide, combines 30 negatives through composite printing: a young man (in two images) is choosing between the paths of virtue or of vice, the latter represented by a half-dozen nudes. The picture created a sensation in 1857 and Queen Victoria herself purchased a print. Rejlander, however, never enjoyed the same success again. He was the most adventurous photographer of his time and soon turned to other subjects less in keeping with prevailing taste.

ROBINSON. The mantle of art photography fell to Henry Peach Robinson (1830–1901), who became the most famous photographer in the world. He established his reputation with *Fading Away* (fig. 1014), which appeared a year after Rejlander's *The Two Paths of Life.* With six lines from Shelley's

1014. Henry Peach Robinson. *Fading Away.* 1858. Combination print. Royal Photographic Society, London

"Queen Mab" printed below on the mat, it is typical of Robinson's sentimental scenes. Like *The Two Paths of Life,* it is a photomontage, but of only five negatives, and the scene is as carefully staged as any Victorian melodrama. At first Robinson made detailed drawings of his scenes before photographing the individual components. He later renounced multiple-negative photography, but still contrived to imitate contemporary genre painting in his pictures. When treating elevated subject matter he continued to distinguish between fact and truth, which to him was a mixture of the real and the artificial.

CAMERON. The photographer who pursued ideal beauty with the greatest passion was Julia Margaret Cameron (1815–1879). An intimate of leading poets, scientists, and artists, she took up photography at the age of 48 when she was given a camera. She went on to create a remarkable body of work. In her own day Cameron was known for her allegorical and narrative

1015. Julia Margaret Cameron. *Ellen Terry, at the Age of Sixteen.*
c. 1863. Carbon print, diameter 9¹/₂" (24 cm). The Metropolitan Museum of Art, New York
Alfred Stieglitz Collection, 1949

pictures, but now she is remembered primarily for her portraits of the men who shaped Victorian England. Many of her finest photographs, however, are of the women who were married to her closest friends. An early study of the actress Ellen Terry (fig. 1015) has the lyricism and grace of the Pre-Raphaelite aesthetic that shaped Cameron's style (compare fig. 946).

Naturalistic Photography

EMERSON. The cudgel against art photography was taken up by Peter Henry Emerson (1856–1936), who became the bitter enemy of Robinson. Emerson espoused what he called naturalistic photography, based on scientific principles and Constable's landscapes. Nevertheless, he too contrasted realism with truth, defining truth in terms of sentiment, aesthetics, and the selective arrangement of nature. Using a single negative, Emerson composed his scenes with the greatest care, producing results that were sometimes similar to Robinson's, though of course he never acknowledged this. Most of Emerson's work was devoted to scenes of rural and coastal life which are not far removed from early documentary photographs.

In his best prints, nature predominates. He was a master at distributing tonal masses across a scene, and his photographs (fig. 1016) are equivalent to fine English landscape paintings of the period. Although the effect is rarely apparent in his work, Emerson advocated putting the lens slightly out of focus, in the belief that the eye sees sharply only the central area of a scene. When he gave up this idea a few years later, he decided that photography was indeed science instead of art because it was machine-made, not personal.

Photo-Secession

The issue of whether photography could be art came to a head in the early 1890s with the Secession movement (see page 763), which was spearheaded in 1893 by the founding in London of the Linked Ring, a rival group to the renamed Royal Photographic Society of Great Britain. Stimulated by Emerson's ideas, the Secessionists sought a pictorialism independent of science and technology. They steered a course between academicism and naturalism by imitating every form of late Romantic art that did not involve narrative. Equally antithetical to their aims were Realist and Post-Impressionist painting, then at their zenith. In the group's approach to photography as Art for Art's Sake, the Secession had the most in common with Whistler's aestheticism.

To resolve the dilemma between art and mechanics, the Secessionists tried to make their photographs look as much like paintings as possible. Rather than resorting to composite or multiple images, however, they exercised total control over the printing process, chiefly by adding special materials to their printing paper to create different effects. Pigmented gum brushed on coarse drawing paper yielded a warm-toned, highly textured print that in its way approximated Impressionist painting. Paper impregnated with platinum salts was especially popular among the Secessionists for the clear grays in their prints. Their subtlety and depth lend a remarkable ethereality to *The Magic Crystal* (fig. 1017) by Gertrude Käsebier (1854–1934), in which spiritual forces are almost visibly sweeping across the photograph.

STEICHEN. Through Käsebier and Alfred Stieglitz, the Linked Ring had close ties with America, where Stieglitz

1016. Peter Henry Emerson. *Haymaking in the Norfolk Broads.* c. 1890. Platinum print. Société Française de Photographie, Paris

1017. Gertrude Käsebier. *The Magic Crystal.* c. 1904. Platinum print. Royal Photographic Society, Bath

opened his Photo-Secession gallery in New York in 1905. [See Primary Sources, no. 97, page 941.] Among his protégés was the young Edward Steichen (1879–1973), whose photograph of Rodin in his sculpture studio (fig. 1018) is without doubt the finest achievement of the entire Photo-Secession movement. The head in profile contemplating *The Thinker*

1018. Edward Steichen. *Rodin with His Sculptures "Victor Hugo" and the "Thinker."* 1902. Gum print, 14^{1}/4 x 12^{3}/4" (36.3 x 32.4 cm). The Art Institute of Chicago
Alfred Stieglitz Collection

1019. Eadweard Muybridge. *Female Semi-Nude in Motion,* from
Human and Animal Locomotion, vol. 2, pl. 271. 1887. George Eastman House, Rochester, New York

expresses the essence of the confrontation between the sculptor and his work of art. His brooding introspection hides the inner turmoil evoked by the ghostlike monument to Victor Hugo which rises dramatically like a genius in the background. Not since *The Creation of Adam* by Michelangelo (fig. 612), who was Rodin's ideal, have we seen a more telling use of space or an image that penetrates the mystery of creativity so deeply.

The Photo-Secession movement achieved its goal of gaining wide recognition for photography as an art form, but by 1907 its artifices were regarded as stilted. Though the movement lasted for a few more years, it was becoming clear that the future of photography did not lie in the imitation of painting, for painting was then being drastically reformed by modernists. Yet the legacy of the Photo-Secession was valuable, its limitations notwithstanding, for it taught photographers much about the control of composition and the response to light.

Motion Photography

MUYBRIDGE. An entirely new direction was charted by Eadweard Muybridge (1830–1904), father of motion photog-

raphy. He wedded two different technologies, devising a set of cameras capable of photographing action at successive points. Photography had grown from such marriages. Another instance had occurred earlier when Nadar used a hot-air balloon to take aerial shots of Paris (fig. 926). After some trial efforts, Muybridge managed in 1877 to get a set of pictures of a trotting horse which forever changed artistic depictions of the horse in movement. Of the 100,000 photographs he devoted to the study of animal and human locomotion, the most astonishing were those taken from several vantage points at once (fig. 1019). The idea was surely in the air, for the art of the period occasionally shows similar experiments, but Muybridge's photographs must nevertheless have come as a revelation to artists. The simultaneous views present an entirely new treatment of motion across time and space that challenges the imagination. Like a complex visual puzzle, they can be combined in any number of ways that are endlessly fascinating.

Muybridge left it to others to pursue these possibilities further. Much of his later work was conducted at the University of Pennsylvania in Philadelphia with the support of Eakins, then the head of the Academy of the Fine Arts. Eakins was already adept at using a camera, and it provided the subjects for several of his paintings; soon his interest in science led him

1020a, b. Étienne-Jules Marey. *Man in Black Suit with White Stripes Down Arms and Legs, Walking in Front of a Black Wall.* c. 1884. Chronophotograph

to take up motion photography. Unlike Muybridge's succession of static images, Eakins' multiple exposures show sequential motion on one plate. In the end, photography for Eakins was simply a means of depicting figures more realistically.

MAREY.   It was Étienne-Jules Marey (1830–1904) who developed motion photography into an art. A noted French physiologist, Marey, like Muybridge, with whom he was in direct contact, saw the camera as a tool for demonstrating the mechanics of bodily movement, but he soon began to use it so creatively that his photographs have a perfection not equaled

for another 60 years (compare fig. 1222). Indeed, his multiple exposure of a man walking (fig. 1020a, b) satisfies both scientific and aesthetic truth in a way that Emerson and the Secessionists never imagined.

The photographs of Muybridge and Marey convey a peculiarly modern sense of dynamics reflecting the new tempo of life in the Machine Age. However, because the gap was then so great between scientific fact on the one hand and visual perception and artistic representation on the other, their far-reaching aesthetic implications were to be realized only by the Futurists (see page 794).

CHAPTER FOUR

TWENTIETH-CENTURY PAINTING

PAINTING BEFORE WORLD WAR I

In our account of art in the modern era, we have already discussed a succession of "isms": Neoclassicism, Romanticism, Realism, Impressionism, Post-Impressionism, Divisionism, and Symbolism. There are many more to be found in twentieth-century art—so many, in fact, that nobody has made an exact count. These "isms" can form a serious obstacle to understanding: they may make us feel that we cannot hope to comprehend the art of our time unless we immerse ourselves in a welter of esoteric doctrines. Actually, we can disregard all but the most important "isms." Like the terms we have used for the styles of earlier periods, they are merely labels to help us sort things out. If an "ism" fails the test of usefulness, we need not retain it. This is true of many "isms" in contemporary art. The movements they designate either cannot be seen very clearly as separate entities, or have so little importance that they can interest only the specialist. It has always been easier to invent new labels than to create a movement in art that truly deserves a new name.

Still, we cannot do without "isms" altogether. Since the start of the modern era, the Western world (and, increasingly, the rest of the world) has faced the same basic problems everywhere, and local artistic traditions have steadily given way to international trends. Among these we can distinguish three main currents, each comprising a number of "isms," that began among the Post-Impressionists and have developed greatly in our own century: Expressionism, Abstraction, and Fantasy. The first stresses the artist's emotional attitude toward himself and the world; the second focuses on the formal structure of the work of art; the third explores the realm of the imagination, especially its spontaneous and irrational qualities. We must not forget, however, that feeling, order, and imagination are all present in every work of art. Without imagination, it would be deadly dull; without some degree of

order, it would be chaotic; without feeling, it would leave us unmoved.

These currents are not mutually exclusive, and we shall find them interrelated in many ways. An artist's work often belongs to more than one, which may in turn embrace a wide range of approaches, from the realistic to the completely non-representational (or non-objective). Our three currents, then, do not correspond to specific styles but to general attitudes. They represent parallel responses to the realization, intuitive as well as intellectual, that after 1900 people were living in a different age. The primary concern of Expressionism is the human community; of Abstraction, the structure of reality; and of Fantasy, the labyrinth of the mind. And we shall find that Realism, which is concerned with the appearance of the world around us, has continued to exist independently of the other three, especially in the United States, where art has often pursued a separate course. These strands bear a shifting relation to each other that reflects the complexity of modern life. To be understood, they must be seen in their proper historical context. Beginning in the mid-1930s, however, the distinction between them begins to break down, so that after 1945 it is no longer meaningful to trace their evolution separately.

In examining twentieth-century art, we shall find it anything but tidy. On the contrary, we quickly discover the visual arts are like soldiers marching to different drummers. A purely chronological approach would reveal just how out of step they have generally been with each other—but at the cost of losing sight of their internal development. Does this mean that the other visual arts have shared none of the same concerns? No, that is not the case either. The three main currents we outlined in painting—Expressionism, Abstraction, and Fantasy—may be found as well in sculpture, architecture, and photography before 1945. But they are present in

1021. Henri Matisse. *The Joy of Life*. 1905–6. Oil on canvas, 5'8¹/₂ x 7'9³/₄" (1.74 x 2.38 m).
The Barnes Foundation, Merion, Pennsylvania

EXPRESSIONISM

The Fauves

The twentieth century may be said to have begun five years late, so far as painting is concerned. Between 1901 and 1906, several comprehensive exhibitions of the work of Van Gogh, Gauguin, and Cézanne were held in Paris, as well as Germany. For the first time the achievements of these masters became accessible to a broad public. The young painters who had grown up in the "decadent," morbid mood of the 1890s (see page 761) were profoundly impressed by what they saw. Several of them formulated a radical new style, full of the violent color of Van Gogh and bold distortions of Gauguin, which they manipulated freely for pictorial and expressive effects. When their work first appeared in 1905, it so shocked critical opinion that they were dubbed the Fauves (wild beasts), a label they wore with pride. Actually, it was not a common program that brought them together, but their shared sense of liberation and experiment. As a movement, Fauvism comprised a number of loosely related individual styles, and the group dissolved after a few years, most of its members unable to sustain their inspiration or adapt successfully to the challenges posed by Cubism. It was nevertheless a decisive breakthrough, for it constituted the first unequivocally modern movement of the twentieth century in both style and attitude, one to which every important painter before World War I acknowledged a debt.

MATISSE. Its leader was Henri Matisse (1869–1954), the oldest of the founders of twentieth-century painting. *The Joy of Life* (fig. 1021), probably the most important picture of his long career, sums up the spirit of Fauvism better than any other single work. It obviously derives its flat planes of color, heavy undulating outlines, and the "primitive" flavor of its forms from Gauguin (see fig. 981). Even its subject suggests the vision of humanity in a state of Nature that Gauguin had pursued in Tahiti. But we soon realize that Matisse's figures are not Noble Savages under the spell of a native god. The subject is a pagan scene in the classical sense: a bacchanal like Titian's (compare fig. 632). The poses of the figures have for the most part a classical origin, and in the apparently careless draftsmanship resides a profound knowledge of the human body. (Matisse had been trained in the academic tradition.) What makes the picture so revolutionary is its radical simplicity, its

1022. Henri Matisse. *The Red Studio.* 1911. Oil on canvas,
5'11¹/4" x 7'2¹/4" (1.81 x 2.19 m). The Museum of Modern Art, New York

Mrs. Simon Guggenheim Fund

cf. Vermeer Velasquez

"genius of omission." Everything that possibly can be has been left out or stated by implication only, yet the scene retains the essentials of plastic form and spatial depth. What holds the painting together is its firm underlying structure. (Matisse venerated Cézanne and owned one of his paintings.)

Painting, Matisse seems to say, is not a representation of observed reality but the rhythmic arrangement of line and color on a flat plane. But it is not only that. How far can the image of nature be pared down without destroying its basic properties and thus reducing it to mere surface ornament? "What I am after, above all," he once explained, "is expression . . . [But] . . . expression does not consist of the passion mirrored upon a human face. . . . The whole arrangement of my picture is expressive. The placement of figures or objects, the empty spaces around them, the proportions, everything plays a part." [See Primary Sources, no. 98, pages 941–42.] What, we wonder, does *The Joy of Life* express? Exactly what its title says. Whatever his debt to Gauguin, Matisse was never stirred by the same agonized discontent with the decadence of our civilization. He instead shared the untroubled outlook of the Nabis, with whom he had previously associated, and the canvas derives its decorative quality from their work (compare fig. 983). He was concerned above all with the act of painting. This to him was an experience so profoundly joyous that he wanted to transmit it to the beholder.

Matisse's "genius of omission" is again at work in *The Red Studio* (fig. 1022). By reducing the number of tints to a minimum, he makes color an independent structural element. The result is to emphasize the radical new balance he struck between the "two-D" and "three-D" aspects of painting. Ma-

tisse spreads the same flat red color on the tablecloth and wall as on the floor, yet he distinguishes the horizontal from the vertical planes with complete assurance using only a few lines. Equally bold is Matisse's use of pattern. By repeating a few basic shapes, hues, and decorative motifs in seemingly casual, but perfectly calculated, array around the edges of the canvas, he harmonizes the relation of each element with the rest of the picture. Cézanne had pioneered this integration of surface ornament into the design of a picture (see fig. 969), but Matisse here makes it a mainstay of his composition.

ROUAULT. The other important member of the Fauves, Georges Rouault (1871–1958), would hardly have agreed with Matisse's definition of "expression." For him this had still to include, as it had in the past, "the passion mirrored upon a human face"—as we can tell from his *Head of Christ* (fig. 1023). But the expressiveness does not reside only in the "image quality" of the face. The savage slashing brushstrokes speak equally eloquently of the artist's rage and compassion. If we cover the upper third of the picture, it is no longer a recognizable image. Yet the expressive effect is hardly diminished.

Rouault was the true heir of Van Gogh's and Gauguin's concern for the corrupt state of the world. However, he hoped for spiritual renewal through a revitalized Catholic faith. His pictures, whatever their subject, are personal statements of that ardent hope. Trained in his youth as a stained-glass worker, he was better prepared than the other Fauves to share Gauguin's enthusiasm for medieval art. Rouault's later work, such as *The Old King* (fig. 1024), has glowing colors and compartmented, black-bordered shapes inspired by Gothic stained-glass win-

1023. Georges Rouault. *Head of Christ.* 1905.
Oil on paper, mounted on canvas, 39 x 25¼" (99.1 x 64.2 cm).
The Chrysler Museum, Norfolk, Virginia
Gift of Walter P. Chrysler, Jr.

1024. Georges Rouault. *The Old King.* 1916–37.
Oil on canvas, 30¼ x 21¼" (76.8 x 54 cm). The Carnegie
Museum of Art, Pittsburgh
Patrons Art Fund

1025. Ernst Ludwig Kirchner. *Self-Portrait with Model.* 1907.
Oil on canvas, 59¼ x 39⅜" (150.5 x 100 cm). Kunsthalle, Hamburg

German Expressionism

Fauvism exerted a decisive influence on the Expressionist movement that arose at the same time in Germany. Because Expressionism had deep historical roots that made it especially appealing to the Northern mind, it lasted far longer in Germany, where it proved correspondingly broader and more diverse than in France. For these reasons, Expressionism is sometimes applied to German art alone, but such a limit ignores the close ties and numerous similarities between them. To be sure, Fauvism was generally less neurotic and morbid, but although German Expressionism was characterized by greater emotional extremes and a more spontaneous approach, the two branches were not separated by any fundamental difference in style or content.

DIE BRÜCKE. Expressionism in Germany began with *Die Brücke* (The Bridge), a group of like-minded painters who lived in Dresden in 1905. Through its totally bohemian lifestyle, *Die Brücke* cultivated a sense of immanent disaster that is one of the hallmarks of the modern avant-garde. Their early work not only reveals the direct impact of Van Gogh and Gauguin but also shows elements derived from Munch, who was then living in Berlin and deeply impressed the German Expressionists. *Self-Portrait with Model* (fig. 1025) by Ernst

dows (compare fig. 494). Within this framework he retains a good deal of the pictorial freedom we saw in the *Head of Christ,* which he uses to express his profound understanding of the human condition. The old king's face conveys a mood of resignation and inner suffering that reminds us of Rembrandt, Daumier, and Van Gogh.

1026. Erich Heckel. *Woman Before a Mirror.* 1908. Woodcut,
16⁵/8 x 8⁷/8" (42.2 x 22.5 cm). Brücke Museum, Berlin

1027. Emil Nolde. *The Last Supper.* 1909. Oil on canvas,
32¹/2 x 41³/4" (82.6 x 106.1 cm). Stiftung Seebull Ada und
Emil Nolde, Neukirchen, Schleswig, Germany

1028. Oskar Kokoschka. *Self-Portrait.* 1913.
Oil on canvas, 32 x 19¹/2" (81.7 x 49.7 cm). The Museum
of Modern Art, New York
Purchase

Ludwig Kirchner (1880–1938), the group's leader, reflects Matisse's simplified, rhythmic line and loud color. Yet the contrast between the coldly aloof artist and the brooding model, who looks as if she has been violated, has a peculiar expressiveness that can have come only from Munch, whose work was often fraught with a palpable sexual tension.

HECKEL.   The artists of *Die Brücke* were idealists who sought to revive German art. Toward that end, they took up woodcuts, which they regarded as a uniquely national medium. The first to do so was Kirchner, but the finest printmaker of the group was Erich Heckel (1883–1970). Under the influence of ethnographic art and Gauguin's woodcuts (see fig. 982), Heckel's prints, such as our *Woman Before a Mirror* (fig. 1026), imitate the straightforward manner of the early German "primitives" (compare figs. 692 and 700) rather than the example of Dürer that had originally inspired *Die Brücke.* Heckel's woman before a mirror is "primitive" in another sense as well: her ponderous fleshiness lends her the primeval quality of ancient fertility goddesses (compare figs. 43 and 44), but with a sensuous charm that is utterly disarming.

1029. Oskar Kokoschka. *The Bride of the Wind.* 1914. Oil on canvas,
5'11¼" x 7'2⅝" (1.81 x 2.20 m). Öffentliche Kunstsammlung Basel, Kunstmuseum, Switzerland

NOLDE. One *Brücke* artist, Emil Nolde (1867–1956), stands somewhat apart. Older than the rest, he was already working in an Expressionist style when he was invited to join the movement in 1906. Nolde shared Rouault's preference for religious themes, and his figures show a like sympathy for the suffering of humanity. The thickly encrusted surfaces and deliberately clumsy draftsmanship of *The Last Supper* (fig. 1027) reject pictorial refinement in favor of a primeval, direct expression inspired by Gauguin. Ensor's grotesque masks, too, come to mind (see fig. 988), as does the blocklike monumentality of Barlach's peasants (see fig. 998).

KOKOSCHKA. Another artist of highly individual talent was the Austrian painter Oskar Kokoschka (1886–1980). In 1910, he was invited to Berlin by the publisher of *Der Sturm* (The Storm), which soon attracted members of *Die Brücke* and *Der Blaue Reiter* (see below). His main contribution is the portraits he painted before World War I, such as the moving *Self-Portrait* in figure 1028. Like Van Gogh, Kokoschka sees himself as a visionary, a witness to the truth and reality of his inner experiences (compare fig. 979). The hypersensitive features seem lacerated by a great ordeal of the imagination. We

may find in this tortured psyche an echo of the cultural climate that also produced Sigmund Freud.

Kokoschka's most memorable work is *The Bride of the Wind* (fig. 1029). Based on Romantic paintings of Dante's tragic lovers Paolo and Francesca, it shows the artist with Alma Mahler, the "muse" who inspired so many of Germany and Austria's leading cultural figures. The awesome canvas is a monument to the power of love: echoing the impassioned brushwork, the entire universe resounds in a great chord of exaltation at their embrace.

KANDINSKY. The most daring and original step beyond Fauvism was taken in Germany by a Russian, Wassily Kandinsky (1866–1944), the leading member of a group of Munich artists called *Der Blaue Reiter* (The Blue Rider) after one of his early paintings. Formed in 1911, it was a loose alliance united only by its mystical tendencies. Kandinsky began to forsake representation as early as 1910 and abandoned it altogether several years later. Using the rainbow colors and the free, dynamic brushwork of the Paris Fauves, he created a completely non-objective style. These works have titles as abstract as their forms: our example, one of the most striking, is called

1030. Wassily Kandinsky. *Sketch I for "Composition VII."* 1913.
Oil on canvas, 30³/4 x 39³/8" (78 x 100 cm). Private collection

Sketch I for "Composition VII" (fig. 1030). Perhaps we should avoid the term *abstract,* because it is often taken to mean that the artist has analyzed and simplified visible reality into geometric forms. (Compare Cézanne's dictum that all natural forms are based on the cone, sphere, and cylinder.) Kandinsky did indeed derive his shapes from the world around him—landscapes that he freely invented—but by transforming rather than reducing them.

As the first part of his book *Concerning the Spiritual in Art,* published in 1912, makes clear, Kandinsky's aim was to charge form and color with a purely spiritual meaning (as he put it), one that expressed his deepest feelings, by eliminating all resemblance to the physical world. [See Primary Sources, no. 99, page 942.] To him, the only reality that mattered was the artist's inner reality. Kandinsky acknowledged the Symbolists as his ancestors. Like Gauguin, he wanted to create an art of spiritual renewal. But in contrast to Rouault or Nolde, his was an art without a specific spiritual program, though it has close affinities with the theosophy of Rudolf Steiner, which influenced many early modern artists in Germany. Kandinsky, like Steiner, believed that humanity had lost touch with its spirituality through attachment to material things, and he sought to rekindle that dreamlike consciousness through his art.

The second part of the book is concerned exclusively with the formal aspects of painting, above all color. Kandinsky studied the color theories of Seurat and his followers (see page 751), as did many other Expressionists, but the meaning he attached to specific hues was no less individual than Van Gogh's. However, not until after his return from Russia in 1922 were the implications of his discussion of form fully realized when he adopted geometric abstraction (see page 759).

What does all this have to do with Kandinsky's paintings themselves? The character of his art is best summed up by his later statement: "Painting is the vast, thunderous clash of many worlds, destined, through a mighty struggle, to erupt into a totally new world, which is creation. And the birth of a creation is much akin to that of the Cosmos. There is the same vast and cataclysmic quality belonging to that mighty symphony—the Music of the Spheres."

Kandinsky's antinaturalism was inherent in Expressionist theory from the very beginning. Whistler, too, had spoken of "divesting the picture from any outside sort of interest." He even anticipated Kandinsky's "musical" titles (fig. 949). But it was the liberating influence of the Fauves that permitted Kandinsky to put this approach into practice: when the upper third of Rouault's *Head of Christ* (fig. 1023) is covered, we recall, the rest becomes a nonrepresentational composition strangely similar to Kandinsky's in its slashing brushwork and charged forms.

How valid is the analogy between painting and music? Although Kandinsky was careful to acknowledge the differences between the two art forms, he sought a painting that,

1031. Franz Marc. *Animal Destinies*. 1913. Oil on canvas, 6'4¹/₂" x 8'7" (1.94 x 2.62 m).
Öffentliche Kunstsammlung Basel, Kunstmuseum, Switzerland

like music, was an absolute because it was divorced entirely from the "objective," material realm. When a painter like Kandinsky carries it through so uncompromisingly, does he really lift his art to another plane? Or could it be that his declared independence from representational images now forces him instead to "represent music," which limits him even more severely? Kandinsky's advocates like to point out that representational painting has a "literary" content, and they deplore such dependence on another art. But they do not explain why the "musical" content of non objective painting should be more desirable. Is painting less alien to music than to literature? They seem to think music is a higher art than literature or painting because it is inherently nonrepresentational. This point of view has an ancient tradition that goes back to Plato and includes Plotinus, St. Augustine, and their medieval successors. The attitude of the non-objectivists might thus be termed "secular iconoclasm." They do not condemn images as wicked, but denounce them as non-art.

The case is difficult to argue, and it does not matter whether this theory is right or wrong, for the proof of the pudding is in the eating, not in the recipe. Kandinsky's—or any artist's—ideas are not important to us unless we are convinced of the importance of the work itself. The painting reproduced here has such density and vitality that it impresses us with its radiant freshness of feeling, even though we may be uncertain what exactly the artist has expressed.

MARC. The subject matter of Franz Marc (1880–1916) was the unconscious life of animals in nature. Motivated by the pantheistic feeling of the Romantics, which was heightened by his association with Kandinsky, the artist's paintings represent humanity's desire to return to a state of harmony with the universe—a central concept of Rudolf Steiner's theosophy. Marc devised a color symbolism as personal as that of Van Gogh, who had inspired his early work (see page 757). He wrote: "Blue is the masculine principle, robust and spiritual. Yellow is the feminine principle, gentle, serene, sensual. Red is matter, brutal and heavy." But it was the Orphism of Robert Delaunay (see page 793), with whom he formed a friendship in 1912, that showed Marc the full potential of color to express his mystical beliefs. Later that year, Futurism enabled him to depict the dynamism of nature by creating rhythms that echo those of the cosmos, or so he believed. In *Animal Destinies* (fig. 1031), Marc's poetic vision has attained apocalyptic intensity. With its interpenetrating crystalline forms looking like so many pieces of jagged stained glass, the picture is even more terrifying than Stubbs' *Lion Attacking a Horse* (fig. 848) in evoking the cataclysmic forces that overwhelm these uncomprehending beasts. Here the artist was indeed on the verge of depicting a "higher" symbolic reality. A year later he abandoned representation almost entirely for an abstract style no less advanced than Kandinsky's. Soon, however, he was drafted into the war, which claimed his life.

1032. Marsden Hartley. *Portrait of a German Officer.* 1914.
Oil on canvas, 68¼ x 41⅜" (173 x 104 cm). The Metropolitan
Museum of Art, New York
The Alfred Stieglitz Collection, 1949

ABSTRACTION

The second of our main currents is Abstraction. When discussing Kandinsky, we said that the term is usually taken to mean the process (or the result) of analyzing and simplifying observed reality into geometric shapes. Literally, it means "to draw away from, to separate." Actually, abstraction goes into the making of any work of art, whether the artist knows it or not, since even the most painstakingly realistic portrayal can never be an entirely faithful replica. The process was not conscious and controlled, however, until the Early Renaissance, when artists first analyzed the shapes of nature in terms of mathematical bodies (see page 432). Cézanne and Seurat revitalized this approach and explored it further. They are the direct ancestors of the abstract movement in twentieth-century art. The difference, as one critic has noted, is that for the latter, abstraction has been both a premise and a goal, not simply a reductive refinement. Abstraction has been the most distinctive and consistent feature of modern painting to which even its most vocal opponents have responded.

PICASSO'S DEMOISELLES D'AVIGNON. It is difficult to imagine the birth of modern abstraction without Pablo Picasso. About 1905, stimulated as much by the Fauves as by the retrospective exhibitions of the great Post-Impressionists, he gradually abandoned the melancholy lyricism of his Blue Period (see fig. 991) for a more robust style. He shared Matisse's enthusiasm for Gauguin and Cézanne, but he viewed these masters very differently. In 1907 he produced his own counterpart to *The Joy of Life,* a monumental canvas so challenging that it outraged even Matisse (fig. 1033). The title, *Les Demoiselles d'Avignon* ("The Young Ladies of Avignon"), does not refer to the town of that name, but to Avignon Street in a notorious section of Barcelona. When Picasso started the picture, it was to be a temptation scene in a brothel, but he ended up with a composition of five nudes and a still life. But what nudes! Matisse's generalized figures in *The Joy of Life* (see fig. 1021) seem utterly innocuous compared to this savage aggressiveness.

The three on the left are angular distortions of classical figures, but the violently dislocated features and bodies of the other two have all the barbaric qualities of ethnographic art. Following Gauguin's lead, the Fauves had discovered the aesthetic appeal of African and Oceanic sculpture and had introduced Picasso to this material. Nonetheless it was Picasso, not the Fauves, who used primitivist art as a battering ram against the classical conception of beauty. Not only the proportions, but the organic integrity and continuity of the human body are denied here, so that the canvas (in the apt description of one critic) "resembles a field of broken glass."

Picasso, then, has destroyed a great deal. What has he gained in the process? Once we recover from the initial shock, we begin to see that the destruction is quite methodical. Everything—the figures as well as their setting—is broken up into angular wedges or facets. These, we will note, are not flat, but shaded in a way that gives them a certain three-dimensionality. We cannot always be sure whether they are concave or convex. Some look like chunks of solidified space, others like fragments of translucent bodies. They constitute a unique kind of

HARTLEY. Americans became familiar with the Fauves through exhibitions from 1908 on. After the pivotal Armory Show of 1913, which introduced the latest European art to New York, there was a growing interest in the German Expressionists as well (see page 783). The driving force behind the modernist movement in the United States was the photographer Alfred Stieglitz (see page 898), who almost single-handedly supported many of its early members. To him, modernism meant abstraction and its related concepts. Among the most significant works by the Stieglitz group are the canvases painted by Marsden Hartley in Munich during the early years of World War I under the direct influence of Kandinsky. *Portrait of a German Officer* (fig. 1032) is a masterpiece of design from 1914, the year Hartley (1887–1943) was invited to exhibit with *Der Blaue Reiter.* He had already been introduced to Futurism and several offshoots of Cubism (see page 794), which he used to discipline Kandinsky's supercharged surface. The emblematic portrait is testimony to the militarism he encountered everywhere in Germany. It incorporates the insignia, epaulets, Maltese cross, and other details from an officer's uniform of the day.

1033. Pablo Picasso. *Les Demoiselles d'Avignon.* 1907.
Oil on canvas, 8' x 7'8" (2.44 x 2.34 m). The Museum of Modern Art, New York
Acquired through the Lillie P. Bliss Bequest

If any one event announced the arrival of twentieth-century music, it was the ballet *The Rite of Spring* (1913) by the Russian-born composer Igor Stravinsky (1882–1971), the last of three scores commissioned in 1910–13 by the impresario Sergei Diaghilev for his Ballets Russes (see box page 795). While a pupil of the nationalist composer Nikolai Rimsky–Korsakov (1844–1908) in St. Petersburg, Stravinsky had revealed a striking gift for melody in the Russian tradition and an unusual sense of rhythm. These were evident in his first two ballets, *The Firebird* and *Petrushka*, which created a sensation in Paris because of their exoticism. The primitivism and eroticism of the *Rite of Spring* caused a famous riot at its premiere, although there is evidence that it was staged. Stravinsky was the musical counterpart to Picasso as a giant of his time. Indeed, the *Rite* may be compared to Picasso's *Demoiselles d'Avignon* (fig. 1033) in its impact. Like Picasso, Stravinsky turned to classicism after 1920. Finally, toward the end of his long life, he successfully adopted the serialism of Arnold Schoenberg.

Just as the art of the twentieth century was distinguished by abstraction from an early date, so its music has often been marked by atonality, a rejection of the major and minor diatonic scales, the rules of harmony in general, and especially the importance of the tonic (the first tone of the scale in which a given piece was written; see box page 624). From about 1550, most European music had centered around the tonic note, in effect a musical "home base" to which the melody tended to return. However, a frequent return to the tonic note is not actually required by the rules of harmony or the tempered scale (see page 624)—a fact that had already been exploited by a number of German composers, starting with Wagner. It was almost inevitable that the final break with tonality—the importance of the tonic—would be made by a Post-Romantic.

The final step was taken by Arnold Schoenberg (1874–1951). The hypersensitive content of his early work, like Mahler's, sometimes brings to mind the world of neurosis explored by his great contemporary in Vienna Sigmund Freud, the pioneer of modern psychology. His *Transfigured Night* (1899) has the sensuality of the famous *Liebestod* duet in Wagner's opera *Tristan and Isolde*. Schoenberg, an Expressionist by inclination, later became a friend of Kandinsky and a capable artist in his own right. Schoenberg, however, moved almost immediately into complete atonality. In 1912 he took the further step of abandoning the pitches used in

normal singing for "speech-song" (German, *Sprechstimme*). Schoenberg nevertheless continued to make use of other traditional techniques of composition, which he built into pieces of extraordinary complexity. Finally, in 1923, he took another step when he produced his first "serial" works based on the so-called "twelve-tone row" (also called the "series") utilizing the same devices he had been working with for some time. Each row uses all the notes of the tempered scale just once, except for a few "free" notes that do not conform to the sequence. It thus constitutes a self-contained musical realm representing the final overthrow of tonalism. By subjecting it to various techniques for modifying and extending it (including such as devices as retrogrades, inversions, and transpositions), the row can be built into a large-scale composition without repeating any sequence. Serialism was, then, simply a means of organizing Schoenberg's compositions, and although others were to extend its principles, he

Pablo Picasso. *Portrait of Igor Stravinsky.* 1920. Pencil on paper, 24³/8 x 19¹/8" (62 x 48.5 cm). Musée Picasso, Paris

matter, which imposes a new integrity and continuity on the entire canvas. The *Demoiselles,* unlike *The Joy of Life,* can no longer be read as an image of the external world. Its world is its own, analogous to nature but constructed along different principles. Picasso's revolutionary "building material," compounded of voids and solids, is hard to describe with any precision. The early critics, who saw only the prevalence of sharp edges and angles, dubbed the new style Cubism.

Analytic Cubism

That the *Demoiselles* owes anything to Cézanne may at first seem incredible. However, Picasso had studied Cézanne's late work (such as fig. 971) with great care, finding in Cézanne's abstract treatment of volume and space the translucent structural units from which to derive the faceted shapes of Analytic (or Facet) Cubism. The link is clearer in *Portrait of Ambroise Vollard* (fig. 1034)—Vollard was one of the leading print publishers and dealers of the time—which Picasso painted three always stressed the personal nature of his work, which was no less individual than that of his contemporaries. He remained an Expressionist at heart. *A Survivor from Warsaw* (1948), written after the composer had fled Austria and settled in California (as did Stravinsky), conveys the nightmare of the Holocaust with almost unbearable anguish.

Needless to say, Schoenberg's music made extraordinary demands on musician and listener alike. Yet he was able to attract talented disciples almost as soon as he settled in Vienna in 1903. Chief among them was Anton Webern (1883–1945), who, like Gustav Mahler before him, was better known as a conductor during his lifetime. Webern's mature compositions, all small in scale, are miracles of rigor, conciseness, and purity. For over a decade his music retained aspects of Schoenberg's expressionism, making it a counterpart to the hypersensitive manner of his friend Oscar Kokoschka. Hence, serialism initially had little impact on his style and, as with Schoenberg, was little more than a convenient means of organizing his music more coherently. However, he gradually began to apply its principles to other aspects of music, not just tone rows. Much of Webern's work consists of songs and choral music that treat the voice as simply another instrument, for he was as devoted to his serial system as Bach had been to counterpoint. At first Webern's literary sources differed little in character from Mahler's, but his terse atonality can be regarded as the antidote to the inflated rhetoric of his predecessor's song cycles, such as *The Youth's Magic Horn.* Despite their serial technique, Webern's later songs are remarkably successful settings of mystical poems by his friend Hildegard Jone.

The main contributions of Alban Berg (1885–1935), Schoenberg's other important pupil, are the Expressionist operas *Wozzeck* (1923), based on the play by Georg Büchner, and the unfinished *Lulu* (1935), derived from two plays of 1895 by Franklin Wedekind. Both are emotionally harrowing explorations of the dark side of human existence in a world of unrelenting evil: *Wozzeck* becomes a terrifying symbol of modern man trapped by forces he cannot comprehend that ultimately destroy him, while *Lulu* traces the descent of the protagonist into prostitution and her murder at the hands of Jack the Ripper as a tragic metaphor for the unbridled lust and avarice in contemporary society. In Berg's vocal writing one can still hear the last vestiges of Wagnerian opera, but stripped of its mythical trappings so that it evokes a disturbing, yet haunting, vision of twentieth-century life.

1034. Pablo Picasso. *Portrait of Ambroise Vollard.* 1910. Oil on canvas, 36¹/4 x 25⁵/8" (92 x 65 cm). The Pushkin State Museum of Fine Arts, Moscow

years later. The facets are now small and precise, more like prisms, and the canvas has the balance and refinement of a fully mature style.

Contrasts of color and texture, so pronounced in the *Demoiselles,* are now reduced to a minimum; the subdued tonality of the picture approaches monochrome, so as not to compete with the design. The structure has become so complex and systematic that it would seem wholly cerebral if the

"imprismed" sitter's face did not emerge with such dramatic force. Indeed, this is as commanding a portrait as Ingres' *Louis Bertin* (fig. 871), one that fully conveys the power of his complex personality. Of the "barbaric" distortions in the *Demoiselles* there is no trace; they had served their purpose. Cubism has become an abstract style within the purely Western sense, but its distance from observed reality has not significantly increased. Picasso may be playing an elaborate game of hide-and-seek with nature, but he still needs the visible world to challenge his creative powers. The non-objective realm held no appeal for him, then or later.

1035. Pablo Picasso. *Still Life with Chair Caning.* 1912. Collage of oil, oilcloth,
and pasted paper simulating chair caning on canvas, 10^1/2 x 13^3/4" (26.7 x 35 cm). Musée Picasso, Paris

1036. Georges Braque. *Newspaper, Bottle, Packet of Tobacco (Le Courrier).* 1914.
Collage of charcoal, gouache, pencil, ink, and pasted paper on cardboard, 20^5/8 x 25" (52.4 x 63.5 cm).
Philadelphia Museum of Art
A. E. Gallatin Collection

Synthetic Cubism

By 1910 Cubism was well established as an alternative to Fauvism, and Picasso had been joined by a number of other artists, notably Georges Braque (1882–1963), with whom he collaborated so intimately that their work at that time is difficult to tell apart. Both of them (it is not clear to whom the chief credit belongs) initiated the next phase of Cubism, which was even bolder than the first. Usually called Synthetic Cubism because it puts forms back together, it is also known as Collage Cubism, after the French word for "paste-up," the technique that started it all. We see its beginnings in Picasso's *Still Life with Chair Caning* of 1912 (fig. 1035). Most of the painting shows the now-familiar facets, except for the letters; these, being already abstract signs, could not be translated into prismatic shapes. But from beneath the still life emerges a piece of imitation chair caning, which has been pasted onto the canvas, and the picture is "framed" by a piece of rope. This intrusion of alien materials has a most remarkable effect: the abstract still life appears to rest on a real surface (the chair caning) as if it were on a tray, and the substantiality of this tray is further emphasized by the rope.

Within a year, Picasso and Braque were producing still lifes composed almost entirely of cut-and-pasted scraps of material, with only a few lines added to complete the design. In *Le Courrier* by Braque (fig. 1036) we recognize strips of imitation wood graining, part of a tobacco wrapper with a contrasting stamp, half the masthead of a newspaper, and a bit of newsprint made into a playing card (the ace of hearts). Why did Picasso and Braque suddenly prefer the contents of the wastepaper basket to brush and paint? In wanting to explore their new concept of the picture as a tray on which to "serve" the still life, they found the best way was to put real things on the tray. The ingredients of a collage actually play a double role. They have been shaped and combined, then drawn or painted upon to give them a representational meaning, but they do not lose their original identity as scraps of material—they remain "outsiders" in the world of art. Their function is both to represent (to be a part of an image) and to present (to be themselves). In this latter capacity, they endow the collage with a self-sufficiency that no Analytic Cubist picture can have. A tray, after all, is a self-contained area, detached from the rest of the physical world. Unlike a painting, it cannot show more than is actually on it.

The difference between the two phases of Cubism may also be defined in terms of picture space. Analytic Cubism retains a certain kind of depth, so that the painted surface acts as a window through which we still perceive the remnants of the familiar perspective space of the Renaissance. Though fragmented and redefined, this space lies behind the picture plane and has no visible limits. Potentially, it may even contain objects that are hidden from our view. In Synthetic Cubism, on the contrary, the picture space lies in front of the plane of the "tray." Space is not created by illusionistic devices, such as modeling and foreshortening, but by the actual overlapping of layers of pasted materials. The integrity of the nonperspective space is not affected when, as in *Le Courrier*, the apparent thickness of these materials and their distance from each other are increased by a bit of shading here and there. Synthetic Cubism, then,

1037. Robert Delaunay. *Simultaneous Contrasts: Sun and Moon.* 1913. Oil on canvas, diameter 53" (134.5 cm). The Museum of Modern Art, New York
Mrs. Simon Guggenheim Fund

offers a basically new space concept, the first since Masaccio. It is a true landmark in the history of painting.

Before long Picasso and Braque discovered that they could retain this new pictorial space without the use of pasted materials. They only had to paint as if they were making collages. World War I, however, put an end to their collaboration and the further development of Synthetic Cubism, which reached its height in the following decade.

Orphism

THE DELAUNAYS. The Cubism of Picasso and Braque was little concerned with color—an issue addressed finally by Robert Delaunay (1885–1941) and his wife, Sonia Delaunay-Terk (1885–1979). They evolved a totally abstract style, called Orphism, after the legendary Orpheus, by the poet Apollinaire (1880–1918), the chief theorist of the movement. Following the concepts of Chevreul, Seurat, and Gauguin, they sought to produce pure color harmonies as independent of nature as music. Late in 1912, Delaunay began to paint his series *Simultaneous Contrasts* (fig. 1037), in which the swirling movement is meant to evoke the rhythms pulsating throughout the universe. The idea was in the air: at almost the same time the Czech painter Frantisek Kupka (1871–1957), working independently in Paris, came to the identical solution. It was soon taken up as well by the Americans Stanton Macdonald-Wright (1890–1973) and Morgan Russell (1886–1953), also active in Paris, who called their movement Synchromism. Orphism proved to be short-lived, however. Even the Delaunays were able to maintain this non-objective style for only a few years and soon turned to Futurism. Nevertheless, the movement proved of great importance. Among its early members were Marcel

1038. Umberto Boccioni. *Dynamism of a Cyclist.* 1913.
Oil on canvas, 27⁵/8 x 37³/8" (70 x 95 cm). Collection Gianni Mattioli, Milan

Duchamp and his brother Raymond Duchamp-Villon. In addition to Franz Marc, it also affected Fernand Léger, Marc Chagall, and even Paul Klee.

Futurism

As originally conceived by Picasso and Braque, Cubism was a formal discipline of subtle balance applied to traditional subjects: still life, portraiture, the nude. Other painters, however, saw in the new style a special affinity with the geometric precision of engineering that made it uniquely attuned to the dynamism of modern life. The short-lived Futurist movement in Italy exemplifies this attitude. In 1909–10 its disciples, led by the poet Filippo Tommaso Marinetti, issued a series of manifestos violently rejecting the past and exalting the beauty of the machine. [See Primary Sources, no. 100, pages 942–43.]

BOCCIONI. At first they used techniques developed from Post-Impressionism to convey the surge of industrial society, but these were otherwise static compositions, still dependent upon representational images. By adopting the simultaneous views of Analytic Cubism in *Dynamism of a Cyclist* (fig. 1038), Umberto Boccioni (1882–1916), the most original of the Futurists, was able to communicate the energy of furious pedaling across time and space far more tellingly than if he had actually depicted the human figure, which could be seen in only one time and place in traditional art. In the flexible vocabulary provided by Cubism, Boccioni found the means of expressing the twentieth century's new sense of time, space, and energy that Albert Einstein had defined in 1905 in his special theory of relativity. Moreover, Boccioni suggests the unique quality of the modern experience. With his pulsating movement, the cyclist has become an extension of his environment, from which he is now indistinguishable.

Cubo-Futurism

As its name implies, Cubo-Futurism, which arose in Russia a few years before World War I as the result of close contacts with the leading European art centers, took its style from Picasso and based its theories on Futurist tracts. The Russian Futurists were, above all, modernists. They welcomed industry, which was spreading rapidly throughout Russia, as the foundation of a new society and the means for conquering that old Russian enemy, nature. Unlike the Italian Futurists, however, the Russians rarely glorified the machine, least of all as an instrument of war.

Central to Cubo-Futurist thinking was the concept of *zaum,* a term which has no counterpart in English. Invented by Russian poets, zaum was a trans-sense (as opposed to the Dadaists' nonsense; see page 806) language based on new word forms and syntax. In theory, zaum could be understood universally, since it was thought that meaning was implicit in the basic sounds and patterns of speech. When applied to painting, zaum provided the artist with complete freedom to redefine the style and content of art. The picture surface was now seen as the sole conveyer of meaning through its appearance. Hence, the subject of a work of art became the visual elements and their formal arrangement. However, because Cubo-Futurism was concerned with means, not ends, it failed to provide the actual content that is found in modernism. Although the Cubo-Futurists were more important as theorists than artists, they provided the springboard for later Russian movements.

The new world envisioned by the Russian modernists led to a broad redefinition of the roles of man and woman, and it was then in Russia that women emerged as artistic equals to an extent not achieved in Europe or America until considerably later. The finest painter of the group was Liubov Popova (1889–1924), who studied in Paris in 1912 and visited Italy in 1914. The combination of Cubism and Futurism that she

By far the most adventurous theater before World War I was to be found in Russia, thus preparing the way for even more radical experiments after the Russian Revolution of 1917. The most famous of the Russian reformers remains Konstantin Stanislavsky (1863–1938), who was a co-founder of the Moscow Art Theater with Vladimir Nemirovich-Danchenko (1858–1943). His legacy is clouded by a lack of fully authentic texts, but in general he placed greatest emphasis on the actor, despite the fact that he never adopted the "star" system. Stanislavsky insisted on a rigorous training of body, voice, and mind based on a thorough understanding of stagecraft, reality, and the drama itself, so that the action would unfold naturally and convincingly, though he was by no means a Realist. Stanislavsky's theories were later practiced in America as "method acting" (see box page 825).

The key figure in early Russian modernism, however, was Vsevelod Meyerhold (1874–1940), who considered the director to be the main creative force in the theater. He was employed by every Russian avant-garde theater, including Stanislavsky's Moscow Art Theater, but never lasted very long in any position because his experiments were regarded as too bold. For example, he dispensed with the theatrical curtain and set his productions in symbolic scenery or even on a bare stage. Alexander Tairov (1885–1950) adopted a centrist position: like Stanislavsky, he stressed the importance of the actor but followed Meyerhold in treating the play as the point of departure for the director's creativity. At the same time, he maintained that there is no relationship between art and life and that theater should be like the sacred dances of ancient temples. The ritual effect of his productions, which stressed unity of word, music, and dance, was similar in intent to Classical Greek theater. At the opposite end of the spectrum was the equally innovative Nikolai Evreinov (1879–1953), whose "monodramas," such as *The Theater of the Soul* (1912), sought to lead the audience to a greater understanding by drawing on what he believed was humanity's innate theatricality, which leads people to seek a higher reality.

The Russians had a great impact on French theater. The first to exercise his influence was Sergei Diaghilev (1872–1929), whose publication *The World of Art* promoted Symbolist art, literature, and theater. The ballet company he took to Paris in 1909 met with such success that he formed the Ballets Russes, featuring the great dancer Vasily Nijinsky (1890–1950), the choreography of Mikhail Fokine (1880–1942), the music of Igor Stravinsky and his teacher Nikolai Rimsky-Korsakov, and the designs of Aleksandr Benois (1870–1960) and Léon Bakst (1866–1924). With the onset of the Russian Revolution the company remained in Paris; it later employed Picasso, Braque, and De Chirico among other artists as stage and costume designers.

Under Russian influence, Jacques Rouché (1862–1957) launched the periodical *Modern Theater* simultaneously with the Théâtre des Arts in 1910. His ideas were to bear fruit at the Paris Opéra, where he was appointed director four years later and remained until 1936. It was at the Théâtre des Arts that Jacques Copeau (1879–1949), who became the leading figure in French theater between the wars, got his start. He adopted the opposite position of Meyerhold's in arguing that only the actor was essential and that the director's primary responsibility was the faithful translation of the script into a "poetry of the theater." And whereas Rouché thought primarily in visual terms, Copeau argued for a return to the bare stage.

For all of its inventiveness, early-twentieth-century theater contributed little in the way of new plays. The main impetus in dramatic writing came from Ireland. There plays with a Gaelic focus were produced by the Irish National Theater Society, better known as the Abbey Theater, where it was housed after 1904. The most important playwrights were the poet William Butler Yeats (1865–1939), Lady Augusta Gregory (1863–1935), and John Synge (1871–1909). Yeats' early work sprang from the writing of the French Symbolists he had met in Paris. He was primarily concerned with restoring the importance of writing to theater; thus, his poetic-mythic approach was the opposite of Lady Gregory's, whose style was realistic-domestic. It was Yeats who convinced Synge to return from Paris to write about Irish peasant life. Synge successfully synthesized the best features of Yeats and Lady Gregory in the two finest dramas staged by the Abbey: *Riders to the Sea* (1904) and *The Playboy of the Western World* (1907). Synge was fearless in tackling controversial subjects that went against customary beliefs—*Playboy* caused riots wherever it played—but the real secret of his success was his unique form of poetic prose.

In England, the most important theorist was the director and designer Edward Gordon Craig (1872–1966), the son of Ellen Terry and Edward Goodwin, whose thinking laid the ground for many of the key concepts of modern directing. Like Meyerhold, he conceived of the director as an artist who created theater as a work of art independent of the drama itself by utilizing lights and simply painted screens. No one, however, had more impact on theater than Max Reinhardt (1873–1943), who succeeded Brahm as director of the Deutsches Theater in Berlin. He realized that each play demanded a different approach, without adhering to any single system. In place of the conventions of the day he insisted that the director rethink and control every detail of the production, which was prepared in close collaboration with his actors and designers.

1039. Liubov Popova. *The Traveler*. 1915.
Oil on canvas, 56 x 41¹/2" (142.2 x 105.4 cm). Norton Simon Art
Foundation, Pasadena, California

absorbed abroad is seen in *The Traveler* (fig. 1039). The treatment of forms remains essentially Cubist, but the painting shares the Futurist obsession with representing dynamic motion in time and space. The jumble of image fragments creates the impression of objects seen in rapid succession. The furious interaction of forms with their environment across the plane threatens to extend the painting into the surrounding space. At the same time, the strong modeling draws attention to the surface, lending it a relieflike quality that is enhanced by the vigorous texture.

Suprematism

The first purely Russian art of the twentieth century, however, was Suprematism. In one of the greatest leaps of the symbolic and spatial imagination in the history of art, Kazimir Malevich (1878–1935) invented the *Black Quadrilateral,* as seen in figure 1040. How is it that such a seemingly simple image should be so important? By limiting art to a few elements—a single shape repeated in two tones and fixed firmly to the picture plane—he emphasized the painting as a painting even more radically than had his predecessors. Simultaneously, he transformed it into a concentrated symbol having multiple layers of meaning, thereby providing the content missing from Cubo-Futurism. The inspiration for *Black Quadrilateral* came in 1913 while Malevich was working on designs for the opera *Victory over the Sun,* with music by the composer-painter Mikhail Matiushin and libretto by the poet-painter Alexei Kruchenykh. This production was one of the most important artistic collaborations in the modern era. In the context of the opera, the black quadrilateral represents the eclipse of the sun of Western painting and of everything based on it. Further, the work can be seen as the triumph of the new order over the old, the East over the West, humanity over nature, idea over matter. The black quadrilateral (which is not even a true rectangle) was intended to stand as a modern icon. It supersedes the traditional Christian trinity and symbolizes a "supreme" reality, because geometry is an independent abstraction in itself; hence the movement's name, Suprematism.

According to Malevich, Suprematism was also a philosophical color system constructed in time and space. His space was an intuitive one, with both scientific and mystical overtones. The flat plane replaces volume, depth, and perspective as a means of defining space. Each side or point represents one of the three dimensions, while the fourth side stands for the fourth dimension, time. Like the universe itself, the black surface would be infinite were it not delimited by an outer boundary, the white border and shape of the canvas. *Black Quadrilateral* thus constitutes the first satisfactory redefinition, visually and conceptually, of time and space in modern art. Like Einstein's formula $E=mc^2$ for the theory of relativity, it has an elegant simplicity that belies the intense effort required to synthesize a complex set of ideas and reduce them to a fundamental "law." When it first appeared, Suprematism had much the same impact on Russian artists that Einstein's theory had on scientists: it unveiled a world never seen before, one that was unequivocally modern. The relation between art and science is closer than we might think, for despite the differences in approach, they are united by the imagination. In fact, the key to solving the theory of relativity came to Einstein as a visual image.

Later, Malevich began to tilt his quadrilaterals and simplify his paintings still further in search of the ultimate work of art. Malevich's efforts culminated in *Suprematist Composition: White on White* (fig. 1041), his most famous composition, which limits art to its fewest possible components. It is all too tempting to dismiss such a radical extreme as a *reductio ad absurdum.* Seen in person, however, the canvas is surprisingly persuasive. The shapes, created by two subtly different shades of white, have a revelatory purity that makes even *Black Quadrilateral* seem needlessly complex.

The heyday of Suprematism was over by the early 1920s. Reflecting the growing diversity and fragmentation of Russian art, its followers defected to other movements, above all to the Constructivism led by Vladimir Tatlin (see pages 847–48).

FANTASY

Our third current, Fantasy, follows a less clear-cut course than the other two, since it depends on a state of mind more than on any particular style. The one thing all painters of fantasy have in common is the belief that imagination, "the inner eye," is more important than the outside world. We must be careful how we use the term *fantasy*. It originated in psychoanalytic theory, and meant something very different in the early twentieth century than it does now. It was thought of as mysterious and profound, anything but the lighthearted and superficial view we take of it today.

1040. Kazimir Malevich. *Black Quadrilateral.* c. 1913–15. Oil on canvas, 24 x 17" (61 x 43.3 cm). Copyright the George Costakis Collection, Athens

1041. Kazimir Malevich. *Suprematist Composition: White on White.* 1918. Oil on canvas, 31¼ x 31¼" (79.4 x 79.4 cm). The Museum of Modern Art, New York

Why did private fantasy come to loom so large in twentieth-century art? We saw the trend beginning at the end of the eighteenth century in the art of Goya and Fuseli (see figs. 862 and 884); perhaps this suggests part of the answer. In fact, there seem to be several interlocking causes. First, the cleavage that developed between reason and imagination in the wake of rationalism tended to dissolve the heritage of myth and legend that had been the common channel of private fantasy in earlier times. Second, the artist has a greater freedom—and insecurity—within the social fabric, giving him a sense of isolation and favoring an introspective attitude. Then, too, the Romantic cult of emotion prompted the artist to seek out subjective experience, and to accept its validity. Needless to say, this process took time, so that in early-nineteenth-century painting, private fantasy was still a minor current, but by 1900 it had become a major one, thanks to Symbolism on the one hand and the naïve vision of artists like Henri Rousseau on the other.

DE CHIRICO. The heritage of Romanticism can be seen most clearly in the astonishing pictures painted in Paris just before World War I by Giorgio de Chirico (1888–1978), such as *Mystery and Melancholy of a Street* (fig. 1042). This deserted square with endless diminishing arcades, nocturnally illuminated by the cold full moon, has all the poetry of Romantic reverie—but it has also a strangely sinister air. This is an "ominous" scene in the full sense of the term: everything here suggests an omen, a portent of unknown and disquieting significance. The artist himself could not explain the

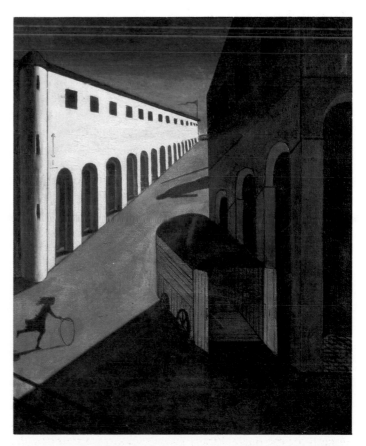

1042. Giorgio de Chirico. *Mystery and Melancholy of a Street.* 1914. Oil on canvas, 34¼ x 28½" (87 x 72.4 cm). Private collection

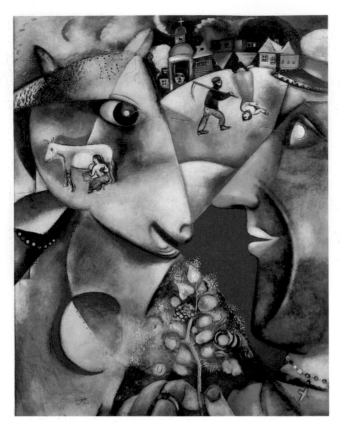

1043. Marc Chagall. *I and the Village.* 1911. Oil on canvas,
6'3⁵/8" x 4'11¹/2"(1.92 x 1.51 m). The Museum of Modern Art,
New York
Mrs. Simon Guggenheim Fund

1044. Marcel Duchamp. *Nude Descending a Staircase No. 2.* 1912.
Oil on canvas, 58 x 35" (147.3 x 89 cm). Philadelphia Museum of Art
Louise and Walter Arensberg Collection

incongruities in these paintings—the empty furniture van, or
the girl with the hoop—that trouble and fascinate us. De
Chirico called this *Metaphysical Painting:* "We who know the
signs of the metaphysical alphabet are aware of the joy and the
solitude which are enclosed by a portico, by the corner of a
street, or even in a room, on the surface of a table, or between
the sides of a box. . . . The minutely accurate and prudently
weighed use of surfaces and volumes constitutes the canon of
the metaphysical aesthetic." Later, after he had returned to
Italy, he adopted a conservative style and repudiated his early
works, as if he were embarrassed at having put his dream world
on display, even though he secretly continued to paint copies
to meet the commercial demand for them.

CHAGALL. The power of nostalgia, so evident in *Mystery
and Melancholy of a Street,* also dominates the fantasies of Marc
Chagall (1887–1985), a Russian who went to Paris in 1910.
I and the Village (fig. 1043) is a Cubist fairy-tale, weaving
dreamlike memories of Russian folk tales, Jewish proverbs,
and the look of Russia into one glowing vision. Here, as in
many later works, Chagall relives the experiences of his childhood. These were so important to him that his imagination
shaped and reshaped them for years without their persistence
being diminished.

DUCHAMP. In Paris shortly before World War I we encounter yet another artist of fantasy, the Frenchman Marcel

Duchamp (1887–1968). After basing his early style on
Cézanne, he initiated a dynamic version of Analytic Cubism,
similar to Futurism, by superimposing successive phases of
movement on each other, much as in multiple-exposure photography (see fig. 1020a, b). His *Nude Descending a Staircase*
(fig. 1044), done in this vein, caused a scandal at the Armory
Show of modern art in New York in 1913 because it went
against all traditional notions of what a nude should look like.
Although his objective was simply to paint "a static representation of movement," this parody of the human figure already
shows the ironic wit that was to underlie his work.

Soon, however, Duchamp's development took a far more
disturbing turn. In *The Bride* (fig. 1045), we look in vain for
any resemblance, however remote, to the human form. What
we see is a mechanism that seems part motor, part distilling
apparatus. It is beautifully engineered to serve no purpose
whatever. The title cannot be irrelevant: by lettering it right
onto the canvas, Duchamp has emphasized its importance. Yet
it causes us real perplexity. Evidently the artist intended the
machine as a kind of modern fetish that acts as a metaphor of

1046. George Bellows. *Stag at Sharkey's*. 1909. Oil on canvas,
36¼ x 48¼" (92.1 x 122.6 cm). The Cleveland Museum of Art
Hinman B. Hurlbut Collection

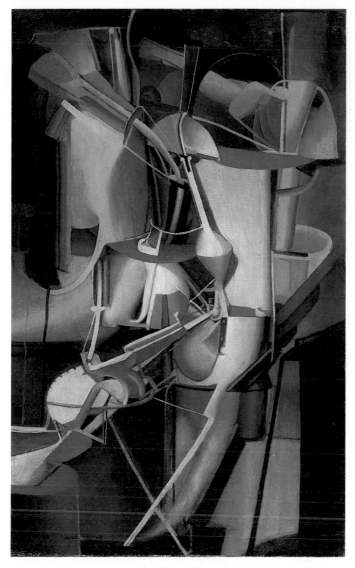

1045. Marcel Duchamp. *The Bride*. 1912. Oil on canvas,
35⅛ x 21¾" (89.4 x 55.2 cm). Philadelphia Museum of Art
Louise and Walter Arensberg Collection

human sexuality. By "analyzing" the bride until she is reduced to a complicated piece of plumbing that seems utterly dysfunctional, physically and psychologically, he satirized the scientific outlook on humanity. Thus the picture represents the negative counterpart of the glorification of the machine, so stridently proclaimed by the Futurists. We may further see in Duchamp's pessimistic outlook a response to the gathering forces that were soon to be unleashed in World War I, toppling the political order that had been created 100 years earlier at the Congress of Vienna.

REALISM

THE ASH CAN SCHOOL. In America, the first wave of change was initiated not by the Stieglitz circle but by the Ash Can School, which flourished in New York just before World War I. Centering on Robert Henri, who had studied with a pupil of Thomas Eakins at the Pennsylvania Academy, this group of artists consisted mainly of former illustrators for Philadelphia and New York newspapers. They were fascinat-

ed with the teeming life of the city slums, and found an endless source of subjects in the everyday urban scene, to which they brought the reporter's eye for color and drama. Despite the socialist philosophy that many of them shared, theirs was not an art of social commentary, but one that felt the pulse of city life, discovering in it vitality and richness while ignoring poverty and squalor. To capture these qualities they relied on rapid execution, inspired by Baroque and Post-Impressionist painting, which lends their canvases the immediacy of spontaneous observation.

BELLOWS. Although not among its founders, George Bellows (1882–1925) became the leading representative of the Ash Can School in its heyday. His masterpiece, *Stag at Sharkey's* (fig. 1046), shows why: no painter in America before Jackson Pollock expressed such heroic energy. *Stag at Sharkey's* reminds us of Eakins' *William Rush Carving His Allegorical Figure of the Schuylkill River* (see fig. 952), for it continues the same Realist tradition. Both place us in the scene as if we were present, and both use the play of light to pick out the figures against a dark background. Bellows' paintings were fully as shocking as Eakins' had been. Most late-nineteenth-century American artists had all but ignored urban life in favor of landscapes, and compared with these, the subjects and surfaces of the Ash Can pictures had a disturbing rawness.

THE ARMORY SHOW. The Ash Can School was quickly eclipsed by the rush toward a more radical modernism set off by the Armory Show held in New York in 1913. It was an outgrowth of the Independents Show three years earlier, which had showcased the talents of a group of rising young artists known as the Eight, who soon founded the American Association of Painters and Sculptors. The Armory Show was intended to foster a "new spirit in art" by introducing Americans to the latest trends from Europe and the United States.

1047. Pablo Picasso. *Three Musicians*. Summer 1921. Oil on canvas, 6'7" x 7'3¾"(2 x 2.3 m). The Museum of Modern Art, New York
Mrs. Simon Guggenheim Fund

The exhibition began with a survey of French painting from the Romantics to the Post-Impressionists, especially the Symbolists. Needless to say, the modern section was also heavily French, with a major emphasis on Matisse and Picasso. There were curious lapses as well: German Expressionism was poorly represented, while Futurism was omitted completely, although Orphism had a prominent place. The selection of sculpture was haphazard at best. The American art, which made up by far the largest part of the exhibition, included works by members of the Ash Can School, the Stieglitz Group, and the Eight. While it failed to promote the interests of its organizers, the Armory Show did succeed in its goal of introducing a new cosmopolitanism into the American art

scene. It proved a *succès de scandale* with the public, who bought an astonishing number of works from the exhibition.

PAINTING BETWEEN THE WARS

The Founders

As we examine painting between the wars, we shall find anything but an orderly progression. World War I had totally disrupted the further evolution of modernism, and its end unleashed an unprecedented outpouring of art after a four-year creative lull. The responses were correspondingly diverse.

1048. Pablo Picasso. *Mother and Child.* 1921–22.
Oil on canvas, 38 x 28" (96.7 x 71 cm). The Alex L. Hillman
Family Foundation, New York

1049. Pablo Picasso. *Three Dancers.* 1925. Oil on canvas,
7'1/2" x 4'81/4" (2.15 x 1.43 m). The Tate Gallery, London

Because they were already fully formed artists, the founders of modern painting—Picasso, Braque, Matisse, Kirchner, and Kandinsky—followed very different paths from those of younger ones who had not yet emerged into maturity by 1914. They broke the "rules" they had established earlier, responding only to the dictates of their sovereign imaginations; hence, their evolution transcends ready categorization. Rather than a simple linear development, we must therefore think in terms of multiple layers of varying depth that bear a shifting relation to each other.

PICASSO. We begin with Picasso, whose genius towers over the period. As a Spanish national living in Paris he was not involved in the conflict, unlike many French and German artists who served in the military and even sacrificed their lives. This was a time of quiet experimentation that laid the foundation for Picasso's art over the next several decades. The results did not become fully apparent, however, until the early 1920s, following a period of intensive cultivation. *Three Musicians* (fig. 1047) shows the fruit of that labor. It utilizes the "cut-paper style" of Synthetic Cubism so consistently that we cannot tell from the reproduction whether it is painted or pasted.

By now, Picasso was internationally famous. Cubism had spread throughout the Western world. It influenced not only other painters, but sculptors and even architects. Yet Picasso

was already striking out in a new direction. Soon after the invention of Synthetic Cubism, he had begun to do drawings in a realistic manner reminiscent of Ingres, and by 1920 he was working simultaneously in two quite separate styles: the Synthetic Cubism of the *Three Musicians,* and a Neoclassical style of strongly modeled, heavy-bodied figures such as his *Mother and Child* (fig. 1048). To many of his admirers, this seemed a kind of betrayal, but in retrospect the reason for Picasso's double-track performance is clear: chafing under the limitations of Synthetic Cubism, he needed to resume contact with the classical tradition, the "art of the museums." The figures in *Mother and Child* have a mock-monumental quality that suggests colossal statues rather than flesh-and-blood human beings, yet the theme is treated with surprising tenderness. The forms, however, are carefully dovetailed within the frame, not unlike the way the *Three Musicians* is put together.

A few years later the two tracks of Picasso's style began to converge into an extraordinary synthesis that was to become the basis of his art. The *Three Dancers* of 1925 (fig. 1049) shows how he accomplished this seemingly impossible feat. Structurally, the picture is pure Synthetic Cubism. It even includes painted imitations of specific materials, such as patterned wallpaper and samples of various fabrics cut out with pinking shears. The figures, a wildly fantastic version of a classical scheme (compare the dancers in Matisse's *The Joy of Life,*

1050. Pablo Picasso. *Guernica*. 1937. Oil on canvas, 11'6" x 25'8" (3.5 x 7.8 m).
Museo Nacional Centro de Arte Reina Sofía, Madrid. On permanent loan from the Museo del Prado, Madrid

fig. 1021), are an even more violent assault on convention than the figures in *Les Demoiselles d'Avignon*. Human anatomy is here simply the raw material for Picasso's incredible inventiveness. Limbs, breasts, and faces are handled with the same sovereign freedom as the fragments of external reality in Braque's *Le Courrier* (fig. 1036). Their original identity no longer matters. Breasts may turn into eyes, profiles merge with frontal views, shadows become substance, and vice versa, in an endless flow of metamorphoses. They are "visual puns," offering wholly unexpected possibilities of expression—humorous, grotesque, macabre, even tragic.

Three Dancers marks a transition to Picasso's experiment with Surrealism (see page 807). Because he did not practice automatism, he never developed into a true adherent of the movement. Nevertheless, the impact of his fellow Spaniard Joan Miró (see page 808) can be seen in the biomorphism of his mural *Guernica* (fig. 1050). Picasso did not show any interest in politics during World War I or the 1920s, but the Spanish Civil War stirred him to ardent partisanship with the Loyalists. The mural, executed in 1937 for the Pavilion of the Spanish Republic at the Paris International Exposition, has truly monumental grandeur. It was inspired by the terror-bombing of Guernica, the ancient capital of the Basques in northern Spain. The painting does not represent the event itself. Rather, it evokes the agony of total war with a series of powerful images.

The destruction of Guernica was the first demonstration of the technique of saturation bombing that was later employed on a huge scale during the course of World War II. The mural was thus a prophetic vision of doom—the doom that threatens us even more in this nuclear age. The symbolism of the scene resists precise interpretation, despite its several traditional elements: the mother and her dead child are the descendants of the *Pietà* (see fig. 479), the woman with the lamp recalls the *Statue of Liberty* (see fig. 908), and the dead fighter's hand, still clutching a broken sword, is a familiar emblem of heroic resistance. We also sense the contrast between the menacing, human-headed bull, surely intended to represent the forces of darkness, and the dying horse.

These figures owe their terrifying eloquence to what they are, not to what they mean. The anatomical dislocations, fragmentations, and metamorphoses, which in the *Three Dancers* seemed willful and fantastic, now express a stark reality, the reality of unbearable pain. The ultimate test of the validity of collage construction (here shown in superimposed flat "cutouts" restricted to black, white, and gray) is that it could serve as the vehicle of such overpowering emotions.

MATISSE. From 1911 on Matisse was influenced increasingly by Cubism, but after the war he, like Picasso, returned to the classical tradition. The lessons he absorbed from Cubism nevertheless had far-reaching consequences for his style. We see this in *Decorative Figure Against an Ornamental Background* (fig. 1051), which has a new luxuriance. At the same time, there is an underlying discipline resulting from his study of Cubism. The carpet provides a firm geometric structure for organizing the composition, so that everything has its place, although the system itself is entirely intuitive. Only in this way could Matisse control all the elements of his elaborate picture. It is among the finest in a long series of odalisques that Matisse painted during the 1920s and 1930s. In them the artist emerges as the titular heir of the French tradition, which he had absorbed through his teacher Gustave Moreau (see page 761). The visual splendor would be worthy of Delacroix himself. Yet in the calm pose and strong contours of the figure, Matisse reveals himself to be a classicist at heart, more akin to Ingres than the Romantics (compare figs. 870 and 874). The picture has overtones of Degas (see fig. 940), who had been trained by a disciple of Ingres and thus formed an important link in the chain of tradition. It breathes the classical serenity of *Seated Woman* by Matisse's friend Maillol (see fig. 994), who early in his career had likewise been inspired by Gauguin. Nevertheless, Matisse's is a distinctly modern classicism.

1051. Henri Matisse. *Decorative Figure Against an Ornamental Background*. 1927. Oil on canvas, 51¹/8 x 38¹/2" (129.9 x 97.8 cm). Musée National d'Art Moderne, Paris

1052. Ernst Ludwig Kirchner. *Winter Landscape in Moonlight*. 1919. Oil on canvas, 47⁵/8 x 47⁵/8" (121 x 121 cm). The Detroit Institute of Arts
Gift of Curt Valentin in memory of the artist on the occasion of Dr. William R. Valentiner's sixtieth birthday

KIRCHNER. Kirchner, too, was affected by Cubism after 1911, when he joined the other members of *Die Brücke* in Berlin. Four years later he was drafted into World War I, which ruined his physical and mental health. Released from the army after six months to recuperate from tuberculosis, he moved to Switzerland, where he turned increasingly to landscapes, as did many other German Expressionists following the war. *Winter Landscape in Moonlight* (fig. 1052), painted in the Swiss Alps, resounds with a sense of peace and wonderment before nature. The painting rivals the ecstatic rhythms of the young Kandinsky (compare fig. 1030), whose work Kirchner came to know while participating in the exhibitions of *Der Blaue Reiter* following the dissolution of *Die Brücke*.

KANDINSKY. Kandinsky himself spent the war years in Russia, where he participated enthusiastically in the Revolution and played an important role in shaping artistic policy. When his pedagogical reforms met with growing hostility, he returned to Germany in 1921 and soon accepted an invitation from Walter Gropius to teach at the Bauhaus (see page 874). Although he had begun to experiment with a more geometric style in Russia under the influence of Constructivism and other related avant-garde movements (see page 847), some of which shared his mystical tendencies, his output was surprisingly small, and it was only after he assumed his position at Weimar that he adopted geometric abstraction once and for all. The lessons and exercises he developed for his students no doubt helped to crystallize his theories of form and structure.

1053. Wassily Kandinsky. *Accented Corners, No. 247*. 1923. Oil on canvas, 51¹/4 x 51¹/4" (130 x 130 cm). Private collection

These he set out systematically in *Point and Line to Plane*, published in 1926, which elaborates concepts that were only nascent in his earlier book *Concerning the Spiritual in Art* (see page 786). His development was perhaps reinforced by the presence at the Bauhaus after 1923 of Laszlo Moholy-Nagy, who came from a Constructivist background, although his approach was otherwise the opposite of Kandinsky's (see page 906). Looking at a typical example of his work from this time (fig. 1053), we seem to have entered a different world from that of his earlier work (fig. 1030). Only when we analyze the

1054. Fernand Léger. *The City*. 1919. Oil on canvas,
7'7" x 9'9" (2.31 x 2.98 m). Philadelphia Museum of Art
A. E. Gallatin Collection

painting do we realize that it embodies the same titanic clash of forces. The artist has clarified the shapes and lines of force that had been buried in a sea of swirling forms. Yet the attitude is still the same, and he admitted that he remained a Romantic to the end.

Abstraction

Picasso's abandonment of strict Cubism signaled the broad retreat of abstraction after 1920 because the utopian ideals associated with it had been largely dashed by "the war to end all wars." In retrospect, abstraction can be seen as a necessary phase through which modern painting had to pass, but it was not essential to modernism as such, even though it has been perhaps the dominant tendency of the twentieth century.

LÉGER. The Futurist spirit nevertheless continued to find adherents on both sides of the Atlantic. Buoyant with optimism and pleasurable excitement, *The City* (fig. 1054) by the Frenchman Fernand Léger (1881–1955) conjures up a mechanized utopia. This beautifully controlled industrial landscape is stable without being static, and reflects the clean geometric shapes of modern machinery. In this instance, the term *abstraction* applies more to the choice of design elements and their manner of combination than to the shapes themselves, since these are "prefabricated" entities, except for the two figures on the staircase.

DEMUTH. The modern movement in America proved short-lived. One of the few artists to continue working in this vein after World War I was Charles Demuth (1883–1935). A member of the Stieglitz group (see pages 898–90), he had been friendly with Duchamp and exiled Cubists in New York during World War I. A few years later, under the impact of Futurism, he developed a style known as Precisionism to depict urban and industrial architecture. We can detect influences from all of these movements in *I Saw the Figure 5 in Gold* (fig. 1055). The title is taken from the poem "The Great Figure" by Demuth's friend William Carlos Williams, whose name also forms part of the design as "Bill," "Carlos," and

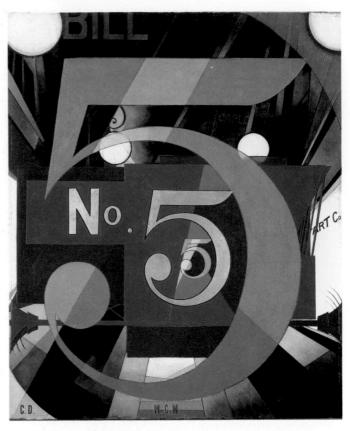

1055. Charles Demuth. *I Saw the Figure 5 in Gold*. 1928.
Oil on composition board, 36 x 29³/4" (91.4 x 75.6 cm).
The Metropolitan Museum of Art, New York
The Alfred Stieglitz Collection, 1949

"W. C. W." In the poem the figure 5 appears on a red fire truck, while in the painting it has become the dominant feature, thrice repeated to reinforce its echo in our memory as the fire truck rushes on through the night:

> Among the rain
> and lights
> I saw the figure 5 in gold
> on a red
> firetruck
> moving
> tense
> unheeded
> to gong clangs
> siren howls
> and wheels rumbling
> through the dark city

STELLA. Poetry was central as well to *Brooklyn Bridge* (fig. 1056) by the Italian-American Joseph Stella (1877–1946). To Stella, who emigrated to America as a young man, the bridge became a symbol of his adopted land, which provided his boldest theme. He wrote in his autobiography: "To realize this towering imperative vision in all its integral possibilities . . . I appealed for help to the soaring verse of Walt Whitman and to the fiery Poe's plasticity. Upon the swarming darkness of the night, I rung all the bells of alarm with the blaze of electricity scattered in lightnings down the oblique cables, the dynamic pillars of my composition, and to render more pungent the mystery of the metallic apparition, through the green and red

1056. *(left)* Joseph Stella.
Brooklyn Bridge. 1917.
Oil on bedsheeting,
7' x 6'4" (2.13 x 1.93 m).
Yale University Art Gallery,
New Haven, Connecticut
Gift of Collection Société
Anonyme

1057. *(below)* Piet Mondrian.
*Composition with
Red, Blue, and Yellow.* 1930.
Oil on canvas, 20 x 20"
(50.8 x 50.8 cm).
Private collection
Courtesy of the Mondrian
Estate/Holtzman Trust/MBI NY

glare of the signals I excavated here and there caves as subterranean passages to infernal recesses." His painting achieves what a contemporary critic perceptively called the apotheosis of the bridge, through a synthesis of Futurism, which he had been exposed to during a visit to Paris in 1912, and Precisionism, which he experimented with as early as 1917. With its maze of luminescent cables, vigorous diagonal thrusts, and crystalline cells of space, the painting is a striking visual counterpart to Hart Crane's famous hymn of 1930, "To Brooklyn Bridge":

O harp and altar, of the fury fused,
(How could mere toil align thy choiring strings!)
Terrific threshold of the prophet's pledge,
Prayer of pariah, and the lover's cry,—
Again the traffic lights that skim thy swift
Unfractioned idiom, immaculate sigh of stars,
Beading thy path—condense eternity:
And we have seen night lifted in thine arms.

MONDRIAN. The most radical abstractionist of our time was a Dutch painter nine years older than Picasso, Piet Mondrian (1872–1944). He arrived in Paris in 1912 as a mature Expressionist in the tradition of Van Gogh and the Fauves. Under the impact of Analytic Cubism, his work soon underwent a complete change, and within the next decade Mondrian developed an entirely nonrepresentational style that he called Neo-Plasticism. The short-lived movement as a whole is also known as *De Stijl*, after the Dutch magazine advocating his ideas, which were formulated with Theo van Doesburg (1883–1931) and Bart van der Leck (1876–1958). Mondrian became the center of the abstract movement in Paris, where he returned in 1919 and remained until the onset of World War II. Indeed, the School of Paris in the 1930s was made up largely of foreigners like him—especially the Abstraction-Création group, which included artists of every persuasion. As a result, the differences between the various movements soon became blurred, although Mondrian himself consistently adhered to his principles.

Composition with Red, Blue, and Yellow (fig. 1057) shows Mondrian's style at its most severe. He restricts his design to

1058. Ben Nicholson. *Painted Relief.* 1939. Synthetic board mounted on plywood, painted, 32⁷/8 x 45" (83.5 x 114.3 cm). The Museum of Modern Art, New York
Gift of H. S. Ede and the artist by exchange

horizontals and verticals and his colors to the three primary hues, plus black and white. Every possibility of representation is thereby eliminated. Yet Mondrian sometimes gave to his works such titles as *Trafalgar Square* or *Broadway Boogie Woogie* (fig. 13) that hint at some degree of relationship, however indirect, with observed reality. Like Kandinsky, Mondrian was affected by theosophy, albeit the distinctive Dutch branch founded by M. J. H. Schoenmaekers. Unlike Kandinsky, however, he did not strive for pure, lyrical emotion. His goal, he asserted, was "pure reality," and he defined this as equilibrium "through the balance of unequal but equivalent oppositions." [See Primary Sources, no. 101, page 943.] For all of their analytic calm, Mondrian's paintings are highly idealistic: "When we realize that equilibriated relationships in society signify what is just, then we shall realize that in art, likewise, the demands of life press forward when the spirit of the age is ready."

Perhaps we can best understand what he meant by equilibrium if we think of his work as "abstract collage" that uses black bands and colored rectangles instead of recognizable fragments of chair caning and newsprint. He was interested solely in relationships and wanted no distracting elements or fortuitous associations. By establishing the "right" relationship among his bands and rectangles, he transforms them as thoroughly as Braque transformed the snippets of pasted paper in *Le Courrier* (fig. 1036). How did he discover the "right" relationship? And how did he determine the shape and number for the bands and rectangles? In Braque's collage, the ingredients are to some extent "given" by chance, but apart from his self-imposed rules, Mondrian constantly faced the dilemma of unlimited possibilities. He could not change the relationship of the bands to the rectangles without changing the bands and rectangles themselves. When we consider his task, we begin to realize its infinite complexity.

Looking again at *Composition with Red, Blue, and Yellow,* we find that when we measure the various units, only the proportions of the canvas itself are truly rational, an exact square. Mondrian has arrived at all the rest "by feel," and must have undergone agonies of trial and error. How often, we wonder, did he change the dimensions of the red rectangle to bring it and the other elements into self-contained equilibrium?

Strange as it may seem, Mondrian's exquisite sense for non-symmetrical balance is so specific that critics well acquainted with his work have no difficulty in distinguishing fakes from genuine pictures. Designers who work with nonfigurative shapes, such as architects and typographers, are likely to be most sensitive to this quality, and Mondrian has had a greater influence on them than on artists (see Chapter 6).

NICHOLSON. Mondrian nevertheless did produce a number of followers among the painters. By far the most original was the English artist Ben Nicholson (1894–1982). A rigorous abstractionist, he bent Mondrian's rules without breaking them in his painted reliefs (fig. 1058), which also show the inspiration of his wife, the sculptor Barbara Hepworth (see page 854). The overlapping shapes violate the integrity of the rectangle and overcome the tyranny of the grid maintained by Mondrian. The geometry is further enlivened by the introduction of the circle. Yet his work, too, relies on the delicate balance of elements. The effect is enhanced by the subdued palette and matte finish, which create harmonies of the utmost refinement. Indeed, compared to Nicholson's, Mondrian's primary colors seem astonishingly bright and exuberant.

Fantasy

DADA. Out of despair over the mechanized mass killing of World War I, a number of artists in Zurich and New York (including Marcel Duchamp) simultaneously launched in protest a movement called Dada (or Dadaism), which then spread to other cities in Germany and France. The term, which means hobbyhorse in French, was reportedly picked at random from a dictionary, although it had actually been used as the title of a Symbolist journal. As an infantile, all-purpose word, however, it perfectly fitted the spirit of the movement. Dada has often been called nihilistic, and its declared purpose was indeed to make clear to the public at large that all established values, moral or aesthetic, had been rendered meaningless by the catastrophe of the Great War. During its short life (c. 1915–22) Dada preached nonsense and antiart with a vengeance. As Hans Arp wrote, "Dadaism carried assent and dissent ad absurdum. In order to achieve indifference, it was destructive." Marcel Duchamp once "improved" a reproduction of Leonardo's *Mona Lisa* with a moustache and the letters LHOOQ, which when pronounced in French, make an off-color pun. Not even modern art was safe from the Dadaists' assaults: one of them exhibited a toy monkey inside a frame with the title "Portrait of Cézanne." Yet Dada was not a completely negative movement. In its calculated irrationality there was also liberation, a voyage into unknown provinces of the creative mind. The only law respected by the Dadaists was that of chance, and the only reality, that of their own imaginations.

ERNST. Although their most characteristic art form was the ready-made (see page 850), the Dadaists adopted the collage technique of Synthetic Cubism for their purposes. Figure 1059 by the German Dadaist Max Ernst (1891–1976), an associate of Duchamp, is largely composed of snippets from illustrations of machinery. The caption pretends to enumerate these mechanical ingredients which include (or add up to)

1059. Max Ernst. *1 Copper Plate 1 Zinc Plate 1 Rubber Cloth 2 Calipers 1 Drainpipe Telescope 1 Piping Man.* 1920. Collage, 12 x 9" (30.5 x 23 cm). Estate of Hans Arp

1060. Max Ernst. *La Toilette de la Mariée.* 1940. Oil on canvas, 51 x 37⁷/8" (129.5 x 96.2 cm). Peggy Guggenheim Collection, Venice

"1 Piping Man." Actually, there is also a "piping woman." These offspring of Duchamp's prewar *Bride* (see fig. 1045) stare at us blindly through their goggles.

SURREALISM. In 1924, after Duchamp's retirement from Dada, a group led by the poet André Breton founded Dada's successor, Surrealism. They defined their aim as "pure psychic automatism . . . intended to express . . . the true process of thought . . . free from the exercise of reason and from any aesthetic or moral purpose." [See Primary Sources, no. 102, page 943.] Surrealist theory was larded with concepts borrowed from psychoanalysis, and its rhetoric cannot always be taken seriously. The notion that a dream can be transposed by "automatic handwriting" directly from the unconscious mind to the canvas, bypassing the conscious awareness of the artist, did not work in practice. Some degree of control was unavoidable. Nevertheless, Surrealism stimulated several novel techniques for soliciting and exploiting chance effects.

ERNST'S DECALCOMANIA. Max Ernst, the most inventive member of the group, often combined collage with "frottage" (rubbings from pieces of wood, pressed flowers, and other relief surfaces—the process we all know from the children's pastime of rubbing with a pencil on a piece of paper covering, say, a coin). In *La Toilette de la Mariée* (fig. 1060), he has obtained fascinating shapes and textures by another technique: "decalcomania" (the transfer, by pressure, of oil paint to the canvas from some other surface). This procedure is in essence anoth-

1061. Salvador Dalí. *The Persistence of Memory.* 1931. Oil on canvas, 9¹/2 x 13" (24.1 x 33 cm). The Museum of Modern Art, New York
Given anonymously

er variant of that recommended by Alexander Cozens (see fig. 849) and Leonardo da Vinci. Ernst certainly found, and elaborated upon, an extraordinary wealth of images among his stains. The end result has some of the qualities of a dream, but it is a dream born of a strikingly Romantic imagination.

DALI. The same can be said of *The Persistence of Memory* (fig. 1061) by Salvador Dali (1904–1989). The most notorious of

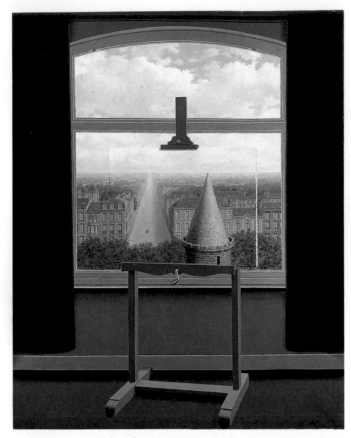

1062. René Magritte. *Les Promenades d'Euclid.* 1955. Oil on canvas, 64¹/8 x 51¹/8" (163 x 130 cm). The Minneapolis Institute of Arts
The William Hood Dunwoody Fund

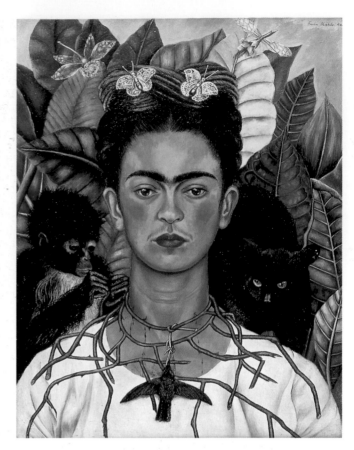

1063. Frida Kahlo. *Self-Portrait with Thorn Necklace.* 1940. Oil on canvas, 24¹/2 x 18³/4" (62 x 47.5 cm). Art Collection, Harry Ransom Research Center, University of Texas at Austin

the Surrealists because of his self-promotion, Dali used a meticulous verism to render a "paranoid" dream in which time, forms, and space have been distorted in a frighteningly real way.

MAGRITTE. The Belgian artist René Magritte (1898–1967) also employed detailed realism, but for completely different ends. Although he found his early inspiration in the work of De Chirico, his naturalism stems from the tradition of Magic Realism that flourished in Belgium in the late nineteenth and early twentieth centuries. Magritte's goal was "poetic painting": illusionistic pictures that transform objects into images having completely different meaning through astonishing transformations, changes in scale, juxtapositions, and the like. *Les Promenades d'Euclid* (fig. 1062) shows one of his favorites devices, the picture within a picture. The title, added after the fact through free association, only compounds the mystery of the painting by failing to explain it. This divorce of word and image prevents us from finding any literal (or literary) meaning. The painting's charm lies not simply in this visual and verbal puzzle but in the presentation itself: the beautifully simple, abstract design, and the artist's way of subtly heightening reality while ultimately denying its plausibility.

KAHLO. A number of women, including Meret Oppenheim (see page 850), were associated with the Surrealist movement. Today the best known is Frida Kahlo (1910–1954), who was first discovered by the poet André Breton during a visit to Mexico in 1938 and then rediscovered in recent years by feminist art historians. [See Primary Sources, no. 103, pages 943–44.]

She owes her reputation as much to her troubled life as to her work, for they are inseparable. Her paintings are frankly autobiographical, yet so laden with personal meaning and couched in such enigmatic terms that the exact circumstances must be known in order to decipher their content. *Self-Portrait with Thorn Necklace* (fig. 1063) is similar in style to traditional Mexican devotional images. It was painted in 1940, when her tempestuous marriage to the painter Diego Rivera (1886–1957) was interrupted for a year by divorce. The necklace, an allusion to the crown of thorns worn by Christ during the Passion, is a symbol of her humiliation by her husband. From it hangs a dead hummingbird, a traditional amulet worn in Mexico by people seeking love. On her shoulders are two demons in the guise of the artist's pets: death, who appears as a black cat, and the devil, seen as a monkey. In context, it is clear that Kahlo must have been contemplating suicide: she has been a martyr to love while hoping for a resurrection like the Lord's, as signified by the butterflies overhead.

MIRÓ. Surrealism also has a boldly imaginative branch. Some works by Picasso, such as *Three Dancers* (fig. 1049), have affinities with it, and its greatest exponent was also Spanish: Joan Miró (1893–1983), who painted the striking *Composition* (fig. 1064). His style has been labeled "biomorphic abstraction," since his designs are fluid and curvilinear, like organic forms, rather than geometric. Actually, "biomorphic concretion" might be a more suitable name, for the shapes in Miró's pictures have their own vigorous life. They seem to change before our eyes, expanding and contracting like amoebas

1064. Joan Miró. *Composition.* 1933. Oil on canvas, 51¼ x 63½" (130.5 x 161.3 cm). Wadsworth Atheneum, Hartford, Connecticut
Ella Gallup Sumner and Mary Catlin Sumner Collection

until they approach human individuality closely enough to please the artist. Their spontaneous "becoming" is the very opposite of abstraction as we defined it above (see page 788), though Miró's formal discipline is no less rigorous than that of Cubism. (He began as a Cubist.)

KLEE. The German-Swiss painter Paul Klee (1879–1940) was decisively influenced early in his career by *Der Blaue Reiter,* and shared many of the same ideas as his friends Kandinsky and Marc. He was, for example, fascinated with music and was himself a talented violinist. His theories of art also have much in common with those of Kandinsky. (They were colleagues at the Bauhaus.) He nevertheless went in the opposite direction. Instead of a higher reality, he wanted to illuminate a deeper one from within the imagination which parallels nature but is independent of it. Thus natural forms are essential to his work, but as pictorial metaphors filled with hidden meaning rather than as representations of nature. He was affected, too, by Cubism and Orphism, but ethnographic art and the drawings of small children held an equally vital interest for him.

During World War I, he molded these disparate elements into a pictorial language of his own, marvelously economical and precise. *Twittering Machine* (fig. 1065), a delicate pen-and-ink drawing tinted with watercolor, demonstrates the

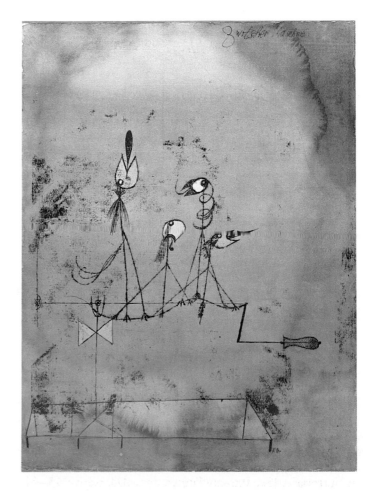

1065. *(right)* Paul Klee. *Twittering Machine.* 1922. Watercolor and pen and ink on oil transfer drawing on paper, mounted on cardboard, 25¼ x 19" (64.1 x 48.3 cm). The Museum of Modern Art, New York
Purchase

1066. Paul Klee. *Park near Lu(cerne).* 1938. Oil and newsprint on burlap, 39¹/₂ x 27¹/₂" (100.3 x 69.7 cm). Fondation Paul Klee, Musée des Beaux-Arts de Berne, Bern, Switzerland
Copyright 1986 COSMOPRESS, Geneva

1067. Käthe Kollwitz. *Never Again War!* 1924. Lithograph, 37 x 27¹/₂" (94 x 70 cm). Courtesy Galerie St. Etienne, New York

unique flavor of Klee's art. With a few simple lines, he has created a ghostly mechanism that imitates the sound of birds, simultaneously mocking our faith in the miracles of the Machine Age and our sentimental appreciation of bird song. The little contraption is not without its sinister aspect: the heads of the four sham birds look like fishermen's lures, as if they might entrap real birds. It thus condenses into one striking invention a complex of ideas about present-day civilization.

The title has an indispensable role. It is characteristic of the way Klee worked that the picture itself, however visually appealing, does not reveal its full evocative quality unless the artist tells us what it means. The title, in turn, needs the picture: the witty concept of a twittering machine does not kindle our imagination until we are shown such a thing. This interdependence is familiar to us from cartoons, but Klee lifts it to the level of high art without relinquishing the playful character of these verbal-visual puns. To him art was a "language of signs," of shapes that are images of ideas as the shape of a letter is the image of a specific sound, or an arrow the image of the command, "This way only." He also realized that in any conventional system the sign is no more than a "trigger." The instant we perceive it, we automatically invest it with meaning, without stopping to ponder its shape. Klee wanted his signs to impinge upon our awareness as visual facts, yet also to share the quality of "triggers."

Toward the end of his life, he immersed himself in the study of ideographs of all kinds, such as hieroglyphics, hex signs, and the mysterious markings in prehistoric caves—"boiled-down" representational images that appealed to him because they had the twin quality he strove for in his own graphic language. This "ideographic style" is clearly articulated in figure 1066, *Park near Lu(cerne).* As a lyric poet may use the plainest words, these deceptively simple shapes sum up a wealth of experience and sensation: the innocent gaiety of spring, the clipped orderliness peculiar to captive plant life in a park. Has it not also a relationship, in spirit if not in fact, with the Romanesque *Summer Landscape* in the manuscript of *Carmina Burana* (fig. 422)? Klee's attitude soon changed. Shortly before his death, the artist's horror at World War II led him to abandon this lighthearted vein in favor of a bleakly pessimistic manner that drew close to Miró's darkest fantasies of the same time.

Expressionism

KOLLWITZ. The experience of World War I filled German artists with a deep anguish at the state of modern civilization, which found its principal outlet in Expressionism. The work of Käthe Kollwitz (1867–1945) consists almost exclusively of

1068. George Grosz. *Germany, a Winter's Tale.* 1918.
Formerly Collection Garvens, Hannover, Germany

prints and drawings that parallel those of Kokoschka, whose work she admired. Her graphics had their sources in the nineteenth century. Munch, Klimt, and the German artist Max Klinger (1857–1920) were early inspirations, as was her friend Ernst Barlach (see page 768). Yet Kollwitz pursued a resolutely independent course, devoting her art to themes of inhumanity and injustice. To articulate her social and ethical concerns, she adopted an intensely expressive, naturalistic style that is as unrelenting in its bleakness as her choice of subjects. Gaunt mothers and exploited workers provided much of Kollwitz's thematic focus, but her most eloquent statements were reserved for war. World War I, which cost her oldest son his life, made her an ardent pacifist. Her lithograph *Never Again War!* (fig. 1067) is an unforgettable image of protest.

GROSZ. George Grosz (1893–1959), a painter and graphic artist who had studied in Paris in 1913, joined the Dadaist movement in Berlin after the end of the war. Inspired by the Futurists, he used a dynamized form of Cubism to develop a bitter, savagely satiric style that expressed the disillusionment of his generation. In *Germany, a Winter's Tale* (fig. 1068), the city of Berlin forms the kaleidoscopic and chaotic background for several large figures, which are superimposed on it as in a

1069. Max Beckmann. *The Dream.* 1921. Oil on canvas,
71 x 35" (180.3 x 89 cm). Collection Morton D. May,
St. Louis, Missouri

collage. They include the marionettelike "good citizen" at his table, and the sinister forces that molded him: a hypocritical clergyman, a general, and a schoolmaster.

BECKMANN. Max Beckmann (1884–1950), a robust descendant of *Die Brücke* artists, did not become an Expressionist until after he had lived through World War I, which filled him with such despair at the state of modern civilization that he took up painting to "reproach God for his errors." *The Dream* (fig. 1069) is a mocking nightmare, a tilted, zigzag world as disquieting as those in Bosch's Hell (see fig. 684). It is crammed with maimed, puppetlike figures that reflect his experience in the army medical corps: the handless swimmer, carrying a fish, who climbs a ladder that leads only to another

German Expressionism in art had a counterpart in Expressionist drama, which compressed as much emotion as possible into a play, eliminating anything not needed to convey the central message of the piece. It initially took the form of subjective truth and utopian vision in *The Beggar* (1912) by Reinhard Sorge (1892–1916) but soon turned to antiwar sentiment in *One Race* (1918) by Fritz von Unruh (1885–1970). Expressionist theater was also promoted by Herwarth Walden (1878–1941), publisher of the journal *Der Sturm*, which attracted many of the leading painters to Berlin, including Oskar Kokoschka, who was also a dramatist. The trilogy *Gas* (1917–20) by Georg Kaiser (1878–1945) characteristically expressed utopian ideals by reducing its characters to symbols of social forces, such as the Engineer and the Billionaire's Son.

Under the Weimar Republic (1920–33), Germany was the most vibrant center of theater in all of Europe, with a dazzling variety that reflected the turmoil of the postwar years. The most important German drama produced between the wars was *Man and the Masses* (1921) by Ernst Toller (1893–1939), featuring a kaleidoscopic production by the director Jürgen Fehling (1890–1968). It already shows the pessimism that led to the decline of Expressionism a few years later. In its place rose Epic Theater, promoted by Erwin Piscator (1893–1966), who championed proletarian theater. He instituted a deliberately episodic style of drama that, in contrast to Expressionism, encouraged psychological distance in the viewer through using divided stages, incorporating film clips, and having characters speak to the audience directly. These devices, later to become standard, thus broke the traditional theatrical illusion that the audience is watching actual events as they are taking place.

The main exponent of Epic Theater was Bertholt Brecht (1898–1956), a confirmed communist who spent much of his career in exile in America. He remains best known for *The Three Penny Opera* (1928), with cabaret-style music by Kurt Weill (1900–1950), that is even more profoundly cynical than the original opera by John Gay on which it is based (see page 623). Brecht's best play, however, is *Mother Courage and Her Children* (1938–39), the story of the destruction of a family during the Thirty Years' War. It provoked viewers to think about its meaning by setting contemporary events in the past (a process known as historification) and presenting them as a series of disjointed episodes, while adding strange effects to induce a sense of alienation. Thus, theater would illuminate the action by commenting on it.

The 1920s were also a time of technical innovation in Germany. The Bauhaus conducted important experiments under Walter Gropius, its longtime director, who devised a stage that could be reconfigured to place the audience in the center of the action. Oskar Schlemmer (1888–1943), head of the theater workshop, designed abstract costumes that made actors into architectural units to be placed at will within the stage space by rigorously controlling their every movement. *Neue Sachlichkeit* (New Objectivity) also found an outlet in theater in documentary dramas dealing with a variety of social issues, but the only playwright of note was Ferdinand Bruckner (1891–1958).

In France, the major contribution was Surrealist theater. In addition to Jarry's *Ubu Roi*, *The Breasts of Tiresias* (1903–17) by Guillaume Apollinaire (1880–1918) was the early prototype of Surrealist drama, mingling popular theater with music and dance in an illogical free form. The poet Jean Cocteau (1892–1963) used many of these devices in *Parade* (1917), a ballet presented by Diaghilev's Ballets Russes that was one of the great collaborations of the time, with costumes by Picasso and music by Erik Satie (1866–1925). Cocteau's finest efforts were restatements of Classical Greek dramas transposed to modern times and treated with all kinds of Surrealist effects. He also worked for the Ballet Suédois (Swedish Ballet), a rival company active in the early 1920s that attracted the painters Léger and De Chirico.

Although the Surrealists mounted numerous absurdist events in the 1920s and 1930s, the most important work was done by André Breton's disciple Antonin Artaud (1896–1948) after he abandoned Surrealism in 1931. Rather than appealing to the mind, his Theater of Cruelty rejected language as impotent and mounted a concerted assault on all the senses to drain the "abscesses" of civilization by "providing the spectator with the true sources of his dreams, in which his taste for crime, his erotic obsessions, his savagery . . . would surge forth." Surrealism also stimulated Henri-René Lenormand (1882–1951) to write *Time is a Dream* (1919) and *The Eater of Dreams* (1922), whose distortions of time and space anticipate effects seen later in Dali's *The Persistence of Memory* (fig. 1061). Perhaps the most interesting Surrealist play was *No Exit* (1944), written during World War II by the existentialist philosopher Jean-Paul Sartre (1905–1980). It is a drama about interpersonal relations in which a man and two women pursue each other vainly as they seek self-validation in the eyes of others, whom they try to control but who in turn have their own agenda. Sartre's "theater of situations" sought to "explore the state of man in its entirety, and to present to modern man a portrait of himself" through his choices and actions.

Although it was short-lived, Italian Futurism was notable for its extreme rejection of traditional staging through the use of multimedia techniques to promote its glorification of the machine, achieve simultaneous effects, and break down barriers between the arts. World War I saw the equally brief Theater of the Grotesque in the plays of Luigi Chiarelli (1880–1947). By far the greatest Italian playwright of the century was Luigi Pirandello (1867–1936), a novelist who turned his hand to drama only after 1910. *Six Characters in Search of an Author* (1921) intermixes fantasy and reality so completely that truth becomes entirely subjective and unknowable, since it varies according to the perspective of each character and spectator. The finest dramatist in Spain was the novelist and poet Federico García Lorca (1898–1936). He worked with the theater group La Barraca in the early 1930s to create updated versions of popular theater dealing with the time-honored Spanish themes of love and honor, as did Alejandro Casona (1903–1966), who directed a similar touring group, The People's Theater.

After the Revolution, theater in Russia continued to be a hotbed of experimentation. The most powerful director was Meyerhold, who now emphasized biomechanics: machine-like movement as the chief means of expression. His sets, designed by the Constructivists, were the most boldly imaginative the world has ever seen. Meyerhold collaborated with Vladimir Mayakovsky (1893–1930), the only true literary genius produced by the Communist Revolution, in which he, like Tatlin, believed wholeheartedly. However, his last plays, such as *The Bedbug* (1929), were acerbic satires on Soviet bureaucracy which were received so badly that he committed suicide. Yevgeny Vakhtangov (1883–1922), who trained many of the leaders of the next generation, managed to successfully combine the seemingly opposite approaches of Meyerhold and Stanislavsky.

Theater thrived in England after World War I. Not since the Elizabethan era were there so many great directors and actors, or so many major theaters. The list of legendary stars includes Tyrone Guthrie, Barry Jackson, Laurence Olivier, John Gielgud, Michael Redgrave, Alec Guinness, Elsa Lanchester, Charles Laughton, and Sybil Thorndike, to name only the most famous. English playwriting of the time is remembered now chiefly for comedies by the novelist W. Somerset Maugham (1874–1965) and Noël Coward (1899–1973), who was a consummate man of the theater. There was considerable dramatic writing by serious authors as well. A notable example is *I Have Been Here Before* (1937) by the novelist J. B. Priestley (1894–1984), which deals with the effect of previous incarnations on the present. The poet W. H. Auden (1907–1973) and the novelist Christopher Isherwood (1904–1986) collaborated on several plays in expressionistic verse, including *The Dog Beneath the Skin* (1935), which was presented at the Group Theater. The American-born poet T. S. Eliot (1888–1965) was also a founder of the Group Theater, which staged his *Sweeney Agonistes* (1932), an "Aristophanic melodrama" which he considered a poem in dialogue, and *Murder in the Cathedral* (1935), about the death of Thomas à Becket. Both were attempts to restore verse to theater using popular forms and music-hall techniques, though Eliot abandoned this approach toward the end of the decade. The early dramas written for the Abbey Theater in the mid-1920s by Sean O'Casey (1880–1964) dealt with the impact of the Irish rebellion on people's lives, but his style later veered toward Expressionism in the pacifist play *The Silver Tassie* (1928), which led to a break with the Abbey, despite support from Yeats.

In the United States, new groups sprang up everywhere, many of them later subsidized by the government during the Depression under the Federal Theater Project. Stagecraft underwent radical changes at the hands of the designers Lee Simonson (1888–1967) and Robert Jones (1887–1954) and the producers Arthur Hopkins (1878–1950) and Norman Bel Geddes (1893–1958), all of whom were well versed in the latest European techniques. The Group Theater, begun in 1931 by Lee Strasberg (1901–1982) and others along the lines of the Moscow Art Theater, included such stars as Stella Adler (1904–1992) and Elia Kazan (born 1909). It was also the golden age of Hollywood films. Orson Welles, Laurence Olivier, his wife, Vivien Leigh, John Gielgud, Elsa Lanchester, Vincent Minelli, and his wife, Judy Garland, were among the actors and directors who were equally successful on stage and screen.

For the first time in its history, America had writers who were fully the equal of those in Europe, and many of them wrote for the stage. The finest was unquestionably Eugene O'Neill (1888–1953), the son of the actor James O'Neill (1846–1920), whose powerful dramas *Desire Under the Elms* (1925), *Mourning Becomes Electra* (1931), and *The Iceman Cometh* (1940/46) remain the great American classics of the era. Their only rivals are the plays written by Clifford Odets (1906–1963) in 1935 for the Group Theater—*Waiting for Lefty, Awake and Sing!,* and *Paradise Lost*—all scripted in intense, graphic language. Odets' most popular work remains *Golden Boy* (1937), about a young violinist who becomes a boxer to earn money, which is a thinly veiled reference to his own decision to move to Hollywood, where his talents soon petered out. The novelist John Steinbeck (1902–1968) adapted three of his books for the stage; much the best is *Of Mice and Men,* done in collaboration with George S. Kaufman (1889–1961), a story of strength, weakness, and human dignity among migrant workers in a Midwest farming town during the Depression. Maxwell Anderson (1888–1959) achieved critical acclaim during the 1930s, when he won the Pulitzer Prize for *Both Your Houses* (1933) and the Drama Critics' Circle Award for *Winterset* (1935). Much of his work dealt with war or the great monarchs and political leaders of the past. Other notable contributions to the American theater were *Street Scene* (1929) by Elmer Rice (1892–1967), about oppression and dehumanization; *The Time of Your Life* (1939) by William Saroyan (1908–1981), a witty and colorful story about life in San Francisco; *Mulatto* (1935) by Langston Hughes (1902–1967), the great writer of the Harlem Renaissance; and *The Cradle Will Rock* (1937) by Marc Blitzstein (1905–1964), whose rejection by the Federal Theater Project led Welles and John Houseman (1902–1988) to form the Mercury Theater.

1070. Max Beckmann. *Departure*. 1932–33. Oil on canvas, center panel
7'3/4" x 3'93/8" (2.15 x 1.15 m); side panels each 7'3/4" x 3'31/4" (2.15 x 1 m). The Museum of Modern Art, New York
Given anonymously by exchange

ladder on the ceiling; the crippled clown whose open hat protects his eyes but not his head from the nonexistent sun; the woman singing ecstatically to herself as she plays a stringless cello; and the beggar frantically cranking his hurdy-gurdy and blaring his trumpet to this unreceptive audience. All are blind except the blond girl in the center. (Note the mirror that reflects nothing and the lantern that illuminates nothing.) Evidently a recent arrival, to judge from her trunk, she observes everything with detachment and gestures as if to say, "Behold this Ship of Fools," while the puppet she holds mockingly applauds the absurd performance. Her innocence is underscored by the plant, which rudely pushes aside her dress as she tries to stop its advance with one foot. The forms show the inspiration of early German prints, which Beckmann shared with the members of *Die Brücke* (compare figs. 692–95).

The claustrophobic space, which comes from the same source, is essential to the image, which radiates an oppressive aura. It was, he said, "how I defend myself against the infinity of space . . . the great spatial void and uncertainty that I call God." Beckmann has created a powerful image whose meaning is conveyed by evocative symbolism which is necessarily subjective. How indeed could Beckmann have expressed the chaos in Germany after that war with the worn-out language of traditional symbols? "These are the creatures that haunt my imagination," he seems to say. "They show the true nature of

the modern condition—how weak we are, how helpless against ourselves in this proud era of so-called progress."

Some elements from this grotesque and sinister sideshow recur in altered guise more than a decade later in the wings of Beckmann's triptych *Departure* (fig. 1070), a painting that reflects Beckmann's admiration for Grünewald. The right panel incorporates a blind man holding the fish, a lantern, and a mad musician. The left panel shows a scene of almost unimaginable torture. What are we to make of these brutal images? We know from letters written by the artist and a close friend that they represent life itself as endless misery filled with all manner of physical and spiritual pain. The woman trying to make her way in the dark with the aid of the lamp is carrying the corpse of her memories, evil deeds, and failures, from which no one can ever be free so long as life beats its drum. The center panel signifies the departure from life's illusions to the reality behind appearances. The crowned figure seen from behind perhaps represents the legendary Fisher King from the legend of the Holy Grail, whose health and that of his land is restored by Parsifal.

In the hindsight of today, *Departure* acquired the force of prophecy. It was completed when, under Nazi pressure, the artist was on the verge of leaving his homeland. The topsy-turvy quality of the two wing scenes, full of mutilations and meaningless rituals, well captures the flavor of Hitler's Ger-

1071. Arthur G. Dove. *Foghorns.* 1929. Oil on canvas,
18 x 26" (42.7 x 66 cm). Colorado Springs Fine Arts Center
Anonymous gift

1072. José Clemente Orozco. *Victims.* Detail of fresco cycle. 1936.
University of Guadalajara, Mexico

many. The stable design of the center panel, in contrast, with its expanse of blue sea and its sunlit brightness, conveys the hopeful spirit of an embarkation for distant shores. [See Primary Sources, no. 104, page 944.] After living through World War II in occupied Holland under the most trying conditions, Beckmann spent the final three years of his life in America.

DOVE. After 1920 in the United States, most of the original members of the Stieglitz group concentrated on landscapes, which they treated in representational styles derived from Expressionism. Alone among them, Arthur G. Dove (1880–1946) consistently maintained a form of abstraction, one based loosely on Kandinsky's style. The difference between the two artists is that Dove sought to reveal the inner life of nature, whereas Kandinsky tried to rid his images of readily recognizable subject matter. Dove's paintings possess a monumental spirit that belies their typically modest size. *Foghorns* (fig. 1071) epitomizes the intelligence and economy of his mature landscapes. To evoke the diffusion of sound, Dove utilized the simple but ingenious device of irregular concentric circles of color that grow paler as they radiate outward.

OROZCO. During the 1930s, the center of Expressionism in the New World was Mexico. The Mexican Revolution began in 1911 with the fall of the dictator Porfirio Díaz and continued for more than two decades. It inspired a group of young painters to search for a national style incorporating the great native heritage of Pre-Columbian art. They also felt that their art must be "of the people," expressing the spirit of the Revolution in large mural cycles in public buildings. Although each developed his own distinctive style, they shared a common point of departure: the Symbolist art of Gauguin, which had shown how non-Western forms could be integrated with the Western tradition. The flat, decorative quality of this art was particularly suited to murals. However, the involvement of these artists in the political turmoil of the day often led them to overburden their works with ideological significance. The artist least subject to this imbalance of form and subject matter was José Clemente Orozco (1883–1949), a passionately independent artist who refused to get embroiled in factional politics. The detail from the mural cycle at the University of Guadalajara (fig. 1072) illustrates his most powerful trait: a deep humanitarian sympathy with the silent, suffering masses.

Realism

DIX. In 1923 the director of the Mannheim museum organized an exhibition with the title *Die Neue Sachlichkeit* (The New Objectivity; sometimes also known as Magic Realism).

The most important composer to emerge between the world wars was Béla Bartók (1881–1945). In 1905 he met the composer Zoltán Kodály (1882–1967); together they began to collect the ethnic music of Hungary and ran the Budapest Academy of Music. While utilizing folk melodies, rhythms, and modes, Bartók incorporated the complex rhythms and the percussive effects of Stravinsky, as well as the dissonance and atonality of Schoenberg. His music was intensely personal, uniting Expressionism and Surrealism to convey the searing emotionalism apparent in the opera *Bluebeard's Castle* (1918), the ballet *The Mandarin Prince* (1926), and especially the six string quartets (1908–39), which equal Beethoven's in profundity and innovation. Bartók was a famous piano virtuoso, whose three concertos (1926–45) exploit the full potential of that instrument. The final piano concerto and the *Concerto for Orchestra* (1943) are more melodic and accessible to a wide audience, without diluting the composer's unique vision.

The Russian piano virtuoso Sergei Prokoviev (1891–1953) began his career as a member of the avant-garde with two dissonant concertos for piano, although the heart of his music remained melody. He left for Europe following the Russian Revolution of 1917. Soon after his return to Russia in 1934, he composed his great ballet *Romeo and Juliet* and an orchestral fairy tale for children, *Peter and the Wolf.* Although he tried his best to meet the demands of Soviet authorities for propaganda music in such works as the Fifth Symphony (1944), he suffered terrible privation and repression, as did the younger Dmitri Shostakovich (1906–1975), whose private works are uncompromising in their integrity. Fittingly enough, no one today listens to the composers who were approved by Russian officials.

The United States produced two composers of note during the first part of the twentieth century: Charles Ives (1874–1954) and Henry Cowell (1897–1965). Ives received a conventional academic music training at Yale University, but even before then he had begun to experiment with effects that were to become the hallmarks of his music. They reach their height in *Symphony No. 4* (1916), which employs several themes played simultaneously in different keys by different groups under separate conductors that create a clashing, kaleidoscopic effect; and in the *Concord Sonata* for piano (1920), which uses elbows as well as wood blocks to play the notes. He was nevertheless a gifted melodist. *Three Places in New England* (1914) is a consciously American piece in its choice of themes and alternately festive and haunting atmosphere.

Ives did little composing after 1918. He spent the rest of his life as a successful insurance salesman, and shared his music with only a few friends, such as Cowell and Carl Ruggles (1876–1971). Cowell, like Ives, was a pioneer in experimental music for the piano. He wrote several pieces for "prepared piano," an instrument made ready for performance by having objects attached to or placed on its strings, some of which might also be tuned unconventionally. He was the first American composer to show a consistent interest in the music of other cultures, which he incorporated into his numerous symphonies. Ruggles was a resolute individualist whose few works, such as *Sun Treader* (1932), deal with Symbolist themes. Although their treatment sometimes has a nearly post-Romantic massiveness, they consistently show an obsession with perfection of form and sound achieved through the most concentrated means. (He once spent the afternoon repeating the same note on the piano in search of "the perfect C.")

Aaron Copland (1900–1990) studied under Nadia Boulanger (1887–1979) during the early 1920s in Paris, where he came under the influence of Stravinsky. Upon his return to the United States, he adopted themes and rhythms inspired by jazz. Enthused by liberal ideology, he sought to create music that would speak to all the people, not simply those of one region. As a result, Copland, more than any other composer, defined our concept of "American" music across a wide spectrum, including Latin, Mexican, Appalachian, and Western. His three ballets—*Billy the Kid* (1838), *Rodeo* (1942), and above all *Appalachian Spring* (1944)—are justifiably popular works that combine touching lyricism with rhythmic vivacity in almost irresistible combination. Copland's work also includes a number of challenging serious works, such as *Variations* for piano (1930) and the Third Symphony (1946), composed in the Neoclassical manner of Stravinsky.

England also had an important school of composers before 1945, starting with the Victorian Romantic Edward Elgar (1857–1934). Elgar's cantata, *A Dream of Gerontius* (1900), based on a poem about a soul's journey to heaven by the theologian John Henry Newman, conveys the idealism of the English school. Equally characteristic was the love of nature found in the work of Gustav Holst (1874–1934), best-known for *The Planets* (1916). Perhaps the finest composer was Ralph Vaughan Williams (1872–1958), whose compositions, such as the *Serenade to Music* (1938), set to a text from Shakespeare's *Othello,* epitomize English lyricism.

This, he explained, was "a label for the new realism bearing a socialist flavor. Cynicism and resignation are the negative side of New Objectivity; the positive side expresses itself in the enthusiasm for immediate reality." Its principal representatives were George Grosz, who by this time had abandoned his slashing style for a more realistic manner no less biting in its sarcasm, and Max Beckmann, whose naturalism was simply a vehicle for expressing his disillusionment. But it was the meticulous verism of Otto Dix (1891–1969), another Expressionist who had also been a member of Dada, that defined the essential characteristics of the New Objectivity. Its roots lay in German Renaissance art and the Romanticism of Runge, which Dix used to expose the ills of modern Germany with obsessive detail. Dix's best works are his portraits, such as that of Dr. Mayer-Hermann (fig. 1073). The image has a supernatural clarity that lends an almost nightmarish intensity to

1073. Otto Dix. *Dr. Mayer-Hermann*. 1926.
Oil and tempera on wood, 58³/4 x 39" (149.2 x 99.1 cm).
The Museum of Modern Art, New York
Gift of Philip Johnson

1074. Georgia O'Keeffe. *Black Iris III*. 1926. Oil on canvas,
36 x 29⁷/8" (91.4 x 75.9 cm). The Metropolitan Museum of Art,
New York
The Alfred Stieglitz Collection, 1949

this seemingly straightforward image of the doctor seated impassively before his instruments, which echo his bulbous shape. In the process, they have acquired the alien character of the devices in Max Ernst's *1 Piping Man* (fig. 1059), so that they become strangely menacing. For a comparably overwhelming portrayal, we must turn to Ingres' *Louis Bertin* (fig. 871). That Dix fares remarkably well in the comparison is testimony to his powers of characterization.

O'KEEFFE. The New Objectivity soon succumbed to realism for its own sake tinged with Romantic nostalgia as part of a widespread conservative reaction on both sides of the Atlantic. The naturalism that characterized American art as a whole during the 1920s found its most important representative in Georgia O'Keeffe (1887–1986). Throughout her long career, she covered a wide range of subjects and styles. Like Arthur Dove, she practiced a form of organic abstraction indebted to Expressionism, but she also adopted the Precisionism of Charles Demuth (see page 804), so that she is sometimes considered an abstract artist. Her work often combined aspects of both approaches: as she assimilated a subject into her imagination, she would alter and simplify it to convey a personal meaning. Nonetheless, O'Keeffe remained a realist at heart. *Black Iris III* (fig. 1074) is the kind of painting for which she is best known. The image is marked by a strong

sense of design uniquely her own. The flower, however, is deceptive in its decorative treatment. Observed close up and magnified to large scale, it is a thinly disguised symbol of female sexuality.

AMERICAN SCENE PAINTING. The dominance of realism during the 1930s signaled the retreat of progressive art everywhere in response to the economic depression and social turmoil that gripped both Europe and the United States. Often realism was linked to the reassertion of traditional values. Most American artists split into two camps, the Regionalists and the Social Realists. The Regionalists sought to revive idealism by updating the American myth, defined, however, largely in midwestern terms. The Social Realists, on the other hand, captured the dislocation and despair of the Depression era, and were often concerned with social reform. But both movements, although bitterly opposed, drew freely on the Ash Can School (see page 799).

HOPPER. The one artist who appealed to all factions alike, including that of the few remaining modernists, was a former pupil of Robert Henri, Edward Hopper (1882–1967). He focused on what has since become known as the "vernacular architecture" of American cities—store fronts, movie houses, all-night diners—which no one else had thought worthy of an

1075. Edward Hopper. *Early Sunday Morning.* 1930.
Oil on canvas, 35 x 60" (88.9 x 152.4 cm). Whitney Museum of American Art, New York

artist's attention. *Early Sunday Morning* (fig. 1075) distills a haunting sense of loneliness from the all-too-familiar elements of an ordinary street. Its quietness, we realize, is temporary; there is hidden life behind these facades. We almost expect to see one of the window shades raised as we look at them. Apart from its poetic appeal, the picture also shows an impressive formal discipline. We note the strategy in placing the fireplug and barber pole, the subtle variations in the treatment of the row of windows, the precisely calculated slant of sunlight, the delicate balance of verticals and horizontals. Obviously, Hopper was not unaware of Mondrian.

LAWRENCE. The 1920s brought about a cultural revival among African-Americans known as the Harlem Renaissance. Although its promise was dashed by the economic catastrophe of the Depression, this brief flowering did produce the first black artists to gain national recognition. By far the most famous remains Jacob Lawrence (born 1917), who rose to prominence around 1940. Motivated by rage at the injustices inflicted on African-Americans, Lawrence treated historical themes and the major social issues of the day. His series "From Every Southern Town . . ." (see fig. 1076) focuses on the great exodus of blacks from the south. Despite its small size, our panel has an impressive monumentality, thanks to the simplified forms and flat color, which express his intent with admirable directness. So powerful was Lawrence's impact that

his art continues to define the prototype of African-American painting for many people, although he retired in 1983.

PAINTING SINCE WORLD WAR II

Abstract Expressionism: Action Painting

The world, having survived the most serious economic calamity and the greatest threat to civilization in all of history, now faced a potentially even greater danger: nuclear holocaust. This central fact conditioned the entire Cold War era, which has only recently come to an end. Ironically, it was also a period of unprecedented prosperity in much of the West, but not in the rest of the world, which, with the notable exception of Japan, has struggled until recently to compete successfully.

The painting that prevailed for about 15 years following the end of World War II arose in direct response to the anxiety brought on by these historical circumstances. The term *Abstract Expressionism* is often applied to this style, which was initiated by artists living in New York City. Under the influence of Surrealism and existentialist philosophy, Action painters, the first of the Abstract Expressionists, developed a new approach to art. Painting became a counterpart to life itself, an ongoing process in which artists face comparable risks and overcome the dilemmas confronting them through a

1076. Jacob Lawrence. *The Migration of the Negro,* panel 3, "From Every Southern Town Migrants Left by the Hundreds to Travel North." 1940–41. Tempera on masonite, 11¹/2 x 17¹/2" (29.2 x 44.4 cm). The Phillips Collection, Washington, D.C.

series of conscious and unconscious decisions in response to both inner and external demands. The Color Field painters in turn coalesced the frenetic gestures and violent hues of the Action painters into broad forms of poetic color that partly reflect the spirituality of Oriental mysticism. In a sense, Color Field Painting resolved the conflicts expressed by Action Painting. They are, however, two sides of the same coin, separated by the thinnest differences of approach.

GOTTLIEB. During World War II, the poet André Breton and other Surrealists found refuge in New York, where their work was enthusiastically received by critics and exhibited at museums and galleries such as Peggy Guggenheim's Art of This Century. Soon the early Abstract Expressionists evolved their own form of Surrealism that allowed them to express their sense of horror at the pervasive evil of a chaotic world. Distraught by the carnage, which threatened the very existence of civilization, they became myth-makers who sought to evoke images that expressed their sense of impending disaster. In this they were strongly affected by the theory of the collective subconscious formulated by Freud's disciple Carl Jung, who believed that universal archetypes are imbedded in our psyches.

The breakthrough came in a discussion between Adolph Gottlieb (1903–1974) and Mark Rothko (1903–1970), who suggested they try Classical themes. Gottlieb consequently began to paint pictographs based on Sophocles and the other Greek tragedians. Pictographs are a form of picture writing found in prehistoric art; no longer intelligible to us, they continue to exercise a mysterious, instinctive appeal. Few prehistoric images, however, have the impact of Gottlieb's pictographs (fig. 1077), which conjure up something more elemental than even the most ancient relic. The canvas owes its power to his uncanny ability to cast the viewer back into the dark, primitive realm of the subconscious. Painted in an uncompromisingly severe style, it radiates a menacing evil that is a truly frightening evocation of the war. Composed in a grid system derived from Mondrian, it contains Surrealist forms influenced by the grimmest works of Picasso, Miró, and Klee from the same years. At face value the picture seems a confusing jumble of human anatomy cut up and reassembled by a

1077. Adolph Gottlieb. *Descent into Darkness.* 1947. Oil on masonite, 30 x 25" (76.2 x 63.5 cm). Smith College Museum of Art, Northampton, Massachusetts
Acquired by exchange, 1951

lunatic. It demands to be read section by section, yet it does not yield a literal meaning. Instead, the accumulation of intuitive responses through free association to this enigmatic image provides an experience at once overwhelming and profoundly disturbing.

GORKY. Arshile Gorky (1904–1948), an Armenian who came to America at 16, was the pioneer of the movement and the single most important influence on its other members. It

1078. Arshile Gorky. *The Liver Is the Cock's Comb.* 1944. Oil on canvas,
6'1¼" x 8'2" (1.86 x 2.49 m). Albright-Knox Art Gallery, Buffalo, New York
Gift of Seymour H. Knox, 1956

took him 20 years, painting first in the manner of Cézanne, then in the vein of Picasso, to arrive at his mature style. We see it in *The Liver Is the Cock's Comb* (fig. 1078), his greatest work. The enigmatic title suggests Gorky's close contact with the Surrealists during the war. Gorky developed a personal mythology that underlies his work; each form represents a private symbol within this hermetic realm. Everything here is in the process of turning into something else. The treatment reflects his own experience in camouflage, gained from a class he conducted earlier. The biomorphic shapes clearly owe much to Miró, while their spontaneous handling and the glowing color reflect Gorky's enthusiasm for Kandinsky (see figs. 1064 and 1030). Yet the dynamic interlocking of the forms, their aggressive power of attraction and repulsion are uniquely his own.

POLLOCK. The most important of the Action painters proved to be Jackson Pollock (1912–1956). His huge canvas entitled *Autumn Rhythm: Number 30, 1950* (fig. 1079) was executed mainly by pouring and spattering the colors, instead of applying them with a brush. [See Primary Sources, no. 105, page 944.] The result, especially when viewed at close range, suggests both Kandinsky and Max Ernst (compare figs. 1030 and 1060). Kandinsky's nonrepresentational Expressionism and the Surrealists' exploitation of chance effects are indeed the main sources of Pollock's work, but they do not sufficiently

account for his revolutionary technique and the emotional appeal of his art. Why did Pollock "fling a pot of paint in the public's face," as Ruskin had accused Whistler of doing? It was surely not to be more abstract than his predecessors, for the strict control implied by abstraction is exactly what Pollock relinquished when he began to dribble and spatter. Rather, he came to regard paint itself not as a passive substance to be manipulated at will but as a storehouse of pent-up forces for him to release.

The actual shapes visible in our illustration are largely determined by the internal dynamics of his material and his process: the viscosity of the paint, the speed and direction of its impact upon the canvas, its interaction with other layers of pigment. The result is a surface so alive, so sensuously rich, that all earlier painting looks pallid in comparison. When he "aims" the paint at the canvas instead of "carrying" it on the tip of his brush—or, if you will, releases the forces within the paint by giving it a momentum of its own—Pollock does not simply "let go" and leave the rest to chance. He is himself the ultimate source of energy for these forces, and he "rides" them as a cowboy might ride a wild horse, in a frenzy of psychophysical action. He does not always stay in the saddle, yet the exhilaration of this contest, which strains every fiber of his being, is well worth the risk. Our simile, though crude, points up the main difference between Pollock and his predecessors: his total commitment to the act of painting. Hence his pref-

1079. Jackson Pollock. *Autumn Rhythm: Number 30, 1950.* 1950.
Oil on canvas, 8'8" x 17'3" (2.64 x 5.26 m). The Metropolitan Museum of Art, New York
George A. Hearn Fund, 1957

1080. Lee Krasner. *Celebration.* 1959–60. Oil on canvas, 7'8¹/4" x 16'4¹/2" (2.3 x 4.9 m). Private collection
Courtesy Robert Miller Gallery, New York

erence for huge canvases that provide a "field of combat" large enough for him to paint not merely with his arms, but with the motion of his whole body.

The term *Action Painting* conveys the essence of this approach far better than does Abstract Expressionism. To those who complain that Pollock was not sufficiently in control of his medium, we reply that this loss is more than offset by a gain—the new continuity and expansiveness of the creative process that gave his work its distinctive mid-twentieth-century stamp. Pollock's drip technique, however, was not in itself essential to Action Painting, and he stopped using it in 1953.

KRASNER. Lee Krasner (1908–1984), who was married to Pollock, never abandoned the brush, although she was unmistakably influenced by Pollock. She struggled to establish her artistic identity, emerging from his shadow only after undergoing several changes in direction and destroying much of her early work. After Pollock's death, she succeeded in doing what he had been attempting to do for the last three years of his life: to reintroduce the figure into Abstract Expressionism while retaining its automatic handwriting. The potential had always been there in Pollock's work: in *Autumn Rhythm,* we can easily imagine wildly dancing people. In *Celebration* (fig. 1080),

1081. Willem de Kooning. *Woman II*. 1952. Oil on canvas, 59 x 43" (149.9 x 109.2 cm). The Museum of Modern Art, New York

Gift of Mrs. John D. Rockefeller 3rd

Krasner defines these nascent shapes from within the tangled network of lines by using the broad gestures of Action Painting to suggest human forms without actually depicting them.

DE KOONING. The work of Willem de Kooning (born 1904), another prominent member of the group and a close friend of Gorky, always retains a link with the world of images, whether or not it has a recognizable subject. In some paintings, such as *Woman II* (fig. 1081), the image emerges from the jagged welter of brushstrokes as insistently as it does in Rouault's *Head of Christ* (see fig. 1023). De Kooning has in common with Pollock the furious energy of the process of painting, the sense of risk, of a challenge successfully—but barely—met. In reality, the artist worked on the canvas for two years, constantly repainting it until he got it right. What are we to make of his wildly distorted *Woman II*? It is as if the flow of psychic impulses in the process of painting has unleashed this nightmarish specter from deep within the artist's subconscious, much as it did in Adolph Gottlieb's pictographs (compare fig. 1077). For that reason, he has sometimes been accused of being a woman-hater, a charge he denied. Rather, she is like a primordial goddess, cruel yet seductive, who represents the dark, primitive side of our makeup. We have met her before, for example in *"The Mistress of the Animals"* from Thera (fig. 123). At the same time, De Kooning's woman is

intended as a humorous caricature of modern movie stars such as Marilyn Monroe. Yet he shared with Max Beckmann an Old World horror of empty space, which to him signified the existential void. Only after he moved to Long Island from the confines of New York City was he able to overcome this deep-seated anxiety.

Expressionism in Europe

Action Painting marked the international coming-of-age for American art. The movement had a powerful impact on European art, which in those years had nothing to show of comparable force and conviction. One French artist, however, was of such prodigal originality as to constitute a movement all by himself: Jean Dubuffet, whose first exhibition soon after the Liberation electrified and antagonized the art world of Paris.

DUBUFFET. As a young man Dubuffet (1901–1985) had formal instruction in painting, but he responded to none of the various trends he saw around him, nor to the art of the museums. All struck him as divorced from real life, and he turned to other pursuits. Only in middle age did he experience the breakthrough that permitted him to discover his creative gifts. Dubuffet suddenly realized that for him true art had to

1082. Jean Dubuffet. *Le Métafisyx,* from the *Corps de Dames* series. 1950. 45³/4 x 35¹/4" (116.2 x 89.5 cm). Private collection

1083. Karel Appel. *Burned Face.* 1961. Oil on canvas, 9'10" x 6'6³/4" (3 x 2 m). Private collection

come from outside the ideas and traditions of the artistic elite, and he found inspiration in the art of children and the insane. The distinction between "normal" and "abnormal" struck him as no more tenable than established notions of "beauty" and "ugliness." Not since Marcel Duchamp (see page 798) had anyone ventured so radical a critique of the nature of art.

Dubuffet made himself the champion of what he called *l'art brut,* "art-in-the-raw," but he created something of a paradox besides: while extolling the directness and spontaneity of the amateur as against the refinement of professional artists, he became a professional artist himself. Duchamp's questioning of established values had led him to cease artistic activity altogether, but Dubuffet became incredibly prolific, second only to Picasso in output. Compared with Klee, who had first utilized the style of children's drawings (see pages 809–10), Dubuffet's art is "raw" indeed. Its stark immediacy, its explosive, defiant presence, are the opposite of the older painter's formal discipline and economy of means. Did Dubuffet perhaps fall into a trap of his own making? If his work merely imitated the *art brut* of children and the insane, would not these self-chosen conventions limit him as much as those of the artistic elite?

We may be tempted to think so at our first sight of *Le Métafisyx* (fig. 1082) from his *Corps de Dames* series. Even De Kooning's wildly distorted *Woman II* (fig. 1081) seems gentle when matched against this shocking assault on our inherited sensibilities. The paint is as heavy and opaque as a rough coating of plaster, and the lines articulating the blocklike body are

scratched into the surface like graffiti made by an untrained hand. Appearances are deceiving, however. The fury and concentration of Dubuffet's attack should convince us that his demonic female is not "something any child can do." In an eloquent statement the artist has explained the purpose of images such as this: "The female body . . . has long . . . been associated with a very specious notion of beauty which I find miserable and most depressing. Surely I am for beauty, but not that one . . . I intend to sweep away everything we have been taught to consider—without question—as grace and beauty [and to] substitute another and vaster beauty, touching all objects and beings, not excluding the most despised . . . I would like people to look at my work as an enterprise for the rehabilitation of scorned values, and . . . a work of ardent celebration."

APPEL. *L'art brut* and Abstract Expressionism provided the mainsprings for the COBRA group in Denmark, Belgium, and Holland, which took its name from Copenhagen, Brussels, and Amsterdam, the capitals of those countries. The Dutch artist Karel Appel (born 1921), one of the group's co-founders, soon distinguished himself as the finest pure painter of his generation in postwar Europe. To the subject matter of Dubuffet he added the slashing brushwork and vivid colors of De Kooning. During several extended visits to the United States in the late 1950s and early 1960s, Appel was directly exposed to the Action painters and inspired by jazz musicians. As a result, his palette became even more sonorous, the texture more sensuous, and the space more complex. *Burned Face* (fig. 1083), one of

The end of World War II brought an explosion of theater in response to pent-up cultural energy and popular demand. In Europe heavy government subsidies were used to restore national theaters and establish new ones. French theater initially adhered to concepts and practices that had been developed during the war years. Most new dramas were by established writers, such as Jean Anouilh (1910–1987), the most popular playwright in France through the 1970s, whose work centered on the dilemma of maintaining youthful integrity in an adult world based on compromise. But the essential contribution of postwar France was the Theater of the Absurd, which, appropriately enough, was never an organized movement and was named by the critic Martin Esslin only in 1961, when its heyday was over. The term derives from the essay "The Myth of Sisyphus" written in 1943 by Albert Camus (1913–1960), who considered the universe to be chaotic and irrational and considered the search for meaning to be as "absurd" as the futile task of the Corinthian king who was condemned to pushing the same boulder up a hill in Hades forever. Camus' outlook was closely related to the existentialism of Jean-Paul Sartre, which held that truth in any absolute sense is unknowable, and that meaning must be self-created by each individual. Camus, however, rejected Sartre's call for political engagement as a necessary, albeit irrational, act, thereby prompting a long and bitter feud between the two men.

This attitude was a response to the horrors of the war and the anxiety created by the ensuing Cold War, with its omnipresent threat of nuclear holocaust. In fact, *End Game* (1957) by Samuel Beckett (1906–1989), the greatest of the absurdists, takes place at the end of the world and uses the metaphor of chess to represent the human condition through four characters who alternately torment and console each other in their incomprehensible predicament, over which they have no control. Although he was Irish, Beckett spent much of his career in Paris, and *End Game* was originally written in French. Paris was also home to the Romanian-born Eugène Ionesco (1912–1994), whose early one-act dramas, such as *The Bald Soprano* (1949), which was inspired by an English phrase book, were "antiplays" using the conventions of language to convey irrational, anguished states of mind. His later works, notably *Rhinoceros* (1960), are more conventional in form and character delineation, but they are no less hallucinatory in their effect. Of all the absurdists, the most disturbing was Jean Genet (1910–1986). Like many of his plays, Genet's masterpiece *The Balcony* (1956) deals with outcasts—he himself was a criminal and a homosexual—caught in a web of perverse and destructive relationships, but nevertheless reveals a surprisingly compassionate, if pessimistic, view of humanity. Genet's plays are extremely powerful in their impact on the viewer. In this he reveals himself a disciple of Artaud's Theater of Cruelty, which exercised a pervasive influence on French theater after the war, including the director Roger Blin (1907–1984), who staged numerous absurdist plays in experimental theaters across the country. By far the most important recent development has come from the Théâtre du Soleil, founded in 1964, with Ariane Mnouchkine (born 1940) at its helm. Her productions of Shakespeare, Euripides, and Aeschylus freely incorporate elements from India, Japan, and Asia to striking effect.

In Germany, the most powerful influence came from Bertholt Brecht, whose Berlin Ensemble, directed by his wife, Helene Weigel (1900–1971), was widely regarded as among the finest of the time in Europe. Despite heavy state support on both sides of the iron curtain, not until the 1960s did Germany produce its first postwar dramatist of note: Peter Weiss (1916–1982), whose *Marat/Sade* (the customary shortened title) unites Brecht and Artaud to treat an insane asylum as a metaphor of the world. Of the German playwrights born around the end of the war, the foremost is Botho Strauss (born 1944), whose drama *Big and Little* (1978), in which characters try unsuccessfully to establish contact with one another, are close to absurdist theater but replete with political overtones. Throughout the 1970s German theater was heavily leftist in its orientation, especially the productions of director Peter Stein (born 1937), which were critiques of the ideologies underlying traditional plays and examinations of their historical roots. Since then a more conventional ideology and approach have been adopted, as much out of self-preservation as conviction.

England rebuilt its fabled theater system, including the Old Vic and the Stratford Festival Company, and reestablished the important festivals such as Glyndebourne. Experimental theater, however, came only in the mid-1950s, when the English Stage Company, under George Devine (1910–1966), was established and produced two epoch-making plays by John Osborne (1929–1994): *Look Back in Anger* (1956), an attack on the inherited class system and its injustices, and *The Entertainer* (1957), starring Laurence Olivier as the fading music-hall actor Archie Rice, who symbolizes the decline of England. At about the same time, the Theatre Workshop began to reach its height under Joan Littlewood (born 1914), its director until 1961, who wanted to create a working-class theater. Her most famous productions were *The Quare Fellow,* written in 1945 by the Irish poet and novelist Brendan Behan (1923–1964), about the impending execution of an Irish Republican Army sympathizer; and *A Taste of Honey* (1958), written at the age of 17 by Shelagh Delaney (born 1939), about a teen-aged mother who rears her child with the help of a gay man. Under Peter Hall (born 1930) and Peter Brook (born 1925), the most experimental of all English directors, the newly chartered Royal Shakespeare Company became the leading venue for avant-garde theater in the 1960s. By far the most significant English playwright of the postwar era has been Harold Pinter (born 1930), whose enigmatic "comedies of menace," such as *The Caretaker* (1960), have more than a little in common with Beckett's dramas but are filled with a sense of mystery and fear that makes them psychologically gripping. The generation born in the 1930s continues to dominate English drama. Typically their work is radical, both socially and morally. Among them, Edward Bond (born 1935) gained particular notoriety for the shock value of his early plays written in 1965–68, which use violence and bizarre plots to emphasize the moral depravity of modern existence.

Poland's contribution to contemporary theater has been no less important than in music. Jerzy Grotowski (born 1933) emerged as a leading director in the mid-1960s, when the Polish Laboratory Theater toured Europe, but it was as a theorist that he made his mark with the publication in 1968 of *Towards a Poor Theater,* which advocated eliminating every nonessential element from theater, until it was reduced to the only components that could not be omitted without destroying theater itself—the actor and the audience. The heavy physical and psychic demands of his acting method drew mainly on the Russians, while his approach to stagecraft makes the audience play a role in the drama unself-consciously through its psychological response. Eventually he took the final step of eliminating theater itself in favor of rituals re-creating the archetypal experiences on which he believed theater was ultimately based.

In contrast to Europe, the United States government gave little support to theater after the war. American theater nonetheless prospered in small houses across the land, thanks to a revival of the Little Theater movement, which had struggled during the Great Depression. In New York experimental theater thrived off-Broadway. Major new regional companies were formed as well, particularly the Tyrone Guthrie Theater in Minneapolis, established in 1963. The most prominent organization was the Actors Studio, which was co-founded in 1947 by the director Elia Kazan, although Lee Strasberg soon became the key figure. It was the first theater to promote the "method acting" of Stanislavsky (see page 795), which dominated the American stage into the 1960s. It also staged the first classics of American postwar drama: *A Streetcar Named Desire* (1947) by Tennessee Williams (1911–1983), and *Death of a Salesman* (1949) by Arthur Miller (born 1916). The former, featuring the actor Marlon Brando in his first important role as the brutish Stanley Kowalski, is an unforgettable play about sex, madness, and violence in the South, while the latter, which focuses on the American dream of success, was written as a classical tragedy about the common man. As in the other arts, the period since 1945 has witnessed the high tide of writing for the American stage.

The most important playwright of the 1960s was Edward Albee (born 1928), who began as an absurdist, then turned to dramas (*Who's Afraid of Virginia Woolf,* 1962) about how people deal psychologically with inner and external reality, before becoming an iconoclast whose meanings are ambiguous (*The Marriage Play,* 1987). In 1964 Sam Shepard (born 1943) won an Obie Award for his first play, *Cowboy,* centering on his favorite theme, the American West, treated in archetypal terms. The late 1960s and early 1970s were a time of turmoil everywhere. In addition to student riots in France and America in 1968, there were protests against the Vietnam War, which found expression in such plays as *America Hurrah!* (1967) by Jean-Claude van Itallie (born 1936) and *Sticks and Bones* (1971) by David Rabe (born 1940).

1084. Francis Bacon. *Head Surrounded by Sides of Beef.* 1954. Oil on canvas, 50³/4 x 48" (129 x 122 cm). The Art Institute of Chicago
Harriott A. Fox Fund

the personages that inhabits Appel's work from that period, is an explosion of color applied with a brilliant technique that at first hides the figural elements lurking within the painting. In maintaining the importance of content while thoroughly integrating it with the style of Abstract Expressionism, Appel established a precedent which was followed by many other European artists, as well as by a number of American painters who have become preoccupied with the same problem.

BACON. The English artist Francis Bacon (1909–1992) was allied not with Abstract Expressionism, though he was clearly related to it, but with the Expressionist tradition. For his power to transmute sheer anguish into visual form he had no equal among twentieth-century artists unless it be Rouault (see pages 482–83). Bacon often derived his imagery from other artists, freely combining several sources while transforming them so as to infuse them with new meaning. *Head Surrounded by Sides of Beef* (fig. 1084) reflects Bacon's obsession with Velázquez' *Pope Innocent X* (compare fig. 758), a picture that haunted him for some years. It is, of course, no longer Innocent X we see here but a screaming ghost, inspired by a scene from Sergei Eisenstein's film *Alexander Nevsky,* that is materializing out of a black void in the company of two luminescent sides of beef taken from a painting by Rembrandt. Knowing the origin of the canvas does not help us to understand it, however. Nor does comparison with earlier works such as Grünewald's *The Crucifixion,* Fuseli's *Nightmare,* Ensor's *Christ's Entry into Brussels in 1889,* or Munch's *The Scream* (see figs. 696, 884, 988, and 989), which are its antecedents. Bacon was a gambler, a risk taker, in real life as well as in the way he worked. What he sought are images that, in his

1085. Mark Rothko. *Orange and Yellow.* 1956. Oil on canvas, 7'7" x 5'11" (2.31 x 1.8 m). Albright-Knox Art Gallery, Buffalo, New York
Gift of Seymour H. Knox, 1956

1086. Helen Frankenthaler. *The Bay.* 1963. Acrylic on canvas, 6'8³/4" x 6'9³/4" (2.05 x 2.08 m). The Detroit Institute of Arts
Gift of Dr. and Mrs. Hilbert H. DeLawter

own words, "unlock the deeper possibilities of sensation." Here he competes with Velázquez, but on his own terms, which are to set up an almost unbearable tension between the shocking violence of his vision and the luminous beauty of his brushwork.

Color Field Painting

By the late 1940s, a number of artists began to transform Action Painting into a style called Color Field Painting, in which the canvas is stained with thin, translucent color washes. These may be oil or even ink, but the favored material quickly became acrylic, a plastic suspended in a polymer resin, which can be thinned with water so that it flows freely.

ROTHKO. In the mid-1940s Mark Rothko worked in a style derived from the Surrealists, then adopted the gestures of early Action Painting, but within a few years his forms began to coalesce, until he subdued the aggressiveness of Action Painting so completely that his mature pictures breathe the purest contemplative stillness. *Orange and Yellow* (fig. 1085) consists of two rectangles with blurred edges on a pale red ground. The lower rectangle seems immersed in the red ground, while the upper rectangle stands out more assertively in front of the red. The canvas is very large, over seven and one-half feet high, and the thin washes of color permit the texture of the cloth to be seen. This description hardly begins to touch the essence of the

work, or the reasons for its mysterious power to move us. These are to be found in the delicate equilibrium of the shapes, their strange interdependence, and the subtle variations of hue, which seem to immerse the beholder in the painting. For those attuned to the artist's special vision, the experience can be akin to a trancelike rapture. Yet Rothko sought to convey not a mystical experience but a tragic outlook, for he possessed a melancholy, philosophical cast of mind. The overarching theme of his paintings is the tragedy of the human condition in the face of inevitable death. His bold, simplified forms are intended to function as universal symbols that express the most elemental meaning of life by condensing the drama of existence to its very essence.

FRANKENTHALER. The stained canvas was also pioneered by Helen Frankenthaler (born 1928), who was inspired by Rothko's example as early as 1952. In *The Bay* (fig. 1086) Frankenthaler uses the same biomorphic forms basic to early Action Painting but eliminates the personal handwriting found in the brushwork of Gorky and De Kooning. The results are reminiscent of O'Keeffe's paintings in their lyrical and decorative qualities, and no less impressive (compare fig. 1074).

LOUIS. A visit to Frankenthaler's studio in 1953 proved decisive for Morris Louis (1912–1962), perhaps the most gifted of all the Color Field painters. The following year he painted his first "veil" paintings, then struggled unsuccessfully for several

1087. Morris Louis. *Blue Veil.* 1958–59. Acrylic resin paint on canvas,
7'7³/4" x 13' (2.3 x 4 m). Fogg Art Museum, Harvard University Art Museums, Cambridge, Massachusetts
Gift of Lois Orswell and Purchase from the Gifts for Special Uses Fund

1088. Ellsworth Kelly. *Red Blue Green.* 1963. Oil on canvas,
7'8" x 11'4" (2.34 x 3.45 m). Museum of Contemporary Art, San Diego, La Jolla, California
Gift of Jack and Carolyn Farris

years before inaugurating a second series that proved even more majestic. The successive layers of color in *Blue Veil* (fig. 1087) have been "floated on" without visible marks of the brush. Their harmonious interaction creates a delicately shifting balance, like the aurora borealis, that gives the picture its mysterious beauty. How did Louis achieve this mesmerizing effect, so akin to late paintings by Monet (see fig. 943)? We do not know for certain, but he seems to have poured his gossamer-thin paints down the canvas, which he tilted and turned to give direction to their flow. Needless to say, it took a great deal of experimentation to arrive at the seemingly effortless perfection seen in our example.

Late Abstract Expressionism

KELLY. Many artists who came to maturity in the 1950s turned away from Action Painting altogether in favor of hard-edge painting. *Red Blue Green* (fig. 1088) by Ellsworth Kelly

1089. Frank Stella. *Empress of India*. 1965. Metallic powder in polymer
emulsion on canvas, 6'5" x 18'8" (1.9 x 5.7 m). The Museum of Modern Art, New York
Gift of S. I. Newhouse, Jr.

(born 1923), an early leader of this tendency, abandons Roth-ko's impressionistic softness. Instead, flat areas of color are circumscribed within carefully delineated forms as part of the formal investigation of color and design problems for their own sake.

This radical abstraction of form is known as Minimalism, which implies an equal reduction of content. It was a quest for basic elements representing the fundamental aesthetic values of art, without regard to issues of content. Minimalism was a necessary, even valuable phase, of modern art. At its most extreme, it reduced art not to an eternal essence but to an arid simplicity. In the hands of a few artists of genius like Kelly, however, it yielded works of unprecedented formal perfection.

STELLA. The brilliant and precocious Frank Stella (born 1936) began as an admirer of Mondrian, then soon evolved a nonfigurative style that was even more self-contained. Unlike Mondrian (see pages 805–6), Stella did not concern himself with the vertical-horizontal balance that relates the older artist's work to the world of nature. Logically enough, he also abandoned the traditional rectangular format, to make quite sure that his pictures bore no resemblance to windows. The shape of the canvas had now become an integral part of the design. In one of his largest works, the majestic *Empress of India* (fig. 1089), this shape is determined by the thrust and counterthrust of four huge chevrons, identical in size and shape but sharply differentiated in color and in their relationship to the whole. The paint, moreover, contains powdered metal which gives it an iridescent sheen. This is yet another way to stress the impersonal precision of the surfaces and to remove the work from any comparison with the "handmade" look of easel pictures. In fact, to call *Empress of India* a picture is something of a misnomer. It demands to be thought of as an object, sufficient unto itself.

African-American Painting

Following World War II, blacks began to attend art schools in growing numbers, at the very time that Abstract Expressionism marked the coming of age of American art. The civil rights movement helped them to establish their artistic identities and find appropriate styles for expressing them. The turning point proved to be the assassinations of Malcolm X in 1965 and Martin Luther King, Jr., in 1968, which provoked an outpouring of African-American art.

Since then, black artists have pursued three major tendencies. Mainstream Abstractionists, particularly those of the older generation, tend to be concerned primarily with seeking a personal aesthetic, maintaining that there is no such thing as African-American, or black, art, only good art. Consequently, they have been denounced by activist artists who, stirred by social consciousness as well as by political ideology, have adopted highly expressive representational styles as the means for communicating a distinctive black perspective directly to the people in their communities. Mediating between these two approaches is a more decorative form of art that frequently incorporates African, Caribbean, and even Mexican motifs. Abstraction has proved the most fruitful path, for it has opened up avenues of expression that allow black artists, however private their concerns may be, to achieve a universal, not only an ethnic, statement.

BEARDEN. No hard-and-fast rules separate these alternatives, however, and aspects of each have often been combined into individual styles. Certainly the most successful synthesis was realized by Romare Bearden (1911–1988). [See Primary Sources, no. 106, pages 944–45.] Although he got his start in the 1930s, it was not until the mid-1950s that he decided to devote his career entirely to art. Over the course of his long life, he pursued interests in mathematics, philosophy, and

1090. Romare Bearden. *The Prevalence of Ritual: Baptism.* 1964. Collage of photochemical reproduction, synthetic polymer, and pencil on paperboard, 9¹/8 x 12" (23.2 x 30.5 cm). Hirshhorn Museum and Sculpture Garden, Smithsonian Institution, Washington, D.C.

Gift of Joseph H. Hirshhorn, 1966

music that enriched his work. Bearden was inevitably affected by Abstract Expressionism but, dissatisfied with the approach, abandoned it in favor of a collage technique, although abstraction remained the underpinning of his art. His reputation was established during the mid-1960s by photomontages such as *The Prevalence of Ritual: Baptism* (fig. 1090). Bearden's aim, as he put it, was to depict "the life of my people as I know it, passionately and dispassionately as Brueghel. My intention is to reveal through pictorial complexities the life I know." He had a full command of the resources of Western and African art. Our example is as intricate in its composition as Terbrugghen's *The Calling of St. Matthew* (fig. 771), but it is couched in the familiar forms of tribal masks. The picture fulfills Bearden's goals so completely that it exercises an immediate appeal to people of all races. His widespread popularity was a breakthrough that inspired other African-American artists.

WILLIAMS. William T. Williams (born 1942) belongs to the generation of African-Americans born around 1940 who have brought black painting and sculpture to artistic maturity. He was initially a member of the "lost" generation of the lyrical Expressionists from the early 1970s whose contribution has been largely overlooked. After a period of intense self-scrutiny, he developed the sophisticated technique seen in *Batman* (fig. 1091). His method can be compared to jazz improvisation, a debt that the artist himself has acknowledged. He interweaves his color and brushwork within a contrasting two-part structure that permits endless variations on the central theme. Although Williams is concerned primarily with formal issues, the play of color across the encrusted surface evokes the light,

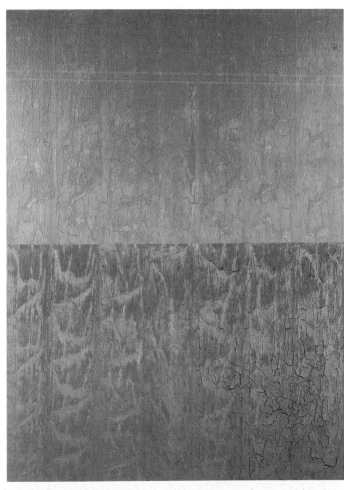

1091. William T. Williams. *Batman.* 1979. Acrylic on canvas, 6'8" x 5' (2.03 x 1.52 m). Collection the artist

1092. Raymond Saunders. *White Flower Black Flower.* 1986. Mixed media on canvas,
6'7" x 8'9³/4" (2.00 x 2.53 m). Private collection

patterns, and texture of a landscape, one that is deeply rooted in the artist's memory of the rural South where he spent his childhood.

SAUNDERS. With Williams, it is the intense effort to build up meaning through dense layers of paint within a clear framework that impresses. By contrast, the work of Raymond Saunders (born 1934) has a spontaneous creativity that emanates equally from his reservoir of memories. He was among the first artists to explore the urban African-American environment. Graffiti, church facades, store signs, restaurant menus, and other commercial images—these and like motifs are grist for his mill. The specific combination in *White Flower Black Flower* (fig. 1092) holds no literal meaning and arises purely through free association. By the same token, there is no precise order, despite the formal presentation. A brilliant technician, Saunders feels at liberty to juxtapose the representational and the abstract, "real" collage elements and "imitation" graffiti, pure geometry and painterly gesture. These components are nevertheless related thematically and aesthetically through their origin in Saunders' experience. We may see this approach as a stratagem that permits him to have the best of both worlds by fusing the unique features of black culture with a singular form of abstraction in a way that resists ready categorization.

Op Art

A trend that gathered force in the mid-1950s was known as Op Art because of its concern with optics: the physical and psychological process of vision. Op Art has been devoted primarily to optical illusions. Needless to say, all representational art from the Old Stone Age onward has been involved with optical illusion in one sense or another. What is new about Op Art is that it is rigorously nonrepresentational. It evolved partly from hard-edge abstraction, although its ancestry can be traced back still further to Mondrian (see page 904). At the same time, it seeks to extend the realm of optical illusion in every possible way by taking advantage of the new materials and processes constantly supplied by science, including laser technology. Much Op Art consists of constructions or "environments" (see page 867) that are dependent for their effect on light and motion and cannot be reproduced satisfactorily in a book.

Because of its reliance on science and technology, Op Art's possibilities appear to be unlimited. The movement nevertheless matured within a decade of its inception and developed little thereafter. The difficulty lies primarily with its subject. Op Art seems overly cerebral and systematic, more akin to the sciences than to the humanities. Op Art often involves the beholder with the work of art in a truly novel, dynamic way. But although its effects are undeniably fascinating, they encompass a relatively narrow range of concerns that lie for the

1093. Josef Albers. *Apparition*, from *Homage to the Square* series. 1959. Oil on masonite, 47¹/₂ x 47¹/₂" (120.7 x 120.7 cm). Solomon R. Guggenheim Museum, New York

1094. Richard Anuszkiewicz. *Entrance to Green.* 1970. Acrylic on canvas, 9' x 6' (2.74 x 1.83 m). Collection the artist

most part outside the mainstream of modern art. Only a handful of artists have enriched it with the variety and expressiveness necessary to make it a viable tradition.

ALBERS. Josef Albers (1888–1976), who came to America after 1933, when Hitler closed the Bauhaus school at Dessau (see page 874), became the founder of the mainstream of Op Art. He preferred to work in series that allowed him to explore each theme fully before moving on to a new subject. Albers devoted the latter part of his career to color theory. *Homage to the Square* (fig. 1093), his final series, is concerned with subtle color relations among simple geometric shapes, which he reduced to a few basic types. Within these confines, he was able to invent almost endless combinations based on rules he devised through ceaseless experimentation. Basically, Albers relied on color scales in which primary hues are desaturated in perceptually even gradations by giving them higher values (that is, by diluting them with white or gray). A step from one color scale can be substituted for the same step in another; these in turn can be combined by following the laws of color mixing, complementary colors, and so forth. This approach requires the utmost sensitivity to color, and even though the paint is taken directly from commercially available tubes, the colors bear a complex relation to each other. In our example, the artist creates a strong optical push-pull through the play of

closely related colors of contrasting value. The exact spatial effect is determined not only by hue and intensity of the pigments but by their sequence and the relative size of the squares.

ANUSZKIEWICZ. Albers was an important teacher as well as theorist. His gifted pupil Richard Anuszkiewicz (born 1930) developed his art by relaxing Albers' self-imposed restrictions. In *Entrance to Green* (fig. 1094), the ever-decreasing series of rectangles creates a sense of infinite recession toward the center. This is counterbalanced by the color pattern, which brings the center close to us by the gradual shift from cool to warm tones as we move inward from the periphery. Surprising for such an avowedly theoretical work is its expressive intensity. The resonance of the colors within the strict geometry heightens the optical push-pull, producing an almost mystical power. The painting can be likened to a modern icon, capable of providing a deeply moving experience to those attuned to its vision.

Pop Art

Other artists who made a name for themselves in the mid-1950s rediscovered what the public continued to take for granted despite all efforts to persuade otherwise: that a picture is not "essentially a flat surface covered with colors," as Maurice

1095. Richard Hamilton. *Just What Is It That Makes Today's Home So Different, So Appealing?*
1956. Collage on paper, 10¼ x 9¼" (26 x 24.8 cm).
Kunsthalle Tübingen. Sammlung Zundel, Germany

Denis had insisted, but an image wanting to be recognized. If art was by its very nature representational, then the modern movement, from Manet to Pollock, was based on a fallacy, no matter how impressive its achievements. Painting, it seemed, had been on a kind of voluntary starvation diet for the past hundred years, feeding upon itself rather than on the world around us. It was time to give in to the "image-hunger" thus built up—a hunger from which the public at large had never suffered, since its demand for images was abundantly supplied by photography, advertising, magazine illustrations, and comic strips.

The artists who felt this way seized on the products of commercial art catering to popular taste. Here, they realized, was an essential aspect of our century's visual environment that had been entirely disregarded as vulgar and antiaesthetic by the representatives of "highbrow" culture, a presence that cried out to be examined. Only Marcel Duchamp and some of the Dadaists, with their contempt for all orthodox opinion, had dared to penetrate this realm (see page 806). It was they who now became the patron saints of Pop Art, as the new movement came to be called.

HAMILTON. Pop Art actually began in London in the mid-1950s with the Independent Group of artists and intellectuals. They were fascinated by the impact on British life of the American mass media, which had been flooding England ever since the end of World War II. The first work that can be called an unequivocal statement of Pop Art was a small collage (fig. 1095) made in 1956 by Richard Hamilton (born 1922), a follower of Marcel Duchamp, which already incorporates most of the themes that were taken up by later artists: comic

strips, cinema, commercial design, nudes, cheap décor, appliances, all tokens of modern materialistic culture.

It is not surprising that the new art had a special appeal for America, and that it reached its fullest development there during the following decade. In retrospect, Pop Art in the United States was an expression of the optimistic spirit of the 1960s that began with the election of John F. Kennedy and ended at the height of the Vietnam War. Unlike Dada, Pop Art was not motivated by despair or disgust at contemporary civilization. It viewed commercial culture as its raw material, an endless source of pictorial subject matter, rather than as an evil to be attacked. Nor did Pop Art share Dada's aggressive attitude toward the established values of modern art.

JOHNS. The work of Jasper Johns (born 1930), one of the pioneers of Pop Art in America, raises questions that go beyond the boundaries of the movement. Johns began by painting, meticulously and with great precision, such familiar objects as flags, targets, numerals, and maps (see fig. 24). His *Three Flags* (fig. 1096) presents an intriguing problem: just what is the difference between image and reality? We instantly recognize the Stars and Stripes, but if we try to define what we actually see here, we find that the answer eludes us. These flags behave "unnaturally." Instead of waving or flopping they stand at attention, as it were, rigidly aligned with each other in a kind of reverse perspective. Yet there is movement of another sort: the reds, whites, and blues are not areas of solid color but subtly modulated. Can we really say, then, that this is an image of three flags? Clearly, no such flags can exist anywhere except in the artist's head. The more we think about it, the more we begin to recognize the picture as a feat of the

1096. Jasper Johns. *Three Flags.* 1958. Encaustic on canvas, 30⁷/8 x 45¹/2 x 5" (78.4 x 115.6 x 12.7 cm). Whitney Museum of American Art, New York

imagination—probably the last thing we expected to do when we first looked at it.

LICHTENSTEIN. Revolutionary though it was, Johns' use of flags, numerals, and similar elements as pictorial themes had to some extent been anticipated 30 years before by another American painter, Charles Demuth, in such pictures as *I Saw the Figure 5 in Gold* (fig. 1055). Roy Lichtenstein (born 1923), in contrast, has seized on comic strips—or, more precisely, on the standardized imagery of the traditional strips devoted to violent action and sentimental love, rather than those bearing the stamp of an individual creator. His paintings, such as *Drowning Girl* (fig. 1097), are greatly enlarged copies of single frames, including the balloons, the impersonal, simplified black outlines, and the dots used for printing colors on cheap paper. [See Primary Sources, no. 107, page 845.]

These pictures are perhaps the most paradoxical in the entire field of Pop Art. Unlike any other paintings past or present, they cannot be accurately reproduced in this book, for they then become indistinguishable from real comic strips. Enlarging a design meant for an area only a few inches square to one several hundred times greater must have given rise to a host of formal problems that could be solved only by the most intense scrutiny: how, for example, to draw the girl's nose so it would look "right" in comic-strip terms, or how to space the colored dots so they would have the proper weight in relation to the outlines.

Clearly, our picture is not a mechanical copy, but an interpretation. In fact, it is excerpted from the original panel. It nevertheless remains faithful to the spirit of the original because of the countless changes and adjustments of detail that

1097. Roy Lichtenstein. *Drowning Girl.* 1963. Oil and synthetic polymer paint on canvas, 67⁵/8 x 66³/4" (171.6 x 169.5 cm). The Museum of Modern Art, New York
Philip Johnson Fund and Gift of Mr. and Mrs. Bagley Wright

the artist has introduced. How is it possible for images of this sort to be so instantly recognizable? Why are they so "real" to millions of people? What fascinates Lichtenstein about comic strips—and what he makes us see for the first time—are the rigid conventions of their style, as firmly set and as remote from life as those of Byzantine art.

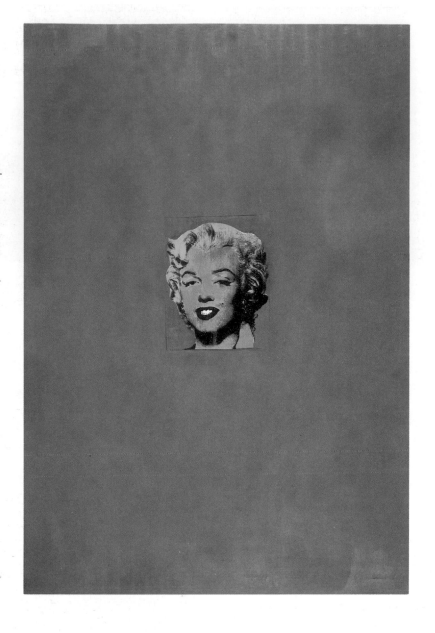

1098. Andy Warhol.
Gold Marilyn Monroe. 1962.
Synthetic polymer paint,
silkscreened, and oil on
canvas, 6'11¼" x 4'7"
(2.12 x 1.4 m).
The Museum of Modern
Art, New York
Gift of Philip Johnson

WARHOL. Andy Warhol (1928–1987) used this very quality in ironic commentaries on modern society. A former commercial artist, he made the viewer consider the aesthetic qualities of everyday images, such as soup cans, that we readily overlook. He did much the same thing with the subject of death, an obsession of his, in silk-screened pictures of electric chairs and gruesome traffic accidents, which demonstrate that dying has been reduced to a banality by the mass media. Warhol had an uncanny understanding of how media shape our view of people and events, creating their own reality and larger-than-life figures. He became a master at manipulating the media to project a public persona that disguised his true character. These themes come together in his *Gold Marilyn Monroe* (fig. 1098). Set against a gold background, like a Byzantine icon, she becomes a modern-day Madonna. Yet Warhol conveys a sense of the tragic personality that lay behind the famous movie star's glamorous facade. The color, lurid and off-register like a reproduction in a sleazy magazine, makes us realize that she has been reduced to a cheap commodity. Through mechanical means, she is rendered as impersonal as the Virgin that stares out from the thousands of icons produced by hack artists through the ages.

Photorealism

Although Pop Art was sometimes referred to as "the new realism," the term hardly seems to fit the painters we have discussed. They are, to be sure, sharply observant of their sources. However, their chosen material is itself rather abstract: flags, numerals, lettering, signs, badges, comic strips. A more recent offshoot of Pop Art is the trend called Photorealism because of its fascination with camera images. Photographs had been utilized by nineteenth-century painters soon after the "pencil of nature" was invented (one of the earliest to do so, surprisingly, was Delacroix) but they were no more than a convenient substitute for reality. For the Photorealists, in contrast, the photograph itself is the reality on which they build their pictures.

EDDY. Their work often has a visual complexity that challenges the most acute observer. *New Shoes for H* (fig. 1099) by

1099. Don Eddy. *New Shoes for H.* 1973–74. Acrylic on canvas, 44 x 48"(111.7 x 121.9 cm). The Cleveland Museum of Art
Purchased with a grant from the National Endowment
for the Arts and matched by gifts from members of The Cleveland Society
for Contemporary Art

1100. Don Eddy. Photograph for *New Shoes for H.* 1973–74.
The Cleveland Museum of Art
Gift of the artist

Don Eddy (born 1944), shows Photorealism at its best. Eddy grew up in southern California. As a teenager he learned to do fancy paint jobs on cars and surfboards with an air brush, then worked as a photographer for several years. When he became a painter, he used both earlier skills. In preparing *New Shoes for H,* Eddy took a series of pictures of the window display of a shoe store on Union Square in Manhattan. One photograph (fig. 1100) served as the basis for the painting. What intrigued him, clearly, was the way glass filters and alters everyday reality. Only a narrow strip along the left-hand edge offers an unobstructed view. Everything else—the shoes, bystanders, street traffic, buildings—is seen through one or more layers of glass, all of them at oblique angles to the picture surface. The familiar scene is transformed into a dazzlingly rich and novel visual experience by the combined displacement, distortion, and reflection of these panes.

When we compare the painting with the photograph, we realize that they are related in much the same way as Lichtenstein's *Drowning Girl* (fig. 1097) is to the original comic-strip frame from which it derives. Unlike the photograph, Eddy's canvas shows everything in uniformly sharp focus, articulating details lost in the shadows. Most important of all, he gives pictorial coherence to the scene through a brilliant color scheme whose pulsating rhythm plays over the entire surface. At the time he painted *New Shoes for H,* color had become newly important in Eddy's thinking. The H of the title pays homage to Henri Matisse and to Hans Hofmann, an Abstract Expressionist whom Eddy had come to admire.

ESTES. The acknowledged grand master of Photorealism is Richard Estes (born 1936). His work is marked by its technical perfection, which turns Photorealism into a form of Magic Realism. Masterful though it be, this ability is no better than that of any competent illustrator; nor does it distinguish him from the earlier Precisionists who often used

1101. Richard Estes. *Food Shop.* 1967. Oil on linen,
65 5/8 x 48 1/2" (166.7 x 123.2 cm). Museum Ludwig, Cologne

photographs as the basis for their paintings. What, then, is the key to his success? It lies in his choice of subject and composition. Estes has a predilection for store fronts of an earlier time that evoke nostalgic memories. In this he is like an archaeologist of modern urban life. His best paintings, such as *Food Shop* (fig. 1101), show the same uncanny ability to

1102. Audrey Flack. *Queen.* 1975–76. Acrylic on canvas, 6'8" (2.03 m) square. Private collection
Courtesy Louis K. Meisel Gallery, New York

strike a responsive chord as Hopper's *Early Sunday Morning* (see fig. 1075). The more we look at it, the more we realize that the gridlike composition is as subtly balanced as a painting by Mondrian (compare fig. 1057). In this way Estes elevates his humble store front to an arresting visual experience fully worthy of our attention.

FEMINISM. Photorealism was part of a general tendency that marked American painting in the 1970s: the resurgence of realism. It took on a wide range of themes and techniques, from the most personal to the most detached, depending on the artist's vision of objective reality and its subjective significance. Its flexibility made realism a sensitive vehicle for the feminist movement that came to the fore in the same decade. Beyond the organizing of groups dedicated to a wider recognition for women artists, feminism in art has shown little of the unity that characterizes the social movement. Many feminists, for example, turned to "traditional" women's crafts, particularly textiles, or incorporated crafts into a collage approach known as Pattern and Decoration. In painting, however, the majority pursued different forms of realism for a variety of ends.

FLACK. Women artists such as Audrey Flack (born 1931) have used realism to explore the world around them and their relation to it from a personal as well as a feminist viewpoint. Like most of Flack's paintings, *Queen* (fig. 1102) is an extended allegory. The queen is the most powerful figure on the chessboard yet she remains expendable in defense of the king.

Equally apparent is the meaning inherent to the queen of hearts, but here the card also refers to the passion for gambling in members of Flack's family, who are present in the locket with photos of the artist and her mother. The contrast of youth and age is central to *Queen:* the watch is a traditional emblem of life's brevity, and the dewy rose stands for transience of beauty, which is further conveyed by the makeup on the dressing table. The suggestive shapes of the bud and fruits can also be taken as symbols of feminine sexuality.

Queen is successful not so much for its statement, however provocative, as for its imagery. Flack creates a purely artistic reality by superimposing two separate photographs. Critical to the illusion is the gray border, which acts as a framing device and also establishes the central space and color of the painting. The objects that seem to project from the picture plane are shown in a different perspective from those on the tilted tabletop behind. The picture space is made all the more active by the play of its colors within the neutral gray.

LATE MODERNISM

Neo-Expressionism

The art we have looked at since 1945, although distinctive to the postwar era, is so closely related to what came before it that it was clearly cut from the same cloth, and we do not hesitate to call it modernist. At long last, however, twentieth-century painting, to which everything from Abstract Expressionism to

1103. Francesco Clemente. *Untitled.* 1983. Oil and wax on canvas, 6'6" x 7'9" (1.98 x 2.36 m)
Courtesy Thomas Ammann, Zurich

Photorealism made such a vital contribution, began to lose vigor. The first sign of decline came in the early 1970s with the widespread use of "Neo-" to describe the latest tendencies, which came and went in rapid succession and are all but forgotten today. Only one of these movements has made a lasting contribution: Neo-Expressionism, which arose toward the end of the decade and became the dominant current of the 1980s. Indeed, imagery of all kinds completely overshadowed Neo-Abstraction (also known as "Neo-Geo"), to the point that abstraction itself was declared all but dead by the critics. In its place was left a feeble imitation, which signified that modern art had turned its back to the mainstream. And despite the fact that Neo-Expressionism is deeply rooted in modernism, there can be little question that it represents the end of the tradition we have traced throughout this chapter.

Europe

CLEMENTE. The Italian Francesco Clemente (born 1952) is representative in many respects of his artistic generation in Europe. His association with the *Arte Povera* ("Poor Art") movement in Italy led him to develop a potent Neo-Expressionist style. His career took a decisive turn in 1982 when he decided to go to New York in order "to be where the great painters have been," but he also spends much of his time in India, where he has been inspired by Hinduism. His canvases and wall paintings sometimes have an ambitiousness that can assume the form of allegorical cycles addressed directly to the Italian painters who worked on a grand scale, starting with

Giotto. His most compelling works, however, are those having as their subject matter the artist's moods, fantasies, and appetites. Clemente is fearless in recording urges and memories that the rest of us repress. Art becomes for him an act of cathartic necessity that releases, but never resolves, the impulses that assault his acute self-awareness. His self-portraits (fig. 1103) suggest a soul bombarded by drives and sensations that can never be truly enjoyed. Alternately fascinating and repellent, his pictures remain curiously unsensual, yet their expressiveness is riveting. Since his work responds to fleeting states of mind, Clemente utilizes whatever style or medium seems appropriate to capturing the transient phenomena of his inner world. He is unusual among Italians in being influenced heavily by Northern European Symbolism and Expressionism with an occasional reminiscence of Surrealism. Here indeed is his vivid nightmare, having the masklike features of Ensor, the psychological terror of Munch, and the haunted vision of De Chirico.

KIEFER. The German artist Anselm Kiefer (born 1945) is the direct heir to Northern Expressionism, but rather than investigating personal moods he confronts moral issues posed by Nazism that have been evaded by other postwar artists in his country. By exploring the major themes of German Romanticism from a modern perspective, he has attempted to reweave the threads broken by history. That tradition, which began as a noble ideal based on a similar longing for the mythical past, ended as a perversion at the hands of Hitler and his followers because it lent itself readily to abuse.

At first glance, postwar music, like postwar art, seems almost chaotic in its diversity. Composers after 1945 have vastly extended the experiments of their early-twentieth-century predecessors. Many have resorted to extreme dissonance, incorporated chance (aleatory, from the Latin work for dice) events, treated music as a form of noise, and abandoned traditional notation. Others have written for newly invented electronic instruments, turned to repetitive motifs, or looked to non-Western music for inspiration. While these innovations have widened the scope of contemporary music, they often, like Abstract Expressionist painting, place extreme demands on the audience, requiring that it discard traditional standards to judge each work on its own terms. Nevertheless, certain sounds, textures, intervals, and rhythms are so widely used as to be virtual signatures of later twentieth-century music. Moreover, contemporary music is no more alien to twentieth-century ears than that of the late Middle Ages or Early Renaissance.

The most important composer of the postwar era was the Frenchman Olivier Messiaen (1908–1992). Like his predecessor Francis Poulenc (1899–1963), Messiaen was a devout Catholic, and his music bears witness to his faith, which remained remarkably pure even in the face of great adversity. Despite his position as a leader of the avant-garde, Messiaen created music of a haunting beauty that makes it remarkably accessible. Nowhere is Messiaen's cosmic vision more fully realized than in *Colors of the Heavenly City* (1963) for piano and ensemble, a kaleidoscopic yet ethereal evocation of the Apocalypse that uses exotic instruments and compositional modes from India and the Orient to suggest a universal spirituality. His music radiates an enchantment with God's creation that led him to incorporate transcriptions of bird songs in the delightful *Exotic Birds* (1955–56), for he delighted in and revered these simple creatures much as St. Francis of Assisi had before him. There is an intimate connection between these works: Messiaen associated the colors of the heavenly city with the brilliant plumage of birds, whose songs provided the inspiration for his music.

Messiaen was one of the first composers to apply the principles of serialism to timbre (tone color), time, rhythm, and dynamic level. His interest in twelve-tone techniques was stimulated by his pupils Pierre Boulez (born 1925) and Karlheinz Stockhausen (born 1928), on whom he in turn exerted a decisive influence. Boulez, the most intellectual composer on the scene today, has likewise extended serialism in all directions, but came to reject the twelve-tone row for a themeless (athematic) style that also permits carefully calculated "chance" effects and sometimes incorporates "concrete" (recorded) music (see below). *The Hammer Without a Master* (1954), inspired by the Surrealist poetry of René Char (1907–1988), has a rhythmic liveliness that belies its highly theoretical conception; by contrast, *Pli selon pli* (*Fold by Fold;* 1957–62), a sustained work for soprano and orchestra utilizing poems by Mallarmé, demands the utmost concentration to absorb its subtleties. The choice of Mallarmé is significant in itself. Not only was his Symbolist poetry the point of departure for Surrealists such as Char, but he was the first to allow reciters the opportunity to vary the choice and sequence of poems at will, a technique which Boulez used in *Pli selon pli* and which Stockhausen exploited around the same time.

Stockhausen's compositions, though no less complex than Boulez's, are more visceral in their power. He became associated early on with Pierre Schaeffer (born 1910), the leader of "concrete" music consisting of recorded natural sounds. Soon after it was invented in Germany in 1950, Stockhausen turned to the electronic synthesizer while continuing to compose for traditional instruments. These strands merged in the mid-1950s, when he experimented with multiple orchestras and choruses placed in different arrays under separate conductors. He also explored a succession of moments in time as a replacement for form, which he subsequently abandoned for free form that allowed players to improvize on brief texts.

The Polish composer Witold Lutoslawski (1913–1994) turned to serialism and aleatory music in 1958, despite the fact that such Western techniques were officially frowned on by Communist authorities. His mature instrumental and orchestral works, such as *Venetian Games* (1961), accord well with the music of Messiaen and Boulez, and he became among the most respected composers of the European avant-garde. After 1975 he pursued a more personal style that culminated in his fourth and final symphony, written in 1992, which begins with an evocation of haunting mystery and ends with a thunderous climax. Lutoslawski began his career in the mold of Bartók, who exercised considerable influence on the Polish school. Krzysztof Penderecki (born 1933) is a miniaturist at heart noted for his discrete use of dissonance. He shares spiritual concerns with Henryk Górecki (born 1933), whose tonalism and traditional religious emphasis have made him very popular in the West in recent years.

From the beginning the French-born composer Edgar Varèse (1883–1965) was a consummate maverick. Influenced by the "Brutism" of the Futurists, he became fascinated by sounds of all sorts, and soon began to utilize sirens and unusual percussion instruments to create novel effects. His major early contribution was three works written between 1918 and 1927 after he emigrated to the United States—*Amériques, Arcana,* and *Intégrales*—that treat the orchestra as a form of organized noise. All are marked by extreme dynamism in rhythm and volume. It is suggestive of Varèse's role in overturning tradition that *Arcana* is the kind of music Sibelius would have written if he had been a modernist composer in the vein of Stravinsky. Though he was a ceaseless experimenter, he never developed a system, which he considered a sign of impotence. It was not until the invention of the tape recorder in 1948 and the synthesizer two years later that Varèse found a medium ideally suited to his extraordinary vision. (He had tried to convince Bell Laboratories to set up an experimental research center around 1930, and even stopped composing around 1937 because he could not achieve the sounds he wanted.) Electronics allowed him to create and mix sounds of every conceivable sort into a new kind of total sound experience: the *poème électronique,* for the 1958 Brussels World's Fair, which stands as the first great masterpiece of American electronic music.

Varèse was precocious not only in coming to America at an early date but also in advocating experimental techniques far in advance of their time. American music reached maturity simultaneously with American art in the early 1950s and for many of the same reasons. During World War II many of Europe's leading composers—Stravinsky, Bartók, and Schoenberg among them—came to the United States, where they exercised considerable influence. The most important American composer of the postwar era was John Cage (1912–1992), who studied with Cowell, Varèse, and Schoenberg. Cage nevertheless owed his unique approach to music primarily to his wide range of interests: he made prints, composed scores for and toured with the avant-garde choreographer Merce Cunningham (born 1919), and organized light shows, among his many activities. During the 1940s he extended Cowell's use of the "prepared" piano by adding bits of "debris" from everyday life to produce unusual sounds. Like many American intellectuals during the 1950s he became interested in Zen Buddhism, which helped stimulate his fascination with chance events. "Chance" for Cage, however, must be understood not as total randomness but as improvisation within a defined context, since Cage considered music a kind of organized noise within the stream of life itself. For example, *Imaginary Landscape No. 4* (1951) uses 12 radios tuned to different frequencies established by the score, though the final result was unpredictable because what each radio was playing could not be predetermined. Such an attitude, we realize, comes very close to that of the Abstract Expressionists, particularly Jackson Pollock, who also relied on chance as a reflection of life. Like Messiaen, Cage sought a spiritual experience in his music; toward that end, silence—what is not there—is often just as important as the sounds themselves.

The foremost disciple of the synthesizer in America has been Milton Babbitt (born 1916), who helped to found the Columbia-Princeton Electronic Music Center in 1959. Like Boulez, he seeks to apply serialism to all aspects of music, including his quartets and compositions for orchestra, which incorporate synthesized sounds. Despite its profoundly logical basis, his music can be surprisingly expressive, almost in spite of itself. Babbitt studied under Roger Sessions (1896–1985), an early pioneer of modernism with Copland. The symphonies and chamber music Sessions composed after adopting the twelve-tone system in 1953 established him as one of America's leading composers. His masterpiece is the cantata *When Lilacs Last in the Dooryard Bloom'd* (1970), a haunting evocation of verses by Walt Whitman (1819–1892), the greatest of all American poets, dedicated to John F. Kennedy and Martin Luther King. Of equal stature is *Time Cycle* (1960) by Lukas Foss (born 1922), who was born in Europe and educated in Paris but came at the age of 15 to the United States, where he completed his training in

Philadelphia. Commissioned for the soprano Adele Addison, it consists of four extended songs based on English and German poetry that includes improvised interludes. Perhaps the most gifted member of the American school to emerge since World War II is Elliott Carter (born 1908). His four quartets are the finest since Bartók's, while *Variations for Orchestra* is the outstanding contribution to orchestral music in the United States from the 1950s.

The compositions of Luciano Berio (born 1925), a former associate of Stockhausen who emigrated to the United States, are mini-dramas (he often composes for the stage as well), which utilize every available modernist technique. He often treats the human voice as another instrument while employing speechlike sounds to suggest different emotional states. Of particular interest are the works he wrote for his wife, the soprano Cathy Berberian (1925–1983), notably *Recital* (1971), which deals with the nervous collapse of a singer. George Crumb (born 1929) has also used the human voice in new ways. *Ancient Voices of Children* (1970), inspired by the poetry of Federico García Lorca, is one of the great masterpieces of the twentieth century. It utilizes motifs similar to those of South and Central American Indians to conjure up a primeval state with unforgettable power. Crumb's work belongs to no school. Neither did that of Samuel Barber (1910–1981), a romantic with an extraordinary gift for melody. Although he felt the influence of Stravinsky's Neoclassicism, Barber's compositions for voice use dissonance discreetly to emphasize the text, to which he had a unique sensitivity. *Knoxville: Summer of 1915* (1947), commissioned by the soprano Eleanor Steber and set to a famous poem by James Agee, is surely the most purely beautiful vocal work by any American composer of the twentieth century.

The main tendency to emerge in recent years has been dubbed Minimalism, which uses many of the same devices as the art movement of the same name, albeit for different ends. It relies on the repetition of simple motifs that are gradually varied over time to create a hypnotic, almost mystical, effect, as in *Drumming* (1970–71) by Steve Reich (born 1936) and *In C* (1964) by Terry Riley (born 1943). These techniques were first explored by Stockhausen, whose music shares an inspiration in Eastern religion with Riley's. The most sophisticated products of Minimalism are the operas of Phillp Glass (born 1937), above all *Satyagraha* ("truthforce," a Sanskrit word that refers to the philosophy of nonviolent resistance practiced by Mahatma Gandhi and Martin Luther King). Minimalism is ideally suited to the text, which is drawn from the *Bhagavad-Gita* that forms part of the major Hindu religious epic known as the *Mahabharata.* Minimalism responds to the music and philosophy of other cultures, from Africa to Asia, but it also represents a "crossover" music that incorporates jazz and popular music, including rock and roll. It reinvests contemporary music with a tonality and accessibility that have won new audiences for the concert hall. In the process, it has enjoyed increasing influence—the recent symphonies of Górecki use Minimalist devices, for example.

1104. Anselm Kiefer. *To the Unknown Painter.* 1983.
Oil, emulsion, woodcut, shellac, latex, and straw on canvas, 9'2" (2.79 m) square. The Carnegie Museum of Art, Pittsburgh
Richard M. Scaife Fund; A. W. Mellon Acquisition Endowment Fund

To the Unknown Painter (fig. 1104) is a powerful statement of the human and cultural catastrophe presented by World War II. Conceptually as well as compositionally it was inspired by the paintings of Caspar David Friedrich (see page 692), of which it is a worthy successor. To express the tragic proportions of the Holocaust, Kiefer works on an appropriately epic scale. Painted in jagged strokes of predominantly earth and black tones, the charred landscape is made tangible by the inclusion of pieces of straw. Amid this destruction stands a somber ruin: it is shown in woodcut to proclaim Kiefer's allegiance to the German Renaissance and to Expressionism. The fortresslike structure is a suitable monument for heroes in recalling the tombs and temples of ancient civilizations (see figs. 56 and 87). But instead of being dedicated to soldiers who died in combat, it is a memorial to the painters whose art was equally a casualty of Fascism.

United States

ROTHENBERG. Neo-Expressionism has found its most gifted American representative in Susan Rothenberg (born 1945). In the mid-1970s the contours of the horse seen in profile provided a thematic focus and personal emblem for her highly formal paintings, but toward the end of the decade she turned to more emotive subjects. The sheer beauty of the surface in *Mondrian* (fig. 1105) belies the intensity of her vision. The figure emerges from the welter of feathery brushstrokes like an apparition from a nightmare. The face, which bears Mondrian's unmistakable features, conjures up a vision of madness. We have seen its like before in Bacon's *Head Surrounded by Sides of Beef* (fig. 1084). The picture, then, announces Rothenberg's allegiance to Expressionism and constitutes a highly charged commentary on Mondrian, whose rigorous discipline is so antithetical to her painterly freedom.

1105. Susan Rothenberg. *Mondrian*. 1983–84. Oil on canvas, 9'1" x 7' (2.8 x 2.1 m). Private collection
Courtesy Sperone Westwater Gallery, New York

1106. Jennifer Bartlett. *Water*. 1990. Oil on canvas, 7' x 7' (2.13 x 2.13 m). Private collection, Honolulu, Hawaii

BARTLETT. Jennifer Bartlett (born 1941) has long been recognized as a talented painter; absent, however, was content worthy of her ability. Like Audrey Flack before her (see page 836), she recently turned to a traditional motif which supplies that missing material. The four elements, a popular subject with artists during the Baroque and Rococo, has provided the focus for an extensive series that is as rich in meaning as it is in appearance. *Water* (fig. 1106), though reminiscent of Monet's *Water Lilies* (fig. 943), is no mere evocation of nature: floating half-in, half-above the water is a skeleton. Indeed, the real subject here is Vanitas, another theme associated with the elements and, in turn, the senses and the seasons (see pages 588–90). References to Fate, inexorable and quixotic, are found in the cards, dominoes, and other devices used in games and fortune-telling. These are seemingly "stuck" onto the canvas, along with illusionistic swatches of plaid material, which serve to deny the illusionism of the scene and emphasize the surface as an independent, formal entity; hence, too, the red container that seems to hover nonsensically in midair. This play between "two-D" and "three-D" has much the same effect as in Flack's *Queen* (fig. 1102), and it shares a similar meaning: it both enlivens the painting and places it at one remove from everyday reality, so that we are forced to contemplate its message instead of seeing it simply as a picture.

1107. Elizabeth Murray. *More Than You Know*. 1983.
Oil on ten canvases, 9'3" x 9' x 8" (2.8 m x 2.7 m x 20.3 cm).
The Edward R. Broida Trust
Courtesy PaceWildenstein, New York

1108. Kay WalkingStick. *On the Edge.* 1989. Acrylic, wax, and oil on canvas, 32 x 64 x 3½" (81.3 x 162.6 x 9 cm)
Courtesy M-13 Gallery, New York

MURRAY. Neo-Expressionism has a counterpart in Neo-Abstraction, which has yielded less impressive results thus far. The greatest success in the Neo-Abstractionist vein has been achieved by those artists seeking to infuse their formal concerns with the personal meaning of Neo-Expressionism. Elizabeth Murray (born 1940) has emerged since 1980 as the leader of this crossover style in America. *More Than You Know* (fig. 1107) makes a fascinating comparison with Audrey Flack's *Queen* (fig. 1102), for both are replete with autobiographical references. While it is at once simpler and more abstract than Flack's, Murray's composition seems about to fly apart under the pressure of barely contained emotions. The table will remind us of the one in Picasso's *Three Musicians* (fig. 1047), a painting she has referred to in other works from the same time. The contradiction between the flattened collage perspective of the table and chair and the allusions to the distorted three-dimensionality of the surrounding room establishes a disquieting pictorial space. The more we look at the painting, the more we begin to realize how eerie it is. Indeed, it seems to radiate an almost unbearable tension. The table threatens to turn into a figure, surmounted by a skull-like head, that moves with the explosive force of Picasso's *Three Dancers* (fig. 1049). What was Murray thinking of? She has said that the room reminds her of the place where she sat with her ill mother. At the same time, the demonic face was inspired by Munch's *The Scream* (fig. 989), while the sheet of paper

recalls Vermeer's paintings of women reading letters (fig. 789), which to her express a combination of serenity and anxiety.

WALKINGSTICK. An artist who has managed to combine Neo-Expressionism and Neo-Abstraction in a particularly fruitful way is Kay WalkingStick (born 1935). Part Cherokee, she was deeply affected by her Indian spiritual heritage, especially its reverence for the earth, although she was raised in white culture. The death of her husband in 1989 brought forth the literal outpouring of grief seen in *On the Edge* (fig. 1108), which combines two separate landscape forms in a format that she had experimented with briefly several years earlier. The two halves respond to entirely different impulses. The left panel, built up in thick coats of paint applied mainly with her hands, pursues the abstract manner she had developed successfully for more than a decade. In the center is a fan shape, which both suggests a man-made feature in a primitive landscape, like those of the ancient mound builders, and acts as a sign, investing the canvas with mysterious emblematic significance. The right half, painted in an Expressionist style, unleashes a torrent of anguish that is further expressed by the violent color. This duality has several layers of meaning. It can be seen as describing the contrasting aspects of nature as spiritual center and generative force, of order and chaos, of calm contemplation and powerful emotion. Thus both parts of the diptych are necessary to give the painting its full import.

CHAPTER FIVE

TWENTIETH-CENTURY SCULPTURE

SCULPTURE BEFORE WORLD WAR I

Sculpture, the most conservative of the arts throughout most of the nineteenth century, found it difficult to cast off the burden of tradition. It has remained far less adventurous on the whole than painting, which often influenced it. Indeed, the American sculptor David Smith (see page 856) claimed that modern sculpture was created by the painters, and to a remarkable degree he was right. Sculpture has successfully challenged the leadership of painting in our time only by following a separate path.

France

MATISSE. Some of the most important experiments in sculpture were conducted by Matisse in the years 1907–14, when he was inspired by ethnographic sculpture, although there had been a growing interest in "primitive" art on the part of painters like Gauguin even before the first major public collections began to be formed in 1890. At first glance, *Reclining Nude I* (fig. 1109) seems utterly removed from Matisse's paintings. Yet sculpture was a natural complement to his pictures, which often share its "savage" element. It allowed him to investigate problems of form that in turn provided important lessons for his canvases. While the bulging distortions in the anatomy of the *Nude* create an astonishing muscular tension, the artist was concerned above all with "arabesque": the rhythmic contours that define the nude. We will recognize the statuette's kinship with the recumbent figures in *The Joy of Life* (fig. 1021), which were also conceived in outline. But now these rhythms are explored plastically and manipulated for expressive effect. Remarkably, Matisse accomplishes this without diminishing the fundamentally classical character of the nude.

1109. Henri Matisse. *Reclining Nude I.* 1907.
Bronze, 13⁹/₁₆ x 19⁵/₈ x 11" (34.5 x 49.9 x 28 cm).
The Baltimore Museum of Art
The Cone Collection, formed by Dr. Claribel Cone and
Miss Etta Cone of Baltimore, Maryland

BRANCUSI. Sculpture remained only a sideline for Matisse. Perhaps for that reason, Expressionism was a much less important current in sculpture than in painting. This may seem surprising, since the rediscovery of ethnographic sculpture by the Fauves might have been expected to evoke a strong response among sculptors. Yet the only one who shared in this interest was Constantin Brancusi (1876–1957), a Romanian who went to Paris in 1904. However, he was more concerned with the formal simplicity and coherence of primitive carvings than with their savage expressiveness. This is evident in *The Kiss* (fig. 1110), executed in 1909 and now placed over a tomb in a Parisian cemetery.

The compactness and self-sufficiency of this group are a radical step beyond Maillol's *Seated Woman* (see fig. 994), to which it is related much as the Fauves are to Post-Impressionism. Brancusi has a "genius of omission" not unlike Matisse's. And his attitude toward art expresses the same optimistic faith so characteristic of early modernism: "Don't look for mysteries," he said. "I give you pure joy." To him, a monument is a permanent marker, like the steles of the ancients: an upright slab, symmetrical and immobile, and he disturbs this basic shape as little as possible. The embracing lovers are differentiated just enough to be separately identifiable, and seem more primeval than primitive. They are a timeless symbol of generation, innocent and anonymous—the exact opposite of Rodin's *The Kiss* (see fig. 956), where the contrast of flesh and stone mirrors the dualism of guilt and desire. Herein lies the genius of Brancusi: he posed the first successful alternative to Rodin, whose vast authority overwhelmed the creativity of many younger sculptors. In the process, Brancusi gave modern sculpture its independence.

Brancusi's work took another daring step about 1910, when he began to produce nonrepresentational pieces in marble or metal. (He reserved his "primeval" style for wood and stone.) The former fall into two groups: variations on the egg shape and soaring, vertical "bird" motifs. In concentrating on two basic forms of such uncompromising simplicity, Brancusi strove for essences, not for Rodin's illusion of growth. He was fascinated by the antithesis of life as potential and as kinetic energy: the self-contained perfection of the egg, which hides the mystery of all creation, and the pure dynamics of the creature released from this shell. *The Newborn* (fig. 1111) is a marvelously concise and witty, yet surprisingly sympathetic, portrayal of an infant's first cry upon entering the world.

Bird in Space (fig. 1112), made more than a decade later, is the culmination of Brancusi's art. It began as the figure of a mythical bird that talks, which he gradually simplified until it is no longer the abstract image of a bird. Rather, it is flight itself, made visible and concrete: "All my life I have sought the essence of flight," Brancusi stated, and he repeated the motif in variants of ever greater refinement. Its disembodied quality is emphasized by the high polish that gives the surface the reflectivity of a mirror, thus establishing a new continuity between the molded space within and the free space without.

CUBISM. In the second decade of the century a number of artists tackled the problem of body-space relationships with the formal tools of Cubism—no simple task, since Cubism was a painter's approach more suited to shallow relief and not

1110. Constantin Brancusi. *The Kiss.* 1909. Stone, height 35¼" (89.5 cm). Tomb of T. Rachevskaia, Montparnasse Cemetery, Paris

1111. Constantin Brancusi. *The Newborn.* 1915. Marble, length 8⅛" (20.7 cm). Philadelphia Museum of Art
Louise and Walter Arensberg Collection

1113. Raymond Duchamp-Villon. *The Great Horse.* 1914.
Bronze, height 39¼" (99.7 cm). The Art Institute of Chicago
Gift of Miss Margaret Fisher in memory of her parents,
Mr. and Mrs. Walter L. Fisher

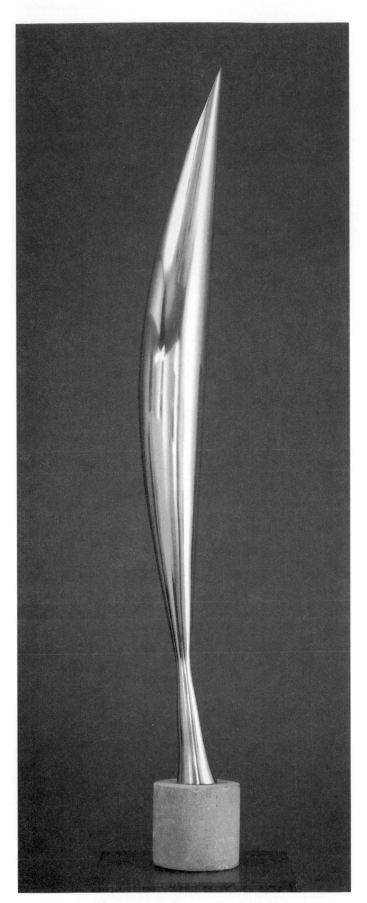

1112. Constantin Brancusi. *Bird in Space* (unique cast). 1928.
Bronze, 54 x 8½ x 6½" (137.2 x 21.6 x 16.5 cm).
The Museum of Modern Art, New York
Given anonymously

easily adapted to objects in the round. Most of the Cubist painters essayed at least a few sculptures, but the results were generally timid. Picasso's tentative efforts at sculpture attest to the difficulties he faced, yet they were of fundamental importance nonetheless. His attempts to translate the Analytic Cubism seen in *Portrait of Ambroise Vollard* (fig. 1034) into three-dimensional form succeeded only partially in breaking up the solid surface. Precisely because its facets are ambiguous in density and location, painting afforded an infinitely richer experience both visually and expressively.

DUCHAMP-VILLON. The boldest solution to the problems posed by Analytic Cubism in sculpture was achieved by the sculptor Raymond Duchamp-Villon (1876–1916), an elder brother of Marcel Duchamp, in *The Great Horse* (fig. 1113). He began with abstract studies of the animal, but his final version is an image of "horsepower," wherein the body has become a coiled spring and the legs resemble piston rods. Because of this very remoteness from their anatomical model, these quasi-mechanical shapes have a dynamism that is altogether persuasive.

Italy

BOCCIONI. In 1912 the Futurists suddenly became absorbed with making sculpture, which they sought to redefine as radically as painting. They used "force-lines" to create an "arabesque of directional curves" as part of a "systematization of the interpenetration of planes." Hence, as Umberto Boccioni declared, "We break open the figure and enclose it in

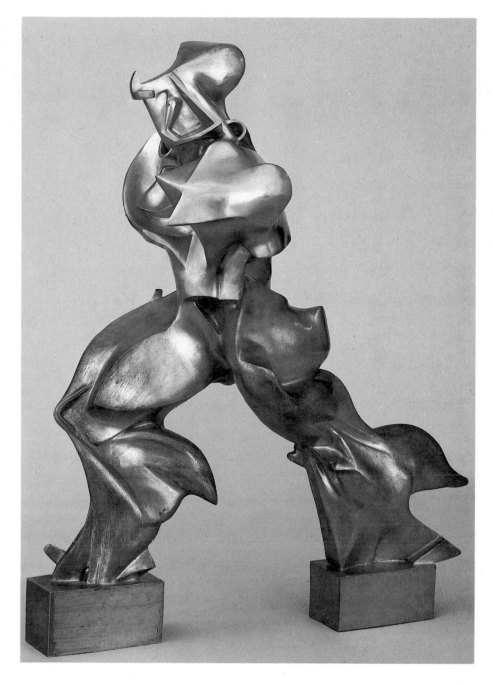

1114. Umberto Boccioni. *Unique Forms of Continuity in Space*. 1913. Bronze (cast 1931), 43⁷/8 x 34⁷/8 x 15³/4" (111.4 x 88.6 x 40 cm). The Museum of Modern Art, New York
Acquired through the Lillie P. Bliss Bequest

SCULPTURE BETWEEN THE WARS

Russia

environment." His running figure entitled *Unique Forms of Continuity in Space* (fig. 1114) is as breathtaking in its complexity as Brancusi's *Bird in Space* is simple. Boccioni has attempted to represent not the human form itself, but the imprint of its motion upon the medium in which it moves. The figure itself remains concealed behind its "garment" of aerial turbulence. The picturesque statue recalls the famous Futurist statement that "the roaring automobile is more beautiful than the Winged Victory," although it obviously owes more to the *Winged Victory* (the *Nike of Samothrace,* fig. 214) than to the design of motor cars. (Fins and streamlining, in 1913, were still to come.)

CONSTRUCTIVISM. In Analytic Cubism, concave and convex were postulated as equivalents. All volumes, whether positive or negative, were "pockets of space." The Constructivists, a group of Russian artists led by Vladimir Tatlin (1895–1956), applied this principle to relief sculpture and arrived at what might be called three-dimensional collage.

TATLIN. Eventually the final step was taken of making the works free-standing. According to Tatlin and his followers, these "constructions" were actually four-dimensional: since they implied motion, they also implied time. Suprematism (see page 796) and Constructivism were therefore closely

1115. Vladimir Tatlin. Project for *Monument to the Third International*. 1919–20. Wood, iron, and glass, height 20' (6.1 m). Destroyed; contemporary photograph

1116. Naum Gabo. *Linear Construction #1* (smaller version). 1942–43. Plexiglass and nylon thread on plexiglass base, 12¼ x 12¼ x 2¾" (31.1 x 31.1 x 6.9 cm). Hirshhorn Museum and Sculpture Garden, Smithsonian Institution, Washington, D.C.
Gift of Joseph H. Hirshhorn, 1966

related, and in fact overlapped, for both had their origins in Cubo-Futurism. They were nonetheless separated by a fundamental difference in approach. For Tatlin, art was not the Suprematists' spiritual contemplation but an active process of formation that was based on material and technique. He believed that each material dictates specific forms that are inherent in it, and that these must be followed if the work of art was to be valid according to the laws of life itself. In the end, Constructivism won out over Suprematism because it was better suited to the post-Revolution temperament of Russia, when great deeds, not great thoughts, were needed.

Cut off from artistic contact with Europe during World War I, Constructivism developed into a uniquely Russian art that was little affected by the return of some of the country's most important artists, such as Kandinsky and Chagall. The Revolution galvanized the modernists, who celebrated the overthrow of the old regime with a creative outpouring throughout Russia.

Tatlin's model for a *Monument to the Third International* (fig. 1115) captures the dynamism of the technological utopia envisioned under Communism. Pure energy is expressed as lines of force that establish new time-space relationships as well. The work also implies a new social structure, for the Constructivists believed in the power of art literally to reshape society. This extraordinary tower revolving at three speeds was conceived on a monumental scale, complete with Communist

Party offices. Like other such projects, however, it was wildly impractical in a society still recovering from the ravages of war and revolution and was never built.

Constructivism subsequently proceeded to a Productivist phase, which ignored any contradiction between true artistic creativity and purely utilitarian production. After the movement had been suppressed as "bourgeois formalism," a number of its members emigrated to the West, where they joined forces with the few movements still espousing abstraction.

GABO.   The most important of these was Naum Gabo (1890–1977), who went first to Berlin, then to England, before settling in America after World War II. His main contribution to modern art came in the early 1940s, when he created a new kind of plastic construction strung with nylon filament (fig. 1116) that comes very close to mathematical models. Although he arrived at it through intuition, the parallels to contemporary scientific theory are astonishing, for his work embodies much the same spatiality as modern physics. Gabo was fascinated by the links between art and science, which, he said, "arise from the same creative source and flow into the same ocean of the common culture." Like Kandinsky's, his motives were purely spiritual, and he saw Constructivism as a vehicle of change. None of this, however, accounts for the elegance of Gabo's linear constructions, which embody an entirely modern sensibility.

1117. Georges Vantongerloo. *Métal: $y=ax^3-bx^3+cx$*. 1935.
Argentine, height 15" (38 cm). Emanuel Hoffmann Foundation,
Basel, on loan to Kunstmuseum Basel

France

VANTONGERLOO. Soon after arriving in Berlin, Gabo was in touch with *De Stijl,* the Dutch group. Its only true sculptor was the Belgian Georges Vantongerloo (1886–1965), who settled in Paris. He, too, was obsessed with the problem of how to represent space. *Métal: $y=ax^3-bx^3+cx$* (fig. 1117) is a daring prefiguration of Minimalist sculpture of the 1950s and 1960s. Whereas Mondrian's grids were never governed by strict ratios, Vantongerloo used the same bands to articulate space by establishing precise relationships as defined by the algebraic formula. The artist, however, saw this method as a means of expressing an intuition of creation, which is infinite

1118. Jacques Lipschitz. *Figure.* 1926–30 (cast 1937). Bronze, height 7'1¼" (2.17 m). The Museum of Modern Art, New York
Van Gogh Purchase Fund

and is perceived only through our sensitivity. His was indeed an ecstatic vision: "O! The incommensurable is never the same; if it were, it would be commensurable. And as the universe is incommensurable, what we need is an expression that would have neither end nor beginning; and this too exists." Ultimately this realization led him to abandon his sparse geometry for a curvilinear approach, based not on classical Euclidian geometry but on Cartesian analytical geometry, to describe parabolic equations.

LIPSCHITZ. Contrary to what one might have expected, the everyday materials of Synthetic Cubism proved of far greater interest to painters than to the Cubist sculptors, who maintained a traditional allegiance to bronze. After World War I sculptors in France largely forsook abstraction and abandoned Expressionism altogether. Only the Lithuanian-born Jacques Lipschitz (1891–1973), a friend of both Picasso and Matisse, continued to explore the possibilities offered by Cubism. He also shared in Brancusi's primevalism, and in the mid-1920s he achieved a remarkable synthesis of these two tendencies. With its intently staring eyes, *Figure* (fig. 1118) is a haunting

1119. Marcel Duchamp. *In Advance of the Broken Arm.* 1945, from the original of 1915. Snow shovel, length 46³/₄" (118.7 cm). Yale University Art Gallery, New Haven, Connecticut
Gift of Katherine S. Dreier for the Collection Société Anonyme

1120. Meret Oppenheim. *Object.* 1936. Fur-covered cup, saucer, and spoon; diameter of cup 4³/₄" (12.1 cm); diameter of saucer 9³/₈" (23.8 cm); length of spoon 8" (20.3 cm). The Museum of Modern Art, New York
Purchase

evocation in Cubist terms of African sculpture. Consisting of two interlocking figures, it creates a play of open and closed forms that relieves Brancusi's austere simplicity through arabesque rhythms akin to those of Matisse. Not surprisingly, the patron who commissioned it as a garden sculpture found it difficult to live with *Figure.* No other sculptor at the time was able to rival Lipschitz for sheer power, and he set an important example for the generation of sculptors that reached maturity a decade later (see pages 853–55).

DUCHAMP. Lipschitz's disciplined abstraction was the very antithesis of Dada, which fostered nontraditional approaches that have both enriched and confounded modern sculpture ever since. Playfulness and spontaneity are the impulses behind the ready-mades of Marcel Duchamp, which he created by shifting the context of everyday objects from the utilitarian to the aesthetic. The artist would put his signature, and a provocative title, on ready-made objects such as bottle racks and snow shovels and exhibit them as works of art. *In Advance of the Broken Arm* (fig. 1119) pushed the spirit of ready-mades to a new height: Duchamp "re-created" the lost original version of 1915 with this one made in 1945. Some of Duchamp's examples consist of combinations of found objects. These "assisted" ready-mades approach the status of constructions or of three-dimensional collage. This technique, later baptized "assemblage" (see pages 863–67), proved to have unlimited possibilities, and numerous younger artists have explored it since, especially in junk-ridden America (see fig. 1144).

SURREALISM. Ready-mades are certainly extreme demonstrations of a principle: that artistic creation depends neither on established rules nor on manual craftsmanship. The principle itself was an important discovery, although Duchamp abandoned ready-mades after only a few years. The Surrealist contribution to sculpture is harder to define. It was difficult to apply the theory of "pure psychic automatism" to painting, but still harder to live up to it in sculpture. How indeed could solid, durable materials be given shape without the sculptor being consciously aware of the process?

OPPENHEIM. A breakthrough came in 1930, when the Surrealists met in response to a growing crisis within the movement. They issued a new manifesto drafted by André Breton that called for the "profound and veritable occultation of Surrealism." It further required "uncovering the strange symbolic life of the most ordinary and clearly defined objects." The result was a new class of Surrealist object: neither ready-made nor sculpture, it constituted a kind of three-dimensional collage assembled not out of aesthetic concerns using traditional techniques but according to "poetic affinity" following dictates of the subconscious. Like *Object* (fig. 1120) by Meret Oppenheim (1913–1985), which created a sensation when it was exhibited in 1936, many were intended to be repulsive and unsettling in the extreme, yet proved all the more fascinating for that very reason.

ARP. Perhaps the purest form of Surrealist sculpture, however, was created by Hans Arp (1887–1966). Around 1930 he began to translate his reliefs, which arose from his experiments

1121. Hans Arp. *Human Concretion.* 1935.
Original plaster, 19¹/2 x 18³/4 x 25¹/2" (49.5 x 47.6 x 64.7 cm).
The Museum of Modern Art, New York
Gift of the Advisory Committee

with collage, into three-dimensional forms. These evolved a few years later into the *Human Concretion* series (fig. 1121), a term that aptly describes their character (see also page 808). In contrast to Brancusi's abstractions, which reduce things to their absolute essence, Arp's biomorphic forms seem to grow organically as they are built up. Regardless of medium, the concretions are notable for their perfection. (They were almost always modeled in clay or plaster, although many were later carved in marble and wood, or sometimes cast in bronze, by skilled artisans.) Small wonder they have influenced countless sculptors since then.

PICASSO. As in painting, Picasso's sovereign genius provided much of the impetus for sculpture during the 1930s. In 1928 it emerged as a serious interest for him, and for the next five years he concentrated intensively on making sculptures of all sorts. They demonstrate an amazing variety that testifies to the fertility of his imagination. *Head of a Woman* (fig. 1122) is an especially appealing example of his work from this period. This arresting figure, made from a colander and other discarded materials, shows Picasso's fascination with ethnographic sculpture in its "primitive" quality. Its kinship with the head in *Girl Before a Mirror* of about the same time (see fig. 11) suggests why the artist turned to sculpture in the first place. On the one hand, his painted shapes have a solidity that practically demands to be translated into three-dimensional form.

1122. Pablo Picasso. *Head of a Woman.* 1930–31. Painted iron, sheet metal, springs, and colanders, 39³/8 x 14¹/2 x 23¹/4" (100 x 37 x 59 cm). Musée Picasso, Paris

1123. Alberto Giacometti. *The Palace at 4 A.M.* 1932–33.
Construction in wood, glass, wire, and string, 25 x 28¹/₄ x 15³/₄"
(63.5 x 71.8 x 40 cm). The Museum of Modern Art, New York
Purchase

1124. Julio González. *Head.* c. 1935. Wrought iron, 17³/₄ x 15¹/₄"
(45.1 x 38.7 cm). The Museum of Modern Art, New York
Purchase

On the other, his work is so replete with startling transformations that the process of metamorphosis involved in sculpture became highly intriguing. Here there can be little doubt that Picasso's involvement with Surrealism stimulated his imagination and allowed him to approach sculpture without preconception. As he put it, "One should be able to take a bit of wood and find it's a bird." That is what allowed him to see the possibilities in the debris of modern civilization—an attitude that culminated in *Bull's Head* (fig. 2).

GIACOMETTI. Picasso's impact can be seen in *The Palace at 4 A.M.* (fig. 1123) by Alberto Giacometti (1901–1966), a Swiss sculptor and painter who lived in Paris. In 1928 Picasso had made a number of wire constructions, including a maquette for a monument to the poet Apollinaire, that are its immediate forerunners. Giacometti, however, has transformed them into an airy cage that is the three-dimensional equivalent of a Surrealist picture. Unlike earlier pieces of sculpture, it creates its own spatial environment that clings to it as though this eerie miniature world were protected from everyday reality by an invisible glass bell. The space thus trapped is mysterious and corrosive and gnaws away at the forms until only their skeletons are left. And even they, we feel, will disappear before long.

GONZÁLEZ. Picasso also stimulated the astonishing sculptural imagination of Julio González (1872–1942). Trained as a wrought-iron craftsman in his native Catalonia, González had gone to Paris in 1900. Although he was a friend of both Brancusi and Picasso, he produced little of consequence until the 1930s, when his creative energies suddenly came into focus after Picasso called him for technical advice in working with wrought iron. It was González who established this medi-

um as an important one for sculpture, taking advantage of the very difficulties that had discouraged its use before. *Head* (fig. 1124) combines extreme economy of form with an aggressive reinterpretation of anatomy that is derived from Picasso's work after the mid-1920s. As in the head of the figure on the left in Picasso's *Three Dancers* (see fig. 1049), the mouth is an oval cavity with spikelike teeth, the eyes two rods that converge upon an "optic nerve" linking them to the tangled mass of the "brain." González has produced a gruesomely expressive metaphor, as if the violence of his working process mirrored the violence of modern life.

CALDER. The early 1930s, which brought Giacometti and González to the fore, produced still another important development: the mobile sculpture of the American Alexander Calder (1898–1976). Called mobiles for short, they are delicately balanced constructions of metal wire, hinged together and weighted so as to move with the slightest breath of air. They may be of any size, from tiny tabletop models to the huge *Lobster Trap and Fish Tail* (fig. 1125). Kinetic sculpture had been conceived by the Constructivists, and their influence is evident in Calder's earliest mobiles, which were motor-driven and tended toward abstract geometric configurations. Calder was also affected early on by Mondrian, but it was his contact with Surrealism that made him realize the poetic possibilities of "natural" rather than fully controlled movement. He borrowed biomorphic shapes from Miró and began to think of mobiles as analogues of organic structures: flowers on flexible stems, foliage quivering in the breeze, marine animals floating in the sea. Unpredictable and ever-changing, such mobiles incorporate the fourth dimension as an essential element of their structure. Infinitely responsive to their environment, they are more truly alive than any fabricated thing.

1125. Alexander Calder. *Lobster Trap and Fish Tail*. 1939. Painted steel wire and sheet aluminum, approx. 8'6" x 9'6" (2.6 x 2.9 m). The Museum of Modern Art, New York
Commissioned by the Advisory Committee for the stairwell of the Museum

England

The effects produced by Calder can be compared directly with those of Surrealist painting. The same cannot be said of two English sculptors who represent the culmination of the modern sculptural tradition before 1945: Henry Moore (1898–1986) and Barbara Hepworth (1903–1975), the preeminent woman sculptor of the twentieth century. The presence of Gabo, Kokoschka, Mondrian, Gropius, and other émigrés helped give rise to modern art in England during the mid-1930s, when Moore and Hepworth were emerging as mature artists. In consequence, they absorbed the full spectrum of earlier twentieth-century sculpture, but in different measure, reflecting their contrasting personalities. Moore was the more boldly inventive artist, but Hepworth may well have been the better sculptor. However, the two were closely associated as leaders of the modern movement in England, and influenced one another.

MOORE. The majestic *Two Forms* (fig. 1126), an early work by Moore, may be regarded as the second-generation offspring of Brancusi's *The Kiss* done a quarter-century earlier (see fig. 1110), although there is no direct connection between them. [See Primary Sources, no. 108, page 946.] Abstract and subtle in shape, they are nevertheless "persons" in much the same vein

1126. *(right)* Henry Moore. *Two Forms*. 1936.
Stone, height approx. 42" (106.7 cm).
Collection Mrs. H. Gates Lloyd, Haverford, Pennsylvania

1127. Henry Moore. *Recumbent Figure.* 1938.
Green Hornton stone, length approx. 54" (137.2 cm). The Tate Gallery, London

as Lipschitz's *Figure* (fig. 1118), even though they can be called "images" only in the metaphoric sense. This family group—the forked slab evolved from the artist's studies of the mother-and-child theme—is mysterious and remote like the monoliths of Stonehenge, which greatly impressed the sculptor (see fig. 47). And like Stonehenge, Moore's figures are meant to be placed in a landscape, so architectural are they in character.

Through biomorphic abstraction, his *Recumbent Figure* (fig. 1127) retains both a classical motif—one thinks of a reclining river-god (see fig. 6)—and a primeval look. The design is in complete harmony with the natural striations of the stone, as if the forms had resulted from slow erosion over a thousand years. Moore has evoked the essence of the human figure so successfully that if we were to succumb to the natural temptation to run our hand over the sculpture, it would seem filled with inner life, so convincingly do the forms swell and undulate. Moore was originally inspired by a Mayan statue of the rain spirit Chac Mool. Interestingly enough, the nearest relative of Brancusi's *The Kiss* is a Pre-Columbian pottery figurine group, which, however, the artist cannot have known, since it was a later discovery. The coincidence nevertheless serves to underscore the fundamental kinship between Brancusi and Moore. Moore's figure also suggests an awareness of Arp's *Human Concretions* from about the same time (see fig. 1121). The difference is that Arp suggests anatomical forms without specifically referring to them, as Moore does. The total effect is not unlike the arabesques achieved by Matisse in *Reclining Nude I* (fig. 1109). In addition, the liberties Moore takes with the human figure are unthinkable without Picasso (compare fig. 1050). In this way, Moore unites the strands of early modern sculpture into a seamless whole of incomparable beauty and subtlety.

1128. Barbara Hepworth. *Sculpture with Color (Deep Blue and Red).* 1940–42. Wood, painted white and blue, with red strings, on a wooden base, 11 x 10¼" (27.9 x 26 cm). Collection Alan and Sarah Bowness, London

HEPWORTH. In common with Moore's, Hepworth's sculpture had a biological foundation, but her style became more abstract after her marriage to the painter Ben Nicholson (see page 806), her association with the Constructivist Naum Gabo, and her contact in Paris with Brancusi and Arp. For a time she was practicing several modes at once under these influences. With the onset of World War II, she moved to St. Ives in Cornwall, where she initiated an individual style that emerged in the early 1940s. *Sculpture with Color (Deep Blue and Red)* flawlessly synthesizes painting and sculpture, Surrealist biomorphism and organic abstraction, and the molding of space and shaping of mass (fig. 1128). Carved from wood and immaculately finished, it modifies the shape of an egg to a timeless ideal that has the lucid perfection of a classical head, yet the elemental expressiveness of a primitive mask. Hepworth's egg undoubtedly owes something to Brancusi's (see fig. 1111), although their work is very different. The colors accentuate the play between the interior and exterior of the hollowed-out form, while the strings, a device first used by Moore, seem to suggest a life force within. As a result of its open forms, *Sculpture with Color* enters into an active relationship with its surroundings. Like Moore, Hepworth was concerned with the relationship of the human figure in a landscape, but in an unusually personal way. After moving to a house overlooking St. Ives Bay, she wrote, "I was the figure in the landscape and every sculpture contained to a greater or lesser degree the ever-changing forms and contours embodying my own response to a given position in that landscape. I used colour and strings in many of the carvings of this time. The colour in the concavities plunged me into the depth of water, caves, or shadows deeper than the carved concavities themselves. The strings were the tension I felt between myself and the sea, the wind or the hills."

SCULPTURE SINCE 1945

Primary Structures and Environmental Sculpture

Like painting, sculpture since 1945 has been notable for its epic proportions. Indeed, scale assumed fundamental significance for a sculptural movement that extended the scope—the very concept—of sculpture in an entirely new direction. "Primary Structure," the most suitable name suggested for this type, conveys its two salient characteristics: extreme simplicity of shapes and a kinship with architecture. Another term, "Environmental Sculpture" (not to be confused with the mixed-medium "environments" of Pop), refers to the fact that many Primary Structures are designed to envelop the beholder, who is invited to enter or walk through them. It is this space-articulating function that distinguishes Primary Structures from all previous sculpture and relates them to architecture. They are the modern successors, in structural steel and concrete, to such prehistoric monuments as Stonehenge (see figs. 46 and 47).

GOERITZ. The first to explore these possibilities was Mathias Goeritz (born 1915), a German working in Mexico City. As early as 1952–53, he established an experimental museum, The Echo, for the display of massive geometric compositions, some of them so large as to occupy an entire patio (fig. 1129). His ideas have since been taken up on both sides of the Atlantic.

BLADEN. Often, these sculptors limit themselves to the role of designer and leave the execution to others, to emphasize the impersonality and duplicability of their invention. If no patron is found to foot the bill for carrying out these costly structures, they remain on paper, like unbuilt architecture. Sometimes such works reach the mock-up stage. *The X* (fig. 1130), by the Canadian Ronald Bladen (1918–1988), was originally built with painted wood substituting for metal for an exhibition inside the two-story hall of the Corcoran Gallery in Washington, D.C. Its commanding presence, dwarfing the Neoclassic

1129. Mathias Goeritz. *Steel Structure*. 1952–53. Height 14'9" (4.5 m). The Echo (Experimental Museum), Mexico City

1130. Ronald Bladen. *The X* (in the Corcoran Gallery, Washington, D.C.). 1967. Painted wood, later constructed in steel, 22'8" x 24'6" x 12'6" (6.9 x 7.3 x 3.8 m)
Courtesy Fischbach Gallery, New York

1131. David Smith. *Cubi* series (at Bolton Landing, New York). Stainless steel. *(left) Cubi XVIII.* 1964.
Height 9'8" (2.9 m). Museum of Fine Arts, Boston; *(center) Cubi XVII.* 1963. Height 9'2" (2.7 m). Dallas Museum of Fine Arts;
(right) Cubi XIX. 1964. Height 9'5" (2.9 m). The Tate Gallery, London

colonnade of the hall, seems doubly awesome in such a setting.

SMITH. Not all Primary Structures are Environmental Sculptures, of course. Most are free-standing works independent of the sites that contain them. Bladen's *The X,* for example, was later constructed of painted steel as an outdoor sculpture. They nevertheless share the same monumental scale and economy of form. The artist who played the most influential role in defining their character was David Smith (1906–1965). His earlier work had been strongly influenced by the wrought-iron constructions of Julio González (fig. 1124), but during the last years of his life he evolved a singularly impressive form of Primary Structure in his *Cubi* series. Figure 1131 shows three of these against the open sky and rolling hills of the artist's farm at Bolton Landing, New York. (All are now in major museums.) Only two basic components are employed: cubes (or multiples of them) and cylinders. Yet Smith has created a seemingly endless variety of configurations. The units that make up the structures are poised one upon the other as if they were held in place by magnetic force, so that each represents a fresh triumph over gravity. Unlike many members of the Primary Structure movement, Smith executed these pieces himself, welding them of sheets of stainless steel whose shiny surfaces he finished and controlled with exquisite care. As a result, his work

displays an "old-fashioned" subtlety of touch that reminds us of the polished bronzes of Brancusi.

JUDD. Donald Judd (1928–1994) carries the implications of Primary Structures to their logical conclusion: Minimalism. Unlike Environmental Sculpture, his works serve to articulate interior space without shaping it. In search of the ultimate unity, he separated Smith's *Cubi* into its two components, reducing the geometry to a single cube or cylinder. Judd established the proportions through precise mathematical formulas and eliminated any hint of personal intervention by contracting the work out to industrial fabricators. Having gained total control over all his elements, he soon began to elaborate on them. The most involved pieces produce a decorative opulence by repeating the shape serially at set intervals and adding an intense primary color to one or more sides (fig. 1132). Judd's strict guidelines permit few variations, only greater refinement, but within these limitations the results are often impressive. Why this should be so is not easily explained, although the artist is an eloquent spokesman. In the end, the success of his work depends on its subtle proportions and flawless finish, which enable him to achieve a degree of perfection attained by few other sculptors who share the same approach.

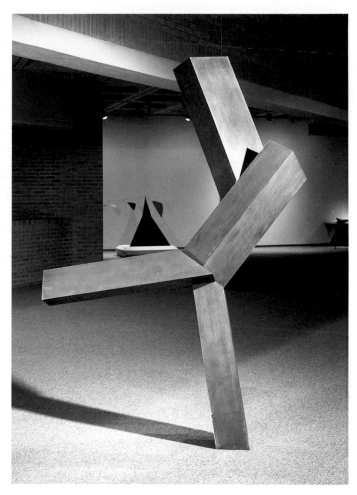

1133. Joel Shapiro. *Untitled.* 1989–90.
Bronze, 8'5½" x 3'6" x 6'6" (2.57 x 1.06 x 1.98 m).
North Carolina Museum of Art, Raleigh
Purchased with funds from various donors, by exchange

1132. Donald Judd. *Untitled.* 1989. Copper with red plexiglass;
ten units, each 9 x 39½ x 31" (23 x 100.3 x 78.8 cm)
Courtesy The Pace Gallery, New York

SHAPIRO. A number of sculptors gradually began to move away from Minimalism without entirely renouncing it. This trend, called Post-Minimalism to denote its continuing debt to the earlier style, has as its leading exponent Joel Shapiro (born 1941). After fully exploring the possibilities of small pieces having great conceptual intensity and aesthetic power, he suddenly began to produce sculptures of simple wood beams that refer to the human figure but do not directly represent it. They assume active "poses," some standing awkwardly off-balance, others dancing or tumbling, so that they charge the space around them with energy. Shapiro soon began casting them in bronze, which retains the impress of the rough wood grain (fig. 1133). These are hand-finished with a beautiful patina by skilled artisans, reasserting the craftsmanship traditional to sculpture. By freely rearranging the vocabulary of David Smith, who actually experimented with a similar figure before his death, Shapiro has given Minimalist sculpture a new lease on life. Nevertheless, his remains one of the few successful attempts at reviving contemporary sculpture, which as a whole has found it especially difficult to seek a new direction.

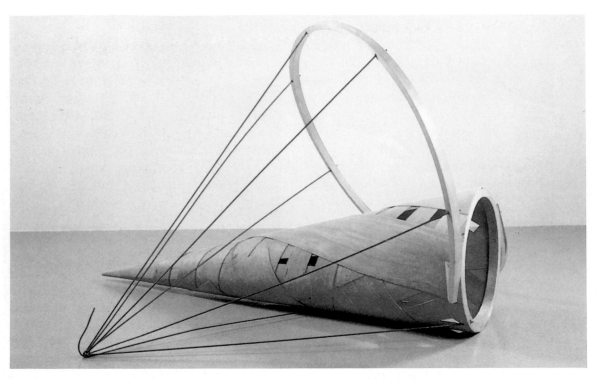

1134. Martin Puryear. *The Spell.* 1985. Pine, cedar, and steel,
4'8" x 7' x 5'5" (1.42 x 2.13 x 1.65 m). Collection the artist

African-American Sculpture

Minimalism was also a decisive influence on a group of talented African-American sculptors who came to maturity in the 1960s, although their contribution has only recently begun to receive critical attention. Their work has helped to make the late twentieth century the first great age of African-American art. While the artists themselves show a variety of style, subject matter, and approach, all address the black experience in America within a contemporary abstract aesthetic. Thus they have the advantage over African-American painters, who have often been burdened by representationalism and traditional styles.

PURYEAR. Martin Puryear (born 1941), the leading black sculptor on the scene today, draws on his experience with the woodworkers of both Sierra Leone in western Africa, where he spent several years in the Peace Corps, and Sweden, where he attended the Royal Academy. Puryear manages to weld these disparate sources into a seamless unity. He adapts African motifs and materials to the modern Western tradition, relying on meticulous craftsmanship to bridge the gap. His forms, at once bold and refined, have an elegant simplicity that contrasts the natural and man-made, the finished and unfinished. They may evoke a saw, bow, fishnet, anthill, or in this case a basket (fig. 1134)—whatever his memory suggests—each restated in whimsical fashion.

MITCHELL. Tyrone Mitchell (born 1944), like Puryear, spent a pivotal sojourn in Africa, where Dogon culture had a profound impact on him. His mature work, too, presents a flawless synthesis of Western and African sources. *Horn for Wifredo* (fig. 1135) reduces an antelope to its essence using Minimalist forms and the spare simplicity of Brancusi, who influenced him at the beginning of the 1980s. Yet the diversity of materials creates a rich array of textures and colors that shows the artist's respect for time-honored materials and craftsmanship. This compound object, we realize, is suffused with a vital energy that makes of it a Surrealist creature. Indeed, the title refers to the Cuban-born Surrealist Wifredo Lam (1902–1982), an important early inspiration for Mitchell.

EDWARDS. Melvin Edwards (born 1937), who has also paid homage to Lam, was equally affected by his visits to Africa. He may be regarded as the purist among contemporary African-American sculptors. An artist in the mold of David Smith, he continues to maintain an allegiance to the Primary Structure and the vocabulary of Minimalism, but invests them with uniquely personal meaning and social content. *To Listen* (fig. 1136) is a totemic figure reminiscent of Moore's *Two Forms* (fig. 1126) in its elemental shape but with the rugged strength that defines Edwards' work. Attached to it is the fragment of a chain, a favorite motif which recurs in his "Lynch Fragment Series"—small works that radiate a truly frightening menace. In addition to denoting slavery, however, the chain has a positive meaning for the artist, to whom it signifies links with the past and the larger community. Likewise, abstraction helps him get in touch with his roots while providing a common ground of experience. In this he is close to the painter William T. Williams (see page 829), a personal friend. Edwards revels in the labor of sculpture, the very feel of metal, which is reflected in the vigorous, handmade finish, a further debt to Smith. The result is a powerful monument to the African-American struggle for freedom and equality that possesses the dignity of the man himself and reflects the artist's strong sense of social responsibility.

1135. Tyrone Mitchell. *Horn for Wifredo.* 1987. Wood, copper, plaster, and pigment, 65 x 49 x 7" (165 x 124.5 x 17.8 cm). Collection of the Schomburg Center for Research in Black Culture, The New York Public Library, Art and Artifacts Division

1136. Melvin Edwards. *To Listen.* 1990. Stainless steel, 7'5¹/2" x 1'3¹/2" x 3'1" (2.27 x .39 x .93 m) Courtesy CDS Gallery, New York

Monuments

OLDENBURG. On a large scale, most Primary Structures are obviously monuments. But just as obviously they are not monuments commemorating or celebrating anything except their designer's imagination. To the uninitiated, they offer no ready frame of reference, nothing to be reminded of, even though the original meaning of "monument" is "a reminder." Monuments in the traditional sense died out when contemporary society lost its consensus of what ought to be publicly remembered, yet the belief in the possibility of such monuments has not been abandoned altogether.

The Pop artist Claes Oldenburg (born 1929) has proposed a number of unexpected and imaginative solutions to the problem of the monument. He is, moreover, an exceptionally precise and persuasive commentator on his ideas. All his monuments are heroic in size, though not in subject matter. And all share one feature: their origin in humble objects of everyday use.

In 1969 Oldenburg conceived his most unusual project. For a piece of outdoor sculpture he wanted a form that combined hard and soft and did not need a base. An ice bag met these demands, so he bought one and started playing with it. He soon realized, he says, that the object was made for manipulation, "that movement was part of its identity and should be used." He then executed a work shaped like a huge ice bag (fig. 1137) with a mechanism inside to make it produce "movements caused by an invisible hand," as the artist described them. He sent the *Giant Ice Bag* to the U.S.

1137. Claes Oldenburg. *Ice Bag—Scale B.* 1970. Programmed kinetic sculpture of polyvinyl, fiberglass, wood, and hydraulic and mechanical movements, 16 x 18 x 18' (4.9 x 5.5 x 5.5 m). National Gallery of Art, Washington, D.C.

1138. Barnett Newman. *Broken Obelisk.* 1963–67.
Steel, height 25'1" (7.7 m). Rothko Chapel, Houston

Pavilion at EXPO 70 in Osaka, Japan, where crowds were end-lessly fascinated to watch it heave, rise, and twist like a living thing, then relax with an almost audible sigh.

What do such monuments celebrate? Part of their charm, which they share with ready-mades and Pop Art, is that they reveal the aesthetic potential of the ordinary and all-too-famil-iar. But they also have an undeniable grandeur.

NEWMAN. There is one dimension, however, that is miss-ing in Oldenburg's monuments. They delight, astonish, amuse—but they do not move us. Wholly secular, wedded to the here and now, they fail to touch our deepest emotions. In our time, one of the rare monuments successful in this is *Bro-ken Obelisk* (fig. 1138) by Barnett Newman (1905–1970). An artist inspired by profound religious and philosophical con-cerns which he struggled throughout his life to translate into visual form, Newman conceived *Broken Obelisk* in 1963 but could not have it executed until four years later, when he found the right steel fabricator. Rising from the center of a shallow reflecting pool, it consists of a square base plate sup-porting a four-sided pyramid whose tip meets and supports that of the up-ended broken obelisk.

Obelisks are slender, four-sided pillars of stone erected by the ancient Egyptians. The Romans brought many of them to Italy; one marks the center of the colonnaded piazza of St. Peter's (see fig. 739). These gave rise to a number of later mon-uments in Europe and America. The two tips in Newman's sculpture have exactly the same angle (53 degrees, borrowed from that of the Egyptian pyramids, which had long fascinat-ed the artist) so that their juncture forms a perfect X. Why this monument has such power to stir our feelings is difficult to put into words. Is it the daring juxtaposition of two age-old shapes that have contrary meanings, the one symbolizing timeless stability, the other a thrust toward the heavens? Sure-ly, but what if the obelisk were intact? Would that not reduce the whole to an improbable balancing feat? The brokenness of the obelisk, then, is essential to the pathos of the monument. It speaks to us of our unfulfilled spiritual yearnings, of a quest for the infinite and universal that persists today as it has for thousands of years.

NOGUCHI. The search for meaning also preoccupied the Japanese-American sculptor Isamu Noguchi (1904–1988). Influenced early on by the Surrealists, as well as by Brancusi, he did not confront Oriental culture until a prolonged stay in Japan in 1952 that proved decisive to his formation. From then on, he developed into one of the most diverse sculptors of this century whose rich imagination fed on both heritages. His role in mediating between East and West was of incalculable importance. To the Japanese he introduced modern Western ideas of style; to Americans he rendered traditional Japanese concepts of art visually comprehensible at a time when there was a growing fascination with Zen Buddhism. We see this fusion in his fountain for the John Hancock Insurance Company in New Orleans (fig. 1139). Like much of Zen thought, it is an elegantly simple statement of a paradoxical idea. Atop a grooved column recalling the primitive Doric of ancient Greece, where the Western sculptural tradition of which Noguchi felt himself a part originated, sits a "capital" rather like the wood-beam supports in a Japanese temple. Except for the flat faces on either side of the capital, the finish has been left rough, out of the age-old Japanese respect for the natural materials and the unadorned in the crafts. It gives the fountain a primeval look that emphasizes the stone's origin in the earth, for which Noguchi acquired an Oriental veneration. The contrast to the sleek modern lines of the Hancock building could hardly be greater. Yet the placement of the fountain shows not only a Japanese sensitivity to space but a fundamental understanding of the logic of modern architecture that Japanese critics recognized as distinctly Western.

LIN. Part of the problem confronting the monument maker in our era is that, unlike a century ago, there is so little worth commemorating in the first place—no event, no cause unites our fragmented world, despite the momentous changes going on everywhere—and no artistic vocabulary that we readily agree on. It is all the more ironic that the memorial to American soldiers killed in Vietnam should turn out to be not an embarrassing reminder of one of the most bitterly divisive chapters in recent history, but eloquent testimony to the universal tragedy of war (fig. 1140). Designed by Maya Lin (born

1139. Isamu Noguchi. Fountain for the John Hancock Insurance Company, New Orleans. 1961–62. Granite, 16' (4.88 m)

1140. *(below)* Maya Lin. *Vietnam Veterans Memorial.* 1982. Black granite, length 500' (152 m). The Mall, Washington, D.C.

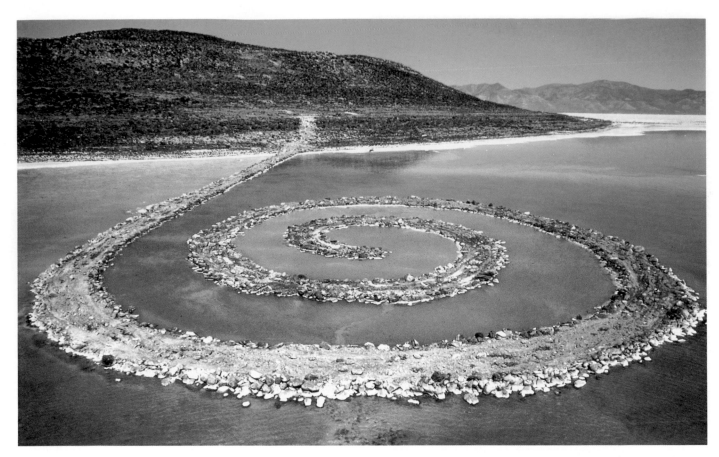

1141. Robert Smithson. *Spiral Jetty.* As built in 1970. Total length 1,500' (457.2 m); width of jetty 15' (4.6 m). Great Salt Lake, Utah

1959), it casts a spell on all those who see it. What is its secret? The very simplicity of the architectural form and its setting are disarming. By comparison, all other war memorials of recent times seem trite and needlessly elaborate, especially those incorporating realistic figures. It evokes a solemn mood while precluding the inflated rhetoric that mars most memorials. The triangular shape, although embedded in tradition and fraught with historical connotations (compare fig. 900), permits viewers to form their own associations because of its abstractness. Moreover, the reflective quality of the polished granite draws the viewer into the work. Yet these attributes alone cannot account for the extraordinary impact. Like Labrouste before her (see page 738), Lin seized on the simple but brilliant idea of inscribing names—thousands of them—whose cumulative effect is to bring home the full enormity of the tragedy with awesome power. This device does not tell the story either, since names inscribed on walls or tombs rarely move us, least of all those of people we never knew. In the end, the *Vietnam Veterans Memorial* is that rare instance of perfect consonance between form and idea. So unique is this achievement that no artist has been able to duplicate its success.

Earth Art

Because of its space-articulating function we might be tempted to call the *Vietnam Veterans Memorial* a work of architecture, like Stonehenge; yet it is so sculptural that it belongs equally well to Primary Structures. The two categories merge in "Earth Art," which is the ultimate medium for Environmental Sculpture, since it provides complete freedom from the limitations of the human scale. Logically enough, some designers of Primary Structures have turned to it, inventing projects that stretch over many miles. These latter-day successors to the mound-building Indians of Neolithic times have the advantage of modern earth-moving machinery, but this is more than outweighed by the problem of cost and the difficulty of finding suitable sites on our crowded planet.

SMITHSON. The few projects of theirs that have actually been carried out are mostly found in remote regions of western America, so that the finding is itself often difficult enough. *Spiral Jetty,* the work of Robert Smithson (1938–1973), jutted out into Great Salt Lake in Utah (fig. 1141) and is now partly submerged. Its appeal rests in part on the Surrealist irony of the concept: a spiral jetty is as self-contradictory as a straight corkscrew. But it can hardly be said to have grown out of the natural formation of the terrain like the Great Serpent Mound (see fig. 49). No wonder it has not endured long, nor was it intended to. The process by which nature is reclaiming *Spiral Jetty,* already twice submerged, was integral to Smithson's design from the start. The project nevertheless lives on in photographs.

CHRISTO. By way of contrast, the projects of Christo (Christo Javacheff, born 1935), who first gained notoriety for wrapping things, are deliberately short-lived. They enhance the environment only temporarily instead of altering it per-

Handwritten annotations on the drawing:

Surrounded Islands (Project for Biscayne Bay, Greater Miami, Florida) Venetian Causeway, J. Tuttle Causeway, 79 th. street Causeway, Broad Causeway and Bakers Haulover Inlet — Christo 1982

Covering the Surface of the water, woven polypropylene Fabric (7x7mm inch. Cm. 0.18) extending into the Bay — 200 Feet — Boom in sections of 100 Feet

Island #12 length 650 Feet and Width 300 Feet

Boom 7'.9 and anchor 7'.0

the Floating Fabric attached to a long Boom/etc

1142. Christo (Christo Javacheff). *Surrounded Islands, Project for Biscayne Bay, Greater Miami, Florida*. 1982.
Drawing in two parts, 1'3" x 8' (.38 x 2.44 m) and 3'6" x 8' (1.06 x 2.44 m).
Pencil, charcoal, pastel, crayon, enamel paint, aerial photograph, and fabric sample. Private collection
Copyright Christo 1982

manently. *Surrounded Islands, Biscayne Bay, Miami*, his most satisfying project to date, was installed for all of two weeks in the spring of 1983. Part Conceptual Art, part Happening (see pages 870–71), this ambitious repackaging of nature was a public event involving a small army of assistants. While the emphasis was on the campaign itself, the outcome was a triumph of epic fantasy.

Photographs hardly do justice to the results. Our collage of Christo's drawings, an aesthetic object in its own right, gives a clearer picture of the artist's intention by presenting the project in different ways and conveying the complexity of the experience it provided (fig. 1142). (Drawings such as this helped to fund the project.) In effect, Christo turned the islands into inverse lily pads of pink fabric. If Smithson's *Spiral Jetty* suggests the futility of grandiose undertakings, Christo's visual pun is as festive and decorative as Monet's water-lily paintings (fig. 943), an inspiration the artist has acknowledged.

Constructions and Assemblage

Constructions present a difficult problem. If we agree to restrict the term *sculpture* to objects made of a single substance, then we must put "assemblages" (that is, constructions using mixed mediums) in a class of their own. This is probably a useful distinction, because of their kinship with ready-mades. But what of Picasso's *Bull's Head* (fig. 2)? Is it not an instance of

assemblage, and have we not called it a piece of sculpture? Actually, there is no inconsistency here. The *Bull's Head* is a bronze cast, even though we cannot tell this by looking at a photograph of it. Had Picasso wished to display the actual handlebars and bicycle seat, he would surely have done so. Since he chose to have them cast in bronze, this must have been because he wanted to "dematerialize" the ingredients of the work by having them reproduced in a single material. Apparently he felt it necessary to clarify the relation of image to reality in this way—the sculptor's way—and he used the same procedure whenever he worked with ready-made objects.

Nevertheless, we must not apply the "single-material" rule too strictly. Calder's mobiles, for instance, often combine metal, string, wood, and other substances. Yet they do not strike us as being assemblages, because these materials are not made to assert their separate identities. Conversely, an object may deserve to be called an assemblage even though composed of essentially homogeneous material. Such is often true of works known as "junk sculpture," made of fragments of old machinery, parts of wrecked automobiles, and similar discards, which constitute a broad class that can be called sculpture, assemblage, or environment, depending on the work itself.

RAUSCHENBERG. Robert Rauschenberg (born 1925) pioneered assemblage as early as the mid-1950s. Much like a composer making music out of the noises of everyday life, he

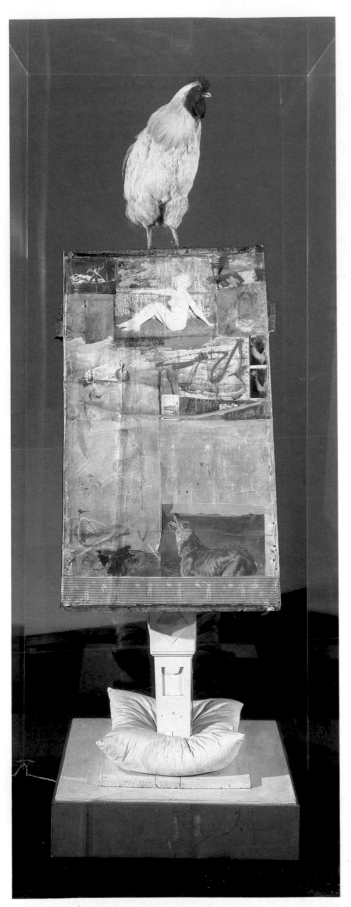

1143. Robert Rauschenberg. *Odalisk.* 1955–58. Construction, 6'9" x 2'1" x 2'1" (2.06 x .64 x .64 m). Museum Ludwig, Cologne

constructed works of art from the trash of urban civilization. *Odalisk* (fig. 1143) is a box covered with a miscellany of pasted images—comic strips, photos, clippings from picture magazines—held together only by the skein of brushstrokes the artist has superimposed on them. The box perches on a foot improbably anchored to a pillow on a wooden platform and is surmounted by a stuffed chicken.

The title, a witty blend of "odalisque" and "obelisk," refers both to the nude girls among the collage of clippings as modern "harem girls" and to the shape of the construction as a whole, for the box shares its verticality and slightly tapering sides with real obelisks. Rauschenberg's unlikely "monument" has at least some qualities in common with its predecessors: compactness and self-sufficiency. We will recognize in this improbable juxtaposition the same ironic intent as the readymades of Duchamp, whom Rauschenberg had come to know well in New York.

CHAMBERLAIN. A most successful example of junk sculpture, and a puzzling borderline case of assemblage and sculpture, is *Essex* (fig. 1144) by John Chamberlain (born 1927). The title refers to a make of car that has not been on the market for many years, suggesting that the object is a kind of homage to a vanished species. But we may well doubt that these pieces of enameled tin ever had so specific an origin. They have been carefully selected for their shape and color, and composed in such a way that they form a new entity, evoking Duchamp-Villon's *The Great Horse* (fig. 1113) rather than the crumpled automobiles to which they once belonged. Whether we prefer to call *Essex* assemblage or sculpture is of little importance, but in trying to reach a decision we gain a better insight into the qualities that constitute its appeal.

NEVELSON. Although it is almost always made entirely of wood, the work of Louise Nevelson (1900–1988) must be classified as assemblage, and when extended to a monumental scale, it acquires the status of an environment. Before Nevelson, there had not been any important women sculptors in twentieth-century America. Sculpture had traditionally been reserved for men because of the manual labor involved. Thanks to the women's suffrage movement in the second half of the nineteenth century, Harriet Hosmer (1830–1908) and her "White Marmorean Flock" (as the novelist Henry James called her and her followers in Rome) had succeeded in legitimizing sculpture as a medium for women. This school of sculpture lapsed, however, when the sentimental, idealizing Neoclassical style fell out of favor after the Philadelphia Centennial of 1876.

In the 1950s Nevelson rejected external reality and began to construct a private one from her collection of found pieces of wood, both carved and rough. At first these self-contained realms were miniature cityscapes, but they soon grew into large environments of free-standing "buildings," encrusted with decorations that were inspired by the sculpture on Mayan ruins. Nevelson's work generally took the form of large wall units that flatten her architecture into reliefs (fig. 1145). Assembled from individual compartments, the whole is always painted a single color, usually a matte black to suggest the shadowy world of dreams. Each compartment is elegantly

1144. John Chamberlain. *Essex*. 1960. Automobile body parts and other metal, 9' x 6'8" x 3'7" (2.74 x 2.03 x 1.09 m). The Museum of Modern Art, New York
Gift of Mr. and Mrs. Robert C. Scull and purchase

1145. Louise Nevelson. *Black Chord*. 1964. Painted wood, 8' x 10' x 11½" (2.44 x 3.05 x .29 m), Collection Joel Ehrenkranz

1146. *(right)* Barbara Chase-Riboud. *Confessions for Myself.* 1972.
Bronze, painted black, and black wool, 10' x 3'4" x 1'
(3.05 x 1.02 x .30 m). University Art Museum, University of
California at Berkeley
Purchased with funds from the H. W. Anderson Charitable Foundation

designed and is itself a metaphor of thought or experience.
While the organization of the ensemble is governed by an
inner logic, the entire statement remains an enigmatic monument to the artist's fertile imagination.

CHASE-RIBOUD. Nevelson's success has encouraged other
American women to become sculptors. Barbara Chase-
Riboud (born 1939), a prize-winning poet who lives in Paris,
belongs to a generation of remarkable black women who have
made significant contributions to several of the arts at once.
She is heir to a unique American tradition. It is a paradox that
whereas black women never carve in traditional African cultures, in America they found their first artistic outlet in sculpture. They were attracted to it by the example set by Harriet
Hosmer at a time when abolitionism and feminism were closely allied liberal causes.

Chase-Riboud received a traditional training in her native
Philadelphia, the first center of minority artists. The monumental sculpture she developed in the early 1970s makes an
indelible impression. In *Confessions for Myself* (fig. 1146) she
has conjured up a demonic archetype of awesome power. Her
highly individual aesthetic utilizes a combination of bronze,
either polished or with a black patina, and braided fiber. Similar qualities can be found in cast bronze figures from Benin
and in carved wooden masks by the Senufo tribe, which are
sometimes embellished with textiles. The form can be compared to a poem: each fold is like a strophe that contributes to
the total meaning of the work. Nor is the analogy an accident,
for Chase-Riboud's progress as an artist was in tandem with
her development as a poet. The title, too, is deliberate in this
case; she began the sculpture with it in mind, which accounts
for the extremely personal nature of the work. On the one
hand, her sculpture expresses a distinctly ethnic sensibility and
feminist outlook. On the other, she is like an archaeologist,
peeling back layer after layer of personal memory to reveal a
human meaning from deep within our collective subconscious
that transcends limitations of race and culture. Thus, she
achieves a universality in keeping with her cosmopolitan view
of art and life. Ironically, her art has found wider acceptance
in Europe than in the United States, where her sophisticated
vision does not meet preconceived stereotypes of black art.

HESSE. A special case is formed by Eva Hesse (1936–1970).
Although her work stands on its own, she had just begun to
hit her stride when her life was cut short by cancer. Moreover,
it is impossible to separate her work from her life, which is
known in considerable detail, thanks to her diaries and many

1147. Eva Hesse. *Accession II.* 1967. Steel and
rubber tubes, 30³/4 x 30³/4 x 30³/4" (78 x 78 x 78 cm).
The Detroit Institute of Arts
Founders Society Purchase, Friends of Modern Art and Miscellaneous Gifts Fund

interviews. [See Primary Sources, no. 109, page 946.] While not a feminist, she has been treated as a heroine by the women's liberation movement because of her inner and artistic struggles. In many respects she represented the very prototype of the feminist artist, one who was later to provide inspiration to others. Her sculpture, too, defies convenient categories. It began to develop rapidly only in 1966 as the result of a stay in Germany, where she was influenced by Joseph Beuys and his Zero Group (see page 871). For her as for Beuys, art had healing powers through its revelatory function, only they were private rather than social in nature. Her artistic milieu was nevertheless the New York circle of Minimalists that included her closest friends. Her work derives its best features from both, but restates matters in an entirely individual way.

To look at Hesse's sculpture is to see a central mystery unveiled through its often paradoxical, mythic character. Thus *Accession II* (fig. 1147) has aptly been described as "suggesting a stylistic collision between one of Donald Judd's minimalist aluminum boxes and Meret Oppenheim's Surrealist fur-covered teacup of 1936." (Compare figs. 1132 and 1120.) Aesthetically it has the spareness of Minimalist art, but with infinitely richer content, for Hesse has reinvested her industrial object with personal meaning. It at once possesses all the enigma of Pandora's box and the piquancy of an erotic fetish, a quality found throughout her mature work, which is laden with unmistakable sexual overtones.

Environments and Installations

A number of artists associated with Pop Art have also turned to assemblage because they find the flat surface of the canvas too confining. In order to bridge the gap between image and reality, they often introduce three-dimensional objects into their pictures. Some even construct full-scale models of everyday things and real-life situations, utilizing every conceivable kind of material in order to embrace the entire range of their physical environment, including the people, in their work. These "environments" combine the qualities of painting, sculpture, collage, and stagecraft. Being three-dimensional, they can claim to be considered sculpture, but the claim rests on a convention which Pop Art itself has helped to make obsolete. According to this convention, a flat or smoothly curved work of art covered with colors is a painting (or, if the surface is not covered, a drawing). Everything else is sculpture, whether or not the surface is colored and regardless of the material, size, or degree of relief—unless we can enter it, in which case we call it architecture.

Our habit of using the term *sculpture* in this sense is only a few hundred years old. Antiquity and the Middle Ages had separate terms to denote various kinds of sculpture according to the materials and working processes involved, but no single term that covered them all. Maybe it is time to revive such distinctions and to modify the all-inclusive definition of sculpture by acknowledging "environments" as a separate category, distinct from both painting and sculpture in its use of heterogeneous materials ("mixed mediums") and blurring of the borderline between image and reality. The differences are underscored by "installations," which are expansions of environments into room-size settings.

1148. George Segal. *Cinema.* 1963. Plaster, metal, plexiglass, and fluorescent light, 9'10" x 8' x 3'3" (3 x 2.4 x .99 m). Albright-Knox Art Gallery, Buffalo, New York
Gift of Seymour H. Knox

SEGAL. George Segal (born 1924) creates three-dimensional lifesize pictures showing people and objects in everyday situations. The subject of *Cinema* (fig. 1148) is ordinary enough to be instantly recognizable: a man changing the letters on a movie-theater marquee. Yet the relation of image and reality is far more subtle and complex than the obvious authenticity of the scene suggests. The man's figure is cast from a live model by a technique of Segal's invention and retains its ghostly white plaster surface. Thus it is one crucial step removed from our world of daily experience, and the neon-lit sign has been carefully designed to complement and set off the shadowed figure. Moreover, the scene is brought down from its natural context, high above the entrance to the theater, where we might have glimpsed it in passing, and is presented at eye level, in isolation, so that we grasp it completely for the first time.

THE KIENHOLZES. Some environments can have a shattering impact on the viewer. This is certainly true of *The State Hospital* (fig. 1149) by the West Coast artists Edward Kienholz (1927–1994) and Nancy Kienholz (born 1944), which shows a cell in a ward for senile patients with a naked old man strapped to the lower bunk. He is the victim of physical cruelty, which has reduced what little mental life he had in him almost to the vanishing point. His body is little more than a skeleton covered with leathery, discolored skin, and his head

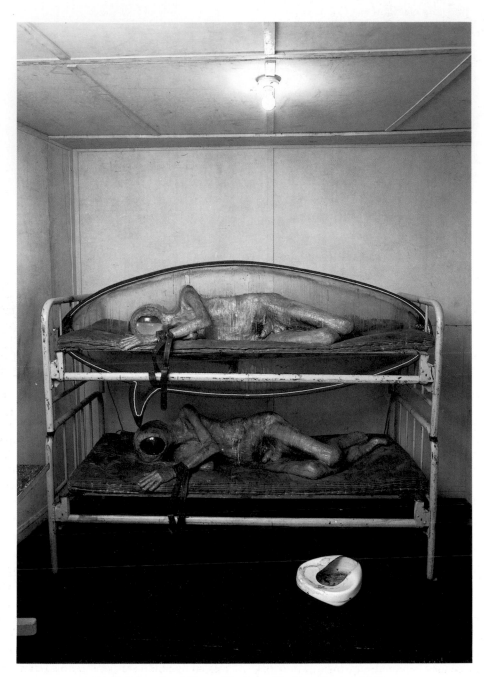

1149. Edward and Nancy Kienholz. *The State Hospital.* 1966.
Mixed mediums, 8 x 12 x 10' (2.4 x 3.7 x 3.1 m). Moderna Museet, Stockholm

is a glass bowl with live goldfish, of whom we catch an occasional glimpse. The horrifying realism of the scene even has an olfactory dimension. When the work was displayed at the Los Angeles County Museum of Art, it exuded a sickly hospital smell. But what of the figure in the upper bunk? It almost duplicates the one below, with one important difference: it is a mental image, since it is enclosed in the outline of a comic-strip balloon rising from the goldfish bowl. It represents, then, the patient's awareness of himself. The abstract devices of the balloon and the metaphoric goldfish bowl are both alien to the realism of the scene as a whole; yet they play an essential part in it, for they help to break the grip of horror and pity. They make us think as well as feel. The Kienholzes' means may be Pop, but their aim is that of Greek tragedy. As witnesses to the unseen miseries beneath the surface of modern life, they have no equal.

1150. Judy Pfaff. *Dragons.* Installation at the Whitney Biennial, February–April 1981. Mixed mediums. Whitney Museum of American Art, New York

Courtesy Holly Solomon Gallery, New York

1151. Joseph Kosuth. *One and Three Chairs.* 1965. Wooden folding chair, photographic copy of chair, and photographic enlargement of dictionary definition of chair; chair $32^3/8$ x $14^7/8$ x $20^7/8$" (82.2 x 37.8 x 53 cm); photo panel 36 x $24^1/8$" (91.5 x 61.1 cm); text panel 24 x $24^1/8$"(61 x 61.3 cm). The Museum of Modern Art, New York

Larry Aldrich Foundation Fund

PFAFF. The installations of Judy Pfaff (born 1946) can be likened to exotic indoor landscapes. The inspiration of nature is apparent in the junglelike density of *Dragons* (fig. 1150), aptly named for its fiery forms and colors. Pfaff uses painting together with sculptural and other materials to activate architectural space. The treatment of the wall surface will remind us of the collage in Rauschenberg's *Odalisk* (fig. 1143), but Pfaff's work is characterized by playfulness rather than ironic wit. The nearest equivalent to Pfaff's spontaneous energy is the Action Painting of Jackson Pollock. It is as if the poured paint had been released from the canvas and left free to roam in space. The swirling profusion around the viewer makes for an experience that is at once pleasurable and vertiginous.

Conceptual Art

Conceptual Art has the same "patron saint" as Pop Art: Marcel Duchamp. It arose during the 1960s out of the Happenings staged by Alan Kaprow (born 1927) in which the event itself became the art. Conceptual Art challenges our definition of art more radically than Pop, insisting that the leap of the imagination, not the execution, is art. According to this view, works of art can be dispensed with altogether, since they are incidental by-products of the imaginative leap. So too can galleries and, by extension, even the artist's public. The creative process need only be documented in some way. Sometimes this is in verbal form, but more often it is by still photography, video, or cinema displayed within an installation.

Conceptual Art, we will recognize, is akin to Minimalism as a phenomenon of the 1960s, but instead of abolishing content, it eliminates aesthetics from art. This deliberately antiart approach, stemming from Dada (see page 806), poses a number of stimulating paradoxes. As soon as the documentation takes on visible form, it begins to come perilously close to more traditional forms of art (especially if it is placed in a gallery where it can be seen by an audience), since it is impossible fully to divorce the imagination from aesthetic matters.

KOSUTH. We see this in *One and Three Chairs* (fig. 1151) by Joseph Kosuth (born 1945), which is clearly indebted to Duchamp's ready-mades (fig. 1119). It "describes" a chair by

ART HISTORY

A young artist had just finished art school. He asked his
instructor what he should do next. "Go to New York," the
instructor replied, "and take slides of your work around to
all the galleries and ask them if they will exhibit your work."
Which the artist did.

He went to gallery after gallery with his slides. Each director picked up his slides one by one, held each up to the light
the better to see it, and squinted his eyes as he looked.
"You're too provincial an artist," they all said. "You are not
in the mainstream." "We're looking for Art History."

He tried. He moved to New York. He painted tirelessly,
seldom sleeping. He went to museum and gallery openings,
studio parties, and artists' bars. He talked to every person
having anything to do with art; travelled and thought and read
constantly about art. He collapsed.

He took his slides around to galleries a second time. "Ah,"
the gallery directors said this time, "finally you are historical."

Moral: Historical mispronounced sounds like hysterical.

1152. John Baldessari. *Art History,* from *Ingres and Other Parables.* 1972. Photograph and typed text.
Collection Angelo Baldassarre, Bari, Italy

combining in one installation an actual chair, a full-scale photograph of that chair, and a printed dictionary definition of a
chair. Whatever the Conceptual artist's intention, this making
of the work of art, no matter how minimal the process, is as
essential as it was for Michelangelo. In the end, all art is the
final document of the creative process, because without execution, no idea can ever be fully realized. Without such "proof
of performance," the Conceptual artist becomes like the
emperor wearing new clothes that no one else can see. And, in
fact, Conceptual Art has embraced all of the mediums in one
form or another.

BALDESSARI. Like Dada, Conceptual Art is notable for its
ironic humor—whose bark is admittedly worse than its bite,
however. It reached its high point with *Art History,* from *Ingres
and Other Parables* by John Baldessari (born 1931), which is
both a witty spoof on art-history texts such as this book and a

telling commentary on the difficulties young artists face in
finding acceptance (fig. 1152). The juxtaposition of a great
monument, mock-serious narrative, and absurd moral is
meant to deride traditional value judgments about art. Yet it
remains strangely innocuous, as if the artist were too self-consciously aware of his mischievous role.

Performance Art

Performance art, which originated in the early decades of
this century, belongs to the history of theater, but the form
that arose in the 1970s combines aspects of Happenings and
Conceptual Art with installations. In reaction to Minimalism, artists now sought to assert their presence once again
by becoming, in effect, living works of art. The results, however, have relied mainly on the shock value of irreverent
humor or explicit sexuality. Nonetheless, Performance art

1153. Joseph Beuys. *Coyote.* Photo of performance at
Rene Block Gallery, New York, 1974. Photograph © 1974 Caroline Tisdall
Courtesy Ronald Feldman Fine Arts, New York

emerged as perhaps the most characteristic art form of the 1980s.

BEUYS. The German artist Joseph Beuys (1921–1986) managed to overcome these limitations, though he, too, was a controversial figure who incorporated an element of parody into his work. Life for Beuys was a creative process in which everyone is an artist. He assumed the guise of a modern-day shaman intent on healing the spiritual crisis of contemporary life caused, he believed, by the rift between the arts and sciences.

To find the common denominator behind such polarities, he created objects and scenarios which, though often baffling at face value, were meant to be accessible to the intuition. In 1974, Beuys spent one week caged up in a New York gallery with a coyote (fig. 1153), an animal sacred to the American Indian but persecuted by the white man. His objective in this "dialogue" was to lift the trauma caused to an entire nation by the schism between the two opposing world views. That the attempt was inherently doomed to failure does not in any way reduce the sincerity of this act of conscience.

CHAPTER SIX

TWENTIETH-CENTURY ARCHITECTURE

ARCHITECTURE BEFORE WORLD WAR I

Modernism in twentieth-century architecture has meant first and foremost an aversion to decoration for its own sake, without a trace of historicism. Instead, it favors a clean functionalism, which expresses the Machine Age, with its insistent rationalism. Yet modern architecture demanded far more than a reform of architectural grammar and vocabulary. To take advantage of the expressive qualities of the new building techniques and materials that the engineer had placed at the architect's disposal a new philosophy was needed. The leaders of modern architecture have characteristically been vigorous and articulate thinkers, in whose minds architectural theory is closely linked with ideas of social reform to meet the challenges posed by industrial civilization. To them, architecture's ability to shape human experience brings with it the responsibility to play an active role in molding modern society for the better.

WRIGHT. The first indisputably modern architect in this sense was Frank Lloyd Wright (1867–1959), Louis Sullivan's great disciple. If Sullivan, Gaudí, Mackintosh, and Van de Velde could be called the Post-Impressionists of architecture, Wright took architecture to its Cubist phase. This is certainly true of his brilliant early style, which he developed between 1900 and 1910 and had broad international influence. (For an example of his late work, see figs. 21 and 22). In the beginning Wright's main activity was the design of suburban houses in the upper Midwest. These were known as Prairie School houses, because their low, horizontal lines were meant to blend with the flat landscape around them.

Frank Lloyd Wright's last, and most accomplished, example in this series is the Robie House of 1909 (figs. 1154 and 1155). The exterior, so unlike anything seen before, instantly proclaims the building's modernity. However, its "Cubism" is not merely a matter of the clean-cut rectangular elements composing the structure, but of Wright's handling of space. It is designed as a number of "space blocks" around a central core, the chimney. Some of the blocks are closed and others are open, yet all are defined with equal precision. Thus the space that has been architecturally shaped includes the balconies, terrace, court, and garden, as well as the house itself. Voids and solids are regarded as equivalents, analogous in their way to Analytic Cubism in painting, and the entire complex enters into an active and dramatic relationship with its surroundings.

Wright did not aim simply to design a house, but to create a complete environment. In the Francis W. Little House (fig. 1156), he even took command of the details of the interior and designed stained glass, fabrics, and furniture. The controlling factor here was not so much the individual client's special wishes as Wright's conviction that buildings have a profound influence on the people who live, work, or worship in them, making the architect, consciously or unconsciously, a molder of people. [See Primary Sources, no. 110, page 947.]

LOOS. In Europe modern architecture developed more slowly and unevenly, and came to a head only on the eve of World War I, which effectively halted its further growth for nearly a decade. One of the first priests of modernism, Adolf Loos (1870–1933), spent several years working in Chicago

1154. Frank Lloyd Wright. Robie House, Chicago. 1909

1155. Plan of the Robie House

1156. Frank Lloyd Wright. Installation of the living room from the Francis W. Little House. 1913.
The Metropolitan Museum of Art, New York

1157. Adolf Loos. Steiner House, Vienna. 1910

1159. Walter Gropius and Adolf Meyer. Fagus Shoe Factory, Alfeld, Germany. 1911–14

1158. Peter Behrens. A.E.G. Turbine Factory, Berlin. 1909–10

during the 1890s and returned to Vienna a convert to functionalism. The garden side of his Steiner House of 1910 (fig. 1157), one of the first private houses built of ferroconcrete (concrete reinforced with steel), is free of decoration, and retains its striking modern appearance to this very day. (The front represents an awkward compromise with local building authorities.)

DEUTSCHER WERKBUND. Central to the early development of modernism in Germany was the Deutscher Werkbund, an alliance of "the best representatives of art, industry, crafts and trades" founded in 1907 by Hermann Muthesius (1861–1927). His mission was to translate the Arts and Crafts Movement into a machine style using the most advanced techniques of industrial design and manufacturing.

BEHRENS. The way was led by Peter Behrens (1869–1940), the chief architect and designer for the electrical firm A.E.G. His Turbine Factory of 1909–10 (fig. 1158) transforms the factory shed into a monument to industry through the unmistakable reference to Greek temples (compare fig. 169). Yet it does so without resorting merely to a historicist veneer. Rather, it articulates a modern aesthetic stemming from Mackintosh's Glasgow School of Art (fig. 1003). The result is an austere simplicity surpassing that of Sullivan's Carson Pirie Scott & Company store (fig. 1010). Structurally there is little new here. Reinforced concrete had been in use since the later nineteenth century; even the wall of glass does not advance beyond Paxton's Crystal Palace (see fig. 962). Yet the building was of critical importance for Behrens' three disciples, who became the founders of modern architecture: Walter Gropius, Ludwig Mies van der Rohe, and Le Corbusier.

GROPIUS. The first to cross that threshold fully was Gropius (1883–1969). The Fagus Shoe Factory (fig. 1159), designed with Adolf Meyer (1881–1929), represents the crucial step toward modernism in European architecture. The most dramatic feature is the walls, which are a nearly continuous surface of glass. This radical innovation had been possible ever since the introduction of the structural steel skeleton several decades before, which relieved the wall of any load-bearing function. Sullivan had approached it, but he could not yet free himself from the traditional notion of the window as a "hole in the wall." Far more radically than Sullivan or Behrens, Gropius frankly acknowledged, at last, that in modern architecture the wall is no more than a curtain or climate barrier, which may consist entirely of glass if maximum daylight is desirable. Only in the classically conceived entrance did he pay a nod to the past.

1162. Max Berg. Interior of the Centennial Hall, Breslau, Germany. 1912–13

1160. Bruno Taut. Staircase of the "Glass House," Werkbund Exhibition, Cologne. 1914

1161. Bruno Taut. The "Glass House," Werkbund Exhibition, Cologne. 1914

TAUT. The Werkbund exhibition of 1914, which featured Van de Velde's theater (fig. 1005), was a showcase for a whole generation of young German architects who were to achieve prominence after World War I. Many of the buildings they designed for the fairgrounds anticipate ideas of the 1920s. Among the most adventurous is the staircase of the "Glass House" (fig. 1160) by Bruno Taut (1880–1938), made magically translucent by the use of glass bricks, then a novel material. The structural steel skeleton is as thin and unobtrusive as the great strength of the metal permits. The total effect precociously suggests Stella's *Brooklyn Bridge* (see fig. 1036) translated into three dimensions.

If the interior seems astonishingly prophetic, the exterior of the "Glass House" (fig. 1161) was shaped like a multifaceted bulbous crystal not unlike those on John Nash's Brighton pavilion (fig. 912). It was inspired, oddly enough, not by technology but by the widespread mystical fascination with crystal. To Taut, architecture "consists exclusively of powerful emotions and addresses itself exclusively to the emotions." We may call this approach Expressionism, because it stresses the artist's emotional attitude toward himself and the world (see page 781). Taut's mysticism was shared by the members of *Der Blaue Reiter.* Does modern architecture not incorporate the spontaneous and irrational qualities of Fantasy as well? Indeed it does. But because the modern architect shares the Expressionist's primary concern with the human community, rather than the labyrinth of the imagination, Fantasy plays a much lesser role than Expressionism, which has subsumed it.

BERG. The visionary side that distinguishes Expressionist architecture is best seen in the Centennial Hall (fig. 1162) built by Max Berg (1870–1948) in Breslau to celebrate Germany's liberation from Napoleon in 1812. Berg, for the first time, has taken full advantage of reinforced concrete's incredible flexibility and strength. The vast scale is not simply an engineering marvel but a visionary space that fulfills the grandest dream of Boullée (compare fig. 857). The immediate ancestry of Centennial Hall can be traced back to the Bank

1163. Antonio Sant'Elia. Central Station project for Città Nuova (after Banham). 1914

of England by John Soane (see fig. 916), while the exterior is strangely reminiscent of Ledoux's tollgate (fig. 858). Ultimately, the interior looks back to the Pantheon (fig. 246), but with the solids and voids in reverse, so that we are reminded of nothing so much as the interior of Hagia Sophia (fig. 328). That Centennial Hall further recalls the soaring spirituality of a Gothic cathedral (such as our fig. 439) is not a coincidence: Berg shared with Rouault and Nolde an intense religiosity, which later led him to abandon his profession for Christianity.

SANT'ELIA. The final component of modernist architecture—its utopian side—was added by the Futurist Antonio Sant'Elia (1888–1916), who declared that "we must invent and reconstruct the Futurist city as an immense, tumultuous yard and the Futurist house as a gigantic machine." The Central Station project for his Città Nuova (New City; fig. 1163) is treated in terms of circulation patterns that determine the relationships between buildings, establishing a restless perpetual motion that fulfills the Futurist vision announced in Boccioni's work (see figs. 1038 and 1114). But it is the enormous scale, dwarfing even the most grandiose complexes of the past, that makes this a uniquely modern conception. It even includes a runway for airplanes, impractical as that may seem.

ARCHITECTURE BETWEEN THE WARS

By the onset of World War I, the stage was set for a modern architecture. But which way would it go? Would it follow the impersonal standard of the machine aesthetic advocated by Muthesius or the artistic creativity espoused by Van de Velde? Ironically, the issue was decided by Van de Velde's choice of

Behrens' disciple Walter Gropius as his successor at Weimar. Yet the beginning of the war effectively postponed the further development of modern architecture for nearly a decade. When this development resumed in the 1920s, the outcome of the issues posed at the Cologne Werkbund exhibition in 1914 was no longer clear-cut. Rather than a simple linear progression, we find a complex give-and-take between modernism and competing tendencies representing traditional voices and alternative visions. This varied response has its parallel in the art of the period, which largely rejected abstraction in favor of Fantasy, Expressionism, and Realism.

RIETVELD. The work of Frank Lloyd Wright attracted much attention in Europe by 1914. Among the first to recognize its importance were some young Dutch architects who, a few years later, joined forces with Mondrian in the *De Stijl* movement (see page 805). Among their most important experiments is the Schröder House, designed by Gerrit Rietveld (1888–1964) in 1924. The facade looks like a Mondrian painting transposed into three dimensions, for it utilizes the same rigorous abstraction and refined geometry (fig. 1164). The lively arrangement of floating panels and intersecting planes is based on Mondrian's principle of dynamic equilibrium: the balance of unequal but equivalent oppositions, which expresses the mystical harmony of humanity with the universe. Steel beams, rails, and other elements are painted in bright, primary colors to articulate the composition. Unlike the elements of a painting by Mondrian, the exterior parts look as if they can be shifted at will, though in fact they fit as tightly as interlocking pieces of a jigsaw puzzle. Not a single element could be moved without destroying the delicate balance of the whole.

Rietveld's approach to the interior (figs. 1165 and 1166) reveals his background as a cabinetmaker in his use of unadorned "boxes" of space. However, the upper story can be left open or configured into different work and sleeping areas through a system of sliding partitions that fit neatly together when moved out of the way. While this flexible treatment of the living quarters was devised with the owner, herself an artist, to suit her individual life-style, the decentralized plan also incorporates a continuous, "universal" space which is given a linear structure by the network of panel dividers.

Despite the fact that it retains an allegiance to traditional materials and craftsmanship, which were equated by *De Stijl* with the self-indulgent materialism of the past, Schröder House proclaims a utopian ideal widely held in the early twentieth century. The machine would hasten our spiritual development by liberating us from nature, with its conflict and imperfection, and by leading us to the higher order of beauty reflected in the architect's clean, abstract forms. The harmonious design of Schröder House owes its success to the insistent logic of this aesthetic, which we respond to intuitively even without being aware of its ideology. Yet the design, far from being impersonal, is remarkably intimate.

THE BAUHAUS. Schröder House was recognized immediately as one of the classic statements of modern architecture. The *De Stijl* architects represented the most advanced ideas in European architecture in the early 1920s. They had a decisive

1164. Gerrit Rietveld. Schröder House, Utrecht, Holland. 1924

1165. Plan of the Schröder House

1166. Interior, Schröder House

1167. Walter Gropius. Shop Block, the Bauhaus, Dessau, Germany. 1925–26

1168. Plan of the Bauhaus

influence on so many architects abroad that the movement soon became international. The largest and most complete example of this International Style of the 1920s is the group of buildings created in 1925–26 by Walter Gropius for the Bauhaus in Dessau, the famous German art school of which he was the director. [See Primary Sources, no. 111, page 947.] The most dramatic is the shop block, which is a fully mature statement of the principles announced ten years earlier in Gropius' Fagus Shoe Factory (see fig. 1159). The structure is a four-story box with walls that are a continuous surface of glass (fig. 1167). The result is rather surprising: since the glass walls reflect as well as transmit light, their appearance depends on the interplay of these two effects. They respond, as it were, to any change of conditions without and within and thus introduce a strange quality of life into the structure. In this way, the facade serves a similar purpose to the mirrorlike finish of Brancusi's *Bird in Space* (fig. 1112).

More important than this individual structure, however, is the complex as a whole and what it stood for. Initially during its Weimar phase, the Bauhaus (which was the result of merging two separate schools) tried to fulfill the goals of the Arts and Crafts Movement, but the traditional attitudes toward the arts and crafts were too different for this romantic dream to succeed, and there developed a deep split between the Workshop Masters, who were responsible for practical crafts, and the Masters of Form, whom Gropius invited to teach theory, such as Kandinsky and Klee. The arrival of László Moholy-Nagy (see page 907), a Hungarian follower of Tatlin's Constructivism (see page 847), and then Josef Albers (see page 831) gave the curriculum a far more rational basis. But it was the move to Dessau, which invited the school to transfer there when it was closed down for a while by Weimar, that proved decisive. The definitive character of the Bauhaus is reflected in Gropius' design. The plan consists of three major blocks (fig. 1168) for classrooms, shops, and studios, and a student center, the first two linked by a bridge of ferroconcrete contain-

ing offices. Its curriculum embraced all the visual arts, linked by the root concept of "structure" (Bau). It included, in addition to an art school, departments of industrial design under Marcel Breuer (see page 883), graphic art under Herbert Bayer (see page 907), and architecture, whose chief representative was Mies van der Rohe (see below), the Bauhaus' last director.

Gropius' buildings at Dessau incorporate elements of *De Stijl* and Constructivism, just as the school accommodated a range of temperaments and approaches. The Shop Block proclaims the Bauhaus' frankly practical approach, yet the complex as a whole promoted a remarkable community spirit, both of which were entirely different in character from what Gropius had inherited from Van de Velde at Weimar. The Bauhaus thus embodied Gropius' tolerant, yet unified vision. Not surprisingly, the school did not long outlast his departure in 1929 to pursue architecture full time. After his hand-picked successor, Hannes Meyer (1889–1954), was forced to resign because of his Marxist leanings, Mies van der Rohe tried vainly to revive the school's fortunes, but it was shut down by the Dessau parliament. By then, most of its leaders had left, and after a final attempt to reopen it as a private school in Berlin, the Bauhaus was closed by the Nazis in 1933.

MIES VAN DER ROHE. Equally prophetic was the German Pavilion designed by Ludwig Mies van der Rohe (1886–1969) for the International Exposition of 1929 in Barcelona (figs. 1169 and 1170), unfortunately dismantled soon after the fair closed. The structure was a daringly low-slung affair elevated on a marble base, with enclosed courtyards at the front and rear, and even more radically simple in appearance than Wright's Robie House (see figs. 1154 and 1155), out of which it clearly developed. Its walls were constructed of different-colored marble slabs, arranged like so many "dominoes" in a grid system with such precision that not a single element could be moved without disturbing the balance. Here is the great spiritual counterpart to Mondrian among contemporary

1169. Ludwig Mies van der Rohe. German Pavilion,
International Exposition, Barcelona. 1929

1170. Ludwig Mies van der Rohe. Interior, German Pavilion,
International Exposition, Barcelona. 1929

designers, possessed of the same "absolute pitch" in determining proportions and spatial relationships. Flooded with light from the great expanse of windows, the interior was wonderfully open and fluid, yet with a sparse cleanness that still seems irrepressibly modern.

LE CORBUSIER'S EARLY WORK. In France, the most distinguished representative of the International Style during the 1920s was the Swiss-born architect Le Corbusier (Charles Édouard Jeanneret, 1886–1965). At that time he built only private houses—from necessity, not choice—but these are as

important as Wright's Prairie School houses. Le Corbusier called them *machines à habiter* (machines to be lived in), a term intended to suggest his admiration for the clean, precise shapes of machinery, not the Futurist desire for "mechanized living." (The paintings of his friend Fernand Léger during those years reflect the same attitude; see fig. 1054. Le Corbusier was himself an excellent painter in this vein.) Perhaps he also wanted to imply that his houses were so different from conventional homes as to constitute a new species.

Such is indeed our impression as we approach the most famous of them, the Savoye House at Poissy-sur-Seine (fig.

1171. Le Corbusier. Savoye House, Poissy-sur-Seine, France. 1929–30

1172. Interior, Savoye House

1171). It resembles a low, square box resting on stilts—pillars of reinforced concrete that form part of the structural skeleton and reappear to divide the "ribbon windows" running along each side of the box. The flat, smooth surfaces deny all sense of weight and stress Le Corbusier's preoccupation with abstract "space blocks."

In order to find out how the box is subdivided, we must enter it (fig. 1172). We then realize that this simple "package" contains living spaces that are open as well as closed, separated by glass walls. Within the house, we are still in communication with the outdoors: views of the sky and the surrounding terrain are everywhere to be seen. Yet we enjoy complete privacy, since an observer on the ground cannot see us unless we stand next to a window. The functionalism of the Savoye House thus is governed by a "design for living," not by mechanical efficiency.

AALTO. Although its style and philosophy were codified about 1930 by a committee of Le Corbusier and his followers, the International Style was by no means monolithic. Soon all but the most purist among them began to depart from this standard. One of the first to break ranks was the Finnish architect Alvar Aalto (1898–1976), whose Villa Mairea (figs. 1173 and 1174) reads at first glance like a critique of Le Corbusier's Savoye House of a decade earlier. Like Rietveld's Schröder House, Villa Mairea was designed for a woman artist; her second-story studio, covered with wood slats, dominates the view of the house from three directions. This time, however, the architect was given a free hand by his patron, and the building is a summation of ideas Aalto had been developing for nearly ten years. He adapted the International Style to the traditional architecture, materials, life-style, and landscape of Finland. Aalto took the opposite approach of Le Corbusier's in order to arrive at a similar end. Aalto's primary concern was human needs, both physical and psychological, which he sought to harmonize with functionalism. The modernist heritage, which extends back to Wright, is unmistakable in his vocabulary of forms and massing of elements; yet everywhere there are romantic touches that add a warmth absent from the Savoye House. Wood, brick, and stone are employed in various combinations throughout the interior and exterior, in contrast to Le Corbusier's pristine classicism. Free forms are introduced at several places to inject an element of playfulness, as well as to break up the cubic geometry and smooth surfaces favored by the International Style.

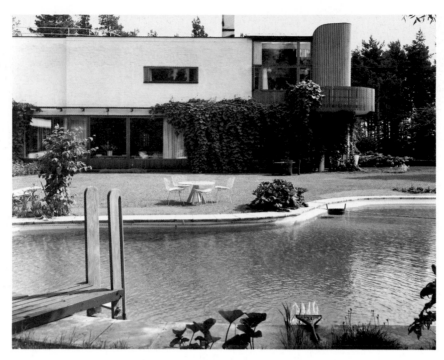

1173. Alvar Aalto. Villa Mairea, Noormarkku, Finland. 1937–38

1174. Interior, Villa Mairea

Aalto's importance is undeniable, but his place in twentieth-century architecture remains unclear. His infusion of nationalist elements in Villa Mairea has been interpreted both as a rejection of modernism and as a fruitful regional variation on the International Style. Today his work can be seen as a direct forerunner of Late Modern architecture (see pages 890–93).

EXPRESSIONISM. Architecture between the wars is sometimes labeled Expressionist if it does not conform to the International Style. Such a view is valid only insofar as it represents the assertion of the right of the individual to express a personal point of view against the norms of modernism. The International Style based its ideals on standardization for the sake of universality. As such, it represents the triumph of classicism. In reality, however, it was never the dominant approach after 1917, any more than abstraction was in painting. It seems best, then, to limit Expressionism in architecture following World War I to the few years around 1920.

MENDELSOHN. Inspired by the Arts and Crafts Movement's liberal politics and utopian ideals, a number of German

1175. Erich Mendelsohn. Einstein Tower, Potsdam. 1921

1176. Auguste Perret. Notre Dame, Le Raincy, France. 1923–24

architects gave free rein to their imaginations. The most eccentric building from this period is the Einstein Tower at Potsdam (fig. 1175) by Erich Mendelsohn (1887–1953), which has an organic quality that looks back to the Art Nouveau architecture of Antoní Gaudí and Henry van de Velde (see figs. 1001 and 1005). Despite this retrospective element, Mendelsohn was no reactionary, and the Einstein Tower, which functioned as an observatory, has also been hailed as the forerunner of Le Corbusier's later work (see fig. 1183).

PERRET.   Even more important for Le Corbusier was the precedent set by Auguste Perret (1874–1954). Early in the century he had been among the first to make effective use of recent advances in reinforced concrete and to define its architectural character. His greatest achievement is the Church of Notre Dame at Le Raincy outside Paris (fig. 1176). It is an astonishingly successful translation of Romanesque architectural forms (compare fig. 385) into ferroconcrete, while the vast expanses of glass "walls" are counterparts to the stained-glass windows of Gothic cathedrals (see fig. 423). This feat is not important in itself—it could, after all, readily be dismissed as mere historicism. Yet Perret has brilliantly solved one of the thorniest problems facing the modern architect: how to create a suitable expression of traditional spirituality in our secular Machine Age using a twentieth-century vocabulary. Le Raincy is so pivotal that all later church architecture in the West is indebted to its example, no matter how different the results.

THE SKYSCRAPER IN AMERICA.   The United States, despite its early position of leadership, did not share the exciting growth that took place in European architecture during the 1920s. The impact of the International Style did not begin to be felt on its side of the Atlantic until the very end of the decade. A pioneer example is the Philadelphia Savings Fund Society Building of 1931–32 (fig. 1177) by George Howe (1886–1954) and William E. Lescaze (1896–1969). It is the

1177. George Howe and William E. Lescaze. Philadelphia Savings Fund Society Building, Philadelphia. 1931–32

first skyscraper built anywhere to incorporate many of the features evolved in Europe after the end of World War I. The skyscraper was of compelling attraction to modernist architects in Europe as the embodiment of the idea of America, and during the 1920s Gropius and Mies van der Rohe designed several prototypes that were remarkably advanced for their time. Yet none were erected, while those constructed in the United States were sheathed in a variety of revivalist styles. (The Gothic was preferred.) Although they quickly became the most characteristic form of American architecture, even the skyscrapers of the 1930s—when many of the most famous ones, such as the Empire State Building, were built—are in the tradition of Sullivan, and do little to expand on the Wainwright Building (fig. 1009) except to make it bigger. Despite the fact that it is not entirely purist, the skyscraper of Howe and Lescaze is a landmark in the history of architecture that, remarkably enough, was not to be surpassed for 20 years (compare fig. 1181).

DESIGN

Like their predecessors in the Rococo, many of the great architects since Gaudí and Mackintosh have also been important designers who exercised an incalculable influence on others. The reason is not hard to find: they have had a unique, even privileged, understanding of modernism, its meaning, materials, and techniques. Their designs, like their buildings, have generally expressed the Machine Age through clean lines and cubic shapes bereft of unnecessary decoration. This was particularly true of the Bauhaus, where architecture and design were closely linked. The Bauhaus nevertheless failed in its goal of unifying the arts and putting the decorative arts on the same level as the fine arts. The main reason was that its members were far more gifted in architecture and painting than in design, despite the considerable emphasis placed on this area.

Gropius himself considered Bauhaus designs as models for the future that would fulfill his goal of providing high-quality wares to everyone through mass-manufacturing techniques, although only under Hannes Meyer was design placed at the service of people's practical needs. The interiors of the Masters' Houses designed by Marcel Breuer (1902–1981) reflect the school's outlook (fig. 1178). They have an almost monastic asceticism that is further emphasized by the stark simplicity of the furnishings. Breuer's famous chair in the right foreground is a marvel of elegant geometry for its own sake—without regard to comfort, as anyone who has ever sat in it can attest. Here, then, is the chief limitation of so much of twentieth-century design: the tyranny of form over human considerations.

Art Deco

The Bauhaus style was not the only major form of early-twentieth-century design, however. Art Deco is the name commonly given to the style that dominated the decorative arts between the world wars. In France it was called *Le Style Moderne*. Like the Bauhaus, Art Deco arose out of the work of the Glasgow school. Charles Rennie Mackintosh (see page 770), his wife Margaret Macdonald-Mackintosh (1865–1933), and her sister Frances Macdonald (1874–1921) had a great impact after 1900 on the Secession movements in Munich and especially Vienna, where the next phase of modern design took place (see page 763). Art Deco received its official baptism at the Exhibition of Decorative and Industrial Arts held in Paris in 1925, two years after the Bauhaus scored a great success at its initial design show in Weimar. The Paris exposition had actually been conceived ten years earlier, but like the progress of the style itself, it was postponed by World War I, when the movement was already well under way. The hit of the show was the Hôtel du Collectionneur pavilion assembled by Emil-Jacques Ruhlmann (1879–1933), the last of the truly great French furniture designers (fig. 1179).

In common with the Bauhaus, Art Deco attempted to resolve the dilemma between quality design and mass

1178. Marcel Breuer. The living room of Josef and Anni Albers, Masters' house, Dessau, Germany. c. 1929

1179. Emil-Jacques Ruhlmann. Grand Salon of the Hôtel du Collectionneur at the 1925 Exposition, Paris

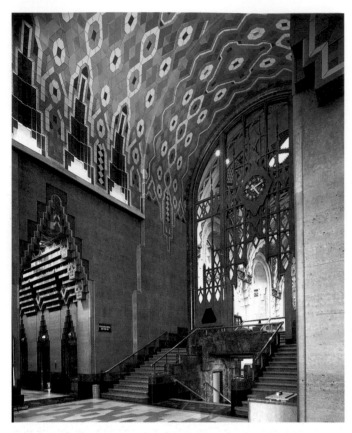

1180. Wirt Rowland, with Smith, Hinchman & Grylls, Associates Inc. (Tiles designed by Thomas Dilorenzo and made by Rookwood, Cincinnati). Main Lobby, Union Trust Company, Detroit. 1929

production, which both the Arts and Crafts Movement and Art Nouveau had also failed to reconcile. It, too, created a geometric style that could be applied to anything from teacups to building facades, a tendency that reached its climax in the following decade when everything became streamlined. The difference is that Art Deco never made the decisive break from Art Nouveau, of which it was a direct outgrowth.

Because it never developed the fully defined machine aesthetic that distinguishes the International Style, Art Deco cannot be called a modernist movement in the same sense, although they evolved in parallel to each other and sometimes achieved strikingly similar results. With its idealistic program of social and artistic reform, the International Style proved far bolder in redefining the decorative arts, despite its failure to achieve those goals. Art Deco, in contrast, was a decorative veneer that did not address the substance of modern existence. Instead, it responded to the changing taste of society during the "Jazz Age," without consciously intending to shape it. Whereas the Bauhaus came to adhere to a rigorous machine style, Art Deco was broadly eclectic in its scope, which included a taste for the exotic ranging from the art of ancient Egypt and Native American to the Russian Ballet of Sergei Diaghilev—whatever could be incorporated into its geometric framework. The virtue of Art Deco is that it embodied the very feature so conspicuously lacking in the International Style: fantasy, which permitted highly individual expression. Perhaps for that reason, it proved widely popular. Moreover, it enjoyed the commercial backing of the major manufacturers and department stores. Needless to say, much of what filtered down to everyday

objects catered to the lowest common denominator. But at its finest Art Deco could be brilliantly innovative.

Because it was essentially a decorative "skin," Art Deco lent itself readily to architecture. (Even the streamlined style associated with it was adapted from Dutch architecture of the early 1920s.) It proved especially popular in the United States, where it reached its most flamboyant phase during the 1930s. A spectacular example is the interior of the Union Trust Company in Detroit (fig. 1180). Resembling a gigantic Indian feather headdress, the ceiling of ceramic tiles has the honeycomb pattern of a beehive to symbolize Thrift and Industry.

ARCHITECTURE FROM 1945 TO 1980

High Modernism

Following the rise of the Nazis, the best German architects, whose work Hitler condemned as "un-German," came to the United States and greatly stimulated the development of American architecture. Gropius, who was appointed chairman of the architecture department at Harvard University, had an important educational influence. Ludwig Mies van der Rohe, his former colleague at Dessau, settled in Chicago as a practicing architect. Following the war, they were to realize the dream of modern architecture, contained in germinal form in their buildings of the 1930s but never fully implemented. We may call the style that dominated architecture for 25 years after World War II "High Modernism," for it was indeed the culmination of the developments that had taken place during the first half of the twentieth century. High Modernism was never monolithic even at its zenith. Yet its unified spaces, be they geometric or organic, embodied a harmonious vision that developed in a consistent way as the style was disseminated in countless buildings throughout the world. Like the International Style before it, High Modernism permitted considerable local variation within established guidelines, although the process of elaboration led almost inevitably to its dissolution.

MIES VAN DER ROHE. The crowning achievement of American architecture in the postwar era was the modern skyscraper, defined largely by Mies van der Rohe. The Seagram Building in New York, designed with his disciple Philip Johnson (fig. 1181), carries the principles announced in Gropius' design for the Bauhaus to their ultimate conclusion by using the techniques developed by Louis Sullivan and Frank Lloyd Wright, Mies van der Rohe's great predecessors in Chicago, to extend the structure to a vast height. Yet the building looks like nothing before it. Though not quite a pure box, it exemplifies Mies van der Rohe's famous dictum that "less is more." This alone does not explain the difference, however. Mies van der Rohe discovered the perfect means to articulate the skyscraper in the I-beam, its basic structural member, which rises continuously along nearly the entire height of the facade. (The actual skeleton of the structure remains completely hidden from view.) The effect is as soaring as the responds inside a Gothic cathedral (compare fig. 435)—and with good reason, for Mies van der Rohe believed that "structure is spiritual." He achieved it through the lithe proportions, which create a perfect balance between the play of horizontal and vertical forces.

1181. Ludwig Mies van der Rohe and Philip Johnson. Seagram Building, New York. 1954–58

1182. Le Corbusier. Unité d'Habitation Apartment House, Marseilles, France. 1947–52

This harmony expresses the idealism, social as well as aesthetic, that underlies High Modernism in architecture.

LE CORBUSIER'S LATER WORK. Abandoning the abstract purism of the International Style, Le Corbusier's postwar work shows a growing preoccupation with sculptural, even anthropomorphic, effects. Thus the Unité d'Habitation, a large apartment house in Marseilles (fig. 1182), is a "box on stilts" like the Savoye House, but the pillars are not thin rods. Their shape now expresses their muscular strength in a way that makes us think of Doric columns. The exposed staircase on the flank, too, is vigorously sculptural, and the flat plane of the all-glass facade has a honeycomb screen of louvers and balconies that forms a sunbreak but also enhances the three-dimensional quality of the structure. This projecting screen has proved to be an invention of great importance, practically and aesthetically: it is now a standard feature of modern architecture throughout the tropics. (Le Corbusier himself introduced it in India and Brazil.)

The most revolutionary building of the mid-twentieth century, however, is Le Corbusier's church of Notre-Dame-du-Haut at Ronchamp in eastern France (figs. 1183–85). Rising like a medieval fortress from a hillcrest, its design is so irrational that it defies analysis, even with the aid of perspective diagrams. The play of curves and countercurves is here as insistent as in Gaudí's Casa Milá, though the shapes are now simple and more dynamic. The massive walls seem to obey an unseen force that makes them slant and curl like paper. And the overhanging roof suggests the brim of an enormous hat, or the bottom of a ship split lengthwise by the sharp-edged buttress from which it is suspended.

This evocation of the dim, prehistoric past is quite intentional: asked to create a sanctuary on a hilltop, Le Corbusier must have felt that this was the primeval task of architecture, placing him in a direct line of succession with the builders of Stonehenge, the ziggurats of Mesopotamia, and the Greek temples. Hence, he also consciously avoids any correlation between exterior and interior. The doors are concealed; we must seek them out like clefts in a hillside. To pass through them is much like entering a secret—and sacred—cave.

Only inside do we sense the specifically Christian aspect of Ronchamp. The light, channeled through stained-glass windows so tiny that they seem hardly more than slits or pinpricks on the exterior, cuts widening paths through the thickness of the wall, and thus becomes once more what it had been in medieval architecture: the visible counterpart of the Light Divine. There is true magic in the interior of Ronchamp, but also a strangely disquieting quality, a nostalgia for the certainties of a faith that is no longer unquestioned. Ronchamp mirrors the spiritual condition of the modern age, which is a measure of its greatness as a work of art.

KAHN. Le Corbusier belongs to the same heroic generation as Gropius and Mies van der Rohe: all were born in the 1880s. It was these giants who in the course of their long, fruitful careers coined the language of twentieth-century architecture. Their successors continued to employ many aspects of its vocabulary in new building types and materials. Nor did they forget its fundamental logic.

1183. Le Corbusier.
Notre-Dame-du-Haut
(from the southeast),
Ronchamp, France.
1950–55

1184. Interior, Notre-Dame-du-Haut

1185. Bird's-eye perspective diagram of
Notre-Dame-du-Haut (from the northeast)

Louis Kahn (1901–1974) used bare concrete to great effect in the Jonas Salk Institute of Biological Studies in La Jolla (fig. 1186). Salk, inventor of the first polio vaccine, had been deeply impressed by his visit to Assisi and conceived of the center as analogous to the Franciscan monastery there. Kahn, who was in complete sympathy with his patron's views, carried out this scheme brilliantly. He treated the offices as a series of monastic cells attached to the central work spaces formed by the laboratories—or, as he put it, servant and server spaces. Like so many others, the ambitious project proved too costly (it included, among other things, separate living quarters for the scientists and their families) and was halted before it could be completed. It nevertheless remains the fullest statement of Kahn's principles.

1186. Louis Kahn. Jonas Salk Institute of Biological Studies,
La Jolla, California. 1959–65

1187. Eero Saarinen. Trans World Airlines Terminal, John F. Kennedy Airport, New York. 1956–63

1188. Interior, Trans World Airlines Terminal, John F. Kennedy Airport

SAARINEN. There is, however, an alternate tradition of reinforced concrete dating back to Berg's Centennial Hall (see fig. 1162). This Expressionist vision continued to provide a dialogue with the International Style that enriched modern architecture. The Trans World Airlines Terminal at Kennedy Airport in New York (figs. 1187 and 1188) by Eero Saarinen (1910–1961) is the great statement of postwar Expressionism. Saarinen, whose father had been a well-known architect in his own right, was a skilled practitioner of the International Style. Here he has used the full potential of concrete in order to express the very essence of flight. Yet the inspiration, rather than mechanical, was purely organic. The swelling, saillike

forms of the four "flying" roofs create the impression of a gigantic bird, while the free-flowing spaces conduct the visitor through the graceful interior with astonishing force, as if pulled along by a vortex.

NERVI. Saarinen is linked to Berg by Pier Luigi Nervi (1891–1979), who during the 1930s and 1940s pioneered the investigation of ferroconcrete in designs for aircraft hangars that provided the point of departure for all future developments in this vein. Nervi was the twentieth-century counterpart to Gustave Eiffel: a structural engineer with a bold sense of form and an even more daring vision. The culmination of

1189. Pier Luigi Nervi and Annibale Vitellozzi. Sports Palace, Rome. 1956–57

1190. Interior, Sports Palace, Rome

Nervi's efforts was the Sports Palace designed with Annibale Vitellozzi for the 1960 Olympics in Rome (figs. 1189 and 1190). From the outside, the roof appears as a thin covering whose light weight and flexibility are emphasized by the scalloped edges, so that it seems to have been draped over the Y-shaped supports radiating outward like flying buttresses. The effect inside is even more remarkable. The honeycombed roof, nearly 200 feet in diameter, recalls the interior of the Pantheon, with its great oculus (see fig. 246). A marvel of engineering, it seems to float effortlessly, like the dome of Hagia Sophia, in a pool of light without visible support (compare fig. 328).

URBAN PLANNING. To some architects, the greatest challenge is not the individual structure but urban design. Urban planning is probably as old as civilization itself (which, we recall, means "city life"). We have caught only occasional glimpses of it in this book, since its history is difficult to trace by direct visual evidence. Cities, like living organisms, are ever-changing, and to reconstruct their pasts from their present appearances is not an easy task.

With the advent of the industrial era two centuries ago, cities began to grow explosively and have continued to do so ever since. Much of this growth was uncontrolled, beyond the laying out of a network of streets. Worse, housing standards were poor or poorly enforced. The unfortunate result can be seen in the overcrowded, crumbling apartment blocks that are the blight of huge urban areas. They were taken over by the poor, while those who could afford it fled to the dormitory

1191. Oscar Niemeyer. Brasilia, Brazil. Completed 1960

decaying cities with housing that will provide a socially health-ful environment for very large numbers of people.

NIEMEYER. Nowhere are the issues facing modern civilization put into sharper relief than in the grandiose urban projects conceived by twentieth-century architects. These utopian visions may be regarded as laboratory experiments which seek to redefine the role of architecture in shaping our lives and to pose new solutions. Limited by their very scope, few of these ambitious proposals make it off the drawing board. Among the rare exceptions is Brasilia, the inland capital of Brazil built entirely since 1960. Presented with an unparalleled opportunity to design a major city from the ground up and with vast resources at its disposal, the design team, headed by the Brazilian Oscar Niemeyer (born 1907), achieved undeniably spectacular results (fig. 1191). Like most projects of this sort, Brasilia has a massive scale and insistent logic that make it curiously oppressive, so that despite the lavish display, the city provides a chilling glimpse of the future (compare fig. 1163).

SAFDIE. One particularly thorny problem is how to develop an alternative to the conventional high-rise apartment block in densely populated areas: a housing pattern that will be less deadeningly uniform (but no more expensive) and provide more light and air, safer access, and a multitude of other desirable features. A promising approach, by the Israeli architect Moshe Safdie (born 1938), was demonstrated in the Habitat complex at the Montreal EXPO 67 (fig. 1192). The individual apartments consist of prefabricated "boxes" that can be combined into units of several sizes and shapes, attached to a zigzagging concrete framework that can be extended to fit any site. Nevertheless, this lead, which proceeds from the work of Louis Kahn, has hardly been pursued by other architects.

towns of suburbia. This exodus, accelerated by the automobile, has produced the dangerous tensions that lend urgency to the cry for urban renewal today. Such renewal, needless to say, must involve the political, social, and economic resources of an entire society, rather than the architect alone. Yet the architect has an essential role in the process, that of translating the schemes of the planning agencies into reality. However, they have generally failed in their social mandate to replace the slums of our

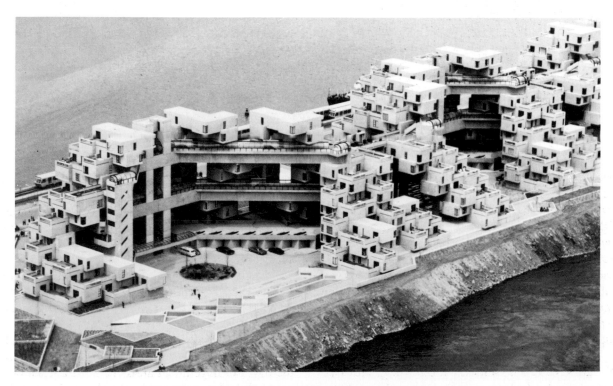

1192. Moshe Safdie and others. Habitat, EXPO 67, Montreal. 1967

1193. Richard Meier. The Atheneum, New Harmony, Indiana. 1975–79

Late Modernism

Since 1970 architecture has been obsessed with breaking the tyranny of the cube—and the High Modernism it stands for. In consequence, a wide range of tendencies has arisen, representing almost every conceivable point of view. They have made architecture perhaps the most vital of the arts in the last quarter of the twentieth century. Like so much else in contemporary art, architecture has become theory-bound. Yet once the dust has settled, we may simplify these bewildering categories, with their equally confusing terminology, into Late Modernism, Postmodernism, and Deconstructivism (see Chapter 8). They are separated only by the degree to which they challenge the basic principles of High Modernism.

MEIER. Late Modernism began innocuously enough as an attempt to introduce greater variety of form and material, but ended in the segmentation of space and use of "high-tech" finishes that are the hallmarks of late-twentieth-century buildings. An important early example of this process is The Atheneum at New Harmony, Indiana (fig. 1193), by Richard Meier (born 1934). In its departure from the idealism of High Modernism, it seemingly constitutes an ironic commentary on the utopian vision of this historic settlement, which was founded in 1815 by George Rapp and sold ten years later to the Scottish reformer Robert Owen, who established a short-lived Socialist society. The Atheneum reflects Meier's principal

concerns: program and site, entry and circulation, structure and enclosure. Its placement within the landscape has been judiciously calculated, with equally careful consideration given to its function as a visitors' center. The inspiration of Le Corbusier's Savoye House (fig. 1171) of nearly a half-century earlier is evident in the pristine white surfaces, which lend the building a sense of clarity. The vocabulary, too, remains essentially Cubist (compare fig. 1047).

To that extent, the Atheneum falls well within the modern tradition. Yet it looks like Le Corbusier's classic statement exploded from within. The building fairly bristles with external stairways and ramps, intersecting planes and jutting walls, and false structural elements that "frame" the view. These conspire to disrupt the facade and dissolve the boundary with the surrounding environment, so that the structure lacks the self-containment of the International Style. As we might expect, the interior is an equally dynamic play on Savoye House: spatial relations are skewed by distorting forms and rotating them off-axis. Clearly Meier has pushed the syntax of High Modernism to its limits. Beyond this lies only Postmodernism.

PEICHL. In contrast to the centralized authority proclaimed by the Seagram Building, Late Modernist corporate architecture may be seen as a reflection of today's global economy, in which the major companies are based on rapid technological

1194. Gustav Peichl. Austrian Radio and Television Studio, Salzburg. 1970–72

1195. Interior, Austrian Radio and Television Studio, Salzburg

advances and dispersed in far-flung smaller units. The Austrian Radio and Television studios designed by Gustav Peichl (born 1928) in 1970 have sharply contrasting wings radiating out from a central core to suggest their different functions (fig. 1194). The core itself has been conceived as a witty parody of spaceships, while the astonishing interior (fig. 1195) looks like a futuristic movie set. Everything gleams with polished metal tubing clustered like the pipes of a rocket, which "blasts off" above the skylight. This space-age motif is continued on the rear of the auditorium, which sports exhaust pipes that curiously resemble the artillery of an aircraft carrier, as if to protect its flanks from some imaginary attack.

1196. Richard Rogers and Renzo Piano. Centre National d'Art et Culture Georges Pompidou, Paris. 1971–77

ROGERS AND PIANO. Among the freshest, as well as most controversial, results of Late Modernism is the Centre Georges Pompidou, the national arts and cultural center in Paris, which rejects the formal beauty of the International Style without abandoning its functionalism (fig. 1196). Selected in an international competition, the design by the Anglo-Italian team of Richard Rogers (born 1933) and Renzo Piano (born 1937) looks like a building turned inside-out. The architects have eliminated any trace of Le Corbusier's elegant facades (fig. 1171), exposing the building's inner mechanics while disguising the underlying structure. The interior itself has no fixed walls, so that temporary dividers can be arranged to meet any need. This stark utilitarianism expresses a populist sentiment current in France. Yet it is enlivened by eye-catching colors, each keyed to a different function. The festive display is as vivacious and imaginative as Léger's *The City* (fig. 1054), which, with Paris' Eiffel Tower (fig. 964), can be regarded as the Pompidou Center's true ancestor.

FOSTER. Rogers helped to bring Late Modernism to a head in a series of buildings around London that inspired the wrath of Prince Charles. We can see why in the Hongkong Bank, designed by Norman Foster (born 1935), one of Rogers' former associates (figs. 1197 and 1198). It testifies to the bank's desire to have the most beautiful building in the world. (It is certainly the most expensive that money can buy.) Everything about the structure is extreme. The huge scale represents the megalomania of today's corporations and the architects who work for them. The edifice was intended quite consciously as a cathedral of banking. Like a Gothic cathedral, the reinforcing members of this capitalist "church" are located on the exterior in the form of bizarre struts (compare fig. 429). The cavernous interior, with its elaborately articulated structural skeleton, may likewise be compared to that of a Gothic cathedral (see fig. 451), although the immediate antecedents of the vast atrium lie in the early work of Frank Lloyd Wright. The Hongkong Bank has been hailed as a brilliant architectural feat, and condemned as a monstrosity that offers a nightmarish vision of the future. In any event, there can be little doubt that both the principles and the vocabulary of the International Style have been abandoned so completely that it may be considered an example of Late Modernism or Postmodernism with equal justification. Whatever we choose to call it, we have clearly reached the end of High Modernist architecture.

1197. Foster Associates.
Hongkong Bank, Hong
Kong. 1979–86

1198. Interior, Hongkong
Bank, Hong Kong

CHAPTER SEVEN

TWENTIETH-CENTURY PHOTOGRAPHY

THE FIRST HALF-CENTURY

During the nineteenth century, photography struggled to establish itself as art but failed to find an identity. Only under extraordinary conditions of political upheaval and social reform did it address the most basic subject of art, which is life itself. In forming an independent vision, photography would combine the aesthetic principles of the Secession and the documentary approach of photojournalism with lessons learned from motion photography. At the same time, modern painting, with which it soon became allied, forced a decisive change in photography by undermining its aesthetic assumptions and posing a new challenge to its credentials as one of the arts. Like the other arts, photography responded to the three principal currents of our time: Expressionism, Abstraction, and Fantasy. But because it has continued to be devoted for the most part to the world around us, modern photography has adhered largely to realism and, hence, has followed a separate evolution. We must therefore discuss twentieth-century photography primarily in terms of different schools and how they have dealt with those often-conflicting currents.

The course pursued by modern photography was aided by technological advances. It must be emphasized, however, that these have increased but not dictated the photographer's options. George Eastman's invention of the hand-held camera in 1888 and the advent of 35mm photography with the Leica camera in 1924 made it easier to take pictures that had been difficult but by no means impossible to take with the traditional view camera.

Surprisingly, even color photography did not have such revolutionary importance as might be expected. It began in 1907 with the introduction of the "autochrome" by Louis Lumière (1864–1948), who with his brother had created a new art form, the cinema, in 1894. The autochrome was a glass plate covered with grains of potato starch dyed in three colors which acted as color filters, over which was applied a coating of silver bromide emulsion; it yielded a positive color transparency upon development and was not superseded until Kodak began to make color film in 1932, using the same principles but more advanced materials. The autochrome was based on the color theories used by Seurat and even achieved

Divisionist effects, as we can see if we look hard enough at *Young Lady with an Umbrella* (fig. 1199), an early effort. Except for its color, the picture differs little from photographs by the Photo-Secessionists, who were the first to turn to the new process. Color, in fact, had little immediate impact on the content, outlook, or aesthetic of photography, even though it removed the last barrier cited by nineteenth-century critics of photography as an art.

The School of Paris

ATGET. Modern photography began quietly in Paris with Eugène Atget (1856–1927), who turned to the camera only in 1898 at the age of 42. From then until his death, he toted his heavy equipment around Paris, recording the city in all its variety. Atget was all but ignored by the art photographers, for whom his commonplace subjects had little interest. He himself was a humble man whose studio sign read simply, "Atget—Documents for Artists," and, indeed, he was patronized by the fathers of modern art: Braque, Picasso, Duchamp, and Man Ray, to name only the best known. It is no accident that these artists were also admirers of Henri Rousseau, for Rousseau and Atget had in common a naïve vision, though Atget found inspiration in unexpected corners of his environment rather than in magical realms of the imagination.

Atget's pictures are marked by a subtle intensity and technical perfection that heighten the reality, and hence the significance, of even the most mundane subject. Few photographers have equaled his ability to compose simultaneously in two- and three-dimensional space. Like *Versailles* (fig. 1200),

1199. *(opposite, above)* Louis Lumière. *Young Lady with an Umbrella.* 1906–10. Autochrome. Société Lumière

1200. *(opposite, below)* Eugène Atget. *Versailles.* 1924. Albumen-silver print, 7 x 9³/₈" (17.8 x 23.9 cm). The Museum of Modern Art, New York
Abbott-Levy Collection. Partial gift of Shirley C. Burden

1201. André Kertész. *Blind Musician.* 1921.
Gelatin-silver print, 16³/8 x 13¹/4" (41.6 x 33.7 cm).
The Museum of Modern Art, New York
Gift of the artist

1202. Brassaï. *"Bijou" of Montmartre.* 1933. 11⁷/8 x 9¹/4"
(30.2 x 23.5 cm). The Museum of Modern Art, New York
The Ben Schultz Memorial Collection. Gift of the artist

his scenes are often desolate, bespeaking a strange and individual outlook. The viewer has the haunting sensation that time has been transfixed by the stately composition and the photographer's obsession with textures. While Atget's work is marginally in the journalistic tradition of Nadar, Brady, and Riis (see pages 715, 717, and 774), its distinct departure from that earlier photography can only be explained in relation to late-nineteenth-century art. His pictures of neighborhood shops and street vendors, for example, are virtually identical with slightly earlier paintings by minor realists whose names are all but forgotten. Moreover, his photographs are directly related to a strain of Magic Realism that was a forerunner of Surrealism. Atget has been called a Surrealist, and while this characterization is misleading, it is easy to understand why he was rediscovered by Man Ray, the Dada and Surrealist artist-photographer, and championed by Man Ray's assistant, Berenice Abbott (see page 907). As a whole, however, Atget's work is simply too varied to permit convenient classification.

KERTÉSZ. Atget's direct successors were two East Europeans. The older of them, André Kertész (1894–1985), began photographing in his native Hungary as early as 1915, and his style was already defined when he came to Paris ten years later. *Blind Musician* (fig. 1201), made in Hungary in 1921, is the kind of picture Atget sometimes took, and it uses much the same

devices, above all the careful composition that isolates the subject within just enough of its surroundings to set the scene.

BRASSAÏ. The photographic style of Gyula Halasz, known simply as Brassaï (1899–1984), Atget's other successor, was also conditioned by Paris, its views and its habits. He was born in Transylvania and studied art in Budapest, but was a Frenchman at heart even before arriving in Paris in 1923. Several years later, while working there as a journalist, he borrowed a camera from Kertész and took a series of evocative photographs of the city by night. He soon turned to the nightlife of the Parisian cafés, where he had an unerring eye for the exotic characters who haunt them. *"Bijou" of Montmartre* (fig. 1202) shows the same sense of the typically aberrant as *At the Moulin Rouge* (see fig. 975) by Toulouse-Lautrec, whose art certainly influenced him.

CARTIER-BRESSON. The culmination of this Paris school is Henri Cartier-Bresson (born 1908), the son of a wealthy thread manufacturer. He studied under a Cubist painter in the late 1920s before taking up photography in 1932. Strongly affected at first by Atget, Man Ray (see page 906), Kertész, and even the cinema, he soon developed into the most influential photojournalist of his time, and he still thinks of himself primarily as one. His purpose and technique are nevertheless those of an artist.

1203. Henri Cartier-Bresson. *Mexico, 1934.* 1934. Gelatin-silver print

Cartier-Bresson is the master of what he has termed "the decisive moment." This to him means the instant recognition and visual organization of an event at the most intense moment of action and emotion in order to reveal its inner meaning, not simply to record its occurrence. Unlike other members of the Paris school, he seems to feel at home anywhere in the world and always to be in sympathy with his subjects, so that his photographs have a nearly universal appeal. His photographs are distinguished by an interest in composition for its own sake, derived from modern abstract art. He also has a particular fascination with motion, which he invests with all the dynamism of Futurism and the irony of Dada.

The key to his work is his use of space to establish relations that are suggestive and often astonishing. Indeed, although he deals with reality, Cartier-Bresson is a Surrealist at heart and has admitted as much. The results can be disturbing, as in *Mexico, 1934* (fig. 1203). By omitting the man's face, Cartier-Bresson prevents us from identifying the meaning of the gesture, yet we respond to its tension no less powerfully.

DOISNEAU. If Cartier-Bresson has a peer in any area, it is in the ironic wit of Robert Doisneau (1912–1994). His subject matter is human foibles, which he unmasks with the best of humor. Who has not seen the man in *Side Glance* (fig. 1204), sneaking a glimpse of the voluptuous nude while his wife comments on the more serious painting before them?

1204. Robert Doisneau. *Side Glance.* 1953. Gelatin-silver print

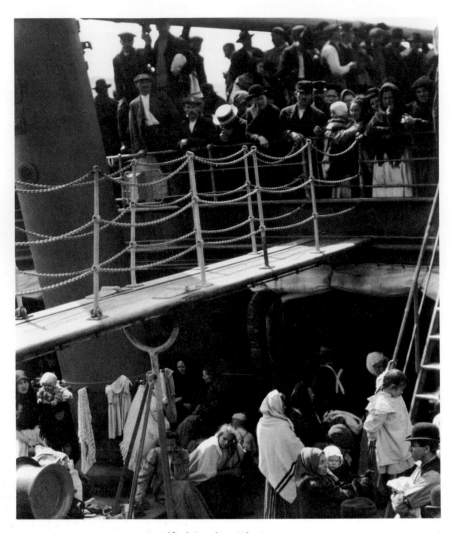

1205. Alfred Stieglitz. *The Steerage.* 1907.
Chloride print, $4^3/8$ x $3^5/8$" (11.1 x 9.2 cm). The Art Institute of Chicago
Alfred Stieglitz Collection

The Stieglitz School

STIEGLITZ. The founder of modern photography in the United States was Alfred Stieglitz, whose influence remained dominant throughout his life (1864–1946). From his involvement with the Photo-Secession onward (see page 776), he was a tireless spokesman for photography-as-art, although he defined this more broadly than did other members of the movement. He backed up his words by publishing the magazine *Camera Work* and supporting the other pioneers of American photography by exhibiting their work in his New York galleries, especially the first one, known as "291." The bulk of his early work adheres to Secessionist conventions, treating photography as a pictorial equivalent to painting. During the mid-1890s, however, he took some pictures of street scenes that are harbingers of his mature photographs.

His classic statement, and the one he regarded as his finest photograph, is *The Steerage* (fig. 1205), taken in 1907 on a trip to Europe. Like Ford Madox Brown's *The Last of England* (see fig. 944), painted more than a half-century earlier, it captures the feeling of a voyage, but does so by letting the shapes and composition tell the story. The gangway bridge divides the

scene visually, emphasizing the contrasting activities of the people below in the steerage, which was reserved for the cheapest fares, and the observers on the upper deck. If the photograph lacks the obvious sentiment of Brown's painting, it possesses an equal drama by remaining true to life.

This kind of "straight" photography is deceptive in its simplicity, for the image mirrors the feelings that stirred Stieglitz. For that reason, it marks an important step in his evolution and a turning point in the history of photography. Its importance emerges only in comparison with earlier photographs such as Steichen's *Rodin* (see fig. 1018) and Riis' *Bandits' Roost* (see fig. 1012). *The Steerage* is a pictorial statement independent of painting on the one hand and free from social commentary on the other. It represents the first time that documentary photography achieved the level of art in America.

Stieglitz' straight photography formed the basis of the American school. It is therefore ironic that it was Stieglitz, with Steichen's encouragement, who became the champion of abstract art against the urban realism of the Ash Can school (see page 799), whose paintings were at face value often simi-

1206. Alfred Stieglitz. *Equivalent*. 1930.
Chloride print. The Art Institute of Chicago
Alfred Stieglitz Collection

lar in content and appearance to his photographs. The resemblance is misleading. For Stieglitz, photography was less a means of recording things than of expressing his experience and philosophy of life, much as a painter does.

This attitude culminated in his "Equivalents." In 1922 Stieglitz began to photograph clouds to show that his work was independent of subject and personality. A remarkably lyrical cloud photograph from 1930 (fig. 1206) corresponds to a state of mind waiting to find full expression rather than merely responding to the moonlit scene. The study of clouds is as old as Romanticism itself, but no one before Stieglitz had made them a major theme in photography. As in Käsebier's *The Magic Crystal* (see fig. 1017), unseen forces are evoked that make *Equivalent* a counterpart to Kandinsky's *Sketch I for "Composition VII"* (see fig. 1030).

WESTON. Stieglitz' concept of the Equivalent opened the way to "pure" photography as an alternative to straight photography. The leader of this new approach was Edward Weston (1886–1958), who, although not Stieglitz' protégé, was decisively influenced by him. During the 1920s he pursued abstraction and realism as separate paths, but by 1930 he fused them in images that are wonderful in their design and miraculous for their detail.

Pepper (fig. 1207) is a splendid example that is anything but a straightforward record of this familiar fruit. Like Stieglitz' "Equivalents," Weston's photography makes us see the mundane with new eyes. The pepper is shown with preternatural sharpness and so close up that it seems larger than life. [See Primary Sources, no. 112, pages 947–48.] Thanks to the tightly cropped composition, we are forced to contemplate the

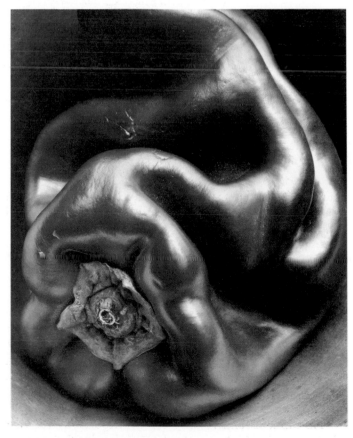

1207. Edward Weston. *Pepper*. 1930. Center for
Creative Photography, Tucson, Arizona

1208. Ansel Adams. *Moonrise, Hernandez, New Mexico.* 1941.
Gelatin-silver print, 15 x 18¹/₂" (38.1 x 47 cm). The Museum of Modern Art, New York
Gift of the photographer

form, whose every undulation is revealed by the dramatic lighting. *Pepper* has the sensuousness of *Black Iris III* by O'Keeffe (see fig. 1074) that lends the Equivalent a new meaning. Here the shapes are intentionally suggestive of the photographs of the female nude that Weston also pioneered.

ADAMS.   To achieve uniform detail and depth, Weston worked with the smallest possible camera lens openings, and his success led to the formation, in 1932, of the West Coast society known as Group f/64, for the smallest lens opening. Among the founding members was Ansel Adams (1902–1984), who soon became the foremost nature photographer in America. He can rightly be regarded as the successor to Timothy O'Sullivan (see fig. 927), for his landscapes hark back to nineteenth-century American painting and photography.

Adams was a meticulous technician, beginning with the composition and exposure and continuing through the final printing. His justifiably famous work *Moonrise, Hernandez, New Mexico* (fig. 1208) came from pure serendipity which could never be repeated, a perfect marriage of straight and Equivalent photography. As in all of Adams' pictures, there is a full range of tonal nuances, from clear whites to inky blacks. The key to the photograph lies in the low cloud that divides

1209. Margaret Bourke-White. *Fort Peck Dam, Montana.*
1936. Time-Life, Inc.

1210. Edward Steichen. *Greta Garbo.* 1928 (for *Vanity Fair* magazine). The Museum of Modern Art, New York
Gift of the photographer

the scene into three zones, so that the moon appears to hover effortlessly in the early evening sky.

BOURKE-WHITE. Stieglitz was among the first to photograph skyscrapers, the new architecture that came to dominate the horizon of America's growing cities. In turn, he championed the Precisionist painters (see pages 804–5) who began to depict urban and industrial architecture around 1925 under the inspiration of Futurism. Several of them soon took up the camera as well. Thus, painting and photography once again became closely linked. Both were responding to the revitalized economy after World War I which led to an unprecedented industrial expansion on both sides of the Atlantic. During the subsequent Depression, industrial photography continued surprisingly to grow with the new mass-circulation magazines that ushered in the great age of photojournalism and, with it, of commercial photography. In the United States, most of the important photographers were employed by the leading journals and corporations.

Margaret Bourke-White (1904–1971) was the first staff photographer hired by *Fortune* magazine and then by *Life* magazine, both published by Henry Luce. Her cover photograph of Fort Peck Dam in Montana for the inaugural

November 23, 1936, issue of *Life* remains a classic example of the new photojournalism (fig. 1209). The decade witnessed enormous building campaigns, and with her keen eye for composition, Bourke-White drew a visual parallel between the dam and the massive constructions of ancient Egypt (compare fig. 74), an idea that had already appeared in a painting of 1927 by Charles Demuth, *My Egypt.* In addition to their architectural power, Bourke-White's columnar forms have a remarkable sculptural quality and an almost human presence, looming like colossal statues at the entrance to a temple. But unlike the pharaohs' passive timelessness, these "guardian figures" have the spectral alertness of Henry Moore's abstract monoliths (see fig. 1126). Bourke-White's rare ability to suggest multiple levels of meaning made this cover and her accompanying photo essay a landmark in photojournalism.

STEICHEN. The flourishing magazine business also gave rise to fashion and glamour photography, which was developed into an art in its own right by Edward Steichen, America's most complete photographer to date. Steichen's talent for portraiture, seen in his early Photo-Secession photograph of Rodin (see fig. 1018), makes *Greta Garbo* (fig. 1210) a worthy successor to Nadar's *Sarah Bernhardt* (see fig. 925). The young

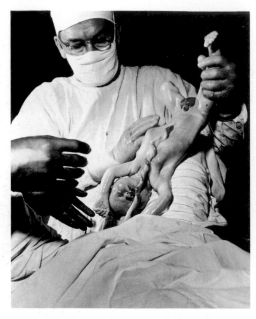

1211. Wayne Miller. *Childbirth.* "Family of Man" exhibition. 1955

film actress would have her picture taken countless times, despite her desire "to be alone," but none captures better the magnetic presence and complex character seen in her movies. The photograph owes much to its abstract black-and-white design, which focuses attention on her wonderfully expressive face. But Steichen's stroke of genius was to have Garbo put her arms around her head in order to suggest her enigmatic personality.

MILLER.   One of Steichen's contributions to photography was to organize the "Family of Man" exhibition, which opened in New York in 1955. Wayne Miller's picture of childbirth (fig. 1211) from this epoch-making show captures the miracle of life in one dramatic image. It records with shocking honesty the newborn infant's abrupt entry into the world we all share. At the same time, the hands that reach out to help him are a moving affirmation of human existence.

VAN DER ZEE.   The nature of the Harlem Renaissance, which flourished in the 1920s (see page 818), was hotly debated by black critics even in its own day. While its achievement

1212. James Van Der Zee. *At Home.* 1934. James Van Der Zee Estate

in literature is beyond dispute, the photography of James Van Der Zee (1886–1983) is often regarded today as its chief contribution to the visual arts. Much of his work is commercial and variable in quality, yet it remains of great documentary value and, at its best, provides a compelling portrait of the era. Van Der Zee had an acute understanding of settings as reflections of people's sense of place in the world, which he used to bring out a sitter's character and dreams. Though posed in obvious imitation of fashionable photographs of white society, his picture of the wife of the Reverend George Wilson Becton (fig. 1212), taken two years after the popular pastor of the Salem Methodist Church in Harlem was murdered, shows Van Der Zee's unique ability to capture the pride of African-Americans during a period when their dreams seemed on the verge of being realized.

Germany

With the New Objectivity movement in Germany during the late 1920s and early 1930s (see page 815), photography achieved a degree of excellence that has not been surpassed. Fostered by the invention of superior German cameras and the boom in publishing everywhere, this German version of straight photography emphasized materiality at a time when many other photographers were turning away from the real world. The intrinsic beauty of things was brought out through the clarity of form and structure in their photographs. This approach accorded with Bauhaus principles except with regard to function (see page 876).

RENGER-PATZSCH. *Potter's Hands* (fig. 1213) by Albert Renger-Patzsch (1897–1966), New Objectivity's leading exponent, is a marvel of technique and design that deliberately avoids any personal statement by reducing the image to an abstraction; the content lies solely in the cool perfection of the presentation and the orderly world it implies.

SANDER. When applied to people rather than things, the New Objectivity could have deceptive results. August Sander (1876–1964), whose *Face of Our Time* was published in 1929, concealed the book's intentions behind a disarmingly straightforward surface. The 60 portraits provide a devastating survey of Germany during the rise of the Nazis, who later suppressed the book. Clearly proud of his position, the man in Sander's *Pastry Cook, Cologne* (fig. 1214) is the very opposite of the timid figure in George Grosz' *Germany, a Winter's Tale* (see fig. 1068). Despite their curious resemblance, this "good citizen" seems oblivious to the evil that Grosz has depicted so vividly. While the photograph passes no individual judgment, in the context of the book the subject's unconcern stands as a strong indictment of the era as a whole.

Czechoslovakia

SUDEK. Josef Sudek (1896–1976) was the most diverse photographer of his time. The work of this one-armed photographer (he lost his right arm in World War I and had to struggle to take his pictures) incorporated nearly the full range of modern photography before 1945, except photojournalism,

1213. Albert Renger-Patzsch. *Potter's Hands.* 1925. Gelatin-silver print, 11³/4 x 15¹/8" (29.8 x 38.2 cm). The Museum of Modern Art, New York
Gift of the photographer

1214. August Sander. *Pastry Cook, Cologne.* 1928. August Sander Archiv/SK-Stiftung Kultur, Cologne, Germany

1215. Josef Sudek. *View from Studio Window in Winter.* 1954.
Gelatin-silver print, 8¹/₂ x 11¹/₁₆" (21.6 x 28.1 cm). The Museum of Modern Art, New York
Gift of Harriette and Noel Levine

which is concerned with passing moments that to him were merely incidental. Sudek was the Atget of Prague, which provided his main subject matter. From pictorialism, he learned to become a master of light, which he invested with the poetry of Vermeer, while the New Objectivity taught him to photograph simple objects with the reverence of Chardin. A romantic at heart, he sought to reveal the secret life of nature. Sudek preferred to work in series over the years and would often return to the same place to document its changing face and uncover new meanings. He was a recluse who became even more secretive during World War II, when his movement was severely restricted by the German occupation of Czechoslovakia. The most characteristic photographs from his later years are of private worlds, be they the cluttered studio where he lived, or gardens, his own as well as those of the artists, writers, and musicians who were his friends. Branches of a tree in snow seen through his window (fig. 1215) may be taken as a metaphor of the photographer himself. To Sudek, trees were primordial symbols of life that weather life's difficulties, much as he had survived personal tragedy.

The Heroic Age of Photography

CAPA. The period from 1930 to 1945 can be called the heroic age of photography for its photographers' notable response to the challenges of their times. Their physical bravery was exemplified by the combat photographer Robert Capa (1913–1954), who covered wars around the world for 20 years before being killed by a land mine in Vietnam. While

barely adequate technically, his picture of a Loyalist soldier being shot during the Spanish Civil War (fig. 1216) captures fully the horror of death at the moment of impact. Had it been taken by someone else, it might seem a freak photograph, but it is altogether typical of Capa's battle close-ups; he was as fearless as Civil War photographer Mathew Brady.

LANGE. Photographers in those difficult times demonstrated moral courage as well. Under Roy Stryker, staff photographers of the Farm Security Administration compiled a comprehensive photodocumentary archive of rural America during the Depression. While the FSA photographers presented a balanced and objective view, most of them were also reformers whose work responded to the social problems they confronted daily in the field. The concern of Dorothea Lange (1895–1965) for people and her sensitivity to their dignity made her the finest documentary photographer of the time in America.

At a pea-pickers' camp in Nipomo, California, Lange discovered 2,500 virtually starving migrant workers and took several pictures of a young widow with her children, much later identified as Florence Thompson; when *Migrant Mother, California* (fig. 1217) was published in a news story on their plight, the government rushed in food, and eventually migrant relief camps were opened. More than any Social Realist or Regionalist painting (see page 817), *Migrant Mother, California* has come to stand for that entire era. Unposed and uncropped, this photograph has an unforgettable immediacy no other medium can match.

1216. Robert Capa. *Death of a Loyalist Soldier.* September 5, 1936

1217. Dorothea Lange. *Migrant Mother, California.* February 1936. Gelatin-silver print. Library of Congress, Washington, D.C.

Fantasy and Abstraction

"Impersonality," the very liability that had precluded the acceptance of photography in the eyes of many critics, became a virtue in the 1920s. Precisely because photographs are produced by mechanical devices, the camera's images now seemed to some artists the perfect means for expressing the modern era. This change in attitude did not stem from the Futurists who, contrary to what might be expected, never fully grasped the camera's importance for modern art, despite Marey's in-

fluence on their paintings (see page 779). The new view of photography arose as part of the Berlin Dadaists' assault on traditional art.

Toward the end of World War I, the Dadaists "invented" the photomontage and the photogram, although these completely different processes had been practiced early in the history of photography. In the service of antiart they lent themselves equally well to fantasy and to abstraction, despite the apparent opposition of the two modes.

PHOTOMONTAGE. Photomontages are simply parts of photographs cut out and recombined into new images. Composite negatives originated with the art photography of Rejlander and Robinson (see page 775), but by the 1870s they were already being used in France to create witty impossibilities that are the ancestors of Dada photomontages. Like *1 Piping Man* (see fig. 1059) by Max Ernst (who, not surprisingly, became a master of the genre), Dadaist photomontages utilize the techniques of Synthetic Cubism to ridicule social and aesthetic conventions.

These imaginative parodies destroy all pictorial illusionism and therefore stand in direct opposition to straight photographs, which use the camera to record and probe the meaning of reality. Dada photomontages might be called "ready-images," after Duchamp's ready-mades. Like other collages, they are literally torn from popular culture and given new meaning. Although the photomontage relies more on the laws of chance, the Surrealists later claimed it to be a form of automatic handwriting on the grounds that it responds to a stream of consciousness.

Most Surrealist photographers have been influenced by the Belgian painter René Magritte, whose mystifying fantasies (see fig. 1062) are treated with a magic realism that is the opposite of automatic handwriting. Since Magritte's pictorial style was already highly naturalistic, he only experimented with the camera. Nevertheless, he had a considerable impact on photography because his illusionistic paradoxes can be readily emulated in photographs, such as the photomontage

1218. Herbert Bayer. *lonely metropolitan.* 1932. Photomontage, 14 x 11" (35.6 x 28 cm). Collection the artist (copyright)

1219. John Heartfield. *As in the Middle Ages, so in the Third Reich.* 1934. Poster, photomontage. Akademie der Künste, John Heartfield Archiv, Berlin

1220. Man Ray. *Untitled* (Rayograph). 1928. Gelatin-silver print, 15¹/₂ x 11⁵/₈" (39.4 x 29.5 cm). The Museum of Modern Art, New York
Gift of James Thrall Soby

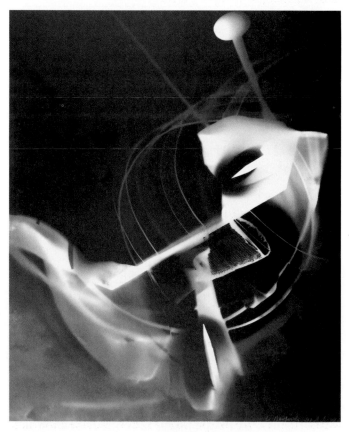

1221. László Moholy-Nagy. *Untitled.* Photogram, silver bromide print, 19¹/₂ x 15³/₄" (49.5 x 40 cm). The Art Institute of Chicago
Gift of George Bancroft, 1968

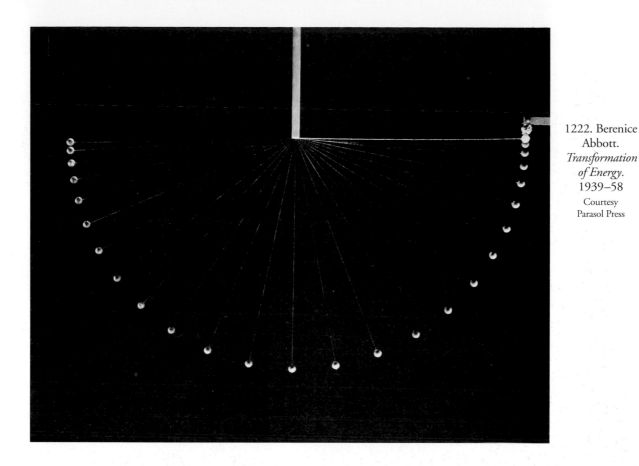

1222. Berenice
Abbott.
*Transformation
of Energy.*
1939–58
Courtesy
Parasol Press

lonely metropolitan (fig. 1218) by the German-born Herbert Bayer (1900–1985). The purpose of such visual riddles is to challenge our conception of reality, showing up the discrepancy between our perception of the world and our irrational understanding of its significance.

POSTERS. Photomontages were soon incorporated into carefully designed posters as well. In Germany, posters became a double-edged sword in political propaganda, used by Hitler's sympathizers and enemies alike. The most acerbic anti-Nazi commentaries were provided by John Heartfield (1891–1968), who changed his name from the German Herzfeld as a sign of protest. His horrific poster of a Nazi victim crucified on a swastika (fig. 1219) appropriates a Gothic image of humanity punished for its sins on the wheel of divine judgment. Obviously, Heartfield was not concerned about misinterpreting the original meaning in his montage, which communicates its new message to powerful effect.

PHOTOGRAMS. The photogram does not take pictures but makes them: objects are placed directly onto photographic paper and exposed to light. Nor was this technique new. Fox Talbot (see pages 713–14) had used it to make negative images of plants which he called "photogenic drawings." The Dadaists' photograms, however, like their photomontages, were intended to alter nature's forms, not to record them, and to substitute impersonal technology for the work of the individual. Since the results in the photogram are so unpredictable, making one involves even greater risks than does a photomontage.

Man Ray (1890–1976), an American working in Paris, was not the first to make photograms, but his name is the most closely linked to them through his "Rayographs." Fittingly enough, he discovered the process by accident. The amusing face in figure 1220 was made according to the laws of chance by dropping a string, two strips of paper, and a few pieces of cotton onto the photographic paper, then coaxing them here and there before exposure. The resulting image is a witty creation that shows the playful, spontaneous side of Dada and Surrealism as against Heartfield's grim satire.

THE CONSTRUCTIVISTS. Because the Russian Constructivists had a comparably mechanistic conception of society, they soon followed Dada's lead in using photograms and photomontages as a means to integrate industry and art, albeit for quite different purposes. László Moholy-Nagy (1895–1946), a Hungarian teaching at the Bauhaus who was deeply affected by Constructivism, successfully combined the best features of both approaches. By removing the lens to make photograms, he transformed his camera from a reproductive into a productive instrument; photography could now become, at least in theory if not in practice, a technological tool for fostering creativity in mass education.

Like many of the Russian artists in the 1920s, Moholy-Nagy also saw light as the embodiment of dynamic energy in space. The effects conjured up by the superimposition and interpenetration of forms in his photographs are fascinating (fig. 1221). We feel transported in time and space to the edges of the universe, where the artist's imagination gives shape to the play of cosmic forces created by a supreme cosmic will.

ABBOTT. One of the principal educational purposes of Moholy-Nagy's images was to extend sense perception in new ways. Similar goals have been achieved by taking pictures through microscopes and telescopes. Such photographs have helped to open our eyes to the invisibly small and the infinitely far. Wondrous scientific photographs were taken from 1939 to 1958 by Berenice Abbott (1898–1991), Man Ray's former pupil and assistant, to demonstrate the laws of physics (fig. 1222).

1223. Aaron Siskind. *New York 2.* 1951. Collection the artist

Like Marey's motion photographs of 50 years earlier (see fig. 1020a, b), they are arresting images, literally and visually. Their formal perfection makes them aesthetically compelling and scientifically valid, and they have proved to be even more educational than Moholy-Nagy's photograms.

PHOTOGRAPHY SINCE 1945

Abstraction

SISKIND. Photography after World War II was marked by abstraction for nearly two decades, particularly in the United States. Aaron Siskind (1903–1991), a close friend of the Abstract Expressionist painters, recorded modern society's debris and decaying signs. Hidden in these details he discovered cipherlike figures (fig. 1223) that are ironically similar to the ideographs of some forgotten civilization no longer intelligible to us.

WHITE. Minor White (1908–1976) approached even closer to the spirit of Abstract Expressionism. An associate of Adams and Weston, he was decisively influenced by Stieglitz' concept of the Equivalent. During his most productive period, from the mid-1950s to the mid-1960s, White evolved a highly individual style, using the alchemy of the darkroom to transform reality into a mystical metaphor. His *Ritual Branch* (fig. 1224) evokes a primordial image: what it shows is not as important as what it stands for, but the meaning we sense there remains elusive.

Documentary Photography

SMITH. The continuing record of misery that photography provides has often been the vehicle for making strong personal statements. W. Eugene Smith (1918–1978), the foremost photojournalist of our time, was a compassionate cynic who commented on the human condition with "reasoned passion," as he put it. *Tomoko in Her Bath* (fig. 1225), taken in 1971 in the Japanese fishing village of Minamata, shows a child crippled by mercury poisoning being bathed by her mother. Not simply the subject itself but Smith's treatment of it makes this an intensely moving work. The imagery lies deep in our heritage: the mother holding her child's body goes back to the theme of the German Gothic *Pietà* (see fig. 479), while the dramatic lighting and vivid realism recall a painting of another martyr in his bath, Jacques-Louis David's *The Death of Marat* (see fig. 844). But what engages our emotions above all in making the photograph memorable is the infinite love conveyed by the mother's tender expression.

FRANK. The birth of a new form of straight photography in the United States was largely the responsibility of one man, Robert Frank (born 1924). His book *The Americans,* compiled from a cross-country odyssey made in 1955–56, created a sensation upon its publication in 1959, for it expressed the same restlessness and alienation as *On the Road* by his traveling companion, the Beat poet Jack Kerouac, published in 1957. As this friendship suggests, words have an important role in Frank's photographs, which are as loaded in their meaning as Demuth's *I Saw the Figure 5 in Gold* (fig. 1055). Yet Frank's

1224. Minor White. *Ritual Branch.* 1958. Gelatin-silver print, 10³/8 x 10⁵/8" (26.4 x 27 cm).
The International Museum of Photography at George Eastman House, Rochester, New York

1225. W. Eugene Smith. *Tomoko in Her Bath.* December 1971.
Gelatin-silver print. Aileen and W. Eugene Smith–Black Star

1226. Robert Frank. *Santa Fe, New Mexico.* 1955–56. Gelatin-silver print. Collection Pace-MacGill Gallery, New York

1227. Bill Brandt. *London Child.* 1955
Copyright Mrs. Noya Brandt

1228. Jerry Uelsmann. *Untitled.* c. 1972.
Collection the artist

social point of view is often hidden behind a facade of disarming neutrality. It is with shock that we finally recognize the ironic intent of *Santa Fe, New Mexico* (fig. 1226): the gas pumps face the sign save in the barren landscape like members of a religious cult vainly seeking salvation at a revival meeting. Frank, who subsequently turned to film, holds up an image of American culture that is as sterile as it is joyless. Even spiritual values, he tells us, become meaningless in the face of vulgar materialism.

1229. Joanne Leonard. *Romanticism Is Ultimately Fatal,* from *Dreams and Nightmares.* 1982. Positive transparency selectively opaqued with collage, 9³/4 x 9¹/4" (24.8 x 23.5 cm). Collection M. Neri, Benicia, California

Fantasy

Fantasy gradually reasserted itself on both sides of the Atlantic in the mid-1950s. Photographers first manipulated the camera for the sake of extreme visual effects by using special lenses and filters to alter appearances, sometimes virtually beyond recognition. Since about 1970, however, they have employed mainly printing techniques, with results that are frequently even more startling.

BRANDT. Manipulation of photography was pioneered by Bill Brandt (1904–1983). Though regarded as the quintessential English photographer, he was born in Germany and did not settle in London until 1931. He decided on a career in photography during psychoanalysis and was apprenticed briefly to Man Ray. Consequently, Brandt remained a Surrealist who manipulated visual reality in search of a deeper one, charged with mystery. His work was marked consistently by a literary, even theatrical, cast of mind which drew on the cinema for some of its effects. His early photodocumentaries were often staged as re-creations of personal experience for the purpose of social commentary based on Victorian models. Brandt's fantasy images manifest a strikingly romantic imagination. Yet, there is an oppressive anxiety implicit in his landscapes, portraits, and nudes. *London Child* (fig. 1227) has the haunting mood of novels by the Brontë sisters, Charlotte, Emily, and Anne. At the same time, this is a classic dream image fraught with troubling psychological overtones. The spatial dislocation, worthy of De Chirico, expresses the malaise of a person who is alienated from both himself and the world.

UELSMANN. The American Jerry Uelsmann (born 1934), a more recent leader of this movement, was inspired by Oscar Rejlander's multiple-negative photographs, as well as by Stieglitz' Equivalents. While Uelsmann's work also has a playful side, for the most part he involuntarily expresses archetypal images from deep within the subconscious. [See Primary Sources, no. 113, page 948.] The nude lying within the soil in *Untitled* (fig. 1228) identifies the fecundity of nature, signified by the tree of life, with woman as earth goddess. At the same time, the photograph seemingly conveys a dream in which the psyche retreats into the womblike sanctuary of primal nature. Each part of the print is a faithful record; it is their astonishing juxtaposition that gives the image a new reality.

Uelsmann once participated in one of Minor White's classes, and their photographs are not as far removed visually or expressively from each other's as they might seem. The principal difference lies in their approach to the Equivalent as a means of achieving a poetical inner truth: White, like Stieglitz, recognizes his symbols in received images from nature, whereas Uelsmann creates his symbols from the imagination in the dark room. Paradoxically, it is Uelsmann's imagery, not *Ritual Branch,* that is instantly recognizable, but, like the paintings of René Magritte (see fig. 1062) that inspired him, it refuses to yield an ultimate meaning.

LEONARD. Contemporary photographers have often turned to fantasy as autobiographical expression. Both the image and the title of *Romanticism Is Ultimately Fatal* (fig. 1229) by Joanne Leonard (born 1940) suggest a meaning

1230. David Wojnarowicz. *Death in the Cornfield.* 1990. Silver print, 26 x 38" (66 x 96.5 cm)
Courtesy of P.P.O.W. Gallery, New York

that is personal in its reference; it was made during the breakup of her marriage. We will recognize in this disturbing vision something of the tortured eroticism of Fuseli's *The Nightmare* (see fig. 884). The clarity of the presentation turns the apparition at the window into a real and frightening personification of despair. This is no romantic knight in shining armor, but a grim reaper whose ancestors can be found in Dürer's woodcut *The Four Horsemen of the Apocalypse* (see fig. 700).

WOJNAROWICZ. Even more shocking is *Death in the Cornfield* (fig. 1230) by David Wojnarowicz (1954–1992). Gifted with a singularly bizarre imagination, he was obsessed with the horrific, which consistently informs his work. At the time of this photograph, Wojnarowicz was already afflicted with AIDS, which claimed his life two years later. Of the countless images devoted to this dread disease by painters and pho-

tographers, none so fully captures its nightmarish terror. The macabre costume, made by Wojnarowicz himself, conjures up an awesome demon of death from some primitive tribal ritual that appears out of nature as if by magic. Like Munch's *The Scream* (fig. 989), here is an expression of irrational fear so gripping in its power as to lift personal suffering to a universal plane. It serves as an unforgettable reminder that, just as in the art world, soon virtually everyone will have been touched by the loss of cherished friends and colleagues to AIDS.

Artists as Photographers

HOCKNEY. The most recent demonstrations of photography's power to extend our vision have come, fittingly enough, from artists. The photographic collages that the English painter David Hockney (born 1937) has been making since 1982 are like revelations that overcome the traditional limita-

1231. David Hockney. *Gregory Watching the Snow Fall, Kyoto, Feb. 21, 1983*. 1983.
Photographic collage, 43¹/₂ x 46¹/₂" (110.5 x 118 cm). Collection the artist
© 1983 David Hockney

tions of a unified image, fixed in time and place, by closely approximating how we actually see. In *Gregory Watching the Snow Fall, Kyoto, Feb. 21, 1983* (fig. 1231), each frame is analogous to a discrete eye movement containing a piece of visual data that must be stored in our memory and synthesized by the brain. Just as we process only essential information, so there are gaps in the matrix of the image, which becomes more fragmentary toward its edges, though without the loss of acuity experienced in vision itself. The resulting shape of the collage is a masterpiece of design. The scene appears to bow curiously as it comes toward us. This ebb and flow is more than simply the result of optical physics. In the perceptual process, space and its corollary, time, are not linear, but fluid. Moreover, by including his own feet as reference points to establish our position clearly, Hockney helps us to realize that vision is less a matter of looking outward than an egocentric act that defines the viewer's visual and psycholog-

ical relationship to the surrounding world. The picture is as expressive as it is opulent. Hockney has recorded his friend several times to suggest his reactions to the serene landscape outside the door.

Hockney's approach is embedded in the history of modern painting, for it shows a self-conscious awareness of earlier art. It combines the faceted views of Picasso (see fig. 1034) and the sequential action of Duchamp (see fig. 1044) with the dynamic energy of Popova (see fig. 1039). *Gregory Watching the Snow Fall* is nonetheless a distinctly contemporary work, for it incorporates the fascinating effects of Photorealism and the illusionistic potential of Op Art. Hockney has begun to explore further implications inherent in these photo collages, such as continuous narrative. No doubt others will be discovered as well. Among these is the possibility of showing an object or scene simultaneously from multiple vantage points to let us see it completely for the first time.

CHAPTER EIGHT

POSTMODERNISM

We began Part Four with a discussion of modernism. It is appropriate that we end, for now, with its antithesis: postmodernism. We live in the postmodern era. How can that be, if modern is what is today? The term itself suggests the quizzical nature of the trend, which seeks out incongruity. To resolve this paradox, we must understand modern in a dual sense: modernity and modernism. Postmodernism as a trend not only supersedes modernism but, as we shall see, is opposed to the world order as it exists today and to the values that created it.

What, then, is postmodernism and when did it begin? Critics are in little agreement on these questions, which is hardly surprising, given how recent the phenomenon is. Generally speaking, postmodernism is marked by an abiding skepticism that rejects modernism as an ideal defining twentieth-century culture as we have known it. In challenging tradition, however, postmodernism resolutely refuses to provide a new meaning or impose an alternative order in its place. It represents a generation consciously not in search of its identity. Hence, it is not a coherent movement at all, but a loose collection of tendencies which, all told, reflect a new sensibility. Each country has a somewhat different outlook and terminology; nevertheless all may be grouped under the rubric of postmodernism. We must therefore resort to a composite picture. Though broadly painted as a matter of necessity, it will provide us with a general idea of postmodernism's peculiar character. Our treatment of postmodern art is likewise intended to be suggestive by discussing representative examples, albeit at the cost of omitting a great deal that is also of interest.

As the term *post* suggests, our world is in a state of transition—without telling us where we will land. Although "postmodern" was coined by a historian in the late 1940s to denote a late stage of the civilization initiated by the Renaissance, it has been used mainly by literary critics since the mid-1960s, a significant fact in itself. We may indeed trace the first symptoms back to that time, but in retrospect they appear to have been essentially a late phase of modernism, without making a decisive break from the mainstream of the twentieth century.

What is the difference? Postmodernism springs from post-industrial society, which is passing rapidly into the Information Age (the so-called "Third Wave"). According to this view, the political, economic, and social structures that have governed the Western world since the end of World War II are either changing, undergoing attack from within, or breaking down altogether, ironically at the same time as the collapse of Communism in eastern Europe. This institutional erosion has resulted in a corresponding spiritual crisis that reflects the disarray of people's lives. Postmodernism is a product of the disillusion and alienation afflicting the middle class. At the same time, bourgeois culture has exhausted its possibilities by absorbing its old nemesis, the avant-garde. Strangely enough, the avant-garde's mission was ended by its very success. During the 1950s the media made the avant-garde so popular that the middle class accepted it and began to hunger for ceaseless change for its own sake. By the following decade, modernism was reduced to a "capitalist" mode of expression by large corporations, which adopted it not just in architecture but in painting and sculpture.

Postmodernism celebrates the death of modernism, which it regards as not only arrogant in its claim to universality but also responsible for the evils of contemporary civilization. Democracy, based on Enlightenment values, is seen in turn as a force of oppression to spread the West's hegemony throughout the world. In common with most earlier avant-garde movements (including existentialism) postmodernism is antagonistic to humanism, which it dismisses as bourgeois. Reason, with its hierarchies of thought, is abandoned in order to liberate people from the established order. This opens the way for nontraditional approaches, especially those from the Third World, emphasizing emotion, intuition, fantasy, contemplation, mysticism, and even magic. Science is no better than any other system, since it has failed to solve today's problems. And because scientific reality does not conform to human experience, it is useless in daily life.

Truth is rejected as neither possible nor desirable on the grounds that it is used by its creators for their own power ends. Subjective and conflicting interpretations are all that can be offered, and these may vary freely according to the context. Since no set of values can have more validity than any other, everything becomes relative. Bereft of all traditional guidelines, the postmodernist drifts aimlessly in a sea without meaning or reality. To the extent that the world makes any sense, it is at the local level, where the limited scale makes understanding possible in human terms.

The only escape from an existence in which nothing has intrinsic worth is inaction or hedonism on the one hand and spirituality on the other. The latter is rarely an option, however, since religions impose their own authority and self-discipline; thus, only the most extreme forms of mysticism, lacking all rational control, are acceptable. Postmodern people are thus fated to become pleasure-seeking narcissists without any strong identity, purpose, or attachments. Avowedly cynical and amoral, they live for the moment, unburdened by any concern for larger issues, which are imponderables in the first place. Rather than vices, however, these traits are considered virtues, for they grant postmodernists a flexible approach to life that allows them to pursue new modes of existence, free from all restraints or authority.

In the brave new world of postmodernism, the individual is no longer anchored in time or space. Both have been rendered obsolete in life as they have in science, because they are beyond normal human comprehension and based on assumptions that are subject to doubt. Traditional definitions of time and space, moreover, were based on hierarchies of thought that served the purposes of colonialism, but the new "hyper-space" created by global communication makes it impossible to position oneself within customary boundaries.

Just as time and space have lost all meaning, so has history. The view of history as progressive was likewise tied to the established power centers of the capitalist system and used as a tool to oppress the Third World. Furthermore, its very premise is fallacious: if linear logic is inherently invalid, there can be no linear history either. Since conventional knowledge and structures are suspect, nothing can be learned from history in the first place, and its "facts" are therefore of little interest.

Postmodernism, of course, makes no attempt to pose new answers to replace the old certitudes it destroys. Instead it substitutes pluralism in the name of multicultural diversity. Pluralism leads inevitably to eclecticism, with which it is virtually interchangeable, since no one aesthetic is better than any other. Not only are they functions of each other, they become ends in themselves.

By the same token, postmodernism does not try to make the world a better place. In its resolute antimodernism, it is socially and politically ambivalent at best, self-contradictory at worst. Its operating principle is anarchism. But although it is surpassingly liberal in its range of possibilities—witness the rise of "political correctness" in the United States—to Marxists it is simply a decadent late phase of capitalism, while to conservatives it goes against traditional values. To the extent that it does offer an alternative, postmodernism espouses any new doctrine as superior to the one it seeks to displace. Radical politics becomes a game that is played for its own sake. In the end, however, postmodernism remains essentially a form of cultural activism motivated by intellectual theory, not political causes, to which it is ill-suited.

Postmodernism has all the classic earmarks of a self-appointed avant-garde, despite the fact that it vigorously disavows any such connection. Its resolute opposition to modernity makes it the latest adversary of conventional authority, which it is dedicated to overthrowing. Like all avant-gardes, postmodernism is a "degenerate" movement that foments an atmosphere of crisis in order to sustain and

justify itself. In character it comes closest to Dada and Surrealism, but lacks their high-pitched hysteria. Its antielitism is simply another means of attacking the cultural establishment, which it desires to supplant. The relativism and anarchism of postmodernism are patently subversive in their intent. This nihilism reflects the prevailing skepticism of the late twentieth century, when very little is deemed to have any significance or worth.

Postmodernism might well take its credo from Edgar Allan Poe:

All that we see or seem
Is but a dream within a dream.

Such a position is not without its problems. As we examine it, we realize that the postmodernist rejection of reality is a philosophical construct, just as its rejection of truth is an *a priori* value judgment. Even if we grant that everything is ultimately unknowable, reality must nonetheless be capable of being apprehended in a functional sense; otherwise people could not survive. Postmodernism, then, is comparable to that higher understanding sought by mystics, for whom reason alone is insufficient.

Because it has so many meanings, postmodernism itself becomes a meaningless term, posing the kind of hopeless double bind that it delights in. In fact, postmodernism as a whole is riddled with contradictions. But if nothing is valid, then the values it often espouses—feminism, pluralism, and the like—must be fallacious as well. Seen in this light, postmodernism is a sterile philosophy that reflects the impotence of the intelligentsia to act.

In the end, postmodernism cannot escape the very laws of history it claims to deny. As a parody of modernity, it has its parallels—indeed, its origins—in the avant-garde of a hundred years ago. The same "decadence" and nihilism can be found toward the end of the nineteenth century in the Symbolist movement, with its apocalyptic vision of despair. Like pluralism, for example, Gauguin's quest for the spiritual presumed the superiority of "alternative" knowledge systems and asserted a belief in magic, which was widely shared by other Symbolists. More generally, postmodernism espouses the same destructive values as the German philosopher Friedrich Nietzsche, who was one of the principal sources of the avant-garde. Although it offers nothing in exchange, people will no doubt devise a new system to replace the old one that postmodernism strives to overturn.

SEMIOTICS AND DECONSTRUCTION. The Information Age is obsessed with meaning—and the lack thereof. Like the intellectual disciplines, nearly all branches of culture have come under the spell of semiotics—the study of signs—also known as semiology (though a distinction is sometimes made between the two). And with good reason, for semiotics is part of philosophy, linguistics, science, sociology, anthropology, communications, psychology, art, literature, cinema: any sphere of human endeavor that involves symbols. (There are other classes of signs that are the subject of semiotic inquiry as well.) Semiotics in turn has been attacked from within by Deconstruction, which constitutes undoubtedly the most potent attack mounted to date by postmodernism. As the term suggests, deconstruction is destructive, not constructive. It tears a text apart by using the text against itself, until the text finally "deconstructs" itself. For those interested in exploring the issues further, we have supplied a brief overview in the Postscript at the end of this chapter. For our purposes it is not the theories, interesting though they may be, but their effect on art that counts.

POSTMODERN ART

We are, in a sense, the new Victorians. A century ago, Impressionism underwent a like crisis, from which Post-Impressionism emerged as the direction for the next 20 years. Behind its elaborate rhetoric, postmodernism can be seen as a strategem for sorting through the past while making a decisive break with it that will allow new possibilities to emerge. Having received a rich heritage, artists are faced with a wide variety of alternatives. The principal features of the new art are a ubiquitous eclecticism and a bewildering array of styles. Taken together, these pieces provide a jigsaw puzzle of our times. Another indication of the state of flux is the reemergence of many traditional European and regional American art centers.

Art since 1980 has been called postmodern, but not all of it fits under this umbrella. We shall find that the participation of the visual arts in the postmodern adventure has varied greatly and taken some surprising turns. In particular, the traditional mediums of painting and sculpture have played a secondary role. Much of the reason is that painting and sculpture are closely identified with the modernist tradition; by extension they are tainted as tools of the ruling class. Meanwhile, nontraditional forms, such as installations and photography, have come to the forefront and become highly politicized in the process.

Much of the basis for postmodern art can be traced back to Conceptualism, which led the initial assault on modernism (see pages 869–70). Indeed, it has been argued that the beginnings of postmodernism can be dated to the rise of Conceptualism in the mid-1960s. The two, however, are products of two distinctly different generations. Furthermore, Conceptualism itself derived from Dada, which has provided an "antimodern" alternative since early in the twentieth century. In the context of the 1960s, it was simply part of that ongoing dialogue, in which Pop also participated. Such a date, moreover, seems decidedly too early for the onset of what is fundamentally a late-twentieth-century phenomenon.

Installations and performance art have been around that long as well. What has clearly changed is the content of these art forms as part of a larger shift in viewpoint. Focused as it was on matters of art, early Conceptualism seems almost innocent in retrospect. Postmodernists, in contrast, attack modern art as part of a larger offensive against contemporary society. They are far more issue-oriented than their predecessors, and their work cuts across a much wider spectrum of concerns than ever before.

From all the recent ferment a new direction in art has begun to appear, at least for the time being. The principal manifestation of postmodernism is appropriation, which looks back self-consciously to earlier art, both by imitating previous styles and by taking over specific motifs or even entire images. Artists, of course, have always borrowed from tradition, but rarely so systematicals as now. Such plundering is nearly always a symptom of deepening cultural crisis, suggesting bankruptcy. (The same thing is going on in popular culture, with its perpetual "retro" revivals.) Unbound as it is to any system, postmodernism is free not only to adopt earlier imagery but also to alter its meaning radically by placing it in a new context. The traditional importance assigned to the artist and object is furthermore de-emphasized in this approach, which stresses content and process over aesthetics. The other main characteristic of postmodernism is the merging of art forms. Thus there is no longer a clear difference between painting, sculpture, and photography, and we maintain the distinction mainly as a matter of convenience.

Although it has an anti-intellectual side, postmodernism is preoccupied with theory. In consequence, art (and, along with it, art history) has become theory-bound. Yet, despite a growing body of writing and criticism, it lags far behind literature and poetry in developing a postmodern approach. Compared to language, the visual arts are traditionally poor vehicles for theory. Perhaps they have become so word-oriented of late in an attempt to keep pace with other disciplines.

Postmodernism is undeniably a fascinating phenomenon. Yet it has an Achilles' heel: it has produced little art that is memorable—it is merely "symptomatic" of our age. But for that very reason it is worthy of our interest. Fittingly enough, the most devastating critique of postmodernism comes from that apostle of modernism, Charles Baudelaire: "Eclecticism has at all periods and places held itself superior to past doctrines because, coming last on to the scene, it finds the remotest horizons already open to it; but this impartiality only goes to prove the impotence of the eclectics. People who are so lavish with their time for reflection are not complete men: they lack the element of passion. No matter how clever he may be, an eclectic is but a feeble man; for he is a man without love. Therefore he has no ideal . . . ; neither star nor compass. Doubt has led certain artists to beg the aid of all the other arts. Experiment with contradictory means, the encroachment of one art upon another, the importation of poetry, wit, and sentiment into painting—all these modern miseries are vices peculiar to the eclectics."

ARCHITECTURE

We begin with architecture, which not only initiated the postmodern dialogue in the arts but also puts the issues literally in concrete form.

Postmodernism

Postmodernism in art was first coined to denote an eclectic mode of architecture that arose around 1980. Because it is a style, we shall capitalize it to distinguish it from the larger phenomenon of postmodernism, to which it is intimately related. As the term implies, Postmodernism constitutes a broad repudiation of the mainstream of twentieth-century architecture. Although it uses the same construction techniques, Postmodernism rejects not only the vocabulary of

1232. Michael Graves. Public Services Building, Portland, Oregon. 1980–82

Gropius and his followers, but also the social and ethical ideals implicit in their lucid proportions. Looking at the Seagram Building (fig. 1181), we can well understand why: as a statement, it is overwhelming in its authority, which is so immense as to preclude deviation and so cold as to be lacking in appeal. The Postmodernist critique of the International Style was, then, essentially correct: in its search for universal ideals, it failed to communicate with people, who neither understood nor liked it. Postmodernism represents an attempt to reinvest architecture with the human meaning so conspicuously absent from the self-contained designs of High Modernism. It does so by reverting to what can only be called premodernist architecture.

The chief means of introducing greater expressiveness has been to adopt elements from historical styles rich with association. All traditions are assumed to have equal validity, so that they can be combined at will; but in the process, the compilation itself becomes a conscious parody characterized by ironic wit. This eclectic historicism is nevertheless highly selective in its sources. They are restricted mainly to various forms of classicism (notably Palladianism) and some of the more exotic strains of Art Deco, which, as we have seen (page 883), pro-

vided a viable alternative to modernism during the 1920s and 1930s. Architects have repeatedly plundered the past in search of fresh ideas. What counts is the originality of the final result.

VENTURI AND BROWN. The immediate antecedents of Postmodernism can be found in the work of Robert Venturi (born 1925) and his wife, Denise Scott Brown (born 1931). They realized that architecture in America had become so laden with pictorial and commercial imagery that they advocated overturning the modernist credo of "form follows function" by divorcing the symbolic quality of a facade from the building's purpose and structure. To accomplish that end, they created an architecture of banality, whose very triteness was proclaimed by ironic paraphrases of historical clichés from both the recent and distant past. Although few architects followed their lead in design, the theories of Venturi and Brown were important for opening the debate that led to Postmodernism.

GRAVES. The Public Services Building in Portland, Oregon (fig. 1232), by Michael Graves (born 1934) is exemplary of

1233. SITE Projects Inc. with Maple-Jones Associates. Best Stores Showroom, Houston. 1975

Postmodernism. Elevated on a pedestal, it mixes classical, Egyptian, and assorted other motifs in a whimsical building-block paraphrase of Art Deco, which shared an equal disregard for historical propriety. In this way, Graves relieves the building of the monotony imposed by the tyranny of the cube that afflicts so much modern architecture. Although the lavish sculptural decoration was never added, the exterior has a surprising warmth that continues inside. At first glance, it is tempting to dismiss the Public Services Building as mere historicism. To do so, however, ignores the fact that no earlier structure looks at all like it. What holds this historical mix together is the architect's personal style. [See Primary Sources, no. 114, pages 948–49.] It is based on a mastery of abstraction that is as systematic and inimitable as Mondrian's. Indeed, Graves was a skilled Late Modernist who first earned recognition in 1969 at the same exhibition held by the Museum of Modern Art in New York that showcased Richard Meier (see page 890).

Today Postmodern buildings are being erected everywhere. They are instantly recognizable by their ubiquitous reliance on keyhole arches, round "Palladian" windows, and other relics from the architectural past. They are also marked by their ostentation. Postmodernism may be characterized as architecture for the rich that has since been translated downward to the middle class, surrounding it with an aura of luxury bespeaking the egocentricity and hedonism that spawned the "me" generation of the 1980s, one of the most prosperous and extravagant decades in recent history. Nevertheless, the retrospective eclecticism of Postmodernism soon became dated through the repetitious quotation of standard devices that were reduced to self-parodies lacking both wit and purpose. In a larger sense, however, this quick passage reflects the restless quest for novelty and, more important, a new modernism that has yet to emerge to replace the old.

SITE. In its playfulness and complexity Postmodernism has rightly been compared to Mannerist architecture, which similarly introduced a note of decadence into the classical vocabulary inherited from the Renaissance. Both share an element of self-conscious burlesque as well that reaches a climax in the designs by SITE Inc. for Best Stores, such as one in a Houston mall (fig. 1233) that looks for all the world to be crumbling into ruins (compare fig. 660). This droll takeoff on standard commercial architecture is enhanced by the bleakness of the location itself.

The differences are equally profound, however. Postmodernism arises out of the general sense of disillusionment that bedevils our age and prevents the architect from seeing either the past or the present with innocent eyes. Such a claim might well be made of Mannerist architecture, of course. But because architects today must design for different "taste-cultures," the eclecticism of Postmodernism is intended as a reflection of our "social and metaphysical reality." Historicism, then, is part of the new pluralism, which can even incorporate a parody of modernism itself. But such parodies also change old meanings into new ones through "double-coding," which combines modernist techniques and traditional styles to communicate on a new plane with the public and architects alike. The result is a content that is entirely up-to-date, despite the apparent familiarity of its hybrid style.

STIRLING. The Postmodernist critique of Late Modernism is that the latter is committed to the tradition of the new and therefore maintains modernism's integrity of invention and usage. Moreover, it lacks both pluralism and a complex relation to the past, so that it fails to transform meaning. We may test this for ourselves by comparing the Pompidou Center (fig. 1196) with the Neue Staatsgalerie in Stuttgart (fig. 1234), which was immediately recognized as a classic example of

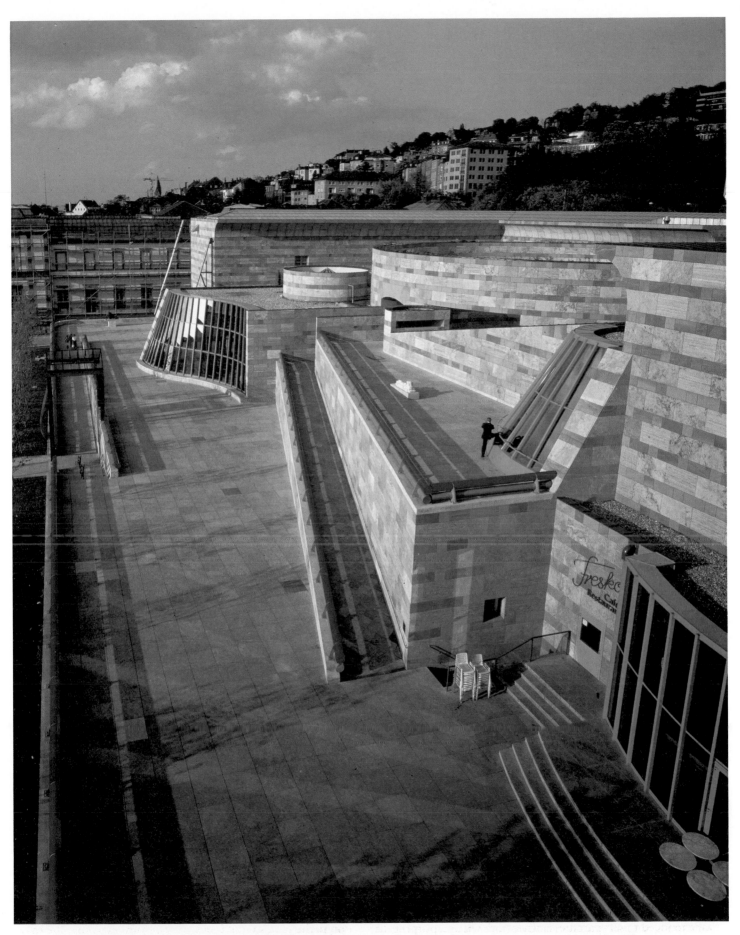

1234. James Stirling, Michael Wilford and Associates. Neue Staatsgalerie, Stuttgart, Germany. Completed 1984

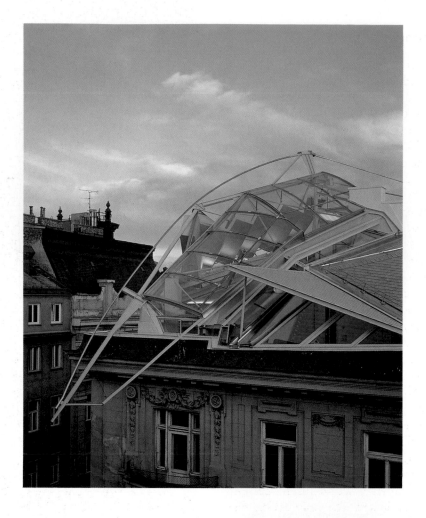

1235. Coop Himmelblau. Roof Conversion Project, Vienna. 1983–88

Postmodernism. The latter has the grandiose scale befitting a "palace" of the arts, but instead of the monolithic cube of the Pompidou Center, English architect James Stirling (born 1926) incorporates a greater variety of shapes within more complex spatial relationships. There is, too, an overtly decorative quality that will remind us, however indirectly, of Garnier's Paris Opéra (fig. 920). The similarity does not stop there. Stirling has likewise invoked a form of historicism through paraphrase that is far more subtle than Garnier's opulent revivalism, but no less self-conscious. The primly Neoclassical masonry facade, for example, is punctured by a narrow arched window recalling the Italian Renaissance (compare fig. 566) and by a rusticated portal that has a distinctly Mannerist look. At the same time, there is an exaggerated quoting of modernism through the use of such "high-tech" materials as painted metal. This eclecticism is more than a veneer—it lies at the heart of the building's success. The site, centering on a circular sculpture court, is designed along the lines of ancient temple complexes from Egypt through Rome, complete with a monumental entrance stairway. This plan enables Stirling to solve a wide range of practical problems with ingenuity and to provide a stream of changing vistas that fascinate and delight the visitor. The results have been compared not inappropriately to the Altes Museum of Karl Friedrich Schinkel (fig. 909), among the most insistently classical structures of the nineteenth century. By comparison, the Pompidou Center is arguably a far more radical building!

1236. Behnisch and Partner. Hall between Laboratory Wings, Hysolar Research Institute, University of Stuttgart. 1987

Deconstructivism

Although it claims to deal with the substance as well, in the end Postmodernist historicism addresses only the decorative veneer of the International Style. Spurred by more radical theories, Deconstructivism, another tendency that has been gathering momentum since 1980, goes much farther in challenging its substance. It does so by likewise engaging in appropriation. Oddly enough, it returns to one of the earliest sources of modernism: the Russian avant-garde. The Russian experiment in architecture proved short-lived, and few of its ideas ever made it beyond the laboratory stage. Recent architects, inspired by the bold sculpture of the Constructivists and the graphic designs of the Suprematists, seek to violate the integrity of modern architecture by subverting its internal logic, which the Russians themselves did little to undermine. Nevertheless, Deconstructivism does not abandon modern architecture and its principles altogether, and remains an architecture of the possible based on structural engineering.

Deconstructivism is a new term that combines Constructivism and deconstruction. Strictly speaking there can be no architecture of deconstruction, because building puts things together instead of taking them apart. Deconstructivism nevertheless follows similar principles and is symptomatic of postmodernism as a whole. It does so by dismembering modern architecture, then reassembling it again in new ways. Although it claims Michelangelo, Bernini, and Guarini as its ancestors, Deconstructivism goes far beyond anything that can be found in earlier architecture. We will find little common ground among its practitioners. The main devices they have in common are superimpositions of clashing systems or layers of space, and distortions from within that subvert the normal vocabulary and purposes of modern architecture.

COOP HIMMELBLAU. Although Deconstructivist designs have won major awards, their experimental approach and ambitious scale have discouraged actual construction. The most advanced designs to get off the drawing board have generally been relatively modest affairs, but no less exciting for that fact. The roof conversion for a Viennese lawyer's office by Coop Himmelblau (fig. 1235) has well been described as "a writhing, disruptive, animal breaking through the corner." The internal disturbances are incorporated into the structure itself: "It is as if some kind of parasite has infected the form and distorted it from the inside." This is directly akin to how deconstruction uses language.

BEHNISCH AND PARTNER. An equally brilliant example is the Hysolar Research Institute at the University of Stuttgart (fig. 1236) by the firm of Behnisch and Partner. The hall between the laboratory wings both reflects and parodies the scientific work being carried on. The materials suggest the "high-tech" purpose of the project, which is to investigate energy based on hydrogen produced by solar power, while the free-flowing passage indicates the collaborative exchange of ideas. Yet the sensation produced by the collision of twisted forms is not unlike careening down a roller coaster. Nothing, it seems, works the way it should in the orderly world of modern science!

1237. Bernard Tschumi Architects. Plan of Parc de La Villette, Paris. 1983

TSCHUMI. One of the first architects avowedly influenced by deconstruction is Bernard Tschumi (born 1944). The most complete embodiment of his Deconstuctivism is the Parc de La Villette in Paris, for which the founder of deconstruction, Jacques Derrida (see Postscript), later wrote an essay in the brochure explaining the project. The park's program was set by the fact that it had to include a variety of functions (workshop, baths, gymnasium, playground, concert facilities) and other parks and buildings already on the site. Tschumi's solution is directly related to this fact and presents an intelligent solution to what could have been a hopelessly complex problem that would have overwhelmed any traditional approach.

To describe the Parc de La Villette, we must resort to the coded terminology of Deconstructivism itself. The architect began by laying out the grounds in a simple abstract grid to provide a strong, yet flexible conceptual framework for change, improvisation, and substitution; he then subverted it by superimposing two other grid systems on it (fig. 1237), so as to

1238. Bernard Tschumi Architects. *Folie* P6, Parc de La Villette, Paris. 1983

prevent any dominant hierarchy or clear relation between the program and the solution. This multiple grid is deliberately antifunctional, anticontextual, and infinite. (In principle, it could be extended in any direction indefinitely.) Tschumi creates highly unorthodox relationships through decentralization, fragmentation, combination, and superimposition of elements, so that the architecture appears to serve no purpose. He further supplants form, function, and structure with contiguity, substitution, and permutation. To undermine the traditional rules of composition, hierarchy, and order, he uses crossprogramming (using space for a different purpose than intended), transprogramming (combining two incompatible programs and spaces), and disprogramming (combining two programs to create a new one from their contradictions). The functions are dispersed through a series of buildings (*folies*) whose components, appearance, and uses are interchangeable. The play between free and rigid form within this multiplicity leads to ambiguity, disorder, impurity, imperfection. The result denies any inherent meaning to the forms, structure, or organization.

What does all this theory have to do with the actual experience? Surprisingly little. The ensemble is meant to induce a sense of disassociation, both within and between its elements, that conveys an unstable programmatic madness (*folie*) through a form of cinematic montage inspired by the films of the Russian Sergei Eisenstein and others. However, the visitor is hardly aware of this effect. On the contrary, the system creates an order and rhythm of its own, whether Tschumi intended it or not. We are left only with a feeling of enchantment, which suggests the more playful meaning of *folie*, not just madness. The *folies* themselves resemble large-scale sculptures extended almost to the breaking point (fig. 1238). Yet the tension between the reality of the built structures and their "impossibility" results in an architecture of rare vitality. It is especially fitting that two of the most captivating *folies* are for

use by children. Although the architect insists that he was not expressing himself, this effect is perhaps the ultimate test of the park's success. Tschumi himself acknowledges the fact indirectly by speaking of affirmative deconstruction—a self-contradiction if ever there was one!

We may yet see one Deconstructivist deconstructing the work of another Deconstructivist. Peter Eisenman (born 1932) has designed a second garden for the Parc de La Villette that poses what might be called "the battle of the grids": Tschumi's versus Eisenman's version of Deconstructivist point grid, which the latter claims to have discovered first. And in this case, it was designed with Derrida's collaboration from the start. To pull it off, Eisenman has added new layers of ever more complex rhetoric (called "tropes" in the current parlance) to justify what amounts to skillful one-upmanship. Since the plan has yet to be built, it remains to be seen whether the results will support the dense verbiage.

POSTMODERN VS. DECONSTRUCTIVISM. Try as their adherents might to deny it, Postmodernism and Deconstructivism are really two sides of the same postmodernist coin, which has pushed modern architecture to its limits. As a style Postmodern challenges it from the outside, while Deconstructivism as an approach corrupts it from within. It is a measure of how far things have proceeded that in 1988 Philip Johnson, who helped to design the interior of the Seagram Building and was himself the architect of one of the most controversial Postmodern buildings (the AT&T Building in New York), declared modern architecture to be dead and mounted an exhibition of Tschumi, Eisenman, and several other Deconstructivists. This sort of questioning has gone on before. Postmodernism is a transition much like Art Nouveau at the turn of the century, which provided part of the foundation for modern architecture. It is a necessary part of the process that will redefine architecture as we have come to know it.

1239. Luciano Fabro. *The Birth of Venus.* 1992.
Onyx and marble, 8'7¹/2" x 2'3¹/2"x 3'10¹/2" (2.63 x .70 x 1.18 m).
Courtesy of Galeric Durand-Dessert, Paris

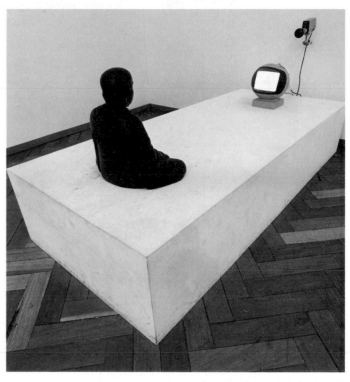

1240. Nam June Paik. *TV Buddha.* 1974.
Video installation with statue. Stedelijk Museum, Amsterdam

SCULPTURE

FABRO. Traditional sculpture has such a little role in post-modernism that it seems almost out of place when it does make an appearance. A rare example is *The Birth of Venus* (fig. 1239) by Luciano Fabro (born 1936), an original member of the *Arte Povera* movement (see page 837) who works in a wide variety of styles and techniques. The roughed-out "figure" is attached like a misshapen cocoon to the eroded capital atop the smooth column drums, all of contrasting color. What might she look like? Unlike Michelangelo's *Awakening Slave* (fig. 3), Fabro's *Venus* remains imprisoned within the marble forever, with no more than the barest outlines to hint at her possible shape. Curiously enough, the column more closely resembles a statue, the Archaic Greek "Peplos" Kore in figure 152, than does this strange appendage. Although some would deny it, *The Birth of Venus* is clearly a postmodern work. What makes it so is the improbable juxtaposition, which is a know-ing misquotation of the past. Yet the ironic takeoff is accom-plished with all the gravity of an artist for whom sculpture is both a living tradition and a dead language to be revived—a serious business that nevertheless does not preclude an ele-ment of irreverence for this vestigial relic. The real surprise is that the piece is so effective, for in its muteness it contains a spellbinding mystery.

PAIK. Sculpture today descends mainly from the work of Joseph Beuys, who, with Andy Warhol and John Baldessari, may be regarded as the patron saint of postmodern art (see pages 871, 834, and 870). The notes and photographs that document Beuys' performances and installations hardly do them justice. His chief legacy today lies perhaps in the stimu-lation he provided his many students and collaborators. Among them was Nam June Paik (born 1932). The sophisti-cated video displays of the Korean-born Paik fall outside the scope of this book; but his installation with a Buddha con-templating himself on television (fig. 1240) is a memorable image uniquely appropriate to the Information Age, in which the fascination with electronic media has replaced transcen-dent spirituality as the focus of life.

LONGO. The work of Robert Longo (born 1953) is the direct outgrowth of his experience in Performance art. Longo addresses disturbing issues in his large tableaux. These usually consist of wall pieces incorporating a variety of mediums, sometimes sound as well, but may also extend into space, so that they fall somewhere between assemblage and environ-ments. Notable for their formal elegance, they are produced with the aid of collaborators, though the conception generally

1241. Robert Longo. *Now Everybody (For R. W. Fassbinder).* 1982–83. Charcoal, graphite, and ink on paper,
8 x 16' (2.4 x 4.8 m); cast bronze, 6'7" x 2'4" x 3'9" (2.01 x .71 x 1.14 m). National Gallery, Budapest, Hungary

remains his. The effect produced by these conflicting elements can be unsettling, in keeping with the provocative subject matter. Longo's characteristic theme is violence and alienation in the artificial world of the urban middle class. The figure in *Now Everybody* (fig. 1241) is seen in a pose inspired by discothèques that, upon closer inspection, is strangely contorted, as if he had been shot or struck by an unseen force. He is engaged, we realize, in the universal dance of death that belies his sheltered life. Despite Longo's attempt to give the subject a larger meaning, it seems strangely characteristic of the 1980s, a decade memorable chiefly for its shallowness.

INSTALLATIONS. Why have installations become such a focal point of postmodernism? They may be regarded as the ideal manifestations of the deconstructionist idea of the world as "text," whose intent can never be fully known even by its author so that "readers" are free to interpret it in light of their own understanding (see Postscript). The installation artist creates a separate world that is a self-contained universe, at once alien and familiar. Left to their own devices to wander this microcosm, viewers bring their own understanding to bear on the experience in the form of memories that are elicited by the novel environment. In effect, then, they help to write the "text." In themselves, installations are empty vessels: they may contain anything that "author" and "reader" wish to put into them. Hence, they serve as ready vehicles for expressing social, political, or personal concerns, especially those that satisfy the postmodern agenda. The installation as text can become deliberately literal: it is often linked to a text that makes the program explicit.

KABAKOV. Russian artists have a special genius for installations. Cut off for decades from contemporary art in the West, they developed mostly provincial forms of painting and sculpture. Yet that very isolation allowed them to cultivate a unique brand of Conceptual Art that in turn provided the foundation for their installations. The first to gain international acclaim was Ilya Kabakov (born 1933), who now keeps his studio in New York. "Ten Characters" was a suite of rooms like those of a seedy communal apartment, each inhabited by an imaginary person possessed of an "unusual idea, one all-absorbing passion belonging to him alone." The most spectacular was *The Man Who Flew into Space from His Apartment* (fig. 1242): he achieved his dream of flying into space by being hurled from a catapult suspended by springs while the ceiling and roof are blown off at the precise moment of launching. Like the other rooms, it was accompanied by a text of Dostoyevskian darkness written by the artist, reflecting the Russian talent for story-telling. The installation was more than an elaborate realization of this bizarre fantasy, however. The extravagant clutter was a sardonic commentary encapsulating a wealth of observations that reflect the peculiar dilemmas of life in the former Soviet Union—its tawdry reality, its broken dreams, the pervasive role of central authority.

1242. Ilya Kabakov. *The Man Who Flew into Space from His Apartment,* from "Ten Characters."
1981–88. Mixed-media installation at Ronald Feldman Fine Arts, New York, 1988

Courtesy Ronald Feldman Fine Arts

POSTMODERNISM *925*

1243, 1244. Ann Hamilton. *parallel lines*. Two parts of an installation in two rooms,
São Paulo Bienal, September–December 1991. Mixed media

Courtesy Richard Ross

HAMILTON. Kabakov was inspired in part by the example of Beuys, who was also an influence on the young American installation artist Ann Hamilton (born 1956). Her work is about loss, be it from personal tragedy or distortion of a natural relationship. Unlike Beuys, she seeks only to raise issues, not to resolve them, a matter that is left to the visitor. Yet she uses many of the same means: her installations involve all of the senses through the use of unusual materials, often in disturbing ways, in order to present a paradox that lies at the center of each work. She exercises these choices through a train of free association until the idea crystallizes. Her installations are labor-intensive—obsessively, even ritualistically, so. Thus *parallel lines* for the 1991 São Paulo Bienal (figs. 1243 and 1244) began with assistants coating the walls of one gallery with soot from burning candles, then attaching sequentially numbered copper tags to the floor (an interest in seriality that is basic to Conceptual Art). Finally, a huge bundle of candles was placed in the room, so as to dominate it. A second room, covered entirely in the same copper tags, held nothing but two glass library cases containing turkey carcasses that were slowly devoured by beetles. This assault on the viewer's senses—and sensibilities—was intended to pose a number of questions. What is collected, why, and by whom? What is the moral difference between showing candles made by people from the fat of dead animals and exhibiting a dead bird with beetles carrying out their natural role as scavengers? Although death was treated matter-of-factly, there was a strangely mournful air to the entire installation, which invited viewers to ponder these matters and to arrive at their own conclusions.

HOWARD. Mildred Howard (born 1945) uses many of the same principles as Hamilton, but constructs her installations as specifically African-American statements. A social activist, she draws chiefly on her own life to define the black experience. To her, memory is both individual and ethnic. Thus *Tap: Investigation of Memory* (fig. 1245) resonates with multiple layers of personal and cultural meaning. It celebrates the importance of this dance form to the artist's family during her childhood, as well as the special contribution African-Americans have made to it. The taps, labeled "Traveler" significantly enough, are lined up ritualistically in rows, with

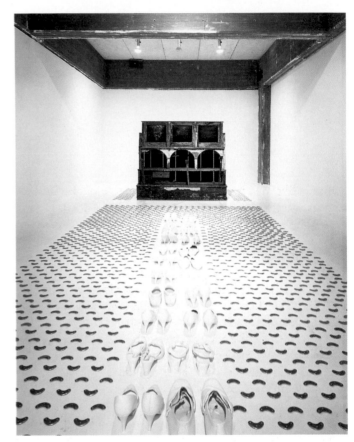

1245. Mildred Howard. *Tap: Investigation of Memory*. 1989. Travelers' shoe taps, in antique 3-seat shoeshine stand, assorted painted shoes, and delayed playback of an ambient sound,
10' x 13'6" x 51'6" (3 x 4 x 15.5 m). Collection the artist

Courtesy Gallery Paule Anglim, San Francisco

shoes in solemn procession down the center aisle, before a beat-up shoeshine stand which becomes a shrinelike altar. The spiritual references are intentional. Movement is closely identified in Howard's mind with African-American worship—especially as practiced in store-front churches, the subject of another of her installations—in contrast to the somber introspection traditional to Western churches. Yet *Tap* succeeds precisely because of the contemplative atmosphere, which evokes a broad range of associations.

1246. David Salle. *Miner*. 1985. Oil, wood, metal tables, and fabric, 8' x 13'7" (2.4 x 4.1 m). Collection Philip Johnson, New Canaan

Courtesy Gagosian Gallery, New York

1247. A. R. Penck. *The Demon of Curiosity*. 1982. Acrylic on canvas, 9'2¼" x 9'2¼" (2.8 x 2.8 m). The Rivendell Collection of Late-Twentieth Century Art on permanent loan to the Center for Curatorial Studies, Bard College, Annandale-on-Hudson, New York

Courtesy Michael Werner Gallery, New York and Cologne

PAINTING

Painting, like sculpture, is a traditional medium that does not lend itself well to postmodernism. Indeed, it is arguable that most of what passes as postmodern painting is really late modernism in disguise. In any event, there is no fixed boundary between the two. To the extent that it can be said to exist at all, however, postmodern painting is an outgrowth of Conceptualism, Pop Art, and Neo-Expressionism. Yet it differs from them in a fundamental respect: now painting acts like a deconstructed text gutted of all significance, except for whatever we choose to add by way of free association from the reservoir of our own experience.

How did painting come to be so barren of content? Traditional vehicles such as allegory require a shared culture. However, this is hardly possible in the postmodern age, despite the concept of the "global village," for our civilization is more fractured than ever. Deconstruction, moreover, proclaims the death of the author and subject matter as unnecessary vestiges of humanism, thus rendering meaning null and void. It argues instead that representation in its broadest sense is both unnecessary and undesirable on the grounds that it strives to re-create a fraudulent reality, and therefore can never provide an authentic experience. Such an attitude is not confined to deconstruction, however. It is inherent in postmodernism as a whole.

SALLE. The postmodern approach to painting is demonstrated by the work of David Salle (born 1952), a controversial figure who often incorporates racy images of nude women. (He worked for a while as a layout artist for a pornographic magazine.) An appropriation artist by nature, he derived everything in *Miner* (fig. 1246) from other sources: the Depression-era picture of a miner with two diamond rings superimposed on his jacket, and the bust of a girl hovering like a neon sign in front of the partial view of an interior. Although his technique is conventional enough, the treatment is novel. The miner's head, for example, is flanked by two smashed metal tables, as if to represent his "thoughts." By combining different objects and materials, the diptych becomes a pictorial counterpart to installations by his friend Robert Longo (see fig. 1241), and in principle there is very little difference between them. Salle's disregard for art-historical decorum in juxtaposing unrelated elements is as great as Michael Graves' (see fig. 1232), and reflects his training under the Conceptual artist John Baldessari, for whom anything goes (compare fig. 1152). Salle is clearly a gifted painter, so that we are forced to take him seriously, despite reservations that his reputation (like that of so many other artists in the 1980s) was driven by the art market's need to find a new "star." Yet the syntax is so disjunctive that *Miner* refuses to yield a satisfactory meaning, try as we might to discover one.

PENCK. Salle had much in common with a group of postmodern artists from the former German Democratic Republic who have helped to make Germany the leading school of painting in the West today. Perhaps the most interesting among them is A. R. Penck (born 1939). Penck is the pseudonym adopted by Ralf Winkler from a famous geologist whose specialty was the Ice Age. In fact, the artist lived in East Germany throughout most of the Cold War, a political "ice age" of its own, before emigrating to the West in 1980. The "primitive" and "childish" quality in *The Demon of Curiosity* (fig. 1247), with its colorful directness, is deceptive. Although

1248. Mark Tansey.
Derrida Queries De Man.
1990. Oil on canvas,
6'11" x 4'7"
(2.13 x 1.4 m).
Collection Michael and
Judy Ovitz,
Los Angeles
Courtesy Curt Marcus Gallery,
New York

Postmodernism in Music and Theater

It is hardly possible to discuss Postmodernism in music, which to date has not yielded significant results on matters of appropriation and deconstruction. The closest it has come to is Minimalism. The composer Lukas Foss, who has been practicing a form of Minimalism since the late 1970s, describes his *Quintets for Orchestra* (1979) in terms very similar to deconstruction: "A five-note chord dominates the composition. It is endlessly repeated, varied, permutated, transposed, and inverted, invading the entire piece . . . like a wound." Theater, by contrast, is ideally suited to appropriation and deconstruction, especially the latter, since it readily permits viewers to participate actively in creating the text as they perceive it. The main tendency has been to reinterpret existing classics, as well as works of recent vintage, in extremely untraditional ways that challenge conventional ("received") ideas about their content and meaning. Such is the case with the Romanian director Andrei Serban (born 1943), who was strongly affected by Peter Brook; Peter Sellars (born 1957), former director of the American National Theater at the Kennedy Center in Washington, D.C.; Les Breuer (born 1937), director of the Mabou Mines company, who was influenced by Beckett, Brecht, and Grotowski, among others; and Robert Wilson (born 1942), who worked with Philip Glass and the choreographers Andrew de Groat and Lucinda Childs on *Einstein on the Beach* (1976). Wilson's own works, stemming from his collaboration with the autistic teen-ager Christopher Knowles, juxtapose elements of different cultures and media in surreal fashion. Perhaps the most important contribution has been made by the Environmental Theater of Richard Schechner (born 1934), who conceives of theater as a public event that can take place in any environment and assigns an active role to the audience. Every element of theater becomes independent of text—indeed, there need not be any text at all. None of these ideas is new in itself. Rather, it is the combination that matters.

largely self-taught, Penck uses a fluid technique that is, in fact, very sophisticated, making it a wonderfully sensitive vehicle for expressing every possible meaning. But what are we to make of the picture's content? At first glance, it seems as bewildering as the rock engraving at the Cave of Addaura. Upon closer inspection we realize that the artist's "code" can be broken, at least enough for us to understand the basic intent. The demon, as fierce as anything conjured up by Gauguin (compare fig. 980), is surmounted by a bird looking both ways that signifies inquisitiveness, to which the small crucified figure at the left has been sacrificed. The figures swim in a sea of hex-like signs, letters, and numbers, symbolizing knowledge, which fills up the man to the point where he seems literally "pregnant (or at least bloated) with meaning." The painting reflects Penck's fascination with cybernetics, the science of information systems. Indeed, to him the artist is a kind of scientist, and he sees little difference between the two.

TANSEY. If Penck follows in the footsteps of artists such as Paul Klee by inventing a personal vocabulary of pictographs, Mark Tansey (born 1949) uses the Roman alphabet to accomplish the seemingly impossible: construct representational images that are literally made up of texts following the principles of deconstruction. *Derrida Queries De Man* (fig. 1248) shows the founder of deconstruction with his chief American disciple, Paul de Man. If we look closely, we see that the landscape consists of typeset lines that merge to form the steep cliffs. Here the texture of the paint serves to bridge the gap between text and illustration by embedding the idea within the image. In this sense, the painting functions as an illustration of a metaphor. But what is it saying? Certainly it makes a serious point about the relation between content, picture, and reality. Yet it does so with surprising wit, beginning with the very idea of building a painting out of words. And, in a gesture of supreme irony, Tansey has appropriated the image from a famous illustration showing the death of Sherlock Holmes at the hands of his archenemy, Professor Moriarty! We have seen such humor before, in the work of René Magritte (see fig. 1062), who served as an early inspiration for Tansey. By precluding a literal reading of the painting, this astonishing juxtaposition opens up new lines of questioning for the viewer that never fully resolve themselves.

PHOTOGRAPHY

Photography, too, has taken up the theme of image as "text." Given the close association of words and photographs in Conceptual Art, such a move was perhaps inevitable. It was abetted, however, by the new importance attached to semiotics, which has opened up fruitful new avenues of investigation for the artist. How do signs acquire public meaning? What is the message? Who originates it? What (and whose) purpose does it serve? Who is the audience? What are the means of disseminating the idea? Who controls the media?

Photographers, especially in the United States, raise these questions in order to challenge our received notions of the world we live in and the social order it imposes. Unlike Joanne Leonard or David Hockney, postmodern photographers are "re-photographers" who for the most part do not take their

1249. Barbara Kruger. *You Are a Captive Audience.*
1983. Gelatin-silver print, 48 x 37³/4" (122 x 96 cm).
Courtesy the artist and Annina Nosei Gallery, New York

own pictures but appropriate them from other mediums. To convey their message, these new Conceptualists often follow the formula established by Baldessari of placing image and text side by side (compare fig. 1152). Sometimes their pictures are intended as counterparts to paintings, and are enlarged on an unprecedented scale, using commercial processes developed for advertisements, which may also serve as sources. Here it is the choice of image that matters, since the act of singling it out and changing its context from billboard to gallery wall constitutes the comment. In both cases, however, we are asked to base our judgment on the message; the means of delivery deliberately shows so little individuality that it is often impossible to tell the work of one artist from another. In the process, however, the message often becomes equally forgettable.

KRUGER. That is not a problem with Barbara Kruger (born 1945), whose pictures are instantly recognizable for their confrontational approach. *You Are a Captive Audience* (fig. 1249) exemplifies her style. It usually involves a tightly cropped close-up in black and white taken from a magazine or newspaper and blown up as crudely as possible to monumental proportions, so that the viewer cannot escape its presence or the message, which is stenciled in white letters against a red background. The conjoining of unrelated text and image is clearly intended for radical ends. The challenging statement is intended to provoke acute anxiety by playing on people's latent fears in our society of being controlled by nameless forces, especially such large, impersonal power centers as the government, the military, or corporations.

1250. Annette Lemieux. *Truth*. 1989. Latex and acrylic on canvas, 7' x 11'1" x 1¹/₂" (213.4 x 337.8 x 3.8 cm)
Courtesy Josh Baer Gallery, New York

LEMIEUX. Kruger's work is like a sharp blow to the solar plexus: the message is direct, the response immediate, especially the first time around. The themes of Annette Lemieux (born 1957) are quieter but correspondingly more thought-provoking. Centering on social issues, they address the human condition without engaging in polemic. Lemieux has a particular gift for perceiving new possibilities of meaning in old photographs and illustrations. *Truth* (fig. 1250) is an image about sound—or, rather, the lack of it. The photograph, derived from a book on the history of radio, is a visual counterpart to the saying, "Hear no evil, speak no evil, see no evil." Transferred to canvas, it acquires a very different meaning in its new context. Stenciled in bold letters is the Russian proverb, "Eat bread and salt but speak the truth," which means roughly, "Be frank when accepting someone's hospitality." The lettering transforms the image from an amusing publicity photograph into an ominous-looking propaganda poster. Contrary to initial impressions, the issue is neither Russia nor Communism—the photograph features the famous American entertainer Jack Benny—but the role of the media in modern life. They enter our homes as guests without being candid: here the performer covers his mouth in order to speak no evil. Shielded by the medium itself, he distorts truth by selectively concealing information, not by telling a deliberate falsehood. Truth emerges as a matter of relative perspective, determined both by who controls it and who hears it.

SHERMAN. Not all postmodern photography is attached to words, nor is it taken simply from other sources. A curious in-between case is provided by Cindy Sherman (born 1954). [See Primary Sources, no. 115, page 949.] Among her best works are the early photographs that were staged in imitation of old movie stills. They are so skillfully realized that they look like the real thing. In them she fulfills the secret American dream of being star, caster, set designer, producer, and photographer, except that she does so almost vicariously. As her own star, she can assume any role she wants, and the choice is illuminating. Figure 1251 shows her predilection for 1940s and 1950s movies portraying beautiful women as vulnerable heroines. The picture is a perfect period piece, down to the last detail of costume, setting, and lighting. Only after we have looked at it for a while do we realize that the photograph raises intriguing questions about the image of women projected on the silver screen. Whether the message is feminist has been the subject of considerable debate. Is Sherman's use of herself merely an exercise in narcissism and her reliance on stereotypes no more than an example of shallow consumerism? Or is there a feminist sense of irony in her posing? However we choose to interpret it, the photograph is strangely affecting in its aura of nostalgia and the sense of mystery it communicates. Here the timeless image of the woman looking in the mirror is updated to receive among its most provocative—and puzzling—expressions ever. Sherman

1251. Cindy Sherman. *Untitled Film Still #2.* 1977.
Photograph, 18 x 10" (45.5 x 25.5 cm)
Courtesy Metro Pictures, New York

offers voyeurism at second hand, so to speak, a fantasy compounded that forever precludes authentic experience. In that sense, it is a paradigm of postmodernism.

POSTSCRIPT: POSTMODERN THEORY

SEMIOTICS. Semiotics (the study of signs) may be regarded ultimately as a branch of philosophy. It has its foundations in ancient philosophy, as well as medieval theology, and its modern form is a direct outgrowth of Enlightenment rationalism. Moreover, the American school of semiotics was founded by a philosopher, Charles Sanders Pierce. Despite its seemingly endless diversity, semiotics retains some key features of all philosophical systems: it seeks a universal understanding, and its theoretical constructs frequently follow classical exemplars. It typically acts as a closed body of ideas, one that is concerned primarily with its inner logic, rather than presenting a corpus of knowledge.

It is impossible to summarize such a vast field here: to do so would require a book as long as this, since there are virtually innumerable permutations. In essence, semiotics provides a stimulating approach to the age-old conundrum: What does the mind know, and how does it know it? In an ultimate sense, the mind is elusive. To a Buddhist, for example, the mind cannot grasp itself, since it lacks physical substance and is ever-changing; hence, it also has an almost endless capacity for self-delusion. Like most hermetic systems, semiotics generally assumes that the mind can know only itself through the concepts it builds. These act as filters through which all experience, internal as well as external, is interpreted. Semiotics is therefore little concerned with objective reality—if it exists at all—since it remains inherently unknowable and meaningless in itself, although some semiologists postulate meaning stemming from God or some form of pure Idea.

Modern semiotics begins with Ferdinand de Saussure. Like many revolutionary intellectuals, he came late in life to rebel against the very ideas he had devoted much of his career to—in his case, philology, the study of language. His contribution lay in the intuitive realization that language cannot be explained simply in terms of its development, because it always functions as a coherent system. For the dynamic (diachronic) paradigm of philology he substituted a static (synchronic) model. At the center of Saussure's system is his definition of a sign as consisting of a concept (signified) and its sound-image (signifier), which is a purely mental impression, not the sound itself. Identity is defined purely by difference, a philosophically suspect approach. Most are binary oppositions (for example, good and evil), built up into larger structures of increasing complexity. As against traditional grammar, meaning is determined by structure and the relationships it imposes. Thus context becomes critical to understanding. Saussure further distinguished between the everyday speech of the individual (*parole*) and language as a socially shared linguistic system (*langue*). Because there are no concrete objects in language, external reality has no place in his analysis—it is simply assumed to lie parallel to, or else to be unknowable outside of, *langue*. The problem with Saussure's semiology is that it proves incapable of dealing with language as an evolving system, which requires a more organic model, and thus with time in general, both as past and as future.

Semiotics constitutes a form of system analysis that in principle can be applied to almost anything. (Saussure's theories, for example, are comparable to those of Talcott Parsons in sociology; interestingly enough, both are indebted partly to the sociologist Émile Durkheim.) What counts is the coherence of the theory itself, not its basis in reality, which, as we have seen, is of secondary importance at best. Data are merely the point of departure for constructing the conceptual model, thus raising the question whether it has any relevance to real life. This suggests the main weakness of the structuralist approach to semiology: if the structure is undermined, then its related concepts are deprived of meaning, which is only an abstraction without independent existence. Logically the result must inevitably be chaos, an important point that we shall soon return to. We may nevertheless wonder whether this is necessarily so in actual fact.

In most cases, the relationship between sign and meaning is extremely complex. In human society it is arbitrary at face value and assigned only as a matter of convention; otherwise most symbols could not possibly be understood and would remain entirely private. This points to a fundamental difficulty besetting semiotics. Like most bodies of theory, it is encumbered by a torturous thought process and tedious jargon. Even granting the inadequacy of normal language to express the formal rhetoric of intellectual disciplines, it functions as a need-lessly complex code system deliberately accessible only to "those in the know." The same critique may be taken to apply to the role of semiotics in contemporary art and art history.

DECONSTRUCTION. The assault on structuralist semiology that began in the late 1960s by the French philosopher Jacques Derrida soon blossomed into a wholesale war on traditional learning in all fields. Similar controversies have raged in philosophy before. The antecedents of deconstruction can be traced back to medieval Scholasticism, both the nominalism of thinkers like William of Ockham, which rejected universals, and supposition theory, in which context determines meaning. In fact, virtually all of its lines of argumentation are to be found in the catalogue of Scholasticism's infamous errors in logic, which are familiar to every student of philosophy. More intriguing still is the relation to music of the fourteenth century, which featured tropes (added pieces of texts and music), as well as suspensions and ambiguities of rhythm, that exactly parallel Derrida's usage. Deconstruction nonetheless has a peculiar flavor that is specifically postmodern.

Derrida considered the structuralist approach to be inadequate to explain the human condition, which he investigated by exploring his own consciousness. As we have seen, Saussure's semiotics contains the seeds of its own destruction. To Derrida language is structure to be dismantled. Against the structuralists, he asserted the primacy of the written word over the spoken, which it at first supplements, then supplants. Since all cultural products are texts in the sense of documents, everything—history, life itself—becomes a text. However, texts never mean what they seem to say, because sign and meaning are entirely separate. This contradicts the fundamental assumption of all semiotics; yet it is a possibility that semiotics itself allows, because of the arbitrary relation between sign and meaning in the first place. In deconstruction theory, everything is intertextual; that is, it is dependent on everything else, to the point where no trait can be isolated and no order or causality can exist. Furthermore, any term ("supplement") can be substituted for any other, so that it can pass for the original one, which it "infects" from inside. Because they are free to recombine, no element can be a self-sufficient sign and must refer to another one that is not present. This gives the reader a new latitude to create his or her own meaning by mixing fragments of text and varying their context, regardless of the author's intent, which can never be truly ascertained anyway. Language thus becomes "meaning-less," and truth a mere linguistic convention that implies an author and a subject, both of which deconstruction also rejects.

Deconstruction is adamantly against all forms of logocentrism (the belief that there are abstract truths that have a basis in reality), which is seen as an instrument of ethnocentrism (the belief that one's own culture is superior to others). It also rejects standard binary oppositions like good versus evil. To undermine such beliefs, it seeks out words that have multiple, even contradictory, meanings that are "undecidables," although these in turn sometimes become binary oppositions themselves!

Deconstruction relies on exceptions to disprove a principle. By focusing on weak points around the fringes where everything can be doubted and become unknowable, it creates an unending series of questions that cannot be answered. In addition to using obscure terms, a favorite technique of deconstruction is to invent new words ("neologisms") that combine bits of old ones to create unusual, often illogical meanings. A case in point is "différance," which compounds "to differ" and "to defer" to produce an "undecidable" by "suspending" between the two. Différance in this sense requires uniqueness of parts rather than coherence of whole. It ostensibly means the implicit reference to other "texts" which change or postpone indefinitely the meaning of the original one. This slip-pery concept of time exploits, we will recall, an intrinsic limitation of structuralism, which is turned against itself.

As this suggests, deconstruction is subversive in its methodology. By destabilizing time and, with it, meaning, suspending permits deconstructionists to change the rules at will to suit their purpose, which is ultimately to overturn the structure of language in order to subvert logical thought. Not only does it go against all the accepted laws of reason, it disallows all exceptions or criticisms. It furthermore utilizes (and openly advocates) the deliberate misuse of terms, inappropriate synonyms, willful misquotes, irrational positions, extreme interpretations, and even personal attacks against its opponents.

To a deconstructionist, texts, not facts, are what count. Reality is at best a mental construct whose apparent meaning is determined by context (as opposed to structure). As a result, everything becomes ultimately unknowable—including one's own feelings, even though the individual is left to arrive at a purely subjective understanding. Hence, every understanding or interpretation is inherently false. Deconstruction denies the priority of any viewpoint, but implicitly holds its own above all others. It conveniently ignores the fact that despite its relativism, even deconstruction cannot fully escape the inherent authoritarianism of language, which creates its own logic structures. Moreover, it rarely, if ever, deconstructs its own texts, for it claims to be a "logic beyond all forms of reason."

Needless to say, deconstruction has provoked a storm of outrage from traditional intellectuals. It has been condemned as everything from irrational sophistry and contrived obscurantism to arid nihilism. Nevertheless deconstruction has had an extraordinary impact on contemporary thought, and remains a fascinating historical phenomenon. Of all the critiques mounted against deconstruction, perhaps the most telling is its predictability: once its unwritten rules are understood, the game is simple to play and each step easy to anticipate.

Primary Sources for Part Four

The following is a selection of excerpts from original texts by writers, critics, artists, architects, and photographers from the late eighteenth to the twentieth century. These readings are intended to supplement the main text and are keyed to it. Full citations are given in the Credits section at the end of the book.

78

Johann Joachim Winckelmann (1717–1768)

From *Thoughts on the Imitation of Greek Works in Painting and Sculpture*

Winckelmann's influential publications on classical antiquities, including Thoughts . . . *(1755) and the* History of Ancient Art *(1764), laid the foundation for modern scientific archaeology.*

To take the ancients for models is our only way to become great. . . . Their masterpieces reveal not only nature in its greatest beauty, but . . . certain ideal beauties of nature which . . . exist only in the intellect.

The most beautiful bodies found among us today might, perhaps not be more similar to the Greek bodies than Iphicles was to Hercules, his brother. . . . Take a young Spartan, bred, by a hero and heroine, never bound by swaddling clothes, who has slept on the bare ground from the age of seven and has been trained in wrestling and swimming from earliest infancy; put him beside a young Sybarite of our day and then decide which one the artist would choose as a model for a youthful Theseus. . . .

Through these exercises the bodies, free from superfluous fat, acquired the noble and manly contours that the Greek masters gave to their statues. . . . Everything that disfigured the body was carefully avoided; Alcibiades refused to play the flute in his youth because it might distort his face. . . . Furthermore, the clothing of the Greeks was so designed as not to interfere with the natural growth of the body, while today our tight and binding dress makes the natural beauty of our bodies suffer, especially at the neck, waist, and thighs. Even the fair sex of the Greeks refused any restricting fashions. . . .

The school of the artist was the gymnasium, where the youths, ordinarily clothed because of modesty, exercised quite naked. It was the gathering place of philosophers as well as artists: Socrates visited it to teach Charmides, Artolycus and Lysis; Phidias went there to enrich his art with these magnificent figures. There one learned the movement of muscles, and studied the contours of the body. . . . The most beautiful aspects of the nude revealed themselves here in many varied and noble poses unattainable by hired models such as are used in our academies. . . .

These frequent opportunities for observing nature caused the Greek artists to go even further: they began to form general concepts of beauty for the individual parts of the body as well as for its proportions: concepts that were meant to rise above nature, being taken from a spiritual realm that existed only in the mind.

In this way Raphael formed his Galathea. As he says in his letter to Count Balthasar Castiglione, "Since beauty is rare among women, I follow a certain idea formed in my imagination. . . ."

The imitation of natural beauty either focuses upon a single model or it collects data from many models and combines them. The first produces a faithful copy, a portrait; it leads to the shapes and figures of Dutch art. The second, however, leads to universal beauty and its ideal images, and this is the path taken by the Greeks.

79

Étienne-Louis Boullée (1728–1799)

From *Architecture, Essay on Art*

Boullée's philosophy was in the Romantic tradition of Jean-Jacques Rousseau. In this introduction to an undated manuscript, he set down his visionary ideas on architecture.

TO MEN WHO CULTIVATE THE ARTS

Dominated by an excessive love for my profession, I have surrendered myself to it completely. But although I have yielded to this overweaning passion, I have made it a rule that I shall work for the benefit of society and thus merit public esteem.

I should confess straightaway that I have refused to confine myself to the exclusive study of our ancient masters and have instead tried, through the study of Nature to broaden my ideas on my profession which, after much thought, I consider to be still in its infancy.

What little attention has been paid in the past to the poetry of architecture, which is a sure means of adding to man's enjoyment and of bestowing on artists the fame they deserve!

That is my belief. Our buildings—and our public buildings in particular—should be to some extent poems. The impression they make on us should arouse in us sensations that correspond to the function of the building in question. It seemed to me that if I was to incorporate in my Architecture all the poetry of which it was capable, then I should study the theory of volumes and analyse them, at the same time seeking to understand their properties, the power they have on our senses, their similarities to the human organism. I flattered myself that if I went back to the source of all the fine arts I should find new ideas and thus establish principles that would be all the more certain for having their source in nature.

You who are fascinated by the fine arts, surrender yourselves completely to all the pleasure that this sublime passion can procure! No other pleasure is so pure. It is this passion that makes us love to study, that transforms our pain into pleasure and, with its divine flame, forces genius to yield up its oracles. In short, it is this passion that summons us to immortality.

It is to you who cultivate the arts that I dedicate the fruits of my long vigils; to you who, with all your learning, are persuaded—and doubtless rightly so—that we must not presume that all we have left is to imitate the ancients!

80

Jean-Auguste-Dominique Ingres (1780–1867)
From "The Doctrine of Ingres"

Maurice Denis, a member of the Nabis, compiled these aphorisms from Ingres' notebooks and from the reminiscences of his students.

Art should only depict beauty. . . .

Do you believe that I send you to the Louvre to find ideal beauty, something different from that which is nature? Similar idiocies in ill-fated epochs brought about the decadence of art. I send you there because you will learn from the ancients to see nature because they are themselves nature; one must be nourished by them. . . .

And no matter what your genius, if you paint to the last stroke not according to nature, but your model, you will always be its slave; your manner of painting will smack of servitude. The proof of the contrary is seen in Raphael. He tamed the model to such a point and possessed it so thoroughly in his memory, that instead of the model giving him orders, one would say that the model obeyed him. . . .

To form yourself in beauty, . . . walk with your head raised to the sky instead of keeping it toward the earth like pigs searching in the mud. . . .

The figures of antiquity are only beautiful because they resemble the beauty of nature. . . . And nature will always be beautiful when it resembles the beauties of antiquity. . . .

Study vases, it was with them that I began to understand the Greeks. . . .

I will write on the door of my studio: School of drawing, and I will make painters.

Drawing is the probity of art. . . .

Smoke itself should be expressed by a line.

Drawing is everything; it is all of art. The material processes of painting are very easy and may be learned in eight days. . . .

There is neither correct nor incorrect drawing; there is only beautiful or ugly drawing. That is all! . . .

Colour [is] one of the ornaments of painting, the lady with her sister's finery, because it is colouring which brings the amateurs and the admirers to the more important perfections of art.

In front of Rubens, put on blinders like those a horse wears.

81

Eugène Delacroix (1798–1863)
From his *Journal*

Delacroix began his Journal *in 1822 and maintained it irregularly until his death in 1863. He wrote it, he said, "for myself alone" in the hope that it would "do me a lot of good." This entry, dated October 20, 1853, was recorded at Champrosay.*

What an adoration I have for painting! The mere memory of certain pictures, even when I don't see them, goes through me with a feeling which stirs my whole being. . . .

The impressions produced by the arts on sensitive organisms are a curious mystery: confused impressions, if one tries to describe them, clear-cut and full of strength if one feels them again, and if only through memory! I strongly believe that we always mix in something of ourselves with feelings which seem to come from the objects that strike us. It is probable that the only reason why these works please me so much is that they respond to feelings which are my own. . . .

The type of emotion peculiar to painting is, so to speak, *tangible;* poetry and music cannot give it. You enjoy the actual representation of objects as if you really saw them, and at the same time the meaning which the images have for the mind warms you and transports you. These figures, these objects, which seem the thing itself to a certain part of your intelligent being are like a solid bridge on which imagination supports itself to penetrate to the mysterious and profound sensation for which the forms are, so to speak, the hieroglyph, but a hieroglyph far more eloquent than a cold representation, a thing equivalent to no more than a character in the printer's font of type. . . .

They are strangely deceived if they think that when they have written: *a foot or a hand,* they have given to my mind the same emotion as the one I experience when I see a beautiful foot or a beautiful hand. The arts are not algebra, in which the abbreviation of the figures contributes to the success of the problem; success in the arts is by no means a matter of abridging, but of amplifying, if possible, and prolonging the sensation by all possible means. What is the theater? One of the most certain witnesses to man's need for experiencing the largest possible number of emotions at one time. It gathers together all the arts so that each may make us feel their combined effect more strongly.

82
Rosa Bonheur (1822–1899)
From *Reminiscences of Rosa Bonheur*

Bonheur's father, Raymond, was a landscape painter and a disciple of the utopian socialist Henri de Saint-Simon, who considered the artist the priest of his "new Christianity" and thought the Messiah of the future would be, as Bonheur states here, a woman. These reminiscences were published in 1910.

I have never counseled my sisters of the palette to wear men's clothes in the ordinary circumstances of life.

If, however, you see me dressed as I am, it is not in the least in order to make me into an original, but simply to facilitate my work. Consider that, at a certain period in my life, I spent whole days at the slaughterhouse. . . . I also had the passion for horses. Now where better to study these animals than in the fairs. . . . I was forced to recognize that the clothing of my sex was a constant bother. That is why I decided to solicit the authorization to wear men's clothing from the prefect of police.

But the suit I wear is my work attire, and nothing else. The epithets of imbeciles have never bothered me. . . .

Two years ago (October 8, 1896) on the occasion of the reception of the Russian royalty in Paris, the minister of the fine arts had the desire to introduce to them the leading figures of French art. . . . I wore my beautiful suit of black velvet and my little feathered bonnet. . . .

From the moment I arrived at the Louvre, I would have given I do not know what to have had on my head my gray felt hat. I was the only woman, in the middle of a crowd of men. . . . All the eyes turned toward me; I didn't know where to hide myself. This was a harsh test, and that day I really missed my masculine attire, I can assure you. . . .

In spite of my metamorphosis of costume, there is no daughter of Eve who appreciates more than I the nuances; my brusque and almost savage nature never prevented my heart from always remaining perfectly feminine. . . .

Why wouldn't I be proud of being a woman? My father, that enthusiastic apostle of humanity, repeated to me many times that woman's mission was to uplift the human race, that she was the Messiah of future centuries. I owe to his doctrines the great and proud ambition that I conceived for the sex to which I take glory in belonging and whose independence I will uphold until my last day. Moreover, I am persuaded that the future belongs to us.

83
John Constable (1776–1837)
From a letter to John Fisher

Fisher, the archdeacon of Salisbury Cathedral, was a lifelong friend of the artist. This letter of October 23, 1821, reflects Constable's sensitivity to the beauties of the English landscape.

How much I wish I had been with you on your fishing excursion in the New Forest! What river can it be? But the sound of water escaping from mill-dams, etc., willows, old rotten planks, slimy posts, and brickwork, I love such things. Shakespeare could make everything poetical; he tells us of poor Tom's haunts among "sheep cotes and mills." As long as I do paint, I shall never cease to paint such places. They have always been my delight, and I should indeed have been delighted in seeing what you describe, and in your company, "in the company of a man to whom nature does not spread her volume in vain." Still I should paint my own places best; painting is with me but another word for feeling, and I associate "my careless boyhood" with all that lies on the banks of the Stour; those scenes made me a painter, and I am grateful; that is, I had often thought of pictures of them before I ever touched a pencil.

84
John Ruskin (1819–1900)
The Stones of Venice, from Chapter 6, "The Nature of the Gothic"

Ruskin's Stones of Venice, *published in 1853, praised Venetian Gothic architecture while condemning its Renaissance buildings. The Gothic was very popular in the nineteenth century.*

It is verily this degradation of the operative into a machine, which, more than any other evil of the times, is leading the mass of the nations everywhere into vain, incoherent, destructive struggling for a freedom of which they cannot explain the nature to themselves. . . .

For observe, I have only dwelt upon the rudeness of Gothic, or any other kind of imperfectness, as admirable, where it was impossible to get design or thought without it. . . . In art, delicate finish is desirable from the greatest masters, and is always given by them. . . . But lower men than these cannot finish, for it requires consummate knowledge to finish consummately, and then we must take their thoughts as they are able to give them. . . . Above all, demand no refinement of execution where there is no thought, for that is slaves' work. . . .

We are always in these days endeavoring to separate the two; we want one man to be always thinking, and another to be always working, and we call one a gentleman, and the other an operative; whereas the workman ought often to be thinking, and the thinker often to be working, and both should be gentlemen, in the best sense. As it is, we make both ungentle, the one envying, the other despising, his brother; and the mass of society is made up of morbid thinkers, and miserable workers. Now it is only by labor that thought can be made healthy, and only by thought that labor can be made happy, and the two cannot be separated with impunity. . . .

Enough, I trust, has been said to show the reader that the

rudeness or imperfection which at first rendered the term "Gothic" one of reproach is indeed, when rightly understood, one of the most noble characters of Christian architecture, and not only a noble but an essential one. It seems a fantastic paradox, but it is nevertheless a most important truth, that no architecture can be truly noble which is *not* imperfect. . . .

Wherever the workman is utterly enslaved, the parts of the building must of course be absolutely like each other; for the perfection of his execution can only be reached by exercising him in doing one thing, and giving him nothing else to do. The degree in which the workman is degraded may be thus known at a glance, by observing whether the several parts of the building are similar or not; and if, as in Greek work, all the capitals are alike, and all the mouldings unvaried, then the degradation is complete; . . . if, as in Gothic work, there is perpetual change both in design and execution, the workman must have been altogether set free.

85
Charles Baudelaire (1821–1867)
"The Modern Public and Photography,"
from Part 2 of *The Salon of 1859*

Baudelaire, now known for his controversial poems The Flowers of Evil *(1857), was an important Parisian art critic at mid-century. The photographer Nadar was one of his close friends.*

In this country, the natural painter, like the natural poet, is almost a monster. Our exclusive taste for the true . . . oppresses and smothers the taste for the beautiful. Where only the beautiful should be looked for . . . our people look only for the true. They are not artistic, naturally artistic. . . .

In the domain of painting and statuary, the present-day credo of the worldly wise, especially in France . . . is this: I "believe in nature, and I believe only in nature. . . . I believe that art is, and can only be, the exact reproduction of nature. . . . Thus if an industrial process could give us a result identical to nature, that would be absolute art." An avenging God has heard the prayers of this multitude; Daguerre was his messiah. And then they said to themselves: "Since photography provides us with every desirable guarantee of exactitude . . . art is photography." From that moment onwards, our loathsome society rushed, like Narcissus, to contemplate its trivial image on the metallic plate. . . .

I am convinced that the badly applied advances of photography, like all purely material progress for that matter, have greatly contributed to the impoverishment of French artistic genius. . . . Poetry and progress are two ambitious men that hate each other, with an instinctive hatred, and when they meet along a pathway one or other must give way. If photography is allowed to deputize for art in some of art's activities, it will not be long before it has supplanted or corrupted art altogether, thanks to the stupidity of the masses, its natural ally. Photography must, therefore, return to its true duty, which is that of handmaid of the arts and sciences. . . . Let photography quickly enrich the traveller's album, and restore to his eyes the precision his memory may lack; let it adorn the library of the naturalist, magnify microscopic insects, even strengthen, with a few facts, the hypotheses of the astronomer; let it, in short, be the secretary and record-keeper of whomsoever needs absolute material accuracy for professional reasons. . . . But if once it be allowed to impinge on the sphere of the intangible and the imaginary, on anything that has value solely because man adds something to it from his soul, then woe betide us!

86
Charles Baudelaire
"On the Heroism of Modern Life,"
from Part 18 of *The Salon of 1846*

Baudelaire thought that painters and sculptors should reject subjects drawn from history and choose those from contemporary life. His ideas influenced the work of a number of later painters, including his close friend Édouard Manet.

To return to our principal and essential problem, which is to discover whether we possess a specific beauty, intrinsic to our new emotions, I observe that the majority of artists who have attacked modern life have contented themselves with public and official subjects—with our victories and our political heroism. Even so, they do it with an ill grace, and only because they are commissioned by the government which pays them. However, there are private subjects which are very much more heroic than these.

The pageant of fashionable life and the thousands of floating existences—criminals and kept women—which drift about in the underworld of a great city . . . all prove to us that we have only to open our eyes to recognize our heroism.

Suppose that a minister, baited by the opposition's impertinent questioning, has given expression once and for all—with that proud and sovereign eloquence which is proper to him—to his scorn and disgust for all ignorant and mischief-making oppositions. The same evening you will hear the following words buzzing around you on the Boulevard des Italiens: "Were you in the Chamber today? And did you see the minister? Good Heavens, how handsome he was! I have never seen such scorn!"

So there *are* such things as modern beauty and modern heroism! . . .

All these words that fall from your lips bear witness to your belief in a new and special beauty, which is neither that of Achilles nor yet of Agamemnon.

The life of our city is rich in poetic and marvellous subjects. We are enveloped and steeped as though in an atmosphere of the marvellous; but we do not notice it.

87
Gustave Courbet (1819–1877)
From his letter to a group of students

A band of students who had withdrawn in protest from the state-run École des Beaux-Arts had invited Courbet to direct the alternative school they were hoping to open. In this letter dated December 25, 1861, he rejected their offer, but did agree to give instruction and criticism for about a year in a rented studio, where the model was usually a peasant with a farm animal.

I do not have, and I can not have, students.

I who believe that every artist should be his own master. . . .

I can not teach my art . . . because I deny that art can be taught and because . . . I maintain that art is completely individual, and the talent of each artist is only the result of his own inspiration and his own study of tradition. . . .

Especially, art in painting can only consist of the representation of objects that are visible and tangible to the artist.

No age can be depicted except by its own artists. . . . I believe that the artists of one century are completely incompetent when it comes to depicting the objects of a preceding or future century. . . .

It is in this sense that I deny the term historical art as applied to the past. Historical art is, by its very essence, contemporary. Every age should have its artists, who will express it and depict it for the future. . . .

The true artists are those who take up their epoch at exactly the point to which it has been carried by preceding ages. To retreat is to do nothing. . . . This explains why all archaic schools have always ended by reducing themselves to the most useless compilations.

I also believe that painting is an essentially CONCRETE art and can only consist of the representation of REAL AND EXISTING objects. . . . Imagination in art consists in knowing how to find the most complete expression of an existing object, but never in imagining or in creating the object itself.

Beauty is in nature, and in reality is encountered under the most diverse forms. As soon as it is found, it belongs to art, or rather to the artist who is able to perceive it. . . . The beauty based on nature is superior to all artistic conventions.

88
Lilla Cabot Perry (1848?–1933)
From "Reminiscences of Claude Monet from 1889 to 1909"

Perry was an American expatriate painter. Monet, a strict empiricist, had a horror of artistic theory and therefore refused to systematize his ideas on art. Perry's reminiscences, published in 1927, provide our best evidence of those ideas.

He never took any pupils, but he would have made a most inspiring master if he had been willing to teach. I remember his once saying to me:

"When you go out to paint, try to forget what objects you have before you—a tree, a house, a field, or whatever. Merely think, here is a little square of blue, here an oblong of pink, here a streak of yellow, and paint it just as it looks to you, the exact color and shape, until it gives your own naïve impression of the scene before you."

He said he wished he had been born blind and then had suddenly gained his sight so that he could have begun to paint in this way without knowing what the objects were that he saw before him. He held that the first real look at the motif was likely to be the truest and most unprejudiced one, and said that the first painting should cover as much of the canvas as possible, no matter how roughly, so as to determine at the outset the tonality of the whole. . . .

Monet's philosophy of painting was to paint what you really see, not what you think you ought to see; not the object isolated as in a test tube, but the object enveloped in sunlight and atmosphere, with the blue dome of Heaven reflected in the shadows.

89
Mary Cassatt (1845–1926)
From a letter to Harrison Morris

Between 1874 and 1886 a loosely affiliated group of artists in France, who became known as the Impressionists, organized eight exhibitions outside the official Salon. These "independent" exhibitions soon inspired other artists in western Europe, thereby contributing significantly to the demise of the academic system that had dominated European art since the mid-seventeenth century. Cassatt's letter of March 15, 1904, to Morris, Managing Director of the Pennsylvania Academy of the Fine Arts, is in response to a prize she had been awarded.

Our first exhibition was held in 1879 and was a protest against official exhibitions and not a grouping of artists with the same art tendencies. We have been since dubbed "Impressionists" a name which might apply to Monet but can have no meaning when attached to Degas' name.

Liberty is the first good in this world and to escape the tyranny of a jury is worth fighting for, surely no profession is so enslaved as ours. Gérôme [an academic painter] who all his life was on the Jury of every official exhibition said only a short time before his death that if Millet were then alive, he, Gérôme would refuse his pictures, that the world has consecrated Millet's genius made no difference to him. I think this is a good comment on the system. . . . When I was at home a few years ago it was one of the things that disheartened me the most to see that we were slavishly copying all the evils of the French system, evils which they deplore and are trying to remove.

90
James Abbott McNeill Whistler
(1834–1903)
From *The Gentle Art of Making Enemies*

Whistler's book, published in 1893, also contains his account of the famous libel suit he brought against John Ruskin in 1878.

As music is the poetry of sound, so is painting the poetry of sight, and the subject-matter has nothing to do with harmony of sound or of colour.

The great musicians knew this. Beethoven and the rest wrote music—simply music; symphony in this key, concerto or sonata in that.

On F or G they constructed celestial harmonies . . . as combinations, evolved from the chords of F or G and their minor correlatives.

This is pure music as distinguished from airs—commonplace and vulgar in themselves, but interesting from their associations, as, for instance, "Yankee Doodle. . . ."

Art should be independent of all clap-trap—should stand alone, and appeal to the artistic sense of eye or ear, without confounding this with emotions entirely foreign to it, as devotion, pity, love, patriotism, and the like. All these have no kind of concern with it, and that is why I insist on calling my works "arrangements" and "harmonies."

Take the picture of my mother, exhibited at the Royal Academy as an "Arrangement in Grey and Black." Now that is what it is. To me it is interesting as a picture of my mother; but what can or ought the public to care about the identity of the portrait?

91
Auguste Rodin (1840–1917)
From "Conversations" with Paul Gsell

The following remarks, recorded in 1911, reveal Rodin as an exponent of the unconventional idea that the beauty or ugliness of a work of art centers on its inherent "character," or "truth."

The vulgar readily imagine that what they consider ugly in existence is not fit subject for the artist. They would like to forbid us to represent what displeases and offends them in nature.

It is a great error on their part.

What is commonly called *ugliness* in nature can in art become full of great beauty.

In the domain of fact we call *ugly* whatever is deformed, whatever is unhealthy, whatever suggests the ideas of disease, of debility, or of suffering, whatever is contrary to regularity, which is the sign and condition of health and strength: a

hunch-back is *ugly*, only who is bandy-legged is *ugly*, poverty in rags is *ugly*. . . .

But let a great artist or a great writer make use of one or the other of these uglinesses, instantly it is transfigured. . . .

To the great artist, everything in nature has character. . . . And that which is considered ugly in nature often presents more *character* than that which is termed beautiful, because in the contractions of a sickly countenance, in the lines of a vicious face, in all deformity, in all decay, the inner truth shines forth more clearly than in features that are regular and healthy.

And as it is solely the power of *character* which makes for beauty in art, it often happens that the uglier a being is in nature, the more beautiful it becomes in art.

There is nothing ugly in art except that which is without character, that is to say, that which offers no outer or inner truth.

Whatever is false, whatever is artificial, whatever seeks to be pretty rather than expressive, whatever is capricious and affected, whatever smiles without motive, bends or struts without cause, is mannered without reason; all that is without soul and without truth; all that is only a *parade* of beauty and grace; all, in short, that lies, is *ugliness* in art.

92
Joris-Karl Huysmans (1848–1907)
From "Iron"

Huysmans, author of the radical antinaturalist novel Against the Grain *(1884), was also an important art critic in Paris at the end of the nineteenth century. The following is taken from a selection of his art criticism entitled* Certaines *(1889).*

In architecture, the situation is now this.

The architects build absurd monuments whose parts, borrowed from all ages, constitute in their ensemble the most servile parodies that one could see. . . .

One fact is certain: the age has produced no architect and is characterized by no style. . . . Another undoubted fact is that stone, considered until now the fundamental material of building, has foundered, drained by repetition. . . .

But our period may yet incarnate itself in buildings that symbolize its activity and its sadness, its cunning and its money, in works sullen and hard, in any case, new.

And the material is here named, it is iron.

Since the reign of Louis Philippe [1830–48], iron structure has been attempted many times, but . . . no new form has been discovered; the metal remains . . . linked to stone, a subordinate agent, incapable of creating by itself a monument that is not a railway station or a greenhouse, a monument that aesthetic criticism may cite. . . .

Iron's role is thus practical and limited, purely internal.

This was the state of architecture when the exposition of 1889 was resolved upon.

It is interesting to see if, in . . . the Eiffel Tower [fig. 964], iron-making has come out of its gropings, and . . . has finally invented a new style. . .

In a touching unanimity, . . . the entire press, flat on its stomach, exalts the genius of M. Eiffel.

And yet his tower resembles a factory chimney under construction, a carcass that waits to be filled with cut stone or bricks. One cannot imagine that [it] is finished, that this solitary suppository riddled with holes will remain as it is. . . .

The Eiffel Tower is truly of a disconcerting ugliness, and it is not even enormous! Seen from below, it does not seem to attain the height cited for it. . . .

From afar, from the center of Paris, from the depths of the suburbs, the effect is identical. The emptiness of this cage diminishes it; the lathing and the meshwork make of this trophy of iron a horrible bird cage. . . .

It is 300 meters tall and appears one hundred; it is finished and appears barely begun. . . .

Finally, one must ask oneself, what is the fundamental purpose for the existence of this tower?

93
Vincent van Gogh (1853–1890)
From a letter to his brother, Theo

Theo, who worked for an art dealer in Paris, provided Vincent's chief emotional and economic support. This letter, dated April 30, 1885, was written from their father's house in Neunen.

I have tried to emphasize that those people, eating their potatoes in the lamplight, have dug the earth with those very hands they put in the dish, and so it speaks of *manual labor,* and how they have honestly earned their food [fig. 977].

I have wanted to give the impression of a way of life quite different from that of us civilized people. Therefore I am not at all anxious for everyone to like it or to admire it at once. . . .

It would be wrong, I think, to give a peasant picture a certain conventional smoothness. If a peasant picture smells of bacon, smoke, potato steam—all right, that's not unhealthy; if a stable smells of dung—all right, that belongs to a stable; if the field has an odor of ripe corn or potatoes or of . . . manure—that's healthy, especially for city people.

94
Vincent van Gogh
From an undated letter to Theo

I am returning to the ideas I had in the country before I knew the impressionists. And I should not be surprised if the impressionists soon find fault with my way of working, for it has been fertilized by Delacroix's ideas rather than by theirs.

Because instead of trying to reproduce exactly what I see before my eyes, I use color more arbitrarily, in order to express myself forcibly. . . .

I should like to paint the portrait of an artist friend, a man who dreams great dreams, who works as the nightingale sings, because it is his nature. He'll be a blond man. I want to put my appreciation, the love I have for him, into the picture. So I paint him as he is, as faithfully as I can, to begin with.

But the picture is not yet finished. To finish it I am now going to be the arbitrary colorist. I exaggerate the fairness of the hair, I even get to orange tones, chromes and pale citron-yellow.

Behind the head, instead of painting the ordinary wall of the mean room, I paint infinity, a plain background of the richest, intensest blue that I can contrive, and by this simple combination of the bright head against the rich blue background, I get a mysterious effect, like a star in the depths of an azure sky

95
Paul Gauguin (1848–1903)
From a letter to J. F. Willumsen

The Danish painter J. F. Willumsen was a member of Gauguin's circle in Brittany. Gauguin wrote this letter in the autumn of 1890, before his departure for the South Seas.

As for me, my mind is made up. I am going soon to Tahiti, a small island in Oceania, where the material necessities of life can be had without money. I want to forget all the misfortunes of the past, I want to be free to paint without any glory whatsoever in the eyes of the others and I want to die there and to be forgotten there. . . . A terrible epoch is brewing in Europe for the coming generation: the kingdom of gold. Everything is putrefied, even men, even the arts. There, at least, under an eternally summer sky, on a marvellously fertile soil, the Tahitian has only to lift his hands to gather his food; and in addition he never works. When in Europe men and women survive only after unceasing labor during which they struggle in convulsions of cold and hunger, a prey to misery, the Tahitians, on the contrary, happy inhabitants of the unknown paradise of Oceania, know only sweetness of life. To live, for them, is to sing and to love. . . . Once my material life is well organized, I can there devote myself to great works of art, freed from all artistic jealousies and with no need whatsoever of lowly trade.

96
Louis Sullivan (1856–1924)
From "The Tall Office Building Artistically Considered"

Sullivan had already completed several skyscrapers, including the

Wainwright Building (fig. 1009) and the Guaranty Building, when he recorded these ideas in an essay of 1896.

The architects of this land and generation are now brought face to face with something new under the sun—namely, . . . a demand for the erection of tall office buildings. . . .

Offices are necessary for the transaction of business; the invention and perfection of the high-speed elevators make vertical travel, that was once tedious and painful, now easy and comfortable; development of steel manufacture has shown the way to safe, rigid, economical constructions rising to a great height; continued growth of population in the great cities, consequent congestion of centers and rise in value of ground, stimulate an increase in number of stories. . . . Thus has come about that form of lofty construction called the "modern office building. . . ."

Problem: How shall we impart to this sterile pile, . . . this stark, staring exclamation of eternal strife, the graciousness of those higher forms of sensibility and culture that rest on the lower and fiercer passions? . . .

What is the chief characteristic of the tall office building? . . . It is lofty. This loftiness is to the artist-nature its thrilling aspect. . . . It must be every inch a proud and soaring thing, rising in sheer exultation that from bottom to top it is a unit without a single dissenting line. . . .

Certain critics . . . have advanced the theory that the true prototype of the tall office building is the classical column, consisting of base, shaft and capital. . . .

Other theorizers, assuming a mystical symbolism as a guide, quote the many trinities in nature and art, and the beauty and conclusiveness of such trinity in unity. . . .

Others, seeking their examples and justification in the vegetable kingdom, urge that such a design shall above all things be organic. . . . They point to the pine-tree, its massy roots, its lithe, uninterrupted trunk, its tuft of green high in the air. Thus, they say, should be the design of the tall office building: again in three parts vertically.

Others still, more susceptible to the power of a unit than to the grace of a trinity, say that such a design should be struck out at a blow, as though by a blacksmith or by mighty Jove. . . .

I shall, with however much of regret, dissent from [these critics] as touching not at all upon . . . the quick of the entire matter, upon the true; the immovable philosophy of the architectural art. . . .

Unfailingly in nature [its] shapes express the inner life, the native quality, of the animal, tree, bird, fish, that they present to us; they are so characteristic, so recognizable, that we say, simply, it is "natural" it should be so. . . .

It is the pervading law of all things organic, and inorganic, . . . that form ever follows function. . . .

Shall we, then, daily violate this law in our art? . . .

Does this not . . . conclusively show that the lower one or two stories [of the tall office building] will take on a special character suited to the special needs, that the tiers of typical offices, having the same unchanging function, shall continue

in the same unchanging form, and that as to the attic, . . . its function shall equally be so in force, in . . . outward expression? From this results, naturally, . . . a three-part division, not from any theory, symbol, or fancied logic.

97
Georgia O'Keeffe (1887–1986)
From "Stieglitz: His Pictures Collected Him"

O'Keeffe met Alfred Stieglitz in 1908, and had her first show at his gallery in 1916. She married him in 1924. These remarks, published in 1949, were made after his death.

Stieglitz grew up during the period when photography was young, began working at it while studying mechanical engineering at the Berlin Polytechnic. . . . He soon decided to make himself an authority on photography and went about it by sending his photographs everywhere to exhibitions to get all the medals that were given in the world at that time. . . .

Although the photographs that he was making at this time were very much admired by painters and artists generally, the artists seemed to have the idea that photography could never be accepted as one of the arts. Stieglitz denied this. As he was naturally a fighter, he began to work for its recognition as one of the arts, not particularly for himself but for the idea of photography. . . . Painters would often say they wished they had painted what he had photographed. He always said he never regretted that he had not photographed what they were painting.

In 1890 Stieglitz returned to America from his European student period, twenty-six years old. Years of feverish activity with photography followed. He finally decided that for photography to be recognized as one of the arts, the work of a group could bring about this recognition better than the work of an individual. . . .

The Photo-Secession group was formed in 1902, . . . Stieglitz . . . was the leader. In 1905 they began having photographic exhibitions at the little gallery known as "291". . . . Here the beginnings of modern art were also shown. . . .

I was sent, like all the other students, by the instructors of the Art Students League to see the first showing of Rodin drawings at "291." . . .

I very well remember the fantastic violence of Stieglitz's defense when the students with me began talking with him about the drawings.

98
Henri Matisse (1869–1954)
From "Notes of a Painter"

This 1908 article, Matisse's most complete statement on his art, reflects the transition from his early Fauve phase to his mature, post-Fauve period.

Often when I settle down to work I begin by noting my immediate and superficial color sensations. Some years ago this first result was often enough for me—but today if I were satisfied with this, my picture would remain incomplete. I would have put down the passing sensations of a moment; they would not completely define my feelings and the next day I might not recognize what they meant. I want to reach that state of condensation of sensations which constitutes a picture. . . .

There are two ways of expressing things; one is to show them crudely, the other is to evoke them artistically. In abandoning the literal representation of movement it is possible to reach toward a higher ideal of beauty. . . .

Suppose I set out to paint an interior: I have before me a cupboard; it gives me a sensation of bright red—and I put down a red which satisfies me; immediately a relation is established between this red and the white of the canvas. If I put a green near the red, if I paint in a yellow floor, there must still be between this green, this yellow and the white of the canvas a relation that will be satisfactory to me. But these several tones mutually weaken one another. It is necessary, therefore, that the various elements that I use be so balanced that they do not destroy one another. To do this I must organize my ideas; the relation between tones must be so established that they will sustain one another. A new combination of colors will succeed the first one and will give more completely my interpretation. . . . I cannot copy nature in a servile way; I must interpret nature and submit it to the spirit of the picture. When I have found the relationship of all the tones the result must be a living harmony of tones, a harmony not unlike that of a musical composition. . . .

What I dream of is an art of balance, of purity and serenity devoid of troubling or depressing subject matter, an art which might be for every mental worker, be he businessman or writer, like an appeasing influence, like a mental soother, something like a good armchair in which to rest from physical fatigue.

99
Wassily Kandinsky (1866–1944)
Concerning the Spiritual in Art, from Chapter 5, "The Effect of Color"

Kandinsky hoped to inaugurate a new spiritual era for modern man through his art. These remarks first appeared in 1912.

If you let your eye stray over a palette of colors, you experience two things. In the first place you receive *a purely physical effect,* namely the eye itself is enchanted by the beauty and other qualities of color. You experience satisfaction and delight, like a gourmet savoring a delicacy. Or the eye is stimulated as the tongue is titillated by a spicy dish. But then it

grows calm and cool, like a finger after touching ice. These are physical sensations, limited in duration. They are superficial, too, and leave no lasting impression behind if the soul remains closed. Just as we feel at the touch of ice a sensation of cold, forgotten as soon as the finger becomes warm again, so the physical action of color is forgotten as soon as the eye turns away. On the other hand, as the physical coldness of ice, upon penetrating more deeply, arouses more complex feelings, and indeed a whole chain of psychological experiences, so may also the superficial impression of color develop into an experience. . . .

And so we come to the second result of looking at colors: their psychological effect. They produce a correspondent spiritual vibration, and it is only as a step towards this spiritual vibration that the physical impression is of importance. . . .

Generally speaking, color directly influences the soul. Color is the keyboard, the eyes are the hammers, the soul is the piano with many strings. The artist is the hand that plays, touching one key or another purposively, to cause vibrations in the soul.

It is evident therefore that color harmony must rest ultimately on purposive playing upon the human soul.

100
Filippo Tommaso Marinetti (1876–1944)
From "The Foundation and Manifesto of Futurism"

After Marinetti's example of 1908, the manifesto became a popular device for innovative twentieth-century artists to publicize their views.

We declare our primary intentions to all living men of the earth:

1. We intend to glorify the love of danger, the custom of energy, the strength of daring. . . .

3. Literature having up to now glorified thoughtful immobility, ecstasy, and slumber, we wish to exalt the aggressive movement, the feverish insomnia, running, the perilous leap, the cuff, and the blow.

4. We declare that the splendor of the world has been enriched with a new form of beauty, the beauty of speed. A race-automobile adorned with great pipes like serpents with explosive breath . . . a race-automobile which seems to rush over exploding powder is more beautiful than the Victory of Samothrace. . . .

7. There is no more beauty except in struggle. No masterpiece without the stamp of aggressiveness. Poetry should be a violent assault against unknown forces to summon them to lie down at the feet of man. . . .

9. We will glorify war—the only true hygiene of the world—militarism, patriotism, the destructive gesture of anarchist, the beautiful Ideas which kill, and the scorn of woman.

10. We will destroy museums, libraries, and fight against

moralism, feminism, and all utilitarian cowardice. . . .

It is in Italy that we hurl this overthrowing and inflammatory declaration, with which today we found Futurism, for we will free Italy from her numberless museums which cover her with countless cemeteries.

Museums, cemeteries! . . . Identical truly. . . .

To admire an old picture is to pour our sentiment into a funeral urn instead of hurling it forth in violent gushes of action and productiveness. . . .

The oldest among us are thirty; we have thus at least ten years in which to accomplish our task. When we are forty, let others—younger and more daring men—throw us into the wastepaper basket like useless manuscripts!

101

Piet Mondrian (1872–1944)
From "Plastic Art and Pure Plastic Art"

This essay, published in 1937, is the culmination of Mondrian's attempts to work out his aesthetic theories in written form.

Although Art is fundamentally everywhere and always the same, nevertheless two main human inclinations, diametrically opposed to each other, appear in its many and varied expressions. One aims at the *direct creation of universal beauty,* the other at the *esthetic expression of oneself.* . . . The first aims at representing reality objectively, the second subjectively. . . . This latter attempt must of necessity result in an individual expression which veils the pure representation of beauty. Nevertheless, both the two opposing elements (universal-individual) are indispensable if the work is to arouse emotion. Art had to find the right solution. . . . For the artist the search for a unified expression through the balance of two opposites has been, and always will be, a continual struggle. . . .

The only problem in art is to achieve a balance between the subjective and the objective. . . .

Gradually art is purifying its plastic means and thus bringing out the relationships between them. Thus, in our day two main tendencies appear: the one maintains the figuration, the other eliminates it. While the former employs more or less complicated and particular forms, the latter uses simple and neutral forms, or, ultimately, the free line and the pure color. It is evident that the latter (nonfigurative art) can more easily and thoroughly free itself from the domination of the subjective than can the figurative tendency.

102

André Breton (1896–1966)
From "What is Surrealism?"

The first Surrealist manifesto appeared in 1924, the second in 1930, and this one, considered the third, in 1934. Although the Surrealist movement was dedicated to the freedom of the individual, its founder, Breton, was both moralistic and highly authoritarian. Because he sometimes excommunicated members of the group, he became known as "the Pope of Surrealism."

We still live under the reign of logic, but the methods of logic are applied nowadays only to the resolution of problems of secondary interest. The absolute rationalism which is still the fashion does not permit consideration of any facts but those strictly relevant to our experience. Logical ends, on the other hand, escape us. Needless to say that even experience has had limits assigned to it. It revolves in a cage from which it becomes more and more difficult to release it. Even experience is dependent on immediate utility, and common sense is its keeper. Under color of civilization, under the pretext of progress, all that rightly or wrongly may be regarded as fantasy or superstition has been banished from the mind, all uncustomary searching after truth has been proscribed. It is only by what must seem sheer luck that there has recently been brought to light an aspect of mental life—to my belief by far the most important—with which it was supposed that we no longer had any concern. All credit for these discoveries must go to Freud. Based on these discoveries a current of opinion is forming that will enable the explorer of the human mind to continue his investigations, justified as he will be in taking into account more than mere summary realities. The imagination is perhaps on the point of reclaiming its rights. If the depths of our minds harbor strange forces capable of increasing those on the surface, or of successfully contending with them, then it is all in our interest to canalize them, to canalize them first in order to submit them later, if necessary, to the control of the reason. . . .

I am resolved to render powerless that *hatred of the marvelous* which is so rampant. . . . Briefly: The marvelous is always beautiful, anything that is marvelous is beautiful; indeed, nothing but the marvelous is beautiful.

The admirable thing about the fantastic is that it is no longer fantastic: there is only the real.

103

Frida Kahlo (1910–1954)
From a letter to Nickolas Muray

Kahlo, wife of the muralist Diego Rivera, met André Breton when he came to Mexico in 1938 to give some lectures and visit the exiled Russian Communist Leon Trotsky. Kahlo, who had looked forward to meeting Breton, found him pretentious, boring, vain, and arrogant. This letter of February 16, 1939, recounts the Paris exibition Breton arranged for her.

The question of the exhibition is all a damn mess. . . . Until I came the paintings were still in the custom house, because the s. of a b. of Breton didn't take the trouble to get them out.

... So I had to wait days and days just like an idiot till I met Marcel Duchamp ... who is the only one who has his feet on the earth, among all this bunch of coocoo lunatic sons of bitches of the surrealists. He immediately got my paintings out and tried to find a gallery. Finally there was a gallery called "Pierre Colle" which accepted the damn exhibition. . . .

[A] few days ago Breton told me that the associate of Pierre Colle, an old bastard and son of a bitch, saw my paintings and found that only *two* were possible to be shown, because the rest are too "*shocking*" for the public!! I could of kill[ed] that guy and eat it afterwards, but I am so sick and tired of the whole affair that I have decided to send every thing to hell, and scram from this rotten Paris before I get nuts myself. . . . You have no idea the kind of bitches these people are. They make me vomit. They are so damn "intellectual" and rotten that I can't stand them any more. . . . They sit for hours in the "cafes" warming their precious behinds, and talk without stopping about "culture," "art," "revolution," and so on and so forth, thinking themselves the gods of the world, dreaming the most fantastic nonsenses, and poisoning the air with theories and theories that never come true. . . . I never seen Diego [Rivera, her husband] or you wasting their time on stupid gossip and "intellectual" discussions. That is why you are real *men* and not lousy "artists."

104
Max Beckmann (1884–1950)
From "On My Painting"

This excerpt is from a lecture delivered in London in July of 1938.

In my opinion all important things in art since Ur . . . have always originated from the deepest feeling about the mystery of Being. Self-realization is the urge of all objective spirits. It is this self which I am searching in my life and in my art.

Art is creative for the sake of realization, not for amusement; for transfiguration, not for the sake of play. It is the quest of our self that drives us along the eternal and never-ending journey we must all make. . . .

I have always on principle been against the artist speaking about himself or his work. Today neither vanity nor ambition causes me to talk about matters which generally are not to be expressed even to oneself. But the world is in such a catastrophic state, and art is so bewildered that I, who have lived the last thirty years almost as a hermit, am forced to leave my snail's shell to express these few ideas which, with much labor, I have come to understand in the course of the years.

The greatest danger which threatens mankind is collectivism. Everywhere attempts are being made to lower the happiness and the way of living of mankind to the level of termites. I am against these attempts with all the strength of my being. . . .

And for this reason I am immersed in the phenomenon of the Individual, the so-called whole Individual, and I try in every way to explain and present it. What are you? What am I? Those are the questions that constantly persecute and torment me and perhaps also play some part in my art.

105
Jackson Pollock (1912–1956)
From "My Painting"

In 1947, when these remarks were recorded, Pollock rejected the usual easel format by placing his unstretched canvases directly on the floor. Using ordinary house paint, he claimed that he was not just throwing paint but delineating some real thing in the air above the canvas.

My painting does not come from the easel. I hardly ever stretch my canvas before painting. I prefer to tack the unstretched canvas to the hard wall or the floor. I need the resistance of a hard surface. On the floor I am more at ease. I feel nearer, more a part of the painting, since this way I can walk around it, work from the four sides and literally be *in* the painting. This is akin to the method of the Indian sand painters of the West.

I continue to get further away from the usual painter's tools such as easel, palette, brushes, etc. I prefer sticks, trowels, knives and dripping fluid paint or a heavy impasto with sand, broken glass and other foreign matter added.

When I am *in* my painting, I'm not aware of what I'm doing. It is only after a sort of "get acquainted" period that I see what I have been about. I have no fears about making changes, destroying the image, etc., because the painting has a life of its own. I try to let it come through. It is only when I lose contact with the painting that the result is a mess. Otherwise there is pure harmony, an easy give and take, and the painting comes out well.

The source of my painting is the unconscious. I approach painting the same way I approach drawing. That is direct—with no preliminary studies. The drawings I do are relative to my painting but not for it.

106
Romare Bearden (1911–1988)
From two interviews

In interviews conducted by Myron Schwartzman in 1983 and 1986, Bearden discussed the wide range of artistic influences on his working methods and ideas.

MYRON SCHWARTZMAN: So [collage] gets improvisational. . . .

ROMARE BEARDEN: Well, it's like jazz; you do this and then you improvise. You know Manet (I think) said, "A painting isn't finished; sometimes you get on the surface." He meant, "Well, you've got it under control." Maybe sometimes a third of the way through [a painting], I'll say, "I know this is coming out." You get that feeling that the thing is going to be all right. And other things you just have to surrender. As my friend Carl Holty used to say, "Don't close your picture too quickly; keep it open until the very last, and that gives you room to maneuver." You reach a point when all the elements seem to focus, so that the colors and the forms will set. And at that point you can relinquish the painting. . . .

MS: What triggers [a] series, Romie?

RB: Well, the memories are just there; they're just really with me. It's strange, the memories are there. For instance, you see the Vermeer [reproduction of *The Concert*] up there on the wall? I'll say, "Well, I saw something like this; this used to be so-and-so." Because I guess art is made from other art. Yes, I've been in places like this; I've gone in with the same kind of stillness, and the light coming in from this source.

Those people [of Vermeer's time] moved on, and the people from Mecklenburg [North Carolina, Bearden's birthplace] have come in there; they stayed a while and now there is something else.

MS: Let's explore the theme of relationships. What does it mean to you in painting?

RB: In discussing relationships, we have to consider many disparate factors, or seemingly disparate factors, in the way a painting is put together, such as scale, space, line, and so forth. And the idea of my thinking is that everything has a certain correspondence. . . . For instance, a Chinese painter, in the classic days, when he looked at the rocks and trees, felt a certain oneness with them. . . . I think this is one of the most important things that Matisse talks about—the relationships, how one does things—and it changes. . . .

In the Cloisters [museum] I saw some old Spanish frescoes, and I thought—Picasso. In the icons, and in African sculpture, they bring everything to a very beautiful shape. So long as you can get everything in a nice shape, the picture will be all right—you're just shaping it, not worrying so much about the anatomy. If you do that and it all moves in the right rhythms, you have a painting. We get deceived so much by appearances. You sometimes just have to forget about that, because you are working in another world here. And so you could easily take these [canvases] as being completely non-representational.

Take Vermeer's drawings—you turn them upside down, and there's real, great abstraction. The wrinkles in the clothes, for instance; you turn the drawing upside down, and you see something else, the great relationships. This is the abstracting of things. People think abstraction means that you don't have figurative objects in a work. So a more accurate word is "non-representational" rather than "abstract," because Poussin, Ingres are great abstractionists. . . .

The thing is that the artist confronts chaos. The whole thing of art is, how do you organize chaos? . . . Probably, if you take it symbolically, there is no greater chaos than in the inferno, down in hell. Dante, in his *Inferno,* meets Virgil. . . .

He's lost and confused there, and Virgil says, "I'll guide you, . . . " to me he is like the artist. This is the help that he needs in understanding what is going on, . . . some kind of organization that he finds. And he's talking about sin, and the rest of these things. But he needs that guide.

So I think it's the same thing with the artist.

107
Roy Lichtenstein (born 1923)
From "What is Pop Art?"

This interview with Gene R. Swenson appeared in 1963, the same year as Lichtenstein's Drowning Girl *(fig. 1097).*

GENE R. SWENSON: What is Pop Art?

ROY LICHTENSTEIN: I don't know—the use of commercial art as subject matter in painting, I suppose. It was hard to get a painting that was despicable enough so that no one would hang it. . . . The one thing everyone hated was commercial art; apparently they didn't hate that enough either.

GRS: Is Pop Art despicable?

RL: . . . Well, it is an involvement with what I think to be the most brazen and threatening characteristics of our culture, things we hate, but which are also powerful in their impingement on us. I think art since Cézanne has become extremely romantic and unrealistic, feeding on art. . . . It has had less and less to do with the world. . . . Outside is the world; it's there. Pop Art looks out into the world; it appears to accept its environment. . . .

I suppose I would still prefer to sit under a tree with a picnic basket rather than under a gas pump, but signs and comic strips are interesting as subject matter. There are certain things that are usable, forceful and vital about commercial art. We're using those things—but we're not really advocating stupidity, international teenagerism and terrorism. . . .

I think my work is different from comic strips—but I wouldn't call it transformation. . . . What I do is form, whereas the comic strip is not formed in the sense I'm using the word; the comics have shapes but there has been no effort to make them intensely unified. The purpose is different, one intends to depict and I intend to unify. And my work is actually different from comic strips in that every mark is really in a different place, however slight the difference seems to some. The difference is often not great, but it is crucial. . . .

GRS: A curator at the Modern Museum has called Pop Art fascistic and militaristic.

RL: The heroes depicted in comic books are fascist types, but I don't take them seriously in these paintings—maybe there is a point in not taking them seriously, a political point. I use them for purely formal reasons, and that's not what those heroes were invented for. . . .

The techniques I use are not commercial, they only appear to be commercial—and the ways of seeing and composing and unifying are different and have different ends.

108

Henry Moore (1898–1986)
From "The Sculptor Speaks"

Moore's sculpture in the 1930s began to reveal the tension between solid and void. His interest in the human figure and in natural forms remained paramount, however, as is evident in these comments published in 1937.

It is a mistake for a sculptor or a painter to speak or write very often about his job. It releases tension needed for his work. By trying to express his aims with rounded-off logical exactness, he can easily become a theorist whose actual work is only a caged-in exposition of conceptions evolved in terms of logic and words.

But though the nonlogical, instinctive, subconscious part of the mind must play its part in his work, he also has a conscious mind which is not inactive. . . .

Since the Gothic, European sculpture had become overgrown with moss, weeds—all sorts of surface excrescences which completely concealed shape. It has been Brancusi's special mission to get rid of this overgrowth, and to make us once more shape-conscious. To do this he has had to concentrate on very simple direct shapes, to keep his sculpture, as it were, one-cylindered, to refine and polish a single shape to a degree almost too precious. Brancusi's work, apart from its individual value, has been of historical importance in the development of contemporary sculpture. But it may now be no longer necessary to close down and restrict sculpture to the single (static) form unit. We can now begin to open out. To relate and combine together several forms of varied sizes, sections, and directions into one organic whole.

Although it is the human figure which interests me most deeply, I have always paid great attention to natural forms, such as bones, shells, and pebbles, etc. Sometimes for several years running I have been to the same part of the seashore—but each year a new shape of pebble has caught my eye, which the year before, though it was there in hundreds, I never saw. . . . A different thing happens if I sit down and examine a handful one by one. I may then extend my form-experience more, by giving my mind time to become conditioned to a new shape.

There are universal shapes to which everybody is subconsciously conditioned and to which they can respond if their conscious control does not shut them off.

Pebbles show nature's way of working stone.

109

Eva Hesse (1936–1970)
From an interview

An abbreviated version of this interview with Cindy Nemser was published in 1970, shortly before her death. Hesse resisted the impersonal formalism of 1960s art.

CINDY NEMSER: Tell me about your family background.

EVA HESSE: . . . I was told by the doctor that I have the most incredible life he ever heard. . . . It's not a little thing to have a brain tumor at thirty-three. Well my whole life has been like that. I was born in Hamburg, Germany. My father was a criminal lawyer. He had just finished his two doctorates and I had the most beautiful mother in the world. She looked like Ingrid Bergman and she was manic depressive. She studied art in Hamburg. My sister was born in 1933 and I was born in 1936. Then in 1938 there was a children's pogrom. I was put on a train with my sister. We went to Holland where we were supposed to be picked up by my father's brother and his wife in Amsterdam but he couldn't do it, so we were put in a Catholic children's home and I was always sick. So I was put in a hospital and I wasn't with my sister. My parents were hidden somewhere in Germany and then they came to Amsterdam and had trouble getting us out. Somehow they got us to England. My father's brother and his wife ended up in concentration camps. No one else in my family made it. . . . No one in my family has lived. I have one healthy sister. There's not been one normal thing in my life—not one—not even my art. . . .

CN: . . . Looking at your works they seem, to me, to be filled with sexual impulses or organic feeling. I feel there are anthropomorphic inferences.

EH: It's not a simple question for me. First when I work it's only the abstract qualities that I'm really working with, which is to say the material, the form it's going to take, the size, the scale, the positioning. . . . However, I don't value the totality of the image on these abstract or esthetic points. For me it's a total image that has to do with me and life. It can't be divorced as an idea or composition or form. I don't believe art can be based on that. . . . I don't want to make that my problem. . . . Those problems are solvable, I solve them, can solve them *beautifully*. In fact, my idea now is to discount everything I've ever learned or been taught about those things and to find something else. So it is inevitable that it is my life, my feelings, my thoughts. And there I'm very complex. I'm not a simple person and the complexity . . . is the total absurdity of life. I guess that's where I relate, if I do, to certain artists who I feel very close to, and not so much through having studied their writings or works, but because, for me, there's this total *absurdity* in their work.

CN: Which artists are they?

EH: Duchamp, Yvonne Rainer, Ionesco, Carl Andre.

CN: Let's talk about some of your early sculptures.

EH: There was a piece I did for that show in the Graham Gallery . . . in 1965 or '66. It was called Hang-Up—a dumb name . . . but I can't change it. I think it was about the fifth piece I did and I think the most important statement I made. It's close to what I feel I achieve now in my best pieces. It was the first time where my idea of absurdity or extreme feeling came through.

110
Frank Lloyd Wright (1867–1959)
From "A Philosophy of Fine Art"

Wright delivered these remarks at a meeting of the Architectural League of the Art Institute of Chicago in 1900.

We feel and find in Nature always, an accord of form and function with Life principle. . . . But, however much we love the oak and pine in a state of nature in pristine freedom, their freedom is not for us. It does not belong to us now, however much the relic of barbarism within us may yearn for it. Civilization means for us a conventionalizing of our original state of nature. . . . For Art is the great conservator of the finer sensibilities of a people. . . . I wish I might use another word than "conventionalizing," to convey the idea of this magic process, for only an artist or one with some genuine artistic training, will realize precisely what that means. To know a thing, what we can call knowing, a man must first love the thing, sympathize with it. So the Egyptians "knew" the Lotus and translated the Lotus to the dignified stone forms of their Architecture: this was the Lotus "conventionalized!" The Greeks "knew" and idealized the Acanthus in stone translations. This was the Acanthus conventionalized. Of all Art, whatsoever, perhaps Architecture is the Art best fitted to teach this lesson, for in its practices this problem of "conventionalizing" Nature is worked out at its highest and best. . . . A work of Architecture is . . . in no sense naturalistic—it is the highest, most subjective, conventionalization of Nature known to man, and at the same time it must be organically true to Nature.

111
Walter Gropius (1883–1969)
From *Scope of Total Architecture*

Gropius was interested in the social and aesthetic implications of housing and city planning, as these remarks of 1943 suggest.

Every thinking contemporary searches his mind now trying to figure out what may be the ultimate value of our stupendous scientific progress. We roar with new techniques and new inventions for speedier means of transportation. But what do we do with all the time saved? Do we use it for contemplation of our existence? No, we plunge instead into an even more hectic current of activity, surrendering to that fallacious slogan: time is money. We obviously need a clarification as to what exactly our spiritual and intellectual aims are. . . .

I should like, therefore, to attempt to outline the potential strategic aim of planning for my own profession, architecture, within the cultural and political context of our industrial civilization. . . .

Our scientific age, by going to extremes of specialization, has obviously prevented us from seeing our complicated life as an entity. The average professional man, driven to distraction by the multiplicity of problems spread out before him, seeks relief from the pressure of general responsibilities by picking out one single, rigidly circumscribed responsibility in a specialized field and refuses to be answerable for anything that may happen outside this field. A general dissolution of context has set in and naturally resulted in shrinking and fragmenting life. As Albert Einstein once put it: "Perfection of means and confusion of aims seem to be characteristic of our age. . . ."

But there are indications that we are slowly moving away from overspecialization and its perilous atomizing effect on the social coherence of the community. . . . In the gigantic task of its reunification, the planner and architect will have to play a big role. He must be well trained not ever to lose a total vision, in spite of the infinite wealth of specialized knowledge which he has to absorb and integrate. He must comprehend land, nature, man and his art, as one great entity. In our mechanized society we should passionately emphasize that we are still a world of men, that man in his natural environment must be the focus of all planning. We have indulged our latest pets, the machines, to such an extent that we have lost a genuine scale of values. Therefore, we need to investigate what makes up the really worthwhile relationships among men, and between men and nature, instead of giving way to the pressure of special interests or of shortsighted enthusiasts who want to make mechanization an end in itself. . . .

There is no other way toward progress but to start courageously and without prejudice new practical tests by building model communities in one stroke and then systematically examining their living value. What a wealth of new information for the sociologist, the economist, the scientist and the artist would be forthcoming, if groups, formed of the most able planners and architects available, should be commissioned to design and build completely new model communities! Such information would also offer most valuable preparatory data to solve the complicated problem of rehabilitating our existing communities.

112
Edward Weston (1886–1958)
From "Photographic Art"

Weston insisted that the photographer should previsualize the final print before making the exposure and not crop or trim the print. This excerpt from an encyclopedia entry published in 1942 attempts to synthesize some of the reflections on photography that he kept in his Daybooks.

The camera lens sees too clearly to be used successfully for recording the superficial aspects of a subject. . . .

But if the camera's innate honesty works any hardship on the photographer by limiting his subject matter in one direction, the loss is slight when weighed against the advantages it provides. For it is that very quality that makes the camera expressly fitted for examining deeply into the meaning of things. The discriminating photographer . . . can reveal the essence of what lies before his lens with such clear insight that the beholder will find the recreated image more real and comprehensible than the actual object.

The photograph isolates and perpetuates a moment of time: an important and revealing moment, or an unimportant and meaningless one, depending upon the photographer's understanding of his subject and mastery of his process. The lens does not reveal a subject significantly of its own accord. On the contrary, its vision is completely impartial and undiscriminating. It makes no distinction between important detail and meaningless detail. Selection, emphasis, and meaning must be provided by the photographer in his composition. . . . To compose a subject well means no more than to see and present it in the strongest manner possible. . . . Its capacity for rendering fine detail and tone makes photography excel in recording form and texture. Its subtlety of gradation makes it admirably suited to recording qualities of light or shadow. . . . The photographer cannot depend on rules deduced from finished work in another medium. He must learn to see things through his own eyes and his own camera; only then can he present his subject in a way that will transmit his feeling for it to others.

An intuitive knowledge of composition in terms of the capacities of his process enables the photographer to record his subject at the moment of deepest perception; to capture the fleeting instant when the light on a landscape, the form of a cloud, the gesture of a hand, or the expression of a face momentarily presents a profound revelation of life.

The appeal to our emotions manifest in such a record is largely due to the quality of authenticity in the photograph. The spectator accepts its authority and, in viewing it, perforce believes that he would have seen that scene or object exactly so if he had been there. We know that the human eye is capable of no such feat, and furthermore that the photographer has not reproduced the scene exactly; quite possibly we would not even be able to identify the original scene from having seen the photograph. Yet it is this belief in the reality of the photograph that calls up a strong response in the spectator and enables him to participate directly in the artist's experience.

113
Jerry Uelsmann (born 1934)
From "Some Humanistic Considerations of Photography"

Uelsmann's approach to photography—postvisualization—is the opposite of Edward Weston's previsualization. This excerpt is

from a speech given by Uelsmann to the Royal Photographic Society of Great Britain in 1971.

As you may know the dominant aesthetic in photography has been called previsualization. This means that the image is essentially fully previsioned at the time the shutter is clicked. Now I propose that photographers keep themselves open to in-process discovery. . . .

It seems to me that all other areas of art allow for in-process discovery. The painter does not begin with a fully-conceived canvas, the sculptor with a fully-conceived piece. They allow for a dialogue to evolve, to develop, and as far as I'm concerned the darkroom is truly capable of being a visual research laboratory, a place for discovery, observation and meditation. . . .

Some of my photographs I don't understand. This disturbs some people. I would like to think that today we are sophisticated enough to realize that first of all there are systems of knowledge which are not necessarily verbal. There are levels of consciousness that we can engage ourselves in when we are encountering the world of photography that are not easy to talk about. . . . I think many times we are pressured into a verbalization of things that we don't fully understand but somehow the words are important. . . .

One recent photograph disturbs me a great deal. Literally I know what's happening: there is a wave and an organic form that was washed up on the beach after a hurricane. . . . But there is some strange thing happening, some strange statement within that I am in no way capable of articulating. I think the sooner that we as photographers become aware of this phenomenon that we can perhaps address each other visually at times, I think the happier we'll all be, because so many times I am pressed to have verbal responses to things that I can't defend verbally.

114
Michael Graves (born 1934)
From "What is the Focus of Post-Modern Architecture?"

This 1981 interview with Michael McTwigan appeared while Graves was designing the Public Services Building (fig. 1232), which was dubbed the "Post-Modern building of the year."

MICHAEL MCTWIGAN: It's interesting that you use the word "figural." By that, do you mean related to human scale . . . ?

MICHAEL GRAVES: Those things, as well as a range of architectonic ideas—elements like a door or a window, a configuration of space that is anthropomorphically related. For instance, if I make a Greek cross plan . . . there's no doubt where the primary space is for us in a room like that. If you look at De Stijl architecture, on the other hand, there is no clear identity of the human body within the plan. I can't locate the figure of myself within the work.

MM: That is presumably why so many people have felt alienated by modern architecture; it stands on its own and doesn't really have a relationship to the human being. . . .

Architect Robert Stern said not too long ago, "We're not in the business of educating and transforming human nature; we're in the business of responding to the human condition. We're not reformers or revolutionaries." That seems to be quite a statement, quite a change from the Bauhaus days. . . .

MG: . . . In part, what Robert is saying is that this is not a time of manifestos. I remember in the early '60s, when Peter Eiseman and I were working together, we wanted to write a manifesto. We wanted to be modern architects and say, "This is what ought to be, not what is. . . ."

We wanted to make clear our own ideas in a general sense, rather than in the peculiarities of site or client or whatever. It's not that one has softened today, but the manifesto is much more gentle now. I would not say we are not reformers, however. We are, in the best sense of the word, re-formers. We are trying to establish form as it relates to us more than to the machine. . . . We are reformers in the sense that we don't want to return to something, but, rather, to reestablish the language of architecture. That's where the manifesto comes.

Although literature can use the window as a metaphor, architecture possesses the window. It's the modern architect who wants to throw the window out. It's people like myself who want to say simply, "The window exists, and I will use the window." The window relates to the human body and it relates to the wall for very specific aesthetic, technical, and cultural reasons. It's not for nothing that the window existed for 2,000 years or more. That's a crucial issue.

So I would vary that rather dramatic statement of Robert's and say I'm interested in reestablishing the language of architecture. . . .

MM: So it's not just a matter of reeducating. It's a matter of teaching old skills as well. . . . It could be said that people almost forgot how to paint in the '60s, and the same could be said about architecture.

MG: Sure. There's an architect by the name of Leo Krier in London who says he won't build, because there's no craft tradition from which to build his buildings. His political standing is that we must dissolve the Industrial Revolution. So he does his drawings. He says, "Let's go back to the craft tradition."

115
Cindy Sherman (born 1954)
From an interview

In these excerpts from a 1988 interview with Jeanne Siegel, Sherman discusses her photographic role-playing.

CINDY SHERMAN: I still wanted to make a filmic sort of image, but I wanted to work alone. I realized that I could make a picture of a character reacting to something outside the frame so that the viewer would assume another person.

Actually, the moment that I realized how to solve this problem was when Robert [Longo] and I visited David Salle, who had been working for some sleazy detective magazine. Bored as I was, waiting for Robert and David to get their "art talk" over with, I noticed all these 8 by 10 glossies from the magazine which triggered something in me. (I was never one to discuss issues—after all, at that time I was "the girlfriend.")

JEANNE SIEGEL: In the "Untitled Film Stills," what was the influence of real film stars? It seems that you had a fascination with European stars. You mentioned Jeanne Moreau, Brigitte Bardot and Sophia Loren in some of your statements. Why were you attracted to them?

CS: I guess because they weren't glamorized like American starlets. When I think of American actresses from the same period, I think of bleached blonde, bejeweled and furred sex bombs. But, when I think of Jeanne Moreau and Sophia Loren, I think of more vulnerable, lower-class types of characters, more identifiable as working-class women.

At that time I was trying to emulate a lot of different types of characters. I didn't want to stick to just one. I'd seen a lot of the movies that these women had been in but it wasn't so much that I was inspired by the women as by the films themselves and the feelings in the films.

JS: And what is the relationship between your "Untitled Film Stills" and real film stills?

CS: In real publicity film stills from the 40s and 50s something usually sexy/cute is portrayed to get people to go see the movie. Or the woman could be shown screaming in terror to publicize a horror film.

My favorite film images (where obviously my work took its inspiration) didn't have that. They're closer to my own work for that reason, because both are about a sort of brooding character caught between the potential violence and sex. However, I've realized it is a mistake to make that kind of literal connection because my work loses in the comparison. I think my characters are not quite taken in by their roles so that they couldn't really exist in any of their so-called "films," which, next to a real still, looks unconvincing. They are too aware of the irony of their role and perhaps that's why many have puzzled expressions. My "stills" were about the fakeness of role-playing as well as contempt for the domineering "male" audience who would mistakenly read the images as sexy. . . .

JS: Another critical issue attached to the work was the notion that the stereotypical view was exclusively determined by the "male" gaze. Did you see it only in this light or did it include the woman seeing herself as well?

CS: Because I'm a woman I automatically assumed other women would have an immediate identification with the roles. And I hoped men would feel empathy for the characters as well as shedding light on their role-playing. What I didn't anticipate was that some people would assume that I was playing up to the male gaze. I can understand the criticism of feminists who therefore assumed I was reinforcing the stereotype of woman as victim or as sex object.

	1800–1820	1820–1840	1840–1850
HISTORY AND POLITICS	**1802** First child labor laws, in England **1803** United States purchases Louisiana from France for $15 million **1804** Napoleon crowned emperor of France, ending the republic established by the French Revolution; 1805–9, occupies Italy and Spain. He wins battles against allied England, Austria, Russia, and Sweden until he retreats from Moscow, 1812, losing the bulk of his army; 1814, successes of allies force him to abdicate; he is exiled to Elba War of 1812 (European allies against Napoleon) draws United States into conflict with Britain; 1814, Washington, D.C. burned **1814** Allies at Congress of Vienna redivide Europe. Louis XVIII, Bourbon king of France (r. 1814–24), establishes a constitutional monarchy; 1815, Napoleon returns; allies defeat him at Waterloo; he abdicates again and, 1821, dies a prisoner of war. Bourbon kings return to power until 1830 **1819–21** Spain sells Florida to United States	**1822** Simon Bolívar (1783–1830) leads revolution in Latin America: six countries gain independence from Spain **1823** Monroe Doctrine claims United States sphere of influence in the Western Hemisphere **1833** Factory Act abolishes slavery in British colonies **1830** July Revolution in France; republican mobs riot against the monarchy; Louis Philippe, nominated as new king (r. 1830–48, the July Monarchy), continues conservative policies. This change of power mandated by popular acclaim spawns revolutionary movements across Europe Queen Victoria (r. 1837–1901) rules Great Britain **1838** "Trail of Tears": Thousands of Cherokee and other Indians are moved by United States government on a forced march from the Southeast to Indian Territory (now Oklahoma); one in four dies	**1842** Oregon Trail opens western lands of North America for settlement **1846–48** War between United States and Mexico over territories of Texas and New Mexico Revolution of 1848 in France; 1848–52, Second Republic declared after abdication of Louis Philippe. Bloody insurrection leads to the election of Louis Napoleon, nephew of Napoleon I, as constitutional monarch; 1852, he overthrows republic and becomes Emperor Napoleon III (Second Empire, 1852–70); 1861–67, disastrous attempt by France to annex Mexico **1848** Revolutions throughout Europe; 1848–61, unification of Italy begins with a revolt led by Giuseppe Garibaldi against Austrian and French rule **1848** Discovery of gold in American West encourages westward expansion
RELIGION	Pope Pius X (r. 1803–14) reforms church law, music, texts, and administration		
	 THÉODORE GÉRICAULT *The Raft of the "Medusa,"* 1818–19	 JOHN CONSTABLE *Salisbury Cathedral from the Meadows,* 1829–34	 JOSEPH MALLORD WILLIAM TURNER *Rain, Steam and Speed—The Great Western Railway,* 1844
MUSIC, LITERATURE, AND PHILOSOPHY	**1800s** English Romantic poets: Wordsworth, Byron, Shelley, Keats; novelists: Thackeray, Austen, Dickens, Trollope, the Brontës, Eliot, Kipling **1807** Georg Wilhelm Friedrich Hegel (1770–1831) writes *Phenomenology of Mind* **1819–37** Jacob and Wilhelm Grimm, brothers, collect authoritative versions of German folktales and myths	Emily Dickinson (1830–86), American poet **1833** Carl von Clausewitz, a general in the Napoleonic Wars, writes *On War,* a treatise on modern warfare **1840** Edgar Allan Poe publishes suspenseful and macabre short stories in United States	**1842** Honoré de Balzac completes *The Human Comedy,* a series of novels and stories Modern economic theories: 1848, Karl Marx and Friedrich Engels write *The Communist Manifesto* and John Stuart Mill publishes *Principles of Political Economy;* 1867, Marx's *Capital*
SCIENCE, TECHNOLOGY, AND EXPLORATION	**1800** Estimated world population nears 1 billion; that of Europe is 180 million; Alessandro Volta (1745–1827) constructs the first battery and demonstrates electric currents **1804–6** Lewis and Clark cross the American continent to the Pacific Ocean **1811** Invention of tin cans for food storage **1814** Steam locomotive, in England, used to power early railroad travel **1819** First steamship crossing of the Atlantic	**1825** Opening of the Erie Canal, allowing passage of ships from the Atlantic Ocean to the Great Lakes **1831** Invention of mechanical McCormick reaper; 1837, John Deere plow **c. 1837** Development of armaments: rifles, artillery, shrapnel, revolvers, and torpedoes by the 1880s **1839** First forms of photography: daguerreotype and negative-positive system	**1844** Samuel Morse's telegraph transforms communications by allowing transmission and reception of a coded signal through wires; 1866, transatlantic cable laid **1846** Sewing machine invented by Elias Howe; William Morton uses ether anesthesia in surgery **1847** First Law of Thermodynamics formulated by Julius von Mayer and James Joule; 1850, Second Law, by Rudolf Clausius

1850–1860	1860–1870	1870–1880

1853–55 Crimean War; England and France halt the advance of Russia into the Balkans
1854 Commodore Matthew Perry of the United States signs treaty opening Japan to foreign trade

1861 Russia abolishes serfdom
1861–65 Civil War in the United States, centering on the issue of slavery; 1863, Emancipation Proclamation frees slaves; 1865, assassination of President Abraham Lincoln
1864 First International Workingman's Association led by Karl Marx, in England
1869 Susan B. Anthony organizes American

1870 Franco-Prussian War; 1871, defeat of French brings collapse of the Second Empire government. Paris populace sets up Third Republic (1870–1914)—at first ruling through the short-lived, radical Paris Commune—opposed to the monarchy. In German states, Prussian victory leads to a nationalist movement for unification (declared 1871) under Otto von Bismarck, Chancellor of Prussia (r. 1862–90) and a conservative (antisocialist) government
1876 Battle of Little Bighorn, in Montana: troops of George Armstrong Custer (1839–76), United States general, defeated and killed by forces of Sitting Bull (Tatanka Iotake, c. 1831–90), Sioux leader
1876–1914 Peak of European colonialism worldwide

> **1848: Nationalism in Europe** The year 1848 may be said to mark the beginning of the modern political world. In France the collapse of the monarchy and the establishment of a republic in February of that year started a chain reaction across Europe. In the capitals of Germany, Spain, Italy, Hungary, Austria, and the Balkans, a general discontent with conservative politics found expression in public demonstrations by masses of students, peasants, and soldiers and in a general cry for the overthrow of monarchies. The anxieties of the working classes (the Industrial Revolution having created an urban bourgeoisie), incipient socialist ideas, and a popular desire for constitutional, representative government added fuel to these fires. In many countries, the revolutions of 1848 led to a permanent change in the form of government. Among the profound cultural effects of this rapid transition were a new sense of national identity, which encouraged the development of national styles in art, and a new sense of the value of freedom of expression.

CAMILLE COROT
Morning: Dance of the Nymphs, 1850

HONORÉ DAUMIER
The Third-Class Carriage, c. 1862

EDWARD BURNE-JONES
The Wheel of Fortune, 1877–83

Mid-1800s Russian literature: Gogol (1809–52?), Turgenev (1818–83), Dostoyevsky (1821–81), Tolstoy (1828–1910), Chekhov (1860–1904)
1851 Melville's *Moby Dick;* Stowe's antislavery novel *Uncle Tom's Cabin;* 1853, Ruskin's *The Stones of Venice;* 1857, *Madame Bovary,* by Flaubert; *The Flowers of Evil,* by Baudelaire

Impressionist composers: Claude Debussy (1862–1918), Maurice Ravel (1875–1937); Romantics: Frédéric Chopin (1810–49), Robert Schumann (1810–56), Franz Liszt (1811–86), Johannes Brahms (1833–97). The Romantic work of Richard Wagner (1813–83) transforms opera
1862 Victor Hugo's novel *Les Misérables*

Carl G. Jung (1875–1961), Swiss psychologist, explores the concept of the collective unconscious
Thomas Mann (1875–1955), German novelist
1878–80 Friedrich Nietzsche, German philosopher, develops idea of an *Übermensch* (superman)

1855 First plastic material, celluloid, discovered by Alexander Parkes
c. 1856–63 Steel manufacturing processes invented; experimentation with alloys proliferates; 1890, first steel-frame skyscraper built, in Chicago
1859 Charles Darwin publishes *The Origin of Species,* formulating the theory of evolution

1863 First subways built, in London
1864 In France, Louis Pasteur's germ theory alters medical research and practice; 1865, antiseptic techniques introduced in surgery
1865 Genetic experiments of Gregor Mendel published in Austria
1866 Invention of dynamite by Alfred Nobel
1869 American transcontinental railroad completed; Suez Canal opens; periodic table of elements formulated by Dmitri Mendeleev

1872 Heinrich Schliemann excavates Troy
1876 Alexander Graham Bell patents the telephone
1876–85 In Germany, internal-combustion engine, running on gasoline fuel, developed
1877 Thomas Edison invents phonograph; 1879, incandescent bulb; 1894, motion pictures
1879 Ivan Pavlov explores the relationship between psychology and physiology

	1880–1890	1890–1900	1900–1910
HISTORY AND POLITICS	**1881–82** First pogroms against Jews in Russia **1886** Labor unrest in United States: Haymarket riot, Chicago, leads to the foundation of the American Federation of Labor, first national labor union; 1892, Carnegie steel strike, Pennsylvania **1886** Zionism, a doctrine calling for the establishment of a Jewish state in Palestine, appears in Europe; 1897, first Zionist Congress called by Theodor Hertzl, in Basel, Switzerland	**1890** Battle of Wounded Knee, between Sioux nation and United States Army, effectively ends Indian resistance **1893** World's Columbian Exposition, Chicago **1894–1906** Dreyfus Affair: a charge of treason brought fraudulently against a Jewish army officer stirs antisemitism and popular unrest in France **1895–98** Wars in Cuba and America weaken Spanish kingdom and result in losses in territory and prestige **1899–1902** Boer War in South Africa; British defeat South Africans and annex territory	Edward VII of England (r. 1901–10), whose government passes sweeping education reforms (1902) **1904–5** Russian–Japanese War over territory on the Pacific coast ends in humiliating defeat for the Russians and heightened unrest among the population; 1905, Bloody Sunday massacre of demonstrating workers in St. Petersburg leads to first Russian revolution; the Great General Strike gives birth to organized labor movement and the first *soviets,* or workers' councils

Early Modernism In Europe and America around the turn of the nineteenth century, just as visual artists were beginning to experiment with the concepts of collage and abstraction, and composers were testing unusual tonal systems and atonality in music, a number of writers were trying something parallel in prose and poetry: stream of consciousness, rhythmic language, fragmentation of form, and radical play with grammatical structures. Many were explicitly interested in the connections among art forms: the relationship between sound and color, for example, fascinated both the poet Charles Baudelaire and, later, the painter Wassily Kandinsky. Arthur Rimbaud shocked France in 1873 with the publication of the poem *A Season in Hell;* in 1896, Alfred Jarry's absurdist play *King Ubu* caused a riot in a Paris theater. In England in the 1880s Gerard Manley Hopkins invented "sprung rhythm" in poetry. The American Gertrude Stein, also in Paris, wrote *Three Lives* in 1908; Ezra Pound, in London, published the poems *Personae* in 1909. Thus, the pre–World War I radicalism of such artists as the painters Kandinsky, Pablo Picasso, and Kazimir Malevich and the architect Frank Lloyd Wright may be seen in the broader context of other revolutionary and visionary creative ideas.

(left) AUGUSTE BARTHOLDI, *Statue of Liberty (Liberty Enlightening the World)*, 1875–84

(right) GEORGES SEURAT
A Sunday on La Grande Jatte—1884, 1884–86

PAUL GAUGUIN
Where Do We Come From? What Are We? Where Are We Going?, detail, 1897

CLAUDE MONET
Water Lilies, Giverny, 1907

	1880–1890	1890–1900	1900–1910
MUSIC, LITERATURE, AND PHILOSOPHY	French Symbolist poets: Stéphane Mallarmé (1842–98), Paul Verlaine (1844–96), Arthur Rimbaud (1854–91) **1881** *Portrait of a Lady,* by Henry James **1884** *The Adventures of Huckleberry Finn,* by Mark Twain; *Against the Grain,* by Joris-Karl Huysmans	**1890–1903** Erik Satie composes *Three Small Pieces in the Form of a Pear* **1891** Oscar Wilde writes *The Picture of Dorian Gray* **1897** Bram Stoker publishes *Dracula* Jorge Luis Borges (1899–1986), Argentine Surrealist author **1900** Joseph Conrad publishes *Lord Jim*	Pablo Neruda (1904–73), Chilean poet **1906** Upton Sinclair publishes *The Jungle,* an American documentary novel that exposes the injustices of the industrial system **1908** Filippo Tommaso Marinetti writes the *Futurist Manifesto;* the composer Arnold Schoenberg uses atonality in composition Ferdinand de Saussure (1857–1913), French philologist, founds modern linguistics
SCIENCE, TECHNOLOGY, AND EXPLORATION	**c. 1880** Barbed-wire fences of galvanized iron patented and used to fence in much of the open range in American West **c. 1885** First automobiles invented, by Karl Benz and Gottlieb Daimler, in Germany	**c. 1890** Reinforced concrete begins to be used as a primary building material **1892–95** Sigmund Freud, Austrian physician, formulates the theory and method of psychoanalysis **1895** X-rays discovered by Wilhelm Röntgen; Guglielmo Marconi invents wireless telegraph, a precursor of radio **1897** Joseph Thomson discovers the electron **1898** Marie Curie discovers radium	**1903** First aircraft flight, made by Orville and Wilbur Wright, in North Carolina **1905** Albert Einstein (1879–1955), pioneering physicist, formulates the theory of relativity, radically changing modern views of space and time; 1953, Unified Field Theory **1909** American Robert Peary reaches North Pole; 1912, Robert Scott's American expedition reaches the South Pole (discovered by the Norwegian Roald Amundsen, 1911)

1910–1920	1920–1930	1930–1940

1911 Revolution in China: emperor deposed, Sun Yat-sen establishes a republic
1912 British ocean liner *Titanic* sinks
1914 Outbreak of World War I: assassination of Archduke Ferdinand of Austria in Sarajevo leads to war between Germany, Austro-Hungarian Empire, and allies on one side, and Serbia, Russia, France, England, and allies on the other; most of Europe and its colonies become involved; 1917, United States enters; 1918, defeat of Germany. Yugoslavia, Poland, Turkey, Czechoslovakia, Hungary, and Austria become independent nations; Syria, Iraq, and Palestine become mandates controlled by France and Britain
1916 Easter Rebellion in Ireland attempts to gain independence from Britain, but fails
1917 Bolshevik Revolution in Russia, under Lenin, inaugurates first communist state
1919 Foundation of the League of Nations, an international congress to promote peace, forerunner of the modern United Nations

1920 Women enfranchised in the United States; 1928, in England; 1945, in France
1920 With the passage of the Home Rule Bill, the British concede autonomy to southern Ireland; Mohandas Gandhi initiates peaceful mass protests (*satyagraha,* or passive resistance) in India against British rule
1922 Fascists under Benito Mussolini seize power in Italy
1926–53 Joseph Stalin controls Soviet Union; his government is a rigid totalitarian state marked by purges, pogroms, and radical collectivization of farms and industries
1929 Stock-market crash in United States inaugurates the Great Depression, worldwide economic crisis, during the 1930s

1931–41 Japanese wage undeclared war on China, annexing Manchuria
1933 In United States: the New Deal, a program of government spending to end the Depression; in Germany: Adolf Hitler's National Socialist (Nazi) Party seizes power
1934–35 Long March: 90,000 communist rebels led by Mao Tse-tung flee Chiang Kai-shek across China; less than half survive
1936–39 Spanish Civil War, won by Fascists
1938 Germany annexes Austria; 1939, occupies Czechoslovakia
1939–45 World War II: 1939, Germany invades Poland; 1940, Belgium and France; Italy enters war as ally of Germany. 1941, Germany attacks Russia. Japan, allied with Germany, bombs American fleet at Pearl Harbor; United States enters war. Holocaust in Europe: Nazis systematically exterminate over 6 million Jews, communists, homosexuals, gypsies, and others. 1945, defeat of Germans and Japanese by Allies

---

1917 British government, in control of much of the Middle East following World War I, promulgates the Balfour Declaration supporting the establishment of a Jewish state in Palestine

1923 Martin Buber, German Jewish theologian, writes *I and Thou*

1939–43 Rampant persecution of Orthodox church in Soviet Union

---

(left) PABLO PICASSO
Still Life with Chair Caning, 1912

(right) FRANZ MARC
Animal Destinies, 1913

PABLO PICASSO
Three Dancers, 1925

(left) MÉRET OPPENHEIM
Object, 1936

(right) FRIDA KAHLO
Self-Portrait with Thorn Necklace, 1940

1910 Wassily Kandinsky publishes *Concerning the Spiritual in Art*
c. 1912–15 John Dewey (1859–1952) and Maria Montessori (1870–1952) pioneer new ideas about education
1913–28 Marcel Proust, French critic and novelist, writes *Remembrance of Things Past*
1919 *The Cabinet of Dr. Caligari,* innovative German Expressionist silent film

1920s American free-verse and modernist poets: Robert Frost (1874–1963), Ezra Pound (1885–1972), T. S. Eliot (1888–1965)
1926 Franz Kafka's *The Castle;* Ernest Hemingway's *The Sun Also Rises;* 1927, Virginia Woolf's *To the Lighthouse;* Abel Gance makes the film *Napoléon;* 1928, D. H. Lawrence's *Lady Chatterly's Lover;* 1929, William Faulkner's *The Sound and the Fury*

Russian modernist composers: Rachmaninoff (1873–1943), Stravinsky (1882–1971), Prokoviev (1891–1953), Shostakovich (1906–1975)
1932 Aldous Huxley's *Brave New World* describes a pseudo-utopian future
1930s Gertrude Stein explores the forms and structure of language; 1939, James Joyce publishes *Finnegans Wake,* further experimenting with language

---

1911 First model of atomic structure made, by Ernest Rutherford, in Britain
By 1913 Diesel engines replace steam locomotives on many railways
1914 Henry Ford's fully mechanized mass-production plant for the Model T car marks the beginning of American industrialization
1915 Birth-control movement, led by Margaret Sanger in the United States, advocates family planning

1920 Radio programs broadcast, Pittsburgh
1922 Howard Carter discovers the tomb of Tutankhamen in Egypt
1925–26 Werner Heisenberg and Erwin Schrödinger's theories of quantum mechanics
1926 Sound motion pictures and television demonstrated
1927 Charles Lindbergh flies an aircraft solo across the Atlantic
1929 Alexander Fleming discovers penicillin

1931 Radio waves from space detected by the American electrical engineer Karl Jansky: beginning of radio astronomy, using radio waves to trace objects; c. 1935–36, radar discovered by the Scottish physicist Robert Watson-Watt, and others
1935 C. F. Richter, American, devises scale for measuring earthquakes

	1940–1950	1950–1960	1960–1970

HISTORY AND POLITICS

1940–1950

1945 United Nations founded as an international advisory and peacekeeping council; Yalta Conference: British prime minister Winston Churchill, American president Franklin D. Roosevelt, and Marshal Joseph Stalin of the Soviet Union plan division of Germany into zones of occupation and Europe into spheres of influence

1947 Marshall Plan, proposed to aid recovery of European states devastated by World War II, enacted by the United States. Division of Germany into East and West states

1948 Israel achieves nationhood with recognition by the United Nations; India gains independence from Britain

1949 Communist People's Republic of China founded, under Mao Tse-tung

1950–1960

1954 American civil-rights movement begins: United States Supreme Court outlaws racial segregation in public schools; 1955, Montgomery, Alabama, bus boycott by African-Americans, led by Martin Luther King, Jr.

c. 1955–c. 1989 Cold War among Soviet Union, China, and United States: a period of mutual hostilities, espionage, arms escalation, and political maneuvering for influence in other countries by the three world powers; most other nations align themselves with one of the three. Conflicts center upon the opposition between communism and democracy; 1961, Berlin Wall built, isolating West Berlin within East Germany; 1962, Cuban Missile Crisis, Soviet Union attempts to install missiles in Cuba, threatening United States

1959 Fidel Castro establishes communist government in Cuba

1960–1970

1963 Assassination of United States President John F. Kennedy

1965 America enters Vietnam War

1965–76 Cultural Revolution in China: hardline Maoist Red Guards formed; educators, local governments, and other elements seen as "enemies of the Revolution" attacked; thousands are killed, millions sent to reeducation camps; many artworks and religious sites are destroyed

1967 Egypt and Israel at war; Egypt is defeated, Israel controls Sinai peninsula

1968 Prague Spring, an attempt by Czechoslovakia to win freedom from Soviet control, crushed by Soviet troops; in United States, presidential candidate Robert F. Kennedy and civil-rights leader Martin Luther King, Jr., assassinated; mass protests in United States against Vietnam War

RELIGION

1948 Thomas Merton, American Trappist monk, poet, and philosopher, writes *The Seven Story Mountain*

1950s In some Protestant and Jewish denominations, women become ministers. Chinese invade Tibet and destroy over 6,000 ancient temples and monasteries; 1959, Dalai Lama, head of state and of Tibetan Buddhism, forced into exile in India

1962–65 Pope John XXIII's Second Vatican Council institutes use of vernacular in church ritual and other reforms

1964 Pope Paul VI and Patriarch Athenagoras attempt to resolve differences between Eastern and Western Christian churches

ADOLPH GOTTLIEB
Descent into Darkness, 1947

MARK ROTHKO
Orange and Yellow, 1956

(left) ROY LICHTENSTEIN
Drowning Girl, 1963

(right) ROMARE BEARDEN
The Prevalence of Ritual: Baptism, 1964

MUSIC, LITERATURE, AND PHILOSOPHY

1941 Charlie Chaplin makes the film *The Great Dictator*

1942 Albert Camus publishes *The Stranger*

1943 Jean-Paul Sartre writes *Being and Nothingness*, statement of Existentialism

1949 George Orwell's novel *1984* creates a futuristic totalitarian world

1949–50 Simone de Beauvoir authors the key feminist text *The Second Sex*

1950s Beat Generation: artists influenced by jazz whose works criticize American postwar materialism and complacency: 1952, John Cage composes *4'33"*, 1956, Allen Ginsberg writes the narrative poem *Howl*; 1957, Jack Kerouac writes *On the Road*

1955 *Lolita*, by Vladimir Nabakov, humorously explores the erotic relationship between an older man and a young girl

1960 Richard Wright writes *Native Son*, on the African-American experience

c. 1965 British Invasion in popular music: the Beatles, the Rolling Stones, and other rock-and-roll groups sell millions of albums

1967 In Colombia, Gabriel Garcia-Marquez writes *One Hundred Years of Solitude*

1969 Woodstock Festival in New York draws 500,000 fans of rock and roll

SCIENCE, TECHNOLOGY, AND EXPLORATION

The Atomic Age: 1942, in United States, first nuclear chain reaction; 1943, first nuclear fission bomb; 1945, United States drops atomic bombs on Japanese cities, killing over 100,000 instantly. 1949, first Soviet nuclear bomb; 1956, first nuclear electrical generators built in England; by 1970s, nuclear power in widespread commercial use

1946 Radio-carbon dating

1947 Dead Sea Scrolls discovered in Israel

c. 1950 Nuclear-powered submarines and ships in United States and Soviet Union

1953 In England, James Watson and Francis Crick publish a model of the structure of DNA and hypothesize the transmission of genetic codes

1954 Jonas Salk invents polio vaccine

Space Age begins: 1957, Sputnik, first satellite, launched by Soviet Union; 1961, first human orbit of the earth by Yuri Gagarin

1960 Laser technology developed

1963 Research in genetic engineering begins in United States; 1976, synthesis achieved

1967 First human heart transplant, by Dr. Christiaan Barnard, in South Africa

1969 United States' Apollo XI mission: Neil Armstrong and Edwin Aldrin walk on the moon; 1976, solar probe launched

1970–1980	1980–1990	1990–2000

1973 Egypt and Syria attack Israel and are defeated. United States withdraws from Vietnam War, having failed militarily and in response to increasing public criticism. In Chile, Salvador Allende, a socialist, becomes president; he is murdered and a military dictatorship under Augusto Pinochet takes power, until 1989. In Washington, D.C., Watergate scandal: President Richard Nixon is implicated in illegal activities; 1974, he resigns

1975 South Vietnam falls, ending the war; nation is unified under a communist regime

1978 Iranian revolution: Islamic fundamentalists rebel against the shah; the Ayatollah Khomeini takes power

1979 Afghan War: Soviet troops invade Afghanistan; they are forced to withdraw ten years later. Camp David Accords brokered by United States: Egypt formally recognizes Israel and regains Sinai territory

1979–81 Iran holds 52 Americans hostage

1981 Assassination of President Anwar Sadat of Egypt, advocate for peace in the Middle East; 1982, Israel invades Lebanon, whose government falls, causing war among Lebanese and Palestinian factions

1985 Mikhail Gorbachev is premier of Soviet Union: policies of *glasnost* and *perestroika* permit economic, political, and cultural liberalization

1986 In United States, Iran-*contra* scandal: secret, illegal sale of arms to Iran and diversion of funds to Nicaraguan rebels implicates high government officials

1989 Berlin Wall torn down; 1989–90, Soviet Union breaks up into independent states, with mostly noncommunist governments, along old ethnic and political boundaries; Yugoslavia and Czechoslovakia divide; student demonstrations (estimated over 1 million) in favor of democracy, in Tiananmen Square, Beijing, China, suppressed violently by Chinese military

1990–91 Gulf War: Iraq invades Kuwait, is repulsed by combined United Nations and United States armies

1990 Nelson Mandela, leader of the African National Congress and South African anti-apartheid movement, is freed from jail after 27 years; Germany reunifies

1991 Boris Yeltsin elected premier of Russia

1992 Civil war in states of the former Yugoslavia: ethnic and territorial disputes, some of ancient origin, in Bosnia, Croatia, and Serbia

1993 Israeli–Palestinian peace accord ratified; threatened by extremist terrorist activity

1994 South Africa holds first multiracial elections: Nelson Mandela is president; apartheid laws are abandoned; civil war in Rwanda kills over 500,000 civilians in a few months; Palestine Liberation Organization, under Yasir Arafat, gains self-rule from Israel in Jericho and Gaza

---

1977 End of Catholicism as state religion of Italy

1978 Pope John Paul II of Poland elected, first non-Italian pope in 455 years

1980s Rise of religious fundamentalism, especially among Moslems in the Middle East and Central Asia, Hindus in India, and some Christian sects in the United States

---

DON EDDY
New Shoes for H, 1973–74

RAYMOND SAUNDERS
White Flower Black Flower, 1986

AIDS and Art The disease known as Acquired Immune Deficiency Syndrome was first noticed in the United States in about 1981, and first identified by its current name in 1985. Its rapid spread throughout the world population in the succeeding ten years, its fatal nature, and its resistance to treatment or cure make it a powerful and terrible force in culture at the end of the second millennium, comparable in some ways (if not in scale) to the devastating bubonic plague (Black Death) that swept through Europe in 1348–49. Like that plague, AIDS has become a key subject for the art world in the 1990s. Many in the fields of visual arts, dance, theater, music, and film have died of AIDS by mid-decade.

1974 Aleksandr Solzhenitsyn (b. 1918), Russian writer whose novels describe life in a Soviet prison camp and criticize the government, is exiled to the United States

1981 MTV (music television), introduced on cable television, brings the new medium of video music to a mass audience

1989 Anglo-Indian novelist Salman Rushdie's *Satanic Verses* outrages Islamic fundamentalists, who place him under a death threat and force him into hiding

---

1973 Three babies born in England through invitro fertilization

c. 1978 Personal computers widely available

1979 Near-meltdown of nuclear reactor at Three Mile Island electrical-power plant, in Pennsylvania; 1986, explosion of Chernobyl nuclear-power plant in Ukraine devastates the area and causes severe radiation poisoning, as well as contamination of atmosphere over much of Europe

1981 First Space Shuttle, a reusable manned rocket, launched by United States

1982 First artificial heart implanted

c. 1985 AIDS, identified as a new, incurable disease, spreads throughout the world and begins to claim thousands of lives; by 1995, HIV infection levels reach epidemic proportions

1989 Voyager II space probe passes Neptune and discovers a new moon

1990s New office technology: fax for transmission of documents; modem for electronic transmission of information; rapid development of computer programs with many applications; fiber-optic technology in widespread use

1990 Hubble space telescope launched

BOOKS FOR FURTHER READING

by Max Marmor

In the literature of art—as in art itself—the best is not always the newest. We have, therefore, sought to achieve a judicious balance between standard works and current publications. Some works listed here are valuable chiefly for their reproductions, the text being outdated. We have not tried to indicate which titles are currently in print. But most listed here should be available in the art section of a local public or academic library. Your librarian can help you determine whether any specific title is readily available for purchase.

In the literature of art, the best is not always a book. But this list is limited to books, despite the fact that much important art-historical literature appears in periodicals and other types of publications. We have listed below a few of the standard indexes to art periodicals. These, too, should be available in a local library.

In the literature of art, the best is not always written in English. This list is, however, limited to books published in English. If, therefore, some areas of art history seem less well served here than others, readers may assume that the appropriate English literature on those subjects is similarly limited. In an era of multiculturalism and global scholarship, the student of art history is obliged to learn to read foreign languages.

In the literature of art, the best is not always obvious. To help the interested reader explore beyond the self-imposed limits of this list, we include below a list of several general art bibliographies; and more specialized bibliographies may be found throughout, in their appropriate places. We also include a list of standard art dictionaries and encyclopedias.

In the literature of art, the best is not infrequently the artists' own words or those of their contemporaries. We have therefore included a selective list of anthologies of "sources and documents" readily available in English translation.

In the literature of art, the best is not always printed at all. We therefore include a brief list of some electronic resources of interest to the student of art history.

A final note. Monographs on individual artists are legion, and only a handful are included here. Because greatness is established over time, we have been especially economical about listing monographs on individual twentieth-century artists. Your librarian can help you identify scholarly books on artists not included here.

REFERENCE RESOURCES IN ART HISTORY

1. ANTHOLOGIES OF SOURCES AND DOCUMENTS

Documents of Modern Art. 14 vols. Wittenborn, New York, 1944–61. A series of specialized anthologies.

The Documents of Twentieth-Century Art. G. K. Hall, Boston. A new series of specialized anthologies, individually listed below.

Goldwater, R., and M. Treves, eds. *Artists on Art, from the Fourteenth to the Twentieth Century.* 3rd ed. Pantheon, New York, 1974.

Holt, E. G., ed. *A Documentary History of Art.* Vol. 1, *The Middle Ages and the Renaissance.* Vol. 2, *Michelangelo and the Mannerists. The Baroque and the Eighteenth Century.* Vol. 3, *From the Classicists to the Impressionists.* 2nd ed. Princeton University Press, Princeton, 1981.

Sources and Documents in the History of Art Series. General ed. H. W. Janson. Prentice Hall, Englewood Cliffs, N.J. Specialized anthologies, listed individually below.

2. BIBLIOGRAPHIES AND RESEARCH GUIDES

Arntzen, E., and R. Rainwater. *Guide to the Literature of Art History.* American Library Association, Chicago, 1980.

Barnet, S. *A Short Guide to Writing About Art.* 4th ed. HarperCollins College, New York, 1993.

Chiarmonte, P. *Women Artists in the United States: A Selective Bibliography and Resource Guide to the Fine and Decorative Arts, 1750–1986.* G. K. Hall, Boston, 1990.

Ehresmann, D. *Architecture: A Bibliographical Guide to Basic Reference Works, Histories, and Handbooks.* Libraries Unlimited, Littleton, Colo., 1984.

———. *Fine Arts: A Bibliographical Guide to Basic Reference Works, Histories, and Handbooks.* 3rd ed. Libraries Unlimited, Littleton, Colo., 1990.

Freitag, W. *Art Books: A Basic Bibliography of Monographs on Artists.* Garland, New York, 1985.

Goldman, B. *Reading and Writing in the Arts: A Handbook.* Wayne State Press, Detroit, 1972.

Kleinbauer, W., and T. Slavens. *Research Guide to Western Art History.* American Library Association, Chicago, 1982.

Reference Publications in Art History. G. K. Hall, Boston. Specialized bibliographies, individually listed below.

3. DICTIONARIES AND ENCYCLOPEDIAS

Baigell, M. *Dictionary of American Art.* Harper & Row, New York, 1979.

Chilvers, I., and H. Osborne, eds. *The Oxford Dictionary of Art.* Oxford University Press, New York, 1988.

Dictionary of Art, The. 34 vols. Grove's Dictionaries, New York, 1996.

Duchet-Suchaux, G., and M. Pastoureau. *The Bible and the Saints.* Flammarion Iconographic Guides. Flammarion, Paris and New York, 1994.

Encyclopedia of World Art. 14 vols., with index and supplements. McGraw-Hill, New York, 1959–68.

Fleming, J., and H. Honour. *A Dictionary of Architecture.* 4th ed. Penguin, Baltimore, 1991.

———. *The Penguin Dictionary of Decorative Arts.* New ed. Viking, London, 1989.

Hall, J. *Illustrated Dictionary of Symbols in Eastern and Western Art.* HarperCollins, New York, 1994.

———. *Subjects and Symbols in Art.* 2nd ed. Harper & Row, New York, 1979.

Havlice, P. P. *World Painting Index.* 2 vols. Scarecrow Press, Metuchen, N.J., 1977. 2 vols. supplement, 1982.

Hutchinson Dictionary of the Arts, The. Helicon, London, 1994.

Janson, H. W., and D. J., eds. *Key Monuments of the History of Art.* Harry N. Abrams, New York, 1959.

Lever, J., and J. Harris. *Illustrated Dictionary of Architecture, 800–1914.* Faber & Faber, Boston, 1993.

Mayer, Ralph. *The HarperCollins Dictionary of Art Terms & Techniques.* 2nd ed. HarperCollins, New York, 1991.

———. *The Artist's Handbook of Materials and Techniques.* 5th ed. Viking, New York, 1991.

McGraw-Hill Dictionary of Art. Ed. B. S. Myers. 5 vols. McGraw-Hill, New York, 1969.

Millon, H. A., ed. *Key Monuments of the History of Architecture.* Harry N. Abrams, New York, 1964.

Murray, P. and L. *A Dictionary of Art and Artists.* 5th ed. Penguin, New York, 1988.

Osborne, H., ed. *Oxford Companion to Art.* Oxford, Clarendon Press, 1970.

Pierce, J. S. *From Abacus to Zeus: A Handbook of Art History.* 5th ed. Prentice Hall, Englewood Cliffs, N.J., 1995.

Placzek, A. K., ed. *Macmillan Encyclopedia of Architects.* 4 vols. Macmillan, New York, 1982.

Reid, J. D., ed. *The Oxford Guide to Classical Mythology in the Arts 1300–1990.* 2 vols. Oxford University Press, New York, 1993.

Teague, E. *World Architecture Index: A Guide to Illustrations.* Greenwood Press, New York, 1991.

Worldwide Bibliography of Art Exhibition Catalogues, 1963–1987, The. 3 vols. Kraus, Millwood, N.Y., 1992.

West, S., ed. *The Bulfinch Guide to Art History.* Little, Brown and Company, Boston, 1996.

Wright, C., comp. *The World's Master Paintings: From the Early Renaissance to the Present Day: A Comprehensive Listing of Works by 1,300 Painters and a Complete Guide to Their Locations Worldwide.* 2 vols. Routledge, New York, 1991.

4. INDEXES, PRINTED AND ELECTRONIC

Increasingly, the standard indexes to art literature are being made available by computer.

Art Index. 1929 to present. A standard quarterly index to more than 200 art periodicals. Data since 1984 also available electronically.

ART bibliographies MODERN. 1969 to present. A semi-annual publication indexing and annotating more than 300 art periodicals, as well as books, exhibition catalogues, and dissertations. Data since 1984 also available electronically.

Avery Index to Architectural Periodicals. 1934 to present. 15 vols., with supplementary vols. G. K. Hall, Boston, 1973. Also available electronically.

BHA: Bibliography of the History of Art. 1991 to present. The merger of two standard indexes: *RILA* (*Répertoire International de la Littérature de l'Art/ International Repertory of the Literature of Art*, vol. 1, 1975) and *Répertoire d'Art et d'Archéologie* (vol. 1, 1910). Like those indexes, scheduled to be available electronically in the near future.

5. GENERAL SOURCES

Barasch, M. *Theories of Art: From Plato to Winckelmann.* New York University Press, New York, 1985.

Baxandall, M. *Patterns of Intention: On the Historical Explanation of Pictures.* Yale University Press, New Haven, 1985.

Bois, Y.-A. *Painting as Model.* MIT Press, Cambridge, 1990.

Broude, N., and M. Garrard, eds. *Feminism and Art History: Questioning the Litany.* Harper & Row, New York, 1982.

———. *The Expanding Discourse: Feminism and Art History.* Harper & Row, New York, 1992.

Bryson, N., ed. *Vision and Painting: The Logic of the Gaze.* Yale University Press, New Haven, 1983.

———, et al., eds. *Visual Theory: Painting and Interpretation.* Cambridge University Press, New York, 1991.

Cahn, W. *Masterpieces: Chapters on the History of an Idea.* Princeton University Press, Princeton, 1979.

Chadwick, W. *Women, Art, and Society.* Thames and Hudson, New York, 1990.

Freedberg, D. *The Power of Images: Studies in the History and Theory of Response.* University of Chicago Press, Chicago, 1989.

Gage, J. *Color and Culture: Practice and Meaning from Antiquity to Abstraction.* Little, Brown, Boston, 1993.

Gombrich, E. H. *Art and Illusion.* 4th ed. Pantheon, New York, 1972.

Harris, A. S., and L. Nochlin. *Women Artists, 1550–1950.* Knopf, New York, 1976.

Kemal, S., and I. Gaskell. *The Language of Art History.*

Cambridge Studies in Philosophy and the Arts. Cambridge University Press, New York, 1991.

Kleinbauer, W. E. *Modern Perspectives in Western Art History: An Anthology of Twentieth-Century Writings on the Visual Arts.* Reprint of 1971 ed., University of Toronto Press, Toronto, 1989.

Kostof, S. A. *History of Architecture: Settings and Rituals.* 2nd ed. Oxford University Press, New York, 1995.

Kris, E. *Psychoanalytic Explorations in Art.* International Universities Press, New York, 1962.

———, and O. Kurz. *Legend, Myth, and Magic in the Image of the Artist: A Historical Experiment.* Yale University Press, New Haven, 1979.

Kultermann, U. *The History of Art History.* Abaris Books, New York, 1993.

Nochlin, L. *Women, Art, and Power, and Other Essays.* Harper & Row, New York, 1988.

Panofsky, E. *Meaning in the Visual Arts.* Reprint of 1955 ed., University of Chicago Press, 1982.

Parker, R., and G. Pollock. *Old Mistresses: Women, Art, and Ideology.* Pantheon, New York, 1981.

Penny, N. *The Materials of Sculpture.* Yale University Press, New Haven, 1993.

Podro, M. *The Critical Historians of Art.* Yale University Press, New Haven, 1982.

Pollock, G. *Vision and Difference: Feminity, Feminism, and the Histories of Art.* Routledge, New York, 1988.

Rees, A. L., and F. Borzello. *The New Art History.* Humanities Press International, Atlantic Highlands, N.J., 1986.

Roth, L. *Understanding Architecture: Its Elements, History, and Meaning.* Harper & Row, New York, 1993.

Shikes, R. E. *The Indignant Eye: The Artist as Social Critic in Prints and Drawings from the Fifteenth Century to Picasso.* Beacon Press, Boston, 1969.

Summerson, J. *The Classical Language of Architecture.* MIT Press, Cambridge, 1963.

Tagg, J. *Grounds of Dispute: Art History, Cultural Politics, and the Discursive Field.* University of Minnesota Press, Minneapolis, 1992.

Trachtenberg, M., and I. Hyman. *Architecture: From Prehistory to Post-Modernism.* Harry N. Abrams, New York, 1986.

Watkin, D. *The Rise of Architectural History.* University of Chicago Press, Chicago, 1980.

Wittkower, R. and M. *Born Under Saturn: The Character and Conduct of Artists: A Documented History from Antiquity to the French Revolution.* Norton, New York, 1963.

Wölfflin, H. *Principles of Art History: The Problem of the Development of Style in Later Art.* Dover, New York, 1932.

Wolff, J. *The Social Production of Art.* 2nd ed. New York University Press, New York, 1993.

Wollheim, R. *Art and Its Objects.* Cambridge University Press, New York, 1980.

PART THREE: THE RENAISSANCE THROUGH THE ROCOCO

GENERAL REFERENCES

De Winter, P. *European Decorative Arts, 1400–1600: An Annotated Bibliography.* G. K. Hall, Boston, 1988.

Hartt, F. *Italian Renaissance Art.* 4th ed. Harry N. Abrams, New York, 1993.

Haskell, F., and N. Penny. *Taste and the Antique: The Lure of Classical Sculpture, 1500–1900.* Yale University Press, New Haven, 1981.

Held, J., and D. Posner. *Seventeenth and Eighteenth Century Baroque Painting, Sculpture, Architecture.* Harry N. Abrams, New York, 1971.

Hind, A. *History of Engraving and Etching.* Reprint of 1923 3rd ed., Dover, New York, 1963.

———. *An Introduction to a History of Woodcut.* 2 vols. Reprint of 1935 ed., Dover, New York, 1963.

Ivins, W. M., Jr. *How Prints Look: Photographs with a Commentary.* Beacon Press, Boston, 1987.

Landau, D., and P. Parshall. *The Renaissance Print.* Yale University Press, New Haven, 1994.

Martin, J. R. *Baroque.* Penguin, Harmondsworth, England, 1989.

Millon, H. *Baroque and Rococo Architecture.* Braziller, New York, 1961.

Norberg-Schultz, C. *Baroque Architecture.* Harry N. Abrams, New York, 1971.

———. *Late Baroque and Rococo Architecture.* Harry N. Abrams, New York, 1983.

Snyder, J. *Northern Renaissance Art: Painting, Sculpture, the Graphic Arts, from 1350–1575.* Harry N. Abrams, New York, 1985.

Wiebenson, D., ed. *Architectural Theory and Practice from Alberti to Ledoux.* 2nd ed. University of Chicago Press, Chicago, 1983.

Wittkower, R. *Architectural Principles in the Age of Humanism.* 4th ed. St. Martin's, New York, 1988.

1. THE EARLY RENAISSANCE IN ITALY

Alberti, L. B. *On Painting.* Trans. C. Grayson, introduction and notes M. Kemp. Penguin, New York, 1991.

———. *On the Art of Building, in Ten Books.* Trans. J. Rykwert, et al. MIT Press, Cambridge, 1991.

Ames-Lewis, F. *Drawing in Early Renaissance Italy.* Yale University Press, New Haven, 1981.

Battisti, E. *Filippo Brunelleschi: The Complete Works.* Rizzoli, New York, 1981.

Baxandall, M. *Painting and Experience in Fifteenth-Century Italy: A Primer in the Social History of Pictorial Style.* 2nd ed. Oxford University Press, New York, 1988.

Blunt, A. *Artistic Theory in Italy, 1450–1600.* Reprint of 1940 ed., Oxford University Press, New York, 1983.

Bober, P., and R. Rubinstein. *Renaissance Artists and Antique Sculpture: A Handbook of Sources.* Oxford University Press, New York, 1986.

Borsook, E. *The Mural Painters of Tuscany: From Cimabue to Andrea del Sarto.* 2nd ed. Oxford University Press, New York, 1980.

Campbell, L. *Renaissance Portraits: European Portrait-Painting in the 14th, 15th, and 16th Centuries.* Yale University Press, New Haven, 1990.

Chambers, D. S., comp. and trans. *Patrons and Artists in the Italian Renaissance.* University of South Carolina Press, Columbia, 1971.

Dunkelman, M. *Central Italian Painting, 1400–1465: An Annotated Bibliography.* G. K. Hall, Boston, 1986.

Edgerton, S. *The Renaissance Rediscovery of Linear Perspective.* Basic Books, New York, 1975.

Gilbert, C. E. *Italian Art, 1400–1500: Sources and Documents.* Prentice-Hall, Englewood Cliffs, N.J., 1980.

Goldthwaite, R. *Wealth and the Demand for Art in Italy, 1300–1600.* Johns Hopkins University Press, Baltimore, 1993.

Gombrich, E. H. *Norm and Form: Studies in the Art of the Renaissance.* Phaidon, London, 1966.

———. *Symbolic Images: Studies in the Art of the Renaissance.* 3rd ed. Phaidon, London, 1972.

———. *The Heritage of Apelles: Studies in the Art of the Renaissance.* Phaidon, London, 1976.

Heydenreich, L., and W. Lotz. *Architecture in Italy, 1400–1600.* Pelican History of Art. Penguin, Harmondsworth, England, 1974.

Humfreys, P., and M. Kemp, eds. *The Altarpiece in the Renaissance.* Cambridge University Press, New York, 1990.

Huse, N., and W. Wolters. *The Art of Renaissance Venice: Architecture, Sculpture, and Painting, 1460–1590.* University of Chicago Press, Chicago, 1990.

Janson, H. W. *The Sculpture of Donatello.* 2 vols. Princeton University Press, Princeton, 1957.

Joannides, P. *Masaccio and Masolino: A Complete Catalogue.* Harry N. Abrams, New York, 1993.

Jones, R., and N. Penny. *Raphael.* Yale University Press, New Haven, 1983.

Karpinsky, C. *Italian Printmaking, Fifteenth and Sixteenth Centuries: An Annotated Bibliography.* G. K. Hall, Boston, 1987.

Kempers, B. *Painting, Power, and Patronage: The Rise of the Professional Artist in the Italian Renaissance.* Penguin, New York, 1992.

Lavin, M. A. *Piero della Francesca.* Harry N. Abrams, New York, 1992.

Lightbown, R. *Sandro Botticelli.* 2 vols. University of California Press, Berkeley, 1978.

———. *Mantegna: With a Complete Catalogue of the Paintings.* University of California Press, Berkeley, 1986.

Murray, P. *The Architecture of the Italian Renaissance.* The World of Art. Rev. ed. Thames and Hudson, New York, 1986.

Panofsky, E. *Renaissance and Renascences in Western Art.* Humanities Press, New York, 1970.

———. *Perspective as Symbolic Form.* Zone Books, New York, 1991.

Pope-Hennessy, J. *The Portrait in the Renaissance.* Pantheon, New York, 1966.

———. *Italian Renaissance Sculpture.* 3rd ed. Oxford University Press, New York, 1986.

———. *Donatello.* Abbeville, New York, 1993.

Rosenberg, C. *Fifteenth-Century North Italian Painting and Drawing: An Annotated Bibliography.* G. K. Hall, Boston, 1986.

Seymour, C. *Sculpture in Italy, 1400–1500.* Pelican History of Art. Penguin, Harmondsworth, England, 1966.

Turner, A. R. *The Vision of Landscape in Renaissance Italy.* Princeton University Press, Princeton, 1974.

Vasari, G. *The Lives of the Painters, Sculptors, and Architects.* Trans. G. du C. De Vere. 2 vols. Everyman's Library. Knopf, New York, 1996.

Wackernagel, M. *The World of the Florentine Renaissance Artist: Projects and Patrons, Workshop and Art Market.* Princeton University Press, Princeton, 1981.

Wilk, S. *Fifteenth-Century Central Italian Sculpture: An Annotated Bibliography.* G. K. Hall, Boston, 1986.

2. THE HIGH RENAISSANCE IN ITALY

Ackerman, J., and J. Newman. *The Architecture of Michelangelo.* 2nd ed. Penguin, Harmondsworth, England, 1986.

Boase, T. S. R. *Giorgio Vasari: The Man and the Book.* Princeton University Press, Princeton, 1979.

Brown, P. *Venice and Antiquity: The Venetian Sense of the Past.* Yale University Press, New Haven, 1997.

Bruschi, A. *Bramante.* Thames and Hudson, New York, 1977.

Clark, K. *Leonardo da Vinci.* Revised and introduced by M. Kemp. Viking, New York, 1988.

Cole, A. *Virtue and Magnificence: Art of the Italian Renaissance Courts.* Perspectives. Harry N. Abrams, New York, 1995.

De Tolnay, C. *Michelangelo.* 4 vols. 2nd ed. Princeton University Press, Princeton, 1969–71.

Freedberg, S. *Painting of the High Renaissance in Rome and Florence.* 2 vols. Harvard University Press, Cambridge, 1961.

———. *Painting in Italy, 1500–1600.* Pelican History of Art. 3rd ed. Yale University Press, New Haven, 1993.

Hibbard, H. *Michelangelo.* 2nd ed. Harper & Row, New York, 1985.

Kemp, M. *Leonardo da Vinci: The Marvellous Works of Nature and Man.* Harvard University Press, Cambridge, 1981.

———, ed. *Leonardo on Painting: An Anthology of Writings.* Yale University Press, New Haven, 1989.

Klein, R., and H. Zerner. *Italian Art, 1500–1600: Sources and Documents.* Reprint of 1966 ed., Northwestern University Press, Evanston, Ill., 1989.

Panofsky, E. *Studies in Iconology: Humanist Themes in the Art of the Renaissance.* Harper & Row, New York, 1972.

Partridge, L. *The Art of Renaissance Rome.* Perspectives. Harry N. Abrams, New York, 1997.

Pietrangeli, C., et al. *The Sistine Chapel: A Glorious Restoration.* Harry N. Abrams, New York, 1992.

Pope-Hennessy, J. *Italian High Renaissance and Baroque Sculpture.* 3 vols. 3rd ed. Oxford University Press, New York, 1986.

Rosand, D. *Painting in Cinquecento Venice: Titian, Veronese, Tintoretto.* Yale University Press, New Haven, 1982.

Wölfflin, H. *Classic Art: An Introduction to the High Renaissance*. Reprint of 1952 ed., Cornell University Press, Ithaca, 1980.

3. MANNERISM AND OTHER TRENDS

Ackerman, J. *Palladio*. 2nd ed. Penguin, Harmondsworth, England, 1977.

Cellini, B. *The Life of Benvenuto Cellini*. Ed. J. Pope-Hennessy. 3rd. ed. Phaidon, London, 1960.

Friedlaender, W. *Mannerism and Anti-Mannerism in Italian Painting*. Reprint of 1957 ed., Columbia University Press, New York, 1990.

Gould, C. H. M. *The Paintings of Correggio*. Cornell University Press, Ithaca, 1976.

Kaufmann, T. DaCosta. *Art and Architecture in Central Europe, 1550–1620: An Annotated Bibliography*. Reference Publications in Art History. G. K. Hall, Boston, 1988.

Mann, R. *El Greco and His Patrons: Three Major Projects*. Cambridge University Press, New York, 1986.

Rearick, W. R. *The Art of Paolo Veronese, 1528–1588*. Cambridge University Press, Cambridge, 1988.

Shearman, J. *Mannerism*. Penguin, Harmondsworth, England, 1967.

Smyth, C. H. *Mannerism and Maniera*. 2nd ed. IRSA, Vienna, 1992.

Tavernor, R. *Palladio and Palladianism*. The World of Art. Thames and Hudson, New York, 1991.

Valcanover, F., and T. Pignatti. *Tintoretto*. Harry N. Abrams, New York, 1984.

4. "LATE GOTHIC" PAINTING, SCULPTURE, AND THE GRAPHIC ARTS

Blum, S. *Early Netherlandish Triptychs: A Study in Patronage*. University of California Press, Berkeley, 1969.

Davies, M. *Rogier van der Weyden: An Essay with a Critical Catalogue of Paintings*. Phaidon, New York, 1972.

Dhanens, E. *Hubert and Jan van Eyck*. Alpine Fine Arts Collection, New York, 1980.

Friedländer, M. *Early Netherlandish Painting*. 14 vols. Praeger, New York, 1967–73.

———. *From Van Eyck to Bruegel: Early Netherlandish Painting*. 3rd ed. Cornell University Press, Ithaca, 1981.

Frinta, M. S. *The Genius of Robert Campin*. Studies in Art, 1. Mouton, The Hague, 1966.

Gibson, W. *Hieronymus Bosch*. Praeger, New York, 1973.

Mâle, E. *Religious Art in France, the Late Middle Ages: A Study of Medieval Iconography and Its Sources*. Princeton University Press, Princeton, 1986.

Mellinkoff, R. *Outcasts: Signs of Otherness in Northern European Art of the Late Middle Ages*. University of California Press, Berkeley, 1993.

Muller, T. *Sculpture in the Netherlands, Germany, France, and Spain, 1400–1500*. Pelican History of Art. Penguin, Harmondsworth, England, 1966.

Panofsky, E. *Early Netherlandish Painting*. 2 vols. Harvard University Press, Cambridge, 1958.

Scott, K. *Later Gothic Manuscripts, 1395–1495*. Survey of Manuscripts Illuminated in the British Isles. 2 vols. Miller, London. Forthcoming.

5. THE RENAISSANCE IN THE NORTH

Baxandall, M. *The Limewood Sculptors of Renaissance Germany*. Yale University Press, New Haven, 1980.

Benesch, O. *The Art of the Renaissance in Northern Europe*. Rev. ed. Phaidon, London, 1965.

Bialostocki, J. *The Art of the Renaissance in Eastern Europe*. The Wrightsman Lectures, 8. Cornell University Press, Ithaca, 1976.

Chastel, A., et al. *The Renaissance: Essays in Interpretation*. Methuen, London, 1982.

Ganz, P. *The Paintings of Hans Holbein the Younger*. Phaidon, London, 1956.

Harbison, C. *The Mirror of the Artist: Northern Renaissance Art in Its Historical Context*. Perspectives. Harry N. Abrams, New York, 1995.

Hitchcock, H.-R. *German Renaissance Architecture*. Princeton University Press, Princeton, 1981.

Hutchison, J. C. *Albrecht Dürer: A Biography*. Princeton University Press, Princeton, 1990.

Koerner, J. *The Moment of Self-Portraiture in German Renaissance Art*. University of Chicago Press, Chicago, 1993.

Lane, B. *Flemish Painting Outside Bruges, 1400–1500: An Annotated Bibliography*. G. K. Hall, Boston, 1986.

Melion, W. *Shaping the Netherlandish Canon: Karel van Mander's Schilder-Boeck*. University of Chicago Press, Chicago, 1991.

Moxey, K. *Peasants, Warriors, and Wives: Popular Imagery in the Reformation*. University of Chicago Press, Chicago, 1989.

Mundy, E. *Painting in Bruges, 1470–1550: An Annotated Bibliography*. G. K. Hall, Boston, 1985.

Osten, G. von der, and H. Vey. *Painting and Sculpture in Germany and the Netherlands, 1500–1600*. Pelican History of Art. Penguin, Harmondsworth, England, 1969.

Panofsky, E. *The Life and Art of Albrecht Dürer*. 4th ed. Princeton University Press, Princeton, 1971.

Parshall, L. and P. *Art and the Reformation: An Annotated Bibliography*. G. K. Hall, Boston, 1986.

Stechow, W. *Northern Renaissance Art, 1400–1600: Sources and Documents*. Prentice-Hall, Englewood Cliffs, N.J., 1966.

———. *Pieter Bruegel, the Elder*. Harry N. Abrams, New York, 1969.

Van Mander, K. *Lives of the Illustrious Netherlandish and German Painters*. Ed. H. Miedema. 6 vols. Forthcoming.

Wood, C. *Albrecht Altdorfer and the Origins of Landscape*. University of Chicago Press, Chicago, 1993.

6. THE BAROQUE IN ITALY AND SPAIN

Blunt, A. *Borromini*. Harvard University Press, Cambridge, 1979.

Brown, J. *Velázquez: Painter and Courtier*. Yale University Press, New Haven, 1986.

———. *Francisco de Zurbaran*. Harry N. Abrams, New York, 1991.

———. *The Golden Age of Painting in Spain*. Yale University Press, New Haven, 1991.

Enggass, R., and J. Brown. *Italy and Spain, 1600–1750: Sources and Documents*. Reprint of 1970 ed., Northwestern University Press, Evanston, Ill., 1992.

Freedberg, S. *Circa 1600: A Revolution of Style in Italian Painting*. Harvard University Press, Cambridge, 1983.

Haskell, F. *Patrons and Painters: A Study in the Relations Between Italian Art and Society in the Age of the Baroque*. Rev. ed. Yale University Press, New Haven, 1980.

Hibbard, H. *Bernini*. Reprint of 1965 ed., Penguin Books, Baltimore, 1980.

———. *Caravaggio*. Harper & Row, New York, 1983.

Kubler, G., and M. Soria. *Art and Architecture in Spain and Portugal and Their American Dominions, 1500–1800*. Pelican History of Art. Penguin, Harmondsworth, England, 1959.

Levey, M. *Giambattista Tiepolo: His Life and Art*. Yale University Press, New Haven, 1986.

Montagu, J. *Roman Baroque Sculpture: The Industry of Art*. Yale University Press, New Haven, 1989.

Nicolson, B. *Caravaggism in Europe*. Ed. L. Vertova. 2nd ed., rev. and enl. 3 vols. Allemandi, Turin, 1989.

Posner, D. *Annibale Carracci*. 2 vols. Phaidon, London, 1971.

Smith, G. *Architectural Diplomacy: Rome and Paris in the Late Baroque*. MIT Press, Cambridge, 1993.

Spear, R. *Caravaggio and His Followers*. Harper & Row, New York, 1976.

Varriano, J. *Italian Baroque and Rococo Architecture*. Oxford University Press, New York, 1986.

Waterhouse, E. *Italian Baroque Painting*. 2nd ed. Phaidon, London, 1969.

Wittkower, R. *Art and Architecture in Italy, 1600–1750*. Pelican History of Art. 3rd ed. Penguin, Harmondsworth, England, 1980.

———. *Gian Lorenzo Bernini: The Sculptor of the Roman Baroque*. 3rd ed. Cornell University Press, Ithaca, 1981.

7. THE BAROQUE IN FLANDERS AND HOLLAND

Alpers, S. *The Art of Describing: Dutch Art in the Seventeenth Century*. University of Chicago Press, Chicago, 1983.

Blankert, A. *Vermeer of Delft: Complete Edition of the Paintings*. Dutton, New York, 1978.

Bruyn, J., et al. *A Corpus of Rembrandt Paintings*. 3 vols. (to date). Nijhoff, The Hague, 1982–.

Gerson, H., and E. Ter Kuile. *Art and Architecture in Belgium, 1600–1800*. Pelican History of Art. Penguin, Baltimore, 1960.

Haak, B. *The Golden Age: Dutch Painters of the Seventeenth Century*. Harry N. Abrams, New York, 1984.

Rembrandt: The Master and His Workshop. Ed. S. Salvesen. 2 vols. Exh. cat. Yale University Press, New Haven, 1991.

Rosenberg, J., S. Slive, and E. Ter Kuile. *Dutch Art and Architecture, 1600–1800*. 3rd ed. Yale University Press, New Haven, 1997.

Rosenberg, J. *Rembrandt: Life and Work*. Rev. ed. Cornell University Press, Ithaca, 1980.

Schama, S. *The Embarrassment of Riches*. University of California Press, Berkeley, 1988.

Schwartz, G. *Rembrandt: His Life, His Paintings*. Viking, New York, 1985.

Slive, S. *Dutch Painting, 1600–1800*. Pelican History of Art. Yale University Press, 1995.

———. *Frans Hals*. 3 vols. Phaidon, New York, 1970–74.

Stechow, W. *Dutch Landscape Painting of the Seventeenth Century*. Reprint of 1966 ed., Cornell University Press, Ithaca, 1980.

Strauss, W. L., et al., comps. *The Rembrandt Documents*. Abaris, New York, 1979.

Sutton, P. *The Age of Rubens*. Exh. cat. Museum of Fine Arts, Boston, 1993.

Walford, F. *Jacob van Ruisdael and the Perception of Landscape*. Yale University Press, New Haven, 1992.

Westermann, M. *A Worldly Art: The Dutch Republic 1585–1718*. Perspectives. Harry N. Abrams, New York, 1996.

Wheelock, A. K., et al. *Anthony van Dyck*. Exh. cat. Harry N. Abrams, New York, 1990.

Wheelock, A K., ed. *Johannes Vermeer*. Exh. cat. Yale University Press, New Haven, 1995.

White, C. *Peter Paul Rubens*. Yale University Press, New Haven, 1987.

8. THE BAROQUE IN FRANCE AND ENGLAND

Blunt, A. *Nicolas Poussin*. 2 vols. Princeton University Press, Princeton, 1967.

———. *Art and Architecture in France, 1500–1700*. Pelican History of Art. 4th ed. Penguin, Harmondsworth, England, 1981.

Downes, K. *The Architecture of Wren*. Rev. ed. Redhedge, Reading, England, 1988.

Garreau, M. *Charles Le Brun: First Painter to King Louis XIV*. Harry N. Abrams, New York, 1992.

Liechtenstein, J. *The Eloquence of Color: Rhetoric and Painting in the French Classical Age*. University of California Press, Berkeley, 1993.

Mérot, A. *French Painting in the Seventeenth Century*. Yale University Press, New Haven, 1995.

———. *Nicolas Poussin*. Abbeville, New York, 1990.

Röthlisberger, M. *Claude Lorrain: The Paintings*. 2 vols. Yale University Press, New Haven, 1961.

Summerson, J. *Architecture in Britain, 1530–1830*. Pelican History of Art. 6th ed., rev. Penguin, Harmondsworth, England, 1977.

Waterhouse, E. K. *Painting in Britain, 1530–1790*. Pelican History of Art. 4th ed. Penguin, Harmondsworth, England, 1978.

———. *The Dictionary of Sixteenth and Seventeenth*

Century British Painters. Antique Collectors' Club, Woodbridge, Suffolk, 1988.

Whinney, M. *English Art, 1625–1714.* Oxford History of English Art. Clarendon Press, Oxford, 1957.

9. THE ROCOCO

Baillio, J. *Elisabeth Louise Vigée Le Brun, 1755–1842.* Exh. cat. Kimbell Art Museum, Fort Worth, 1982.

Brunel, G. *Boucher.* Vendome, New York, 1986.

Brusatin, M., et al. *The Baroque in Central Europe: Places, Architecture, and Art.* Marsilio, Venice, 1992.

Conisbee, P. *Painting in Eighteenth-Century France.* Cornell University Press, Ithaca, 1981.

———. *Chardin.* Bucknell University Press, Lewisburg, Pa., 1985.

Cormack, M. *The Paintings of Thomas Gainsborough.* Cambridge University Press, New York, 1991.

Cuzin, J. P. *Jean-Honoré Fragonard: Life and Work: Complete Catalogue of the Oil Paintings.* Harry N. Abrams, New York, 1988.

Gaunt, W. *The Great Century of British Painting: Hogarth to Turner.* 2nd ed. Phaidon, London, 1978.

Levey, M. *Rococo to Revolution: Major Trends in Eighteenth-Century Painting.* The World of Art. Reprint of 1966 ed., Thames and Hudson, New York, 1985.

———. *Painting and Sculpture in France, 1700–1789.* Pelican History of Art. New ed. Yale University Press, New Haven, 1993.

Links, J. *Canaletto.* Oxford University Press, New York, 1982.

Paulson, R. *Hogarth: His Life, Art, and Times.* 2 vols. Yale University Press, New Haven, 1971.

Penny, N., ed. *Reynolds.* Exh. cat. Harry N. Abrams, New York, 1986.

Pointer, M. *Hanging the Head: Portraiture and Social Formation in Eighteenth-Century England.* Yale University Press, New Haven, 1993.

Posner, D. *Antoine Watteau.* Cornell University Press, Ithaca, 1984.

PART FOUR: THE MODERN WORLD

GENERAL REFERENCES

Arnason, H. H. *History of Modern Art.* 3rd ed., rev. and enl. Harry N. Abrams, New York, 1988.

Baigell, M. *A Concise History of American Painting and Sculpture.* Harper & Row, New York, 1984.

Barasch, M. *Modern Theories of Art.* Vol. 1, *From Winckelmann to Baudelaire.* New York University Press, New York, 1990.

Battcock, G., and R. Nickas, eds. *The Art of Performance: A Critical Anthology.* Dutton, New York, 1984.

Benevolo, L. *History of Modern Architecture.* MIT Press, Cambridge, 1971.

Boime, A. *A Social History of Modern Art.* 2 vols. (5 vols. planned). University of Chicago Press, Chicago, 1987–.

Brown, M., et al. *American Art: Painting, Sculpture, Architecture, Decorative Arts, Photography.* Prentice-Hall, Englewood Cliffs, N.J., 1979.

Campbell M., et al. *Harlem Renaissance: Art of Black America.* Harry N. Abrams, New York, 1987.

Castelman, R. *Prints of the Twentieth Century: A History.* Oxford University Press, New York, 1985.

Chipp, H., ed. *Theories of Modern Art: A Source Book by Artists and Critics.* University of California Press, Berkeley, 1968.

Crary, J. *Techniques of the Observer: On Vision and Modernity in the Nineteenth Century.* MIT Press, Cambridge, 1990.

Crook, J. *The Dilemma of Style: Architectural Ideas from the Picturesque to the Post Modern.* University of Chicago Press, Chicago, 1987.

Crow, T. *Modern Art in the Common Culture.* Yale University Press, New Haven, 1996.

Documents of Modern Art. 14 vols. Wittenborn, New York, 1944–61.

The Documents of Twentieth-Century Art. G. K. Hall, Boston. Cited individually below.

Driskell, D. *Two Centuries of Black American Art.* Exh. cat. Knopf, New York, 1976.

Eitner, L. *An Outline of Nineteenth-Century European Painting: From David through Cézanne.* 2 vols. Harper & Row, New York, 1986.

Frampton, K. *Modern Architecture: A Critical History.* 3rd ed. Thames and Hudson, New York, 1992.

———, and Y. Futagawa. *Modern Architecture, 1851–1945.* 2 vols. Rizzoli, New York, 1983.

Frascina, F., ed. *Modern Art and Modernism: A Critical Anthology.* Harper & Row, New York, 1982.

———. *Pollock and After: The Critical Debate.* Harper & Row, New York, 1985.

———, and J. Harris, eds. *Art in Modern Culture: An Anthology of Critical Texts.* Harper & Row, New York, 1992.

Gernsheim, H. and A. *The History of Photography: From the Camera Obscura to the Beginning of the Modern Era.* McGraw-Hill, New York, 1969.

Goddard, D. *American Painting.* Macmillan, New York, 1990.

Goldberg, R. *Performance Art: From Futurism to the Present.* Rev. and enl. ed. Harry N. Abrams, New York, 1988.

Goldberg, V., ed. *Photography in Print: Writings from 1816 to the Present.* Simon & Schuster, New York, 1981.

Goldwater, R. *Primitivism in Modern Art.* Enl. ed. Harvard University Press, Cambridge, 1986.

Hamilton, G. H. *Nineteenth and Twentieth Century Art: Painting, Sculpture, Architecture.* Harry N. Abrams, New York, 1970.

Harrison, C., and P. Wood, eds. *Art in Theory, 1900–1990: An Anthology of Changing Ideas.* Blackwell, Oxford, 1992.

Hertz, R., ed. *Theories of Contemporary Art.* Prentice-Hall, Englewood Cliffs, N.J., 1985.

———, and N. Klein, eds. *Twentieth-Century Art Theory: Urbanism, Politics, and Mass Culture.* Prentice-Hall, Englewood Cliffs, N.J., 1990.

Hitchcock, H. R. *Architecture: Nineteenth and Twentieth Centuries.* Pelican History of Art. 2nd ed. Penguin, Harmondsworth, England, 1971.

Hunter, S., and J. Jacobus. *Modern Art: Painting, Sculpture, Architecture.* Harry N. Abrams, New York, 1992.

Janson, H. W. *Nineteenth-Century Sculpture.* Harry N. Abrams, New York, 1985.

———, and R. Rosenblum. *Nineteenth-Century Art.* Harry N. Abrams, New York, 1984.

Joachimides, C., et al. *American Art in the Twentieth Century: Painting and Sculpture, 1913–1933.* Exh. cat. Prestel, Munich, 1993.

Johnson, W. *Nineteenth-Century Photography: An Annotated Bibliography, 1839–1879.* G. K. Hall, Boston, 1990.

Kaplan, P., and S. Manso, eds. *Major European Art Movements, 1900–1945: A Critical Anthology.* Dutton, New York, 1977.

Licht, F. *Sculpture, Nineteenth and Twentieth Century.* New York Graphic Society, Greenwich, 1967.

McCoubrey, J. *American Art, 1700–1960: Sources and Documents.* Prentice-Hall, Englewood Cliffs, N.J., 1965.

McShine, K. *An International Survey of Recent Painting and Sculpture.* Exh. cat. Museum of Modern Art, New York, 1984.

Newhall, B. *The History of Photography from 1830 to the Present Day.* 5th ed., rev. New York Graphic Society, Greenwich, 1982.

Nochlin, L. *The Politics of Vision: Essays on Nineteenth-Century Art and Society.* Harper & Row, New York, 1989.

Norman, G. *Nineteenth-Century Painters and Painting: A Dictionary.* University of California Press, Berkeley, 1977.

Osborne, H., ed. *Oxford Companion to Twentieth-Century Art.* Oxford University Press, New York, 1981.

Phaidon Dictionary of Twentieth-Century Art. Phaidon, Oxford, 1973.

Pierson, W., and W. Jordy. *American Buildings and Their Architects.* 4 vols. Doubleday, Garden City, N.Y., 1970–78.

Pingeot, A., et al. *Sculpture: The Adventure of Modern Sculpture in the Nineteenth and Twentieth Centuries.* Rizzoli, New York, 1986.

Prown, J. D., and B. Rose. *American Painting: From the Colonial Period to the Present.* New ed. Rizzoli, New York, 1977.

Robins, C. *The Pluralist Era: American Art, 1968–1981.* Harper & Row, New York, 1984.

Rose, B., ed. *Readings in American Art Since 1900: A Documentary Survey.* Praeger, New York, 1968.

———. *American Art Since 1900.* Rev. ed. Praeger, New York, 1975.

Rosen, C., and H. Zerner. *Romanticism and Realism: The Mythology of Nineteenth-Century Art.* Viking, New York, 1984.

Rosenblum, N. *A World History of Photography.* Rev. ed. Abbeville, New York, 1989.

Roth, L. *A Concise History of American Architecture.* Harper & Row, New York, 1980.

Sayre, H. *The Object of Performance: The American Avant-Garde Since 1970.* University of Chicago Press, Chicago, 1990.

Schapiro, M. *Modern Art: Nineteenth and Twentieth Centuries.* Braziller, New York, 1982.

Scharf, A. *Art and Photography.* Rev. ed. Penguin, Harmondsworth, England, 1974.

Scully, V. *Modern Architecture.* Rev. ed. Braziller, New York, 1974.

Selz, P. *Art in Our Times: A Pictorial History, 1890–1980.* Harry N. Abrams, New York, 1981.

Stangos, N. *Concepts of Modern Art.* 2nd ed. Harper & Row, New York, 1981.

Tafuri, M. *Modern Architecture.* 2 vols. Rizzoli, New York, 1986.

Taylor, J. *The Fine Arts in America.* University of Chicago Press, Chicago, 1979.

———, ed. *Nineteenth-Century Theories of Art.* University of California Press, Berkeley, 1991.

Tomkins, C. *Post to Neo: The Art World of the 1980s.* Holt, New York, 1988.

Walker, J. *Glossary of Art: Architecture and Design Since 1945.* 3rd ed. G. K. Hall, Boston, 1992.

Weaver, M. *The Art of Photography, 1839–1989.* Exh. cat. Yale University Press, New Haven, 1989.

Weintraub, L. *Art on the Edge and Over.* Art Insights, Litchfield, Connecticut; dist. D.A.P., 1997.

Weiss, J. *The Popular Culture of Modern Art.* Yale University Press, New Haven, 1994.

Wilmerding, J. *American Art.* Pelican History of Art. Penguin, Harmondsworth, England, 1976.

Witzling, M., ed. *Voicing Our Visions: Writings by Women Artists.* Universe Books, New York, 1991.

Wood, P., et al. *Modernism in Dispute: Art Since the Forties.* Yale University Press, New Haven, 1993.

1. NEOCLASSICISM AND ROMANTICISM

Bindman, D. *Blake as an Artist.* Dutton, New York, 1977.

Boime, A. *The Academy and French Painting in the Nineteenth Century.* New ed. Yale University Press, New Haven, 1986.

Braham, A. *The Architecture of the French Enlightenment.* University of California Press, Berkeley, 1980.

Bryson, N. *Word and Image: French Painting in the Ancien Régime.* Cambridge University Press, Cambridge, 1981.

———. *Tradition and Desire: From David to Delacroix.* Cambridge University Press, Cambridge, 1984.

Crow, T. *Painters and Public Life in Eighteenth-Century Paris.* Yale University Press, New Haven, 1985.

Eitner, L. *E. A. Géricault: His Life and Work.* Cornell University Press, Ithaca, 1982.

———. *Neoclassicism and Romanticism, 1750–1850: Sources and Documents.* Reprint of 1970 ed., Harper & Row, New York, 1989.

Fried, M. *Absorption and Theatricality: Painting and Beholder in the Age of Diderot.* University of Chicago Press, Chicago, 1980.

Friedlaender, W. *From David to Delacroix*. Reprint of 1952 ed., Schocken Books, New York, 1968.

Gaunt, W. *The Restless Century: Painting in Britain, 1800–1900*. Phaidon, London, 1972.

Goncourt, E. and J. de. *French Eighteenth-Century Painters*. Reprint of 1948 ed., Cornell University Press, Ithaca, 1981.

Goya and the Spirit of Enlightenment. Exh. cat. Little, Brown, Boston, 1989.

Herrmann, L. *British Landscape Painting of the Eighteenth Century*. Oxford University Press, New York, 1974.

Honour, H. *Neoclassicism*. Reprint of 1968 ed., Penguin, London, 1991.

———. *Romanticism*. Harper & Row, New York, 1979.

Johnson, E. *The Paintings of Eugène Delacroix: A Critical Catalogue, 1816–1831*. 4 vols. Clarendon Press, Oxford, 1981–86.

Koerner, J. *Caspar David Friedrich and the Subject of Landscape*. Yale University Press, New Haven, 1990.

Licht, F. *Canova*. Abbeville, New York, 1983.

———. *Goya: The Origins of the Modern Temper in Art*. Harper & Row, New York, 1983.

Mainardi, P. *Art and Politics of the Second Empire: The Universal Expositions of 1855 and 1867*. Yale University Press, New Haven, 1987.

———. *The End of the Salon: Art and the State in the Early Third Republic*. Cambridge University Press, Cambridge, 1993.

Middleton, R., and D. Watkin. *Neoclassical and Nineteenth-Century Architecture*. Rizzoli, New York, 1977.

Miles, E. G., ed. *The Portrait in Eighteenth-Century America*. University of Delaware Press, Newark, 1993.

Novotny, F. *Painting and Sculpture in Europe, 1780–1880*. Pelican History of Art. Penguin, Harmondsworth, England, 1971.

Pelles, G. *Art, Artists, and Society: Origins of a Modern Dilemma: Painting in England and France, 1750–1850*. Prentice-Hall, Englewood Cliffs, N.J., 1963.

Prown, J. D. *John Singleton Copley*. 2 vols. Exh. cat. Harvard University Press, Cambridge, 1966.

Reynolds, G. *Turner*. The World of Art. Thames and Hudson, New York, 1985.

Rosenblum, R. *Transformations in Late Eighteenth Century Art*. Princeton University Press, Princeton, 1967.

———. *Jean-Auguste-Dominique Ingres*. Harry N. Abrams, New York, 1990.

Saisselin, R. G. *The Enlightenment Against the Baroque: Economics and Aesthetics in the Eighteenth Century*. University of California Press, Berkeley, 1992.

Solkin, D. *Painting for Money: The Visual Arts and the Public Sphere in Eighteenth-Century England*. Yale University Press, New Haven, 1993.

Tomlinson, J. *Goya in the Twilight of Enlightenment*. Yale University Press, New Haven, 1992.

Vaughan, W. *German Romantic Painting*. Yale University Press, New Haven, 1980.

Watkin, D., and T. Mellinghoff. *German Architecture and the Classical Ideal*. MIT Press, Cambridge, 1987.

Wilton, A. *J. M. W. Turner: His Life and Art*. Rizzoli, New York, 1979.

2. REALISM AND IMPRESSIONISM

Adler, K., and T. Garb. *Manet*. Phaidon, Oxford, 1986.

Broude, N. *Impressionism: A Feminist Reading*. Rizzoli, New York, 1991.

Clark, T. J. *The Absolute Bourgeois: Artists and Politics in France, 1848–1851*. Princeton University Press, Princeton, 1982.

———. *The Painting of Modern Life: Paris in the Art of Manet and His Followers*. Princeton University Press, Princeton, 1984.

Denvir, B. *The Impressionists: A Documentary Study*. Thames and Hudson, New York, 1986.

———. *The Thames and Hudson Encyclopaedia of Impressionism*. Thames and Hudson, New York, 1990.

———. *The Chronicle of Impressionism: A Timeline History of Impressionist Art*. Little, Brown, Boston, 1993.

Fried, M. *Courbet's Realism*. University of Chicago Press, Chicago, 1990.

Goodrich, L. *Thomas Eakins*. 2 vols. Exh. cat. Harvard University Press, Cambridge, 1982.

Hamilton, G. H. *Manet and His Critics*. Reprint of 1954 ed., Yale University Press, New Haven, 1986.

Herbert, R. *Impressionism: Art, Leisure, and Parisian Society*. Yale University Press, New Haven, 1988.

Higonnet, A. *Berthe Morisot*. Harper & Row, New York, 1990.

Hilton, T. *The Pre-Raphaelites*. The World of Art. Reprint of 1970 ed., Thames and Hudson, London, 1985.

House, J. *Monet: Nature into Art*. Yale University Press, New Haven, 1986.

Jenkyns, R. *Dignity and Decadence: Victorian Art and the Classical Inheritance*. Harvard University Press, Cambridge, 1991.

Kendall, R., and G. Pollock, eds. *Dealing with Degas: Representations of Women and the Politics of Vision*. Universe, New York, 1992.

Lipton, E. *Looking into Degas*. University of California Press, Berkeley, 1986.

Miller, D., ed. *American Iconology: New Approaches to Nineteenth-Century Art and Literature*. Yale University Press, New Haven, 1993.

Mosby, D. *Henry Ossawa Tanner*. Exh. cat. Rizzoli, New York, 1991.

Needham, G. *Nineteenth-Century Realist Art*. Harper & Row, New York, 1988.

Nochlin, L. *Realism and Tradition in Art, 1848–1900: Sources and Documents*. Prentice-Hall, Englewood Cliffs, N.J., 1966.

———. *Impressionism and Post-Impressionism, 1874–1904: Sources and Documents*. Prentice-Hall, Englewood Cliffs, N.J., 1976.

Novak, B. *American Painting of the Nineteenth Century: Realism and the American Experience*. Harper & Row, New York, 1979.

———. *Nature and Culture: American Landscape Painting, 1825–1875*. Oxford University Press, New York, 1980.

Pollock, G. *Mary Cassatt*. Harper & Row, New York, 1980.

Reff, T. *Manet and Modern Paris*. Exh. cat. National Gallery of Art, Washington, D.C., 1982.

Rewald, J. *The History of Impressionism*. 4th ed., rev. New York Graphic Society, Greenwich, 1973.

Spate, V. *Claude Monet: Life and Work*. Rizzoli, New York, 1992.

Tucker, P. *Monet at Argenteuil*. Yale University Press, New Haven, 1981.

———. *Monet in the '90s: The Series Paintings*. Exh. cat. Yale University Press, New Haven, 1989.

Walther, I., ed. *Impressionist Art, 1860–1920*. 2 vols. Forthcoming.

Weisberg, G. *Beyond Impressionism: The Naturalist Impulse*. Harry N. Abrams, New York, 1992.

Wilmerding, J. *Winslow Homer*. Praeger, New York, 1972.

Wood, C. *The Pre-Raphaelites*. Viking, New York, 1981.

3. POST-IMPRESSIONISM, SYMBOLISM, AND ART NOUVEAU

Brettell, R., et al. *The Art of Paul Gauguin*. Exh. cat. Little, Brown, Boston, 1988.

Broude, N. *Georges Seurat*. Rizzoli, New York, 1992.

Cachin, F., I. Cahn, et al., *Cézanne*. Exh. cat. Harry N. Abrams, New York, 1995.

Denvir, B. *Post-Impressionism*. The World of Art. Thames and Hudson, New York, 1992.

Gaunt, W. *Renoir*. Notes by K. Adler. Rev. and enl. ed. Phaidon, Oxford, 1982.

Goldwater, R. *Symbolism*. Harper & Row, New York, 1979.

———. *Paul Gauguin*. Concise ed. Harry N. Abrams, New York, 1983.

Hamilton, G. H. *Painting and Sculpture in Europe, 1880–1940*. Pelican History of Art. 6th ed. Yale University Press, New Haven, 1993.

Hulsker, J. *The Complete Van Gogh*. Harry N. Abrams, New York, 1980.

Rewald, J. *Post-Impressionism: From Van Gogh to Gauguin*. 2nd ed. Museum of Modern Art, New York, 1962.

Roskill, M. *Van Gogh, Gauguin, and the Impressionist Circle*. New York Graphic Society, Greenwich, 1970.

Schapiro, M. *Van Gogh*. Rev. ed. Harry N. Abrams, New York, 1982.

———. *Paul Cézanne*. Concise ed. Harry N. Abrams, New York, 1988.

Shiff, R. *Cézanne and the End of Impressionism: A Study of the Theory, Technique, and Critical Evaluation of Modern Art*. University of Chicago Press, Chicago, 1984.

Silverman, D. *Art Nouveau in Fin-de-Siècle France*. University of California Press, Berkeley, 1989.

Varnedoe, K. *Vienna 1900: Art, Architecture, and Design*. Exh. cat. Museum of Modern Art, New York, 1986.

4. TWENTIETH-CENTURY PAINTING

Ades, D., et al., eds. *In the Mind's Eye: Dada and Surrealism*. Abbeville, New York, 1986.

Ashton, D. *American Art Since 1945*. Oxford University Press, New York, 1982.

Baker, K. *Minimalism*. Abbeville, New York, 1989.

Battcock, G., comp. *Minimal Art: A Critical Anthology*. Dutton, New York, 1968.

———. *Idea Art: A Critical Anthology*. New ed. Dutton, New York, 1973.

Beardsley, J., and J. Livingston. *Hispanic Art in the United States: Thirty Contemporary Painters and Sculptors*. Exh. cat. Abbeville, New York, 1987.

Breton, A. *Manifestoes of Surrealism*. Trans. R. Seaver and H. R. Lane. University of Michigan Press, Ann Arbor, 1969.

Brown, M. *The Story of the Armory Show*. Rev. ed. Abbeville, New York, 1988.

Celant, G. *Unexpressionism: Art Beyond the Contemporary*. Rizzoli, New York, 1988.

Chadwick, W. *Women Artists and the Surrealist Movement*. Thames and Hudson, New York, 1991.

Crane, D. *The Transformation of the Avant-Garde: The New York Art World, 1940–1985*. University of Chicago Press, Chicago, 1987.

Crow, T. *The Rise of the Sixties: American and European Art in the Era of Dissent*. Perspectives. Harry N. Abrams, New York, 1996.

Duchamp, M. *Marcel Duchamp, Notes*. Trans. P. Matisse. The Documents of Twentieth-Century Art. G. K. Hall, Boston, 1983.

Fer, B., et al. *Realism, Rationalism, Surrealism: Art Between the Wars*. Modern Art—Practices and Debates. Yale University Press, New Haven, 1993.

Gilbaut, S. *How New York Stole the Idea of Modern Art*. University of Chicago Press, Chicago, 1983.

———, ed. *Reconstructing Modernism: Art in New York, Paris, and Montreal, 1945–1964*. MIT Press, Cambridge, 1990.

Golding, J. *Cubism: A History and an Analysis, 1907–1914*. 3rd ed. Harvard University Press, Cambridge, 1988.

Goldwater, R. *Primitivism in Modern Art*. Enl. ed. Belknap Press, Cambridge, Mass., 1986.

Gordon, D. *Expressionism: Art and Idea*. Yale University Press, New Haven, 1987.

Gray, C. *The Russian Experiment in Art, 1863–1922*. Harry N. Abrams, New York, 1970.

Green, C. *Cubism and Its Enemies*. Yale University Press, New Haven, 1987.

Greenberg, C. *Clement Greenberg, The Collected Essays and Criticism*. Ed. J. O'Brian. 4 vols. University of Chicago Press, Chicago, 1986–93.

Herbert, J. *Fauve Painting: The Making of Cultural Politics*. Yale University Press, New Haven, 1992.

Hoffman, K., ed. *Collage: Critical Views*. UMI Research Press, Ann Arbor, 1989.

Kandinsky, W. *Kandinsky, Complete Writings on Art*. Eds. K. C. Lindsay and P. Vergo. The Documents of Twentieth-Century Art. 2 vols. G. K. Hall, Boston, 1982.

Krauss, R. *The Originality of the Avant-Garde and Other Modernist Myths*. MIT Press, Cambridge, 1986.

Kuspit, D. *The Cult of the Avant-Garde Artist*. Cambridge University Press, New York, 1993.

Langer, C. *Feminist Art Criticism: An Annotated Bibliography*. G. K. Hall, Boston, 1993.

Leggio, J., and S. Weiley, eds. *American Art of the 1960s*. Studies in Modern Art, 1. Museum of Modern Art, New York, 1991.

Leja, M. *Reframing Abstract Expressionism: Subjectivity and Painting in the 1940s*. Yale University Press, New Haven, 1993.

Lewis, H. *The Politics of Surrealism*. Paragon, New York, 1988.

Lippard, L. R., et al. *Pop Art*. Praeger, New York, 1966.

———, ed. *From the Center: Feminist Essays on Women's Art*. Dutton, New York, 1976.

———. *Overlay: Contemporary Art and the Art of Prehistory*. Pantheon, New York, 1983.

Livingstone, M. *Pop Art: A Continuing History*. Harry N. Abrams, New York, 1990.

Lodder, C. *Russian Constructivism*. Yale University Press, New Haven, 1983.

Martin, M. *Futurist Art and Theory, 1909–1915*. Clarendon Press, Oxford, 1968.

Meisel, L. K. *Photorealism*. Harry N. Abrams, New York, 1980.

Miró, J. *Joan Miró: Selected Writings and Interviews*. Ed. M. Rowell. The Documents of Twentieth-Century Art. G. K. Hall, Boston, 1986.

Mitchell, W. J. T. *The Reconfigured Eye: Visual Truth in the Post-Photographic Era*. MIT Press, Cambridge, 1992.

Mondrian, P. *The New Art, the New Life: The Complete Writings*. Eds. and trans. H. Holtzmann and M. James. The Documents of Twentieth-Century Art. G. K. Hall, Boston, 1986.

Motherwell, R., ed. *The Dada Poets and Painters: An Anthology*. 2nd ed. Harvard University Press, Cambridge, 1989.

———. *Collected Writings*. Ed. Stephanie Terenzio. Oxford University Press, New York, 1992.

Nadeau, M. *History of Surrealism*. Harvard University Press, Cambridge, 1989.

Pincus-Witten, R. *Postminimalism into Maximalism: American Art, 1966–1986*. UMI, Ann Arbor, 1987.

Polcari, S. *Abstract Expressionism and the Modern Experience*. Cambridge University Press, New York, 1991.

Richter, H. *Dada: Art and Anti-Art*. McGraw-Hill, New York, 1965.

Rosen, R., and C. Brawer, eds. *Making Their Mark: Women Artists Move into the Mainstream, 1970–85*. Exh. cat. Abbeville, New York, 1989.

Rosenblum, R. *Cubism and Twentieth-Century Art*. Prentice-Hall, Englewood Cliffs, N.J., 1976.

Roskill, M. *Klee, Kandinsky, and the Thought of Their Time: A Critical Perspective*. University of Illinois Press, Urbana, 1992.

Ross, C. *Abstract Expressionism: Creators and Critics: An Anthology*. Harry N. Abrams, New York, 1990.

Rubin, W. S. *Dada and Surrealist Art*. Harry N. Abrams, New York, 1968.

———. *Picasso and Braque: Pioneering Cubism*. Exh. cat. Museum of Modern Art, New York, 1989.

Sandler, I. *The Triumph of American Painting: A History of Abstract Expressionism*. Praeger, New York, 1970.

———. *The New York School: The Painters and Sculptors of the Fifties*. Harper & Row, New York, 1979.

Seitz, W. *Abstract Expressionist Painting in America*. Harvard University Press, Cambridge, 1983.

Silver, K. E. *Esprit de Corps: The Art of the Parisian Avant-Garde and the First World War, 1914–1925*. Princeton University Press, Princeton, 1989.

Varnedoe, K., and A. Gopnik. *High and Low: Modern Art/ Popular Culture*. Harry N. Abrams, New York, 1990.

Washton, R.-C., ed. *German Expressionism: Documents from the End of the Wilhelmine Empire to the Rise of National Socialism*. The Documents of Twentieth-Century Art. G. K. Hall, Boston, 1993.

5. TWENTIETH-CENTURY SCULPTURE

Bach, F., T. Bach, and A. Temkin. *Constantin Brancusi*. Exh. cat. MIT Press, Cambridge, 1995.

Beardsley, J. *Earthworks and Beyond: Contemporary Art in the Landscape*. Enl. ed. Abbeville, New York, 1989.

Beaumont, M., et al. *Sculpture Today*. St. Martin's, New York, 1987.

Elsen, A. *Origins of Modern Sculpture*. Braziller, New York, 1974.

Krauss, R. *Passages in Modern Sculpture*. MIT Press, Cambridge, 1977.

Kultermann, U. *The New Sculpture: Environments and Assemblages*. Praeger, New York, 1968.

Lucie-Smith, E. *Sculpture Since 1945*. Universe Books, New York, 1987.

Read, H. *Modern Sculpture: A Concise History*. The World of Art. Reprint of 1964 ed., Thames and Hudson, London, 1987.

Selz, J. *Modern Sculpture: Origins and Evolution*. Braziller, New York, 1963.

Senie, H. *Public Sculpture: Tradition, Transformation, and Controversy*. Oxford University Press, New York, 1992.

Tucker, W. *The Language of Sculpture*. Reprint of 1974 ed., Thames and Hudson, New York, 1985.

Waldman, D. *Collage, Assemblage, and the Found Object*. Harry N. Abrams, New York, 1992.

6. TWENTIETH-CENTURY ARCHITECTURE

Bayer, H., et al., eds. *Bauhaus, 1919–1928*. Reprint of 1938 ed., New York Graphic Society, Boston, 1986.

Collins, G. R. *Antonio Gaudí*. The Masters of World Architecture. Braziller, New York, 1960.

Curtis, W. *Modern Architecture Since 1900*. 2nd ed. Prentice-Hall, Englewood Cliffs, N.J., 1987.

Fitch, J. *American Building: The Historical Forces that Shaped It*. 2 vols. 2nd ed. Houghton Mifflin, Boston, 1966–72.

Franciscono, M. *Walter Gropius and the Creation of the Bauhaus in Weimar*. University of Illinois Press, Urbana, 1971.

Hitchcock, H. R. *In the Nature of Materials: The Buildings of Frank Lloyd Wright, 1887–1941*. Duell, Sloane & Pierce, New York, 1942.

———, and P. Johnson. *The International Style*. 2nd ed. Norton, New York, 1966.

Jencks, C. *Le Corbusier and the Tragic View of Architecture*. Harvard University Press, Cambridge, 1973.

Johnson, P. *Mies van der Rohe*. 3rd ed., rev. New York Graphic Society, Greenwich, 1978.

Kultermann, U. *Architecture in the Twentieth Century*. Van Nostrand Reinhold, New York, 1993.

Lane, B. *Architecture and Politics in Germany, 1918–1945*. New ed. Harvard University Press, Cambridge, 1985.

Le Corbusier. *Towards a New Architecture*. Dover, New York, 1986.

Magnago Lampugnani, V. *Encyclopedia of Twentieth-Century Architecture*. Harry N. Abrams, New York, 1986.

Ockman, J., ed. *Architecture Culture, 1943–1968: A Documentary Anthology*. Rizzoli, New York, 1993.

Pehnt, W. *Expressionist Architecture*. Thames and Hudson, London, 1973.

Pevsner, N. *The Sources of Modern Architecture and Design*. Oxford University Press, New York, 1977.

Russell, J. *Art Nouveau Architecture*. Rizzoli, New York, 1979.

Sharp, D. *Modern Architecture and Expressionism*. Braziller, New York, 1966.

Troy, N. J. *Modernism and the Decorative Arts in France: Art Nouveau to Le Corbusier*. Yale University Press, New Haven, 1991.

Wright, F. L. *Frank Lloyd Wright, Collected Writings*. 2 vols. Rizzoli, New York, 1992.

7. TWENTIETH-CENTURY PHOTOGRAPHY

Ades, D. *Photomontage*. Pantheon, New York, 1976.

Ansel Adams: Images, 1923–1974. Foreword W. Stegner. New York Graphic Society, Boston, 1974.

August Sander: Photographs of an Epoch, 1904–1959. Aperture, Millerton, N.Y., 1980.

Burgin, V., ed. *Thinking Photography*. Communications and Culture. Macmillan Education, Houndsmills, England, 1990.

Callahan, S., ed. *The Photographs of Margaret Bourke-White*. New York Graphic Society, Boston, 1972.

Coke, V. D. *The Painter and the Photograph: From Delacroix to Warhol*. Rev. ed. University of New Mexico Press, Albuquerque, 1972.

Dorothea Lange: Photographs of a Lifetime. Aperture, Millerton, N.Y., 1982.

Ducrot, N., ed. *André Kertész: Sixty Years of Photography, 1912–1972*. Grossman, New York, 1972.

Gidal, T. *Modern Photojournalism: Origin and Evolution, 1910–1933*. Collier, New York, 1972.

Green, J. *American Photography: A Critical History, 1945 to the Present*. Harry N. Abrams, New York, 1984.

Greenough, S., and J. Hamilton. *Alfred Stieglitz, Photographs and Writings*. National Gallery of Art, Washington, D.C., 1983.

Haus, A. *Moholy-Nagy: Photographs and Photograms*. Pantheon, New York, 1980.

Henri Cartier-Bresson, Photographer. Foreword E. Bonnefoy. New York Graphic Society, Boston, 1979.

Krauss, R. *L'Amour Fou: Photography and Surrealism*. Abbeville, New York, 1985.

Longwell, D. *Steichen: The Master Prints, 1895–1914*. New York Graphic Society, Boston, 1978.

Maddow, B. *Edward Weston: Fifty Years*. Aperture, Millerton, N.Y., 1973.

Marzona, E., and R. Fricke. *Bauhaus Photography*. MIT Press, Cambridge, 1987.

Naef, W. *Fifty Pioneers of Modern Photography: The Collection of Alfred Stieglitz*. Viking Press, New York, 1978.

Petruck, P., ed. *The Camera Viewed: Writings on Twentieth-Century Photography*. 2 vols. Dutton, New York, 1979.

Phillips, C., ed. *Photography in the Modern Era: European Documents and Critical Writings, 1913–1940*. Metropolitan Museum of Art, New York, 1989.

Sontag, S. *On Photography*. Farrar, Straus and Giroux, New York, 1973.

Szarkowski, J., and M. Hambourg. *The Work of Atget*. 4 vols. Museum of Modern Art, New York, 1981–84.

Walsh, G., et al. *Contemporary Photographers*. St. Martin's Press, New York, 1983.

8. POSTSCRIPT: POSTMODERN THEORY

Barthes, R. *The Pleasure of the Text*. Blackwell, Oxford, 1990.

Brunette, P., and D. Wills, eds. *Deconstruction and the Visual Arts: Art, Media, Architecture*. Cambridge University Press, New York. Forthcoming.

Derrida, J. *Writing and Difference*. University of Chicago Press, Chicago, 1978.

Eco, U. *A Theory of Semiotics*. Indiana University Press, Bloomington, 1976.

Foster, H., ed. *The Anti-Aesthetic: Essays on Postmodern Culture*. Bay Press, Seattle, 1983.

Jameson, F. *The Prison House of Language*. Princeton University Press, Princeton, 1972.

Jencks, C. *Post-Modernism: The New Classicism in Art and Architecture*. Rizzoli, New York, 1987.

———. *Architecture Today*. Rev. and enl. ed. Harry N. Abrams, New York, 1988.

———. *What is Post-Modernism?* 3rd ed. St. Martin's Press, New York, 1989.

Norris, C., and A. Benjamin. *What is Deconstruction?* St. Martin's Press, New York, 1988.

Papadakes, A., et al., eds. *Deconstruction: The Omnibus Volume*. Rizzoli, New York, 1989.

Portoghesi, P. *Postmodern: The Architecture of the Post-Industrial Society*. Rizzoli, New York, 1983.

Risatti, H., ed. *Postmodern Perspectives*. Prentice-Hall, Englewood Cliffs, N.J., 1990.

Tafuri, M. *Contemporary Architecture*. Harry N. Abrams, New York, 1977.

Wallis, B., ed. *Art After Modernism: Rethinking Representation*. Documentary Sources in Contemporary Art, 1. Godine, Boston, 1984.

GLOSSARY

ABACUS. A slab of stone at the top of a classical CAPITAL, just beneath the ARCHITRAVE.

ABBEY. 1) A religious community headed by an abbot or abbess. 2) The buildings which house the community. An abbey church often has an especially large CHOIR to provide space for the monks or nuns.

ACADEMY. A place of study, the word coming from the Greek name of a garden near Athens where Plato and, later, Platonic philosophers held philosophical discussions from the 5th century B.C. to the 6th century A.D. The first academy of fine arts, properly speaking, was the Academy of Drawing, founded 1563 in Florence by Giorgio Vasari. Important later academies were the Royal Academy of Painting and Sculpture in Paris, founded 1648, and the Royal Academy of Arts in London, founded 1768. Their purpose was to foster the arts by systematic teaching, exhibitions, discussion, and occasionally by financial assistance.

ACANTHUS. 1) A Mediterranean plant having spiny or toothed leaves. 2) An architectural ornament resembling the leaves of this plant, used on MOLDINGS, FRIEZES, and Corinthian CAPITALS.

ACRYLIC. A plastic binder MEDIUM for pigments that is soluble in water. Developed about 1960 (fig. 1086).

AERIAL PERSPECTIVE. See PERSPECTIVE.

AISLE. See SIDE AISLE.

ALLA PRIMA. A painting technique in which pigments are laid on in one application with little or no UNDERPAINTING.

ALTAR. 1) A mound or structure on which sacrifices or offerings are made in the worship of a deity. 2) In a Catholic church, a tablelike structure used in celebrating the Mass.

ALTARPIECE. A painted or carved work of art placed behind and above the ALTAR of a Christian church. It may be a single panel (fig. 41) or a TRIPTYCH or a POLYPTYCH having hinged wings painted on both sides (figs. 671, 675). Also called a reredos or retable.

AMBULATORY. A covered walkway. 1) In a BASILICAN church, the semicircular passage around the APSE. 2) In a CENTRAL-PLAN church, the ring-shaped AISLE around the central space (fig. 744). 3) In a CLOISTER, the covered COLONNADED or ARCADED walk around the open courtyard.

ANNULAR. From the Latin word for ring. Signifies a ring-shaped form, especially an annular barrel VAULT.

APOCALYPSE. The Book of Revelation, the last book of the New Testament. In it, St. John the Evangelist describes his visions, experienced on the island of Patmos, of Heaven, the future of humankind, and the Last Judgment.

APOSTLE. One of the 12 disciples chosen by Jesus to accompany him in his lifetime, and to spread the GOSPEL after his death. The traditional list includes Andrew, Bartholomew, James the Greater (son of Zebedee), James the Less (son of Alphaeus), John, Judas Iscariot, Matthew, Peter, Philip, Simon the Canaanite, Thaddaeus (or Jude), and Thomas. In art, however, the same 12 are not always represented since "apostle" was sometimes applied to other early Christians, such as St. Paul.

APSE. 1) A semicircular or polygonal niche terminating one or both ends of the NAVE in a Roman BASILICA. 2) In a Christian church, it is usually placed at the east end of the nave beyond the TRANSEPT or CHOIR (figs. 667, 811); it is also sometimes used at the end of transept arms.

AQUATINT. A print processed like an ETCHING, except that the ground or certain areas are covered with a solution of asphalt, resin, or salts which, when heated, produces a granular surface on the plate and rich gray tones in the final print (fig. 849). Etched lines are usually added to the plate after the aquatint ground is laid.

AQUEDUCT. Latin for duct of water. 1) An artificial channel or conduit for transporting water from a distant source. 2) The overground structure which carries the conduit across valleys, rivers, etc.

ARCADE. A series of ARCHES supported by PIERS or COLUMNS (fig. 542). When attached to a wall, these form a blind arcade.

ARCH. A curved structure used to span an opening. Masonry arches are built of wedge-shaped blocks, called voussoirs, set with their narrow side toward the opening so that they lock together. The topmost voussoir is called the keystone. Arches may take different shapes, as in the pointed Gothic arch (fig. 915), or the rounded classical arch (fig. 914), but all require support from other arches or BUTTRESSES.

ARCHBISHOP. The chief BISHOP of an ecclesiastical district.

ARCHITRAVE. The lowermost member of a classical ENTABLATURE, i.e., a series of stone blocks that rest directly on the COLUMNS (figs. 665, 666, 860).

ARCHIVOLT. A molded band framing an ARCH, or a series of such bands framing a TYMPANUM, often decorated with sculpture (fig. 593).

ARRICCIO. See SINOPIA.

ATMOSPHERIC PERSPECTIVE. See PERSPECTIVE.

ATRIUM. 1) The central court of an ancient Roman house, or its open entrance court. 2) An open court, sometimes COLONNADED or ARCADED, in front of a church.

ATTIC. A low upper story placed above the main CORNICE or ENTABLATURE of a building, and often decorated with windows and PILASTERS (fig. 622).

AUTOCHROME. A color photograph invented by Louis Lumière in 1903, using a glass plate covered with grains of starch dyed in three colors to act as filters, then a silver bromide emulsion (fig. 1199).

BACCHANT (fem. **BACCHANTE**). A priest or priestess of the wine god, Bacchus (in Greek mythology, Dionysus), or one of his ecstatic female followers, who were sometimes called maenads (fig. 632).

BALUSTRADE. A railing supported by short pillars called balusters (fig. 617). Occasionally applied to any low parapet (fig. 601).

BAPTISTERY. A building or a part of a church, often round or octagonal, in which the sacrament of baptism is administered. It contains a baptismal font, a receptacle of stone or metal which holds the water for the rite.

BARREL VAULT. See VAULT.

BASE. 1) The lowermost portion of a COLUMN or PIER, beneath the SHAFT. 2) The lowest element of a wall, DOME, or building, or occasionally of a statue or painting (see PREDELLA).

BASILICA. 1) In ancient Roman architecture, a large, oblong building used as a hall of justice and public meeting place, generally having a NAVE, SIDE AISLES, and one or more APSES. 2) In Christian architecture, a longitudinal church derived from the Roman basilica, and having a nave, apse, two or four side aisles or side chapels, and sometimes a NARTHEX (fig. 543). 3) One of the seven main churches of Rome (St. Peter's, St. Paul Outside the Walls, St. John Lateran, etc.), or another church accorded the same religious privileges.

BATTLEMENT. A parapet consisting of alternating solid parts and open spaces designed originally for defense and later used for decoration (fig. 910).

BAY. A subdivision of the interior space of a building, usually in a series bounded by consecutive architectural supports.

BISHOP. The spiritual overseer of a number of churches or a diocese. His throne, or cathedra, placed in the principal church of the diocese, designates it as a cathedral.

BLIND ARCADE. See ARCADE.

BLOCK BOOKS. Books, often religious, of the 15th century, containing WOODCUT prints in which picture and text were usually cut into the same block (compare fig. 693).

BOOK COVER. The stiff outer covers protecting the bound pages of a book. In the medieval period, frequently covered with precious metal and elaborately embellished with jewels, embossed decoration, etc.

BOOK OF HOURS. A private prayer book containing the devotions for the seven canonical hours of the Roman Catholic church (matins, vespers, etc.), liturgies for local saints, and sometimes a calendar (fig. 40). They were often elaborately ILLUMINATED for persons of high rank, whose names are attached to certain extant examples.

BRACKET. A stone, wooden, or metal support projecting from a wall and having a flat top to bear the weight of a statue, CORNICE, beam, etc. The lower part may take the form of a SCROLL: it is then called a scroll bracket.

BROKEN PEDIMENT. See PEDIMENT.

BRUSH DRAWING. See DRAWING.

BURIN. See ENGRAVING.

BUTTRESS. 1) A projecting support built against an external wall, usually to counteract the lateral THRUST of a VAULT or ARCH within. 2) FLYING BUTTRESS. An arched bridge above the aisle roof that extends from the upper nave wall, where the lateral thrust of the main vault is greatest, down to a solid pier.

BYZANTIUM. City on the Sea of Marmara, founded by the ancient Greeks and renamed Constantinople in 330 A.D. Today called Istanbul.

CAESAR. The surname of the Roman dictator, Caius Julius Caesar, subsequently used as the title of an emperor; hence, the German *Kaiser*, and the Russian *czar (tsar)*.

CALVARY. The hill outside Jerusalem where Christ was crucified, the name being taken from the Latin word *calvaris*, meaning skull (Golgotha is the Greek transliteration of skull in Aramaic). The hill was thought to be the spot where Adam was buried, and was thus traditionally known as "the place of the skull."

CAMERA OBSCURA. Latin for dark room. A darkened enclosure or box with a small opening or lens on one wall through which light enters to form an inverted image on the opposite wall. The principle had long been known, but was not used as an aid in picture making until the 16th century.

CAMPAGNA. Italian word for countryside. When capitalized, it usually refers to the countryside near Rome.

CAMPANILE. From the Italian word *campana*, meaning bell. A bell tower, either round or square in plan, and sometimes freestanding (fig. 666).

CAMPOSANTO. Italian word for holy field. A cemetery near a church, often enclosed.

CANOPY. In architecture, an ornamental, rooflike projection or cover above a statue or sacred object (fig. 740).

CAPITAL. The uppermost member of a COLUMN or PILLAR supporting the ARCHITRAVE.

CARDINAL. In the Roman Catholic church, a member of the Sacred College, the ecclesiastical body which elects the pope and constitutes his advisory council.

CARTOON. From the Italian word *cartone*, meaning cardboard. 1) A full-scale DRAWING for a picture or design intended to be transferred to a wall, panel, tapestry, etc. (fig. 597). 2) A drawing or print, usually humorous or satirical, calling attention to some action or person of popular interest (fig. 876).

CARVING. 1) The cutting of a figure or design out of a solid material such as stone or wood, as contrasted to the additive technique of MODELING. 2) A work executed in this technique (figs. 609, 610).

CASTING. A method of duplicating a work of sculpture by pouring a hardening substance such as plaster or molten metal into a mold. See CIRE-PERDU PROCESS.

CAST IRON. A hard, brittle iron produced commercially in blast furnaces by pouring it into molds where it cools and hardens. Extensively used as a building material in the early 19th century (figs. 961, 962), it was superseded by STEEL and FERROCONCRETE.

CATHEDRA, CATHEDRAL. See BISHOP.

CELLA. 1) The principal enclosed room of a temple, to house an image. Also called the naos. 2) The entire body of a temple as distinct from its external parts.

CENTERING. A wooden framework built to support an ARCH, VAULT, or DOME during its construction.

CENTRAL-PLAN CHURCH. 1) A church having four arms of equal length. The CROSSING is often covered with a DOME (figs. 572–74). Also called a Greek-cross church. 2) A church having a circular or polygonal plan (fig. 602).

CHANCEL. See CHOIR.

CHAPEL. 1) A private or subordinate place of worship (figs. 544–47). 2) A place of worship that is part of a church, but separately dedicated (figs. 561, 611).

CHASING. 1) A technique of ornamenting a metal surface by the use of various tools. 2) The procedure used to finish a raw bronze cast.

CHÂTEAU (pl. CHÂTEAUX). French word for castle, now used to designate a large country house as well (fig. 720).

CHIAROSCURO. Italian word for light and dark. In painting, a method of modeling form primarily by the use of light and shade (figs. 594, 632, 726).

CHOIR. In church architecture, a square or rectangular area between the APSE and the NAVE or TRANSEPT. It is reserved for the clergy and the singing choir, and is usually marked off by steps, a railing, or a CHOIR SCREEN. Also called the chancel. See PILGRIMAGE CHOIR.

CHOIR SCREEN. A screen, frequently ornamented with sculpture and sometimes called a rood screen, separating the CHOIR of a church from the NAVE or TRANSEPT.

CIRE-PERDU PROCESS. The lost-wax process of CASTING. A method in which an original is MODELED in wax or coated with wax, then covered with clay. When the wax is melted out, the resulting mold is filled with molten metal (often bronze) or liquid plaster.

CITY-STATE. An autonomous political unit comprising a city and the surrounding countryside.

CLERESTORY. A row of windows in the upper part of a wall that rises above an adjoining roof; built to provide direct lighting, as in a BASILICA or church (fig. 542).

CLOISTER. 1) A place of religious seclusion such as a monastery or nunnery. 2) An open court attached to a church or monastery and surrounded by a covered ARCADED walk or AMBULATORY. Used for study, meditation, and exercise.

CODEX (pl. CODICES). A manuscript in book form made possible by the use of PARCHMENT instead of papyrus. During the 1st to 4th centuries A.D., it gradually replaced the roll or SCROLL previously used for written documents.

COFFER. 1) A small chest or casket. 2) A recessed, geometrically shaped panel in a ceiling. A ceiling decorated with these panels is said to be coffered (figs. 743, 914).

COLLAGE. A composition made of cut and pasted scraps of materials, sometimes with lines or forms added by the artist (fig. 1036).

COLONNADE. A series of regularly spaced COLUMNS supporting a LINTEL or ENTABLATURE (fig. 601).

COLOSSAL ORDER. COLUMNS, PIERS, or PILASTERS which extend through two or more stories (figs. 567, 621).

COLUMN. An approximately cylindrical, upright architectural support, usually consisting of a long, relatively slender SHAFT, a BASE, and a CAPITAL (fig. 542). When imbedded in a wall, it is called an engaged column (fig. 567). Columns decorated with spiral RELIEFS were used occasionally as freestanding commemorative monuments.

COMPOUND PIER. See PIER.

CONCRETE. A mixture of sand or gravel with mortar and rubble, invented in the ancient Near East and further developed by the Romans. Largely ignored during the Middle Ages, it was revived by Bramante in the early 16th century for St. Peter's. Reinforced concrete: see FERROCONCRETE.

CONTÉ CRAYON. A crayon made of graphite and clay used for DRAWING. Produces rich, velvety tones (fig. 973).

CONTRAPPOSTO. Italian word for set against. A method developed by the Greeks to represent freedom of movement in a figure. The parts of the body are placed asymmetrically in opposition to each other around a central axis, and careful attention is paid to the distribution of the weight (fig. 535).

CORINTHIAN ORDER. See ORDER, ARCHITECTURAL.

CORNICE. 1) The projecting, framing members of a classical PEDIMENT, including the horizontal one beneath and the two sloping or "raking" ones above (fig. 569). 2) Any projecting, horizontal element surmounting a wall or other structure, or dividing it horizontally for decorative purposes (fig. 550).

COUNTER-REFORMATION. The movement of self-renewal and reform within the Roman Catholic church following the Protestant REFORMATION of the early 16th century, and attempting to combat its influence. Also known as the Catholic Reform. Its principles were formulated and adopted at the Council of Trent, 1545–63.

CRENELATED. See BATTLEMENT.

CROSSHATCHING. See HATCHING.

CROSSING. The area in a church where the TRANSEPT crosses the NAVE, frequently emphasized by a DOME (fig. 548), or crossing tower.

CROSS SECTION. See SECTION.

CRYPT. In a church, a VAULTED space beneath the CHOIR, causing the floor of the choir to be raised above the level of that of the NAVE.

DAGUERREOTYPE. Originally, a photograph on a silver-plated sheet of copper which had been treated with fumes of iodine to form silver iodide on its surface and, after exposure, was developed by fumes of mercury. The process, invented by L. J. M. Daguerre and made public in 1839 (fig. 923), was modified and accelerated as daguerreotypes gained worldwide popularity.

DEËSIS. From the Greek word for entreaty. The representation of Christ enthroned between the Virgin Mary and St. John the Baptist, frequent in Byzantine MOSAICS and depictions of the Last Judgment (fig. 672); refers to the roles of the Virgin Mary and St. John as intercessors for humankind.

DIPTYCH. 1) Originally a hinged two-leaved tablet used for writing. 2) A pair of ivory CARVINGS or PANEL paintings, usually hinged together.

DISGUISED SYMBOLISM. "Hidden" meaning in the details of a painting that carry a symbolic message (fig. 671).

DOME. A true dome is a VAULTED roof of circular, polygonal, or elliptical plan, formed with hemispherical or ovoidal curvature (figs. 601, 743). May be supported by a circular wall or DRUM, and by PENDENTIVES or related constructions. Domical coverings of many other sorts have been devised (figs. 547, 749).

DONOR. The patron or client at whose order a work of art was executed; the donor may be depicted in the work (figs. 671, 687).

DORIC ORDER. See ORDER, ARCHITECTURAL.

DRAWING. 1) A work in pencil, pen and ink, charcoal, etc., often on paper (fig. 986). 2) A similar work in ink or WASH, etc., made with a brush and often called a brush drawing. 3) A work combining these or other techniques. A drawing may be large or small, a quick sketch or an elaborate work. Among its various forms are: a record of something seen (fig. 597); a study for all or part of another work (figs. 590, 872; see also OIL SKETCH; SINOPIA); an illustration associated with a text (fig. 599); a technical aid.

DRUM. 1) A section of the SHAFT of a COLUMN. 2) A wall supporting a DOME (fig. 622).

DRYPOINT. See ENGRAVING.

ELEVATION. 1) An architectural drawing presenting a building as if projected on a vertical plane parallel to one of its sides. 2) Term used in describing the vertical plane of a building.

ENAMEL. 1) Colored glassy substances, either opaque or translucent, applied in powder form to a metal surface and fused to it by firing. Two main techniques developed: "champlevé" (from the French for raised field), in which the areas to be treated are dug out of the metal surface; and "cloisonné" (from the French for partitioned), in which compartments or "cloisons" to be filled are made on the surface with thin metal strips. 2) A work executed in either technique (fig. 657).

ENGAGED COLUMN. See COLUMN.

ENGRAVING. 1) A means of embellishing metal surfaces or gemstones by incising a design on the surface. 2) A PRINT made by cutting a design into a metal plate (usually copper) with a pointed steel tool known as a burin. The burr raised on either side of the incised line is removed; ink is then rubbed into the V-shaped grooves and wiped off the surface; the plate, covered with a damp sheet of paper, is run through a heavy press (fig. 694). The image on the paper is the reverse of that on the plate (figs. 824, 825). When a fine steel needle is used instead of a burin and the burr is retained, a drypoint engraving results, characterized by a softer line (fig. 695). 3) These techniques are called, respectively, engraving and drypoint.

ENTABLATURE. 1) In a classical order, the entire structure above the COLUMNS; this usually includes ARCHITRAVE, FRIEZE, and CORNICE. 2) The same structure in any building of a classical style (fig. 855).

ENTASIS. A swelling of the SHAFT of a COLUMN.

ETCHING. 1) A PRINT made by coating a copperplate with an acid-resistant resin and drawing through this ground, exposing the metal with a sharp instrument called a STYLUS. The plate is bathed in acid, which eats into the lines; it is then heated to remove the resin, and finally inked and printed on paper (fig. 778). 2) The technique itself is also called etching.

EUCHARIST. 1) The sacrament of Holy Communion, the celebration in commemoration of the Last Supper (fig. 564). 2) The consecrated bread and wine used in the ceremony.

EVANGELISTS. Matthew, Mark, Luke, and John, traditionally thought to be the authors of the GOSPELS, the first four books of the New Testament, which recount the life and death of Christ. They are usually shown with their symbols, which are probably derived from the four beasts surrounding the throne of the Lamb in the Book of Revelation or from those in the vision of Ezekiel: a winged man or angel for Matthew (fig. 651), a winged lion for Mark, a winged ox for Luke, and an eagle for John. These symbols may also represent the evangelists.

FAÇADE. The principal face or the front of a building.

FERROCONCRETE. Reinforced CONCRETE, strengthened by STEEL rods and mesh placed in it before hardening. Introduced in France c. 1900, and widely used today (figs. 1167, 1171, 1181, 1192).

FIBULA. A clasp, buckle, or brooch, often ornamented.

FINIAL. A relatively small, decorative element terminating a GABLE, PINNACLE, or the like (fig. 719).

FLUTING. In architecture, the ornamental grooves channeled vertically into the SHAFT of a COLUMN or PILASTER (fig. 577). They may meet in a sharp edge, as in the Doric ORDER, or be separated by a narrow strip or fillet, as in the Ionic, Corinthian, and Composite orders.

FLYING BUTTRESS. See BUTTRESS.

FONT See BAPTISTERY.

FORESHORTENING. A method of reducing or distorting the parts of a represented object which are not parallel to the PICTURE PLANE, in order to convey the impression of three dimensions as perceived by the human eye (figs. 794, 871).

FRESCO. Italian word for fresh. 1) True fresco is the technique of painting on moist plaster with pigments ground in water so that the paint is absorbed by the plaster and becomes part of the wall itself (fig. 36). Fresco secco is the technique of painting with the same colors on dry plaster. 2) A painting done in either of these techniques.

FRIEZE. 1) A continuous band of painted or sculptured decoration (fig. 965). 2) In a classical building, the part of the ENTABLATURE between the ARCHITRAVE and the CORNICE. A Doric frieze consists of alternating TRIGLYPHS and METOPES, the latter often sculptured. An Ionic frieze is usually decorated with continuous RELIEF sculpture.

FROTTAGE. See RUBBING.

GABLE. 1) The triangular area framed by the CORNICE or eaves of a building and the sloping sides of a pitched roof. In classical architecture, it is called a PEDIMENT. 2) A decorative element of similar shape, such as the triangular structures above the PORTALS of a Gothic church.

GALLERY. A second story placed over the SIDE AISLES of a church and below the CLERESTORY, or, in a church with a four-part ELEVATION, below the TRIFORIUM and above the NAVE ARCADE which supports it on its open side.

GENIUS (pl. GENII). A winged semi-nude figure, often purely decorative (fig. 577) but frequently representing the guardian spirit of a person or place, or personifying an abstract concept (fig. 900).

GENRE. French word for kind or sort. A work of art, usually a painting, showing a scene from everyday life that is represented for its own sake (fig. 821).

GESSO. A smooth mixture of ground chalk or plaster and glue, used as the basis for TEMPERA PAINTING and for OIL PAINTING on PANEL.

GILDING. 1) A coat of gold or of a gold-colored substance that is applied mechanically or chemically to surfaces of a painting, sculpture, or architectural decoration (figs. 537, 834). 2) The process of applying same.

GLAZE. 1) A thin layer of translucent oil color applied to a painted surface or to parts of it in order to modify the tone. 2) A glassy coating applied to a piece of ceramic work before firing in the kiln, as a protective seal and often as decoration.

GLORIOLE or **GLORY.** The circle of radiant light around the heads or figures of God, Christ, the Virgin Mary, or a saint. When it surrounds the head only, it is called a halo or nimbus (fig. 38); when it surrounds the entire figure with a large oval, it is called a *mandorla* (the Italian word for almond). It indicates divinity or holiness, though originally it was placed around the heads of kings and gods as a mark of distinction.

GOLD LEAF, SILVER LEAF. 1) Gold beaten into very thin sheets or "leaves," and applied to ILLUMINATED MANUSCRIPTS and PANEL paintings (fig. 38), to sculpture, or to the back of the glass TESSERAE used in MOSAICS. 2) Silver leaf is also used, though ultimately it tarnishes. Sometimes called gold foil, silver foil.

GOLGOTHA. See CALVARY.

GOSPEL. 1) The first four books of the New Testament. They tell the story of Christ's life and death, and are ascribed to the EVANGELISTS Matthew, Mark, Luke, and John. 2) A copy of these, usually called a Gospel Book, often richly ILLUMINATED.

GREEK-CROSS CHURCH. See CENTRAL-PLAN CHURCH.

GROIN VAULT. See VAULT.

GROUND PLAN. An architectural drawing presenting a building as if cut horizontally at the floor level.

HALLENKIRCHE. German word for hall church. A church in which the NAVE and the SIDE AISLES are of the same height. The type was developed in Romanesque architecture, and occurs especially frequently in German Gothic churches.

HALO. See GLORIOLE.

HATCHING. A series of parallel lines used as shading in PRINTS and DRAWINGS (fig. 590). When two sets of crossing parallel lines are used, it is called crosshatching.

HIGH RELIEF. See RELIEF.

HÔTEL. French word for hotel, but used also to designate an elegant town house (fig. 814).

ICON. From the Greek word for image. A PANEL painting of one or more sacred personages such as Christ, the Virgin (fig. 31), a saint, particularly venerated in the ORTHODOX Catholic church.

ICONOSTASIS. See CHOIR SCREEN.

ILLUMINATED MANUSCRIPT. A MANUSCRIPT decorated with drawings or with paintings in TEMPERA colors.

ILLUSIONISM. In artistic terms, the technique of manipulating pictorial or other means in order to cause the eye to perceive a particular reality. May be used in architecture (fig. 749) and sculpture (figs. 753, 754), as well as in painting (figs. 736, 737).

IMPASTO. From the Italian word meaning "in paste." Paint, usually oil paint, applied very thickly (figs. 759, 978).

IONIC ORDER. See ORDER, ARCHITECTURAL.

JAMBS. The vertical sides of an opening. In Romanesque and Gothic churches, the jambs of doors and windows are often cut on a slant outward, or "splayed," thus providing a broader surface for sculptural decoration.

JESUIT ORDER. The "Society of Jesus" was founded in 1534 by Ignatius of Loyola (1491–1556), and especially devoted to the service of the pope. The order was a powerful influence in the struggle of the Catholic COUNTER-REFORMATION with the Protestant REFORMATION, and also very important for its missionary work, disseminating Christianity in the Far East and the New World. The mother church in Rome, Il Gesù (figs. 668–70), conforms in design to the preaching aims of the new order.

KEYSTONE. See ARCH.

LABORS OF THE MONTHS. The various occupations suitable to the months of the year. Scenes or figures illustrating these were frequently represented in ILLUMINATED manuscripts (fig. 40); sometimes with the symbols of the ZODIAC signs, CARVED around the PORTALS of Romanesque and Gothic churches.

LANTERN. A relatively small structure crowning a DOME, roof, or tower, frequently open to admit light to an enclosed area below (fig. 622).

LAY BROTHER. One who has joined a monastic ORDER but has not taken monastic vows, and therefore belongs still to the people or laity, as distinguished from the clergy or religious.

LIBERAL ARTS. Traditionally thought to go back to Plato, they comprised the intellectual disciplines considered suitable or necessary to a complete education, and included grammar, rhetoric, logic, arithmetic, music, geometry, and astronomy. During the Middle Ages and the Renaissance, they were often represented allegorically in painting, engravings, and sculpture.

LINTEL. See POST AND LINTEL.

LITHOGRAPH. A PRINT made by drawing a design with an oily crayon or other greasy substance on a porous stone or, later, a metal plate; the design is then fixed, the entire surface is moistened, and the printing ink which is applied adheres only to the oily lines of the drawing. The design can then be transferred easily in a press to a piece of paper. The technique was invented c. 1796 by Aloys Senefelder, and quickly became popular (figs. 876, 987). It is also widely used commercially, since many impressions can be taken from a single plate.

LOGGIA. A covered GALLERY or ARCADE open to the air on at least one side. It may stand alone or be part of a building (fig. 661).

LONGITUDINAL SECTION. See SECTION.

LOUVERS. A series of overlapping boards or slats which can be opened to admit air, but are slanted so as to exclude sun and rain (fig. 1182).

LOW RELIEF. See RELIEF.

LUNETTE. 1) A semicircular or pointed wall area, as under a VAULT or above a door or window. When it is above the PORTAL of a medieval church, it is called a TYMPANUM (fig. 45). 2) A painting (fig. 731), relief sculpture (fig. 576), or window of the same shape (fig. 853).

MAESTÀ. Italian word for majesty, applied in the 14th and 15th centuries to representations of the Madonna and Child enthroned, and surrounded by her celestial court of saints and angels (fig. 32).

MAGUS (pl. MAGI). 1) A member of the priestly caste of ancient Media and Persia. 2) In Christian literature, one of the three Wise Men or Kings who came from the East bearing gifts to the newborn Jesus (fig. 41).

MANDORLA. See GLORIOLE.

MANUSCRIPT. From the Latin word for handwritten. 1) A document, scroll, or book written by hand, as distinguished from such a work in print (i.e., after c. 1450). 2) A book produced in the Middle Ages, frequently ILLUMINATED.

MAUSOLEUM. 1) The huge tomb erected at Halicarnassus in Asia Minor in the 4th century B.C. by King Mausolus and his wife Artemisia. 2) A generic term for any large funerary monument.

MEANDER. A decorative motif of intricate, rectilinear character, applied to architecture and sculpture.

MEDIUM. 1) The material or technique in which an artist works. 2) The vehicle in which pigments are carried in paint, PASTEL, etc.

METOPE. In a Doric FRIEZE, one of the panels, either decorated or plain, between the TRIGLYPHS. Originally it probably covered the empty spaces between the ends of the wooden ceiling beams.

MINIATURE. 1) A single illustration in an ILLUMINATED manuscript. 2) A very small painting, especially a portrait on ivory, glass, or metal (fig. 712).

MODEL. 1) The preliminary form of a sculpture, often finished in itself but preceding the final CASTING or CARVING (figs. 806, 807, 907). 2) Preliminary or reconstructed form of a building, made to scale. 3) A person who poses for an artist.

MODELING. 1) In sculpture, the building up of a figure or design in a soft substance such as clay or wax (fig. 815). 2) In painting and drawing, producing a three-dimensional effect by changes in color, the use of light and shade, etc.

MOLDING. In architecture, any of various long, narrow, ornamental bands having a distinctive profile, which project from the surface of the structure and give variety to the surface by means of their patterned contrasts of light and shade (figs. 577, 593).

MOSAIC. Decorative work for walls, VAULTS, ceilings, or floors, composed of small pieces of colored materials (called TESSERAE) set in plaster or CONCRETE. The Romans, whose work was mostly for floors, used regularly shaped pieces of marble in its natural colors. The early Christians used pieces of glass whose brilliant hues, including gold, and slightly irregular surfaces produced an entirely different, glittering effect. See also GOLD LEAF.

MURAL. From the Latin word for wall, *murus*. A large painting or decoration, either executed directly on a wall (FRESCO) or done separately and affixed to it (fig. 984).

MUSES. In Greek mythology, the nine goddesses who presided over various arts and sciences. They are led by Apollo as god of music and poetry, and usually include Calliope, muse of epic poetry; Clio, muse of history; Erato, muse of love poetry; Euterpe, muse of music; Melpomene, muse of tragedy; Polyhymnia, muse of sacred music; Terpsichore, muse of dancing; Thalia, muse of comedy; and Urania, muse of astronomy.

NARTHEX. The transverse entrance hall of a church, sometimes enclosed but often open on one side to a preceding ATRIUM.

NAVE. 1) The central aisle of a Roman BASILICA, as distinguished from the SIDE AISLES. 2) The same section of a Christian basilican church extending from the entrance to the APSE or TRANSEPT (fig. 542).

NIKE. The ancient Greek goddess of victory, often identified with Athena, and by the Romans with Victoria. She is usually represented as a winged woman with windblown draperies.

NIMBUS. See GLORIOLE.

OBELISK. A tall, tapering, four-sided stone shaft with a pyramidal top. First constructed in ancient Egypt; certain examples since exported to other countries (fig. 739).

ODALISQUE. Turkish word for a harem slave girl or concubine (figs. 870, 874).

OIL PAINTING. 1) A painting executed with pigments mixed with oil, first applied either to a panel prepared with a coat of GESSO (as also in TEMPERA PAINTING), later to a stretched canvas primed with a coat of white paint and glue. The latter method has been usual since the late 15th century. Oil painting also may be executed on paper, parchment, copper, etc. 2) The technique of executing such a painting.

OIL SKETCH. A work in oil painting of an informal character, sometimes preparatory to a finished work (figs. 763, 887).

ORDER, ARCHITECTURAL. An architectural system based on the COLUMN and its ENTABLATURE, in which the form of the elements themselves (CAPITAL, SHAFT, BASE, etc.) and their relationships to each other are specifically defined. The five classical orders are the Doric, Ionic, Corinthian, Tuscan, and Composite. See also COLOSSAL ORDER, SUPERIMPOSED ORDER.

ORDER, MONASTIC. A religious society whose members live together under an established set of rules. See JESUIT, THEATINE.

ORTHODOX. From the Greek word for right in opinion. The Eastern Orthodox church, which broke with the Western Catholic church during the 5th century A.D. and transferred its allegiance from the pope in Rome to the Byzantine emperor in Constantinople and his appointed patriarch. Sometimes called the Byzantine church.

PALAZZO (pl. PALAZZI). Italian word for palace (in French, *palais*). Refers either to large official buildings (fig. 621), or to important private town houses (fig. 550).

PALETTE. 1) A thin, usually oval or oblong board with a thumbhole at one end, used by painters to hold and mix their colors. 2) The range of colors used by a particular painter. 3) In Egyptian art, a slate slab, usually decorated with sculpture in low RELIEF.

PANEL. 1) A wooden surface used for painting, usually in TEMPERA, and prepared beforehand with a layer of GESSO. Large ALTARPIECES require the joining together of two or more boards (fig. 690). 2) Recently panels of Masonite or other composite materials have come into use (fig. 1093).

PANTHEON. A temple dedicated to all the gods, or housing tombs of the illustrious dead of a nation, or memorials to them (fig. 856).

PARCHMENT. From PERGAMUM, the name of a Greek city in Asia Minor where parchment was invented in the 2nd century B.C. 1) A paperlike material made from thin bleached animal hides, used extensively in the Middle Ages for MANUSCRIPTS. Vellum is a superior type of parchment, made from calfskin. 2) A document or miniature on this material.

PASSION. 1) In ecclesiastic terms, the events of Christ's last week on earth. 2) The representation of these events in pictorial, literary, theatrical, or musical form (figs. 636, 679, 762).

PASTEL. 1) A color of a soft, subdued shade. 2) A drawing stick made from pigments ground with chalk and mixed with gum water. 3) A drawing executed with these sticks (fig. 939).

PEDESTAL. An architectural support for a statue, vase, column, etc.

PEDIMENT. 1) In classical architecture, a low GABLE, typically triangular, framed by a horizontal CORNICE below and two raking cornices above; frequently filled with relief sculpture (fig. 856). 2) A similar architectural member, either round or triangular, used over a door, window, or niche (fig. 616). When pieces of the cornice are either turned at an angle or broken, it is called a broken pediment (fig. 617).

PENDENTIVE. One of the spherical triangles which achieves the transition from a square or polygonal opening to the round BASE of a DOME or the supporting DRUM (fig. 574).

PERIPTERAL. An adjective describing a building surrounded by a single row of COLUMNS or COLONNADE.

PERISTYLE. 1) In an ancient Roman house, an open garden court surrounded by a COLONNADE. 2) A colonnade around a building or court (fig. 602).

PERSPECTIVE. A technique for representing spatial relationships and three-dimensional objects on a flat surface so as to produce an effect similar to that perceived by the human eye. In "atmospheric" or aerial perspective, this is accomplished by a gradual decrease in the intensity of local color and in the contrast of light and dark, so that everything in the far distance tends toward a light bluish-gray tone (fig. 672). In one-point linear perspective, developed in Italy in the 15th century, a mathematical system is used, based on orthogonals (all lines receding at right angles to the picture plane) that converge on a single vanishing point on the horizon. Since this presupposes an absolutely stationary viewer and imposes rigid restrictions on the artist, it is seldom applied with complete consistency (figs. 534, 563).

PHOTOGRAM. A shadowlike photograph made without a camera by placing objects on light-sensitive paper and exposing them to a light source (fig. 1220).

PHOTOGRAPH. The relatively permanent or "fixed" form of an image made by light that passes through the lens of a camera and acts upon light-sensitive substances. Often called a PRINT.

PHOTOMONTAGE. A photograph in which prints in whole or in part are combined to form a new image (fig. 1219). A technique much practiced by the Dada group in the 1920s.

PIAZZA (pl. PIAZZE). Italian word for public square (in French, *place*; in German, *Platz*).

PICTURE PLANE. The flat surface on which a picture is painted.

PICTURESQUE. Visually interesting or pleasing, as if resembling a picture (fig. 855).

PIER. An upright architectural support, usually rectangular, and sometimes with CAPITAL and BASE. When COLUMNS, PILASTERS, or SHAFTS are attached to it, as in many Romanesque and Gothic churches, it is called a compound pier.

PIETÀ. Italian word for both pity and piety. A representation of the Virgin grieving over the dead Christ. When used in a scene recording a specific moment after the Crucifixion, it is usually called a Lamentation.

PILASTER. A flat, vertical element projecting from a wall surface, and normally having a BASE, SHAFT, and CAPITAL. It has generally a decorative rather than structural purpose (figs. 569, 572).

PILGRIMAGE CHOIR. The unit in a Romanesque church composed of the APSE, AMBULATORY, and RADIATING CHAPELS.

PILLAR. A general term for a vertical architectural support which includes COLUMNS, PIERS, and PILASTERS.

PINNACLE. A small, decorative structure capping a tower, PIER, BUTTRESS, or other architectural member, and used especially in Gothic buildings.

PLAN. See **GROUND PLAN.**

PODIUM. 1) The tall base upon which rests a temple. 2) The ground floor of a building made to resemble such a base (fig. 799).

POLYPTYCH. An ALTARPIECE or devotional work of art made of several panels joined together (fig. 673), often hinged.

PORCH. General term for an exterior appendage to a building which forms a covered approach to a doorway. See PORTICO for porches consisting of columns.

PORTA. Latin word for door or gate.

PORTAL. A door or gate, usually a monumental one with elaborate sculptural decoration.

PORTICO. A columned porch supporting a roof or an ENTABLATURE and PEDIMENT, often approached by a number of steps (fig. 853). It provides a monumental covered entrance to a building, and a link with the space surrounding it.

POST AND LINTEL. A basic system of construction in which two or more uprights, the "posts," support a horizontal member, the "lintel." The lintel may be the topmost element, or support a wall or roof (fig. 1004).

PREDELLA. The base of an ALTARPIECE, often decorated with small scenes which are related in subject to that of the main panel or panels (fig. 41).

PRINT. A picture or design reproduced, usually on paper and often in numerous copies, from a prepared wood block, metal plate, or stone slab, or by photography. See AQUATINT, ENGRAVING, ETCHING, LITHOGRAPH, PHOTOGRAPH, WOODCUT.

PSALTER. 1) The book of Psalms in the Old Testament, thought to have been written in part by David, king of ancient Israel. 2) A copy of the Psalms, sometimes arranged for liturgical or devotional use, and often richly ILLUMINATED.

PULPIT. A raised platform in a church from which the clergy deliver a sermon or conducts the service. Its railing or enclosing wall may be elaborately decorated.

PUTTO (pl. PUTTI). A nude, male child, usually winged, often represented in classical and Renaissance art. Also called a cupid or *amoretto* when he carries a bow and arrow and personifies Love (figs. 628, 764).

PYLON. Greek word for gateway. 1) The monumental entrance building to an Egyptian temple or forecourt, consisting of either a massive wall with sloping sides pierced by a doorway, or of two such walls flanking a central gateway. 2) A tall structure at either side of a gate, bridge, or avenue, marking an approach or entrance.

QUATREFOIL. An ornamental element composed of four lobes radiating from a common center.

RADIATING CHAPELS. Term for CHAPELS arranged around the AMBU-LATORY (and sometimes the TRANSEPT) of a medieval church.

REFECTORY. 1) A room for refreshment. 2) The dining hall of a monastery, college, or other large institution.

REFORMATION. The religious movement in the early 16th century which had for its object the reform of the Catholic church, and led to the establishment of Protestant churches. See also COUNTER-REFORMATION.

REINFORCED CONCRETE. See FERROCONCRETE.

RELIEF. 1) The projection of a figure or part of a design from the background or plane on which it is CARVED or MODELED. Sculpture done in this manner is described as "high relief" or "low relief" depending on the height of the projection. When it is very shallow, it is called *schiacciato*, the Italian word for flattened out (fig. 532). 2) The apparent projection of forms represented in a painting or drawing.

RESPOND. 1) A half-PIER, PILASTER, or similar element projecting from a wall to support a LINTEL, or an ARCH whose other side is supported by a free-standing COLUMN or pier, as at the end of an ARCADE. 2) One of several pilasters on a wall behind a COLONNADE (fig. 542) which echoes or "responds to" the columns, but is largely decorative. 3) One of the slender shafts of a COMPOUND PIER in a medieval church which seems to carry the weight of the VAULT.

RIB. A slender, projecting archlike member which supports a VAULT either transversely, or at the GROINS, thus dividing the surface into sections. In Late Gothic architecture, its purpose is often primarily ornamental.

RIBBED VAULT. See VAULT.

ROOD SCREEN. See CHOIR SCREEN.

RUBBING. A reproduction of a relief surface made by covering it with paper and rubbing with pencil, chalk, etc. Also called frottage.

RUSTICATION. A masonry technique of laying rough-faced stones with sharply indented joints (figs. 550, 662).

SACRA CONVERSAZIONE. Italian for holy conversation. A composition of the Madonna and Child with saints in which the figures all occupy the same spatial setting, and appear to be conversing or communing with each other (figs. 593, 633).

SACRISTY. A room near the main altar of a church, or a small building attached to a church, where the vessels and vestments required for the service are kept. Also called a vestry.

SALON. 1) A large, elegant drawing or reception room in a palace or a private house. 2) Official government-sponsored exhibition of paintings and sculpture by living artists held in the Louvre at Paris, first biennially, then annually. 3) Any large public exhibition patterned after the Paris Salon.

SANCTUARY. 1) A sacred or holy place or building. 2) An especially holy place within a building, such as the CELLA of a temple, or the part of a church around the altar.

SARCOPHAGUS (pl. **SARCOPHAGI**). A large stone coffin usually decorated with sculpture and/or inscriptions. The term is derived from two Greek words meaning flesh and eating, which were applied to a kind of lime stone in ancient Greece, since the stone was said to turn flesh to dust.

SATYR. One of a class of woodland gods thought to be the lascivious companions of Dionysus, the Greek god of wine (or of Bacchus, his Roman counterpart). They are represented as having the legs and tail of a goat, the body of a man, and a head with horns and pointed ears. A youthful satyr is also called a faun (fig. 584).

SCRIPTORIUM (pl. **SCRIPTORIA**). A workroom in a monastery reserved for copying and illustrating MANUSCRIPTS.

SCROLL. 1) An architectural ornament with the form of a partially unrolled spiral, as on the CAPITALS of the Ionic and Corinthian ORDERS. 2) A form of written text.

SCUOLA. Italian word for school. In Renaissance Venice it designated a fraternal organization or confraternity, dedicated to good works, usually under ecclesiastic auspices.

SECTION. An architectural drawing presenting a building as if cut across the vertical plane, at right angles to the horizontal plane. Cross section: a cut along the transverse axis. Longitudinal section: a cut along the longitudinal axis.

SEXPARTITE VAULT. See VAULT.

SFUMATO. Italian word meaning gone up in smoke, used to describe very delicate gradations of light and shade in the MODELING of figures; applied especially to the work of Leonardo da Vinci and his followers (fig. 598).

SHAFT. In architecture, the part of a COLUMN between the BASE and the CAPITAL.

SIBYLS. In Greek and Roman mythology, any of numerous women who were thought to possess powers of divination and prophecy. They appear in Christian representations, notably in Michelangelo's Sistine ceiling, because they were believed to have foretold the coming of Christ.

SIDE AISLE. A passageway running parallel to the NAVE of a Roman BASILICA or Christian church, separated from it by an ARCADE or COLONNADE (fig. 744). There may be one on either side of the nave, or two, an inner and outer.

SILENI. A class of minor woodland gods in the entourage of the wine god, Dionysus (or Bacchus). Like Silenus, the wine god's tutor and drinking companion, they are thick-lipped and snub-nosed, and fond of wine. Similar to SATYRS, they are basically human in form except for having horses' tails and ears.

SILVER LEAF. See GOLD LEAF.

SILVER SALTS. Compounds of silver—bromide, chloride, and iodide—which are sensitive to light and are used in the preparation of photographic materials. This sensitivity was first observed by Johann Heinrich Schulze in 1727.

SINOPIA (pl. **SINOPIE**). Italian word taken from Sinope, the ancient city in Asia Minor which was famous for its brick-red pigment. In FRESCO paintings, a full-sized, preliminary sketch done in this color on the first rough coat of plaster or "arriccio."

SKETCH. See DRAWING, OIL SKETCH.

SPANDREL. The area between the exterior curves of two adjoining ARCHES, or, in the case of a single arch, the area around its outside curve from its springing to its keystone (fig. 633).

SPHINX. 1) In ancient Egypt, a creature having the head of a man, animal, or bird, and the body of a lion; frequently sculpted in monumental form. 2) In Greek mythology, a creature usually represented as having the head and breasts of a woman, the body of a lion, and the wings of an eagle. It appears in classical, Renaissance, and Neoclassical art.

STANZA (pl. **STANZE**). Italian word for room.

STEEL. Iron modified chemically to have qualities of great hardness, elasticity, and strength. For use in sculpture, see figs. 1131, 1138. For architectural use, see STRUCTURAL STEEL.

STELE. From the Greek word for standing block. An upright stone slab or pillar with a CARVED commemorative design or inscription.

STEREOBATE. The substructure of a classical building, especially a Greek temple.

STEREOSCOPE. An optical instrument which enables the user to combine two pictures taken from points of view corresponding to those of the two eyes into a single image having the depth and solidity of ordinary binocular vision (fig. 928). First demonstrated by Sir Charles Wheatstone in 1838.

STILTS. Term for pillars or posts supporting a superstructure; in 20th-century architecture, these are usually of FERROCONCRETE (figs. 1171, 1182). Stilted, as in stilted arches, refers to tall supports beneath an architectural member.

STRUCTURAL STEEL. STEEL used as an architectural building material either invisibly (fig. 1009) or exposed (fig. 1160). See FERROCONCRETE.

STUCCO. 1) A CONCRETE or cement used to coat the walls of a building. 2) A kind of plaster used for architectural decorations, such as CORNICES, MOLDINGS, or for sculptured RELIEFS (fig. 658).

STUDY. See DRAWING.

STYLOBATE. A platform or masonry floor above the STEREOBATE forming the foundation for the COLUMNS of a classical temple.

STYLUS. From the Latin word *stilus*, the writing instrument of the Romans. 1) A pointed instrument used in ancient times for writing on tablets of a soft material such as clay. 2) The needlelike instrument used in drypoint or etching. See ENGRAVING, ETCHING.

SUPERIMPOSED ORDERS. Two or more rows of COLUMNS, PIERS, or PILASTERS placed above each other on the wall of a building (fig. 661).

TABERNACLE. 1) A place or house of worship. 2) A CANOPIED niche or recess built for an image (fig. 530). 3) The portable shrine used by the ancient Jews to house the Ark of the Covenant.

TEMPERA PAINTING. 1) A painting made with pigments mixed with egg yolk and water. In the 14th and 15th centuries, it was applied to PANELS which had been prepared with a coating of GESSO; the application of GOLD LEAF and of underpainting in green or brown preceded the actual tempera painting (fig. 35). 2) The technique of executing such a painting.

TERRACOTTA. Italian word for baked earth. 1) Earthenware, naturally reddish-brown but often GLAZED (fig. 576) in various colors and fired. Used for pottery, sculpture, or as a building material or decoration. 2) An object made of this material. 3) Color of the natural material.

TESSERA (pl. **TESSERAE**). A small piece of colored stone, marble, glass, or gold-backed glass used in a MOSAIC.

THEATINE ORDER. Founded in Rome in the 16th century by members of the recently dissolved Oratory of Divine Love. Its aim was to reform the Catholic church, and its members were pledged to cultivate their spiritual lives and to perform charitable works.

THRUST. The lateral pressure exerted by an ARCH, VAULT, or DOME, which must be counteracted at its point of greatest concentration either by the thickness of the wall or by some form of BUTTRESS.

TRACERY. 1) Ornamental stonework in Gothic windows. 2) Similar ornamentation using various materials and applied to walls, shrines, etc. (fig. 691).

TRANSEPT. A cross arm in a BASILICAN church, placed at right angles to the NAVE, and usually separating it from the CHOIR or APSE.

TREE OF KNOWLEDGE. The tree in the Garden of Eden from which Adam and Eve ate the forbidden fruit which destroyed their innocence.

TREE OF LIFE. A tree in the Garden of Eden whose fruit was reputed to give everlasting life; in medieval art it was frequently used as a symbol of Christ.

TRIFORIUM. The section of a NAVE wall above the ARCADE and below the CLERESTORY. It frequently consists of a BLIND ARCADE with three openings in each bay. When the GALLERY is also present, a four-story ELEVATION results, the triforium being between the gallery and clerestory. It may also occur in the TRANSEPT and the CHOIR walls.

TRIGLYPH. The element of a Doric FRIEZE separating two consecutive METOPES, and being divided by channels (or glyphs) into three sections. Probably an imitation in stone of wooden ceiling beam ends.

TRIPTYCH. An ALTARPIECE or devotional picture, either CARVED or painted, with one central panel and two hinged wings (fig. 684).

TRIUMPHAL ARCH. 1) A monumental ARCH, sometimes a combination of three arches, erected by a Roman emperor in commemoration of his military exploits, and usually decorated with scenes of these deeds in RELIEF sculpture. 2) The great transverse arch at the eastern end of a church which frames ALTAR and APSE and separates them from the main body of the church. It is frequently decorated with MOSAICS or MURAL paintings.

TROPHY. 1) In ancient Rome, arms or other spoils taken from a defeated enemy and publicly displayed on a tree, PILLAR, etc. 2) A representation of these objects, and others symbolic of victory, as a commemoration or decoration.

TRUSS. A triangular wooden or metal support for a roof which may be left exposed in the interior, or be covered by a ceiling.

TURRET. 1) A small tower, part of a larger structure. 2) A small tower at an angle of a building, frequently beginning some distance from the ground.

TYMPANUM. 1) In classical architecture, the recessed, usually triangular area, also called a PEDIMENT, often decorated with sculpture. 2) In medieval architecture, an arched area between an ARCH and the LINTEL of a door or window, frequently carved with RELIEF sculpture (fig. 45).

UNDERPAINTING. See **TEMPERA PAINTING.**

VAULT. An arched roof or ceiling usually made of stone, brick, or CONCRETE. Several distinct varieties have been developed; all need BUTTRESSING at the point where the lateral THRUST is concentrated. 1) A barrel vault is a semicylindrical structure made up of successive ARCHES. It may be straight or ANNULAR in plan. 2) A groin vault is the result of the intersection of two barrel vaults of equal size which produces a BAY of four compartments with sharp edges, or "groins," where the two meet. 3) A ribbed groin vault is one in which RIBS are added to the groins for structural strength and for decoration. When the diagonal ribs are constructed as half-circles, the resulting form is a domical ribbed vault. 4) A sexpartite vault is a ribbed groin vault in which each bay is divided into six compartments by the addition of a transverse rib across the center. 5) The normal Gothic vault is quadripartite with all the arches pointed to some degree. 6) A fan vault is an elaboration of a ribbed groin vault, with elements of TRACERY using conelike forms. It was developed by the English in the 15th century, and was employed for decorative purposes.

VEDUTA (pl. **VEDUTE**). A view painting, generally a city landscape (fig. 840).

VELLUM. See **PARCHMENT.**

VESTRY. See **SACRISTY.**

VICES. Often represented allegorically in conjunction with the seven VIRTUES, they include Pride, Avarice, Wrath, Gluttony, Unchastity (Luxury), Folly, and Inconstancy, though others such as Injustice are sometimes substituted.

VILLA. Originally a large country house (fig. 665), but in modern usage also a detached house or suburban residence.

VIRTUES. The three theological virtues, Faith, Hope, and Charity, and the four cardinal ones, Prudence, Justice, Fortitude, and Temperance, were frequently represented allegorically, particularly in medieval manuscripts and sculpture.

VOLUTE. A spiral architectural element found notably on Ionic and Composite CAPITALS, but also used decoratively on building FACADES and interiors (fig. 670).

VOUSSOIR. See **ARCH.**

WASH. A thin layer of translucent, highly diluted color or ink used to model forms in WATERCOLOR PAINTING and BRUSH DRAWING, and occasionally in OIL PAINTING.

WATERCOLOR PAINTING. Painting, usually on paper, in pigments suspended in water (figs. 699, 1065).

WING. The side panel of an ALTARPIECE which is frequently decorated on both sides, and also hinged, so that it may be shown either open or closed. (figs. 673, 675).

WOODCUT. A PRINT made by carving out a design on a wooden block cut along the grain, applying ink to the raised surfaces which remain, and printing from those (figs. 694, 700, 966).

WROUGHT IRON. A comparatively pure form of iron which is easily forged and does not harden quickly, so that it can be shaped or hammered by hand (fig. 1124), in contrast to molded CAST IRON.

ZODIAC. An imaginary belt circling the heavens, including the paths of the sun, moon, and major planets, and containing 12 constellations and thus 12 divisions called signs, which have been associated with the months. The signs are: Aries, the ram; Taurus, the bull; Gemini, the twins; Cancer, the crab; Leo, the lion; Virgo, the virgin; Libra, the balance; Scorpio, the scorpion; Sagittarius, the archer; Capricorn, the goat; Aquarius, the water-bearer; and Pisces, the fish. They are frequently represented around the PORTALS of Romanesque and Gothic churches in conjunction with the LABORS OF THE MONTHS.

ART AND ARCHITECTURE WEB SITE GAZETTEER

The directory below is comprised mainly of the significant museum collections and monuments illustrated in this book. A few additional non-illustrated art sites are also listed. All efforts have been made to gather up-to-date addresses, phone numbers, and Web sites. Contact information is current as of time of printing.

UNITED STATES

ARIZONA

The Heard Museum, 22 E. Monte Vista Rd., Phoenix 85004. (602)252–8840. hanksville.phast.umass.edu/defs/independent/Heard/Heard.html

Phoenix Art Museum, 1625 N. Central Ave., Phoenix 85004. (602)257–1880. aztec.asu.edu/AandE/phoenix.art

Center for Creative Photography, University of Arizona, 843 E. University Blvd., Tuscon 85721. (520)621–7968. www.library.arizona.edu/branches/ccp/ccphome.html

CALIFORNIA

University Art Museum and Pacific Film Archive, University of California, 2626 Bancroft Way, Berkeley 94704. (510)642–0808. www.uampfa.berkeley.edu

Los Angeles County Museum of Art, 5905 Wilshire Blvd., Los Angeles 90036. (213)857–6111. www.lacma.org

The Museum of Contemporary Art, Los Angeles, 250 S. Grand Ave. at California Plaza, Los Angeles 90012. (213)382–6622, 621–2766. www.MOCA-LA.org

University of California, Los Angeles, Frederick S. Wright Art Gallery, 405 Hilgard Ave., Los Angeles 90024. (213)825–1461

The J. Paul Getty Museum, 17985 Pacific Coast Hwy., Malibu 90265. (310)458–2003. ca.living.net/trav/museums/carjpgm.htm

Stanford University Museum and Art Gallery, Lomita Dr. & Museum Way, Palo Alto 94305. (415)725–4177. www.leland.stanford.edu/dept/SUMA/

Norton Simon Museum, 411 W. Colorado Blvd., Pasadena 91105. (818)449–6840; 449–3730. www.citycet.com/CCC/Pasadena/nsmuseum.htm

Crocker Museum of Art, 216 O St., Sacramento 95814. (916)264–5423

Museum of Contemporary Art, San Diego, 1001 Kettner Blvd., San Diego 92101, 700 Prospect St., La Jolla 92037. (619)454–3541

San Diego Museum of Art, Balboa Park, 1450 El Prado, San Diego 92101. (619)232–7931. www.sddt.com/sdma.html

The Fine Arts Museums of San Francisco, www.famsf.org: **California Palace of the Legion of Honor,** Lincoln Park, near 34th Ave. and Clement St., San Francisco 94121. (415)863–3330; **M. H. de Young Memorial Museum,** Golden Gate Park, San Francisco 94118. (415)221–4811

San Francisco Museum of Modern Art, 151 3rd St., San Francisco 94103. (415)357–4000. www.sfmoma.org/

San Jose Museum of Art, 110 S. Market St., San Jose 95113. (408)294–2787. www.sjliving.com/sja

Huntington Library, Art Collections, and Botanical Gardens, 1151 Oxford Rd., San Marino 91108. (818)405–2141

Santa Barbara Museum of Art, 1130 State St., Santa Barbara 93101. (805)963–4364. www.artdirect.com/sbma/

COLORADO

The Denver Art Museum, 100 W. 14th Ave. Pkwy., Denver 80204. (303)640–2793

Colorado Springs Fine Arts Center, 30 W. Dale St., Colorado Springs 80903. (719)634–5581

CONNECTICUT

Wadsworth Atheneum, 600 Main St., Hartford 06103. (203)278–2670

Yale Center for British Art, 1080 Chapel St., New Haven 06520. (203)432–2800

Yale University Art Gallery, 1111 Chapel St. at York, New Haven 06520. (203)432–0600

DELAWARE

Delaware Art Museum, 2301 Kentmere Pkwy., Wilmington 19806. (302)571–9590. www.udel.edu/delart

DISTRICT OF COLUMBIA

The Corcoran Gallery of Art, 500 17th St. NW, 20006. (202)638–1903. www.corcoran.org

Freer Gallery of Art, Smithsonian Institution, Jefferson Dr. at 12th St. SW, 20560. (202)357–4880. www.si.edu/

Hirshhorn Museum and Sculpture Garden, Smithsonian Institution, Independence Ave. at 7th St. SW, 20560. (202)357–2700. www.si.edu/

National Gallery of Art, 4th St. at Constitution Ave. NW, 20565. (202)737–4215; (202)842–6176 (TDD). www.nga.gov

National Museum of American Art, 8th and G Sts., 20560 (202)357–2700. www.nmaa.si.edu

National Museum of American Art, Renwick Gallery, Pennsylvania Ave. at 17th St. NW, 20006. (202)357–2700

National Museum of Women in the Arts, 1250 New York Ave. NW, 20005, (202) 783–5000. www.nmwa.org

National Portrait Gallery, 8th and F Sts. NW, 20560. (202)357–2700. www.npg.si.edu

The Phillips Collection, 1600 21st St. NW, 20009. (202)387–0961

Vietnam Veterans Memorial, The Mall

FLORIDA

Lowe Art Museum, University of Miami, 1301 Stanford Dr., Coral Gables 33124. (305)284–3535

John and Mable Ringing Museum of Art, 5401 Bay Shore Rd., Sarasota 34243. (813)359–5700. www.sarasotaonline.com/ringling/welcome.html

Museum of Fine Arts, Saint Petersburg, Florida, 255 Beach Dr. NE, Saint Petersburg 33701. (813)896–2667

GEORGIA

Georgia Museum of Art, University of Georgia, Jackson St., North Campus, Athens 30602. (706)542–GMOA or 4662

High Museum of Art, 1280 Peachtree St. NE, Atlanta 30309. (404)733–HIGH or 4444. www.high.org

HAWAII

Honolulu Academy of Arts, 900 S. Beretania St., Honolulu 96814. (808)532–8700; 532–8701

ILLINOIS

Krannert Art Museum, University of Illinois, 500 E. Peabody Dr., Champaign 61820. (217)333–1861. www.art.uiuc.edu/kam/

The Art Institute of Chicago, 111 S. Michigan Ave. at Adams St., Chicago 60603. (312)443–3600; 443–3500. www.artic.edu/aic/firstpage.html

Museum of Contemporary Art, 220 E. Chicago Ave., Chicago 60611. (312)280–2660; 280–5161. www.webcore/chicago/thingsplaces/museums/mca/mca-home.html

Oriental Institute Museum, The University of Chicago, 1155 E. 58th St., Chicago 60637. (773)702–9520

Terra Museum of American Art, 666 N. Michigan Ave., Chicago 60611. (312)664–3939

INDIANA

Indianapolis Museum of Art, 1200 W. 38th St., Indianapolis 46208. (317)923–1331. web.ima-art.org/ima

IOWA

Des Moines Art Center, 4700 Grand Ave., Des Moines 50312. (515)277–4405

University of Iowa Museum of Art, 150 N. Riverside Dr., Iowa City 52242. (319)335–1727

KANSAS

Spencer Museum of Art, University of Kansas, 1301 Mississippi St., Lawrence 66045. (913)864–4710

Wichita Art Museum, 619 Stackman Dr., Wichita, 67203. (316)268–4921

KENTUCKY

J. B. Speed Art Museum, 2035 S. 3rd St., Louisville 40208. (502)636–2920. www.gatech.edu/CARLOS/AAMDO/Speedext.htm

LOUISIANA

New Orleans Museum of Art, 1 Collins Diboll Circle, City Park, New Orleans 70124. (504)488–2631

MAINE

Bowdoin College Museum of Art, Walker Art Building, Brunswick 04011. (207)725–3275

Portland Museum of Art, 7 Congress Sq., Portland 04101. (207)775–6148

MARYLAND

The Baltimore Museum of Art, Art Museum Dr. at North Charles and 31st Sts., Baltimore 21218. (410)396–7100. www.world-arts-resources.com/cgi-bin/access?mu269

Walters Art Gallery, 600 N. Charles St., Baltimore 21201. (410)547–9000; 547–ARTS

MASSACHUSETTS

Mead Art Museum, Amherst College, Amherst 01002. (413)542–2335

Addison Gallery of American Art, Phillips Academy, Andover 01810. (508)749–4015. www.andover.edu/addison/home.html

Isabella Stewart Gardner Museum, 280 The Fenway, Boston 02115. (617)566–1401. www.boston.com/gardner

Museum of Fine Arts, Boston, 465 Huntington Ave., Boston 02115. (617)267–9300. www.mfa.org

Harvard University Art Museums, Cambridge 02138. (617)495–9400 www.fas.harvard.edu/~artmuseums/: **Busch-Reisinger Museum,** 32 Quincy St.; **Fogg Art Museum,** 32 Quincy St.; **The Arthur M. Sackler Museum,** 485 Broadway

Smith College Museum of Art, Elm St. at Bedford Terrace, Northampton 01063. (413)585–2760

Peabody Essex Museum, East India Sq., Salem 01970. (508)745–1876. www.pem.org

Mount Holyoke College Art Museum, South Hadley 01075. (413)538–2245

Rose Art Museum, Brandeis University, 415 South St., Waltham 02254. (617)736–3434

Davis Museum and Cultural Center, Wellesley College, 106 Central St., Wellesley 02181. (617)283–2051

Sterling and Francine Clark Art Institute, 225 South St., Williamstown 01267. (413)458–9545

Williams College Museum of Art, Main St., Williamstown 01267. (413)597–2429

Worcester Art Museum, 55 Salisbury St., Worcester 01609. (508)799–4406

MICHIGAN

The University of Michigan Museum of Art, 525 S. State St., Ann Arbor 48109. (313)764–0395

The Detroit Institute of Arts, 5200 Woodward Ave., Detroit 48202. (313)833–7900. www.dia.org

Grand Rapids Art Museum, 155 Division North, Grand Rapids 49503. (616)459–4677

MINNESOTA

The Minneapolis Institute of Arts, 2400 3rd Ave. S., Minneapolis 55404. (612)870–3131; 870–3200. www.artsMIA.org

Walker Art Center, Vineland Pl., Minneapolis 55403. (612)375–7622. www.walkerart.org

MISSOURRI

The Nelson-Atkins Museum of Art, 4525 Oak St., Kansas City 64111. (816)561–4000

The Saint Louis Art Museum, 1 Fine Arts Dr., Forest Park, St. Louis 63110. (314)721–0072. www.slam.org

NEBRASKA

University of Nebraska-Lincoln/Sheldon Memorial Art Gallery and Sculpture Garden, 12th and R Sts., Lincoln 68588. (402)472–2461

Joslyn Art Museum, 2200 Dodge St., Omaha 68102. (402)342–3300. www.gatech.edu/CARLOS/AAMDO.cenreg.htm

NEW HAMPSHIRE

Hood Museum of Art, Dartmouth College, Wheelock St., Hanover 03755. (603)646–2808

NEW JERSEY

The Montclair Art Museum, 3 S. Mountain Ave. at Bloomfield Ave., Montclair 07042. (201)746–5555. www.interactive.net/~upper/mam.html

The Newark Museum, 49 Washington St., Newark 07101. (201)596–6500

Jane Zimmerli Art Museum, Rutgers The State University of New Jersey, Hamilton and George Sts., New Brunswick 08903 (201)932–7237

The Art Museum, Princeton University, Princeton 08544. (609)258–3788

NEW MEXICO

Millicent Rogers Museum, 1504 Millicent Rogers Rd., Taos 87571. (505)758–2462

NEW YORK

The Brooklyn Museum, 200 Eastern Pkwy., Brooklyn 11238. (718)638–5000. wwar.com/brooklyn_museum/index.html

Albright-Knox Art Gallery , 1285 Elmwood Ave., Buffalo 14222. (716)882–8700

Herbert F. Johnson Museum of Art, Cornell University, Ithaca 14853. (607)255–6464

Storm King Art Center, Old Pleasant Hill Rd., Mountainville 10953. (914)534–3115

American Craft Museum, 40 W. 53rd St., New York 10019. (212)956–3535

The Cloisters, Fort Tryon Park, New York 10040. (212)923–3700

Cooper-Hewitt National Museum of Design, Smithsonian Institution, 2 E. 91st St., New York 10128. (212) 860–6868

The Frick Collection, 1 E. 70th St., New York 10021. (212)288–0700

The Grey Art Gallery and Study Center, New York University Art Collection, 33 Washington Pl., New York 10003. (212)998–6780

Guggenheim Museum SoHo, 575 Broadway, New York 10012. (212)423–3500

International Center of Photography, 1130 5th Ave., New York 10028. (212)860–1777

International Center of Photography Midtown, 1133 6th Ave., New York 10036. (212)860–1783

The Jewish Museum, 1109 5th Ave., New York, 10128. (212)423–3200

The Metropolitan Museum of Art, 5th Ave. at 82nd St., New York 10028. (212)879–5500. www.metmuseum.org

The Museum of Modern Art, 11 W. 53rd St., New York 10019. (212)708–9400. www.moma.org

The New Museum of Contemporary Art, 583 Broadway, New York 10012. (212)219–1222. www.newmuseum.org

The Pierpont Morgan Library, 29 E. 36th St., New York 10016. (212)685–0008

Solomon R. Guggenheim Museum, 1071 5th Ave., New York 10128. (212)423–3500.www.mediabridge.com/nyc/museums/guggenheim.html

The Studio Museum in Harlem, 144 W. 125th St., New York 10027. (212)864–4500

Whitney Museum of American Art, 945 Madison Ave., New York 10021. (212)570–3676. www.echonyc.com/~whitney

Neuberger Museum of Art, Purchase College, State University of New York at Purchase, 735 Anderson Hill Rd., Purchase 10577. (914)251–6133

George Eastman House/International Museum of Photography and Film, 900 E. Ave., Rochester 14607. (716)271–3361

Memorial Art Gallery of the University of Rochester, 500 University Ave., Rochester, NY 14607. (716)473–7720

Everson Museum of Art of Syracuse and Onondaga County, 401 Harrison St., Syracuse 13202. (315)474–6064

Munson-Williams-Proctor Institute Museum of Art, 310 Genesee St., Utica 13502. (315)797–0000

The Hudson River Museum of Westchester, 511 Warburton Ave., Yonkers 10701. (914)963–4550

NORTH CAROLINA

The Ackland Art Museum, University of North Carolina, Chapel Hill, Columbia and Franklin Sts., Chapel Hill 27599. (919)966–5736

Duke Univerisity Museum of Art, Buchanan Blvd. at Trinity, East Campus, Durham 27708. (919)684–5135. www.duke.edu/duma

Weatherspoon Art Gallery, University of North Carolina, Greensboro, Spring Garden and Tate Sts., Greensboro 27412. (910)334–5770

North Carolina Museum of Art, 2110 Blue Ridge Rd., Raleigh 27607. (919)833–1935

OHIO

Great Serpent Mound, Adams County

Cincinnati Art Museum, Eden Park, Cincinnati 45202. (513)721–5204

The Taft Museum, 316 Pike St., Cincinnati 45202. (513)241–0343

The Cleveland Museum of Art, 11150 E. Blvd., Cleveland 44106. (216)421–7340. www.clemusart.com

The Columbus Museum of Art, 480 E. Broad St., Columbus 43215. (614)221–6801

Wexner Center for the Arts, The Ohio State University, North High St. at 15th Ave., Columbus 43210. (614)292–3535

Dayton Art Institute, 456 Belmonte Park North, Dayton 45405. (513)223–5277. www.gatech.edu/CARLOS/AAMDO/Daytext.htm

Allen Memorial Art Museum, Oberlin College, 87 N. Main St., Oberlin 44074. (216)775–8665. www.oberlin.edu/wwwmap/allen_art.html

The Toledo Museum of Art, 2445 Monroe St., Toledo 43620. (419)255–8000; (800)644–6862

The Butler Institute of America, 524 Wick Ave., Youngstown 44502. (216)743–1711. www.butlerart.com

OKLAHOMA

Gilcrease Museum, 1400 Gilcrease Museum Rd., Tulsa 74127. (918)596–2700

The Philbrook Museum of Art, 2727 S. Rockford Rd., Tulsa 74114. (918)749–7941

OREGON

Portland Art Museum, 1219 SW Park Ave, Portland 97205. (503)226–2811. www.pam.org/~pam/index.html

PENNSYLVANIA

Brandywine River Museum, Brandywine Conservancy, Rt. 1 at PA Rt. 100, Chadds Ford 19317. (610)388–2700

Barnes Foundation, 300 North Natch's Ln., Merion Station 19066. (610)667–0290

Institute of Contemporary Art, University of Pennsylvania, 118 S. 36th St., Philadelphia 19104. (215)898–7108

Museum of American Art of the Pennsylvania Academy of the Fine Arts, 118 N. Broad St., Philadelphia 19102. (215)972–7600. www.pond.com/~pafa

Philadelphia Museum of Art, 26th St. and Benjamin Franklin Pkwy., Philadelphia 19130. (215)763–8100. liber tynet.org/~pma/pmahome.html

University of Pennsylvania Museum, 33rd and Spruce Sts., Philadelphia 19104. (215)895–4000

The Andy Warhol Museum, 117 Sandunsky St., Pittsburgh 15212. (412)237–8300. www.clpgh.org/warhol

The Carnegie Museum of Art, 4400 Forbes Ave., Pittsburgh 15213. (412)622–3131. www.clpgh.org/moa

The Frick Art Museum, 7227 Reynolds St., Pittsburgh 15208. (412)371–0600

RHODE ISLAND

Museum of Art, Rhode Island School of Design, 224 Benefit St., Providence 02903. (401)454–6500. www.gatech.edu/CARLOS?AAMDO/RISDext.htm

SOUTH CAROLINA

Greenville County Museum of Art, 420 College St., Greenville 29601. (803)271–7570

TENNESSEE

Knoxville Museum of Art, 410 10th Ave., World's Fair Park, Knoxville 37916. (615)525–6101. www.esper.com/kma/index.html

Memphis Brooks Museum of Art, Overton Park, 1934 Poplar, Memphis 38104. (901)722–3500

TEXAS

Dallas Museum of Art, 1717 N. Harwood, Dallas 75201. (214)922–1200. www.unt.edu/dfw/dma/www/dma.htm

Amon Carter Museum, 3501 Camp Bowie Blvd., Fort Worth 76107. (817)738–1933. cartermuseum.org

Kimbell Art Museum, 3333 Camp Bowie Blvd., Fort Worth 76107. (817)332–8451. www.corbis.com/features/secure/kimbell

Modern Art Museum of Fort Worth, 1309 Montgomery St. at Camp Bowie Blvd., Fort Worth 76107. (817)738–9215

Contemporary Arts Museum, 5216 Montrose Blvd., Houston 77006. (713)526–0773. riceinfo.rice.edu/projects/cam

The Menil Collection, 1515 Sul Ross, Houston 77006. www.menil.org/~menil

The Museum of Fine Arts, Houston, 1001 Bissonnet St., Houston 77005. (713)639–7300. www.mfah.org

Rothko Chapel, 1409 Sul Ross, Houston 77006. (713)524–9839

Marion Koogler McNay Art Museum, 6000 N. New Braunfels Ave., San Antonio 78209. (210)824–5368

San Antonio Museum of Art, 200 W. Jones St., San Antonio 78215. (210)978–8100. www.samuseum.org

VIRGINIA

Monticello, Charlottesville. www.monticello.org/

Hampton University Museum, Hampton 23668. (804)727–5308

The Chrysler Museum, 245 W. Olney Rd., Norfolk 23510. (804)664–6200. www.whro.org/cl/cmhh

Virginia Museum of Fine Arts, 2800 Grove Ave., Richmond 23221. (804)367–0844

WASHINGTON

Seattle Art Museum, 100 University St., Seattle 98101. (206)625–8900; 654–3100. www.pan.ci.seattle.wa.us/sam

Tacoma Art Museum, 12th and Pacific Ave., Tacoma 98402. (206)272–4258

WISCONSIN

Milwaukee Art Museum, 750 N. Lincoln Memorial Dr., Milwaukee 53202. (414)224–3200. www.mam.org

OUTSIDE
THE UNITED STATES

AUSTRIA

Graphische Sammlung Albertina, Augustinerstr. 1, Vienna 1010. (0222)534830

Kunsthistoriches Museum, Burgring 5, Vienna 1010. (0222)525240

Österreichische Galerie Belvedere, Prinz. Eugen. Str. 27, Vienna 1037. (01) 79557

BELGIUM

Musées Royaux des Beaux-Arts de Belgique: Musée d'Art Ancien, 3 Rue de la Régence, Brussels 1000. (32)25083211; **Musées d'Art Moderne,** 1-2, Place Royale, Brussels 1000. (32) 25083211

Musée Royaux d'Art et d'Histoire, Parc du Cinquantenaire 10, Brussels 1040. (02)7417211

CANADA

Edmonton Art Gallery, 2 Sir Winston Churchhill Sq., Edmonton, Alberta T5J 2C1. (403)422–6223

Glenbow, 130 9th Ave., Southeast, Calgary, Alberta T2G 0P3. (403)268–4100. www.glenbow.org

Vancouver Art Gallery, 750 Hornby St., Vancouver, British Columbia V6Z 2H7. (604)682–4668. www.vanartgallery.bc.ca

National Gallery of Canada, 380 Sussex Dr., Ottawa, Ontario K1N 9N4. (800)319–ARTS; (613)990–1985. national.gallery.ca

Art Gallery of Ontario, 317 Dundas St. W., Toronto, Ontario M5T 1G4. (416)977–6648. www.ago.on.ca

Royal Ontario Museum, 100 Queen's Park, Toronto, Ontario M5S 2C6. (416)586–5551. www.rom.on.ca/

Canadian Center for Architecture, 1920, rue Baile, Montréal, Quebec H3H 2S6. (514)939–7000; 939–7026

Montréal Museum of Fine Arts, 1379-80 Sherbrook St. W., Montréal, Quebec H36 2T9. (514)285–1600; 285–2000. www.mmfa.qc.ca

CZECH REPUBLIC

National Gallery in Prague. (42)2 53 08 95. (43)5132782.

Sternberg Palace, Hradcanske namesti 15, Prague 1-Hradcany. (42)23524413

DENMARK

Ny Carlsberg Glyptotek, Dantes Plads 7, Copenhagen 1556. (45)33418141. www.europe-today.com/denmark/museum2.html#carlsberg2

Louisiana Museum of Modern Art, Gl. Strandvej 13, Humlebaek 3050 (nr. Copenhagen). (45)42190719. www.europe-today.com/denmark/museum2.html#Louisiana

EGYPT

Egyptian Museum, Cairo University. Midan el Tahrir, Cairo. (2)760390

The Great Sphinx, Giza

Pyramids of Menkaure, Khafre, Khufu, Giza

Temple Complex of Amun-Mut-Khonsu, Luxor

ENGLAND

Birmingham Museum and Art Gallery, Chamberlain Sq., Birmingham B3 3DH. (0121)2352834

Durham Cathedral, Durham

Banqueting House, Whitehall Palace, London

British Library Exhibition Galleries, Great Russell St., London WC1B 3DG. (0171)4127595

British Museum, Great Russell St., London WC1B 3DG. (0171)6361555

Westminster Abbey, London

Courtauld Institute Galleries, Somerset House, Strand, London WC2R ORN. (0181)8732538

The Houses of Parliament, London

The National Gallery, Trafalgar Sq., London WC2N 5DN. (0171)8393321

Royal Academy of Arts, Burlington House, Piccadilly, London WIV ODS. (0171) 439-7438

Sir John Soane's Museum, 13 Lincoln's Inn, London WC2A 3BP. (0171)4052107

Tate Gallery, Millbank, London SWIP 4RG. (0171)8878000

Victoria and Albert Museum, Cromwell Rd., South Kensington, London SW7 2RL. (0171)9388500. www.vam.ac.uk

Wellington Museum, Apsley House, 149 Piccadilly, Hyde Park Corner, London N1V 9FA. (0171)4995676

Ashmolean Museum of Art and Archaeology, Beaumont St., Oxford 0X1 2PH. (01865)278000. www.ashmol.ox.ac.uk

Salisbury Cathedral, Salisbury

Stonehenge, Salisbury Plain (Wiltshire)

Blenheim Palace, Woodstock 0X7 1PX. (01993)811325

FRANCE

Chauvet cave, Vallon-pont-d'Arc

Chartres Cathedral, Chartres

Château de Fontainebleau, Fontainebleau. (1)60715070

Musée Claude Monet, rue Claude Monet, Giverny 27620. 32512821. giverny.org/monet/welcome.htm

Musée des Beaux-Arts de Lyon, Palais St. Pierre, 20 place des Terreaux, 69001 Lyon. 78280766

Bibliothèque Nationale de France, 25 rue de Richelieu, Paris 75002. (1)47038126

Galeries Nationales du Grand Palais, 3 avenue du Général Eisenhower, Paris 75008. (1)42895410

Musée Auguste Rodin, 77 rue de Varenne, Paris 75007. (1)47050134

Musée du Louvre, rue de Rivoli, 75001 Paris. (1)40205009. www.Louvre.Fr

Musée National d'Art Moderne—Centre National d'Art et de Culture

Georges Pompidou, Centre Beaubourg, Paris 75191. (1)781233. www.paris.org/Musees/Beaubourg

Musée d'Orsay, 1 rue de Bellechasse, Paris 75007. (1)40494814. www.paris.org.:80/Musees/Orsay/

Musée Picasso, Hôtel Salé, 5 rue de Varenne, Paris 75003. (1)42712521

Notre-Dame, Paris

The Opéra, Paris

Château de Versailles, Versailles. (1)30847400

GERMANY

Ägyptisches Museum und Papyrussammlung, Staatliche Museeun zu Berlin-Preussischer Kulturbesitz, Schlossstr. 70, Berlin 14059. (030)32091261. fub46.zedat.fu-berlin.de:8080/˜kurtwagn/gendir/aegy-pap/aegychar.html

Schloss Charlottenburg, Berlin. peri.pericont.in-berlin.de/cgi-bin/cg/museummuseumshow.pl?80;land=Berlin

Staatliche Museen zu Berlin, Gemäldegalerie. peri.pericont.in-berlin.de/cgi-bin/cg/museummuseumshow.pl?80;land=Berlin

Staatliche Museen zu Berlin, Preussischer Kulturbesitz, Stauffenbergstr. 41, Berlin 10785. (030)2666. peri.pericont.in-berlin.de/cgi-bin/cg/museummuseumshow.pl?80;land=Berlin

Museum Ludwig, Bischofsgartenstr. 1, Cologne 50667. (0221)2212379. www.blackbox.de/kunst/museen/mlu.htm

Städelsches Kunstinstitut und Städtische Galerie, Schaumainkai 63, Frankfurt 60596. (069)6050980. peri.pericont.in berlin.de/cgi-bin/cg/museumcity search.pl?city=Frank furt_am_Main

Hamburger Kunsthalle, Glockengiesser-wall, 20095 Hamburg. (040)24862612. www.hamburg.de/Behoerden/Museen/kh/

Hildesheim Cathedral, Hildesheim

Staatliche Kunsthalle, Hans-Thoma-Str. 2, Karlsruhe 76133. 1353370. www.rz.uni- karlsruhe.de/Nick/Karlsruhe/

Alte Pinakothek, Barer Str. 27, Munich 80333. (089)238050. server.StMUK WK.bayern.de/kunst/museen/pinalt.html

Bayerische Staatsgemäldesammlungen, Barrer Str. 29, Munich 80799. (089)238050

Staatliche Graphische Sammlung, Meis-erstr. 10, Munich 80333. (089)5591490

Staatliche Antikensammlungen und Glyptothek, Konigspl 1–3, Munich 80333. (089)1598359

Staatsgalerie Stuttgart, Konrad-Ade-nauer Str. 30, Stuttgart 70173. (0711) 212 4050. macserver.zedat.fu- berlin.de:1080/index.html

GREECE
Acropolis, Athens

Acropolis Museum, Athens. www.culture.gr

National Archaeological Museum, Od Tosita 1, Athens 10682. (01)8217717. www.culture.gr

Archaeological Museum, Corfu. www.culture.gr

Archaeological Museum, Heraklion, Crete. www.culture.gr

Palace of Minos, Knossos, Crete

Archaeological Museum, Delphi 33054. (0265)82313. www.culture.gr

HUNGARY
National Gallery, Budapest

IRAN
Archaeological Museum, Teheran

IRAQ
Iraq Museum, Karkh Museum Sq., Baghdad. 361215

IRELAND
National Gallery of Ireland, Merrion Sq. W., Dublin 2. (01)6615133

ITALY
Museo Civico Archeologico, Via del-l'Archiginnasio 2, Bologna 40124. (051)233849. www.dsnet.it/Bologna/engl_musei.html

Florence Cathedral and Baptistery of S. Giovanni, Florence

Galleria dell'Academia, Via Ricasoli 60, Florence 50122. (055)214375

Galleria degli Uffizi, Piazza degli Uffizi 6, Florence 50122. (055)2388651. www.televisual.it/uffizi/

Museo Nazionale del Bargello, Via del Proconsolo 4, Florence 50122. 055210801

Sta. Maria delle Grazie, Milan

Museo Archeologico Nazionale, Via Museo 19, Naples 80135. (081)440166

Museo e Gallerie Nazionale di Capodi-monte, Palazzo di Capodimonte, Naples 80136. (081)7410801

House of the Vettii, Pompeii

Villa of the Mysteries, Pompeii

S. Apollinare in Classe, Ravenna

S. Vitale, Ravenna

Arch of Constantine, Rome

Arch of Titus, Rome

The Colosseum, Rome

Column of Trajan, Rome

Galleria Borghese, Piazzale Scipione Borghese 5, Rome 00197. (06)858577

Musei Capitolini, Piazza del Campidog-lo, Rome 00186. (06)67102475

Museo dei Conservatori, Piazza del Campidoglio, Rome 00186. (06)67102475

Museo delle Terme, Rome

Museo Nazionale di Villa Giulia, Piazza di Villa Giulia 9, Rome 00195. (06)350719

Palazzo Farnese, Rome

The Pantheon, Rome

St. Peter's, Rome

Sta. Maria Maggiore, Rome

Sta. Maria della Vittoria, Rome

Vatican Museums, Viale Vaticano, Città del Vaticano 00120, Rome. (06)69883333

Villa Medici, Rome

Tombs, Tarquinia

Peggy Guggenheim Collection, Palazzo Venier dei Leoni, 701 Dorsoduro, 30123 Venice. (041)5206288

Galleria dell'Academia, Campo della Carità, Venice 30121. (041)22247

St. Marks, Venice

Villa Rotonda, Vicenza

JORDAN
Jordan Archaeological Museum, Amman. 638795

THE NETHERLANDS
Rijksmuseum, Stadhouderskade 42, Amsterdam 1070. (020)6732121. www.nbt.nl/holland/museums/home.htm

Stedelijk Museum of Modern Art, Paulus Potterstraat 13, Amsterdam 1070. (020)5732911. art.cwi.nl

Kröller-Müller Museum, Otterlo 6730.

08382. www.nbt.nl/holland/museums/home.htm

Museum Boymans-van Beuningen, Museumpark 18-20, Rotterdam 3015. 010441400. www.nbt.nl/holland/museums/home.htm

Centraal Museum Utrecht, Agnietenst. 1, Utrecht 3500. (030)362362. www.nbt.nl/holland/museums/home.htm

NORWAY
Nasjonalgalleriet, Universitestgaten 13, Oslo 0033. 22200404

ROMANIA
National Museum, Str. Stirbei Vida, nr. 1–3, Bucharest 70733. (01)6155193

RUSSIA
Pushkin Museum of Fine Arts, Ul. Volkhonka 12, Moscow. (095)2037412. www.rosprint.ru/art/museum/pushkin

Hermitage Museum, 36 Dvortsovaya Naberezhnaya, Saint Petersburg, (812)3113420

SCOTLAND
National Gallery of Scotland, The Mound, Edinburgh EH2 2EL. (0131)5568921

SPAIN
Church of the Sagrada Familia, Barcelona

Museo Nacional del Prado, Paseo del Prado, Madrid 28014. (91)4680950

Museo Nacional Centro de Arte Reina Sofía, Santa Isabel 52, Madrid 28012. (1)4675062

SWEDEN
Moderna Museet, Spårvagnshallarna, Box 16382, Stokholm 10327. (08)6664250

Nationalmuseum, S. Blasieholmsham-nen, Stockholm 10324. (08)6664250

SWITZERLAND
Öffentliche Kunstsammlung Basel, Kunstmuseum, St. Alban-Graben 16, Basel 4010. (41)612710828. www.access.ch/bsweb/museum/e/kusa_ku/index.htm

Musée d'Art et d'Histoire, 2 Rue Charles Gallard, Geneva 1211. (022)3114340

TURKEY
Archaeological Museum, Ankara

Archaeological Museum of Istanbul, Gülhane Sultanahmet, Istanbul 34400. (520)7742

Hagia Sophia, Istanbul

INDEX

Works ascribed to a specific artist are indexed under the artist's name, shown in SMALL CAPITAL letters. Insofar as possible, works, including buildings and archeological remains, are also indexed by site of origin. Buildings whose name begins with "Palace," "Villa," "Cathedral," and such generic names are listed under the next significant part (e.g., Versailles, France, Palace). Illustration references, shown in *italic* type, are to *figure numbers,* not page numbers.

PHOTOGRAPH CREDITS and COPYRIGHTS

The author and publisher wish to thank the libraries, museums, galleries, and private collections for permitting the reproduction of works of art in their collections and for supplying the necessary photographs. Photographs from other sources are gratefully acknowledged below. All numbers refer to figure numbers.

PHOTOGRAPH CREDITS and COPYRIGHTS

J.S. Ackerman, *The Architecture of Michelangelo*: 618; ACL, Brussels: 673–75, 693; Archivi Alinari, Florence: 530, 540, 541, 542, 550, 566, 569, 574, 578, 589, 594, 621, 635, 661, 662, 670, 732, 743, 746, 755; Arcaid/David Churchill, Kingston upon Thames, U.K.: 910, 911; Art Co. Limited, Nassau, Bahamas: 1040; Artothek/Joachim Blauel, Peissenberg, Germany: 561, 636, 701, 705, 707, 713, 763, 776, 896; Cameraphoto-Arte, Venice/Art Resource, New York: 633, 653, 663; Foto Marburg/Art Resource, New York: 45, 719, 745, 798, 960–62, 1158, 1159, 1162, 1169; Scala/Art Resource, New York: 544, 562, 588, 606, 627, 631; The Tate Gallery, London/Art Resource, New York: 945, 969, 1049, 1127; Bank of England, London: 916; Herbert Bayer Studio, Montecito, California: 1218; Bildarchiv Preussischer Kulturbesitz, Berlin: 529, 680, 687, 773, 893, 909; Paul Bitjebier, Brussels: 1034; Black Star, New York: 1225; Boyan & Shear, Glasgow: 1003; The Bridgeman Art Library, London: 803; British National Tourist Office, New York: 912; F. Bruckmann Verlag, Munich: 930; Martin Bühler, Basel: 993, 1117; Photographie Bulloz, Paris: 723, 724, 906; Bundesdenkmalsamt, Vienna: 900; Caisse Nationale des Monuments Historiques et des Sites/© Arch.Phot.Paris: 43, 609, 610, 907; F. Camard, *Ruhlmann, Master of Art Deco*: 1194; Canali Photobank, Capriolo: 32, 34, 35, 36, 37, 44, 46, 532, 534, 538, 551, 558, 561, 564, 567, 572, 581, 586, 587, 596, 601, 617, 622, 626, 628, 637, 638, 644, 646, 647, 654, 659, 660, 682, 710, 718, 725–27, 729, 731, 734–36, 740, 741, 756, 753, 758, 886, 902; Canali Photobank/Bertoni, Capriolo: 41, 531, 537, 560, 579, 607; Canali Photobank/Codato: 536, 582, 593; Chicago Historical Society: 929; Cinématique Française, Paris: 1020; Alschwill-Basel: 993; Paula Cooper Gallery, New York: 1106, 1107; The Conway Library/Courtauld Institute of Art, University of London: 850, 937; Culver Pictures, New York: 928; D. James Dee, New York: 1242; Eric De Maré, © Gordon Fraser Gallery, London: 1008; M. Droste, *Bauhaus 1919–1933*: 1178; *Du Atlantis*, Zurich (September 1965): 966; E. Du Cerceau, *Les Plus Excellent Batissement . . .*: 721; Galerie Durand-Dessert, Paris: 1239; English Heritage Photograph Library, London: 847, 859; ESTO/© Peter Aaron, Mamaroneck, N.Y.: 1232; ESTO/© Peter Mauss, Mamaroneck, N.Y.: 1238; ESTO/© Ezra Stoller, Mamaroneck, N.Y.: 1139, 1181, 1186–88, 1193; Ronald Feldman Fine Arts, New York: 1242; Fischbach Gallery, New York: 1130; Fotocielo, Rome: 739; Peter Fowles, Glasgow: 1004; © Klaus Frahm, Hamburg: 1236; John R. Freeman, Limited, London: 590; French National Tourist Board, Paris: 904; Gabinetto Fotografico Nazionale, Rome: 624, 669, 730, 752, 806; Gabinetto Nazionale delle Stampe, Rome: 619, 620; G.E.K.S., New York: 747, 1173, 1174, 1182, 1206; Philip Gendreau, New York: 963; G. Gherardi/A. Fioretti, Rome: 1189, 1190; Photographie Giraudon, Paris: 600, 722, 816, 851, 856, 918, 921, 964, 976; P. Gössel and G. Leuthäuser: *Architecture in the Twentieth Century*: 1195, 1233; © Gianfranco Gorgoni, New York: 1141; Foto Grassi, Siena: 33; Peter Grosz, Princeton, N.J.: 1068; Hedrich-Blessing/Bill Engdahl, Chicago: 1154, 1170; Lucien Hervé, Paris: 1172; Hirmer Fotoarchiv, Munich: 28, 575, 608, 616, 663, 694; H.R. Hitchcock, *Architecture: Nineteenth and Twentieth Century*: 919, 1002; © Angelo Hornak Library, London: 665; Christian Huelsen, *Il Libro di Giuliano da Sangallo*: 547; Timothy Hursley: 1234; L'Institut de France, Paris: 600; The Iveagh Bequest, Kenwood, London: 847; *Jahrbuch des Deutschen Werkbundes (1915)*: 1005, 1006, 1160, 1161; Anthony Janson: 858, 1092; H.W. Janson: 552, 995, 1094; Bruno Jarrett/ARS, New York/ADAGP, Paris: 956, 958; A.F. Kersting, London: 799, 809; Jörg Klam, Berlin: 1026; © Studio Kontos, Athens: 1, 19; Balthazar Korab,

Troy, Michigan: 1138; Ian Lambot, Haslemere, Surrey: 1197, 1198; Kurt Lange, Oberdorf, Allgäu, Germany: 528; Jacques Lathion, Oslo: 989; Lautman Photography, Washington, D.C.: 860; William Lescaze, New York: 1177; Library of Congress, Washington, D.C.: 885; Lichtbildwerkstätte Alpenland, Vienna: 591, 639, 655, 657, 708, 716, 717; Maya Lin, New York: 1140; Jannes Linders, Rotterdam: 1164, 1166; Magnum, New York: 1203, 1211, 1216; Marlborough Gallery, New York: 1146; Maryland Historical Society, Baltimore: 915; Arxiu MAS, Barcelona: 684, 685, 649, 759, 764, 863, 864, 876; Foto Mayer, Vienna: 691; © Rollie McKenna, Stonington, Connecticut: 548; H. Millon, *Key Monuments in the History of Art*: 568, 605, 623, 748; Ministry of Public Buildings and Works, London: 853, 854; André Morin, Paris: 1239; © Museum of Modern Art, New York: 1167, 1168; National Buildings Record, London: 810, 812, 917; Otto Nelson, New York: 1091; Richard Nickel, Chicago: 1007, 1009–11; Nippon Television Network Corporation, Tokyo: 9, 611–15; © Takashi Okamura, Shizuoka City, Japan: 539, 545, 559, 576, 577, 629; Bill Orcutt Studios, New York: 1248; Oroñoz, Madrid: 632, 714, 839, 1001; Pace Wildenstein Gallery/Bill Jacobsen, New York: 1132; Gustav Peichl, Vienna: 1194; Robert Perron, New York: 1192; N. Pevsner, *Outline of European Architecture*: 549; Erich Pollitzer, New York: 979; Winslow Pope/Michigan Consolidated Gas Company, Detroit, Michigan: 1180; Port Authority, New York: 908; Foto Positiv, Vienna: 833; © Museo del Prado: 679; Provinciebestuur van Antwerpen: 777; Antonio Quattrone (Courtesy of Olivetti), Florence: 553–56; Mario Quattrone Fotostudio, Florence: 30, 583, 640, 643; Rapho, Paris: 1204; Carl Reiter: 751; Studio Rémy, Dijon, France: 39; © Réunion des Musées Nationaux, Paris: 4, 585, 595, 597, 598, 625, 634, 690, 709, 711, 733, 767, 784, 791, 792, 808, 817, 818, 820, 821, 842, 865–68, 870–73, 880, 883, 905, 931, 932, 936, 938, 939, 947, 948, 984, 985, 1035, 1051; Rheinisches Bildarchiv, Cologne: 1101, 1143; Photographie Roger-Viollet, Paris: 720, 803, 920, 1000, 1176; Richard Ross: 1243, 1244; Jean Roubier, Paris: 29; Routhier/Studio Lourmel, Paris: 940; The Royal Collection Enterprises, Windsor Castle: 599, 652, 840; Sächsische Landesbibliothek, Deutsche Fotothek, Dresden: 1190; Galerie St. Etienne, New York: 1067; Armando Salas, Portugal: 1129; Toni Schneiders, Lindau, Germany: 835, 837; Fotostudio Schoenen & Junger, Aachen: 1241; Silvestris Photo-Service, Kastl, Germany: 832; Aaron Siskind: 1223; Haldor Sochner, Munich: 648; Société Française de Photographie, Paris: 923; Holly Solomon Gallery, New York: 1150; Sperone Westwater Gallery, New York: 1105; Franz Stoedtner, Düsseldorf: 999; A. Stratton: *Life. . .*: 811; Adolph Studley, Pennsburg, Pennsylvania: 998; Wim Swaan: 3, 656, 737, 749, 800–02, 830; © Jean Clottes, SYGMA, New York: 28; © 1974 Caroline Tisdall: 1168; Marvin Trachtenberg, New York: 570, 666, 804, 834, 1171, 1183, 1184; Bernard Tschumi Architects, New York: 1237; University Library, Uppsala, Sweden: 715; Robert Villani: 1155, 1165; John B. Vincent, Berkeley, California: 668; Wolfgang Volz © Christo: 1142; © Elke Walford, Hamburg: 894, 895, 1025; Denise Walker, Baltimore: 913, 914; © Lewis Watts Anselmo, California: 1245; Etienne Weil, Jerusalem: 1110, 1196; Whitaker Studios, Richmond, Virginia: 852; Joachim Wilke, Stuttgart: 855; David Wilkins, Pittsburgh: 535; Ole Wodbye, Copenhagen: 903; © Arq. Sergio Zepeda C., Guadalajara, Mexico: 1072; O. Zimmerman, Colmar, France: 696, 697; © Gerald Zugmann, Vienna: 1235; Foto Zwicker-Berberich, Gerchsheim/Würzburg, Germany: 823.

ARTIST COPYRIGHTS